2013 NHL BLACK BOOK
PROSPECT SCOUTING REPORTS AND DRAFT RANKINGS

by HockeyProspect.com

© 2013 by The Hockey Press

ALL RIGHTS RESERVED.

ISBN-13: 978-0991677528 (The Hockey Press)

ISBN-10: 0991677528

HOCKEYPROSPECT.COM

Table of Contents

1. **2013 NHL DRAFT RANKINGS.43**

2. **2013 NHL DRAFT PROSPECTS.51**

   ★ Ahlgren, Jake – FW – Sioux Falls Stampede (USHL) – 6'1" 173..52

   ★ Aldworth, Thomas – RW – Cushing Academy (Prep-MA) – 6'0, 179..52

   ★ Allen, Evan – LW – US NTDP Under-18 Team – 5'10, 195 .52

   ★ Allen, Mitchell – RC – Kent School (Prep-CT) – 6'2 180..52

   ★ Amorosa, Terrance – LD – Holderness School (Prep-NH) – 6'2, 190..53

   ★ Andrighetto, Sven – RW – Rouyn-Noranda Huskies (QMJHL) – 5'10" 180..53

   ★ Antonen, Joose – LW – JYP-Akatemia (FIN-2) – 6'2, 183 .54

   ★ Arnesson, Linus – LD – Djurgarden (SAL) – 6'2" 190 .54

   ★ Ast, Anthony – RC – Vancouver Giants (WHL) – 5'8" 170..54

   ★ Auger, Justin – RW – Guelph Storm (OHL) – 6'7" 223..55

   ★ Ausmus, Gage – LD – US NTDP Under-18 Team – 6'1, 211..55

   ★ Babintsev, Sam – RW – Mississauga Steelheads (OHL) – 5'10" 167..55

   ★ Baddock, Brandon – RW – Edmonton Oil Kings (WHL) – 6'3" 200 .56

   ★ Bailey, Justin – RC – Kitchener Rangers (OHL) – 6'3" 186..56

   ★ Baptiste, Nicholas – RW – Sudbury Wolves (OHL) – 6'1" 190..57

   ★ Barkov, Aleksander – LC – Tappara (SM-liiga) – 6'3 209..57

   ★ Barrick, Brodie – G – Sarnia Sting (OHL) – 6'2" 171 .58

   ★ Bateman, Adam – RD – Windsor Spitfires (OHL) – 5'11" 185..58

   ★ Bauman, Chadd – LD – Guelph Storm (OHL) – 6'2" 203..58

   ★ Bauml, Kohl – LC – Everett Silvertips (WHL) – 5'8" 164..59

   ★ Beaton, Bronson – RC – Cape Breton Screaming Eagles (QMJHL) – 6'1" 182 .59

   ★ Beaulieu, Anthony – LD – Victoriaville Tigres (QMJHL) – 6'5" 203 .59

   ★ Beckstead, Marc – LW – Kingston Frontenacs (OHL) – 6'0" 174 .59

   ★ Bellerive, Matt – RW – Red Deer Rebels (WHL) – 5'11" 188 .59

2013 NHL DRAFT BLACK BOOK

- ★ Berisha, Aaron – Belleville Bulls (OHL) – 5'10" 183 ..60
- ★ Bertuzzi, Tyler – LW – Guelph Storm (OHL) – 6'0" 178 .60
- ★ Besse William (Grant) - Benilde-St. Marg. – (Minn. HS) – 5'9" 177 .61
- ★ Betker, Ben – LD – Everett Silvertips (WHL) – 6'5" 200 ..61
- ★ Betz, Nick – RW – Erie Otters (OHL) – 6'5" 210 ..61
- ★ Betzold, Greg – LW – Peterborough Petes (OHL) – 6'1.5" 195 ..61
- ★ Bibeau, Antoine – G – PEI Rocket (QMJHL) – 6'2" 213 ..62
- ★ Bigras, Chris – LD – Owen Sound Attack (OHL) – 6'0.5" 186 .62
- ★ Bjorkstrand, Oliver – RW – Portland Winterhawks (WHL) – 5'11" 164 .63
- ★ Blomqvist, Axel – LW – Lethbridge Hurricanes (WHL) – 6'5" 194 .63
- ★ Boland, Connor – LD – Peterborough Petes (OHL) – 6'2" 200 .64
- ★ Boudens, Matthew – LC – Drummondville Voltigeurs (QMJHL) – 5'11" 199 .64
- ★ Bowey, Madison – RD – Kelowna Rockets (WHL) – 6'1" 194 .64
- ★ Bowles, Parker – LW – Tri-City Americans (WHL) – 5'11" 180 .65
- ★ Brouillard, Nikolas – LD- Drummondville Voltigeurs (QMJHL) – 5'10" 148 ..65
- ★ Buchnevich, Pavel - C- Russia - 6'0" 157 .66
- ★ Brace, Cameron – RW – Owen Sound Attack (OHL) – 5'9.5" 176 ..66
- ★ Bradford, Erik – LC – Barrie Colts (OHL) – 5'11.25" 178 .66
- ★ Brassard, Connor – RD – Cushing Academy (Prep-MA) – 6'0, 165 ..67
- ★ Bristedt, Leon – RW – Linkoping J20 (SWE J20) – 5'8" 180 .67
- ★ Broadhead, Gavin – RC – Medicine Hat Tigers (WHL) – 5'11" 180 ..67
- ★ Brodzinski, Michael – RD – Muskegon Lumberjacks (USHL) – 5'11" 193 .68
- ★ Johnny Brodzinski – C – ST.Cloud State (NCAA) – 6'0" 202 .68
- ★ Brown, Connor – LW – Ottawa 67's (OHL) – 5'11" 186 ..68
- ★ Brown, Davis – LW – Sarnia Sting (OHL) – 5'9" 185 ..68
- ★ Buckles, Matt – RW – 6'2" – 210lb. – St. Michael's Buzzers (OJHL) .69
- ★ Burakovsky, Andre – LW – Malmo (SAL) – 6'1" 178 .69
- ★ Burke, Brendan – G – Portland Winterhawks (WHL) – 6'3" 174 .69
- ★ Burnside, Josh – LW – Mississauga Steelheads (OHL) – 5'11" 176 ..70
- ★ Burroughs, Kyle – RD – Regina Pats (WHL) – 5'11" 175 .70

- ★ Butcher, Will – LD – US NTDP Under-18 Team – 5'10, 191 ..70
- ★ Calderone, Tony – FW – Sioux Falls Stampede (USHL) – 5'11" 202 ..71
- ★ Cammarata, Taylor – FW – Waterloo Blackhawks (USHL) 5'7" 156 .71
- ★ Carlisle, Chris – LD – Oshawa Generals (OHL) – 5'11" 178 .72
- ★ Carnevale, Alex – LW – Sarnia Sting (OHL) – 5'11" 170 ..72
- ★ Carrier, William – LW – Cape Breton Screaming Eagles (QMJHL) – 6'1" 198 ..72
- ★ Cassels, Cole – RC – Oshawa Generals (OHL) – 6'0" 178 ..73
- ★ Cave, Colby – LC – Swift Current Broncos (WHL) – 6'0" 188 .74
- ★ Cederholm, Anton – LD – Rogle (SEL) – 6'2" 205 .74
- ★ Peter Cehlarik – LW – Lulea (Elitserien) - 6'2" 192 .74
- ★ Chapman, Joshua – RD – Sarnia Sting (OHL) – 6'4" 208 ..75
- ★ Chase, Greg – RC – Calgary Hitmen (WHL) – 6'0" 195 .75
- ★ Cianfrone, Bryson – FW – Cedar Rapids RoughRiders (USHL) – 5'8" 169 .75
- ★ Clapperton, Christopher – LW – Blainville-Boisbriand Armada (QMJHL) – 5'10" 180 .76
- ★ Clifton, Connor – RD – US NTDP Under-18 Team – 5'11, 175 ..76
- ★ Cloonan, Ryan – LC – Boston Jr. Bruins (EJHL) – 5'9, 145 .77
- ★ Clutsam, Mac – LD – Sault Ste. Marie Greyhounds (OHL) – 5'9" 172 ..77
- ★ Compher, JT – RC – US NTDP Under-18 Team – 5'11, 184 ..77
- ★ Comrie, Eric – G – Tri-City Americans (WHL) – 6'1" 170 ..78
- ★ Cook, Dawson – LW – US NTDP Under-18 Team – 6'1, 197 ..78
- ★ Cooper, Olivier – LW – Saint-John Sea Dogs (QMJHL) – 6'2" 197 .78
- ★ Corbett, Jeff – RD – Sudbury Wolves (OHL) – 6'1" 180 .79
- ★ Couturier, Joshua – LD – Boston Jr. Bruins (EJHL) – 6'2, 175 .79
- ★ Cox, Trevor – LW – Medicine Hat Tigers (WHL) – 5'7" 150 .79
- ★ Crisp, Connor – LC – Erie Otters (OHL) – 6'4" – 225 .79
- ★ Crunk, Taylor – LW – Victoria Royals (WHL) – 6'0" 201 .80
- ★ Crus Rydberg, Viktor – LC – Linköping (SEL) – 5'11, 190 ..80
- ★ Dauphin, Laurent – LC – Chicoutimi Saguenéens (QMJHL) – 6'0" 166 ..81
- ★ Davis, Taylor – RD – Ottawa 67's (OHL) – 6'0" 205 .81
- ★ De Jong, Nolan – LD – Victoria Grizzlies (BCHL) – 6'2" 188 .82

- de Haan, Evan – LD – Sudbury Wolves (OHL) – 5'11" 150 .82
- Dea, Jean-Sébastien – RC – Rouyn-Noranda Huskies (QMJHL) – 6'0" 160 ..82
- Dedenbach, Jared – FW – Fargo Force (USHL) – 5'8" 170 ..83
- DeKort, Jordan – G – Windsor Spitfires (OHL) – 6'4" 192 .83
- de la Rose, Jacob – LW – Leksand – Sweden – 6'2" 190 ..83
- DeLuca, Anthony – LW – Rimouski Océanic (QMJHL) – 5'9" 198 ..84
- Dempsey, Mitchell – LW – Soo Greyhounds (OHL) – 6'4" 202 ..84
- Desautels, Matthew – RD – Ottawa 67's (OHL) – 5'11" 190 .84
- Descheneau, Jaedon – RW – Kootenay Ice (WHL) 5'8" 177 ..85
- Desrochers, Danny – LW – Sudbury Wolves (OHL) – 6'0" 182 .85
- Desrosiers, Philippe – G – Rimouski Océanic (QMJHL) – 6'1" 187 ..85
- Diaby, Jonathan – LD – Victoriaville Tigres (QMJHL) – 6'5" 231 .86
- Dichiara, Frank – LW – Dubuque (USHL) - 6'05" 215 .87
- Dickinson, Jason – LW – Guelph Storm (OHL) – 6'1.25" 178 .87
- DiFruscia, Anthony – LW – Niagara Ice Dogs (OHL) – 5'10.5" 190 .88
- Dikushin, Grigory – FW – Green Bay Gamblers (USHL) – 5'8" 150 .88
- Doetzel, Kayle – RD – Red Deer Rebels (WHL) – 6'3" 191 .88
- Domi, Max – LC – London Knights (OHL) – 5'9.25" 197 .89
- Dorantes, Tyler – LD – Des Moines Buccaneers (USHL) – 6'1" 179 .90
- Downing, Michael – LD – Dubuque Fighting Saints (USHL) – 6'3" 190 ..90
- Drouin, Jonathan – LW – Halifax Mooseheads (QMJHL) – 5'11" 176 ..90
- Duclair, Anthony – LW - Québec Remparts (QMJHL) – 5'11" 182 ..91
- Dunn, Vincent – LC – Val D'Or Foreurs (QMJHL) – 5'11" 181 ..92
- Dupuy, Jean – RW – Kingston Frontenacs (OHL) – 6'2.25" 190 ..92
- Eastman, Kyle – FW – Tri-City Storm (USHL) – 5'11" 195 ..92
- Ebbing, Thomas – FW – Chicago Steel (USHL) – 5'11" 165 ..93
- Elie, Remi – LW – London Knights (OHL) – 6'0.5" 203 .93
- Ellis, Eddie – LC – Phillips Andover Academy (Prep-MA) – 6'1, 190 ..94
- Erkamps, Macoy – RD – Lethbridge Hurricanes (WHL) – 5'11" 193 ..94
- Erne, Adam – RW – Québec Remparts (QMJHL) – 6'1" 198 ..94

★ Etchegary, Kurt – LC – Québec Remparts (QMJHL) – 5'11" 185 ..95

★ Evans, Jake – LC – Erie Otters (OHL) – 6'0" 185 ..96

★ Fasching, Hudson – RW – US NTDP Under-18 Team – 6'2, 214 .96

★ Fisher, Logan – LC – Victoria Royals (WHL) – 6'2" 175 ..96

★ Fitzgerald, Ryan – LC – Valley Jr. Warriors (EJHL) – 5'9, 170 .97

★ Fitzmorris, Mitchell – LC – Niagara Ice Dogs (OHL) – 5'11" 180 .97

★ Florentino, Anthony – RD – South Kent School (HIGH-CT) – 6'1 227 ..97

★ Ford, Dakota – LD – Middlesex Islanders (EJHL) – 6'2, 185 .98

★ Fram, Jason – RD – Spokane Chiefs (WHL) – 6'0" 180 ..98

★ Fucale, Zachary – G – Halifax Mooseheads (QMJHL) – 6'1" 176 ..98

★ Gabor, Gilbert – LW – Owen Sound Attack (OHL) – 6'3" 192 ..99

★ Gamez, Garrett – FW – Tri-City Storm (USHL) – 5'11" – 180 .99

★ Ganly, Tyler – RD – Sault Ste. Marie Greyhounds (OHL) – 6'2" 197 .99

★ Garlent, Hunter – RC – Guelph Storm (OHL) – 5'8.25" 164 .100

★ Gauthier, Frédérick – LC – Rimouski Oceanic (QMJHL) – 6'4" 215 ..101

★ Geertsen, Mason – LD – Vancouver Giants (WHL) – 6'4" 203 .101

★ Genovese, Cory – LD – Sudbury Wolves (OHL) – 6'2" 201 ..102

★ Gilbert, Jared – LD – Kitchener Rangers (OHL) – 5'11" 189 ..102

★ Girard, Félix – RC – Baie-Comeau Drakkar (QMJHL) – 5'11" 190 ..103

★ Gisonti, Vincent – LC – Westminster (Prep-CT) – 5'9, 178 .103

★ Giugovaz, Michael – G – Peterborough Petes (OHL) – 6'0" 172 ..104

★ Goldberg, Andrew – RW – Mississauga Steelheads (OHL) – 5'11" 199 ..104

★ Golonka, Will – LW – Belmont Hill (Prep-MA) – 5'10, 185 .104

★ Gore, Bryson – RC – Moose Jaw Warriors (WHL) – 5'10" 182 .104

★ Gravel, Maxime – RD – Rimouski Océanic (QMJHL) – 6'0" 182 ..105

★ Graves, Ryan – LD – PEI Rocket (QMJHL) – 6'4" 225 ..105

★ Green, Taylor – LD – Seattle Thunderbirds (WHL) – 6'7" 220 ..105

★ Grégoire, Jérémy – C – Baie-Comeau Drakkar (QMJHL) – 6'0" 188 .106

★ Gross, Jordan – RD – Green Bay Gamblers (USHL) – 5'10" 178 ..106

★ Guénette, Justin – LD Rouyn-Noranda Huskies (QMJHL) – 5'11" 185 .107

2013 NHL DRAFT BLACK BOOK

- ★ Guentzel, Jake – FW – Sioux City Musketeers (USHL) – 5'9" 153..107
- ★ Guertler, Gabe – FW – Fargo Force (USHL) – 5'9" 178 .107
- ★ Guindon, Louis-Philip – G – Drummondville Voltigeurs (QMJHL) – 6'0" 167 .108
- ★ Guy, Nevin – LD – Ottawa 67's (OHL) – 5'10" 165..108
- ★ Hagg, Robert – LD – MODO (SEL) – 6'2" 204..108
- ★ Halagian, Nick – LW – Sault Ste. Marie Greyhounds (OHL) – 6'1" 199..109
- ★ Hall, Zach – LC – Barrie Colts (OHL) – 5'10.5" 172 .109
- ★ Hallisey, David – RW – Westminster (Prep-CT) – 5'10, 170..110
- ★ Hamilton, Trevor – RD – US NTDP Under-18 Team – 6'0, 181 .110
- ★ Hansen, Carter – RW – Moose Jaw Warriors (WHL) – 6'2" 191 .110
- ★ Hansson, Niklas – RD – Rögle BK (SEL) - 6'0, 173..110
- ★ Harms, Brendan – FW – Fargo Force (USHL) – 5'11" 169 .111
- ★ Harmsworth, Colby – LD – Calgary Hitmen (WHL) – 6'1" 188 .111
- ★ Harper, Stephen – LW – Erie Otters (OHL) – 6'1.25" 200..111
- ★ Harpur, Ben – LD – Guelph Storm (OHL) – 6'5.5" 210..112
- ★ Harris, Jacob – RC – Sudbury Wolves (OHL) – 6'0" 185..112
- ★ Hart, Jayden – RC – Prince Albert Raiders (WHL) – 6'1" 188..113
- ★ Hartman, Ryan – LW – Plymouth Whalers (OHL) – 5'11" 181 .113
- ★ Hauf, Jared – LD – Seattle Thunderbirds (WHL) – 6'6" 216..114
- ★ Hayden, John – RW – US NTDP Under-18 Team – 6'2, 185 .114
- ★ Heatherington, Dillon – LD – Swift Current Broncos (WHL) – 6'4" 196 .114
- ★ Heinrich, Blake – LD – Sioux City Musketeers (USHL) – 5'11" – 192 .115
- ★ Henriksson, Alexander – LW – Farjestad J20 (SWE J20) – 6'2" 190 .115
- ★ Hill, Tyler – FW – Chicago Steel (USHL) – 6'5.75" 220 .116
- ★ Hope, Brandon – G – Owen Sound Attack (OHL) – 6'0" 197 .116
- ★ Horvat, Bo – LC – London Knights (OHL) – 6'0" 206..117
- ★ Houck, Jackson – RW – Vancouver Giants (WHL) – 6'0" 184..117
- ★ Hurley, Connor – FW – Muskegon Lumberjacks (USHL) – 6'2" 175..118
- ★ Hutchison, Nick – LC – Avon Old Farms (Prep-CT) – 6'2, 180..118
- ★ Hutchinson, Ryan – RD – Kingston Frontenacs (OHL) – 6'1" 204..119

- ★ Ikonen, Jusso – RW – Blues (SM-liiga) – 5'9" 170 ..119
- ★ Ilvonen, Mika – LD – Blues U20 (Jr. A SM-liiga) – 5'8, 152 .119
- ★ Jarry, Tristan – G – Edmonton Oil Kings (WHL) – 6'2" 181 ..119
- ★ Jenkins, Jack – FW – Des Moines Buccaneers (USHL) – 5'10" 165 .120
- ★ Jensen, Spencer – RD – Medicine Hat Tigers (WHL) – 6'3" 193 ..120
- ★ Johnson, Luke – FW – Lincoln Stars (USHL) – 5'11" 178 .121
- ★ Jones, Mitch – LD – Plymouth Whalers (OHL) – 5'11" 185 ..121
- ★ Jones, Seth – RD – Portland Winterhawks (WHL) – 6'4" 206 .121
- ★ Josephs, Troy – LW – 6'1"– 180lb. – St. Michael's Buzzers (OJHL) ..122
- ★ Kahun, Dominik – LW – Sudbury Wolves (OHL) – 5'9" 160 ..122
- ★ Kanzig, Keegan – LD – Victoria Royals (WHL) – 6'5" 238 .123
- ★ Kavanagh, Shane - F, Cushing Academy (Prep-MA) – 5'11, 195 .123
- ★ Kelleher, Tyler – RC – US NTDP Under-18 Team – 5'6, 164 ..123
- ★ Kelly, Broderick – RD – Niagara Ice Dogs (OHL) – 5'11" 195 .124
- ★ Kile, Alex – FW – Green Bay Gamblers (USHL) – 5'11" 180 ..124
- ★ Kivihalme, Teemu – Burnsville (High-MN) and Fargo (USHL) – 6'0, 161 .124
- ★ Kirkup, Ryan – LC – Sault Ste. Marie Greyhounds (OHL) – 5'8" 182 ..125
- ★ Klimchuk, Morgan – LW – Regina Pats (WHL) – 5'11" 180 .125
- ★ Koivistoinen, Eetu – LC – Blues U20 (Jr A SM-liiga) – 6'2" 201 .126
- ★ Koledov, Pavel – RD – Lokomotiv Yaroslavl-2 (VHL) – 6'0" 181 ..126
- ★ Kopta, Ondrej – LW – Niagara Ice Dogs (OHL) – 6'2" 180 .127
- ★ Kostalek, Jan – RD – Rimouski Océanic (QMJHL) – 6'0" 182 .127
- ★ Krueger, Mason – LW – Avon Old Farms (Prep-CT) – 6'0, 193 ..128
- ★ Kubalik, Dominik – LW – Sudbury Wolves (OHL) – 6'1" 175 .128
- ★ Kujawinski, Ryan – LC – Kingston Frontenacs (OHL) - 6'1.5" 205 ..129
- ★ Kulda, Edgars – LW – Edmonton Oil Kings (WHL) – 5'11" 180 .129
- ★ Kuleshov, Artem – LD – Erie Otters (OHL) - 6'3" 200 .129
- ★ Kuster, Clark – RD – Cedar Rapids RoughRiders (USHL) – 5'10" 180 .130
- ★ L'Esperance, Joel – FW – Tri-City Storm (USHL) – 6'1" 195 .130
- ★ Labbé, Dylan – LD – Shawinigan Cataractes (QMJHL) – 6'2" 189 ..130

2013 NHL DRAFT BLACK BOOK

- ★ Laffin, Michael – LW – New York Apple Core (EJHL) – 5'11, 172 .131

- ★ Lafontaine, Raphael – LW – Acadie-Bathurst Titan (QMJHL) – 5'10" 176 .131

- ★ Laplante, Yan Pavel – C – PEI Rocket (QMJHL) – 6'0" 172..131

- ★ Latour, Bradley – RW – Oshawa Generals (OHL) – 5'10" 182 .132

- ★ Lazar, Curtis – RC – Edmonton Oil Kings (WHL) – 6'0" 198 .132

- ★ Lees, Jesse – RD – Kelowna Rockets (WHL) – 6'0" 180..133

- ★ Artturi Lehkonen – LW – KalPa (SM-Liiga) - 5'10" 152..133

- ★ Lemmon, Mack – RW – Niagara Ice Dogs (OHL) – 5'10" 195 .134

- ★ Lettieri, Vinni – FW – Lincoln Stars (USHL) – 5'8" 170..134

- ★ Lewington, Tyler – RD – Medicine Hat Tigers (WHL) – 6'1" 191 .135

- ★ Lewis, Clint – LD – US NTDP Under-18 Team – 6'2, 181..135

- ★ Liberati, Miles – LD – London Knights (OHL) – 5'11.5" 195 .135

- ★ Light, Connor – LD – Phillips Andover Academy (Prep-MA) – 6'5, 198..136

- ★ Liljendahl, Tobias – RC – Djurgarden J20 (SWE J20) – 6'2" 214 .136

- ★ Linaker, Cole – RC – Kelowna Rockets (WHL) – 6'1" 165..136

- ★ Lindholm, Elias – RC – Brynas (Elitserien) - 6'0" 192..137

- ★ Lipon, J.C. – RW – Kamloops Blazers (WHL) – 6'0" 181..137

- ★ Lipsbergs, Roberts – LW – Seattle Thunderbirds (WHL) – 5'11" 195..138

- ★ Locke, Eric – LC – Saginaw Spirit (OHL) – 5'9" 182..138

- ★ Lodge, Jimmy – RC – Saginaw Spirit (OHL) – 6'2" 165 .139

- ★ Lotz, Austin – G – Everett Silvertips (WHL) – 6'0" 185..139

- ★ Louis, Anthony – LW – US NTDP Under-18 Team – 5'6, 142 .140

- ★ Lysenko, Vladislav – LD – Sherbrooke Phoenix (QMJHL) – 6'0" 198 .140

- ★ MacDonald, Josh – LW – Barrie Colts (OHL) – 5'10" 186 .141

- ★ Mackey, Kyle – FW – Youngstown Phantoms (USHL) – 6'0" 167 .141

- ★ MacKinnon, Nathan – RC – Halifax Mooseheads (QMJHL) – 5'11" 179..141

- ★ Maguire, Geordie – LW – Brandon Wheat Kings (WHL) – 6'0" 165 .142

- ★ Makinen, Atte – RD – Tappara U20 (Jr A SM-liiga) – 6'3" 206..142

- ★ Maletta, Jordan – RW – Niagara Ice Dogs (OHL) – 6'3" 215..143

- ★ Malone, Sean – LC – US NTDP Under-18 Team – 5'11, 183 .143

- ★ Mansfield, Ian – FW – Sioux Falls Stampede (USHL) – 5'11" 188 .143
- ★ Mantha, Anthony – RW – Val D'Or Foreurs (QMJHL) – 6'3" 200..144
- ★ Martin, Jon – RC – Kootenay Ice (WHL) – 6'2" 201 .144
- ★ Martin, Spencer – G – Mississauga Steelheads (OHL) – 6'2.25" 198..145
- ★ McAdam, Eamon – G – Waterloo Blackhawks (USHL) – 6'2" 182..145
- ★ McCarron, Michael – RW – US NTDP Under-18 Team – 6'5, 229 .145
- ★ McCoshen, Ian – LD – Waterloo Blackhawks (USHL) – 6'3" 207..146
- ★ McCue, Beau – RW – Tri-City Americans (WHL) – 6'1" 200 .146
- ★ McGauley, Tim – LC – Brandon Wheat Kings (WHL) – 6'0" 177 .146
- ★ McGlynn, Conor – FW – Sioux City Musketeers (USHL) – 6'2" 193 .147
- ★ McIntosh, Jeremy – LD – Spokane Chiefs (WHL) – 6'2" 190..147
- ★ McLaughlin, Dylan – FW – Cedar Rapids RoughRiders (USHL) – 5'10" 171..147
- ★ McNulty, Marc – LD – Prince George Cougars (WHL) – 6'6" 189..147
- ★ Melanson, Drew – FW – Omaha Lancers (USHL) – 5'10" 160 .148
- ★ Merkley, Jay – RC – Swift Current Broncos (WHL) – 5'11" 187..148
- ★ Millette, Cory – LW – Red Deer Rebels (WHL) – 5'11" 188..148
- ★ Milne, Brody – LW – Guelph Storm (OHL) – 6'1" 157..148
- ★ Monahan, Sean – LC – Ottawa 67's (OHL) – 6'2.25" 187..149
- ★ Moore, Trevor – LW – Tri-City Storm (USHL) – 5'9 170..149
- ★ Morin, Samuel – LD – Rimouski Océanic (QMJHL) – 6'6" 203 .150
- ★ Morrissey, Josh – LD – Prince Albert Raiders (WHL) – 6'0" 185 .150
- ★ Motte, Tyler – LW – US NTDP Under-18 Team – 5'9, 184..151
- ★ Moutrey, Nick – RW – Saginaw Spirit (OHL) – 6'3" 208 .151
- ★ Moy, Tyler – FW – Omaha Lancers (USHL) – 6'1" 178..152
- ★ Mueller, Mirco – LD – Everett Silvertips (WHL) – 6'4" 185 .152
- ★ Murphy, Matt – LD – Halifax Mooseheads (QMJHL) – 6'1" 200..153
- ★ Murphy, Trevor – LD – Windsor Spitfires (OHL) – 5'10" 173 .153
- ★ Mylchreest, Michael – RD – Prince George Cougars (WHL) – 6'3" 198 .154
- ★ Nastasiuk, Zach – RW – Owen Sound Attack (OHL) – 6'1.25" 190..154
- ★ Needham, Matt – RC – Kamloops Blazers (WHL) – 5'10" 187..155

2013 NHL DRAFT BLACK BOOK

- ★ Nemecek, David – LD – Sarnia Sting (OHL) – 6'4" 206 .155
- ★ Nichols, Justin – G – Sault Ste. Marie Greyhounds (OHL) – 5'11" 150..156
- ★ Nichushkin, Valeri – RW – Traktor Chelyabinsk (KHL) – 6'4" 202 .156
- ★ Nikandrov, Daniel – LC – Sarnia Sting (OHL) – 6'2" 191..157
- ★ Nikkel, Ayrton – LD – Everett Silvertips (WHL) – 6'1" 195 .157
- ★ Norell, Robin – LD – Djurgården J20 (Superelit) – 5'11, 192 .158
- ★ Nosad, Stephen – RW – Peterborough Petes (OHL) – 5'11" 188 .158
- ★ Nurse, Darnell – LD – Sault Ste. Marie Greyhounds (OHL) – 6'5" 192..158
- ★ Oglevie, Andrew – FW – Cedar Rapids RoughRiders (USHL) – 5'9" 156 .159
- ★ Ohman, Victor – LC – MODO J20 (SWE J20) – 5'9" 170 .160
- ★ Olofsson, Gustav – LD – Green Bay Gamblers (USHL) – 6'2" 185 .160
- ★ Olsson, Ross – FW – Cedar Rapids RoughRiders (USHL) – 6'4" 200..160
- ★ Paul, Nicholas – LW – Brampton Battalion (OHL) – 6'2" 202 .161
- ★ Pawley, Corey – LW – London Knights (OHL) – 5'8" 163 .161
- ★ Pedersen, Brent – LW – Kitchener Rangers (OHL) – 6'2" 205 .161
- ★ Pellah, Bo – LD – Alberni Valley Bulldogs (BCHL) – 5'11" 139 .162
- ★ Brett Pesce – RD – University of New Hampshire (NCAA) - 6'3" 174 .162
- ★ Petan, Nicolas – LC – Portland Winterhawks (WHL) – 5'9" 166 .163
- ★ Petersen, Calvin – G – Waterloo Blackhawks (USHL) – 6'1" 175..163
- ★ Petersen, Trevor – LW – Niagara Ice Dogs (OHL) – 5'11" 200..163
- ★ Peterson, Avery – FW – Grand Rapids H.S. (USHS-MN) – 6'2" 181..164
- ★ Peterson, Elliot – LW – Calgary Hitmen (WHL) – 5'10" 188 .164
- ★ Petrash, Corey – FW – Cedar Rapids RoughRiders (USHL) – 5'9" 160 .164
- ★ Pezzetta, Stefano – LW – Owen Sound Attack (OHL) – 5'11" 190..164
- ★ Pieper, Bo – FW – Indiana Ice (USHL) – 5'11" 177..165
- ★ Pinho, Brian – RC – St. John's Prep (High-MA) – 6'1, 175..165
- ★ Pionk, Neal – RD – Sioux City Musketeers (USHL) – 5'11" 160 .165
- ★ Pittman, Zack – LD – Lincoln Stars (USHL) – 6'1" 190 .166
- ★ Platzer, Kyle – RW – London Knights (OHL) – 5'11" 185..166
- ★ Poirier, Émile – LW – Gatineau Olympiques (QMJHL) – 6'1" 183..166

- ★ Polino, Patrick – FW – Chicago Steel (USHL) – 5'8" 164 .167
- ★ Pope, David – LW – West Kelowna Warriors (BCHL) – 6'2" 193 .168
- ★ Popoff, Carter – RC – Vancouver Giants (WHL) – 5'9" 180 ..168
- ★ Possler, Gustav – LW – MODO (SEL) – 5'11" 181 ..168
- ★ Potomak, Brandon – RW – Moose Jaw Warriors (WHL) – 5'11" 165 .169
- ★ Povorozniouk, Sam – Kingston Frontenacs (OHL) – 5'10" 183 .169
- ★ Pulock, Ryan – RD – Brandon Wheat Kings (WHL) – 6'1" 211 .169
- ★ Rafikov, Rushan – LD – Yaroslavl (MHL) – 6'1 185 .170
- ★ Rankin, Connor – LC – Tri-City Americans (WHL) – 6'0" 195 .170
- ★ Reway, Martin – LW – Gatineau Olympiques (QMJHL) – 5'9" 173 .171
- ★ Ripley, Luke – LD – Powell River Kings (BCHL) – 6'3" 195 .171
- ★ Ristolainen, Rasmus – RD – TPS (SM-Liiga) - 6'3" 207 .171
- ★ Roos, Alex – FW – Chicago Steel (USHL) – 5'9" 168 .172
- ★ Roy, Eric – LD – Brandon Wheat Kings (WHL) – 6'3" 190 ..172
- ★ Roy, Marc-Olivier – RW – Blainville-Boisbriand Armada (QMJHL) – 6'1" 180 ..173
- ★ Rychel, Kerby – LW – Windsor Spitfires (OHL) – 6'1" 200 .174
- ★ Salerno, Brandon – FW – Waterloo Blackhawks (USHL) – 5'7" 169 .174
- ★ Sanche, Phillipe – RW – Blainville-Boisbriand Armada (QMJHL) – 5'5" 150 .174
- ★ Sanford, Zachary – LW – Middlesex Islanders (EJHL) – 6'3, 190 ..175
- ★ Santini, Steve – RD – US NTDP Under-18 Team – 6'2, 205 ..175
- ★ Saros, Juuse – G – HPK U20 (Jr A SM-liiga) – 5'10" 178 .176
- ★ Schiller, Landon – RW – Sault Ste. Marie Greyhounds (OHL) – 6'1" 187 .176
- ★ Schueneman, Corey – LD – Des Moines Buccaneers (USHL) – 6'3" 187 .176
- ★ Scott, Justin – RW – Barrie Colts (OHL) – 6'1" 189 ..177
- ★ Segalla, Ryan – LD – Salisbury School (Prep-CT) – 6'05", 190 .177
- ★ Shea, Brandon – LC – South Shore Kings (EJHL) – 6'2", 201 ..177
- ★ Sheen, Riley – LW – Seattle Thunderbirds (WHL) – 5'11" 156 ..178
- ★ Sherman, Wiley – LD – Hotchkiss School (Prep-CT) – 6'6", 206 ..178
- ★ Shields, Mack – G – Calgary Hitmen (WHL) – 6'3" 190 .178
- ★ Shinkaruk, Hunter – LW – Medicine Hat (WHL) – 5'11" 175 .179

2013 NHL DRAFT BLACK BOOK

- Shiplo, Luke – LD – Des Moines Buccaneers (USHL) – 5'8" 159 .179
- Silk, Brody – LW – Sudbury Wolves (OHL) – 6'0" 185 .179
- Sills, Connor – RW – Plymouth Whalers (OHL) – 6'4" 202 .180
- Siroky, Ryan – FW – Green Bay Gamblers (USHL) – 5'11" 190 .180
- Smith, Alex – RD – Indiana Ice (USHL) – 6'0" 177 ..180
- Smith, Jerret – RD – Seattle Thunderbirds (WHL) – 6'2" 198 ..181
- Smith, Hunter – RW – Oshawa Generals (OHL) – 6'7" 218 .181
- Sorensen, Nick – RW – Québec Remparts (QMJHL) – 6'1" 175 .181
- Souto, Chase – RW – Kamloops Blazers (WHL) – 5'11" 176 .182
- Stadnyk, Carson – LC – Everett Silvertips (WHL) – 6'2" 170 .182
- Stanton, Ty – LD – Medicine Hat Tigers (WHL) – 6'3" 173 ..182
- Sterk, Josh – LC – Kitchener Rangers (OHL) – 5'10" 161 ..183
- Stork, Luke – FW – Youngstown Phantoms (USHL) – 5'11" 175 ..183
- Studnicka, Sam – RW – Windsor Spitfires (OHL) – 6'1" 193 .183
- Subban, Jordan – Belleville Bulls (OHL) – 5'9" 175 ..184
- Talcott, Alex – FW – Indiana Ice (USHL) – 6'1" 198 .185
- Tambellini, Adam – LC – Surrey Eagles (BCHL) – 6'1" 174 .185
- Tanus, Jonatan – LC – Peterborough Petes (OHL) – 5'9" 184 .185
- Teskey, Scott – RW – Mississauga Steelheads (OHL) – 6'0" 186 ..186
- Theodore, Shea – LD – Seattle Thunderbirds (WHL) – 6'2" 175 .186
- Thompson, Keaton – LD – US NTDP Under-18 Team – 6'0, 185 ..187
- Tiffels, Frederik – FW – Muskegon Lumberjacks (USHL) – 6'0" 186 .187
- Tkatch, Jordan – LC – Prince George Cougars (WHL) – 5'11" 196 ..187
- Toffey, Will – LD – Salisbury School (HIGH-CT) – 6'1 185 ..187
- Tolchinsky, Sergey – LW – Soo Greyhounds (OHL) – 5'9" 160 ..188
- Topping, Joel – RD – Lethbridge Hurricanes (WHL) – 6'0" 184 ..189
- Tremblay, Simon – LW – Chicoutimi Saguenéens (QMJHL) – 6'1" 190 .189
- Tringale, Devin – LW – Valley Jr. Warriors (EJHL) – 6'0, 193 ..189
- Ully, Cole – LW – Kamloops Blazers (WHL) – 5'11" 165 .189
- Urbanic, John – RW – Ottawa 67's (OHL) – 5'11" 196 .190

- ★ Valiyev, Rinat – LD – Indiana Ice (USHL) – 6'1, 190 .190
- ★ Vanderwiel, Danny – LW – Plymouth Whalers (OHL) – 6'0" 210 .190
- ★ Tommy Vannelli – RD – Minnetonka (MN High School) - 6'2" 170 .191
- ★ Varga, Steven – LD – Peterborough Petes (OHL) – 6'3" 214 ..192
- ★ Veilleux, Tommy – LW – Victoriaville Tigres (QMJHL) – 6'0" 186 .192
- ★ Verhaeghe, Carter – LC – Niagara Ice Dogs (OHL) – 6'1" 181 .192
- ★ Vlajkov, Michael – LD – Ottawa 67's (OHL) – 6'2" 185 .193
- ★ Voltin, Luke – FW – Des Moines Buccaneers (USHL) – 6'0" 180 .193
- ★ Wallmark, Lucas – LC – Karlskrona HK (SAL) – 6'0, 176 .193
- ★ Watson, Jamal – RW – Lethbridge Hurricanes (WHL) - 6'0" 176 ..194
- ★ Webster, Michael – LD – Barrie Colts (OHL) – 6'0" 183 ..194
- ★ Weegar, Mackenzie – RD – Halifax Mooseheads (QMJHL) – 5'11" 181 ..194
- ★ Westermarck, Felix – LW – Blues U20 (Jr. A SM-liiga) – 6'1, 204 .195
- ★ Westlund, Wilhelm – LD – Färjestad (SEL) – 5'11, 185 .195
- ★ Weis, Matthew – FW – Green Bay Gamblers (USHL) – 5'10" 194 .195
- ★ Wennberg, Alexander – LW – Djurgarden (SAL) – 6'1" 183 .195
- ★ Wheaton, Mitchell – RD – Kelowna Rockets (WHL) - 6'5" 225 ..196
- ★ Whistle, Jackson – G – Kelowna Rockets (WHL) – 6'1" 185 .196
- ★ White, Torrin – RW – Moose Jaw Warriors (WHL) – 5'9" 163 ..197
- ★ Widmar, Joseph – FW – Indiana Ice (USHL) – 6'0" 199 .197
- ★ Williams, Brian – RW – Tri-City Americans (WHL) – 5'8" 170 .197
- ★ Williams, Colby – RD – Regina Pats (WHL) – 5'11" 182 ..197
- ★ Witala, Chase – LW – Prince George Cougars (WHL) – 6'0" 157 .198
- ★ Wolanin, Christian – LD – Green Bay Gamblers (USHL) – 6'0" 172 .198
- ★ Wood, Miles – LW - Nobles (HIGH-MA) - 6'1" 160 .198
- ★ Worden, Nash – LD – Omaha Lancers (USHL) – 6'0" 196 .198
- ★ Yakimov, Bogdan – RC – Dizel Penza (VHL) – 6'4" 201 .199
- ★ Yuill, Alex – LD – Barrie Colts (OHL) – 5'8" 167 ..199
- ★ Zadorov, Nikita – LD – London Knights (OHL) – 6'5.25" 221 .199
- ★ Zdrahal, Patrik – RW – Acadie-Bathurst Titan (QMJHL) – 5'11" 178 ..200

2013 NHL DRAFT BLACK BOOK

- ★ Zottl, Nick – LD – Mississauga Steelheads (OHL) – 6'4" 215..200
- ★ Zykov, Valentin – RW - Baie-Comeau Drakkar (QMJHL) – 6'1" 215..201

3. 2014 NHL DRAFT TOP 30.203

4. 2014 NHL DRAFT PROSPECTS.205

- ★ Abou-Assaly, Andrew – Ottawa 67's (OHL) – 5'11" 172 .206
- ★ Addesi, Jordan – LW – Sarnia Sting (OHL) – 6'2" – 194 .206
- ★ Atwal, Arvin – RD – Vancouver Giants (WHL) – 6'0" 188 .206
- ★ Aubé-Kubel, Nicolas – RC - Val D'Or Foreurs (QMJHL) – 5'11" 180 .207
- ★ Audette, Daniel – LC – Sherbrooke Phoenix (QMJHL) – 5'9" 168..207
- ★ Ayotte, Mathieu – RW – Victoriaville Tigres (QMJHL) – 5'10" 144..207
- ★ Baillie, Tyson – RC – Kelowna Rockets (WHL) – 5'10" 185 .207
- ★ Bahl, Julien – RD – Blainville-Boisbriand Armada (QMJHL) – 5'11" 170 .208
- ★ Baltisberger, Phil – LD – GC Kusnacht Lions (NLB) – 6'0" 210 .208
- ★ Barbashev, Ivan –LW – Moncton Wildcats (QMJHL) – 6'1" 185 .208
- ★ Bennett, Sam – LC – Kingston Frontenacs (OHL) – 6'0" 168 .209
- ★ Bergman, Julius – RD – Karlskrona (SAL) – 6'1" 187 .209
- ★ Bilia, Julio – G – Chicoutimi Saguenéens (QMJHL) – 5'11" 152..209
- ★ Bishop, Clark – LC – Cape-Breton Screaming Eagles (QMJHL) – 5'11" 173 .210
- ★ Bleackley, Connor – RC – Red Deer Rebels (WHL) – 6'0" 199 .210
- ★ Boivin, Christophe – LW – Seminaire Saint-François Blizzard (MAAA) – 5'6" 141..211
- ★ Boucher, Félix – LD – Victoriaville Tigres (QMJHL) – 6'2" 177 .211
- ★ Bourne, Damian – LW – Mississauga Steelheads (OHL) – 6'4" 211..211
- ★ Bratina, Zach – LW – Saginaw Spirit (OHL) – 6'1" 170 .211
- ★ Brown, Graeme – LD – Windsor Spitfires (OHL) – 6'1" – 184 .212
- ★ Carrier, Scott – RD – Chicoutimi Saguenéens (QMJHL) – 5'9" 170 .212
- ★ Chartier, Rourke – LW – Kelowna Rockets (WHL) – 5'10" 165 .212
- ★ Chatham, Connor – FW – Omaha Lancers (USHL) – 6'1" – 187l..213
- ★ Clarke, Blake – LW – Brampton Battalion (OHL) – 6'1" 190..213
- ★ Cornel, Eric – RC – Peterborough Petes (OHL) – 6'2" 172 .213

- ★ Côté, Vytal – RD – Acadie-Bathurst Titan (QMJHL) – 6'2" 190 .213
- ★ Cramarossa, Michael – LC – Belleville Bulls (OHL) – 6'0" 190 .214
- ★ Cummins, Conor – LD – Sudbury Wolves (OHL) – 6'2" – 205..214
- ★ Dal Colle, Michael – LW – Oshawa Generals (OHL) – 6'2" – 171..214
- ★ De Leo, Chase – LC – Portland Winterhawks (WHL) – 5'9" 172..214
- ★ De Sousa, Daniel – RD – Belleville Bulls (OHL) – 5'11" 175 .215
- ★ DeAngelo, Anthony – RD – Sarnia Sting (OHL) – 5'11" – 167 .215
- ★ Delisle-Houde, Alex – RW – Seminaire Saint-François Blizzard (MAAA) – 5'11" 164..216
- ★ Draisaitl, Leon – LC – Prince Albert Raiders (WHL) – 6'1" 198..216
- ★ Deschamps, Jonathan – LD – Sherbrooke Phoenix (QMJHL) – 6'2" 192 .216
- ★ DiPerna, Dylan – RD – Kingston Frontenacs (OHL) – 6'1" 187 .217
- ★ Dodero, Christopher – FW – Chicago Steel (USHL) – 5'8" 165..217
- ★ Donaghey, Cody – RD – Québec Remparts (QMJHL) – 6'1" 182..217
- ★ Duchesne, Jonathan – LD – Ottawa 67's (OHL) – 6'1" 204..217
- ★ Ekblad, Aaron – RD – Barrie Colts (OHL) – 6'4" 213..218
- ★ Fabbri, Robby – LC – Guelph Storm (OHL) – 5'10" 160..218
- ★ Fleury, Haydn – LD – Red Deer Rebels (WHL) – 6'3" 204..219
- ★ Foster, Thomas – LC – Vancouver Giants (WHL) – 5'10" 160 .219
- ★ Friedman, Mark – RD – Waterloo Blackhawks (USHL) – 5'10" 180 .219
- ★ Gardiner, Reid – RC – Prince Albert Raiders (WHL) – 5'10" 179 .220
- ★ Garland, Conor – RW – Moncton Wildcats (QMJHL) – 5'6" 150 .220
- ★ Goldobin, Nikolay – RW – Sarnia Sting (OHL) – 5'11" – 165..220
- ★ Hargrave, Brett – RC – Sarnia Sting (OHL) – 6'4" – 206..221
- ★ Hawryluk, Jayce – RC – Brandon Wheat Kings (WHL) – 5'10" 186 .221
- ★ Haydon, Aaron – RD – Niagara Ice Dogs (OHL) – 6'3" 185 .221
- ★ Hiddink, Brook – RW – Niagara Ice Dogs (OHL) – 5'11" 195..221
- ★ Highmore, Matthew – LW – Saint-John Sea Dogs (QMJHL) – 5'11" 172..222
- ★ Hodgson, Hayden – RW – Erie Otters (OHL) – 6'1" 190..222
- ★ Honka, Julius – RD – JYP U20 (Jr. A SM-liiga) – 5'10" 167 .222
- ★ Hore, Tyler – RD – Sarnia Sting (OHL) – 6'3" – 182..223

2013 NHL DRAFT BLACK BOOK

- ★ Ho-Sang, Joshua – RW – Windsor Spitfires (OHL) – 5'11" – 160 .223
- ★ Iverson, Keegan – RC – Portland Winterhawks (WHL) – 6'0" 215..223
- ★ Jacobs, Joshua – RD – Indiana Ice (USHL) – 6'2" 190 .224
- ★ Jammes, Jacob – RW – London Knights (OHL) – 5'10" 180..224
- ★ Jenkins, Kyle – LD – Sault Ste. Marie Greyhounds (OHL) – 6'0" – 160 .224
- ★ Kapanen, Kasperi – LW – KalPa (SM-liiga) – 5'10" 165 .224
- ★ Karlsson, Anton – RW – Frolunda (SEL) – 6'0" 190 .225
- ★ Kempe, Adrian – LC – MODO J20 (SWE J20) – 6'1" 170 .225
- ★ Keskitalo, Miro – LD – Jokerit U18 (Jr B SM-liiga) – 6'1" 168 .225
- ★ Kiviranta, Joel – RW – Jokerit U20 (Jr. A SM-liiga) – 5'10" 154..226
- ★ Larkin, Dylan – LC – USNTDP (USHL) – 6'0" 172..226
- ★ Lazarev, Maxim – LW – AK Bars Kazan (MHL) – 5'9" 148 .226
- ★ Leblanc, Olivier – LD – Saint-John Sea Dogs (QMJHL) – 5'11" 166..226
- ★ Lee, Payton – G – Vancouver Giants (WHL) – 6'0" 175..227
- ★ Lemieux, Brendan – LW – Barrie Colts (OHL) – 6'0" 194 .227
- ★ Leone, Luca – RW – Vancouver Giants (WHL) – 6'0" 190 .228
- ★ Lindblom, Oskar – RW – Brynas J18 (SWE J18) – 6'0" 185 .228
- ★ Lindo, Jaden – RW – Owen Sound Attack (OHL) – 6'1" – 194 .228
- ★ Linhart, Jake – LD – Green Bay Gamblers (USHL) – 5'9" 152 .228
- ★ Llewellyn, Darby – RW – Kitchener Rangers (OHL) – 6'1" 173..229
- ★ Locke, Kyle – RD – Guelph Storm (OHL) – 6'2" 195..229
- ★ Lyamkin, Nikita – LD – Kuznetskie Medvedi (MHL) – 6'3" 165..229
- ★ MacDonald, Mason – G – Acadie-Bathurst Titan (QMJHL) – 6'3" 170..230
- ★ MacIntyre, Bobby – LW – Mississauga Steelheads (OHL) – 5'8" 175 .230
- ★ MacInnis, Ryan – LC – USNTDP (USHL) – 6'3" 161..230
- ★ MacIntyre, Duncan – LD – Quebec Remparts (QMJHL) – 5'11" 189..230
- ★ MacSorley, Mac – FW – Youngstown Phantoms (USHL) – 5'10" 201..231
- ★ Maheux, Raphaël – LD – Shawinigan Cataractes (QMJHL) – 6'1" 216..231
- ★ Mallette, Trent – RW – Sault Ste. Marie Greyhounds (OHL) – 5'10" – 165 .231
- ★ Malone, Seamus – FW – Dubuque Fighting Saints (USHL) – 5'9" 158..231

- ★ Mantha, Ryan – RD – Sioux City Musketeers (USHL) – 6'4" 208 .232
- ★ Mappin, Ty – RC – Everett Silvertips (WHL) – 5'11" 170..232
- ★ Martin, Brycen – LD – Swift Current Broncos (WHL) – 6'1" 181 .232
- ★ Mayo, Dysin – RD – Edmonton Oil Kings (WHL) – 6'0" 173..233
- ★ McCann, Jared – LC – Sault Ste. Marie Greyhounds (OHL) – 6'0" – 174 .233
- ★ McKeown, Roland – RD – Kingston Frontenacs (OHL) – 6'1" 186 .234
- ★ McSween, Guillaume – LD – Chateauguay Grenadiers (MAAA) – 6'4" 215..234
- ★ Middleton, Jacob – LD – Ottawa 67's (OHL) – 6'3" 194..234
- ★ Mikulovich, Alexander – LD – Belie Medvedi Chelyabinsk (MHL) 6'3" 179 .235
- ★ Milan, Cody – FW – Sioux Falls Stampede (USHL) – 6'0" – 163lb..235
- ★ Milano, Sonny– LW – USNTDP (USHL) – 5'10" 159..235
- ★ Mistele, Matthew – LW – Plymouth Whalers (OHL) – 6'2" – 183 .236
- ★ Moody, Zach – LC – Cape Breton Screaming Eagles (QMJHL) – 6'1" 160..236
- ★ Moran, Brent – G – Niagara Ice Dogs (OHL) – 6'3" 180..236
- ★ Morrison, Tyler – LD – Vancouver Giants (WHL) – 5'11" 183 .236
- ★ Nantel, Julien – LW – Laval-Montréal Rousseau-Royal (MAAA) – 6'0" 168 .237
- ★ Nasybullin, Eduard – RD – Irbis Kazan (MHL B) – 5'9" 148 .237
- ★ Nedeljkovic, Alex – G – Plymouth Whalers (OHL) – 6'0" – 186..237
- ★ Neil, Carl – RD – Sherbrooke Phoenix (QMJHL) – 6'1" 195..238
- ★ Nikolishin, Ivan – LC – CSKA Moskva (MHL) – 5'8" 148 .238
- ★ Nylander Altelius, William – LW – Sodertalje (SAL) – 5'10" 170 .238
- ★ Ollas Mattsson, Adam – LD – Djurgarden J18 (SWE J18) – 6'3" 192..239
- ★ Pastorious, Nick – Sault Ste. Marie Greyhounds (OHL) – 6'1" – 194..239
- ★ Pépin, Alexis – LC – PEI Rocket (QMJHL) – 6'2" 196..239
- ★ Petti, Niki – LC – Belleville Bulls (OHL) – 6'0" 175 .240
- ★ Pettit, Kyle – LC – Erie Otters (OHL) – 6'3" 175 .240
- ★ Philp, Luke – RC – Kootenay Ice (WHL) – 5'9" 169 .240
- ★ Point, Brayden – RC – Moose Jaw Warriors (WHL) – 5'8" 155 .240
- ★ Poganski, Austin – RW – St. Cloud Cathedral (USHS-MN) – 6'1" 195 .241
- ★ Prophet, Brandon – LD – Saginaw Spirit (OHL) – 6'2" 196 .241

2013 NHL DRAFT BLACK BOOK

- ★ Ratelle, Joey – LW – Drummondville Voltigeurs (QMJHL) – 5'10" 163 .241
- ★ Reinhart, Sam – RC – Kootenay Ice (WHL) – 6'0" 182 .242
- ★ Renaud, Alexandre – LW – Sarnia Sting (OHL) – 6'4" – 214 ..242
- ★ Ritchie, Nick – LW – Peterborough Petes (OHL) – 6'2" 218 ..242
- ★ Sadowy, Dylan – LW – Saginaw Spirit (OHL) – 6'2" 180 ..243
- ★ Sandhu, Tyler – RC – Everett Silvertips (WHL) – 5'10" 155 ..243
- ★ Sanvido, Patrick – LD – Windsor Spitfires (OHL) – 6'6" – 220 ..243
- ★ Schmalz, Matt – RC – Sudbury Wolves (OHL) – 6'5" – 186 ..244
- ★ Schmaltz, Nick – FW – Green Bay Gamblers (USHL) – 5'11" 160 ..244
- ★ Serebryakov, Nikita – G – Saginaw Spirit (OHL) – 5'11" 162 ..244
- ★ Sergeyev, Dmitri – LD – Belie Medvedi Chelyabinsk (MHL) – 6'0" 172 ..244
- ★ Shirley, Colin – LC – Kootenay Ice (WHL) – 6'1" 172 ..245
- ★ Spinozzi, Kevin – LD – Sault Ste. Marie Greyhounds (OHL) – 6'2" – 195 .245
- ★ Subban, Marselis – RD – Saginaw Spirit (OHL) – 6'0" 193 .245
- ★ Thrower, Josh – RD – Calgary Hitmen (WHL) – 6'0" 194 .246
- ★ Tuch, Alex – RW – USNTDP (USHL) – 6'3" 219 ..246
- ★ Turgeon, Dominic – LC – Portland Winterhawks (WHL) – 6'1" 191 ..246
- ★ Vanier, Alexis – LD – Baie-Comeau Drakkar (QMJHL) – 6'4" 210 .247
- ★ Verbeek, Ryan – LC – Windsor Spitfires (OHL) – 5'11" – 181 .247
- ★ Vickerman, Taylor – LW – Vancouver Giants (WHL) – 6'1" 181 .247
- ★ Virtanen, Jake – RW – Calgary Hitmen (WHL) – 6'1" 190 ..248
- ★ Watson, Matthew – LD – Kingston Frontenacs (OHL) – 5'10" 157 .248
- ★ Watson, Spencer – RW – Kingston Frontenacs (OHL) – 5'10" 157 .248
- ★ Wesley, Joshua – RD – USNTDP (USHL) – 6'2" 188 ..249
- ★ Wilkie, Chris – RW – USNTDP (USHL) – 5'10" 172 .249
- ★ Wood, Travis – LD – Erie Otters (OHL) – 5'11" 175 ..249
- ★ Yetman, Nathan – LC – PEI Rocket (QMJHL) – 5'8" 165 ..249
- ★ Zalitach, Reid – RD – Vancouver Giants (WHL) – 6'0" 175 .250
- ★ Zinoviev, Ilya – RW – Belie Medvedi Chelyabinsk (MHL) – 5'10" 185 ..250

5. 2015 NHL DRAFT PROSPECTS.251

- ★ Addison, Jeremiah – RW – Saginaw Spirit (OHL) – 6'0" 183 .252
- ★ Alain, Alexandre – RW – Blizzard du Saint-François (LHMAAAQ) – 5'10" 157 ..252
- ★ Baer, Alec – RC – Vancouver Giants (WHL) – 5'10" 150 ..252
- ★ Baird, Mike – LW – Southern Tier Admirals (OMHA) – 6'1" 171 ..253
- ★ Barwell, Jesse – LC – Oakville Rangers (OMHA) – 5'10" 175 .253
- ★ Barzal, Mathew – RC – Seattle Thunderbirds (WHL) – 5'11" 170 ..253
- ★ Beauvillier, Anthony – C – Collège Antoine-Girouard (LHMAAAQ) – 5'9" 159 .254
- ★ Bell, Jason – LD – Laval-Montréal Rousseau-Royal (LHMAAAQ) – 6'1" 185 ..254
- ★ Birdsall, Chris – G – Cedar Rapids RoughRiders (USHL) – 5'10" 160 .254
- ★ Bittner, Paul – LW – Portland Winterhawks (WHL) – 6'4" 194 .255
- ★ Booth, Callum – G – Salisbury Prep School (USHS) – 6'2" 185 .255
- ★ Bracco, Jeremy – RC – NJ Rockets (AJHL) – 5'9" 137 ..255
- ★ Bricknell, Jake – RC – Central Ontario Wolves (OMHA) – 5'11" 194 ..255
- ★ Brisebois, Guillaume – LD – Collège Antoine-Girouard (LHMAAAQ) – 5'11" 152 ..256
- ★ Bruce, Riley – RD – Ottawa Valley Titans (ODHA) – 6'4" 182 ..256
- ★ Burns, Andrew – LD – Oakville Rangers (OMHA) – 5'11" 165 .256
- ★ Bushnell, Noah – RW – Sun County Panthers (MHAO) – 6'2" 200 .256
- ★ Capobianco, Kyle – LD – Oakville Rangers (OMHA) – 6'0" 155 .257
- ★ Cascagnette, Jacob – LW – Kitchener Jr. Rangers (MHAO) – 6'2" 179 .257
- ★ Chabot, Thomas – LD – Commandeurs de Levis (LHMAAAQ) – 6'0" 169 ..257
- ★ Ciccarelli, Matteo – RC – Sarnia Sting (OHL) – 5'9" 181 .258
- ★ Connor, Kyle – FW – Youngstown Phantoms (USHL) – 6'0" 160 .258
- ★ Coyle, Josh – C – Elgin-Middlesex Chiefs (MHAO) – 6'3" 195 ..258
- ★ Craievich, Adam – RW – Oakville Rangers (OMHA) – 6'0" 189 ..258
- ★ Crawford, Marcus – LD – South Central Coyotes (OMHA) – 5'10" 178 ..259
- ★ Crouse, Lawson – LW – Elgin-Middlesex Chiefs (MHAO) – 6'3" 189 .259
- ★ Davies, Michael – LW – Southern Tier Admirals (OMHA) – 6'1" 198 .259
- ★ De Farias, Joshua – LD – Toronto Marlboros (GTHL) – 5'11" 172 .259

2013 NHL DRAFT BLACK BOOK

- ★ Deschenes, Luc – RD – Fredericton Canadiens (NBPEIMMHL) – 5'11" 197 .260
- ★ Eichel, Jack – RC – USNTDP (USHL) – 6'1" 177 ..260
- ★ Fanjoy, Ben – C – Ottawa Jr. Senators (ODHA) – 6'1" 174 ..260
- ★ Franzen, Gustav – RC – HV71 J20 (SWE J20) – 5'11" 161 .261
- ★ Galipeau, Olivier – LD – Phénix du Collège Esther-Blondin (LHMAAAQ) – 6'1" 190 ..261
- ★ Gerhart, Austin – RW – Barrie Colts AAA (OMHA) – 6'0" 175 .261
- ★ Greenway, Jordan – LW – Shattuck St. Mary's (USA) – 6'5" 205 ..261
- ★ Hanifin, Noah – LD – St. Sebastian's School (Prep-MA) – 6'3" 185 .262
- ★ Harding, Sam – C – York-Simcoe Express (OMHA) – 6'0" 161 ..262
- ★ Henley, David – LD – Forestiers d'Amos (LHMAAAQ) – 6'2" 174 .262
- ★ Holmes, Michael – LD – Barrie Colts (OMHA) – 6'2" 166 ..262
- ★ Helvig, Jeremy – G – Toronto Red Wings (GTHL) – 6'3" 194 ..263
- ★ Henley, Troy – RD – Oakville Rangers (OMHA) – 5'11" 186 .263
- ★ Kaura, Rocky – RD – Mississauga Rebels (GTHL) – 6'2" 200 .263
- ★ Knott, Graham – LW – York-Simcoe Express (OMHA) – 6'2" 158 .264
- ★ Konecny, Travis – C – Elgin-Middlesex Chiefs (MHAO) – 5'9" 162 .264
- ★ Korostelev, Nikita – RW – Toronto Jr. Canadiens (GTHL) – 6'0" 187 ..264
- ★ Kovacs, Robin – LW – AIK J18 (SWE J18) – 6'0" 157 .265
- ★ Kreis, Matthew – LC – Halton Hurricanes (OMHA) – 5'10" 155 .265
- ★ Kreis, Mitchell – RD – Halton Hurricanes (OMHA) – 5'11" 139 .265
- ★ Laishram, Adam – RW – Whitby Wildcats (OMHA) – 5'8" 155 .265
- ★ Lemcke, Justin – RD – Whitby Wildcats (OMHA) – 6'2" 192 .266
- ★ Lizotte, Cameron – LD – Nickel City Sons (NOHA) – 6'1" 185 ..266
- ★ MacArthur, Tyler – RD – Barrie Jr. Colts (OMHA) – 6'3" 174 ..266
- ★ Marner, Mitchell – RC – Don Mills Flyers (GTHL) – 5'8" 130 .266
- ★ Mayo, Cole – RD – Elgin-Middlesex Chiefs (MHAO) – 6'0" 200 .267
- ★ McCool, Hayden – C – Whitby Wildcats (OMHA) – 6'3" 190 .267
- ★ McDavid, Connor – LC – Erie Otters (OHL) – 5'11" 175 ..267
- ★ McFadden, Garrett – LD – Grey-Bruce Highlanders (OMHA) – 5'10" 195 .268
- ★ McKenzie, Brett – LC – Oakville Rangers (OMHA) – 6'1" 181 ..268

- ★ Meloche, Nicolas – RD – Vikings de St-Eustache (LHMAAAQ) – 6'1" 200..268
- ★ Mercer, Cullen – RC – Huron-Perth Lakers (MHAO) – 5'11" 168 .269
- ★ Miller, David – RC – Sault Ste. Marie Greyhounds (OHL) – 5'10" 155..269
- ★ Moore, Ryan – C – Detroit Belle Tire (USA T1) – 5'8" 150 .269
- ★ Murray, Liam – LD – Eastern Ontario Wild (ODMHA) – 6'0" 191 .269
- ★ Musil, Adam – RC – Red Deer Rebels (WHL) – 6'1" 182 .270
- ★ Myllari, Kris – LD – Ottawa Jr. Senators (ODHA) – 6'1" 173 .270
- ★ Noel, Nathan – C – Shattuck St-Mary's Midget Prep (USHS) – 5'10" 158..270
- ★ Orban, Ryan – LD – Ottawa Valley Titans (ODHA) – 6'2" 205..270
- ★ Petawabano, Cody – LW – Oakville Rangers (SCTA) – 6'3" 225..271
- ★ Pilon, Ryan – LD – Lethbridge Hurricanes (WHL) – 6'2" 197 .271
- ★ Rantanen, Mikko – RW – TPS (SM-liiga) – 6'1" 179..271
- ★ Robertson, Daniel – LD – Windsor Jr. Spitfires (MHAO) – 6'0" 155 .272
- ★ Roy, Jeremy – RD – Collège Antoine-Girouard (LHMAAAQ) – 5'11" 186 .272
- ★ Roy, Nicolas – C/RW – Forestiers d'Amos (LHMAAAQ) – 6'3" 168..272
- ★ Saarela, Aleksi – RW – Lukko U20 (Jr. A SM-liiga) – 5'10" 187..273
- ★ Saban, Jesse – LD – Toronto Red Wings (GTHL) – 6'2" 195 .273
- ★ Salituro, Dante – RC – Ottawa 67's (OHL) – 5'8" 187..273
- ★ Schlichting, Connor – LD – York-Simcoe Express (OMHA) – 6'2" 192 .273
- ★ Senyshyn, Zachary – RW – Ottawa Jr. Senators (ODMHA) – 6'1" 175 .274
- ★ Speers, Blake – C – SOO Thunder (NOHA) – 5'10" 157..274
- ★ Spencer, Matthew – RD – Oakville Rangers (OMHA) – 6'1" 192..274
- ★ Sprong, Daniel – RW – Tigres du Lac Saint-Louis (Midget Esp) – 5'10" 165..275
- ★ Stephens, Mitchell – RC – Toronto Marlboros (GTHL) – 5'10" 166 .275
- ★ Strome, Dylan – C – Toronto Marlboros (GTHL) – 6'2" – 170 .276
- ★ Svechnikov, Yevgeni – RW – AK Bars Kazan (MHL) – 6'0" 170..276
- ★ Szypula, Ethan – RC – London Jr. Knights Gold (MHAO) – 5'10" – 154lb..276
- ★ Thompson, Will – RD – Rothesay Netherwood (CAHS) – 5'10" 152..277
- ★ Tretiak, Maxim – G – CSKA Moskva (MHL) – 6'3" 206..277
- ★ Vande Sompel, Mitchell – London Jr. Knights Gold (MHAO) – LD – 5'10" 171 .277

- ★ Webb, Jack – LW – Toronto Marlboros (GTHL) – 6'2" 170..277
- ★ Webb, Mitchell – LW – Toronto Marlboros (GTHL) – 6'1" 174 .278
- ★ Werenski, Zack – RD – Detroit Little Caesars (HPHL) – 6'2" 200..278
- ★ White, Colin – RW – Noble and Greenough School (Prep-MA) – 6'1" 175 .278
- ★ White, Colton – LD – London Jr. Knights Gold (MHAO) – 5'11" 177 .278
- ★ Wilkie, Zach – RD – Toronto Jr. Canadiens (GTHL) – 6'0" 166 .279
- ★ Worrad, Drew – LC – Elgin-Middlesex Chiefs (MHAO) – 5'11" 146..279
- ★ Yetman, Bryce – RW – Whitby Wildcats (OMHA) – 6'1" 147 .279
- ★ Zeppieri, David – C – Mississauga Rebels (GTHL) – 6'1" 182..280

6. 2016 NHL DRAFT PROSPECTS.281

- ★ Allard, Frédéric – RD – Blizzard du Séminaire Saint-François (LHMAAAQ) – 5'11" 152 .282
- ★ Bastien, Nathan – C – Kitchener Jr. Rangers (MHAO) – 6'0" 157..282
- ★ Brookshaw, Carson – LW – Elgin-Middlesex Chiefs (MHAO) – 5'9" 174 .282
- ★ Brunet, Brody – RC – Nickel City Sons (NOHA) – 5'10" 193 .282
- ★ Carroll, Noah – RD – Elgin-Middlesex Chiefs (MHAO) – 6'0" 159..283
- ★ Cormier, Evan – G – Clarington Toros (OMHA) – 6'2" 176 .283
- ★ Day, Sean – LD – Detroit Compuware (HPHL) – 6'1" 180..283
- ★ Gauthier, Julien – RW – Rousseau-Royal de Laval-Montréal (LHMAAAQ) 6'2" 205 .283
- ★ House, Brent – RW – London Jr. Knights Gold (MHAO) – 6'0" 156..284
- ★ Kirwan, Luke – LW – Middlesex Islanders (EJHL) – 6'1" 216 .284
- ★ Morin, Alex – LD – Sault Ste. Marie Thunder (NOHA) – 5'10" 177..284
- ★ Timpano, Troy – Toronto Titans (GTHL) – 5'11" 174 .284
- ★ Tkachuk, Matthew – LW – St. Louis Blues AAA – 5'11" 165 .285
- ★ Verbeek, Hayden – C – Sun County Panthers (MHAO) – 5'9" 155 .285

7. SCOUTS GAME REPORTS.287

- ★ April 14, 2012, Finland vs. Canada (U18 World Championship)..289
- ★ April 16, 2012, Czech Republic vs. Canada (U18 World Championships) .289
- ★ April 17, 2012, Finland vs. Czech Republic (U18 World Championships)..290
- ★ April 17, 2012, Sweden vs. Russia (U18 World Championship)..291

- April 19, 2012, Canada vs. Russia (U18 World Championship)..291
- April 20, 2012, Czech Republic vs. Latvia (U18 World Championships)..292
- June 24, 2012, USA Black vs. USA Orange (US Select 17) .293
- June 24, 2012, USA Royal Blue vs. USA Red (US Select 17) .293
- June 24, 2012, USA Kelly Green vs. USA Grey (US Select 17)..294
- June 24, 2012, USA Columbia Blue vs. USA Gold (US Select 17)..295
- June 24, 2012, USA Forest Green vs. USA White (US Select 17)..296
- June 25, 2012, USA Kelly Green vs. USA Gold (US Select 17) .297
- June 25, 2012, USA Columbia Blue vs. USA White (US Select 17) .297
- June 25, 2012, USA Forest Green vs. USA Orange (US Select 17) .298
- June 25, 2012, USA Black vs. USA Red (US Select 17) .298
- August 4, 2012, Team Red vs. Team White (Team Canada U18 Camp) .299
- August 5, 2012, Team Red vs. Team White (Team Canada U18 Camp) .301
- August 24, 2012, Victoriaville Tigres vs. Drummondville Voltigeurs (QMJHL)..303
- August 25, 2012, Chatham Maroons @ Sarnia Legionnaires (GOJHL)..304
- September 7, 2012, Sherbrooke Phoenix vs Victoriaville Tigres (QMJHL)..304
- Sept 7, 2012 Chilliwack Chiefs vs. Penticton Vees (BCHL)..306
- Sept 7, 2012, Victoria Grizzlies vs. Coquitlam Express (BCHL) .307
- Sept 8, 2012, Prince George Spruce Kings vs. Merritt Centennials (BCHL) .308
- Sept 8, 2012, Salmon Arm Silverbacks vs. West Kelowna Warriors (BCHL)..309
- Sept 8, 2012, Cowichan Valley Capitals vs. Trail Smoke Eaters (BCHL)..309
- Sept 9, 2012, Vernon Vipers vs. Powell River Kings (BCHL) .310
- Sept 9, 2012, Coquitlam Express vs. Cowichan Valley Capitals (BCHL)..311
- Sept 9, 2012, Prince George Spruce Kings vs. Langley Rivermen (BCHL)..311
- September 9, 2012, Drummondville Voltigeurs vs Victoriaville (QMJHL) .312
- September 19, 2012, Dubuque Fighting Saints v Tri-City Storm (USHL) .313
- Sept 19, 2012, Cedar Rapids vs. Des Moines (USHL) .314
- Sept 21, 2012, Green Bay Gamblers vs. Fargo Force (USHL) .315
- September 21, 2012, Chicoutimi Saguenéens vs. Québec Remparts (QMJHL) .316
- September 21, 2012, Rimouski Oceanic vs Sherbrooke (QMJHL) .318

2013 NHL DRAFT BLACK BOOK

- Sep 21 2012, Québec Remparts @ Chicoutimi Saguenéens, (QMJHL)..319
- Sep 22 2012, Gatineau Olympiques @ Chicoutimi Saguenéens (QMJHL)..320
- September 21, 2012, USA U18 v Sioux City Musketeers (USHL)..320
- September 21, 2012, Belleville Bulls @ Sarnia Sting (OHL) .322
- September 22, 2012, Muskegon Lumberjacks v Lincoln Stars (USHL)..323
- September 22, 2012 Portland Winterhawks @ Seattle Thunderbirds (WHL) .324
- September 23, 2012 Prince George Cougars @ Everett Silvertips (WHL)..325
- September 23, 2012, Kitchener Rangers @ Sarnia Sting (OHL) .326
- Sep 23 2012, Drummondville Voltigeurs @ Sherbrooke Phoenix, (QMJHL) .327
- Sep 26 2012, Victoriaville Tigres @ Chicoutimi Saguenéens, (QMJHL)..328
- Sept 28, 2012, Shawinigan Cataractes @ Victoriaville Tigres, (QMJHL) .329
- Sept 28, 2012, Québec Remparts @ Sherbrooke Phoenix, (QMJHL) .330
- September 28, 2012, Rouyn-Noranda Huskies vs. Drummondville Voltigeurs (QMJHL)..331
- September 28, 2012, Sault Ste. Marie Greyhounds @ Sarnia Sting (OHL) .332
- Sept 28, 2012, Vancouver Giants vs Everett Silvertips .333
- Sept 29 CCM All-American Prospects Game (Buffalo New York) .334
- September 29, 2012, Baie-Comeau Drakkar vs. Victoriaville Tigres (QMJHL)..335
- September 29, 2012, Val-D'Or Foreurs vs. Drummondville Voltigeurs (QMJHL) .336
- Sept 30, 2012, Vancouver Giants vs Spokane Chiefs (WHL)..337
- Oct 04, 2012, Victoriaville Tigres @ Rimouski Océanic. (QMJHL)..338
- Oct. 05 2012, Moncton Wildcats @ Chicoutimi Saguenéens, (QMJHL)..338
- October 5, 2012, Youngstown Phantoms vs Waterloo Blackhawks (USHL) .339
- October 5, 2012, Owen Sound Attack @ Sarnia Sting (OHL)..340
- October 5, 2012, Portland Winterhawks @ Brandon Wheat Kings (WHL) .341
- October 5, 2012, Acadie- Bathurst Titan @ Baie-Comeau Drakkar (QMJHL)..342
- October 6th, 2012 Everett Silvertips @ Seattle Thunderbirds (WHL)..343
- October 6, 2012, US NTDP Under-18 at University of Wisconsin..344
- October 7, 2012, US NTDP Under-18 at University of Notre Dame..344
- October 9, 2012, Portland Winterhawks @ Regina Pats (WHL) .345
- October 10, 2012, Baie-Comeau Drakkar vs. Victoriaville Tigres (QMJHL)..346

- ★ October 12, 2012, Boston Jr. Bruins vs. Valley Jr. Warriors (EJHL) .347
- ★ October 12, 2012, South Shore Kings vs. Portland Jr. Pirates (EJHL) .348
- ★ October 12, 2012, Plymouth Whalers @ London Knights (OHL) .348
- ★ Oct 12, 2012, Vancouver Giants vs Seattle Thunderbirds (WHL) ..349
- ★ Oct 12, 2012, Prince Albert Raiders vs. Portland Winterhawks (WHL) .350
- ★ October 13, 2012, Baie-Comeau Drakkar @ Rimouski Oceanic (QMJHL) ..351
- ★ October 13, 2012, Niagara Ice Dogs @ Sarnia Sting (OHL) ..352
- ★ October 13, 2012, Halifax Mooseheads vs. Drummondville Voltigeurs (QMJHL) .353
- ★ October 13, 2012, Halifax Mooseheads vs. Shawinigan (QMJHL) ..354
- ★ OCT 13, 2013, Swift Current Broncos vs. Portland Winterhawks (WHL) ..355
- ★ October 14, 2012, Sault Ste. Marie Greyhounds @ Sarnia Sting (OHL) .356
- ★ Oct 16, 2012, USNTDP U18 vs Muskegon Lumberjacks (USHL) ..357
- ★ October 17, 2012, Indiana Ice @ Green Bay Gamblers (USHL) ..358
- ★ Oct 17, 2012, Lethbridge Hurricanes vs. Brandon Wheat Kings (WHL) ..359
- ★ October 18, 2012, Mississauga Steelheads @ Sarnia Sting (OHL) ..360
- ★ October 19, 2012, Everett Silvertips @ Prince Albert Raiders (WHL) ..362
- ★ October 19, 2012, Québec Remparts vs. Victoriaville Tigres (QMJHL) .362
- ★ October 19, 2012, Sarnia Sting at Guelph Storm (OHL) ..364
- ★ Oct 19, 2012, Sioux City Musketeers vs. Youngstown Phantoms (USHL) .364
- ★ Oct 20, 2012, Chicago Steel vs Muskegon Lumberjacks (USHL) .366
- ★ Oct 20, 2012, Kingston Frontenacs vs Niagara IceDogs (OHL) ..366
- ★ October 20, 2012, London Knights at Barrie Colts (OHL) .367
- ★ October 20, 2012, Kitchener Rangers @ Sarnia Sting (OHL) ..368
- ★ Oct 20, 2012, Swift Current Broncos vs. Tri-City Americans (WHL) ..369
- ★ Oct 21, 2012, Kingston Frontenacs vs Kitchener Rangers (OHL) .370
- ★ Oct 23, 2012, Indiana Ice vs. USNTDP (USHL) .370
- ★ Oct 24, 2012, Vancouver Giants vs Brandon Wheat Kings (WHL) ..372
- ★ October 25, 2012, Windsor Spitfires @ Sarnia Sting (OHL) ..373
- ★ October 24, 2012, Saginaw Spirit at Erie Otters (OHL) ..375
- ★ October 25, 2012, Acadie-Bathurst Titan vs. Victoriaville Tigres (QMJHL) ..375

2013 NHL DRAFT BLACK BOOK

- ★ October 26, 2012, Sault Ste. Marie Greyhounds at Erie Otters (OHL) .376
- ★ October 26, 2012, Guelph Storm @ London Knights (OHL) ..377
- ★ Oct 27, 2012, Waterloo Blackhawks vs. USNTDP U 17 (USHL) ..378
- ★ Oct 27, 2012, Sioux City Musketeers vs. Chicago Steel (USHL) .379
- ★ Oct 28, 2012, Green Bay Gamblers vs. USNTDP U 17s (USHL) .380
- ★ November 1, 2012, Oshawa Generals @ Peterborough Petes (OHL) .382
- ★ Oct 27, 2012, Medicine Hat Tigers vs. Regina Pats (WHL) ..383
- ★ Oct 27, 2012, Edmonton Oil Kings vs. Kelowna Rockets (WHL) .384
- ★ Oct 31, 2012, Portland Winterhawks vs. Everett Silvertips (WHL) .385
- ★ November 2, 2012, Val d'Or Foreurs @ Victoriaville Tigres (QMJHL) .386
- ★ November 2nd 2012, Val-D'Or Foreurs vs. Victoriaville Tigres (QMJHL) .387
- ★ November 3, 2012, Halifax Mooseheads vs. Drummondville Voltigeurs (QMJHL) .388
- ★ November 3, 2012, Halifax Mooseheads @ Drummondville (QMJHL) .389
- ★ Nov. 3, 2012, Sudbury Wolves vs. Ottawa 67s (OHL) ..389
- ★ Nov 4, 2012, Rimouski Oceanic vs. Halifax Mooseheads (QMJHL) ..391
- ★ November 4, 2012, Val d'Or Foreurs @ Gatineau Olympiques (QMJHL) ..392
- ★ Nov 5, 2012, Czech Republic vs. Russia (World Junior A Challenge) ..393
- ★ Nov 5, 2012, QMJHL vs. Russia (Subway Super Series Game 1) ..394
- ★ Nov 5, 2012, Team USA vs. Team Canada East (World Junior A Challenge) .395
- ★ Nov 6, 2012, Barrie Colts vs. Peterborough Petes (OHL) ..396
- ★ Nov 6, 2012, Mississauga Steelheads vs. Kitchener Rangers (OHL) ..397
- ★ Nov. 6, 2012, USNTDP U18 vs. Team Finland U18 (U18 Four Nations) ..398
- ★ November 6, 2012, Team Sweden vs. Team Switzerland (U18 Four Nations) ..400
- ★ November 6, 2012, Team Finland vs. Team USA (U18 Four Nations) .401
- ★ Nov 7, 2012, Russia vs. QMJHL (Subway Super Series Game 2) ..402
- ★ Nov. 7, 2012, Team Sweden vs. Team Finland U18 (U18 Four Nations) .403
- ★ Nov. 7, 2012, Team Switzerland vs. USNTDP U18 (U18 Four Nations) ..404
- ★ November 7, 2012, Team Sweden vs. Team Finland (U18 Four Nations) ..405
- ★ November 8, 2012, Des Moines @ Sioux City Musketeers (USHL) .407
- ★ Nov 8, 2012, Russia vs. OHL (Subway Super Series Game 3) ..407

HOCKEYPROSPECT.COM

- ★ Nov 9, 2012, Switzerland vs. Team USA (World Junior A Challenge)..408
- ★ November 9, 2012, Team Finland vs. Team Switzerland (U18 Four Nations) .409
- ★ November 9, 2012, Team Sweden vs. Team USA (U18 Four Nations)..410
- ★ Nov 9, 2012, Vancouver Giants vs. Portland Winterhawks (WHL)..411
- ★ November 9, 2012, Cap-Breton Screaming Eagles vs. Victoriaville Tigres..412
- ★ Nov 10 2012, Acadie-Bathurst Titan @ Sherbrooke Phoenix, (QMJHL)..415
- ★ November 10 2012, Halifax Mooseheads vs. Victoriaville Tigres (QMJHL) .416
- ★ November 10, 2012, Team Finland vs. Team Switzerland (U18 Four Nations)..417
- ★ November 10, 2012, London Knights @ Plymouth Whalers (OHL)..418
- ★ Nov 10, 2012, Czech Republic vs. Russia (World Junior A Challenge) .419
- ★ Nov. 10, 2012, USNTDP U18 vs. Team Sweden (U18 4 Nations Gold Medal)..420
- ★ November 11, 2012, Sudbury Wolves @ Sarnia Sting (OHL)..422
- ★ November 11, 2012, Cap-Breton Screaming vs. Québec Remparts (QMJHL)..423
- ★ November 12, 2012, Russia @ OHL Game #4 Subway Super Series .423
- ★ November 15, 2012, Oshawa Generals @ London Knights (OHL) .424
- ★ Nov 12, 2012, Team OHL vs. Russia (Subway Super Series Game 4)..426
- ★ Nov 14, 2012, WHL vs. Russia (Subway Super Series Game 5)..427
- ★ Nov 15, 2012, Russia vs. WHL (Subway Super Series Game 6)..427
- ★ Nov 16, 2012, Peterborough Petes vs. Kingston Frontenacs (OHL)..428
- ★ Nov 16, 2012, Sault Ste. Marie Greyhounds vs. Brampton Battalion (OHL) .430
- ★ November 16, 2012, Owen Sound Attack @ London Knights (OHL)..431
- ★ November 20, 2012, Leamington Flyers @ Sarnia Legionnaires (GOJHL)..432
- ★ Nov 17, 2012, Belleville Bulls vs. Plymouth Whalers (OHL)..433
- ★ November 18, 2012, Halifax Mooseheads vs. Val D'or Foreurs (QMJHL) .434
- ★ Nov. 18, 2012, Barrie Colts vs. Sudbury Wolves (OHL)..435
- ★ Nov 18, 2012, Kitchener Rangers vs. London Knights (OHL) .436
- ★ Nov 18, 2012, Windsor Spitfires vs. Owen Sound Attack (OHL)..438
- ★ Nov 18, 2012, Sarnia Sting vs. Sault Ste. Marie Greyhounds (OHL) .439
- ★ Nov. 20, 2012, Kingston Frontenacs vs. Ottawa 67s (OHL)..440
- ★ Nov 20, 2012, Medicine Hat Tigers vs Everett Silvertips (WHL) .441

2013 NHL DRAFT BLACK BOOK

- ★ Nov 21, 2012, Kootenay Ice vs Seattle Thunderbirds (WHL)..442
- ★ November 22, 2012, London Knights @ Sarnia Sting (OHL) .443
- ★ November 23, 2012, Moose Jaw Warriors @ Edmonton Oil Kings (WHL) .444
- ★ November 24, 2012, Peterborough Petes @ Sarnia Sting (OHL)..444
- ★ November 24 2012, Chicoutimi Saguenéens vs. Victoriaville Tigres (QMJHL) .445
- ★ Nov 25, 2012, Owen Sound Attack vs. Mississauga Steelheads (OHL) .447
- ★ November 26 2012, Drummondville Voltigeurs vs. Victoriaville Tigres (QMJHL) .448
- ★ November 27, 2012, PEI Rocket vs. Drummondville Voltigeurs (QMJHL) .449
- ★ Nov 28, 2012, Vancouver Giants vs. Moose Jaw Warriors (WHL)..450
- ★ November 29, 2012, LaSalle Vipers @ Sarnia Legionnaires (GOJHL)..451
- ★ November 30, 2012, Saginaw Spirit @ Sarnia Sting (OHL)..452
- ★ Dec 1st, 2012, Portland Winterhawks vs Everett Silvertips (WHL) .453
- ★ Dec 1, 2012, Green Bay Gamblers vs. Indiana Ice (USHL) .454
- ★ Dec 4, 2012, Guelph Storm vs. Kitchener Rangers (OHL) .455
- ★ Dec 4, 2012, Portland Winterhawks vs. Everett Silvertips (WHL) .456
- ★ Dec 5, 2012, Kelowna Rockets vs. Swift Current Broncos (WHL) .457
- ★ Dec 05, 2012, Lethbridge Hurricanes vs. Edmonton Oil Kings (WHL)..458
- ★ Dec 5, 2012, Belleville Bulls vs. Peterborough Petes (OHL) .459
- ★ Dec 6, 2012, Peterborough Petes vs. Kingston Frontenacs (OHL)..460
- ★ December 6, 2012, Rimouski Oceanic vs Sherbrooke Phoenix (QMJHL) .461
- ★ December 7 2012, Moncton Wildcats vs. Victoriaville Tigres (QMJHL) .462
- ★ Dec 7, 2012. Guelph Storm vs. Owen Sound Attack (OHL) .463
- ★ December 7, 2012, Windsor Spitfires @ Sarnia Sting (OHL)..464
- ★ Dec 7, 2012, Guelph Storm vs. Owen Sound Attack (OHL)..465
- ★ Dec 7, 2012, Sarnia Sting vs. Windsor Spitfires (OHL) .466
- ★ Dec 8, 2012, Kingston Frontenacs vs. Barrie Colts (OHL)..467
- ★ Dec 8th, 2012, Vancouver Giants vs Everett Silvertips (WHL)..469
- ★ December 8, 2012, PEI Rocket vs. Victoriaville Tigres (OHL) .470
- ★ December 8, 2012, Boston Jr. Bruins vs. New York Apple Core (EJHL)..470
- ★ December 8, 2012, South Shore Kings vs. Jersey Hitmen (EJHL) .471

- December 8, 2012, Middlesex Islanders vs. Philadelphia Revolution (EJHL) .471
- December 8, 2012, Portland Jr. Pirates vs. Rochester Stars (EJHL)..471
- December 8, 2012, Valley Jr. Warriors vs. New York Apple Core (EJHL)..471
- Dec. 9 2012, Cape-Breton Screaming @ Chicoutimi Saguneéens (QMJHL)..472
- December 9, 2012, Sault Ste. Marie Greyhounds @ Sarnia Sting (OHL) .473
- Dec. 11 2012, Rouyn-Noranda Huskies @ Val D'Or Foreurs, (QMJHL) .475
- Dec 12, 2012, Red Deer Rebels vs. Calgary Hitmen (WHL) .476
- December 12, 2012, Kelowna Rockets @ Lethbridge Hurricanes (WHL)..477
- Dec 12, 2012, Ottawa 67s vs. Belleville Bulls (OHL)..478
- Dec 13, 2012, Erie Otters vs. Niagara IceDogs (OHL)..479
- Dec 13, 2012, Oshawa Generals vs. Barrie Colts (OHL) .480
- Dec 14, 2012, Plymouth Whalers vs. Sudbury Wolves (OHL)..481
- December 14, 2012, Guelph Storm @ Sarnia Sting (OHL) ..483
- Flood-Marr Holiday Hockey Tournament (December 14th-16th 2012):..484
- Dec 15, 2012, Coquitlam Express vs. Powell River Kings (BCHL)..486
- Dec 15, 2012. Guelph Storm vs. London Knights (OHL) .486
- Dec 16, 2012, Prince Albert Raiders vs. Brandon Wheat Kings (WHL) .487
- Dec 15, 2012, Barrie Colts vs. Plymouth Whalers (OHL)..488
- Dec 15, 2012, Niagara IceDogs vs. Sudbury Wolves (OHL)..489
- December 16, 2012, Kingston Frontenacs @ London Knights (OHL) .490
- Dec 18, 2012, Indiana Ice vs. USNTDP U18 (USHL)..491
- December 20, 2012, Quebec Remparts @ Victoriaville Tigres (QMJHL)..493
- Dec 27, 2012, Germany vs. USA (2013 WJHC) .494
- Dec 28, 2012, Czech Republic vs. Finland (2013 WJHC) .494
- Dec 28, 2012, Sweden vs. Switzerland (2013 WJHC)..495
- December 28, 2012, Peterborough Petes @ Kingston Frontenacs (OHL)..496
- December 29, 2012, Team Ontario vs. Team USA – (World U17)..497
- December 29, 2012, Team Pacific vs. Team Russia – (World U17) .499
- December 29 2012, Team Sweden vs. Team Ontario (World U17 –Exhibition)..500
- Dec 29, 2012, Sweden vs. Latvia (2013 WJHC)..502

2013 NHL DRAFT BLACK BOOK

- ★ December 30 2012, Team Sweden vs. Team Finland (World U17)..503
- ★ December 30, 2012, Team Sweden vs. Team Finland (World U17) .504
- ★ December 30, 2012, Rimouski Oceanic @ Victoriaville Tigres (QMJHL)..505
- ★ December 31, 2012, Team Pacific vs. Team Sweden – (World U17) .506
- ★ December 31, 2012, Team Quebec vs. Team USA (World U17) .507
- ★ January 1, 2013, Team Pacific vs. Team Finland – (World U17)..509
- ★ January 1, 2013, Team Russia vs. Team Sweden (World U17) .510
- ★ January 2, 2013, Team Russia vs. Team Finland (World U17)..512
- ★ January 2, 2013, Team Pacific vs. Team West (World U17)..513
- ★ Jan 2, 2013, Vancouver Giants vs. Kamloops Blazers (WHL)..514
- ★ Jan 3, 2013, Canada vs. USA (2013 WJHC) .515
- ★ January 3, 2013, Team Ontario vs. Team Pacific – (World U17) .516
- ★ January 3, 2013, Team Russia vs. Team USA (World U17)..517
- ★ Jan, 4, 2013, Chicago Steel vs. Green Bay Gamblers (USHL)..518
- ★ Jan 4, 2013, Fargo Force vs. Omaha Lancers (USHL)..519
- ★ Jan 5, 2012, Waterloo Blackhawks vs. Cedar Rapids Roughriders (USHL)..520
- ★ Jan 5, 2012, USNTDP U18 vs. MSOE Raiders..521
- ★ Jan 10, 2012, Owen Sound Attack vs. Niagara IceDogs (OHL) .522
- ★ Jan 11, 2012, Omaha Lancers vs. Dubuque Fighting Saints (USHL) .523
- ★ January 11th, 2013. London Knights vs. Ottawa 67's .524
- ★ Jan 12, 2013, Vancouver Giants vs. Kelowna Rockets (WHL)..525
- ★ January 12, 2013, Ottawa 67's @ Sarnia Sting (OHL)..526
- ★ Jan 13, 2013. Guelph Storm vs. Kingston Frontenacs (OHL) .527
- ★ January 13, 2013, Shawinigan Cataractes @ Rimouski Oceanic (QMJHL)..528
- ★ Jan 16, 2013, Vancouver Giants vs. Tri-City Americans (WHL)..529
- ★ Jan 16, 2013, Team Cherry vs. Team Orr (CHL Top Prospects Game) .530
- ★ Jan 18, 2013, P.E.I. Rocket vs. Baie-Comeau Drakkar (QMJHL)..532
- ★ Jan 18, 2013, Halifax Mooseheads vs. Quebec Remparts (QMJHL)..533
- ★ Jan 18, 2013, Vancouver Giants vs. Victoria Royals (WHL) .534
- ★ January 18, 2013, Erie Otters @ Sarnia Sting (OHL)..535

- January 18, 2013, Halifax Mooseheads at Quebec Remparts (QMJHL) .536
- January 19, 2013, Val-d'Or Foreurs at Blainville-Boisbriand (QMJHL) .536
- Jan 19, 2013, P.E.I. Rocket vs. Chicoutimi Sagueneens (QMJHL) .537
- January 20, 2013, Owen Sound Attack at Ottawa 67s (OHL) .538
- January 20, 2013, Halifax Mooseheads @ Blainsville-Boisbriand (QMJHL) ..538
- January 21, 2013, Erie Otters at Plymouth Whalers (OHL) ..539
- Jan. 22 2013, Gatineau Olympiques @ Chicoutimi Saguenéens, (QMJHL) ..540
- Jan. 22 2013, Gatineau Olympiques @ Chicoutimi Saguenéens, (QMJHL) ..540
- January 23, 2013, USHL Top Prospects Game (Muskegon, MI) .541
- Jan 23, 2013, Team East vs. Team West (USHL Top Prospects Game) Prospects Breakdown: ..542
- Jan 24, 2013, Cape Breton vs. Quebec Remparts (QMJHL) ..543
- January 24, 2013, Plymouth Whalers at Windsor Spitfires (OHL) ..544
- Jan. 24 2013, Rouyn-Noranda Huskies @ Val D'Or Foreurs, (QMJHL) .545
- January 25, 2013, Sioux Falls Stampede at US NTDP Under-17 (USHL) .546
- Jan 25, 2013, Kelowna Rockets vs Seattle Thunderbirds (WHL) ..547
- January 25, 2013, Plymouth Whalers @ Sarnia Sting (OHL) .547
- January 26, 2013, Dubuque Fighting Saints at US NTDP Under-17 (USHL) ..548
- Jan. 26 2013, Québec Remparts @ Halifax Mooseheads, (QMJHL) .549
- January 27, 2013, Dubuque Fighting Saints at US NTDP Under-17 (USHL) ..551
- Jan 29th, 2013, Portland Winterhawks vs Everett Silvertips (WHL) .551
- Jan 30, 2013, Vancouver Giants vs. Prince Albert Raiders (WHL) ..552
- Jan 30, 2013, Saint Johns Sea dogs vs. Victoriaville Tigers (QMJHL) ..553
- Jan 31, 2013, Youngstown Phantoms vs. USNTDP U18 (USHL) .554
- Feb 1, 2013, Swift Current Broncos vs. Edmonton Oil Kings (WHL) ..555
- Feb. 1, 2013, Waterloo Blackhawks vs. Green Bay Gamblers (USHL) .556
- Feb 1, 2013, Red Deer Rebels vs. Lethbridge Hurricanes (WHL) .557
- Feb 1, 2013, Vancouver Giants vs. Kelowna Rockets (WHL) ..558
- Feb 1, 2013, Moose Jaw Warriors vs. Medicine Hat Tigers (WHL) .559
- February 1st, 2013. Guelph Storm vs. Windsor Spitfires .560
- Feb 1st, 2013, Tri City Americans vs Everett Silvertips (WHL) .561

2013 NHL DRAFT BLACK BOOK

- ★ Feb 2nd, 2013, Kamloops Blazers vs Everett Silvertips (WHL)..562
- ★ Feb 2, 2013, Brandon Wheat Kings vs. Regina Pats (WHL) .562
- ★ Feb 2, 2013, Sioux City Musketeers vs. Sioux Falls Stampede (USHL)..563
- ★ February 6, 2013, Kitchener Rangers @ Guelph Storm (OHL) .565
- ★ February 6, 2013, USA vs. Finland (5 Nations Tournament)..565
- ★ February 6, 2013, Sweden vs. Czech Republic (5 Nations Tournament)..567
- ★ Feb. 6 2013, Blainville-Boisbriand Armada @ Chicoutimi Saguenéens, (QMJHL)..568
- ★ February 6th, 2013. Guelph Storm vs. Kitchener Rangers (KIT 5-2) .568
- ★ February 7th, 2013. Sault Ste. Marie Greyhounds vs. Brampton Battalion..569
- ★ February 7, 2013, Finland vs. Czech Republic (5 Nations Tournament)..570
- ★ February 7, 2013, Sweden vs. Russia (5 Nations Tournament) .571
- ★ February 7, 2013, Sarnia Sting @ London Knights (OHL) .572
- ★ February 8, 2013, Owen Sound Attack @ London Knights (OHL) .573
- ★ February 8, 2013, Finland vs. Russia (5 Nations Tournament)..574
- ★ February 8, 2013, Czech Republic vs. USA (5 Nations Tournament)..575
- ★ Feb 8, 2013, Halifax Mooseheads vs. Moncton Wildcats (QMJHL) .577
- ★ February 9, 2013, Sweden vs. Finland (5 Nations Tournament)..578
- ★ February 9, 2013, Owen Sound Attack @ Plymouth Whalers (OHL) .579
- ★ February 10, 2013, Barrie Colts @ Sarnia Sting (OHL)..579
- ★ February 10, 2013, Czech Republic vs. Russia (5 Nations Tournament) .580
- ★ February 10, 2013, Sweden vs. USA (5 Nations Tournament)..581
- ★ Feb. 10, 2013, Cedar Rapids Roughriders vs. Green Bay Gamblers (USHL) .583
- ★ Feb 11, 2013, Rimouski Oceanic vs. Moncton Wildcats (QMJHL)..584
- ★ Feb 15, 2013, Sioux City Musketeers vs. Tri-City Storm (USHL)..585
- ★ Feb 15 2013, Val D'Or Foreurs @ Chicoutimi Saguenéens, (QMJHL) .586
- ★ Feb. 23 2013, Sherbrooke Phoenix @ Chicoutimi Saguenéens, (QMJHL)..587
- ★ February 15th, 2013. Guelph Storm vs. Owen Sound Attack (OHL) .588
- ★ February 15, 2013, Rouyn-Noranda Huskies @ Drummondville Voltigeurs (QMJHL)..589
- ★ February 16, 2013, Oshawa Generals @ Sarnia Sting (OHL)..590
- ★ Feb 16, 2013, Cedar Rapids Roughriders vs. Green Bay Gamblers (USHL)..591

- ★ February 16, 2013, Des Moines Buccaneers vs. Sioux City Musketeers (USHL)..592
- ★ Feb 17, 2013, Calgary Hitmen vs. Regina Pats (WHL)..593
- ★ February 18, 2013, Plymouth Whalers @ Sarnia Sting (OHL)..594
- ★ February 20, 2013, Choate Rosemary at Loomis-Chaffee (New England Prep School) .595
- ★ February 21, 2013, Sault Ste. Marie Greyhounds @ Sarnia Sting (OHL) .596
- ★ February 22, 2013, Erie Otters @ Sarnia Sting (OHL)..597
- ★ February 22, 2013, St. Paul's at Dexter (New England Prep School) .598
- ★ February 27, 2013, Westminster at Belmont Hill (New England Open Quarterfinal)..599
- ★ Feb 22, 2013, Vancouver Giants vs. Kamloops Blazers (WHL)..600
- ★ February 22, 2013, Sherbrooke Phoenix @ Baie-Comeau Drakkar (QMJHL)..601
- ★ Feb 26, 2013, Seattle Thunderbirds vs. Edmonton Oil Kings (WHL) .602
- ★ February 26, 2013, Lincoln Stars vs. Sioux City Musketeers (USHL)..603
- ★ Feb 27, 2013, Brandon Wheat Kings vs. Swift Current Broncos (WHL) .604
- ★ February 28, 2013, Holderness at Rivers (New England Small School Quarterfinal)..605
- ★ March 1, 2013, Sarnia Sting @ London Knights (OHL) .606
- ★ March 1st, 2013, Gunnery vs. Kent (New England Open Semifinal)..607
- ★ March 1st, 2013, Salisbury vs. Westminster (New England Open Semifinal) .608
- ★ March 1, 2013, Calgary Hitmen vs Swift Current Broncos (WHL)..609
- ★ Mar. 1st 2013, Moncton Wildcats @ Rimouski Océanic, (QMJHL) .609
- ★ Mar 1, 2013, Vancouver Giants vs. Lethbridge Hurricanes (WHL) .611
- ★ Mar 1, 2013, USNTDP U18 vs. Muskegon Lumberjacks (USHL)..612
- ★ Mar 1, 2013, Moncton Wildcats vs. Rimouski Oceanic (QMJHL) .613
- ★ Mar 1, 2013, Sioux Falls Stampede vs. Green Bay Gamblers (USHL)..614
- ★ March 2, 2013, Moncton Wildcats @ Quebec Remparts (QMJHL) .615
- ★ March 2nd, 2013, Kents Hill vs. Holderness (New England Small School Semifinal)..615
- ★ March 2nd, 2013, Brooks vs. Tilton (New England Small School Semifinal) .616
- ★ March 2nd, 2013, Cushing vs. Exeter (New England Big School Semifinal) .616
- ★ March 2nd, 2013, Avon vs. Thayer (New England Big School Semifinal) .617
- ★ March 3rd, 2013, Avon vs. Cushing (New England Big School Final)..618
- ★ March 3rd, 2013 Kent vs. Salisbury (New England Open Final)..619

2013 NHL DRAFT BLACK BOOK

- ★ Mar 3, 2013, Regina Pats vs. Brandon Wheat Kings (WHL)..620
- ★ Mar 3, 2013, Medicine Hat Tigers vs. Calgary Hitmen (WHL)..621
- ★ Mar 3, 2013, Chicago Steel vs. USNTDP U17 (USHL) .622
- ★ Mar 5, 2013, Red Deer Rebels vs. Kootenay Ice (WHL)..623
- ★ Mar 5, 2013, Prince George Cougars vs. Tri-City Americans (WHL)..624
- ★ March 5, 2013, Quebec Remparts @ Baie-Comeau Drakkar (QMJHL)..625
- ★ Mar 6, 2013, Prince Albert Raiders vs. Calgary Hitmen (WHL)..626
- ★ March 8th, 2013.   Sault Ste. Marie Greyhounds vs. Guelph Storm..627
- ★ March 8, 2013, Gatineau Olympiques vs. Val-d'Or Foreurs (QMJHL) .628
- ★ March 8th, 2013, Québec Remparts vs. Victoriaville Tigres (QMJHL) .629
- ★ March 9, 2013, Gatineau Olympiques vs. Chicoutimi Saguenéens (QMJHL)..629
- ★ Mar 9, 2013, Swift Current Broncos vs. Brandon Wheat Kings (WHL) .630
- ★ Mar 9, 2013, Vancouver Giants vs. Victoria Royals (WHL)..631
- ★ Mar 10, 2013, Youngstown Phantoms vs. Green Bay Gamblers (USHL)..632
- ★ March 13, 2013, New Jersey Hitmen vs. Middlesex Islanders (EJHL Finals Game 1)..633
- ★ March 13 2012, Gatineau Olympiques @ Rimouski Océanic, (QMJHL) .633
- ★ March 13-15, 2013, Beantown Spring Classic (Marlboro, MA) .634
- ★ 3/14 New Jersey Hitmen vs. Middlesex Islanders (EJHL Finals Game 2) .635
- ★ Mar 14, 2013, Cedar Rapids Roughriders vs. USNTDP U18 (USHL)..636
- ★ Mar 15, 2013, Dubuque Fighting Saints vs. Sioux City Musketeers (USHL)..637
- ★ Mar 15, 2013, Red Deer Rebels vs. Edmonton Oil Kings (WHL)..638
- ★ Mar 15, 2013, Vancouver Giants vs. Kelowna Rockets (WHL) .639
- ★ Mar 16, 2013, Sioux City Musketeers vs. Sioux Falls Stampede (USHL) .640
- ★ March 17 2013, Rimouski Océanic @ Québec Remparts, (QMJHL) .641
- ★ Mar. 19, 2013, Tri-City Storm vs. Sioux City Musketeers (USHL) .642
- ★ Mar. 19, 2013, Youngstown Phantoms vs. USNTDP U18 (USHL) .643
- ★ Mar. 21, 2013, Saskatoon Blades vs. Medicine Hat Tigers (WHL) .644
- ★ March 21, 2013, Acadie-Bathurst Titan at Blainville-Boisbriand Armada (QMJHL) .645
- ★ Mar 22, 2013, Portland Winterhawks vs. Everett Silvertips (WHL) .645
- ★ March 22nd, 2013. London Knights vs. Saginaw Spirit..647

- Mar. 22, 2013, Niagara IceDogs vs. Oshawa Generals (OHL) .647
- March 23rd, 2013. Owen Sound Attack vs. Sault Ste. Marie Greyhounds .648
- March 23, 2013, Mississauga Steelheads at Belleville Bulls (OHL) ..649
- March 24, 2013, Sudbury Wolves at Brampton Battalion (OHL) ..650
- March 24, 2013, Guelph Storm at Kitchener Rangers (OHL) .651
- Mar 24, 2013, Fargo Force vs. Green Bay Gamblers (USHL) .651
- Mar. 24, 2013, Saginaw Spirit vs. London Knights (OHL) .652
- Mar 24, 2013, Youngstown Phantoms vs. USNTDP U18 (USHL) ..654
- March 26, 2013, London Knights at Saginaw Spirit (OHL) .655
- March 26th, 2013. Guelph Storm vs. Kitchener Rangers (OHL) ..656
- March 27 2013, Moncton Wildcats vs. Victoriaville Tigres (QMJHL) .657
- March 29th, 2013. Owen Sound Attack vs. Sault Ste. Marie Greyhounds (OHL) ..657
- Mar 30, 2013, Sioux City Musketeers vs. Omaha Lancers (USHL) ..658
- Apr 1, 2013, Mississauga Steelheads vs. Belleville Bulls (OHL) ..659
- Apr 1, 2013, Portland Winterhawks vs. Everett Silvertips (WHL) .660
- Apr 2, 2013, Waterloo Blackhawks vs. Green Bay Gamblers (USHL) .662
- April 5, 2013, Calgary Hitmen vs. Red Deer Rebels (WHL) ..663
- Apr 5, 2013, Kitchener Rangers vs. London Knights (OHL) .664
- April 5, 2013, Sudbury Wolves vs. Belleville Bulls (OHL) ..665
- April 5, 2013, Val D'or Foreurs @ Blainsville-Boisbriand Armada (QMJHL) .666
- April 5, 2013, Calgary Hitmen vs Red Deer Rebels (WHL) .667
- Apr 7, 2013, Kelowna Rockets vs. Kamloops Blazers (WHL) .668
- April 7, 2013, Sudbury Wolves vs. Belleville Bulls (OHL) ..669
- April 8, 2013, London Knights vs. Kitchener Rangers (OHL) ..670
- Apr 9, 2013, Gatineau Olympiques vs. Halifax Mooseheads (QMJHL) .671
- Apr 9, 2013, Barrie Colts vs Oshawa Generals (OHL) ..673
- Apr 10, 2013, Gatineau Olympiques vs Halifax Mooseheads (QMJHL) .674
- Apr 20, 2013, Finland vs. Russia (World U18 Championships) .675
- April 23, 2013. Team Russia vs. Team Czech Republic (World U18 Championships) ..676
- April 24, 2013, Calgary Hitmen vs Edmonton Oil Kings (WHL) ..677

- April 8, 2013, Baie-Comeau Drakkar vs. Victoriaville Tigres (2nd round playoff) .678
- April 17, 2012, Youngstown Phantoms @ Green Bay Gamblers (USHL)..679
- April 18, 2012, Youngstown Phantoms @ Green Bay Gamblers (USHL)..680
- April 23, 2013, Baie-Comeau Drakkar at Blainville-Boisbriand Armada (QMJHL) .681
- April 24, 2013, Baie-Comeau Drakkar at Blainville-Boisbriand Armada (QMJHL) .682
- Calgary Hitmen vs Edmonton Oil Kings (WHL) .683

8. CREDITS 687

Part 1
2013 NHL DRAFT RANKINGS

2013 NHL DRAFT BLACK BOOK

Rank	CS	PLAYER	Team	League	Pos.	Ht	Wt
1	2	NATHAN MACKINNON	HALIFAX	QMJHL	RC	6' 0"	182
2	1	SETH JONES	PORTLAND	WHL	RD	6' 3.5"	205
3	3	JONATHAN DROUIN	HALIFAX	QMJHL	LW	5' 10.5"	186
4	2	VALERI NICHUSHKIN	CHELYABINSK	RUSSIA	RW	6' 4"	202
5	1	ALEKSANDER BARKOV	TAPPARA	FINLAND	LC	6' 3"	209
6	5	SEAN MONAHAN	OTTAWA	OHL	LC	6' 2.25"	187
7	3	ELIAS LINDHOLM	BRYNAS	SWEDEN	RC	6' 0"	192
8	22	NIKITA ZADOROV	LONDON	OHL	LD	6' 5.25"	221
9	4	RASMUS RISTOLAINEN	TPS	FINLAND	RD	6' 4"	207
10	19	MAX DOMI	LONDON	OHL	C/LW	5' 9.25"	197
11	15	BO HORVAT	LONDON	OHL	LC	6' 0"	206
12	5	ALEXANDER WENNBERG	DJURGARDEN	SWEDEN-2	LC	6' 1"	190
13	7	VALENTIN ZYKOV	BAIE-COMEAU	QMJHL	LW	5' 11.75"	209
14	1	ZACH FUCALE	HALIFAX	QMJHL	G	6' 1"	181
15	32	MADISON BOWEY	KELOWNA	WHL	RD	6' 0.75"	195
16	4	DARNELL NURSE	SOO	OHL	LD	6' 3.5"	185
17	27	JOSHUA MORRISSEY	PRINCE ALBERT	WHL	LD	5' 11.75"	186
18	23	SAMUEL MORIN	RIMOUSKI	QMJHL	LD	6' 6.25"	202
19	10	ANTHONY MANTHA	VAL-D'OR	QMJHL	RW	6' 3.75"	190
20	16	RYAN HARTMAN	PLYMOUTH	OHL	RW	5' 11"	181
21	20	CURTIS LAZAR	EDMONTON	WHL	C/RW	5' 11.75"	190
22	26	ADAM ERNE	QUEBEC	QMJHL	LW	6' 0.5"	210
23	25	MORGAN KLIMCHUK	REGINA	WHL	LW	5' 11.25"	180
24	6	HUNTER SHINKARUK	MEDICINE HAT	WHL	C/LW	5' 10.25"	181
25	33	NICOLAS PETAN	PORTLAND	WHL	LC	5' 8.5"	165
26	14	CHRIS BIGRAS	OWEN SOUND	OHL	LD	6' 0.5"	186
27	39	EMILE POIRIER	GATINEAU	QMJHL	LW	6' 0.75"	183
28	17	KERBY RYCHEL	WINDSOR	OHL	LW	6' 0.75"	205
29	8	FREDERIK GAUTHIER	RIMOUSKI	QMJHL	LC	6' 4.5"	214
30	12	RYAN PULOCK	BRANDON	WHL	RD	6' 0.5"	211
31	8	ROBERT HAGG	MODO JR.	SWEDEN-JR.	LD	6' 2.25"	204
32	36	OLIVER BJORKSTRAND	PORTLAND	WHL	RW	5' 10.75"	166
33	34	JT COMPHER	USA U-18	USHL	LW	5' 10.5"	184
34	47	STEVEN SANTINI	USA U-18	USHL	RD	6' 1.5"	207
35	35	MICHAEL MCCARRON	USA U-18	USHL	RW	6' 5"	228

Rank	CS	PLAYER	Team	League	Pos.	Ht	Wt
36	28	LAURENT DAUPHIN	CHICOUTIMI	QMJHL	LC	6' 0"	165
37	7	JACOB DE LA ROSE	LEKSAND	SWEDEN-2	LW	6' 2.25"	190
38	10	PAVEL BUCHNEVICH	CHEREPOVETS 2	RUSSIA-JR.	LW	6' 1"	176
39	11	SHEA THEODORE	SEATTLE	WHL	LD	6' 1.75"	178
40	9	MIRCO MUELLER	EVERETT	WHL	LD	6' 3.25"	184
41	31	DILLON HEATHERINGTON	SWIFT CURRENT	WHL	LD	6' 3"	196
42	30	JASON DICKINSON	GUELPH	OHL	LC	6' 1.25"	179
43	9	ARTTURI LEHKONEN	KALPA	FINLAND	LW	5' 11"	163
44	44	THOMAS VANNELLI	MINNETONKA	HIGH-MN	RD	6' 2"	165
45	71	REMI ELIE	LONDON	OHL	LW	6' 0.5"	203
46	6	ANDRE BURAKOVSKY	MALMO	SWEDEN-2	LW	6' 1"	178
47	24	IAN MCCOSHEN	WATERLOO	USHL	LD	6' 2.5"	205
48	28	PETER CEHLARIK	LULEA JR.	SWEDEN-JR.	LW	6' 2"	192
49	58	NICK MOUTREY	SAGINAW	OHL	C/LW	6' 2"	208
50	21	JAMES LODGE	SAGINAW	OHL	RC	6' 0.5"	166
51	49	MICHAEL DOWNING	DUBUQUE	USHL	LD	6' 2.75"	192
52	13	LINUS ARNESSON	DJURGARDEN	SWEDEN-2	LD	6' 2"	187
53	NR	PAVEL KOLEDOV	LOKOMOTIV	VHL	RD	6' 0"	181
54	45	CONNOR HURLEY	EDINA HIGH	HIGH-MN	LC	6' 1.25"	174
55	42	ADAM TAMBELLINI	SURREY	BCHL	LC	6' 2.25"	169
56	61	NICHOLAS BAPTISTE	SUDBURY	OHL	RW	6' 0.75"	189
57	3	TRISTAN JARRY	EDMONTON	WHL	G	6' 1.25"	183
58	13	ZACH NASTASIUK	OWEN SOUND	OHL	RW	6' 1.25"	190
59	14	VIKTOR CRUS RYDBERG	LINKOPING JR.	SWEDEN-JR.	RC	5' 11"	190
60	63	RYAN KUJAWINSKI	KINGSTON	OHL	LC	6' 1.5"	204
61	40	BRETT PESCE	NEW HAMPSHIR	H-EAST	RD	6' 2.75"	170
62	56	RYAN FITZGERALD	VALLEY	EJHL	RC	5' 9.5"	170
63	51	GUSTAV OLOFSSON	GREEN BAY	USHL	LD	6' 2.75"	185
64	7	PHILIPPE DESROSIERS	RIMOUSKI	QMJHL	G	6' 1.25"	182
65	48	NICK SORENSEN	QUEBEC	QMJHL	RW	6' 0.75"	174
66	15	WILHELM WESTLUND	FARJESTAD JR.	SWEDEN-JR.	LD	5' 11.25"	184
67	2	ERIC COMRIE	TRI-CITY	WHL	G	6' 0.75"	167
68	12	MARKO DANO	BRATISLAVA	RUSSIA	LC	5' 11"	183
69	26	NIKLAS HANSSON	ROGLE JR.	SWEDEN-JR.	RD	6' 0.5"	175
70	37	JONATHAN DIABY	VICTORIAVILLE	QMJHL	LD	6' 5"	223

2013 NHL DRAFT BLACK BOOK

Rank	CS	PLAYER	Team	League	Pos.	Ht	Wt
71	1	JUUSE SAROS	HPK Hameenlinna	FINLAND	G	5'10"	180
72	100	GREG BETZOLD	PETERBOROUGH	OHL	C/LW	6'1.5"	195
73	7	SPENCER MARTIN	MISSISSAUGA	OHL	G	6'2.25"	198
74	38	JUSTIN BAILEY	KITCHENER	OHL	RW	6'3"	186
75	18	WILLIAM CARRIER	CAPE BRETON	QMJHL	LW	6'1.5"	198
76	55	JORDAN SUBBAN	BELLEVILLE	OHL	RD	5'9"	175
77	53	KEATON THOMPSON	USA U-18	USHL	LD	6'0.25"	187
78	64	TEEMU KIVIHALME	BURNSVILLE	HIGH-MN	LD	5'11.25"	161
79	23	JUUSO IKONEN	BLUES	FINLAND	LW	5'9"	169
80	109	BRIAN PINHO	ST. JOHN'S PREP	HIGH-MA	RC	6'0"	173
81	11	BOGDAN YAKIMOV	NIZHNEKAMSK 2	RUSSIA-JR.	LC	6'5"	202
82	29	JOHN HAYDEN	USA U-18	USHL	RC	6'2.5"	210
83	NR	SVEN ANDRIGHETTO	ROUYN-NORANDA	QMJHL	RW	5'10"	180
84	57	ANTHONY DUCLAIR	QUEBEC	QMJHL	LW	5'11"	177
85	113	JEFF CORBETT	SUDBURY	OHL	LD	6'1.5"	170
86	88	CONNOR CLIFTON	USA U-18	USHL	RD	5'10.75"	175
87	21	RUSHAN RAFIKOV	YAROSLAVL 2	RUSSIA-JR.	LD	6'2"	181
88	64	GUSTAV POSSLER	MODO JR.	SWEDEN-JR.	RW	6'0"	183
89	25	ANTON CEDERHOLM	ROGLE JR.	SWEDEN-JR.	LD	6'1.5"	204
90	51	JOOSE ANTONEN	JYP 2	FINLAND-2	LW/RW	6'1.5"	183
91	50	YAN PAVEL LAPLANTE	PEI	QMJHL	LC	6'0"	178
92	70	HUDSON FASCHING	USA U-18	USHL	RW	6'1.75"	213
93	60	ZACHARY SANFORD	ISLANDERS	EJHL	LW	6'3"	185
94	73	VINCENT DUNN	VAL-D'OR	QMJHL	LC	5'11"	172
95	18	CARL DAHLSTROM	LINKOPING JR.	SWEDEN-JR.	LD	6'3.25"	211
96	89	ATTE MAKINEN	TAPPARA JR.	FINLAND-JR.	RD	6'3"	206
97	NR	CONNOR CRISP	ERIE	OHL	LC/LW	6'4"	225
98	166	TYLER GANLY	SOO STE. MARIE	OHL	RD	6'1"	201
99	135	DANIEL NIKANDROV	SARNIA	OHL	LC	6'1.5"	191
100	139	DOMINIK KUBALIK	SUDBURY	OHL	LW	6'1"	181
101	110	KYLE PLATZER	LONDON	OHL	RC	5'11"	185
102	54	MARC-OLIVIER ROY	BLAINVILLE	QMJHL	LC	6'0"	175
103	16	LUCAS WALLMARK	SKELLEFTEA JR.	SWEDEN-JR.	LC	5'10.5"	175
104	145	ERIK BRADFORD	BARRIE	OHL	LC	5'11.25"	178
105	108	TIM BENDER	MANNHEIM JR.	GERM JR.	LD	6'0"	174

Rank	CS	PLAYER	Team	League	Pos.	Ht	Wt
106	124	NICHOLAS PAUL	BRAMPTON	OHL	LW	6' 2.25"	202
107	150	MILES LIBERATI	LONDON	OHL	LD	5' 11.5"	195
108	79	JEREMY GREGOIRE	BAIE-COMEAU	QMJHL	C/LW	5' 11.75"	190
109	41	ERIC ROY	BRANDON	WHL	LD	6' 2.5"	180
110	43	JAN KOSTALEK	RIMOUSKI	QMJHL	RD	6' 0.5"	181
111	153	GREGORY CHASE	CALGARY	WHL	C/RW	6' 0"	195
112	102	CARTER VERHAEGHE	NIAGARA	OHL	LC	6' 1"	181
113	207	TYLER BERTUZZI	GUELPH	OHL	LW	6' 0"	178
114	85	ROBERTS LIPSBERGS	SEATTLE	WHL	LW	5' 10"	192
115	193	TAYLOR CAMMARATA	WATERLOO	USHL	C/LW	5' 7"	156
116	65	JACKSON HOUCK	VANCOUVER	WHL	RW	6' 0"	186
117	59	MASON GEERTSEN	VANCOUVER	WHL	LD	6' 3"	199
118	104	WILEY SHERMAN	HOTCHKISS	HIGH-CT	LD	6' 5.75"	206
119	101	BEN HARPUR	GUELPH	OHL	LD	6' 5.5"	210
120	72	KURT ETCHEGARY	QUEBEC	QMJHL	LC	5' 11"	185
121	75	ANTHONY FLORENTINO	SOUTH KENT	HIGH-CT	RD	6' 1"	227
122	17	ANDREI MIRONOV	DYNA MOSCOW	RUSSIA	LD	6' 2"	176
123	4	CALVIN PETERSEN	WATERLOO	USHL	G	6' 2.0"	183
124	52	GAB PAQUIN-BOUDREAU	BAIE-COMEAU	QMJHL	LW	5' 11"	167
125	39	NIKOLAI GLUKHOV	OMSK 2	RUSSIA-JR.	RD	6' 2"	178
126	54	DAVID KAMPF	CHOMUTOV JR.	CZREP-JR.	RW	6' 0"	168
127	41	DMITRI YUDIN	ST. PTSBURG 2	RUSSIA-JR.	LD	6' 1"	179
128	128	STEPHEN HARPER	ERIE	OHL	LW	6' 1.25"	200
129	120	COLE CASSELS	OSHAWA	OHL	RC	6' 0"	178
130	90	KAYLE DOETZEL	RED DEER	WHL	RD	6' 2.25"	190
131	80	JAKE GUENTZEL	SIOUX CITY	USHL	LC	5' 9.5"	157
132	118	SERGEY TOLCHINSKY	SOO STE. MARIE	OHL	LW	5' 7.25"	152
133	NR	FELIX GIRARD	BAIE-COMEAU	QMJHL	RC	5'11"	190
134	92	COLE ULLY	KAMLOOPS	WHL	LW	5' 10.75"	164
135	125	BRENT PEDERSEN	KITCHENER	OHL	LW	6' 2"	205
136	123	JOSHUA BURNSIDE	MISSISSAUGA	OHL	LW	5' 11.0"	171
137	87	WILL BUTCHER	USA U-18	USHL	LD	5' 9.5"	191
138	101	TOBIAS LILJENDAHL	DJURGARDE JR.	SWEDEN-JR.	RC	6' 1.75"	214
139	67	DAVID POPE	WEST KELOWNA	BCHL	LW	6' 2.25"	187
140	172	JERRET SMITH	SEATTLE	WHL	RD	6' 1.5"	198

2013 NHL DRAFT BLACK BOOK

Rank	CS	PLAYER	Team	League	Pos.	Ht	Wt
141	8	PATRIK BARTOSAK	RED DEER	WHL	G	6' 1.0"	187
142	NR	DANNY VANDERWIEL	PLYMOUTH	OHL	LW	6' 0"	210
143	NR	RINAT VALIYEV	INDIANA	USHL	LD	6' 01"	190
144	6	EAMON MCADAM	WATERLOO	USHL	G	6' 2.25"	188
145	74	DYLAN LABBE	SHAWINIGAN	QMJHL	LD	6' 1"	180
146	83	JC LIPON	KAMLOOPS	WHL	RW	5' 11.5"	180
147	66	TYLER LEWINGTON	MEDICINE HAT	WHL	RD	6' 1.0"	189
148	58	ROBIN NORELL	DJURGARDE JR.	SWEDEN-JR.	LD	5' 11"	189
149	158	ZACH HALL	BARRIE	OHL	LC	5' 10.5"	172
150	24	ALEXANDER HENRIKSSON	FARJESTAD JR.	SWEDEN-JR.	LW	6' 1.75"	190
151	NR	FREDERIK TIFFELS	MUSKEGON	USHL	LW	6' 0	185
152	161	BRODY SILK	SUDBURY	OHL	LC	5' 11.75"	185
153	201	THOMAS ALDWORTH	CUSHI ACADEMY	HIGH-MA	RW	5' 11.5"	179
154	9	ANTOINE BIBEAU	PEI	WHL	G	6' 02.5"	207
155	24	SEAN ROMEO	YOUNGSTOWN	USHL	G	5' 11.75"	166
156	68	LEON BRISTEDT	LINKOPING JR.	SWEDEN-JR.	RW	5' 7.5"	180
157	114	MATTHEW MURPHY	HALIFAX	QMJHL	LD	6' 2"	197
158	136	ALEX KILE	GREEN BAY	USHL	LW	5' 11.25"	190
159	192	TREVOR MOORE	TRI-CITY	USHL	LW	5' 9.25"	170
160	62	SEAN MALONE	USA U-18	USHL	LC	5' 11"	183
161	78	TY STANTON	MEDICINE HAT	WHL	LD	6' 3.5"	173
162	14	ALEXANDRE BELANGER	ROUYN-NORANDA	QMJHL	G	6' 0.5"	170
163	69	MITCHELL WHEATON	KELOWNA	WHL	LD	6' 4"	228
164	187	TYLER HILL	CHICAGO	USHL	LW	6' 5.75"	220
165	86	LUKE RIPLEY	POWELL RIVER	BCHL	LD	6' 3.75"	181
166	98	CONNOR RANKIN	TRI-CITY	WHL	LW	5' 11.75"	194
167	29	VICTOR OHMAN	MODO JR.	SWEDEN-JR.	LC	5' 8.5"	170
168	164	MACKENZIE WEEGAR	HALIFAX	QMJHL	RD	5' 11.75"	183
169	NR	SHANE KAVANAGH	CUSHING ACADEM	HIGH-MA	RW	5' 11"	195
170	144	CAMERON BRACE	OWEN SOUND	OHL	C	5' 9.5"	176
171	199	STEPHEN NOSAD	PETERBOROUGH	OHL	RW	5' 11"	188
172	148	GAGE AUSMUS	USA U-18	USHL	LD	6' 0.75"	211
173	156	HUNTER GARLENT	GUELPH	OHL	RC	5' 8.25"	164
174	132	JONNY BRODZINSKI	ST. CLOUD STATE	WCHA	C	6' 0"	202
175	91	MARTIN REWAY	GATINEAU	QMJHL	LW	5' 8"	158

Rank	CS	PLAYER	Team	League	Pos.	Ht	Wt
176	77	AVERY PETERSON	GRAND RAPIDS	HIGH-MN	LC	6' 2"	194
177	84	TYLER MOTTE	USA U-18	USHL	LC	5' 9.25"	190
178	157	EVAN ALLEN	USA U-18	USHL	RC	5' 9.75"	201
179	152	JEAN-SEBASTIEN DEA	ROUYN-NORAND	QMJHL	RC	6' 0"	155
180	185	CONNOR LIGHT	ANDOVER	HIGH-MA	LD	6' 4.75"	198
181	32	VYACHESLAV LESCHENKO	MYTISCHI 2	RUSSIA-JR.	RW	5' 11"	165
182	186	ROSS OLSSON	CEDAR RAPIDS	USHL	RW	6' 4.5"	207
183	12	EVAN COWLEY	WICHITA FALLS	NAHL	G	6' 3.75"	182
184	195	DANIEL LAFONTAINE	AVON OLD FARM	HIGH-CT	RC	5' 9.5"	160
185	NR	WILL TOFFEY	SALISBURY	HIGH-MA	LD	NA	NA
186	76	SPENSER JENSEN	MEDICINE HAT	WHL	RD	6' 4"	191
187	NR	MACOY ERKAMPS	LETHBRIDGE	WHL	RD	5' 11"	193
188	111	NOLAN DE JONG	VICTORIA	BCHL	LD	6' 2"	173
189	169	RYAN SEGALLA	SALISBURY	HIGH-CT	LD	6' 0.5"	190
190	105	MARC MCNULTY	PRINCE GEORGE	WHL	LD	6' 5.75"	185
191	10	AUSTIN LOTZ	EVERETT	WHL	G	6' 0.0"	188
192	117	MATT BUCKLES	ST. MICHAELS	OJHL	RC	6' 1.25"	205
193	37	FILIP SANDBERG	HV 71 JR.	SWEDEN-JR.	RW	5' 9"	172
194	NR	SAM POVOROZNIOUK	KINGSTON	OHL	LW	5' 10"	183
195	42	TIMOTEJ SILLE	SKALICA JR.	SLOVAK-JR.	RW	6' 3"	183
196	138	MILES WOOD	NOBLES	HIGH-MA	LW	6' 0.75"	160
197	NR	JESSE LEES	KELOWNA	WHL	RD	6'0"	180
198	NR	BO PELLAH	ALBERNI VALLEY	BCHL	LD	5'11"	150
199	81	LUCA FAZZINI	LUGANO	SWISS	LW	5' 9"	185
200	96	LUKE JOHNSON	LINCOLN	USHL	C	5' 11"	179
201	112	KEEGAN KANZIG	VICTORIA	WHL	D	6' 7"	241
202	93	BRENDAN HARMS	FARGO	USHL	RW	5' 11.5"	174
203	171	TOMMY VEILLEUX	VICTORIAVILLE	QMJHL	LW	6' 0"	188
204	20	ANTON SLEPYSHEV	UFA	RUSSIA	LW	6' 2"	194
205	NR	ERIC LOCKE	SAGINAW	OHL	LC	5' 9"	182
206	94	NICK HUTCHISON	AVON OLD FARM	HIGH-CT	LC	6' 1.75"	178
207	NR	CONNOR BOLAND	PETERBOROUGH	OHL	LD	6' 02"	200
208	81	BLAKE HEINRICH	SIOUX CITY	USHL	D	5' 10.75"	194
209	13	BRENDAN BURKE	PORTLAND	WHL	G	6' 3.0	176
210	122	EETU KOIVISTOINEN	BLUES JR.	FINLAND-JR.	C/LW	6' 2"	201

Part 2

2013 NHL DRAFT PROSPECTS

Ahlgren, Jake – FW – Sioux Falls Stampede (USHL) – 6'1" 173

Ahlgren played his rookie season with Sioux Falls and had 8 points in the 32 games that he played in. He is not much of an offensive force but does get himself in lanes to block shots from the point and he puts good pressure on the puck carrier. He protects the puck pretty well from the opposition and has some moves to get around defenders off the wide drive. He can make good passes to lead teammates into the offensive zone with speed and he drives hard to the net looking for loose pucks and rebounds. He needs to try and drive the puck down low more often to try to create opportunities in tight rather than taking long outside shots on the rush.

Aldworth, Thomas – RW – Cushing Academy (Prep-MA) – 6'0, 179

The lanky, Texas-bred winger plays the game the right way, skating well and involving himself in the play at both ends of the rink. He plays with a lot of intensity, especially with the puck where he gets up to speed quickly and can beat defenders with deft stick handling or brute strength down the outside. He protects the puck well and shows off an excellent wrist shot that he releases deceptively, though he could stand to shoot more. He forechecks and back checks with vigor and takes the body hard. He's aggressive and capably defensively with a good compete level along the boards and strong penalty killing. He does too much at times with the puck, trying to make fancy plays instead of putting it on net or taking the easy pass, which can cause him problems. His tools and skill set are suited to the professional game, and he has the frame to be a force when he bulks up.

Allen, Evan – LW – US NTDP Under-18 Team – 5'10, 195

If you ranked the forwards in this draft class based on shooting ability alone, Allen would be in the top 30. There were times this season when the NTDP power play consisted of repeatedly feeding Allen passes for one-timers, to the extent that teammates were forcing pucks through traffic trying to get him the shot. He can absolutely rifle it and is a threat to score from anywhere in the offensive zone, though he's more of a close-your-eyes-and-shoot type than a guy who picks his spots. He also made a positive impression with his work ethic this season, showing on numerous occasions that he's willing to do the little things to win hockey games.

He forechecks, back checks, and shows good situational and positional awareness. On the downside, he's really a complementary player and projects as such in the future as well. Though from time to time he shows good jump, his skating is average. What really holds him back is his lack of puck handling ability. He's not proven that he can consistently take the puck through the neutral zone with poise or create space for himself in the offensive zone, and as a result has a hard time being effective as anything but a triggerman. That doesn't make him a bad prospect, but he's not a real difference-maker offensively as he has to rely on his teammates to be productive, which limits his upside.

Allen, Mitchell – RC – Kent School (Prep-CT) – 6'2 180

Though still very raw, Allen intrigues with good skating and skill to go along with a projectable frame. He shows good acceleration and control on his feet, with quality straight-line speed when given space to get going. He shows good stick handling ability, with very quick hands for his size. He distributes the puck well with crisp, intelligent passes in all situations, especially on the power play where he works better when given room to operate.
He flashes power forward skills from time to time, using his reach to drive wide and power to the net, but overall he shies away from contact a bit. He lacks consistent finishing ability and has games where his decision-making with the puck as a whole is questionable. He also needs to keep his feet moving, as he has a tendency to float, especially in the neutral zone. He's a good back checker when he puts his energy into it. He might be a late-round flier in this draft, but likely hasn't shown a strong enough work ethic to be selected.

Amorosa, Terrance – LD – Holderness School (Prep-NH) – 6'2, 190

Terrance is a big-bodied offensive defenseman who carried his team for much of this season. Down the playoff stretch and into the playoffs, he was playing more than half of each game and the entirety of every power play. He's a great power play quarterback with outstanding puck skills including accurate passes, a great variety of effective shots from the point, and the stick handling ability to carry up ice and make fore checkers miss. He's not especially dynamic but he's very effective at protecting the puck and reacting to pressure. When he doesn't have a lane to break the play out himself, his outlets and stretch passes are excellent. His skating is strong and efficient forward and back, and he shows good lateral agility, especially at the point in the offensive zone with keeps and good movement.

His defensive zone play is very rough, as he has trouble identifying his check and is much too aggressive in outnumbered situations. His physical play is inconsistent but he does have the frame to be effective when he does use his body. He isn't assertive enough in front of his net and along the boards and needs to better utilize his size. He tries to do too much at times and causes headaches for his teammates, as his misplays often lead to outnumbered attacks the other way, but part of that is likely coaching as he was the only player on Holderness with consistent game breaking ability, especially from the back end.

Andrighetto, Sven – RW – Rouyn-Noranda Huskies (QMJHL) – 5'10" 180

After getting passed on during his first two years of eligibility at the NHL Draft, the Swiss forward has had a tremendous 2012-2013 season with the Rouyn-Noranda Huskies, totaling 98 points in 53 games. We feel that the third time's going to be the charm for the highly skilled forward.

Andrighetto possesses elite offensive tools and is one of the most talented players in the QMJHL. His skating abilities are just great, whether it's his rarely matched top speed, superb acceleration in two footsteps or his fantastic agility on skates, twisting and turning abruptly. The puck-control is amazing and it seems like the puck is glued to his stick, especially when he gets to that top speed and cruises easily around players. He will get past defenders by using speed instead of trying to go through the players with a slick move which is something we really like to see. His hands are quick and fluid and with the agility he possesses, he's able to get rapidly to places where he has space in the offensive zone. He possesses a rocket of a shot, whether it's the lethal release on the wrist shot that doesn't give a chance to any goalie or his powerful slapshot, Andrighetto really has all the tools to score frequent goals in professional hockey. Although he's really quick, he loves to delay the play and poise with the puck, using his good passing skills to find teammates. He will rarely give the puck away under pressure, preferring to try something offensively, whether it's a shot on goal with no angle, passing the puck in the slot or use his speed to get a lane to the net. He is a great powerplay player, firm at the blue line with Rouyn, he sees the play well and chooses the right options at the right times, showing good offensive hockey sense.

Andrighetto has improved his defensive game a lot in the past season, showing more maturity his position and in the way he will rarely cheat or skip a backcheck to take a chance offensively. He is willing to battle on the boards to retrieve the puck and is not afraid of getting hit, using a low center of gravity to his advantage. He's not a big player and will need to bulk up to be as effective in pro hockey, but has proven that he can physical abuse and keep the puck against bigger players on multiple occasions. We like the character he has, being able to produce and make big plays whether they are defensive or offensive in high pressure situations.

The 19 year old undrafted Swiss player doesn't have glaring flaws in his game. Some will certainly question the size and durability of that kind of player in professional hockey, but he has shown no fear in our viewings when he played against physical teams. We believe he could benefit from playing a couple of years in the AHL. With the speed and skills he possesses, he can play an East-West game in the QMJHL and can gain space and time easily for himself. We believe that he'll need big adjustments to his game to be as effective in the North-South type of game of the NHL. We have never seen him play a chip-and-chase game in our viewings with regularity and will rarely simplify his game to this point, which is something he could benefit on some nights. But those are things you can learn, Andrighetto has had a great learning curve in his QMJHL career possessing many natural intangibles that only great offensive players have.

Quotable: "Andrighetto has been a favorite of mine since his arrival in QMJHL last season. He always finds ways to create something when he is on the ice and he makes his linemates look better." - Simon Larouche

Antonen, Joose – LW – JYP-Akatemia (FIN-2) – 6'2, 183

Joose is talented, but enigmatic. He has the size and skill to play an excellent power game. He can bring the puck down the wing with great speed and protection, and flashes talent with deft stick handling, quality passes through sticks and bodies, and an excellent wrist shot. He is smart with the puck along the boards and can shield defenders off well. However, the effort level is not always there. Often, he looks sluggish on the ice with labored movement, whiffed shots, and at times neglects to put in any kind of back checking or fore checking effort. Even when he gets his shots off, his accuracy is questionable. His attention to detail is sorely lacking. He teases with shifts where he turns it on and looks like a prospect, but doesn't consistently show a strong enough compete level.

Arnesson, Linus – LD – Djurgarden (SAL) – 6'2" 190

Arnesson is a steady defensive defenseman who does an excellent job of keeping plays to the outside and limiting the offensive chances that opponents create whenever he is out on the ice. The best asset of Arnesson is probably his skating ability. He is very quick on his skates, and when you combine that with his size, opponents have a very difficult time in trying to get inside positioning on him off the rush. He has good lateral movement, and is able to keep up with opponents as they try to go wide on him. Along the walls, Arnesson possesses very quick starts and stops, which comes useful as opponents try to shake him off and get a lane to the net.

He is not particularly physical, but he has displayed good overall strength to fight off opposing forwards for loose pucks, and stay on his feet even when he gets hit. Arnesson is consistently in good position to take away dangerous chances in the slot. He does not run around in his own end, and plays a very composed game without the puck. Offensively, Arnesson will probably never really become much of a threat. His outlet passes are above average, but lacks creativity. He keeps it safe when moving the puck, and thinks about defense first whenever his team is on the attack. He does a good job of keeping pucks in the offensive zone by moving down the walls when he sees the opportunity, but he will not take a chance if he does not see a clear chance. He does not like to use his shot very much either.

Arnesson may not provide many points in his career, but he will be a valuable piece to any defense unit as all teams need a shutdown defenseman to rely on when trying to hold onto leads. The one positive aspect of his game is that because he is so dependable defensively, teams can put him out there in any situation and trust that he will keep the puck out of their net.

Quotable: "I question his hockey sense, I may have him lower than some other guys have him." - NHL Scout

Ast, Anthony – RC – Vancouver Giants (WHL) – 5'8" 170

A former first round pick in the WHL bantam draft, Ast has been a big disappointment for the Giants organization so far into his junior career. He has not been able to develop into a top 6 forward, mainly because of his size. He is a great skater who can reach top end speed in a hurry, but he does very little with the puck. Ast looks nervous for the most part out on the ice in the offensive zone, and tries to do things too fast and does not read the play particularly well. Ast is far too weak along the boards and in the slot, and has had a few injury issues this season.

Auger, Justin – RW – Guelph Storm (OHL) – 6'7" 223

Justin was selected in the 6th round of the 2010 OHL Priority Selection Draft by the Guelph Storm out of the Waterloo Wolves Minor Midget program. Justin played his 16 year old season with his hometown Waterloo Siskins Jr. B team putting up impressive numbers obtaining a 20+ goal season. Justin made the Guelph Storm right out of camp for his 2011-2012 OHL season, while receiving limited ice behind a lot of talented forwards. He made a good argument towards getting selected in the 2012 NHL Entry Draft, but was ultimately passed over. He returned for his second OHL season, and thanks to his massive size and performance this season, he's back on the radar for the 2013 NHL Entry Draft.

Auger is a massive winger who excels at puck control in the offensive zone and dominates along the boards on the cycle. He is very effective at using his size to shield opponents from the puck and can lean on smaller players knocking them off the puck very easily. He is good at standing in front of the net creating a big screen on opposing goaltenders and does not get bothered by defenders taking hacks at him to move. Justin has a deceptive first step when coming off the cycle and surprises defenders with a quick drive to the net. His skating has generously improved from last year and he works hard to keep up with the rush and back checks when needed.

There is room for improvement on his finishing skills as he needs to be consistent burying the numerous chances his size gains him. He possesses a strong wrist shot and would benefit from quickening his release and working to get it off quicker in limited amounts of space. Auger sometimes starts drifting into the center or left wing side of the ice and needs to work at staying in his lanes and remaining in position. Justin needs to improve his playmaking skills and sometimes holds onto the puck too long instead of moving it up ice to his line mates in better scoring positions. Auger has shown a ton of improvement from last season and if he continues to work on his skating and vision, he should certainly become a key player for the Storm in 2013-2014. Auger is a good candidate to be selected in the re-entry draft position.

Quotable: "I like Auger, but more as a kid who can be a good OHL'er than as an NHL Prospect." - NHL Scout

Ausmus, Gage – LD – US NTDP Under-18 Team – 6'1, 211

Gage has a habit of blending into the background, playing a steady game with smart defensive positioning and safe plays with the puck in his zone. Then, all of a sudden, he's laying a guy out at the blueline or pinching into the attack. One time this season, he jumped up and ended up with a shorthanded breakaway. These moments are fleeting and interspersed, and he sometimes goes a whole game without making himself noticeable. He's a smart player that picks his spots well. His end comes first, but if he sees a sure-thing opportunity to provide a little extra, he can do it. He lacks dynamic skating and puck skills, but seems to have a good handle on his limitations and knows how to keep things simple. He has the potential to be an NHL defenseman based on his humble approach and intelligence on the ice.

Babintsev, Sam – RW – Mississauga Steelheads (OHL) – 5'10" 167

Sam may not be an elite top talent player heading into the draft and he may not have the size to play in an NHL bottom-6 role, however, Babintsev knows his role for the Mississauga Steelheads and plays how he needs to in order to be effective. Babintsev can be quite a physical presence, which is somewhat surprising for a player of his size. He is at his best when he's moving the puck effectively, as he can distribute it well, either on the rush through the neutral zone or moving it around to create opportunities in the offensive zone. However, he has the tendency to turn the puck over trying to force passes through the opposition at times. Babintsev is able to come down off the wing with great speed to put some good low shots on net to try to generate rebounds and opportunities for teammates in front. He can find the man in front with some good passes off the side wall. He puts some pressure on the fore-check, can cycle the puck in deep, and will go to the net with his stick down to try to get chances in front.

What he needs to try to do more often, however, is drive to the net with the puck, and try to play through the middle rather than being a perimeter player who likes to move the puck towards the middle.

Baddock, Brandon – RW – Edmonton Oil Kings (WHL) – 6'3" 200

Baddock is a physical depth winger who loves to punish opponents with some big hits. He plays a north-south game and every time he steps out onto the ice he is looking to land a punishing body check. He is strong along the wall, and is effective when cycling the puck. He is in poor position to receive passes, and has a difficult time finding open areas in coverage. He also has limited passing abilities, and will probably never be much of a scorer at any level that he plays in. His responsibility is to be responsible defensively and create turnovers for his line mates to take advantage of and try to score.

Bailey, Justin – RC – Kitchener Rangers (OHL) – 6'3" 186

Justin was selected in the 7th round of the 2011 OHL Priority Selection Draft by the Kitchener Rangers out of the Buffalo Regals U16 program. Justin showed off his talents with the Long Island Royals of the AYHL last season scoring almost a goal per game and putting up 34 points in 22 games. Justin also got a brief two game experience with the Indiana Ice (USHL) scoring 1 goal. Justin more than doubled his games played when he joined the Kitchener Rangers this season and entered the league with tremendous hype and expectations. While he may not have quite lived up to the unfair and lofty expectations, Justin certainly had a very successful rookie season. Things started out slowly for Justin receiving ice primarily on the 4th line. He never really moved beyond the 3rd line this season due to the tremendous depth and veteran presence on the Rangers, but he worked well with his line mates providing some depth scoring down the stretch. Bailey's work ethic improved and he battled for loose pucks and attempted to create turnovers.

Justin likes to have the puck on his stick and is always looking for scoring opportunities in the offensive zone. He has shown some flashes of creativity with the puck. He works hard to be reliable in the defensive zone and is good at assisting his defenders down low and can play a full 200 feet. He has a tremendous shot that fools many goaltenders. His skating stride is fairly choppy and he has issues generating speed in his first few steps. While he is capable of reaching a good speed for a 6'3" forward, he needs to continue to work on his skating in the offseason. Although he's a big kid, Bailey rarely gets involved in the physical aspect of the game, which may be a confidence issue at this point. He should look to add strength to his frame in the offseason in preparation for next year. Bailey will be looked upon to play a much larger role in the Rangers offensive plans next season as they graduate a number of key veterans.

Quotable: "I keep waiting to be blown away by this kid but I keep leaving the rink wanting more. He's a 3rd rounder for me." - NHL Scout

Quotable: "I spoke to Justin this year and I really like the kid. He was well spoken, gave thoughtful answers, and was realistic about where his game was at that point of the season. As for his game, it was hit and miss, he lacked consistency. I thought he was turning a corner at one point of the season but I thought that he continued to struggle to keep an upward trend in his progression. I think he is behind others when it comes to thinking the game. He seemed a step behind at times, especially when he played with some of Kitchener's top forwards." - Mark Edwards

Baptiste, Nicholas – RW – Sudbury Wolves (OHL) – 6'1" 190

Nicholas is a player we've seen a ton of potential in, even before his OHL Draft season began. Unfortunately multiple shoulder injuries slowed his development that year. He was still selected first round, 6th Overall, by the Sudbury Wolves out of the Ottawa Jr. Senators Minor Midget Program. He is a very quick, agile player that is physical and puts great pressure on the forecheck. Baptiste's biggest asset as a player is his speed.

He possesses good hands and the ability to create time and space for himself to make a play. He has a great work ethic, battles really hard for the puck and can protect it very effectively on the wide drive. He competes to get to the front of the net, cycles the puck really well and puts great pressure on the fore-check, making sure to finish his hits. His best asset is definitely his speed, as he is the fastest player on the ice most nights. He has some creativity to make plays with the puck, is not intimidated to go to the dirty areas and doesn't panic when he has the puck.

He needs to watch some of the turnovers trying to force passes at times. He also needs to hit the net with more consistency. Like many players he will need to get stronger so that he can become a forceful power forward with great speed and quickness. Baptiste is a sure fire pick in the 2013 NHL Entry Draft and it wouldn't be a surprise to us to see a team use a second round pick on him..

Quotable: "We had many internal discussions about when Baptiste was going to start playing to the expectations we had for him. He showed flashes late in the season. I thought he had some good games in Sochi." - Mark Edwards

Quotable: "Nick stood out to us in Minor Midget, but we were waiting to see him show his potential at the OHL level as a true NHL prospect. As the 2012-2013 season went on, Nick finally started to show his true potential." - Ryan Yessie

Barkov, Aleksander – LC – Tappara (SM-liiga) – 6'3 209

Aleksander has been on the radar for the 2013 NHL Entry Draft for a few years now. It's hard to believe if Barkov was born just two weeks later he would be ineligible until the 2014 NHL Entry Draft. In 2010-2011 a 15 year old Barkov really had his giant bridge in development rapidly rising through the U16 and U18 programs posting nearly a point per game in the U20 league. In 2011-2012 as a 16 year old Barkov posted 16 points in 32 games in Finland's top mens league showing his true potential, also participating in the 2012 World Junior Championships. Aleksander can't even be considered an adult in North America until September 2013, but he looked like a man amongst boys finishing in the top 10 scoring in Finland's top men's league this past season.

Barkov is a big strong forward who showed particularly in the World Junior Championships when matched up against players his own age that he is capable of asserting himself with his size. He is strong on the puck, protecting it effectively and can possess the puck for long periods of time. This is increasingly dangerous because of the high level of creativity Barkov possesses. He can produce points very well, but he does so using a great combination of shooting and passing ability. He is an unpredictable player because if you play his shot, he'll make a great pass, and if you play the pass he'll fire a hard, accurate shot on net. Barkov is capable of taking up space out front of the opposing net. Because of his size he is very difficult to move out front. This is something he's had to learn because he was a bit more on the perimeter. If you can move him from the front, Barkov will find good positioning in the offensive zone. He is great along the boards and wins a lot of battles showing strength and relentlessness along the boards. He also forechecks hard creating turnovers. Barkov's skating ability needs to improve. It is expected at his size and age that it is something that needs work and will be the biggest area of focus during the summer to help Barkov be NHL ready come September. He shows good backcheck and competes hard defensively. He has also shown well in the face-off circle winning a lot of key draws for his teams.

Barkov is expected to be one of the first names called at the 2013 NHL Entry Draft. He shows a ton of upside as a forward who could walk onto an NHL roster immediately and help a team at the NHL level right away. He has a big upside and whichever team selects Aleksander will be very happy on June 30th

Barrick, Brodie – G – Sarnia Sting (OHL) – 6'2" 171

Brodie has taken a bit of a long road to get to Sarnia but he's impressed us along the way. We've been able to see Barrack in training camps and were particularly impressed with his quickness at his size. Brodie played with the Pittsburgh Hornets U18 team and put up strong performances and good numbers. Last season Barrick got a good amount of starts with the Carleton Place Canadians (CCHL). This past season he made the jump to the OHL and looked good early on. Brodie's lower body quickness appears to be his best asset and he is tough to beat down low. He has a good glove hand and usually makes the first save. He has an odd side to side movement that is effective but it looks more like a stepping movement.

Brodie's season was limited to only four games due to a broken ankle. While he recovered in time to assume the back-up role in a few games, he wasn't able to get back into game action the rest of the season. Brodie is a late birth date which works against him in regards to the amount of time he has to prove himself. He showed flashes of an NHL draftable goaltender, but with limited viewings he can only be regarded so high at this point. He may get selected late or get an invite. Brodie will have a shot at being a starter for the Sting next season, and if he stays healthy, he could show his true potential because he has certainly been one of the most intriguing goaltending prospects pre-Christmas.

Bateman, Adam – RD – Windsor Spitfires (OHL) – 5'11" 185

Adam was selected in the first round of the 2011 OHL Priority Selection Draft by the Niagara Ice Dogs. After Niagara was unable to come to terms with Bateman he was traded to Windsor. Things looked bright for him early on but as the season went on he actually declined a bit. The 2012-2013 season was a new opportunity for Bateman. However, he didn't quite play at the level that was expected of him. Adam is a good skater who rushes the puck up ice effectively. He makes some good passes but can be pressured into making mistakes.

For a defenseman who is looked towards to provide offense, he just didn't provide enough as the season went on. Adam shows a strong compete level but needs to get physically stronger in order to win more battles. Defensively, he was hit or miss. We saw him make some good smart plays, but also saw him get burned badly at times as well. Adam is a player who we don't expect to get drafted in 2013, but if he continues to improve, he isn't a player to count out. He showed a ton of potential in Minor Midget, and much like others before him, may just need a little extra time.

Bauman, Chadd – LD – Guelph Storm (OHL) – 6'2" 203

Chadd was selected in the 4th round of the OHL Priority Selection Draft by the Guelph Storm out of the Waterloo Wolves Minor Midget Program. As a 16 year old, Chadd joined the Guelph Hurricanes Jr. B Organization and provided a physical, stay-at-home presence to the team, showing maturity beyond his years. Bauman saw limited ice time in his first season with the Storm due to a veteran loaded defense core. Chad was good in the action that he did see over the course of the season. He kept things simple and did not try to force any plays or take any major risks. He is good at getting pucks out of the defensive zone and uses the glass when needed in a hurry. Chad is a smooth skater and has enough speed to keep defenders to the outside.

Bauman needs to work at adding some strength to his frame so that he can add more of a physical element to his game in the corners and in front of the net. He showed enough promise throughout the season to earn the chance to play a bigger role on the Storm blue line next season. Bauman is not expected to be selected in this draft but has excellent size and appears to understand himself as a player showing promise for the future.

Bauml, Kohl – LC – Everett Silvertips (WHL) – 5'8" 164

Bauml may be an undersized centre, but he was depended on to play in every important situation for Everett this year. He out wills his opponents in the defensive zone to beat them for loose pucks and block shots to help his team win. He is good at reading the play without the puck, and is consistently in good position to make a play and provide some impact for the Silvertips. Offensively, Bauml has shown the ability to drive to the net and score dirty goals. He is not afraid of sacrificing his body to try to score from in tight. He has a good release to his shot, but needs to work on hitting the net more often and improve the velocity on his shots. He has limited playmaking abilities as he lacks the vision to make creative plays. The issue with Bauml's size combined with his lack of offensive abilities will really make it difficult for him to make much of an impact at the pro level. As a centre, he will have to go up against much more skilled and stronger opponents that he may not be able to cover and be a reliability as a result.

Beaton, Bronson – RC – Cape Breton Screaming Eagles (QMJHL) – 6'1" 182

Playing with the youngest team in the CHL was not an easy task for anyone this season, but many young players should become solid major junior performers in the next seasons, Bronson Beaton being one of them. A good puckhandler, the 6,01 182 pounds center has fluid hands and surprised us in many of our viewings with some slick moves when bringing the puck up. He makes is way well in traffic around the net and loves to use his body to shield the puck effectively. He has solid hockey sense, understanding his role as a center, supporting his defensemen and using his teammates well with his passing game. His biggest weakness is skating, with below average top speed and weak explosiveness; Beaton just can't get away easily from opposing players. He gets late to many plays whether they are offensive or defensive. We would also like to see more competitiveness from him, in his one-on-one battles and when he's around the net, more intensity and desire.

Beaulieu, Anthony – LD – Victoriaville Tigres (QMJHL) – 6'5" 203

Beaulieu was an interesting case to scout: he's a bad and slow skater with a huge body and a long reach. While he doesn't look very good and was far from being in control, it seems he found a way to make a safe defensive play 80% of the time. The problem is the other 20%. He has a lot of trouble defending speedy players and his slow footing doesn't allow him to be much of a physical threat. His play with the puck is also an area of weakness: very nervous with the puck and is limited in what he can do on the transition. He gave the puck away too often and he needs to make a more secure first pass out of his zone.

Beckstead, Marc – LW – Kingston Frontenacs (OHL) – 6'0" 174

Beckstead was an excellent selection by the Kingston Frontenacs going in the 14th round of the 2011 OHL Priority Selection Draft out of the Upper Canada Cyclones Minor Midget Program. Marc plays a very simple game. He likes to get pucks deep and is willing to hit. He battles hard in the corner and shows a consistent work ethic.

He has shown flashes of offensive potential with some smooth passes and getting the puck on the net but it just isn't enough at this point to consider him a potential offensive prospect. Beckstead certainly has a shot at being picked, but he's likely bunched in with a large group of bottom six potential players. Many of which have better offensive statistics and are either stronger skaters, possess bigger frames, or both. Marc will need to continue working hard to be a bigger part of this up and coming Frontenacs organization.

Bellerive, Matt – RW – Red Deer Rebels (WHL) – 5'11" 188

Bellerive started the season with his hometown Vancouver Giants, but requested for a trade earlier in the year because of lack of ice time. He immediately grabbed a hold of a permanent spot in the line up with the Rebels, and proved to be a good player at this level. The best attribute of Bellerive is his speed. He plays the game at a very quick pace and is at his best when he is moving his feet to make things happen. He has a good release to his shots, but needs to really work on hitting the net more often. He possesses above average vision, but will probably never really become a great playmaker around the net. The biggest detriment to Bellerive's game is his poor play along the wall. He gets beat in puck battles on a regular basis, and has a difficult time tying up opponents along the wall. He just does not make enough of an impact on a night to night basis to be considered as an NHL prospect at this point in his career.

Berisha, Aaron – Belleville Bulls (OHL) – 5'10" 183

Berisha was a 4th round pick in the 2011 OHL Priority Selection Draft after he lead his Toronto Marlboros to an OHL cup and was named the tournament MVP. Aaron joined Salisbury Prep High School for the 2011-2012 season putting up impressive numbers. He worked hard and was able to crack the Bulls roster out of training camp. Throughout his rookie season he was able to demonstrate his good hands, skating and a good sense for the game. He cycles the puck well and goes hard to the net while protecting it to create chances in tight. He puts good pressure on the fore-check, hustles nicely to get on loose pucks and plays the puck carrier with an element of physicality. He can make some good passes on the breakout to start the rush up through the neutral zone and is able to center the puck in the offensive zone to get it to the slot to create scoring chances. He can move around to find space in the offensive zone, opens up to provide his teammates with scoring options and can read the play well in both aspects of the game to make a smart play, whether it be picking up a long pass off the boards or coming back to cover for a defenseman who may have been jumping up on a pinch. He is fairly strong on the puck, battles well for it but just needs to watch the turnovers trying to force passes through the opposition and needs to get his shots through to the net on chances off the rush. Aaron is a player we don't expect to be drafted, but could see being selected late in the 2013 NHL Entry Draft due to the energetic game he was able to bring the Bulls this season. He shows some good offense, but not enough to project him as a top six forward at the next level.

Bertuzzi, Tyler – LW – Guelph Storm (OHL) – 6'0" 178

Tyler was selected in the 4th Round of the 2011 OHL Priority Selection Draft by the Guelph Storm out of the Sudbury Wolves Minor Midget Program. Tyler joined the Storm and used his tenacious physical play to earn a spot on the roster as a 16 year old, however, caught behind many talented forwards, he received limited ice time. Bertuzzi then had an up and down 2012-2013 season for the Storm. He was just getting into a solid stride when he was forced to miss a large number of games due to an upper body injury through the middle of the season. The Storm are a different team with Tyler in the lineup as he is constantly setting the physical tone and firing up his teammates with his aggressive style of play. He can generate a good amount of space when given room to skate north and south along the boards and shows flashes of offensive creativity in one on one situations. Bertuzzi is at his best when he is driving to the net and outworking opposing defenders battling for rebound opportunities. He is always keeping his feet moving and likes to get in on the forecheck and dish out punishment to opposing defenders. Tyler is built very solid and he is very effective at getting under the skin of the opposition and works hard to draw penalties in scrums after the whistle.

On the other edge of that sword, however, he can sometimes let his emotions get the best of him and take penalties himself. He is a little undersized and will need to get even stronger to consistently play the same role at the NHL level. He has limited offensive upside at the pro level and will get many of his points from driving the net and working hard. Bertuzzi also needs to learn when to reign in his game and not allow himself to get out of position constantly chasing hits.

Quotable: "Tyler overcame some injuries and became the player we thought he would be. He's a tough physical, agitating forward who teams don't like to face. His offensive upside is not very high, but every team needs a player who plays the way Bertuzzi does." - Ryan Yessie

Quotable: "Unfortunately Tyler missed a large chunk of the season due to injuries, however when he was in the line-up for the Storm he was certainly quite noticeable. He fits the pest role to a tee, and is constantly getting under the skin of opponents. He sometimes crosses the line however and perhaps took a few too many penalties.- Kevin Thacker

Besse William (Grant) - Benilde-St. Marg. – (Minn. HS) – 5'9" 177

Really good talent but he left us wanting more. He's not big but he has a great shot and is a natural goal scorer. He's a good skater and you can see a ton of natural ability. He had some shifts that looked kind of lazy. He has good instincts and knows how to finish. Heading to Wisconsin.

Betker, Ben – LD – Everett Silvertips (WHL) – 6'5" 200

Betker is a tall, lanky stay at home defenseman with limited puck skills. He plays with a chip on his shoulder and plays a tough, physical game. There are a number of improvements that Betker needs to make. Firstly, his skating is below average and has a lot of trouble handling any amount of speed off the rush. He has a long reach, but does not position himself properly to utilize it. He is not very good along the corners because he has a tough time with quick starts and stops and trying to turn quickly to keep up with opponents. Another improvement Betker needs to make is his ability to read the play. There are often times when he looks overwhelmed and confused with the play down low. He must do a better job of staying in his position and taking away passing lanes. He also needs to make better passes out of the zone and have some poise with the puck.

Betker will give opponents a difficult time around the ice as he loves to dish out hits and be in their faces all game long. He will fight anybody, and stand up for teammates when necessary. He sacrifices his body to block shots on a regular basis as well.

Betz, Nick – RW – Erie Otters (OHL) – 6'5" 210

Nick was selected in the 6th Round of the 2011 OHL Priority Selection Draft out of the Detroit Little Caesars U16 program. Despite being drafted in the 6th Round, Nick did a great job in camp and made the Erie Otters as a 16 year old playing almost every game during the 2011-2012 season. Everything looked promising for Nick entering the 2012-2013 season, however, he really didn't reach his potential this season which is likely going to affect his draft status. Nick is a huge winger who has a huge frame. He generally played 3rd and 4th line for the Otters and hasn't been much of a point producer in that role. Nick showed an effective work ethic and handles the puck moderately well in the slot area. He doesn't have a big offensive upside and while he may put up decent numbers in the OHL later on in his career, it's not expected to translate at the pro level. Nick's greatest asset is his size, although we were a little disappointed in this area. Not because he doesn't use it, he just doesn't use it often enough to maximize his effectiveness on the ice or for his team.

We believe Nick has a small outside shot at being drafted. Of course, a player his size has potential for a free agent invite, or to be picked up as a re-entry, but he simply has to play more consistently to his perceived strengths. He needs to be more mean, more physical and finish his checks regularly. On a nightly basis Nick is one of, if not the biggest body on the ice. He needs to play like he is and make himself a difficult player to play against every night. If he does this he's going to have NHL scouts putting a star next to his name as a re-entry. A team may still pick him up with the feeling they can help get him on track, but it's more likely he will have to learn this on his own before being picked up.

Betzold, Greg – LW – Peterborough Petes (OHL) – 6'1.5" 195

A native of Bel Air, Maryland, Greg spent two seasons at Shattuck St. Mary's. He then received an invite to the Peterborough Petes Rookie Camp. After impressing at the camp, Greg signed with the Petes and became a valuable contributor for them all season. Greg often plays a pro style game and is at his best when he sticks to it. He works hard and wins tons of 1 on 1 battles, he cycles the puck well, and does a good job getting the puck to the scoring areas. While he did not have many goals this season, we believe they are going to come. All of his goals were "goal-scorer's goals" and we think with more confidence and experience, those numbers will improve.

His best skill is his ability to control the puck, beat defenseman and then use his creativity to create scoring chances. With these skills, he was able to effectively play up and down the lineup. Besides his offensive abilities, Greg displayed a fantastic work ethic all season. He came into the OHL raw, and by the end of the season was a strong three zone player, and consistently one of the hardest workers on the ice. Greg showed some clutch ability in playing some of his best hockey in Peterborough's final 2 weeks of the season.

Greg could stand to finish more of his checks. He had games where this was a strength and others where he left hits on the ice. Sometimes Greg looks rushed to get rid of the puck. We would like to see him trust his possession skills a little more. We think it may have been a result of worrying too much about turnovers, which can lead to reduced ice time, especailly for a rookie.

Overall, we see Betzold as a player with tremendous upside. With added strength, and a whole summer to work on his skating ability and overall training, Betzold has a chance to be part of the solution next year in Petrborough and a solid NHL prospect.

Quotable: "Greg sent me DVD's of a couple of his games late last May. I was very impressed with what I saw on tape, so I made a few calls and Peterborough ended up being where he attended camp. He was signed quickly and the rest, as they say, is history. I watched the Petes a lot this year and Greg impressed me. He had never played at a speed close to the OHL but adjusted nicely. He has more scoring skills than he showed this year. I want to see him play more to his size more often next season." - Mark Edwards

Quotable: "I can see the upside in this kid, for a rookie coming where he came from, he could really impress in year two. He's an intriguing player." - NHL Scout

Bibeau, Antoine - G - PEI Rocket (QMJHL) - 6'2" 213

It took Antoine Bibeau some time before becoming stellar 1st goalie in QMJHL, but at 18 years old that's what he was able to do in a surprising PEI Rocket team in 2012-2013. Antoine is a big kid, taking out tons of space in front of his net. For a goalie his size, his athleticism and flexibility is impressive, he made a lot of spectacular saves in our viewings of him. He is a quick and agile goalie, butterfly based but his technique is not his strongest asset and he will rely on reflexes to make saves, even some that are easier than they look to be. He has quick hands and although he is quick on knees sometimes his reactions are accurate and quick with the glove. Bibeau likes to be agressive, challenge shooters and obviously that's when he is at his best and most confident. Bibeau's biggest weakness is his work ethic during a game, sometimes will get lazy in his positioning, will over move and rely too much on his reflexes to make saves. His angle coverage, butterfly base positioning and rebound countrol will get inaccurate and pucks will get through him because of that. He certainly has some natural physical abilities that are interesting, but for us it remains to be seen if he can keep the same kind of confidence and level of performances that he had this season with PEI with the low level of work ethic we've seen.

Bigras, Chris - LD - Owen Sound Attack (OHL) - 6'0.5" 186

Chris was selected 2nd round, 41st overall at the 2011 OHL Priority Selection draft out of the Barrie Colts Minor Midget program. The Attack made a great pick in selecting Chris who improved at an alarming rate throughout his rookie season. Despite Owen Sound being one of the best teams in the Western Conference last year, Chris was used on the power play as a 16 year old and looked like one of the better young offensive defensemen coming up from his age group. What was really impressive came early on this season. Chris had greatly improved his defensive game and was extremely reliable in a shutdown role. He doubled his points total from last season, despite being used in a stronger defensive role.

Chris enters the 2013 NHL Entry Draft as one of the most well rounded defenders eligible for the draft. Chris sticks with his man very well along the boards and is rarely evaded even by the shiftiest of skaters. He moves very well in all directions and is extremely tough to beat in one on one situations. His positional play is generally strong, but he does have an occasional tendency to lose his positioning. This is something he's improved at throughout the year and is really our only concern defensively, besides Chris getting stronger. Offensively he was a lot more tame and selective in when he would use his puck skills. However, when he did choose to rush the puck he was very effective going end to end evading checkers. He is a smooth puck mover who makes intelligent decisions and rarely makes a mistake.

Bigras projects to be a player who isn't going to be a star in the NHL, but he's going to be an all game situations player. He won't be the #1 penalty killer, or power play quarterback, but he will be able to play both of those roles effectively in the NHL. He isn't projected to be a top pairing guy, but he would be a compliment to a team's top four. He's one of the most well rounded defenseman in the 2013 NHL Entry Draft and should be a popular player in the second half of the first round.

Quotable: "One of my risers this year. I liked him every time I saw him. He has more offensive ability than he gets credit for. He is a smart player. He logged a ton of minutes and shutdown the best the league had to offer. Other than not being a huge kid, I don't see any real weaknesses." - Mark Edwards

Quotable: "He does everything well, he is smart as hell, I have him ranked higher than Nurse." - NHL Scout

Bjorkstrand, Oliver – RW – Portland Winterhawks (WHL) – 5'11" 164

Bjorkstrand came into the league as an import forward and quickly adjusted to the North American style of play. He mostly played on the 3rd line on a very deep team, but was able to make a good impact consistently and gave teams a nightmare in terms of matching lines every game. The first thing you notice about Bjorkstrand is that he plays bigger than his size. He is very good along the boards and drives to the net hard. He may not be involved in many scrums after the whistles, but whenever he is out on the ice, he gives his full effort in tough areas. Another strength of Bjorkstrand is his skating abilities. He is so tough to tie up along the wall because he can make quick tight turns with the puck and buy his line mates some time to get open. He has very impressive acceleration and opponents have a difficult time keeping him to the outside. Offensively, Bjorkstrand has very good overall skill. He possesses a good touch around the net, and a quick release. He positions himself well everywhere out on the ice, and constantly moves into open areas to receive passes. He is a good playmaker himself, and sees the ice quite well. Defensively, Bjorkstrand works hard in his own end without the puck, but still has work to do in regards to positioning. He has a tendency to lose track of his point man, and has a difficult time getting into shooting lanes and taking away passes as a result.

Quotable: "I liked him when I saw him last year and I have been impressed with him this season. The kid has an NHL release and he has impressed me with his compete level all over the ice. I like his scoring upside at the next level."

- Mark Edwards

Quotable: "This kid will score a ton next season with Rattie gone." - NHL scout

Blomqvist, Axel – LW – Lethbridge Hurricanes (WHL) – 6'5" 194

Blomqvist is a big forward with some skills with the puck. He was mostly depended on to provide a net front presence, but his lack of toughness and willingness to take punishment in the slot does not allow him to make much of an impact. He must work on his skating, particularly his acceleration and overall speed. He does not read the play quickly, and combined with lack of quickness, it makes it difficult for him to get into the right areas of the ice. He has to use his body to his advantage more by providing a more physical presence along the walls and in front of the net. He has shown above average stick handling abilities, but will have to develop his game further to have any sort of an impact.

Boland, Connor – LD – Peterborough Petes (OHL) – 6'2" 200

Connor was selected in the 2nd round of the 2010 OHL Priority Selection Draft out of the Whitby Wildcats Minor Midget program. Connor showed good development in his rookie season playing regularly in the third pairing. Unfortunately for Boland he suffered a shoulder injury that limited his 2011-2012 season to just 13 games. However, due to a late birth date, he was not eligible for the NHL Draft until 2013 allowing him to get his third OHL season in before becoming a first year eligible.

Connor's issues continued at the start of this season when he was diagnosed with mononucleosis. However, when he came back from it, he immediately provided a very steady presence on the blueline for Peterborough. His ice and subsequently his play showed great improvements after Slater Koekkoek was moved from Peterborough to Windsor opening up ice time on the Petes. He is not flashy, but he is a strong skater, provides physical play and generally makes the smart play. With his size and skating ability, we think Boland could be a valuable pick in the late rounds of the 2013 NHL Entry Draft. He projects to be a steady safe, third pairing defenseman at the NHL level.

Boudens, Matthew – LC – Drummondville Voltigeurs (QMJHL) – 5'11" 199

Boudens quickly became a favorite of ours ever since he joined the QMJHL from Ontario. He quickly established himself as one the best grinders in the league. He moves surprisingly well for a big man and he is all over the ice running over people. He plays a simple game and is very effective in all areas. He also plays a very physical game, willing to throw the body, his hits are heavy and punishing. He is a character player showing up every night, getting his nose dirty and willing to sacrifice his body for his team. He will be an active player in scrums and is a proven pugilist. His skating has improved significantly over the 2011-2012 season which has helped him play his role with more energy and effectiveness. He doesn't have an astonishing top speed but it's fairly good for major junior, it will need to be better for pro hockey. While it's not the best part of his game, Boudens can play with the puck and will try to make things happens around the opposition's net. He can hold on to the puck, protect it and likes to drive the net. His upper body strength is really good and only few defensemen in the Q can match him on the boards. He plays a simple dump and chase game with the vast majority of his offensive puck possession time cycling the puck effectively. He also displayed an interesting wrist shot in our viewings, getting himself close to the 20 goals mark this season with 18. He will jump on rebounds, deflect pucks and be a great net presence. A strong presence defensively, Boudens plays a clever and simple game. His work ethic makes him a great defensive forward, playing with desire and winning most of his battles to get the puck out.

Bowey, Madison – RD – Kelowna Rockets (WHL) – 6'1" 194

Bowey is a dynamic defenseman who has continued to improve his overall game. His best asset is his skating abilities, which he uses with and without the puck to be a force for the Rockets every game. In an interview with HockeyProspect, Madison has acknowledged that he has been focusing on playing a more solid game in his own end this season and letting the play come to him, which he has definitely improved on since last year. Offensively, Bowey is very fun to watch. He loves to skate with the puck and add another dimension to the Rockets' transition attack with his speed. He moves the puck very well when necessary, and is an important piece to their power play. Bowey sees the ice well and identifies open lanes and makes very good back door passes. He takes some risks at times that does not always pay off, but they are rarely terrible mistakes that result in great scoring chances for the other team. Bowey is mobile along the blueline, and makes it difficult for opposing forwards to cover him because he could move laterally or move down the boards with the puck in a hurry. He has so many options due to his speed, that opponents are half a step late in trying to read what his next move will be.

Bowey's game without the puck has come a long way from the start of the season. He does not chase the puck as much as he did, and lets the play come to him instead. He has done a great job in playing between the dots instead of trying to land big open ice hits and getting caught out of position. He still likes to take chances in the neutral zone to create turnovers and start a transition the other way, but he takes low risk, high reward gambles. He is strong along the walls and has a bit of an edge to his game, and is not afraid to get into an opponent's face and make it difficult to play against him. The aspect of his game that is fun to watch is that he plays with such a great level of energy. Even when he may be playing his 3rd game in 3 nights, he plays with the same enthusiasm consistently and it looks like he really enjoys playing the game. He back checks hard if he is ever caught in a bad position in the neutral zone, and quickly jumps into the play when he sees a lane that he can attack. He is hard to ignore when he is out on the ice, and will surely be a fan favorite wherever he goes.

Quotable: "I love the feet, his skating is high end. I have seen flashes of a physical game which I like. He has PP 2 upside and moves the puck well. I think he has lots of room to get even better. Has the occasional brain cramp. He was good in Sochi at the U18." - Mark Edwards

Quotable: "Bowey's game only got better as the season went on especially his ability to read the play and step up in the neutral zone to make an open ice hit. I also don't think people talk enough about his play on the PP. I also love the confidence that he plays with every shift." - Charles An

Quotable: "I like his upside. He has raised his stock in this tournament." - NHL scout (during U18 in Sochi)

Bowles, Parker – LW – Tri-City Americans (WHL) – 5'11" 180

Parker Bowles is a fast, offensive minded winger who loves to carry the puck and try to score highlight reel goals. He is able to take advantage of slow defensemen or opponents that are caught flat footed or in a poor position and be able to burn them off the rush. Bowles' favorite move in the offensive zone is to skate the puck up to the point from the corner, then quickly cut to the middle in the high slot and snap a shot. He also loves to pick up the puck from the defensive zone with speed and try to go through the entire opposing line up to get to the net. He only possesses above average hands, which he will need to work on if he wants to do the same thing at the pro level. Opponents will be bigger and faster, which will give him less opportunities to wheel around the ice. He has below average playmaking abilities, and his wrist shot is not very good either. Defensively, Bowles is poor in his own end. He is almost invisible in the defensive zone, and does not do a very good job along the boards. He is quite soft to play against, and he has to commit to blocking shots more often. He likes to cheat and seldom comes down low to help out his defensemen.

Brouillard, Nikolas – LD – Drummondville Voltigeurs (QMJHL) – 5'10" 148

In his rookie season, Brouillard made a good impression on us with his understanding of the game and offensive abilities. He put that to good use this season, racking up an impressive 57 points. He likes to rush the puck up the ice and organize the transition. A great passer, he has solid offensive vision, making long accurate feeds on the transition look easy, being able to execute high risk plays with great confidence. He is not an explosive skater but he has great top speed and tremendous footwork, gets his wheels going with little footsteps over the more effective power skating driven approach. When he doesn't have the puck, he loves to act as the fourth man on the rush, often leading up to odd-man rushes. He often goes all the way to the net with his group of forwards, thus resulting in many points. His mobility enables him to join the rush but react quickly in the case of a turnover. He has great offensive hockey sense, rarely staying stationary, always keeping the feet moving. He has a strong accurate wrist shot, his great footwork helps him find shooting lanes easily. A fantastic powerplay performer, Nikolas Brouillard is really well suited for games with time and space. Defensively Brouillard is good enough to be an effective defender, following his man easily and winning the footraces to loose pucks. His positional game has been significantly better this season, but he still tends to run around too much. His extremely small frame puts him serious trouble. He is often bounced around in front of his net and along the boards. He needs to get stronger to handle big forwards and his duty as defenseman. In addition, the fact he lacks high end speed as a puck-moving defenseman, we see Brouillard going in the later rounds of the draft, if drafted at all.

Buchnevich, Pavel - C - Russia - 6'0" 157

We saw him in Windsor last year at the U17 and again this year at the U18 in Sochi. While he didn't tear it up in Windsor last year he left an impression this year in Sochi. He is a highly skilled player who stood out on multiple shifts. He centred a line with Nichushkin and was veru good all tournament long. He has skill, playmaking abilities and has proven he can score. Although we have limited viewings he has made an impression. Heard some NHL guys talking about some concerns with him but we liked what we saw from him, especially at the U18. He needs to get stronger in order to progress to the NHL. His phyical attributes are his weakness.

Quotable: " I watched him a few times in his home country and he impressed me in each game." - Mark Edwards

Brace, Cameron - RW - Owen Sound Attack (OHL) - 5'9.5" 176

Brace has spent his entire four year OHL Career with the Attack. He saw marginal action in his rookie season. In his second year he was consistently used in a bottom six role. He became more of an impact player during their OHL Championship stretch and provided a consistent work ethic with scoring touch. After going unselected, Cameron came back and became a go to guy for the Attack offensively, while still showing his chippy two-way play. Again he went unselected. He stayed consistent in his role this season looking very similar as he did last season. He is very speedy and quick. He is capable of driving the wing and taking some damage from defensemen while protecting the puck. Brace is more of a shooter than a passer and he has a quick release. He also has a knack for scoring big goals. He scored 10 goals, 7 in the first 10 games of the season. He also had three game winning goals just six games into the OHL season this year.

Cameron may not be the biggest player in the ice, but he's not afraid to play physical or go head first into puck battles. What separates Brace from the average small, speedy goal scorer is his commitment to the defensive game. We've seen many occasions where Cameron has been willing to get down and block shots, where he's been a key contributor to the team's penalty kill, and he's come away with some short handed goals thanks to his ability to force turnovers. Cameron is a player who we really feel may get drafted late. Should he go unselected, he should be pursued for an NHL camp invite.

Quotable: " I'd like to see him play gritty more often, when he does he looks a lot more like a legit prospect." - NHL Scout

Bradford, Erik - LC - Barrie Colts (OHL) - 5'11.25" 178

Bradford was selected in the 10th Round of the 2010 OHL Priority Selection Draft out of the Markham Waxers Minor Midget Program. This turned out to be an outstanding pick by the Colts organization. Bradford received a handful of games as a 16 year old, but started to really come onto the scene in the second half of the 2011-2012 season. Due to his late birth date he was ineligible for the 2012 NHL Entry Draft. The Colts really benefitted from Erik's smart two-way play heading into the playoffs, and while his ice time really didn't increase much due to the number of returning veterans, Erik has only become a stronger presence in the two-way style consistently placed on the third line in Barrie. Regardless, Erik had a decent season statistically. 18 goals, 46 penalty minutes, and was +8 in 68 games this season, which represents his style of game.

Bradford plays a hard-nosed game with great work ethic mixed with an element of skill. He is a physical presence, puts great pressure on the puck carrier, especially on the fore-check, and makes sure to finish all his hits along the boards. He is willing to go to the dirty areas, battles well for pucks in front of the net, and gets many of his opportunities off loose pucks and rebounds. He provides his defensemen with good support in his own end, tying up the opposition in front of the net as well as going down to get in lanes and block shots. He can cycle the puck effectively, brings a decent net-front presence in the offensive zone and possesses pretty good speed and agility to distance himself from the opposition's pressure when he has the puck. He moves the puck around well to start the rush, and likes to drive it wide with good protection, then throw it to the front of the net to teammates driving down the middle. He opens up nicely down low to take passes, then put good shots on net and will drive the puck to the net to create chances in tight.

What makes him such an intriguing prospect is his level of hockey sense and ability to read and understand the play so quickly. Bradford projects to be a highly capable two-way forward who provides a wide range of talent and possesses some legitimate untapped offensive potential that may be exposed as he plays a bigger role next season in junior. Erik has been one of our favorite under appreciated prospects in the 2013 NHL Entry Draft. We expect Bradford to be selected.

Quotable: "Erik was stuck on the third line all year in Barrie because of how many older forwards the Colts had. They always seemed to call upon Erik in the final minute of the game, especially in the playoffs whether they needed a goal, or to hold down a lead. He's so reliable defensively but has a lot of offensive upside that has yet to be tapped by the Colts." - Ryan Yessie

Brassard, Connor – RD – Cushing Academy (Prep-MA) – 6'0, 165

Connor is a big, smooth-skating defenseman who plays with a lot of poise. He was selected by Val-d'Or in the 2012 QMJHL Draft, but played this year with Cushing and was selected by Chicago in the 2013 USHL Draft at the season's conclusion. He plays a refined two-way game, with deft stick handling and good puck decisions to go along with smart positional play in his zone. He's not physical, but uses his stick well and can utilize his frame to box forwards out along the boards and in front of the net. He can carry the puck up ice and make plays though he takes care of his end first and foremost. He defends well against the rush and makes intelligent decisions overall. He looks like a possible late-round flier, but it could be that scouts are waiting to see how he does when he steps up a level, as the prep game can be flattering.

Bristedt, Leon – RW – Linkoping J20 (SWE J20) – 5'8" 180

Leon is an undersized yet ultra talented and competitive forward who has developed up through the Linkoping system the past two years. Leon is very creative offensively with the puck. He has the ability to elude multiple defenders but also possesses a calm and patience with the puck that allows him to create plays for his teammates. He also has the ability to possess the puck for long periods of times, evading checkers, sometimes forcing them to take a stick or holding infraction just to slow him down. Bristedt also will drive the net hard with the puck and try to finish himself. He has a powerful shot and lets to let it go in the offensive zone. Leon is sometimes one of, if not the smallest player on the ice. He overcomes this regularly with a tremendous work ethic, tenacious energy and a never quit attitude. Defensively he gets all over the puck carrier and is capable of forcing turnovers. Leon is the type of player NHL teams would love to have, but wished he was much bigger. There is little doubt some team will take a shot at him at some point, but he will likely go off the board where there isn't much risk to the pick. There's concern about his 5'8" frame, but little to no concern about his skill set.

Broadhead, Gavin – RC – Medicine Hat Tigers (WHL) – 5'11" 180

Broadhead is a depth, high energy centre for the Tigers. He has very limited offensive skills, and will probably never be counted on to provide much offense at any level of hockey. He has very little playmaking abilities and does not show much poise with the puck, and his puck protection is quite poor. Broadhead is most effective when he is on the forecheck and creating turnovers with his hits and speed. He is quick to loose pucks, and allows his team to get set in the offensive zone. He plays a good role on the PK, and does a good job of blocking shots. Unfortunately, due to his lack of offense, there will probably be very little interest in him on draft day.

Brodzinski, Michael – RD – Muskegon Lumberjacks (USHL) – 5'11" 193

Brodzinski played his first 3 games in the USHL last year where he registered his first point with an assist after being selected 7th overall in the 1st round by Des Moines Buccaneers. He followed it up with a full season playing in 61 games and scoring 33 points including 16 goals, which was the most in the league as a defenseman for the Muskegon Lumberjacks. He possesses great hands to rush the puck up the ice into the offensive zone and he finds lanes to get to the slot to put great shots on net. He is really calm with the puck and he gets his shot through to the net on a fairly consistent basis. He has decent size and skating, moves the puck well on the breakout and can hold on to the puck in the offensive zone to keep the cycle alive. He plays with an element of physicality on the puck carrier. Brodzinski demonstrated this year that he can be effective in the offensive zone but needs to translate that success to his own end moving forward. He needs to make sure he is hard to play against in his own end.

Johnny Brodzinski – C – ST.Cloud State (NCAA) – 6'0" 202

He got a lot of exposure with plenty of scouts in his rink. He has a cannon of a shot and can rattle some cages going bar down from the slot. He's not the best skater but he gets around. He's a pretty smart player and plays a simple game winning puck battles and going about his business. We expect him to get drafted in the later rounds.

Brown, Connor – LW – Ottawa 67's (OHL) – 5'11" 186

Connor was selected in the 9th round of the 2011 OHL Priority Selection by the Ottawa 67's out of the Halton Hurricanes Minor Midget Program. Connor spent his 2011-2012 season with the Halton Hurricanes Major Midget AAA team before cracking the rebuilding 67's lineup. Connor posted 6 points in 68 games this season. He is a blue collar role player who brings a physical element, blocks shots and puts good pressure on the puck carrier. He makes all his hits along the wall and is a reasonably tough player that is willing to drop the gloves. He keeps to a simple game all around, can cycle the puck well and gets to the front of the net looking for rebounds in tight.

He gets the puck in deep on simple dump and chase plays, but has to watch some of the turnovers trying to get too fancy and force passes through the opposition. Connor is not expected to be selected at the 2013 NHL Entry Draft. Instead he needs to continue working hard, getting stronger and playing a simple tough style of hockey. He needs to come out of the board battles more often with the puck and get to the front of the net as much as he can to try to score some dirty goals.

Brown, Davis – LW – Sarnia Sting (OHL) – 5'9" 185

Davis was a third round pick by the Sarnia Sting in the 2011 OHL Priority Selection Draft. As a 16 year old, Davis was one of the most dangerous goal scorers in the GOJHL for the Strathroy Rockets Jr. B team scoring 45 goals in 49 games. Davis saw limited action with the Sting in 2011-2012 playing 14 games but was primarily used as a fourth line forward. This season Davis played full time with the Sting. Just as Davis seemed to be getting things going he received an elbow to the head in open ice. This kept Davis out of action for weeks and it really seemed like he had to go back to square one when he returned.

Davis' strongest assets are his shot and his compete level. He has a laser quick shot so six goals is a large underachievement for him. To his credit he was used more for his hard work and checking than his shot playing on a line that didn't produce much offense overall. Davis is a little undersized but he hits surprisingly hard. He forces turnovers and plays much bigger than his size. He is also a very good skater and uses his speed when carrying the puck. The NHL will be an uphill battle, as he must overcome his size. Davis is one of those players that could break out in an increased role due to his shot and his willingness to put the work in to get into good scoring areas.

Buckles, Matt – RW – 6'2" – 210lb. – St. Michael's Buzzers (OJHL)

Buckles had a strong sophomore campaign for the OJHL champion Buzzers. After being selected in the 4th round by the Sault Ste. Marie Greyhounds in 2011, Buckles decided to go the NCAA route and committed to Cornell University. Matt was named the Top NHL prospect from the OJHL and participated for Canada East at the World Junior A. Challenge U19. He brings a blend of size and speed to his game and is very effective in the power forward position. He is very good at driving the net and has the offensive statistics to prove that he is a reliable goal scorer. Matt is lethal on the power play when setting up for the one timer at the top of the circle, and beats many goaltenders top shelf when given space to shoot. Buckles is not afraid to get into the corners and battle against bigger defenders and can turn up the physical intensity when necessary. He needs to work on consistency because there are some nights where he struggles to get much offence going. Matt also needs to work on defensive zone positioning and ensuring that he work to win board battles instead of making fancy outlet passes or flying the zone too early.

Burakovsky, Andre – LW – Malmo (SAL) – 6'1" 178

Andre has been a product of the Malmo system ever since he played for the U16 team as a 14 year old. He worked up to the J18 and J20 receiving an impressive 10 game tryout with the men's league team which started when he was just 16 years old. Andre has participated in two straight IIHF World U18 Championships in 2012 and 2013. He was also a gamebreaker for Team Sweden at the 2012 World U17 Challenge. Andre really jumped out to us at this tournament and we saw a player with a great deal of potential. Unfortunately since then he hasn't quite reached that level of play in our viewings. Andre displays very good playmaking ability. He is creative with the puck and makes his linemates better with his puck movement. He always finds a way to slip into scoring positioning but he forechecks hard battling for pucks and showing strong skating ability to get to the wall and the corners very fast. While he has a decent shot, in our viewings he seemed to lean more towards passing and creating rather than finishing. There really isn't a glaring weakness in his game. We would like to see him get stronger but the concern seems to be with the consistency in which he shows these skills. While he's a well rounded player, there have been too many instances where he simply did not show up to games or was invisible for long stretches. The potential is there but the consistency needs to follow for Andre to truly reach his potential.

Burke, Brendan – G – Portland Winterhawks (WHL) – 6'3" 174

Brendan Burke is the son of long time NHL goaltender and current goaltending coach of the Phoenix Coyotes, Sean Burke. He was initially awarded the starting job with Portland to start the year, but because he struggled, and with the return of Mac Carruth from the AHL, Burke has been assigned to the bench for most of the season. Burke fills up a lot of the net with his big frame. Once he challenges shooters coming down the wing, they do not have the chance to see much of the net. He uses his size to his advantage by standing tall and keeps his legs under his shoulders to give himself maximum power as he pushes off on his skates. He also has a wide butterfly, and takes up a lot of space when down on his knees. The problem with Burke seems to be his mental game. He is prone to giving up easy goals, and allows them to rattle him and allows the game to slip away for his team. He is not very good when the puck is around his feet and starts to flop around and gets on his back, which makes it difficult for him to recover afterwards. He really needs to work on his rebound control as well.

Quotable: "I saw two games early in the season, he struggled in both." – Mark Edwards

Burnside, Josh – LW – Mississauga Steelheads (OHL) – 5'11" 176

After playing just 13 games last season and registering only a single point, Burnside found a role on this team and ended up being a big piece of the puzzle. He was used extensively in an offensive role and played quite a bit of power play minutes. He possesses great speed, is really quick when he gets going and is very willing to bring a net-front presence on the power play. He hustles well in both ends of the ice, can cycle the puck effectively and then gets himself to the front of the net to try to create chances from in tight. He has an element of agility and shiftiness to his game, puts excellent pressure on the puck and protects the puck well to be able to take a hit and still hold on to it. Burnside also has shown good offensive instincts to be able to get in good position in the offensive zone, to be able to receive a pass then get a shot off, and he makes pretty quick decisions with the puck. He can read the play to determine when the opposition's defense are giving him a bit too much space, which allows him to make a play and take advantage of that time he is given. He is willing to go to the dirty areas, competes well for the puck and plays the game with a good energy and compete level.

He needs to work on how he controls and handles the puck, as he often appears to be playing on the edge and mishandles it when he is not able to control it at the speed and pace he likes to play at. Moving forward he will need to continue to show a responsible 200 foot game, where he can be effective offensively and contribute on a nightly basis, but at the same time take care of business in his own end and not be a liability. He has the speed and some size to try to be a good power forward and should try to model his game after a player like Blake Wheeler, who uses his speed to drive the puck hard to the net and create those opportunities within a few feet of the goal. He might not have as much size as Wheeler, but this type of game would make him most effective.

Quotable: "He's a mucker. Ugly but effective, not a ton of skill but he may be worth a late round selection." - NHL Scout

Burroughs, Kyle – RD – Regina Pats (WHL) – 5'11" 175

Burroughs was depended on to play some significant minutes for Regina this season, which has really helped his development. His overall play has improved steadily throughout the year, and will be counted on to be a key contributor for his team again next season as Regina's depth on defense is quite poor. Burroughs is not exceptionally skilled at any particular area of his game. He is an above average skater who likes to step up in the neutral zone to land open ice hits and try to get a counter attack started. He stays aggressive between the blue lines with his gap control, and gives opponents very little room to try to go wide on him. He needs to improve on his lateral mobility to take away space more quickly in the slot. Defensively, Burroughs is good without the puck along the walls, but he could be more patient and hold his position in between the faceoff circles to take away dangerous chances. The one attribute that stands out for Burroughs is his puck moving skills. When he is at his best, he makes crisp and simple outlet passes to get the attack going. There are times when he tries to thread the needle through a number of opponents, which more often than not gets intercepted. He needs to keep it simple all the time and cut back on the unnecessary passes. Burroughs should also try to shoot more from the point to keep opponents from easily predicting what he will do with the puck.

Butcher, Will – LD – US NTDP Under-18 Team – 5'10, 191

Will was the only defenseman able to consistently produce from the blueline for the NTDP this season. He was a factor in the offense every game. The stocky blueliner possesses great skating puck skills, able to accelerate from his zone into open space up ice with poise and navigate neutral zone traffic. He deals well with forecheck pressure and is smart about making safe plays to clear the zone when necessary, but can kick start the offense by head manning the puck with crisp feeds. He isn't afraid to take hits to make plays with the puck. His point work in the offensive zone is excellent. Thanks to quick feet and good awareness, he's good at keeping the puck in the zone at the point. He likes to pinch into the attack to keep the other team on their toes and has good finishing ability. His wrist shot is excellent. He can snap the puck with a quick release and precise accuracy. Also has a good one-timer that he's unafraid to use, frequently acting as the triggerman on the power play. Shows a good awareness of open shooting lanes and gets the puck on net frequently. Defensive play is mixed. He keeps his stick active and tracks the play with his head up, but sometimes has trouble finding the middle ground between overaggressive and passive positioning. Even when he does read the play correctly and plays the body, he lacks the strength to be effective on the boards and in front of the net against bigger players. His strong skating allows him to cover the rush well, but has trouble keeping tabs on forwards who try to beat him strong down the wing. Butcher's stock has dropped this season, which is more indicative of projection than his performance on the ice. He's an excellent defenseman against other under-18 teams and most USHL and college players, but lacks the defensive awareness and size to project him as a sure thing at the professional level right now.

Quotable: "I'm not sure he has developed all that much over the past couple of years. I like things in his game but upside is probably limited." - NHL Scout

Calderone, Tony – FW – Sioux Falls Stampede (USHL) – 5'11" 202

Calderone was a 1st overall pick by the Sioux Falls Stampede in the 2012 USHL Entry Draft and he played his rookie year in the USHL this year where he had a solid offensive performance with 44 points in 64 games played. Calderone protects the puck well in deep in the offensive zone and can get a pretty nice cycle started. He goes hard to the net looking for loose pucks and opportunities and he battles really well for his chances. He brings a nice net-front presence in the offensive zone, getting in the goaltender's face and trying to tip pucks to give his team a greater chance of scoring on their point shot opportunities. He takes far too many long outside shots on the rush when he has teammates and options available to move the puck, but at least he follows up the shot by going to the net or the slot to try and pick up on rebounds. He can distribute the puck pretty well in the offensive zone then gets himself to the slot to open up and provide scoring options and he also finds space to work with in the high slot to take passes and put good shots on net. He finds lanes on the power play to move the puck to open teammates down low in scoring positions and for the most part he gets his shots through to the net to generate opportunities in tight. The most desirable quality about his game is that he gets to the net and is not scared to go to those dirty areas and battle for his chances and loose pucks in tight to score the grinder type goals. He just needs to start trying to drive the puck down low rather than taking the long outside shots so often and has to have more creativity to move the puck and try and make a play off the rush when he has teammates and options available to him. Tony was also selected in the 13th round by the 2010 OHL Priority Selection Draft by the Windsor Spitfires. Calderone has committed to play for Princeton University.

Cammarata, Taylor – FW – Waterloo Blackhawks (USHL) 5'7" 156

Taylor and his line mates, Justin Kloos and Zach Stepan, dominated the USHL this year. The diminutive forward drove the Waterloo attack and led the league in goals and points. He scored with freakish consistency, going two straight games without a point just once. His production is largely based on his unpredictability. With the puck, Cammarata is a wizard with elite stick handling and lateral movement. He can evade checks with fantastic precision in the neutral and offensive zones and is extremely difficult to pin down. He's aware of everything happening on the ice and has the ability to alter the tempo of the game with the puck on his stick, showing outstanding vision and puck control in the process. He is nearly unstoppable on the power play when he has room to work with and shows off excellent passing, a great variety of hard, accurate shots, and fantastic poise. However, even at the USHL level, his size is clearly a limiting factor. Now known league-wide, Cammarata faces tough coverage on a nightly basis and is forced to endure serious physical punishment. He takes hits well but cannot be expected to continue to absorb contact at the same right against professionals. He eludes many checks but continuing to improve that aspect of his game will be essential if he wants to be productive in the future, much less prevent serious injury on a game-by-game basis.

Quotable: "Always an enjoyable player to watch. I wish he had he size to put him up with the top guys in this class." - NHL Scout

Carlisle, Chris – LD – Oshawa Generals (OHL) – 5'11" 178

Carlisle was a well hidden secret for the Generals playing for the NYC Cyclones U16 program and was selected in the 15th and final round of the 2010 OHL Priority Selection Draft. Despite this he played about half of the season for Oshawa in a limited role last season. This season he was more of a regular, but still limited due to the number of talented defensemen ahead of him. Chris showed his skating ability this season and while he's a slightly undersized defenseman he can rush the puck if given the opportunity. He competes hard and is willing to play with a little physicality. His puck play is where he is most valuable when he carries it and when he moves it.

He has a moderately strong point shot but it's not always on target. He battles hard but he does get caught trying to do too much at times, forcing plays and making mistakes that cause him to rush back in transition. We do not expect Chris to be selected at this year's NHL Draft. Instead, we look for him to continue to raise his competitiveness and be more consistent with his decision making and take advantage of the ice he's going to gain with the multiple big minute defensemen on the Generals moving on to the professional ranks next season. While this may be Chris' draft year, next year may be his chance to shine if he can make those adjustments.

Carnevale, Alex – LW – Sarnia Sting (OHL) – 5'11" 170

Alex was a third round pick at the 2011 OHL Priority Selection Draft. He was able to crack the Belleville Bulls lineup and worked hard regularly in a minimal role. A few games into this season, Alex hadn't moved up the depth chart. Seeing the potential in Carnevale, Sarnia acquired the forward and Alex spent the majority of his season in a third line role.

Alex is most noticeable with his hard working play. He wins a little more than his share of battles along the boards. He finishes his checks every time and provides good energy. Alex also works in his own zone and is able to force turnovers. He's shows flashes of hands around the net and will need to finish more of his chances out front. Alex is not expected to be selected in this draft but provides plenty of energy and has the potential to be a solid two-way player as he develops.

Carrier, William – LW – Cape Breton Screaming Eagles (QMJHL) – 6'1" 198

After a strong sophomore season in the QMJHL getting 27 goals and 70 points that put him on the radar for the 2013 NHL Draft, the late-birth Carrier only played 34 games in 2012-2013 due to injuries but managed to get 42 points and still be first scorer on Cape Breton's active roster at the end of the season.

Carrier is one of the strongest prospects you will find at the 2013 NHL Draft. A type of player highly sought for professional hockey, Carrier has a great mix of skating, skills, power and goal scoring abilities. He makes all of these abilities look effortless. His puck protection is one of the best in the QMJHL. We've rarely seen Carrier get pushed off the puck by an opponent when he leans on his inside leg and pushes his opponent with his inside shoulder. He has a great variety of shots that he can release quickly. He showed great accuracy on the wrister finding the net when releasing it in traffic. He finds the spaces that the goalie doesn't have covered easily. A powerful slapshot, quick release on a strong backhand and superb forehand-to-backhand move are also keys to Carrier's potential. He is a talented young man with the puck, having good puck control and looking smooth and relaxed while executing sweet moves with the puck. He handles the puck well in traffic and his large frame also gives him an extra second to make his play on the boards. He has long skating strides and gains his top speed quickly. He should still need improvement in those two areas to play in pro hockey but for such a big body it's still a rarity to see such a big guy skate this well. An underrated passer, William Carrier sees the ice well and can execute some intricate plays on the rush and when he controls the play on he powerplay. Again the big frame helps him cruise around the offensive zone and see his options showing great poise with the puck before setting up his teammates. Carrier's biggest weakness and what has been worrying us all year in our viewings is the lack of effort and passion he displays on the ice. In his own zone, he rarely moved his feet and showed a satisfying compete level. He picked his spots when he would move his feet and give maximum effort. We didn't see a game of William Carrier this year where he showed consistency in his effort.

Although he should improve drastically his work ethic, we also feel that playing for a team that as won only 55 games in the past 3 season could also have its effect on him and that his effort level could be better in a motivating winning environment.

Defensively, Carrier still has a lot to learn, being more caring, making the necessary sacrifices and keeping his position better. He made some costly turnovers and got in the wrong position covering his man at the blue line, giving him the inside of his own zone. We feel he needs to be smarter in his decisions in all 3 zones as he has turned the puck over and tried complex plays when he shouldn't have. For his size, he doesn't play a physical game and we would like to see his aggressiveness go up in his battles.

Carrier is a diamond that needs polishing. His raw talent mixed with his size makes him really attractive and it remains to be seen if his poor work ethic is just a question of circumstances or something that's going to hold him back in his career. He's a power forward playing a pretty soft game based on skills and puck protection for the moment. If there are changes in his mental game and intensity, he could end up being be a huge steal at the draft if he starts sliding.

Cassels, Cole – RC – Oshawa Generals (OHL) – 6'0" 178

Cole was selected 1st round, 16th Overall by the Oshawa Generals out of the Ohio Blue Jackets U16 program. He is also the son of former NHLer Andrew Cassels. His rookie season could be best described as a learning process. He didn't get a great deal of ice, but did his best with it and played a reliable two-way game. Cole's role increased greatly this season playing primarily on the third line, with spot action on the second line. He consistently received top penalty killing minutes and was very strong in this role.

Any team looking at selecting Cole will likely look primarily to his ability to shut down the opposition. He constantly maintains excellent defensive zone positioning and gets his sticks in lanes. He's willing to get down and block shots and pressures the puck carrier very well. He also engages regularly in battles. Cole has really improved his skating ability over the last two years and he's turned this area into an asset to his game. He wins races to a lose puck and can carry it deep into the offensive zone. He engages in puck battles in all three zones, however, has experienced mixed results in this area primarily due to a lack of strength.

Offensively he doesn't appear to have a great amount of upside at the pro level. Many of his plays around the goal area with the puck revolve around throwing the puck into the slot and hoping for the best, and he doesn't show a very high level of puck skills. He has shown some moves on the breakaway, and gets many of his goals around the slot. We undoubtedly believe an NHL team will be interested in Cassels and we see him being selected. However, we see him being a penalty killing specialist who plays a bottom six role, should he make the next level. Cole will be a key contributor to the Generals who are losing much of their top talent. He will have a great opportunity to reach career highs statistically and play in every game situation for his team.

Quotable: "I never saw Cole with 1st round value in the OHL Draft and he struggled a bit in some of my viewings this season. He's not without value in this draft, but I don't see him as a high end selection." – Mark Edwards

Quotable: "He is a little bit all over the place, he sometimes looks like he is playing as if his hair is on fire." – NHL Scout

Quotable: "Cole got talked about quite a bit, I just don't see the offensive upside. For me, Cole projects to be a solid two-way forward who an NHL team can put on their PK one day." – Ryan Yessie

Cave, Colby – LC – Swift Current Broncos (WHL) – 6'0" 188

Colby Cave is a 2 way forward who found some success offensively this season for the Broncos. Cave is an above average skater who still has some work to do in terms of speed and acceleration. He is strong on his feet, which is useful as much of his play is around the boards and cycling the puck. He is good along the walls to keep pucks deep, but could learn to manage the puck better and improve his puck protection. He has a tendency to throw the puck away, and also needs to cut down on the turnovers. He has a good release to his shots, and likes to shoot whenever he gets the puck in the slot. When Cave does manage the puck well, he has displayed good vision and playmaking abilities. He likes to find the trailer on the rush and drive the net to give his teammate some more room to score. Another improvement that Cave could make to his game is to play with more intensity. There are times when opponents out battle him for loose pucks easily, and he needs to be tougher to play against on a consistent basis.

Cederholm, Anton – LD – Rogle (SEL) – 6'2" 205

Anton has worked his way up the Rogle system playing U16, J18 and J20 games as a 15 year old and didn't look back playing in the J20 since with the exception of a few games here and there. He worked his way up to the Elitserien this season playing 12 games in the men's league. Unfortunately Rogle was relegated to the Allsvenskan league for the 2013-2014 season. Anton is a big bodied defenseman who loves to play physical and use his size to intimidate his opponents. He makes some huge open ice hits and destroys opponents along the boards. In one on one situations he utilizes both his stick and his body to make good plays and is reliable defensively. Anton moves the puck incredibly well and shows the ability to create breakout situations moving the puck over two lines and hitting his man tape to tape. He moves the puck intelligently in all three zones, but generally doesn't do much more offensively other than move the puck well. He needs to work on his skating ability but it's not a major concern at this point. He will never put up a ton of offensive points but he plays a solid, mean, physical defensive game and chips in with his smart puck moving ability.

Peter Cehlarik – LW – Lulea (Elitserien) - 6'2" 192

Cehlarik is a big two-way forward who plays a smart game. He seems to be in good position consistently to make a play at both ends of the ice and uses his size to his advantage on a consistent basis.

Cehlarik has good hockey sense. He is in good position on the forecheck time and time again, and is able to find open areas out on the ice offensively. He is not very quick out on the ice, so this ability is crucial for him to be involved in the play on a consistent basis. He possesses a good quick release, and is not afraid to go to the net for scoring opportunities. Cehlarik could be a little more physical, but he does a good job of protecting the puck and using his reach to try to create turnovers in the neutral zone.

The biggest weakness for Cehlarik is his skating ability. He is not very quick out on the ice, and if opponents have a step on him off the rush, he has a very difficult time catching up to the play and making an impact. Once the puck gets by him, he can be eliminated from the play at times.

If Cehlarik can work on his quickness, he could be a good defensively responsible winger at the pro level in North America one day who provides offense once in a while. He certainly has the size that NHL teams look for, and the hockey sense without the puck.

Quotable: "He is a kid that made an impression on me in Sochi. He worked hard, played smart and flashed a quick release on his shot. Made a few poor decisions with the puck on a few occasions but nothing crazy. He made up for it with a few great passes in a game vs Germany. - Mark Edwards

Chapman, Joshua – RD – Sarnia Sting (OHL) – 6'4" 208

Joshua is a late birth date who has spent some time with the Sting in 2010-2011 while splitting time with the Sarnia Legionnaires Jr. B (GOJHL) team. Last season Joshua opted to join the Stoufville Spirit (OJHL) and put up surprisingly good numbers for them with 13 points in 28 regular season games. Then, on their big playoff run he added 10 points in 25 games. Joshua made the Sting playing full time minutes. After a few moves were made Joshua was used on the second pairing for the Sting. The biggest thing Joshua has going for him is his tremendous size. He uses it in front of his own net to clear space for his goaltender and is rather effective. In the playoffs Chapman really was the only player on Sarnia who was physically able to move the big Whaler forwards from the front of the net or match their physicality. Joshua finishes his hits regularly and plays very tough. He was willing to drop the gloves regularly early on this season but this cooled down significantly as the season went on. Joshua has moderate puck skills and became more consistent throughout the season with his passes, but generally is very basic in this area and can make mental errors. Joshua's skating ability has also seen improvements as his ice time increased this season. It is still below average but when you consider his size he's certainly better than some of the other 6'4" defensemen we've seen in the OHL.

The biggest frustration we had with Joshua is the amount of times he was down on the ice after a hit or a play that could be perceived as a potential injury. Either he was the most targeted player in the league, has a low pain threshold or was trying to sell the hits to gain power plays. While we suspect the latter, which at times was effective in turning a 2 minute into a 4 or 5, the frequency of it was felt to be a little ridiculous by our staff and is discouraging to see. Joshua has a legitimate shot at being picked in the final rounds or at least invited to an NHL camp due to his size and his physical strength. He projects to be a simple reliable shutdown defenseman who asserts his size regularly.

Chase, Greg – RC – Calgary Hitmen (WHL) – 6'0" 195

Chase is a playmaking forward who is at his best when he is moving his feet and playing with an edge. He likes to get involved physically and be in the middle of scrums, but needs to control himself to not take undisciplined penalties. He has been able to positively contribute to the success of the team and has received valuable minutes throughout the year. Greg Chase's best attribute is his playmaking ability. He has very good vision in the offensive zone, and makes good accurate passes for his teammates to receive great scoring chances. He uses his good speed down the wing to try to create some separation from opposing defensemen. He is able to read opposing coverage well and take advantage of any holes. Chase is deceptively quick on the ice. He does not move with great explosiveness out on the ice, but he is able to get from one area to another in a hurry. He is always in a battle for loose pucks, and has shown good strength. One issue with Chase's game is his inconsistency. He could be an offensive force in one game, then completely disappear the next game. He needs to consistently make a difference to have a better chance of playing at higher levels.

Quotable: "Going back to last season at the U17 in Windsor I thought he played some great hockey. I have only seen him a few times since and all on tape. Our WHL guys including Calgary based Scott McDougall have watched him be hot and cold." - Mark Edwards

Cianfrone, Bryson – FW – Cedar Rapids RoughRiders (USHL) – 5'8" 169

After an outstanding season as the captain of the Toronto Marlboros Minor Midget team, Bryson was selected in the 16th round of the 2011 USHL Entry Draft and in the 3rd round of the 2011 OHL Priority Selection Draft. Bryson chose to play his 2011-2012 season in the OJHL. Bryson opened with the Oakville Rangers, but later joined the Toronto Jr. Canadiens posting impressive numbers as a 16 year old. Bryson then made the decision to join the USHL's Cedar Rapids RoughRiders as his USHL rights were transferred. Bryson put together a successful season receiving good ice time. Bryson displays very good skating handling the puck well at top speed. He is quick and shifty and is capable of creating offense for himself and his teammates.

Maybe his strongest asset is his work ethic. He works hard every single shift and rarely if ever takes a shift off. He puts everything into his games. Really the only single reason Bryson isn't talked about much in regards to the 2013 NHL Draft due to his his lack of size. If he was even at 5'10" NHL teams might be more likely to take a chance on him. Bryson has committed to join the University of Michigan for this fall of 2013.

Quotable: "Bryson is a player we've watched for the last three years. It's really unfortunate about his size because he shows so much heart and is such a great leader. He's a kid we'd love to see get selected, because he has so many good attributes, but the size makes it a real tough case for him." - Ryan Yessie

Clapperton, Christopher – LW – Blainville-Boisbriand Armada (QMJHL) – 5'10" 180

The Cap - d'Espoir native went undrafted last year, but has impressed our staff over the last two years with his competitiveness and maturity on the ice. Clapperton played on the Armada top line with Cedric Paquette (TB fourth rounder in 2012) and fellow draft eligible Marc-Olivier Roy most of the year. He's a hard worker and doesn't shy away from the physical game and will go in the tough areas of the ice. Solid in all three zones and he's a smart player that doesn't put his team in trouble. His smarts help him get open for goals as he follows the play really well and finds soft ice easily. Like last season, his skating will hurt him come draft day, he has quick feet but lacks high end speed, something you like to see from a small player. His offensive game would be limited at the next level as he doesn't have big strengths: his skill set is pretty average, lacking size and high end speed, he doesn't possess a particularly lethal shot, his passing game is simple and effective but again just average. He'd be well worth an invitation after the NHL draft though like he had last year with the Philadelphia Flyers.

Clifton, Connor – RD – US NTDP Under-18 Team – 5'11, 175

Connor was tabbed for the NTDP from the Eastern Junior Hockey League, where he came up with the Jersey Hitmen. He is committed to Quinnipiac University for the 2013-14 season, and was also selected by the Peterborough Petes in the 4th round (75th overall) of the 2013 OHL Priority Selection.

Clifton isn't the biggest kid but he's strong, physical, and keeps other teams honest with his ability to throw momentum-changing hits. He's also diligent about clearing the front of his net and playing heavy on the boards. He's a hard worker and rarely takes a shift off. Clifton's game is tied together with excellent skating. He accelerates quickly and is very strong on his feet, allowing him to fight off checks and pin players against the boards. Against the rush, he shows good balance, an active stick, and smart gap control. He moves well with the puck and is agile laterally. Clifton's offensive game is evolving. He shows flashes of dynamic puck-rushing ability and can go end-to-end with poise and determination, though he had a hard time producing points this year. His stick handling is a bit sloppy, but he's skilled enough to evade a forecheck and navigate neutral zone traffic. He likes to join the rush and pinch into the attack and, for the most part, does so without being a liability. He has a good wrister and can bomb it with a one-timer, though his accuracy is inconsistent. The biggest question here is discipline. Clifton can be overzealous in his pursuit of contact and sometimes crosses the line with excessive roughness or after-the-whistle antics.

He has gotten better about picking his spots as the year has gone by, but the lapses in judgment and coverage are still there. He has the tools to be an excellent professional defenseman, and based on his progress this season it's fair to predict that he'll continue to refine his game, but he's still very raw. There's a lot of upside here for a team willing to be patient.

Quotable: "Connor really impressed our whole staff with his improvements this season. He plays a game that projects well at the next level. The size, or lack there of will be the only thing that holds him back at this point." - Ryan Yessie

Quotable: "Clifton improved by leaps and bounds this season, and really brought a high level of play at the Five Nations Tournament in Jönköping. Though he still lacks consistency, he shows flashes of being a force with game-breaking hits and puck-rushing ability." - Josh Deitell

Cloonan, Ryan – LC – Boston Jr. Bruins (EJHL) – 5'9, 145

On pure skill alone, Cloonan ranks near the top of the 2013 draft class. His hands are elite and with the puck he can be an unstoppable force, navigating traffic with incredible awareness and making numerous players miss en route to scoring chances. He's able to create space for himself and maintain possession for extended periods of time, carrying the puck with authority. He can be an absolutely explosive player when he asserts himself. The downside is, he's not a great team player. He can't do everything alone but often insists on trying, leading to turnovers and frustration. He can play very well defensively when motivated, with strong pickpocket skills on the back check and the occasional hit, but rarely puts in the work. More often than not, he floats around waiting for his teammates to recover the puck. He takes shifts off and generally looks passive and bored without the puck. When he does come back to his defensive zone, he doesn't look like he understands where to be. On the upside, he's young and could stand to add about 40 pounds to his frame, so there's plenty to work with here, but he needs to seriously alter his attitude on the ice before he can be taken earnestly as a professional prospect. He'll suit up for the University of Maine starting in the fall.

Clutsam, Mac – LD – Sault Ste. Marie Greyhounds (OHL) – 5'9" 172

Mac was drafted in the 7th Round of the 2011 OHL Priority Selection Draft by the Sault Ste. Marie Greyhounds out of the Hamilton Jr. Bulldogs Minor Midget Program. Mac saw a handful of games with the Greyhounds in the 2011-2012 season but spent most of his 16 year old season with the Elmira Sugar Kings Jr. B program. Clutsam struggled to crack a veteran laden defense corps for the Greyhounds in 2012-2013.

He is an undersized defender who struggles facing bigger power forwards in the corners and front of the net. He is a strong skater and brings a good element of speed. Mac keeps things simple in the defensive zone and does not hold onto the puck for very long before moving it up the boards. He is good at making smart plays and rarely takes any risks in the offensive zone. Clutsam should have a chance to crack the top 6 defense role in 2013-2014 as the Greyhounds graduate a number of veteran defenders. However, we do not expect him to be selected in the 2013 NHL Draft. We would love to see him grow and get stronger to better suit his game and we like his never quit attitude on the ice.

Compher, JT – RC – US NTDP Under-18 Team – 5'11, 184

JT was the captain of the U18 team and did an excellent job of leading by example with his intelligent, two-way play. He's a Swiss army knife of sorts, the type of player coaches are happy to put on the ice in any situation at any time of a game. Need a goal in the last minute? He's your guy. Need to keep the puck out of your net with the lead? He can do that too. Power play, penalty kill, 4-on-4, you name it. He can do it all with a consistently strong effort. He very rarely takes shifts off and plays the full rink. His skating is excellent with swift acceleration and agility. With quick starts and stops, he can dart around the offensive zone and is very effective in a cycle. In flashes, he shows outstanding stick handling ability and creativity. He can be very deceptive. He has a nice selection of shots and shows good variety with a sharp wrister, good one-timer, big slap shot, and a nice backhand. He gets good lift on his shots in tight. He takes the puck to the net and goes to the dirty areas to battle.

His defensive game is very strong. He's aggressive on the back check, forcing turnovers in the neutral zone with good pressure from behind and acting quickly after regaining possession to catch defenders flat-footed going the other way. He helps his defensemen out whenever possible with an honest effort in his zone, an active stock, and shot blocking. He's a strong penalty killer with good positioning and is a threat to score shorthanded. Compher missed time early on in the season with injury, bringing up questions of durability with his sometimes-reckless play, but was a fixture in the lineup from the end of November onwards. His excellent all-around play makes him one of the safest picks in this draft class, and he has been consistent enough offensively this year to say that he could very well still be a solid offensive contributor at the professional level, though at this point that's not quite a sure thing.

Quotable: "I don't see top six skills. He will probably go off the board between 25 & 35. Love his heart." - NHL Scout

Quotable: "I spoke to Compher at the Combine and was very impressed. This kid knows his game and how he will need to play to be effective in the NHL." - Mark Edwards

Comrie, Eric – G – Tri-City Americans (WHL) – 6'1" 170

Comrie was the undisputed number 1 goaltender for the Americans this season before he went down with a hip injury for the year. His game has been rock solid and it is rare to see such a young player play such a composed game. The technical game of Comrie is quite solid. He has a good, wide butterfly and is very quick on his knees to go post to post. He has good active arms to knock rebounds away to the corners, and is good at catching pucks coming to his glove hand. He has the ability to quick recover after giving up a rebound and making a huge save because of his quickness. He is good at tracking pucks through traffic, but it is something that he will have to keep working on. Comrie plays with such poise, that any amount of bodies in front of him will not rattle his game, and he solely focuses on stopping pucks. He also seems to have a short memory as he does not let bad goals effect him either. A great example is the number of times that he got pulled this season. Out of 37 starts, he was only pulled once against a lethal Portland team. He managed to finish every other game that he started, and it is pretty clear that his focus is at an elite level at such a young age already. An area of improvement for Comrie would be his puck handling abilities. He could make it easier for his defensemen by stopping pucks behind the net and making passes to one of his teammates to get a break out going. He struggles with making passes, particularly on his backhand. He also does not have the ability to clear pucks high and off the glass to clear the zone when necessary. It will be interesting if Comrie's athleticism has regressed due to his hip surgery. His injury was actually considered to be minor, and it seems like Tri-City are just being cautious to ensure that he has a long, successful career. Any team that drafts him are getting a polished goaltender who seems to have the mental strength to be a good starting goaltender in the NHL one day.

Quotable: "Impressed me when I saw him last season. Only saw him on tape this season before the injury. Our west guys really like him." - Mark Edwards

Quotable: "I'm not as sold on him as some people." - NHL Scout

Cook, Dawson – LW – US NTDP Under-18 Team – 6'1, 197

Dawson is a character forward. He brings good size and work ethic to the rink. He back checks and forechecks hard and is a good teammate, helping out along the boards and backing up his teammates in scrums. He goes hard to the net and is strong on the puck along the boards. Unfortunately, the hands and offensive sense just aren't there. He hasn't shown the ability to make plays individually or make his teammates better. There's a chance that he carves out an NHL future for himself as a bottom six forward, but as he stands it looks like he'll need to prove himself at the University of Notre Dame before a team takes serious notice.

Cooper, Olivier – LW – Saint-John Sea Dogs (QMJHL) – 6'2" 197

A big player with soft hands, Oliver Cooper had troubles adjusting from playing a support role in the top team in the CHL in 2011-2012 to taking the offensive leadership in a rebuilding Saint-John team in 2012-2013. Cooper has soft hands and a polished finishing touch around the net. His puck control is above average and he can gain a few more seconds with his size and puck protection skills. He has shown some glimpses here and there during the season of a power forward which is something we really liked, but most of the time he was undisciplined. He made inept decisions with the puck, showing poor hockey sense multiple times, giving the puck away and not seeing the easy options. He lacks skating ability and has a tough time creating distance from opponents when he has the puck. We don't think he has what he takes to get drafted at the 2013 NHL Draft with what he's shown this season.

Corbett, Jeff – RD – Sudbury Wolves (OHL) – 6'1" 180

Jeff came on to our radar later on in the season and we like what we saw. Played some smart minutes and didn't show any big gaps in his game. He played smart and moved the puck effectively. Seemed to get better as the game progressed. Skating was solid and he showed good feet.

Quotable: "Maybe a little raw at this point of his development, but I see some potential in his game." – Mark Edwards

Couturier, Joshua – LD – Boston Jr. Bruins (EJHL) – 6'2, 175

Joshua is a big defenseman with a projectable frame, but lacks the poise and positioning necessary to project him as a future NHL talent. He plays with an active stick and can be physical in the corners, but routinely chases the play and doesn't use his size consistently. He has slow feet and poor footwork, causing him trouble against the cycle and the rush. He lacks poise against the forecheck with the puck and has a hard time getting the puck out of his zone cleanly. Has some tools, but he's a major project and his hockey sense is a concern. He has committed to Northeastern for 2014.

Cox, Trevor – LW – Medicine Hat Tigers (WHL) – 5'7" 150

Cox is a quick playmaker who generates offense off the half wall. Despite his size, Cox is not afraid to go to the net and try to score dirty goals. His size is a detriment to his play along the walls and in the slot, but he fights through it and does not allow it to stop him from working hard and trying to create offense. Cox is quick with the puck in the neutral zone, and is able to push opponents back into their own zone. Defensively, Cox is far too easy to play against. His back check is terrible, and he does not put enough effort into his own zone. He has a lot of improvements to make in his game, especially with his lack of size, to ever play as a professional.

Crisp, Connor – LC – Erie Otters (OHL) – 6'4" – 225

Connor was selected in the 2nd round of the 2010 OHL Priority Selection Draft by the Erie Otters out of the York-Simcoe Express Minor Midget Program. Connor made the Otters as a 16 year old and scored 5 goals in his rookie season. Connor was primed to enter the 2012 NHL Draft but a shoulder injury kept him out of all but six games last year, one of which he spent playing goalie for Erie after they went into a game in Niagara with only one netminder. That one goaltender was promptly run by Alex Friesen during his first shift, causing injury, which saw Connor play goal for the entire game, minus the first few seconds. This was a once in a lifetime experience and Connor actually made 30+ saves in this game. Entering the 2012-2013 season, Connor was healthy and ready to show what he's capable of in hopes of being a re-entry selection at the NHL Draft.

Connor did a good job posting a 20+ goal season on the fourth lowest scoring team in the OHL. Connor played top power play minutes for the Otters and can consistently be found in the crease area. He battles extremely hard out front making life difficult for goaltenders and defenders due to his huge frame. He has pretty good hands in the goal area and finishes many of his goals using his frame and his hands to put the puck in the back of the net. He also displays good physicality. He finishes his checks regularly and isn't afraid to drop the gloves. He hit double digits for fights this past season and took on some of the better fighters in the league. Connor's ability to read plays and make quick decisions seems to go underrated because of his size and physicality but he regularly makes smart plays with the puck, but will have the occasional miscue. He contributed defensively, and while he wasn't exceptional in this area of the game, he was usually reliable.

Connor has a few things working against him. Of course, the loss of most of a whole year of development with a shoulder injury does hurt him. The second is his skating ability. Connor has a huge frame and has the strength that will get him through junior, and should even help him at the pro level, but his skating is simply not fast enough. He doesn't have very good quickness, he looks heavy on his feet, and this is an area that may scare off some teams. It will take a great deal of work for him to get his skating up to average. It likely will never be an asset, but this is a major area of improvement for Connor. He has the high end upside of a low end top six power forward. He plays the game he would need to in order to be effective in that role. He knows how to use his size and has the ability to score some goals. This, however, is only a reality if his skating improves.

Quotable: "Connor looked a lot more comfortable this season. He's shown with or without goalie pads he's willing to get in front of some shots, but he's at his best when he's in the slot. Tough to move, causes disruptions and can put the puck in the back of the net. I just hope his skating improves." - Ryan Yessie

Quotable: "He was passed over last year but gets a free pass for a second look. He has size and work ethic." - Mark Edwards

Crunk, Taylor – LW – Victoria Royals (WHL) – 6'0" 201

Crunk is a physical depth forward for the Royals who provided a good presence out on the ice with his speed and physicality. He makes the most impact on the forecheck when he quickly closes the gap between him and the opposing defensemen and lands a solid hit and create a turnover. He brings a consistent effort out on the ice at all times, and coaches trust him and know what they are getting from him at all times. Defensively, Crunk covers his point man quite well, and does not make any huge mistakes without the puck, and as a result he can be relied upon on the penalty kill regularly. Offensively, Crunk is inconsistent when he has the puck on his stick. There are times when he would make good plays with the puck, then other times he would make careless plays and give it away on a poor pass. He needs to cut down on the number of bad chances that he takes when making passes and play it safe. He has average stick handling abilities, and will need to improve on it to be more effective with his speed on the rush. He also does not have a very good shot, and needs to work on getting himself open more often.

Crus Rydberg, Viktor – LC – Linköping (SEL) – 5'11, 190

Though he possesses outstanding two-way ability, Crus Rydberg is still very inconsistent. He has whole games where he's invisible, and turns in dominant performances in others. He's an excellent skater with great straight-line speed that can turn on the jets to get behind a defense. He carries the puck up ice with poise at high speed to back off defenders and create space. He's good in the cycle game with agile stops and starts, and an excellent passer in all situations. He has a shot-first mentality with hard, accurate one-timers, snapshots, and wrister shots. He back checks hard and plays physical in his zone. He shows an active stick while defending to take away lanes all over the ice. His defensive coverage is overaggressive at times, but earnest. Crus Rydberg is an excellent talent, but needs to find a way to bring his A-game every night.

Quotable: "Viktor was maybe the most pleasant surprise of any player we saw at the Four Nations Cup. He didn't come in with a big reputation but he showed his potential NHL upside through skating, work ethic and great play in all three zones." - Ryan Yessie

Dauphin, Laurent – LC – Chicoutimi Saguenéens (QMJHL) – 6'0" 166

Playing his rookie season in the QMJHL, Dauphin consistently had strong showings after strong showings, impressing Hockey Prospect's scouting staff. He had good offensive numbers with 25 goals and 57 points in 62 games played and led all players in the Q with 9 winning goals.
First thing that really stands out in Dauphin's game is his puck control. A very creative puck handler, Dauphin has quick hands and is very unpredictable when he comes in front of an opponent. He uses every inch opponents give him, finding space where there doesn't seem to be any. Dauphin has good top speed and he uses long strides to get that speed in neutral zone. He showed great East-West mobility as well. He twists and turns very quickly when battling on the boards easily creating space for himself. He has strong legs which also helps him win several battles on the boards and crash the net effectively. The Repentigny native has a natural goal scorer's instinct, registering 200 shots this season, using his elusiveness to get those shooting lanes from the slot, especially on the powerplay. Dauphin shoots a lot and doesn't wait for the perfect opportunity to let it go. He likes to cut aggressively to the front of the net, not afraid to get hit or roughed up when he does so.

A very smart player, Dauphin played in every situation with Chicoutimi in 2012-2013, with an important role 5-on-5, playing on the first PP unit as well as regular shifts on the PK, where he registered 3 goals. He is not particularly physical but rather he is willing to get hit to make a play. Responsible defensively, he will get into shooting lanes and pay a physical price to accomplish defensive missions. Dauphin will work twice as hard to correct a mistake that he or a teammate did, especially in the defensive zone. He showed tremendous work ethic and determination throughout numerous situations during the season, battling pain to stay in position or working through checks to get to the puck. He got hit very hard a couple of times this season but kept getting back up and playing hard with intensity.

Dauphin's biggest weakness is his ability to accelerate. He has a tough time distancing players when he takes a puck away from his opponents and needs to work through players sometimes because he lacks the explosiveness to go around them. An improved explosiveness would make his 2-way game go from good to great. Another weakness of Dauphin is his poor use of his teammates. He has good vision and sees plays well, but with his skill level and elusiveness, he will sometimes try to do it all by himself which appears selfish. In his case, given his smarts, he's demonstrated that he can utilize teammates defensively but will too often choose to wait until he's in trouble or out of options with the puck before passing to a teammate offensively.

Dauphin's pro potential is great, with more maturity and minor inherent weaknesses corrected. He could be a smart 2-way center or winger with natural goal scoring instincts.

Quotable: "One thing that impresses me the most with Dauphin is his compete level. He is a clutch performer and thrives on pressure, the consistency of his 2nd and 3rd efforts is terrific." – Simon Larouche

Davis, Taylor – RD – Ottawa 67's (OHL) – 6'0" 205

Taylor joined the 2012-2013 Ottawa 67's as a free agent after spending his 2011-2012 season with the Buffalo Jr. Blades Jr. B team in the GOJHL. Davis posted 6 points and a -10 rating in 43 games played this season. He is a defenseman who can play a physical game, keeps the opposition to the outside, and likes to direct the play with his stick then squeezes his man out along the boards. He is able to protect the puck well from the opposition's pressure, holds the offensive line effectively and is calm with the puck. He is able to move the puck up out of the zone to start the rush, but still has to watch some of the neutral zone turnovers on breakout passes. He ties up the opposition well in his own end and likes to get involved with opponents after whistles, demonstrating good aggression at times.

Davis most likely will not be drafted in the upcoming draft and really needs to improve in his skating as he has been beaten by faster forwards who can drive the puck wide around him to get to the net for opportunities, and needs to try to keep the turnovers to a minimum. He has decent size and needs to use it more effectively to play the body and keep the opposition from gaining the inside track to the net.

De Jong, Nolan – LD – Victoria Grizzlies (BCHL) – 6'2" 188

De Jong is a defensive defenseman who plays a very composed game. He is not very physical, but his play without the puck was quite impressive as opponents had a tough time trying to create scoring chances when he was on the ice. De Jong is not a particularly great skater, but can certainly keep up with opponents off the rush and do a decent job of maintaining a good gap. There are times when he does give players too much room because he respects their speed, but when he feels like he can be aggressive, he is quite effective off the rush. He has a very good stick that he uses to knock away passes into the slot, and does a nice job of holding his position and letting the play come to him. Offensively, De Jong's play is quite limited. He makes good first passes out of the zone, but lacks creativity and offensive skill to do much damage. He keeps it very simple with the puck, and does not try to take many chances from the blue line. He has below average hands, and his shooting ability is just average. De Jong will be a long term project for NHL teams, but his size and defensive game should attract some interest in the draft. He will have plenty of time to develop under a very impressive program with the University of Michigan.

de Haan, Evan – LD – Sudbury Wolves (OHL) – 5'11" 150

Evan was selected in the 2nd round of the 2011 OHL Priority Selection Draft by the Sudbury Wolves out of the Ottawa Valley Titans Minor Midget program. Evan is the younger brother of New York Islanders prospect Calvin de Haan. As a 16 year old Evan spent the season with the Pembroke Lumber Kings of the CCHL. de Haan was able to crack the Wolves lineup to open the 2012-2013 season and hasn't looked back.

de Haan is a two-way defenseman who likes to jump up on the rush and join the attack. He likes to drive the puck wide into the zone when he spots his opportunity, then goes around behind the opposition's net to look for his passing options to make a play, or just centers the puck to the middle off the side wall. He picks off turnovers in the neutral zone then rushes the puck back up into the offensive zone. He possesses great skating, vision and passing abilities off the rush to get the puck up the ice. In his own end he gets in lanes to break up passes then makes the simple play to move the puck out of the zone up along the boards. He uses his body and stick to try to keep the opposition to the outside and plays the opposition with a pretty good gap control.

He needs to get much stronger on the puck, as there were way too many times this season when he was battled off the puck fairly easily, especially at critical times. He needs to watch that he isn't getting caught trying to play the puck rather than the body in his own end at times. He also has to watch some of the turnovers on puck mishandles in his own end. Evan has a bit of an outside chance at being selected. Having a brother who was drafted in the first round in the NHL won't hurt his case either. If a team selects Evan they will likely do so with the hope and potential that he grows a little bit. He has a great amount of room to add muscle and will need to hit the gym hard to have a chance at handling the more powerful forwards more effectively.

Dea, Jean-Sébastien – RC – Rouyn-Noranda Huskies (QMJHL) – 6'0" 160

Jean-Sébastien Dea is what you can call a late bloomer, those kids that for whatever reason take more time than others before reaching their potential. He went from 17 goals scored in 2011-2012 to 45 in 2012-2013. He racked up 85 points for the Huskies and formed a tremendous duo in the QMJHL with Sven Andrighetto. Dea is a very smart centerman who knows how to make himself available for teammates. He has great offensive execution and his finishing touch is just tremendous. He scored numerous goals on the powerplay and around the net. He anticipates where the play is headed before his teammates executes his play, which is a sign of his great hockey sense. He has an accurate wrist shot that can be released quickly on the rush or on a one-timer. Dea doesn't have great high end speed, dazzling skills or amazing passing skills; but, he has an above-average skills set of all those named atributes. He wins numerous faceoffs and again uses great smarts in his own zone to support his defensemen. His positioning without the puck is great and he will use an active stick to block the passing lanes. We think Dea's high number of points this season is partially due to the fact he was playing with a tremendous passer in Sven Andrighetto. He was also lined with a great overager Gabriel Desjardins. He deserves credit for scoring those goals, but we don't think he will be able to do a repeat performance in 2013-2014. His level of competitiveness in his one-on-one battles is not consistent and he can start gliding at times. Not a physical player, Dea is also a slight stature player and should fill in that frame completely before playing in pro hockey. We don't think Dea should be drafted.

Dedenbach, Jared – FW – Fargo Force (USHL) – 5'8" 170

Dedenbach was selected in the 5th round, 70th overall by Fargo force in 2012 and then played his first year in the USHL this season where he had 12 points in 46 games played. He is a player who keeps it simple for the most part and just tries to get the puck in deep. He battles hard for the puck in the corners, puts great pressure on the fore-check and can make some good little passes to start the breakout with speed, however there are still times when he has trouble getting the puck out of his own end along the boards. In his own end he puts good pressure on the point on the penalty kill and ties up his man pretty well. Dedenbach doesn't have the skills to be an offensive force and therefore needs to establish himself as a player who takes care of his own end. He is a small player and needs to add a lot of size and strength and also has to play the puck carrier with more of a physical edge along the boards. What he does well is keeps it simple and pressures the puck carrier but he needs to cycle the puck in the offensive zone more often and get to the net to try and score on tough goals from in tight.

DeKort, Jordan – G – Windsor Spitfires (OHL) – 6'4" 192

Jordan was selected in the second round of the 2011 OHL Priority Selection Draft out of the Markham Majors program. DeKort spent the majority of last season with the LaSalle Vipers Jr. B team receiving the majority of the team's starts. He also appeared in a handful of games for the Spitfires. This season, Jordan received more action, however, on a rebuilding team, his numbers were not very strong. Jordan is a big goaltender who has great size and uses it effectively to make the first shot hit him almost every time.

While he's great on the first save, when teams make him move around, he gets into trouble. His recovery is below average and he will need to get quicker side to side. He also has a tendency to kick rebounds into dangerous areas. While he appears to have made some improvements it's an area he needs to continue to work on. This may or may not affect Jordan's ability to get drafted. Goaltenders can develop late and with less than 30 games of OHL experience, Jordan may be a late bloomer. NHL teams are more likely to lean towards a 6'4" late bloomer than most, so he may be a goaltender to get picked up late and gets developed by an OHL team, as all his flaws are potentially correctable.

de la Rose, Jacob – LW – Leksand – Sweden – 6'2" 190

Jacob is a power forward prospect who needs to be physical to be his best. We have seen these games and he was impressive in them, but we have seen the games where he wasn't physical as well. He does a good job closing gaps and taking away time and space. He dis show us some smart positional play and has shown some flashes of beating defenders 1 on 1. We like the straight line skating and the work ethic he has shown us. He plays well in all three zones. Jacob is very aware of his need to work on his shot and his scoring ability. If can can improve in those areas going forward it will surely raise his stock.

Quotable: "I went into this season with a goal of figuring out Jacob's potential as a potential top 6 forward in the NHL. It took a while for me to see enough of him, but I think I got my answer. While he showed me some flashes of scoring skills, I'm not sure he has enough to give me confidence that they would translate well to the next level. I was a big fan of the kid last year and liked a lot *of things in his game. I still think he has 2nd round value in this draft." — Mark Edwards*

DeLuca, Anthony – LW – Rimouski Océanic (QMJHL) – 5'9" 198

After a tremendous 2011-2012 season in Midget AAA where he had 48 goals in 43 goals, the young sniper made his debut in the QMJHL with Rimouski and displayed great offensive qualities. Anthony De Luca has an elite skillset and can dazzle a defenseman at any time in a one-on-one situation with his magic hands. He seems to be able to get through most defenders with those dekes and although we would like him to simplify his game on multiple occasions, he was still able to have his share of success this season while using this type of game. He also possesses a lethal release on the wrist shot, having great velocity, which gives little to no time for goaltenders to react. He has the instincts of a natural goal scorer, always trying to get in the slot to take a shot. When you're as skilled as De Luca, it is sometimes difficult to simplify your play feeing you can get through everybody with ease. We've observed that problem with De Luca on many occasions throughout the season. He can get overconfident and try fancy moves at the wrong places or times in a game.

Physically, he is small but somewhat wide and tough to knock off his feet as his center of gravity is low. He is not explosive, but his top speed is great with impressive puck control when he attains it. He is not a physical player on a regular basis, but can throw some good hits when he wants to play aggressively and move his feet. The major problem of Anthony De Luca is his work ethic. He tends to move his feet only in the offensive zone and will often be lazy and gliding in the defensive zone. He won't sacrifice his body to block shots and will sometimes cheat in his defensive position to get in neutral zone early. Although this major weakness has improved significantly, there's still room for improvement in his defensive game and intensity. We would also like to see him show character by going in front of the net to get the goals and to have the will to get hit or slashed to score that goal, something we haven't observed often.

Dempsey, Mitchell – LW – Soo Greyhounds (OHL) – 6'4" 202

Mitchell was selected 1st round, 11th Overall by the Plymouth Whalers at the 2011 OHL Priority Selection Draft out of the Cambridge Hawks program. Mitchell received some unfair hype that he wasn't likely to live up to, as he wasn't an overwhelming offensive talent in Minor Midget. He was also playing behind many veteran players in Plymouth and did moderately well for a 16 year old playing limited ice in the OHL. Dempsey was traded north to Sault Ste. Marie during the offseason. The fresh start looked great for him at first, but his play quickly declined below the level he is capable of producing. Dempsey struggled to crack the veteran laden forward lineup for the Greyhounds on a game by game basis.

He possesses a very strong wrist shot but really needs to work harder to get into the necessary positioning to use it. Mitchell protects the puck effectively when driving the net thanks to his big frame, and is generally the way he is able to create chances. Dempsey has the benefit of possessing the natural size that many NHL prospects would love to have. He needs to put in some work in the offseason, and hopefully will come back rejuvenated with an opportunity to move up the Greyhounds depth chart, as some key forwards are graduating. Mitchell needs to continue to work on his skating but also needs to focus more mentally at working hard on a shift by shift basis. We do not expect Mitchell to be selected at the 2013 NHL Entry Draft.

Desautels, Matthew – RD – Ottawa 67's (OHL) – 5'11" 190

Matthew was passed over at the 2011 and 2012 OHL Priority Selections after spending the last two years with Eastern Ontario Wild Minor Midget and the Ottawa Jr. Senators of the CCHL. Matthew signed in July of 2012 and immediately joined the 67's posting 2 assists and a -25 rating. However, he did play on a team where the majority of the players were all minuses. Desautels possesses some decent good hands and agility with the puck to get away from the opposition's pressure, then move it up the ice quickly. He has good speed to his game and gets in lanes really well on the back check to come back and break up the opposition's opportunities.

There are times in the game that he can use his stick well to check the puck away from the opposition, but other times when he is quite ineffective and allows the opposition to walk around him or is careless with his stick and takes a tripping penalty. His best asset is the ability to get in lanes in the defensive zone and he needs to continue to do that to pick off turnovers, then move the puck up the ice to start a quick transition game. Desautels will probably not be selected in this year's NHL draft and needs to use his body much more to keep the opposition to the outside and away from his team's goal.

Descheneau, Jaedon – RW – Kootenay Ice (WHL) 5'8" 177

Descheneau is a skilled winger who was able to form dangerous chemistry with teammate Sam Reinhart this season, and helped carry the Ice offensively this season. He loves to shoot from anywhere, and Reinhart is able to find him whenever he has any open space. Descheneau is at his best when he is moving his feet and identifying open areas in coverage in the slot. He has a good release to his shots, and opposing goaltenders have a tough time making saves when he is so close to the net combined with his shot. He loves to shoot from anywhere, and could take some more time to figure out some more options that he has with the puck. He is not very strong along the walls, and will definitely need to work on his game along the boards to be more effective off the walls on the cycle. Descheneau makes good passes, but needs to identify opportunities quicker. If his first option is taken away, he just quickly releases a shot on net.

Defensively, Descheneau has a lot of work to do. He is weak along the walls, and regularly loses battles for loose pucks. He commits too many turnovers, and needs to be more responsible in his own end and his the neutral zone. He does not receive ice time on the penalty kill as his positioning without the puck is not very good. He is soft to play against, which is something that he will have to change with his lack of size.

Desrochers, Danny – LW – Sudbury Wolves (OHL) – 6'0" 182

Danny was selected in the 3rd round of the 2011 OHL Priority Selection Draft by the Sudbury Wolves out of the North Bay Trappers of the GNML. Danny received 8 games with the Wolves while playing most of his season in the NOJHL with the North Bay Trappers. Danny made the jump full time this season and displayed a hard working, blue collar type of game. He is also able to chip in offensively occasionally, which lead to his 13 points in 58 games this season, his first full season in the OHL.

He battles very effectively for the puck to force turnovers and keeps his game simple by just trying to get the puck in deep off the rush. He puts great pressure on the forecheck, finishes his hits along the boards and gets down really well to block shots on the penalty kill. He works hard in both ends of the ice and tries to make the safe play to get the puck out of his own end. He protects the puck well by using his body and can get a good cycle going in deep in the offensive zone. He is a decent skater with an element of speed to his game and he gets back well on the back-check to provide support in his own end. Desrochers isn't likely to be selected at the 2013 NHL Entry Draft. Any interest a team will have in him will come from his hard working two-way style. He has some flashes of offensive potential but not enough to persuade a team. If he makes it to the NHL level he projects to be a bottom six physical player who is effective in all three zones.

Desrosiers, Philippe – G – Rimouski Océanic (QMJHL) – 6'1" 187

Philippe Desrosiers has been a steady performer for the young Rimouski Océanic squad. Coming from AAA Midget where he was a stellar goalie at 16 years old, Desrosiers started the season as a backup goalie with Rimouski, supporting veteran Carl Hozjan in his work by putting solid effort after solid effort gave no choice to Rimouski's management but to put him as the number one goalie on the team.

There's little to dislike in Desrosiers' game. He plays a fairly robotic standard butterfly style with tremendous attention to details and accurate positioning. He is calm in front of his net and compacted. Pucks will rarely get through his body he appears big, shoulders high, displaying a picture perfect butterfly standing position. He plays the angles and positional game like very few 17 years old goalie do. He is waiting for the puck to touch him and gives himself the least reaction necessary to make the play. This great positioning helps him tremendously in regards to rebound control. He is already one of the best goalies in that area, rarely giving away any rebounds, pucks will be absorbed by his body and pushed aside lower shots in the corners. He handles the puck fairly well and likes to go out of his net to play the puck and initiating the transition himself. His reads are great and his anticipation is a very strong quality in Desorisiers' game. These attributes help him again move laterally at the right moments to get in great position. His pushes are accurate and they assist him in making great point leg saves.

Desrosiers has good reflexes, but still need to practice the catching glove. Developing quicker reflexes would help, as most of his saves with both hands are made because of his tremendous positioning. We would like to see him put more effort in finding pucks through traffic. He can be beat on scramble plays and he ought to use that 6,01 frame to see and compete harder to find the puck at his feet when he doesn't see where it is. His mental toughness is great, performing well at the most important times and quickly forgetting a bad goal he allowed. He has consistency that teams will look for, rarely stealing a game on his own but as well, rarely having a terrible game. He's been a HP favourite. We have him positioned closely to Fucale regarding his professional potential.

Quotable:" Saw him mid season and he had a rough game, much different story at the top prospects game and my viewings in Sochi. Cool customer who played great hockey in big games. His skill playing the puck is elite but he needs to learn when to play it and where to put the pucks. That should come with time." - Mark Edwards

Diaby, Jonathan – LD – Victoriaville Tigres (QMJHL) – 6'5" 231

Here is a player who took advantage of his late birthday to develop his game properly. In his third season in the QMJHL (second complete season), Diaby established himself as a force on the blue line with his solid defensive play and physical attributes.

What caught our eye first about him is his ability to play in a 1-on-1 situation, whether it's on the rush or along the boards. His improved mobility allows him to react well and make an excellent use of his body and stick to stop his opponents. He showed good synchronism in his approach defensively, often poke-checking the puck to subsequently deliver a perfectly timed hit. A prime example was in a game against the Halifax Mooseheads when he spent all night defending Nathan Mackinnon and Jonathan Drouin. Diaby was a step-ahead of them the entire time and did a great job defending them. He also displays impressive strength along the board and in front of the net, where he can move players and retrieve pucks for his team. It's also worth mentioning that Diaby is an accomplished fighter and took on the biggest players in the league, although his focus was primarily his hockey play in the second half of the season.

His play with the puck has always been an issue for us since he entered the league, but it has improved drastically this year. He now plays safely with the puck from his own end and can execute a solid transition most of the time. While he is still prone to make a few mistakes, he is confident in his abilities and can still execute high level plays. While we don't envision him in this role at the professional level, Diaby showed he could play on the power play this year where he kept things under control and scored quite a few nice goals with his strong shot.

The main component missing from his game that prevents us from ranking him higher is his hockey sense at times. He struggles with his decision making while defending 3-on-2 or 2-on-1 situations. He doesn't always react properly and will often give the other team too many options. He has a tendency to freeze, which makes him look bad, instead of covering one of the many options the other team has. There is no doubt in our mind Diaby is an interesting project that could develop into a solid physical shutdown in the NHL. He has to acquire experience defensively and continue to improve his play with the puck in order to succeed at the next level. He also needs to maintain the improvement we have seen in his skating since coming into the league.

Quotable: "I saw this kid play some good games this year, he is still very raw and a project but he has some potential to be a hard nosed blue liner at the NHL level." - Mark Edwards

Dichiara, Frank – LW – Dubuque (USHL) – 6'05" 215

Frank is a strong kid who posted 30 goals and added 30 more assists. His feet are getting better all the time and he is really strong on the puck. He has a pro shot and a quick release to along with it. He is good along the walls down low and is effective when he gets pucks on his tape in the slot.

Quotable: "This is a player I like in the late rounds. There is some good elements to his game." - Mark Edwards

Dickinson, Jason – LW – Guelph Storm (OHL) – 6'1.25" 178

Jason was selected in the 2nd round of the 2011 OHL Priority Selection Draft by the Guelph Storm out of the Halton Hurricanes Minor Midget program. He really wasn't a big standout in Minor Midget but he really elevated his game as a 16 year old putting together one of the more impressive rookie seasons of any 16 year old in the 2011-2012 season. Jason looked to build upon this in his draft year and opened up a great start to the season. He opened his first 11 games of the season with 8 goals and 8 assists. He looked like an undisputed first round pick in this 2013 NHL Entry Draft. He declined in our rankings in the second half of the season. As opposed to his first 11 games, he posted just 1 goal and 1 assist in 12 games from January 26th to February 23rd. While his offensive game had a massive contrast from hot to cold, what should keep him up in the 2013 NHL Entry Draft is he's always strong defensively and takes care of his own zone.

Jason is a very smooth skater and is able to generate a good level of speed when given space to carry the puck down the wing or up the middle. He works hard to play all 200 feet of the ice and can be counted on in the defensive zone either helping out down low or winning battles along the boards to get pucks into the neutral zone. Jason is constantly working to keep body positioning on the D side of the puck and thus is seldom caught out of position. He has solid recovery speed that helps combat any time he is out of position.

Around December, Dickinson noticeably started to really ramp up his physical play which carried over to the second half of the season. Jason was constantly finishing checks in both open ice and along the boards and showed deceptive strength knocking a number of bigger opponents off of pucks with ease. He is good at using his body to shield opponents from the puck and will drive to the net with speed when given space. He generally worked along the wall on the power play and possesses a very powerful wrist shot from the top of the circle when coming in off the wall. Dickinson was also an exceptionally strong penalty killer for the Storm and was great at getting into both passing and shooting lanes and he blocked a number of shots throughout the season. He struggled in the face-off circle when forced to take the draw and is much better suited playing the wing. The biggest issue with Jason is the lack of offensive consistency over the season. There were games where his offensive skills would be on full display and he would dominate defenders both on and off the puck, and then there would be games where we saw little to no offensive pressure.

If he could improve consistency and feature his strong offensive skills on a nightly basis he will become quite the prospect in the years to come. Jason is considered to have very good character and is a player who is knowledgeable about the areas in which he needs to improve. The high end, if he can show his offense consistently, would see him being a potential second liner in the NHL. Dickinson can be a reliable two-way forward who shows flashes of productivity and plays a key penalty killing role. The safety of a Dickinson pick by an NHL team lies in his defensive abilities, but his high end intrigue will come if he can play a more consistent offensive game.

Quotable: "The biggest thing I look for every time I see him is his ability to score. He is smart and plays a good 200 foot game. I want to see him show me consistent scoring ability." - Mark Edwards

Quotable: "Getting the chance to see the Storm quite a bit this season I really had the chance to fully see the up and down season that Jason had. He would dazzle me with offensive ability one night and then disappear in the offensive zone for the next 4 or 5 games. He is great at playing the full 200 feet of the rink and is strong defensively. If he could ever get some offensive consistency he will be a great depth forward at the NHL level" - Kevin Thacker

DiFruscia, Anthony – LW – Niagara Ice Dogs (OHL) – 5'10.5" 190

Anthony was selected in the 2nd round, 40th overall pick by the Niagara Ice Dogs in the 2011 OHL Priority Selection Draft out of the Welland Tigers Minor Midget program. Anthony decided to go to Salisbury Prep. High School in 2011-2012 and did a very good job of adding muscle and preparing himself for the OHL. The 2012-2013 season was his rookie season with the Ice Dogs, and one that was fairly successful. He registered a respectable 15 goals and 30 points in 68 games.

DiFrucia's game is built on a drive and desire to win. When he takes shifts off or tries to rely on natural skill and abilities, he becomes nearly a non-factor. He is not easily intimidated, will get involved in scrums and will cut towards the middle of the ice in order to create opportunities in tight. He will take a hit to still make a play and is willing to take a beating to stand in front of the net in the goaltender's face.

At times a lack of offensive awareness is evident, as he makes poor reads on where to go in the offensive zone. In his own end he gets in lanes to block shots and positions himself well. He does not shy away from any physical play and is good both forechecking and on the penalty kill. He may not have all the skill in the world, but is a hard worker.

Dikushin, Grigory – FW – Green Bay Gamblers (USHL) – 5'8" 150

Grigory joined the Green Bay Gamblers for the 2011-2012 season. He made a good adjustment to North America while playing a limited role. He also put on a very solid performance at the World U-17 Challenge in Windsor posting 9 points in 5 games en route to winning gold. Grigori has gained some extra ice time in his second season with Green Bay and displays an array of talents. First and foremost, Grigory is a very solid skater who moves well up and down the ice and is capable of handling the puck very well. He tends to shoot first, but is a capable passer. He is very dangerous on the breakaway and possesses some very good moves. Dikushin works hard forcing turnovers and puts great pressure on the puck carrier. He also uses his quickness in all three zones making him an effective two-way player. Grigory can sometimes get too carried away with his skating ability and actually work himself out of good scoring positions or ideal positioning in the offensive zone. He also made some questionable decisions in our viewings putting some concern on his hockey sense. Dikushin's biggest battle will come from his lack of size.

Doetzel, Kayle – RD – Red Deer Rebels (WHL) – 6'3" 191

Kayle Doetzel is a fairly mobile, physical defenseman who had a solid season for the Rebels this year. He was counted on to play some big minutes, and he was able to respond with a great performance on a consistent basis and gain the trust of the coaching staff. Doetzel is known for his work in the defensive zone. He provides a physical presence at all times, and is difficult to play against along the wall. He is constantly in good position to protect the slot from dangerous situations, and has a good stick, but it is something he can work on. He is more than willing to take a hit to make a play with the puck when there is forecheck pressure, and is very strong on his skates. Doetzel is able to stay on his feet with the puck and quickly get the puck out of trouble. Offensively, Doetzel has shown limited potential. He will probably never regularly put up points, but has the ability to make good passes out of the zone. However, he often has more time than he thinks, and should look to make a pass to a teammate instead of putting the puck off the glass and out. He also does a good job of pinching down the walls when necessary to keep the offensive pressure going. Teams looking for a dependable defenseman for the future will take a long look at Doetzel. He has the size to take on big forwards at the pro level, and the potential defensively to at least be a bottom pairing defenseman if he continues to work on his skating abilities and poise with the puck.

Quotable: "Sometimes a performance sticks with you, in this case it was viewing him at the Hlinka camp." - Mark Edwards

Quotable: "He was average in my viewings." - NHL Scout

Domi, Max – LC – London Knights (OHL) – 5'9.25" 197

Max was selected in the 1st round, 8th Overall by the Kingston Frontenacs in the 2011 OHL Priority Selection Draft out of the Don Mills Flyers Minor Midget program. Max was arguably the best player available in the draft, however fell due to potential NCAA commitments. After a little negotiating, Max was traded to London from Kingston and would begin his career with the Knights on schedule. Max is the son of former NHLer Tie Domi. While he possesses the grit and resiliency of his father, he plays a much more skilled dynamic style of game fueled by his physical talents and high level hockey sense.

Max instantly became a contributing player on a veteran London squad. Max was a productive player in his rookie season and was one of the most talented rookies in the entire CHL. Leading into Max's NHL Draft Year the question was whether he'd be able to take on a leadership role and produce at a rate that would help London remain among the top teams in the league. He answered that question rather emphatically, finishing the season as a top 10 scorer in points, goals, power play goals and plus/minus (also finished 1 assist out of the top 10). Max not only produces points but he comes through at the most critical moment in the game. London had many come from behind victories and often, when the game was on the line, Max elevated his play to a higher level. Domi handles the puck extremely well and shows great shiftiness. He is extremely difficult to contain because he is an excellent skater. He accelerates quickly, changes directions on a dime and can fly around the ice.

Along with his skating he is built very solid. He's not a big player but possesses exceptional core strength allowing him to absorb contact and keep going. Max has an excellent shot which is very accurate and he is capable of finishing consistently. He displays excellent vision and while he's more than capable of putting the puck in the net, he can create and set up scoring chances in ways that few other prospects can. In terms of improvements, Max can get into slumps where he occasionally tries to do too much and gets caught turning over some pucks in the grey zones. We see Max as a sure fire first round pick and while his size may drop him on some teams draft boards, it wouldn't be out of the realm of possibilities for Max to find his way into the top 10 or 15 picks.

Max projects to be a skilled top six forward at the next level who has a very high potential ceiling. He has proven to us over many viewings that he excels in clutch situations. Max will also benefit from his character, which is highly regarded as an individual.

Quotable: "I expect Max to be even better as an NHL'er. I think that once he starts to play with more players who are as smart as he is, he will really shine. Max is at his best when he is moving the puck with that elite vision. He tends to get the puck back on his tape anyway and that's when he is most dangerous. He is relentless hounding pucks and doesn't get enough credit for how strong he is in puck protection and winning battles." - Mark Edwards

Quotable: "He is a highly skilled player with elite vision. It's a nice combination to go along with his motor that never seems to stop." - NHL Scout

Quotable: "When you're undersized like Max is, you need a specific combination of hockey sense, puck skills, skating ability and fearlessness to be successful. Safe to say Max has all of these abilities, and then some. Not to mention he's a kid who has great character and a good teammate." - Ryan Yessie

Dorantes, Tyler – LD – Des Moines Buccaneers (USHL) – 6'1" 179

Dorantes played in the Detroit system with Bell Tire U16 in midget then with Detroit Compuware U18 the following year. He joined Des Moines Buccaneers of the USHL this year to play his rookie season and had 7 points in 38 games but an overwhelming 132 penalty minutes. Dorantes is a tough kid who plays with an edge on the ice, but has to watch some of the unwarranted penalties that cost his team. He is pretty calm with the puck, can hold the offensive line well and gets his shot through to the net from the point. He can distribute the puck pretty well in the offensive zone and has the capability to find lanes to move the puck to teammates down low, however still needs to watch some of the offensive zone turnovers that he makes by trying to force passes through the opposition. He is also able to make a pretty decent 1st pass out of the zone to start the rush.

Dorantes can make a name for himself by playing a tough, physical style of hockey and being a defenseman that forwards hate to play against. He needs to finish all his hits along the boards and be tough with his stick on opponents, however needs to use his edge that he is in a way that will be effective and help the team, rather than by taking costly penalties. Tyler is committed to Ferris State this fall of 2013.

Downing, Michael – LD – Dubuque Fighting Saints (USHL) – 6'3" 190

Michael is a hard-working two-way defenseman with a mean streak and upside. He plays with great awareness, tracking the play with his head up and keeping his feet moving. He joins the attack frequently and intelligently. He wants the puck and wants to be a difference maker. His pinches are aggressive but sometimes ill advised. He's a rover on the power play, taking advantage of his strong skating, smart passing, and great point shot. He tries to get into the head of his opponents with questionable stick work and chirping. He loves to throw big hits and is willing to drop the gloves. Overall, he needs to watch his discipline and temper his aggressiveness. He makes mistakes in coverage, especially in outnumbered attack situations, by forcing the issue instead of allowing the play to come to him. He's also guilty of taking needless, badly timed penalties. The big blueliner is headed to Michigan in the fall.

Quotable: "He got better as the season went on. He was not good early this season. He probably raised his stock late with improved play." - NHL Scout

Drouin, Jonathan – LW – Halifax Mooseheads (QMJHL) – 5'11" 176

What an amazing season it was for Jonathan Drouin, from start to finish. He left a strong impression on us at our first viewing early in the year and he kept accumulating solid outings from that moment on.

Drouin's play with the puck is clearly special and he would seem to be a lock as a point producer at the NHL, level. His game is about elite speed, vision and puck handling abilities combined with perhaps the smartest player in the draf t. He has extremely quick feet and a very good explosiveness that allows him to transition from one zone to another in a hurry. Drouin is also extremely creative using his quick hands that creates the opportunity to elude extra defenders on his way to the offensive zone. As a puck carrier, he was not stopped often this season. Regardless of some risky plays he tries at times, he always manages to get the puck back on his stick and keep going.

Drouin excels when managing the puck in the offensive zone, where he is just as good shooting the puck as passing it. He showed off his laser wrist shot on numerous occasions this season, leaving the goalies little chance when he lets it go. It's a very quick and accurate shot that he rapidly fires. Drouin can also set up magnificent plays for his teammates with great vision and accuracy. He is a very natural player with the puck and the decisions he makes are always quick and in the flow of the game. His offensive instincts are extremely sharp, allowing him to play with great confidence.

Defensively, Drouin was fairly dedicated and has made some good progress. It was not rare to see Drouin create a few turnovers in a game with his strong sense of anticipation.

Quotable:" One things that stood out for me in my early viewings of him was his ability to create time and space for himself. I saw him hold of defenders dogging him all over the offensive zone and he used his feet, creativity and puck handling skills to buy himself time until he could make a smart play. Drouin is up with my fave prospects I have ever scouted because he provides so much excitement. I'll remember a goal he scored in Drummondville for a long time. He could easily have been the first player taken in a draft without guys named Seth Jones and Nathan MacKinnon.

Duclair, Anthony – LW – Québec Remparts (QMJHL) – 5'11" 182

After a highly impressive rookie season in QMJHL where he was able to rack up 31 goals and 66 points, Anthony had a tough time doing the same this season with the Remparts. Scoring only 20 goals and only showing some chunks of the level at times, he can be off and on during the season.
Anthony Duclair is a tremendous skater blessed with amazing explosive ability. This makes him a great neutral zone player as he can go through a tight defensive system by putting pucks just behind players using his blazing speed to recover the puck before his opponents can. His elite quickness gave him an edge against most defensemen in the QMJHL, creating more space than most forwards achieve. He has quick hands and can dangle the puck quite well at top speed. He will get many scoring chances simply by retrieving loose pucks before his opponents and getting to soft areas of the ice before the defense can adjust. Although we feel he can still improve his finish, Anthony Duclair generates multiple scoring chances for himself and could have doubled his number of goals scored with better opportunism. He prefers to use his speed out wide to get around the net and try a wrap around or a pass in the slot. He has scored many goals this way since the start of his career. He has great puck protection skills and uses his reach effectively to get the puck to an area where it can't be poke checked by his opponent. He is a strong player and will not be easily be pushed off the puck. Duclair has great hands in tight spaces and can get pucks through skates and sticks efficiently. He can execute great passing plays at top speed, whether those are shot feeds off a cycle or long cross ice passes. He's an underrated passer, setting up many plays with crisp and accurate passes.

The Québec Remparts forward has had some up and down moments during season. He had his best moments while playing with North-South players, driving the net and playing a cycling game. He showed more intensity, work ethic and dedication when he took this approach to the game. With the speed he has in his skating and execution, he dominated as a forward when he played this way. His worst moments were when he played a soft peripheral game, choosing to rely on skills and East-West play. He subsequently appeared overconfident, gliding and not especially focused in the decisions he was making with the puck. He has to show better consistency in the way he plays and the intensity he brings each night.

Anthony Duclair needs improvement defensively. His offensive hockey sense is great, but defensively he will cause turnovers by trying dangerous plays at his blue-line demonstrating poor defensive hockey sense on multiple occasions. He's not the type of player that will go out of his way to block a shot and further, we would like to see the same kind of speed he uses offensively put to use defensively, to press his opponents. Unfortunately, Duclair is often seen gliding and stationary in his own zone and we've watched him cheat in neutral zone to get easy soft ice. He needs to play a better positional game and stay cautious in his own zone, we haven't seen enough from him this year to call him a 2-way forward. He has many tools of a great offensive players in professional hockey, but needs to be more consistent in his efforts and smarter in his own zone.

Dunn, Vincent – LC – Val D'Or Foreurs (QMJHL) – 5'11" 181

Vincent Dunn came into the QMJHL at 16 years old in 2011-2012 and made a name for himself by playing a rarely seen aggressive and intense game, never backing down from anybody. In fact, in his first two season, Dunn has accumulated close to 200 penalty minutes while being a pretty good hockey player.

Dunn displays a great level of energy when he is on the ice which makes him very noticeable, rarely taking a shift off. He will try to get under the skin of his opponents, bantering after whistles, starting scrums, giving a little more on the body check and just knocking them off their game. Although he is not the biggest player at 5'11", Dunn will rarely refuse a fight and he is a proven fighter in that realm. He is a player you don't like to come up against because of his level of competitiveness and associated intensity will expose a soft player. He doesn't necessary lay out the big hit often, but will be physical on the forecheck with high energy. He has an above-average top speed and great power in his first few strides to quickly reach max speed. He is not an East-West player by any means, but has quick feet and will use them to gain time and space laterally. He has quick hands and more than a decent skill set that he uses well in tight spaces to get pucks around the net to generate a scoring chance or simply keep the puck in battles. A strong player, Dunn has good puck protection and his tenacity makes him tough to knock off the puck. He will score goals around the net, jumping on rebounds but he also scores some solid goals off the rush. His offensive vision is impressive, finding teammates quickly and executing skilled setups on the rush. He is also effective when delaying the play because of those good passing skills.

Defensively, Dunn has never stopped progressing, working hard and supporting his defensemen well. He needs to play a better positional game as he tends to be a little too aggressive at times. Dunn can overreact and be undisciplined also, he needs to have control of his temper. His hits can be dangerous at times. Dunn doesn't possess a big frame or high end offensive potential for the next level, but his intensity and character mixed with his above-average abilities make him a very interesting pick come draft day.

Quotable: "Impressed me with some good vision and playing ability in a couple viewings this season" - Mark Edwards

Dupuy, Jean – RW – Kingston Frontenacs (OHL) – 6'2.25" 190

Jean was another solid late round selection for the Kingston Frontenacs in the 13th Round of the 2010 OHL Priority Selection Draft. He had a tough route working his way up, he split his time between AA and AAA hockey even in Minor Midget, but was selected out of the Ottawa Jr. 67's Minor Midget Program. He went on to play Major Midget with them as well as Hawkesbury Hawks in CCHL action before joining the Frontenacs. Jean plays a pretty simple game. He has great size and is very assertive physically. He delivers to big hits and he works hard in the corners. He's also shown a distinct willingness to drop the gloves. He hasn't particularly faired well in every fight, but he appears comfortable with the fighting aspect of the game. Jean is a late 1994 birth date who has applied himself physically and shown moderately effective defensive play. He's certainly a player that may hear his name called in the final rounds of the draft, but with limited offensive upside, a team will need to pick his name out of the large group of bottom six players that are looking to get picked in the 2013 NHL Entry Draft.

Eastman, Kyle – FW – Tri-City Storm (USHL) – 5'11" 195

Eastman was developed in the Buffalo Regals U16 program. He was then selected by the Tri-City Storm in the 3rd round at 38th overall. He played in 2 games for Tri-City last year in the USHL, then played his first full year in the league this season and registered 10 points in 54 games but was a -14. He is a player who is willing to bring a net-front presence in the offensive zone and opens up pretty well next to the net to provide scoring options to his teammates down low. He can move the puck around pretty well, finds lanes to get the puck to teammates but needs to start driving the puck to the net more often rather than continuously taking long outside shots.

Ebbing, Thomas – FW – Chicago Steel (USHL) – 5'11" 165

Ebbing was drafted into the USHL in the 3rd round by the Chicago Steel after playing for Brother Rice High School in 2011-2012 where he scored 67 points in just 30 games. He played in his rookie season with Chicago this year and had 26 points in 60 games but was also a -26 player. He had a chance to play for USA in the World Junior A Challenge as well and was invited to play in the USHL top prospects game. Ebbing possesses good hands and speed to gain the offensive zone off the rush and puts good shots on net. He protects the puck really effectively along the wall in the offensive zone and cycles the puck very well. Ebbing may be drafted late in the 2013 NHL entry draft. The most important thing for him moving forward is to take the off-season to get bigger and stronger and hopefully his skills will translate into more offensive production next year at Michigan State University.

Quotable: "In my opinion his play dropped off after the Junior A Challenge. His stock dropped for me. He went from a player I was quite high on, to a fringe prospect who will need to get back to work in order to regain NHL prospect status." - Mark Edwards

Elie, Remi – LW – London Knights (OHL) – 6'0.5" 203

Remi was selected in the 5th round of the 2011 OHL Priority Selection Draft by the London Knights out of the Eastern Ontario Wild Minor Midget program. Remi stayed close to home last season playing for the Hawkesbury Hawks of the CCHL where he put up nearly a point per game and scored over 20 goals as a 16 year old. Remi came to London Knights camp and made an immediate impact on our scouts causing us to watch him closely right from day one. Remi has spent the majority of the season playing on the Knights fourth line due to the tremendous depth of the team. His only escape from this has been when an injury occurs or someone in the top 9 has been underperforming. Usually this would result in Remi being promoted to a higher line that game. This has affected his numbers making Remi one of those players you have to watch closely to truly appreciate his level of talent. He had a bit of a coming out party early in the playoffs, scoring three goals in London's four game sweep of Saginaw.

While we see Remi posting a big point increase next season, what he brings goes well beyond stats. Remi plays a great power game where he wins battles along the boards and provides a relentless work ethic allowing him to win more than his share of battles. He plays a very physical game and will finish his checks. He also battles in his own zone winning along the wall. He reads the play well and can break up potential scoring chances with a stick check or to separate an opposing player from the puck. What helps Elie be as successful as he has been in his first OHL season, is his hockey sense. Remi has the ability to read the play. He's a big player, who knows he's big and knows how to use his size intelligently to give himself an advantage. While he competes in all three zones, he shows offensive potential with his shot. He has a cannon of a slap shot which was used at different times this season on the point of the Knights' power play. He also has a quick release on his wrist shot. Sometimes it takes him a little too long to make puck decisions, but he has creativity with his passing.

Remi didn't play a lot of minutes, didn't put up many points, but with the way he projects at the pro level and the potential he displays, it would not be the least bit surprising to see him picked inside the Top 60.

Quotable: "I love the way he plays a pro game already. He does all the little things right. You won't see him turnover pucks on failed dangles. You will see soft chips and relentless fore checking. This kid finishes every check. His shot is a cannon. Remi has a lot of upside. I love watching him play. I spoke to him earlier this season, he had played the point on the power play that day. He said Dale just decided to throw him out there, the kid let a few bombs go that day." - Mark Edwards

Quotable: "I saw you did a front page story on Elie, so much for him being under the radar." - NHL Scout

Quotable: "On the very first day of London Knights training camp I took one look at this kid and 'wow' was my first reaction. London is doing a great job developing Remi, just wait until some of the older Knights graduate and his ice time goes up. He's going to show his true potential then. Some NHL team is going to steal this kid." - Ryan Yessie

Ellis, Eddie – LC – Phillips Andover Academy (Prep-MA) – 6'1, 190

After coming into the year as one of the top draft prospects in New England, Ellis has seen his stock plummet due to struggles with consistency. He can intimidate offensively with speed, skill, and intensity, but very rarely brings his A-game. More often than not, he's indecisive, unsure on his feet, and tries to do too much. His skating is a major question mark, as at times he looks like he's stuck in cement. He has a good selection of shots but can't always get into position to use them. He shows good hands in flashes, especially on the power play when he's given more time and space. His defensive coverage is poor, as he floats and fixates on the puck. He doesn't get involved enough in battles and frequently gives the puck away. At this point, it would be surprising to see him get drafted.

Erkamps, Macoy – RD – Lethbridge Hurricanes (WHL) – 5'11" 193

Macoy Erkamps is a smart, physical defenseman who plays much bigger than he actually is out on the ice. He likes to throw his body around in the neutral zone whenever he gets the opportunity, while making good plays with the puck on a consistent basis. Erkamps really likes to involve himself in all areas of the ice. He likes to be aggressive in between the blue lines and try to start counter attacks for his team. He also makes very good first passes out of the zone, and does a good job of staying in between the dots and staying patient when necessary. He has a good stick that he uses to pick off passes and to stir opponents to the outside. Erkamps is quite strong along the boards, and consistently wins battles for pucks. An area of improvement for Erkamps is his ability to read the play without the puck. There are times when he is caught watching the puck and not reacting to how opposing forwards are positioned in the slot. One of Erkamps' best attributes is his puck moving abilities. He may not be flashy or catch anybody's attention, but he is solid with the puck in all areas, and makes good decisions with it consistently. He quarterbacks the power play for Lethbridge and does a good job for them, but he will probably never be good enough to have that role as a pro. He does not possess elite vision or a heavy shot from the point.

Erne, Adam – RW – Québec Remparts (QMJHL) – 6'1" 198

Without making big waves, Erne has put yet another solid season this year in the QMJHL. He was a reliable force on offense for the Quebec Remparts as he improved his production from last year.
Erne's play fits in between a highly talented player and a power forward. He is a good skater with impressive explosion for a big player and he uses that to his advantage. He is not as dynamic as some highly skilled players in this draft, but he does a good job exploding on the wing and cutting to the

net. Erne possesses tremendous top speed and can make even the best defensemen look vulnerable. His feet are quick and they make him an agile skater, twisting and turning with ease on the boards. That fact, mixed with his size, gives him amazing tools to create space. In the neutral zone, he won't hesitate to carry the puck for extended periods of time and does a good job of letting it go at the right moment. Indeed, his puck distribution is very good and Erne shows developed maturity and intelligence in his passing game, able to execute tremendous cross-ice feeds and quick short passes. His hands are definitely not elite but he handles the puck well whether at top speed or stationary. With a quick rolling movement of the wrists and can fire a rapid wrist shot. His shot is released in a hurry and gives no time for the goalie to control the rebound. It's a powerful shot that he prefers to use in the lower part of the net. A natural goal scorer, Erne is strong on his stick when battling for a loose puck in front of the net. He showed great offensive hockey sense on multiple occasions, getting into a scoring position when teammates control the puck. Erne is dangerous around the net, his bread and butter all season long, crashing and feeding open teammates, trying the wrap around or simply jumping on rebounds.

One of the reasons why the words power forward are used when talking about Erne is because of his blend of grit and physical play. He can impose a nasty physical presence along the boards with his size and good motor skills. We have seen him absolutely destroy some of his opponents with punishing hits, whether they are in his own zone or on the forecheck, Erne can be a very intimidating player when he plays this way. He will initiate physical contact and rarely have we seen Erne get over powered when engaging in a body positioning battle in a race for a loose puck. He has created soft ice for his teammates in many of our viewings by using is big frame to play this way. Defensively, Erne has progressed well, using great anticipation to play his positional game and physical intensity to make sure the puck gets out. When there is a pass to be made he will do it, but rarely will he cause a turnover near his own blue line.

One of Adam's few weaknesses is his consistency. He can get away with a non-physical approach to his game in the Q by using his speed, good hands around the net and finishing touch to have an impact on the game. We feel it's a commitment he will have to make every night in professional hockey to be successful. On some nights this season, Erne was a beast, crashing the net, banging bodies and displaying a tremendous work ethic. On other nights, he played a softer game and that's an area where he needs to be better. His finishing touch could be better, Erne could have had more than 40 goals this season with better opportunism around the net, he needs to stay aggressive and keep practicing the accuracy of his hard shot and maybe add more variety to his shooting game.

Erne has been a favourite of ours in his last two seasons with the Québec Remparts. His mix of hockey sense, physical ability and good hockey tools makes him one of the top prospects in this draft class. We've rarely had one bad viewing of Adam Erne and although he didn't have as impressive of an offensive production as many of other 2013 NHL Draft eligible, we feel Erne's game is already polished and ready for the next level. His affect on a hockey game goes way beyond statistics, he is an impact player.

Quotable: "If you take him you might get one of the top scorers in the draft. I'm a little worried about what he's going to do at the combine." NHL Scout

Quotable "Really liked this kid last year and again this year. I expect big powerful players to be at a premium in this draft based on what I have heard all season long from scouts. I heard from multiple scouts that Adam was less than stellar in his combine interview with them. I saw Adam at the combine, don't know his test results yet, but he is man.

Etchegary, Kurt – LC – Québec Remparts (QMJHL) – 5'11" 185

The Newfoundland native has been injured for more than half of the 2012-2013 season but had an impact when he was in the lineup with the Québec Remparts. He is a gritty center with a very good hockey sense on offense and defense. Etchegary plays a smart game in his own zone, always on time for the backcheck. He is willing to get hit to make a play and willing to sacrifice the body to block shots. He plays a smart positional game as he is not the fastest skater and will look bad if he starts running around. The 5'11" center will be physical and strong in his battles even against bigger opponents. He has showed a lot of character by dropping the gloves against bigger opponents throughout his career. He plays defensive situations with smarts, determination and dedication. Kurt possesses great passing skills as he sees the ice very well. He can pass through skates and sticks with ease, finding teammates in traffic. He likes to delay the play when he enters the offensive zone, put his head up and create plays with his passing skills. He also showed his great offensive vision on the powerplay at multiple times in our viewings, creating scoring chances with superb cross-ice feeds. He will get goals when he crashes the net but he doesn't have a really good shot or the skating abilities to get in the slot before the opponent's defensive coverage is on him. He's not a gifted t puck handler and doesn't have the best puck control, regardless, he can still create some nice plays to keep the puck in tight space areas. His skating strides are not the most fluid or well-executed but gives him an average explosion and above-average speed. He should improve his skating to play at a higher level.

Evans, Jake – LC – Erie Otters (OHL) – 6'0" 185

Jake was selected in the 2nd round of the 2011 OHL Priority Selection Draft by the Erie Otters. In his rookie season he put together some impressive numbers with 12 goals and 23 points. He was expected to elevate his game even further this year, however, he really didn't produce the way we were expecting. Consistently playing in a bottom six role, his numbers took a step back and he played more of a hard working game. Jake is a very good skater and gets going quickly with some good size. He's most effective when playing simple and getting the puck deep then chasing. He cycles the puck effectively and keeps it simple along the boards. He has shown some flashes of elusiveness but generally didn't generate much offense. He was also used regularly on Erie's penalty kill showing the ability to get into passing lanes and willing to block shots. Jake is not a player we expect to get drafted although it wouldn't be a shock either. He has a fair amount of untapped offensive ability. When you combine that with his speed, size and willingness to hit, he might be worth taking a shot at late in the draft. Jake will look to take on a bigger role with the Otters and hopefully put up career numbers while continuing to play physical.

Fasching, Hudson – RW – US NTDP Under-18 Team – 6'2, 214

Hudson has seen his stock plummet since this time last year, and rightly so. He teases with great size and great flashes of offensive talent, but his hockey sense is questionable and infrequently gives his best effort. When he's on his game he moves well for his size, controls the puck well, shows good hands along the boards, and plays an intelligent, physical defensive game. More often than not, he has a hard time handling the puck and tries to force plays, leading to frustration and the rest of his game falling apart. It's easy to tell what kind of game Fasching will have based on his first shift. Part of his issues this year seemed to draw from puck luck as well, as he went stretches where he was ridiculously snake bitten with frequent goalposts and near misses. He also dealt with a concussion at the beginning of the season, and it's possible that the lingering effects of that were also a factor. Such negatives do have a way of snowballing. Fasching will surely be drafted and will be looking at next year as a clean slate, which could be just the thing he needs to get his game back together.

Quotable: "Some games he seems to have it all together, other games he's not a factor. Physically he has all the tools. I just don't see him putting it all together. I have coached some players in the past who were just too nice. It's difficult to make a nice kid be something he's not comfortable being. I see some of that in Hudson." – Mark Edwards

Fisher, Logan – LC – Victoria Royals (WHL) – 6'2" 175

Fisher is a 4th line centre for the Royals who received limited ice time this year and was counted on to not get scored on whenever he was out on the ice. Fisher is a good skater who is primarily a north-south player. He works hard to win battles for lose pucks, and must give everything that he has on a nightly basis to stay in the lineup. Fisher has limited skill with the puck, and does not think the game particularly well. He is not able to really find open areas out on the ice and get free from coverage, or read the play in the defensive zone to get into good position to takeaway passes or get in front of a quick shot in the slot. He also has a tough time handling any sorts of breakout passes from his defensemen, and will definitely need to work on his hands.

Fitzgerald, Ryan – LC – Valley Jr. Warriors (EJHL) – 5'9, 170

Despite his small stature, Fitzgerald oozes skill and hockey sense. He plays a smooth two-way game with great awareness of time, space, and pressure. He's a shifty skater with quick hands and is very deceptive with the puck, able to beat defenders 1-on-1 with swift changes of direction and outstanding skill. He plays with a lot of jump, keeps his feet moving and his head up, actively tracking the play. He is apt at finishing plays as he can pick spots with quick shots. He's excellent at receiving passes, even errant ones, in a manner that allows him to continue the attack without missing a beat. His penalty killing is solid and he covers well in his own zone. He shows an active stick in all three zones. He's good on the dot with a refined technique.

His size is an issue at times, as bigger players can overpower him. He generally shows good evasiveness but when keyed in on by the opposing team, he can have a tough time making an impact. He is guilty of trying to do too much at times, which though not a major issue at the EJHL level due to his ability to quickly cover his mistakes with strong back checking could become a concern as he progresses. He'll suit up for Boston College in the fall, where he'll look to add strength and continue to refine his all-around game. He's still very raw, but even playing against weak competition has shown enough to merit serious attention.

Quotable: "In most EJHL games this year, Fitzgerald was head-and-shoulders above the competition, but I was most impressed with the way he played for the NTDP U18 team in October. He stepped in as an undersized player and didn't look out of place skating against college teams." - Josh Deitell

Fitzmorris, Mitchell – LC – Niagara Ice Dogs (OHL) – 5'11" 180

Mitchell was selected in the 3rd round of the 2011 OHL Priority Selection Draft by the Kingston Frontenacs out of the Elgin-Middlesex Chiefs program. Fitzmorris got a handful of games with the Frontenacs as a 16 year old, but played the majority of his season with the St. Mary's Lincolns Jr. B. organization. To open the 2012-2013 season, Mitchell had more success making the Frontenacs regular lineup. As the trade deadline was approaching Mitchell was moved a little closer to home joining the Niagara Ice Dogs. Fitzmorris will not overwhelm you with any offensive numbers, with only 7 points this year in his first full season split between Kingston and Niagara, however, he is a really high-energy, up-tempo player who finishes his checks and puts good pressure on the puck carrier on the fore-check.

He is a blue-collar player who can cycle the puck, protect it on the wide drive and follows up the play to get to the slot for rebound chances. He takes too many weak outside shots off the rush, most of which do not even get through to the net. He could improve on his skating stride as he moves his legs very quickly, but not effectively. His best chance for success is to continue to demonstrate a penalty killing ability, stick to a simple game and do all the dirty work on the ice that is necessary to give a team a chance for success.

Florentino, Anthony – RD – South Kent School (HIGH-CT) – 6'1 227

The stocky blueliner had a nice season for the Selects, playing physical, defensive-minded hockey on a nightly basis and flashing a little offensive ability in the process. He's not the most agile skater, but he moves well for his size and can carry the puck up ice while building speed like a freight train. His hands are quick enough to make some plays and he gets good shots on net from the point, though he probably won't be a big point producer at the next level. He'll be able to clear danger with safe outlets and occasionally lug the puck, but his bread and butter is hard-nosed, positional defensive coverage. He impresses with smart reads against the rush, maintaining an active stick and stepping up to play the body when he can. He's aggressive behind his net and protects his crease with intensity, though he can get so caught up with laying contact in his end that he loses focus on the play and floats out of position. His footwork is an issue at times, especially when he jumps into the attack and doesn't hustle back to his end. He's strong enough positionally that his skating will do him fine if he doesn't try to do too much out there, but he could stand to add a step. He'll suit up for Providence next season and looks like the type of blueliner who'll benefit greatly from the physicality of the college game.

Ford, Dakota – LD – Middlesex Islanders (EJHL) – 6'2, 185

Dakota improved by leaps and bounds this season, and was a major stabilizing force on the Islanders back end. He skates well for his size and plays a steady two-way game. He's smart in his zone with smooth outlet passes and good physical play. He covers the rush well with good backwards skating and clears his net front with vigor. He shows an active stick in shooting and passing lanes and keeps his head up to track the play. His offensive upside shows from time to time, as he can join the rush with strong skating and picks his spots well. He won't be a scoring dynamo as a professional, but shows the tools to be reliable in his zone with the occasional offensive contribution. He was selected by Cedar Rapids in the 2013 USHL Draft, and will likely make the jump there this fall. He could be a late-round flier in the 2013 NHL Draft. At the very least, he put himself on a lot of radars this year.

Fram, Jason – RD – Spokane Chiefs (WHL) – 6'0" 180

Fram is a solid defenseman in his own zone. He does not do anything particularly well, but is good in all areas of the game defensively. He does not make many glaring mistakes without the puck, and does a good job of maintaining a tight gap at all times. Fram's skating abilities are good, but his lateral mobility needs to improve. He has good north-south speed, but whenever opponents make a move inside, he has a difficult time staying on them. He is in good position to protect the slot and once in a while pick off some passes, but his work with his stick could improve. Fram's physical play is not very good, and it is an area of his game that he really needs to improve on. Offensively, Fram shows good instincts in the offensive zone. He likes to pinch down the wall and keep the puck in the zone, and has a good shot from the point. He makes very good first passes out of the zone and is efficient with the puck. He limits the turnovers, and keeps it simple. He does not possess any elite skills, and will probably never score any highlight reel goals or make any amazing plays with the puck.

Fucale, Zachary – G – Halifax Mooseheads (QMJHL) – 6'1" 176

Zachary Fucale has been a part of the big 3, with MacKinnon and Drouin in Halifax that hockey people have been raving about for this year's draft. He has piled up 77 wins in 123 games in his young career and has been one of the major reasons why Halifax have been such a major junior power house in 2012-2013.

Fucale stands at 6'1", 176 pounds giving him a fairly decent size for a goaltender. He plays a standard butterfly game, focusing on covering his angles and trying to stop more pucks by doing less. What separates him from others is his mental toughness. Zachary Fucale is unshakable, nothing seems to get into his head in a hockey game. His composure is always disarming. He forgets a bad goal quickly, doesn't lose his focus when players crash his net, impressively keeps the same level of focus whether he receives 15 or 45 shots and just never seems to have mental fatigue even when playing back to back games. One thing we really like about him is the way he can control his emotions and make the key save when games are on the line. He just has that quality that clutch goaltenders have. Fucale is not an aggressive goalie, limiting the movements he needs to do to make a save, he will rarely overreact when making his lateral movements, showing tremendous control on his body when moving. He is a really smart goalie with great anticipation; always finding a way to track pucks and knowing what are the puck carrier's options, helping him getting in position in time in the case of a pass. A great athlete, Fucale is a very quick goalie. We have seen him make saves on superb post-to-post movements displaying his flexibility. His legs are strong and quick helping him in the rebound control area and in his lower-net coverage.

We would like to see Fucale be more aggressive as his calm and cool can be his own worst nightmare exemplified by staying too deep in his crease which forces him to make reactionary saves instead of coming in front of his crease and letting the puck touch him. Some pucks might get through because of that bad habit, making him look vulnerable at times. Fucale also needs to get a better catching glove, sometimes putting it too low. We also feel his reflexes with both hands need to get better for professional hockey.

Quotable: "Mental toughness is mandatory for goalies in the NHL and Fucale has it. I have seen him look awkward and shaky in some games, but he will always find a way to get his confidence back and make the big save at the right moment, which speaks volumes about the mental side of his game. - Simon Larouche

Quotable: " Best attribute for me after the obvious talent he has physically and reading the play, is his poise between the pipes. Nothing rattles this kid - Like water rolling of a ducks Back. Finally spoke to him at the combine, good sense of humor and an easy kid to like. Seems like people predict goalies to the Devils yearly of late, I think this is the year. I Think they may attempt to trade back a couple spots if the opportunity arrises, but I don't think they think twice over taking him with their own pick if no trade rears it's head." - Mark Edwards

Gabor, Gilbert – LW – Owen Sound Attack (OHL) – 6'3" 192

Gilbert came over from Stockholm, Sweden despite representing Slovakia at the World U17 Challenge last year. Gilbert posted over a point per game for AIK's J18 team last season but made the jump across the pond to play for the Attack. He came with moderate expectations but took a little while to get rolling. He has excellent size and is generally at his best when he utilizes it. Despite his size he's an effective skater and gets around well. He forechecks hard and provides a good work ethic. He has a decent shot and generally takes a shoot first approach when he has the puck in the offensive zone. Gilbert has shown flashes of his ability but hasn't progressed quite as expected. We don't expect to see him get selected in this draft, but he has size and a progressed willingness to engage physically. Gilbert will need to find his role and continue to improve and work hard in the offseason to hopefully have a better season next year and turn some heads.

Gamez, Garrett – FW – Tri-City Storm (USHL) – 5'11" – 180

Gamez was selected in the 1st round at 8th overall in the 2012 USHL Entry Draft and he played in his rookie season in the USHL this year, playing in 46 games and earning himself a solid 18 points. He is a player with good speed and quickness and he is willing to drive the middle towards the net with his stick down to provide his teammates with scoring options in tight. His best quality is his ability to get down low and drive the net with the puck. He has hands and moves to get by defenders or to beat the goaltender and he also is willing to bring a net-front presence on the power play. He can rush the puck up the ice with pretty good speed and distributes the puck to gain the offensive zone off the wing.

Ganly, Tyler – RD – Sault Ste. Marie Greyhounds (OHL) – 6'2" 197

Tyler was selected in the 5th round of the 2011 OHL Priority Selection Draft by the Sault Ste. Marie Greyhounds out of the Toronto Jr. Canadiens Minor Midget program. Ganly has been one of our favorite players and stories in this 2013 NHL Entry Draft. Ganly played Major Midget for the Toronto Jr. Canadiens last season with a handful of performances for the Brampton Capitals of the OJHL. When he was selected he was a true project that needed to put in a ton of work to reach his potential as of the 2011 OHL Draft. He certainly put in that work and looked excellent in our viewings this season. He also started to show a great improvement in his confidence as the season progressed.

Tyler started the season by keeping things simple and ensuring a complete defense first attitude. As the season progressed he began to show more of a willingness to contribute to the offensive rush and take more chances with the puck. He is a big strong defender and is good at getting physical in the corners and front of the net in the defensive zone. He has been one of the most effective defensemen eligible in the draft in one on one situations and rarely got beat. He is a hard worker and generally makes strong simple crisp breakout passes and moves the puck quickly when pressured. Ganly is effective on the penalty kill and has shown a willingness to block shots and do whatever it takes to get the puck out of the defensive zone. He has also shown a willingness to stand up for teammates and dropped the gloves on a number of occasions over the season. Tyler needs to work on improving his offensive shot and adding some strength to his frame in order to really be able to dominate physically down low.

Ganly may end up being one of the young leaders from the blueline for the Greyhounds next season as the Greyhounds graduate multiple defenders and has some excellent potential moving forward. We really believe NHL teams are going to be looking at this kid as a potential shutdown defenseman who can play big minutes and kill penalties. As his puck moving abilities have improved, he's shown to be a player that's reliable in making the intelligent plays and handles the puck better than many big defensemen out there. We would like to see Ganly fill out his frame, get stronger and further improve his skating. We're very excited to see where he gets selected and how he develops as he shows a lot of intriguing potential.

Quotable: "Tyler wasn't the kind of player you'd call home about back in Minor Midget. He had size and did ok. I think you had to see him in Minor Midget to really appreciate the great deal of improvements Tyler has made over the past two years. He's come miles and the Greyhounds have done a great job developing him into a legitimate NHL prospect." - Ryan Yessie

Quotable: "Tyler had his ups and downs as a rookie in the OHL. I really liked how he kept things simple in the defensive zone and seemed to constantly improve and gain confidence as the season progressed. He would consistently stand up for his teammates and showed a willingness to drop the gloves with anyone in the league. He will be looked upon to play a larger role on the Greyhounds blue line next season and I think he will be up to the task." - Kevin Thacker

Garlent, Hunter – RC – Guelph Storm (OHL) – 5'8.25" 164

Hunter was selected first round, 11th Overall by the Guelph Storm at the 2011 OHL Priority Selection Draft out of the Welland Tigers Minor Midget program. Hunter had to come in to the OHL at 16 and prove himself capable of overcoming his size. He did an excellent job putting up 42 points in 60 games as a rookie. He also played a key part of Team Ontario's World U17 Challenge Team in Windsor, Ontario. Hunter came into this season hoping to further improve on his statistics, however, he actually took a step back in terms of his numbers.

Garlent is a small shifty forward for the Storm. He skates like a water bug and is constantly zipping in and out all over the ice. Hunter brings a good level of speed to his game and can beat defenders with a quick outside move. He works hard and always strives to keep his feet moving when he is on the ice, which occasionally earns him the chance to create turnovers from the opposition. He is average in the face-off circle and generally ends up close to even most nights. Hunter shows flashes of offensive creativity but struggles to bring it consistently night in and night out. Garlent is not afraid to go to the hard areas of the ice to make a play despite his usual size disadvantage to most opponents. He is constantly buzzing around the net and jumps all over rebound opportunities when they become available. Hunter saw time on the 2nd power play unit for the Storm primarily on the blue line as the 4th forward showcasing good playmaking ability by working one timers with his defense partner. He also possesses a rocket of a wrist shot and is able to get it off with a deceptively fast release, fooling goaltenders a number of times top shelf.

Hunter also had the chance to represent Team Canada at the U18 world championships and was effective against international competition. He will play a large role in the success of the Storm in 2013-2014. Hunter is expected to go outside the first few rounds. He shows a lot of intriguing skills but will have to overcome his size and show a little more production offensively to reach his potential. However, he works extremely hard and has shown some real flashes of talent which will work in his favor later on in the draft with a team willing to take a chance on him.

Gauthier, Frédérick – LC – Rimouski Océanic (QMJHL) – 6'4" 215

Perhaps Gauthier lived in the shadows of other QMJHL rookies this season, at least on the score sheet, but he managed to put together a solid performance throughout the year. When talking about Gauthier, the one word we continually go back to is intelligence. He displays it in all phases of the game and reading the play extremely well. He knows where to position himself to be effective and showed to be one step ahead of his opponents on numerous occasions. If takeaways were to be counted by the QMJHL, there is no doubt you would find Gauthier's name at the top. He creates many turnovers in the defensive and neutral zone with his long reach and more specifically his awareness. His play on defense and the penalty kill was stellar; his positioning was excellent and he did a good job using his big body defensively.

His play with the puck is also very good, but not near the top regarding offensive contribution. Gauthier has all the basics covered with solid hands, a strong wrist shot and again, good hockey sense that allows him to make the right decisions and set up good plays. He likes to cycle the puck in the offensive zone and he protects the puck well with his body and solid hands. Gauthier is neither a dynamic playmaker nor a dangerous shooter, but he is very effective in his decisions as mentioned. In addition, he positions himself properly to be productive.

We identified two areas of improvement while watching Gauthier play. The first one is his skating. He moves well enough to play his two-way game effectively but he doesn't have the explosiveness required to apply additional pressure defensively or to power his way through the offensive zone. Second, he needs to make a greater use of his body along the board to punish opponents to maximize his potential.

Quotable: "You don't see many players coming from the QMJHL who have Gauthier attention to detail in the defensive zone. He has a terrific defensive game and is very raw in the offensive end." – Jerome Berube

Quotable: "I was much higher on this player early on in the season. I am scared off a bit about his lack of willingness to play physical and overall compete level. In Sochi I thought he had a few very poor games. He barely even touched the puck in one game. I see him as a very smart 3rd line centre but I have more 'bust' fears than I did a few months ago." – Mark Edwards

Geertsen, Mason – LD – Vancouver Giants (WHL) – 6'4" 203

Geertsen joined the Giants midway through the season following a trade from Edmonton, and it has really helped him develop into a good defenseman. He received limited minutes on a stacked Oil Kings team, but with Vancouver, he has been counted on to eat big minutes and has looked quite good doing so. His leadership abilities are evident as he was presented with the "A" shortly after he arrived, and he sets a good example to all of his teammates on the ice. Geertsen is tough to play against in the defensive zone. He has a mean streak to his game, and will physically punish opponents in the slot and along the boards. He protects his teammates when necessary and is not afraid to get into scrums. He is good at reading the play without the puck, but he still has some improvements to make particularly when his goalie gives up a rebound and he has a tough time tracking it and trying to tie up opponents. He has let a few passes go cross crease which also led to dangerous chances. On the rush, Geertsen is a bit of a hit or miss. He has a good reach that he uses well, but when elite offensive players come down his wing with speed, he has difficulty at times of keeping them to the outside and not getting danced around by them. He definitely needs to work on his footwork and using his stick better to knock away pucks. A big change in Geertsen's playing time has come from receiving power play minutes with the Giants. He has received the opportunity to quarterback the power play, and has not looked great doing so. He makes good, simple passes, but he does not read the play too well and does not make the greatest decisions with the puck. He also does not have the speed or skating abilities to rush the puck himself. He has an above average shot that he needs to work on, and make better passes from the blueline to prevent them from getting intercepted and having a play go the other way.

Quotable: "A fight from last season where he took on and older player comes to mind every time I hear his name. He is a tough kid." - Mark Edwards

Genovese, Cory – LD – Sudbury Wolves (OHL) – 6'2" 201

Cory was selected in the 13th round of the 2010 OHL Priority Selection Draft by the Kitchener Rangers out of the Cambridge Hawks Minor Midget Program. Due to his late birth date he has been able to play three years of junior hockey before being eligible for the NHL Entry Draft. Cory spent his first year of junior with the Elmira Sugar Kings which was a big experience for him as he got plenty of action in the playoffs and at the Sutherland Cup. He was able to make a stacked Kitchener Rangers blueline for the 2011-2012 season, however was a healthy scratch for some games. To open the 2012-2013 season, he played a more regular role with the Rangers before being part of a blockbuster deal to Sudbury. Genovese is a defenseman with good size and keeps to a fairly simple game, sticking to the basics. This was his second season in the league and was traded to Sudbury from Kitchener part way through the year, and in 115 career OHL games he has a whopping 175 penalty minutes. He is very calm with the puck, moves it around the boards nicely to get it out of the zone and avoids a lot of high risk plays up the middle. He plays with some good physicality to finish his hits along the boards and does a good job of getting his stick in shooting lanes to deflect shots out of play. He misses his target on some of his breakout passes and at times when he goes in for a puck battle he tries to reach around the opponent rather than taking a direct root and trying to attack the puck with his stick.

Genovese may be a late draft selection in the upcoming draft, due to his size, toughness and physical nature. He is willing to drop the gloves and stick up for teammates and keeps his mistakes to a minimum. He has to establish himself as a defenseman who can play a very reliable game in his own end, continue to play physical and tie up his man to keep them from getting opportunities in tight in front of the net. Cory will likely get some consideration at the 2013 NHL Entry Draft, but isn't expected to be selected. Cory projects to be a player who could play a minimal role at the top level using his size and safe simple style of play to shut down opposing forwards.

Gilbert, Jared – LD – Kitchener Rangers (OHL) – 5'11" 189

Jared was selected in the 3rd round of the 2011 OHL Priority Selection Draft out of the Toronto Marlboros Minor Midget Program. Jared split time last season between the OHL Rangers and the Kitchener Dutchmen Jr. B program. Jared got ice that prepared him for a more regular role in the OHL. This season Gilbert saw a regular shift generally in the 3rd pairing of Kitchener's top 6 Rangers defensemen, but failed to generate much offensive output and primarily concentrated on playing the role of a shutdown defender. He makes sound breakout passes and rarely takes much risk when moving the puck up the ice. Jared is a decent skater and is good at transitioning from forward to backwards skating and vice versa. He shows adequate hockey sense and focuses on a defense first aspect when he is on the ice. Jared will need to improve on playing a more consistent game. There were too many times where he would make the unnecessary mental mistake or get beat one on one defensively. Gilbert is a thick kid and needs to add some strength to his frame in order to become more of a physical presence on the back end.

Girard, Félix – RC – Baie-Comeau Drakkar (QMJHL) – 5'11" 190

Félix Girard is all about heart, dedication and commitment to his sport. He was passed on last year at the draft in his first eligibility year, a season where he was relinquished to an exclusively defensive role with defensive players. With a much better season offensively in 2012-2013, he has been the heart and soul of the Baie-Comeau Drakkar and deserves to be drafted at 18 years old without a doubt.

Girard plays with a rarely seen intensity and his natural enthusiasm leads by example. In our numerous viewings, we have never seen Félix Girard get outworked in any area on the ice. He wins his battles, completes every body check legally when he's in pursuit of the puck, plays a tremendous "in your face" type of game and is very good at getting under the skin of players. Not a really tall player at 5'11", but considerably big and strong. Girard has no fear and won't give an inch to even the biggest of opponents. He is the kind of player you want on the ice against the opposition's top players. He will make these players pay the price and will get them off their game. Defensively, Girard is outstanding, winning the important face offs, laying down in front of shots, blocking passing lanes with a smart stick positioning and paying attention to the details. He's always the first forward back and always comes in hard on support for his teammates. He keeps his head up on a swivel, staying well aware of what's around him, reading and reacting displaying intelligence defensively.

His stamina and energy are a notch higher than most players, never appearing winded or unable to complete a longer shift if he had to. A very good skater with a great top speed, Girard has good explosiveness that serves him well to press. His quick feet allow him to follow just about anybody in defensive coverage. Offensively, he uses his top speed well to create lanes to the net and space for himself. Possessing a good wrist shot, Félix Girard gets most of his goals from smart positioning around the offensive net and pushing rebounds or teammates strategies into the net. Not a highly skilled player by any means, he still has above average puck control and fairly quick hands. He plays a high energy dump-and-chase, North-South game very well creating opportunities coming off the cycle. He consistently uses nice passing skills and again intelligence to his advantage.

There are no overt weaknesses right now in Félix Girard's game for junior hockey, he is one of the hardest players to be matched against, a natural leader who possesses unrivaled intensity. His lack of high end talent may raise some doubts whether he can adjust to a quicker game in professional hockey. He will certainly need to improve his puck handling abilities and puck control to play up there. Regardless, he has shown a superb progression already this year with more confidence and more offensive responsibilities. His explosiveness could improve as he gains speed, which will benefit him in hitting his opponents, as relentless as they are at the next level. We don't think he has the potential to have an offensive impact in professional hockey rather, he could settle into an energy role with defensive minutes to play. You always want to give individuals with such character and passion for the game a second chance.

Gisonti, Vincent – LC – Westminster (Prep-CT) – 5'9, 178

It's hard to watch Gisonti and come away unimpressed. He's an honest hockey player that plays an excellent two-way game. His skating is excellent. He's strong on his skates and shows top-end burst quickness and agility. He's an outstanding stick handler who can make plays at high speed. Despite his size, he's unafraid to go hard to the net, and can beat defenders with dangles or by taking the puck wide and eluding checks. He's creative in the offensive zone, working well in a cycle with smart positioning and passing. His shot is dangerous with a quick release and good placement. He forechecks hard, pressing the defense aggressively. His defensive game is refined with smart back checking and good play in his end. His only red flag is consistency, as he can disappear for shifts or whole periods at a time. It's hard to fathom how Gisonti has gone without a DI college offer, and he's not a legitimate professional prospect, but his work this season deserves mention here.

Giugovaz, Michael – G – Peterborough Petes (OHL) – 6'0" 172

Michael was selected in the 10th round of the 2011 OHL Priority Selection Draft by the Peterborough Petes out of the Toronto Red Wings Minor Midget program. Michael joined the Georgetown Raiders of the OJHL for his 16 year old season and put on an outstanding performance posting great numbers and helping the Raiders to a successful 2011-2012 season. Michael came to the Petes' camp and made the team right off the bat. It was a bit of a tale of two seasons for Michael. He started the season great, and while he opened the season as the back-up, he arguably earned the starting role. However, after the Christmas break, his play dropped off a bit.

Giugovaz has tools to be a successful goalie. Michael's glove positioning was really our biggest concern about his game as he would drop his glove and quicker shooters could beat him high glove side seemingly at will. Also as the season went on, he appeared to become fatigued and focus was a bit of an issue, which to be fair to Michael is not an uncommon occurrence for players in their first season of CHL play. Giugovaz is certainly worthy of a late round pick for a team who could take Michael and help him develop into a potential NHL goaltender. He has excellent athleticism which is a great thing to build off of.

The one down side is he is in tough to earn the starting job for the Peterborough Petes and will be in a bit of an uphill battle. He has shown the potential of being a starting goaltender in this league, and is in for a great battle with D'Agostini come September.

Quotable: "I made a long trek to see this kid on a recommendation. He has talent but is very raw." – NHL Scout

Goldberg, Andrew – RW – Mississauga Steelheads (OHL) – 5'11" 199

Goldberg was able to chip in with 9 goals this season in 61 games. He plays a pretty simple game by getting the puck in deep off the rush and put some pressure and physicality on the fore-check to try to force turnovers. He brings a net-front presence in the offensive zone and works pretty hard in both ends of the ice. He needs to pick up the speed and tempo of his game, get stronger on the puck and has to start driving the puck down low rather than just throwing weak outside shots on net from bad scoring positions. He also needs to move the puck around quicker and watch some of the turnovers trying to force passes through the opposition.

Golonka, Will – LW – Belmont Hill (Prep-MA) – 5'10, 185

Will's line at Belmont Hill, which saw him skating alongside Dartmouth recruit Carl Hesler and DIII-bound Mike Najjar, was among the best in prep hockey this year. Golonka plays a flashy, offensive style with excellent skating and stick handling to go along with good awareness. He reads the play well, burning up ice immediately after turnovers to create options and positioning himself well in the offensive zone. He can beat players 1-on-1 with great maneuverability and carries the puck at speed with great poise. He's a fairly one-dimensional player as he lacks a refined defensive game, but is worth consideration for his skill alone.

Gore, Bryson – RC – Moose Jaw Warriors (WHL) – 5'10" 182

Gore is a quick moving centre who provided an inconsistent performance throughout the year. He has troubles at times handling the puck and commits turnovers in the neutral zone, even on easy outlet passes. Then in other times, he is able to take control of difficult, off target passes and get the attack going for his team. Gore needs to go to the net with more authority, and not be scared to take punishment while driving the net. He pursues loose pucks with good energy, and really uses his speed to his advantage. He displays above average hands in the offensive zone when he has some room in tight, and when given the opportunity he has the ability to quick roof the puck. Defensively, Gore needs to commit himself more to playing without the puck. He has shown that he does not like to block shots, and he is really everywhere in the defensive zone. He could be better at reading the play down low to be a better assistance for his defensemen. Gore has not shown enough offensive or defensive capabilities to put his name into consideration to be drafted by an NHL team this year. He has to work on being a more consistent player at both ends of the ice, and play with more tenacity to make up for his lack of size.

Gravel, Maxime – RD – Rimouski Océanic (QMJHL) – 6'0" 182

Gravel entered his rookie season with Rimouski after spending 2 years in AAA Midget with the Collège Esther-Blondin along Frédérik Gauthier and Laurent Dauphin. He is an offensive defenseman with great tools for that style of play. He moves very well, having an above-average overall speed and strong explosiveness. His fluidity could be better, as his strides don't seem natural. We like the puck-moving abilities he posesses, making hard accurate passes, having quick hands with solid puck control. He also has a strong slap shot, and he is not afraid of letting go in traffic. Gravel is confident in his abilities, rushing the puck well and not afraid to force the play. The Blainville native likes to be agressive, whether it's in physical confrontation, in his gap coverage defensively or even in neutral zone. We doubt Gravel's level of hockey sense. He plays a high risk offensive game and can cause multiple turnovers, although he has shown improvement over the course of the season. He needs to improve his game management, as to when he can take chances and when he needs to stay back. His defensive awareness and positional game are below average, sometimes forgetting opponents behind him and making the wrong decisions in slot coverage creating opportunities for opponents to get there. We feel he has shown nice improvement this season and should be drafted for his offensive potential in the later rounds of the draft.

Graves, Ryan – LD – PEI Rocket (QMJHL) – 6'4" 225

Graves is what you don't get much of in the QMJH, a 6'4", 225 pound defenseman. Graves would get more recognition if he was playing in the WHL. Graves is a project no doubt about it, but he has shown consistent progression this season. He wants to be aggressive and punishing but for the moment, he doesn't have the skating abilities to do an effective job playing this style. That problem manifests as getting caught out of position and beat in one-on-one situations by agile skaters. Moving that frame around is not an easy task at 17 years old. Graves will be a better player when his legs develop and generate more power in each skating stride. He plays a simple game offensively, with developed basic skills that coupled with solid decisions with the puck have helped him get points sporadically during the season. He can be mean and intimidating down-low in his own zone and that's the nasty side we've loved from Ryan Graves this season. We think he could become a shutdown physical defenseman on a 3rd pairing in professional hockey if his footwork progresses enough.

Green, Taylor – LD – Seattle Thunderbirds (WHL) – 6'7" 220

Taylor Green was the most raw, undeveloped defenseman on the Seattle defense unit that is full of rookies. To his credit, he has probably made the most progress in terms of overall skill, and went from a player who looked very overwhelmed by the pace of the play whenever he was out on the ice to a quiet but dependable defenseman. One aspect that Green had to really work on was his skating. He was extremely sluggish, and had a difficult time keeping up with anybody. He has since worked on his foot speed, and while it is still quite below average, he has improved on it to the point where he is not a huge liability. He also needs to work on his balance as he is easy to knock off the puck at times. He still had difficulties with speedy forwards, but when he is out against 3rd and 4th lines, he can hold his own in the corners with starts and stops and skating backwards to angle them to the outside with his good stick. He was also getting dangled time and time again, but has since improved on that immensely, and he uses his stick much more effectively and uses his reach to his advantage. He is okay at reading the play without the puck, and is better at positioning himself in the slot to take away any dangerous chances.

Offensively, Green is still very limited with his play with the puck. He fumbled the puck regularly on breakout passes, but has since improved his outlet passes and while they are very simple and short, he has been able to show some poise with the puck. He is bad at generating offense from the point, and it is very doubtful that he will develop any kind of an offensive game at this point.

Grégoire, Jérémy – C – Baie-Comeau Drakkar (QMJHL) – 6'0" 188

After a promising rookie season with Chicoutimi in 2011-2012 when he scored 15 goals, Jérémy Grégoire had issues getting his confidence back in the first half of the year in Chicoutimi. He was subsequently dealt to Baie-Comeau in a blockbuster trade at Christmas time and finally started to regain his confidence and identity back at the end of the season, specifically during the QMJHL playoffs.

Jeremy Grégoire is all about work ethic and going to the dirty areas. Most of his offensive production comes from tenacity around the net whether those are quick passing plays, finding soft areas to release shots or banging away on rebounds until they cross the goal line. He is able to produce extra intensity in front of the net to be the man jumping on the rebounds and holding his body position against older players. A big strong player, Grégoire competes really hard and has natural goal scoring instincts. He has a strong wrist shot, knows how to position himself and his stick to tip pucks or generate a shooting lane. He has an above-average skill set with very good puck control. He has an effective, dextrous forehand to backhand move that is very quick allows him to shield the puck effectively in the offensive zone. Possessing a great work ethic, Grégoire is willing to hit and take a hit from an opponent to make a play. He generates scrums, pushing and shoving with his intensity, he likes to agitate and provoke his opponents. Grégoire can drop the gloves and is a fairly accomplished fighter at only 17 years old. He has great character and dedication which he has displayed often in the season, willing to block shots and skate as hard as he can to backcheck. As a natural leader, the enthusiasm he brings to the game is catching for his teammates. He has already played as a centerman for long periods in his major junior career. However, with his skating deficiencies and a personal style that suits him best, Grégoire is at his optimum on the wing.

Grégoire's biggest weakness is his skating. His top speed is below average for major junior and his explosiveness will needs improvement. He is limited in what he can do on the ice because of poor speed. He's in late to the puck pursuit and late to defensive coverage although he works hard to get there and experiences a tough time creating space for himself with such slow feet. He still has a tough time drawing a line between getting under the skin of players with intensity and being undisciplined. He will let his emotions get the best of him at times which will result for additional trouble for him. His passing game is not well developed which result in turnovers. He could turn develop into a nice surprise playing a specific goal-scoring role in professional hockey if his skating improves significantly. Possessing such character and intensity, Grégoire should get drafted at the 2013 NHL Draft.

Gross, Jordan – RD – Green Bay Gamblers (USHL) – 5'10" 178

Jordan was a first round pick, 6th Overall by the Green Bay Gamblers at the 2011 USHL Futures Draft. Jordan played his first full season in the USHL after spending the past few seasons at Maple Grove High School. He had a very strong run there and started to get his name out there, but really put his name on the radar at the US Select 17 Camp in Rochester, NY. Jordan possesses excellent skating ability and he is capable of skating the puck out of trouble and is very adept at rushing the puck up the ice, identifying options and making good decisions with speed heading up the ice. Jordan was very good on the point for Green Bay's power play. He looked very comfortable and knows when to shoot, when to pass and made quick decisions. He also possesses a deceptive slap pass that resulted in a few power play goals for Green Bay.

He generally works hard defensively but he has also made some clear mental lapses. He usually has good gap control but has been absolutely walked by forwards despite his skating ability. He shows a knowledge of how to use his stick. Jordan is a player who, at times looks like one of the most underrated USHL prospects, but there have been many frustrating moments along the way with Jordan making mistakes unbecoming of his skill level. Jordan has committed to play for Notre Dame University this fall of 2013.

Guénette, Justin – LD Rouyn-Noranda Huskies (QMJHL) – 5'11" 185

A small defenseman whom may be of interest to a few teams in the late rounds of the 2013 NHL Draft is Justin Guénette. He's not flashy by any means, rather he is very effective and steady on defense in our viewings of Rouyn-Noranda. He doesn't show much offensively, having barely received power play minutes during the season, a place where most young defensemen develop confidence in their offensive abilities. Guénette is a small, yet solid D physically, tough to knock off the puck with his great upper body strength to control players on the walls. Managing physical play is no problem for Justin Guénette, as he is willing to take a hit while still protecting the puck maintaining a physical presence on players coming in on him. Rarely will Guénette give up in a 1-on-1 battle. He's been steady and reliable this season for Rouyn, a consistency we attribute to his strong work ethic. He has a highly developed hockey sense and displays it well when paired with his solid positional game and quick decisions while under pressure. He will rarely get caught turning the puck over, demonstrating his composure. He makes crisp passes to his teammates, preferring the safe option as opposed to a long stretch pass. His awareness is very good, always showing maturity and intelligence on the ice. His play with the puck is controlled in tight spaces. He is able to maintain puck possession by carrying the puck through traffic. He joins the rush at the right times and makes safe decisions at the offensive blue line, rarely exposing his team to risk, while skating well to hold the blue line and maintain puck possession. He has good footwork and overall speed in his game, but continues to lack explosiveness. He doesn't have elite skills, great creativity or confidence to use his shot often. However, his slapshot is very powerful. We feel it's a matter of confidence for Guénette as far as offense goes, although he will never be an offensive defenseman. The hockey sense and work ethic in Guénette's game make him worth the risk in the last rounds of the draft for sure.

Guentzel, Jake – FW – Sioux City Musketeers (USHL) – 5'9" 153

Jake Guentzel had an incredibly impressive 73 points in 60 games in his rookie season in the USHL this year and was named USHL rookie of the year and also had the opportunity to play in the USHL top prospects game. Guentzel was a dangerous offensive force every time he stepped on the ice and he is a player who has really nice hands and moves to skate the puck up the ice on an end-to-end rush then can make a great pass to move the puck to a man driving hard to the net for a great opportunity in tight. He protects the puck really well along the boards, gets a good cycle game going in deep and distributes the puck very effectively on odd-man rush chances

His hands are incredible and the ability to find lanes to move the puck unmatched. He is not scared or intimidated to drive the puck to the net and he opens up so well to take passes and provide his teammates with scoring options. He has great offensive instincts to get to the slot, find space and open up for passes and he also has the vision and ability to get the puck to the right areas. Guentzel is a smaller forward which will make it difficult for him moving forward and he therefore needs to add size and strength if he ever wants to play at the next level. He has fantastic skills with the puck, a great sense of the game and can create a scoring chance each time he is on the ice. Jake is committed to join the University of Nebraska-Omaha this fall of 2013.

Quotable: "I like a lot about him. He's a gamer with great hands and good hockey sense, but he is an average skater. The skating and his size and strength will work against him. He's got 2nd round type talent but I'd select him later because of the lack of the size and strength. It's behind other small guys." - Mark Edwards

Guertler, Gabe – FW – Fargo Force (USHL) – 5'9" 178

Guertler was a top selection at #2 overall by Fargo Force in the 2011 USHL Futures Draft and got the opportunity this year to play in the USHL top prospects game. He played his first year in the USHL last year where he had 28 points in 57 games before earning himself an impressive 51 points in 60 games this season and had a +21 rating. Guertler is a bit of a smaller player but he can protect the puck very well to gain the offensive zone and is willing to bring a nice net-front presence. He does a great job of getting himself open down low next to the net on the power play and holds the puck in the offensive zone very effectively to keep the attack alive. He has a quick release on his shot that can fool goaltenders at times and gets the puck in deep into the offensive zone for the most part off the rush. He distributes the puck really well on the rush to start the breakout and will drive the puck hard towards the net to create chances in tight. He can read the play well to pick off turnovers in the neutral zone to rush the puck back into the offensive zone and puts great pressure on the puck carrier on the fore-check to try and force turnovers. He possesses great agility with the puck to twist from the opposition's pressure and create room to work with in order to make a play.

Guertler has good offensive instincts to find space in the offensive zone and open up to provide his teammates with a passing option. He has a good shot and can move the puck around well too, which makes him quite a threat to create scoring chances. He has to watch some of the turnovers trying to force passes through the opposition in the offensive zone and he also tries some high risk passes at times through the neutral zone up the middle.

Guindon, Louis-Philip – G – Drummondville Voltigeurs (QMJHL) – 6'0" 167

Guidon has been a huge surprise in 2012-2013 season of the QMJHL, after being selected in the 9th round by the Voltigeurs at the 2012 Q Draft. Guindon came in and stole the spotlight from a struggling Domenic Graham whom Drummondville had place their hopes on in net. Guindon is one of the quickest, most athletic goalies you will find. At 6'0" 165 pounds, he doesn't have much to carry around. His lateral movements are advanced, allowing him to move from post to post in a split second. He has made tremendous leg saves because of that quickness this season. His reflexes are great and with Louis-Philip Guindon, it's not a matter of how, it's only a matter of results. He will stop pucks in an unorthodox manner, yet still maintaining great consistency in his own style during the season. His catching gloves is as good and steady as his blocker which is rare in the era of the butterfly style. He is a great competitor working hard to track pucks through traffic, spot pucks at his feet when he gives up rebounds and will rarely back down during a game whether it's 1-1 or 5-1. His work ethic is another one of his strongest qualities, rarely letting a bad goal affect him while keeping the intensity high fighting for every save he makes even though his confidence may not be at the same level at that moment. His technique has improved significantly this year, but Guindon remains a reactive goalie. His standing position can look awkward at times and pucks will get by him because he isn't always square to the puck. He will give away bad rebounds and forcing himself to make a difficult save as a result. His lower net could also be better, especially the five hole, an area where he can be vulnerable. We believe that with better technique, with all the reflexes and competitiveness he possesses, Guindon could prove doubters wrong again.

Guy, Nevin – LD – Ottawa 67's (OHL) – 5'10" 165

After going unselected in the 2011 and 2012 OHL Priority Selection Drafts, Nevin was signed as a free agent by the Ottawa 67's in July 2012. Nevin spent his 2011-2012 season in the EOMHL with the Winchester Hawks while enjoying a brief stint with the Kemptville 73's of the CCHL. Guy registered 11 points in 66 games with a -23 rating in his OHL rookie season. He was a defenseman who was used in a forward role at times this season which displayed some desirable versatility in this player. When he played forward he just got pucks in deep by dumping it then chasing after it, kept to a simple game and put great pressure on the fore-check. When he played defense he liked to pressure the puck and use his stick to try to knock it off the opposition.

He is a smaller player who is going to have to add some size and strength to be more effective and learn to play the body more in a physical fashion. He has to be a player who can make a really good 1st pass out of the zone to start the rush on the breakout for a quick transition game. Nevin isn't a player we expect to be selected at the 2013 NHL Entry Draft and hope to see him continue to improve in his second season in the OHL.

Hagg, Robert – LD – MODO (SEL) – 6'2" 204

Robert has shown us a wide array of play in our viewings. He has looking both outstanding and invisible in different games, and sometimes in the same game. He has has excellent size but generally only seems to use it when he feels it's absolutely necessary. In the defensive zone he shows good positioning and knowledge of the play going on around him, but can get a little lazy and look uninterested resulting in unnecessary turnovers in his own end. He is capable of passing the puck from long distances but also effectively in the offensive zone. When he loses his focus, that is generally where the puck playing mistakes come. One of Robert's strongest assets is his shot. He has a big blast he can unload from the point and usually chooses good shooting options. He gets so much power behind it, when it doesn't beat the goaltender generally it results in a nice big rebound for his forwards to jump on. Hagg is a player who we've felt all season long possesses the tools to be a great defenseman but lacks the mindset to be a great defenseman. Robert has the upside to be one of the best defensemen in the entire 2013 NHL Entry Draft. However his downside is just as drastic in the opposite direction. He will be a bit of a risky pick for this draft, but one that could potentially pay off big time.

Quotable: "This is a player that extends scouting meetings. I think he has top 10 ability but he only occasionally flashed it for me. I'd see one shift and love what I saw and then on the next shift he would leave me wondering what he was doing. His compete level was on and off. This was another player I had plenty of conversations about with NHL scouts. It seemed like most teams staffs had a wide range of opinions. Everywhere from top 10 to late 30's." - Mark Edwards

Quotable: "Early in the season my reports were negative, late in the year they were all positive." - NHL Scout

Quotable: "At the Hlinka he played like he had a piano on his back. He got much better in my viewings later on this season. I really like him." - NHL Scout

Halagian, Nick – LW – Sault Ste. Marie Greyhounds (OHL) – 6'1" 199

Nick was a 3rd round pick of the Sault Ste. Marie Greyhounds at the 2011 OHL Priority Selection Draft out of the St. Catherine's Falcons Minor Midget program. Nick proved himself as a 16 year old in the Greyhounds camp and earned himself a roster spot. Nick played a limited role as a 16 year old and used the 2011-2012 season as a chance to adjust to the OHL level. We expected good things from him in 2012-2013 but he didn't quite finish the season as strongly as we had hoped. Nick is a player who remained in the bottom six due to a veteran presence among the forwards in Sault Ste. Marie. He showed great work ethic early on, working hard night in and night out. Later in the season, he started to let up on his efforts, which seemed to minimize his impact with the Hounds.

Halagian does not possess as much pure offensive skill as some of his teammates but certainly works hard in order to make things happen. He is good at getting in on the fore check and forcing opposing defenders into making turnovers or bad puck decisions. He is a fairly thick kid and likes to finish checks when given the opportunity. Halagian skates with long powerful strides and is good at back checking and being responsible in the defensive zone. He works hard to win puck battles along the boards. Nick is good on the penalty kill and will generally do whatever it takes to make a play for his teammates. He is at his best when he is creating turnovers down low with hustle and hard work before driving the net with authority.

Halagian will be looked upon to take a bigger role next season with the graduation of a number of key forwards from the Greyhounds lineup. We believe it's unlikely that Halagian will be selected at the NHL Draft, although it is certainly not out of the realm of possibility. Nick has the potential upside of a very solid bottom six forward at the NHL level. We would like to see him continue to improve his play with the puck, getting stronger and faster and showing what he can do in an increased role. NHL teams looking at Nick will be intrigued primarily by his work ethic.

Hall, Zach – LC – Barrie Colts (OHL) – 5'10.5" 172

Zach is being featured by us for a third straight season entering his final year of NHL Draft eligibility. Zach once again showed great improvements, this time leading the Barrie Colts in scoring during the regular season. Zach has shown his durability playing both centre and wing. He has excellent speed and absorbs contact well, eluding checkers. He's good with the puck and shows the knowledge of when to pass and when to shoot. Zach is likely to be drafted late in this draft due to his potential. If he is not, then we fully expect an NHL team to give him a long look as he is eligible to play in the AHL next year.

Hallisey, David – RW – Westminster (Prep-CT) – 5'10, 170

David plays the game the right way. The Princeton recruit is an honest, hard-working two-way player. He's a great skater with a lot of quickness and uses his feet to get in hard on the forecheck to create havoc. He plays the body hard with consistency, throwing his weight around like a much bigger player. He's a strong penalty killer, always giving a great effort, keeping his stick in lanes, and laying out to block shots. He back checks hard and helps out his defense along the boards and in front of the net. He shows offensive upside as well, with good cycling ability and passing. He navigates traffic well with quick hands and flashes a strong wrist shot with a quick release, and can also play a power game by fearlessly driving the puck hard to the net. He makes the occasional mental mistake but for the most part his game is very polished. Having already been passed over in 2012, it is likely Hallisey goes unselected again, but he's a safe bet to have an excellent college career and plays a pro-style game.

Hamilton, Trevor – RD – US NTDP Under-18 Team – 6'0, 181

Trevor joined the NTDP in 2011, at the time spurning offers to play with Fargo and London of the USHL and OHL. He was a productive two-way defenseman in midget, but has since changed his game and now plays a simple, defense-first role. He plays the game with poise, using solid positioning to keep the other team in check. He shows an active stick and uses his body well defensively, but is not a strong physical presence. He makes an OK first pass but as a whole his puck skills are lacking and he is prone to the odd giveaway. Hamilton's game is vanilla. There's not much to hate about him, but there's not much to get excited about either. He will suit up for Miami University in the fall and should be a solid depth defenseman in college, but at this point he probably does not do anything well enough to project as a future NHL talent.

Hansen, Carter – RW – Moose Jaw Warriors (WHL) – 6'2" 191

Hansen is a defensive forward with limited offensive abilities. He uses his big frame and above average skating abilities to dish out good hits and be difficult to play against along the walls as he is able to create some turnovers. He is good on the PK with his hustle and puck blocking abilities. Offensively, Hansen's development has not progressed much. He has limited offensive instincts, and just is not able to find any open areas out on the ice. He uses his body effectively to protect the puck along the walls, but he has not been able to produce much offense with the puck. He has a difficult time handling hard passes in the neutral zone. He does not get many shots on net as he is not able to separate himself from opponents very much.

Hansson, Niklas – RD – Rögle BK (SEL) – 6'0, 173

Niklas is a two-way defenseman who lacks polish but has plenty of upside. He's strong offensively. His outlet passes are excellent, whether long bombs or short, safe dishes. He plays the point well on the power play with good keeps and a hard one-timer, though he could stand to improve his accuracy as he frequently misses the target. He can skate the puck with poise when given room and stickhandles well, but his skating lacks explosiveness, which makes it difficult for him to beat defenders outright. In his own zone, his unrefined footwork can cause him problems tracking the cycle, with slow starts and stops, and evading the forecheck when picking up a loose puck. His coverage is generally good, with particularly strong positioning against the rush where he angles off effectively and finishes his checks well. He's not the most physical player but he plays the body capably. Bigger forwards give him trouble, especially in front of his net. He still has a lot of room to add onto his frame, which will not only improve his strength but should also boost his confidence and in turn improve all aspects of his game.

Harms, Brendan – FW – Fargo Force (USHL) – 5'11" 169

Harms played for the Portage Terriers of the MJHL where he had great success of being over a point a game player for two seasons straight before being drafted in the 6th round at 80th overall in 2011 and joining the Fargo Force of the USHL for 64 games where he registered an impressive 70 points and +33 rating.

Harms can make great passes to move the puck out of his own end to start the breakout and he drives hard to the net with his stick down for chances in tight. He battles hard for the puck in front of the net to win it in good scoring positions and can cycle it effectively in deep in the offensive zone. He is patient with the puck, can hold up to wait for a shooting lane before getting shots through to the net and he distributes the puck really well on the rush into the offensive zone. He brings a nice net-front presence, battles for his territory in the dirty areas and opens up really well in the slot to take passes and put good one-timers on net from scoring areas, demonstrating some great offensive instincts. He can make great passes to find open teammates in the offensive zone to create scoring chances and can find a man in behind the opposition's defense to spring a break opportunity. He finishes his hits along the boards and just needs to watch the turnovers trying to dangle his way through the opposition or by trying to force passes through. He is a highly skilled player who still needs to get bigger and stronger, but plays the game the right way and is not intimidated to go to the dirty areas to score tough goals. He has great skills, offensive sense of the game and vision to spot his options to create chances.

Quotable: " Looked like he needs to get stronger as it hurts his skating, but this is a smart hockey player. Has good hands, good skill overall and he is a gamer willing to block shots and do the little things." – Mark Edwards

Harmsworth, Colby – LD – Calgary Hitmen (WHL) – 6'1" 188

Harmsworth is a steady defenseman who was able to gain more ice time as the season went on. He has become an effective option for the Hitmen as he has been able to consistently bring a good effort. He does not take many chances in the defensive zone and just lets the play come to him. He does not land many hits, and leaves a big gap between himself and opponents off the rush. He has an average first pass out of the zone, and will not pick up many assists with his passing skills. Harmsworth is still quite raw and has a lot of improvements to make in his game to ever play as a professional.

Harper, Stephen – LW – Erie Otters (OHL) – 6'1.25" 200

Stephen was selected in the first round, 12th overall by the Erie Otters at the 2011 OHL Priority Selection Draft out of the Burlington Eagles Minor Midget program. Stephen was a bit of a surprise pick in the first round, a player who projected to be taken in the second, but showed great speed and scoring ability at the Minor Midget level, he was able to lure the Otters in. Stephen put together an excellent rookie season scoring 24 goals as a 16 year old in the OHL on what turned out to be the worst team in the league in 2011-2012. Stephen received a Team Canada Ivan Hlinka Camp tryout and looked primed to have a strong draft year and make a push for the second round. However, this season didn't quite go the way he was hoping and he scored less goals this year (18) than his rookie season.

Stephen generally lives and dies on the ice by his two strongest attributes. He is a very smooth skater who is able to fly up and down the ice. He also has a very powerful shot which he is able to unload quickly and with power. Stephen has also shown a physical side. He's delivered some solid hits in our viewings but isn't one to drop the gloves or spend much time in the penalty box. Stephen was generally used on the point of the Otters power play due to his big shot. He was able to unload one-timers and get shots through traffic to create rebounds and occasionally score. Unfortunately he needs to be a little more accurate with his shot and more precise with his decisions to shoot and pass.

Ultimately our biggest concern with Stephen has been his decision making process. He can be a little risky with the puck at times and mistakes can go back the other way. We would also like to see him show more hustle in order to get back defensively. Playing on the third line primarily down the stretch did affect his numbers, but he got enough ice to produce. He put forward adequate numbers, but not what we expected out of him considering his skill set. Stephen is a player who we think, with zero doubt, will get selected. However, it most likely won't be as high as expected back a year ago. A team who takes him a little higher will likely look at his speed and shot and feel they can build upon these talents.

Harpur, Ben – LD – Guelph Storm (OHL) – 6'5.5" 210

Ben was selected in the 3rd round of the 2011 OHL Priority Selection Draft by the Guelph Storm out of the Niagara Falls Canucks Minor Midget program. Ben made the Storm as a 16 year old but received limited action due to the depth on the Storm blueline. Harpur had a steady sophomore season for the Storm. He is a big bodied presence on the blue line and is good at using his size to lean on smaller forwards and clear out the front of the net. He needs to work at bringing a consistent physical presence to his game and finish more checks when given the opportunity.

He is a good skater despite being such a big guy and has adequate speed to jump into the offensive rush when available. However, he has struggled in one on one situations at times due to a late pivot. He is good at using his long stick to keep opponents to the outside and is effective at getting into passing lanes and intercepting passes. Harpur is sometimes caught standing around in the defensive zone and needs to consistently pressure opposing forwards rather than let the play come to him. He takes good angles when he does pressure forwards and is good at keeping his body to the net so that driving lanes are kept to a minimum. He occasionally steps up and effectively holds the offensive blue line strong but is sometimes slow transitioning from forwards to backwards and would benefit from improved foot speed. Harpur is good at getting his shots on net through traffic but needs to work at walking the line to create better shooting lanes.

Ben shows flashes of potential but also needs to further improve and become more comfortable in his size. He will need to become a better skater and play a more tenacious game at his size. He does a variety of things well but nothing that stands out as exceptional. Harpur is a player we see going outside the first few rounds and selected to become a reliable defensive defenseman at the next level. One that doesn't play huge minutes but can be relied upon in his own end, and to hopefully play a penalty killing role as well.

Quotable: " Ben had a few games that really impressed me. He kept the game simple and had some error free games. I'd like to see more consistency and better feet would help his game going forward." - Mark Edwards

Harris, Jacob – RC – Sudbury Wolves (OHL) – 6'0" 185

Jacob was selected in the 2nd round of the 2011 OHL Priority Selection Draft by the Sudbury Wolves out of the Halton Hurricanes Minor Midget program. Jacob made the Wolves right out of camp as a 16 year old, however, he missed a few games after taking an unsuspecting hit in the middle of the ice when he didn't have the puck and struggled to get back on the strong pace he opened with. Harris took on a slightly larger role with the Wolves and did well producing 30 points in 54 games in his second season in the OHL.

He is at his best when he is all around the net and battling hard in front for loose pucks. He comes out of board battles with the puck, then is able to get it out to the front of the net quickly to create good opportunities. He puts good pressure on the puck carrier and pressures the point on the penalty kill, then is able to clear the puck out of the zone. He hustles hard for loose pucks, pressures on the fore-check and comes back well on the back-check showing the ability to play a full 200-foot game. He can distribute the puck decently off the rush, moves it out of the zone to start the breakout and will put a shot low on net off the wide drive to try to create a rebound for out front. He goes to the net to get in the goaltender's face and look for tips. He can also find space in the offensive zone, then open up to take passes and put one-timers on net. He puts shots on net from just about everywhere to try to create rebound opportunities. He is very responsible in both ends of the ice and will need to establish himself as that solid two-way forward who can kill penalties and tie up his man in his own end if he wants to have a shot at playing at the next level.

Hart, Jayden – RC – Prince Albert Raiders (WHL) – 6'1" 188

Hart initially started the season with the Medicine Hat Tigers and was given a top 6 spot with the team. He was using his size, speed and grit to contribute on a consistent basis. However, he was traded to Prince Albert due to character issues. Once he got traded, Hart continued to provide much of the same spark and put up a decent amount of points. Hart gets into the forecheck hard and always looks to separate an opponent from the puck. He is effective when he is moving his feet and uses his body to provide a physical presence out on the ice. He is difficult to move from the slot, and gives teams a tough time by providing a good screen. He does not possess great offensive skills, as he is not really able to do much with the puck in speed. A concern with Hart's game is that his development has been stagnant since last season. He has not been able to make much improvement in all areas of his game. There is certainly potential in his game with his skill set to develop into a bottom 6 forward one day, but he will have to commit himself to being a better teammate and improving his game to play as a pro.

Hartman, Ryan – LW – Plymouth Whalers (OHL) – 5'11" 181

Ryan is hands down one of the hardest working players available in this 2013 NHL Entry Draft. He was selected in the 5th Round of the 2010 OHL Priority Selection Draft out of the Chicago Mission U16 program. Ryan opted to join the U.S. National Development Program and he has done an outstanding job representing his country. He's not even eligible to be drafted until June of this year and he already owns a U17, U18 and U20 Gold medal for Team USA. He also posted a point per game or better at both the World Under 17 Challenge and the IIHF U18 Championships. Due to his late birth date, while many of his USNTDP teammates went on to be selected at the 2012 NHL Entry Draft, Hartman weighed his options and chose to join the Plymouth Whalers this season. Ryan was in tough heading into camp. Plymouth was loaded at forward with several NHL Picks. He started out on the third line, but worked tremendously hard. By the time the trade deadline came and went, Ryan was on Plymouth's top line contributing on a nightly basis.

What we like most about Ryan is how hard he works every shift, every game. He plays whistle to whistle and battles for every inch. He has a tenacious forecheck and forces tons of turnovers. He hits and despite his average size, he packs a lot of power in his physical game. He has also shown a willingness to drop the gloves from time to time. He competes hard in all three zones and will work defensively creating turnovers and ending potential scoring chances against his team. Ryan was one of Plymouth's go to penalty killers and did an excellent job getting in passing lanes and sacrificing his body to block shots. The only question for Hartman going forward is whether his offensive game will translate at the next level. He shows good instincts in the offensive zone and is capable of reacting quickly and staying patient with the puck. He has an above average shot and is capable of creating plays not just with puck skills and hands, but also going back to his work ethic and just wanting the puck more than the opposition. There's little doubt that Ryan will be taken in the first round of the NHL Draft. He's a very popular player among scouts and he is highly regarded for his character. While he projects to go in the late teens or early 20's of the first round, a team that wants him bad enough may not take a chance and take him earlier.

Quotable: "I can't even put what I think of him into words, he's just a hockey player. He will go to a good team drafting late and be a star for years." NHL Scout

Quotable: "Ryan reminds me a bit of Andrew Shaw, he is a gamer and just gets it done. He is a player that every coach wants on his team, and opposing coaches hate to go up against." - Mark Edwards

Hauf, Jared – LD – Seattle Thunderbirds (WHL) – 6'6" 216

Hauf is a big, shutdown defenseman whose defensive abilities continued to develop throughout the year due to the ice time he was receiving. He was out on the ice in most important defensive situations, and seemed to have really learned by repetition and became a nice presence from the backend. One reason why Hauf received so much crucial ice time was because he was one of the most dependable defensemen in a group that was filled with very raw players. While Hauf is no all-star by any means, he had some experience and had some of the best defensive abilities. He used his stick quite well off the rush, and provided a good physical presence when necessary. He holds his position well, and does not like to chase the play because he knows that his skating abilities do not allow him to do so. He really uses his reach to his advantage, and it comes in handy along the walls as he is able to quickly poke pucks loose. He could improve his gap control, but that will come along if he can get faster, and he has more confidence to be able to stick to opponents off the rush. Hauf provided very little offense for the Thunderbirds this season. He does not have very good poise with the puck, and will need to improve on his passing abilities. He panics when there is any sort of pressure on him, and jumps dumps it out of the zone even when he has a good option in the neutral zone. He is not very mobile on the blue line, and does not take any chances to keep pucks in the offensive zone.

Hayden, John – RW – US NTDP Under-18 Team – 6'2, 185

John is a tough, two-way forward who is nasty to play against. His fore checking ability is excellent with good timing and great hitting, and he has shown the resolve to battle tooth and nail for loose pucks, many times forcing turnovers through sheer force of will. He also back checks hard, plays the body in the neutral and defensive zones, and is strong on the penalty kill. Even though American junior leagues do everything possible to dissuade players from fighting in regular season games, he proved to the scouts on hand at the USHL Top Prospects Game that he will drop the gloves for teammates when necessary and showed well in the bout. He brings the same type of energy offensively, but lacks touch. He's at his most effective in the dirty areas but when it comes to finishing plays, hitting open teammates with passes, and carrying the puck through the neutral zone, he's inconsistent. He can bulldoze the puck to the net from behind or the corners and can screen the goaltender, so he can be useful even without finesse. He's a safe bet to be an effective professional in a bottom-six role, and could eventually slot into a top-six role with the right line mates but realistically his offensive upside is limited.

Quotable: "I expect him to impress at the combine. I don't see a natural goal scorer, I see a 3rd or 4th line type guy. Could see him going in the 2nd round but just as easily as I could see him slip to the 4th" - Mark Edwards

Heatherington, Dillon – LD – Swift Current Broncos (WHL) – 6'4" 196

Heatherington is one of the biggest risers for the upcoming NHL Entry Draft from the WHL. His defensive game has progressed steadily throughout the year, and is definitely one of the most defensively sound players available. He has size, grit and hockey intelligence that he uses on a nightly basis to shut down the best opposing forwards.

The most impressive aspect of Heatherington's game is his ability to read the play. He is very composed and lets the play come to him. He stays in good position in front of the net, and makes sure that he is always in between the puck and an opponent so he can intercept passes easily and not allow any scoring opportunities. He is very physical along the boards, and is hard to knock off the puck. He uses his size to his advantage, and keeps opponents to the outside with his long reach. He plays with an edge at all times, and will mix it up with opponents when necessary. Offensively, Heatherington makes solid passes out of the zone. He will never dominate a game offensively, but he does a good job of pinching when he sees an opportunity, and come down the boards to hold the puck and keep the offense going. He rarely takes risks with the puck, and ensures that he is able to start the attack for his team with a good first pass. An area of improvement for Heatherington would be his skating abilities. He is a good skater given his size, but he will need to add speed and explosiveness in his speed to keep up with speedy forwards at the pro level. He is constantly in solid position and uses his reach to force opponents to the outside in the WHL, but it will get much tougher when players are faster and bigger.

Heatherington is a type of player that every team would love to have in crucial defensive situations. He can match up with the best forwards on a consistent basis and give them a tough time when they have the puck. He is a very efficient player who has all the tools to be a successful pro one day with more development.

Quotable: "I'm really high on him. He's a player I have liked all season long. Size and a steady game" - NHL Scout

Quotable: "I think his compete level is up with the top guys in the draft. He logged good minutes in Sochi. I like his range in the D-Zone and he's a character guy. My concerns are hockey sense and play with the puck on his tape under pressure. The comments were decent amongst NHL guys in some post-game chatter in the hotel lounge in Sochi." - Mark Edwards

Heinrich, Blake – LD – Sioux City Musketeers (USHL) – 5'11" – 192

Sioux City picked Heinrich in the 3rd round at 34th overall in the 2011 USHL Futures Draft and he played in his first USHL game with Sioux City in the 2011-2012 season where he had an assist in that game. He then played his first full year in the league this year and registered 20 points in 42 games while also receiving the opportunity to play in the World Junior A Challenge for Team USA and had 2 points in 4 games in the tournament and got the opportunity this year to also play in the USHL top prospects game. Heinrich is a defenseman who can make a good 1st pass out of his zone to start the breakout and he gets his shot through to the net from the point. He will jump up on a play to come into the high slot to take a pass and put a great shot on net, and he also distributes the puck really well from the point on the power play.

He has to work on getting his shots through to the net with much greater consistency and needs to watch the offensive zone turnovers trying to force passes through the opposition. He also needs to watch the neutral zone turnovers on breakout passes and can't cross the line so much with his aggression and physicality and take penalties. Blake was selected in the 12th round of the 2012 WHL Bantam Draft by the Portland Winterhawks. Heinrich is committed to join the University of Minnesota-Duluth.

Quotable: "He's a strong kid for his size and I like the aggressiveness he shows in his game. I questioned some decision making from time to time. Skating looked good north/south but not as good east/west." Mark Edwards

Henriksson, Alexander – LW – Farjestad J20 (SWE J20) – 6'2" 190

Alexander has developed up through the Skovde IK club early in his career playing in a J20 league as a 14 year old but eventually moved over to the more established Farjestad program working his way up starting with the J18 eventually joining the J20 full time. Alexander is a threat in the offensive zone primarily due to his shot. He utilizes his size well when driving the puck into the zone protecting it and taking it to the net. He forechecks hard and can force turnovers and finish some checks taking the puck away and turning it into a chance. Alexander just needs to play this game more consistently. While he has offensive skills, we're not convinced to this point he'll turn into a big offensive producer. However he does show some abilities that could translate to him playing a support role forechecking and chipping in offensively.

Hill, Tyler – FW – Chicago Steel (USHL) – 6'5.75" 220

The hulking offensive forward shows flashes of greatness, but has yet to develop consistency. He can use his long reach and frame to protect the puck well and is surprisingly shifty for his size with good agility and excellent hands, but doesn't always utilize his abilities. He floats too often and has a hard time carrying the puck against physical checking, especially at the USHL level this year where he lacked the first step quickness to pick up the pick and carry it up ice without immediately being pressured. He has a hard, accurate wrist shot and he likes to put the puck on net from all over the offensive zone. He works well on the boards with his size and fights through checks though he lacks killer instinct overall. He can forecheck, back check, and penalty kill well, utilizing his reach and playing the body hard, but doesn't always do so with intensity. He can play mean and outright ragdoll opposing players, but mostly seems unwilling. He's an intriguing prospect based on his combination of skill, size, and speed, but is incredibly raw and may have actually hurt his stock by playing the second half of the season in the USHL. With Holderness, one of the worst prep teams in New England, it was thought that his team was holding him back. At the junior level, it became clear that despite his tremendous tools, he still has a ton of work to do before he can be considered a legitimate professional prospect.

Quotable: "He obviously has size but I'm not seeing anything close to the 1st round ranking I saw out there earlier this season." - Mark Edwards

Hope, Brandon – G – Owen Sound Attack (OHL) – 6'0" 197

Brandon Hope was selected in the 3rd round by the Sarnia Sting in the 2010 OHL Priority Selection. This pick was a little risky due to Brandon being a well pursued goaltender by NCAA teams. Sarnia to their credit was able to persuade him to commit to the OHL. Hope made the team as a 16 year old, after putting together a very strong performance in camp, combined with the organization's confidence in his ability. Hope went on to play 29 games in 2010-2011; more than any 16 year old rookie in the entire CHL. Everything was looking up for Brandon going into the 2012 NHL Entry Draft. However, a lack of playing time, quickly being pulled when he struggled and a few tough starts derailed Brandon's draft year. During the offseason Brandon was dealt to the Owen Sound Attack which proved to be a great move for him. Statistically alone he put up impressive numbers and improved in virtually every area. He really got a chance to shine when he was the Attack's temporary starter while Jordan Binnington was in Russia for the World Junior Championship. Hope went 4-1 in December posting a 1.85 GAA.

Brandon displays excellent leg movement. He is very quick and drops down to make saves, recovering quickly. He also moves very well in the crease. His reflexes are strong and he has shown good recovery ability to make those highlight reel saves when it appears a sure goal will be scored. We still see the occasional mental lapse on goals that should not get past him, but generally he is able to let those bad goals go and not let it snowball into something bigger. Brandon has shown good puck skills and is capable of playing the puck well. Rebound control is likely the biggest area of improvement for Brandon, not only the number in rebounds but in directing them away from the scoring area. Brandon is still a very interesting prospect.

He has shown to be worthy of an NHL pick. Goaltenders tend to develop later on, and with the improvements shown over the course of this season, combined with the fact that he will be called upon to carry the bulk of the Owen Sound schedule next season, the 2013 NHL Draft may see Brandon either get selected or get picked up as a camp invitee so that a team can get him at a value should he excel in his first starting role and reaching the high potential he was touted with as a 15 year old.

Quotable: "He may finally get his chance to play a large number of games next season. Looks like the rookie tender the Attack drafted will back him up." - Mark Edwards

Horvat, Bo – LC – London Knights (OHL) – 6'0" 206

Horvat was selected 1st Round, 9th Overall out of the 2011 OHL Priority Selection Draft by the London Knights out of the Elgin-Middlesex Chiefs Minor Midget program. Bo really impressed us in Minor Midget and we were impressed with this pick. There was no question of his work ethic, but there was a question if he would be able to produce at the OHL level. While it took him a little bit to get rolling, he put up a respectable 30 points as a 16 year old playing a bottom six role with the Knights. Horvat really became more known after he was named captain of Team Ontario at the World Under 17 Challenge and put on a great performance putting up more than a point per game. He really hit his stride as a hard working two-way player who played with maturity beyond his years. While quiet on the scoresheet, his forecheck, defensive play and competitiveness is evident in every shift.

With a new season came new responsibilities for Horvat this year. He started out in and out of the top six but it didn't take long for him to establish himself as a game by game top six all situations kind of guy. Bo isn't a flashy player although he is capable of making a few moves and beating defenders. He also has tremendous focus and hand/eye coordination, making him very dangerous in the goal area. He has excellent positioning in all three zones, but in the offensive zone he moves around from the front of the net, and sliding off to the side setting up for scoring chances. He has an excellent forecheck and competes hard in corners, along the walls and wins more battles than he's expected to. Bo is also very solid defensively. He blocks shots and gets in lanes on the penalty kill. Defensively, he hurries back in transition and can break up scoring chances. He is smart, positionally, and isn't afraid to go down low to compensate for a defensive mistake by a teammate.

Bo's game projects extremely well for the pro level and he has the size closely similar to a power forward. Skating has always been an area of Horvat's needing improvement. He has shown improvement over the last two years, but will need to get even better to reach his potential at the pro level. Bo is a safe pick in the 2013 NHL Entry Draft and is secure in the first round. It wouldn't be a shock to see him creep into the top 10 or 12 players selected in this draft.

Quotable: "He had a slump this year that seemed to end about the same time that he changed his (brand of) skates. He started beating Dmen wide and played with more confidence. He made more plays with the puck. Bo is a complete player, the kind that coaches rely on in the last minute of tight games. I expect him gone by pick number fifteen or twenty at the latest." - Mark Edwards

Houck, Jackson – RW – Vancouver Giants (WHL) – 6'0" 184

A physical, hard working forward who has been the go-to offensive player for the Giants this season. Houck definitely has the intangibles to be a good bottom 6 NHL player one day and plays the game with an edge at all times. He is one of the hardest working player on the team, and is consistently praised for his work ethic by those around him. Offensively, Houck has had to do a little bit of everything for the Giants this season. His skill set suits him in front of the net to bang home rebounds and provide a screen, but due to the lack of depth on the team, he has had to try to create offense for his team and play on the half wall on the power play for much of the year, which he clearly struggled with. Whenever he was responsible for providing net front presence, Houck often came up with goals and showed above average hands in tight and the ability to take a beating but hold his ground. He has an average shot that he likes to use off the rush, and needs to hit the net more often. He is good along the boards and comes away with pucks on a consistent basis. Houck has played a key role in his own end for the Giants. He is not afraid to block shots, and reads the play well without the puck. He played centre a few times this year and did not look out of place defensively.

Houck is difficult to play against when he is on the forecheck and delivers some big hits. The biggest improvement he needs to make is his skating. He has average speed, and when he plays against opponents that are faster than him, he has a difficult time catching up to them and his physical game disappears completely. He will definitely need to get faster to reach the pro level one day and be a difficult player to play against.

Quotable: "I got to watch Houck play a lot over the last 2 seasons, and I am impressed with his work ethic and physical play. However, his skating is a big detriment to his game as if he faces a team with speedy players or they are able to move the puck around quite well, then he has trouble using his body to make any sort of an impact in games." - Charles An

Hurley, Connor – FW – Muskegon Lumberjacks (USHL) – 6'2" 175

Connor has played the last two seasons for Edina High School proving to be a key offensive contributor for his school. He has also enjoyed stints with the U.S. National Team Development Program and finished the season playing with his brother on the Muskegon Lumberjacks of the USHL. Connor really jumped out at us in our early viewings of him. He is capable of doing so many different things in a shift. He handles the puck well and displays good vision creating offense for his team. He provides an excellent work ethic when he's on his game forcing turnovers regularly and displaying a solid physical game finishing his checks. Hurley has had a few moments of inconsistency where we noticed him taking a shift off here and there, but it wasn't a major concern.

Connor has the high end upside of a power forward who can play a second line role. However to reach that potential he has a long way to go. He is fairly lanky and needs to add a lot of muscle to his frame. He has certainly shown us clear top six offensive potential at times, but these have been flashes and they have not occurred on a consistent basis. Connor likes to pass the puck, but has a laser of a shot and needs to utilize it more often. A safer and more reliable projection would be to see Connor ending up as a third line winger who uses his size and shows flashes of offensive production. He also has provided a very steady two-way presence in viewings of him playing with the USNTDP and Muskegon. Regardless, Connor has a lot of potential at the top level and is committed to Notre Dame University this coming fall of 2013.

Quotable: "No doubt his stock dropped after a poor showing at a December tournament. I liked what I saw in my viewings. I think he is a kid worth drafting and waiting out his development. He has upside as a strong two-way forward playing smart minutes down the middle." - Mark Edwards

Quotable: "Connor really jumped out at us at the U.S. Select 17 camp. He plays a hard working game and has told us that he sees himself as a playmaker. We found this a little surprising because of how good his shot is. Connor might take a little more time than some to develop, but should fill out and become a very good prospect." - Ryan Yessie

Quotable: "I go all the way to Minnesota for a Christmas tourney and the kid doesn't even get a point in 3 high school games. There was nothing to see there." - NHL Scout

Hutchison, Nick – LC – Avon Old Farms (Prep-CT) – 6'2, 180

The Hicksville, New York native is a big, lanky two-way forward with a mean streak. He shows skill in bursts, with nifty dekes and a quick-release shot, but his puck handling needs refining, as he's prone to giveaways. His board work is strong and he drives the net hard. He's physical defensively and plays body hard in all three zones. He can be intimidating to play against, with targeted physical play and chippiness after whistles. His skating needs work as he's strong on his feet but moves awkwardly. He was selected by Tri-City in the 2012 USHL Draft and played a handful of games there this season

Hutchinson, Ryan – RD – Kingston Frontenacs (OHL) – 6'1" 204

Hutchinson was selected in the 4th round of the 2011 OHL Priority Selection Draft out of the Chicago Young Americans program. Hutchinson is a very mean defenseman who didn't quite develop the way we expected considering the work the Frontenacs have done on developing players recently. Ryan plays with a very nasty edge and doesn't always know when to draw the line. He's the kind of player where, when you wake up the next morning, you know you played against him. He is very physically strong and always has been ever since minor midget. He's not afraid to drop the gloves, in fact he appears to enjoy it.

His play undoubtedly revolves around the physical areas of the game. However, he is pretty well positioned in his own zone, getting his stick in passing lanes and following the play effectively. He does have the occasional mental error, but he has been very reliable. He does get into a little trouble when handling the puck and will need to improve in this area to be able to advance to the next level. This will never be an asset, but needs to be brought up to par.

Ryan is effective one on one and will eliminate the puck with his stick, then the man with his body. The only problem is he's not a great skater and can be evaded at times by more elusive players. He can also engage a little too aggressively and can get beat due to making the first move. Hutchinson has a ways to go in his development but it would not be a surprise to see an NHL team select him. His upside is more so as a third pairing physical beast who will destroy opponents, drop the gloves, and play a simple defensive game. However despite all the size and strength he will need to improve his puck play, skating, and a few adjustments to his positional play.

Ikonen, Jusso – RW – Blues (SM-liiga) – 5'9" 170

Ikonen is an undersized Finnish winger who possesses a good skating ability and is generally pretty strong on his feet for a smaller player. He is fairly easy to move off the puck but almost always stays on his feet although bigger opponents win majority of puck battles along the boards. Jusso is good at making smart passes and moves the puck effectively up the ice although he sometimes has a habit of trying to be too fancy which can sometimes result in turnovers. He needs to improve his positioning and awareness in the defensive zone as he sometimes is caught standing around or flying the zone too early before the puck is in total possession.

Ilvonen, Mika – LD – Blues U20 (Jr. A SM-liiga) – 5'8, 152

Mika is an undersized offensive defenseman. He has quick feet and can accelerate quickly up ice with the puck to kick start the offense but tries to force the play at times with ill-advised jumps into the attack and poorly-timed stretch passes, leading to turnovers. He has a hard time dealing with bigger fore checkers and can be pushed off the puck too easily. He is skilled at the offensive point with creative passing and a good shot that he places for tips and rebounds. He pinches aggressively to keep the puck in and get shots on net but takes too many hard hits for a player of his stature. His game doesn't project well to the North American game though he should eventually be a quality player in Europe with his skill set.

Jarry, Tristan – G – Edmonton Oil Kings (WHL) – 6'2" 181

Jarry has been a backup to goaltender Laurent Brossoit for the last 2 seasons, and has developed into a solid prospect for the upcoming NHL Entry Draft. Although he has a great team playing in front of him, he has been able to showcase his abilities and the potential to become a very good goaltender at the professional level one day.

Jarry looks very poised and confident when he is on the ice. He does not waste much energy flopping around the crease, but rather keeps his movements quite efficient. He has shown good athletic ability to be able to quickly move post to post and make some big saves when necessary. He can comfortably move around the net on his feet and get in front of the puck as opponents pass it around for a scoring chance. Jarry has also displayed good hands and the ability to catch any pucks and deflect away shot to the corner with his blocker. He could still work on his overall mechanics to kick away rebounds better or to give opponents less chances after the initial shot. Another intriguing factor of Jarry's play is his ability to look like he has been playing regularly whenever he gets the start. He does not look rusty at all despite the fact that he receives very limited minutes. He seems to be mentally focused at all times to play, and it could safely be assumed that he consistently practices hard.

It will be very interesting to see how Jarry responds to being the starter for the Oil Kings next season. Judging by his mental game this season, it seems that he will be solid mentally even when he has games in which he struggles and be able to carry on with his solid play throughout the year. Teams will be taking a bit of a gamble when he has played in such a limited amount of games, but it could be well worth it in the future.

Quotable: "My top goalie in this draft." - NHL Scout

Quotable: "I thought he had the best camp of all the goalies at the Hlinka camp in August. There were some good goalies there. - Mark Edwards

Jenkins, Jack – FW – Des Moines Buccaneers (USHL) – 5'10" 165

Jenkins was drafted into the USHL in the 4th round, 60th overall by Des Moines Buccaneers in 2012. Jenkins played in his rookie season in the USHL this year where he played in 62 games and had 26 points, 21 of those points coming as assists. Jenkins has good speed, hustle and puts good pressure on the puck carrier. He can get a good cycle going in deep and opens up well to take passes down low beside the net for shot opportunities from scoring positions. He likes to come down on the wing then cut to the middle for chances in tight and can make really good passes in the offensive zone to set up one-timers for open teammates. He puts good pressure on the fore-check, uses his stick well to poke the puck loose to force turnovers and he also plays the puck carrier with a nice element of physicality. He needs to get much stronger on the puck as he gets knocked off it way too easily and also has to watch the turnovers trying to skate the puck up the ice through the neutral zone.

He does not have the offensive production to be considered a potential top-6 forward at the next level and does not have the size or strength to be effective in a physical, defensive role yet. Jenkins has to use the off season to add much needed size and strength and needs to come back next season showing that he can play a role that would be most effective for a team moving forward. He needs to demonstrate he is willing to play the puck carrier hard and physical, tie him up in the defensive zone and get in lanes to block shots and break-up passing plays for the opposition. He needs to battle hard for the puck in the corners and come out with the puck most of the time as well.

Jensen, Spencer – RD – Medicine Hat Tigers (WHL) – 6'3" 193

Jensen is a defensive defenseman who provides a strong, physical presence from the backend. His game is mostly depended on his work ethic and being a tough player to play against in the defensive zone. Jensen is an average skater, and will be something that he has to improve on for the future. His lateral movement is quite poor, and he has a tendency to get beat to the inside by a quicker player with a nice move to get around him off the rush. Jensen is not an enforcer, but he will get into scrums and protect his teammates when necessary. He likes to use his body to land big hits along the boards and to be hard to play against in the slot. He is not afraid to block shots, and is more than willing to stand in front of shots to help his goaltender out. His best asset is his stick, as he does a very good job of creating takeaways and protecting the slot. He stirs opponents to the outside quite well, with his stick, but needs to give quicker opponents a larger gap off the rush to not get beat to the net.

Jensen is very limited with the puck. His outlet passes need some work as they are not always easy and accurate for his teammates to receive them. He is quite stationary on the blue line, and does not really provide an option for forwards if they ever want to pass it to him to relieve some pressure down low. An NHL team looking for a reliable defensive defenseman for the future will take a long look at Jensen. He will have to take a few years to develop his game, particularly his skating, but they may be rewarded in the end with a good penalty killer who can eat up some valuable minutes to protect the lead.

Johnson, Luke – FW – Lincoln Stars (USHL) – 5'11" 178

Johnson was picked in the 1st round at #11 by the Lincoln Stars in 2010 and played in the USHL top Prospects game in both the 2011-2012 and the 2012-2013 season. Johnson played in his rookie season with Lincoln in the USHL in 2011-2012 where he was a point a game player with 55 points in 55 games and had a +22 rating. His offensive production dipped slightly this year to 46 points and a +17 rating; however he also played in 4 games for USA in the World Junior A Challenge where he had 4 assists in the tournament. He will cut to the middle off the rush to get shots on net and can get open and park himself right in front of the opposition's goal for chances in tight. He goes to the net to pick up rebounds and loose pucks, but has to watch that he isn't always taking long outside shots rather than driving the puck to the net. He has the offensive instincts, but can't be intimidated to get the puck to the dirty areas to try and score some tough goals from in tight. Johnson is pretty strong on his feet but still needs to add some size and strength.

Quotable: "I'd like to see more compete level from him. He's an average skater with average size but has really good hands and a good shot. He had a good line mate last year which may have helped his numbers." - Mark Edwards

Jones, Mitch – LD – Plymouth Whalers (OHL) – 5'11" 185

Jones was selected by the Plymouth Whalers in the 11th round of the 2011 OHL Priority Selection Draft. Jones is one of only three players to be selected in the 11th round in 2011 to play in the OHL. He is also the son of former NHLer Brad Jones. He received some ice time last season, also receiving an invite to the USA Select 17 camp in Rochester, NY. Jones received marginal ice for the Whalers, but as veterans returned, Mitch found himself caught in a numbers game.

Mitch plays a very simple defensive game. He uses his stick well, but is also capable of delivering some solid hits. He has a decent shot from the point and is good with making the simple pass, but struggles with turnovers when he over handles the puck or tries to do too much with it. While we don't expect Mitch to be selected at the 2013 NHL Entry Draft, he's a player we would like to see improve upon in his skating and his puck skills. He needs to continue to play simple and continue to play a physical game if he wants to become an everyday player in the OHL, and see where things go from there.

Jones, Seth – RD – Portland Winterhawks (WHL) – 6'4" 206

It is rare to find a complete package in a defenseman like Seth Jones. He can make an impact at both ends of the ice in every game he plays with his size, athleticism, intelligence and hockey skills. He has caught the attention of the entire hockey world it seems with his play this year, and which ever team that is able to pick him up in the NHL Entry Draft this year will have their hands on a franchise defenseman for years to come.

One of the most impressive attributes of Seth Jones is his skating ability given his size. He is very mobile in all areas of the ice. He can make quick pivots and fast stops and starts along the walls to contain an opponent, quickly accelerate and reach top end speed to go coast to coast for a scoring chance or quickly skate backwards and maintain an excellent gap on the quickest players in the league. Offensively, Jones seems to have all the tools. He has very good vision and quarterbacks a lethal power play. He recognizes when he can push the play, and when to be patient and wait for his forwards to get into position. He makes excellent passes to get the attack going, but he does have the tendency to try to force plays at times. Jones also has a rocket of a shot from the point, and makes it miserable on opposing goaltenders, especially when there is a screen in front of them as Jones does a good job of getting shots on net. Jones has also been able to score a few coast to coast goals this year. He uses his speed, long reach and stick handling abilities to get around opponents and score some nice goals.

Jones is a force in his own zone. He maintains an excellent gap and uses his long reach. He is able to be aggressive because of his speed. He consistently uses his great stick to take away passing lanes and deflect away anything that comes to the slot. He is so strong along the boards, and is great at tying up opponents. He has the abilities to land big hits in the neutral zone and force opponents to be wary as they enter the neutral zone. The biggest concern for Jones is his lack of intensity in his play at times. He certainly shows up for big games, as evident by his performance in the World Juniors. He needs to be the best player on his team every night and will surely be counted on to be a leader on his team wherever he goes, but without the high level of intensity and interest in every game, it may be a concern in the future.

Quotable: "I was sold at the World Juniors. He was a man amongst boys there." - NHL Scout

Quotable: "The first time I saw him was the USHL fall classic two years ago. To say he stood out would be putting it mildly." - Mark Edwards

Quotable: "I don't think he dominates a game enough from the back end, I like Mackinnon." - NHL Scout

Josephs, Troy – LW – 6'1"– 180lb. – St. Michael's Buzzers (OJHL)

Josephs had a strong sophomore campaign for the OJHL champion Buzzers. After being selected in the 15th round of the 2010 OHL draft by the Belleville Bulls, Josephs decided to follow the NCAA route and eventually committed to Clarkson University. Josephs finished 2nd in the voting for OJHL Top NHL prospect behind teammate Matt Buckles. Troy was a bit of a late bloomer but really began to earn attention this season in the OJHL. He brings solid size and a good skating ability to his game allowing him to be effective on the fore check and work at creating offensive zone turnovers with smarts and positioning. While not as offensively gifted as his teammate Buckles, Josephs works hard to overcome this with a consistent effort and constant pursuit of the puck. He is a good playmaker and works well with his linemates to provide solid depth scoring for the Buzzers. Troy needs to improve his scoring touch so that he can benefit further from the chances his work ethic brings him. He would also benefit from adding some strength to his frame in order to improve his shot and ability to win battles along the boards. Josephs will be looking to continue his development when he joins the Clarkson Golden Knights next season.

Kahun, Dominik – LW – Sudbury Wolves (OHL) – 5'9" 160

Dominik was born in Czech Republic, but moved to and developed in Germany, which is the country he represents nationally. He became known for scoring over 200 points in just 30 games as a 15 year old in Germany's U16 league. In 2011-2012 he joined the U18 league putting up respectable numbers and had a great playoff performance helping his team win the championship of the German U18 division. He also participated in the 2012 World U-17 Challenge in Windsor as well as the 2012 IIHF World U-18 Championships. Dominik joined the Wolves after being selected in the 1st round of the 2012 CHL Import Draft. He came over to Canada to play for Sudbury while for the second year in a row representing his country twice. First, at the 2013 World Junior Championships and once again at the 2013 IIHF World U18 Championship. Kahun managed to get 40 points and was named to Germany's World Junior team where he had 3 assists in 6 games.

Kahun has good speed on the rush to come down off the wing and step in towards the net to put a great shot on. He can make good passes to move the puck out of his zone to start the breakout, and has the agility to stop-up quickly then create space in the offensive zone. He puts good pressure on the puck carrier and can get to the slot with the puck for good scoring opportunities. He opens up well on odd-man rushes to provide teammates with scoring options and just needs to watch his turnovers, both on trying to be too fancy with moves entering the zone or by trying to force passes through the opposition.

This was Kahun's first year playing on North American ice after dominating some German leagues, and adjusted well. He still has a lot to learn moving forward and needs to recognize the time and place to make certain moves or passes, but he has the skill and a great work ethic to continue to contribute. He has the potential to be selected at the 2013 NHL Entry Draft, but struggled through some of our viewings, and unfortunately lacks both size and strength. He would need to make the jump as an offensive player, but while he showed us some good moments, we don't believe there is quite enough there to be an impactful offensive player at the NHL level.

Kanzig, Keegan – LD – Victoria Royals (WHL) – 6'5" 238

Kanzig is a big, physical defenseman with very limited offensive abilities. He plays in a lot of key defensive situations for the Royals, and does an admirable job for the team. He makes the life of opposing forwards miserable with his nasty streak. He will not back down from anybody, and will take on anybody in a fight. The biggest issue with Kanzig's game is his poor skating abilities. He is quite slow out on the ice, and depends on good positioning and his reach to keep opponents away from the slot on the rush and along the boards. He looks quite awkward on his skates, and could also improve on his lower body strength to stay on his feet.

Offensively, Kanzig possesses average passing abilities and has a difficult time reading the play and making good, solid passes. He often goes glass and out if he ever feels pressure from a fore checker. He does not put himself in a position to be open for passes along the blueline, and due to his poor skating abilities, he often backs off instead of being aggressive to try to keep pucks in the offensive zone. Kanzig has a lot of developing to do if he ever wants to play hockey at the professional level. He certainly has the size that NHL teams are looking for, but with other parts of his game being in the shape that they are currently now, he will have a difficult time making it to the next level in the future.

Kavanagh, Shane – F, Cushing Academy (Prep-MA) – 5'11, 195

A sparkplug two-way forward with good hands and goal-scoring instincts, Kavanagh is well rounded and a nightmare to deal with. He relishes the pest role, laying consistently heavy, legal contact in the forecheck and in the neutral zone and drawing the ire of opposing teams. He has shifts were he outright lays out multiple players, sometimes even bigger guys who he has no business going after, much less overpowering. As a result, he gets targeted physically and can have some trouble dealing with serious contact. Was knocked out of New England Prep championship game after being bent over the boards awkwardly when an opponent took a run at him, illustrating the potential for injury that will continue to exist for him as long as he plays the way he does.

He plays with a lot of jump and is an excellent skater with a powerful stride. With the puck, he mostly plays a power forward game, taking the puck strong down the wing and hard to the net, which probably won't work for him much longer as he progresses to playing against bigger players, but he also possesses a great shot and can get open in the slot area. Has the tools to be an excellent two-way player and should be on the draft radar this year, though it's likely that he won't be selected.

Quotable: "On heart and effort alone, Kavanagh is an absolute stud, but he also brings a solid two-way game and an excellent skill-set. He's the type of player that jumps out at you on his first shift and forces you to take notice." - Josh Deitell

Kelleher, Tyler – RC – US NTDP Under-18 Team – 5'6, 164

It's difficult not to be impressed with Kelleher's skill set. Many games, he's the most talented player on the ice. His hands are outstanding and he makes plays at high speed in addition to handling the puck well along the boards. His feet are excellent. He possesses great burst quickness and can evade checks with swift stops and starts. He's determined to win loose pucks and shakes off contact well, popping back to his feet after getting leveled to rejoin the play. His consistency is just not there, as he can disappear for periods at a time. It's not due to a lack of work ethic, but has to do with his lack of size and strength, which limits his effectiveness against heavy defending. He didn't prove this season that he can deal with

Kelly, Broderick – RD – Niagara Ice Dogs (OHL) – 5'11" 195

Broderick was selected in the 5th Round of the 2011 OHL Priority Selection Draft by his hometown Niagara Ice Dogs out of the St. Catharines Falcons Minor Midget program. Kelly split time in the 2011-2012 season with the St. Catharines Falcons of the GOJHL and the Niagara Ice Dogs, playing in 13 games and registering a goal and 2 assists. This was his first full season in the OHL and finished with 2 goals and 2 assists in 61 games and a -17 rating. Kelly had a pretty slow start to the season and it took him some time to look comfortable on the ice, but his confidence started to grow as the season went on.

He is willing to jump up on the rush and will step in off the point as well to provide his teammates with passing options to put some good shots on net. He plays with a degree of physicality in his own end, will use his stick to knock the puck from the opposition and can make some good simple little chip plays to move the puck out of the zone along the boards. There were times throughout the year when he let his man get away from him a bit, giving too much time and space, which resulted in great chances or goals for the opposition. He needs to tie up his man as best as he can in his own zone. Kelly probably will not hear his name get called this year at the NHL draft. To have a chance in the future, he is going to need to tighten up his defensive play in his own zone and be a reliable defenseman who can move the puck up and make that great 1st pass out of the zone to start the rush with ease. He will need to get shots through to the net with more consistency to create offensive chances and needs to use his body more to have a physical edge on opponents.

Kile, Alex – FW – Green Bay Gamblers (USHL) – 5'11" 180

After showing some intriguing flashes of talent last year, Alex really took his game to another level and was a key player for the Gamblers all season long. Alex developed through the Detroit Honeybaked system after joining the USHL's Green Bay Gamblers for the 2011-2012 season. Alex handles the puck very well and displays intriguing creativity with the puck at this level he is capable of creating offense for himself and his teammates. He also has a fairly effective shot. Alex isn't an overly physical player but will finish his checks and displays a willingness to battle. Alex is a re-entry player for the 2013 NHL Entry Draft and has a chance of being drafted. Alex has a very tough decision to make next season. He was selected in the 2010 OHL Priority Selection Draft by the London Knights.

The Knights are going to host the 2014 Memorial Cup and Alex is the type of player who would really benefit playing on a team like London as his offensive creativity would probably see him teamed with some talented forwards. His former teammate Alex Broadhurst has also experienced success there. He has also committed to the University of Michigan which is an excellent program and would give Alex four more years to develop under their system. Both are excellent options and the future looks very bright for Alex who should have every opportunity to succeed over the next few years.

Quotable: "He's an interesting player. He's a good skater and he has plenty of skill. He plays a bit too much of a solo game for my liking at times and he needs to work to become a complete player but you can't deny the talent this kid has."
- Mark Edwards

Kivihalme, Teemu – Burnsville (High-MN) and Fargo (USHL) – 6'0, 161

Teemu is Finnish by name, but was born and raised in Minnesota, where he plays his high school hockey for Burnsville. He holds dual citizenship but has suited up for the USA in international play. He also suited up for a handful of games for Fargo of the USHL this year. His game revolves around excellent skating, which he uses to maneuver swiftly around the ice with and without the puck. He's a smooth stickhandler with excellent offensive upside, able to rush the puck end-to-end with poise.

He excels at running an offense from the point, especially on the powerplay, where he uses quick footwork and good puck skills to make plays. He frequently looks to jump into the attack and is responsible about dropping back when he should. His defensive zone play needs some refining. He sometimes lacks urgency with the puck in his end, either with weak passes or by holding onto the puck for too long, leading to giveaways and chances against. He shows an active stick but his positioning can be off by a step or two, especially against the rush where his gap control is inconsistent and although he's improved in this area, he can still be overly aggressive at times. He's not physically involved enough on the boards and in front of the net, though shows an edge from time to time. Adding bulk will really help improve his game, as he's still very lean and lanky. His tools are excellent, but he's still raw. He's a definite project but also a great talent. He's a scout tester for sure. He'll suit up for Colorado College in the fall.

Quotable: "I like Teemu, he is a player that I liked going back to the select 17 camp last summer. He was raw but I liked the upside. He's needs to gain a lot of weight, so he may take longer than other prospects to get where you want him to be. I think he may be worth the wait. He's smart, his skating is NHL caliber, puck skills are great and he's already improved quite a bit since last summer. He was a great kid to talk to, outgoing and realistic about the work ahead of him to get stronger. He will have time to develop at the NCAA level." - Mark Edwards

Kirkup, Ryan – LC – Sault Ste. Marie Greyhounds (OHL) – 5'8" 182

Ryan was selected in the 8th Round of the 2011 OHL Priority Selection Draft by the Sault Ste. Marie Greyhounds out of the Markham Waxers Minor Midget program. Ryan spent his 16 year old year on a long playoff run with the OJHL's Whitby Fury. Ryan was an effective depth center for the Greyhounds in 2012-2013 earning his spot through hard work and determination. He was effective at understanding his role on the team and stuck to it whenever he was one the ice. Ryan kept things simple and made sure to be reliable in the defensive zone.

He is a good skater and works hard on the back check to pick up the trailing forward. He works hard and is good at keeping his feet moving. Kirkup makes smart simple plays in the offensive zone and does not try to get too fancy. He is more of a straight forward offensive player and works tirelessly, battling for rebounds against bigger defenders. He is undersized but is not afraid to take a hit or block a shot to make a play for the Greyhounds. Kirkup is the type of depth forward that is important for any team to have.

Klimchuk, Morgan – LW – Regina Pats (WHL) – 5'11" 180

Morgan Klimchuk enjoyed a big break out season this year for the Pats, who as a team really struggled. Klimchuk was able to put up solid offensive numbers all season long while taking care of his defensive game too.

The first thing you notice about Klimchuk is his speed and tenacity. He plays the game at such a quick pace, and is not afraid to get into corners and try to win battles for pucks. He is constantly moving his feet, and really uses his speed to his advantage. He can turn on a dime with the puck while maintaining full control, and is able to make quick starts and stops. Offensively, Klimchuk is difficult to contain. He uses his speed and puck handling abilities off the rush to get good chances, and in the offensive zone he has the special ability to be able to disappear and find open areas in coverage to unleash his deadly one timer from the high slot. He is dangerous off the half wall on the power play because he can skate to the net and place a perfect shot in just about any areas of the net.

Klimchuk is fearless when he drives the net, and is willing to sacrifice his body for his team. He will likely not become much of a playmaker at the next level as his vision is limited.

An area of Klimchuk's game that he is improving is his work in the defensive zone. He is still working on his positioning and reading the play without the puck. It has improved steadily as the season has progressed, but he still has work to do to not be a liability as a professional. One encouraging sign of his defensive play is his willingness to block shots. Time and time again Klimchuk would dive in front of one timers from the point to help his team win. The combination of speed, heart and offensive abilities will be tough to ignore for teams drafting in the late first round. Klimchuk will see a ton of ice time with the Regina Pats next season, which will only help with his development. It is clear that he is more than willing to play without the puck and do anything for his team to win, and teams definitely cannot have enough of players like Klimchuk in their lineup.

Quotable: "He's been solid every time I have seen him." - NHL Scout

Quotable: "Klimchuk added an element of physicality to his game this year, and drove to the net with authority. Time and time again he was able to find a soft area in coverage and show off his impressive shot. I really like his combination of offensive skill and work ethic." - Charles An

Quotable: "I am a fan of this kid. Liked him all year long and I liked his energy in Sochi, minus a few lapses. I often refer to players that coaches will like and want to have on their teams. I think he's one of those guys. He was one of my favorite interviews at the combine and I heard all good things about his interviews from NHL teams as well." - Mark Edwards

Quotable: "I'm not sure he always competes hard enough and I question his skating." - NHL Scout

Koivistoinen, Eetu – LC – Blues U20 (Jr A SM-liiga) – 6'2" 201

Eetu has worked his way up the ranks of the Blues over the past few seasons. He played full time with the Blues U20 team this past season posting 24 points in 42 games. Eetu also played internationally at the Four Nations Cup in Ann Arbor, Michigan. He has a huge frame and surprisingly good skating ability for his size. He is capable of rushing the puck in open ice, and will chase them deep into the zone and win battles. He displays some intriguing offensive upside creating plays for his teammates moving the puck very effectively on the rush and in the offensive zone. He has a powerful shot when he gets it off. He is capable of getting to the front of the net and competing in the slot disrupting things for the defense and goaltenders. Koivistoinen has size and shows intelligence and skills making him an intriguing prospect for an NHL team at the 2013 NHL Entry Draft.

Koledov, Pavel – RD – Lokomotiv Yaroslavl-2 (VHL) – 6'0" 181

Pavel played primarily in the VHL for Lokomotiv Yaroslavl-2 putting on a strong performance at the World Junior Championships for Russia bumping some talented defensemen from the roster and played well for Russia. Pavel really impressed us throughout our viewings of him. His size is average at best but he's very reliable defensively. He is effective in one on one situations showing a good gap control and good balance between a willingness to use strength and his stick. He competes very hard down low and has the ability to stick with his man along the wall. He battles hard and wins in the corners a surprising percentage of the time. He also maintains strong positioning in the defensive zone on a regular basis. He was also strong on the penalty kill forcing turnovers and getting the puck out of the zone while under pressure. Pavel reads the play quickly and effectively and will jump up and intercept passes and take the m the other way. He has effective skating ability that allows him to carry the puck up ice. He makes good decisions on the rush around carrying and passing the puck off. He displays good hockey sense and always seems to be in ideal positioning in all three zones. Pavel made a real impression on our scouts and could an a steal in the 2013 NHL Entry Draft.

Kopta, Ondrej – LW – Niagara Ice Dogs (OHL) – 6'2" 180

Kopta was selected 1st round, 55th Overall at the 2012 CHL Import Draft after developing up through the U16 and U18 programs of HC Plzen. He then joined the Texas Tornado posting 8 points in 41 games in the NAHL as a 16 year old. He did not overwhelm anyone offensively in his first season with the Niagara Ice Dogs with 3 goals and 11 points in 51 games and was a -17.

He is a very patient player with the puck, protects it pretty well from the opposition's pressure and goes hard to the net to follow up shots for rebound opportunities. He likes to take long shots on net and use defenders as screens to try to fool the goaltender and can play a pretty decent cycle game off the fore-check. He tracks the puck in the defensive zone to get in lanes and block passes and uses his body well to keep the opposition from the puck. He possesses good size, is willing to be physical and finish his hits and gets right in the middle of scrums. Kopta will most likely not be drafted this year and needs to demonstrate that he can play a very solid, physical, blue-collar game effectively to create energy and grind out the opposition. He has to use his big frame to drive the puck down low and get the cycle going in deep.

Kostalek, Jan – RD – Rimouski Océanic (QMJHL) – 6'0" 182

Entering his rookie season in the Q with the rebuilding Rimouski Océanic, Jan Kostalek was given huge responsibilities. He's been a consistent presence on defense for Rimouski and was a nice surprise amongst this year's 2013 NHL Draft eligible players.

Kostalek plays a smart game in all 3 zones with simple yet effective execution. He is the best defenseman without a doubt for this year's draft. He is always well positioned and executes details well in one-on-one situations. His top speed is good but will need to get better for professional hockey while his explosiveness is already pretty good and well suited for the game he plays. His game is typified by always pressing on the puck carrier, so many short bursts of speed. He has great footwork which helps him adjust to a player trying to change his speed or trying to deke him out of position. He will rarely give the slot to a player coming down his side, keeping him on the outside wall. Even when he was matched against bigger and stronger opponents, he was able to keep them on the outside resulting from his footwork, speed and great angling with his body. His positioning defensively is something you rarely see from a defenseman his age, always mindful of the slot coverage and in position to block shots. His physical play never stopped developing this season, throwing the body with more consistency as the season went on. Using his speed and hockey sense, he can play a physical and aggressive game without making too many positional mistakes. His awareness on the ice is good, always adjusting to his opponent's positioning in all 3 zones, staying on the defensive side of the puck. The Czech defenseman has character and intensity in his game, willing to pay the price to make a play and we've seen him take significant punishment physically and stay in the play regardless, showing tremendous toughness.

His play with the puck is not spectacular yet really effective, rarely causing turnovers. For transition, he will use a well executed crisp accurate pass to the nearest viable teammate, rarely going for the long risky feed. He will use the safe chip play on the boards if there are no safe options available. He rejoins the rush very wisely and when he doesn't have the puck on the breakout, will offer himself as a great passing option for his teammate without hesitating to jump in the play. He has turned in many of these breakouts on odd-man rushes because of the high level of hockey sense he has. He knows where to go when he doesn't have the puck to create offensive opportunities. In the offensive zone, his passes are well executed on tape, but he's not considered a creative passer. He has a good slapshot and we would like him to shoot more on net as he tends to wait for the perfect option before letting it go.

We would like to see Jan Kostalek get better and more confident with the puck and develop better puck controlling skills. We've seen him lose the puck by himself on some occasions. He can panic when he is pressured and shoot the puck away by the boards, causing turnovers. With better puck control and more confidence, we feel that Kostalek will gain poise and will have better puck management when he is under pressure in his own zone. He still managed to get 18 points in 48 games played in his rookie season without being overly skilled or offensively minded. He achieved this by using good hockey instincts, so we feel there's huge potential for Jan Kostalek in professional hockey.

Krueger, Mason – LW – Avon Old Farms (Prep-CT) – 6'0, 193

Mason is not the fleetest of foot, but he's a sniper. He has a bullet shot with a lightning quick release and places his shots well, finding tiny holes in goaltenders from a variety of spots on the ice. He works well in the cycle and makes intelligent passes all over the ice. He battles through contact, using his body well to protect the puck and create space. His defensive game needs improvement, especially in regards to his back checking effort. He also needs to work on his skating, as he moves sluggishly and coasts too often. He was selected by Waterloo in the 2013 USHL Draft, and could make the jump there in the fall.

Kubalik, Dominik – LW – Sudbury Wolves (OHL) – 6'1" 175

Dominik spent the 2010-2011 and 2011-2012 rising up the ranks of HC Plzen from the U16 program all the way up to the Men's Czech Extraliga, scoring his first pro goal as a 16 year old.

The Sudbury Wolves decided to use their first of two 1st round picks in the 2012 CHL Import Draft to select Dominik and he has made a great debut in North America this year. He posted 34 points this season and added another 6 points in 9 games in the playoffs. He protects the puck really well to get a good cycle going in the offensive zone and has excellent moves to beat defenders and create space for himself and teammates. He is willing to go to the net to try to tip the puck and will play physical and make the big hits. He battles well for the puck to come out of the corners with it and gets down in lanes displaying a great willingness to block shots. He moves the puck around really well in the offensive zone to find lanes to get the puck to teammates which create good chances, and can find teammates in the slot with good passes. He can also move the puck to the high slot pretty well off the rush and will drive the puck towards the net. He rushes the puck up the ice pretty effectively with good speed and opens up nicely in the slot to take passes and put one-timers on from good scoring positions.

We expect Dominik to be selected at the 2013 NHL Entry Draft and feel he's one of the better prospects out there that are not talked about at all. He plays a power game in North America which makes him well suited for different scenarios at the NHL level. The move to the OHL turned out to be a very good one for Dominik because it allowed him to show he can play that style on the small ice. Dominik may not have the offensive upside of a top six forward, but he has certainly shown flashes that prove he should be able to be moderately productive at higher levels while providing a physical mindset to any team.

Quotable: "He had a fantastic game in Sochi, I loved what he did all game long. I'd like to see games like that from him more often. He was physical and played smart, he moved the puck really well. The next game was not so good." - Mark Edwards

Quotable: "There were definitely moments this year where you'd forget Dominik was an import pick. His game is so well suited for the small ice. He finishes his checks and plays with a lot of aggression in his game. Can't wait for him to get stronger" - Ryan Yessie

Kujawinski, Ryan – LC – Kingston Frontenacs (OHL) - 6'1.5" 205

Ryan was selected 1st Round, 4th Overall by the Sarnia Sting in the 2011 OHL Priority Selection Draft from the Sudbury Wolves Minor Midget program. Ryan joined a very deep Sarnia Sting forward group as they were looking to make a big playoff run. He gained limited ice in Sarnia as a 16 year old but when the trade deadline approached he was dealt to the rebuilding Frontenacs where he received primarily 2nd line minutes. He also went on a nice statistical run showing what he's capable of.

This season was expected to be a huge coming out for the potential first rounder. However, Ryan really didn't play up to the expectations that were set out for him at the start of the season. When he's on he's a very dangerous offensive player. He displays very strong and creative passing ability. He can also make some good moves in one on one situations to beat defensemen and goaltenders. He has fairly quick hands and an effective shot. When he's on his game he engages very well along the boards and wins more than his share of battles.

The major issue with Kujawinski is his consistency. He has shown us these strengths in brief flashes, generally over a few shifts, then will disappear for long extents. He likely has the biggest combination of inconsistency and talent of any player entering the 2013 NHL Entry Draft. A consistent work ethic will be a huge improvement for Ryan and will likely be the difference of whether or not he makes it at the next level. We also need him to play more physical. Hits were generally few and far between in our viewings of Kujawinski. He's a tough player to gauge heading into this draft because he has shown glimpses of being a potential low end top six player, He will need to show this game in, game out, shift in, shift out, if he wants to reach his true potential which we believe, quite frankly, is higher than some of the players we see going ahead of him at the draft.

Quotable: "I found myself liking many of the 2014 eligible players on his team more than him during many of my viewings. Although in fairness to Ryan, that happened quite a bit this season around the OHL." - Mark Edwards

Kulda, Edgars – LW – Edmonton Oil Kings (WHL) – 5'11" 180

This fast, import rookie winger made some nice contributions for Edmonton this season. He was defensively reliable, and created a few offensive chances here and there for the Oil Kings. The issue with Kulda's game is his lack physical game and difficulty to generate much offense along the boards. He also has average stick handling abilities that he did not use very well. He did show some good positioning without the puck, and was fairly responsible in his own end has he received regular ice time throughout the year. Kulda will really have to work on his offensive game and strength to receive any attention from pro teams in the future.

Kuleshov, Artem – LD – Erie Otters (OHL) - 6'3" 200

Artem was selected in the 2nd round, 63rd Overall of the 2012 CHL Import Draft and immediately made the jump to Erie and the OHL to open the season. Things looked promising for the big blueliner, however, he struggled to keep up with the level of play the OHL provided. He hung in there and played a regular role for the Otters, but will need to keep improving to stay at this level.

Artem has excellent size and is willing to play physical. He is at his best when making the simple plays with the puck, moving it up ice to Erie's talented forwards and letting them do their thing. He can get himself in trouble being unnecessarily aggressive both physically and in one on one situations causing him to either wind up out of the play, getting beat or both. Artem gets into trouble when he tries to do too much with the puck and needs to continue to keep it simple. Artem is not expected to be selected at the NHL Draft. If this is his target then he will need to improve on his skating, continue to get stronger and keep his game simplified. He is at his best when he just makes the basic play with the puck and maintains strong defensive positioning.

Kuster, Clark – RD – Cedar Rapids RoughRiders (USHL) – 5'10" 180

Kuster played for the St. Louis Blues AAA system in Minor Midget before being drafted by Cedar Rapids in round 2 of the USHL Futures Draft in 2012. He played for Cedar Rapids this year for his rookie season in the USHL and had a pretty impressive 25 points in 53 games for a defenseman.

What is great about Kuster's game is that he can both skate the puck out of his zone to start the rush, or can make a good breakout pass to move it up the ice as well. He is willing to jump down low into the slot in the offensive zone to provide scoring options off the rush and then can also get back to tie-up his man on the back-check to nullify the opposition's opportunity. He can take a hit to make a play and move the puck up the boards to get it out of his own end and gets his stick in lanes to breakup passes for the opposition on some of their odd-man rush chances. He can close his man off along the boards to separate him from the puck and at times throughout the year has displayed a willingness to get in lanes to block shots in the defensive zone and will also put good pressure on the puck carrier. He has a nice hard shot from the point that he can get through with a degree of consistency and he also distributes the puck well on the rush through the neutral zone. He can hold the offensive line pretty well and protect the puck from the opposition's pressure and tries to keep his shot down low to generate rebound opportunities for teammates in front of the net.

L'Esperance, Joel – FW – Tri-City Storm (USHL) – 6'1" 195

L'Esperance played a few years in the Detroit Compuware system where he was just under a point per game player before being selected in the 3rd round by Des Moines and then joining the Tri-City Storm for 2 games in the 2011-2012 season. He played his first full year this season in the USHL where he registered 19 points in 49 games. He plays with a pretty nice element of physicality on the puck carrier and he uses his stick well to knock the puck free off the opposition. He will take the puck off the sidewall to come in towards the slot to put shots on net and he is wiling to bring a nice net-front presence on the power play to get in the goaltender's face and tip pucks to try and score. He battles hard for his territory in front of the net and puts great pressure on the puck carrier on the point in his own end, then gets in lanes to block shots. He can move the puck out of his zone on the breakout to start the rush, but needs to hit his target on his passes with more consistency. He also has to tie-up his man much more effectively on the back-check in his own zone. Joel has committed to Michigan Tech for the fall of 2013.

Labbé, Dylan – LD – Shawinigan Cataractes (QMJHL) – 6'2" 189

Joining the rebuilding Memorial Cup champions, the Shawinigan Cataractes, Dylan Labbé was immediately given big minutes and important responsibilities as the season started. He impressed us during the whole season with his offensive aptitudes.

He likes to carry the puck and is really confident when starting the breakout on his own. His puck handling abilities are good, he can make his way around players easily with slick moves, displaying confidence when bringing the puck up. He will rarely lose handling of the puck and can maneuver comfortably in traffic. His forward speed for a 6,02 189 pounds player is great, using long powerful strides to reach top speed quickly, which helps him get away from pressure and start transition effectively. His shot is tremendous, powerful and accurate, preferring a great release with the wrist shot to a slapshot. He got numerous scoring chances with the hard wrister on the powerplay this season, but needs to put more pucks on net 5-on-5. His passing game is also above-average, finding teammates easily and quickly in the offensive zone with hard passes on tape. He was used on the powerplay for the vast majority of the season and showed a nice puck-moving potential. We like the physical attributes Labbé possess, being able to play a physical game down-low, rarely getting beat in restricted areas. We like to see him play with an aggressive edge, something he didn't do with enough consistency this season.

Dylan Labbé still has major issues in his game. The first one is his limited defensive hockey sense. He had one of the worst plus-minus ratings in the Q in 2011-2012 with a -40. Part of that atrocious rating could be attributed to having faced opposing team's top lines at only 17 years old. In most of our viewings he had a tough time making the right decision in his own zone. He still seems to have difficulty playing in an elaborate system, looking lost positionally in his own zone resulting in bad decisions. Those choices caused a high number of turnovers, thus creating doubts about his level of hockey sense. He needs to improve his footwork, while his forward speed is good, his lateral movements are still sluggish and at times he can lose his coverage easily against agile skaters. We like the improvement we've seen from him in this particular area during the season. Labbé certainly has an attractive toolbox with the size and existing abilities and should be drafted near the 5th round at the 2013 NHL Draft.

Laffin, Michael – LW – New York Apple Core (EJHL) – 5'11, 172

The feisty New York native had a noteworthy season, with good play at the EJHL level and a two-game stint with the NTDP U18 team. He's quick and shows good goal-scoring instincts. He accelerates quickly into open ice and carries the puck with poise. He has the hands to draw coverage and the passing ability to hit teammates through seams. He frequently acts as a triggerman on the power play, taking advantage of his dangerous shot. He shows strong stick work along the boards and in front of the net, but needs to be more involved with his body. Overall, he's much too stationary without the puck in the offensive zone. He needs to keep his feet moving to draw coverage and give his teammates options. His positioning is strong and he has good offensive instincts, but he doesn't play with an edge and lacks consistent intensity. He has an outside shot at being taken late in the 2013 NHL Draft, but still has plenty to prove.

Lafontaine, Raphael – LW – Acadie-Bathurst Titan (QMJHL) – 5'10" 176

Lafontaine was traded at the start of the season from Gatineau and had an immediate impact with the Titan. On the ice he scored important goals while off the ice he was named captain shortly after his arrival. His leadership and work ethic are two of his biggest qualities, showing up every game, willing to sacrifice his body for his team. A winger with a gritty identity, Lafontaine has a great nose for the net. He has scored most of his goals in tight around the net; comprised of rebounds, puck deflections and crashing the net. He has a ton of heart as a great defensive forward making him tough to play against. He's physical on the boards, although he is not an intimidating player. He can play the defensive situations such as PK and final minutes of the game with great determination, protecting a lead. His skating is just average and his strides are not fluid. He has below average puck skills and will be mostly satisfied offensively playing a dump-and-chase, North-South game with little creativity. Raphael Lafontaine could earn an invitation next summer to an NHL camp for the dedication and work ethic he brings on the ice.

Laplante, Yan Pavel – C – PEI Rocket (QMJHL) – 6'0" 172

Yan Pavel Laplante came into the 2012-2013 season with a lot of ice time waiting for him with the PEI Rocket, a team finally leaving the shallows of the QMJHL rankings. Unfortunately, Laplante injured his shoulder seriously at the Ivan Hlinka Under-18 tournament in August and had to wait until February to play his first game of the season. He came back in top shape and impressed us in our viewings with both the PEI Rockets and at the World Under-18 Hockey Championship.

Laplante is a gifted puck handler with great speed and goal scoring instincts. He has quick hands and could dangle in a phone booth. An elusive and creative puck handler, he can easily put a defenseman attempting to play the puck off balance with his skill set. He possesses a great wrist shot with a lethal release to go with it. He has a shoot first mentality and you can see the enthusiasm when he scores goals. He uses his skills and high end skating agility to get into great shooting positions. His top speed is great but he needs to develop more lower body and core strength to be explosive, although it is at an acceptable level at the moment. He gets in a scoring position when he doesn't have the puck, whether he is in the high slot or crashing the net for a chance to jump on a rebound. He plays a spectacular brand of hockey and will score a lot of highlight reel goals in his major junior career. He can execute some high quality passing plays, but will always prefer the shot.

We like the improvement in his competitiveness during the 2012-2013 season, as he was not previously known as a hard working player. This season he put more effort in the offensive and i defensive zones, consistently moving his feet. He showed the will to block shots, back check hard, support his defensemen and get involved in the physical side of the game. He still needs to improve his consistency as he tends to wait for the important moments before doing those little details.

Laplante needs to put on some mass as he is still really small statured and can be pushed off the puck by big defensemen. His durability could also improve with pounds added to his frame. Yan Pavel possesses a very good skill set and he displays a lot of confidence when he is carrying the puck. He can be selfish at times, hanging on to the puck for too long and over using his wrist shot. We feel Yan Pavel has made the most out of his limited games played this season and should be drafted in the 4th round.

Latour, Bradley – RW – Oshawa Generals (OHL) – 5'10" 182

Bradley was selected in the fourth round of the 2011 OHL Priority Selection Draft by the Oshawa Generals out of the Barrie Colts Minor Midget Program. Bradley joined the Stayner Siskins, a Georgian Mid-Ontario Jr. C team, putting up over a point per game and nearly 100 penalty minutes. He was rewarded with a couple games with the Generals last season. This season Bradley wasn't going to accept anything less than an OHL roster spot and he worked extremely hard earning a spot on the Generals. Bradley spent a fair amount of time on Oshawa's second line behind some very talented forwards and did an excellent job playing within his role. Latour was a very well liked prospect from our staff based on his ability to do the little things. At 5'10" he's not the biggest guy on the ice, he's not the most talented player on the ice, but he will do what it takes to help his team win.

Bradley drives the net hard when he has the puck on his stick and has a powerful shot. He's much more of a shoot first player and already possesses a slightly above average shot. Generally he will try to put the puck on net, or go to the net and jam at the rebounds. He hits hard and despite his size packs a lot of power in his checks. He's smart positionally in the offensive zone. He also gets back defensively and shows good positional awareness in the defensive zone getting his stick in lanes and blocking shots. Bradley is a very intriguing prospect for the later rounds of this draft. Bradley has proven himself deserving of one of those late round picks. His upside is limited, but he already does all the things that would make him a very successful bottom six forward at the next level. He was one of the unsung contributors to Oshawa's strong season, and as some of their top forwards graduate, he will be given a great opportunity to be an all game situation player for the Generals next year.

Lazar, Curtis – RC – Edmonton Oil Kings (WHL) – 6'0" 198

Lazar entered this season with a lot of hype surrounding his game. His play without the puck was very impressive for such a young player, while his offensive game was starting to improve. He has not been able to put up the offensive numbers that usually garner the amount of attention that he is getting now, but there is certainly potential in his game to be an effective 2 way forward in the NHL one day.

The best attribute of Lazar's game is his play without the puck. He is always in such good position in his own end, and is very strong along the boards. He is always out on the ice in crucial defensive situations, and will positively impact the game in some way. He fearlessly blocks shots to help his team win games, and seems to be able to consistently be in the shooting lane. His coverage down low is very good, and displays good anticipation to be able to knock away passes and tie up opponents. Offensively, Lazar has a very impressive wrist shot. He has a nice quick release off the rush in speed. He is not much of a playmaker, and most of his offensive contribution will come in the form of goals and scoring chances. He is able to get into good position in dangerous scoring areas, and make himself available for passes. Lazar has a bit of work to do with his hands around the net, as he could further develop his scoring touch. He has also shown that he is a streaky scorer. He may go a long stretch of not picking up any point, then go on a long streak where he seems to score whenever he is around the net.

Lazar will have to be able to consistently put up points to be a more dangerous player as a pro. Lazar is by no means a slow player, but he does have some work to do in terms of his acceleration. It takes him a bit longer to reach his good top end speed, and it inhibits him from being a more dangerous player than he could be. Any team that is looking for a heart and soul, future captain will not have to look further than Curtis Lazar. He may not put up more than 50 points a year in his prime, but he is able to impact the game in more ways than just offensively. He plays the game with such a passion, that it will be contagious within the dressing room. If he can continue to play a 200 ft game while improving his strength and speed and chip in offensively, he will put up a long NHL career.

Quotable: "He can do everything at high speed. He is a player. Top 10 pick for me." - NHL Scout

Quotable: "He grew on me. I still don't have him as a top 20 but I didn't have him as a top 40 a few months ago." - NHL Scout

Quotable: "Probably the best defensive forward available from the WHL this year. I have never seen him take a shift off over the last 2 seasons. He may not put up a point per game at the NHL level, but teams need players like Lazar to win in the playoffs." - Charles An

Lees, Jesse – RD – Kelowna Rockets (WHL) – 6'0" 180

An offensive minded defenseman, Lees has played to his strengths this season and has been relatively good for the Rockets. If he does get drafted, Lees will definitely be a project for an NHL team for a few years due to his defensive play. Lees is a perfect example that the +/- stat is a bad indicator of how good a player is in his own end. He has a very good plus rating, but he is all over the ice when he does not have the puck and does not read the play well. He makes bad pinches in the offensive zone, which leads to odd man chances and chases the puck and makes unnecessary gambles in his own end, leaving his goaltender out to dry consistently. He is not particularly strong along the boards, and has a lot of work to do without the puck.

The offensive zone is where Lees looks comfortable. He makes very good outlet passes and has been able to spring teammates on breakaways consistently. He has good vision on the blueline and has contributed immensely on the Rockets' power play with his passes. He has a good shot that he could use more often, but he still needs to work on changing the angles of his shots. He is often planted in one area of the ice when he could take the puck to the middle to give himself a better angle and to make it harder for opponents to block his shots.

Artturi Lehkonen – LW – KalPa (SM-Liiga) - 5'10" 152

Lehkonen is a skilled, speedy winger who must improve his physical game to be an effective player in North America. He is able to use his speed and stickhandling abilities so well because of the open ice available in the big rinks, but he is quite weak on his skates, which will hinder him from contributing much at the NHL level because of the lack of open ice.

Lehkonen may not be very strong, but he is certainly not afraid to battle for loose pucks and get in on the forecheck. The problem is that he rarely wins these battles, and is often knocked onto the ice quite easily. He needs to really work on his strength level to come away with the puck more often, as he will have to be much more involved physically at the AHL or NHL level to be successful. One clear strength of Lehkonen's game is his speed. He has very good top end speed, and is able to get from point A to B in a hurry. As a result, he is so successful in the bigger rinks as his speed allows him to create more separation from opponents and utilize his good stickhandling ability as well. He can make quick stops as he is moving at full speed while maintaining control of the puck, which throws opponents off guard as they have to quickly adjust and take away time and space from him.

Offensively, Lehkonen loves to shoot from anywhere. He is not afraid to go to the net to sniff out any rebounds, but he needs to be in a better position at times to take advantage of opportunities around the net and provide a better screen for his teammates. He possesses very smooth hands, and shows them off in the neutral zone with speed. One area of concern of Lehkonen's game is his inability to find open areas in the offensive zone. He needs to read the play better and get away from coverage to set himself up to receive a pass for a quick scoring opportunity in the slot.

Defensively, Lehkonen uses his stick more than his body, which is something he needs to address. He likes to take a poke with his stick and just skate by the opposition instead of laying a hit and try to knock an opponent off the puck for a quick takeaway. He uses his speed to take away time and space in the neutral zone, but could do a better job of creating turnovers. He is rarely involved physically if he does not see much of a scoring chance coming out of the play.

It will be interesting to see if Lehkonen can find some success offensively on smaller ice. His game is built for lots of space with his speed and stickhandling rather than the "North American" game that he will have to play at the AHL and NHL level. If he does not improve his strength and ability to find open holes in coverage, he will have a difficult time making any sort of an impact for an NHL team in the future.

Lemmon, Mack – RW – Niagara Ice Dogs (OHL) – 5'10" 195

Mack was selected in the 2nd round of the 2011 OHL Priority Selection Draft by the Belleville Bulls out of the Markham Majors Minor Midget program. He played a full season for the Bulls playing in limited action on the fourth line, utilizing the physical play he was heavily noted for in Minor Midget. Mack opened the season with the Bulls but was quickly moved to the Niagara Ice Dogs where he played primarily a third line role. Lemmon posted 6 goals, 5 assists and 186 penalty minutes to show for his 2 year OHL career thus far after 104 games played.

Lemmon is a physical blue collar type role player who battles hard for the puck and is aggressive getting in opponent's faces. He is smart on the fore-check, applying good pressure to force turnovers. He gets in lanes to block passes and breakup plays on the penalty kill. He finishes his hits along the boards and brings a net-front presence in the offensive zone. He keeps to a simple game, dumping the puck in to get it in deep and for the most part always tries to make the safe plays.

He needs to get both quicker with the puck and stronger on it. He is most effective when he is a pest to play against, getting under the opposition's skin and getting involved in scrums after whistles. Lemmon has an outside shot at being selected in the 2013 NHL Entry Draft due to his tough, gritty play and punishing hits, but he needs to continue to show that he can be a nuisance to play against and get the opposition off their game while producing a little more offensively.

Quotable: "He brings a hard hat to the rink" – NHL Scout

Lettieri, Vinni – FW – Lincoln Stars (USHL) – 5'8" 170

Lettieri was picked in the 3rd round at number 42 overall by the Lincoln Stars in the 2011 USHL Futures Draft and played in just 15 games in the USHL last season where he scored 8 points, but played his first full year this season playing in 61 games and scoring an impressive 56 points which went along well with his +29 rating. He gets the puck in deep to start a good cycle and is a player who will hustle really hard to get on loose pucks, then protects it well. He puts good pressure on the fore-check and goes hard to the net to pick up loose pucks and rebounds for chances in tight. He will step in towards the middle off the rush to get shots from scoring position and drives hard to the net looking for his opportunities in tight. Lettieri is also used at the point sometimes on the power play and he can distribute the puck pretty well to create chances from there, as he has good vision to find lanes and good offensive instincts to decide where the puck should go.

Lettieri needs to add size and strength as he is a much smaller player, but what is a promising sign is that he is not intimidated to play down the middle. This is a player who will be most effective playing a tough grinding game in the dirty areas, but also has the skills with the puck to make plays and create offense that way. Vinni is set to return to his home state playing for University of Minnesota this fall of 2013.

Lewington, Tyler – RD – Medicine Hat Tigers (WHL) – 6'1" 191

Lewington is a puck moving defenseman who plays a simple game. He is quite poised with the puck, and is able to escape forechecks and quickly move the puck up to his forwards. Lewington is a competent skater who does not overwhelm opponents with his speed, but does an admirable job carrying the puck. He has average hands and will probably never score a coast to coast goal, but he could certainly carry the puck to the offensive zone and try to set up the attack. Lewington does not possess a very good shot, and will certainly have to improve on it to be more of a threat from the blue line. He does not like to join the rush and try to create an odd man rush, which is something that he could add to his game as well as he has good skating abilities.

Defensively, Lewington is quite inconsistent. There are times when he uses his stick well to knock away pucks and pick off passes, then there are times when he looks like he has bad habits in his own zone, and not be as strong on the puck and on opponents with his body as he could be. There are also times when he is caught out of position and gives up scoring chances in tight. He has to use his body more to block shots and be tougher to play against along the walls and win more puck battles.

Lewington could become a useful player as a pro one day, but his play without the puck will have to improve immensely. He has to be more consistently effective, and put in the effort to provide more impact in his own end. No matter how well he can move the puck, if he cannot play in his own end, no coach will trust him and put him out on the ice.

Lewis, Clint – LD – US NTDP Under-18 Team – 6'2, 181

Clint is a simple, cerebral defenseman. He was an offensive producer in midget but his game is now focused on covering his zone first and foremost, and his puck skills have fallen by the wayside. His positioning in his zone is solid, with an active stick and good reads. He makes few mistakes though he does get burned from time to time. His first pass is OK but he generally takes the safest option possible, either taking advantage of short outlets or putting pucks off the glass to clear. He has a good frame and while he but doesn't always use his size to his advantage. He's not a game breaker by any stretch of the imagination, and doesn't project as an NHL talent at this point, but should have plenty of success in a supporting role at Cornell University starting this fall.

Liberati, Miles – LD – London Knights (OHL) – 5'11.5" 195

Miles was drafted by the London Knights at the 2011 OHL Priority Selection Draft in the 3rd round out of the Pittsburgh Viper Stars U16 program. Showing a commitment to his long term development, Miles joined The Hill Academy Varsity hockey team for the 2011-2012 season helping him refine his skills and prepare him for the OHL. Miles made the Knights out of camp but has had to fight for every minute of ice time playing on a very deep team.

Miles has shown good two-way potential in our viewings of him this season. He likes to jump up in the rush, which he is effective at but needs to be careful at times not to get caught too far up ice. He has a good accurate shot from the point and can get it through. He is also smart and patient with the puck in all three zones. In his own zone he makes intelligent passes and is able to usually minimize turnovers although he does have the occasional mental error. Miles battles very hard in his own zone and shows a very strong compete level. He wins battles and fights for every inch in the defensive zone.

In terms of improvement, Miles is a well rounded player who doesn't do anything particularly great, but doesn't have a single area that is a glaring weakness. We'd like to see him get stronger, faster and a lot of his improvements are going to be made by playing a regular every day shift next season when some of the veterans move on. He is a defenseman that will be looked at outside the first few rounds as he shows good puck skills, good defensive work ethic and can play a very good two-way game. He has average size for a defenseman, but can handle the physical battles at this level. He will need two before being pro ready, but he shows all the signs of developing into a very well rounded defender.

Quotable: "I liked what I saw early in the season when he had more opportunity. The Knights moved him up front when Sefton arrived. I personally would have played him ahead of Sefton on the backend. I liked what I saw offensively when he played defense. I spoke to Miles in November and came away impressed." - Mark Edwards

Light, Connor – LD – Phillips Andover Academy (Prep-MA) – 6'5, 198

Connor possesses an excellent frame and shows some positive attributes on the ice, but is still very raw. His defensive zone positioning is strong and he plays well in front of his net, but has occasional lapses of over aggressiveness. Against the rush, he's hard to beat with good feet and long reach. He can line guys up for big hits along the boards and pinches like a freight train to make plays. His skating is strong and smooth, especially for his size, and does well to skate the puck out of danger and up ice. He shows OK puck skills but his offensive upside is a question mark as his decision-making on the attack is poor at times. Even if his game doesn't completely round out, he's still an intriguing prospect with his combination of size, skating, and physical play. The Omaha Lancers drafted him in the 2013 USHL Draft, and without a college commitment he looks a safe bet to suit up for them in the fall.

Quotable: "Another one of the surprisingly numerous big, mobile defensemen out of New England this year, Light has excellent tools but has yet to really refine his game. He has shifts that make you think, 'Wow, there's really something here,' but rarely strings them together back-to-back." - Josh Deitell

Liljendahl, Tobias – RC – Djurgarden J20 (SWE J20) – 6'2" 214

Tobias is a big forward who has developed through Djurgarden's junior system and represented Sweden internationally multiple times, some of these times as a captain or assistant captain. Tobias plays a pretty simple game. He is a two-way centre who can be used in both offensive and defensive situations. He shows great hockey sense making smart plays with the puck and displays excellent positioning and constantly seems to be where he should be. He doesn't try to force plays and will just choose the smart option with the puck. He also has a powerful shot with a quick release. He can play physical but he isn't overly aggressive and will also use his size to protect the puck. Tobias showed excellent defensively in different situations including penalty kills and was chosen to be the lone forward on a 5 on 3 kill. His calm, never risky demeanor really serves him well on the penalty kill. He quickly gets into good positioning, gets in passing lanes, blocks shot and does a great job in these situations. His top speed is not bad at all for a player his size but his first few steps need work to get him to where he needs to be. Tobias is an emotional player at times, sometimes after the game. We once witnessed after losing a Bronze Medal, he stood respectably for the national anthem. Once it was over, he skated over to his own net, and smashed his stick in half over the net. We feel Tobias is more well suited for a bottom six role and thus may go later in the draft, but he shows a lot of attributes that are worth taking a long look at for the 2013 NHL Entry Draft.

Linaker, Cole – RC – Kelowna Rockets (WHL) – 6'1" 165

Linaker is a depth forward with limited offensive abilities. He is a good skater who can eat up some minutes for Kelowna, but does not provide much impact in games. He received regular minutes because of his dependability in the defensive zone, but he does have moments where he makes big mistakes defensively, which costs his team a goal. He needs to read the play at a much quicker pace, and anticipate where he should be at all times and move his feet to take away good scoring chances. Linaker was able to step up for the Rockets during the playoffs when the team faced a number of injuries and provided a nice presence on the ice. He will need to continue to develop his game to ever be considered by teams for at least a camp invite.

Lindholm, Elias – RC – Brynas (Elitserien) - 6'0" 192

Elias Lindholm first caught the attention of HockeyProspect during the 2011 World Jr. A Challenge Tournament. He was undoubtedly the best player, and has since been touted as the best player available in the 2013 NHL Entry Draft from Sweden by many scouts.

It is difficult to not notice Lindholm when he is out on the ice. He always seems to be around the puck and plays with such a high intensity at all times. He positions himself properly without the puck to give himself a chance to be a target for a pass or to make a great defensive play. Lindholm battles hard for loose pucks, and backchecks extremely hard. He makes smart stick checks from behind and is able to create takeaways after takeaways and get a quick transition play started for his team.

Offensively, Lindholm is a very skilled playmaker. He sees the ice extremely well, and seems to be very aware of everything around him. He is very patient and allows the play to develop before he makes a play with the puck, and he is able to do so because of his good stickhandling abilities and his quickness out in open ice. In terms of his passing ability, he can make tape to tape saucer passes in traffic if necessary, or quickly send a backhand pass to a teammate in the slot from behind the net through a few sticks. He really makes his linemates look better because he is able to find them anywhere out on the ice and give them a chance to score. One area of improvement for Lindholm with the puck would be his ability to finish off plays. He gets very good chances around the net, but just does not seem to be able to score on them as often as he should, and he should also try to look to shoot more often. He could get a little predictable and opponents may start to anticipate passes and intercept them more easily.

Defensively, Lindholm is a very polished player without the puck. Not only does he play with a lot of intensity, but he also possesses a high level of hockey sense. He seems to be able to pick off passes easily as he puts himself in good position, and anticipates the play quite well. He will block shots fearlessly, and displays his high level of competitiveness again and again during battles for loose pucks.

It is only a matter of time before Lindholm is thought of as a star in the NHL by fans and media. His combination of skill and work ethic will allow him to be a fan favorite for a long time, and be a player that coaches can trust in any situations, whether it be to protect a lead or to score a game tying goal late in the game. He has already proven himself to a be a good offensive player in the Elitserien, and we are sure that Lindholm will do the same at the NHL level soon.

Quotable: "When I first watched Lindholm play in the 2011 World Jr. A Challenge Tournament, I couldn't help but to pay attention to him whenever he was out on the ice. His tenacity and skill level were truly incredible to watch. Fans are going to love him if he plays for their team, and hate him if he's playing against their team." - Charles An

Quotable: "I'm still a big fan. He has kept his stock high with us. On February 15th 2012 we ranked him 5th overall for this years draft. 15 months later he has barely moved in our rankings. He blew me away in Brno last year. Great vision and one of the smartest players in this draft." - Mark Edwards

Lipon, J.C. – RW – Kamloops Blazers (WHL) – 6'0" 181

JC Lipon went unselected in the 2011 and 2012 NHL Entry Drafts, but has gained a lot of attention this season with his offensive productivity and his continued strong 2 way game. He was rewarded with a spot on Team Canada for the World Juniors, and provided a good defensive zone presence. His offensive production slowed down around the 2nd half of the season, but picked it up in the playoffs and provided a much boost for the Blazers. Offensively, Lipon just seems to be in the right place at the right time on a consistent basis. He always seems to be around the puck and battles hard for loose pucks on the forecheck and continues the attack for his team. Lipon is not particularly a gifted scorer or playmaker, but seems to be comfortable in both roles. He is not afraid to go to the net to score goals in tight, and he makes smart decisions with the puck and makes quick decisions with it. Opponents seemed to have figured him out in the later parts of the season, but he has been able to out battle opponents and be offensively productive again.

Lipon is one of the most dependable penalty killers on the Blazers. He is always out in crucial situations, and really covers his side of the ice well and quick reads the play and get into proper positioning. He is quite intelligent without the puck, and is not afraid to block shots and dish out hits to get the puck back for his team. One area of concern in Lipon's game Is his undisciplined play. He is prone to taking penalties after the whistle, and plays like a pest out on the ice. He is quick to retaliate and has a tough time keeping his composure. He needs to be able to control himself and not put his team on the penalty kill, and he is a valuable player for the Blazers and does more damage when he is out on the ice than in the penalty box. It will certainly be interesting to see if Lipon can become a defensive forward who can provide timely offense at the NHL level. He certainly has the speed, defensive awareness and grit to be an attractive option for any teams, but if he does not play with more disciplined, he will find himself losing a roster spot in a hurry.

Lipsbergs, Roberts – LW – Seattle Thunderbirds (WHL) – 5'11" 195

Lipsbergs was passed over in the NHL Entry Draft last year as he received little exposure in Europe last year, but his strong play and productivity in the WHL this season has caught the attention of scouts and his name could be chosen this year as a result. The first thing you notice about Lipsbergs is his speed. He uses it to his advantage to get in on the forecheck and try to retrieve pucks. He plays hard at all times, and is not afraid of taking hits to make a play. He was one of the hardest workers for Seattle this season, and it showed as he received more and more important ice time as the season went along.

Lipsbergs has good skills with the puck. He possesses above average playmaking skills, especially off the half wall after winning a battle for the puck, he will quickly move it to an open teammate for a good chance. He also has an above average shot, but it is something that he could improve on. His goals seem to come around the net mostly as he likes to drive the net.

Defensively, Lipsbergs picked up more ice time in his own zone as the season went along. He improved on his coverage of the point and was good at moving around in the defensive zone to cover for teammates and help out when necessary. He could be a better shot blocker and provide some more impact in his own end, but it is pretty clear that he is an offense first type of player.

Locke, Eric – LC – Saginaw Spirit (OHL) – 5'9" 182

Locke was selected by the Windsor Spitfires in the 2009 OHL Priority Selection Draft. He made the Spitfires the following year and scored 19 goals in only 38 games before being dealt to the Barrie Colts. Going into his draft year, he was expected to follow up on his strong rookie season and post some big numbers. That did not happen for him. He found himself traded, this time to the Saginaw Spirit. He contributed to the Spirit in a 3rd line role for the majority of the remaining season, posting respectable numbers.

With the graduation of several key players for Saginaw, Eric was once again able to display his true offensive potential and put himself back on the radar of NHL teams after a huge 44 goal season. He's a very dangerous player to be left alone and has the shot to make the opposition pay. He is fairly creative with the puck and can score some very nice goals. He is a good skater, but tends to stay on the perimeter. Along with his shot, he has surprisingly good passing ability for a player who's much more known to be a goal scorer. One of our bigger concerns was we noticed that he disappeared a little when games got very physical. Combine this with sticking on the perimeter and his lack of size it is likely one of the key things that has prevented him from being selected. However after a huge season in Saginaw we would not be surprised to see Eric selected at the 2013 NHL Entry Draft. If he goes undrafted again we are sure there will be a team that shows interest in him and invites him to camp.

Quotable: "I have watched him going back to minor midget and his Telus Cup season. Eric posted big numbers and at least earned himself a camp invite as far as I'm concerned." - Mark Edwards

Lodge, Jimmy – RC – Saginaw Spirit (OHL) – 6'2" 165

Jimmy was selected in the third round of the 2011 OHL Priority Selection Draft from the Toronto Titans Minor Midget program. Jimmy was able to crack the Saginaw lineup as a 16 year old. However he was caught behind several talented veteran forwards and really played a limited role due to his lack of physicality, but he did chip in a little offensively. Jimmy saw a huge increase in ice time, receiving a ton of minutes with the Spirit playing in every offensive situation with some very talented forwards. Jimmy displays outstanding skating ability especially for a 17 year old who is 6'2". Jimmy has shown us some real flashes of creativity. He uses his size to protect the puck fairly well and has a strong shot. He also showed great urgency to get back defensively and was willing to get his stick in lanes and battles.

The biggest concern about Jimmy is his lack of physicality. He really struggles and sometimes disappears in the more physical games and had a tendency of being taken off his game if matched against a big defenseman who asserted himself on Jimmy. He also didn't come out of enough battles with the puck. Fortunately he's only 165 at 6'2" so he's very lanky and would greatly benefit from adding muscle as soon as possible. He needs to get stronger, he already knows how to use his size, and it's possible that after adding 20, 30 pounds of muscle he will become more comfortable and effective in the physical game.

Jimmy is a player we are sure will be selected at the 2013 NHL Entry Draft. He has the potential upside of a top six forward but unless he gets tougher and adds more sandpaper to his game, he's one of those players that almost has to reach that top six potential to make the top level. Otherwise he'll need to add that toughness and muscle that could make him an effective bottom six player, as he already has the size necessary.

Quotable: "He played a very soft game last year and in minor midget. He has made progress in this area and showed scouts he could post some crooked numbers. In talking to other scouts, opinions were all over the map." - Mark Edwards

Quotable: "Made big jump on my list late this season but I still have him lagging behind plenty of other forwards. The strength level is not close." - NHL Scout

Lotz, Austin – G – Everett Silvertips (WHL) – 6'0" 185

Austin Lotz was given the starting job for the Silvertips early in the year, and has shown some flashes of brilliance in net for a team that is currently going through a rebuilding phase. He was able to stand on his head a few times throughout the season, and give his team a chance to win in games that they had no business of winning.

The best attribute of Lotz is his quickness. He can go post to post in a hurry and quickly recover from his butterfly to his feet to get ready for the next wave of shots. He has a tendency to flop at times and attempt to make acrobatic stops, which gets him out of position. Another one of Lotz's strengths is his ability to play his angles very well. He takes shots off his chest time and time again off the rush, and makes it easy to cover rebounds as pucks land right in front of him. He is also good at looking through heavy traffic and not allowing it to rattle his game.

There are some improvements that Lotz needs to make in his game. One of his weaknesses is his inconsistency. There are times when he would be the best player by far on the ice, then there are games where he would look below average and give up goals after goals. Lotz needs to perform at his best more frequently and allow his coaches and teammates to trust in him more. He also needs to work on his rebound control as other teams get shot after shot on him because he gives up a lot of rebounds in prime scoring areas. Lotz also needs to work on his hands and improve his blocker and glove hand.

Quotable: "He is one of those guys who seems to guess a lot, not on my radar." - NHL Scout

Quotable: "A player that our scout Charles An and I had more than one chat about. I see him the same way I see Giugovaz, just an athletic guy that can get hot and steal you a game. Those goalies tend to scare me off because they seem to lose games all on their own at times as well." - Mark Edwards

Louis, Anthony – LW – US NTDP Under-18 Team – 5'6, 142

The University of Miami-bound forward was a consistent factor in the NTDP offense this year. He's undersized but brave and possesses great tools. His hands are lightning-quick, allowing him to navigate traffic with ease and make plays, and he has a hard shot that he releases quickly. His skating is fluid and dynamic and he plays with a lot of jump. His work ethic is also commendable, as he keeps his feet moving on most every shift and does go out of his way to play the body. He's not afraid to take the puck to the slot or go to the corners but his size becomes a factor frequently, especially in board battles. He hasn't shown the ability to evade contact on an elite level, which considering his stature makes it difficult for him to stay relevant against bigger players. He can be completely shut down if targeted and doesn't have the defensive game to be a difference-maker if he's not creating offense. The college game will be a sink-or-swim test for Louis, who has a chance at being selected this June.

Lysenko, Vladislav – LD – Sherbrooke Phoenix (QMJHL) – 6'0" 198

Coming from Ukriane, Vladislav Lysenko joined the newly minted Sherbrooke Phoenix in the QMJHL and brought a physical style to the table. He likes to hit and even though his play progressed well during the season, his decisions need a lot of polishing. He likes to be aggressive in gap coverage, high in the neutral zone to hit a player and throws the body whenever he can. His hits are spectacular and can change the momentum of a hockey game. He moves fluidly, helping him with timing his hits. At the start of the season he was running around his own zone to throw body checks and got caught out of position many times allowing too much space down-low. He also gave up many odd-man rushes to the opposing team by pinching aggressively in the neutral zone, rather than smartly to hit the puck carrier. He settled into a very good physical defensive game with more intelligence as the season went on, displaying more maturity without the puck and a higher level of hockey sense. He is still far away from the quickness required decision making at the pro level. We like the footwork and his ability to follow his man aggressively on the boards, giving little time and space. He still needs to develop to keep up with the best skaters in the league, but as a 17 year old D, his footwork is very good. You are always more at risk of getting beat playing an aggressive defensive game like Lysneko does, especially when following elusive and agile skaters. His play with the puck is above average, nothing spectacular, but makes good passes and has a hard shot. He needs to put it on net more often, as he tends to wait for the perfect opportunity. Getting 7 goals with little powerplay time during the season is a good indication that Lysenko has some offensive potential. His puck control is good while holding his blueline with confidence and rarely mishandles the puck when starting the breakout. His strength is great, winning many battles easily, pinning players on the boards and clearing the front of the net with authority. With Vladislav Lysenko, it's all about decisions, his hockey sense is still average at the moment and it hurts him in all areas of his game. If not for this weakness he would have been in the top draft eligible defensemen coming from the Q. With the progression he's made throughout the season and the rarely seen physicality he puts into his game, we see him getting drafted in the later rounds of the NHL Draft.

MacDonald, Josh – LW – Barrie Colts (OHL) – 5'10" 186

Josh was a 3rd round pick in the 2010 OHL Priority Selection Draft out of the London Jr. Knights Gold Minor Midget program. As a 16 year old he played for the Elmira Sugar Kings Jr. B team. He posted a respectable 20 goal season but he really put his name on the map in the playoffs with a 17 point in 17 game performance which he followed up with a 17 points in 9 game performance at the 2011 Sutherland Cup. He advanced to the OHL joining the Colts in 2011-2012 and played a minimal role on a veteran Colts team. He jumped between the third and fourth lines in Barrie this season, but is a very, very underrated player due to the depth of the Colts.

You'll be hard pressed to find too many players in this draft that work harder than MacDonald on a shift by shift basis. He makes the most of his ice, finishes every check and he competes in all three zones at all times. He's shown well on the penalty kill understanding his positioning allowing him to get into passing lanes. He also was able to tally 15 goals and 30 points in a limited role.

MacDonald is a re-entry 1994 born player and after his offensive outpour in Jr. B and the style of play and flashes he shows it wouldn't be surprising to see Josh break out a little playing a bigger role next year.

Mackey, Kyle – FW – Youngstown Phantoms (USHL) – 6'0" 167

Mackey was a 2nd round pick by Youngstown and played in 38 games this year for them in his rookie season. He is a defenseman who is willing to pinch and join the rush as a 4th forward to provide his teammates with passing options, or is also willing to skate the puck up himself to lead the attack. He steps into the high slot to provide scoring options in the offensive zone and can make a good lead pass to start the breakout. He possesses good strength and the ability to protect the puck in order to take a hit and still make a play to get the puck out of his zone and was moving the puck well to lead teammates into the offensive zone. He is calm with the puck, has agility to twist away from the opposition's pressure and can get his shot through to the net from the point, although it is in no way the hardest shot around. He has decent size but needs to be much stronger on the puck so it is not battled off him so easily and has to tie up his man better in his own end so that the opposition does not get away from him too easily for a good opportunity.

MacKinnon, Nathan – RC – Halifax Mooseheads (QMJHL) – 5'11" 179

After a tremendous rookie season where he recorded 31 goals in 58 games, Nathan MacKinnon solidified his status as a candidate for the #1 overall draft pick in the 2013 NHL Draft this season. He ended the season with 75 points in 44 games centering a line with top 2013 NHL Draft prospect Jonathan Drouin and 2012 Detroit Red Wings 2nd rounder Martin Frk, culminating one of the top lines in the CHL, perhaps one of the best ever.

Nathan MacKinnon is an elite player. A tremendous skater, his first few strides are really what distinguishes him from other players, he can get to top speed with a few strides and get past a defenseman before he starts thinking about pivoting. He will rarely lose a foot race against an opponent. His top speed is superb and his lateral movements are just as good. He can turn on a dime, stop and start easily or twist and turn abruptly in a one-on-one confrontation to create space. He is blessed with amazing puck handling skills that he uses at top speed. Those two elements combined make him a constant threat when he is skating with the puck. Nathan is a great goal scorer and uses all his offensive abilities to find shooting lanes to get that strong and quick release wrist shot on net from just about anywhere. He will find soft areas quickly and always keeps his feet moving in the offensive zone. He excelled eluding defensive coverage; which is saying something, considering he was always paired against the opposing teams' best defensive duo. He has great passing skills, but is probably viewed as a goal scorer more than a playmaker. He will create plays on the rush and coming off a cycle, but has a shoot first mentality.

The Cole Harbour native is a fantastic competitor and he won't take a shift off, even in a tough game for the Mooseheads, you will never see Nathan MacKinnon gliding and taking it easy. He has a great work ethic. He will get the dirty goals in traffic, he will take a hit to make a play or retrieve a lose puck. MacKinnon can simplify the skills and speed game to a chippy North-South game and be as effective. He's a versatile performer. Defensively, Nathan MacKinnon is dedicated and he has progressed nicely in his play without the puck since his first game in the QMJHL. He still has the tendency to run around at times and use his magnificent skating abilities to be aggressive, but will sometimes lose his position in defensive coverage. His strength is great, which gives him solid balance on his skates, especially in situations where he needs to protect the puck. With his competitive nature and overall core strength, Nathan MacKinnon is tough to beat in a 1-on-1 battle, he will rarely give up. If he loses the puck he will work twice as hard to get it back. While not a menacing physical player, he can lay the body on occasion and he will engage a physical battle on the wall.

Mackinnon will sometimes put too much pressure on himself when things aren't going right. He will still work as hard as he can, but not wisely. He also could improve his game management, meaning the importance of choosing the right times to simplify his game. We think this will get better as he plays more defensive minutes. He was on such a stacked team in Halifax this year, he rarely had to do so.

MacKinnon's professional potential is huge. With the skill, speed and competitive nature he possesses he will become a highly dynamic point producer in the NHL. His work ethic and character should be huge factors for him when facing adversity. With more maturity there is no reason why Nathan MacKinnon won't live up to the hype.

Quotable: "He was our number one ranked player from wire to wire this year. Not only do I love his game on the ice, but I got to know Nathan a little bit this season, he is a quality kid. I think the thing that stands out the most for me, is how much he seems to just love the game combined with as much competitiveness as I have seen in a player. I wish he was going to be drafted to a team closer to home. I'd enjoy seeing him play live more often." - Mark Edwards

Maguire, Geordie – LW – Brandon Wheat Kings (WHL) – 6'0" 165

Maguire is a good skating forward with very limited offensive skills. He likes to play a chip and chase game and try to retrieve pucks and start a cycle. He does not accomplish much with the puck and does not manage the puck well, and makes poor decisions with it. He has a below average shot that is often off target if he ever comes down the wing with the puck, and is not often in the right areas in the slot to grab rebounds to score. Defensively, Maguire does not play with enough intensity to be effective in his own end. He is quick to loose pucks along the walls, but is not very committed to blocking shots. He has much to improve in all aspects of his game to even be an effective player at the junior level.

Makinen, Atte – RD – Tappara U20 (Jr A SM-liiga) – 6'3" 206

Makinen has worked his way up the Tappara program through the U16, U18 and U20's and even appeared in three SM-liiga games as a 16 year old last season. This year he played primarily with the U20's getting a brief experience in Finland's 2nd Men's league playing four games with LeKi. Makinen is a big physical defenseman who takes pleasure in punishing opponents. Atte has arguably one of the best combinations of size and the aggression to hit as often as possible you'll find in this draft. He is tough along the boards and wins a lot of battles. He is very strong in one on one situations and provides a good gap control and very rarely gets beaten. He can go through stretches where he's pretty quiet but that is a good thing for a defenseman who plays the type of game Makinen does. He isn't much of an offensive contributor but he has shown the ability to move the puck well and even a few flashes of puck rushing protecting the puck with his big frame when given space. He can however be susceptible to puck playing mistakes or mishandling it when pressured. What you see is what you get with Makinen. He's physical, reliable, but won't put up too much offensively.

Maletta, Jordan – RW – Niagara Ice Dogs (OHL) – 6'3" 215

Jordan was selected firs round, 13th overall at the 2011 OHL Priority Selection Draft by the Windsor Spitfires out of the St. Catharines Falcons Minor Midget program. Jordan got off to a very slow start with the Spitfires and struggled to find his comfort level in the OHL. He got a great chance in the World U-17 Challenge in front of his home team crowd in Windsor, but suffered a minor injury that limited him to only 2 games. He started to pick things up a bit and look like the player he had the potential to be. Entering the 2012-2013 season, Jordan really didn't elevate his game as expected and just never really looked comfortable out there. He was eventually traded to his hometown Niagara Ice Dogs and finished the season there. After registering 20 points in his first season, he followed that up with an identical 20 point season this year.

Maletta can move the puck around nicely in the offensive zone to find the open man in the slot for some good chances in tight and brings a good net-front presence as well. He will be most successful is to use his big frame much more forcefully to drive the puck to the net to create chances in tight and establish that he can be an effective role player with a solid physical edge as well. We don't see Jordan as player we would draft.

Malone, Sean – LC – US NTDP Under-18 Team – 5'11, 183

Sean plays a gritty style suited to a depth role, but his offensive game has shown gradual improvement. The stocky two-way center will suit up for Harvard in the fall. He's strong in front of the net in the offensive zone and fights for rebounds and loose pucks, as well as taking the pucks to the crease and fighting to score until the whistle blows. He's good at screening the goaltender and redirecting pucks. He also shows finesse from time to time with skill moves, but for the most part keeps things pretty simple. Though he's an average skater, he's strong on his feet and has a good motor that keeps him involved in the play. He forechecks, back checks, and shows the willingness to get involved physically, taking the body defensively and taking hits to make plays with the puck.

Malone is a bit of a wildcard as far as draft status, as it would not be a surprise if there were teams high on him and others who don't consider him a professional prospect. He lacks dynamic enough hands and feet to project him as a real offensive threat at the professional level, and though he has the aggressiveness to be an NHL bottom-six player, he lacks ideal size or speed for that role.

Quotable: " I'm not sure he got all that much better this year which is something that works against him. Having said that, I like his hockey sense and he is a solid PK guy." - Mark Edwards

Mansfield, Ian – FW – Sioux Falls Stampede (USHL) – 5'11" 188

Mansfield joined the USHL in 2011-2012 after he was picked in the 8th round and played his second season this year with the Sioux Falls Stampede, where he scored identical 11 point seasons back-to-back.

When Mansfield is at his best he demonstrates hard work at both ends of the ice and has stick skills to get around defenders then drive the puck to the net to create scoring chances from in tight. There are times however when he turns the puck over at the blue line trying to gain the offensive zone by attempting to dangle his way through the entire opposition and not protecting the puck.. He battles and competes pretty well for the puck, hustles hard to be the first one on loose pucks and can get a pretty good cycle going in deep in the offensive zone. He needs to get the puck out of his zone with more consistency on his chances along the boards and can't turn it over trying to pass through the neutral zone. He needs to be engaged in both ends of the ice and has to use his legs to his advantage

Mantha, Anthony – RW – Val D'Or Foreurs (QMJHL) – 6'3" 200

After having a breakout second half of season in the 2011-2012 season where he put his name on the radar for this year's draft, Anthony Mantha has impressed us again in 2012-2013, a season where he was the lone 50 goals scorer in the QMJHL.

The major strength of the big forward is his shot. He can release from just about anywhere in the offensive zone and create a scoring chance with it. It is very hard, quickly released and he has an amazing accuracy with it and is able to put pucks on net with the intention to create a rebound for teammates. He has mastered a great variety of shots also, scoring many goals with his slapshot or backhand, both very accurate. You don't score 50 goals without puttin pucks on net and Mantha directs a lot of pucks to the net whether it is 5-on-5 or on the powerplay or getting pucks through traffic. He is always trying to get at least one shot when he enters the offensive zone when there's no better option. Mantha uses his long reach well to get around players, get in the slot and play keep away with his opponents in tight spaces. He has good puck handling skills, but he is not the kind of player that will try to get through players with slick one-on-one moves. He will use his puck handling skills and good skating abilities to cut in the slot, delay plays and change his angles before taking a shot. He is a really solid player on skates and we like to see him use that frame to cut to the net and be aggressive. We would also like to see him throw the body more often as he tends to be playing on instincts when he presses but would be even more effective by using the body. He has one of the strongest upper bodies you will find for a player of his age, but needs to make a habit of using it.

Anthony Mantha is one of the smartest players available this year in the draft. His shot is one of the reasons he gets so many goals, but his intelligence on the ice is also a huge factor. He seems to know where the play is going before most players. He finds soft areas in the offensive zone very quickly and by doing so always make himself a passing option for a teammate. He has a shoot first mentality, but is also a great passer and has shown some great playmaking qualities in many of our viewings. His hockey sense is also well displayed in the defensive zone, placing his stick in a perfect position to create turnovers when he pressures opponents, reads the play quickly and anticipates like few can. He always seems to be a step ahead of his opponents, even in the defensive zone.

As talented and smart as Mantha may be, one big setback is his work ethic. On some nights, Anthony Mantha will hit, back check, skate hard and win his 1-on-1 battles. However, on most of our viewings, he will rely on his talent and stay out of the play, will be easy to push of the puck in a battle, even against a smaller player and will tend to glide a lot, trying to use hockey sense only to win back the possession of the puck. The lack of competitiveness and character has been very worrying for us in our viewings of Mantha. He doesn't seem to have a high care level for the win or loss of his team as he has shown those bad habits in critical game situations. He can also start cheating and stop caring about his own zone. He knows how to play well in his own zone, but doesn't always want to. His speed needs to get better especially his explosoin, he has nice long strides to get his top speed but not very good at stops and starts because of the poor explosion. His top speed is fairly good for the upper level and displays agility when doing lateral movements.

Mantha has tremendous upsides but also huge downsides, so he's a pretty risky pick for this year's draft. If the work ethic issues can be resolved, there are no doubts that with the shot and intelligence he has, Anthony Mantha can be a steady goal scorer in professional hockey.

Quotable: "Love him when he has the puck on his stick. I'm not his biggest fan when he doesn't. Looks like a boom or bust guy to me." - Mark Edwards

Quotable: "He reminds me of Benoit Pouliot." - NHL scout

Martin, Jon – RC – Kootenay Ice (WHL) – 6'2" 201

Martin is a physical forward who does not make much of an impact in games on the 3rd line. He possesses above average speed, but his acceleration needs some work. He is willing to sacrifice his body when necessary and make his presence known with his hits on the forecheck, but he has to improve on his speed to close in on opponents more quickly. Offensively, Martin is not very good with the puck. He struggles to make good plays as he shows very limited poise and skill. He is good off the cycle because of his big body, but when he has the puck his option is usually to throw it around the net and hope for the best. Martin just does not make enough impact in the course of a game to warrant any legitimate interest in the NHL Entry Draft at this time.

Martin, Spencer – G – Mississauga Steelheads (OHL) – 6'2.25" 198

Martin got off to a flying start this season and was a huge factor in his teams early success. He is am agile kid with good recovery skills. He does a pretty good job of making himself big and staying square to the shooter. His recovery skills are good although sometimes he seems to overplay a few shots when he goes across his net.
Martin is technically sound and combines that with his great size.. A friend of mine coached him for two years leading up to his OHL draft selection. He raved about both Martin the goalie and the person.

McAdam, Eamon – G – Waterloo Blackhawks (USHL) – 6'2" 182

Eamon got his developmental push out of Team Comcast in 2009-2010 where he made the jump to the junior hockey ranks splitting time between the USHL's Waterloo Blackhawks and the NAHL's Austin Bruins. Eamon received a fair amount of starts for a player who was just 16 to start the season in 2011-2012 and increased his starts again this year getting a lot of exposure and recognition early thanks to his participation at the Junior Club World Cup in August. Eamon has proven to cover the lower part of the net very well. He gets around post to post moderately well and shows good second effort on rebounds. He struggles a little with high shots because he has a tendency to go down a little too early. McAdam also benefitted from playing at the World Jr. A Challenge. Eamon is slated to join Penn State University this fall of 2013.

McCarron, Michael – RW – US NTDP Under-18 Team – 6'5, 229

The hulking, Western Michigan commit is one of the more polarizing players in this draft class. He tantalizes with physical tools and displays of impressive strength but lacks enough consistency, particularly in regards to offensive ability, to label him as a top prospect. He puck-watches too much in the offensive zone when he should be using his size and strength to cause havoc and draw attention. It's easy to look at a big player and wish for more of an edge, that road has been well trod and often ends in disappointment, but even if he were 5'10", he would still be too passive. For a player of his size, he loses 50/50 battles too often and doesn't pursue loose pucks with enough intensity. He has games where he relishes contact and takes it upon himself to hit to hurt, but needs to play like that all the time. He protects the puck extremely well along the boards but doesn't show much creativity with it and has a hard time penetrating into scoring chance areas.

Though he does well to take advantage of what he's given on the ice, he hasn't shown the ability to create his own space. His skating is average, he builds speed like a cruise ship with slow first steps but can eventually get going and is very difficult to stop when he does get to stride. Hockey sense is the big question here. He has the tools, but it remains to be seen whether he has the fundamental understanding of the game to be a successful professional. Adding a bit more mystique to his situation is the fact that his OHL rights are owned by London, who are lobbying to bring him on board for next season. The hard-nosed Hunters won't settle for anything but his best effort, and could be just what he needs to right his ship.

Quotable: "NHL Scouts I spoke to had Mike anywhere from an early second rounder to 3rd round or later. I spoke to him at length at the combine and he impressed me with his honesty about his game. We spoke a lot about his team of choice next season, including his visit to London for game 5 of the OHL Finals. My gut feel after our chat is that he will be in London next season but I honestly feel that as of now it's still up in the air. His interview with me rose his stock a bit." - Mark Edwards

McCoshen, Ian – LD – Waterloo Blackhawks (USHL) – 6'3" 207

The smooth, Boston College-bound defenseman plays a seasoned game and is a calming presence on the blueline. He's a fluid skater, especially for his size. He lacks top-end speed but his positioning is so sound that he rarely needs to churn his legs. He has a long stick that he uses well to cover the rush and cover lanes in his zone. He plays with an edge, making it difficult for forwards to gain net front positioning on him, roughing it up along the boards, and lining up big hits when the opportunity presents itself. He's steady and relaxed on the penalty kill, maintaining a presence without chasing the play. He protects his goalie and teammates, coming to their aid after whistles. He will drop the mitts when necessary.

He has a good point shot that he's not afraid to use and can get the puck on net through traffic. When necessary, he makes the safe play from his end but can also carry the puck out or stretch the play with long bombs. He likes to join the rush and picks his spots well, and also pinches aggressively in the offensive zone. He can run a power play and brings the puck up ice well with good reach and hands, though he lacks the dynamic offensive ability to be a major point-producer at the professional level. He plays with a lot of poise but at times lacks proper urgency when pressured by a strong forecheck and can be forced into errors. McCoshen has tools to be a top four defenseman in the NHL.

McCue, Beau – RW – Tri-City Americans (WHL) – 6'1" 200

McCue is a big two way forward with above average speed. He displays good intelligence on the defensive side of the game on the forecheck, and is able to create some turnovers with his anticipation and good stick. He could use his big frame more often to create turnovers and provide a physical presence. Offensively, McCue has limited skills. He does not have a great shot to overwhelm goaltenders, and is not able to find open areas out on the ice very well. He provides a nice presence along the walls with his big body and quickness to be able to cut off any clear attempts off the boards. He possesses limited playmaking skills, and could learn to take his time with the puck as he often has more time than he thinks. He also does not have very good hands, and even has difficulty handling hard outlet passes. McCue has not really developed his game all season long, and will need to really work on all aspects of his game if he ever wants to continue his career after his junior eligibility runs out.

McGauley, Tim – LC – Brandon Wheat Kings (WHL) – 6'0" 177

Tim McGauley is a playmaking centre who displays good confidence and poise with the puck. He is at his best when he plays with a lot of energy and when he is moving his feet to create some room for himself and his teammates. He is a good skater out in open ice, and looks very poised when carrying the puck. McGauley has shown the ability to be a dangerous passer from the half wall on the power play. He can take advantage of open seams cross ice and quickly exploit it with a tape to tape pass. He is not a particularly good goal scorer as he has a difficult time finding open areas in the offensive zone and does not really go to the net. Another aspect of McGauley's game that he must improve is his defensive game. He is far too lazy in his own end, and does not play with much intensity along the walls. He is poor at covering opponents in the slot, and especially down low if he defensemen ever needs help. He looks quite lost in his own end often.

NHL teams will have some interest in McGauley due to his playmaking skills, but there are many areas of his game that needs a lot of improvement, particularly his work ethic. He will need to work much harder without the puck to be a bigger factor in games, and to not be a liability every time he is in his own end.

McGlynn, Conor – FW – Sioux City Musketeers (USHL) – 6'2" 193

McGlynn was selected in the 4th round by Sioux City and he played for the Oakville blades in the OJHL before joining the Musketeers for 5 games last season. He then played his first full year in the USHL this year and had 10 points in 48 games including 74 penalty minutes and got the opportunity to play in the USHL top prospects game.

McGlynn has great size and is a player who will put excellent pressure and physicality on the puck carrier, finishing all his hits along the boards. He uses his body really effectively to protect the puck from the opposition's pressure and possesses good strength to rush the puck up the ice end-to-end. He battles well for the puck along the boards, gets it deep to start a really great cycle and does possess some decent hands to get around defenders to create some space to make a play. However he has the size, strength and sense of how to play a blue collar game which demonstrates that he can be effective in a different capacity

McIntosh, Jeremy – LD – Spokane Chiefs (WHL) – 6'2" 190

McIntosh is a tough, depth defenseman who likes to throw his body around to make the life of opposing forwards so difficult. He loves to be aggressive along the walls and on the blue line, and there are times when he gets caught in a terrible position, and he has a difficult time recovering because of his poor skating abilities. His acceleration and overall speed really needs to improve, as opponents will take advantage of his lack of speed all game long. McIntosh's puck moving abilities are not very good, and he has a very tough time making any decent passes. His impact from the blue line is quite limited and rarely ever has a chance to do anything with the puck. His potential to play at a higher level is very limited, and he will really have to work on his game if he will ever contribute even at the junior level.

McLaughlin, Dylan – FW – Cedar Rapids RoughRiders (USHL) – 5'10" 171

McLaughlin played for the Buffalo Regals in Minor Midget before being drafted in the 1st round, 9th overall into the USHL Futures Draft by the Sioux Falls Stampede. He played his rookie season in the USHL in the 2011-2012 season, where he scored 7 points in 48 games then came to Cedar Rapids to play in 46 games this year where he increased his offensive production by scoring 15 points.

McLaughlin is a decent defensive forward who comes back really well on the back-check to provide his team with support in his own end and he battles hard for the puck. He can tie up his man and puts really good pressure on the puck carrier. He competes hard for the puck in the corners to force turnovers and gets his stick down in lanes to breakup passes and opportunities for the opposition. He plays a pretty simple dump and chase style off the rush but has the ability to make some good passes to find teammates in tight to the goal for chances.

McLaughlin knows his role on the team very well, keeps to a simple defensively minded game and takes care of business in his own end. He puts pressure on the puck all over the ice and gets the puck in deep to avoid bad turnovers for the most part through the neutral zone. There are times when he has the puck and has the opportunity to make a play but chips it in deep instead of trying to make the pass in order to keep it safe, and needs to have a little bit more confidence in himself to try and create some offense once in a while. Dylan was also selected by the Brampton Battalion in the 7th round of the 2011 OHL Priority Selection Draft and is committed to Providence College.

McNulty, Marc – LD – Prince George Cougars (WHL) – 6'6" 189

McNulty is a big defensive defenseman who plays a simple, but effective game. He has limited puck handling abilities, and will make the most impact in games in his own end with his long reach and strong play along the walls. Opponents have a difficult time trying to get around McNulty off the rush. He is not very quick, but he covers a lot of ground with his long legs and reach. He gives opponents plenty of room off the rush because of his lack of speed. He is physical along the boards and is difficult to knock off the puck. McNulty has a good stick to knock away pucks from the slot, and protects his goaltender well. He does not play with much of a mean streak, and only displays an average level of hockey intelligence. He does not look particularly confident in his play, and definitely looks like he will need some more seasoning to reach his potential.

Offensively, McNulty's game is very limited. His poise with the puck is questionable, and does not make very good outlet passes. He does not take a long look to see if anybody is open, and just quickly fires it away as soon as he feels pressure. He does not make himself available for a shot from the point, and does not possess a great shot either. There is certainly potential in McNulty to become a depth defenseman in the NHL one day. He will have to try to improve his skating while playing with more confidence and a bit of an edge to take advantage of his size. A team could take a chance on him and give him plenty of time to develop into a serviceable player.

Melanson, Drew – FW – Omaha Lancers (USHL) – 5'10" 160

Drew is an excellent skater that shows flashes offensively, but has yet to put it all together. He shows great first-step quickness with a smooth stride and a high top speed. He can stickhandle well and shows good agility in evading contact, but makes poor decisions with the puck too frequently and tries to do too much by himself. He could stand to spend more time in the corners and in front of the net, and needs to bulk up further to be effective there. He shows good forecheck ability on some shifts, using his skating to pressure and laying the body when appropriate. He will suit up for RPI starting in the fall.

Merkley, Jay – RC – Swift Current Broncos (WHL) – 5'11" 187

Jay Merkley is an excellent skating centre who has a lot of speed to burn. He can get to point A to B in a hurry, and it is difficult to find many players in the league who can match him stride for stride in a race. However, Merkley has not been able to use his speed effectively to make an impact on a nightly basis for his team. At the beginning of the season, Merkley was a part of the Lethbridge Hurricanes, but in the middle of the year, they decided to trade him away because of work ethic issues and a lack of development. Merkley initially had a good start with Swift Current, but he slowly started to struggle to be relevant in games again. He floats around far too often, and has a difficult time making any sort of a difference for his team whenever he is out on the ice. When he is at his best, he is always moving his feet, getting into the forecheck and creating turnovers. He has shown limited vision and scoring abilities throughout the season. He is also difficult to trust in defensive situations because he does not show the necessary will and toughness to be a responsible player.

Millette, Cory – LW – Red Deer Rebels (WHL) – 5'11" 188

Millette is a speedy, depth winger for the Rebels. He really takes advantage of his quickness to try to generate offense. He possesses average stick handling abilities, but is not afraid to try to deke out opponents to get to the net. He is not very big, but does a good job of using his body to protect the puck and be effective along the wall. The issue with Millette is his inability to find open areas to score, and a lack of playmaking ability. He does not get much accomplished throughout a game at both ends of the ice. He is not counted on to contribute in crucial situations during a game, and his job is simply to not be liable for a goal against when he is on the ice.

Milne, Brody – LW – Guelph Storm (OHL) – 6'1" 157

Brody was selected in the 4th round of the 2011 OHL Priority Selection Draft by the Guelph Storm out of the Halton Hurricanes Minor Midget program. Brody split the 2011-2012 season with the Guelph Jr. Storm Major Midget AAA team and the Guelph Hurricanes Jr. B team showing some offensive and physical potential scoring 44 goals and 165 penalty minutes in Midget AAA hockey. Milne made the Storm but struggled to consistently get into the Storm lineup this season for a number of reasons. When dressed, Milne primarily played a depth forward role for the Storm. He is good on the fore check and works well with line mates generating a cycle and controlling puck possession deep in the offensive zone. He is reliable in the defensive zone and shows a willingness to take a hit or block a shot to make a play. Brody showed flashes of offensive skill driving to the net and finishing rebound opportunities. Milne is at his best when he is consistently finishing checks and working hard up and down the wing. He should see his ice time improve in 2013-2014. We don't expect Milne to be selected in the 2013 NHL Entry Draft

Monahan, Sean – LC – Ottawa 67's (OHL) – 6'2.25" 187

Monahan was a bright spot on a team that did not have very much of that this season. He projects to be a top ten pick in the 2013 NHL Entry Draft and we believe he has the potential to be selected in the top five. He was drafted 16th overall by the Ottawa 67s at the 2010 OHL Priority Selection Draft out of the Mississauga Rebels Minor Midget program. He made the 67's in his 16 year old season and represented Ontario in the World U-17 Hockey Challenge. Sean went into his sophomore season looking to make an impact and with the departure of key players along with a few injuries, Monahan was launched into the spotlight and did an incredible job helping Ottawa capture the 2012 East Division Title. Due to his late birth date he was ineligible for the draft in his second season and needed to return to Ottawa where his 67's were in full rebuild mode. He was named co-captain of the Ottawa 67s at the beginning of the year with Cody Ceci and he also got an invite to Canada's World Junior team and was a late cut.

Monahan has demonstrated the ability to take control of a game and become a factor in every offensive opportunity that takes place when he is on the ice. He possesses incredible patience with the puck that allows him to get to the slot with the puck and find time and space to work with. He has a very accurate shot that can beat goaltenders clean without traffic in front of the net off the rush which is one reason why he has scored 84 goals in his first 3 seasons in the OHL. It is also a tribute to his positioning as he can slip in and out of areas in the offensive zone undetected and always seems to be in the absolute idea positioning. He has solid speed to come off the wing then lets his deadly shot go and can pick his spots with ease. He has great hands and moves with the puck to create space and cycles the puck very effectively to be able to come off the boards and walk out to the slot for shots on net. He has great offensive instincts to be able to find space then open up to provide his teammates with a scoring option but can also move the puck around well in the offensive zone to create chances. He can find an open man in the slot and get him the puck and also moves it well to find a trailing player in the high slot off the rush. He gets to the front of the net on the power play for opportunities in tight and positions himself properly in both ends of the ice, demonstrating he is a 200-foot player. The 67's coaching staff recognized this and used him both on the power play and the penalty kill throughout the season. On the penalty kill he gets his stick in lanes to deflect passes out of danger and in his own end he can make good breakout passes to start the rush with speed.

Monahan projects to be a top six forward at the NHL level and should become a complete centre who plays hard in all three zones. He may need another year at the junior level to continue developing. However it wouldn't be a surprise to see him get a 9 game tryout and see where it goes from there. If he does return to junior, he will likely be a critical part of the potential success of Canada at the 2014 World Junior Championships.

Quotable: "One of my favorite players in the draft. His maturity level is off the charts. I feel like I could easily be speaking to someone 10 years older when I speak with him. I think it speaks volumes about him by how he handled this season with a very weak 67's team. I expect him to be gone at pick number 5 to Carolina. If they pass on him, he will surely go to Calgary. Sorry Edmonton. - Mark Edwards

Moore, Trevor – LW – Tri-City Storm (USHL) – 5'9 170

Trevor is a flashy offensive talent with good skating and puck skills. He's an excellent stick handler and uses his quickness to dart around defenders, though lacks the extra gear that you'd like to see for a player of his stature and he can be weak on the puck against heavy coverage. His offensive zone positioning is solid and he is able to find soft spots in coverage to get open for shots, but has a hard time fighting for position in front of the net due to his lack of strength. He shoots the puck well with hard, accurate wrister shots and one-timers. He frequently tries to do too much by himself with the puck. His defensive game needs work, but he's active on the forecheck with a good stick and shows decent penalty killing positioning. Despite his strength he has also finished some checks effectively. Though he's an excellent junior forward, he hasn't shown that he has the evasiveness necessary to predict him as a major scoring threat at the NHL level.

Morin, Samuel – LD – Rimouski Océanic (QMJHL) – 6'6" 203

The giant defender will interest many NHL teams at the 2013 draft and there's no question he has a lot of attractive tools for the next level, but we would still qualify Samuel Morin as a project.
At 6'6" and 203 pounds, Morin is an intimidating force on the back end. He improved his footwork this year, thus making it easier for him to play an aggressive, mean and physical game. You know it will hurt to go in a battle down-low with the big defenseman. He will pin you to the board easily and use his long reach to eliminate time and space from skilled players. He got over 100 penalty minutes this season, while he should cut down on undisciplined penalties. He was involved in many scrums, roughing situations in front of the net and fights, displaying his physical side well. He executes well the position game defensively, he blocks a lot of shots and covers a lot of space in slot coverage and he chooses the right moments to press the opposition most times showing good defensive hockey sense. He skates with long strides, making him a good forward skater. He has above-average puck control and agility offensively for a big man. He doesn't hesitate to be aggressive on the pinch, shows great confidence controlling the puck at the blue line and possesses a quality, low wrist shot with good accuracy.

Like most 17 year old defensemen his size, Samuel Morin still has a lot to improve before playing in the big league. Backward skating and gap control are still issues for him although it has progressed nicely in 2012-2013. He still has a hard time dealing with explosive skaters when they come out wide on him because he lacks backward speed and lateral mobility. Aquiring better explosiveness and overall skating abilities will help him play an even more aggressive game in all 3 zones. We would also like to see him take fewer undisciplined penalties, Morin has put his team in trouble more than once during the season with these. He still needs to put some pounds on to fill in that frame completely. With the size, mean streak and surprisingly good offensive potential he has, Samuel Morin is surely an interesting project for this year's draft.

Quotable: "Morin has come a long way since last year, more mean and more confident with the puck. Still does have occasional brain cramps that make you scratch your head but his upside is as high as any defensemen from the QMJHL. Its rare to see 6'7 defensemen has mobile as this kid." – Jerome Berube

Quotable: "I saw him early in the season and he had some shifts where he flashed smart play and skill. The problem was the other half of his shifts where brain cramps led to very poor play. I was impressed with him on big ice in Russia. He still had some weak plays on the puck and had made some poor puck decisions but I saw an improved player. If that upward trend continues he will be a valuable prospect." – Mark Edwards

Morrissey, Josh – LD – Prince Albert Raiders (WHL) – 6'0" 185

Morrissey is a poised, puck moving defenseman who has quarterbacked the power play for Prince Albert for the last 2 seasons. He has a solid overall game, and while he may not be the biggest player, he will catch opponents with their head down in the neutral zone whenever he gets the opportunity. No matter how much pressure Morrissey may face when he has the puck, he always seems to find a way to either calmly skate it out of trouble, or quickly spin away from an opponent and make a laser beam, tape to tape pass to his forward to start the attack. He possesses very impressive vision on the point, and time and time again seems to be able to make difficult passes and threads the needle to go cross ice for good scoring chances. Not only does he have elite passing ability, he is able to read the play quickly and take advantage of any mistakes opponents make or be creative with the puck. He has a good shot from the point that he could use more. He walks the line with ease, and keeps his head up to unleash his shot when he sees an open lane, or to make a pass if an opponent cheats to take his shot away.

Defensively, Morrissey gives opponents very little room to work with. His skating abilities allow him to cover a large area, and his gap control is excellent off the rush. He has a good stick to knock away passes and to take away passing lanes. He does not chase the play, and looks calm under pressure. He also forces opponents to keep their head up and enter the neutral zone with caution because of his ability to step up and land good open ice hits. He quickly sees an opportunity to dish out a hit, and closes the gap in a hurry. The one area of improvement for Morrissey would be his strength. He has a hard time maintaining body position against bigger opponents in the slot, and may have a hard time tying up bigger and physically mature players at the pro level.

Morrissey's consistent level of excellence on the ice could allow his name to be called in the first round of the NHL Entry Draft. It is rare to find a defenseman of his age who is can make such an impact with the puck while not sacrificing his defensive game at all. Teams will have to wait a few years until he could be ready to play in the NHL, but with the proper development, Morrissey can surely turn into a valuable top 4 defenseman one day.

Quotable: "I saw him shut down more than one top line in my viewings. That's a nice addition to his offense." - NHL Scout

Quotable: "I have been a fan since the U17 in Windsor. More recently I liked him in Sochi. We dropped him slightly since our last ranking in February. I wanted to see him win a few more battles physically to show me potential in that area of his game. I had a phone conversation with Josh earlier this season and he was one of the more impressive prospects I have spoken to over the years." - Mark Edwards

Motte, Tyler – LW – US NTDP Under-18 Team – 5'9, 184

Tyler is a shifty two-way forward who can do a lot of things for a hockey team. His skating is outstanding, with fantastic acceleration and agility. He tends to be the first player in on the forecheck and doesn't neglect his own zone either, using great wheels to get back and help his defense. His penalty killing is excellent with sound positioning and a good work ethic, and he's a threat to score shorthanded. He plays physical and doesn't shy away from contact but is limited by his size and sometimes when throwing a hit ends up getting the worst of it. He can make plays with the puck on the rush but at times has trouble creating in the offensive zone. He works well in a cycle, is strong on the puck, and has good hands to go along with a pretty decent shot, but his lack of strength can be a factor against bigger players and he can be shut down completely.

Though Motte is an easy player to like, he's hard to project. Consistency is a major concern, as he can disappear for periods or games at a time. He also appears to have a short fuse and was an easy target for pesky opponents who like to agitate opponents. As detailed, his size is the biggest concern. If he's two inches taller, he's potentially a first round talent, but he may not be big enough to handle the rigors of NHL play at both ends of the rink.

Moutrey, Nick – RW – Saginaw Spirit (OHL) – 6'3" 208

Nick was one of our favorite players to watch in Minor Midget and was selected in the first round 15th Overall at the 2011 OHL Priority Selection Draft by the Saginaw Spirit out of the York-Simcoe Express program. Nick played regularly on the fourth line as a 16 year old, getting brief promotions up to the third line due to strong play or injuries to other players.

Nick really improved over the summer and was used primarily in a second line role. He displays great physicality and usually finishes his checks. Nick is a surprisingly good skater for his size and gets around fairly quickly. He wins battles along the boards and works hard winning more than his share of battles. He is surprisingly creative and can beat defensemen one on one and possesses a strong shot. Nick isn't a flashy player, or a player who brings a lot of attention to himself but he works hard and shows a lot of tools that are intriguing to Nick's potential success at the pro level.

Nick has been pretty effective in his own zone getting in passing lanes, getting in front of shots and clearing the zone well. His final numbers were a little concerning to us considering how well he played and the amount of ice he received. He needs to continue to play his game on a more consistent basis.

Nick should be a lock a to be picked at the 2013 NHL Entry Draft. At his highest potential, Nick could become a second line power forward as he possesses a good shot, and intelligent positioning. However a more safer projection, but what could see him drop in lists is the expectation that Nick will develop into a bottom six forward who plays hard on the boards, wins battles, chips in a little offensively and uses his size.

Moy, Tyler – FW – Omaha Lancers (USHL) – 6'1" 178

The California native plays a respectable two-way game, but is still looking to establish himself at the USHL level. He's a strong skater with a good frame and good playmaking skills. He shows good poise with the puck and shows good passing vision. He has a good wrister but doesn't utilize it enough. He has a hard time getting himself into dangerous positions in the offensive zone as he lacks the assertiveness and strength to outmuscle defenders. He shows good back checking ability with the stick skill to pickpocket but overall his defensive positioning needs work and he tends to chase the play in his zone. He has good tools but is still very raw and lacking killer instinct. He'll suit up for Harvard starting in the fall.

Mueller, Mirco – LD – Everett Silvertips (WHL) – 6'4" 185

The development of Mueller throughout this season has been intriguing to track. He certainly showed potential with his hockey intelligence with and without the puck, but his biggest flaw was the lack of physical play, particularly around the walls and in the slot. He was often pushed around easily, and played much smaller than he actually was. However, it is safe to say that Mueller has greatly improved that area of his game, which has made him one of the biggest risers in the WHL this year for the 2013 NHL Entry Draft.

Mueller's play with the puck is quite underrated. People rave about how good he is defensively, but often forget how good he is when the puck is on his stick. He makes excellent first passes out of the zone, and rarely tries to force a pass to his forwards. He takes his time to read the play, and if he does not have an outlet option, he softly puts it off the glass and into the neutral zone for his forwards to chase after it and try to win a battle for the puck. He receives a lot of time on the PP for Everett, and gets in good position on the blue line, and makes good, smart passes. Mueller could use his slap shot more to keep opponents on their toes however.

Defensively, Mueller is so difficult to play against. He has such a good stick, that opponents have a tough time doing anything when they are on his side of the ice with the puck. He will quickly knock away pucks, and keep everything to the outside. His gap control is very good, and he is able to give opposing forwards very little room because of his great skating abilities. Mueller possesses very good speed for his size, and has nice, quick feet to stick to opponents along the boards. The biggest improvement Mueller made in his game is his toughness. He will not be counted on to stick up for teammates anytime soon, but he looks very strong along the boards, and will not let anybody take him off his game with their forecheck. Mueller plays a very composed game, and will deliver good body checks when he gets the opportunity.

If Mirco Mueller continues to develop his overall game, there is an excellent chance that he will carve out a long, but quiet career in the NHL and be a player that can be depended on in every situation for his team.

Quotable: "He is pretty limited as far as PP ability goes. He plays very smart hockey and does little things well. He struggled on a few shifts in Sochi under some forecheck pressure. That surprised me a little bit. If he had power play ability, he would be up our rankings for sure. I think he can still play a lot of NHL minutes." - Mark Edwards

Quotable: "I love him. Smart and a solid top four in the NHL." - NHL Scout

Quotable: "At the start of the year he was pushed around far too often and he didn't use his size to his advantage. Fast forward to the end of the year, and he is a key piece to the Silvertips' success. He could be a premier shut down defenseman in the NHL one day." - Charles An

Murphy, Matt – LD – Halifax Mooseheads (QMJHL) – 6'1" 200

Matt Murphy has shown the two sides of his game this season, one where he makes poor decisions and is all about offense, will join the rush and cause multiple turnovers carelessly. The good side of Murphy is when he plays a cautious game, waiting for the right times to rush the puck and effectively uses his skating skills. He has good skating abilities for his size, but could work on his explosiveness as he can be beat by quick skaters going out wide. His top speed is impressive and he has displayed the great forward speed he poseses multiple times when rushing the puck. Murphy will play a punishing physical game at times, but has lacked consistency in this area over the whole season. Murphy has a pretty good shot that he doesn't release enough from the blue line, especially when he can set it up on the one-timer. A confident puckhandler, Murphy prefers to pass the puck and use his offensive awareness to find teammates. While we like the offensive potential, we feel Murphy's work in his defensive zone is still just average. He has progressed nicely with the Mooseheads in the 2nd half of the season, but his defensive hockey sense still is lacking. He will make poor decisions with the puck, get attracted by the puck, loosing his positioning and will be aggressive at the wrong times. He's not an easy opponent to beat on the boards, but again will get eluded by good puckhandler's because of his attraction to the puck. We feel Murphy is a high risk pick because of this weakness. If he gets picked in the later rounds of the draft, he should be considered an offensive defenseman project with good size.

Quotable: "There was a weekend this year where Matt may have played himself right off some NHL teams lists. He simply couldn't handle any sort of forecheck pressure. A game in Gatineau turned into a nightmarish day. I'll give him credit for improving his play as the season moved along. - Mark Edwards

Murphy, Trevor – LD – Windsor Spitfires (OHL) – 5'10" 173

Trevor was a high end offensive defenseman in Minor Midget, frequently pairing up with current Barrie Colts defenseman Aaron Ekblad. He scored 39 goals with the Sun County Panthers and was ultimately selected in the third round by the Peterborough Petes (OHL). After receiving a fair amount of ice time in a little over a year in Peterborough, he did not appear to be a good fit on that team. The Petes then dealt him to his hometown Windsor Spitfires and Murphy showed a great amount of improvement over the second half of the season. Sometimes this happens where a player just isn't the right fit in one organization and fits the mould of another. Murphy is a defenseman who is used in offensive and defensive situations, but his greatest strength may be his skating ability. He controls the puck well in the offensive zone and he has a pretty effective point shot.

He has been hit or miss in the defensive zone. He battles hard and shows good compete but he is fairly small and will need to get stronger. His positioning has been very hit or miss. He's made the ideal play at times, but also been way out of position. His greatest area of improvement is patience with the puck. He can be pressured into making many mental errors from turnovers to icings to shooting the puck over the glass when he's under heavy pressure. He needs to use his skating ability to create more time and make safer options when he's pressured. While there are a lot of things stacked against Trevor, he shows some good abilities and improved greatly from our October viewings to our March viewings.

Quotable: "Watched him a ton while still with the Petes and he really struggled. He was hanging his partner out to dry causing odd man rushes. He struggled in his own zone. I thought he was better in all facets of his game after the trade to Windsor." - Mark Edwards

Mylchreest, Michael – RD – Prince George Cougars (WHL) – 6'3" 198

Mylchreest is a defensive defenseman who receives limited minutes of play. He provides a good defensive presence when he is out on the ice with his calm style. He is not very physical, but seems to wait for the play to come to him before he makes a move. He is not very strong on his skates, and his play along the walls is not very good. He is good at poking pucks away with his good reach and does not give opponents much in the slot. Mylchreest is an average skater, but will have troubles with quick players in the corners. He does not react particularly quickly, and will need to improve on his starts and stops and quick turns. Offensively, Mylchreest is quite limited. His breakout passes are below average, and needs to work on handling the puck more efficiently and with much more poise. He doe not like to hold onto the puck, and quickly gets rid of it without much thought.

Nastasiuk, Zach – RW – Owen Sound Attack (OHL) – 6'1.25" 190

Nastasiuk was selected the Owen Sound Attack's 1st round (20th Overall) selection at the 2011 OHL Priority Selection Draft from the Barrie Colts Minor Midget program. Zach got off to a bit of a slow start to his career however by the middle of the year, Zach was starting to show what he could do providing a powerful shot and scoring a few nice goals. This season Zach got off to another slow start and just as he got going he went down with a shoulder injury missing most of October. Once he returned to the lineup, Zach started to heat up and only got better as the season went on. He shows a great compete level along the boards and as he got stronger he began to win even more battles. He controls the puck well and can stickhandle around opponents. He is also a very strong puck protector and uses this ability very well to maintain control or get a little extra time to make a decision with the puck. He loves to shoot the puck and has a very quick reaction time around the net which was key to him reaching the 20 goal mark in his sophomore season with Owen Sound.

While he plays a power game in regard to protecting the puck, playing in the dirty areas, he's not overly physical and he rarely takes a penalty. Zach's penalty killing ability has greatly improved throughout this season. He's intelligent position wise and always gets his stick in the lanes. His quick reaction pays off here as well allowing him to clear the zone when his team is under pressure. He has also sacrificed the body to block shots. So the question is why is a player we regard so highly ranked as low as he is? It all comes down to his skating ability. While he shows the potential to be a very good two-way forward at the next level, he not only has to overcome his skating ability but he will have a very long route to get here. He has trouble with balance, stumbles regularly and has trouble keeping up with the play, not because his talent doesn't allow him to, but because his skating isn't strong enough at times for him to be effective in high speed back and forth action. This needs to be the superior focus in his development process as it will likely hold the key to whether or not he can play at the NHL level. We would not be the least bit surprised to see a team who feels that his skating can be easily corrected to select him late in the first round. We hope he can overcome his skating because he has all the other tools to make him a successful player at the next level.

Quotable: "I think I had more conversations with NHL scouts about Zach than any other player in the draft. In short, we all love so much about his game but are scared off by how far away his skating is at this point of his development. Most NHL guys I spoke to are fans of the kid and watched him extra games to view his skating. As recently as in Sochi, most still thought skating was a large issue. I liked so much about the rest of his game I found myself hoping the skating would be better each time I saw him. The only other thing that stands out for me is that he needs some 'nasty' in his game. He's wins puck battles but I want to see a bit more of an edge in his game. In the end, If you put the skating aside, He's got size, he competes hard and most importantly he's smart" - Mark Edwards

Quotable: "I really like him as a player, he does a lot of good things, but I think his skating just too far away for me." NHL Scout

Quotable: "I saw him last week, have you seen him recently? He looked fantastic in a game versus Oshawa." NHL Scout

Needham, Matt – RC – Kamloops Blazers (WHL) – 5'10" 187

Needham is an undersized, speedy forward who has shown some nice playmaking abilities this year. He plays the game at a very quick pace, and is good at generating chances off the rush with his speed and quick decision making. One concerning area of Needham's game is his inconsistency. There are nights when he disappears and provides 0 impact, and then there are times when he looks inspired to put up points and help his team win. This year's playoffs is a great example of how effective he could be if he plays hard every night. At his best, Needham goes hard into the forecheck, creates turnovers in the neutral zone and starts an odd man rush. He plays with an edge and is not afraid to attack the net and get into scrums after the whistle. Needham's play along the wall will have to improve if he ever wants to play as a pro. He will have to be quicker to slip away from checks, and buy more time for his teammates to get open. He will also have to be able to tie up opponents along the wall in the defensive zone, and continue to improve his play without the puck.

Nemecek, David – LD – Sarnia Sting (OHL) – 6'4" 206

David came over from Czech Republic this season in the import draft. David developed in the HC Plzen organization and joined their U18 program at age 16 after getting a few games in as a 15 year old. He also competed for team Czech Republic in the World Under 17 Challenge. David came over and while he had an awkward skating stride he was moderately quick for a 6'4" defenseman. He isn't very physical but when he chooses to hit he gets a lot of power into his contact. He is willing to battle and puts in the work in his own end. He's not the strongest, quickest or smartest but he will give you 100% when pursuing forwards.

Due to the depth on Sarnia's blueline David saw himself sitting in the stands for half of Sarnia's games this season which hindered his development and his adjustment to the North American game. He was hit or miss in a lot of areas primarily playing forwards one on one, battles in front of the net and in his puck playing decisions. We saw him both make some solid reliable passes and some really bad ones that resulted in turnovers.

We do not expect David to be selected by a team this year. However we feel that if he can get himself into a situation where he's getting a lot of ice at the CHL level he may be able to eventually turn into a solid defenseman. However the only thing that's going to help him at this point is ice and lots of it.

Nichols, Justin – G – Sault Ste. Marie Greyhounds (OHL) – 5'11" 150

Justin was selected in the 3rd round of the 2011 OHL Priority Selection Draft out of the St. Catharines Falcons Minor Midget program. Justin spent the 2011-2012 season with Salisbury Prep High School showing off his potential. Nichols then joined the Greyhounds and had a very strong rookie season as a backup for the Greyhounds and put on some very solid performances. Nichols worked hard down the stretch and was reliable in the second half of the season helping to clinch a playoff spot for the Greyhounds. He shows a calm coolness that is usually not seen as a rookie and does not get flustered facing a big number of shots. Justin showed good lateral movement making a number of strong sliding back door saves. He possesses a strong glove hand and works to make himself appear bigger than he is in the net. Nichols takes good angles and does not get too deep in his net. He also has very quick reflexes and moves well. He needs to work at growing confidence coming out to play the puck and needs to be quicker out of his net stopping dump-ins for his defenders. Nichols also needs to be aware to not drop to his knees quickly as being a smaller goaltender he needs to stay up as long as possible. Justin showed good potential this season and should eventually slide smoothly into the starter role once Murray graduates from the Greyhounds roster.

Justin isn't expected to be selected in the 2013 NHL Entry Draft, but with many goaltenders, they generally show their potential later on.

Nichushkin, Valeri – RW – Traktor Chelyabinsk (KHL) – 6'4" 202

Valeri is a forward who has impressed us over the last two years growing from a good prospect, to a great prospect. Valeri spent last season playing with Belie Medvedi Chelyabinsk of the MHL, but missed playing time throughout the season appearing at the 2011 World Jr. A Challenge, 2012 World U-17 Challenge and finally the IIHF U18 Championships representing Russia.

Every time we saw Valeri he seemed to be improving making the 2012-2013 season very intriguing for him. Valeri moved up the ranks from the MHL to Chelmet Chelyabinsk of the VHL and finally finishing his season and playing most of his games with Traktor Chelyabinsk of the KHL. Valeri continued his international representation of his country playing at the 2013 World Junior Championships and the 2013 IIHF U18 Championships.

Valeri has tremendous size and has an effective skating ability that can best be compared to Alex Galchenyuk's or Evgeni Malkin's skating style where all are big bodied and have a crouched down skating style. All three have deceptive speed to go with their size. Valeri protects the puck and will fearlessly drive the net. Despite his size he is surprisingly elusive and can utilize his hands and some moves to evade checkers and score some absolutely beautiful goals. His physical game has grown a bit over the last few years he's more willing to give and receive hits than he used to be and makes him much more effective. It's still not a big part of his game, but his comfort level is increasing. Valeri is more of a goal scorer and has a shot that is already better than the average NHL players shot and will allow him to score right away in the league. He prefers to shoot the puck way over passing it, which actually results in Valeri having a deceptive ability to pass the puck and create plays. We've watched moments where he simply didn't have a shooting lane, sometimes he will force it, but when he passes he completes some moderately difficult passes tape to tape. Valeri is intelligent with his positioning and makes himself an available shooting option for passers.

Nichushkin has shown us some flashes of competitiveness outside of the offensive zone forcing turnovers and being aggressive on the puck carrier. Valeri is one of the top prospects for the 2013 NHL Entry Draft. His willingness to come to North America to play certainly will alter the shape of this draft near the top and he has shown us clear signs of being able to contribute at the NHL level right away.

Quotable: "No bigger topic as far as players go during the post games in Sochi than this kid. He had some lazy play in his game at the U18 after dominating the Five Nations tourney a couple of months earlier. That said, this kid is an elite talent. He might have as a high a ceiling as any player in this draft. We were all *set to rank him out of the top 6 or 7, until he informed everyone he plans to play in the NHL year. He might go in the top 5 or 6 now. I was told that his team interviews were fine and I listened in on his media availability at the combine. He was quiet but his answers were fine." - Mark Edwards*

Nikandrov, Daniel – LC – Sarnia Sting (OHL) – 6'2" 191

Daniel came into this season essentially as rookie after playing only 7 games last year putting up two points. He spent his first junior season with the Sarnia Legionnaires Jr. B (GOJHL) putting up a point per game as one of the youngest players in the league providing good two-way play. Daniel posted respectable numbers this season starting out in a third line role, but eventually earning his way to the second line.

Daniel's strongest asset is his defensive awareness. He competes hard in his own zone, maintains good positioning and gets his sticks in lanes. Daniel has likely spent plenty of post games with a few bags of ice as he's more than willing to block shots. Daniel was Sarnia's best penalty killing forward by a wide margin this season. Nikandrov also competes along the wall. This developed over the course of the season and will likely improve further with increased strength. Daniel isn't a flashy offensive player but he is creative with the puck. He has good hands and is an excellent passer. He shows good vision. Many of his assists have come from high difficult passes made into easy finishes in the offensive zone. The chemistry he developed with top 2014 NHL Draft prospect Nikolay Goldobin was exceptional this season.

We certainly see Daniel being selected in this year's NHL Draft. His skill set and play suggests that Daniel would be an excellent addition to any NHL team's penalty kill. He's one of the best defensive forwards available in this draft and while he projects to only be a bottom six forward at the NHL level, that defensive acumen should intrigue a few NHL teams that value a forward who will consistently play 200 feet every night.

Quotable: "Daniel is a very under appreciated player for this year's draft. He's not a flashy player but he spent a lot of time playing against the top line of the opposition and was Sarnia's best penalty killing forward. You won't get a ton of offense out of Daniel, but he's always black and blue after the game because he hits, blocks shots and is the guy who does the little things that ever NHL team needs." - Ryan Yessie

Nikkel, Ayrton – LD – Everett Silvertips (WHL) – 6'1" 195

One of the toughest player available from the WHL for this year's NHL Entry Draft, Nikkel makes life miserable for opponents with his physicality, and is not afraid to mix it up with anybody in the league. He has very limited talent in the offensive zone, but could turn into a valuable defensive defenseman as a pro one day. Nikkel makes most of his impact in his own end. He looks quite comfortable without the puck, and provides solid PK minutes every night. He consistently stays in good position, and does not chase the play that will give opponents a good scoring chance as a result. He has a good stick that he uses to poke away pucks and take away passing lanes. On the rush, Nikkel will maintain a good gap, and look to land a hit whenever he can.

The most attractive attribute of Nikkel is his toughness and physical play. He will protect his teammates and goaltender at all costs, and will fight anybody when necessary. He does not constantly take undisciplined penalties, and will not lose his composure easily to go after an opponent and put his team on the PK. He uses his body effectively, and is hard to knock off the puck. One of the improvements Nikkel has to make is his skating. He is an above average skater overall, but could get quicker in open ice and skating backwards. He does not have a problem keeping up with players in corners and in tight areas in regards to quick starts and stops, but if fast opponents come down his wing in open ice, Nikkel has had some trouble keeping them to the outside. Another area of improvement is his puck handling ability. He makes good, simple first passes out of the zone most of the time, but could be more consistent with it, and be better at handling the puck while he is moving with speed.

Norell, Robin – LD – Djurgården J20 (Superelit) – 5'11, 192

Robin is a simple, stocky defenseman who plays a strong defensive game. He's solid in his own end, playing a positional game with an active stick and intelligent contact. He understands the limitations of his size and waits for the right opportunity to play the body, rather than trying to overpower with brute force. He can make big hits standing up at the blueline and his repertoire includes a great hip check. He's sturdy on his feet and though not the strongest skater, positions himself well enough that he rarely has to move quickly to recover. He makes safe outlets and can occasionally stretch the rink with long bomb passes, but tends to keep it pretty simple with the puck and knows when to chip it off the glass and out. He has stretches of over aggressiveness and puck troubles, but for the most part is safe and reliable.

Nosad, Stephen – RW – Peterborough Petes (OHL) – 5'11" 188

Stephen was very highly regarded out of Minor Midget as the captain of the York-Simcoe Express. He was selected in the 2nd round of the 2011 OHL Priority Selection Draft by the Peterborough Petes. His rookie season showed some very, very promising signs. He put together impressive point totals and put up almost a point per game for Team Ontario's World U-17 Challenge team. Nosad entered his NHL Draft Year on a high but this season was a step back for Stephen as he didn't quite elevate his game quite the way we expected. Stephen is one of those players who is capable of doing many things well, but nothing great. When he's on his game he shows off his skating ability and is willing to chase pucks into corners and battle hard winning more than his share of battles. He shows effective intelligence with the puck and knows when to pass or shoot.

The concern with Stephen is he went through multiple stretches where we didn't feel he was working hard enough or playing his style of game. Regardless, we do believe Stephen could be selected late in this draft purely based on his potential alone. He showed some excellent flashes, but those flashes need to be more of a consistent effort to really reach his potential. Stephen has only received 6 minor penalties in 124 OHL games so far which is extremely impressive for a player who can go into the corners and win battles.

Nurse, Darnell – LD – Sault Ste. Marie Greyhounds (OHL) – 6'5" 192

Darnell was picked by the Sault Ste. Marie Greyhounds and he was the top defenseman selected out of the 1995 born group of players at the 2011 OHL Priority Selection Draft. Darnell struggled a little out of the gate with high expectations as a 16 year old. As the season went on things started to fall into place but it really wasn't the rookie season most were expecting from Darnell. Fortunately as he went into Team Canada's U18 Ivan Hlinka camp he showed exactly how much he improved playing an important part in Canada's Gold Medal win.

Nurse is the prototypical shutdown defenseman in the OHL. He is big and can play a mean and nasty style of game punishing opponents in the corners and in front of the net. Nurse works to win battles along the boards and thrives pushing forwards off the puck with a strong physical compete level. Darnell hammers forwards in front of the net and is very effective at allowing his goaltender to see most shots from the point. He also shows a willingness to block shots and excels on the penalty kill setting up strong positioning and utilizing an active stick to disrupt passing lanes. Nurse is a strong skater and can quickly close gaps on rushing forwards crossing the blue line. Nurse shows confidence skating with the puck out of the defensive zone and has the ability to evade pressure with his feet. He generally makes smart outlet passes but needs to work at touch and precision allowing his line mates to receive passes in stride. Darnell began to show some improvement in his offensive game as the season progressed and he was started jumping into the rush and contributing offensively. He needs to continue to work at improving the accuracy of his shot from the blue line, but has a decent wrist shot. He also shows great leadership qualities on and off the ice and works well with his teammates earning an assistant captain letter in only his second season in the league. Nurse is usually effective at puck moving and creating space for his line mates to work. Darnell has shown a willingness to drop the gloves from time to time and will stand up for his teammates.

Nurse struggled a bit in this year's playoffs and had trouble with his decision making. He got away from playing a strong defensive first game. Darnell showed enough however over the course of the season to remain a first round pick in the 2013 NHL Draft. He will be the key player on the Greyhound blue line next season with high leadership expectations for a younger OHL club.

Quotable: "For me Nurse turned a corner in the Czech Republic at the U18. I was not as high on him as others had been coming into the OHL. I felt like he figured out what he was as a player in Brno and that led to much better results on the ice. I don't see him as top 10 pick because I think his offensive ability is limited and I'm not sure he thinks the game as well as some other Dmen in this draft. I love his physical game and he's a gamer. Thoughts from NHL guys are all over the map on Nurse." - Mark Edwards

Quotable: "Nurse is at his best when he is physically manhandling opponents in the corners and in front of the net. When he starts to think too much and try to get overly active in the offensive game is when he starts to run into some trouble. Cutting down on some of these mistakes and keeping things simple will go a long way towards his success at the NHL level" - Kevin Thacker

Quotable: "He's out of my first round." NHL Scout

Quotable: "I take at least four other defenseman ahead of Nurse." Josh Deitell

Quotable: "I see him as a top 10 pick. Early on I never saw what all the fuss was about but he has grown on me." NHL Scout

Quotable: "I heard he was playing injured, I give the kid credit for sucking it up, especially in the playoffs." NHL Scout

Quotable: "So much talk about him, my concern is the hockey sense. I think he has average hockey sense at best. He will play in the NHL but he might top out as nothing all that special." - NHL Scout

Quotable: "I'd take him in the top 5." - NHL Scout

Oglevie, Andrew – FW – Cedar Rapids RoughRiders (USHL) – 5'9" 156

Oglevie was drafted in the 1st round, 14th overall into the USHL Futures draft by the Cedar Rapids Roughriders in 2011 and scored 13 points as a rookie that year which he followed up with 20 points this season in 60 games played. Oglevie distributes the puck pretty effectively on the rush up the ice and drives hard to the net with his stick down. He can make a good 1st pass out of his zone to start the rush and has the puck protection and agility to avoid the opposition's pressure. He uses his body to win puck battles pretty well and will go to the net looking for loose pucks and opportunities. He has good speed to his game, pressures the puck carrier well and can play nice and physical on the fore-check. He can get in behind the opposition's defense to take passes and also gets the puck to the slot to put shots on net. He plays a pretty good cycle game, can get open down low next to the net and has good hands and moves off the rush to get by defenders. He needs to drive the net more often and get his head up to see all his options before moving the puck. Oglevie does not not have much size to him and lacks the offensive skills and production to be considered a top-6 forward at the next level.

Oglevie has some limited skill and speed to his game, but has to be more of a defensive specialist who can chip in offensively and get goals off the cycle by grinding out the opposition's defense. Andrew was also selected by the Tri-City Americans in the 11th round of the 2010 WHL Bantam Draft. Oglevie is committed to join the University of Notre Dame this fall of 2013.

Ohman, Victor – LC – MODO J20 (SWE J20) – 5'9" 170

Victor has been the product of the MODO system for the past few years. He has taken his time working his way up starting with the J18 after a brief appearance at the U16 level and played primarily J18 the past two seasons. This year he played exclusively at the J20 level with a one game exception where he made his Elitserien debut. Ohman is a skilled offensive player who displays excellent skating ability and is able to create plays for himself and his linemates. He shows some clear flashes of offensive ability and even protects the puck well for his size. While he's strong offensively he struggles with both the physical side of the game and the defensive side of the game. While he can skate control and pass the puck well, showing distinctive offensive potential, he may be too far away in other areas of the game. A team may be intrigued by him later on in the draft.

Olofsson, Gustav – LD – Green Bay Gamblers (USHL) – 6'2" 185

Gustav is a Swedish-born, mostly US-raised blueliner who plays a strong all-around game and will suit up for Colorado College in the fall. He takes care of his end first and foremost by making himself hard to play against with strong stick and body checking against the rush, along the boards, and in front of his net. His positioning is sound and he's strong on his feet. He has an affinity for contact, and as such goes for big hits from time to time. He usually picks his spots well but does sometimes take himself out of the play.

He shows good offensive upside with a smart first pass and intelligent reads with the puck in his end. At times, he rushes the puck with poise and can be useful on the power play with smart point play, but his puck skills have yet to manifest on a consistent basis. His point shot in particular needs to be refined as he has a hard time getting it on net. He's a safe pick based on his defensive play and considering his lanky frame and developing offensive game, he has the potential to round out into a solid NHL blueliner.

Quotable: "His shot needs a ton of work but this is a player with plenty of upside. I expect him to be one of the top 75 players selected. - Mark Edwards

Olsson, Ross – FW – Cedar Rapids RoughRiders (USHL) – 6'4" 200

Paquyn-Boudreau, Gabriel – LW - Baie-Comeau Drakkar (QMJHL) – 5'11" 160
A first round selection by the Drakkar at the 2012 QMJHL draft, Paquyn Boudreau didn't take much time establishing his offensive game in the QMJHL. He is fairly slight player at only 160 pounds so his effectiveness is by playing a really smart hockey game based on his playmaking abilities and great hockey sense. He is at his best when playing with a natural goal scorer, setting up magnificent plays, he tracks his teammates and executes his plays very quickly, looking like he has eyes all around his head. He has created some tremendous plays with low-percentage passes and we like his ability to pass through sticks and skates, completing most of his passes to the receiver. The way he took away options in the neutral zone in some of our viewings this season demonstrates his intelligence. He anticipates where passes are going and positions himself well to intercept plays. He has above-average skating abilities and puck handling skills, effectively bringing the puck in neutral zone. His wrist shot is good and very accurate, but he doesn't use it nearly enough, preferring the passing game. His smarts serve him well again in his own zone, using a great positional game and strong awareness to be effective. Gabriel Paquyn-Boudreau is not a big player thus making him an average on the boards. He's also not an aggressive player, rarely recording hits. He should not be considered a character player by any means and we would like to see him make more sacrifices for

the good of his team. He can get pushed off the puck by bigger defensemen and will need to bulk up before he plays professional hockey. He will also need to build consistency and a work ethic. We've seen him have some tremendous shifts energy wise, while minutes later he's gliding and looking disinterested on the ice. He needs to get his competitiveness elevated on some nights and keep moving his feet to be an effective player.

Paul, Nicholas – LW – Brampton Battalion (OHL) – 6'2" 202

Nicholas was selected in the 5th round of the 2011 OHL Priority Selection Draft by the Brampton Battalion out of the Mississauga Senators Minor Midget program. Nicholas continued to develop his game playing for the Mississauga Reps AAA Major Midget and got a brief and successful stint with the Mississauga Chargers of the OJHL.

Nicholas went into the Battalion training camp and earned a spot on the roster. In early and especially mid-season viewings, you could always find Paul playing physical, and showing a nice pair of hands in front of the net. He was not a good skater but was always able to remain involved in the play. However, towards the end of the season, he seemed to hit a wall likely due to playing his first full season at this level of play. He became a little more perimeter oriented and he essentially got away from his strengths. He is a strong player, who has a good chance to hear his name called at the 2013 NHL Entry Draft. When he sticks to his strengths he's an extremely effective player who plays a power game. However he needs to use the next season as an opportunity to elevate his play and show his true potential.

Quotable: " I liked him is my first viewing of the year and he improved as the season progressed. The skating isn't great but he seems to always get there." - Mark Edwards

Pawley, Corey – LW – London Knights (OHL) – 5'8" 163

Corey was selected in the 4th round of the 2011 OHL Priority Selection Draft by the London Knights out of the Lambton Jr. Sting Minor Midget program. Corey got a handful of games as a 16 year old with the Knights, but spent most of his 2011-2012 season with the Lambton Shores Predators Jr. B team.

The adjustment to the OHL has been a little tough for Pawley but he has done an admirable job adapting his game. In Minor Midget and Jr. B he was an extremely creative speedy scorer. However playing for a team as deep as London his offensive displays have been relatively limited and when he's got into the lineup, it's generally been as an energetic winger. Corey has adjusted well showing a willingness to play physical, although with limited effectiveness. He shows good work ethic and despite his size he does win some battles with pure work ethic and compete. He hurries back defensively and he has excellent skating ability and speed. When he does get chances offensively he shows good moves, he's capable of beating defenders one on one but can get caught trying to over handle the puck.

While we don't expect Corey to be selected, we would like to see him get stronger. He is going to get some good opportunities to get some effective ice and if he can move up the depth chart, he may be able to show everyone what he's truly capable of. As for pro hockey he's got a few steep hills to climb, but if he can take it one challenge at a time he can prove many doubters wrong.

Pedersen, Brent – LW – Kitchener Rangers (OHL) – 6'2" 205

Brent was selected first round, 14th Overall by the Kitchener Rangers at the 2011 OHL Priority Selection Draft out of the Waterloo Wolves Minor Midget program. Brent joined his hometown team right out of camp as a 16 year old and split time between the 3rd and 4th lines. Pedersen saw his offensive output double in his second full season in the OHL remaining primarily in a bottom six role.

Pederson has shown improved skating throughout this year with size and a heavy shot. Pedersen reads the ice well enough to effectively use his teammates. He showed flashes of offensive creativity when given the opportunity to play with more skilled line mates. Brent works hard in the offensive zone and is good at using his size shielding opponents from the puck with his body before cutting to the net. He is big enough to withstand a beating in front of the net and is constantly looking for rebound opportunities. He is good at using his size to create space for his line mates and can add a physical side to his game when needed. Pedersen will be looked upon to have a much larger role in the Ranger offense next season and will look to build off of a solid sophomore season.

At the pro level he's projected to be a power forward who is able to produce offensively to a limited extent. He looks very prototypical as a power forward and understands himself and his role very well. He needs to continue to improve skating and work on getting even stronger to be able to be more dominant along the walls and while driving the net.

Quotable: "A bit of a slider for me. I thought he had some better games late in the season but his feet are still an issue." - Mark Edwards

Pellah, Bo – LD – Alberni Valley Bulldogs (BCHL) – 5'11" 139

Pellah is a poised puck moving defenseman who provided a very strong offensive presence from the backend this season and made the power play look quite impressive with his smart decisions with the puck. Pellah does most of his damage offensively with his hockey sense and very impressive passes. He reads the play quite well, and displays good vision from the blue line. He can thread passes through small seams and be mobile to create some space and time to make a play. Pellah does not have a great shot, but he does a good job of getting them on net and creating rebounds by shooting low. He does not carry the puck too often, but does limit the turnovers that he commits and makes a pass or simply dumps the puck in when he feels pressure.

The issue with Pellah's game his is lack of strength and defensive game. He still has a lot of weight to put on, and really lacks the upper body strength to physically handle players along the walls and in the slot. He has to become much stronger to have any sort of a chance to be a professional player one day. Defensively, Pellah is not particularly great without the puck. He does a good job of positioning himself, but when he has to engage physically, he gets beat time and time again, and bigger players easily get positioning around him.

Pellah is not heading to the NCAA until 2014, so he has a lot of time to develop physically and improve on his defensive game. He is definitely another project, and teams may pass on him this year, but if he can get stronger and be a better presence without the puck to go with his impressive offensive skills, an NHL team may sign him to a rookie contract in the future, or draft him this year and give him a lot of time to develop.

Brett Pesce – RD – University of New Hampshire (NCAA) – 6'3" 174

Pesce is a steady defensive defenseman who limits the number of mistakes he commits with his solid positioning and good skating abilities. He will never be much of an offensive threat and will need to be very good in the defensive zone to make it to the pro level.

Pesce rarely takes chances offensively. He is good at coming down the boards in the offensive zone to keep the puck in, but he will only take that chance when he knows that he will win the race for the puck for sure. He rarely joins the rush and will only do so if he sees a clear lane to attack and it is a quick transition play. He makes average first passes out of the zone, and possesses very limited playmaking abilities. His shot on the point definitely needs to improve, particularly getting them on net.

Defensively, Pesce is a very solid presence. He is in good position time and time again, and makes it difficult for opponents to create good scoring chances. He has a very good stick that he uses to knock away passes, and is tough to play against along the walls. He uses his good reach and good speed to create a lot of turnovers with the puck. One area of improvement for Pesce would be his gap control. Despite his good skating ability, at times leaves too big of a gap off the rush. We expect that like many players, once he learns to trust his skating bility and be a little more aggressive, he will become an even more effective defenseman in the future.

Quotable: "Reminds me of Bigras, not quite as good but plays like him." - NHL Scout

Petan, Nicolas – LC – Portland Winterhawks (WHL) – 5'9" 166

Nicolas Petan has been one of the biggest stories to come out of the WHL this year. An undersized centre, Petan came out of nowhere to lead the dominant Winterhawks offensively and burn opponents all year long with his elite offensive skills. Even as the season went along and more and more attention was given to him and his line mates, Petan continued to put up huge numbers and put himself in the talks of being a first round draft pick in the upcoming NHL Entry Draft despite his size.

Petan's best offensive attribute is his vision and playmaking abilities. He is so patient and poised with the puck, and waits for the perfect moment to make a quick pass for an easy goal. He seems to have a pair of eyes on the back of his head, because he made some unbelievable no look passes from behind the goal line to a teammate or passes off the half wall. His confidence with the puck has really made the difference in his game this season. Petan was also very impressive at finding open areas in the slot to score some timely goals. He also displayed very good stick handling skills and showed some nice elusiveness. Simply put, he could not be stopped this season.

The biggest concern with Petan is his lack of size. He has shown some weakness along the walls and for puck battles, but it is not for a lack of effort. He engages physically whenever he has the opportunity, and drives to the net for loose pucks as hard as anybody. He has shown that he can quickly turn away from opponents and make it hard to tie him up, but as a centre he will have to match up with much bigger centres down low on the defensive end. If Petan can outsmart opponents with and without the puck to compensate for his size, he could have some big impact as a pro.

Quotable: "I really like Petan. I had a lot of people ask me why is Domi ranked higher? For me it's two reasons. First, Domi has a very strong core. Secondly, I think Domi helped his line mates more than he was helped. Petan is smart and skilled but I think his line mates helped him out as well. Regardless, he's a first rounder in my books. He's small but elite." Mark Edwards

Petersen, Calvin – G – Waterloo Blackhawks (USHL) – 6'1" 175

Petersen is a massive goaltender for the Waterloo Blackhawks. He is very effective at eliminating the bottom half of the net and is great at using his long legs to shutdown backdoor scoring chances. He shows good lateral movement and is rarely beat with a deke in tight. Cal does go down into the butterfly quick at times and needs to work at standing tall to take away the top half of the net as well. He is good at going from the butterfly to the standing position quickly and hugs the post tight stopping most wraparound situations. He is good at getting out of his net to stop pucks being dumped in from wrapping around for his defenseman and shows the ability to move pucks up the ice when given time and space. Petersen does need to work on improving his rebound control but is generally good at making the first save.

Petersen, Trevor – LW – Niagara Ice Dogs (OHL) – 5'11" 200

Petersen went undrafted in the 2010 and 2011 OHL Priority Selections and was picked up in July of 2011 as a free agent after playing his 16 year old season with The Hill Academy Varsity Hockey. Due to a late birth date, Petersen was able to get two seasons in at the OHL level before being eligible for the NHL Entry Draft. In the 2011-2012 season he registered 6 points in 38 games. In his second season he increased his point totals to 11 in 65 games.

Petersen hustles hard for loose pucks and puts great pressure on the puck carrier. He plays with good energy, physicality and at an up-tempo pace. He can move the puck decently off the rush and protects the puck along the boards. We do not expect that Petersen will be selected in the NHL draft. Petersen needs to be much more responsible in his own end, to cover his points and get in lanes to make sure that shots are not getting through to the net and work on using his quickness to establish a quick transition game to create opportunities off odd-man rushes.

Peterson, Avery – FW – Grand Rapids H.S. (USHS-MN) – 6'2" 181

Petersen played primarily for Grand Rapids High School with a brief 8 game appearance in the USHL with the Sioux City Musketeers joining the team pretty late into the season. He possesses some nice quick hands and drives the puck wide really well into the offensive zone. He put low shots on net to try and generate rebounds for teammates driving the net.

Quotable: "Skating is an issue here. He's hunched over and I don't see much agility. I like his hands but I'm not sure he thinks the game as quickly as I'd like to see. He stayed on the outside and didn't look creative. I probably sound overly negative, but I guess I was just hoping for a lot more because I had heard some talk about him as a possible 2nd rounder. - Mark Edwards

Peterson, Elliot – LW – Calgary Hitmen (WHL) – 5'10" 188

Peterson is a depth player for Calgary, and provides the team with a lot of energy on a nightly basis. He gets into the forecheck and dishes out solid hits to create turnovers and get a cycle going along the boards. He sacrifices his body on a regular basis to block shots and make a difference in the defensive zone. Peterson has shown very limited offensive abilities this year and will probably never make much of a difference on the scoresheet for his team. He will have to make it to the next level by being a successful enforcer or a very effective grinder who can kill penalties well.

Petrash, Corey – FW – Cedar Rapids RoughRiders (USHL) – 5'9" 160

Petrash comes from Manitoba where he played in the MJHL in the 2011-2012 season for the Winnipeg Saints and had 39 points in 51 games. He was also drafted into the USHL in that 2011 year in the 4th round, then played his rookie season this year playing in 57 games with 22 points. Petrash keeps to a really simple game, as he does not have all the speed, size or skill in the world and just likes to get the puck in deep, go hard to the net and battle for loose pucks and opportunities. He needs to play a really effective defensive game and come back next season as a physical force that can play a much bigger, rougher game in order to be harder for opponents to play against. Corey is committed to Bemidji State.

Pezzetta, Stefano – LW – Owen Sound Attack (OHL) – 5'11" 190

Pezzetta was selected in the 12th round of the 2011 OHL Priority Selection Draft out of the Markham Waxers program. Stefano made the Attack against the odds providing good work ethic and competing hard. Owen Sound had a fairly deep group at forward, and Stefano was limited to a limited role and just 27 games. In those games he provided good energy and was a fairly physical player in a bottom six role for the Attack. He is at his best when he keeps it simple, getting the puck deep, playing a dump and chase or cycle game.

Stefano is willing to work hard in the defensive zone but over our viewings we've seen too many costly turnovers. He is not expected to be selected at the 2013 NHL Entry Draft and will need to continue to improve his decision making and refine his game to become a regular energy player in the OHL, which we believe is a realistic and attainable goal for him to achieve this fall, then will go from there in his development.

Pieper, Bo – FW – Indiana Ice (USHL) – 5'11" 177

Pieper played for Shattuck St. Mary's U16 in Midget where he was over a point a game player before joining the USHL in the 2011-2012 season with the Chicago Steel. He had 16 points in his rookie season, which he followed up with the Indiana Ice where his production dropped to 12 points in 63 games, and he had an unfortunate -23 rating.

Pieper keeps it pretty simple and puts good pressure on the puck carrier and will battle well for his territory in front of the opposition's net. He has good speed, hustles for loose pucks and can skate the puck up the ice on the rush. He generally gets the puck in deep on dump and chase plays, then pressures the fore-check and he goes hard to the net looking for loose pucks and rebounds.

He needs to get bigger and stronger to be more effective and has to hit his target more often on his breakout passes as he often passes into feet or behind teammates. Pieper does not have the skill and offensive instincts to be an effective top-6 forward at the next level and therefore needs to try to play a role that he can still be an asset to a team. He needs to add size and strength, work on his breakout passes so that he is not missing his target or turning the puck over and has to play a hard, physical game where he get an effective cycle going in the offensive zone. He needs to play with energy on a consistent basis and battle hard to win the puck along the boards. Bo is committed to Quinnipiac University in fall of 2013.

Pinho, Brian – RC – St. John's Prep (High-MA) – 6'1, 175

The smooth, dynamic Pinho plays a strong two-way game and was head and shoulders above his competition playing high school hockey in Massachusetts this year. He is an absolute force with the puck, acting as quarterback at even strength and on the power play with the skill to take over on every shift. His skating is fluid and precise with great acceleration. He buys time and space with elite stick handling in the neutral and offensive zones, and uses his reach and frame well. He can play the point on the power play and shows off an excellent wrist shot, snapshot, and one-timer.

Pinho could stand to distribute better but is likely acting on coach's orders with St. John's as his finishing ability is strong enough that he can threaten even when keyed on by opponents. He forechecks and back checks intelligently, using an active stick more than his body to capably strip the puck and force mistakes. He battles hard for rebounds and positioning in front of the net and wins pucks along the boards with quick stick work. Best of all, he's still lanky with room to add muscle to his frame.

He'll need to simplify and continue to round out his game at the next level – which for him will likely be with the Indiana Ice, who selected him in the first round of the 2013 USHL Draft – but has the tools and sense to be an outstanding professional. He's committed to Providence College for 2014 onwards.

Quotable: "I like him a lot. He's an excellent skater and is a high character player. He's a good checker and works hard across all 200 feet. He's not an elite skill guy but he's a really good hockey player. I guess I'd call him one of my sleepers." – Mark Edwards

Pionk, Neal – RD – Sioux City Musketeers (USHL) – 5'11" 160

Pionk was a 5th round pick by the Musketeers and managed to play in 12 games this year for Sioux City while picking up a goal and 5 assists. He is a defenseman who possesses a pretty good shot from the point that he can keep down low on net and plays his man with a good element of physicality in his own end by forcing him to the outside then uses his stick effectively to poke the puck away from the opposition. He can make a pretty good breakout pass to start the rush through the neutral zone and also distributes the puck effectively on the power play in the offensive zone. Pionk skates really well and can join the rush up the ice. Good on the PP. He needs to add some size and strength.

Quotable: "He is a firebug." - NHL Scout

Pittman, Zack – LD – Lincoln Stars (USHL) – 6'1" 190

Pittman is in no way an offensive defenseman recording only 7 points with Detroit Belle Tire in his minor midget year and then managed just 5 points in 56 games with the Lincoln Stars in his first season in the USHL, but had 107 penalty minutes and an impressive +24 rating. Pittman was selected by the Lincoln Stars at 58th overall in the 4th round and is a defenseman who has really good size and plays with a nice physical edge from the back end. He protects the puck well from the opposition's pressure then can move it up out of his zone with pretty good passes to start the rush, however he needs to watch some of the turnovers on plays where he panics with the puck or is out-muscled off of it along the boards. He is very tough to play against and will play a tough physical game and always finishes his checks along the wall. Opponents know when they've been paired against Pittman the next day. Zack was also selected in the 9th round of the 2012 OHL Priority Selection Draft.

Platzer, Kyle – RW – London Knights (OHL) – 5'11" 185

Kyle was selected in the 4th round of the 2011 OHL Priority Selection Draft by the London Knights out of the Waterloo Wolves Minor Midget program. Kyle played a handful of games while spending most of his 2011-2012 season with the Waterloo Siskins Jr. B team posting over a point per game including a 30+ goal season. Kyle came to Knights camp and made an impression. He was stuck on the fourth line, he showed great chemistry with his line-mates one of which was fellow 2013 Eligible Remi Elie.

Kyle displayed a strong work ethic and he competes every single shift. He isn't the biggest guy but wins more than his share of battles due to his never quit attitude. He displays good hockey sense and makes intelligent plays and seems to never hurt his team with his decisions even when pressured. Kyle chips in defensively playing very responsibly and maintains strong positioning. Kyle has shown some very good offensive skills at both the Minor Midget and Jr. B level but has just been able to show flashes of it at the OHL level.

Watching Platzer play for 4 years and grow as a player, we feel there is a good chance he will start to show some very good offensive skill when he becomes a more critical offensive player for the Knights. However it may not be enough to make him an offensive player at the NHL level. He projects to be a very good two-way forward that plays a bottom six role. He is regarded for having good character and would be one of those guys who might not help his team every game, but will work hard, compete and rarely if ever hurts his team. We hardly ever have anything negative to say about Kyle because he plays within his game and works hard consistently. He knows what he needs to do to be successful.

Quotable: "Another example of a player in London who is waiting his turn for more minutes. I liked the skills level and think he is worthy of a mid round selection." - Mark Edwards

Quotable: "Kyle is a player we really liked in Minor Midget and felt if he got a chance this year he would prove himself to be an NHL prospect. He showed great chemistry with Remi Elie and provides a smart presence and a strong work ethic." - Ryan Yessie

Poirier, Émile – LW – Gatineau Olympiques (QMJHL) – 6'1" 183

The late-birthdate Émile Poirier has enjoyed a tremendous season with the struggling Gatineau Olympiques, scoring 32 goals in 65 games. He was Gatineau's best forward in most of our viewings and never stopped going up in our monthly rankings as the season progressed.

Émile Poirier has amazed us with his speed and especially the second gear he has, scoring multiple goals and creating chances going wide on defensemen. He is very deceptive and will create space for himself within two skating strides, a great neutral zone player. Poirier doesn't look pretty when he skates, but it is highly effective. A gifted puck handler, he can also undress a defenseman having the wrong gap coverage on him with sweet one-on-one moves. He can stickhandle in tight spaces with ease. The Montreal native is a natural goal scorer who will use his quick hands to beat goalies with great dekes, having the forehand-to-backhand move as his favorite. He also possesses a great wrist shot and has good accuracy. He will always try to get in the slot before shooting pucks on net and will mostly find soft ice in this area, making himself available for teammates. He has great hockey sense and sees his teammates really well in the offensive zone. With his soft hands and great passing skills, Poirier has no problems passing the puck through sticks and skates before reaching teammates. He is a strong player and has nice size at 6'01" 183 pounds.

Poirier is not only a gifted goal-scorer, but a very smart player, he anticipates quickly and is always a threat because of his speed and active stick. He takes away a lot of time for the opposition when they have the puck. He knows where to go immediately when his team recovers the puck to make it an easy and quick transition. He plays on the PK and is well served again by his great anticipation and hockey sense, blocking shots and his position fairly well. He progressed nicely during the season in his defensive play, taking better decisions with and without the puck. He also has shown better implication in the physical department. He's started to hit with more regularity and win more battles than he did last year, he got stronger and improved his puck protection a lot. He also showed more aggressiveness, being more involved in scrums and even dropping the gloves to defend teammates which his something we always like to see.

Émile Poirier has progressed into an impressive complete package for the next level and has never stopped progressing during the season. He had a huge amount of ice-time in Gatineau and made the best of it. His biggest weakness is work ethic and laziness. Poirier will sometimes be seen cheating high in the neutral zone, while his team has not retrieved the puck in the defensive zone. He is at his best when he moves his feet and get his second gear working out wide on defensemen, but will rely from times to times on his skill set only and avoid hits with careless decisions. He will forget to do the defensive details that he does in other games, because he doesn't feel like it. He also has improved this area of his game this year, but is still lacking consistency from shifts to shifts.

We feel that Poirier could have a big impact in professional hockey if he's able to get an irreproachable work ethic. His explosiveness and soft-hands are already above most players his age and with the progression he's had in his defensive game, we see him as a possible steal in the 2013 NHL Draft.

Quotable: "He had two hatricks and a two goal game in my first three viewings. What's not to like?" – Mark Edwards

Polino, Patrick – FW – Chicago Steel (USHL) – 5'8" 164

Polino was a 1st round pick, 4th overall by the Chicago Steel in the 2011 USHL Futures Draft and he played in just 3 games for Chicago at the end of that season scoring his 1st point as an assist. He then played his first full season this year playing in 60 games and registering 24 points however was an unfortunate -16.

Polino has a bit of aggression to him as he will get involved after whistles and he likes to put great pressure on the puck carrier. He can move the puck around pretty well in the offensive zone on the power play, gets a nice cycle going in deep and will get down low next to the net with the puck for chances in tight, he just needs to try to drive the puck more towards the net rather than taking so many outside shots that have little chance of scoring. He likes to drive the puck wide into the offensive zone, can get the puck in deep off the rush and is physical on the fore-check. He can also find lanes to move the puck cross-ice on the power play to find an open teammate but has to watch the turnovers being overly patient and trying to hold on to the puck for too long to make a play. Polino does not have much size which makes it difficult for him to drive the puck down low, but he plays far too much on the perimeter trying to make plays and attempting to shoot around defenders on chances off the rush. He has good vision and passing abilities but will never be at his most effective playing along the boards rather than up the middle.

Polino needs to add a lot of size and strength still and has to become less intimidated of playing in the dirty areas of the ice to try and create offense from tough areas.

Pope, David – LW – West Kelowna Warriors (BCHL) – 6'2" 193

Pope is a big, skilled winger who plays a good all around game. He provided match up problems for opponents because of his mix of skill and size, and when he wanted to, he was able to provide big match up problems for opponents. Pope is at his best when he is moving his feet and attacking the middle of the ice. He can create a lot of scoring chances by skating down the wing then cutting to the slot to get a shot on net. The problem is that he was not always willing to do so. At times he would just skate up and down the wing, and not be much of a factor. Pope has a good slap shot, and is set up to use it on the PP consistently. He needs to work on hitting the net however. Pope needs to be a more consistent factor in games to have more success and put up more points. Pope is also not very good along the walls, especially given his size. His desire to win puck battles is not very high, and he gets beat for pucks time and time again. He needs to develop a mean streak in his game to be successful.

Defensively, Pope is adequate without the puck. He does a good job of maintaining position to limit chances for opposing defensemen, but he could read the play better and help out along the walls as the play comes up towards the blue line. He is average at blocking shots, but does not really go out of his way to get his body in front of a shot. Ultimately, Pope is not skilled enough to succeed without playing with some grit at the pro level. He was able to get away with it at the junior "A" level because he was big, fast and skilled, but players at the next level are as big and strong as him and if Pope is not committed to playing a physical game, he will tumble down depth charts very quickly.

Quotable: "He has the speed, size and hands, but he is really missing a physical element to his game. He does not like to engage in puck battles, and is quite soft along the walls. Pope has to develop a mean streak." Charles An

Popoff, Carter – RC – Vancouver Giants (WHL) – 5'9" 180

Diminutive forward whose best asset is his skating ability. Popoff is a quick centre who is always moving at a high speed. He has had a number of different roles this season, from a top 6 forward to a 4th line centre, and has not really found much success anywhere. He is not particularly skilled enough to consistently put up points, and not strong enough defensively or gritty enough to excel as a defensive forward. Popoff has not been able to use his speed to his advantage mainly because his stick handling is not good enough, and he has a difficult time finding open areas in the offensive zone. He is not strong enough to consistently win puck battles and for most of time, he is going back and forth out on the ice following the play and does not get much accomplished.

Possler, Gustav – LW – MODO (SEL) – 5'11" 181

Possler is a quick sniper who moved up and down between MODO's U20 squad and their men's team. He has a real nose for the net, and is a threat to score from the slot on a consistent basis. The first thing you notice about Possler's game is his offensive abilities. He is very quick off the rush and shows good poise with the puck on his stick. He has above average stick handling abilities, and while he may not overwhelm any defender with his hands, he is able to protect the puck quite well and keep control of it easily as he moves with speed. Possler's best asset is his shooting ability. He has a very good release to his shots, and is also able to place them quite accurately. He is not afraid to crash the net, and show some toughness and be willing to mix it up with opposing defensemen.

The weakness to Possler's game is his defensive abilities. There are times when he floats around the ice without the puck, and will need to really improve on playing with more intensity in his own end.

He certainly has the offensive tools to be a successful pro, but if he cannot be trusted by his coaches in the defensive zone, he will not have the opportunity to show off his skills in the offensive zone.

Quotable: "A player we liked last season who fell off the radar a bit this year. Our scout Charles An had him high on his list last season. He really impressed me last year at the U18 in the Czech Republic." - Mark Edwards

Potomak, Brandon – RW – Moose Jaw Warriors (WHL) – 5'11" 165

Potomak is a 2 way, depth forward who provides a very limited presence out on the ice. He has had good opportunity to contribute for the Warriors this year due to their lack of depth, but he has not been able to make much of an impact. Offensively, Potomak has limited skills. He has below average stick handling abilities and does not handle the puck very much. His playmaking skills are also quite below average as he does not make very good passes and cannot take advantage of open seams in coverage. He does not get many opportunities to score as he is not able to weave through traffic to find open areas.

In his own end, Potomak is good enough to be trusted to kill penalties. He holds shooting lanes well, and is willing to block shots. He could still improve on his ability to read the play and get into the right areas out on the ice, and help down low if necessary. He is average along the walls, and could still improve his strength. He looks like he is putting in good effort, but just does not make much impact.

Povorozniouk, Sam – Kingston Frontenacs (OHL) – 5'10" 183

Sam was selected in the 2nd round of the 2011 OHL Priority Selection Draft by the Saginaw Spirit from the Chicago Steel of the USHL. Sam immediately made the jump to the OHL and contributed in a limited role for Saginaw last season. As this season opened, Sam gained extra ice time, but struggled out of the gate with Saginaw and was ultimately dealt to the Kingston Frontenacs.

In Kingston Sam really found his role and put up excellent numbers spending time on both the second and third lines for Kingston. He shows an above average shot and the speed and agility to beat defenders at times. He provides a good mix of energy and offense to the Kingston lineup on a very consistent basis. He works hard on the forecheck and is able to force turnovers. He's also willing to battle and compete for pucks. Sam also chips in defensively in his own zone getting into lanes and coming out with the puck.

Sam has a good shot at being a late round pick. He falls into the group of players who likely don't have enough offense at the next level but provides the work ethic that an NHL team would like to add. Sam will look to provide more offense while still providing great, consistent effort to his team on a nightly basis next season.

Pulock, Ryan – RD – Brandon Wheat Kings (WHL) – 6'1" 211

Ryan Pulock was clearly the best player for Brandon this season. He carried his team all year long, but unfortunately it was not enough to get them to the playoffs.

In his third full year in the WHL, Pulock has developed into a very good offensive defenseman who provides a steady presence from the backend. Pulock may not be the fastest player on the team, but he can comfortably get around the ice to jump into the play or back check and cover for his mistakes. He is also good around tight areas to make quick starts and stops to stick to his man in coverage. Pulock's best weapon is his slap shot. He was able to record 102 MPH during a skills competition, and it is something that opponents really concentrate on to prevent him from using it. As the season progressed, opposing wingers stuck to him like glue to take him away as an option, which really hurt Brandon's offensive production. However, on the power play Pulock freely snuck down to the slot from the point, which presented him with some nice scoring chances. He was able to find open holes in coverage quite well, and picked the right times to jump into the play. Pulock is also a good passer, but it is something that he can improve on. There were stretches during the season when his hockey sense has come into question by our scouts because of the alarming number of turnovers he was committing. He has given up the puck less in the final 2 months of the season, but it is still something to keep in mind. Pulock has a solid frame, and he likes to use his body to try to separate opponents from the puck quite often. He plays a physical game and makes it tough on opposing forwards along the walls. He will catch a player with the head down in the neutral zone when given the opportunity, so opponents really have to keep their heads up. There are some questions to his play without the puck. He is not always in the right position, and he could do a better job with his stick to knock away passes and shots and to take away lanes. He needs to stay more patient and let the play come to him when he is in the slot.

Teams will definitely give Ryan Pulock a long look in the first round. He certainly has all the tools to be a successful pro, but he just has to improve his play without the puck and find ways to use his slap shot from the point. To his credit, he received very little help from his teammates all season long, and was often left on his own to try to do everything.

Quotable: "A big faller for us. I don't think our scout Charles An has soured on top ranked player more than he did with Ryan. For me, I see the cannon shot, but too many poor decisions really make me question selecting him with a higher pick. It reminds me of last year, I liked Colberg's puck skills but questioned the thinking part of his game." - Mark Edwards

Quotable: "Like the shot but his skating was not as good as I expected based on what I had heard." - NHL Scout

Rafikov, Rushan - LD - Yaroslavl (MHL) - 6'1 185

Rushan is a throwback defender. He plays a strong defensive game with a wicked edge. For forwards trying to come into his corner or camp out in front of the net, he makes life hell with gritty stick work and hard hits. He's difficult to beat wide and steps up at the blueline when he sees the opportunity. He relishes contact and likes to mix it up after the whistles, though he can overdo it and at times takes ill-advised penalties.

His offensive game is limited. He makes a good first pass and has a nice point shot, but lacks real upside with the puck. He pinches decisively and physically, leading with the stick and making heavy contact on 50/50 pucks. He's a good leader and takes few shifts off.

Rankin, Connor - LC - Tri-City Americans (WHL) - 6'0" 195

Connor Rankin is a skilled forward for the Americans whose development has slowed down in the last couple of seasons. He has played an important role offensively for Tri-City, and really has had mixed results so far. Rankin is a good skater who can move quickly up the ice with the puck. He looks comfortable weaving through traffic, and limits his turnovers by quickly moving the puck when he senses trouble. He will never blow past any dependable defenseman with his speed and stick handling abilities, but will be able to push the defense on their heels and give teammates some room to work with and find some open areas out on the ice. He looked to be more of a playmaker in the previous seasons, but has shown that he has a scoring touch to his game and the ability to quickly catch and shoot the puck from anywhere out on the ice.

Defensively, Rankin has shown that he could play a good 2 way game. He has developed good habits in his game, and back checks hard on any type of a counter attack. He is reliable on the PK and does an above average job of getting into shooting lanes. There are times when he gets on the wrong side of the play and needs to take a penalty to prevent a scoring chance. Rankin's good overall game will certainly garner some attention from NHL teams in the later rounds of the draft. He has shown that he could play a consistent game, even though he will not provide big highlight reel plays. He will have to continue to improve on his overall game to be a serviceable pro one day.

Reway, Martin – LW – Gatineau Olympiques (QMJHL) – 5'9" 173

Reway was pick #4 at the 2012 CHL Import Draft and Gatineau made a great one with the small but very talented forward. Reway plays a typical European game, based on more East-West puck movement than the North-South North American game. His biggest asset is his passing skills and vision. He seems to have eyes all over his head and seems to know where his teammates are at all times on the ice. A dynamic and creative puck-handler, he has quick hands and is able to find space where there doesn't seem to be any. He loves to use his offensive skills to create fancy plays, cross-ice passes, behind the back feeds and risky but spectacular plays. He plays an attractive brand of hockey and you have to live with the downside of some of it.

Reway is a quick skater with above-average acceleration. His quick feet gives him great lateral skating abilities again serving him well in the East-West hockey he plays. A great powerplay player, he controls the play with ease and shows tremendous poise with the puck before executing a superb pass or getting space for a shot on goal. With the vision he possesses, Reway also has a great sense of anticipation and will takeaway plays by using good positioning or a well placed stick. Physicality will always be an issue for Reway, with such a small frame it is difficult for him to win 1-on-1 battles effectively and will always take physical abuse from bigger players. He didn't show the will to take a hit and rarely initiated a contact in our viewings. His vision and smarts help him a lot in his defensive zone, he understands the fundamentals of positioning, but was sometimes seen cheating in neutral zone while his team didn't retrieve the puck. In regards to pure talent, Reway is a very talented player with elite passing skills, but will need to settle into a more North-American style of game with better defensive cautiousness and an improved ability to deal with physicality to play in the NHL one day.

Ripley, Luke – LD – Powell River Kings (BCHL) – 6'3" 195

Ripley is a big, defensive defenseman who provides a physical presence from the backend. He was initially draft eligible in 2012, but was passed over mostly due to his poor skating ability. However, he seems to have really concentrated on it for a year, and is no longer a huge weakness in his game. One area of weakness for Ripley is his footwork along the walls and agility. He needs to work on making quicker stops and being able to stick to opponents on the boards and not give them a lane to the net. He has been able to develop good overall speed, but his explosive quickness still needs to be improved on. He also needs to work on being in good position without the puck in the neutral zone so that opponents cannot go wide and have an easy lane to attack. There are times when he is caught standing still in the middle of the ice, and is not able to cut down the angle on an opponent attacking the net.

The best asset of Ripley is his physicality. He dishes out hits often and is difficult to play against along the walls. He uses his long reach to poke away pucks and intercept passes consistently, and because of the improvements he made with his skating, these skills are much more noticeable as he is more often in the play to be able to make an impact. Ripley is headed to the University of Notre Dame next season, and will likely need a few years of seasoning at the NCAA level and then in the minor leagues to become a depth defenseman in the future.

Ristolainen, Rasmus – RD – TPS (SM-Liiga) – 6'3" 207

Ristolainen is an aggressive offensive defenseman who always looks to push the pace whenever he gets the opportunity. He loves to take chances with the puck, and provides a good presence from the backend offensively with his size, hockey sense and puck skills.

The first thing you notice about Ristolainen is his positioning in the defensive zone. Whenever the play is along the half wall or around the blue line, he creeps up to the high slot and waits for his team to get possession of the puck so that he can join the rush. There are times when he gets caught and opponents have a small odd man scoring chance, but more often than not he does pick his spots quite well and is able to create an odd man rush up the ice for his team. Defensively, Ristolainen is physical along the boards, and maintains an excellent gap off the rush. He is very aggressive in the neutral zone, and does not give opponents a free pass to gain the blue line. He uses his stick quite effectively, and is able to knock away pucks on a consistent basis. Ristolainen does a good job of knowing what is happening around him at all times, and puts himself in solid position again and again to be a factor without the puck.

Ristolainen is a very good skater. He does not possess great top end speed, but he uses his edges so well to maneuver through traffic and carry the puck easily. He makes quick starts and stops to stick to opponents well in the defensive end, and does a good job of angling players to the outside and ensuring that they do not get a lane to the net off the rush. His feet allow him to look so smooth out on the ice and also allows him to do all the things that he does every game.

Offensively, Ristolainen is so poised with the puck on his stick. He will exploit holes in the neutral zone and carry the puck when given an opportunity, or make a crisp, tape to tape pass to his teammates to start the rush on a consistent basis. Ristolainen has to be respected by opponents defending him because he can quickly join the attack and be a threat to produce points. He has good vision with the puck and makes smart decisions with the puck time and time again. He also has a very good shot from the point, which allows him to be unpredictable in the offensive zone. He has slick hands, which he displays time and time again when he carries the puck up the ice through defenders. Ristolainen has proven to be a very effective player at the professional level already in Finland. He provides such a unique presence from the backend offensively and defensively with his aggressive mentality. If he can decrease the amount of chances he gives up because of his eagerness to join the rush, he will be a premier offensive defenseman in the NHL one day.

Quotable: "Another guy where the NHL guys I spoke to about him are all over the map. Some say lock for top 10, others say mid 20's. I am a huge fan of this kid. I love the mean streak I saw in my viewings. He's in the upper half of the draft for me. I think Zadorov has slightly more room to get better going forward, but I like Risto's game right now and I think he will be a very good player in the NHL. I spoke to him at the combine and I was impressed. He was shy at first but as he got more comfortable he opened up and even cracked a few jokes. He roomed with Saros and had some fun with that. He joked that Saros was just a kid and so he was the boss." - Mark Edwards

Roos, Alex – FW – Chicago Steel (USHL) – 5'9" 168

Roos was drafted in the 2nd round, 16th overall by Cedar Rapids into the USHL after playing for Team Illinois in the U18s. He joined the Chicago Steel in the 2011-2012 season for 25 games where he had an impressive 22 points without taking a single penalty and then followed that up this year with 64 games and a total of 47 points.

Roos is a smaller forward but is able to really pass the puck well. He opens up really effectively to take passes in the offensive zone to connect on one-timer opportunities and will take the puck to scoring areas to try and get good shot opportunities.. He distributes the puck well on the rush, can make great give-and-go plays to get to scoring areas with the puck with a bit of time and space in order to make a play and uses his speed to blow by defenders for break chances. There are times when he tries to make a play unnecessarily when one may not be available which results in a turnover rather than just getting the puck in deep and he still needs to get much stronger on the puck along the boards. He turns the puck over at times as well in the offensive zone trying to force passes through the opposition and even with all the skills that he has there are also moments when he makes bad decisions with the puck, for example electing to shoot on a 2-on-1 chance when there is a lane to move the puck across and instead the goaltender is able to make an easy save. Alex has committed to Colorado College for this fall of 2013.

Roy, Eric – LD – Brandon Wheat Kings (WHL) – 6'3" 190

Roy is a big, offensive defenseman who has very good puck skills. He is able to move the puck smoothly and quite efficiently from the backend to start the attack for the Wheat Kings. Roy is featured as the power play quarterback, and has done an admirable job since last season. The biggest concern with Roy is his defensive game. He is often caught in the middle of nowhere, and does not provide very good coverage in his own end. Roy seems to be guessing quite often as to whether he should chase the puck or stay where he is, which gives opponents plenty of time to make plays, or exploit his bad decision to chase them behind the net and leave a lane in the slot wide open. He needs to have his head on a swivel and be more aware of his surroundings. Offensively, Roy is quite impressive with and without the puck. He handles the puck smoothly and has very good control of it. Time and time again he is able to make very tight spins to get away from a forecheck to get the rush going up the ice. He makes good, crisp passes to his forwards, and limits the turnovers he commits. Roy has a good shot from the point, but needs to work on getting it on net and to use it if he has an open lane to the net. Roy may not be particularly quick, but he is able to cover a lot of ground with his long strides. He is good in tight areas with the puck, but he is slow to react when on defense. Another concern with Roy is his lack of toughness. He is fairly easy to bump off the puck, and does not show much desire to stand up for teammates in any situations nor be harder to play against, which is something he really needs to work on if he ever wants to play as a professional.

Quotable: "He has some attributes but I'm not seeing enough from him, especially when I compared it to some of the talk out there." - NHL Scout

Roy, Marc-Olivier – RW – Blainville-Boisbriand Armada (QMJHL) – 6'1" 180

The Boisbriand native had his coming out party in last year playoff with 14 points in 11 games as the Armada were eliminated by the league runner up Rimouski Oceanic. Roy has enjoyed a highly productive 2012-2013 season with 29 goals and 67 points in 65 games.

Roy is a great skater with good agility which helps him change direction quickly. His explosion is powerful helping him create space and be the first man to a loose puck. He played on the team's top line most of the year, and produced consistently. Roy has a good work ethic and great anticipation. He can be a very effective 2-way forward when he plays with aggressiveness and keeps moving his feet. The 18 year old has a good quick-release shot and likes to set it up on the half wall on the power play. He has scored numerous times in our observations from that position. His puck handling at top speed is great and he can be elusive when he's coming in a one-on-one situation putting his quick hands to good use. He's just as good at scoring goals as he is at setting up plays. His speed again serves him well as it helps him create passing lanes and get to the slot before the opposing team's defense can adjust. He can execute plays offensively exceptionally well at very high speeds. He sees the ice well and has a high level of hockey sense, serving him both offensively and defensively. Roy has become a complete player in those last 2 years under the tutelage of Jean-Francois Houle, being more cautious in his own zone than he used to be last year when he has the puck. He will also rarely get caught cheating in neutral zone before his team recovers the puck.

Marc-Olivier Roy needs to go in the tough areas of the ice more frequently as he will find more success there than staying out in the perimeter. We have seen some games where Roy was very soft on the puck, gliding and looking disinterested in making or dishing a contact. He needs to keep his level of intensity at a higher level as he is a better player when he keeps his game simpler and plays with more grit. He will need to get stronger as he doesn't look that big on the ice despite being fairly tall, listed at 6'1.

Quotable: "Love the way Roy plays, a good skater and his motor never stops. Has become more reliable without the puck thanks to a great coaching staff they have there. I saw him score goals in different ways this season, either from 5 feet jamming on a rebound or from taking a one-timer from the half wall on the power play." - Jerome Berube

Rychel, Kerby – LW – Windsor Spitfires (OHL) – 6'1" 200

It seems like Kerby has been a Spitfire forever, but he actually went through quite the journey to get to where he was. Kerby was selected in the first round of the 2010 OHL Priority Selection Draft by the Barrie Colts. From there he was traded to the Memorial Cup Host Mississauga St. Michael's Majors where he spent the first half of his rookie season. Kerby was then delt to the Windsor Spitfires and finished his rookie season there. Due to his late birth date, he had one more year to go before he was NHL Eligible and he passed the time quite effectively. As the Spitfires were looking to reload their roster and get working towards a 2014 contender, Kerby was busy notching 41 goals as a sophomore OHLer.

You can really see Kerby's father Warren's influence in his physical play. Warren was always known as a hard working player and Kerby has seemed to learn from that. He finishes his checks very hard whenever possible and generally played his best games on the bigger stages. Along with his physical play, Kerby's best asset has to be his shot. He's not a fancy player who will stickhandle around opposing players. You won't see many highlight reel goals from Rychel. What you will see is a well positioned forward who constantly seems to be in the right spot with a lethal release allowing him to post back to back 40 goal seasons. Kerby is also willing to drop the gloves and has faired moderately well. While Kerby looks like an NHL player it seems the biggest gap is what he is projected to be. His shot suggests he could play a second line power forward type of role. His energy and board play suggests he can play as a third pairing.

Whoever selects Rychel will look for him to improve his skating ability and become that true second line power forward who can play physical and put the puck in the net while having a third line grinder as the safety net if he doesn't pan out the way they expect. With the Spitfires hoping to acquire the 2014 CHL Memorial Cup, Kerby could be the go to guy on a very big stage next year. On what should be a more improved team Kerby will continue to be the go to guy for the Spitfires, but can make the jump to the AHL for the 2014-2015 season thanks to his late birth date.

Quotable: "When Kirby is on, he is very very good. He is best when he mixes in physical play and goes to the dirty areas." - Mark Edwards

Salerno, Brandon – FW – Waterloo Blackhawks (USHL) – 5'7" 169

Brandon made an impression on our scouts as early as his Minor Midget when he stared for the Don Mills Flyers. While small, Brandon made a big impact playing in a supporting offensive role playing behind top 2013 NHL prospects Max Domi and Darnell Nurse. Brandon joined the North York Rangers of the OJHL for his 2011-2012 and put together a solid performance for a 16 year old contributing in all zones. Brandon made the jump to the USHL joining a powerful Waterloo Black Hawks team and providing a powerful forecheck and back check. He's been important supporter for Waterloo in all game situations chipping in on the power play, while playing with a lot of energy on the penalty kill blocking shots and getting into passing lanes. Brandon may not be the biggest guy on the ice but he plays big finishing his checks and showing fearlessness going into the corners.

It will be a huge uphill battle for Salerno overcoming his size heading into the 2013 NHL Entry Draft, but he plays with the heart and desire that teams love. Brandon was also selected in the 3rd round of the 2011 OHL Priority Selection Draft by the Ottawa 67's. Salerno is committed to play for University of Maine.

Sanche, Phillipe – RW – Blainville-Boisbriand Armada (QMJHL) – 5'5" 150

To say Sanche is undersized would be a gross misrepresentation, standing at 5'5 150 he was in fact the smallest player in the QMJHL this season. His size didn't hinder him as he still produce over 50 points in a secondary scoring role for the Armada. He is a very courageous forward that will go in the tough area of the ice and won't back down from anyone, displaying character and intensity. A quick skater always moving his feet, Sanche uses this great speed to make up for his lack of size. He sees the ice well and makes good short passes when working down-low. Quick hands and above-average skill set also gives him good results in the Q. Although Sanche can have a tough time against physical teams and defensive games, he still showed tons of heart and intensity in those games where teams tried to intimidate him. Not likely to get drafted but has already disproved critics and could do it again.

Sanford, Zachary – LW – Middlesex Islanders (EJHL) – 6'3, 190

Perhaps no 2013 NHL Draft prospect has seen his stock rise this season like Sanford. At the onset of the season, he showed physical tools and played a gritty game in bursts, but showed slow feet and had a hard time handling the puck and working together with his teammates. Months later, he's a completely different player.

Sanford shows ever-improving poise with the puck and has learned to better utilize his hands, which are deceptively quick for his size. He's strong on his stick and skates, allowing him to protect the puck well on the boards, though he can expose the puck with poor positioning at times. He makes plays in the offensive zone with intelligent passing, and can take the puck to the net with great force. He forechecks well with good contact and an active stick. His skating needs further improvement, as he's still choppy on his feet. He plays his best when he keeps things simple and focuses on going north-south, rather than trying to create. The Boston College-commit is still very raw, but shows flashes of being a dominant player.

Quotable: "After watching Zach in the fall, it was hard to anticipate his meteoric rise this season. Credit him, and the Islanders coaching staff, for recognizing and working to correct the flaws in his game. There's still plenty of work to do here, but the improvement has been noticeable, at times even on a shift-to-shift basis." - Josh Deitell

Santini, Steve – RD – US NTDP Under-18 Team – 6'2, 205

Mean, strong, and sound at both ends of the rink, Santini is the best defensive prospect from the NTDP this year. A confident leader who brings it for big games and works hard on and off the ice, he rarely goes a shift without making a positive impression and can be iced comfortably in any situation.

A defense-first player, Santini makes life hell on opposing forwards, physically dominating those who come into his corner or try to camp out in front of the net. He makes very few mistakes against the rush and is difficult to beat wide, though he does chase the play from time to time when the opposing team get their offense set up. He steps up when he senses hesitation and can lay big, open-ice hits. He takes few penalties for such an aggressive player, but discipline is an occasional issue. Though he managed to go the entire year without scoring a goal, Santini's puck skills are actually quite good. He's not dynamic, and therefore not an ideal power play quarterback, but he has the ability to skate the puck out of danger and makes a good first pass. His shot is powerful and he keeps his head up when shooting, but his release tends to be slow and his accuracy is lacking. He's not particularly elusive against the forecheck but protects the puck well and shows good instincts under pressure. When he finds himself without an option, he's good about making the safe clearance. Excellent skating ties his game together. He has a powerful stride and is difficult to beat in tight with great edge work.

Santini projects as a top-quality, smooth-skating shutdown defenseman who won't be a liability with the puck. Santini is the type of glue player that helps teams win championships.

Quotable: "Had him really high on my list early this season. I thought he could post some offensive numbers but they never came. He's still a top 40 guy for me, I like the toughness, he moves the puck and can skate." - Mark Edwards

Saros, Juuse – G – HPK U20 (Jr A SM-liiga) – 5'10" 178

Saros has moved up the ranks with HPK rather rapidly and started in goal as a 16 year old in the U20 league posting very good numbers last season. He returned to this league and showed his talents internationally as well. Juuse will need to overcome his size. It's what's made us most cautious about him as 5'10" is a tough height to succeed at the NHL level as a goaltender. However, Juuse seems to be defying the odds at this point of his development. Hands down his best attribute is his leg movement. It looks like someone hit the turbo button every time he drops into the butterfly. What's more impressive is how quickly he gets up. His leg movement is simply outstanding and when you mix it with his vision through traffic and technical abilities it makes him a very talented goaltender. He has excellent reflexes and his glove hand is great. He also has great recovery and looks poised when making multiple saves in succession. He has trouble with rebound control and will need to improve this. He's quick enough to make the save, but it will be more of a concern at a higher level. Juuse is a good puck playing goaltender and doesn't rush or panic making intelligent passes up ice or clearing the zone.

Quotable: "He is an outstanding kid, I enjoyed interviewing him. The first game I saw him was at the Four Nations tourney and I was impressed, but didn't think too much about it because he lacked size. Then I saw him play the rest of the week and he was great game after game. Flash forward to Sochi in April and once again the kid stood on his head. To put it bluntly, he won games for his team. NHL teams like the 6'0" plus goalies but this kid looks good enough to me to be an exception to the rule." – Mark Edwards

Quotable: "If Saros is three inches taller, he's unquestionably the best goaltending prospect in the draft. He has no real weaknesses. Whatever success the Finnish U18 team had this year can be largely attributed to his spectacular play in net." – Josh Deitell

Schiller, Landon – RW – Sault Ste. Marie Greyhounds (OHL) – 6'1" 187

Landon was selected in the 11th round of the 2011 OHL Priority Selection Draft by the Sault Ste. Marie Greyhounds out of the Markham Majors Minor Midget program. He spent his 2011-2012 with the Markham Majors Major Midget AAA team in the GTHL. Landon then came to Greyhounds camp this year and managed to grab up one of the final roster spots. Schiller had an up and down season for the Greyhounds. He missed some time due to a suspension for an illegal hit and was in and out of the lineup from that point forward. Schiller is the typical grinder type forward who likes to punish opposing defenders by finishing every possible check. He is good at getting into opponents faces and does not back down from scrums after the whistle.

Landon did not show much offensive production this season but saw limited shifts when he was dressed. He brings a good element of speed and is good at getting in on the fore check creating turnovers and pressure situations. Schiller is a hard working depth forward who should see improved ice time next season for the Greyhounds.

Schueneman, Corey – LD – Des Moines Buccaneers (USHL) – 6'3" 187

Schueneman is a defenseman who was drafted into the USHL by the Muskegon Lumberjacks in the 4th round in 2011 after he played for Little Caesars U16 in his minor midget year and was a near point a game player as a defenseman. He played in just a single game earlier this year for the Muskegon Lumberjacks before joining Des Moines Buccaneers for 25 games where he managed to register 12 points. He is a defenseman that can make a good long pass out of the zone to find a man at the far blue line to spring him into the offensive zone and he does a good job of holding the offensive blue line. He distributes the puck pretty well on the power play, can find a teammate down low to create some good opportunities and makes good chip plays to create space for teammates with the puck. He gets his stick in lanes for the most part in the defensive end to try and break-up plays and block passes and protects the puck pretty well on the rush as he can take a hit and still hold on to the puck to make a play. Corey is committed to Western Michigan University.

Scott, Justin – RW – Barrie Colts (OHL) – 6'1" 189

Justin was selected in the 4th round of the 2011 OHL Priority Selection Draft by the Barrie Colts out of the Burlington Eagles. In his rookie season, Scott may have not lit up the lamp all that much, however he learned his role on his team and played it effectively. He came up this year from the Burlington Cougars of the OJHL and had 9 points in 55 games this season.

Justin was used mainly as a role player because it is well suited for his skill set. Scott is able to get a good cycle going in the offensive zone and goes hard to the net for opportunities in tight to the net. He puts good pressure on the fore-check, while battling hard for the puck to try to force turnovers and he protects the puck nicely from the opposition's pressure. For the most part he sticks to a simple game, chipping pucks in deep, putting long shots on net and pressuring the puck. He is reasonably physical, plays in the dirty areas of the ice, but needs to improve his speed and quickness and also get stronger on his feet so that he is not knocked off the puck too easily. We do not expect Scott to get drafted at the 2013 NHL Entry Draft, but his strong energy role and size should see him become a regular for the Colts next season.

Segalla, Ryan – LD – Salisbury School (Prep-CT) – 6'05", 190

Ryan is a very strong, defense-first defenseman with some offensive upside. He can be downright nasty and is hard as nails to play against, clearing his net front with intensity and getting seriously involved physically along the boards. He can overdo it with his aggression by taking himself out of position to make contact, and has some trouble controlling his anger at times, but his decision-making has seen marked improvement this season. His stick is active and he's a smooth skater who's very strong on his feet with impressive footwork, which combined with his ability to step up at the blueline makes him difficult to beat on the rush. He has some puck skills but is far from a sure thing to produce as a professional. While he can carry the puck with a lot of vigor and poise through center, he has trouble making the right read when he nears the opposing blueline. He can also be careless with the puck in his zone, trying risky passes instead of making safe plays. He has a booming shot from the point and moves the puck well on the power play.

Ryan plays his best when he keeps his offensive game simple and focuses on his defensive responsibilities. He played with impressive poise in boosting Salisbury to their New England Prep championship win, a performance that undoubtedly boosted his draft stock. He'll play for the University of Connecticut starting in 2014.

Quotable: "I like Ryan, he's a meat and potatoes guy. He skates well and shoots the puck hard." – NHL Scout

Quotable: "Ryan plays angry, which can help or hurt him. I saw fear in the eyes of players who had to go into the corners with him, but I also saw him boil over at the tail end of a Salisbury loss at the Flood-Marr Holiday Tournament and it wasn't pretty. There's a lot of passion in his game. He's at his best when he controls it." – Josh Deitell

Shea, Brandon – LC – South Shore Kings (EJHL) – 6'2", 201

Brandon's career has taken a number of interesting twists and turns. He left Noble and Greenough school in Massachusetts to go to the QMJHL after being selected in the first round of the 2011 Q Draft by Moncton, then quit the team mid-season and sat at home for months without playing hockey, having lost his college eligibility in the process. He was traded to the Quebec Remparts this past summer but after struggling out of the gate, left the team in November. He returned home to play for the South Shore Kings of the EJHL. With the Kings, he played a nice power forward game, acting like a human wrecking ball with a bull-in-a-china-shop approach. He lacks the touch with the puck, skating ability, and two-way ability to be considered a professional prospect. He serves as a cautionary tale in development.

Sheen, Riley – LW – Seattle Thunderbirds (WHL) – 5'11" 156

Sheen is a speedy winger who generates scoring chances using his speed and going hard to the net. He was counted on by his team to provide a good offensive presence, and was able to do so at times. The problem with Sheen this season was his inconsistency. There are shifts when he looks very impressive, then he disappears for long stretches during play. Sheen likes to drive down the wing, quickly stop and turn towards the boards on the half wall and see if he has any options to make a pass to a trailer. When he is interested in playing, he is good at protecting the puck along the boards, and he makes it hard for opponents to pin him to the boards with his quick turns. He has an average shot that he does not use very often. He likes to throw the puck at the net to create chances, and when he does not have the puck, he is at his best when he drives the net and causes havoc. Defensively, Sheen is average in his own end. He has his moments where he seems to pick off passes on a regular basis to get a counter attack going. He needs to be more consistent without the puck, and block more shots and help more often down low when necessary.

Sherman, Wiley – LD – Hotchkiss School (Prep-CT) – 6'6", 206

Wiley intrigues as a huge defenseman who's a great skater for his size. He moves swiftly with a smooth stride and good edges. His defensive game is sharp. He's a calming presence who uses his long stick well to cover lanes and can play nasty, clearing the front of his net and making life difficult for forwards trying to play the puck along the boards. He's very aware and at times looked a step ahead of everybody else on the ice. He has a good shot from the point and can make a safe first pass out of his zone, but lacks the puck skills to say he has serious offensive upside at the next level. He rarely makes mistakes with the puck, but rarely makes things happen either. He played for a poor Hotchkiss team this year, which made it difficult to judge him properly, but showed very well at showcases playing against other top prospects from New England. He showed too many good things this season to pass through this draft unselected.

Quotable: "I like the upside here but he is raw. He didn't do some of the simple things you would expect but I'll give him the benefit of the doubt due to not playing at a higher level. I like his compete level, his long reach and his aggressive playing style. Decision making needs to be better." - Mark Edwards

Quotable: "Rarely do you find a 6'6 defenseman who can skate and play both ends of the rink. It's difficult to judge big players against Prep talent, but Sherman has the tools to be an impact defender at the next level." Josh Deitell

Shields, Mack – G – Calgary Hitmen (WHL) – 6'3" 190

Mac Shields is the back up for Calgary who has received very limited minutes playing behind Chris Driedger this season. Shields has been able to provide a good presence in the net whenever he was called upon. Even when he gives up bad goals, he does not let it effect him mentally, and plays a steady game in net. He does not have great mobility to go post to post to make big saves, and his only real asset is his size. He is a below average puck handler, and is not able to make any good passes to get his team started on the attack.

Shinkaruk, Hunter – LW – Medicine Hat (WHL) – 5'11" 175

There were a lot of questions as to whether Hunter Shinkaruk could put up the same types of numbers with ex-teammate Emerson Etem moving onto the AHL this season. Sure enough, Shinkaruk was able to prove that last season was no fluke, and led the Tigers with his impressive offensive skills.

It is difficult to find a player who is as dynamic offensively as Hunter Shinkaruk. He plays the game at such a high speed, that teammates sometimes have a difficult time keeping up with him. He has very good hands that he is able to use to maneuver around opponents as he is skating at full speed. Shinkaruk has a good release to his shots that is able to fool goaltenders. He has the ability to consistently score highlight reel goals, and really make players around him look so much better. He is relentless on the forecheck, and does a good job of knocking opponents off the puck despite his size.

Defensively, Shinkaruk has made some good strides in his game in that area of his game. He is good at getting into the shooting lanes of opposing defensemen, and is not afraid to block shots when necessary. He has also become a key contributor on the PK for the Tigers, and adds a dangerous scoring element for them. He still needs to work on his physical play along the boards and using his stick more effectively, but it is definitely a good sign to see him improve his play without the puck. It will be interesting to see how Shinkaruk will adjust to the professional level. He is able to get away with trying to get through opponents all the time at the junior ranks, but it will be tough to do so against much more mature players. He will have to develop a knack of getting into open areas to score to contribute to his team. His offensive talent is undeniable, but it will be interesting to see just how successful he will become.

Quotable: "He left me wanting more early at the U18 in Brno last year, but I was jet lagged as well, so I cut him a lot of slack. He got much better. You can't deny the points he puts up. I have heard a lot of talk about him from scouts this year. Seems guys are either really hot or cold on him or have him as a 1st round slider. I had multiple scouts tell me his interview with their team during combine week was not good." - Mark Edwards

Shiplo, Luke – LD – Des Moines Buccaneers (USHL) – 5'8" 159

Shiplo has had to overcome some real adversity to make it into the USHL after being selected in the 20th round at 288th overall in the 2012 Futures Draft. Shiplo played in the OMHA for the Oakville Rangers in minor midget, then played for the Georgetown Raiders and Toronto Lakeshore Patriots in the OJHL the following season. He joined Des Moines Buccaneers this season for his rookie year in the USHL and managed to get 10 points in 46 games. He is a defenseman who skates the puck up too often and needs to make breakout passes more to get the puck up the ice quicker. He has a good shot from the point that he can get through to the net, but needs to keep it down low with more consistency to try and generate chances. Luke was also selected by the Peterborough Petes at the 2011 OHL Priority Selection Draft. Shiplo has committed to Western Michigan University starting this fall of 2013

Silk, Brody – LW – Sudbury Wolves (OHL) – 6'0" 185

Brody was selected in the 2nd round of the 2010 OHL Priority Selection Draft by the Sudbury Wolves out of the New Liskeard Cubs of the GNML. He made the Wolves as a 16 year old allowing him to be one of a very select group to go into their first year of the NHL Draft Eligibility with over 150 games played in the CHL.

Brody has really progressed each year as he was used very limited at 16 but got a great experience playing for Team Ontario at the 2011 World U-17 Challenge. Brody's role increased as he entered his second season, and was a key two-way player for Sudbury and an assistant captain in this his 3rd year. He finished the year with 36 points and 102 penalty minutes in 55 games showing that offensive potential with an aggression and edge as well. He possesses pretty good size and uses it to cycle the puck and go hard to the net for opportunities from in tight. He keeps his game simple, competes for the puck and challenges the point well. He can make good short passes and is a pretty good skater with a good first 3 steps for a quick acceleration. He gets to the front of the net and is not intimidated to play in those dirty areas and the coach likes to use him in critical situations, probably for this reason.

Silk's best chance for success is to continue establishing himself as a solid defensively responsible forward that kills penalties, does the dirty work on the ice, battles and competes hard for the puck and can be an asset for a team moving forward. He may not have the most skill but seems to understand the game well, uses good positioning and instincts in all three zones.

Sills, Connor – RW – Plymouth Whalers (OHL) – 6'4" 202

Connor was selected in the 9th round of the 2011 OHL Priority Selection Draft from the Thunder Bay Kings Minor Midget program. He remained in Thunder Bay working up the ranks at home before joining the Plymouth Whalers this season. He was in and out of the lineup, however he played over half of the games this regular season and a handful of playoff games. He will likely be expected to be an everyday player for the Whalers next season with so many forwards graduating. When this happens, Connor will make his presence known when he's on the ice as he is a very physically imposing player. Sills dropped the gloves 10 times this season, and took on some strong opponents, generally players not quite as big as him.

Without trying to insult Connor we don't exactly see him playing a skilled style of game. He is not great with the puck and will need to work on being better at making the simple plays. He is a player that has great size, a great frame and he understands himself as a player. He gets the puck deep and crashes and bangs in the corners winning his share of the battles. He will drive to the net and create a disruption in the crease. While it wouldn't be an absolute shock to see him selected in the draft or invited to a camp, we aren't expecting it. Generally players that play his role and contain limited offensive upside get invited later on in their careers, and generally are picked to play that game at the pro level. Connor will need to improve his skating and his puck handling abilities to reach his effectiveness. We would also like to see him add more of a defensive element to his game as it would certainly make him more valuable at the junior and pro levels.

Siroky, Ryan – FW – Green Bay Gamblers (USHL) – 5'11" 190

Ryan developed his game in California playing for both the Los Angeles Selects and Los Angeles Jr. Kings U16 programs. From there he joined the Green Bay Gamblers of the USHL experiencing moderate success in his rookie season. Ryan plays with a relentless forecheck presence and is able to force turnovers and make an impact on a shift by shift basis. He provides intelligent positioning in the offensive zone and is always seen hovering around the slot. He posted twice as many goals as assists but this was more so a tribute to his presence around the net as opposed to an unwillingness to pass.

Ryan possesses a physical presence for the Gamblers and always finishes his checks. He works hard in all three zones and puts in a lot of work along the walls. While his offensive instincts are good and have helped him score as a USHL rookie, they likely aren't enough for him to project as a top six forward prospect. Fortunately Ryan shown a willingness to drop the gloves at the junior level. Siroky will be a player to watch moving forward due to his potential. Ryan is committed to join Miami University this fall of 2013.

Smith, Alex – RD – Indiana Ice (USHL) – 6'0" 177

Smith played 47 games for the Muskegon Lumberjacks in the 2011-2012 season after being selected by them in the 1st round at 5th overall, however was only able to play in 12 games for Indiana Ice this year due to injury. Smith is a really good skater and can make a good 1st pass up out of his own zone to start the rush. He jumps up on the rush to join the attack and will come into the high slot to take passes to put good shots on net. He uses his stick really effectively to knock the puck free off the opposition to force turnovers and can distribute the puck really well from the point on the power play. He also has a really hard shot that he can get on target from the point and can make good long passes to find teammates at the blue line to lead them into the offensive zone with speed. He can skate the puck up the ice end-to-end to gain the offensive zone and does a good job of finding those lanes to rush the puck up the ice. He has good vision to spot his options on the breakout then can make a good tape-to-tape pass and in his own end he plays with good gap control and forces the opposition to the outside. He plays the body really well, keeping to a nice physical game on the puck carrier and clears the front of his net well. He can take a hit and still make a play to get the puck out of the zone and reads the play well on the penalty kill to get in lanes to pick off passes and breakup plays in order to get the puck out of the zone.

What is most desirable about his game are his two-way play and the willingness to play the body on the opposition to keep his man from gaining the inside track to the net. Smith has a good sense of how to play the opposition off the rush, and will play them hard and physically along the wall and also has the capability to get the puck up the ice on a quick transition.

Smith, Jerret – RD – Seattle Thunderbirds (WHL) – 6'2" 198

Smith is a good defensive defenseman who is developing into a good shut down defenseman for the future. Like most of the young defensemen that Seattle used this year, he started the season quite raw, but received consistent ice time and has since really improved his overall game. Smith is actually one of the smaller defensemen on Seattle, but he probably has the best stick among his partners. He gives very little opportunities in the slot, and he is quite good at picking off passes and knocking away pucks as opponents come down his wing on the rush. Smith is solid along the walls, and really gives opponents very little to work with. He could work on being more physical in front of the net and be a tougher presence to play against. His gap control also needs work because of his lack of foot speed. He gives opponents some room to come into the zone, and is not able to close the gap and land a good hit on them.

Offensively, Smith will probably never develop into a dependable offensive player. He really needs to work on handling the puck in pressure and make good outlet passes. His play with the puck is quite mediocre, and it is definitely something that he will have to fix. He does not take much time handling the puck, and more often than not goes glass and out of the defensive zone.

Smith, Hunter – RW – Oshawa Generals (OHL) – 6'7" 218

Smith was selected by his hometown Windsor Spitfires in the 2nd round pick in the 2011 OHL Priority Selection Draft after spending the past season with the Windsor Jr. Spitfires Minor Midget program. He has played marginally over the last two years due to injuries and depth reasons. If he was born 5 days later he would not be eligible for the NHL Draft until 2014.

We have seen Hunter play in limited action. The kid is built like a house and will hit every opportunity he gets. He has shown the willingness to drop the gloves but doesn't excel in fights. Hunter can best be described as a "project" for an NHL team. His skating and puck skills are well below average and he will need to put in a lot of work to get these up to par. Hunter would really benefit from another year of experience. He needs to improve his skating before he can start to see his potential. We don't expect him to get selected, but you can never count out a 6'7" monster like Hunter and we hope to see him continue to improve.

Sorensen, Nick – RW – Québec Remparts (QMJHL) – 6'1" 175

Following a rookie season that ended after only 9 games with a knee injury, Nick Sorensen returned stronger and even quicker this season with the highly talented Québec Remparts. He enjoyed a highly productive offensive season with 47 points in 46 games played.

Nick Sorensen is a great skater, possessing a tremendous explosion which makes him a dangerous player when he has the puck or when he crashes the net. A dynamic skater that is tough to stop when he handles the puck at his top speed. He is a very good finisher and finds countless ways to put the puck in the back of the net. He is not afraid of high traffic areas, being able to position his stick at the right place and doing the little details that a good goal scorer can. He doesn't shoot a lot and prefers to choose the right moment and use his intelligence to get the goals. His wrist shot is released quickly with great accuracy, he will rarely miss a shot on net. He has very good sense and makes a solid decision quickly showing high hockey IQ. He is not a selfish player and will use his good passing skills to create a scoring chance for a teammate. He's not a physical player by any means, but will use his good puck protection to control the puck when he gets hit. He has great puck handling skills but will use speed and reach most of the times to get around players rather than try to go through them. Sorensen's defensive instincts are solid which makes him a good 2-way player when he's focused in the game. He showed the willingness to take a hit to get the puck out or to sacrifice the body to block a shot. He still needs to get bigger and stronger to win those battles on the boards, but his progression throughout the year in this particular area is undeniable. He seems to be able to elevate his play in the crucial moments of the game.

The Denmark native had a bad tendency to rely on his talent in some of our viewings this year. In those games Sorensen was reactive instead of proactive which made him look bad in all 3 zones. He's not the kind of player that can rely only on his talent to have success. Skating is such a big part of his game, that he becomes pretty average when he starts gliding. Sorensen needs to play with energy every night if he wants to be an effective player in professional hockey. I would also like to see him more aggressive in his battles and when he crashes the net. Some will certainly question his durability as he only played 51 regular season games in 2 seasons and seems like a player that could be categorized as injury prone, but those injuries didn't seem to affect the style he plays in the viewings we had of him.

Souto, Chase – RW – Kamloops Blazers (WHL) – 5'11" 176

Souto is a 2 way forward with some offensive abilities while providing a good defensive presence. He will definitely need to work on his speed as he is not particularly big or strong. Souto has demonstrated his very good wrist shot off the rush. He has a quick release as he comes down the wing, but could work on locating his shots more accurately. He has limited playmaking abilities, but does seem to be able to find open areas out on the ice to receive passes. Defensively, Souto is in good position consistently, but could do a better job of blocking shots. The issue with Souto's game is his lack of impact. He is not able to get much accomplished on a consistent basis, and he is not particularly tough to play against in his own zone either. He has to be more committed to blocking shots on a nightly basis. He gets a couple scoring chances a game, and has a difficult time finishing opportunities off.

Stadnyk, Carson – LC – Everett Silvertips (WHL) – 6'2" 170

Stadnyk was used as a bottom 6 forward for much of the season for Everett. He struggled to receive much ice time due to his struggles at both ends of the ice. He has a big frame that he does not use very well, and was not much of a factor for the Silvertips.

Stadnyk has a lot of improvements to make in his game. His skating is not good enough to be an effective shut down centre, and he is not good in his own zone at all. He runs around in the defensive zone, and makes mistake after mistake. Offensively, he does not have a good touch around the net, and his playmaking abilities are below average.

Stanton, Ty – LD – Medicine Hat Tigers (WHL) – 6'3" 173

Stanton is a skilled defenseman who brought a good offensive presence for the Tigers in the backend when he was in the line up. He was bothered by small injuries throughout the year, which has effected his development. The best asset of Stanton is probably his puck moving abilities. He makes very good passes from the backend to get the attack going for his team. He has the ability to carry the puck up the ice to provide another threat off the rush, and makes good decisions with the puck. He walks the blue line quite well to create some space to get a shot off, but he is definitely more of a passer than a shooter.

Defensively, Stanton definitely has to get much stronger. He gets pushed off the puck too easily, and does not win enough battles along the walls. He needs to add muscle to his height to have a chance of playing as a pro one day. Stanton shows above average skating abilities, and will have to keep improving his use of his reach to keep opponents to the outside. He is quite soft to play against, and will have to provide a more physical presence in games.

Sterk, Josh – LC – Kitchener Rangers (OHL) – 5'10" 161

Joshua was selected in the 5th round from the Mississauga Senators program at the 2011 OHL Priority Selection draft by the Kitchener Rangers. Josh had a fairly successful rookie season making the Rangers out of camp as a 16 year old playing a bottom six forward role.

Sterk played a bottom six role for most of this season for the Rangers before being scratched for the majority of their playoff run. Sterk is slightly undersized but makes up for it with excellent speed and skating ability and by constantly moving his feet to outwork his opponents. He brings grit and effort whenever he is on the ice and is not afraid to go into the corners and battle for the puck with much bigger opponents. Josh showed flashes of offensive skill in a limited ice time role and is good at getting into the slot before fooling goaltenders with a silky quick release wrister. Sterk needs some work on his defensive zone positioning and sometimes runs around too much trying to make a play. He has shown a willingness to block shots and is good at getting into passing and shooting lanes. Sterk showed areas of potential over the course of the season, and should expect to see a larger role in the Rangers offensive lineup next season.

While Sterk has shown some good potential at the junior level, we don't expect him to be selected at the 2013 NHL Entry Draft. If he does, he will be selected out of a large group of players who's potential lies as a bottom six grinder who can contribute in a defensive role and is reliable in a defensive/penalty kill role. Sterk does have his skating to rely upon and displays the clear willingness to work hard. We would like to see him continue to get stronger and be more difficult to play against. Sterk is a player who could potentially break out if the right situation presents itself.

Stork, Luke – FW – Youngstown Phantoms (USHL) – 5'11" 175

Luke Stork played for the Pittsburgh Hornets in minor midget and was a near point a game player before he was selected in the 3rd round by the Youngstown Phantoms. He then played in 2 games for Youngstown last year then followed it up with his first full season in the USHL with 30 points in 64 games this year.

Stork is a player who can get the puck in deep to start the cycle and has decent size and physicality to finish some big hits along the boards. He brings a net-front presence and is very willing to stand in the dirty areas to look for tips. He moves the puck around pretty well in the offensive zone, will crash the net hard and keep to a simple, effective grinding game. In his own end he challenges the puck carrier at the point, gets in lanes and shows a willingness to block shots. He comes back to his own end for good support, has great pressure and battle for the puck and plays with good speed, hustle and compete for loose pucks. He has an agility to stop-up quickly off the rush to distance himself somewhat from the opposition then moves the puck to a trailing player in the high slot for good shot opportunities. He has to hit the net on his chances off the rush and needs to watch when he turns the puck over on the rush on puck mishandles. Stork's best quality is how well he pressures on the fore-check, plays hard along the boards and finishes all his hits on the puck carrier. He may still need to add size and strength to be more of a force on the ice, but needs to stick to the tough grinding game that has made him successful. Luke has committed to Ohio State University for this fall of 2013.

Studnicka, Sam – RW – Windsor Spitfires (OHL) – 6'1" 193

Studnicka was selected in the 5th round of the 2011 OHL Priority Selection out of the Sun County Panthers Minor Midget organization. Despite being selected in the 5th round, Sam was just one of a handful of 5th rounders to see action as a 16 year old and made the most of it. When he wasn't up with Windsor he spent last season with the Chatham Maroons Jr. B team posting respectable numbers.

Sam is a very simplified hard working player. He goes hard into the corners, finishes his checks, and drops the gloves from time to time. He plays in a limited role for Windsor, one that will likely increase as he develops as a player, but will likely be limited offensively and will survive off of his physical play. Sam makes basic offensive plays but isn't really a threat to score. He will play a two-way game and we'd like to see him become a more intense defensive forward to maximize his potential. Sam appears to be a player who understands his role which is very important for these hard working grinder types as they are able to focus on their role as a prospect and a player and be of the most potential value of their team.

Sam is a player who may go late, he may be a camp invite, or he may need to work hard another year before getting an opportunity. The key for Sam will be to keep getting stronger, keep working hard and keep playing a two-way game. We would also like to see him become a better skater as it will help him in all of these areas.

Subban, Jordan – Belleville Bulls (OHL) – 5'9" 175

Subban had quite a sophomore season in the OHL registering an impressive 51 points in 68 games as a defenseman and was a solid +22. He won a gold medal with Canada in the 2012 Ivan Hlinka tournament and also played in this season's top prospects game.

His style of game resembles that of his older brother P.K. Subban, a smooth skating, puck rushing defenseman who likes to jump in on the attack and provide the team with offense from the back end. He is a quick defenseman who finds lanes to skate the puck up the ice effectively and holds the offensive line well to keep the attack alive. He is agile with good moves to get around defenders or create space to work with from the opposition and reads the play well to step off the point and come down into the high slot to put good shots on net. He is able to get to the slot with the puck to put shots on and finds lanes to move the puck around in the offensive zone. He makes a great 1st pass out of the zone to start the rush and gets his shots through to the net from the point kept down low to try to generate rebounds. He has demonstrated a good two-way hustle on many occasions to get back after he gets caught on a pinch to help out in his own end, and he uses his stick effectively to take the puck away from the opposition. He gets in lanes to breakup some plays in his own end and he can cycle the puck in the offensive zone or drive it hard to the net. Jordan also provides a gritty agitating style of game and has a great ability to get under the skin of his opposition and throw them off their game. He needs to watch some of the turnovers trying to force passes through the opposition and is also a bit soft on the puck at times, getting knocked off it too easily. He also gives up a bit too much space sometimes in his own end, leaving the opposition with the opportunity to get a pretty good shot off with time and space.

Subban is a sure fire pick in the 2013 NHL Entry Draft, however he may not go as high as some may believe because of the last name. He shows many of the assets P.K. has, but he requires a lot of physical and mental maturation before reaching the level he's capable of. We see his high end as an offensive defenseman at the next level who can play average minutes spending time on the power play. It would be great if he could grow a bit, but will need to get much stronger to play the style he does at the junior level without getting into trouble. He will also need to find a way to be more reliable defensively while remaining an offensive threat. Jordan has shown us in a few shootouts that he would make a tremendous option at the NHL level, as he is already extremely difficult to stop in the shootouts at the junior level.

Quotable: "I think he will make it to the NHL but I'm not sure he will end up playing a large amount of games." NHL Scout

Quotable: "We really liked him in his OHL Draft year and ranked him very high. I'm not sure he has grown very much since that time. Is his overall game good enough to make up for his size, that is my biggest concern. The offense is still developing and improving." – Mark Edwards

Talcott, Alex – FW – Indiana Ice (USHL) – 6'1" 198

In 2011-2012 Talcott played in 5 games last year for the Muskegon Lumberjacks registering his first point as an assist after being selected in the 2nd round, then played his first full season in the league this year with the Indiana Ice, playing in 51 games and scoring 15 points, however had a forgettable -21 rating in his plus/minus.

Talcott has to show that with his size and lack of offensive production that he can be an effective role player for a team. He needs to play the puck carrier hard and physical, be reliable in his own end and establish himself as a top-tier penalty killer. He needs to keep the game simple in the offensive zone, just get the puck in deep, cycle it with his great puck protection and get the puck to the front of the net for some grinder type goals. Alex was also drafted in 2011 OHL Priority Selection Draft by the Sarnia Sting. Alex is committed to the University of Michigan for this fall of 2013.

Tambellini, Adam – LC – Surrey Eagles (BCHL) – 6'1" 174

Adam is the son of long time NHL executive Steve Tambellini and the younger brother of former 1st rounder Jeff Tambellini. Adam plays the game at a very quick pace, and is a very impressive skater for his size. Tambellini is very dangerous in the offensive zone because of his size, speed and skill. He has good vision, a nice release and is able to do everything with the puck at a high pace.

Opponents had a very tough time containing him this season because not many players in the league can play the game at the same speed as him. Tambellini can easily drive to the net and score around the net because teams did not have a defenseman who could match him with size and speed at once. He can play in so many different areas on the power play because of his unique skill set. There were times when during the same game, Tambellini would provide the screen on the PP, then the next opportunity play on the half wall and be a shooter, and then play on the point to be a playmaker. Teams really had to create game plans around Tambellini to try to stop him on a consistent basis.

The big knock on Tambellini's game at this point is his lack of a physical game. He could provide a more physical presence with his size, but stays away from contact when possible. He is not very gritty, and is not particularly strong along the walls. He will need to add an element of toughness to his game and increase his work ethic in order to maximize his high end potential.

Quotable: "He has first round talent but work ethic varies from shift to shift." - NHL Scout

Quotable: "Always tough to rank players like this. I didn't see him live but Charles An saw him a few times. NHL guys mostly said the same thing, elite talent but needs to put it all together." - Mark Edwards

Tanus, Jonatan – LC – Peterborough Petes (OHL) – 5'9" 184

Jonatan has worked his was up Tappara's development program starting at just 13 on Tappara's U16 team. The following season at the age of just 14 he became the captain of their U16 team, and even received some action with the U18 team. Then as a 15 year old he played primarily in the U20 league playing against players up to 5 years older than him. Jonatan also played at the 2011 World U-17 Hockey Challenge posting 2 points in 5 games. Jonatan again played full time with Tappara's U20 team putting on a great performance. At the 2012 CHL Import Draft Jonatan was selected in the first round by the Peterborough Petes. Jonatan decided it was time for a new challenge and he made the jump overseas to play for Peterborough of the OHL and while he got off to a bit of a slow start, he put up some solid numbers.

Tanus certainly had his moments this season however consistency was an issue for Tanus all season long. When playing well, Tanus is gritty and creative, with a nose for the net. However, when he is not playing at his best, he can be invisible. Tanus's did receive a bit of a boost playing regularly with overagers Brett Findlay and Nick Czinder. Despite that he has very good hands, he skates well and he's surprisingly strong for an undersized import. Jonatan has a moderately good chance at being selected at the 2013 NHL Entry Draft. He has proven to be capable of producing at multiple levels through his development and moderately well in Peterborough, but the likelihood of his success at the NHL level isn't very high.

Teskey, Scott – RW – Mississauga Steelheads (OHL) – 6'0" 186

For Scott there were many nights this season that he was not very noticeable and was unable to create very much in the way of offense. He seems to be trying to establish himself as a player who is defensively responsible and will cover for his defensemen when they step up but if he is going to do this he needs to play the puck carrier harder and play the body to keep him from walking out front for good scoring chances.

Teskey does not project to get drafted this year and he is going to need to show an ability to score. He needs to play physically in the dirty areas of the ice and able to win board battles to have a chance of success moving forward to the next level.

Theodore, Shea – LD – Seattle Thunderbirds (WHL) – 6'2" 175

Teams will have a difficult time finding a defenseman who is as skilled with the puck as Shea Theodore in the upcoming NHL Entry Draft. He has the ability to go coast to coast and score a goal to change the momentum of the game, and provide a strong offensive presence from the backend.

Theodore is excellent at using his long reach to keep pucks away from opponents as he quickly picks up speed. He has the ability to quickly identify open lanes, and changes his direction in a hurry to drive to the net and forces his opponents to be caught flat footed. He can control the puck so effortlessly and even when he is skating at a very high speed, while keeping his head up to identify any open teammates. Theodore can also turn on a dime to get away from defenders, and buy his team more time to get open. He often stays on the ice for the entire power play for the Thunderbirds and does a very admirable job. He moves the puck quickly and accurately, but may give up a few turnovers throughout a game as he gambles and tries to connect on long stretch passes. Theodore is definitely a pass-first player who can improve on his shot from the point. His slap shot could have more velocity on it, while he could get them on net more often.

The biggest concern of Theodore is his defensive abilities. He has a tough time getting into proper position without the puck, and often gets caught sleeping in his own end. He has to be more aware of his surrounding, and know where he should be in certain situations. One factor of his poor positioning may be his ice time. He eats up a lot of minutes for Seattle, which may get him fatigued and affect his play. Theodore uses his good reach to poke pucks away and keep opponents to the outside on a consistent basis. The upside in Shea Theodore is undeniable. He could make a huge impact as an offensive defenseman in the league, but he will need to be better defensively to not be a liability out on the ice at the pro level. Coaches need to be able to trust him in any situation that they put him in. He certainly has all the tools to become an NHL defenseman one day, but his play without the puck and his ability to think the game will determine just how successful he can be.

Quotable: "I think his offensive potential is off the charts but there is little doubt he has a bust factor attached to him as well." – NHL Scout

Quotable: "He is one of those players that the more I saw of him, the more flaws I saw and dropped him in my rankings. No debating the offense he brings, it's a bit similar to the type of game Ryan Sproul had in his draft year, Ryan was bigger and had a much better shot." – Mark Edwards

Thompson, Keaton – LD – US NTDP Under-18 Team – 6'0, 185

Keaton is a tough nut to crack. Catch the Devil's Lake, North Dakota native on the right day and he looks like a top-15 pick that's sure to have success with the University of North Dakota Fighting Sioux next season. He's an excellent skater and when he's on his game, his decision-making is near perfect. He's not overly physical, but intelligent, aware, poised, and fundamentally sound, with pinches at the right times, puck-rushing ability, excellent passing, the ability to quarterback a power play and get pucks on net, and instinctive and smooth defensive zone positioning. The superlatives go on. Unfortunately, he hasn't shown that he can play at his peak on a consistent basis. Far from it. Most games, Thompson frustrates with consistently bad reads and giveaways.

The tools are still there, but the decision-making is lacking. Thompson played his best hockey in early season viewings and by the end of the campaign, was having a rough go of it just about every single night. A poor showing at the U18 World Junior Championships in Sochi put a disappointing cap on his season. His footwork is borderline elite and has carried him quite far, and the tools are certainly there, but his hockey IQ remains a major question mark.

Quotable: "At this point, Keaton is all tools. He has fleeting moments where he puts it all together and teases with unbelievable upside, but he also tends to disappoint you multiple times per game with his decision-making and sometimes goes whole periods without making a correct play." - Josh Deitell

Tiffels, Frederik – FW – Muskegon Lumberjacks (USHL) – 6'0" 186

Tiffels was picked in the 2nd round, 17th overall by the Muskegon Lumberjacks and came to the USHL from Germany to play in 50 games for the Lumberjacks registering 25 points.

Tiffels plays with good speed and agility and will hustle to get on loose pucks, using his body to protect it and get a good cycle going in deep in the offensive zone. He can move the puck very effectively, possesses exceptional vision and passing and brings good speed to the game as well. He likes to come down the wing with speed on the outside, protects the puck well but the most noticeable attribute of this player by far is his passing. He has vision to see all his options, is creative, can read the play well and guys himself time before moving the puck. He plays the game with an element of physicality, but still needs to get stronger on the puck along the boards. Tiffels also needs to work on shooting the puck more often.

Tkatch, Jordan – LC – Prince George Cougars (WHL) – 5'11" 196

Tkatch is a depth forward for the Cougars, and does an admirable job as a checker. He provides some good coverage down low when his defensemen ever need help. He has above average speed, but is not able to use it to his advantage very much as he has poor stick handling abilities. Tkatch likes to chip and chase or dump the puck in for his teammates to chase and try to retrieve. His offensive game is very limited, and he will not overwhelm anybody with his skills. Tkatch does not shy away from contact, but is not a great hitter. He is average along the boards without the puck, and is not always able to out will opponents to get pucks out of the defensive zone.

Toffey, Will – LD – Salisbury School (HIGH-CT) – 6'1 185

Though prep champion Salisbury was a deep team this year, Will was in many ways the straw that stirred the drink. He brings an excellent two-way skillset with top-end skating and shows flashes of gamebreaking ability. He can absolute fly up the ice and is comfortable with the puck at high speed, able to navigate neutral zone traffic and make plays. Though he's overzealous at times with his end-to-end efforts, it's encouraging to see him consistently try to make things happen and he recovers well when he does overcommit himself. He frequently pinches into the attack and can play like a forward with good positioning along the boards. On the powerplay, he can act as quarterback and shows good puck distribution and low shots from the point. He's difficult to beat on the rush with intelligent gap control and good reads, with patience and aggression at the right times. He has the tools to defend well in his zone and generally does so, showing pinpoint footwork, an active stick, and good physical play, but has occasional shifts where he's too lax or chases the play. If he can remove the sporadic gaffes from his game, Toffey has the upside to be an excellent defenseman.

Quotable: " "Every time I saw Salisbury this year, Will was the driving force. He had this one heroic shift I remember in particular where he went end-to-end through three defenders to create a scoring chance, then hurdled a sprawled out player while in full-flight and burned back down the ice to get back into position. It was one of the more impressive individual displays of skill and effort that I saw all season." - Josh Deitell*

Tolchinsky, Sergey – LW – Soo Greyhounds (OHL) – 5'9" 160

Sergey was selected 1st Round, 12th Overall at the 2012 CHL Import Draft by the Sault Ste. Marie Greyhounds. Sergey spent his 2011-2012 season with CSKA-Krasnaja Armija Moskva of the MHL in Russia. He really jumped onto the scene at the 2012 World U17 Challenge. Tolchinsky scored some very dynamic goals in this event and left an impression with our scouts. After much consideration, Sergey decided to come to North America and join the Sault Ste. Marie Greyhounds to mixed results in his rookie season.

Tolchinsky is an undersized forward for the Greyhounds. He is an exceptional skater and possesses a strong top gear that catches many unsuspecting defenders flat footed coming off the rush. Sergey is riveting to watch when he is skating with the puck and can stickhandle inside of a phone booth. He is very shifty and shows good awareness keeping himself out trouble by keeping his head up and knowing who is around him on the ice. He shows creativity in one on one situations and has a strong inside move cutting to the slot before putting pucks on net. Tolchinsky has a tendency to try to do too much on his own and would benefit from moving the puck to his line mates creating more space for him to skate in the open. The majority of his rushes end up in the corner of the offensive zone and more than half the time does not result in solid scoring chances, which could be improved by distributing the puck and creating give-and-go situations. Sergey plays with a very shoot first mentality and does have a strong wrist shot that can get upstairs very quickly and fools goaltenders with a quick release.

Tolchinsky had a solid playoff series for the Greyhounds and continually improved as the season progressed and he got acclimatized to the North American game. He went on to join Team Russia at the IIHF World U-18 Championships and put forward a respectable performance. He will be a key forward for the Greyhounds next season after the graduation of a number of important veterans.

Sergey projects to be a top six or bust type of player. He is not suited whatsoever for the grinder, bottom six role and will need to play an offensive role at the NHL level in order to make it to that level. Sergey is a player we see getting selected in the 2013 NHL Entry Draft outside the top 60 due to the risk that comes with picking an undersized forward who has limited options at the pro game. He has NHL top six skills, however he is very small and has been shut down too regularly at the junior level for us to feel comfortable with an early ranking. This will be a risk/reward style of pick which generally favors teams with deep prospect pools that can take the risk and hope Sergey rewards them.

Quotable: "Tolchinsky's skill level alone could be arguably in the top 10 of this draft. Unfortunately his size really affects him and is the reason he could fall in this draft. Too often he was contained and neutralized by bigger, stronger defenders, but if he gets some space, he can fly." - Ryan Yessie*

Topping, Joel – RD – Lethbridge Hurricanes (WHL) – 6'0" 184

Topping is a dependable 3rd pairing defenseman at the junior level. He is an above average skater, and plays the game with poise in his own end. Topping does a good job with gap control, but does not like to step up and try to land a hit in transition. He is not very physical, and just uses his stick to keep opponents to the outside. He does not do anything particularly well, but does his job when playing against less skilled opponents. He has limited skills with the puck, and will probably never be much of an offensive presence from the backend.

Tremblay, Simon – LW – Chicoutimi Saguenéens (QMJHL) – 6'1" 190

A late player for this year's draft, Simon Tremblay sustained a very serious concussion on January 4, 2012 in Blainville-Boisbriand and played only few games before the 2011-2012 season ended. It took a while for him to get his game back this season but eventually he showed very nice qualities in the second half of the season. He plays with grit and determination when he's at his best. Tremblay likes to play rough on the boards and never backs down from a physical challenge, winning most of his 1-on-1 battles. He's a great character player with tons of energy. He has a nose for the net and showed good goal scoring abilities around the net in some of our viewings this season. Simon Tremblay has surprisingly good puck handling abilities but is willing to play a simple chip and chase game with intensity. He will rarely try a creative play when he has the puck. His defensive game is a big part of this game, showing good hockey sense in his positioning and performances on the PK throughout the season. He is willing to block shots and fight with second efforts to get the puck safely out of his zone. Tremblay lacks a 2nd gear in his skating ability and could also improve his top speed. He doesn't have high end skills or very high offensive potential for professional hockey, but he showed great progression in his overall game this year and had a strong showing in the 1st round of the playoffs.

Tringale, Devin – LW – Valley Jr. Warriors (EJHL) – 6'0, 193

Devin was passed over in the 2012 NHL Draft even after being named the Independent School League MVP for driving Lawrence Academy to their elite prep championship win last year. He made the jump to the EJHL this season to try to prove that all 30 NHL teams made a mistake, and won a scholarship to Harvard in the process. He's a good player at the junior level, but he's still choppy. He plays a determined game, based around work ethic rather than skill. He's solid around the offensive crease and shows a good scoring touch. He's strong on his skates and takes the puck hard to the net, but lacks refined skating ability and finesse stick skills. He can carry the puck and passes well, but his motions aren't smooth and, at times, unnatural. As he's still not a sure thing, it's likely at this point that teams will wait to see how he plays at Harvard, rather than taking a flier on him this year. His work ethic is commendable but he's still very raw.

Ully, Cole – LW – Kamloops Blazers (WHL) – 5'11" 165

Cole Ully is a very good 2 way forward who had a productive season with the Blazers in a top 6 forward role. He has stepped up his game immensely at both ends of the ice and his development has really soared this year. Ully plays the game at a quick pace. He is always on the pursuit of loose pucks, and quickly joins the rush off the wing to provide another option. When he handles the puck, his hands look loose and smooth as he stickhandles his way through traffic. He identifies open lanes quickly, and shifts his direction to attack any open seams. Ully is an average playmaker from the wall, but limits his turnovers with the puck. The one area of improvement for his game would be his ability to get shots off quickly from the slot. Ully takes too long to release his shots when he is covered, and lacks the size to be able to protect the puck and his stick from opponents to prevent them from disrupting his shots. Defensively, Ully is a good penalty killer who has a very good stick. He is skilled at intercepting passes, and always being in the right position to do so. He is fearless when it comes to blocking shots, and is willing to take a hit to make a play along the boards. He is not overly aggressive, but rather depends on his intelligence to be good defensively. Ully's game could allow him to be a 3rd line winger with a scoring touch at the pro level. He has to get stronger along the boards to be effective on the cycle, and continue to work on his speed to allow him to have an advantage over opponents. If he can also improve his scoring touch around the net and slot, he could become a good player in the NHL one day.

Urbanic, John – RW – Ottawa 67's (OHL) – 5'11" 196

John was selected in the 8th round of the 2011 OHL Priority Selection Draft out of the Russell Stover U16 program. For the 2011-2012 season Urbanic split time between the Russell Stover U18 program and the Oshawa Generals of the OHL. John opened the 2012-2013 season with Oshawa was traded mid-season from the Generals to the Ottawa 67's where he played primarily a third line role. Urbanic was very impressive in a penalty killing role in our viewings of him, particularly with the 67's where he was out on every kill.

John has excellent defensive zone positioning, intercepts passes and clears the zone very effectively. John has always seemed to bring a physical style of game and has pretty good skating ability allowing him to add some power to his physical side and allows him to get up and down the ice effectively. John isn't a very offensive player, but he displays intelligent positioning in the offensive zone which has lead to some scoring chances, however he didn't finish.

While we don't expect Urbanic to be selected at the 2013 NHL Entry Draft, he shows many valuable assets to his game between his defensive play and his willingness to play a hard physical game. He doesn't project to be anything more than a bottom six grinder and really seems to lack the offensive tools despite having the positional knowledge in all three zones.

Valiyev, Rinat – LD – Indiana Ice (USHL) – 6'1, 190

The Russian blueliner made the jump to North American hockey this year with Indiana, and showed well with the team despite their last place finish. He plays a sound two-way game with plenty of upside. His defensive game is strong with an intelligent, active stick and tight coverage. He's not a bruiser but he plays physical and closes gaps quickly. His positioning, especially against the rush, is excellent. He had an excellent showing for Russia at the Five Nations U18 tournament, where he led all defensemen in scoring. He makes a good first pass but can also carry the puck when given a lane. He's an excellent skater and, while he doesn't project as a top pairing power play defenseman as a professional, can quarterback the man advantage well. He pinches and joins the rush at the right times, and shows a good wrister with smart placement, either shooting to score or aiming for tips and rebounds. He doesn't have a booming shot but it's still effective. He can rush the puck and does well to evade fore checkers, but makes the safe play under pressure if necessary. He suffered a season-ending injury in February, which may affect his stock come draft time, but there's a lot to like about his polished and responsible play.

Vanderwiel, Danny – LW – Plymouth Whalers (OHL) – 6'0" 210

Danny was selected in the 8th round of the 2011 OHL Priority Selection draft from Team Illinois U16 program. This turned out to be a valuable pick for the Whalers as Vanderwiel committed to them and joined their team as a 16 year old. He put up a respectable 6 goals and 9 points while playing in the bottom six and providing energy. This year was supposed to be a little more of a breakout year for Danny, however he saw some time as a healthy scratch this year, and played primarily on the fourth line. Despite this he never quit. He always worked extremely hard and was like a big ball of energy in all of our viewings.

Vanderwiel is an energetic physical winger who plays every moment of every shift at full speed. He hits hard in open ice and along the boards. Whenever there is an opportunity to finish a check he takes it. He always wins more than his share of battles along the wall. He also forces turnovers helping his team generate puck control and he cycles the puck intelligently. Danny is very solid positionally in all three zones and we saw him grow as one of Plymouth's best penalty killers due to this. He's willing to sacrifice himself for his team. At times while even strength he almost looked like he was the third defenseman for the Whalers going deep into the zone and doing his best to shut down the opposition. He's a fairly effective skater for his size. His offensive upside is not very high and he doesn't show signs of growing into an offensive talent. However Vanderwiel seems to know exactly who he is and what he needs to do to make the NHL. He's an energetic, lunch pail grinder type of player who plays bottom six minutes and kills penalties.

Danny is a player who we expect to see selected in this NHL Draft. He won't be a widely talked about guy, but when you have his size, playing the style of game he plays, playing with the kind of heart he shows, teams will be lining up to spend one of their final picks to bring in a guy who looks like a pretty safe bet as a role player.

Quotable: "Every time Danny set foot on the ice it was like taking a dog off his leash. He plays with great energy and loves to finish his checks. He doesn't have any high end skills and won't mark up the scoresheet but he can hit hard and has a motor that doesn't quit." - Ryan Yessie

Tommy Vannelli - RD - Minnetonka (MN High School) - 6'2" 170

Vannelli is a quick skating defenseman who loves to join the rush and provides a lot of offense from the backend. He looks so effortless as he skates around the ice and gives opponents a difficult time trying to handle his speed.

It is difficult to not notice the impact Vannelli provides in games on a consistent basis for his team. Opponents always have to be aware of him joining the rush and to create an odd man opportunity. He is able to make a seamless transition from defense to offense with his very impressive skating ability, whether or not he has possession of the puck. He is able to quickly recover if a turnover ever occurs and get back into his defensive position before a scoring opportunity occurs for the opposing team.

Vannelli is not highly skilled with the puck, but he displays very good poise. He may be pressured heavily on the blueline, but he is so mobile that he can either move laterally to give himself more time or make a quick spin move. He possesses good vision and makes good passes, but his passing could be a little quicker. He also has a hard shot from the point, but he needs to do a better job of hitting the net. He does not have elite stickhandling abilities to deke through opponents at the pro level, and will likely have to make an impact offensively by joining the rush and being a good PP player.

Defensively, Vannelli's skating ability really allows him to thrive. He can maintain a good tight gap and drive opponents to the wall and not give them a lane to the net and maintain good positioning along the boards so that they will not be able to get past him and make a play. Vannelli is able to use his stick very effectively and knock away passes time and time again. The one big issue of his game is physical play. Vannelli is not very physical, and will need to add that element to his game as he has a very good frame. He still has some bulking up to do, which may allow him to be a more physical presence on the defensive end.

Vannelli is committed to the University of Minnesota and will have a very good opportunity to develop his game in a program that has produced so many NHLers over the years. His offensive abilities may not quite translate to the pros as he lacks the elite skill level, but he can certainly still make an impact with his skating and poise from the blueline. He just needs to use his frame to his advantage in the defensive end, and if he can do that he can be a good defenseman at the pro level one day.

Quotable: "I spoke with Vannelli at the NHL combine and came away impressed. It was one of the best player interviews of the day. He knows his game, was well spoken, kew his weaknesses and where he improved. He said all the right things about his teammates with sounding like it was just agent speak. He told me if the NHL team who drafts hints towards him playing in the CHL he would most likely go because the NHL is his ultimate goal." - Mark Edwards

Varga, Steven – LD – Peterborough Petes (OHL) – 6'3" 214

Steven was selected in the 2nd round of the 2011 OHL Priority Selection Draft by the Peterborough Petes out of the York-Simcoe Express Minor Midget program. Steven came out of Minor Midget very highly regarded. He was a solid shutdown defenseman with great size and a promising future against bigger and stronger players. However he stumbled a bit in his rookie season getting beat defensively on a regular basis and got beat in battles too often. The Petes' were hoping for a better result, however there simply weren't enough improvements. He has only received 5 minor penalties in two seasons with the Petes

Varga loses quite a few battles and appears to lose his positioning. He has shown the ability to make effective passes up ice and has great size but simply needs to use it a whole lot more. For a player the size of Varga he is a good skater with a great frame. We don't expect Steven to be selected at the 2013 NHL Entry Draft. However, he has a lot going for him, he not only needs to continue to get stronger and improve his skating but he needs to add a mean streak to his game. We need to see him more physical and become a player that teams hate to play against. The positive thing for Steven is that he still has time, players develop later and we hope that he is one of those players, because he has the potential to be a very effective defenseman, but needs to play the style of game that will make him the most successful.

Veilleux, Tommy – LW – Victoriaville Tigres (QMJHL) – 6'0" 186

Veilleux was a first round pick for Victoriaville in the 2011 QMJHL entry draft after putting up a strong offensive season at the lower midget level. Praised for his goal scoring ability and physical play, he displayed more of the later in the two seasons he played with the Tigres leading up to the 2013 NHL Draft. Veilleux proved to be a valuable grinder for Victoriaville, playing with energy and passion every night.

Tommy is at his best when he plays a simple game with a straightforward approach. He is limited in what he can do with the puck, regarding speed and maneuverability. Although he improved his skating considerably since he joined the league, he is best suited to play a dump and chase type of game, using his physical approach to win puck battles deep in the offensive zone. He also showed limited hockey sense in distributing the puck and setting up plays for teammates. The best aspect of his game as we mentioned is his physical play and intensity. He loves to play this role and he pushes it to the limit sometimes. He brings energy and passion when he is on the ice and that showed to be valuable asset for Victoriaville, as it assisted them in gaining momentum quite a few times throughout the season. The biggest improvement in his game apart from skating is his approach to the game. Instead of going all-in and trying to destroy everything on the ice, he picks his moments wisely and doesn't take himself out of the play as much as he used to.

In the long run, Veilleux will be categorized as a physical grinder who brings energy and can fight from time to time. His future at the professional level would be on the 4th line and it's still a long shot he makes it that far with his limited hockey sense and play with the puck. Therefore, we don't see him as a player who will be drafted.

Verhaeghe, Carter – LC – Niagara Ice Dogs (OHL) – 6'1" 181

Carter was selected in the 2nd round of the 2011 OHL Priority Selection Draft by the Niagara Ice Dogs out of the Hamilton Jr. Bulldogs Minor Midget program. Carter received limited ice with a very talented Niagara Ice Dogs team that would go on to win the 2012 OHL Eastern Conference Championship resulting in low point totals and ice in his 16 year old season. Verhaeghe moved up the draft rankings late in this season and finished the regular season with 6 goals, 9 points in his final 6 games. He posted 44 points in 67 games this season. Carter then joined Team Canada at the IIHF World U-18 Championship putting up 4 assists in 7 games playing a defensive role and helping Canada to a Gold Medal.

Carter has been noticeably strong in the defensive zone and has been able to be a penalty killing specialist for the Ice Dogs at times. His most glaring weakness at the moment is his skating, which is an awkward style to say the least. We do expect that he will hear his name announced at the 2013 NHL Entry Draft. He projects to be a forward that can help his team out at both ends. However his skating simply has to improve. He will likely be a project who requires a few more seasons in the OHL and likely even a few AHL seasons to reach his potential.

Quotable: "Did a nice job stepping up from the 13th forward role after injuries to his teammates in Sochi. He is an energy guy, a worker ant, I thought he was a contributor at the U18." - Mark Edwards

Vlajkov, Michael – LD – Ottawa 67's (OHL) – 6'2" 185

Michael was selected in the 2nd round of the 2011 OHL Priority Selection Draft by the Ottawa 67's out of the St. Catharines Falcons Minor Midget program. Michael played a minimal role with the 67's during their strong 2011-2012 season as a 16 year old. Heading into the 2012-2013 season, although at age 17 Vlajkov has to be considered one of the veterans on the blueline on this rebuild to give an idea of how young this team was.

Vlajkov played key minutes defensively but was also used as a forward at times throughout the year. He works hard in both ends of the ice, back-checking really well and he puts good pressure on the puck carrier. He possesses good offensive instincts to be able to read the play to come in off the point into the high slot when the opportunity is available to become a good passing option because he has an absolute cannon of a point shot. He uses his stick well to challenge the puck carrier and plays with decent physicality in his own end to separate his man from the puck along the boards. He likes to play the body to keep the opposition to the outside and just needs to try to cut down on some of the turnovers on breakout passes. Because he is so hard working, versatile player with a physical element and good size Vlajkov puts himself in a position where he could be selected at the 2013 NHL Entry Draft. However his skating is clearly the most glaring of his weaknesses and has really affected his play so far. This area of his game absolutely has to improve for him to reach his potential.

Voltin, Luke – FW – Des Moines Buccaneers (USHL) – 6'0" 180

Last year Voltin played for Des Moines Buccaneers for 24 games, as well as the USNTDP and USA U17 in the World Hockey Championship. This season he played his first full year in the USHL with Des Moines and had 26 points in 60 games played and also earned the opportunity to play in the USHL top prospects game. Voltin can get a good cycle going in deep in the offensive zone and finds lanes to get the puck back to the point for shot opportunities. He puts good pressure on the fore-check and will play with an element of physicality but has to get his shots through to the net with more consistency on chances from the high slot and needs to watch the turnovers trying to get the puck out of his own end along the boards. Voltin has pretty decent size but still needs to add some strength and needs to have a bigger role playing in his own end. He has good skills with the puck and can create opportunities offensively, and now just needs to demonstrate that he is a full 200-foot player. He has good offensive instincts and opens up really well for passes but has to try and also create chances off the cycle rather than just creating opportunities off the rush. Luke is committed to the University of North Dakota for this fall of 2013.

Wallmark, Lucas – LC – Karlskrona HK (SAL) – 6'0, 176

After starting off the year with Skellefteå, Wallmark was loaned to Karlskrona down the stretch where he was a factor in helping them stave off relegation, at times playing in the team's top six in crucial games. He is an excellent playmaker with fantastic hands, able to create time and space for his teammates with deft stick handling along the boards. He reads coverage patterns and can find holes in defenses with well-timed pinpoint passes. He has a good shot but tends to look for a passing option first, and when he does put the puck on the net it's often looking to create chances off rebounds. He's a good back checker and has a good understanding of his defensive zone responsibility. Where he's limited is with his skating. He's agile in the offensive zone with good starts and stops, but in open ice he's slow-footed and awkward, limiting his ability to carry the puck up ice, forecheck, and back check.

Watson, Jamal – RW – Lethbridge Hurricanes (WHL) – 6'0" 176

Jamal Watson is a speedy winger for the Hurricanes whose game at both ends of the ice failed to develop this season. He received regular ice time on the 2nd and 3rd line, but just was not able to improve his game much. When Watson touches the ice, you cannot help but notice him because of how quick he is out on the ice. He is very difficult to hit in the neutral zone when he is moving down the ice with the puck, but the problem is that he cannot do much with it afterwards. Watson possesses below average hands, and is not a very good stick handler, especially when he's moving with speed. When he has some room down the wing, he creates good scoring opportunities. He needs to get to the net more often, and be better at protecting the puck. He is pretty strong on his feet, and he has moments where he looks good along the walls. Unfortunately, Watson is far too inconsistent with his game. He disappears far too often in games, and needs to be able to make impact in more than just with his speed. He relies on his speed too much, and he will have to improve his other aspects of his game to have any success at the pro level.

Webster, Michael – LD – Barrie Colts (OHL) – 6'0" 183

Michael was selected in the 12th Round of the 2011 OHL Priority Selection Draft out of the Vaughan Kings Minor Midget program. Webster thus far has turned out to be a steal by the Colts scouting staff. Webster had a successful rookie season even though he did not register a single goal, he was able to create some offense through his passes and finished the season with 11 assists and a +14 rating in 63 games played.

Webster plays with a decent gap control, uses his stick very effectively to check the puck away from the opposition and gets down in lanes to block passes to breakup plays in his own end. He uses his body to protect the puck well from the opposition's pressure and is able to take a hit and still hold on to the puck to make a play and move the puck up out of the zone. He can close the gap to squeeze his man off the puck along the boards, plays the puck carrier with a nice element of physicality and has some aggression as well getting involved in scrums after whistles. At times he needs to play with more patience, to wait for the play to come to him rather than chasing it down and has to watch both the neutral zone turnovers and suicide passes that he makes which leaves teammates vulnerable to big hits in open ice.

Michael needs to bring a more consistent effort. as our viewings have contrasted overall between some good and some not so good viewings .Webster is a defensive first defenseman who focuses on his own end and making the intelligent passes up ice.

Quotable: "I try not to ever read too much into one single game but I can't shake a game in the playoffs. He really struggled." - Mark Edwards

Weegar, Mackenzie – RD – Halifax Mooseheads (QMJHL) – 5'11" 181

Coming from the CCHL where he racked up 50 points in 53 games in 2011-2012, Mackenzie Weegar started his QMJHL career at 18 years old with the CHL's top team, the Halifax Mooseheads. He has been a huge surprise for us this season and deserves to have his name on the radar for this year's NHL Draft.

Weegar is a 2-way defenseman, he was an asset all season long for the Mooseheads. He skates smoothly and follows the play really well. He doesn't have a whole lot of explosiveness but his overall speed is very good. Weegar is a really smart player. With the puck, he sees the ice well and finds teammates easily on the breakout, making the transition very quickly. He follows the game at a high pace and makes great plays when he is under pressure showing his high level of hockey sense. He has soft hands and can carry the puck himself to the neutral zone without issues. We like the poise and composure he shows when he has the puck on his stick, rarely making dumb decisions and waiting for the right moment before executing his play.

Although he's a little undersized for a defenseman at 5-11, Weegar has several other tools to win the battles and make up for that downside. We've never seen him in trouble because of his size. He has a pretty accurate wrist shot but he's still tentative of using it instead waiting for a perfect opportunity. Without the puck, Weegar positions himself very well and will rarely lose his coverage. He will initiate a body contact and we've even seen good body checks from the Ottawa native. He blocks shots due to great positioning, his stick will take away space from the opposition. His footwork is good enough to follow most of the league's skaters, but should get better to play at the next level. He is dedicated and has a good work ethic. Mackenzie Weegar is a tough player to get away from, always staying in movement and making sure he eliminates time and space from his opponents.

Weegar is good at just about every aspect of the game but he doesn't have much upside, most of his game coming from hockey sense and work ethic.

His lack of natural skating ability, elite talent with the puck and size might hurt him at the professional level, but as far as the 2012-2013 goes, Mackenzie Weegar was one of the top defensemen in QMJHL and probably deserves a good hard look by teams for the NHL Draft.

Westermarck, Felix – LW – Blues U20 (Jr. A SM-liiga) – 6'1, 204

Felix is a bulky forward that plays a power game. He takes the puck down the wing with good protection and takes the direct lane to the net with it. He also likes to bring the puck to the net from the corners and behind the net. He can cycle the puck well but lacks agility, limiting his ability to evade defensemen. His skating is average overall and lacking in quickness. He flashes good hands and a hard wrist shot from time to time, but overall his offensive game is fairly simple and predictable, and if he doesn't have a lane to the net he has a hard time making things happen. He shows up and flashes but is not a consistent threat. He's not a major factor defensively.

Westlund, Wilhelm – LD – Färjestad (SEL) – 5'11, 185

He has games where he plays excellent hockey, but Westlund is in many ways still trying to put it all together. At his best, he plays mistake free hockey. He made the jump to the Elitserien this year and has not looked out of place, keeping it simple in generally limited ice time. He shows a good active stick, especially against the rush, and keeps his head on a swivel at all times. His skating is strong, with good agility and first step quickness. He shows a lot of poise for his age, evading the forecheck and making a solid first pass. With Sweden at U18 tournaments this year, he showed offensive upside with puck-rushing ability and a good selection of shots. At times, sometimes for whole games, his defensive coverage is off a step. He can have trouble with speed to the outside and can be too tentative. He could stand to play more physically in his end, but is limited in part by his size. He lacks elite upside, but has played well against men this year and projects as a strong two-way player.

Weis, Matthew – FW – Green Bay Gamblers (USHL) – 5'10" 194

Matthew had an excellent year for Green Bay after struggling to get his footing in the USHL last season. The stocky forward is excellent with the puck. He shows great distribution skills and excels on the power play when he has more time and space to make plays. He makes crisp, accurate passes and reads defensive coverage intelligently. He's apt at setting up behind the net and finding teammates through sticks in front. He has a good snapshot but is a pass-first player. His skating needs work as he lacks quickness and is slow out of the gates. He's good on the penalty kill with an active stick and smart positioning, but could stand to be more involved physically. His defensive coverage is spotty, as he generally knows where to be but doesn't always work as hard as he should, especially on the back check. He has a chippy side that comes out occasionally, as he takes runs and mixes it up after whistles.

Wennberg, Alexander – LW – Djurgarden (SAL) – 6'1" 183

Wennberg is a strong 2 way forward who displayed a very good combination of size, skill and hockey intelligence at the 2013 World Junior Tournament. He initially started on the 4th line, but played his way up onto a top 6 role with his consistent effort.

Wennberg is most effective along the walls. He is strong on his skates and wins a lot of battles for loose pucks. He uses his edges well to quickly change directions to buy himself some time to make a pass or to walk towards the slot and get a scoring chance. He is at his best when playing a physical game and outworking opponents to win battles and be tough to play against in front of the net. Wennberg has very good vision, and manages the puck well. He does not make poor decisions with the puck and allows the play to develop before making a pass. He is able to protect the puck with his frame and drive to the net when possible. He has a good release to his shot, but will need to shoot the puck more to add another dimension to his game.

Defensively, Wennberg plays with his head on a swivel and is very aware of the situation out on the ice. He puts himself in a good position to take away plays from the point. He is tough to play against because of his physical game, and consistently outworks opponents without the puck to help his team win games. Aside from his work with his body, Wennberg thinks the game well, and plays with good confidence and makes quick reads. Teams will definitely be interested in Wennberg's solid overall game. He may not have elite offensive abilities, but his intensity and physical game makes up for it. He has some work to do for his overall game, but he has had good success offensively this season while playing on Djurgarden's men's team. He should be used to the speed of playing with older players, which puts him in a good position to succeed in the future at the NHL level.

Quotable: "I got my first chance to speak to Alex at the combine. It was easy to see why I got several rave reviews about his interviews from scouts. He was as impressive as any player I have spoken to. On the ice I always look for smart players and Wennberg is a very intelligent hockey player. - Mark Edwards

Wheaton, Mitchell – RD – Kelowna Rockets (WHL) – 6'5" 225

Wheaton is a big defensive defenseman who stepped into the Rockets' line up this season and provided a solid presence in the backend. His season was cut short by a shoulder injury, but came back in the second round of the playoffs, and played a limited role because his shoulder was not fully healed. Wheaton possesses a good stick and the ability to be in good position to cover a lot of area to try to prevent good scoring chances. He uses his long reach to his advantage and does a good job to knocking away pucks and keeping opponents to the outside. He is very strong along the boards, and his physical abilities seem to be ready for the pro level already.

Offensively, Wheaton's game is quite limited. His outlet passes are average, and has shown limited playmaking abilities. He has an average shot and he is not particularly good at walking the line to get shots through traffic. Wheaton will also need to work on his skating abilities. He is good at quick starts and stops along the corner, but his overall speed will need to be improved to be more effective on the rush at the professional level. He has had some troubles with keeping quick players to the outside at the junior level as well.

Whistle, Jackson – G – Kelowna Rockets (WHL) – 6'1" 185

Jackson Whistle started the season with the Vancouver Giants but was traded during the pre-season simply because of too many bodies in net. He struggled mightily as the backup for the Giants last year, and it seems that a change of scenery has really benefited his career. Whistle is a good athletic goaltender. He is quick on his feet and on his knees and recovers quickly after making a save to prepare for the next shot on rebounds. He can go post to post to make highlight reel saves. He has average glove and blocker hands, and has to work on his mechanics to be more efficient in the crease. He does not play the puck particularly well, and is only able to simply move the puck to one of his defensemen in the corners. He could also work on looking through traffic better as he is not particularly tall. His game mentally seems to be a little shaky as he is prone to occasionally give up goals after goals.

White, Torrin – RW – Moose Jaw Warriors (WHL) – 5'9" 163

White is a skilled, small winger who has displayed some good goal scoring ability in tight when he is in the line up. He has the ability to quickly get a shot on net as soon as he picks up the puck from in tight and catch goaltenders off guard. He has also shown some above average play making abilities, but he needs to manage the puck much better and limit the number of turnovers that he commits. He takes unnecessary chances in the neutral zone and in the defensive zone at times to try to go up the middle, which gets picked off most often than not. Defensively, White is often a liability in his own end. He is weak along the boards, and he does not do a good enough job to cover the point man on his side. Opponents have a lot of time to get a shot off from the point as he is sometimes caught watching the puck in the middle of nowhere. He has to be more willing to take hits to make a play, and that may have something to do with the fact that he's been injured a few times throughout the season.

Widmar, Joseph – FW – Indiana Ice (USHL) – 6'0" 199

Widmar played his rookie season this year in the USHL starting out with the Chicago Steel after they selected him in the 2nd round, then finished off with the Indiana Ice for the final 25 games. Widmar has pretty good size to him and will to the little things to keep to a pretty simple game. He puts pressure on the puck carrier, brings a nice net-front presence and battles for his territory in the dirty areas. He finishes his hits on the fore-check, will drive hard to the net and can rush the puck up the ice to gain the offensive zone with speed. He does possess some decent offensive instincts, with good vision and passing abilities and will drive the puck on the outside with great protection then move it towards the front of the net to try and create chances for teammates in front. Widmar needs to focus more on the defensive aspects of the game, by getting in lanes and tying up the opposition in front of his own net. He has to play the puck carrier hard and physical and get his stick in lanes to breakup passes and plays as well in his own end. He has good size and just needs to try to use it more to his advantage.

Williams, Brian – RW – Tri-City Americans (WHL) – 5'8" 170

Brian Williams is a quick, undersize forward who displays good confidence with the puck and loves to pick up speed from the defensive zone and try to carry the puck into the offensive zone. He is slippery along the walls, and is difficult to check in the neutral zone when he is going at top speed and quickly changes directions to keep opponents flat footed. Williams possesses above average hands as he is able to maneuver through traffic well when skating at a high speed. However, he gets quite predictable as he loves to skate with the puck, and opponents could predict that he will as games go on, and adjust their games to try to stop him in the neutral zone and angle him to the boards. Williams has an average shot, but will need to work a lot of the accuracy of his shots. He also is prone to turning the puck over, and needs to improve his decision making. Defensively, Williams does not provide much help in his own end. He likes to cheat and get to the neutral zone before his opponents for a breakaway opportunity. He does not block many shots, and is not strong along the walls either. He has to commit himself more to being tougher to play against in his own end to provide more impact in games.

Williams, Colby – RD – Regina Pats (WHL) – 5'11" 182

Colby Williams had a quiet, but effective season for the Pats. He was depended on for his steady presence in the defensive zone and was out in crucial situations whenever his team was trying to hold onto a lead. Williams is a good skater, and used it effectively to maintain a good gap. He would stir opponents to the wall with his stick consistently, and play a patient game to hold his position to try to take away dangerous scoring chances. One area of his game that must be improved on is his strength along the walls. Williams is pushed around far too easily, and has a difficult time trying to tie up opponents and win puck battles. Offensively, Williams showed limited potential in the offensive zone. He is an average puck handler, and just makes quick, simple outlet passes. He does not have great vision or confidence with the puck on his stick too. His shot from the point is just average, and he does not hold onto the puck for too long.

Witala, Chase – LW – Prince George Cougars (WHL) – 6'0" 157

Witala is a hard nosed winger who has been able to provide a lot of energy for the Cougars with his speed and defensive play. On a better team, Witala would probably have played a bottom 6 role, but with the Cougars he had the opportunity to play a key role in their offense and was able to put up some decent numbers. Offensively, Witala does not have very good skills. He receives a lot of ice time, but is quite unproductive with the time that he receives. He is good on the forecheck and causes a lot of havoc, but he is not able to create many chances with the puck. He provides a good net front presence, but needs to work on staying on his feet despite the physical punishment he may take. He is good along the boards, as he is able to use his body effectively to protect the puck, but does not have much skill to do anything after. Witala is most effective in his own zone with his tenacity and speed. He plays hard without the puck and is quite responsible in his own end. He is good at chasing down loose pucks and quickly getting it out of the defensive zone along the walls. He is not afraid to block shots, and does an above average job of taking away shooting lanes.

Wolanin, Christian – LD – Green Bay Gamblers (USHL) – 6'0" 172

Christian developed through the Detroit Little Caesars U16 and U18 programs and is the son of former NHLer Craig Wolanin. Christian was selected in the 2nd round of the 2012 USHL Entry Draft by the Green Bay Gamblers. He possesses good size and is capable of providing a pretty steady reliable presence on the blue line while adding in a few offensive flashes. He likes to jump up in the play here and there but can get caught up ice appearing to not fully understand his limits. Christian has shown some ability to play a shutdown role and wins an acceptable amount of battles along the wall. He generally can make the simple pass and has played effectively at the USHL level but hasn't really stood out to us in any viewings. Christian was also selected in the 13th round of the 2011 OHL Priority Selection Draft by the Plymouth Whalers.

Wood, Miles – LW - Nobles (HIGH-MA) - 6'1" 160

Had injury issues but he's a player we like. Good frame to grown into as he is a lanky kid. Wood has game and drives the middle lane and the net as hard as anyone. He's a good skater and he has a good compete level. Not a player we saw much but we liked him quite a bit. He has some intangibles to his game that make is raise his stock.

Worden, Nash – LD – Omaha Lancers (USHL) – 6'0" 196

Worden took quite a route to get to the USHL after he played in the NAHL for the Wichita Falls Wildcats in 2011 he was selected in the 20th round at 297th overall. Worden played his first season this year in the USHL and was not much of an offensive producer with just 6 points in 51 games played, however he showed a real edge to his game racking up 124 penalty minutes over the course of the year. He is a pretty big body defenseman who skates decently and can rush the puck up the ice by skating it out. He is willing to jump in on the attack to put pressure on the fore-check and he also distributes the puck pretty well on the rush into the offensive zone. He plays with a pretty decent gap control in order to force the opposition to chip the puck past him and can make some decent stretch passes to start the breakout, however has to watch the neutral zone turnovers as well. He has good versatility as there were times throughout the year the coach used him as a winger and he was able to skate the puck into the offensive zone with decent puck protection then come down low to drive towards the net.

Nash played with a physical element on the fore-check, finished his hits along the boards on the dump and chase play and then he came back for good support in his own end, showing that defenseman mentality to take care of your own end first and fore-most. He needs to watch the turnovers on puck mishandles through the neutral zone and has to be stronger on the puck along the boards more often to not lose those board battles. There are times in his own end where he looks lost as far as coverage. Worden combines good size and physical play and works hard; however he still needs to get a better sense of the game playing in his own zone.

Yakimov, Bogdan – RC – Dizel Penza (VHL) – 6'4" 201

Yakimov spent all of last season, and the first part of this season with Reaktor Nizhnekamsk of the MHL. During that time he also played for Team Russia at the 2011 and 2012 IIHF World U18 Championships. Due to a late birthdate, Bogdan wasn't eligible until the 2013 NHL Entry Draft. After opening this season in the MHL, he split the remainder of the season with Dizel Penza (21 games) and Izhstal Izhevsk (16 games) both of the VHL playing 5 more games with Dizel Penza. The first thing you notice on Bogdan Yakimov is his size. He's a big forward with a huge frame and he protects the puck well. Despite lacking skating ability he has the hands to evade defensemen in one on one situations, but likely won't be able to do that against talented defensemen he'll find at higher levels. Yakimov shows no hesitation using his size to battle for pucks but unfortunately loses far too many battles for someone his size. He needs to get better in these battles because he gets right in there and fights for pucks in all three zones. Skating is the biggest area of improvement. He struggles getting up and down the ice and will likely be what drops him out of the spot his size and puck skills could have him. He has a very hard shot and seems to be his go to offensive weapon as he shoots a lot more than passes.

Quotable: "Skating is the issue, he is a train when he gets rolling but that takes a few too many steps." - Mark Edwards

Yuill, Alex – LD – Barrie Colts (OHL) – 5'8" 167

Alex was selected in the first round, 21st Overall in the 2011 OHL Priority Selection Draft out of the Quinte Red Devils. Alex has been a prospect we've liked since before even his Minor Midget season. He has represented Ontario in both the Canada Games and at the World U-17 Challenge in Windsor. Alex has shows us a great skill set that would make him a reliable shutdown defenseman, if only he was 4 or 5 inches taller. There's no way around it, the biggest hindrance onto Alex's career is his size. Very few 5'8" defensemen are capable of making an impact at all let alone defensively. Alex finds a way to do this with his excellent hockey sense, ability to process the play quickly and make the smart play up ice. Alex also has a relentless stick which he uses extremely well in one on one situations. He is capable of starting the rush and possesses strong skating ability. He has agility to twist from the opposition's pressure to make a play and is also surprisingly strong on the puck, protecting it effectively from the opposition's pressure. He uses his stick really well to check the puck off the opposition and battles well to take it and force turnovers. He also has a nice element of aggression and physicality to his game, playing the puck carrier hard along the boards. He is able to get his shots through to the net, but has to watch some of the turnovers trying to force passes through the opposition.

Alex is a player we wish could say he has a chance to get drafted at the 2013 NHL Entry Draft, but the reality is he's a very long shot to get picked. Not because he isn't capable but because his size is a big enough of a disadvantage that it wouldn't be logical for a team to use one of their draft picks. It would be intriguing to see how he would do against bigger and stronger opponents in a pro camp, but he will need to work on adding more muscle to his frame, and enhance his offensive game. It's a very steep road uphill for Alex, but he has a ton of natural ability.

Zadorov, Nikita – LD – London Knights (OHL) – 6'5.25" 221

Nikita was selected 9th Overall in the 2012 CHL Import Draft by the London Knights. Nikita spent his 2011-2012 season with CSKA-Krasnaja Armija Moskva of the MHL in Russia. He first showed what he was capable of in North America at the 2012 World U17 Challenge. He had a fairly strong performance for Team Russia en route to helping them win Gold. He also participated in the IIHL World U18 Championships scoring twice as an under-ager at the tournament. He impressed the Knights who were willing to take him very high and bring him over to the OHL. The Knights placed him in the 3rd pairing to start the season and slowly increased his minutes as the season moved along.

The first things you notice about Nikita is his skating and his size. He is very good skater and we expect he will continue to improve as he gains strength. Nikita is also a very physical player who takes pride in finishing his hits. This was an area we saw tremendous improvements this season.

Early in the season, he would chase hits and put himself out of position, making his team outnumbered down low. Now he regularly lets the play come to him, maintaining much better one on one positioning. He will still use his body effectively, but will pick his spots and do it at intelligent times. Nikita has underrated puck skills and is capable of skating the puck up ice and gaining the offensive zone. Another area he has improved is his puck handling ability. He was hit or miss early in the year but now he's a lot more consistent and intelligent with both his decisions and actual puck skills. He's effective holding the offensive line and generally can get his shot through from the point with smart shooting decisions. Nikita has provided some offense at the junior level while playing a solid defensive game making him a valuable defenseman at both ends. Right now, Nikita looks more like a physical shutdown defenseman who is just now discovering his offensive potential. His overall shooting ability needs improvement.

Quotable: "If Nurse goes before this kid it will be a mistake." - NHL Scout

Quotable: "I really liked him coming into the season, much like Maatta he struggled a bit early on. I like the way the Knights eased him into the league playing 3rd pairing early in the season. He kept improving. I liked it when he stopped chasing hits and started lugging the puck. He was one of my favorite players I spoke to this season. I think he may surprise a few folks down the road with his offensive contributions. He told me that in Russia he was told to play defense, now he is discovering his offensive game" - Mark Edwards

Quotable: "He was in my top 30 coming into the season, dropped out and than played his way up to being a high pick." NHL Scout

Zdrahal, Patrik – RW – Acadie-Bathurst Titan (QMJHL) – 5'11" 178

The first round selection at the CHL Import Draft of the Titan, Patrik Zdrahal showed some good offensive flashes during his rookie season. The Czech showed his quick hands and pretty good offensive hockey sense. He's at his best in offensive games where he can let the hands and his talent speak. A pretty good player on the powerplay, using his creativity and skill set to control the play and create opportunities with his vision. He has very good agility on skates and plays a fairly European game, still far from the North-South approach of the North American game. He will score goals using his intelligence to find soft ice and make himself available for teammates. He doesn't have a powerful shot but it's pretty accurate. His physical implication is still lacking and he can rapidly become invisible when games get tight and become about going on the boards to grind. He's not a powerful skater but has decent top speed for major junior. He didn't show much character or glimpses of a 2-way game in our viewings of him this season. He will need substantial maturing and growth in his game to get to professional hockey.

Zottl, Nick – LD – Mississauga Steelheads (OHL) – 6'4" 215

Nick was selected in the 11th round of the 2011 OHL Priority Selection Draft out of the Lambton Jr. Sting Minor Midget Program. After spending a year playing for Lambton Jr. Sting Major Midget AAA team he made the move to Mississauga and split time between the OHL Steelheads and the OJHL's Mississauga Chargers. Zottl who used to play forward when he was younger is still adjusting to the defensive position, where he is more suited to play. He has a big frame and an active stick and he uses both effectively. He likes to finish his checks, and is constantly capable of deflecting away scoring chances.

He needs to improve his skating ability, and he won't ever be a puck moving specialist at the NHL level. He needs to work on just making the basic simple play and be a stay at home physical defenseman. Big defensemen like Zottl aren't always easy to find, especially with his learning curve of the defensive position which suggests he should continue to improve and develop as he has just completed his first year of play above the AAA level. He does have a long path in order for him to reach his potential.

Zykov, Valentin – RW – Baie-Comeau Drakkar (QMJHL) – 6'1" 215

Zykov was a 2nd round import draft by the Baie-Comeau Drakkar last June. After playing last season in the MHL recording 11 points and 105 penalty minutes in 52 games, Zykov made his debut in North American soil in 2012-2013 and has been a terrific goal-scoring force in QMJHL with 40 goals scored in his rookie season.

The St. Petersburg native has a huge frame at 6'01" 215 pounds and uses it very well to protect the puck and create time to maintain puck possession in favor of his team. He is already one of the strongest players in the league in 1-on-1 situations and we have rarely seen him get knocked off the puck when he uses this asset along the boards. He loves to crash the net and is not afraid of getting hit while doing so. Zykov also possesses tremendous puck control and has made some magnificent plays in tight spaces. He changes direction abruptly, twisting and turning on a dime, and has shown tremendous control of the puck, executing complex maneuvers quickly and effectively through or around players. An unpredictable player to follow in coverage, Zykov has undressed many players and goaltenders during the season displaying a great skill set and nice elusiveness. He has natural goal scoring instincts, shooting on net whenever he can and positioning himself in goal scoring areas when he doesn't have the puck. He has a rocket of a wrist shot and is really accurate with it even when shooting one-timers.

Valentin Zykov is not a selfish player and will make good use of teammates when cycling the puck or working around the net, although his playmaking abilities are not near his goal scoring abilities. He will hit players on the forecheck and get physical in front of the net, being an active part of scrums. Although he has tons of skills, Zykov can play an aggressive, gritty game when he is asked to, which shows a lot of versatility in his game. Defensively, he understands his role and will rarely be caught cheating, playing strongly on the wall, winning the important battles and hardly causing any turnovers at his own blue line. We like the intensity, consistency and character he has shown in our multiple observations of him. He has rarely backed down from a challenge and was a big time performer in important moments for Baie-Comeau this season,

Valentin Zykov's speed has improved as the season progressed, but it's still hindering him in defensive coverage at times. The fact that he's been having such success without having any high end speed speaks volume about the his natural talent with the puck, goal-scoring instincts and defensive awareness. Skating should be something Valentin Zykov gets as his legs get stronger and when he gets that speed, he'll be something special.

Quotable: "Skating was really the only issue for me and our Q guys all year. We waited and watched and I liked him more as the season went on. Many of you know I don't like to do many comparable but Logan Couture comes to mind as far as the skating situation as a draft eligible. That would work." - Mark Edwards"

Part 3

2014 NHL DRAFT TOP 30

2013 NHL DRAFT BLACK BOOK

RANK	PLAYER	POS	TEAM	LEAGUE	HEIGHT	WEIGHT
1	REINHART, SAM	RC	KOOTENAY	WHL	6'0"	182
2	NYLANDER, WILLIAM	LW	SODERTALJE J20	SWEDEN	5'10"	170
3	EKBLAD, AARON	RD	BARRIE	OHL	6'4"	213
4	MCKEOWN, ROLAND	RD	KINGSTON	OHL	6'1"	186
5	BARBASHEV, IVAN	LW	MONCTON	QMJHL	6'1"	185
6	LYAMKIN, NIKITA	LD	KUZNETSKIE MEDVEDI	RUSSIA	6'3"	165
7	MCCANN, JARED	LC	SAULT STE. MARIE	OHL	6'0"	174
8	DRAISATL, LEON	LC	PRINCE ALBERT	WHL	6'1"	198
9	GOLDOBIN, NIKOLAY	LW	SARNIA	OHL	5'11"	165
10	SCHMALTZ, NICK	RC	GREEN BAY	USHL	5'11"	160
11	CLARKE, BLAKE	LW	BRAMPTON	OHL	6'1"	190
12	DAL COLLE, MICHAEL	LW	OSHAWA	OHL	6'2	171
13	RITCHIE, NICK	LW	PETERBOROUGH	OHL	6'2"	216
14	VRANA, JAKUB	LC	LINKOPING J20	SWE	6'0"	165
15	BENNETT, SAM	LC	KINGSTON	OHL	6'0"	168
16	KARLSSON, ANTON	RW	FROLUNDA J20	SWE	6'0"	185
17	PEPIN, ALEXIS	RC	P.E.I.	QMJHL	6'2"	196
18	LINDBLOM, OSKAR	RW	BRYNAS J20	SWE	6'0"	185
19	MIDDLETON, JACOB	LD	OTTAWA	OHL	6'3"	194
20	BLEACKLEY, CONNOR	RC	RED DEER	WHL	6'0"	199
21	FLEURY, HAYDN	LD	RED DEER	WHL	6'3"	204
22	MARTIN, BRYCEN	LD	SWIFT CURRENT	WHL	6'3"	179
23	VIRTANEN, JAKE	LW	CALGARY	WHL	6'1"	190
24	KAPANEN, KASPER	RW	KALPA	FIN	5'11"	172
25	MISTELE, MATTHEW	LW	PLYMOUTH	OHL	6'2"	183
26	BUKARTS, RIHARDS	LW	HK RIGA	MHL	5'10"	185
27	WATSON, SPENCER	LW	KINGSTON	OHL	5'10"	157
28	BALTISBERGER, Phil	LD	GCK LIONS ZURICH	SUI	6'0"	207
29	HONKA, JULIUS	D	JYP JYVASKLA	FIN	5'10	170
30	POINT, BRAYDEN	RC	MOOSE JAW	WHL	5'8"	155

Part 4
2014 NHL DRAFT PROSPECTS

Abou-Assaly, Andrew – Ottawa 67's (OHL) – 5'11" 172

Andrew was selected in the third round of the 2012 OHL Priority Selection draft by his hometown Ottawa 67's after developing in the Ottawa Jr. 67's Minor Midget program. Due to his good grades in school, Andrew was able to consider NCAA options, but decided after being selected at the OHL draft to stay home and play in the OHL for his hometown team. Andrew had a bit of an underwhelming rookie season, however he played on a rebuilding 67's team. Andrew, who was known more so at the minor midget level for his offensive input beyond anything else had to try and adjust to a bit of a grinder role as a 16 year old. It was a bit of a challenge for Andrew, but will only help him moving forward already with a season under his belt in the OHL. Andrew is a player who generally anticipates the play well. He is able to read the play and get in fairly good positioning. He has a strong powerful shot, with a quick release, which made it shocking to see Andrew post only one goal this past season. However he has also shown the ability to include his linemates very well especially on the rush making great passes and set up a few goals this season. Andrew will likely gain some ice heading into the 2013-2014 season and will need to start showing why the Ottawa 67's picked him in the third round in order to be selected at the 2014 NHL Entry Draft.

Addesi, Jordan – LW – Sarnia Sting (OHL) – 6'2" – 194

Jordan was selected in the 4th round of the 2012 OHL Priority Selection from the Vaughan Kings in the GTHL. Jordan impressed our scouts early on with his power game and puck skills however his season ended early due to a shoulder injury. Sarnia picked Addesi very close to our projected rating and he really reached or even surpassed expectations this year. Addesi was regularly used in a fourth line role but saw himself promoted mid game throughout the season by Coach Beaulieu during his stronger games. If there's a hit to be made, Jordan will finish it every single time. We love the physical element he brings and more importantly he does this every single game. Jordan has shown flashes of offensive ability but where he was on the depth chart and the role he was expected to play it's certainly too early to gauge exactly where he is in the offensive department. We would like to see him improve his skating heading into next season. We certainly feel Jordan will hear his name called at the 2014 NHL Entry Draft if he continues this style of play and look forward to seeing what he does with increased ice next season.

Atwal, Arvin – RD – Vancouver Giants (WHL) – 6'0" 188

Atwal is a defenseman whose game has come a long way this season. He received very limited minutes when he first joined the Giants and made mistakes after mistakes, but has moved up to the top defense pairing since then. He is a tough player who is willing to fight anybody and stick up for his teammates. Atwal plays the game with a lot of tenacity and has really caught the organization's attention with his improvements.

Defensively, Atwal committed very many turnovers and ran around the ice like he had very little idea of what he was doing without the puck. He was a liability and had very little trust from the coaching staff. However, he has limited the number of giveaways, which has led to a more composed game. He takes his time with the puck now instead of just blindly throwing it away, and while he still commits turnovers, they are not as dangerous as they were previously. Atwal plays with a lot of energy and is tough to play against. He is relentless in his pursuit for the puck, and sometimes that negatively effects his game. He likes to chase the play instead of being patient and letting the play come to him. Good players take advantage of his energy and find open teammates in the slot for very good scoring chances.

Atwal has shown limited offensive abilities up to this point in his junior career, but it is clearly improving. His outlet passes has gotten better in terms or accuracy and reading the forecheck to make it easier for his team to breakout. He still has limited vision and does not seem like he will be much of a power play quarterback, but he is getting ice time on the power play, and has looked more comfortable on the blueline. He still needs to work on his shots, particularly getting them through in traffic. Atwal is still a project for the Giants, but it is encouraging to see that his play has improved as he is getting more ice time this year.

Aubé-Kubel, Nicolas – RC – Val D'Or Foreurs (QMJHL) – 5'11" 180

Aubé-Kubel was one of the most talented 16 year old players in QMJHL. He had limited minutes on many nights with the Val D'Or Foreurs, he had a tough time getting a rythme and confidence this season. He is a great explosive skater, posessing a blazing top-speed and tremendous agility on skates. He creates a lot of space for himself because of that speed. A great neutral zone player, he eluded many defensemen already at 16 years old by stopping abruptly, changing direction quickly or just twisting and turning. Aubé-Kubel is also very gifted with the puck, dangling through sticks and skates easily. His puck-control is great at top speed making him tough to stop when he is carrying the puck. He is a great player on the rush, using his skills to create scoring opportunities. He has a decent wrist shot, but we feel he will settle into a great playmaker in his career with the vision he displayed during the season. A great powerplay performer this season, we don't think Aubé-Kubel was really able to establish his game 5-on-5, as he was changing lines fairly often and playing with energy players. Aubé-Kubel is a hard-working player, but the way he works is not always good. He will try to do too many fancy plays and beat many players by himself. He looked tentative at times engaging in battles on the boards and although he is not the biggest, Aubé-Kubel still could be more implicated physically in all areas. Defensively, he still needs experience, but his skating has helped him a lot being the first man back as he is a natural center.

Audette, Daniel – LC – Sherbrooke Phoenix (QMJHL) – 5'9" 168

Donald Audette's son, Daniel, is a highly talented small center who was selected at the number 1 spot at the 2012 QMJHL draft. He had a tough time adjusting to the caliber of major junior early in the season but played much better in the second half. Daniel has tremendous puckhandling skills and excels when he has time and space. He is fluid with the puck and will beat defenders 1-on-1 if they try to play the puck against him. An elusive player, Audette is also a very agile skater, twisting and turning to gain space while still keeping control of the puck. He still lacks top speed, explosiveness and will become a threat every time he has the puck as soon as he gets that high end speed. A natural playmaker, his passing skills are great, finding teammates easily through traffic in the offensive zone, with saucer passes, mastering it on the backhand or forehand. An accurate wrist shot, Daniel Audette executes offensively at a higher pace than most players his age. He has a great level of offensive hockey sense, reading and reacting well to find soft ice or create plays. Defensively, he improved as the season went on, showing more intelligence, supporting defensemen and being more cautious in his play with the puck. Where Daniel Audette will need to develop is his work ethic, intensity and physical play. He will shy away from physical contact, losing puck posession and giving big physical forwards and easy time when he's in defensive coverage. We also have doubts about his attitude, as he has been seen making sellfish decisions at times during the season.

Ayotte, Mathieu – RW – Victoriaville Tigres (QMJHL) – 5'10" 144

Ayotte played 32 games for Victoriaville this season before being sent down to his Midget team. He didn't look out of place in the league but struggled to be consistent. The best aspect of his game he displayed during his short stint in the league is his vision and passing skills. He didn't show much speed and agility with the puck but he was good at holding on to it and passing it on to other teammates on the rush. He can be precise with his passes and has a decent shot on goal. One issue that prevented him from doing better offensively and being more consistent was his size. He is useless in puck battles and gets knocked off the puck too easily. He looked slightly better at the U17 tournament with Team Quebec, although he didn't have a big affect. Not considered a viable prospect right now based on what we saw.

Baillie, Tyson – RC – Kelowna Rockets (WHL) – 5'10" 185

Tyson Baillie's offensive production really improved as the season went on. His intensity and confidence with the puck during the second half of the year really allowed him to rise to the occasion and earn a top 6 spot with the Rockets, and provide a very impressive presence offensively.

Baillie may seem a little small out on the ice, but he plays the game like he is 6' tall. He loves to go to the net with the puck, and actually protects the puck quite well with his body. He will take on anybody physically, and proved that he can play against bigger players this year. He has very good patience with the puck, and is able to buy some time off the wing for a play to develop because of his good stickhandling abilities and the way that he can protect the puck. He creates good scoring chances on a consistent basis, and is tough to play against every game.

Baillie's fearlessness really helped to spark the Rockets' season, and he was able to fill a very important role for the team as the team's second line centre. He played a good two way game throughout the season, and was coached well by Ryan Huska as his development continued to improve as he played in more games. An area of improvement for Baillie would be his skating. For his size, he will need to get quicker to avoid checks and to drive to the net more effectively, especially at the next level. Baillie has become a pest to play against, and it will be interesting to see just how much his offensive game can improve next season as he is counted on even more to product points. If he can continue to be physically hard to play against while maintaining his composure, he will surely continue to catch the attention of NHL scouts.

Bahl, Julien – RD – Blainville-Boisbriand Armada (QMJHL) – 5'11" 170

Julien Bahl played the vast majority of the season in the Blainville-Boisbrand line up, earning good ice-time for a 16 year old playing on one of the most experienced defensive squads in QMJHL. Bahl doesn't have much upside offensively or physically, but plays a very smart type of hockey. He rarely makes positional mistakes, skates fluidly and plays simple hockey. His puck skills are average, but are decent enough to make the simple plays quickly without turning the puck over even when he's under pressure, also displaying good hockey sense. Without being agressive or physical, Bahl's a solid player who doesn't shy away from physical play and intense puck battles. A fairly good passer, Bahl uses the board a lot to start transitions if there are no obvious options. Bahl is still undersized, lacks explosiveness and high end speed. He doesn't have a really good shot, but has the smarts to progress and work ethic to progress well in the next seasons.

Baltisberger, Phil – LD – GC Kusnacht Lions (NLB) – 6'0" 210

Phil has moved up the development ranks of ZSC Lions from U15 all the way up to playing in a few playoff games for the men's top league team over the past two years. He moves the puck up ice very effectively. He doesn't show a lot of flash offensively, but he gets the job done with intelligence and poise reading plays well in the offensive zone. He also possesses a cannon of a shot from the point which is very dangerous when he gets it on goal. Phil is at his best when working along the boards. He's got great size and strength and wins a lot of battles in the corners and along the walls. He battles hard and uses his size very intelligently in the defensive zone. He's usually strong in one on one situations but can get burned on his pivot at times. Phil projects to be the top prospect coming out of Switzerland next season. He already has two World Junior Championships under his belt, and could represent Switzerland four times at the WJC by the time he reaches the age of 20. He already possesses good size and strength, although we'd like to see him improve his skating a little.

Quotable: "Liked him in Sochi this year, he was much bigger than when I saw him previously. He played smart hockey. Feet were a little sluggish, perhaps due to the weight gain. He competes hard and wins battles." - Mark Edwards

Barbashev, Ivan –LW – Moncton Wildcats (QMJHL) – 6'1" 185

The top pick in the 2012 CHL Import Draft, Barbashev quickly established himself as a premium offensive player with the contending Moncton Wildcats. He impressed us in all our viewings this year and deserves a place near the top of the early 2014 NHL draft rankings. Barbashev has a complete package of speed, skills and physical abilities. He is a very gifted skater with a good burst of speed that allows him to carry the puck all over the ice and make aggressive approaches in the offensive zone. He likes to use his body to beat the defenders when entering the offensive zone. He also uses his quick hands to elude players and has shown very good puck skills thus far. He is dynamic with his very strong hands and he also takes dangerous shots on goal. He has also displayed his great offensive hockey sense, distributing the puck and creating superb plays around the net for teammates.

Barbashev is considered a threat every time he touches the puck but he also plays a very interesting game without it. He proved to be an intense player and we like his hustle on the ice. He takes a liking to finishing his checks and showed he can deliver some very hard ones. He is hard working and will rarely take a night off, showing heart and desire in his defensive zone. He is willing to battle through traffic to create plays and crash the opposition's crease. All that being said, we feel his high-end attributes and attitude on the ice makes him a player to follow closely for the 2014 NHL Draft.

Quotable: "He was impressive at the U18's in Russia. I didn't see Moncton live this season, so I was happy to see him play in Sochi. Showed off his skill level and played smart hockey. He was one of my fave players in the tourney." - Mark Edwards

Bennett, Sam – LC – Kingston Frontenacs (OHL) – 6'0" 168

Sam was selected 9th Overall by the Kingston Frontenacs at the 2012 OHL Priority Selection Draft out of the Toronto Marlboros Minor Midget program. Bennett really seemed to grow as his Minor Midget season went on and was one of the most improved players over the course of that season. Sam immediately joined the Frontenacs and became a regular player in the top six forwards playing every game situation especially power plays. Sam creates plays extremely well and is able to beat defensemen one on one. He's able to draw in opponents with puck possession and utilizes strong vision to complete difficult pass and create scoring chances. Sam has a pretty strong shot and isn't shy about utilizing it. Sam is a very offensive minded player who is most successful making plays happen, but is also an effective forechecker, can force turnovers. Sam will need to try and limit the number of minor penalties he takes. 87 penalty minutes is ok if you're dropping the gloves, but with only one fight, that's simply too many minor penalties for a player of his talent to take. Sam will once again be a big time contributor to the Kingston Frontenacs who are on the way up.

Bergman, Julius – RD – Karlskrona (SAL) – 6'1" 187

Julius has worked his way up Karlskrona's system and eventually worked his way up to playing almost full time in the men's Allsvenskan league this past season. He was also loaned out to Frolunda's J20 team briefly this season showing well helping their organization out. Julius also participated in the 2013 IIHF World U18 Championship. He is a big reliable defenseman who isn't too flashy but gets the job done. He is a good skater, particularly at his size and is capable and poised enough to skate the puck out of trouble in his own zone. He makes smart solid passes out of the defensive zone and keeps it pretty simple with the puck. He can get into some trouble when trying to do too much with the puck so he generally keeps it simple. Julius works very hard along the boards and is capable of winning battles. He displays good defensive positioning and is capable of breaking up plays. You won't see much offense out of Julius but when he's on his game, he's as reliable and as smart of a defenseman you'll find. Julius has a late birth date which makes him eligible for the 2014 NHL Entry Draft.

Bilia, Julio – G – Chicoutimi Saguenéens (QMJHL) – 5'11" 152

The Chicoutimi rookie goalkeeper started the season in AAA Midget with Laval-Montréal, but then got called up by the Saguenéens and was good enough to be kept in QMJHL playing the backup role to LA Kings' 2011 2nd round draft pick, Christopher Gibson. Bilia is a small goalie with tremendous quickness, looks relaxed in front of his net, rarely over reacting or getting caught out of position. He follows the play very well and never seems to lose eye-contact with the puck, even in traffic. A real fighter in scrambles and in his crease, he will give the 2nd and 3rd efforts to reach for a spectacular save even when he looks beat. Bilia posesses a rare quality in a world of butterfly-driven goalies, great upper net coverage. Both hands are lightning quick with great reflexes and they are both steady, rarely having a night where he is struggling in this area. He likes to play the puck behind his net and he does it very well, communicating well with defensemen and understanding the breakout strategies of his team. Bilia's legs are quick and powerful, enabling him to make great lateral movements and be in position quickly on crisp passing plays. Mentally, Bilia is very strong, making great saves at the right times and showing no effect in his game after a bad goal. His major weakness is his size, pucks will get through him and he is often forced to make tough saves when they would be routine saves for a bigger goalies. His rebound control is decent, but has problem absorbing pucks easily because of his size. He will allow bad goals in the five hole and needs to close out the legs better and be more compact in his butterfly basic positioning.

Quotable: " Impressed our staff this season, with our scout Simon Larouche based in Chicoutimi, he will get plenty of views next season." - Mark Edwards

Bishop, Clark – LC – Cape-Breton Screaming Eagles (QMJHL) – 5'11" 173

The New Foundland native was the Screaming Eagles' first selection (3rd overall) at last year's QMJHL draft. Bishop plays much bigger than his size, protects the puck very well and is excellent at cycling the puck. A dynamic skater, he can gain top speed very quickly and his feet rarely stop moving. Excellent on the forecheck using his speed, he drives the net hard. Bishop loves to hit and his physical game will be even better once he get bigger and stronger. If he was couple inches taller he would be an ideal power forward. A complete player with a very good work ethic, his willingness and intensity lead by example. He is a fairly good puckhandler, Bishop controls the puck really well at top speed and has no problem carrying the play from one end to another. He has a nose for the net and will jump on those available pucks rapidly around the net. His decisions are very good for a 16 years old, with and without the puck, he plays at a very fast pace but shows a good vision and high hockey sense. He is very responsible defensively, backchecking and always supporting his defensemen. Clark was in tough situation with Cape-Breton as the team finished last in the regular season standing, he also played for team Atlantic at the U17 hockey challenge and did very well with 5 points in 5 games.

Quotable: " I love the work ethic he showed even though he didn't get much ice-time with one of the worst teams in QMJHL. Regardless if you give him 5 or 20 minutes, you know he's always having the same attitude and going full tilt on the ice which is something I really like." - Simon Larouche

Bleackley, Connor – RC – Red Deer Rebels (WHL) – 6'0" 199

Bleackley is a physical 2 way centre who displayed good talent at both ends of the ice. He was more and more dependable as the season went on, and was trusted on to shut down opposing teams to protect the lead late into games.

Offensively, Bleackley was not able to get on the scoresheet much this season, but showed some potential with his size and speed. He has a good shot off the rush, but really needs to work on hitting the net more often. He does not have exceptional playmaking skills, but does a good job off the cycle to keep the pressure on in the offensive zone and makes good passes off the rush. Bleackley's issue seems to be his ability to think and read the game. He does not seem to find open areas out on the ice very well, and is a little bit behind in making passes in the offensive zone. His confidence with the puck needs to improve for him to make an impact offensively.

Bleackley made most of his contributions this season in the defensive end. He is strong on his skates, and does little things well, like faceoffs and body positioning to be difficult to play against. His speed allows him to backcheck quickly and get to dangerous areas out on the ice quickly to take away any scoring opportunities. He does not hesitate to block shots and to sacrifice his body to make plays. Another positive attribute of Bleackley is his disciplined play. He rarely takes penalties, and does a good job of controlling his stick and instead being in good position with his body to ensure that opponents do not have a good play to make with the puck.

It will be interesting to see if Bleackley's offensive game could improve at all next season with added responsibilities. He will definitely have to improve his output offensively for the Rebels to improve on their season. If he can gain more poise with the puck and slow down the game in the offensive zone, he could be a dangerous player with his strength and speed.

Quotable: "One of the players who made an impression on several of our scouts at the U17 in December." - Mark Edwards

Boivin, Christophe – LW – Seminaire Saint-François Blizzard (MAAA) – 5'6" 141

Christophe Boivin was a stellar performer with the Blizzard in the 2012-2013 season, he was passed on at the 2012 QMJHL Draft playing minor midget and being even smaller than he is now. Boivin is a tremendous playmaker, controlling the play all season long on his line and creating scoring chances profusely. He is an agile skater, having an easy time creating space, stopping abruptly to delay the play and consider his options and gaining space twisting and turning. A great puck-handler, Boivin makes smart decisions in all 3-zones and is an asset whatever the time and score is in a hockey game. He has a great work ethic and will show up every game. A lightweight player, Boivin didn't shy away from physical play but it still remains to be seen if he will be able to gain muscles and handle physicality at the next level. He will go around the net to score goals and knows how to get open for scoring chances. By gaining some height and some weight, Boivin could be a really interesting player for the 2014 draft, because of the tremendous smarts and passing skills in his game.

Boucher, Félix – LD – Victoriaville Tigres (QMJHL) – 6'2" 177

Boucher is a young defenseman that will benefit from his late birthday to polish his skills leading up to next year's draft. He has likable size for a defenseman and we liked how he handled his defensive duties this season. He has a bit above average footing and he is a smooth skater. He can be very sharp when defending a player one-on-one, maintaining proper gap and using his stick to make plays. As a rookie he made his share of mistakes but he never gave up and did a good job recovering. He is not a very talented player with the puck but he seemed comfortable and was able to make plays from the backhand. The next step for him is getting more experience and sharpening up his defensive game to be able to be more consistent in his zone. He also needs to be more physical and use his body to his advantage. We don't consider him a top prospect for next year's draft but it's also too soon to discard him as well.

Bourne, Damian – LW – Mississauga Steelheads (OHL) – 6'4" 211

Damian was selected first round, 11th overall by the Mississauga Steelheads at the 2012 OHL Priority Selection Draft out of the 2012 OHL Cup Champion Mississauga Rebels. Damian actually got off to a bit of a quick start statistically posting 8 points in his first 12 games. Unfortunately he would only score 4 in his final 38 games of the season. He made adjustments throughout the season playing a bottom six role for the Steelheads.

Damian was always one of the more physically dominant players in the entire age group, but he showed he still has to get stronger as he wasn't quite as assertive as he could have been. He has shown a few flashes of offensive ability but his offensive contributions seem to come from using his size in front and distributing the puck effectively. Damian worked hard in all three zones and contributed to the Steelheads on a regular basis. Heading into Damian's NHL Draft Year in 2014 we hope to see him improve on his skating and develop a bit of a mean streak making him tougher to play against on a more regular basis.

Bratina, Zach – LW – Saginaw Spirit (OHL) – 6'1" 170

Zach was selected in the first round, 19th Overall at the 2012 OHL Priority Selection Draft by the Plymouth Whalers out of the Central Ontario Wolves Minor Midget program. Zach made the jump right away joining the Plymouth Whalers. He only played in limited action for the Whalers as they were stacked with veteran forwards. Zach did what he could with the time he had, but was eventually moved to the Saginaw Spirit as a main part of a deal that sent Florida Panthers prospect Vincent Trocheck to Plymouth. Zach received a little more action on the Spirit who were in a bit of a reloading year. Zach has great size and when he's on his game he displays great knowledge of how to use his size to protect the puck, play physical and drive the net. Zach is actually a better playmaker than a shooter and has shown very good passes on the rush. Zach needs to work on his consistency as there have been games where he has been invisible on the ice and others where he seems to get it. Zach has the build and potential to be a power forward, but has quite a ways to go. Next to his consistency we would like to see Zach add some muscle and get stronger while maintaining his skating ability.

Brown, Graeme – LD – Windsor Spitfires (OHL) – 6'1" – 184

Graeme was the Windsor Spitfires third round selection out of the Kingston Jr. Frontenacs Minor Midget program. He made the move to southwestern Ontario and was designated to the LaSalle Vipers Jr. B team for the majority of this season. He worked hard and earned himself 19 games with the Spitfires in the second half of the season and is very likely to be a regular in the Spitfires line-up next season. Graeme is a smooth skating defenseman for his size who shows good mobility in all directions and puck control. He will need to improve his puck decisions as we have seen him make both smooth solid passes, but also make a few mental errors. Brown is a defenseman who takes care of his own end. He has good physical endurance and solid positioning in his own zone. He was used as a top penalty killer at the Jr. B level and shows positioning and a mindset that will help him at any level. He has excellent reaction time when clearing out rebounds and is intelligent getting in passing lanes. We expect Graeme to be a player to watch playing full time against some good OHL competition. He already has the size we'd like to see for the 2014 Draft, but want him to get a little stronger.

Carrier, Scott – RD – Chicoutimi Saguenéens (QMJHL) – 5'9" 170

Carrier was a 6th round draft pick by Chicoutimi at the 2012 QMJHL Draft and was a nice surprise on a rebuilding Saguenéens' defense. Carrier earned big minutes with Chicoutimi by playing a steady, simple and physical game. He is a smart defenseman, playing the gap well, executing smart plays with the puck from his own zone when he is under pressure and having poise in his game, which you rarely see from a 16 year old. He likes to get his nose dirty, will be involved in scrums, will initiate physical contact and is willing to take hits to make a play. He has a lot of character and intensity. A solid player physically, Carrier doesn't play like he's undersized. He has a great footwork, but lacks speed in his game having to take decisions quickly with the puck because he can't get space with skating and having a tough time containing explosive skater even though the position is good. He has a little confidence offensively, using simple plays by the boards to start transition, he doesn't have a good shot and will use an accurate wrist shot to touch the net. He prefers holding his blue line safely and will rarely take chances offensively.

Chartier, Rourke – LW – Kelowna Rockets (WHL) – 5'10" 165

Chartier is another one of those smaller forwards for the Rockets who seem to play bigger than he actually is. He is not particularly physical, but his work along the walls is exceptional as he does a good job of fighting for loose pucks and protecting the puck in the offensive zone.

Chartier had a tough start to his rookie season in the WHL as he was adjusting to the level of play, but his play improved as the season went on. It may not have showed on the score sheet, but he was creating more chances and was more difficult to play against. He still needs to work on his strength and play with the puck to be more productive. His shot and passing abilities are not particularly great, but are coming along. He needs to work on staying on his feet more and filling up his frame to even be tougher to play against along the walls.

Defensively, Chartier still looks a little overwhelmed with the pace of play without the puck. He is a little late on covering the point at times, and there are also moments when he needs to come down low to support his defensemen, but is a step or two behind. He could also play with some more intensity and be more of a physical presence by finishing his checks and create some turnovers.

It will be interesting to see just how well Chartier could play in his second full year in the WHL. The key for him seems to be to have a good start to the season and play a consistent game. He was playing catch up to his team for a large portion of the year, which hurt his confidence. He was able to prove that he belongs in the line up as the season went along, and it is important to build on that and start to be a regular contributor on the scoresheet.

Chatham, Connor – FW – Omaha Lancers (USHL) – 6'1" – 187

Connor opened his USHL career as part of the U.S. National Team Development Program playing for the U-17's and represented USA internationally at the 2012 World U-17 Hockey Challenge in Windsor, Ontario. Connor had an impressive and successful first year in the program. Connor joined the Omaha Lancers of the USHL this season and put together some very impressive numbers. Connor showed a lot of offensive upside possessing great size and some effective physical play, but could still stand to add some more muscle. He is more of a shooter than a passer and is able to finish plays in the offensive zone with a powerful shot. Despite his size, Chatham displays efficient skating ability. Connor was also selected in the 5th round at the 2011 OHL Priority Selection Draft by the Plymouth Whalers. Chatham is slated to join the University of Denver this fall of 2013. Due to his late birth date he is ineligible until the 2014 NHL Entry Draft.

Clarke, Blake – LW – Brampton Battalion (OHL) – 6'1" 190

A US born, 2014 eligible player, Blake Clarke came on in a big way for the traditionally offensively starved Brampton Battalion. He was thrust into key offensive situations as a top 6 forward and top powerplay player and performed well. He has a great combination of skating ability, hands, and creativity in the offensive end. Moreover, in viewings, he did not look out of place in the defensive zone. While in some games Clarke was not as noticeable for the full 60 minutes as one would like, you can't deny his rookie season production. If he can put together another strong season, he will have to be mentioned with the likes of the highest tier prospects for the NHL 2014 draft.

Cornel, Eric – RC – Peterborough Petes (OHL) – 6'2" 172

Eric was selected first round, 3rd overall at the 2012 OHL Priority Selection Draft by the Peterborough Petes out of the Upper Canada Cyclones Minor Midget program. Eric came to the Petes' providing a great combination of size and speed, but never really found his place with the Petes' showing a few flashes of skill along the way. At 6'2" his skating ability is excellent and he can just fly around the ice. While Cornel is a natural centre, he experienced most of his success when he was moved to the wing. Eric has shown us flashes of offensive potential and he has a powerful shot with a quick release. Overall this past season was a little underwhelming for Cornel, but everything is looking up for him. He has a year of OHL experience under his belt, Peterborough is on the rise and he's going to have a bigger role with the team next season. Eric will be given all the opportunities to succeed next season in his NHL Draft year.

Quotable: "Saw some good signs as the 2013 season ended. The Petes need him to become a key player in their lineup every night. - Mark Edwards

Côté, Vytal – RD – Acadie-Bathurst Titan (QMJHL) – 6'2" 190

Côté started his QMJHL career after the Victoriaville Tigres recruited him south of the border. We thought he showed very decent aptitudes and was off to a promising start. He has decent mobility and he likes to play an aggressive style of hockey. He has a mean streak and it shows in his physical play. He can also handle the puck well and is not a liability on the transition. He seemed to lack hockey sense at times and struggled with the pace of the game a little bit. His struggle prevented him from playing a prominent role and establishing himself consistently in the lineup. He was subsequently traded to the Acadie-Bathurst Titan at the trade deadline where he played a substantial amount of games. While he is no sure thing, his attributes, more specifically his physical play, makes him a player to keep an eye on for next year's draft.

Cramarossa, Michael – LC – Belleville Bulls (OHL) – 6'0" 190

Michael was selected in the third round of the 2012 OHL Priority Selection Draft out of the Toronto Marlboros Minor Midget program. Michael was able to play with his brother Joseph who was selected by the Anaheim Ducks at the 2011 NHL Entry Draft. While his brother didn't play with the most natural skill and worked incredibly hard to acquire everything he has thus far in hockey. Michael on the other hand appears to have a lot of natural ability, but his compete level has been a concern for us going back to his Minor Midget days. Michael skates fairly well and displays good puck skills. He can be dangerous in the offensive zone but we have noticed him going through the motions at times. Michael has a lot of potential, enough to follow in his brothers footsteps at the 2014 NHL Entry Draft, but will need to bring a more consistent effort. Michael was used in a very limited role, so while this season was a good chance for him to get his feet wet, he will get a lot more ice time with graduations from the Bulls' up front, giving Michael the chance to play a skillful hard working game and contribute to his team on a nightly basis.

Cummins, Conor – LD – Sudbury Wolves (OHL) – 6'2" – 205

Conor was selected first round, 14th Overall at the 2012 OHL Priority Selection Draft by the Sudbury Wolves out of the Whitby Wildcats Minor Midget Program. Connor is a tremendous skater for his size and as a defenseman shows the mobility that some 6'2" defensemen never gain even at the top level which alone makes Conor a very intriguing prospect. He received moderate ice as a 16 year old and got a great chance with Team Ontario at the 2013 World U-17 Challenge in Victoriaville/Drummondville. Conor is at his best with the puck on his stick rushing it as he knows how to protect while evading checkers. He has been a little hit or miss with puck decisions and will look to improve in that area with a year of experience. He also has struggled in our viewings getting beat defensively, losing his positioning at time. Also, at his size his physical play is extremely underwhelming. He tends to lose quite a few battles and rarely shows any push back against opposing forwards. Conor has a long way to go, but he has a lot of natural tools in his corner that could see him develop into a very good defenseman.

Dal Colle, Michael – LW – Oshawa Generals (OHL) – 6'2" – 171

Michael was selected 1st Round, 7th Overall by the Oshawa Generals out of the Vaughan Kings Minor Midget program. Michael was one of the premier forwards in all of Ontario leading into the draft. He played ridiculous minutes with Vaughan, so we knew going in he would be well conditioned to play big ice in the OHL.

Early on he established himself showing his potential and winding up on a line with Columbus Blue Jackets' prospect Boone Jenner and Toronto Maple Leafs Tyler Biggs. They maintained this line for the vast majority of this season. Michael is an excellent playmaker and shows creativity with the puck well beyond his years. He visualizes plays well and has a high percentage of success rate on his passing, even in difficult situations. His effort is consistent and he is able to create several scoring chances over the course of a game. Despite his size he's a pretty good skater with efficient quickness. Michael already plays a mature, well rounded game and we hope for him to gain more strength and become a little more physical with his game. Michael is one of the top prospects for the 2014 NHL Entry Draft and will be one of the go to guys for the Generals next season.

De Leo, Chase – LC – Portland Winterhawks (WHL) – 5'9" 172

De Leo is an undersized, but gritty centre who mostly played on the 3rd line this season. He was not really depended on to shut down opponents, but because of the Winterhawks' depth, he was expected to provide offense while being responsible in his own end.

De Leo's size is misleading because he plays much bigger than he is. He does not back down from anybody, and provides a very pesky presence for Portland. He is not afraid to go to the net to try to score off of rebounds, and will go back again and again despite the physical punishment he receives. De Leo is a good, responsible playmaker off the rush. He makes quick decisions with the puck, and also is creative with it. He can pass the puck off to the wing then drive the net, make a quick stop at the faceoff circle to wait for the trailer or drive to the net then quickly make a pass to the slot. De Leo's offensive work mostly occurs off the rush, as he has a difficult time along the boards with protecting the puck due to his size, and is a liability when trying to set up in the offensive zone.

Defensively, De Leo is not particularly good in his own end. He has to read the play better, and try to take away space more rather than just engage physically. He also has a tendency to focus too much on the puck and not be aware of his surroundings, which is a problem as he often plays down the middle and is counted on to watch the slot.

De Leo's lack of size will definitely worry teams, even though he plays a grinding style of game. He has not been able to show the ability to be a consistent offensive threat and tire out opponents with the cycle. He will most likely have to move to the wing as a pro, but his poor work along the walls will not help his cause. If he can get stronger, then teams could take a chance in him.

De Sousa, Daniel – RD – Belleville Bulls (OHL) – 5'11" 175

De Sousa struggled to consistently crack a veteran loaded Bulls lineup in his rookie season. He was selected 31st overall at the 2012 OHL Priority Selection Draft from a strong Toronto Marlboros squad. Daniel is a very strong skater and has the ability to skate himself out of trouble in the defensive zone. He shows good confidence carrying the puck but needs to make quicker decisions on where to move it. He shows good offensive instincts and is constantly looking for opportunities to jump into the offensive rush. He is good at walking the blue line and getting himself into strong shooting lanes but needs to work at finding the net through traffic. De Sousa has a mean streak to him and needs to be careful to not let opponents get him off his game and draw him into taking penalties. He needs to improve his defensive zone work and become stronger so that he can effectively knock opponents off of pucks down low. De Sousa sometimes tries to do too much with the puck and needs to cut down on the risks and turnovers to really excel as a defender. Daniel will see his ice time and opportunity grow next season with the advancement of a few veterans and is a prospect to keep an eye on for the 2013-2014 season.

DeAngelo, Anthony – RD – Sarnia Sting (OHL) – 5'11" – 167

Anthony has been one of the most polarizing players in recent memory. He came in as a second round pick in the 2012 OHL Priority Selection draft from the Cedar Rapids RoughRiders after playing in the USHL as a 15 year old. He came to Sarnia as one of the highest regarded defensemen in recent memory. Anthony really showed his potential as a rookie as he was able to contribute to a very talented Sarnia team starting his OHL career at 15 years old.

As the 2012-2013 season opened Anthony took over a top defenseman role with the Sting and carried that role throughout the season. DeAngelo is an outstanding skater and can go end to end with the puck almost at will. His first few steps are good, he's agile and provides a good top speed. He moves the puck very well most of the time on the power play and shows good vision in the offensive zone. He has a pretty good shot from the point but also will sneak in from the point and has scored a few goals this season making a good read and coming in. He's elusive and talented with the puck. When he's having a good game he's tough to contain and will help Sarnia put points on the board. He has hit or miss moves like the spin-o-rama which he loves to use and it works sometimes. However he overuses it and it can sometimes result in a scoring chance for the opposition because he's off balance, knocked down and out of the play. Anthony shows some aggression and will hit and will battle but he needs to get stronger. Unfortunately over the three years we've watched Anthony play his temper has been the a defining part of his game. He has taken dumb penalties, slammed his stick and let it affect hsi game.

Defensively Anthony has been hit or miss defensively. He's made some good one on one plays, competes and battles but he's also been beat pretty bad and caught out of positioning to the point of being subject to being benched.

Anthony is eligible in 2014 and it is almost impossible to predict what will happen. If he can improve his defensive play while not being too risky with his offense, Anthony could elevate himself back up among the top prospects in 2014. However if the defensive lapses and temper tantrums continue he could be "that guy" in the 2014 draft that sees himself surprise some people and freefall down the list in the 2014 NHL Entry Draft. Fortunately he has a lot of control over what his future holds.

Delisle-Houde, Alex – RW – Seminaire Saint-François Blizzard (MAAA) – 5'11" 164

Alexandre Delisle-Houde is a Shawinigan Cataractes propriety and was one of the smartest forwards in AAA Midget this season playing with the runner-up Blizzard. He is an effortless skater, getting to his top speed quickly. He is a great playmaker making decisions with the puck in a split second and making his linemates look good. He uses his smarts without the puck to post himself in scoring positions and has great offensive execution on complex plays. He has a hard snap shot that he can release on one-timers. He is not a physical player but protects the puck really well and doesn't mind taking a hit when he has the puck, showing good physical strength. He is a 2-way player with smart instincts in his own zone, playing well on the boards and using smart positioning to be effective. Delisle-Houde can be soft at times and lose battles without fighting, he can start to glide and rely on intelligence only in some games but has shown clutch player qualities, being a strong performer in the playoffs.

Draisaitl, Leon – LC – Prince Albert Raiders (WHL) – 6'1" 198

Draisaitl is a big, playmaking centre who plays a very similar game to current NHLer Joe Thornton. He has unbelievable vision out on the ice, uses his body well to protect the puck along the walls and then feeds his teammates with excellent passes when they get open for good scoring chances. As a rookie, Draisaitl has received a lot of attention from opposing teams, but he has consistently been able to produce points regardless of the amount of pressure he faced.

The best asset of Draisaitl is definitely he playmaking ability. He can thread a pass cross ice with a perfect saucer pass, make a one touch pass to an open player in the slot or make a behind the pass to a streaking teammate down the middle. Draisaitl is very unpredictable, and seems to always be able to find a play out on the ice that generates some sort of a chance for the Raiders. Not many players at his age can make the types of plays he can with the puck, and he seems to read the play a step ahead of everybody else. In terms of goal scoring ability, Draisaitl is definitely a pass first player, but he has shown the ability to finish in tight and quickly releasing the puck around the slot when given the opportunity. He has very good stickhandling abilities and is able to deke by opponents and use his long reach to his advantage.

An area of improvement for Draisaitl would be his skating abilities. He needs to work on his acceleration and overall speed. He covers a lot of ground with his long strides, but he could be quicker out on the ice to provide another weapon in his game. Defensively, Draisaitl is not bad in his own end. His ability to read the play without the puck improved, and looked like he was adjusting to the physical game of the league well. He could do a better job of being a more physical player and hit opponents off the puck.

Draisaitl's potential is through the roof with his playmaking abilities. His play in his own end will improve with more experience and coaching as he continues to play. If he can improve his speed, Draisaitl will definitely have a very long and productive NHL career and be a sought after playmaker by every team in the NHL.

Quotable: "One of the top players our radar for next year. He was good this year." - NHL Scout

Quotable: "A player who I like more every time I see him. He showed off some high end potential in Sochi at the U18's." - Mark Edwards

Deschamps, Jonathan – LD – Sherbrooke Phoenix (QMJHL) – 6'2" 192

If you review Jonathan Deschamps' statistics in the 2012-2013 season, you might think he's not worth a look for the 2014 NHL Draft, but his role is far beyond statistics. Deschamps is a stay-at-home defenseman with great size, high defensive hockey sense and decent puck control. He played for one of the worst teams in QMJHL but still was able to show his defensive qualities throughout the season and especially with brilliant performances at the World Under 17 Challenge in December with a surprising Team Québec. He plays a strong positional game, anticipates plays very well, makes the little details that you rarely see from a 16 years old. He wins his battles on the boards and makes the simple plays when he recovers the puck in his own zone. Solid puck control and intelligence help him create a good transition for his team with good hard passes on tape. His offensive game is limited althoughh he posesses a strong shot, he looked tentative joining the rush all season long and still seems to lack the confidence to settle into his game. His biggest weakness is skating, he has average speed although his footwork is decent. His smarts have made up for it during most of the season, but we feel it's a necessary improvement to be considered a top prospect at next year's draft and it would help his overall game.

DiPerna, Dylan – RD – Kingston Frontenacs (OHL) – 6'1" 187

Dylan was selected in the 2nd round of the 2012 OHL Priority Selection Draft by the Kingston Frontenacs out of the 2012 OHL Cup champion Mississauga Rebels. Dylan had a solid rookie season with the Frontenacs and provided a steady presence primarily playing on the third pairing, moving up to the top four when injuries occurred. Dylan plays a physical style of game. Despite this Dylan is fairly mobile for his age and size and handles one on one situations moderately well. He shows some effective puck movement while it's not his game. He does possess a cannon of a shot from the point. Dylan will see his role increase and he looks ready for it as the Frontenacs look to go on a bit of a run up the standings in the OHL's Eastern Conference.

Dodero, Christopher – FW – Chicago Steel (USHL) – 5'8" 165

Dodero was drafted into the USHL in the 3rd round, 36th overall by the Chicago Steel in the 2012 Futures Selection after spending last season with the Chicago Young Americans U16 program. Dodero had 12 points this season in his rookie year for the Chicago Steel. Chris has excellent skating ability, he's very quick and accelerates well. He is a player who keeps can keep it simple and play a hard forecheck, force turnovers and try to help his team out with a lot of energy. Unfortunately he lacks size which will be an ongoing uphill battle for him come the 2014 NHL Entry Draft, as he possesses a lot of skill, but lacks the size. He needs to become quicker in regards to his decision making and show more confidence and elusiveness with the puck. He seems to have lost this playing a minimized role at the USHL level compared to his explosive offensive game at the U16 level. Chris is a player who may have some considerations for the 2014 NHL entry draft, but still has a lot of work to do going into next season. Christopher was also selected by the Windsor Spitfires of the OHL and is committed to Colorado College.

Donaghey, Cody – RD – Québec Remparts (QMJHL) – 6'1" 182

Donaghey was traded to Quebec at the trade deadline after being Rouyn-Noranda 2nd pick in the first round in last year QMJHL draft. Donaghey is an offensive defensemen who likes to join the rush and has tools to play on the power play. He has an above average shot from the point. Hasn't got the chance to play on the man advantage too often yet as he got limited ice time in Rouyn-Noranda and barely played in Quebec. He's a good skater with good lateral mobility. He's not an explosive skater like his Quebec teammate Duncan MacIntyre which is the biggest difference between the two Remparts prospects. He's a smart defender with good hockey IQ, he's got some learning to do in the defensive end but as he get more playing time we're confident he will pick it up. Ice time will be the key for Donaghey next year as he didn't play enough this year, as potential to play in Quebec top 4 next year.

Duchesne, Jonathan – LD – Ottawa 67's (OHL) – 6'1" 204

Jonathan was selected in the 2nd round of the 2012 OHL Priority Selection Draft out of the Vaughan Kings Minor Midget Program. Jonathan came into the 67's organization as a bit of a project. He has size becoming of an NHL prospect let alone an OHL prospect, but made a lot of mental errors which affected his overall efficiency. Jonathan has shown noticeable improvements during his 16 year old season with the Ottawa 67's. He displayed great physicality this season and was more than willing to engage physically. Duchesne is capable of crushing opponents and is more than willing to drop the gloves. He faired well in these fights and can throw some big punches. Duchesne is an average skater for his size which is pretty good considering his age. He needs to improve on his puck play as it is very hit or miss, but is at his best when he makes the simple play and sticks to a reliable physical shutdown role. Jonathan had a moderately successful rookie season in the OHL, and if he can build on this NHL teams may find him an interesting option at the 2014 NHL Entry Draft.

Ekblad, Aaron – RD – Barrie Colts (OHL) – 6'4" 213

Ekblad was selected 1st overall in the 2011 OHL entry draft after he was the second player ever (after John Tavares) to receive exceptional player status drafted a year ahead of other players his age. Aaron was selected out of the Sun County Panthers organization following in his brother's footsteps who was selected by the London Knights in 2009. Ekblad possesses excellent size and entered the league at the age of 15 scoring 10 goals and 29 points in his rookie season, which he followed up with 34 points this year and a +29 rating. He moves up and down the ice effectively but his skating style is rather sloppy. He displays his strength in battles along the walls and infront of his own net. He has been hit or miss one on one, when successful he displays strength and uses his size to edge players out and keep them from gaining the inside track to the net. He can distribute the puck effectively in the offensive zone to create scoring chances and has an excellent shot from the point. Aaron generally looks his best when he's in the offensive zone. Despite his size and the hype he has behind him, he has struggled defensively in our viewings and his reaction time isn't what we'd hope and his positioning is not always idea. He has gained a ton of experience which should only help him. He's expected to be a high pick in the 2014 NHL Entry Draft, but simply needs to clean up his skating and become more consistent in the defensive zone. We've seen a lot of bright spots and a high ceiling in his potential, but there is clearly still work to be done for Ekblad.

Quotable:" I take back what I said earlier, he was not good today." - NHL Scout

Quotable:" I thought he had a few rough shifts at the U17 but logged a lot of minutes and followed up the tourney with a strong run towards the playoffs. Had some great games in the playoffs and some average ones. The potential is obviously off the charts." - Mark Edwards

Fabbri, Robby – LC – Guelph Storm (OHL) – 5'10" 160

Fabbri had a solid rookie season for the Storm after being selected 6th overall in the 2012 OHL Priority Selection from the 2012 OHL Cup Champion Mississauga Rebels. Fabbri is a strong skater and shows confidence carrying the puck through the neutral zone and into the offensive zone. Robby is exceptional in the face-off circle and wins the majority of draws earning the chance to take a number of key face-offs late in the playoffs. He went through sporadic scoring spurts over the course of the season but continued to work hard and make strong plays while adjusting to the OHL. He is very aggressive in going for the puck in the offensive zone and constantly wants to have the puck on his stick. Fabbri has a strong wrist shot and gets into good scoring positions coming off the wall on the cycle. He is also a good playmaker and shows great awareness and vision finding teammates with a variety of creative passes. He is a bit undersized but never backs down from opponents and appeared open to dropping the gloves on a number of occasions.

Robby was one of the best Storm forwards in the playoffs and did not look like a rookie in a number of the playoff games against Kitchener. He was constantly creating scoring chances and working hard to win puck possession in the offensive zone. He needs to work at adding some strength to his frame in the offseason. If he can work on building off his offensive output this season and bring some consistency to his scoring touch and get stronger, Fabbri could potentially hear his name called early on in the 2014 NHL Draft.

Quotable: "Robby had a solid rookie season for the Storm. He had points throughout the season where he just could not seem to find the back of the net, but I liked that he was constantly working and earning both scoring chances and ice time with a fairly older Storm forward core. Fabbri had an excellent playoff series for Guelph and I am looking forward to see him bring that passion and intensity to his second season in the OHL" - Kevin Thacker

Fleury, Haydn – LD – Red Deer Rebels (WHL) – 6'3" 204

Fleury is a physical, good skating defenseman who received more and more ice time as the season went along, and eventually was out on the ice to play against the opponent's top lines on a nightly basis. Fleury's game at both ends is quite impressive for his age, and is well on his way to be a top defenseman in the WHL.

For his size, Fleury has exceptional skating abilities. He has very good speed, and his footwork in tight areas is exceptional. He can maintain a very tight gap off the rush and use his reach to angle opponents to the boards and poke away pucks to create turnovers. He can still learn to take better angles on opposing forwards to take away any sort of offensive opportunities. Fleury plays a physical game, and is very difficult to play against on a consistent basis. He is very strong along the walls, and because of his speed and size, he rarely ever has to hook or trip players to prevent them from having a scoring opportunity. He does not take undisciplined penalties, and understands that he is more valuable to his team when he is out on the ice and not in the penalty box.

Offensively, Fleury is an above average puck mover. He can still improve on his passes out of the zone and allow his team to break out smoothly. He is not afraid to carry the puck himself into the offensive zone and provide another weapon on the rush. He has a good shot from the point, but needs to work on getting it through traffic or having a shorter back swing on his slap shots to get shots off more quickly when necessary. He does not possess elite vision or skills, but has shown that he can handle the puck well enough.

Fleury definitely has all the tools to become an NHL player one day. He still has improvements to make in his game, but much of that comes from more experience. He projects as a top 4 shut down defenseman as his offensive game is not exceptional, but he could certainly fill in some PP time when necessary. He will be counted on to play even more minutes next season, and Fleury will have an excellent opportunity to further raise his draft stock for 2014.

Foster, Thomas – LC – Vancouver Giants (WHL) – 5'10" 160

Foster is another one of those players on the Giants that has really struggled this year and plays like he has very little confidence in his abilities. He just goes through the motions and does not show much effort or desire to win on a consistent basis. He seems to be quite weak, and has a tough time coming away with the puck in any situations. He is not very productive with and without the puck, and is almost invisible out on the ice. He receives very limited ice time, and Foster's work ethic and tenacity will have to improve to have a chance of becoming an integral part of the rebuild in Vancouver in the near future.

Friedman, Mark – RD – Waterloo Blackhawks (USHL) – 5'10" 180

Mark developed up through the Don Mills Flyers' program in the GTHL. He was selected in the 4th round by the Waterloo Blackhawks at the 2011 USHL Entry Draft. Instead of heading to the USHL, Mark joined the North York Rangers in the OJHL putting on an excellent performance as a 16 year old and showing his true potential all season long. Mark joined Waterloo in time to play in the World Junior Club Cup in Russia then played the full season with the Black Hawks. Friedman is an undersized defenseman who isn't afraid to play physical and play bigger than he is along the walls. Mark showed good puck skills and is capable of helping out offensively making smart decisions and getting the puck to the net. Mark was utilized in all game situations and was an effective penalty killer putting pressure on the puck carrier and stick checking them when he was challenged physically negating the play. Mark has an uphill battle with his size heading into the 2014 NHL Entry Draft. He will have to show his potential on a nightly basis at a high level since he is slated to join Bowling Green State University this fall of 2013. Mark was also selected in the 13th round of the 2011 OHL Priority Selection Draft. This ensures he will be up against strong talent one way or the other for his draft year.

Gardiner, Reid – RC – Prince Albert Raiders (WHL) – 5'10" 179

Gardiner is a smart, defensive forward who was an essential piece to the Raiders' PK efforts this season. He displayed very good awareness out on the ice without the puck, and did an excellent job of disrupting breakouts in the neutral zone.

Gardiner does an excellent job with his stick and knowing where to be out on the ice. He is defensively sound, and seems to be in good position on a consistent basis. He is not particularly big or strong, so he uses his intelligence to take away passes and be an asset on the defensive end. He does a good job of taking away shooting lanes from the point, and places his stick strategically to take away any cross ice passes.

Offensively, Gardiner has not been able to show much skill with the puck. He does not have a particularly good set of hands nor does he possess good offensive instincts. Much of his offensive production comes from hard work as he scores goals off the rebound in front of the net and working hard off the cycle and one of his line mates getting lucky and scoring a goal.

Gardiner will definitely need to add some more offensive game to be a much more sought after prospect for the 2014 NHL Entry Draft. Not many players of his age play such a good game defensively, but as a forward he will be counted on to provide some secondary scoring. If he cannot produce once in a while, teams will take their chances on more skilled players whose defensive play can be improved on.

Garland, Conor – RW – Moncton Wildcats (QMJHL) – 5'6" 150

Garland played a couple of games in 2012-2013 with Muskegon before leaving for Moncton in the QMJHL. He was a scoring sensation with the Boston Jr Bruins in the EmJHL last season, completing a fantastic duo with top 2015 prospect Jack Eichel. Garland is a highly talented little player. He uses his skating agility to get space but is also able to undress a defenseman with a sweet skills move. He has quick feet but doesn't posess the high end explosiveness and top speed most smallish players have in professionnal hockey. He likes to control the play and showed nice poise on the Moncton 2nd powerplay unit this season. Garland has a great wrist shot with terrific accuracy. A player with great offensive awareness, he finds teammates easily and is an accomplished playmaker even though he has a shoot-first mentality. He needs to improve in physical games as he doesn't win many battles and only shined on powerplays and offensive games. He is too skinny to be a steady 5-on-5 performer in major junior at the moment and also needs to show better desire without the puck.

Goldobin, Nikolay – RW – Sarnia Sting (OHL) – 5'11" – 165

Goldobin was selected high in two drafts this past summer. Metallurg Novokuznetsk of the KHL selected Nikolay 8th Overall and Sarnia Sting selected him 36th Overall in the CHL Import Draft. Nikolay was a little apprehensive to open the season. You could see his talent but he just didn't apply himself. Every game he played, Nikolay noticeably improved. His strongest asset is his vision. Goldobin sees the ice so well and uses this ability to make absolutely perfect passes through traffic. He makes difficult passes look easy and hits low percentage passes on a regular basis. He's extremely creative and has excellent hands. He was very good on the breakaway including shootouts thanks to his hands and quick release but it was his passing that brought fans out of their seats and got scouts talking. We would like to see Nikolay get an extra gear in his skating. While he moves well he doesn't really have that breakout speed that would make him that much better. He definitely needs to get stronger and be more willing to take physicality. All season he looked a little timid in the neutral zone and would poke at pucks but wouldn't risk getting hit hard in netural ice to make a play and he needs to be more willing to take physicality and hopefully get stronger to more comfortably handle this side of the game. Nikolay has the potential to be the top forward selected out of the OHL at the 2014 NHL Entry Draft.

Hargrave, Brett – RC – Sarnia Sting (OHL) – 6'4" – 206

Brett was selected 13th Overall by the Sarnia Sting at the 2012 OHL Priority Selection and joined the team this season as a fourth liner. After the departure of Alex Galchenyuk to Montreal, Brett was moved up to the third line and played there for the remainder of the season. Brett played a little under expectations but after posting 5 points in 5 games for Team Ontario at the World Under 17 Challenge he started to really show improvements. By the end of the season Brett was a lot calmer with the puck, he was able to possess it for longer periods of time using his huge frame to protect it. He has a powerful shot and needs to let it fly a little more often. He had some success passing the puck well after protecting it allowing options to open up for him. Defensively he works hard and wins battles along the boards. This is an area he improved throughout the year after being so successful in Minor Midget. Brett's skating needs improvement. He generates good speed but his turns and first few steps aren't where they should be. Brett will be looked upon in a much bigger role this coming season and if he can answer the bell, Brett will get a lot of exposure for the 2014 NHL Draft thanks to his natural size.

Hawryluk, Jayce – RC – Brandon Wheat Kings (WHL) – 5'10" 186

Hawryluk is a good 2 way centre who plays hard in all areas of the ice. He is a good skater and really uses his speed to his advantage to get to loose pucks and be tough to play against in the defensive zone.
Offensively, Hawryluk has a nice release to his wrist shots. He likes to come down the wing and quickly get the puck on net if he has any room to get his shot off. He could improve the velocity on his shots and location however. He is a good playmaker, and takes care of the puck quite well. He limits the turnovers that he commits, and does not take unnecessary chances with the puck. He goes to the net with authority, and does a good job of protecting the puck with his body. Hawryluk could pick better opportunities to take his shots, especially as he comes down the wing. With his size, it will also be difficult to translate his current game to the NHL.
Hawryluk is a dependable forward in his own end. He does not take shifts off even without the puck, and does a good job in the neutral zone on set forechecks to make it difficult for opponents to enter the zone. He is not particularly smart in the defensive zone, but does an admirable job of covering the point and chipping pucks out of the zone along the walls.

Haydon, Aaron – RD – Niagara Ice Dogs (OHL) – 6'3" 185

Aaron was selected in the first round, 20th Overall at the 2012 OHL Priority Selection Draft by the Niagara Ice Dogs out of the Detroit Belle Tire U16 program. Hayden has very desirable size in a young player and he moves the puck well and opens up very effectively to get a shot off from the point. Hayden registered 10 points in 42 games in his rookie season this year. He does a great job moving the puck up the ice to start the breakout and can see his options in the offensive zone and lanes to move the puck around. He has a pretty powerful stride, but it is somewhat awkward and could still be improved upon. He also has to relax on his gap control as at times he gets way too aggressive trying to force a play and gets beat and just needs to have more patience and play his gaps properly. Aaron plays a very physical brand of game and understands himself as a player and is generally aware of what he is capable of, and what his limitations are. Haydon is a player who will benefit from a few graduations out of the Ice Dogs program. He received limited ice in the OHL on a deep Niagara blue line, but we've seen him show the flashes of a very dominant blue liner as far back as minor midget. If he can improve his skating and get stronger the sky is the limit for Aaron.

Hiddink, Brook – RW – Niagara Ice Dogs (OHL) – 5'11" 195

Brook was selected in the first round, 21st Overall at the 2012 OHL Priority Slection Draft by the Niagara Ice Dogs out of the Elgin-Middlesex Chiefs Minor Midget program. Brook is a player we've seen a lot of over the last three seasons as he played two years of Minor Midget, the first year as an underager and the second line centre on a team that featured likely NHL first round pick Bo Horvat. Hiddink registered 7 points in 51 games and had a -1 rating. He played primarily as a role player on this team, protecting the puck very well and he can cycle it effectively in the offensive zone. He works hard every shift, knows his role and goes hard to the net. He keeps his game pretty simple, gets it in deep and then tries to get the cycle game going. He still needs to add strength as he can get out-muscled in battles and at times looks lost as to his responsibility in his own end. We would like to see him play with more tenacity and physicality as it will help him win battles because he's fairly mature physically at this age. Hiddink should get more of an offensive role on the team with Strome and Ritchie moving on very soon and will need to take advantage of that opportunity as he has shown the ability to create offense, but will likely remain in a more well suited two-way role for the Ice Dogs. If Brook can get stronger, show some creativity and physicality he should have a good chance at being selected at the 2014 NHL Entry Draft.

Highmore, Matthew – LW – Saint-John Sea Dogs (QMJHL) – 5'11" 172

Highmore was the 8th overall pick in last year's QMJHL draft, he didn't start his season until late November as he was recovering from a shoulder injury he suffered the year before. He's excellent at cycling the puck, using his size well to shield the puck and gaining puck possession time for his team in the offensive zone. Already playing a mature two-way game, he plays well in his own zone and works hard at both ends of the ice. A fierce competitor, Highmore has a high level of hockey sense, which is a good mix. He has a good scoring touch around the crease and a nose for the net, displaying a good shot and quick hands to put pucks behind the red line. Highmore likes to use the center of the ice to bring the puck on net, having an aggressive approach to his one-on-one situations. He will need to work on his skating as it is lacking right now, he will need to improve top speed and explosiveness before he can become a consistent offensive threat. Has been labeled as an injury prone player but he doesn't shy away from the physical game, will initiate physical contact and take a hit for his team.

Hodgson, Hayden – RW – Erie Otters (OHL) – 6'1" 190

Hayden was selected in the 3rd round of the 2012 OHL Priority Selection Draft by the Erie Otters out of the Sun County Panthers Minor Midget Program. Hayden is a talented multi-sport athlete who chose hockey and made a strong debut in the OHL as a 16 year old. Haydon played a bottom six role but he's well adjusted to this style of game. Hayden provided solid physical play finishing his checks whenever possible. He chips in as a grinder but really shows good projection as a potential power forward. He can drive the puck hard to the net and possesses a very powerful shot. Hodgson received some power play ice and showed early on that he is capable of playing different roles. Hodgson will go into his NHL Draft Year with increased ice. We look to see Hayden continue to play a power game and increase his offensive input. His skating is average and we'd like to see him improve it a bit as well.

Honka, Julius – RD – JYP U20 (Jr. A SM-liiga) – 5'10" 167

Julius has worked his way up through JYP's U16 and U18 teams and spent all season this year with the U20 team. He also put together a strong performance at the 2013 IIHF U18 Championships. Julius isn't the biggest defenseman, but he makes up for it with excellent skating ability and a very high level of hockey sense. Julius is an excellent puck rusher who always seems to choose the right option on the rush either to pass the puck off or take the puck deep into the offensive zone. He makes very intelligent decisions with the puck, and very rarely ever misplays it. He pinches in from the point at the right time making him dangerous during sustained pressure. Despite his size and offensive abilities, he's surprisingly strong defensively. His ability to read the play in his own zone is very strong which helps him maintain consistent ideal positioning. He is more than willing to battle in the corners and considering his size, he wins a surprising amount of battles. Julius will need to overcome his size and get stronger, but his hockey sense and puck skills will make him an intriguing prospect for the 2014 NHL Entry Draft.

Quotable: "From the Hlinka and the Four Nations tourney, right through the U18's in Sochi, Honka impressed me every time I watched him. He may not be very big but he is one of the smartest defenders I have seen who is eligible for the 2014 NHL Draft." – Mark Edwards

Hore, Tyler – RD – Sarnia Sting (OHL) – 6'3" – 182

After being selected by the Oshawa Generals in the 9th round of the 2011 OHL Priority Selection Draft out of the Mississauga Reps program, Tyler split time in 2011-2012 with Mississauga Reps Major Midget and the Mississauga Chargers (OJHL). Tyler made the Oshawa Generals right out of camp and was used in a third pairing role. He displayed the ability to contribute at both ends competing defensively and being strong on the line in the offensive zone. The Sting picked up Tyler in a last minute deal at the OHL Trade Deadline and he instantly improved their blueline. While his size suggests a shutdown defenseman, Tyler plays a pretty solid two-way game. He uses his stick really well denfeisvely although he will play physical when needed. We would like to see him pick up his physical play leading into next season. He skates well for his size. His first few steps need work but he was able to evade checkers in the neutral zone with the puck and carry the puck deep. Tyler moved the puck intelligently showing a few flashes of completing higher difficulty passes. He also possesses a good shot from the point. Tyler would be considered a 4-5 defenseman on the Sting this season and split time on the second and third pairing. Hore will need to get stronger on this offseason and improve his first few steps. But he already has NHL scouts talking about him for 2014 and will just need to continue to evolve physically.

Ho-Sang, Joshua – RW – Windsor Spitfires (OHL) – 5'11" – 160

Joshua is one of the most dynamic 16 year olds to debut in the CHL this year and was selected 5th Overall out of the Toronto Marlboros Minor Midget program by the Windsor Spitfires. Ho-Sang got off to a bit of a slow start opening on the third line and took a little while to get things rolling. As the season progressed he became more adjusted to the OHL and in turn he was given more ice time. He is a very flashy player who can be quiet for a couple shifts then in a second turn it on. He has outstanding speed and can score highlight reel goals. His hands are almost as quick as his feet and displays excellent elusiveness. He has a pretty good shot and at times has solid positioning in the offensive zone. While he has all the speed hands and skill you could ask for, he still has a lot of work ahead of him. He still needs to be more willing to utilize his teammates. Too often Joshua turned the puck over at the end of a play where he tried to do too much himself instead of utilizing his teammates before he became overwhelmed. He also needs to be more willing to play a two-way game. While his game is all about speed and putting up points, it will only increase his value to the Spitfires and to NHL scouts looking at him next season to skate hard to get back and show some defensive competitiveness. He will also need to hit the weights and get stronger. Joshua will likely be one of the most watched prospects in the OHL leading into the 2014 NHL Entry Draft.

Iverson, Keegan – RC – Portland Winterhawks (WHL) – 6'0" 215

Iverson is a physical centre who came into the WHL last season with some hype in his game. However, he has not been able to hold a regular spot in the line up throughout the season, and has not been able to score many points, although most of his minutes do come in the 4th line.

Iverson is a hard hitting forward. He needs to keep his arms down to take less penalties, but he has the ability to change the game with his open ice hits. He quickly steps into a vulnerable opponent when given the opportunity, and makes sure to finish them and take them out of the play. Iverson would be more effective on the forecheck if he was quicker. He is an average skater who needs to work on his speed and acceleration. If he can improve his quickness out on the ice, he would be able to land more open ice hits and provide a bigger physical presence for his team.

So far into his WHL career, Iverson has not been able to find an offensive touch. He is certainly not afraid to go to the net, but he has lacked the hockey intelligence to get into the right areas to bury rebounds or pucks thrown to the net and has not shown that he has hands to finish off plays. He does play on the 4th line with offensively limited players, which may hurt his points total. He is definitely more of a scorer than a passer, as he has not been able to create offense by himself.

Iverson will surely receive more opportunities to play next season, and have a bigger role with the team. It will be interesting to see if he can show off an offensive touch to his game, and if he can get faster. If he could add those two elements to go along with his physicality, he will surely draw some interest from NHL teams for 2014.

Jacobs, Joshua – RD – Indiana Ice (USHL) – 6'2" 190

Jacobs played his first year in the USHL for the Indiana Ice and had 15 points in 48 games this season and another 52 penalty minutes to go along with it. He plays with a pretty good gap control, challenges the shooter and directs the play really well with his stick. He also keeps his man to the perimeter and uses his stick to tip shots out of play and gets down in lanes to block passes and breakup the opposition's opportunities. Jacobs possesses excellent size and asserts himself regularly. He is physical and battles hard in the corners. Joshua is also a surprisingly good skater for his size. He rushes the puck up ice very well and possesses a good point shot that he is able to keep low and get it deflected. Josh is considered one of the top American defensemen heading into the 2014 NHL Entry Draft at this point. Joshua was selected at the 2011 OHL Priority Selection Draft in the 4th round by the Sarnia Sting. Jacobs is committed to Michigan State University.

Jammes, Jacob – RW – London Knights (OHL) – 5'10" 180

Jacob was selected in the 2nd round of the 2011 OHL Priority Selection Draft by the London Knights out of the Ottawa Jr. 67's Minor Midget program. Due to a deep Knights forward group Jacob went unsigned and instead joined the Gloucester Rangers of the CCHL and put together a very good performance as a 16 year old. Jacob came to Knights camp and earned himself a spot on the Knights roster, however he spent much of this season as a healthy scratch only cracking the line-up sparingly despite playing fairly well in his first OHL season. Jacob took advantage of every opportunity he got displaying great energy and good skating ability. He is capable of cycling the puck and playing a good hard working game. He is also fairly intelligent with the puck, although got caught shooting from bad angles and needs to pick the moments he utilizes his shot more efficiently. Jacob is going to benefit from having a late birthdate as he has one more season to show what he is capable of in the OHL. He likely would have been selected this season despite the limited action on potential alone, but with the graduation of a few forwards on the Knights, Jacob should get a full season to show what he can do before the 2014 NHL Entry Draft.

Jenkins, Kyle – LD – Sault Ste. Marie Greyhounds (OHL) – 6'0" – 160

Kyle was selected in the 4th round of the 2012 OHL Priority Selection Draft by the Sault Ste. Marie Greyhounds after winning the 2012 OHL Cup with the Mississauga Rebels. Kyle spent the entire season with the Oakville Blades (OJHL) providing some good offensive numbers as a 16 year old. He was signed by the Greyhounds and was called up to join Greyhounds at the end of the season. Kyle shows good offensive instincts and is a smooth puck mover. Kyle also displays very good skating ability and was highly regarded by HockeyProspect going into the 2012 OHL Draft. Kyle will be given every opportunity to crack the top 6 defense corps of the Greyhounds next season.

Kapanen, Kasperi – LW – KalPa (SM-liiga) – 5'10" 165

Kasperi developed all the way up to the men's league with KalPa, the organization currently owned by his father and long time NHLer Sami Kapanen. Kasperi split his season between the U20 team and the men's league team playing alongside his father, who still plays as well as owns KalPa. Kasperi is a good skater who is not shy around the physical game. Although he's a player we feel needs to add muscle he's packs an effective check and we've witnessed him delivering some pretty solid checks. He is capable of providing a relentless forecheck and can force turnovers. When he's on his game he displays some creative puck control and can beat defenders one on one. He's particularly dangerous on breakaways and shootouts and can finish regularly when he comes in alone on a goaltender. He has good awareness on the rush showing the ability to pass, but quite often he's much more comfortable shooting the puck, even if it means forcing the shot sometimes. Kasperi has shown well in the defensive zone battling and even blocking shots in penalty killing situations while being a dangerous option should he steal the puck and get a bit of a break on the defensemen. Really the only concerns for Kasperi is that he is a little undersized, however he really doesn't play like it. Also we have had some concerns with consistency. We've seen him play quite a bit this season, and while he's a key factor in a lot of games, there are some where he just simply disappears and is not very visible. We would like to see him clear this up a little bit moving forward as he leads the charge for Finland towards the 2014 NHL Entry Draft.

Quotable: "Potential is there to be a high end pick in 2014. When he had good shifts he was one of the best 2014's I saw this season, the problem was a few too many average or poor shifts. He is young, plenty of time to gain consistency." - Mark Edwards

Karlsson, Anton – RW – Frolunda (SEL) – 6'0" 190

Anton is the brother of Erik Karlsson who was selected by the Carolina Hurricanes in the 2012 NHL Entry Draft, it appears at least early on that Anton has a much higher ceiling of potential moving forward. Anton has very good size for a player his age and plays an aggressive style of play finishing his checks whenever possible. He plays with a great deal of energy and forechecks hard, forcing turnovers and punishing opponents. While he has excellent work ethic and his turnover numbers are impressive, he's not a flashy offensive player and tends to predatorily work his way into primary scoring areas and gets open for passes, finishing chances around the net. He relies on of his very high level hockey sense and vision which helps him see the play faster than his opponents, giving him the jump on the play. While he has a powerful shot, he is an effective passer and makes some slick passes look effortless. He is really one of those players who always seems to be in the middle of the play, even if you don't notice him at first by the end of the shift he will usually make himself noticeable in a positive way. Anton battles hard in all three zones and will backcheck hard, taking away time and space from opponents in the offensive zone and clear the zone. On the penalty kill he generally puts a lot of pressure on the point and has shown a willingness to block shots.

It is actually very difficult to find a flaw in Anton's game as there really isn't anything glaring, he is a pretty complete player. However we would like to see him improve his skating a little bit. It isn't a flaw, but it's not a big asset either .While he's not as dynamic as fellow countryman William Nylander, he is a much more well rounded player. Combine this with the offensive skillset he possesses, Anton will be a very highly pursued prospect heading into the 2014 NHL Entry Draft.

Quotable: " I saw him quite a few times this year. I was very impressed at times, especially at the U17. I cooled on him slightly at the U18 in April but he is a player I'm looking forward to watching more of next year." - Mark Edwards

Kempe, Adrian – LC – MODO J20 (SWE J20) – 6'1" 170

Adrian worked his way up through the Djurgarden program for the 2011-2012 season moving from the U16 to the J18 team. However he moved to the MODO program opening the first three games with the J18 team then quickly moved up to the J20 SuperElit league where he spent the remaineder of his 2012-2013 season. Adrian has good size but also possesses skating ability and shiftiness that allows him to beat defenders and goaltenders one on one. He seems to prefer shooting the puck much more than passing and has a pretty good shot that he can get off from anywhere in the offensive zone. While he has shown some clear flashes of offensive ability, Adrian also plays an effective penalty kill game. He is willing to block shots and we've seen him take some big blasts off of areas that don't have much padding and watched him hop around and stick with the play instead of laying there trying to get a whistle. He has good positioning in all three zones which he's him contribute in every game situation. We would like to see Adrian get stronger and add a little physicality for his game. With the style he plays, that would make him that much more effective.

Keskitalo, Miro – LD – Jokerit U18 (Jr B SM-liiga) – 6'1" 168

Miro played primarily with Jokerit's U18 team this season while getting a brief experience with the U20 team. Miro displays very good skating ability from the back end showing good skating ability and elusiveness when carrying the puck. Against players his own age Miro showed a few clear flashes of offensive ability moving the puck well and reading plays well. He is also very effective in the defensive zone showing a willingness to take the body whenever the chance came. However he clearly lacks strength and needs to get stronger. He does however possess size, already coming in at

6'1". Keskitalo was a shot blocking machine in our viewings of him and is more than willing to sacrifice the body to get infront of shots. In one game he took a big blast from the point off his leg in an area there was no padding. Miro got up and hopped on one foot remaining in the play making a good play to redirect a pass away from the scoring play despite being in obvious pain. He plays with a lot of heart, determination and puts in the work. The biggest thing for us moving forward is that he hits the weights and gets stronger as it will make him much more effective in his style of play.

Kiviranta, Joel – RW – Jokerit U20 (Jr. A SM-liiga) – 5'10" 154

Joel is a small, skilled forward who has developed at a very quick pace through the ranks in Finland. He has worked his way up the Jokerit program and jumped from the U16 team at the age of 14 to playing regularly for the U20 team at the age of just 15. He finished this season with 20 points in 40 games as a 16 year old in the U20 league and also participated internationally for Finland in the World U-17 Challenge and the IIHF U18 Championships. Joel provides a quick, strong forecheck. He's a pesky player who is able to create turnovers and is a pain to play against. He displays good hands and controls the puck very well under pressure. He has a good shot and he isn't shy about unloading it all over the offensive zone establishing good positioning for his shots. Joel shows a lot of promise as a potential offensive forward. He's a little undersized and we'd ideally like to see him grow a little and get stronger, but he has a lot of skill and has the mindset to contribute in all three zones, and in all game situations as he shows a good defensive presence as well.

Larkin, Dylan – LC – USNTDP (USHL) – 6'0" 172

Dylan participated in the Detroit Belle Tire U16 program over the 2010-2011 and 2011-2012 seasons showing off his true potential and upside over the course of those years. The U.S. National Team Development Program also took notice selecting Larkin for their program. Dylan's best asset is clearly his skating ability. He maintained this ability despite breaking his left ankle at the 2011 Whitby Silver Stick Tournament limiting his last season with Belle Tire significantly. Dylan is able to absolutely fly up ice with the puck and he handles it extremely well in traffic and will go to the net with the puck. He is very intelligent with the puck showing a knowledge of when to make a move and when to get the puck to one of his teammates. He prefers shooting more than passing and possesses a powerful shot. Dylan relies heavily on his skating ability, fortunately he appears to be one of the best skaters in the entire 2014 NHL Draft class. Dylan competes but really would benefit from adding muscle to his frame and being more of an impact along the boards. Dylan was selected in the 10th round of the 2012 OHL Priority Selection Draft

Lazarev, Maxim – LW – AK Bars Kazan (MHL) – 5'9" 148

Maxim has developed in the well known AK Bars Kazan program and put forth a great season this year. He is a dynamic forward who possesses great skating ability and a very powerful shot. He likes to skate with the puck rushing it up ice and isn't afraid to take on defenders one on one where his elusiveness is noticeable. He tends to shoot more than pass utilizing his laser quick release all over the offensive zone. When he does choose to pass however he displays smooth puck movement and generally hits his target accurately. When he's on his game he competes in all three zones forcing turnovers. However we have seen him get a little lazy and ultimately make some very careless turnovers. We're also very concerned about the way he disengages in physical match-up's. Generally when the going gets tough, Maxim appears a little intimidated in these battles which impacted his ability to be effective for his team. Maxim is an intriguing prospect moving forward. He has a lot of skill, but is rather undersized and will need to keep working and getting stronger.

Leblanc, Olivier – LD – Saint-John Sea Dogs (QMJHL) – 5'11" 166

Leblanc had significant ice time in his first season in the QMJHL on a rebuilding Sea Dogs team, learned a lot from veterans Kevin Gagne and Pierre Durepos. Leblanc brings a solid two way game to the ice, contributing offensively joining the rush and showing good hockey IQ when he can do it. He has quick hands and will make solid plays with the puck if rarely spectacular. Although he's undersized, Leblanc brings a solid physical game and can throw some good hits thanks to his mobility and solid upper body strength. His quick feet and great footwork help him be as solid as anybody in 1-on-1 situations, adjusting well to his opponent's speed and giving little time and space. No doubt as he continue to progress Leblanc will need to get bigger and stronger, defensive match-ups will be hard on his small frame. Defensively, Leblanc plays a steady, smart but aggressive game. He likes to press the puck carrier and use his skating abilities effectively, which is something we like to see, his decision with the puck under pressure still need some maturing, but he has been a solid all-around defenseman this season on a struggling rebuilding team. He played for team Quebec at the U17 hockey challenge. Leblanc was the 11th overall pick in this past QMJHL midget draft.

Lee, Payton – G – Vancouver Giants (WHL) – 6'0" 175

Payton Lee has been the backbone for the Giants for most of the year. He has done everything that he can to try to keep his team in games, but constant bad defensive zone breakdowns have made his life miserable for most of the season. Lee had a tough start to the year. He was slated to be the back up for the Giants this year, but he lost the job to Tyler Fuhr, who came out of nowhere in training camp. About a month into the season, Lee was called back up to the Giants, and has taken control of the starting job ever since.
The best asset for Lee is his glove hand. It is lightning quick, and he comfortably catches pucks that come to his glove hand frequently. He looks poised when making glove saves, and tracks the puck all the way to his trapper to ensure that it goes into the netting. His blocker still needs some work, but he looks comfortable making saves on his right hand side too.

Lee's weakness seems to be his 5 hole. He has a tendency of raising his stick when going down to his butterfly at times, or going down too late and letting a puck 5 inches off the ice go through his legs. When pucks do hit his legs, he is good at putting rebounds into the corners, but it is something that can still be worked in his game. His ability to fight through traffic is quite inconsistent, and when he looks like he is into the game mentally, he makes impressive saves, but when he struggles, it is very evident in all parts of his game.

In the latter part of the season, Lee has looked mentally fatigued, and his game has suffered as a result. He has been quite inconsistent, and it is a guessing game to find out which goaltender will show up on a nightly basis. It seems like much of his mental challenge comes from the fact that his team is bad in front of him and he is letting in a number of goals, but he just needs to focus on what he can do and not worry about the team that is playing in front of him. Lee is definitely one of the goaltenders to watch for in the 2014 NHL Entry Draft, and will surely play a key role in the rebuilding Giants.

Lemieux, Brendan – LW – Barrie Colts (OHL) – 6'0" 194

Brendan was selected in the 4th round of the 2012 OHL Priority Selection Draft by the Barrie Colts out of the Toronto Red Wings Minor Midget Program. Despite this, Lemieux signed with the Green Bay Gamblers of the USHL and announced his intention to join the University of North Dakota in the fall of 2014. This lasted a total of 11 games before he decided to return to Ontario and join the Barrie Colts. Lemieux was commonly used on the third line for the Colts and consistently added a very gritty physical presense. Brendan is one who is capable of getting under the skin of the opposition and does a lot of agitating while never giving up a chance to finish his checks. Brendan's best offensive asset is his shot which is at times inaccurate, but is a very dangerous weapon if he is in scoring position. Brendan will need to work on drawing the line as he can at times be caught taking undisciplined and detrimental penalties against his team, and needs to play his physical agitating game. He also has had a short fuse at times and agitating an agitator has, at times backfired on him and actually thrown off his game. We would also like to see him become a better skater as he will likely be one of the players that gets moved up to a top six role with multiple forwards graduating from juniors next season. Brendan is going to be a prospect to watch and has shown very interesting signs of being a forward who can make a physical impact.

Leone, Luca – RW – Vancouver Giants (WHL) – 6'0" 190

Leone joined the Giants midway through the season after leaving the BCHL's Coquitlam Express. He has been receiving regular ice time minutes, and has provided good depth along the wing for Vancouver this season.

Offensively, Leone has not been very successful at the WHL level. He is a good skater and plays a simple chip and chase game, but he has not been able to win many battles for pucks along the boards. He does not find open areas very well, and is not much of a playmaker too. He will need to work on his offensive skills to be an impact player with the Giants. Leone has not been a liability in his own end. He covers the point well, and uses his quickness to cover lanes and limit opposing defensemen's options. He could do a better job along the boards and coming down low to help out teammates though. Leone has another year of developing before he is draft eligible, which he will definitely need to be on NHL teams' radars in the future.

Lindblom, Oskar – RW – Brynas J18 (SWE J18) – 6'0" 185

Oskar developed primarily in the J18 league this season putting up great numbers, also gaining a quick 3 game appearance at the J20 level. Oskar is an excellent offensive talent who has primarily only played against players his own age, but has been dominant in his age group. This was never so prevalent than at the 2013 World U-17 Challenge where he posted 13 points in 6 games. Oskar is much more of a shooter than a passer and displays excellent hands in close and makes plays with the puck in tight areas that few players are able to accomplish. He has the ability to score some highlight reel goals and beat defenders and goaltenders in one on one situations. He doesn't pass a whole lot, but when he does it's generally accurate. His lack of a playmaking presence is primarily due to his preference to shoot the puck rather than an inability to make effective passes. HE really hasn't shown much outside offensive ability and we'd like to see him work hard for the puck and get back defensively more often. He's clearly a gifted offensive player, but what may see him stuck behind others is players with comparable offensive ability who provide another dimension to their game.

Quotable: "One game really stands out for me, it was against Russia at the U17, Oskar showed off high end passing skills, quick inside moves, nice feet walking off the wall, great hand eye and a quick realease on a beautiful goal that went bar down." - Mark Edwards

Lindo, Jaden – RW – Owen Sound Attack (OHL) – 6'1" – 194

Lindo was selected 2nd Round, 26th Overall by the Owen Sound Attack at the 2012 OHL Priority Selection Draft out of the Toronto Marlboros Minor Midget program. Jaden went into Owen Sound already build as solid as some of their veteran forwards and looked like a 19, 20 year old in his first OHL game as supposed to a 16 year old rookie. Jaden plays a pretty simple power forwards game on the ice. He has excellent size and finishes his checks hard. He prides himself on excellent board play and wins more battles than the majority of players his age. Jaden looked like a man amongst boys in the 2013 World U17 Challenge not providing a lot of offense but crushing opponents and helping Ontario maintain puck control. Jaden tends to get a lot of his points out of hard work winning the battles, then passing off to more skilled players. It's a pretty simple game he provides but very effective. Jaden will look to improve his skating ability as he heads into the 2014 NHL Entry Draft. His ability to create offense will also be monitored as he already plays a pretty solid power game, the question will be if he can develop enough offense to go with it.

Linhart, Jake – LD – Green Bay Gamblers (USHL) – 5'9" 152

After spending the last two years developing with the Chicago Mission U16 program, Jacob joined the Green Bay Gamblers putting together a very solid rookie season. Jacob is a slightly undersized defenseman who provides an excellent two-way game. He plays and looks bigger than his listing. Jake likes to finish his checks and packs a surprisingly strong finish to his checks. He was rather solid defensively in our viewings. He also likes to jump up in the rush when possible displaying a moderately effective shot. Jake does a good job in the offensive zone controlling the puck and making decisions fairly quickly. Jake is a very intriguing prospect for the 2014 NHL Entry Draft. He definitely needs to add more muscle and would really benefit from growing a little, but is a prospect to watch next season. Jake was also selected in the 9th round of the 2012 OHL Priority Selection Draft by the Plymouth Whalers. Linhart is committed to the University of Wisconsin.

Llewellyn, Darby – RW – Kitchener Rangers (OHL) – 6'1" 173

Darby was selected in the 4th round of the 2012 OHL Priority Selection Draft by the Kitchener Rangers out of the Detroit Honeybaked U16 Program. Darby joined the Rangers as a 16 year old, however he didn't receive much time due to a very deep, veteran core of forwards in Kitchener. Darby tried to take advantage of the ice he got. He has a very powerful shot and gets it off rather quickly. He finishes his checks and plays a competitive game however he needs to get bigger and stronger over the offseason to give himself the best possible chance to be an effective forward for his team and to get drafted. We also hope he will improve on his skating. It isn't an asset or a deficiency at the moment, but we feel it's something at his size could give him an edge in his sophomore OHL season.

Locke, Kyle – RD – Guelph Storm (OHL) – 6'2" 195

Kyle was selected in the 2nd round of the 2012 OHL Priority Selection Draft by the Guelph Storm out of the York-Simcoe Express Minor Midget program. Locke split his time between the OHL's Guelph Storm and the Sutherland Cup Finalist Cambridge Winterhawks Jr. B team. He is a big strong defender who has the skill set to eventually play a shutdown role at the OHL level. Kyle has slow feet and needs to work at improving his skating and speed of transitions on the blue line. He battles extremely hard in front of the net and does not appear to be intimidated by any player on the ice. Kyle will get a great shot to crack the everyday roster Storm in 2013-2014 and show what he can do en route to a hopeful selection at the 2014 NHL Entry Draft in Philadelphia, PA.

Lyamkin, Nikita – LD – Kuznetskie Medvedi (MHL) – 6'3" 165

Nikita spent the past season in the MHL and enjoyed very successful World U-17 Challenge in Victoriaville/Drummondville, helping Russia to a Silver Medal. Nikita has excellent size and displays an exceptional level of hockey sense. He is extremely strong positionally and always seems to be in the right place on the ice. He is a strong skater with good mobility allowing him to match up against forwards very well one on one. He rarely if ever gets beat. Nikita shows a willingness to battle along the wall with a nastiness in his game. He won the majority of battles, he will win even more as he gets stronger within his big frame.

Nikita isn't PK Subban rushing the puck but he did display the ability to lug it up ice and gain the zone. He makes a very smart first pass and makes quick decisions in all three zones with the puck. He also possesses a good point shot. There is very little negatives in Nikita's game, we were extremely impressed with him in our viewings. He definitely needs to get stronger before he can start realizing his true potential. He has the size but not the strength.

Quotable: "I was really impressed with Nikita at the U17. I noticed him on his 1st shift of the tourney and made a note. I made many more notes after that. He was physical, smart, had good range all over the ice, used his stick well, showed poise in all three zones and on both special teams units. He got away his shot quickly and on net. I saw no panic in his game. Obviously I was limited to a few viewings but I saw a top 10 talent for the 2014 draft. I would select him very high in the CHL Import Draft." - Mark Edwards

MacDonald, Mason – G – Acadie-Bathurst Titan (QMJHL) – 6'3" 170

MacDonald was the backup to Jacob Brennan in Bathurst and had a fairly strong season considering the fact the was playing for a weak defensive team. He has great size and plays an athletic and dynamic butterfly style very well. His best quality is lower net coverage, he possesses quick legs and his pushes are powerful enabling him to cover a lot of space in a short amount of time with accurate lateral movements. We like his athleticism and how he can come out of his crease aggressively to challenge shooters rapidly. He plays an aggressive butterfly game and shows great fighting instincts in front of his net, battling for loose pucks and giving second efforts to make miraculous saves. Both hands are technically solid while reflexes should be quicker, he will rarely make reactionary saves in the upper net, relying mostly on good glove positioning on the butterfly. MacDonald needs to improve his rebound control, as his technique doesn't always seem in control, sometimes putting himself out-of-position. We'd like to see more weight added to his frame and maturity and a poised butterfly style.

MacIntyre, Bobby – LW – Mississauga Steelheads (OHL) – 5'8" 175

Bobby was selected in the 2nd round of the 2012 OHL Priority Selection Draft by the Mississauga Steelheads out of the Whitby Wildcats Minor Midget program. Bobby went up against the odds and made the Steelheads at 16 year old. It was believed he may need another season to get stronger at a lower level of hockey as he is very undersized. However his skating ability, speed and puck skills were enough to convince the Steelheads to bring him in primarily in a bottom six role, although he was seen at times on the power play later on as well. Bobby skates very well with the puck and regularly challenges defensemen one on one showing well against bigger, stronger, older defensemen. He also will drive the net protecting the puck surprisingly well for a small defenseman and is able to get to the net sometimes due to his skating. He has a pretty good shot but will usually use his stickhandling ability when trying to beat the goaltender. He has also shown effective passing ability. Bobby will hopefully grow a little and get stronger. He will face another uphill battle this year as he looks to be selected at the 2014 NHL Entry Draft. The skill is certainly there, but increased viewings of Bobby as a second year player in the OHL will help determine if he has the upside to play at the NHL level as size is going to be the concern for him, not talent.

MacInnis, Ryan – LC – USNTDP (USHL) – 6'3" 161

Ryan, the son of former NHLer Al MacInnis started carving his own path as a highly regarded prospect out of the St. Louis area playing for the Blues AAA U16 team. Ryan chose to join the U.S. National Team Development Program over his father's junior team the Kitchener Rangers of the OHL who selected in him the 3rd round of the 2012 OHL Priority Selection Draft. Ryan opened his first season with the program putting together an adequate performance. His strongest asset is clearly his shot. He is able to get a lot of power behind it without much delay deceiving opponents and prefers shooting much more than passing. Ryan likes to possesses the puck and can protect it with his frame. He will rush it up ice fairly consistently. He has a good top speed, but his first few steps are sluggish and he looks rather awkward while trying to get moving. This is an area that needs work as he is already capable of generating speed, he just needs to do it quicker and more fluidly. Ryan has a lot going for him, bloodlines, a powerful shot and excellent size. However he desparately needs to add muscle to his huge frame. He needs to get stronger and play with a more aggressive style. He does a good job of staying out of the box, racking up only three minor penalties all season long, but it is also a tribute to the lack of competitiveness he has shown in the dirty areas. He plays too perimeter of a game and developing that toughness, willingness to compete and addition of muscle could be the biggest difference between how high Ryan goes in the 2014 NHL Draft.

MacIntyre, Duncan – LD – Quebec Remparts (QMJHL) – 5'11" 189

MacIntyre is a good two-way defenseman who can really help a teams' transition game, very poised with the puck and not much panic in his game. His best attribute might be his skating ability, effortless and very agile. He has great hockey sense and is rarely out of position in his zone, when he is caught off position he can recover nicely because of his footwork. He is a decent puck-mover with natural instincts for joining the rush. His passes are simple, accurate and which make transitions fairly easy. He has solid confidence with the puck and will rarely lose control of it, even under pressure. Although he is not too aggressive or intimidating of a defenseman, we have seen Duncan throw the body beautifully in open-ice this season, showing great timing for this type of hit. He plays a disciplined game mostly using positioning and skating abilities to counter the opposing team's offense. MacIntyre was drafted by the Quebec Remparts in the 2nd round of last year QMJHL draft. Originally from Nova Scotia he also played for team Atlantic at the U17 hockey challenge recording 4 points in 5 games.

MacSorley, Mac – FW – Youngstown Phantoms (USHL) – 5'10" 201

MacSorley played for the Huron Perth Lakers back in minor midget and had 26 goals in just 27 games before getting drafted in the 16th round at 234 overall by Youngstown. He was also selected in the 3rd round of the 2011 OHL Priority Selection Draft by the Brampton Battalion. Despite these options he played for the Stratford Cullitons in the GOJHL in the 2011-2012 season. He then joined the Youngstown Phantoms of the USHL this year playing in 22 games. He was not much of an offensive threat scoring only 3 points in those 22 games but MacSorley has a different role on the team and he realizes it. When you watch him play you realize just how strong he is on his feet, as he is able to take hits without being knocked over or off the puck. He goes down to block shots in his own end and he battles hard to clear the front of his net. He puts good pressure on the puck carrier, is quite aggressive to try and force turnovers, but he needs to be able to get the puck out of his zone on opportunities along the boards. He also has to hit his target on passes with more consistency and watch the turnovers through the neutral zone.

Maheux, Raphaël – LD – Shawinigan Cataractes (QMJHL) – 6'1" 216

A second-round draft pick by Shawinigan at the 2012 QMJHL Draft, Maheux has been a steady, solid player on the back end of the rebuilding 2012 Memorial Cup champions. Possessing a good stature for professional hockey, he plays the game with maturity and tremendous hockey sense. He positions himself well and plays odd-man rushes and defensive zone coverage looking like a veteran. He has corrected many of his teammates' mistakes in the defensive zone because of his anticipation and how quick reaction. We like the mobility and the footwork he has for such a big man, although he should improve his overall speed before being seen as a potential top defenseman in the Q. He has decent puck control and executes smart plays with the puck on the transition. He has a strong shot and will be open to use it even more when he improves his speed. He's not an aggressive or mean defenseman, preferring to play smart with his stick, but should be more physical with the strength he possesses. He's really interesting project that could be a high riser for the 2014 NHL Draft next season.

Mallette, Trent – RW – Sault Ste. Marie Greyhounds (OHL) – 5'10" – 165

Trent was selected in the 4th round of the 2012 OHL Priority Selection Draft by the Sault Ste. Marie Greyhounds from the Copper Cliff Minor Midget program. While undersized, Trent was able to defy the odds and make the Greyhounds out of camp as a 16 year old playing primarily in the 4th line and really excelled in this role working hard and bringing a very energetic attitude to the skilled Greyhounds line up. Trent showed flashes of offensive skills and was good at finishing chances when they came his way. He is reliable in the defensive zone and works hard to chip pucks out into the neutral zone along the boards. Trent needs to work at adding some bulk and strength to his frame so he can consistently compete with bigger opponents. Mallette had a good rookie season and will look to continue to improve and acclimatize to the OHL game next season.

Malone, Seamus – FW – Dubuque Fighting Saints (USHL) – 5'9" 158

After proving his talents in the Chicago Mission U16 program for the 2011-2012 season, Seamus joined the Dubuque Fighting Saints' of the USHL. Malone displays excellent skating ability and is able to elude checkers efficiently. He is a playmaker who is capable of seeing and reading the play well, making smart, accurate passes in the offensive zone. He is constantly able to create offensive chances and posted very good numbers considering he received somewhat limited ice time on one of, if not the deepest team in the USHL this past season. With his first NHL Draft Eligible year coming up in 2014, Seamus is a player we will be watching closely, as he has shown clear potential to be a prospect at the NHL level. Seamus will need to overcome his size and handle physicality a little more consistently. Seamus was also selected by the Plymouth Whalers at the 2012 OHL Priority Selection Draft.

Mantha, Ryan – RD – Sioux City Musketeers (USHL) – 6'4" 208

Ryan, the son of former long time NHLer Moe Mantha made the jump to the USHL right away as a 16 year old after spending last season with the Detroit Belle Tire U16 program. Mantha provided an excellent physical presence for Sioux City this past season. Despite only being 16, he delivers powerful, punishing hits and isn't afraid to drop the gloves in defense of a teammate. Ryan excels at playing a physical reliable defensive game, while maintaining simple intelligent puck moving skills. We expect him to continue to play his style of game and receive increased exposure as he is a very intriguing prospect for the 2014 NHL Entry Draft and should get a lot of attention from NHL teams. We would just like to see him improve on his skating ability which would really maximize his value to his team and as an NHL prospect. Ryan was also selected in the 5th round of the 2012 OHL Priority Selection Draft by the Sault Ste. Marie Greyhounds. Mantha is committed to the University of North Dakota.

Mappin, Ty – RC – Everett Silvertips (WHL) – 5'11" 170

Ty Mappin is a two way forward who plays a very grinding game at both ends of the ice. He may not be particularly talented with the puck, but his intensity often makes up for it, and he is very hard to play against in his own end.

Mappin is an above average skater with good overall speed. He needs to work on his lower body strength to stay on his feet more often as he battles for pucks in the corners. He displayed good defensive presence all year long, as he was in good position in the defensive zone to take away plays in front of the net. He was consistently counted on to kill penalties for the Silvertips, and did an admirable job to take away shooting lanes and ensure that the high slot is covered. An issue with his game defensively is his size. It is difficult to predict if he can play the same kind of a game at the pro level with much faster and stronger players. He will have to put in extra work to increase his overall strength and speed.

Offensively, Mappin displayed average skills with the puck. He is not a particularly great offensive presence, as his playmaking abilities are limited. He is only able to make simple reads, and his poise with the puck is not very good either. He is not able to protect the puck very well to buy himself more time to make a good pass. He goes to the front of the net, but does not have the hands to score from in tight or offensive instincts to get lost in coverage and free himself from opponents to have an easy tap in.

Mappin's limited offensive game is certainly a concern for the future. He may provide good impact in his own end, but a forward has to be able to do much more at the next level. He also does not display the grit and intensity needed to be successful as a grinder in the future.

Martin, Brycen – LD – Swift Current Broncos (WHL) – 6'1" 181

Martin is a poised, puck moving defenseman who really impressed scouts this season with his play with the puck this year. He looked like he was a veteran in the league, and played with confidence that is rarely seen in players at his age in the WHL.

It is fun to watch Martin move the puck and calmly skate out of trouble and buy some more time for himself to make a pass to his teammates. He is always looking to make a play with the puck, and will only go glass and out when his team is in real trouble defensively and they need to eliminate the pressure that they face. Martin is already quarterbacking the PP for the Broncos, and did a very good job of distributing pucks from the blue line. He may not have picked up many points this season, but he displayed above average vision from the point. He needs to work on his shots and using it more often from the point.

Defensively, Martin's game still has some improvements to make. He needs to do a better job of angling opponents along the boards, and not allowing them to get by him. His work with his stick can be improved, as he was not able to knock away passes and shots on a consistent basis. He was out of the shooting lane often to allow his goaltender to take the shot, but did sacrifice his body to block shots once in a while. He could be a little more physical along the walls, and will definitely have to fill out his frame for the future.

Martin will definitely be receiving more ice time and be counted on to provide a more defensive presence next season. He will have to show that he is not a liability out on the ice against the offensively skilled players on a consistent basis, and be tougher to play against. Martin will have adjusted his game to the WHL level, and he will definitely increase his points total and improve his puck moving abilities as the season goes on, which will attract the attention of NHL teams.

Quotable: "His first game at the U17 was fantastic, he looked to tire a bit later in the tourney as he made some mental mistakes. Overall, he made a good impression." - Mark Edwards

Mayo, Dysin – RD – Edmonton Oil Kings (WHL) – 6'0" 173

Dysin Mayo is a poised, puck moving defenseman who would definitely get more playing time on any other team with less depth on the blue line. The Oil Kings are filled with veteran defensemen, which often forces Mayo to be a healthy scratch. When he does have an opportunity to get into the line up however, Mayo has proved that he can play in the WHL, and be a very effective player in the defensive zone and play like he has already been in the league for a few years.

The best asset of Mayo's game is his poise. He is so calm with the puck despite pressure from forecheckers, and calmly moves the puck to a teammate to get the attack going. He does not play an aggressive game, but rather lets the play come to him and he reacts accordingly to try and stop the attack. Mayo is not bad along the boards, as he does not over power opponents with his strength, but uses his stick to create loose pucks and create a turnover. He does a good job of not chasing the play, but holds his position well in the slot and prevents any scoring chances from occurring in the slot.

Mayo has shown limited offensive potential so far at this level. He does not receive any power play time, and he also does not seem to have very good instincts in the offensive zone. Mayo does not join the rush as a trailer and plays a safe game. His shot from the point is average, and likes to just pass it down the wall or go D to D most of the time. He does not have very good vision from the point, and his offensive output seems to be very low at this point.

Dysin Mayo will definitely receive more ice time next season, and have the opportunity to show off his strong defensive play and poise on a consistent basis. He could become an effective shut down defenseman in the future as a pro, and really receive praise for his play without the puck. It would be nice to see him develop his offensive skills to add another dimension to his game.

McCann, Jared – LC – Sault Ste. Marie Greyhounds (OHL) – 6'0" – 174

Jared was selected first round, 4th Overall by the Sault Ste. Marie Greyhounds at the 2012 OHL Priority Selection Draft out of the London Jr. Knights Gold Minor Midget program. Jared was very highly regarded by HockeyProspect and was ranked #2 behind only Connor McDavid in our 2012 OHL Draft Guide.

McCann had an outstanding rookie season for the Greyhounds. He immediately jumped right into the Greyhounds line up and needed a little time to find his groove, but when he did he was a consistently effective player splitting time between the second and third lines. Jared finished his final 9 games of the season posting 16 points in 9 games played. He brings a number of offensive skills to the table and possesses a quick burst of speed when cutting through the middle of the ice that catches many defenders flat footed. Jared displays excellent vision and is particularly so successful because of his very high level of hockey sense. He reads the game at a level higher than most of his peers and it allows him to create, execute and read plays that some players simply cannot. He scored a number of highlight reel goals this season and possesses an absolute rocket of a wrist shot with a lightning quick release that catches many goaltenders off guard.

McCann was very physical in midget and we expect he will bring even more of that side of his game in the OHL. He was not afraid of corners or battles in front of the net against bigger opponents. He is also very reliable in the defensive zone and is more aware than many rookies at helping out defenders down low and moving pucks up ice quickly. He is strong in the face-off circle and wins the majority of draws he takes. Jared provided good scoring depth on the second power play lineup for the Greyhounds displaying good offensive awareness and playmaking abilities. He shows creative one on one moves when skating with the puck. Jared missed time in the playoffs due to concussion reasons but should be ready to go by the start of next season.

McCann will be looking to improve on an impressive rookie season by not only being one of the main contributors in the Greyhounds arsenal but will also expect to hear his name called very early in the 2014 NHL Draft.

Quotable: "That kid in the Soo (McCann) is going high next year. He is a smart player. Where did you guys have him ranked for the OHL Draft?" – NHL Scout

McKeown, Roland – RD – Kingston Frontenacs (OHL) – 6'1" 186

Roland was selected first round, 2nd overall at the 2012 OHL Priority Selection Draft out of the Toronto Marlboros Minor Midget program. Roland came into the OHL Draft as the undisputed top defensive prospect and was able to show why as he made a near seamless transition to the OHL as a 16 year old.

Roland plays an excellent two-way game. He has great combination of size and skating ability. He rushes the puck up ice extremely well and shows fluid ability to evade checkers and acquire the offensive zone. He possesses a strong shot from the point and is an effective puck mover in all three zones identifying passing lanes very quickly in the offensive zone. He is also capable of making a smart play up ice hitting teammates in stride. Thanks to his skating and size Roland is pretty effective regularly in one on one match-up's and when his team is pinned deep he shows good positioning. Roland is a player we'd like to see develop a little more of a mean streak. He will finish his hits but we'd like to see him play with a little more aggression than he does right now. He leads a little more towards the offensive side of the game, but has shown he can be reliable defensively. We'd like to see more of that as he has one season under his belt. We would also like to see more consistency. Roland didn't play to his capabilities in a couple of our viewings this season.

The sky is the limit for McKeown who looks to show he is one of the best defensemen available in the 2014 NHL Entry Draft.

McSween, Guillaume – LD – Chateauguay Grenadiers (MAAA) – 6'4" 215

McSween is a hulking defenseman who played last two seasons for the Chateauguay Grenadier in the Quebec Midget AAA league. He was drafted last year by Rimouski in the 3rd round. The Valleyfield native is a willing to play a physical game but his lack of mobility is hurting him. He can get down right nasty on occasions, playing major junior will help him thrive in his physical game as fighting is not allowed in Midget. His footwork is above-average, fluid for a big man. However, he can't generate a lot of speed overall at the moment. He has decent skills offensively, showing good puck control and confidence in his offensive attributes, has a good shot and can make strong passes but his decision making is lacking. He consistently tries to force a play and he gets in trouble when he does that. A very interesting physical prospect with some offensive upside.

Middleton, Jacob – LD – Ottawa 67's (OHL) – 6'3" 194

Jacob was selected first round, 8th Overall by the Owen Sound Attack at the 2012 OHL Priority Selection Draft out of the Huron-Perth Lakers Minor Midget program. Jacob joined the Attack but quickly suffered an injury limiting his action in the first half of the season. He returned in time to play a prominent role on the blueline for Team Ontario at the World U-17 Challenge in Victoriaville/Drummondville. Jacob then was the key piece traded to the Ottawa 67's in the trade that sent Ottawa Senators prospect Cody Ceci to the Owen Sound Attack.

Jacob played big minutes the rest of the way for the 67's and really took over where he left off from the U-17 Challenge providing an excellent two-way presence for Ottawa. Jacob is very solid in one on one situations. He can get beat, but generally keeps a strong gap control and can win the one on one match-up with both his stick and his body. He displays a physical edge at times and finishes his checks hard, although he doesn't possess much of a mean streak. Jacob moves the puck extremely well up ice and can be relied upon to make the smart decision on the point on the power play. He also possesses a pretty strong shot from the point that he can get through the crowd. Middleton is a pretty complete defenseman. He doesn't really have one single standout ability but doesn't have a major flaw in his game either.

We would like to see Jacob continue to get faster, stronger and prepare to handle big minutes for the 67's next year. We have been high on Middleton for a while. He's considered to have good leadership qualities and should be talked about highly for the 2014 NHL Entry Draft.

Quotable: "I thought he had one of the best showings amongst defenseman at the U17." - Mark Edwards

Mikulovich, Alexander – LD – Belie Medvedi Chelyabinsk (MHL) 6'3" 179

Alexander uses his big frame and will take the body on the opposition as frequently as possible. He's delivered some big open ice hits in our viewings. Despite his size he handles forwards on the rush well and uses both his stick and his body well. He was also noted by our scouts for defending two on ones very effectively and intelligently in our viewings showing strong positional play. He isn't a flashy offensive guy and keeps it pretty simple offensively. He moves the puck up ice very well and can make the strong breakout pass. Otherwise he keeps it pretty simple with the puck.

Milan, Cody – FW – Sioux Falls Stampede (USHL) – 6'0" – 163lb

Cody joined the Sioux Falls Stampede this season after a great run in Michigan high school hockey in his hometown of Orchard Lake. Cody was a highly regarded prospect and was taken 9th Overall at the 2012 USHL Futures Draft by the Stampede and immediately joined their roster. Cody possesses an excellent combination of size and speed already standing at six feet tall with his ability to fly up and down the ice. Although we really want to see Cody add some muscle to his body, he is more than willing to use what size he has effectively and to his advantage. He possesses quick hands but can sometimes get caught rushing the play. Cody will have a great opportunity next season in his draft year to show everyone what he's capable of as he will move up Sioux Falls' depth chart. Cody was also drafted by the Sault Ste. Marie Greyhounds at the 2012 OHL Priority Selection Draft in the 4th round, a team that would also be able to give him good ice and exposure. Milan is committed to Michigan State University.

Milano, Sonny – LW – USNTDP (USHL) – 5'10" 159

Sonny developed with the Cleveland Barons U16 program in 2011-2012 going on to score 87 points in 40 games. Sonny was a rather undersized forward and has grown since opening his season with the Barons and has really become more effective and a more legitimate pro prospect getting himself up to 5'10". Sonny possesses outstanding speed where he can handle the puck and make moves at top speed. He is the kind of player who can make highlight reel plays look easy beating multiple defenders. He has excellent hands and uses it to accurately shoot and pass the puck at high levels. He prefers to shoot over pass, but he does both effectively and we'd like to see him choose the option which gives his team the best chance to score a little more frequently. What holds him back, aside from being 5'10" is that he can disappear at times over the course of the game. He can disappear for a shift or even periods at times. We also would like to see him compete more defensively. Sonny will need to add muscle but heads into the 2014 NHL Entry Draft as a player with intriguing talent and upside. Sonny was selected at the 2011 OHL Priority Selection Draft. Sonny was selected in the 2012 OHL Priority Selection Draft by the Plymouth Whalers. Milano is committed to the University of Notre Dame.

Mistele, Matthew – LW – Plymouth Whalers (OHL) – 6'2" – 183

Matthew was selected in the second round of the 2011 OHL Priority Selection Draft out of the Whitby Wildcats program. He is a late 1995 birthdate, therefore he must wait an extra season before being eligible for the NHL Entry Draft. Matthew was known for his shot in minor midget, however he played in less than half the games for the Whalers as a 16 year old. This season expectations were a little unknown at first. However it wasn't long before he started to make a name for himself putting the puck in the net and becoming a regular for the Whalers alternating between the second and third line. Although the Whalers basically had three #1 lines this year. Matthew has a very quick release on his shot, but what allows him to be so dangerous is his excellent positioning. He always seems to find the right spot in the offensive zone and sets himself up for a great shot if a teammate can get him the puck. Matthew has also shown a physical side to his game. He hits hard and applies pressure along the boards. We would like to see Matthew become a little more consistent. There are games where he's fairly invisible and others where he's an impact player. If he can be more effective on a game by game basis his stock will only rise. He also needs to improve his skating. He has good size but we would like to see him get around the ice quicker.

Moody, Zach – LC – Cape Breton Screaming Eagles (QMJHL) – 6'1" 160

Moody was a 2nd round draft pick by the Screaming Eagles at the 2012 QMJHL draft and has shown decent 2-way potential for the next years in Cape Breton. A lanky center, Moody has average top speed and explosiveness and relies mostly on smarts to have an impact on the game. He plays a solid positional game in his own zone using smart puck distribution offensively. His hockey sense also helps him get open in the right spots to score goals. Moody has fairly good puck control and although he does not qualify as a skilled player, he can use the space an opponent will give him effectively. He has a long reach and is fairly solid in his 1-on-1 battles for his size, displaying nice puck protection. Moody needs better physicality and show more intensity when he's on the ice. He is an interesting project.

Moran, Brent – G – Niagara Ice Dogs (OHL) – 6'3" 180

Brent was selected in the second round of the 2012 OHL Priority Selection Draft out of the Ottawa Jr. 67's Minor Midget program. Brent was one of our biggest surprises this season as he put on an outstanding performance in Minor Midget and really looked physically really for the OHL. However he needless to say stumbled a little out of the gate. In his last 6 performances before Christmas break he allowed 5 or more goals on 4 of those occasions. He joined Team Ontario at the World U-17 Challenge but quickly lost his starting job allowing goals unbecoming of Brent's skill level. By the time March came around, Moran really appeared to start settling in. He went on a three game win streak helping Niagara secure 6th place down the playoff stretch. Brent takes up a lot of the net and plays his angles very well. He follows the play well and has fairly good reflexes. Brent has also shown at a few moments to be a solid puck playing goaltender who is able to come out and make a good pass when the puck comes down the ice. He moves well side to side, but reflexes need to improve, although they aren't a major concern at this point. In our viewings he allowed some goals he should have had, which was a very rare occurrence in Minor Midget, so he deserves the benefit of the doubt. If he continues to be the goaltender who put on a few solid performances consecutively at the end of this season, he has a legitimate chance at the 2014 NHL Entry Draft, because he has all the other natural tools going for him.

Morrison, Tyler – LD – Vancouver Giants (WHL) – 5'11" 183

Defenseman who has looked overwhelmed with the level of play for most of the season. Morrison has not looked very good in all situations presented to him, and has quickly fallen out of favour with the coaching staff. He has received chance after chance on the power play and has been quite consistent. He has shown that he could develop into a puck moving defenseman, but he has to be less of a liability in his own end and limit the number of turnovers he commits by playing with some poise. He panics too much with any amount of pressure from forecheckers. Morrison's confidence level looks quite low, and it is something that he and the team has to raise to help him reach his potential and be a serviceable defenseman for them in the future.

Nantel, Julien – LW – Laval-Montréal Rousseau-Royal (MAAA) – 6'0" 168

A 2nd rounder in 2012 by the Rouyn-Noranda Huskies at the QMJHL draft, Nantel was not able to get a spot in the Huskies' lineup for the 2012-2013 season. However, he was one of the best players in AAA Midget with Laval-Montreal helping them earn 3rd place at the Telus Cup. Nantel is a 2-way player with great skating abilities. His blazing top speed helps him create space offensively but also helps him get back on time for the backcheck. Many times being the first man back in his own zone even if he is not the centerman while in AAA Midget, reacting accurately on turnovers. He possesses superb explosiveness and a nice power skating technique he uses well to elude defenders and find lanes to the net. He possesses very good puck-control at top speed but is also willing to play a gritty dump-and-chase game if he needs to. A player that won't take nights off, always giving his maximum effort on the ice, whether it's in his 1-on-1 battles or in his backchecks. His level of competitiveness is very good. Nantel has a high level of hockey sense and a natural sense of anticipation that helped him create multiple turnovers this season. A lethal release on the wrist shot, Julien Nantel has natural goal scoring instincts and likes to cut abruptly in the slot to take shots. Nantel will probably be bigger when he starts his first season in QMJHL with Rouyn-Noranda, this will help be even better in his aggressive style of play and when he is crashing the net. There's not much we don't like about Nantel's game and we think he could be a huge riser in many scouts' rankings next season. He should have played in the QMJHL this season but with a loaded offensive squad in Rouyn he had no choice but to play a final season in AAA MIdget.

Nasybullin, Eduard – RD – Irbis Kazan (MHL B) – 5'9" 148

Eduard spent this past season in the MHL B league for Irbis Kazan, but don't let that throw you off. He showed his place among the talented upcoming defensemen at the World U-17 Challenge in Victoriaville/Drummondville. Eduard is a good puck rusher. He doesn't have great size but he rushes the puck effectively up ice showing elusiveness acquiring the offensive zone. He has a pretty powerful shot, but his decision making was hit or miss on when he should shoot the puck. Eduard also moves the puck effectively in all three zones. He is capable of unleashing a long distance breakout pass. But he is also capable of making the smart first pass to get things started. Eduard plays with a surprising level of physicality. He's certainly not the biggest defenseman, but he delivered some very big hits in our viewings along the boards. He battles and really wins more puck battles than a 5'9" defenseman should. He plays one on one and 2 on 1 situations very well and utilizes his stick moderately well. Eduard has a lot going for him. He's effective against other players his age at both ends of the ice and plays bigger than he is. Unfortunately the size may hold him back. We'd certainly like to see him grow a little and add some muscle, but it may be a bit of an uphill battle for Eduard in regards to NHL upside, not because of a lack of skill but because of a lack of size for the defensive position.

Nedeljkovic, Alex – G – Plymouth Whalers (OHL) – 6'0" – 186

Alex was a relatively unknown player going into this season. He was selected in the 6th round of the 2012 OHL Priority Selection Draft out of the Detroit Belle Tire U16 program. Alex joined a three goaltender roster including Carolina Hurricanes prospect Matt Mahalak. He didn't even make his OHL Debut until November 17th. He was used as a back-up as expected for a rookie goaltender from there on in. However by February the goaltending controversy boiled over in Plymouth, and Nedeljkovic went over a month without allowing more than two goals in any one game. Over this time he not only established himself as the starting goaltender for Plymouth, but also to end the season with a 19-2-1-1 record. Alex faced criticism once again entering the playoffs; however he responded with impressive performances against Sarnia, Owen Sound and London proving to be a game breaker for the Whalers en route to becoming the Western Conference Championship finalists.

Neil, Carl – RD – Sherbrooke Phoenix (QMJHL) – 6'1" 195

Neil was picked 9th overall in last year QMJHL draft by the Val d'Or Foreurs but didn't report and was traded to the expansion Sherbrooke Phoenix in August. Neil is a strong puck distributor from the point and can quarterback a powerplay, as he did on occasions this season with the Pheonix. The team had an inexperienced blueline and Neil had a good amount of ice time during the year. Carl Neil has very powerful legs and he's a good forward skater but needs some improvement in his backward skating. His footwork should be improved as it's average at the moment, giving him a hard time covering East-West skaters. He needs to make better decisions with and without the puck. He possesses many attributes but we would like to see him develop better hockey sense. On the powerplay his number one weapon is his slapshot from the point, it's lethal and already on a pro level. He likes to join the rush and his offensive passing skills are also very good, creating plays with solid crisp cross-ice passes in the offensive zone. He shows confidence in what he does, can start transition with dangerous plays whether he's carrying the puck or trying long feeds through the neutral zone, but that's how he plays. He has to be more aware of his surroundings as we saw him get caught with a man behind him multiples times this season. His defensive zone coverage also will need some work as he tends to lose his man and get attracted by the puck. He is solid physically down-low, wins most of his battles down-low, had no problems challenging older players on the walls and controlling them physically.

Nikolishin, Ivan – LC – CSKA Moskva (MHL) – 5'8" 148

Ivan is the son of former NHLer Andrei Nikolishin. He put up impressive numbers in the MHL this past season and captained Russia to a Silver Medal at the 2013 World U-17 Challenge. Ivan really impressed us with his skillset. He has explosive skating ability and is able to accelerate exceptionally well. He is elusive when carrying the puck up ice and can beat multiple defenders, although he can also over handle the puck too much. He displays great vision and awareness of the play and makes good decisions around shooting and passing. He has a powerful shot despite his size. With all his offensive skills, it may be surprising to know that Nikolishin has also displayed strong defensive play. He dives in front of shots showing a willingness to block them, but he also maintains good positioning, gets in passing lanes and was a strong penalty killer clearing the zone. Ivan is also dangerous on the PK and can use his skating and puck skills to take a short handed chance in the other direction.

With all these skills and atrributes, Nikolishin isn't without his flaws. The most obvious weakness is his size. At 5'8" the NHL will be an uphill battle unless he grows and can get stronger. Ivan can at times overhandle the puck and play as if he's the only player on the ice. It's nice to see the elusivness but it can be detrimental when he tries to force an individual play when looking off clear offensive opportunities that would result in big scoring chances. Finally, and the most frustrating area is when he fakes injuries. Over the course of the World U-17 Challenge, one where Ivan participated in 6 games, he was seen rolling around the ice back and forth trying to either draw a penalty or get a whistle to blow the play dead elaborately acting out an injury. He never missed a shift afterwards and sometimes just jumped up got back in the play and created a scoring chance despite laying on the ice acting out a serious injury just seconds earlier. This is something that will cause him to drop on draft lists all over the NHL and we certainly hope moving forward Ivan removes this from his game. Ivan has a ton of offensive potential, but size along with some of his decisions will be his biggest battles to overcome.

Nylander Altelius, William – LW – Sodertalje (SAL) – 5'10" 170

William, the son of former NHLer Michael Nylander, is an extremely talented and dynamic forward who spent last season between Sodertalje's J20 team and their men's team playing in the Allsvenskan league. In J20 he put up nearly two points per game and in the men's league, nearly a point per game as a 17 year old. William may in fact be the most absolute dynamic, creative and flashy player you will find in the 2014 NHL Entry Draft. He has exceptional puck skills and can create highlight reel goals on any given shift. He has quick hands and is extremely difficult to contain. He combines this with his skating ability which sports a quick acceleration allowing him to hit top speed very quickly. To top it all off he has an absolute laser of a shot which he can let fly quickly and at a high speed. He has a wealth of natural talent and he has shown clear signs of high level vision and hockey sense making him dangerous every time he steps on the ice. William is not without his flaws however. He can sometimes forget he has teammates and try to take on the other team by himself. These plays showed the flashes of his skill but usually wound up unsuccessful and heading in the opposite direction. When the play does go in the opposite direction, Nylander tends to lack the urgency to get back and defend. Of course at his size, we would like to see him get stronger. He fends off checks fairly well, but he will only become that much better by adding muscle.

Ollas Mattsson, Adam – LD – Djurgarden J18 (SWE J18) – 6'3" 192

Adam started with Varmdo as a youth but quickly moved on to Djurgarden's program playing in the J16 league at the age of 16. He moved up to J18 this season and has played there for a full season breaking only to join Team Sweden at the World U-17 Challenge in Victoriaville/Drummondville, Quebec. Adam plays a pretty simple game. He makes very smart decisions with the puck and is very poised. He is in no ways a flashy player and will stick to making the smart pass and is nearly flawless in this area. Adam is a very big defenseman and uses his size and strength to his advantage and loves to deliver hits both in open ice and along the boards. He plays a very defensive first style of game and is solid on the penalty kill getting into passing plays and shows good hockey sense in reading the play and positioning himself effectively. His positional awareness is that much more critical to his success, because Adam is not a very good skater at all. He struggles a lot in this area and is likely part of the reason he keeps his game so simple. He shows a lot of potential at future levels but simply needs to improve his skating because his intelligence and physical attributes are already prevalent.

Pastorious, Nick – Sault Ste. Marie Greyhounds (OHL) – 6'1" – 194

Pastorious was selected in the 3rd round of the 2012 OHL Priority Selection Draft by the Sault Ste. Marie Greyhounds from the 2012 OHL Cup Champion Mississauga Rebels. Nick was on 3 different rosters this season including Toronto Marlboros Major Midget AAA, SOO Thunderbirds in the NOJHL and of course 6 games with the OHL's Greyhounds. Nick plays an intense physical game and loves to finish his checks. He was one of the absolute best checkers in all of Ontario Minor Midget AAA in 2011-2012 and looked to bring that to the Greyhounds. He is a very hard worker and likes to crash and bang in the offensive zone. He is good on the fore check and works to create turnovers and pressure opposing defenders. Nick works to get under the skin of his opponents and does not back down from post whistle scrums. Pastorious will likely add some good depth to Sault Ste. Marie likely playing a bottom six role providing his great physical presence on a nightly basis.

Pépin, Alexis – LC – PEI Rocket (QMJHL) – 6'2" 196

Alexis Pépin was the number 2 overall selection at the 2012 QMJHL draft, but he wound up being the best 16 year old player in QMJHL. He scored 18 goals, but accomplished more than his offensive statistics. Pépin is a big kid at 6'2" and 196 pounds and does everything on the ice. His hits are already punishing, he likes to play a rough physical game and he doesn't mind to mix it up when it's needed. He is a responsible center with remarkable defensive awareness. He showed impressive maturity in his decisions and support for his defense. He is a strong kid, tough to move off the puck with great puck protection obviously. Pépin possesses tremendous soft hands, controlling the puck with ease through traffic, he has sweet moves in 1-on-1 situations and made experienced defensemen look bad this season. His wrist shot has great power behind it, quick release, but he still lacks accuracy that should come with practice. He is a natural goal scorer, but also has a smart passing game helping him find teammates with nice feeds.

Everything seems easy for Pépin offensively with much fluidity. Pépin is a diamond needing to be polished, but he has many tools to be a high pick at the 2014 NHL Draft : size, skills, intelligence, physicality. His biggest weakness is skating, taking to much time to get to his top speed. He can be neutralized by good skating defensemen because of that. We also didn't like the consistency of his compete level during the season, having great games, but also some games where he was gliding, making bad decision because of his lack of focus and being soft in all-areas.

Petti, Niki – LC – Belleville Bulls (OHL) – 6'0" 175

Niki was selected first round, 10th overall at the 2012 OHL Priority Selection Draft by the Belleville Bulls out of the Southern Tier Admirals program. Niki was drawn to the Bulls with his great skating ability and high energy play, which will work very well at Yardmen Arena's Olympic ice surface. Niki plays with a lot of grit and fire that you love to see out of a player and does so fairly consistently. He always finishes his checks and is capable of forcing a lot of turnovers. He doesn't have the offensive upside of a player drafted where he does, but he provides a style of game that is not always easy to acquire. Niki's best asset is his skating ability and he uses this to skate in all directions regularly competing in all three zones. He has shown us some creativity with the puck as he is able to set up plays and has a moderately effective shot. We would like to see him add more muscle to his frame and feel he is a player that will be watched closely heading into the 2014 NHL Entry Draft. Ideally we would like to see him show more offensive potential, but feel his high energy high speed game is what is going to primarily draw NHL teams in.

Pettit, Kyle – LC – Erie Otters (OHL) – 6'3" 175

Kyle was selected in the 2nd round of the 2012 OHL Priority Selection Draft by the Erie Otters out of the London Jr. Knights Gold Minor Midget program. Kyle played his 16 year old season in the OHL playing primarily in a bottom six role for the Otters. He possesses excellent size already and although he's a bit lanky he does a very good job infront of the opposing net causing disruption and winning battles along the boards. Pettit shows good efficiency in many different roles chipping in defensively, but has also shown moments of creativity to put together scoring chances for his team. Kyle will need to add more muscle to his frame, although he's strong for his size, he's 6'3" and we'd like to see him get thicker. We would also like to see him add another gear to his skating. Pettit projects to be a big bodied forward who can provide a physical presence while chipping in offensively and will get some attention at the 2014 NHL Entry Draft.

Philp, Luke – RC – Kootenay Ice (WHL) – 5'9" 169

Philp is a skilled, undersized forward who was able to put up some good numbers in his first full season in the WHL. He certainly lacks strength and size, but his playmaking skills and vision often made up for it in the offensive zone.

The best attribute of Philp's game is his playmaking abilities. He makes very good passes on a consistent basis, and is able to thread them through a small passing lane right to his teammate. He is a pass first player, but has shown a good release to his shots. His lack of size is a detriment to his game, and he will need to do a much better job along the walls to be able to get loose from hits with the puck instead of being knocked off the puck consistently and turning it over. He could also make up for his lack of size by thinking the game quicker and making plays with the puck more quickly, but that is difficult to do if he needs to buy some more time by holding onto the puck along the walls.

Defensively, Philp actually put in a good performance by reading the play well and quickly getting into open areas. On a team that struggled to keep pucks out of their own net, Philp ended the season with a +4 rating. He did a good job of taking away passes down low, and while he was not much help physically, he was able to get into good areas out on the ice to be a factor.

If Philp can be stronger, he will attract some interest from NHL teams with his play with the puck. He certainly has some offensive potential, but if he cannot go up against big opponents, then he will not be able to show off that offensive game as a pro.

Point, Brayden – RC – Moose Jaw Warriors (WHL) – 5'8" 155

Brayden Point was one of the rare positives that came out of the Warriors' season. He proved himself to be a very good player at the junior level despite his size, and really provided an impressive presence out on the ice for Moose Jaw at both ends of the ice.

Point does not allow his lack of size to be a detriment to his game. He makes sure that he is the hardest working player out on the ice at all times to win battles for pucks, and plays the game with such a high level of intensity on a consistent basis. He was able to earn the "A" this year because of his work ethic as a result. Point is very quick on his feet, and is difficult to hit out in open ice and is slippery along the walls. He has good speed from the outside and is able to drive to the net and create scoring chances. Point displayed good vision with the puck, and was able to create good chances on a consistent basis. He was poised with the puck and took his time when possible to make good plays. He has a good release to his shot and did a good job of finding open areas out on the ice, but his teammates were not able to find him often.

Defensively, Point is fearless when it comes to blocking shots and battling with much bigger opponents for loose pucks along the walls. He received PK time and did a good job of reading plays and taking away passing lanes. He is quick to cover opponents in the slot, but he can do a better job in the slot and by the net to take away scoring chances. His size is an issue in this area, and it will probably prevent him from playing centre as a pro.

Point will have a stronger team to play with, as everybody on his team is a year older and more prepared to play at the WHL level. He will be counted upon once again to be an offensive catalyst for the team, and it looks like he will be well prepared to produce. If he can continue to play with the same intensity while improving his offensive skills next season, NHL teams will surely take a long look at him.

Pomerleau had a good first season in the league. It took him some time to adjust but he played an important role leading up to the playoffs and played regularly role once they started. Pomerleau likes to move the puck and he has some solid puck skills. He is not an explosive puck mover but he uses his hands and body fakes to fool his opponents. Although he did a good job on the transition, he needs to show more awareness and improve his decision making. He is prone to turnovers and that showed as well on the power play where he couldn't establish himself. We also liked the poise he showed defensively and his competition level for an undersized defenseman. All that being said, it's going to be a tough road for Pomerleau to be drafted. He needs to be a better skater, prove he can be a true offensive catalyst from the backhand and show he can handle the defensive duties with his size.

Poganski, Austin – RW – St. Cloud Cathedral (USHS-MN) – 6'1" 195

Austin has played outstanding for St. Cloud Cathedral in his hometown of St. Cloiud, Minnesota. He has left such an impression he was selected to participate for Team USA at the World U-17 Challenge where he scored 6 goals in 6 games. Austin has great size and combines it with excellent elusiveness. He can beat defenders in one on one situations and put some pretty highlight reel moves on. He has great hands and controls the puck in traffic very well. Austin shows great upside moving forward and has already show the ability to dominate at the high school level and against his peers. Austin has committed to the University of North Dakota.

Prophet, Brandon – LD – Saginaw Spirit (OHL) – 6'2" 196

Brandon was selected in the 2nd round of the 2012 OHL Priority Selection Draft by the Saginaw Spirit out of the Upper Canada Cyclones Minor Midget program. Brandon looked physically mature beyond his years, there was little doubt he would be able to make the jump. Brandon possesses NHL ready size and is surprisingly strong for a 16 year old. Brandon plays a physical game and finishes his checks well. He plays a consistently aggressive game and has faired well in one on one match-up's. He makes effective passes up ice and doesn't possess high offensive upside but shows the knowledge and ability to make the smart pass. While his top end upside is somewhat limited, Brandon already looks like a true NHL prospect and will be a player NHL teams will take a long look at next season leading towards the 2014 NHL Entry Draft. We would like to see Brandon improve on his skating and not get caught up trying to do too much, sticking to the game that makes him most successful.

Ratelle, Joey – LW – Drummondville Voltigeurs (QMJHL) – 5'10" 163

The Voltigeurs' second round pick in the Midget draft had a fairly decent rookie season. While he didn't play much on the team's top lines, he certainly did enough to get noticed. Ratelle is not a high-end skater but he moves fairly well and was able to carry the puck effectively on some occasions. He has average skills with the puck but he's a tenacious forward and uses that to make things happen. He seemed to be affected when pressured in the neutral and offensive zone and made some precipitated plays with the puck. He needs to improve his decision making and confidence with the puck as he continues his development. We certainly feel there is room for improvement in his game but he has the potential to become a solid two-way forward with grit. The solid plays he made were on a small scale only this season and we need to see him bring more consistency in his game.

Reinhart, Sam – RC – Kootenay Ice (WHL) – 6'0" 182

In his second season, Sam Reinhart has continued to dominate games offensively despite the lack of help he gets from his teammates. Opposing teams clearly target him and have game plans around him as he is really the only legitimate threat to do any damage for Kootenay, and yet Reinhart has been able to get through it and produce offensively.

Like last season, Reinhart had a bit of a slow start to the year offensively, but really picked up his play as the season went along. His playmaking abilities are already one of the best in the league, and opponents really have a difficult time trying to contain him and take away his time and space. He is able to create chance after chance around the net no matter what kind of pressure he receives. He is very fast on his skates, and opponents have a difficult time trying to pin him up along the walls because he is so strong and quick on his feet to spin away from hits. Reinhart seems to have eyes located in the back of his head, as he makes unbelievable behind the back passes, tape to tape. Reinhart could shoot the puck more as he has very good stickhandling abilities and a good release to his shots, but you cannot question his decisions to pass when they seem to always accomplish something.

Reinhart's play has improved without the puck this season. He has shown more intensity along the walls to win battles for pucks and to get the attack going again. He is not afraid to block shots, but he could block them more often from a game to game basis. He plays so much on the PP and on even strength that he does not receive much PK minutes, but he could probably do an admirable job as his ability to read the play is very good, and he possesses a pretty good stick as well.

There is no question that Reinhart will be a top end pick if he can continue to put up the numbers that he has in the last two seasons. He desperately needs some help in order to help his team win as he cannot be out on the ice every second of the game, but he has been able to make some average players look quite good this season, which is really the ultimate compliment for any player. He comes from a hockey family who will undoubtedly provide good advice to get through any difficult times he may face as a player and as the captain of the Kootenay Ice next season, which is always a positive for any player.

Renaud, Alexandre – LW – Sarnia Sting (OHL) – 6'4" – 214

Alexandre was a player we had rated a little lower for the 2012 OHL Priority Selection but the Sting confidently selected him late in the second round. He has pro ready size right now. Alex seemed to struggle a little early on to find his role with the team. He was doing a little bit of everything but not enough of anything. As he adjusted to the league he become more forceful with his size. While his physical play is still a little inconsistent it has certainly improved throughout the year. Alex has shown a willingness to finish his checks and has added a little more power into these hits. He's also developed a willingness to drop the gloves to stand up for a teammate or to try to get his team going. For a 16 year old he takes a lot of damage and keeps going. He also has thrown some bombs. This could be an attribute that pushes him into a more prominent role with slots opening up higher in the forward depth chart in Sarnia. We would like to see Alex become more noticeable on a game by game basis. We also feel he really needs to improve his skating ability to maximize his potential. Renaud's offensive potential appears fairly limited at this point and appears to be more of a checker, fortunately this is something he does well.

Ritchie, Nick – LW – Peterborough Petes (OHL) – 6'2" 218

Nick was selected first round, 2nd overall by the Peterborough Petes at the 2011 OHL Priority Selection Draft out of the Toronto Marlboros Minor Midget program. Nick made an immediate impact still at the age of 15 due to his late birthdate. Nick had an impressive rookie season including a brief but successful performance at the World U17 Challenge in Windsor. Nick entered the 2012-2013 season unable to enter his NHL Draft year due to his birth date. This turned out to be a positive as Ritchie had multiople issues with his shoulder this season and was limited to 41 games.

Nick is a big power forward. When he's on his game he plays with a great deal of energy, finishes his checks hard and he can be very dangerous in the offensive zone. He has good offensive skills, handles the puck well and gets off a powerful shot. He is a very shoot first type of player who is capable of putting the puck in the net. Unfortunately he struggles with consistency and can be invisible, or even a liability when he is not on his game. Nick has the potential to be a top 5 pick in the 2014 NHL Entry Draft, however needs to become much more consistent and show how dangerous he can be on a nightly basis. The Petes are on the rise, and Nick will need to be one of their leaders.

Sadowy, Dylan – LW – Saginaw Spirit (OHL) – 6'2" 180

Dylan was selected in the 2nd round of the 2012 OHL Priority Selection Draft by the Saginaw Spirit out of the Vaughan Kings Minor Midget program. Dylan was commonly found on Saginaw's fourth line this season with a few boosts up to the third which should only increase as he continues to develop. Dylan rarely if ever passes up a chance to finish his check. He follows through with his size showing strength a little ahead of his development in this physical area. Dylan has shown some flashes of puck skills here and there but is generally most successful keeping it safe and simple with the puck. He cycles effectively and has shown very good two-way play providing a strong presence in his own end. Dylan has a lot going for him heading into the 2014 NHL Entry Draft. His upside appears to be limited, but he possesses size, a willingness to play physical and takes care of his own end. We would like to see him improve on his skating and show a little more offense with increased opportunities.

Sandhu, Tyler – RC – Everett Silvertips (WHL) – 5'10" 155

Tyler Sandhu was depended on for offense for most of the year with Everett in a top 6 role. He displayed average offensive instincts and good speed throughout the year, but just was not able to translate that to much production for the Silvertips.

Sandhu was not able to be an offensive catalyst for the Silvertips this season. They did not really have any player that could single handedly create offense by themselves, which is what Sandhu needed to create more offense. He did not particularly have a great shot that would overwhelm goaltenders, nor be a very good playmaker to set up his teammates for nice goals. He was quite invisible in a number of games that he played because he just could not find open areas or make good plays with the puck. He really needs to work on filling his frame as he is too easy to handle physically, and cannot get around traffic very well. As the season went on, he looked a little bit more confident with the puck on his stick, but he still has a long ways to go before opponents start to target him defensively.
Sandhu will have to play a much more consistent game to make more impact in games and actually be noticeable out on the ice. He is far too easy to play against for shut down defensemen in the league, and they easily covered him out on the ice this season. He will definitely have to improve on his overall play to even be noticed for the 2014 NHL Entry Draft.

Sanvido, Patrick – LD – Windsor Spitfires (OHL) – 6'6" – 220

Patrick is a player we've been watching regularly since Major Bantam. He graduated from the Guelph Jr. Storm Minor Midget program after being selected in the 2nd round of the 2011 OHL Priority Selection Draft. Sanvido has massive size for a defender and is physically imposing without going overboard. He has shown good footwork in small areas, but is very heavy on his feet when attempting to generate speed. Despite his age, he's very good at clearing some strong and older players away from the crease allowing his goaltender to see. He won his share of battles and will need to continue to work at being quicker in these battles as this is a key area to his success. He moves the puck fairly intelligently making the smart simple plays and has an effective shot from the point. One of the best things for Patrick moving forward is he understands that he's a big defenseman with limited mobility and plays to his strength and knows what he needs to do to be successful. We'd love to see his skating improve as he has all the makings of being a smart stay at home defenseman, who is effective in making the simple play and imposing his size on others.

Schmalz, Matt – RC – Sudbury Wolves (OHL) – 6'5" – 186

Matt was selected in the first round, 17th Overall at the 2012 OHL Priority Selection Draft by the Kitchener Rangers out of the Southern Tier Admirals Minor Midget program. Matt opened the season on a very deep Rangers team and struggled to get on the ice because of that depth. When he did he appeared to be adjusting to the OHL game and did his best with what he had available to him. Matt was part of a blockbuster deal that saw him head north to the Sudbury Wolves. The Wolves, while talented, did not have the same forward depth of Kitchener, and Matt saw himself become a regular in the line-up playing a bottom six role and receiving more ice. With increased ice, came increased productivity from Schmalz. He has a good shot and is very difficult to move when he plants his feet, most effectively in front of the opposing net. He is a pretty good skater for his size, and we'd like to see him get quicker while adding some muscle. Matt is a big forward who has a lot going for him, he has moderate puck skills, and needs to continue working on his defensive game. Most importantly we'd love to see him play with more of a mean streak as he can finish his checks, but isn't exactly regarded as a punishing winger. We don't believe he has the upside of a top six forward at the next level, so a power winger who can play both ends of the ice and punish opponents is the type of game we feel will most intrigue NHL teams for next year's draft.

Schmaltz, Nick – FW – Green Bay Gamblers (USHL) – 5'11" 160

Nick is one of the top forwards available heading into the 2014 NHL Entry Draft and he proved exactly why in his second season with the USHL's Green Bay Gamblers. Nick first appeared with the Chicago Mission U16 program at the age of just 13 years old. Nick would spend 3 years with them joining Green Bay at the end of his third year. With some of the Gamblers veterans moving on after their Clark Cup championship, Nick was called upon to be one of their offensive leaders. Schmaltz possesses excellent skating ability and he is very elusive moving up the ice with the puck eluding checkers. He shows poise and confidence with the puck and likes to create scoring chances for his linemates. He is much more of a playmaker than a finisher. He has a pretty good shot, and if anything we would like to see him take the shot a little more often. He could stand to add a little more muscle as he heads into his NHL Draft Year next season. Nick was selected in the 4th round of the 2012 OHL Priority Selection Draft by the Windsor Spitfires. Schmaltz is committed to the University of North Dakota.

Serebryakov, Nikita – G – Saginaw Spirit (OHL) – 5'11" 162

Nikita was selected in the first round of the 2012 CHL Import Draft by the Saginaw Spirit. Although he was also selected 36th round in the 2012 KHL Draft by his hometown Dynamo Moskva, he made the decision to come overseas and join the Saginaw Spirit providing a stable back-up to Detroit Red Wings' prospect Jake Paterson as he adjusted. Nikita really put his name on the map at the 2012 World U-17 Challenge where he overcame a barrage of shots in the final vs. USA making multiple highlight reel saves en route to Russia winning the goal medal. Nikita played in 22 OHL games last season and has really shown a wide range of performances in our viewings. He has had some big performances, making some highlight reel saves and robbing sure goals. He displays excellent recovery ability and very quick reflexes. When he's off his game however he seems to get beat five hole and when he loses his confidence, his positioning quickly follows. Nikita now has a year under his belt in North America, he will be looked upon to play a more consistent game. He is a little undersized for the goaltending position but compensates with quickness, but we need to put together a few more high end performances to move up the draft lists for the 2014 NHL Entry Draft.

Sergeyev, Dmitri – LD – Belie Medvedi Chelyabinsk (MHL) – 6'0" 172

Sergeyev has good size and played for a MHL team that has many good young prospects developing in it's system this past season. He has good size at his age, although he could stand to add some mucle to his frame. He was noticeably strong in one on one situations, in particular using his stick very well. While we want to see him get stronger, he did well against the boards using the strength he has to contain forwards and win battles very effectively. His puck play has been more hit than miss as he shows good patience allowing lanes to open up for him and making the smart accurate pass. He consistently moves the puck up ice well, but there have been a few moments, usually under heavy pressure he'll throw the puck up the middle in a dangerous fashion. Dmitri really left a positive impression on our scouts and will certainly be a player to watch going into the 2014 NHL Entry Draft.

Shirley, Colin – LC – Kootenay Ice (WHL) – 6'1" 172

Shirley is a big, skilled centre for the Kootenay Ice whose game has steadily improved throughout the season, particularly his strength to win loose pucks and using his size to be a more physical presence. His offensive game has not be particularly impressive this season, but on a team with not much skill, Shirley also did not get much help from his teammates.

If Shirley gets to the net, he is a dangerous player. He uses his size and ability to finish to put up some goals on the scoreboard, but he has not been able to get those opportunities very much this season. It is not for a lack of effort, but rather a lack of offensive instincts and not very good line mates throughout the season to create those chances. Shirley plays hard at both ends of the ice, but his lack of a physical game is worrisome for a player with his size. He could get stronger to be knock opponents off the puck more often. Defensively, Shirley has work to do in terms of reading the play. He is not always particularly quick to react to what is happening in his own end, and may be a step or two behind the play, which results in a goal against or a very good scoring chance. He is not afraid to block shots, but he can get caught puck watching and get drawn to the opponent on the half wall, and not be in position to take away a pass to the point or block the point shot.
Shirley has a lot of developing to do to be a more consistent threat, but he has certainly shown some tools that he could be an effective player in the future. The Kootenay Ice are a young team in general, and it will be intriguing to see what they can do as a group next season as everybody comes back older and more experienced in the league.

Spinozzi, Kevin – LD – Sault Ste. Marie Greyhounds (OHL) – 6'2" – 195

Kevin was selected in the 2nd round of the 2012 OHL Priority Selection Draft by the Sault Ste. Marie Greyhounds out of the Kingston Jr. Frontenacs Minor Midget program. Prior to playing with the Jr. Frontenacs Minor Midget team, he dominated from the blueline in France playing in the France U18 league for Amiens and actually lead the U18 league in scoring for defensemen despite playing only half a season at the age of 14. Kevin made the Greyhounds out of camp but saw himself come in and out of the line-up both with healthy scratches and after being suspended after a hit to the head of Davis Brown from the Sarnia Sting. He is a big mean, shutdown defender and really likes to get involved in the physical aspect of the game. He works hard in the corners and in front of the net. Kevin battles extremely hard but needs to know when to draw the line, because we've seen him cross that line a few times. He also needs to ensure that he keeps things simple in the defensive zone and gain some confidence carrying the puck. Spinozzi will play a bigger role on the Greyhound blue line next season after the graduation of a number of key veterans but has shown an intriguing amount of potential going into the 2014 NHL Entry Draft. If he can play his game but keep it within appropriate boundaries, he could be a big riser next season.

Subban, Marselis – RD – Saginaw Spirit (OHL) – 6'0" 193

Marselis was selected in the 5th round of the 2011 OHL Priority Selection Draft by the London Knights out of the Cambridge Hawks Minor Midget program. Marselis joined the Cambridge Winterhawks Jr. B program for the 2011-2012 season to help refine his skills as a 16 year old. He had a fairly successful season overcoming injury posting respectable numbers as a rookie. Marselis joined the London Knights training camp, however due to the incredible blueline depth the Knights possess Marselis was moved to the Saginaw Spirit and he played sparingly throughout the season. Marselis is the cousin of P.K., Malcolm and Jordan Subban, he was more of an offensive defenseman in Minor Midget but has had to try and adjust to playing more of a two-way style. He's very hit or miss out there as he has made some good plays with the puck, smart passes and good defensive plays one on one, but he's also misread plays, missed defensive assignments and been caught out of position. The biggest thing in his favor right now is a late birthdate which makes him ineligible until the 2014 NHL Entry Draft. He has a lot of room for improvement, but we'd like to see him become more consistent, use the size he has better and more reliable in the defensive zone. Next season is a new opportunity for Marselis who has taken a step up in his development every season in his junior career and we hope the 2013-2014 season is no different.

Thrower, Josh – RD – Calgary Hitmen (WHL) – 6'0" 194

Thrower is a hard hitting, physical defenseman who loves to take chances and play a risky game. He plays a similar game to his older brother and Montreal Canadiens draft pick, Dalton Thrower, as Josh also seems to be everywhere that the puck goes. He makes an impact in games by being aggressive and making sure that opponents have their heads up in the neutral zone and be wary of carrying the puck across the blue line down his wing.

Defensively, Thrower makes life miserable for opponents along the walls and in the neutral zone with his crushing hits. He loves to take a gamble and try to knock players off the puck, but this often gets him in trouble as he gets out of position. It is nice to see a physical presence from the backend, but Thrower would be better off trying to contain opponents instead and being in good presence to take away passes across the slot. He is a very good skater who can back check to recover when he does land a solid hit in the neutral zone. Thrower can easily stir opponents to the outside off of a rush, if he does not chase and try to land big hits. He could also improve his stick work and intercept more passes and take away the passing lanes.

Another area of Thrower's game where he excels is when he jumps into the rush to provide offense for the HItmen. He will quickly join the attack whenever he recognizes and opportunity, and provides another weapon for his teammates. His vision with the puck is not particularly good, and does not provide a good power play presence from the backend. He cannot create much offense with his limited puck moving abilities, but he does have the ability to get good shots on net.

Thrower will have to find a good balance of being aggressive and being in good position to receive more ice time next season. He could become a dynamic defenseman in the future if he can improve his puck moving skills, but he certainly has some work to do in that area of his game. His aggressiveness is certainly an asset, but he needs to pick his spots better. Thrower will have an increased role with the Hitmen next year and be counted on to make a positive impact at both ends of the ice. He will have to prove that he can be in good position consistently, and not look like he does not have any idea of where he needs to be out on the ice without the puck.

Tuch, Alex – RW – USNTDP (USHL) – 6'3" 219

Alex got his start in juniors with the Syracuse Jr. Stars of the EmJHL posting a ridiculous 101 points in 40 games all with the frame that NHL prospects would love to possess. Alex was selected to join the U.S. National Team Development Program. As mentioned earlier Alex has excellent size and protects the puck extremely well. There were moments in our viewings where he was absolutely dominant down low against players his age when protecting and controlling the puck. He has a great shot and utilizes it whenever possible. His skating is fairly effective but he looks really uncomfortable skating and has a rather awkward stride. He is positionally sound in the offensive zone when he's not controlling the puck down low opening himself up for shooting options. Alex is a player we'd like to see clean up his skating. He gets around well enough but looks really uncomfortable doing so. We would also like to see him be more of a competitor defensively and be more of a factor in all three zones. Alex was selected by the Guelph Storm in the 5th round of the 2012 OHL Priority Selection Draft. Tuch is committed to Boston College.

Turgeon, Dominic – LC – Portland Winterhawks (WHL) – 6'1" 191

Dominic Turgeon is the son of long time ex-NHLer Pierre Turgeon. Dominic has been used mostly as a defensive specialist this season, and he was able to show off good defensive instincts as a result.

The one area of strength for Turgeon is his faceoffs. He was very strong off the draw for the Winterhawks, and he was able to consistently win draws and allow his team to gain possession to start the play. He was valuable on the PK with his very good positioning and the ability to read the play so well. He does a good job of being aware of his surroundings without the puck and not to chase the play so much. He provides good help for his
teammates and does a good job of covering for them. An area of improvement for Turgeon is to play with more toughness. He does not really assert himself physically, and seems to be soft to play against. This may be one of the reasons why he is not really counted on to play important defensive situations as he needs to show some more intensity when out on the ice.

Turgeon has shown limited offensive abilities. He seems to have below average playmaking abilities, and struggled to control the play in the offensive zone whenever he was out on the ice. His favourite play is to dump and chase and hope that one of his teammates could create a turnover. He does not possess a very good shot, and is not able to get into open areas out on the ice.
Dominic does not seem to have been able to pick up the same offensive skills that made his father Pierre so successful in the NHL. He will definitely have to be better with the puck to have a shot at being drafted in the 2014 NHL Entry Draft.

Vanier, Alexis – LD – Baie-Comeau Drakkar (QMJHL) – 6'4" 210

Vanier looks even bigger than the size he is listed at, a hulking defensemen who was picked up in the first round in last year QMJHL draft. Vanier a December 95 birthday, was used sporadically during the regular season and was mostly a healthy scratch during the Drakkar run in the QMJHL playoff. Mobility is Vanier's biggest issue right now, requires improved footwork and overall skating abilities. His physical game improved as the season progressed as he gained more confidence in his physical ability and as a QMJHL player. He is a very imposing player who developed a nasty streak as the year went on. His lack of mobility makes it hard for him to keep up with smaller quick players in his defensive zone or off the rush. Right now his puck skills are below average, takes too much time to make a decision with the puck and gets in trouble with it. Even though he's not known for his offensive skills, Vanier still likes to take chances when rushing the puck. We wish he would keep his game simpler and cut down on those turnovers.

Verbeek, Ryan – LC – Windsor Spitfires (OHL) – 5'11" – 181

Ryan was Windsor's 3rd round pick in the 2011 OHL Priority Selection Draft out of the Lambton Jr. Sting Minor Midget program. He went in as a slight underdog to make the team however worked his way onto the roster and received a regular shift with the Spitfires. Ryan is very well suited for a bottom six role and appears to be that moving forward at the next level as well. He does a very good job of agitating the opposition and getting under their skin. He is extremely physical and will finish his checks every opportunity he gets. He battles hard and is very relentless along the wall. He's also shown a willingness to drop the gloves from time to time. While he appears very solid in the bottom six checker/grinder style, he has shown flashes of puck handling ability and isn't afraid to shoot the puck when the opportunity arises. It's likely not enough to put him up into a top six role at the NHL level, but if given the opportunity when higher spots on Windsor's depth chart open up, he may provide a little offense at the junior level.

Vickerman, Taylor – LW – Vancouver Giants (WHL) – 6'1" 181

A big forward who has struggled to be much of a factor for the Giants this year. Vickerman has looked overwhelmed with the pace of play in the WHL, and has looked uncomfortable at both ends of the ice this year. The biggest concern with him is that even with his big frame, he is not a presence physically and does not get into the tough areas with authority to create havoc. He is an average skater who will need to get faster to be able to get to loose pucks quickly and do something productive out on the ice. He has to show more desire to compete and to be successful on a team whose coach demands players their best effort every night. If his play does not improve soon, Vickerman's days in the WHL may end in a hurry.

Virtanen, Jake – RW – Calgary Hitmen (WHL) – 6'1" 190

Jake Virtanen is a physical power forward who is quick to get around the ice and possesses very good offensive skills. When he is at his best, opponents have a tough time stopping him from getting to the net and creating havoc. The issue with Virtanen's game is his inconsistency. He has too many games where he is invisible, and makes very little impact out on the ice. He has all the tools to be a high, first round draft pick in 2014, but he has to be able to put it all together on a consistent basis.

Virtanen is very good at getting to the net with his strength and speed, when he wants to. He does not use his body nearly enough to his advantage to create more scoring chances. He possesses good hands and likes to dangle off the rush, but he also needs to dump and chase more often to limit the turnovers that he commits. When he gets in on the forecheck, he has the ability to create a lot of turnovers and make life miserable for opponents. Virtanen also loves to shoot from everywhere, which is something he will need to work on and use his teammates more often in the offensive zone. His ability to think the game does not seem to be at a high level, which may be a concern for the future.

Defensively, Virtanen has some work to do in his own end. He uses his body effectively to land big hits out in the neutral zone and along the boards, but he needs to be better at containing opponents and limiting the plays that they have with the puck, especially at the higher level as players will be much smarter and quicker.

It will be interesting to see the role that Virtanen will receive with Calgary next season, and how he will respond to the added responsibility. He will surely have to produce much more offense than he did this season for the Hitmen to have a successful year, and it may be what Virtanen needed to be a more consistent player. If he can be a dangerous player every game, he will definitely be a first round pick.

Quotable: "I had a lot of conversations with our west guys about this Virtanen. He had one game at the U17's that made him look like a top 5 pick next season. His other games at the tourney were not flattering. His play was more consistent with his Calgary Hitmen team. This is a player who can control much of his own destiny just with work ethic. The tools are there and his potential is high." - Mark Edwards

Watson, Matthew – LD – Kingston Frontenacs (OHL) – 5'10" 157

Matthew was selected in the 5th round of the 2012 OHL Priority Selection Draft by the Kingston Frontenacs. Matthew got a solid 8 game experience with the Frontenacs as a 16 year old, but spent most of his season with the GOJHL's Jr. B Strathroy Rockets. Matthew had a very successful season in the GOJHL. Matthew showed in his OHL appearance and in Jr. B that he has very good potential as a two way defenseman at the junior level. For a defenseman who is 5'10" he has shown very well in one on one defensive situations making up for his size with a good stick and effective skating ability. He handles bigger defensemen very well for his size and is well positioned in his own zone. Matthew has shown the ability more so in Minor Midget and Jr. B his puck rushing ability that will likely translate to the OHL as well. He moves the puck very well in all three zones and can make some tough passes in the offensive zone but makes smart passes in the other two zones. While size will be a huge issue for Watson to overcome, we hope he gets stronger and ideally grow a couple inches.

Watson, Spencer – RW – Kingston Frontenacs (OHL) – 5'10" 157

Spencer was selected by the Kingston Frontenacs in the 2nd round of the 2012 OHL Priority Selection Draft out of the London Jr. Knights Gold Minor Midget Program. Spencer showed his flash and ability on one of the best lines in all of Ontario Minor Midget playing alongside 4th Overall Jared McCann and small but skilled Brett Seney. Before joining the Frontenacs Spencer actually put on an outstanding display as a 15 year old in the playoffs for the London Nationals Jr. B Team of the

GOJHL. Spencer joined the Frontenacs and almost immediately was a top six player for this team playing regularly on the power play. Watson displays tremendous speed, which is clearly his best asset. He is capable of creating outstanding plays with the puck and can score highlight reel goals. He takes on defenders one on one fairly often and has a pretty solid success rate in these situations. Spencer is a strong passer but he also had a great shot and knows how to finish in so many different ways. Spencer competes hard and forces turnovers but isn't very physical and needs to keep improving upon his defensive play. Spencer is not a liability to his team as he recorded only 9 minor penalties all season long. We would like to see Watson get stronger on the offseason as he is still pretty thin and has limited strength.

Wesley, Joshua – RD – USNTDP (USHL) – 6'2" 188

Joshua is the son of former NHLer Glen Wesley. Joshua played for the Carolina Jr. Hurricanes U16 program. He was selected for the U.S. National Team Development program. Joshua displayed a good ability to shutdown opponents on a regular basis during his first season at the program. He shows good physicality and handles opponents well one on one. He's willing to get down and block shots. He is also fairly well positioned when the opposition is bearing down on his team. Unfortunately he can negate some of his strong defensive plays with bad puck decisions after winning battles or when intercepting a puck. He can also freeze up in his own zone at times when pressured resulting in turnovers. We see a lot of upside in Joshua as a defensive defenseman, but needs to improve his puck play and make the strong smart play to reach his potential. Joshua was selected in the 5th round of the 2012 OHL Priority Selection Draft.

Wilkie, Chris – RW – USNTDP (USHL) – 5'10" 172

Chris spent the last two years developing his game as part of the Omaha Lancers U16 program out of his hometown of Omaha, Nebraska. Chris made one appearance in the USHL as a 15 year old for the Lincoln Stars. He was discovered by the U.S. National Team Development Program and had an excellent rookie season playing alongside some talented linemates. Chris looks a lot bigger than his listing on the ice and is a tribute to his style of play. Chris finishes his checks and will go to the dirty areas to force turnovers. He pressures the puck carrier well and battles in front of the net relentlessly causing a disruption. He also possesses strong skating ability and will use his speed to create scoring chances on the rush. He has a powerful shot and picks his spots well providing a quick release. While he provides a fairly strong back-check, we'd like to see him compete a little more defensively. Chris doesn't have many flaws in his game. Ideally we'd like to see him grow just an inch or two, because he has a great frame. One which we hope he adds a little more muscle to in time for the 2014 NHL Entry Draft. Chris was selected in the 4th round of the 2011 WHL Bantam Draft by the Victoria Royals. Wilkie is committed to the University of Notre Dame.

Wood, Travis – LD – Erie Otters (OHL) – 5'11" 175

Travis was selected in the 11th round of the 2011 OHL Priority Selection Draft by the Erie Otters out of Hill-Murray High School. Travis made the jump to the Erie Otters as a 16 year old and put together some very respectable point totals for a young defenseman. Travis looked to duplicate this effort however saw a minor decline statistically. We also saw him moved between defenseman and forward, although he is a natural defenseman. Travis is a smooth skater who shows good puck rushing abilities. He is very offensive minded and possesses a big point shot. He moves the puck moderately well but needs to work on his defensive zone coverage. He can lose his positioning during sustained pressure opening up lanes for opposing forwards to access. He also needs to get stronger in order to win more battles. Due to his late birth date he has an extra year before his eligibility. Travis is a player who will need to provide a little more offense this year while getting better in his own zone to gain a lot of attention at the 2014 NHL Entry Draft.

Yetman, Nathan – LC – PEI Rocket (QMJHL) – 5'8" 165

Nathan Yetman has played a secondary role with the PEI Rocket season, but still showed good 2-way potential and we also like the natural talent with the puck he displayed. He is a good skater and has great agility on skates, finding soft areas well on the ice, handling the puck well at top speed and creating space nicely. His puck control is good, really fluid when he controls the play which he really likes to do while using his vision to find teammates. He is a good passer with tons of smarts, taking already mature decisions with and without the puck. He doesn't shy away from physicality, but will rarely initiate physical contact. He is more of a playmaker than a goal-scorer but has a strong quick-released wrist shot.

Zalitach, Reid – RD – Vancouver Giants (WHL) – 6'0" 175

Zalitach has had an up and down season. Every game it seems like he would show some potential of being an impressive puck moving defenseman, then there were times where he looked like he has not played hockey in years. He needs to learn to be consistent in his play, and cut out the bad mistakes.

Zalitach is a good skater, and has shown that he can be a threat off the rush. He can freeze opponents with his little moves and skate past them and have a clear lane to attack. He is good in tight areas and has quick starts and stops. He needs to use his skating abilities more to his advantage. He is physical along the boards and does not shy away from contact. The big improvement he needs to make in his own end is reading the plays and being in good position to take away chances in the slot. He has played on the power play for most of the year, and could develop into a good power play quarterback. Zalitach needs to take calculated risks, and trust that his teammates will be in the right position and keep it simple on breakouts. He needs to be stronger on the puck and not get it stripped away from behind.

Zinoviev, Ilya – RW – Belie Medvedi Chelyabinsk (MHL) – 5'10" 185

There is no shortage of young talented Russians who love to put the puck in the net. Sometimes it seems there are too many that want to finish and not enough that like to create the play. Zinoviev is one of those players when matched with a goal scorer can be an extremely dangerous combination. Ilya is an excellent playmaker who is able to create goals and create scoring opportunities for his linemates. Ilya is a solid two way presence and he works very hard in his own zone to battle for the puck and is surprisingly strong considering his size, utilizing this to clear the zone. While he prefers to set up goals more than score he has shown the ability to deflect and shoot the puck well enough in the offensive zone to put the puck in the back of the net. However his best asset is clearly his passing.

Part 5
2015 NHL DRAFT PROSPECTS

Addison, Jeremiah – RW – Saginaw Spirit (OHL) – 6'0" 183

Jeremiah was selected in the first round, 12th Overall by the Saginaw Spirit at the 2012 OHL Priority Selection Draft out of the Toronto Marlboros Minor Midget program. Jeremiah brings his high energy never quit attitude to the Spirit. He forechecks relentless and is willing to finish his checks to separate his man from the puck. He has good skating ability which allows him to cut down time and space. He works very hard in all three zones and is very effifcent in the defensive zone pressuring the puck carrier and getting his stick in lanes. We would like to see Jeremiah get stronger as he lost too many battles, not due to a lack of effort but due to a lack of strength. It will also make him a much more punishing checker. Jeremiah showed flashes of puck skills in the offensive zone, but his offensive upside has looked somewhat limited at this point in his development. Due to a late birthdate, Jeremiah has two more seasons in the OHL to show what he can do before becoming eligible for the 2015 NHL Entry Draft.

Alain, Alexandre – RW – Blizzard du Saint-François (LHMAAAQ) – 5'10" 157

Alain suffered from a tumor last January, which was supposed to keep him off the ice for four to six months. Due to great determination and courage, he came back to practice earlier and came back in great form for the Gatorade challenge in early May. The determination he showed off the ice also translates well on the ice. He is a dynamic and energetic player in all the aspects of his game. He is a tireless worker who wins most of his battles for the puck and the games where he is not the hardest worker on his team are fairly rare. A fluid and explosive skater, Alain gets to loose pucks first and is very smart on his forecheck. He is constant in his efforts and shows a good understanding of the game. He is a complete player with a good hockey sense that is equally as good of a passer as he is a shooter. He creates a lot offensively by cycling the puck along the boards and taking his chances at the right time. He executes simple and quick plays and rarely gets into trouble. He has this ability to insert himself in the slot area and works hard to get his hands on rebounds. He also has a good one-timer. His ability level with the puck is good and he can handle himself in traffic although he is not spectacular like other players. Alain is a responsible player defensively where he is well served by his speed and smartness once again. He can shut down the opposition on the penalty kill and blocks a lot of shot. Alain is a good player that is not outstanding in anything except his superior hockey sense and tireless attitude. This leaves some doubts for the next level as far as his offensive potential is concerned.

Baer, Alec – RC – Vancouver Giants (WHL) – 5'10" 150

Baer signed a WHL contract late into the season and was able to play in a few games with the Giants. He immediately left a positive impression on the team, and will be a crucial piece in the rebuilding phase of the Vancouver organization.

The best asset of Baer is his hockey sense. He seems to always make the right play out on the ice, and read the situation well with and without the puck to put himself in a position to succeed. He is smart on the forecheck and is able to create turnovers in the neutral zone. Baer is not particularly quick, but his stickhandling skills combined with his use of edges makes he difficult to catch out in open ice. Baer displayed good vision, and seemed to have been able to develop chemistry quite quickly with players that he did not play with previously. He was able to find open areas in coverage to get quick shots off and be an open target for a pass from teammates.

Baer's main area of improvement is definitely his upper and lower body strength. He had a tough time winning battles for pucks, and was not always able to stay on his feet when taking a beating physically along the walls. Defensively, Baer was in good position consistently, and even killed penalties a few times and did not look out of place. He used his elite hockey sense to read the play and be responsible in his own zone.

It will be interesting to see how good Baer can be over the course of a full WHL season. He certainly has the talent level to have a successful WHL career and open the eyes of scouts that come to watch him on a nightly basis. If he can get stronger and add to his offensive skills, teams will definitely have a hard time stopping him.

Baird, Mike – LW – Southern Tier Admirals (OMHA) – 6'1" 171

Mike was selected 2nd round, 30th Overall by the North Bay Battalion at the 2013 OHL Priority Selection Draft. Mike is very aggressive player and is easily one of the most physical, border lining on dirty, players you'll find in the draft. He has good size at 6'1" and finishes his checks relentlessly. He will go out of his way just to finish a big check. He's not afraid of using his stick to get an extra shot or two in either. He will even drop the gloves. He will definitely need to try to keep himself in check at the next level, but not going too far that makes him such a difficult player to play against. There have been too many games where he has been noticeably taking retaliatory penalties and just putting his team in a bad place all together. He has pretty good speed for his size and protects the puck well. He has limited offensive upside but cycles the puck very effectively. He does appear to have some offensive tools, but perhaps not all of the instincts, as there have been many times where he has an odd-man rush opportunities and chooses to take a long shot on net rather than driving the puck down low or moving it across to a teammate. Mike is a player who opponents hate to play against, but will need to find the right situation at the next level that allows him to be a difficult player to play against, but can teach him the importance of right place, right time with some of the physical things he does on the ice.

Barwell, Jesse – LC – Oakville Rangers (OMHA) – 5'10" 175

Jesse was selected 2nd round, 26th Overall by the Mississauga Steelheads at the 2013 OHL Priority Selection Draft. Barwell possesses really fantastic explosive speed that he uses to blow by defenders to gain the offensive zone off the rush. He is hard to knock off the puck and can protect it along the wall deep in the offensive zone. He has really great passing abilities, whether it be to start the breakout, or to find an open man in the slot to create good chances and has excellent agility to twist and turn from the opposition to get to the slot for opportunities. He opens up well to take passes off the rush and gets to scoring areas with space as well to put his good hard shot on net. He has great hands and puck skills, and is creative with the puck to move it to scoring areas. He puts good pressure on the forecheck and finishes his hits on the wall. Barwell has all the speed, hustle, and skill to be an offensive contributor at the next level, and should be an early pick at this year's OHL draft. He will need to bring a more consistent effort shift to shift. When he's on he's one of the hardest workers on the ice, but can take the odd shift here and there off. He will need to get stronger before jumping up to the OHL level, but should be able to do so this coming season.

Barzal, Mathew – RC – Seattle Thunderbirds (WHL) – 5'11" 170

Barzal is an elite, offensively skilled centre who has put up points at every level that he played in. He initially started the season at the BCHL level with the Coquitlam Express, and it took him about half a game to adjust to the speed and physicality of the league before he started to display his offensive game once again.

The first thing you notice about Barzal is the fact that he always seems to be around the puck. His hockey instincts are very impressive as he seems to be about 3-4 steps ahead of the play every time. He has very soft, quick hands and he can easily maneuver through traffic and make opponents look silly. Barzal is deceptively quick, and is able to reach top speed in a hurry. He uses his edges well and is able to change directions and catch players standing still. He is not afraid to drive to the net, and does a good job along the boards to slip away from a check and quickly make a play. Barzal's best asset is his playmaking ability. His passes are so often tape to tape, whether it be a backhand saucer pass with speed or a cross ice backdoor play for an easy tap in for his teammate.

The issue with Barzal's game and his early dominance is his work ethic at times without the puck. When he loses the puck off the rush, he takes a wide turn to come back on the backcheck, and not always at full speed. He likes to cheat and take off for the neutral zone before his defensemen are even ready, which is something he needs to watch out for as he is often the centre on the line.

The WHL will definitely be a test for Barzal, and it will be interesting to see just how he adjusts to the physical play, especially as players get faster and smarter. He will also have to work hard without the puck to receive regular ice time as he will fall out of favour very quickly if he is a liability out on the ice defensively.

Beauvillier, Anthony – C – Collège Antoine-Girouard (LHMAAAQ) – 5'9" 159

Anthony had a very good 2012-2013 season, leading the league in goals and being named the league MVP with the Gaulois. The younger brother of Rimouski player Francis Beauvillier, he is an offensive threat every time he steps on the ice and also very dangerous on the man advantage. He is a natural goal scorer and has one of the best shots in Midget AAA: he fires it off without warning with rare velocity and precision. He is very agile on his skates and he creates a lot of space for himself with quick direction changes. Beauvillier is just as fast as a skater as he is stick handling the puck. These abilities, along with his creativity, make him a constant threat on the ice. He also showed good vision on the ice and has a superior hockey a sense. He can execute high-level plays and spot teammates easily. He can bring his intensity level up a notch, making him more aggressive and very hard to contain. He also creates more turnovers when he plays this way. Even though he lacks size, Anthony showed us he was willing to work and be involved in puck battles. He is a dedicated player defensively and acts quickly to support his teammates. His tireless attitude defensively eventually earned him a spot on the penalty kill this season. Although his implication is good, he needs to grow bigger in order to be more effective in his defensive duties and puck battles. He also needs to bring this high energy level we were talking about on a more constant basis. He got away with using his talent only at times, but the tactic won't work at the next level. An excellent skater with a knack to score goals, there is no doubt Beauvillier will be able to bring his offensive production with him in the QMJHL.

Bell, Jason – LD – Laval-Montréal Rousseau-Royal (LHMAAAQ) – 6'1" 185

First of all, Jason Bell is gifted with vision and hockey sense that is way above average. He knows how to take advantage of every little inch of space available on the ice. He opens up a lot of passing options on the ice with his powerful and fluid skating ability. He has very impressive abilities with the puck as well and he likes to go up the ice and support the offense. He has very quick hands when he manoeuvres with the puck as well as a terrific slap shot (arguably the best in the league). Bell likes to use the middle of the ice, both when he passes the puck and when he rushes the puck all the way up to the offensive zone. He likes to support the offense and he puts a lot of pressure to keep the offensive movement going. With all this talent with the puck and superior mobility, it goes without saying that Bell is also excellent on the powerplay. Given his mobility, he plays a very aggressive style in coverage and he excels at poke checking his opponents in one-on-one situations. He has a good gap control and he can close in on an opponent very quickly. He has a tendency to go to the puck too often defensively, leaving some players alone in his coverage. We also question his decision-making, as he tries to do it all by himself too often. Taking a simple approach in critical moments doesn't seem to be part of his game and he can give some costly turnovers. He needs to mature a lot in this area to be effective in the QMJHL. We see Bell as a high-risk high-reward type of pick with all the natural talent and offensive abilities he has. It could be hard for him to get a regular shift at five-on-five next season due to those weaknesses.

Birdsall, Chris – G – Cedar Rapids RoughRiders (USHL) – 5'10" 160

Chris got his break playing for the North Jersey Avalanche of the AYHL during the 2011-2012 season. From there Chris joined the Cedar Rapids RoughRiders and played great for a goaltender who was just 15 to start the season. In fact he impressed so much, the U.S. National Development Program Team picked up Chris to play goaltender for them at the World U-17 Hockey Challenge in Victoriaville/Drummondville. Chris returned to Cedar Rapids and wrapped up what was a very successful season. Chris is a little undersized at the goaltending position, but is highlighted by a quick glove and he presents himself to shooters very well. He has quick reflexes and displays patience and always seems to stay in position allowing himself to not only make the first save but the second and third when necessary. He looks very technically sound already factoring in his age. Thanks to a late birth date, Chris will not be NHL eligible until 2015. This past spring the Kitchener Rangers drafted Chris in the 13th round of the 2013 OHL Priority Selection Draft. However Birdsall is already committed to Boston College.

Bittner, Paul – LW – Portland Winterhawks (WHL) – 6'4" 194

Bittner is a hulking power forward whose play has steadily improved throughout the season. He has gained the trust of the coaching staff, and as a result he has been receiving regular minutes on the 4th line, and did a good job of creating match up problems for opponents with his big frame and good offensive skills.

For a player who is so big, Bittner is a good skater. He needs to work on his acceleration and overall speed still, but he still has a lot of time to develop his skating. He is not particularly skilled, but combined with his size, Bittner is already hard to contain when he goes to the net. He protects the puck well, and he may not deke through opponents, but he can definitely create a good scoring chance by taking the puck to the net. He looked more and more comfortable with the puck on his stick as the season went on, and he could play a big role for the Winterhawks next season offensively.

Booth, Callum – G – Salisbury Prep School (USHS) – 6'2" 185

Booth is a big and tall left-handed goalie who inspires confidence for his teammates with his calm on the ice. He has a standard butterfly technique with an almost flawless technique. He is very compact in front of his net and doesn't give up much space to shooters. He likes to confront shooters and does so while displaying solid rebound control. He has calm and precise movements in front of his net and he is just as good defending a solid clear shot than he is against a quick pass play. The Montreal native rarely makes the first movement and waits for the right moment to get on his knees. He is very hard to beat in the bottom of the net because of his precision but not necessarily explosive movements. He has good concentration and he uses his physical attributes to follow the puck well and locate it through heavy traffic. We also liked his flexibility and how he was able to stretch out at times to make some miraculous saves. He posses solid reflexes with both his glove and blocker. He doesn't go out to handle the puck a lot and seems to prefer to stay in his crease. The only thing we would like him to improve is to add some explosion to his already precise movements in front of the net. He is everything a team is looking for in a goalie with calm on the ice, good rebound control, consistency, size and a very sound technique.

Bracco, Jeremy – RC – NJ Rockets (AJHL) – 5'9" 137

Jeremy was selected 5th round, 84th Overall by the Kitchener Rangers at the 2013 OHL Priority Selection Draft. Bracco has really nice hands and moves to get by defenders, then make good passes on odd-man rush opportunities to create chances. He can open up well while driving to the net with his stick down to take passes and put good shots on from in tight. He battles hard for loose pucks in front of the net and competes in board battles too. He shows a really nice creativity off the rush at times and can make some good breakout passes as well. Bracco cycles the puck effectively in deep in the offensive zone and makes sure to get to the net and battle for his territory. Defensively he provides good support, getting his stick in lanes to breakup plays and passes for the opposition, and puts good pressure on the puck carrier. Jeremy has committed to join the U.S. National Team Development Program for the next two seasons which will include his NHL Draft Year.

Bricknell, Jake – RC – Central Ontario Wolves (OMHA) – 5'11" 194

Jake was selected 2nd round, 38th Overall by the Belleville Bulls at the 2013 OHL Priority Selection Draft. Jake was labeled early by HockeyProspect as one of the best pure hard working competitors available for the 2013 OHL Draft ultimately being selected in the second round by the Belleville Bulls. He forechecks and back checks with great pressure. He goes into the corners, competes like crazy and will do whatever it takes to leave with the puck. Jake shows somewhat limited offensive upside providing a decent shot and efficient passing, but has the mentality and attitude of a player who could go very far in the "grinder" role. Jake hits and hits very hard and will even try to sneak in the odd shot with his stick as well. That being said, Jake will need to eliminate the unnecessary penalties moving forward to be as effective as he can for his team. Walking the line between intense and obstruction may be the biggest turning point on how good Jake becomes at the OHL level. He will need to improve his skating ability. This improvement is important for him at the next level, and will make him that much more dangerous in his role.

Brisebois, Guillaume – LD – Collège Antoine-Girouard (LHMAAAQ) – 5'11" 152

Brisebois is two-way defenseman who proved to be very reliable. He played in the shadow of Jeremy Roy and Anthony Beauvillier with the Gaulois but we liked what we saw. Brisebois is an excellent skater with a good top speed and excellent offensive instincts. He is very fluid in his movements and showed excellent agility. As mentioned, he is a good skater with considerable explosion but he could still improve in this area to make the jump to the QMJHL. Very reliable in his own zone, Brisebois relies on intelligence, mobility, positioning and stick work to be effective defensively. We don't view him as a physical player and there is no doubt he needs to get stronger in order to have an impact in the QMJHL in the upcoming seasons. This physical weakness can lead him into trouble against bigger players, although he never backs down from a puck battle. Brisebois is a player that sees the ice well and never panics with the puck. He never gets into trouble on the transition, taking the easy and safe approach all the time. Indeed, he is able to lead the transition quickly and effectively. He also does well on the man advantage where he makes himself available to teammates and creates some options around the ice. He is also able to support the rush smartly without putting his team in trouble. His wrist shot his good but could be released more quickly in order to maximize its efficiency. His offensive potential is hard to gauge because Jeremy Roy had all the main responsibilities with the Gaulois. We feel Brisebois can become a smart and reliable two way defenseman in the QMJHL if he adds some weight to his frame.

Bruce, Riley – RD – Ottawa Valley Titans (ODHA) – 6'4" 182

Riley was selected 3rd round, 50th Overall by the North Bay Battalion at the 2013 OHL Priority Selection Draft. Bruce has outstanding size as a defenseman but is very raw. Despite his size, his skating could be considered average at this point. He shows good gap control in one on one situations and uses his stick effectively. His physical play has been very hit or miss for us. We've seen him assert himself, but also play too passive for his size. He's good in the corners and can dominate at times at this level because of his natural size. Riley handles the puck very well and makes the smart first pass up ice. He holds the line very well offensively but can struggle a bit while under pressure. Riley is very raw and will need to develop and progress as a young defenseman but he has the potential to be a good defenseman over time.

Burns, Andrew – LD – Oakville Rangers (OMHA) – 5'11" 165

Burns was selected 3rd round, 47th Overall by the Windsor Spitfires in the OHL. Burns is a smooth skating defenseman, who has good agility. He can rush the puck up the ice by either passing or skating effectively and can gain the offensive zone well on the wide drive. He is a smart player who reads the play well to pick off neutral zone turnovers and to step in from the point to provide scoring options then get shots through to the net. On the power play he has great vision to spot an open man then distributes the puck well, and is willing to come down and drive the net with his stick down. He is not a physical player by any means, but plays with good hockey sense and uses his stick and speed well to his advantage. His best chance for success at the next level would be to move the puck up the ice quickly on the breakout for a quick transition game, and to demonstrate an ability to move the puck around well in the offensive zone, especially on the power play. He needs to show that he is not a defensive liability and has to add some strength to his frame as well. Burns also has to show that he makes the right decisions when to jump in on the rush to provide scoring options, while also not giving up odd-man rushes by getting caught in the offensive zone if the puck is turned over. He needs to get stronger as well.

Bushnell, Noah – RW – Sun County Panthers (MHAO) – 6'2" 200

Bushnell was selected 2nd round, 33rd Overall by the Sarnia Sting in the OHL. Bushnell has good size and includes plenty of aggression in his game. He hits hard and opposing players commonly know the next day if they've been on the ice regularly against him. While many players at the Minor Midget need to add muscle to be able to make the jump, Noah is pretty good where he's at and is only going to get stronger so long as he keeps applying himself. While he's highlighted by his physical play, Bushnell has shown some offensive upside. He shows good patience with the puck and creates scoring chances for himself and his teammates. Noah shows the ability to make good passes to set up chance, as well as shooting the puck effectively. While there is a lot of positive in his game there have been some concerns in his game. His skating ability needs to improve. He manages to get a good top speed, but his first few steps are a little sluggish and need to improve. While we love his physical play, he needs to pick his spots a little better. We've seen him take unnecessary penalties and land head checks at crucial times putting his team shorthanded or negating a power play. Noah will remind Sarnia Sting fans of New York Islanders forward Matt Martin. We expect him to make the Sting in his rookie season and play a bottom six role while asserting his physicality and improving his skating.

Capobianco, Kyle – LD – Oakville Rangers (OMHA) – 6'0" 155

Kyle was selected 1st round, 7th Overall by the Sudbury Wolves in the 2013 OHL Priority Selection Draft. Capobianco is easily one of the best puck rushing defensemen in this draft, as his skating and ability to find lanes to skate the puck up the ice are just exceptional. He has really nice hands and agility, and can also distribute the puck fairly well. He jumps up in the offensive zone to provide scoring options and can spot an open man next to the net and get him the puck for good scoring chances. He consistently finds those pass options often in the offensive zone to create opportunities. Capobianco also brings good speed on the rush, but at times tries to unnecessarily dangle his way through the entire opposition resulting in bad turnovers. It would be nice to see him pass the puck up more often through the neutral zone and pick his spots a little bit better to skate the puck up the ice. Defensively he can keep his man to the outside and has displayed a decent gap control as well as an element of physicality, but definitely still needs to add some size. He is pretty strong on his feet however, as he is tough to knock off the puck and protects it well. He has good hands and moves to get to the slot as well in order to put great shots on net from scoring areas. Kyle shows a great deal of intelligence and is primed to debut in the OHL as a 16 year old with the Sudbury Wolves.

Cascagnette, Jacob – LW – Kitchener Jr. Rangers (MHAO) – 6'2" 179

Jacob was selected 4th round, 62nd Overall by the Kitchener Rangers at the 2013 OHL Priority Selection Draft. Jacob is an agile skater which he uses to carry the puck into the offensive zone whenever possible. He also has the ability to beat defenders one on one. Cascagnette forechecks hard and possesses a strong work ethic. He doesn't force plays with the puck and generally will use his skating ability to create time and open up options for himself. He looks comfortable making the decision to shoot or pass based on the situation.

Chabot, Thomas – LD – Commandeurs de Levis (LHMAAAQ) – 6'0" 169

Thomas Chabot is a left-handed defenseman who can be noticed quickly with his ability to control the game when he as possession of the puck. He is mostly an offensive defenseman, but due to his excellent understanding of the game and technique, can be quite effective defensively. He rarely gets beaten along the boards or in the middle of the ice. At first glance, it's easy to think he's not a good skater or that he is too slow for the next level. The reality is that his footing and first few steps when he explodes are not very good, but when he gets going, his skating is very good and even above average. His superior hands are what make him effective with the puck, as they allow him to support the rush and elude extra opponents on the way to the offensive zone. We view him as a premium quarter back on the powerplay, where he is very effective. His smartness also makes him a good candidate to play on the penalty kill. His passing ability is among the best in this draft class. He can execute long plays; side-to-side passes and passes through traffic without problem. Chabot also has a good slapshot although he opts to go with the precision instead of the power. His wrist shot is something to improve as it's not very hard and slow to release. Defensively, he makes a good use of his stick and is patient in one-on-one situations. He is rarely taken off guard but his main weakness is his physical force. He needs to get stronger in order to be more effective. His understanding of the game along with his hands and vision as a passer makes him a solid candidate to make the jump to the QMJHL.

Ciccarelli, Matteo – RC – Sarnia Sting (OHL) – 5'9" 181

Due to his late birthdate, Matteo will still have two more seasons in the OHL before being eligible for the NHL Entry Draft. Matteo split time between the Sting and Lambton Shores Predators Jr. B (GOJHL). Matteo is a hard working forward who was able to take advantage of a few injuries in the second half of the season for Sarnia receiving a regular spot on the fourth line when needed. Ciccarelli has a very awkward skating style that needs to be refined but he seems to have the speed to get to where he needs to go quickly enough. He is a little undersized but will go into corners and battle for the puck. He seemed very adept to the energy role forcing turnovers. He was willing to take the hit to make the play and created a few chances over the course of his time in the OHL. Offensively Matteo's strongest asset is his puck moving ability. He has two years before his draft year comes up and we'd like to see him fix his skating stride because he clearly has the quickness to turn a proper stride into an asset. We would like to see him continue to get stronger and hopefully grow an inch or two to make his style of play more effective. If he keeps putting the work in we expect him to play full time in the OHL next year.

Connor, Kyle – FW – Youngstown Phantoms (USHL) – 6'0" 160

After spending two years with the Detroit Belle Tire U16 program, Kyle made the jump to the USHL joining the Youngstown Phantoms. As the level of play increased so did Kyle's play. Connor put together an outstanding rookie season in the USHL playing a surprisingly large role for a player who opened the season as a 16 year old. Kyle Has good size and possesses excellent work ethic. He's able to create turnovers and create scoring chances for his team. He's a fairly good skater and we hope to see him add some muscle to his frame without losing a step. He handles the puck very well under pressure and shows the ability to both pass and score effectively and regularly at the USHL level. Connor is the kind of player you can put in any game situation in any scenario and is effective for his team. Kyle was also selected in the 13th Round of the 2012 OHL Priority Selection Draft by the Saginaw Spirit. Kyle is committed to join the University of Michigan. Due to his late birthdate, Kyle is ineligible to be selected until the 2015 NHL Entry Draft, but if he continues to develop at this pace, he will be a heavily talked about prospect for this draft.

Coyle, Josh – C – Elgin-Middlesex Chiefs (MHAO) – 6'3" 195

Josh was selected 3rd round 48th Overall by the Peterborough Petes at the 2013 OHL Priority Selection Draft. Coyle has great size and gets the most out of it with good speed. He shows good hockey sense and is very smart with the puck. While he can be caught making the odd mistake, he usually makes the right choice with the puck and showed the ability to shoot and pass well. He uses his size very well along the boards and was consistently visible in puck battles. Josh also shows good physicality finishing his checks whenever possible. Josh is a pretty safe selection. While there's no guarantee the offense translates, he shows tremendous work ethic, has excellent size and uses it to best of his ability proving he can contribute in many different ways, even potentially as a 16 year old in the OHL.

Craievich, Adam – RW – Oakville Rangers (OMHA) – 6'0" 189

Adam was selected 3rd round, 52nd Overall by the Guelph Storm at the 2013 OHL Priority Selection Draft. Craievich's niche in this game could be his ability to play the game in the dirty areas, protect the puck and get and effective cycle going. His greatest asset is his extremely powerful shot. He is very willing and most effective when he plays in front of the opposition's net and opens up in the slot to put shots on net. He puts good pressure on the forecheck to force turnovers and battles for the puck along the wall to walk out into the slot to put shots on net. He can get the puck to the front of the net as he makes great passes to find an open man in the slot for opportunities. He is physical, drives hard to the net and looks to pick up loose pucks and rebounds from in deep in the opposition's zone. To be most effective he is going to have to pick up the tempo of his game and play at a quicker pace. He needs to become a better skater and also needs to make quicker decisions with the puck. If Adam can get a bit stronger he should be a player who's difficult to contain in the offensive zone.

Crawford, Marcus – LD – South Central Coyotes (OMHA) – 5'10" 178

Marcus was selected 3rd round, 44th Overall by the Saginaw Spirit in the 2013 OHL Priority Selection Draft. Crawford is comfortable and willing to rush the puck up the ice and does so with a very high success rate. Marcus is really strong on the puck and shows great agility to evade opposing pressure. He's slightly undersized but is built very solid and strong. Marcus also has an absolute cannon of a shot from the point and uses it at intelligent times. He is smooth and smart with the puck displaying good vision moving it up ice when he doesn't have a lane, or moving it around the offensive zone. While he's very reliable with the puck on his stick, he can get a little ahead of the rush at times, and lose his defensive positioning. He will need to improve his defensive zone coverage moving forward because he does have a fair shot of making the jump to the OHL level. However he shows a lot of potential as an offensive defenseman at the next level.

Crouse, Lawson – LW – Elgin-Middlesex Chiefs (MHAO) – 6'3" 189

Lawson was selected 1st round, 5th Overall by the Kingston Frontenacs at the 2013 OHL Priority Selection Draft. Lawson has about as ideal size as you'll find for a talented forward in this draft. He has shown great offensive potential and is extremely dangerous in the goal area. Lawson has a well built frame, but also possesses deceptive speed and explosiveness when flying down the wing with the puck. He protects the puck well and is dangerous every time he enters the offensive zone. He is calm under pressure with the puck allowing options to open up for him if there aren't any all while maintaining control. He has pretty good hands and has good vision. Lawson has good positioning without the puck and finds a way to make himself available. He shows good balance between shooting the puck and passing it and seems to allow the situation to dictate it. Lawson uses his big frame to cycle the puck effectively as well as win battles and escape from those battles to almost instantaneously create a scoring chance for his team. There is no question that Crouse is one of the best forwards in this draft. We really don't have any major concerns moving forward about Lawson. There were games he wasn't able to quite play at the level he's shown most of the time. The most important thing for him will be to perform at the level he's shown on a regular basis.

Davies, Michael – LW – Southern Tier Admirals (OMHA) – 6'1" 198

Michael was selected 1st round, 13th Overall by the Kitchener Rangers at the 2013 OHL Priority Selection Draft. This is a player who's potential is unlimited, but he needs to play at a quicker pace and has to be more consistent. There are nights where Davies just dominates the game in both ends of the ice, with some great end-to-end rushes and power forward moves to cut towards the net on a wide drive to create fantastic opportunities, but then others where is unnoticeable and uninvolved whatsoever. When he is on though he has incredible vision and passing abilities, as he finds lanes to move the puck in the offensive zone and gets the puck to good scoring areas. He has the hands to beat defenders and create space for himself and he is a smart player who isn't scared to drive the puck to dirty areas. He can find space to work with in the offensive zone and opens up well to take passes and put some good shots on net. He gets to the slot to tip pucks and pick up rebounds, cycles the puck well behind the net and distributes it so effectively in the offensive zone. There are some nights where he holds on to the puck a bit too long and needs to move it quicker to try to push the pace a bit.

De Farias, Joshua – LD – Toronto Marlboros (GTHL) – 5'11" 172

Joshua was selected 5th round, 92nd Overall by the London Knights at the 2013 OHL Priority Selection Draft. Josh is a strong skater who uses a combination of quick feet along with a powerful stride to constantly jump into the offensive rush. He is not afraid to skate the puck out of the defensive zone under pressure and shows confidence and poise when controlling the puck. Josh works hard to gain the offensive blue line and starts many offensive chances with his puck carrying ability. He has also shown on several occasions the ability to hold the line extremely well and keep the play going. He is willing to get involved physically but needs to work on finishing checks regularly and being more involved in front of the net. He collapses well in the defensive zone to battle behind the net and battle along the boards taking away time and space forcing mistakes. Once entering the offensive zone Josh shows good awareness and vision along with solid shot from the point which he regularly gets through from the point. He has good recovery speed and works hard to get back into position after entering the offensive rush. Good footwork and an active stick help Josh keep attackers in front of him and his speed prevents many forwards from gaining an outside step or beating him to loose pucks. Josh needs to improve on his defensive ply. He has had a few mental lapses and will need to try to work these out of his game moving forward. De Farias' hockey sense is very apparent when you see him on the ice. He shows maturity beyond his years and is really the offensive defenseman it seems the Knights have been wishing for, for years.

Deschenes, Luc – RD – Fredericton Canadiens (NBPEIMMHL) – 5'11" 197

Luc Deschenes developed very early as we saw him as a thirteen year old player with Team New Brunswick at Canada Games with players two years older than him. He was in his third season of Midget hockey this season with Fredericton and he is clearly ready for the next step. Luc is an extremely strong defenseman who likes to be physical and aggressive along the boards or in the neutral zone. He anticipates well and can synchronise some spectacular hits. However he has a tendency of hitting players without the puck and in vulnerable positions and will need to be more disciplined. He is also a fluid skater with good footing which allows him to play an aggressive style of hockey, noticeably in one-on-one situations. Although he is mobile, he is not an explosive skater and has average speed. He is another player that likes to join the rush and he has very good abilities with the puck. His reads the play very well and finds teammates quickly with accurate passes. Deschenes has a very good wrist shot and he uses his abilities with the puck to find or open shooting lanes. His slapshot is also very powerful but lacks precision. He shows some boldness offensively at times when he goes very deep in the offensive zone to support his forwards. We question his decision making as he can take bad decisions both with and without the puck. He likes to be aggressive defensively which exposes his team to being outnumbered when he misses a play in the neutral zone. Although he has a good vision, he also makes risky plays with the puck and doesn't have the speed to recover on his mistakes. We noticed a lack of effort at times as well and he ends taking bad penalties at times. His potential doesn't leave any doubts but there are also red lights associated with it.

Eichel, Jack – RC – USNTDP (USHL) – 6'1" 177

Jack started his development with the Boston Jr. Bruins during the 2010-2011 and 2011-2012 season proving his talent at this level and becoming a sure pick for the U.S. National Team Development Program. Jack possesses good size already but is a very smooth skater who controls the puck well and can rush up the ice confidently changing directions on a dime. He shows a high level of offensive awareness reading the play faster than most resulting in excellent positioning and an anticipation for the play going on around him. He isn't afraid to get in the goal area and battle although he will need to get stronger. He never seems set in one spot in the ice, if the front of the net doesn't work he'll get into a good shooting position or vice versa. He has an absolute laser of a shot which he gets off quickly and deceptively. He also has good puck moving ability and can create plays to make everyone on the ice better. Jack shows a willingness to use his skating ability to get back defensively in our viewings. He pressures the puck carrier and can take the puck the other way in a hurry. Due to his late birth date, Jack is not eligible until the 2015 NHL Entry Draft. By the time that happens, Jack currently projects to be one of the top picks in that draft. He may not be able to catch Connor McDavid, but he's proven thus far to be hands down one of the most talented players to enter the NHL Draft in 2015. Jack was also selected in the first round of the 2012 QMJHL Entry Draft by the Halifax Mooseheads. Eichel is committed to Boston University.

Fanjoy, Ben – C – Ottawa Jr. Senators (ODHA) – 6'1" 174

Ben was selected 5th round, 89th Overall by the Ottawa 67's at the 2013 OHL Priority Selection Draft. Ben displays good size and he skates well. He protects the puck when rushing up the ice and showed the ability to elude checks very well for having such a big frame. However he does sometimes try to force these rushes when he shouldn't. Ben makes quick decisions with the puck in the offensive zone and makes some very smart plays creating offense for himself and his teammates. He has been great along the boards in battles using the size and the strength he has to win a lot of battles. He is willing to battle defensively and really does plenty of the little things that make him successful. Ben displays a great deal of potential moving forward, however will need to become more consistent. He looks like a complete player on the ice at times, and showed flashes of taking over, but also disappeared at times.

Franzen, Gustav – RC – HV71 J20 (SWE J20) – 5'11" 161

Gustav has really moved up the rankings with HV71 quickly making it to the J20 league last season despite starting the season as a 15 year old. Gustav put up 15 points in 26 games as a 16 year old in the J20 league, finishing with 7 goals in 7 playoff games just one step away from the men's league, despite not being eligible until the 2015 NHL Entry Draft. Gustav likes to shoot a little more than pass, but he is actually a very skilled playmaker who is capable of creating offense for his linemates in the offensive zone. He has shown good anticipation and utilizes this to create turnovers. When he does shoot, Gustav displays good hands and a moderately quick release. He's very dangerous in alone on the goaltender and has excellent moves on the breakaway. Gustav shows a lot of potential due to his offensive abilities, and with a late birth date he could make an impact before an NHL team can even select him.

Galipeau, Olivier – LD – Phénix du Collège Esther-Blondin (LHMAAAQ) – 6'1" 190

Olivier Galipeau is a two-way defenseman that is effective in all three zones. He has good physical abilities defensively, which helps him win one-on-one battles and to protect the puck along the boards. He likes it when the game is physical and delivers a lot of checks in the defensive zone. He likes to intimidate and keeps it going even after the whistle. He also makes the life hard for anyone playing in front of his goalie's crease. He is attracted by the puck at times defensively and leaves his position when he shouldn't have. He is able to recover most of the time with his long reach. He lacks explosion with his skating going forwards and backwards. This allows some forwards to catch him off guard and beat him with speed. His overall mobility and lateral movements are good but require improvements for the next level. With the puck, Galipeau qualifies as a solid player. He makes the simples from his own zone and uses the board nicely to get the puck out. He doesn't have outstanding abilities with the puck, but is patient and reads his options well. He limits mistakes and is able to circle the puck effectively with quick and accurate passes. He has a good shot from the blueline and uses it well on the powerplay. He is a defenseman that we feel will be successful at the next level, both offensively and defensively.

Gerhart, Austin – RW – Barrie Colts AAA (OMHA) – 6'0" 175

Austin was selected 2nd round, 36th Overall by the Mississauga Steelheads at the 2013 OHL Priority Selection Draft. Gerhart possesses great hands that he uses to drive the puck in tight to the slot to create some excellent chances. He is definitely a goal scorer first who is strong in the goal area and gets open in the offensive goal. He is able to get the cycle game going deep in the offensive zone. He drives the puck wide while protecting it off the rush, then either throws the puck low on net to try to generate rebounds, or moves it to a man driving the net. He brings the puck out of his own end pretty well to lead a man through the neutral zone, and can also make excellent cross-crease passes for chances from in tight. He has an acceleration and quickness to his game and will go to the front of the net in the offensive zone. He is a highly skilled player with really nice hands and moves, but needs to add both size and strength so that he is not knocked off the puck so easily. Austin's skating will need some improvements and we'd like to see him add a little more aggression to his game. He's a great goal scorer and should be able to put the puck in the net at the next level, but he needs to add more to his game.

Greenway, Jordan – LW – Shattuck St. Mary's (USA) – 6'5" 205

Greenway was selected 16th Overall in the first round of the 2013 OHL Priority Selection Draft by the Plymouth Whalers out of the Shattuck St. Mary's Program. Greenway has absolutely huge size for someone his age and is one of the most purely talented player in North America among the 1997 birthdates. He already knows how to use his size intelligently to protect the puck. If you can believe it this giant winger is actually a very good skater. He has an excellent skill set and rarely misses when he gets a chance to score. He has good hockey sense and will have a tough choice to make moving forward, but you can believe the Whalers will do everything they can to bring this game changer to

Plymouth. There's a lot to like about Jordan but if there was anything we'd like to see him improve upon it's being more physical.

Hanifin, Noah – LD – St. Sebastian's School (Prep-MA) – 6'3" 185

Noah is a name to remember, as he already shows the tools to be an elite NHL talent. He lacks any distinct weaknesses, with great size, excellent skating, strong puck skills, and a refined defensive game. He plays with an outstanding mixture of poise and aggression, looking calm on the ice while remaining constantly involved in the action. He tracks the play well with strong hockey sense and exceptional positioning, getting in the way of shots and passes with an active stick and playing the body well to separate opponents from the puck. He lacks a consistent mean streak but he can and does play physical. With the puck he is poised and smooth, able to carry end-to-end and make plays or stretch the play with long bomb passes. He makes the safe play when necessary and can also restart the offense by turning back into his defensive zone when he senses pressure, maintaining his composure and allowing his teammates more time to get open. He's an excellent powerplay quarterback with a heavy shot, great lateral movement, and smart puck distribution. If there's a criticism to be made, it's that at times he tries to do too much with the puck, but he's so far ahead of most of his peers that it would be a huge coaching mistake to constrain him too much. Hanifin is slated to play for Boston College starting in 2015, and has committed to the US National Team Development Program for this fall.

Harding, Sam – C – York-Simcoe Express (OMHA) – 6'0" 161

Sam was selected 2nd Round, 31st Overall by the Oshawa Generals in the 2013 OHL Priority Selection Draft. Sam is a speedy player with great skating and is dangerous when he can find open space to work with. He has also shown well controlling the puck under pressure. He moves the puck really well and has good presence in the goal area. He is in great positioning both in the offensive and defensive zone. Sam displays good hockey sense to make good decisions with the puck and created plays for himself and his line mates. Sam will need to add some muscle to his frame and withstand the physical play at the OHL level and become a little stronger. He was a little inconsistent with his work ethic, particularly when the physicality picked up.

Henley, David – LD – Forestiers d'Amos (LHMAAAQ) – 6'2" 174

After brothers Samuel and Cedrick played in the QMJHL, it is time for the younger brother David to make his mark next year. Unlike his two brothers, David is a defenseman and you notice him quickly with his big frame. He is a physical force on the ice and can shut down the opposition with his body and long reach. He is very effective defensively at five-on-five and he rarely loses a one-on-one battle along the boards or deep in his zone. He makes a great use of his sticks and blocks a lot of shots around the net area. His reliability diminishes in the neutral zone and when there is more space due to a lack of mobility, mostly laterally. He struggles covering faster and explosive players and needs to improve his quickness on his pivots. He is a decent skater when going straight forward but lacks explosion. His play with the puck is good as he keeps it under control and makes simple plays. He can contribute on the penalty kill as well with his long reach as he covers a lot of ice and passing lanes. He also has a good slapshot that can be used on the powerplay. Although he can be effective with the puck with simple plays, his decision making is not always good. He takes a lot of chances and the neutral zone and often tries to get the puck out of his zone in risky places. He will need to cut down on those mistakes if he wants a regular spot in the line-up in the QMJHL. Henley represents an interesting project who will be a valuable defenseman once he improves his speed.

Holmes, Michael – LD – Barrie Colts (OMHA) – 6'2" 166

Michael was selected 2nd round, 28th Overall by the Saginaw Spirit in the 2013 OHL Priority Selection Draft. Michael is a smart two-way puck moving defender, he is more of a quiet unassuming type of defenseman that really stands out for having exceptionally strong positioning and rarely making a mistake. He features a strong slap shot from the point when given the opportunity to let fly. Holmes shows good decision making and awareness by constantly making good pinches that keep plays alive and created mismatches down low. He is good at using an active stick and has very strong skating ability which helps him keep defenders to the outside and is strong at getting into passing lanes to break up plays through the middle of the ice. Michael needs to work on incorporating a consistent physical aspect to his game and work at becoming tougher and meaner in the corners and in front of the net. Michael moves the puck really well setting up the breakout and is capable of finding lanes to rush the puck up ice as well. Michael has great size and is a player we feel has a great shot to make the OHL next season thanks to his size and skill. He will however need to get stronger, and we'd like to see him become a little more physically aggressive at the next level.

Helvig, Jeremy – G – Toronto Red Wings (GTHL) – 6'3" 194

Jeremy was selected 3rd round, 45th Overall by the Kingston Frontenacs at the 2013 OHL Priority Selection Draft. Jeremy is a huge goaltender for the Toronto Red Wings. Jeremy is one of the biggest goaltending prospects available in this year's draft and his size helps him cover large areas of the net from all positions. He is good at limiting or controlling rebound opportunities and is good at battling to gain control of any rebounds that he does let out. Jeremy shows great poise and confidence and does not allow goals to get him flustered and off his game. Helvig shows solid lateral movement and excels at sliding across and getting his pads on back door scoring opportunities. He flashes a nice glove hand and is very hard to beat upstairs. He shows solid puck skills and is not afraid of coming out of his net to wrangle pucks on long dump-ins. Jeremy needs to make sure he stays out at the front of the crease and keep good angles as he does occasionally allow himself to get deep into his net which doesn't utilize his excellent size fully. Jeremy stole games all season long for the Red Wings.

Henley, Troy – RD – Oakville Rangers (OMHA) – 5'11" 186

Troy was selected 2nd round, 20th Overall by the Ottawa 67's at the 2013 OHL Priority Selection Draft. Henley has great size, and was quite possibly the most underrated player for the 2013 OHL Draft, proof of this found him falling to the second round where Ottawa stole him. He is physical along the boards and always takes care of business in his own zone. He is excellent in one on one situations, and always seems to have the ideal positioning in the defensive zone. While he is known as a reliable defensive defenseman, part of that is a bias that comes with an offensive talent such as Capobianco. Henley would constantly get into good defensive positioning early as he was the rock that allowed Capobianco to be a little more adventurous in the offensive zone. We feel that Henley has some untapped offensive upside as well. He has a hard shot from the point that he can get on target and will step into the high slot off the point as well for shots. He is intelligent with the puck and very rarely will make the wrong decision with the puck. His skating and agility is very strong as he is built well physically. He gets in lanes to block shots and passes and will step up on his man to take his time, space, and the puck away as well. Troy really doesn't have any flaws. It would be great if he was a little taller, but there really isn't anything to complain about beyond that. His character has been regarded as exceptional and he is very openly considered to be one of the best leaders out of this draft. Troy could take on a captaincy role in the OHL fairly early in his career because of this.

Kaura, Rocky – RD – Mississauga Rebels (GTHL) – 6'2" 200

Rocky was selected 4th round, 63rd Overall by the Barrie Colts at the 2013 OHL Priority Selection Draft. Rocky is a steady stay at home defender for the Mississauga Rebels. Rocky is effective at using his body in the defensive zone to initiate and finish body checks along the walls and in the corners and is able to knock most forwards off of pucks with ease. He utilizes an active stick to keep attackers in front of him and uses a solid backward skating ability to push defenders to the outside while not allowing them a good lane to the net. Rocky does have a strong slap shot although he needs to get into better positions along the blue line to really make it effective. He needs to work on slowing things down in the defensive zone as he sometimes wraps pucks around the boards without looking when he is panicked leading to some risky turnovers. Kaura has an unusual skating style and looks almost as if his head is down when he is skating with the puck, which could prove costly cutting through the neutral zone. He must also work on reading the play in the defensive zone before acting as he sometimes finds himself running around and out of position. He's at his best when he keeps the game as simple as possible. He has shown some good puck decisions but is very inconsistent in this area and will need to improve his skating stride greatly before making the jump to the OHL level.

Knott, Graham – LW – York-Simcoe Express (OMHA) – 6'2" 158

Graham was selected 2nd round, 40th Overall by the Niagara Ice Dogs at the 2013 OHL Priority Selection Draft. Graham missed time this year due to injuries. Unfortunate timing slowed his development a bit but he's still been very noticeable in our viewings of him. Graham has excellent size but still has room to add muscle. He has very good hands and controls the puck well. He drives the net hard with strong puck protection. Graham is extremely difficult to contain in the goal area and has been lethal when picking up rebounds or getting open for passes, rarely missing on his opportunities with a strong shot. Graham is very elusive along the boards despite his size and can protect the puck and elude traffic for extended periods of time. Graham is not just a force in the offensive zone. He's good at forcing turnovers in the neutral zone and has been very efficient on the penalty kill. He puts great pressure on the point and is more than willing to block shots, and blocked a ton consistently in our viewings. While we'd like to see him touch up his skating, we'd like to see him add more muscle, ultimately we feel Graham is ready to make the jump to the OHL next season. He's not the most dynamic or creative player, but he plays a game very well suited not just for the OHL but a pro style of game as well.

Konecny, Travis – C – Elgin-Middlesex Chiefs (MHAO) – 5'9" 162

Travis was selected 1st Overall by the Ottawa 67's at the 2013 OHL Priority Selection Draft. Travis Konecny has shown the potential to be a franchise player in the OHL and has already paved himself a great path leading to potentially being a very high draft pick in a future NHL Entry Draft. Konecny has outstanding speed and has a lot of shiftiness in his game allowing him to change directions on a dime. He eludes contact extremely well. Every year there seems to be players Travis' size who are highly regarded. What separates Konecny from this is his intelligence level with and without the puck. Travis cannot be labeled as a shooter or a passer, he reads situations exceptionally well and makes the decision to give his team the best chance to succeed on the play. He handles contact well and looks to be fairly strong allowing him to control the puck with contact and keep going. Travis shows some impressive physical play despite being slightly undersized he hits fairly hard and isn't shy around this area of the game. He has game breaking tendencies and can take over a game. Even in instances when we try to focus on other players, he will do something special every game we see him play. Travis has shown to be effective defensively and worked hard in his own zone in our viewings. He was put on the penalty kill in our viewings and was capable of pressuring the point well which created turnovers. We expect Travis to be a key member of the Ottawa 67's right out of the gate. He has exceptional talent and can do amazing things with or without the puck.

Korostelev, Nikita – RW – Toronto Jr. Canadiens (GTHL) – 6'0" 187

Korestelev was selected 1st round, 9th Overall by the Sarnia Sting in the OHL. Nikita was an elite offensive talent for the Jr. Canadiens. Nikita shows excellent offensive instincts and is adept at picking off passes through the neutral zone creating quick counter attacks and odd-man rushes. He has many great assets but his greatest may be his shot; one that could arguably be the hardest in the entire draft. Nikita is strong on his feet and possesses a good burst of speed when entering the offensive zone giving him the ability to beat defenders both wide and up the middle. However skating wise Korostelev will need to improve his quickness and footwork. He has an elite scoring touch and is very good at finishing offensive chances in tight or setting up opponents in quality scoring situations. Korostelev uses his body to shield opponents from the puck and is excellent at controlling puck possession in the offensive zone causing defenders to run around to attempt to win it back. Nikita has a laser of a wrist shot and is very good at cutting to the middle before putting it on net. He is effective at making all the little plays that will help him be successful at the next level such as creative offensive movements and putting pucks in good positions for his linemates to make plays with. For being such an elite offensive talent, Korostelev is also not scared to initiate contact with opponents and shows no apprehension battling in the corners or in front of the net. Like many skilled offensive players there is room for improvement in his defensive zone work. Nikita is good at helping out down low but occasionally starts running around and trying to do too much in the defensive zone. Nikita is at his best when he is skating with the puck and using offensive creativity to beat defenders 1-on-1 thus generating numerous offensive opportunities. Consistency will be an important area for

Nikita to improve upon moving forward. Nikita is expected to potentially take on a top six role immediately with the Sting who will likely be taking a step back with the lost of so many key players.

Kovacs, Robin – LW – AIK J18 (SWE J18) – 6'0" 157

Despite not being NHL Eligible until 2015, he already has set foot on the ice in Sweden's top men's league, Elitserien. He spent most of the season with AIK's J18 team where he scored nearly 2 points per game. Robin took his skills to the international stage helping Sweden win Gold at the World U-17 Challenge. Robin shows excellent vision with the puck allowing him to move it well and reading options at a high speed. He is capable of creating chances for his teammates on a regular basis. He skates well and shows good hands in the offensive zone creating offensive chances. Robin has two years before he's eligible for the NHL Draft and will look to gain muscle in that time and continue to play his game. It's exciting to see a prospect at this age show the type of vision he showed at numerous points in our viewings.

Kreis, Matthew – LC – Halton Hurricanes (OMHA) – 5'10" 155

Matthew was selected 1st round, 15th Overall by the Barrie Colts at the 2013 OHL Priority Selection Draft. Kreis plays the game with a great center of gravity, getting down low to the ice so that when combined with his strength it is nearly impossible to knock him off the puck. He has explosive speed that he uses to blow by defenders, and great agility to twist and turn his way out of trouble. He has hands and moves that will keep you mesmerized to watch, while he dangles his way through the opposition on end-to-end rushes. He protects the puck extremely well and is so calm and patient with the puck as well, waiting for his options to open up but he can also make plays at high speed. He has some great vision and passing to find both the open man in the slot and a lane to get him the puck in order to create some fantastic opportunities. What makes him so effective is that he takes all the skills that he has, and uses them effectively, to drive the puck towards the net and makes sure to get to the inside lanes, but is also capable of efficiently working the puck around the perimeter. He competes and battles for the puck and plays a solid two-way game as well, hustling back to provide some good support in his own zone. The only concern with this player may be the fact that at times he tries to do too much himself, as he knows that he is the best player on the ice, and could definitely try to use his teammates more when making plays.

Kreis, Mitchell – RD – Halton Hurricanes (OMHA) – 5'11" 139

Mitchell was selected 3rd round, 49th Overall by the London Knights at the 2013 OHL Priority Selection Draft. Kreis is a smooth skating defenseman with really nice strength and speed to rush the puck up the ice into the offensive zone. He has a great shot that he can keep down low and on target from the point and will step into the high slot to provide options in the offensive zone. He moves the puck very well in the offensive zone and can make some great passes to start the rush but will also join the rush as whenever possible. He is very agile and strong on the puck, as he is so tough to knock off of it. He forces his man to the outside and then finishes him off along the boards to separate them from the puck and uses his stick nicely as well to knock the puck away from the opposition. He needs to watch the turnovers trying to skate the puck out of his own zone, as he turns the puck over far too often when he is the last man back and definitely has a risk factor associated with him, but the upside potential for this defenseman is enormous. Mitchell seemed to get better and better every time we saw him play.

Laishram, Adam – RW – Whitby Wildcats (OMHA) – 5'8" 155

Adam was selected 4th round, 78th Overall by the Belleville Bulls at the 2013 OHL Priority Selection Draft. Adam may not be very big but he plays with a lot of heart and brings his energy every game. He's a great skater who is very difficult to contain. He has shown good skill in our viewings handling the puck well and is capable of putting the puck in the net but is also able to help set up his line mates. Adam is solid in all three zones putting pressure on the puck carrier. He will have the occasional mental lapse, sometimes this occurs at some bad moments, but for the most part he's very reliable with the puck. Moving forward Adam not only has work ethic, but some good puck skills to bring with him to the next level. He skates very well but will need to get stronger to reach his full potential.

Lemcke, Justin – RD – Whitby Wildcats (OMHA) – 6'2" 192

Justin was selected 1st round, 18th Overall by the Belleville Bulls at the 2013 OHL Priority Selection Draft. Lemcke has some really great size, and is an effective skating. He uses his stick really well to check the puck away from the opposition and keep them to the outside. He can move the puck well, and is willing to jump up on the rush to put some low shots on net to try to generate rebounds. He is capable of making some really solid long passes to spring a teammate at the far blue line. He can hold the offensive line and is calm with the puck. He reads plays well and can intercept passes. He will jump up on the rush at times and has some good agility, but just needs to watch some of his turnovers through the middle of the ice. We would also like to see Justin use his size more aggressively and develop a mean streak.

Lizotte, Cameron – LD – Nickel City Sons (NOHA) – 6'1" 185

Cameron was selected 2nd round, 25th Overall by the Peterborough Petes at the 2013 OHL Priority Selection Draft. Cameron displays a great combination of size and skill that could see him emerge as one of the best defensemen out of the 2013 OHL Draft. Cameron has excellent size and likes to use it as often as possible. He's physical along the boards and in open ice. He rarely passes up the opportunity to finish his check. Despite his size and strength, Lizotte is a very good skater and rushes the puck up ice effectively. We've seen moments where he has gone end to end with the puck, eluding checkers then scoring after entering the zone. He's got a quick and accurate shot, but seems to keep it simple with the puck in the offensive zone. Defensively he matches up very well one on one and wins most of these battles using both his stick and his body to separate the opponent from the puck. Cameron such a great array of natural ability, what could push him down the rankings is the puck playing mistakes in his zone. Usually a couple times per game we'll see a frustrating play with the puck resulting in turnovers, some have resulted in goals against. He also can go out of his way to finish his check putting him out of position for the oncoming play. Both of these can be resolved by Cameron simplifying his play a little. He can sometimes try to do too much because more often than not he's the most talented player on the ice. That will change when he reaches the OHL level and he will need to control his decisions and take less chances to make him as successful as he can. We can see Cameron making an immediate impact in the Petes' line-up.

MacArthur, Tyler – RD – Barrie Jr. Colts (OMHA) – 6'3" 174

Tyler was selected 2nd round, 37th Overall by the Owen Sound Attack. MacArthur is calm and patient with the puck, and can lead the rush with some excellent breakout passes for a quick transition. He steps in from the point on the pinch to hold the puck in the zone and keep the attack alive. He also controls the puck deep in the offensive zone well when doing so. He has a good shot that he keeps down low on target from the point. He can find the open man next to the net in the offensive zone with his passes, and has the patience to wait for a lane to open up to get his shot through. He is willing to jump up on the rush and put some good low shots on net to try to generate rebounds. Tyler is not excessively physical but is a fairly effective checker when he chooses to. Our concerns moving forward for Tyler, and what may hold him back is we've seen some questionable decision making with the puck, especially while under pressure. He can lose his positioning and get caught watching the play a little too much. He also loses battles that a defenseman his size should win. There is no doubt in our mind that Tyler's talent and size will make him an attractive option fairly high in the draft, but in saying that we may have him ranked a little lower due to a few of those concerns. Regardless, Tyler should have a great chance at making the OHL next season.

Marner, Mitchell – RC – Don Mills Flyers (GTHL) – 5'8" 130

Mitchell was selected 1st round, 19th Overall by the London Knights at the 2013 OHL Priority Selection Draft. Mitchell showed elite potential offensive talent for the Don Mills Flyers. Mitchell is a good skater and shows acceleration when skating with the puck. Mitchell is very shifty and is constantly making opponents miss putting themselves out of position. He shows excellent puck skills and has the creativity and ability to constantly beat defenders in 1-on-1 situations. Marner also displays an elite scoring touch and is good at beating goaltenders with a variety of different dekes and both slap and wrist shots from all areas of the offensive zone. He shows excellent playmaking skills, constantly making his linemates better by putting setting them up in great scoring situations. He is a threat to score on every shift and if he does not have the puck he is in constant puck pursuit. Marner is also reliable in the defensive zone and is good at helping out down low and uses his skating ability to skate pucks out of trouble situations. He is utilized in both power play and penalty kill situations for the Flyers and works hard to do the little things such as blocking shots in order to get his team the win. Although small in stature, Mitchell is not afraid to take a hit to make a play and does not shy from contact in front of the opposition net. Size is his biggest issue going forward although he has shown that he has the shiftiness and vision to keep out of trouble areas. Mitchell also needs to work on shortening his shifts as he appears tired and lacks back checking towards the end of some shifts.

Mayo, Cole – RD – Elgin-Middlesex Chiefs (MHAO) – 6'0" 200

Cole was selected 3rd round, 42nd Overall by the Erie Otters at the 2013 OHL Priority Selection Draft. Cole has proven over the course of this season to be a very well rounded defenseman for Elgin-Middlesex. It begins with Cole's vision and hockey sense. He reads situations very well allowing him to get into necessary positioning to make the right play. He shows good vision with the puck moving it well in all three zones. Cole occasionally made a mistake with the puck in our viewings, but these were usually few and far between. He shows a lot of potential offensively with his decision making and was a key part of the Chiefs' power play this season. Cole showed a great point shot that found it's way through most of the time and is usually easily deflectable. He has proven to be effective on the penalty kill clearing the zone and winning battles. Although we would like to see him play a little more physical he battles extremely hard in his own zone and is more than capable of winning battles. Cole is a defenseman who we feel can step into the OHL right away and help out the Otters. There really isn't a specific area of weakness for Mayo, we just want to see him continue to refine his game

McCool, Hayden – C – Whitby Wildcats (OMHA) – 6'3" 190

Hayden was selected 1st round, 6th Overall by the Niagara Ice Dogs at the 2013 OHL Priority Selection Draft. Hayden is a big skilled centerman who is a very smooth skater and moves well for his size. He is especially effective picking up the pick in the defensive zone and utilizing a good combination of speed and awareness to carry the puck up ice and enter the offensive zone. He uses his size well in the offensive zone to shield opponents from the puck and usually chooses good options with the puck. He is also very effective on the cycle. McCool shows a good scoring touch and gets into great scoring positions in the offensive zone. He has a very powerful shot which he can get off quickly but also shows solid playmaking abilities. He looked particularly effective on the power play moving the puck to open linemates and setting up scoring opportunities. He is not afraid to engage physically and does not shy away from hits along the boards or in open ice. We've seen him engage in some pretty big physical wars over the course of the season. The only thing that will hold Hayden back at this point is his decision making. While he commonly makes good decisions there have been some major mental lapses at times to the point that hockey sense is a bit of a question mark for us when the game gets faster and tougher. He would like to see him improve his first few steps as well. He generates good speed, and has a powerful stride but his first few steps will make him that much more complete in the skating department. Hayden also needs to become a little more consistent offensively. He has all the making of a great offensive forward in the OHL and beyond, but we need to see him make some of these improvements.

McDavid, Connor – LC – Erie Otters (OHL) – 5'11" 175

Connor was selected first overall at the 2012 OHL Priority Selection Draft after being granted exceptional player status. Connor was selected by the Erie Otters out of the Toronto Marlboros Minor Midget program and made an immediate impact in the Ontario Hockey League.

Connor is indeed an 'exceptional' talent, who has very special skating ability. He is able to reach top gear almost instantaneously, and displays unbelievable elusiveness when opponents try to stop him.

His vision is exceptional as he shows the ability to shoot the puck with a lightning quick release but is also is able to complete passes that seem to be impossible. Connor isn't afraid to go into the corners, although he doesn't play with a lot of toughness, he is willing to finish his check here and there, and can escape from corners with the puck. McDavid needs to be monitored at all times on the ice, as he only needs a split second to make something happen.

Defensively he shows a willingness to get back and help out. He doesn't always rush back and that is something we wouldn't mind seeing a little more of, but he does compete when he gets back. Connor is a player we feel may be the most talented player to come along since Sidney Crosby. It is truly a treat to watch him work his magic. If he was eligible right now we believe any team would select him first overall at either the 2013 or the 2014 NHL Entry Drafts. He is truly developing as a player who only comes along a few times in a generation, and we look forward to watching Connor grow as a young man, and prepare to become a star in the NHL.

McFadden, Garrett – LD – Grey-Bruce Highlanders (OMHA) – 5'10" 195

Garrett was selected 1st round, 12th Overall by the Guelph Storm at the 2013 OHL Priority Selection Draft. McFadden has pretty decent size to his frame, but is also possesses great skating ability with explosive strides and good acceleration. He jumps up on the rush to join the attack and drive hard to the net. He has good hands and can protect the puck well on the rush, and is also able to pass the puck up out of the zone effectively. He creates offense constantly for his team and is very dangerous in the offensive zone. Although he can get too caught up in the offensive game and get caught up ice. He uses his stick nicely to check the puck away from the opposition, and goes down to block shots as well. He has agility to twist away from the opposition, is calm with the puck and finds lanes to rush the puck end-to-end to get it in deep. He is physical along the wall and is able to separate his man from the puck and communicates with his teammates to direct the play. He can read the play to pick off turnovers, holds the offensive zone well and will step into the high slot to take passes and put some great shots on net. This could turn out to be one of the top defensemen to come out of this draft because he possesses the complete package between size, strength, speed, skating, hockey sense and skills.

McKenzie, Brett – LC – Oakville Rangers (OMHA) – 6'1" 181

Brett was selected 1st round, 10th Overall by the North Bay Battalion at the 2013 OHL Priority Selection Draft. McKenzie could turn out to be one of the best players from the 2013 OHL Draft. He has all the tools to be successful including great size, strength, speed, skill and sense. He plays the power forward game with exceptional hands and scoring touch. He has great skill with the puck, but also has a fantastic sense of the game without the puck, to get to scoring areas with space and open up to take passes and put good shots on net. He is willing to drive the puck to the net, protects it really well in doing so and cycles the puck very effectively in the offensive zone. His passing is also exceptional, as he can spot the open man, the lanes that are available to move the puck, and he passes the puck to lead a man into an open space for him to be successful with time and space to shoot the puck from a good scoring area. In other words instead of passing the puck where a player is, he passes it to where they are going, or where they should be. He is very strong and tough to knock off the puck, and can read the play well to pick off passes and force turnovers. The only real area he could use some improvement, might be that he could be hungrier for the puck in battles to come out with the puck more often, which could make him even more of a dominant force than he already is.

Meloche, Nicolas – RD – Vikings de St-Eustache (LHMAAAQ) – 6'1" 200

Meloche is without a doubt one of the most complete defensemen available in the QMJHL draft. When we saw him play, it seems like he didn't have any weaknesses in his strong performances. He is an athletic player who likes to be physical along the boards and in front of his net. He likes to punish his opponents and is an intimidating player on the ice. He has powerful strides when he skates and that allows him to be more aggressive without being scared of making a mistake. His footing is quick and fluid, making him very effective in coverage along with his long reach. He can close the gap between him and an opponent quickly and is able to deliver some perfectly timed hits. He has a rare combination of size and physical ability for a player of his age. Meloche also excels with the puck from the back end: he has a good vision and shows good decision making on the transition. He can execute hard plays but also doesn't mind using simple passes to break out of his zone. He also has the tools and confidence with the puck to rush it out of the zone by himself. His powerful shot also makes him a good candidate for the powerplay, where he can accumulate points. His slapshot needs some work as far as the precision is concerned, but his wrist shot is far more reliable. One weakness that came up to us is his consistency from game to game. He can be the best player on the ice and he can be the worst. All that being said, we view Meloche as a franchise defenseman who will log big minutes in the future.

Mercer, Cullen – RC – Huron-Perth Lakers (MHAO) – 5'11" 168

Mercer was selected 3rd round, 57th Overall by the Plymouth Whalers in the 2013 OHL Priority Selection Draft. Mercer has a tremendous shot and wasn't shy about showing it off as he was one of only five players playing in the Alliance Minor Midget AAA division to reach the 20 goal mark during the Regular Season. He was also the leading goal scorer in the playoffs on the date his Lakers were eliminated from the Alliance Semifinals. Mercer possesses slightly above average skating ability and is a very offensive minded player. He has good patience with the puck and his vision is strong which allows him to take advantage of his offensive ability. He has pretty good size but will need to dedicate himself to adding muscle to give him the best possible chance to make the jump to the OHL in September. He is capable of protecting the puck well down low and fends off defenders effectively. As far as Cullen's game goes, we do need to see him be more dedicated to the defensive side of the game. In our viewings there wasn't a great deal of urgency to get back into positioning. He shows a good compete level but it needs to be more consistent. While his offensive skills are good, he won't be able to survive alone on them. However with some adjustments we see very good OHL level potential in him and believe he can eventually become a strong goal scorer at the next level.

Miller, David – RC – Sault Ste. Marie Greyhounds (OHL) – 5'10" 155

David was selected in the 6th Round of the 2012 OHL Priority Selection Draft by the Sault Ste. Marie Greyhounds from the 2012 OHL Cup Champion Mississauga Rebels. Miller is a player we had ranked higher than he was selected in the OHL Draft and he proved why during the 2012-2013 season. David played the majority of his rookie season with the Georgetown Raiders of the OJHL putting up almost a point per game before joining the Greyhounds. David played a handful of games for Sault Ste. Marie putting up three assists in 5 games giving everyone a preview of what he is capable of. David is an undersized offensive centre but shows good offensive instincts and creative one on one moves. David is a very strong skater and can control the puck well. He is also a very skilled puck mover and although he can hold onto the puck for long periods of times he's more of a passer than a shooter. Miller saw some time in the 2013 OHL Playoffs for the Greyhounds after Jared McCann was knocked out of action and was effective at creating offensive chances and did not look out of place at all. David is expected to make the Greyhounds and will likely get some opportunities in offensive roles. He has the benefit of a late birthdate so he still has two more seasons to go before he's eligible for the NHL Entry Draft.

Moore, Ryan – C – Detroit Belle Tire (USA T1) – 5'8" 150

Due to the Spitfires not having a first round pick, Ryan turned out to be Windsor's first pick selected 2nd round, 35th Overall. Moore looks like one of the ever-increasing number of small, highly skilled players whose lack of size won't be a major hindrance. Ryan is an explosive skater who can blast through open spaces. He's very difficult to contain let alone defend and is very elusive. He displays great puck skills in all aspects, and is very intelligent with his decisions. He competes very hard and also shows a lot of natural creativity and of course the ability to put the puck in the back of the net.

Murray, Liam – LD – Eastern Ontario Wild (ODMHA) – 6'0" 191

Murray was selected 3rd round, 43rd Overall by the Windsor Spitfires in the OHL. Liam provides a good combination of size and skating. He's slightly above average height and skates well in all directions. Liam displayed good puck moving abilities in all three zones. He sends a good hard first pass out of his zone, but was also calm with the puck making the smart decisions. Liam shows the ability to skate end to end with the puck while being elusive in the neutral zone to evade checks. He has a hard shot from the point which he uses well. Liam displays very good physical play but needs to pick his spots a little better to prevent putting himself out of position. Defensively he's good with his stick getting in passing lanes and breaking plays up. He competes hard in his own end but can occasionally lose positioning. Liam is a valuable defenseman who may not go in the first round, but has the upside of a second round pick and has a good chance to play in the OHL next season.

Musil, Adam – RC – Red Deer Rebels (WHL) – 6'1" 182

Musil is a physical forward who was quite impressive when he was called up to play in a handful of games this season. He made his presence felt with his work along the boards as he consistently won puck battles and was able to create good offensive chances. Musil played with good poise, and he was able to keep up with the play admirably. He was not afraid to go to the net to try to score off of rebounds, and while he did not pick up any points in the 6 games that he played in with the Rebels, he was able to consistently create scoring chances for himself and his teammates. He still has some work to do in terms of defensive play to be in good position at all times, especially because he is a centre. Musil certainly has the size and strength to play at the junior level already, and just his skating and hands have to catch up for him to be a force for the Rebels in the future.

Myllari, Kris – LD – Ottawa Jr. Senators (ODHA) – 6'1" 173

Kris was selected 2nd round, 34th Overall by the Kingston Frontenacs at the 2013 OHL Priority Selection Draft. Kris displays excellent size at the defense position. He displays slightly above average skating ability and uses it to rush the puck effectively. He is able to acquire the offensive zone with his skating but also likes to get the puck deep. Maybe his best attribute is his powerful shot from the point but missed the net a little too often. Kris showed well in one on one matchup's. He can at times give too much space but did win most of his one on one matchups taking the body fairly often. He is very strong along the boards and works hard winning the battles. He is pretty tough out front and clears the front of the goal well for his goalie. Kris has improved quite a bit from the start of the season. We want to see him keep getting stronger. He shows smart simple plays on the point, but appears to be more of a shutdown defenseman who can provide flashes of offense.

Noel, Nathan – C – Shattuck St-Mary's Midget Prep (USHS) – 5'10" 158

Although Nathan Noel was born in Newfoundland, he spent the last two seasons playing for the prestigious Shattuck St-Mary's program south of the border. He was able to tally 40 points in the 2012-2013 season, making him the first 15 year old player on the U18 team since Emerson Etem in 2007-2008. Nathan is a smart player with the ability to play at both ends of the ice. He is an outstanding skater with a good explosion and solid top speed. He uses this skating ability to control the offensive game in the neutral zone and to backcheck in the defensive zone and provide some help for his defensemen. He is also an excellent passer, making quick decisions and showing an impressive ease to execute hard plays. He eases the transition phase of the game for his team with this vision. Noel has all the tools to become an impact offensive player at the junior level: quick hands, high-end tools with the puck, elusiveness, good puck control at high speed and a good wrist shot with a quick release. He also excels at gaining and creating space on the ice by using both talent and skating ability. His knack to score spectacular goals makes him an electric player to watch with the puck. Nathan also showed his aptitude to be a physical player and we loved his competition level at the Gatorade Challenge. He showed the work ethic of a leader and seemed to give it all he had. He showed off his physical abilities on numerous occasions, driving the net to score several goals and winning his share of puck battles. When you combine all this with his high-end tools and hockey sense, you have a very complete player. As mentioned, his hockey sense also allows him to anticipate plays and create turnovers. He also uses his intelligence in the defensive zone where has good positioning and is a strong support for his team.

Orban, Ryan – LD – Ottawa Valley Titans (ODHA) – 6'2" 205

Ryan was selected 2nd round, 23rd Overall by the Saginaw Spirit in the 2013 OHL Priority Selection Draft. Ryan has excellent size already for a 15 year old. He is a pretty good skater for his size and matches up well one on one keeping opposing forwards to the outside and sometimes would finish them physically against the boards. Offensively he shows a good strong shot from the point. He is very calm and patient with the puck and generally makes good decisions with it. Ryan is strong in his own zone showing the ability to win battles along the walls and in the corners dominating at times due to his size and strength. Ryan is very raw and will need some time to develop. He has very good potential, but will need to consistently improve in order to reaching it.

Petawabano, Cody – LW – Oakville Rangers (SCTA) – 6'3" 225

Petawabano was born in Montreal, but has played for the Oakville Rangers in Minor Midget last season. Cody possesses fantastic size and strength helping him to put good pressure on the forecheck and having a great reach. He possesses good offensive assets, a fluid skater with correct quickness for his size; he also has an above-average puck control. He protects the puck very effectively on the wide drive, gets a really good cycle going in deep in the offensive zone and is really physical to knock his man over along the boards. He hustles for loose pucks, goes hard to the net looking for rebound opportunities and brings that really desirable net-front presence on the power play. He will need to establish himself as a really physical force that plays consistently in the dirty areas and will need to bring him his work ethic a notch up. We feel sometimes he is uninterested in what's happening on the ice. He has all the tools to be a power forward in major junior, but will need to have better consistency and intensity to do so.

Pilon, Ryan – LD – Lethbridge Hurricanes (WHL) – 6'2" 197

Pilon is a big, 2 way defenseman who has stepped in the Hurricanes' line up this season and was quickly put on the 1st pairing and logged a ton of important minutes. His play was quite impressive at the start of the year, but as the season went on, he looked a little tired and did not play up to the standards that he set.

Given Pilon's size and age, he is quite an impressive skater. He has quick feet and is able to make quick stops and starts in tight areas. He possesses a good reach, and because of his good speed he can maintain a tight gap against opponents and give them very little opportunity to score off the rush. Pilon uses his size to his advantage along the walls, but he could still gain some more muscle and be tougher to play against in his own end. He has good hockey sense without the puck for his age, and while he does still make some mistakes at times and becomes puck focused, he still has a lot of time to improve that area of his game without the puck.

The big issue with Pilon's game is his lack of urgency. He does not seem to play with enough intensity, and seems a little too relaxed when he is out on the ice. When he has the puck, Pilon is able to make good first passes, but there are times when his passes are a little too soft. He also needs to move the puck a little more quickly to prevent his passes from getting intercepted. He has a good shot from the point, and focuses on getting it through traffic with quick shots rather than winding up for a big slapper.

Pilon's game is quite polished for a 16 year old, and if puts in work to improve his awareness out on the ice and play with some more intensity in particular, he will definitely be a high pick in 2015.

Rantanen, Mikko – RW – TPS (SM-liiga) – 6'1" 179

Mikko has quickly climbed up the development charts with TPS in Finland. After successful runs with the U16 and U18 programs, He spent a fair amount of time with the U20 team before making the jump up to the SM-liiga playing 15 games and putting a few points on the board, despite starting the season as a 15 year old. Mikko shows quick reaction time with the puck and has a very powerful shot. He is tough to predict because he shows a clear willingness to move the puck to his teammates and displays the vision possible to make some difficult passes. If you cheat on the pass he has the quick release to make teams pay. He is quick in transition, usually if he gets the puck either he's moving it up ice or carrying it in a hurry. He has smart positioning in the offensive zone and displays good hands as well. Mikko doesn't have blazing speed, but for a 6'1" forward at 16 his skating would be considered above average. Mikko's hockey sense, size and skillset suggest he is going to be a player who is going to make quite the impact at the NHL Entry Draft. However due to his late birthdate, he's ineligible until 2015.

Robertson, Daniel – LD – Windsor Jr. Spitfires (MHAO) – 6'0" 155

Daniel was selected 4th Round, 61st Overall by the Oshawa Generals in the 2013 OHL Priority Selection Draft. Robertson has constantly impressed us throughout this season. He has good skating ability. He is very mobile and walks the line very well keeping the puck in the zone regularly. He uses this ability to skate the puck out of trouble and rushes it very effectively. Daniel is calm and composed with the puck. He chooses intelligent options with the puck and rarely makes a mistake because he will simply get the puck deep if there are no options. He can at times be rushed into taking the first option he sees which has had mixed results. Robertson also possesses an effective shot and he gets it on net more often than not. Robertson is strong defensively as well forcing turnovers and competing hard. He matches up well one on one and can use both his stick and his body to shutdown forwards. Daniel battles well and wins against bigger forwards but simply needs to get stronger before he can be completely effective in these areas, especially in the OHL. He has got beaten at times and will need to get stronger before he can be as effective as he shows the potential to be at the OHL level. Daniel was one of the better all around defensemen in this past draft. He doesn't have one big standout ability except maybe his skating but he shows plenty of talent, hockey sense and the potential to a very durable all situations kind of defenseman who can help at both ends of the ice and in all game situations.

Roy, Jeremy – RD – Collège Antoine-Girouard (LHMAAAQ) – 5'11" 186

Jeremy Roy is another player with gigantic potential and the best eligible defenseman for the QMJHL Draft in the province of Quebec. After being promoted from Bantam to Midget in 2011-2012, Roy played two excellent seasons for the Antoine-Girouard Gaulois. He is gifted with a powerful and natural skating ability, giving him a speed that is already ready for the next level. He also has excellent lateral mobility, which makes it nearly impossible to beat him wide. Roy likes to support his forwards and will often act as the fourth one on the ice. He does it very smartly and it will rarely cost his team. Even if he gets into trouble, he has the speed he needs to recover on some plays. A dominant player on the powerplay, he uses his excellent vision and he is a great puck distributor with his precise passes. He is always moving with the puck and manages the play with natural flair. His passing ability also shows on the transition, where he is very effective, whether it's with short or long range passes. He sees the play develop faster than any defenseman available this year. He also has good puck abilities and is able to rush the puck through traffic while keeping his head up so he knows what is coming to him. Jeremy also uses his terrific slap shot from the blueline to catch goalies off guard when they are moving. Not very tall, Roy is a bulky player that is very solid on his skates and who is hard to move away from the puck. He does an excellent job handling his physical duties in front of his net. He is also physical along the boards and is able to time some solid checks on his opponents. He is aggressive in coverage and likes to pressure the opposition. This sometimes leaves some zone openings for the other team and can get his team into trouble. He definitely has all the tools to become a general at the blueline in the QMJHL. With such great results at the Midget level, he seems like he could have played in the QMJHL this season and still be effective due to his skating ability and physical maturity.

Roy, Nicolas – C/RW – Forestiers d'Amos (LHMAAAQ) – 6'3" 168

Roy won the Mario Lemieux trophy this season, which is given to the best 15 year old prospect in Midget AAA. He accomplished this even though he missed several games due to a shoulder injury. He has great hockey potential and is a rare type of player that will come out of Midget AAA. His biggest quality is his vision and anticipation. He is always in the right place and he is already able to excel in different areas: block shots, covering passing lanes, effective back checks. He creates a lot of turnovers in a game and will use them right away to generate offense. While he already has the frame, he will need to add muscle to it in order to maximize his potential. Offensively, his premium vision allows him to be a great playmaker, finding open teammates from anywhere on the ice with great ease. Here is a player that is easy to play with due to his intelligence. He uses his body well deep in the zone to win puck battles and to create space for teammates. He can use this aspect of his game to gain puck possession time while his team gets organised. He also likes to come down the wing and cut to the middle to attack goalies with his precise wrist shot. Roy handles the puck well and is able to manoeuvre through traffic without losing control of it. He is a fluid skater with a natural ability to generate speed and surprising lateral ability given his size. His speed is above average and uses his big strides to cover a lot of ice. Roy also needs to adjust his intensity level without the puck at five on five because some vigorous players are able to beat him when they use their energy. His hockey comprehension and natural talent makes him a unique player for the 2013 QMJHL Draft.

Saarela, Aleksi – RW – Lukko U20 (Jr. A SM-liiga) – 5'10" 187

Aleksi is a 1997 birthdate, but you would certainly never guess it by watching him play. Aleksi spent most of this season at the U20 level after absolutely lightning up the U18 league early on in the season. He also got a brief 3 game tryout in the SM-liiga, Finland's top men's league where he scored a goal and added an assist in three games. All pretty impressive for a player who, for over the first half of this season was just 15 years old. Aleksi is an excellent skater with great acceleration and he hits his top speed so quickly. He can also catch defencemen flat footed and will just blow by them on the outside. He has gifted hands and can made some excellent plays with the puck. He has shown the ability to score some amazing highlight reel goals. Aleksi, unlike a lot of players with his level of talent has been noticed working hard in the defensive zone forcing turnovers and getting his stick in passing lanes. He is utilized on the penalty kill and is dangerous if the puck is turned over as he can separate himself for short handed scoring chances. Between his explosive acceleration, top end skating and tremendous puck skills, Aleksi is a player we'll be talking about for a while, because he isn't eligible for the NHL Entry Draft until 2015.

Saban, Jesse – LD – Toronto Red Wings (GTHL) – 6'2" 195

Jesse was selected 2nd round, 21st Overall by the Erie Otters at the 2013 OHL Priority Selection Draft. Jesse is a big two-way defender who is also one of the biggest defensive prospects available from the GTHL. He uses his size effectively to win battles in the corners and along the boards and is very good at finishing checks and dishing out punishment in front of his net. Jesse is a solid skater and shows no hesitation from jumping into or leading the offensive rush. He shows solid puck skills when entering the offensive zone and drives the net well for a defender. Saban is also a solid backwards skater and is good at pushing opponents to the outside and not allowing them to back him deep into the zone. Jesse shows good offensive talent from the blue line and is good at putting shots in great areas for tips or deflections. He has a strong slap and wrist shot and is good at walking the line to give himself more shooting time. Jesse is occasionally caught watching the play in the defensive zone and would benefit from keeping his feet moving and ensuring that he closes all gaps. His skating needs improvements as he's a little slow on pivots and needs to work on his acceleration, as is to be expected with a big defenseman his size.

Salituro, Dante – RC – Ottawa 67's (OHL) – 5'8" 187

Dante was selected first round, 18th Overall by the Ottawa 67's in the 2012 OHL Priority Selection Draft out of the Don Mills Flyers Minor Midget program. Dante was a very dynamic player in Minor Midget, which was his way of overcoming his size and making an impact at that level. Dante joined the 67's and struggled a little at first but once he found his groove he put together an excellent rookie season. Dante is quick and elusive showing the ability to beat defenders one on one regularly. He prefers to shoot the puck rather than pass but is effective at both and possesses a bit of a deceptive shot. He is also able to beat goaltenders one on one and has scored some very nice goals. Dante isn't afraid of a little physicality and is willing to finish checks showing a bit of a gritty side to his play. Due to his late birthdate, Dante will have two years to develop and hopefully grow slightly before he is eligible for the NHL Draft.

Schlichting, Connor – LD – York-Simcoe Express (OMHA) – 6'2" 192

Schlichting was selected 3rd round, 41st Overall by the Sarnia Sting in the OHL. Connor is really the story of two different defensemen in one season. He got off to a very rough start, and was sliding down the rankings. However, it seemed like something just clicked with him, and Connor was on a very steep slope to success. Connor is a very well rounded defensemen who can burn you in all three zones. Offensively he has a hard, powerful shot from the point. He is also intelligent with the puck. He doesn't make any high end plays in the offensive zone with the puck, but his vision is good and he rarely turns it over. Connor's most dangerous offensive asset is his breakout pass. He has a great tendency to send passes across two bluelines that land right on the tape and can send teammates on a breakaway. Defensively Connor is physical but he doesn't over do it. He finishes his checks, he puts the body on in one on one situations and is tough in battles along the boards. He has smart defensive positioning and while he will have the odd mental lapse, he's generally very reliable. Connor looked like a completely new player from early season to the OHL Cup. Improvement among 15 and 16 year old players is a common sight, but the gap between where Connor was in September and where he is in March is nothing short of outstanding. Connor was an absolute steal by the Sting where they selected him. He has size although he won't be expected to drop the gloves, he also possesses puck moving skills that should make him a solid two-way defenseman. Sarnia's blueline may have many candidates to return, but we believe there will be room for Connor on that blueline and he will play his first year of junior with the Sting in the OHL.

Senyshyn, Zachary – RW – Ottawa Jr. Senators (ODMHA) – 6'1" 175

Zachary was selected 3rd round, 51st Overall by the Sault Ste. Marie Greyhounds in the 2013 OHL Priority Selection Draft. Zachary is a very offensive minded forward who shows good hands around the goal area. He's an excellent skater and shows excellent moves one on one with the ability to score highlight reel goals. He isn't overly aggressive physically, but does battle and work hard every single shift he plays. Zachary shows great hockey sense and reads the play well making him very dangerous when entering the offensive zone. He always seems to make the right decision with the puck. Zachary went into the 2013 OHL Priority Selection Draft a little underrated, but the Greyhounds did their research and made a great pick. He brings a lot of potential both offensively and with his work ethic. Zach is responsible defensively, but he really needs to get stronger before making the jump to the next level.

Speers, Blake – C – SOO Thunder (NOHA) – 5'10" 157

Blake was selected 1st round, 11th Overall by the Sault Ste. Marie Greyhounds in the 2013 OHL Priority Selection Draft. Blake has proven himself over the course of the season to be one of the most talented players in the draft period. It all starts with his outstanding skating ability. He's very agile when skating through the neutral zone and can elude multiple defenders at once and score some highlight reel goals. Blake seemed to make something happen every time he steps out on the ice. He has a lot of natural ability with the puck and displayed great hockey sense and vision on the ice to find opening either to carry the puck through or to shoot the puck. He is creative with the puck and sometimes very tough to predict. He makes quick decisions with the puck. Speers showed a willingness to compete for the puck getting it deep when necessary and will chase it down and win more battles than his size suggests thanks to his compete level. What separates Blake from most skilled forwards is he competes hard in all three zones and works to help his team defensively. It's hard to find a flaw in Blake's game. We would definitely like to see him get bigger and stronger. There are times when he would pass when he should shoot, or shoot when he should pass, but that was not a prevalent concern just an occasional one in our viewings.

Spencer, Matthew – RD – Oakville Rangers (OMHA) – 6'1" 192

Matthew was selected 1st round, 3rd Overall by the Peterborough Petes at the 2013 OHL Priority Selection Draft. Spencer could turn out to be the best defenseman from the 2013 OHL Draft, but it is a very difficult assessment because at times it looks like a man playing among boys on the ice. His size and skating are on a level that separates him from the rest of his peers and his strength and speed are both assets that make him one of the most desirable defensemen in the draft. He clearly has all the tools, perhaps the best combined skill set matched with size of anyone in the 2013 OHL Draft, however this is a he needs to learn how to play with other good players. There are many things he got away with in Minor Midget because he is so good, however at the next level can't make the same decisions, for example the amount of times he tries to shoot the puck from the point when the lanes are clogged, or the way he skates himself into a corner in the offensive zone off the rush. He is calm and patient with the puck, as he walks along the line and has a really hard booming shot from the point that seems to be able to find the back of the net more often than not when no one is getting in the way trying to block it. He finds lanes to rush the puck up the ice with ease and protects it really well from the opposition. He will jump up on the attack and come down low to create chances and also has the speed to recover from any mistakes by getting back on the back-check to take away the opposition's opportunities. He can pass the puck up on the breakout really effectively and finds lanes in the offensive zone to pass the puck to good scoring areas at times, however other times tries to force the puck through the opposition. He has great hands and moves to create room for both himself and teammates and is so strong that he is almost impossible to knock off the puck. He does a good job defensively forcing his man to the boards then closing him off with big hits and makes sure to finish his checks along the wall. There are times in his own end where he just throws the puck along the boards, resulting in turnovers in the offensive zone and needs to show a bit more patience to wait for his opportunity to pass the puck to a teammate instead of hoping that they will get the puck on the boards.

Sprong, Daniel – RW – Tigres du Lac Saint-Louis (Midget Esp) – 5'10" 165

Daniel Sprong played in Midget Espoir in 2012-2013 and had a season for the ages. Indeed, he beat Alex Killorn's record for most points in a season with 130 in only 30 games. We view Sprong as the player with the most individual talent in this draft class. He is an elite puck handler with extremely quick hands. He is extremely hard to predict and the puck sticks with him all the time. He matches this ability with his superior speed very well, thus creating a lot of space and shooting lanes to the net. He also has a powerful wrist shot with a great release that fooled a lot of goalies this season. Sprong is very elusive and has the ability to put up spectacular plays in a hurry. Although he is a natural scorer, he can also set up plays easily and has a very good vision. He is also a master at organising and controlling the power play. His play with the puck is mostly in an East-West manner and will rarely give up the puck without trying to make a play. He is not very big and not the most intense worker in his battles, but showed good puck protection and the ability to take on a hit while maintaining puck possession. He is solid on his skates and showed interesting potential at times, when he gave some solid checks. His biggest weakness is his work ethic and playing at an inferior level with a talent of his magnitude certainly didn't help. Even at the Gatorade challenge with players of his caliber, he showed some bad habits. He likes to leave the defensive zone prematurely to go cheat on defensemen and he gives up on puck battles easily. Sprong is a diamond in the rough that will need to step up his work ethic to transpose his game to the junior level.

Stephens, Mitchell – RC – Toronto Marlboros (GTHL) – 5'10" 166

Mitchell was selected 1st round, 8th Overall by the Saginaw Spirit in the 2013 OHL Priority Selection Draft. Mitchell has elite quickness and acceleration which can be seen in his first three steps from the stand still position. If given the space to skate Mitchell can generally beat most defenders with an outside move or straight down the middle and thus is always forcing defenseman to back deep into the defensive zone. He also uses this speed to create turnovers and bad decisions by quickly getting onto defenders on the fore-check. Mitchell uses this speed on the back check as well and closes gaps quickly before finishing with good body contact. He is not afraid to initiate or receive contact and goes to the hard areas of the ice in order to make plays. Stephens excels at driving to the net and always has his stick on the ice looking for tips or deflections. Mitchell also possesses a strong scoring touch and is a threat to score from all areas of the offensive zone. This also translates into power play opportunities and Mitchell is effective coming off the half wall and putting shots on net. He also showcases his quick feet and good awareness on the penalty kill getting into passing lanes and forcing defenders to make quick decisions by closing gaps quickly. Consistency has been the biggest issue for Mitchell this season as there have been some stretches where the jump just didn't seem to be in his game. Mitchell also needs to work on his defensive zone awareness as he runs around too much on certain occasions. Mitchell also needs to control his emotions as he can be suckered into taking a bad penalty or the inability to control his temper in certain situations. Stephens is an offensive first forward who offsets the lack of height with a blend of shiftiness and creativity with the puck.

Strome, Dylan – C – Toronto Marlboros (GTHL) – 6'2" – 170

Dylan was selected 1st round, 2nd Overall by the Erie Otters at the 2013 OHL Priority Selection Draft. Dylan, the younger brother of New York Islanders prospect Ryan Stome is bigger and arguably more offensively talented at the minor midget age of 15. Strome is very talented offensively and makes the majority of offensive plays look relatively easy. Puck control and possession are two key factors in his offensive arsenal; Dylan uses his size and soft hands to shield the puck from defenders and is fairly solid on his feet making it quite the hard task to knock him off the puck. Dylan is also effective using his size to win puck battles along the boards and in behind the net or the corners. Strome possesses the ability to read the ice exceptionally well and uses strong vision and creativity to constantly keep defenders guessing his next move. Dylan is a very strong playmaker and is always looking to set up his line mates for easy scoring opportunities. Dylan uses a strong wrist shot when he gets himself in scoring position and would benefit from shooting more often rather than always looking for the extra fancy pass. Dylan is also quite defensively aware and is very strong at helping out his defenseman down low and moving pucks out of the zone. Strome is very strong at doing the little things such as blocking shots and placing pucks in positions with room for his teammates to make something happen that will translate well into his game at the next level. The beginning of the season it appeared that his skating ability might hold Strome back from making the jump to the elite level of prospects for the 2013 OHL draft. However, as the season progressed there has been some big improvement in this area. From Christmas onward, Dylan's skating and acceleration speed has given him that extra boost allowing him to beat defenders wide and win races to loose pucks. That being said there is still room for improvement in this area going forward and his foot speed and edge work will be something he needs to work on to take his game successfully to the next level. Once Dylan enters the offensive zone his exceptional talent is not hard to notice, getting there however is his biggest issue going forward.

Svechnikov, Yevgeni – RW – AK Bars Kazan (MHL) – 6'0" 170

Yevgeni played his past season with the AK Bars Kazan MHL organization putting forward a great performance, in addition he showed very well at the World U-17 Challenge and the IIHF U18 Championships internationally. Svechnikov has good size but is still very elusive and capable of being defensemen regularly. Yevgeni is capable of scoring some highlight reel goals and has a very high upside in regards to his offensive tools. He likes to shoot the puck whenever possible and usually has good positioning in which to get his shot off in high percentage areas. He has good size and skates very well but he also has shown off some intriguing physical play and finished a few opposing players hard along the boards. He is willing to battle out front not allowing opponents to push him around and makes things difficult for goaltenders when doing this. We would like to see him add more muscle to his frame as it would help him with his development and become even more dominant. With the 2015 NHL Entry Draft two years away a lot can change, but Svechnikov is, early on a favorite to go high out of this draft.

Szypula, Ethan – RC – London Jr. Knights Gold (MHAO) – 5'10" – 154lb

Szypula was selected 1st round, 17th Overall by the Owen Sound Attack. Ethan may be one of the best offensive players in the entire 2013 OHL Priority Selection. He is an explosive skater with excellent speed and agility and handles the puck extremely well. He is elusive and very difficult for even the best defensemen in this draft to contain. Szypula possesses a very high level of hockey sense and reads plays and situations very well and quickly. Ethan was a moderately well kept secret until the Alliance All-Star game where he showed everyone how talented he was arguably putting on the best performance of any player. He has excellent offensive tools and makes intelligent decisions around passing and shooting the puck in the offensive zone. He also possesses a quick, powerful shot. His hands may be his best asset and can put on some highlight reel plays. Ethan has at times shown us competitiveness in the defensive zone playing on the penalty kill and blocking shots. To project where Ethan goes, one would have to look at the second half of the first round. He is a skilled player who we fully expected to be selected in the first round, he could have potentially been selected in the top 10, but was a very solid pick for the Attack at 17. With the Attack losing some offensive talent to the pro's next season, Ethan will certainly be able to provide some of this, while chipping in all over the ice as he works his way up the ranks for the Attack. Really the only concern about Ethan would be the occasional off game he would play. This sort if thing was a rarity in our viewings, but it did occur. Szypula will need to add a little muscle in order to be ready for the physical challenges of the OHL, but if he chooses this path there's little stopping him from playing in the league at 16.

Thompson, Will – RD – Rothesay Netherwood (CAHS) – 5'10" 152

Thompson is a right-handed defenseman with excellent mobility. He has the speed it takes to follow the play effectively. He is not an explosive skater, but he has excellent footing and can move quickly in any direction. He stabilizes the play defensively when he's on the ice, as he reads the play extremely well and shows good positioning. His hockey sense and mobility allow him to be effective in one-on-one situations and he can also back up his teammates when they make mistakes. He is also smart enough to support his forwards in the offensive zone. He doesn't take many risks and keeps his game simple. He is solid defensively and very hard to beat deep in his zone. He is not distracted by quick puck movements and always maintains his sound positioning. On the transition, he acts quickly and effectively, using mostly the boards and using the center of the ice only when it's a safe option. He is not a natural and confident puck-handler, but he remains solid and in control. Even though he is not very big, he showed he was very stable on his skates and showed the ability to use his body to create separation between the puck and his opponents. He's not a spectacular hitter, but can deliver some checks at times. The Fredericton native moves the puck well on the powerplay and possesses a good vision. He also makes a good use of his precise slapshot. Here is another defenseman with the potential of becoming a solid two-way player in the QMJHL.

Tretiak, Maxim – G – CSKA Moskva (MHL) – 6'3" 206

Unless you are relatively new to hockey, chances are you've heard of the legendary goaltender Vladislav Tretiak. His grandson, Maxim has arrived on the scene and will be eligible for the 2015 NHL Entry Draft due to a late 1996 birthdate. Maxim at age 15 already grew a few inches taller than his uncle Vladislav and stands 6'3". Maxim uses his tremendous size and frame to cover his angles well. He never gives shooters much to look at and gets around the crease well. His lack of quickness was exposed a bit at the World U-17 Challenge as some of the top shooters exploited a bit of a weakness in his reaction time, he also opens up the five hole quite prominently when shooters make him go side to side. Maxim has ideal size and maybe the best bloodlines a goaltender could ever ask for, but Maxim still has a lot of development to do before becoming an NHL prospect.

Vande Sompel, Mitchell – London Jr. Knights Gold (MHAO) – LD – 5'10" 171

Mitchell was selected 1st Round, 14th Overall by the Oshawa Generals in the 2013 OHL Priority Selection Draft. Mitchell was one of the best defensemen available for the draft period. He is highlighted by his great skating ability. He accelerates very well right on his first step. He rushes the puck up ice with great shiftiness and is very difficult to contain when he carries the puck. We had viewings of Vande Sompel at both forward and defense this year. However he's played primarily defense and that's where we expect him to play moving forward. Mitchell knows when to shoot and when to pass making him effective on the power play. He has a very high hockey IQ in all three zones. While he has shown at times he can be pressured into a few mistakes in his own zone, he's surprisingly good in his own zone considering size and style. He would like to see him continue improving in his own zone, but really what we feel kept him out of the top 10 is his size. Regardless Mitchell will be able to step into the lineup for any next season and help Oshawa out offensively.

Webb, Jack – LW – Toronto Marlboros (GTHL) – 6'2" 170

Jack was selected 5th round 82nd Overall by the Peterborough Petes at the 2013 OHL Priority Selection Draft. Jack is a hard working forward who spent last season with the Toronto Marlboros. Jack works well skating on a line with his twin brother Mitchell to force turnovers and force opponents to make bad decisions in the defensive zone. Jack is not afraid to engage physically in the corners to make the play and finishes his checks with regularity. He's a solid skater and has good closing speed which is evident when he is chasing puck carriers in the offensive and neutral zones. He is reliable in the defensive zone and works hard along the boards to win puck battles and moves the puck up the ice. Like his brother, Jack lacks an elite scoring touch and is at his best when forcing turnovers and moving pucks to more offensively skilled linemates to finish the play. Jack has battled injuries through parts of the season, but has come on strong down the stretch run to the playoffs.

Webb, Mitchell – LW – Toronto Marlboros (GTHL) – 6'1" 174

Mitchell was selected 2nd round 39th Overall by the Peterborough Petes at the 2013 OHL Priority Selection Draft. Mitchell is a very hard working forward who spent last season with the Toronto Marlboros. He works well with his twin brother Jack to constantly get in on the fore-check and is not afraid to initiate physical contact to make a play. Mitchell utilizes good skating ability and awareness to consistently pressure opposing defenseman into turnovers and bad decisions. He is also effective in the defensive zone, working hard to chip pucks out and start counter offensive attacks. Mitchell has very good positioning in front of the opposing net and is always working hard chasing loose pucks. He lacks an elite finishing ability and most of his goals come from rebounds and scrambles in tight of the net. Mitchell is at his best when he gets physical in the corners knocking defenseman off of pucks and then moving them to his more skilled line mates to finish the play.

Werenski, Zack – RD – Detroit Little Caesars (HPHL) – 6'2" 200

Zack was selected 2nd round, 24th Overall by the London Knights at the 2013 OHL Priority Selection Draft. Werenski is a big, smooth skating defenseman and is willing to jump up and join the attack to get the cycle going in the offensive zone. He makes good chip plays, which tend to create space for him and teammates, and is also able to hold the puck in the offensive zone effectively. He battles well for the puck and has really quick hands to get away from pressure then find the space to put shots on net. He distributes the puck nicely in the offensive zone and shows nice creativity at times also to create opportunities. He has speed on the rush to drive the puck wide then put it low on net to try and generate rebounds and can pass the puck on the rush as well to lead a teammate in for a breakout, sometimes even finding a man at the far blue line for a break opportunity. He opens up in the high slot to take passes and put some good shots on net, and protects the puck nicely to get it in deep. He possesses really good hands and moves, and a nice agility as well to avoid the opposition's pressure. He is strong on his feet and pretty calm and patient with the puck. Defensively he has done a good job blocking shots in his own end and uses his stick to challenge the puck carrier and to knock the puck away from the opposition. He plays with some good physicality along the boards to separate his man from the puck and also makes some big hits at times to knock his man over. He can keep his man to the outside pretty effectively and will communicate with his defensive partner to direct the play. He comes back to tie his man up in his own end and closes him off along the boards too. He has to watch however, that he isn't getting caught on pinches when he doesn't have support. Zach has committed to join the USA National Team Development Program for two years. This includes his NHL Draft Year.

White, Colin – RW – Noble and Greenough School (Prep-MA) – 6'1" 175

Colin is a hardworking, power forward type who shows great athleticism and offensive ability. He was one of the top forwards in New England in 2011-12 as an eighth grader, and followed that up with an excellent freshman season in 2012-13. He's an excellent skater who's strong on his feet, able to bring the puck down the wing and shrug off bigger, older players with ease. His puck protection is top-notch as he intelligently shields while in motion through center or along the offensive boards in the cycle. He uses his size well and is unafraid of the corners and net front. He can really shoot the puck, with a good variety of hard, accurate shots that he selects from well. He shows good passing vision with intelligent feeds through sticks and feet, and the ability to make plays in outnumbered attack situations. He shows good defensive awareness and effort most of the time, but his game away from the puck still needs to be refined overall. He should only get better as he continues to physically and mentally mature, which is a scary thought. He has committed to the NTDP for next year and has expressed his intent to play at Boston College down the line.

White, Colton – LD – London Jr. Knights Gold (MHAO) – 5'11" 177

Colton was selected 2nd round, 22nd Overall by the Sault Ste. Marie Greyhounds in the 2013 OHL Priority Selection Draft. Colton has been consistently noted in our viewings for his excellent play with the puck. Colton is composed and shows good vision in all three zones. He moves the puck up ice well from his own zone but can also skate the puck out of trouble when challenged by fore checkers. He makes good decisions on when to carry the puck and when to get in deep in the neutral zone. He was great on the power play and moved the puck well under pressure and chose the right times to shoot the puck. He moves around the point very effectively keeping himself available as a passing option. Colton has average size for the defensive position and above average skating ability making him a good puck rusher and either acquires the offensive zone or gets the puck deep regularly. Moving forward we see Colton as a very good offensive defenseman at the OHL level and had some serious potential in the 1st round, but slipped to the 4th pick in the second round to the Greyhounds. Moving forward we would just like to see Colton refine his defensive game and get a little bit stronger to handle the physicality of the OHL as we expect him to be in the Sault Ste. Marie Greyhounds line-up next year.

Wilkie, Zach – RD – Toronto Jr. Canadiens (GTHL) – 6'0" 166

Zach was selected 2nd round, 29th Overall by the Niagara Ice Dogs at the 2013 OHL Priority Selection Draft. Zach is a very talented two-way defenseman who was one of the most physical defensemen selected in this past OHL Draft and is constantly looking to land massive body checks in all areas of the ice. He uses his strong skating ability to constantly get into good positions to punish forwards who attempt to carry the puck down his wing. Zach also uses his strong skating ability to skate out of trouble in the defensive zone and to lead the offensive rush when given space to skate through the neutral zone. Wilkie is a strong puck handler and shows confidence with the puck in the offensive zone utilizing good passing ability to contribute on a number of goals throughout the season. He also has a big slap shot that has the ability to beat goaltenders from all areas of the offensive zone. Zach's offensive and defensive awareness allow him to be a key contributor on both the penalty kill and the power play. While physicality is one of his best assets Wilkie has occasionally taken himself out of position by trying to throw the perfect body check and would be more effective choosing his spots more wisely. Zach also sometimes lets his aggression get the best of him which has resulted in a fair number of penalties and hitting from behind ejections. Zach is at his best when he keeps his physical abilities in check and uses his strong skating ability to gain puck possession in the defensive zone and jump into the resulting offensive rush.

Worrad, Drew – LC – Elgin-Middlesex Chiefs (MHAO) – 5'11" 146

Worrad was selected 5th round, 90th Overall by the Barrie Colts at the 2013 OHL Priority Selection Draft. Drew looks bigger than his listing. He has excellent speed and uses it to create plays. He has great puck skills and is able to beat multiple defenders at once. Worrad has shown the ability to create some highlight reel goals. He has a powerful shot and can be very dangerous in the offensive zone if opposing defensemen don't keep tabs on him because he can get his powerful shot off quickly. He anticipates plays well reading and reacting quickly and showing a great work ethic allowing him to force many turnovers and win some battles. Drew has also shown in our viewings a willingness to compete in the defensive zone and block shots. Worrad is a player we're confident about making the jump to the OHL because he combines speed and skill with a strong work ethic and possesses a determination to win that we've seen in a few close games. He needs to build muscle and get stronger. While we're confident we'll see him in the league next year if he chooses to go, he's not a lock to make the jump full time as a 16 year old. However being selected by a team who will lose a few forwards to graduation should give him a very good opportunity to be on the Colts' opening night roster.

Yetman, Bryce – RW – Whitby Wildcats (OMHA) – 6'1" 147

Yetman was selected 4th round, 73rd Overall by the Plymouth Whalers in the 2013 OHL Priority Selection Draft. Bryce is a solid two-way winger for the Whitby Wildcats. Bryce uses his size in the offensive zone to effectively shield the puck from opponents and is good at controlling the puck along the boards. He is good at getting to the front of the net and works hard to maintain net presence to screen the goaltender from incoming shots. Yetman utilizes a long stick in the neutral zone to get in passing lanes and create turnovers on the back check. He is reliable in the defensive end and is good at chipping pucks into the neutral zone and making smart outlet passes. Bryce is a hard worker and consistently battles and finishes checks, although he is still very lanky and could stand to add significant muscle to his frame. He would also like him to refine his skating as he needs to get stronger. He shows good potential but needs to play his game on a more consistent basis to reach his potential.

Zeppieri, David – C – Mississauga Rebels (GTHL) – 6'1" 182

David was selected 3rd round, 59th Overall by the Sudbury Wolves in the 2013 OHL Priority Selection Draft. David is a skilled two-way center for the Mississauga Rebels. David is a player that works extremely hard in all three zones of the ice and is in constant pursuit of pucks not in his possession. He is reliable in the defensive zone and is very consistent at pitching in down low helping defenders move pucks up the ice in pressure situations. He shows a good burst of speed, which is impressive at his size and carries the puck into the offensive zone and is capable of beating defenders with an outside step despite his stride being a little ugly. David is good at using his body to shield opponents from pucks and to overpower smaller defenders when driving to the net off the rush. Zeppieri showcases a good variety of puck skills in the offensive zone and is especially strong in tight when he creates space for himself before cutting to the slot. He shows a willingness to battle for loose pucks in hard areas of the ice and does not shy away from scrums after the whistles. Zeppieri is not considered to have high offensive upside and projects more so to be a great two-way contributor with limited offensive production at the OHL level. He needs to improve his starts and stops when the play changes direction as he sometimes is prone to skating in a big loop which occasionally puts him out of position.

Part 6

2016 NHL DRAFT PROSPECTS

Allard, Frédéric – RD – Blizzard du Séminaire Saint-François (LHMAAAQ) – 5'11" 152

Frédéric Allard is a right-handed defenseman who logged important minutes for the Blizzard this season. A fluid skater, Allard has very good footing which allows him to provide great one-on-one coverage and to leave very little space to opponents. He has above-average speed that he uses to get out of his zone as well. He is not an aggressive player nor is he physical, but he relies on positioning and his anticipation sense to be effective. Allard needs to get bigger in order to handle bigger forwards in battles deep in his zone. Offensively, he has good tools, notably his low and effective wrist shot from the blue line. He rarely uses his slapshot but he likes to get involved offensively in the offensive zone and he circles the puck well. He has a good puck-control and fluid hands that allow him to be an effective passer. His biggest weakness is his consistency with his decision making. In some games we have seen he always made the best decisions and on other nights, he panicked and made the life hard on himself and his team. When he does so, he takes too much time to take his decisions and causes a lot of turnovers. He seems to think too much at times and he just needs to execute. With all the tools he has, his potential remains very interesting if he improves his decision making.

Bastien, Nathan – C – Kitchener Jr. Rangers (MHAO) – 6'0" 157

Nathan was selected 7th round, 127th Overall by the Mississauga Steelheads at the 2013 OHL Priority Selection Draft. Nathan is an offensive forward who got off to a bit of a shaky start but seemed to get better and better every time we saw him play. Bastien shows strong net presence, battling hard and creating a disruption while reacting quickly to loose pucks. He works very hard for loose pucks and battles hard along the boards. Nathan has shown us the ability to not only shoot the puck effectively, but finds the open man setting up chances when controlling the puck in all three zones.

Brookshaw, Carson – LW – Elgin-Middlesex Chiefs (MHAO) – 5'9" 174

Brookshaw was selected 3rd round 46th Overall by the Owen Sound Attack. Carson was easily one of the most improved players in Alliance this season. He developed throughout the year going from a player who would check and work, to a player who could produce offensively. He had arguably the best compete level on his team and consistently puts in the work. Carson is effective along the boards playing physical and displaying strength in these battles. He shows some decent skating ability and uses the wing to carry the puck up ice. He has really helped out Elgin-Middlesex offensively going into the slot and jumping on rebounds, crashing the crease and making things disruptive resulting in a lot of offensive opportunities. As the season went on Carson started creating a few more skilled plays for himself and his team. He also contributed well defensively willing to get back and force turnovers. Brookshaw has shown some offensive upside near the end of the season and as a late bloomer there could be some untapped offensive potential that emerges as Carson becomes accustom to the OHL. Even if it doesn't, teams know they're getting a hard working player who will leave it all on the ice for his team. When the Attack selected Carson he immediately gained comparisons to former Attack forward Michael Halmo as the two are of similar size and play a very comparable game.

Brunet, Brody – RC – Nickel City Sons (NOHA) – 5'10" 193

Brody was selected 12th round, 230th Overall by the North Bay Battalion at the 2013 OHL Priority Selection Draft. Brunet displayed some good skating and good skills to help create chances for his team throughout the year. He has a hard shot and is able to skate the puck into the zone and help set things up. His strongest asset offensively would be his hands and they help him win some one on one matchups. He also works hard and battles in the corners. Brody shows a strong compete level and will force turnovers. Brody will need to get stronger to maximize his potential. While his offensive upside is a little questionable he does have good hands, skates well and works hard, and it's his competitiveness that may draw teams in.

Carroll, Noah – RD – Elgin-Middlesex Chiefs (MHAO) – 6'0" 159

Noah was selected 4th round, 77th Overall by the Guelph Storm at the 2013 OHL Priority Selection Draft. Carroll is a player who wasn't talked about much early on in the season, but he was well hidden behind some of the start players on Elgin. By November, he started to really emerge and hasn't looked back. Noah has shown the ability to play in all game situations. Defensively he's very hard working who battles consistently and wins more than his share of pucks in the corners and behind the net. Offensively he's a smart puck mover who likes to jump up on the rush and will carry the puck deep in the offensive zone. He knows when the pinch off the point and read the right times to get back putting himself into position. He has solid skating ability in all directions and shows good overall mobility for a six foot tall defenseman. He's extremely smart with the puck and rarely makes a mistake. He very smoothly advances the puck up ice, makes the smart play under pressure and shows good vision in the offensive zone. He does the little things well like always keeping his feet moving, always putting himself in great positioning. Guelph did a great job stealing Noah in the fourth round of the OHL Draft and with his late birthdate should be very prepared come the 2016 NHL Entry Draft. Moving forward we do feel he needs to fill out more and get stronger.

Cormier, Evan – G – Clarington Toros (OMHA) – 6'2" 176

Evan was selected 5th round, 85th Overall by the North Bay Battalion at the 2013 OHL Priority Selection Draft. Evan has shown the potential to be the first goaltender selected for the 2013 OHL Priority Selection Draft. Evan has excellent size and moves extremely well. He looks very well trained and will challenge shooters well showing effective side to side movement. He doesn't give up a ton of rebounds and can direct them well quite often to avoid creating extra work for himself. Clarington was in the bottom half of the ETA standings and didn't have their best season. Thanks to Evan, Clarington was in some games that they maybe shouldn't have been in and would make some huge saves late in close games to give his team a chance. Evan is going to be intrigued by several teams looking to add a great goaltending prospect this year.

Day, Sean – LD – Detroit Compuware (HPHL) – 6'1" 180

Sean was selected 1st round, 4th Overall by the Mississauga Steelheads at the 2013 OHL Priority Selection Draft. Sean is an elite offensively skilled defenseman for Detroit Compuware. Sean shows exceptional skating ability making it almost seem effortless as he moves around the ice. He has the ability to get back into position with two quick strides and is seemingly never out of a play. Day also shows excellent puck skills and stickhandles with confidence in all three zones of the ice. He uses his size well in the defensive zone controlling the puck and battling for position in front of the net. Day also possesses elite offensive instincts jumping into the rush with ease and shows a strong finishing ability whenever he gets an opportunity. Sean has the ability to beat goaltenders with both a quick release wrist shot and a hard powerful slap shot. He also is very creative when carrying the offensive rush and has good 1-on-1 skills beating opposing defenders and goaltenders with relative ease. There are questions about some decision making in the defensive zone and trying to do too much without using his teammates that need to be improved on to have continued success at the next level. Day also needs to work at getting involved more physically and consistently using his size to finish hits along the boards and in open ice.

Gauthier, Julien – RW – Rousseau-Royal de Laval-Montréal (LHMAAAQ) 6'2" 205

Julien Gauthier will show up at the QMJHL draft with the biggest body but also with one of the biggest potential to work with. Although he is very big for his age, he is an excellent skater and his mobility isn't a weakness in his game. He has a powerful explosion and wins a lot of space with his big strides. He could be more fluid as a skater but it doesn't tamper his skating ability. He has excellent power forward qualities and brings a lot of energy and creates a lot of space on the ice. He excels in puck battles deep in the offensive zone and his puck protection his excellent: very few players were able to move him. Gauthier is very effective when he comes down the wing with an aggressive approach and he creates a lot of confusion among the opposition because of his size. He can force his way through traffic without a problem. He also has a far above-average wrist shot with great speed and precision. He can release quickly and he does a good job at making himself open around the net. The big forward has good aptitudes with the puck and quick hands but is not spectacular by any means. He is an aggressive player who likes to hit but he needs to be more consistent in this area. His biggest weakness is his defensive play. He is fooled by puck movement in the defensive zone and he gives up too much space to the opposing defensemen. His vision and understanding of the game could also use some improvement as he takes a lot of time to take a simple decision on the ice. He needs to react faster, for example on the forecheck. A big player with excellent skating aptitudes is a rare thing in the Province of Quebec and he could become a unique impact player in the years to come.

House, Brent – RW – London Jr. Knights Gold (MHAO) – 6'0" 156

Brent was selected 14th round, 271st Overall by the Sault Ste. Marie Greyhounds in the 2013 OHL Priority Selection Draft. Brent was a player we felt made the most of his ice time whenever he was out there. He has good size and although he needs to add some muscle to his frame he showed excellent competitiveness in puck battles and won more than his share in our viewings. He works incredibly hard down low in the offensive zone His compete level is high and isn't afraid to play physical. He shows good intelligence with the puck in the offensive zone and we've seen him show both good moves and strong passing ability. While we like his potential, it's questionable if he can be an offensive player at the next level. Brent has good size, a good frame and competes hard every night. We certainly aren't counting him out offensively as he has shown tools in this area, but we aren't sold on this area. Brent will need to get stronger in the summer and fill out his frame, but could turn out to be a real steal for the Greyhounds.

Kirwan, Luke – LW – Middlesex Islanders (EJHL) – 6'1" 216

Luke was selected 2nd round, 32nd Overall by the Guelph Storm at the 2013 OHL Priority Selection Draft. Kirwan is a defensively responsible player, who comes back really well on the back-check to tie up his man and puts good pressure on the puck carrier to steal the puck and force turnovers. He gets his stick in lanes to breakup plays defensively and also plays with a nice element of physicality. He starts the breakout with good passes, then holds the puck in the offensive zone and gets a really effective cycle going, protecting the puck along the wall and putting good pressure on the forecheck. He battles hard to come out of the corners with the puck, and uses his body to get the inside track towards the net to open up and take passes for great chances in tight. Kirwan also positions himself well in the defensive zone, especially on the penalty kill, and opens up down low in the offensive zone to provide scoring options. He is willing to bring a net-front presence on the power play, battling for his territory, however still needs to watch the turnovers from panicking when he is under pressure and just throwing the puck up along the boards. Kirwan has committed to the USA National Team Development Program and is expected to spend two years there. Afterwards he will enter his draft year and will either join the Guelph Storm or make an NCAA or USHL commitment.

Morin, Alex – LD – Sault Ste. Marie Thunder (NOHA) – 5'10" 177

Morin was selection 9th round, 174th Overall by the Plymouth Whalers in the 2013 OHL Priority Selection Draft. Alex is a very smooth skating defenseman who is capable of skating the puck out of trouble and up ice. He moves the puck well in the offensive zone and has a decent shot from the point. Alex is defensively responsible and doesn't get caught up ice. He maintains good positioning and will battle for the puck. While we have seen him make many very good passes we question his decision making at times because he's turned the puck over far too many times in his own zone for our liking. Alex projects to be a two-way defenseman at the OHL level who can chip in offensively and will work hard defensively.

Timpano, Troy – Toronto Titans (GTHL) – 5'11" 174

Troy was selected 2nd round, 27th Overall by the Sudbury Wolves in the 2013 OHL Priority Selection Draft. Troy is an athletic goaltender for the Toronto Titans. Troy works extremely hard to fight for loose pucks and never shows any quit no matter what position he is on the ice. He is good getting good angles on shooters and rarely gives them areas to shoot for. He shows great poise and confidence in all situations including handling the puck when needed. Timpano does not allow goals to get him off his game and shows a strong bounce back after conceding the majority of goals he allowed this season. He shows solid lateral movement and works hard to get across to make backdoor saves. Troy always works hard to keep the Titans in the game and has resulted in a number of tight scoring games this season. There is room for improvement in rebound control as he occasionally does let pucks bounce off him although he has improved as the season progressed and became good at directing pucks into the corners of the defensive zone. He also shows a little too much movement at times for our liking but is not a major concern. Troy has shown a lot of character.

Tkachuk, Matthew – LW – St. Louis Blues AAA – 5'11" 165

Mathew was selected 4th round, 64th Overall by the London Knights at the 2013 OHL Priority Selection Draft. Matthew, the son of Keith is committed to Notre Dame University. He is also set to join the USA National Team Development Program. He plays an honest two-way game taking care of his own end. He isn't flashy but does a lot of things well. He goes to the dirty areas along the boards and is difficult to deal with in front of the net. He loves to play physical hockey and takes the puck to the net hard, also causes havoc by crashing the crease without the biscuit. Shows off good hockey sense and decision-making. He's a smart player. He's creative but not highly-skilled, upside isn't sky high but he's a nice player. Due to his late birthdate, he will be eligible for the 2016 NHL Entry Draft and will have one year to play after leaving the USNTDP and will likely do this either in London (OHL) or Notre Dame (CCHA).

Verbeek, Hayden – C – Sun County Panthers (MHAO) – 5'9" 155

Hayden was selected 4th round, 71st Overall by the Sault Ste. Marie Greyhounds in the 2013 OHL Priority Selection Draft. Hayden shows tremendous speed and moves with the puck. He has great hands and excellent mobility allowing him to put together some very highlight reel moves. He is pretty much automatic when he rushes the puck up ice. He has shown on multiple occasions to possess good passing ability. However in our viewings he seems to prefer to shoot much more than pass and if possible will try to finish the play himself. Verbeek is a difficult player to project because he has tons of natural ability but needs to be more willing to use his linemates on a more regular basis. He also needs to compete in his own zone more consistently and at his size he will also need to get stronger. Hayden does bring some risk with him based on everything, but he could turn into a very good player at the OHL level. However he has some work to do both developmentally and physically.

Part 7
SCOUTS GAME REPORTS

2013 NHL DRAFT BLACK BOOK

These game reports are actual reports from our scouts. Keep in mind that they have simply been edited for typos. A large number of the QMJHL reports are written by our french speaking scouts. Please keep that in mind when you are reading them.

The reports can show examples of how prospects can have both great games or bad games in our viewings. We have multiple viewings from multiple scouts. There are the odd Euro players who may only be seen by one scout a handful of times, but for the most part, at least a couple of our scouts see each player.

We included games going back to the 2012 Would U18's in Brno. There were numerous late 1994's in that tournament. We felt it was appropriate to include them in this book for that reason. We also included a few reports from various other tournaments including this years World Under 18's in Sochi Russia, the Four Nations in Sweden & Five Nations in Ann Arbor and we had four scouts in Victoriaville & Drummondville for 7 days, scouting the World U17 Hockey Challenge.

You will also notice some game reports from the Select 17 camp in Rochester, New York. Myself and Ryan Yessie stopped in Rochester on our way home from Pittsburgh (2012 NHL Draft) to watch a few days of the event. I have attended the event the past four years.

Finally, although we have included approximately 400 game reports, there are many more games attended that are not included. We do give a good sampling of reports here though.

Enjoy,

Mark Edwards

April 14, 2012, Finland vs. Canada (U18 World Championship)

FNL # 6, D, Ristolainen, Rasmus (2013) Ristolainen did a really nice job tying up his man, and showed some good strength and 'want to' in his battles for the puck. He displayed some great toughness, but needs to watch that he isn't crossing the line taking dumb penalties. He did a great job protecting the puck to work it down low, and was distributing the puck well in the offensive zone. He takes a hit to make a play, but needs to try to move the puck a bit quicker sometimes. He made some good passes as to start the breakout. Like his mean streak.

FNL # 9, C, Barkov, Aleksander (2013) He is strong on the puck, and showed some hands and creativity with the puck but he was playing a bit too much on the perimeter for most of the game. He had good pressure on the fore-check and was battling hard to force turnovers. He made a good pass across on a 2-on-1 for a great chance, but also missed some of his passes through the neutral zone resulting in turnovers.

FNL # 10, RW, Ikonen, Jusso (2013) Ikonen was getting to the net and in tight on the power play. He can find a lane to move the puck cross-ice. He battled hard for the puck, was competing well and distributing the puck nicely in the offensive zone. He needs to watch the turnovers holding on to the puck too long. He needs to add some size and strength as he was knocked off the puck far too easily.

FNL # 20, C, Antonen, Joose (2013) He made a really nice pass down low to find a man open next to the net, and was hustling really well to get on loose pucks.

CAN # 3, D, Pulock, Ryan (2013) He got caught watching the play and a forward got in behind him for a great chance.

CAN # 8, RW, Shinkaruk, Hunter (2013) Had some great speed rushing the puck up the ice and getting it in deep into the offensive zone. He was throwing pucks to the net from just about everywhere. He made a nice pass down low and was driving to the net with his stick down to provide scoring options. He made a great pass to the point to set up a one-timer for the team's 1st goal of the game.

CAN # 12, LW, Rychel, Kerby (2013) Rychel did a good job on the fore-check, and was cycling the puck well using his big frame to protect the puck.

CAN # 25, LW, Carrier, William (2013) Carrier applied pressure on the puck carrier, and was cycling well protecting the puck along the boards deep in the offensive zone. He made some good breakout passes to start the rush, and was able to get to the slot with the puck but needs to get his shots through to the net. He got caught holding on to the puck for too long through the neutral zone resulting in a turnover.

FINAL SCORE: 4-2 Finland

April 16, 2012, Czech Republic vs. Canada (U18 World Championships)

CZE # 5, D, Kostalek, Jan (2013) Kostalek displayed some good physical play along the boards in his own zone. His passing was somewhat inconsistent as he was able to make some good passes through the neutral zone, but also turned the puck over a few times through passes and by trying to carry the puck through the zone. He also needs to watch the blind turnovers just throwing the puck up the boards when pressured.

CZE # 10, D, Stencel, Jan (2013) Stencel made some good lead passes to start the breakout out of his own end, and is able to move the puck well under pressure. He had some nice battles along the boards in his own end, and was able to rush the puck up to gain the offensive zone as well.

CZE # 13, RW, Vrana, Jacob (2014) Vrana has some fantastic speed that he used on the rush through the neutral zone, and showed off great hands as well. He needs to watch the turnovers when he tries to dangle one guy too many. He was able to take a bad pass behind him at full-speed. He showed some dazzling hands to get by a defender wide, and also made a soft chip plays to get the puck by defenders then used his speed. He was hustling hard on the back-check, coming back for some good support.

CZE # 19, RW, Volek, Dominik (2012 Undrafted) Volek made some good lead passes on the rush, and was driving to the net with his stick down. He put some good pressure on the puck carrier, and was reading the play really well to pick off neutral zone turnovers. He was also able to settle a bouncing puck quickly to get a nice quick shot off from the high slot. He is pretty strong on the puck, and has some really nice hands off the rush. Liked his game but fitness level may have hurt him.

CAN # 6, D, Morrissey, Josh (2013) Morrissey showed some great quickness and agility with the puck to avoid the opposition's pressure, and is a great skater hustling hard to get to loose pucks. He was physical in his own end to take the puck from the opposition, and then showed some great speed to rush the puck back up the ice into the offensive zone. He was also getting involved in post-whistle scrums.

FINAL SCORE: 6-2 Canada

April 17, 2012, Finland vs. Czech Republic (U18 World Championships)

FIN # 6, D, Ristolainen, Rasmus (2013) Ristolainen did a great job spotting an open man in the slot and found a lane to get him the puck for a good shot opportunity. He was distributing the puck very nicely in the offensive zone and had a nice hard shot from the point that he kept down low and was able to hit the net.

FIN # 9, C, Barkov, Aleksander (2013) Barkov possesses fantastic puck protection skills in the corners. He has good strength and competes to win board battles for the puck, but needs to watch both neutral zone turnovers and turnovers entering the offensive zone. He displayed physical toughness on the puck carrier on the fore-check and opened up nicely to provide scoring options down low on the power play. He was able to win face-offs clean. He also fought hard for his territory in front of the net, getting in the goaltender's face, protected the puck very effectively and found lanes on the power play to move the puck cross-ice for some good opportunities.

FIN # 16, LW, Salminen, Saku (2013) Salminen was driving really well to the net with his stick down to deflect a good shot on from in tight. He showed great strength and puck protection to hold on to the puck under pressure, get a pretty nice cycle started in deep in the offensive zone and can take a hit and hold on to the puck to still make a play. He was also distributing the puck well on the rush.

CZE # 5, D, Kostalek, Jan (2013) Kostalek likes to use his stick to direct the play to the outside. He is able to skate the puck up out of his own end well, has some moves to get around the opposition and was physical on the puck carrier in the defensive zone, finishing his hits along the boards. He was skating the puck up well to gain the offensive zone, but has to watch the turnovers up through the middle in the neutral zone.

CZE # 13, RW, Vrana, Jakub (2014) Vrana was able to read the play nicely to pick off a neutral zone turnover and move the puck up to start the rush. He has dynamic speed on the fore-check. He put a nice low shot on net to generate a rebound and a teammate scored on the opportunity. He was back-checking hard all night. He has fantastic quick hands to walk around defenders and he gets to the slot.

FINAL SCORE: 6-2 Finland

April 17, 2012, Sweden vs. Russia (U18 World Championship)

SWE # 19, LW, De La Rose, Jacob (2013) De La Rose was excellent on the forecheck causing turnovers. He had a great rush up the ice to gain the offensive zone and got a good shot off from the high slot. He moved the puck well in the offensive zone. Liked his effort in this one.

SWE # 22, C, Lindholm, Elias (2013) Lindholm has some fantastic speed and agility with the puck. He was distributing the puck well in the offensive zone, giving Forsberg plenty of looks.. He has great offensive instincts, getting to scoring areas, and making great passes to find open men in the slot from behind the net. He had a nice give-and-go play to gain the offensive zone with speed. Looks like an elite playmaker with scoring ability as well.

SWE # 24, RW, Burakowsky, Andre (2013) Burakowsk worked his tail off. He was able to walk out from the sideboards to put a shot on net, but has to get the shot through. He was also able to gain the offensive zone to put a shot on of the rush, but then fanned on his shot. Not sure about his skill level as far as being a top 6 type guy. Looked like a worker ant to me.

SWE # 25, C, Wennberg, Alexander (2013) Wennberg had some great pressure and physicality on the fore-check, and was cycling the puck well. He used his stick well in the Dzone. He made a really nice saucer pass across on a 2-on-1 opportunity. He has some hands, but needs to watch his dangles, a few too many tunovers. He has good agility and was able to get to the slot with the puck to put a great shot on net for an excellent chance. Like this kid, expect him to get better, lots of upside.

RUS # 10, C, Yakimov, Bogdan (2013) Yakimov has some nice hands and moves that were on full display. He takes a while to get rolling but when he does je is like a runaway train. He was coming back well on the back-check, and battling hard for the puck. He showed a willingness to play physical on the fore-check, and got his stick in lanes on the penalty kill. He showed puck distribution off the rush, and has some hands. He uses his stick well on the opposition, and has some good strength to protect the puck along the wall. He provided some good support in his own end tying up his man and playing him physically along the boards.

RUS # 15, C, Kuptsov, Sergei (2013) Kuptsov can protect the puck. He has some speed. Didn't like his hockey smarts.

RUS # 16, D, Zadorov, Nikita (2013) Zadorov showed some really good physical play in his own end. He was clearing the front of his net well keeping the opposition to the outside, and was jumping in on the rush to lead the attack. This kid is the real deal.

RUS # 27, LW, Nichushkin, Valeri (2013) Nichushkin took the puck to the net with good speed and was playing physically on the puck carrier. Got down showing a willingness to block shots in his own end. He was clearing the puck on the penalty kill, and was able to handle some bad passes off the rush. He is able to put shots on net off the rush. He has high end speed and can beat the opposition with some shifty moves, he made look easy on the end-to-end rush. He has high-end moves and puck skills.

April 19, 2012, Canada vs. Russia (U18 World Championship)

CAN # 2, D, Nurse, Darnell (2013) Nurse played this game with some excellent physical play finishing off his man along the boards. He was getting down; showing a willingness to block shots, and was really strong on the puck. He had some great puck battles, and was physical on the puck carrier to take the puck and force turnovers. He made some great passes out of the zone to start the rush, and was playing the body. Where was this all year? Loved him in this game.

CAN # 6, D, Morrissey, Josh (2013) Morrissey once again showed he can skate, but didn't have the best game tonight as he was out-battled for the puck in his own end, and also lost his man defensively in front of the net to give the opposition a good shot from scoring range.

CAN # 8, RW, Shinkaruk, Hunter (2013) He is able to get to the slot with the puck to put shots on net, and was battling well for territory and loose pucks in front of the net. He made a really good pass out front to find a teammate to score the team's 2nd goal. He was willing to play with an element of physicality in his own zone, and was drove the net with the puck finishing off the play with a nice back-hander. He made a nice play along the wall with a somple chip play.

CAN # 12, LW, Rychel, Kerby (2013) Rychel showed some physicality on the fore-check finishing his hits. He played hard and physical on the puck carrier in his own. He took a pass in front of the net to bat in the team's 2nd goal of the game from in tight, and went to the net with his stick down to score the team's 3rd goal of the game as well. He was hustling for loose pucks, competing really well and driving to the net.

RUS # 10, C, Yakimov, Bogdan (2013) Yakimov has decent speed for a big guy once he gets rolling. He showed some moves and puck protection through the neutral zoneand was able to drive the puck down low towards the net. He got in a lane showing a willingness to block shots, and did a good job coming back to his own end to provide some good support. He was winning most of the puck battles.

RUS # 15, C, Kuptsov, Sergei (2013) Kuptsov has some good speed, and was distributing the puck well on the rush through the neutral zone which was something new in my viewings of him. He was driving to the net well and was able to protect the puck and cycle it behind the net. He had a really good wrap-around attempt off the cycle, and showed some speed and creativity with the puck to get by defenders and move it around in the offensive zone. Too many turnovers, he would drive me crazy coaching him.

RUS # 16, D, Zadorov, Nikita (2013) Zadorov displayed aggression in this game getting involved after whistles. Led a rush on a wide drive.. He was finding lanes to skate the puck up the ice into the offensive zone, and was distributing the puck well off the rush. This kid hasn't tipped the iceberg as far as his potential and upside. Looks to be discovering his offensive skills.

RUS # 27, LW, Nichushkin, Valeri (2013) Nichushkin has some excellent speed and was hustling hard to be 1st on loose pucks. He was protecting the puck well taking it wide. Has fantastic hands. Shot is unreal. I want to see more. I like him more with every viewing.

April 20, 2012, Czech Republic vs. Latvia (U18 World Championships)

CZE # 5, D, Kostalek, Jan (2013) He was jumping up on the pinch to keep the attack alive in the offensive zone, and used his stick well to knock the puck free off the opposition, but has to get his shots through to the net with more consistency.

CZE # 13, RW, Vrana, Jakub (2014) Vrana showed fantastic hands that he used on the rush to beat defenders then drive the puck towards the net to put a great shot on net. He made a great pass to move the puck up on the breakout to lead a man with speed into the offensive zone and put good pressure and physicality on the fore-check. He opened up really well in the slot to take a pass for a one-timer and scored. Went hard to the net to pick up a rebound off the post and score from in tight and demonstrated his fantastic hands by getting the puck to the front of the net for a teammate to score. He has incredible hands and vision. I love watching this kid play.

LAT # 18, RW, Golovkovs, Georgs (2013) Showed quick hands and distributed the puck nicely through the neutral zone to get the rush started.

LAT # 9, C, Kondrats, Ricards (2013) He did a great job of coming back for support to pickoff a pass to breakup an opportunity for the opposition and demonstrated some decent puck distribution on a give-and-go play through the neutral zone. He had good speed, battle and puck protection on the wide drive into the offensive zone.

June 24, 2012, USA Black vs. USA Orange (US Select 17)

BLK #3 D Florentino, Anthony (2013) - Showed some flashes throughout game using his skating to create the time necessary for options to open up. Also delivered a few solid hits.

BLK #12 F Basilico, Bryan (2013) - Bryan made several great plays with the puck to advance it into the offensive zone as well to create scoring chances for himself and others. Rushes the puck up ice with speed but takes several steps to reach this speed and it looks a bit awkward/uncomfortable in the process.

ORA #2 D Heinrich, Blake (2013) - Showed great vision moving the puck up ice well, also was effective when rushing the puck himself. Delivered some good hits throughout the game.

ORA #6 D Robert, Alexander (2013) - Alex rushes the puck up ice well using his strong skating ability. However seems to try to do too much at times. He moves the puck up ice well when choosing this option.

ORA #7 – Lopez, Ramon (2013) - Landed some good solid hits early on. However as the game progressed he passed up opportunities to apply himself physically. His skating looks rather awkward.

ORA #12 F Corcoran, Charles (2013) - Very good skating ability, hands looked excellent at times and he used them to create offense. Moves the puck effectively and forechecks hard creating turnovers. While he looked great the first half of the game, he looked very average in the second half.

ORA #17 F Galt, Ryan (2013) - Displayed great skating ability and rushed the puck very well. Ryan has good hands and wasn't afraid to take on defensemen one on one. However the results of this were hit or miss.

Scouts Notes: Defenseman for team black Nicholas Picnic (2013) posted some offensive opportunities moving in from the point under pressure. He also showed a good wrist shot. Meanwhile for team Orange Zachary Diamontoni (2013) who was one of the top scorers in last year's Select 16 camp showed his ability to force the opposition to take penalties to try to contain him. He protected the puck well despite his size and showed strong skating ability.

June 24, 2012, USA Royal Blue vs. USA Red (US Select 17)

RLB #3 D Pomeroy, Stuart (2013) - He has fairly quick feet for a big defenseman but very small strides. Has the sense to skate backwards and create space and time if no option presents itself instead of forcing a play. Cancels out forwards very well in 1 on 1 situations showing the ability to take the body or force them outside.

RLB #17 F Shea, Brandon (2013) - Has good hands and showed great patience with the puck. He can at times turn over the puck carelessly, but works hard to redeem himself and creates turnovers for his team as well.

RED #6 D Streeter, Brandon (2013) - Showed very wide range in play. He made a great pass to set up a goal for his team, and a willingness to play physical. The biggest hit he landed all game may have been himself when he missed on his timing and destroyed himself into the boards. Got beat three times in one shift in different areas of the defensive zone leading to scoring chances for the opposition. He redeemed himself a little bit the next shift, again trapped in his own zone but made smart negating scoring chances.

RED #7 D Coffman, Nikola (2013) - Extremely fast skater he flew all over the ice. He showed off an excellent end to end rush, however looked off several excellent passing options en route to eventually being stopped. Has a quick wrist shot and visibly prefers shooting over passing. Very agile and capable of getting into very good defensive positioning although he kept getting beat even in good position in 1 on 1 situations.

RED #14 F Wood, Miles (2013) - Shows good hands, and loves to drive the net. He constantly crashed the crease, which eventually lead to a penalty. Showed good defensive awareness covering for defensemen who pinched and took on forwards on the rush on a few occasions and faired well.

RED #15 F Hill, Tyler (2013) - His physical play was unpredictable. He absolutely destroyed some guys but passed up on other times where he clearly should have hit. Shows great hands and moves for his size.

RED #19 D Menter, Michael (2013) - Good job getting his stick in lanes. Landed several big solid hits. Battled hard in the slot in front of his own net. Players became afraid to go into the corners with him.

Scouts Notes: Forward Jared Goudreau (2013) showed off an absolute laser top shelf for a goal. He's at his best when shooting, because he seems to try to force plays that aren't there when he passes. Dwyer Tschantz (2013) was a massive forward for Team Red. He showed it off playing a very aggressive style. Late birthdate Jack Ramsey (2014), showed off great hands for the Royal Blue team setting up a goal with a beautiful behind the back pass.

June 24, 2012, USA Kelly Green vs. USA Grey (US Select 17)

KG #8 F Melanson, Drew (2013) - Drew has great skating ability and shows a distinct edge to his game. Very physical, likes to battle particularly in front of the net. Has noticeably small/skinny legs but a good frame.

KG #10 F Erne, Adam (2013) - Rushes up the ice displaying very smooth skating ability and an above average stride. Uses his skating in both directions showing a willingness to get back on defense. Has great, skilled hands and made great moves in 1 on 1 and 2 on 1 situations to create scoring chances for himself and others. Constantly taking the body and shows great physicality down low in the corners.

KG #11 F Bailey, Justin (2013) - Bailey has a huge frame, but needs to grow into it. Drives the net hard protecting the puck well. He outworked opponents on multiple occasions to claim the puck in the offensive zone. Seemed to get ahead of himself fumbling the puck when a lane to the net would appear to him.

KG #12 F Alfred, Riley (2013) - Riley handles the puck well and is very shifty. He shows good speed and can blow by the defense, but generally throws the puck into the crowd of players out front when getting deep in the zone. Goes hard to the net without the puck.

GRY #5 D Gross, Jordan (2013) - Showed off great mobility. He positions himself well making himself an option for the puck carrier in all three zones. Got outworked at times.

GRY #11 F Turner, Michael (2014) - Michael is a very physical winger who takes the body effectively and often. Displayed some very slick passing ability.

GRY #1 G Williams, Devin (2014) - Moves extremely well in the crease, made some great saves anticipating plays well. One of the better goaltenders on day one.

Scouts Notes: Forward for Kelly Green Charlie Gerard (2014) has some time to grow as he's a 2014 Eligible. He is a good skater with a strong forecheck. He needs to work on his 1 on 1 play as he was more successful playing a dump and chase game. Forward Shane Eiserman (2014) is a late birth date but is already very well built and likes to play physical. He drives the net and is dangerous with the puck as he will pass and shoot based on the situation and is equally effective. Another 2014 eligible Biagio Lerario showed off great hands for a goal. For team Grey Nash Worden (2013) showed off his hard physical play throughout the game, although went a little too far taking a very unnecessary and selfish penalty. Mitchell Allen (2013) a forward for Team Grey showed good vision and awareness consistently creating scoring chances.

June 24, 2012, USA Columbia Blue vs. USA Gold (US Select 17)

CB #2 D Schuldt, James (2013) - Good positioning with or without the puck. He showed on numerous occasions the ability to make good, quick decisions with the puck. James works hard and came away with the puck in a lot of battles, and threw a few devastating hits.

CB #7 D Downing, Michael (2013) - Downing really struggled this game. He gave opponents way too much time to make a decision. He has great size, uses it adequately but doesn't use it enough. Took too long to make decisions with the puck. Skating is average.

CB #17 F Hurley, Connor (2013) - Hurley looked like a special player out there today. He makes everyone around him better. It was remarkable how consistently on a shift by shift basis he created offensive chances. Shows great vision along with the ability to react quickly to his surroundings. Very good passer and likes to set up his line mates but his shot is strong as well. Displays great skating ability and likes to get the puck deep, fly in and take it. He battles hard along the walls and the corners, and doesn't get pushed around. Connor shows great two-way ability using his speed to get back defensively and create scoring chances. Best penalty killing forward on either team constantly breaking plays up.

CB #30 G McMenimen, Brendan (2013) - Saw little action but did well when he did he moved well, showed good quickness and covers posts well. Made some lazy plays with the puck.

GLD #2 D Reno, Parker (2013) - Made the right play with the puck for the most part both keeping the puck going in the offensive zone and moving the puck up ice from his own zone.

GLD 17 F Humitz, Michael (2013) - Very smooth skating ability. Had his head up, rushing the puck up ice passing off at the right time. Showed good physicality later on in the game.

Scouts Notes: Columbia Blue Forward Jimmy Lodge (2013) showed off his great skating and can stop or turn on a dime. He moved the puck effectively today. Forward Joel Lesperance (2013) absolutely ran over opposing skaters all game long for Team Columbia Blue. Christopher Javins (2013) a defenseman for Team Gold moved the puck up the ice well showing good skating ability. He also made his mark in the physical game running over players bigger than himself.

June 24, 2012, USA Forest Green vs. USA White (US Select 17)

FG #6 D McCrea, Alec (2013) - Made a solid play with the puck even though he knew he would get rocked. Showed off his strength in the slot area of his own net.

FG #1 G Lee, Andrew (2013) - Played OK, had no chance on the goals scored against him. Good initial positioning but a few holes in his game.

WHT - #4 D Vanelli, Thomas (2013) - Smooth skater who rushed the puck up the ice well; while smooth quickness he lost long distance races to the puck. Made a great long distance pass to set up a scoring chance for his team. Very poised with the puck in all areas of the ice, all his passes are solid tape to tape, even though traffic. Showed a good mean streak in this game.

WHT #5 D Lem, Jason (2014) - Lem threw some huge hits and showed good body position defensively. He moved puck up ice intelligently although his skating needs improvement.

WHT #10 F Yuhasz, Michael (2013) - Great breakout speed, rushes puck up ice and evades checks very well.

WHT #17 F Hajicek, Thomas (2013) - Has Great hands and is very elusive. Showed a laser release getting the puck top shelf in a hurry .Tremendous work ethicic and desire; wanted the puck more than anyone else on the ice. Tries to avoid contact too much despite his strong fore check.

#18 F Cotton, Jason (2013) - Shows great hands and is a very slick passer with great vision, made some excellent passes in this game. Plays with a ton of determination fore checking, back checking and creating a lot of turnovers. Uses his size to protect the puck or to knock the opposition off the puck.

#1 G Pawloski, Jason (2014) - Showed great quickness but didn't get tested much.

June 25, 2012, USA Royal Blue vs. USA Grey (US Select 17)

RB #3 D Pomeroy, Stuart (2013) - Skates well backwards, but pivots too late causing him to get beat. Showed good physicality out front of his own net.

RB #5 D Clifton, Connor (2013) - Delivered two massive hits in this one. Shows the ability to skate the puck out of trouble. Has a good shot, pinched in from the point and wired the puck into the back of the net for a goal.

RB #9 F Labosky, Daniel (2013) - Decisions have been hit or miss in this game. When they are good, they end up being scoring chances. When they're not the puck is going the other way. Showed a hard shot but missed the net from point blank more htan once. Has good elusiveness with a good start/stop making him tough to contain.

RB #14 F Gonzalez, Nicholas (2013) - Relentless on the fore check . Has a good shot and shows some elusiveness. Although he threw the puck away when he was about to get hit. At one point he came in from the corner with no passing option so he roofed a backhand shot. He doesn't like to pass much. During the game he threw a really pointless head check.

RB #15 F Ramsey, Jack (2014) - Skates well rushing puck up ice, made quick puck decisions in offensive zone creating a scoring chance.

RB #18 F Cloonan, Ryan (2013) - Showed good acceleration in small spaces to win pucks and get scoring chance. Has great speed and great skating ability blowing by defenseman on outside. Back checked hard.

GRY #5 D Gross, Jordan (2013) - Battles very hard and is very tough down low in his own zone. Jordan skates well rushes the puck up the ice effectively choosing the right lanes and passing the puck off at the right times. Willing to move the puck up the ice and advances it effectively when pressured.

Scouts Notes: Several players for team Grey made their mark on this game at different points. Defenseman Michael Damien (2013) moved the puck up ice effectively, also showing strong skating ability. Ron Greco (2013) finished his checks regularly despite his small size. Gabe Guertler (2013) forward for Team Grey didn't dominate quite like expected. However he showed his great patience with the puck and strong positional play. He seemed to struggle with the increased strength of the bigger, older players in comparison to our viewings of him at younger ages. Goaltender Devin Williams (2014) continued to show why we felt he was arguably the best goaltender in camp handling traffic very well in and around his crease. Jacob Pritchard (2013) forward for Royal Blue showed off his laser of a shot putting the puck top shelf for a goal.

June 25, 2012, USA Kelly Green vs. USA Gold (US Select 17)

KG #3 D Jones, Mitchell (2013) - Jones looks much bigger than his 5'11" listing. He threw multiple solid hits throughout the game.

KG #10 F Erne, Adam (2013) - Erne absolutely dominated some shifts. Makes difficult plays look easy and is very creative in the way he sees the game. Possesses a lethal shot as well as smooth passing ability. Competed hard all game long. Last game he seemed to take a few breaks throughout the game.

KG #18 F Betz, Nicholas (2013) - Delivered a massive hit in this game. He followed it up with several encores to the point where opposing players became timid when approaching him. Showed some impressive moves and good hands in 1 on 1 situations.

GLD #19 D DeAngelo, Anthony (2014) - Skates very well, likes to come in off point on power play and shoot. Anthony directed the power play very well moving the puck effectively and deceiving the opposition using a great slap pass from the point. He got rocked hard in open ice, got upset and took a selfish and unnecessary penalty on the player who hit him. Holds onto the puck way too long and plays too much like an individual too often.

Scouts Notes: Forward Justin Bailey (2013) didn't have quite as dominant of a performance as yesterday, but showed off great skating and acceleration especially for a player of his size. Shane Eiserman (2014) showed off his skating and made some slick passes today. For Team Gold Christopher Javins (2013) applied himself physically throughout the game. Carlos Fornaris (2013) consistently created offensive chances for himself and others.

June 25, 2012, USA Columbia Blue vs. USA White (US Select 17)

CB #7 D Downing, Michael (2013) - Turned a complete 180 from his performance yesterday compared to today. Pretty good positioning on rush and did well in 1 on 1 situations. He was very physical and won battles, but was also seen drifting off a little in his own zone. Showed decent skating ability for his size and he gets up and down the ice well. Pinched in from the point and buried a goal with his wrist shot.

CB #12 F Widmar, Joseph (2013) - Great skater, who rushes the puck up the ice well, displayed a quick release for goal. Works extremely hard in the defensive zone showing a tireless work ethic, battles hard and hits whenever possible.

CB #14 F Lodge, Jimmy (2013) - Great skating ability, leads rush well, relentless on the puck in the offensive zone and battles hard willing to get involved physically. He set up one goal with a solid pass. A little soft on the puck when trying to clear his own zone.

CB #15 F Lesperance, Joel (2013) - Showed great skating ability driving down the wing, especially for his size. He handles the puck well and displays a good quick release on his shot for a goal.

CB #17 F Hurley, Connor (2013) - Showed off his skating ability and tireless work ethic landing a few good hits taking the body every chance he had. Relentless on the point during the penalty kill making life difficult for the power play. Struggled a little when passing the puck on the rush.

WHT #4 D Vanelli, Thomas (2013) - Handled the puck really well under pressure and moved it well on the power play with a good shot. Body positioning is strong, skating is good in small areas but not on long distances.

Scouts Notes: Unfortunately Jason Cotton (2013) didn't follow through with the same performance he had yesterday taking on a much better team in Columbia Blue. After playing AAA in Colorado, he has still emerged as one of the better big forwards in this camp at 6'3". He used his size well driving to the net with and without the puck, and forces opponents to keep an eye on him at all times.

June 25, 2012, USA Forest Green vs. USA Orange (US Select 17)

ORA #2 D Heinrich, Blake (2013) - Beautiful end to end rush showing the ability to change directions quickly, smooth skater. Blake handles the puck and shows good passing ability.

ORA #4 D Citron, Ken (2013) - Decent skater for his size. He loves to play physical and hit opposing players hard every chance he got. Excellent 1 on 1 play knocking the puck off the forward's stick then stepped up on him. Battles hard for the puck in the corners and along the walls, and won most of the time.

ORA #11 F Schoenborn, Alex (2014) - Likes to carry the puck up ice and showed off good moves in 1 on 1 situations. Makes quick decisions with the puck.

Scouts Notes: Defenseman Ramon Lopez (2013) really picked up his game for Team Orange. He used his size and made excellent defensive plays shutting down the top forwards of Team Forest Green all game long. Connor McGlynn (2013) is a forward we really liked in his OHL Draft Year with the Oakville Rangers. He stood out as one of Forest Green's best forwards today with his skating ability and size. Tyler May (2013) showed moves 1 on 1, at one point making a spectacular play almost finishing on a goal that may have been the best of the camp, if he was able to finish it.

June 25, 2012, USA Black vs. USA Red (US Select 17)

BLK #2 D Kiraly, Danny (2013) - Kiraly moved the puck well on the power play and also showed a good shot from the point. His decision making around when to pinch and when to get back was very good.

BLK #7 D Raskob, Willie (2013) - Displayed a laser of a shot putting the puck top shelf for a goal. He also made a great pass from the point to set up a second goal. Raskob delivered some very solid checks, showing a willingness to finish his opponents whenever possible. Late in the game, down one goal with ten seconds left, Willie won a battle for the puck deep in the offensive zone, then created a scoring chance giving his team one last chance to tie the game.

BLK #10 F Hildenbrand, Nicholas (2013) - Showed good hands and a laser of a shot. He positions himself well on the power play and is effective in front of the net deflecting the puck effectively. Constantly made things happen for his team offensively but got a little over aggressive and got penalized for it.

BLK #11 F Laffin, Michael (2013) - Moved the puck effectively on the power play, not forcing anything showing patience when necessary. Showed great speed when driving the wing and constantly made things happen offensively.

BLK #16 F De Leo, Chase (2014) - De Leo shows great vision and passing ability. On one particular play he made a great drop pass when pressured to get the play going, eventually got the puck back and finished on the play. Showed a bit of an edge later on in the game.

RED #6 D Streeter, Brandon (2013) - Got puck in offensive zone, great positioning and reaction time for goal. Threw huge open ice hit. Treied to force shot after creating an odd man rush.

Scouts Notes: Brian Basilico (2013) forward for Team Black was able to show off his passing ability making a great play to set up a goal. Tyler Sheehy (2014) for Team Black is a late birthdate. He has a hard shot, makes great passes and fights off checkers well despite being slightly undersized. Jared Goudreau (2013) showed off some good hands for Team Red. Meanwhile defenseman Michael Menter (2013) continued to use his size being a physical force for Team Red. He has solid defensive positioning and battles hard. Walker Bass (2014) goaltender for Team Red showed off good reaction time and positioning making several good saves. Tyler Hill has massive size at 6'6" - 225lbs., and scored a massive goal for Team Red with 51 seconds left to elevate them to victory. Interestingly enough Hill was noted in avoiding the physical play in this game despite being the biggest player on the ice.

August 4, 2012, Team Red vs. Team White (Team Canada U18 Camp)

RED #8 LD Morrissey, Josh (2013) - Morrissey is a very smooth skater who moves the puck up ice quickly. He is so calm and composed when rushing the puck, especially out of trouble but doesn't force plays. Reads and reacts to plays and situations extremely quick anticipating plays very effectively. Lightning quick decisions with the puck on the power play helped keep the pressure on the penalty kill.

RED #10 LD Bigras, Chris (2013) - Chris may have shown the best combination of defensive and offensive play of any defenseman in todays scrimmage. Offensively he moved the puck up the ice very effectively and moving it well in the offensive zone. Defensively he stuck on his man extremely well. Whether it was one on one play, or along the boards and he did this on a very consistent basis.

RED #13 RD Subban, Jordan (2013) - Got frustrated on the ice at different points of the game with the extra physical play and the pushing and shoving, he appeared visibly affected by it. Made some good passes, and showed he has one of the stronger shots from the point of any defenseman in this camp.

RED #17 LD Brouillard, Nikolas (2013) - Very smooth skater, rushes the puck extremely well, and is fearless when pushing through small spaces. Tries to force fancy plays on the power play which burned him and got picked off against this type of talent. Didn't adjust and kept trying the same th ings expecting different results.

RED #18 LW Drouin, Jonathan (2013) - Drouin is a great skater and extremely elusive. He gets a away from contact so well along the boards, at one point he evaded about three checks, but then threw the puck away with a no look pass. Very slick passing ability especially on the rush. Did a good job of getting back defensively when the other team is set to push the play up the ice. Put on a great shootout move at the end of the game.

RED #19 RC MacKinnon, Nathan (2013) - Didn't take over the game, but was easily one of the best players. Constantly an offensive threat every time he entered the offensive zone. Great skating ability, exceptional hands and excellent puck control ability. His hockey sense is extremely high and he sees the game very well. Pretty equal between his ability to pass and shoot and he has a very powerful shot. Nathan made defensemen look bad when they went after him as he easily stick handled around opponents. Sometimes plays with his ability will try to do too much but he did a great job of making some excellent plays while not forcing plays that weren't there. Has an excellent shot

RED #21 RW Ritchie, Nicholas (2014) - Nicholas really made an impression right off the bat. He showed his power along the boards and in the corners, while roofing the first goal of the game. He kept it simple when in open ice with good positioning. When he's along the boards or in the corners he punishes the opposing players as much as possible. He crushed several opposing players hard and clean throughout the game, however he did give out a pretty bad hit from behind taking one of the few penalties in this game. Ritchie went to war with Darnell Nurse for the better part of the game along the boards and in the corners.

RED #26 LW Pedersen, Brent (2013) - Powered through two defenders close to the wall so effectively, protecting puck, created scoring chances. Goes to war along the walls and wins a lot of battles. Crashed the net hard took up space out front, quick on rebounds, banged home one goal with net presence. Skating has visibly improved. Pedersen was one of the most consistently effective players of anyone in this game.

WHT #8 LD Nurse, Darnell (2013) - If today's performance is a sign of things to come, then it's safe to say Darnell has really improved over the summer. He was constantly engaging physically includuing an ongoing war he had with Nicholas Ritchie all game long. Had his moments where he rushed the puck effectively showing very good speed for his size.

WHT #13 RD Ekblad, Aaron (2014) - Ekblad was one of the better defensemen throughout the game. He was effective defensively shutting down forwards, but he wasn't overly physical. He moved the puck up the ice extremely well, and knows when to push up the ice himself.

WHT #14 LW Duclair, Anthony (2013) - Great skater with outstanding speed, Anthony handles the puck very well at top speed. He made some puck playing mistakes in the neutral zone which lead to scoring chances against. However in the offensive zone he moved the puck very well showing great patience.

WHT #23 RC Reinhart, Sam (2014) - Very good offensive instincts, forced turnovers and was aware of his surroundings in all three zones. Has a powerful shot and is especially dangerous on the rush.

WHT #24 RW Domi, Max (2013) - Doesn't quit on plays and plays with a lot of determination. At times early on he tried to do too much himself with the puck not willing to pass at times he should. Eventually he corrected this and made some nice set-up's in the offensive zone. Max is very elusive and showed off his powerful shot and good vision. Later on in the game he got upset in a battle and two handed a player on the red team around the ankles. Max was the only player to take two penalties in this game. Showed a very good shootout move after the game.

WHT #29 RC Garlent, Hunter (2013) - He disappeared through atleast half of this game, but when he was on his game he was all over the offensive zone forcing turnovers, landing hits, covering for the defense and creating scoring chances.

Scouts Notes: Team Red was clearly the stronger team posting a 3-0 shutout in the first of three scrimmages at the Team Canada Ivan Hlinka Selection Camp. Zach Fucale (2013) and Tristan Jarry (2013) combined for the shutout, however neither were tested too much. For Team Red Madison Bowey (2013) did very well being paired with Josh Morrissey. They moved the puck smoothly and cleanly between the two. He also showed good skating ability in all directions. Stephen Nosad (2013) wasn't a big standout, but he showed consistent work ethic, finishing his hits. Carter Hanson (2013) skates fairly well for a big kid with a power forward frame. For Team White, Zach Nastasiuk (2013) continued to show how much he's developed. He has a power forward's frame and protects the puck well. He created offense for himself and others a few times this game. However on the negative side both Kayle Doetzel (2013) and Samuel Morin (2013) both really struggled to keep up with the top skilled players of Team Red. Kayle constantly got beat one on one and lost his positioning, whereas Morin kept trying to get too aggressive in 1 on 1 and 2 on 2 situations, went after the forwards and kept getting burned. Both struggled with the concept of trying the same thing over and over expecting different results.

August 5, 2012, Team Red vs. Team White (Team Canada U18 Camp)

RED #8 LD Morrissey, Josh (2013) - The skills that Morrissey shows suggests he is an offensive first defenceman. He made excellent long distance passing tape to tape on a consistent basis. He seems to make the best possible play with the puck every single time he touches it. However Josh battles hard, anticipates plays and intercepts potential scoring chances and defends his own zone well.

RED #9 LD Theodore, Shea (2013) - Moves it up ice well and made good plays with it especially controlling it in the offensive zone. Theodore is a decent skater who was effective in creating scoring chances. Sent a great wrister through traffic which resulted in a goal.

RED #11 RD Bowey, Madison(2013) - Bowey doesn't jump out at you but very quietly does a lot of things right. He helps his team by winning battles, maintaining good defensive positioning and getting the puck up ice quickly and efficiently.

RED #18 LW Drouin, Jonathan (2013) - Created offense at times throughout the game. Scored two goals in this game. He is more than willing to battle but he usually gets beat. As he gets stronger this was start making more of an impact in game. Works hard defensively and usually gets back into his own zone.

RED #21 RW Ritchie, Nicholas (2014) - Ritchie scored a goal very early in this game much like the previous night. Despite not playing with MacKinnon and Drouin, he continued to produce consistently. Played a physical game en route to a two goal performance.

RED #24 RC Needham, Matthew (2013) - Cycles the puck very well and battles consistently hard. Shows good hands, shot and is patient with the puck. Very strong defensively, short handed and 5 on 5.

RED #25 RW Klimchuk, Morgan (2013) - Klimchuk got moved to the top line for his team with MacKinnon and Drouin but really struggled to get it rolling off the bat. He lost a lot of battles and wasn't creating much offense. As the game progressed he did ok, and made a great pass to set up a nice goal. Morgan looks a little bigger than his listing indicates.

RED #26 LW Pedersen, Brent (2013) - Made an excellent deflection out front of the net for a goal. Battled hard, wasn't as noticeable as yesterday, but still making an impact on the fourth line.

RED #30 RW Baptiste, Nicholas (2013) - Baptiste showed off his good skating ability and was good in small areas. He forechecked hard and showed patience with the puck.

RED #29 G Fucale, Zachary (2013) - Showed great lower body quickness preventing anything low from getting past him.

RED #32 G Jarry, Tristan (2013) - Makes very good plays with the puck, and made some solid saves early on.
WHT #8 LD Nurse, Darnell (2013) - Used his strength playing a very aggressive style. Very hard to knock off the puck due to his size and speed. Good puck distribution on the power play. Made a great move in the shootout.
WHT #11 LD Heatherington, Dillon (2013) - Very good skater for size and will get the puck out of harms way when there is no option. Absorbs contact well and shows a good level of aggression.

WHT #12 LD Morin, Samuel (2013) - Made a few good plays one on one early on in the game, but took a bad penalty after losing a battle for the puck. Doesn't look before playing the puck and his turnover rate is very high. He kept struggling all game long with puck decisions.

WHT #13 RD Ekblad, Aaron (2014) - Ekblad showed effective two-way play. He showed matured strength and winning battles in his own zone. Moved the puck effectively up ice fairly consistently. Very good two-way play, overpowering and winning battles in own zone, moving puck very well up ice.

WHT #22 LC Kujawinski, Ryan (2013) - Struggled in battles today losing some when he should have won. He got overpowered out front of the opposing net. Ryan started playing physical and showed some good passing ability as the game went on. There was flashes of talent, but he definitely had his share of struggles. Showed off a great shootout move.

WHT #24 RW Domi, Max (2013) - Won battles against bigger opponents. Showed good passing ability and creativity. Forced turnovers which lead to offensive chances.

WHT #27 RW Nastasiuk, Zach (2013) - Set up scoring chances and created many opportunities for himself and his teammates. Constantly in the mix whenever he was on the ice, and one of the better players for his team tonight.

WHT #31 RW Veilleux, Tommy (2013) - Showed some decent speed but also looked timid at times as he seemed to be trying to sell it when he got hit. He was ok initiating contact, not so much with taking it.

Scouts Notes: A few minor notes for both teams; for Team Red Jordan Subban (2013) looked his best tonight when rushing the puck up the ice. Whereas Nikolas Broulliard (2013) had a little more success keeping it more simple than last night. Nathan MacKinnon (2013) showed great puck distribution and excellent hands. Although he didn't do too much in this game. Stephen Harper (2013) battled sparingly in the corners and didn't get into position to get his powerful shot off. As for team White, Anthony Duclair (2013) pushes the puck up ice with great speed and puck protection to set up the first goal which was scored by Sam Reinhart

(2013). Same went hard to the net and it paid off. Jason Dickinson (2013) made a few nice plays to set up some scoring chances. He had his moments in this game, but wasn't quite as good as yesterday. Curtis Lazar (2013) lost a lot of battles and didn't really do much offensively.

August 24, 2012, Victoriaville Tigres vs. Drummondville Voltigeurs (QMJHL)

Pre Season.

DRU #15 D Brouillard, Nikolas (2013) – Brouillard showed he was the best defenseman on the ice in this game with his strong puck-moving ability. He was always in movement in all three zones and made smart plays to help his team move down the ice. He didn't generate high-end speed and didn't make incredible plays, but they were effective that's for sure. He demonstrated a good arsenal of tools on the power play, where he can pass and shoot the puck fairly well. On two occasions when his shooting lane was blocked he went with a fake shot to reach a teammate that was open beside the goal. It was hard to evaluate him on defense as he had very few one on one situation. He didn't look bigger to the naked eye compared to last (which is still to be seen with official measurements) but he didn't really have to engage physically either in this game because he was one step ahead of his opponents on the puck the whole time.

DRU #31 G Graham, Domenic (2013) – There's not a whole lot to say on Graham in this game as he was tested very few times. He played well allowing 2 goals on 26 shots. The major thing I noticed from him was a change in his style. He used to move a lot in his crease and he would often get caught out of position. Now he seems more laid back and making the right movement at the right time, still with great reflexes.

VIC #3 D Diaby, Jonathan (2013) – Diaby struggled a bit with positioning and timing in this game. He had trouble timing his actions when engaging the attackers coming down the wing, with his stick or his body for instance. The same pattern emerged when he had the puck as he was nervous and made some sloppy plays. Overall he did a good job along the boards and in front of the net where he usually is at his best. Picked up a fight too, landing a couple good punches. He punches hard but not very dynamically.

VIC #19 RW Ayotte, Mathieu (2014) – Hard game to evaluate a forward as puck possession was almost inexistent. Didn't demonstrate anything high end in term of speed but he seemed to have good hands and he takes good decisions with the puck for a young forward. His hockey sense allowed to make quick decision and help his team to keep moving forward.

VIC #57 LW Veilleux, Tommy (2013) – Veilleux was a step behind the whole game in the neutral zone and didn't generate anything offensively. He needs to take decision more quickly with the puck if he can't keep up with the skating, instead of holding on to it. He didn't display his usual physical game either. He seemed rather frustrated by it and took two penalties after the whistle.

Scouts Notes: I thought this was a very hard game to scout as teams were playing ping-pong with the puck. The fact this was a pre-season game also showed a lot in the play of each player. Drummondville seemed to be one step ahead in terms of execution and it showed on the scoreboard with a 4-2 win. I was hoping to see more of Drummondville's import Lukas Balmelli, but he barely played. Brouillard left a good impression with his puck-moving ability, where he was one step ahead of everyone. Jonathan Diaby and Tommy Veilleux didn't leave a strong impression for second year veterans, but like mentioned before, this game is only early pre-season.

August 25, 2012, Chatham Maroons @ Sarnia Legionnaires (GOJHL)

CHA #44 LW Levesque, Michael (2013) Drafted in the 3rd round by the Guelph Storm in the 2011 OHL Priority Selection; Michael has had a reputation for his physical play. Surprisingly there were three fights in this game, none of which Levesque was involved in. Michael played a very hard nosed physical game finishing around a dozen checks while winning battles. You wouldn't expect a player of his size and nature to be as smooth of a skater as he was. He uses his skating and speed to win battles in corners, and while he showed a little offense, it doesn't appear to be a big part of his game going forward at this point. Michael will look to force his way onto the Guelph Storm roster in a bottom six role this coming week.

SAR #3 LD Zottl, Nick (2013) Zottl is a big bodied defenceman drafted in the 11th round by the now Mississauga Steelheads in the 2011 OHL Priority Selection Draft. Nick has massive size, and uses his strength in corners to win battles. He is fairly well positioned against quick forwards and uses his stick very well one on one. He clearly has good strength and we would like to see him land hits on a more regular basis as he seems to prefer to use his strength only when absolutely necessary, and likes to poke the puck away. Shows basic puck movement skills and doesn't get himself in trouble keeping it simple. If Nick continues to play this way he should make a bit of an impact in Steelheads camp.

SAR #4 RD Vandervaart, P.J. (2013) P.J. went undrafted in the 2011 and 2012 OHL Priority Selection much to our surprise. Our scouts were extremely impressed with his potential. We felt he was worthy of a 6th-10th round selection in the 2011 Draft. P.J. Stood out in Sarnia Sting rookie camp and thus received an invite to their main camp. P.J. stood out again tonight in GOJHL action. He finished his checks whenever possible with power and strength. He matches up extremely well in 1 on 1 situations and is able to stick with smaller forwards due to his good skating ability in both directions. Where his game has really evolved is offensively. P.J. made a few excellent breakout passes but also was very effective in the offensive zone moving the puck around. His night ended early as a Chatham player lured him into the fight much to his dismay. Vandervart handled himself very well and won the fight easily. P.J. may be one of the most unknown 95 players up for the 2013 NHL Entry Draft, but if he gets his chance in the OHL he has the potential to surprise some people.

SAR #9 LW Ciccarelli, Matt (2015) A late '96 birthdate, Matt is an undersized forward who will be given every moment he needs to grow as he isn't eligible until 2015. Ciccarelli was drafted in the 5th round by the Sarnia Sting, and will likely see a year of Jr. B action before jumping up with the OHL's Sting full time. Matt likes to do everything at a high speed. He rushes the puck up ice well, drives hard into corners and generally prefers to set up his linemates rather than take the shot himself. He has improved in his corner play, but will need to get stronger and hopefully a little bigger before he sees great success in that area, because the effort is already there. He will be an interesting player to watch progress over the next few years.

SAR #12 RC Kestner, Josh (2013*) Josh was not a player we were really keeping an eye on, but he really forced us to take a long look at him this game, as the puck seemed to gravitate towards him. A late 93 made him available for the 2012 NHL Entry Draft however was looked over as he was playing in the NA3HL for the Flint Jr. Generals. While we are not sure there is an NHL future for him, he has certainly emerged onto atleast the NCAA scene with his play. Kestner has an exceptional work ethic and won battles all over the ice in all three zones. Anticipating players he was able to intercept passes and when he went in along on the goaltender he showed great moves offensively. Josh is going to be an interesting player to watch, as he was hands down one of the best players in this game, and really left an impression.

September 7, 2012, Sherbrooke Phoenix vs Victoriaville Tigres (QMJHL)

(Pre-Season Game)

VIC #3 D Diaby, Jonathan (2013) I thought Diaby played an excellent game with a great impact in the physical department. He showed his usual strength along the boards and in front of the net where he was very effective. He made a great use of his long stick and even his legs to block passing or shooting lanes. This proved to be particularly helpful on the penalty kill. He had good foot speed and it allowed him to unleash some devastating open ice hits. He had a fight as well where he never really was in danger. I liked how mean he was on the ice, punishing his opponents and playing effective defense. It will be interesting to see if he can keep up with this when he faces players with more speed and talent (Sherbrooke doesn't have a lot of depth upfront).

VIC #12 C/W Rehak, Dominik (2013) – Didn't leave a strong impression as far as the whole game is concerned but he had some good flashes where you could see the talent. He had the puck a few times in the neutral zone where he showed good explosion combined with fine hand speed. He did a good job getting involved defensively and positioning properly in order to make plays (Covering a player, cutting a passing lane etc.). He seems to have the potential to play a good two-way game, but he needs to be more physical and find is rhythm.

VIC #55 D Côté, Vytal (2013) - Côté was a force alongside Jonathan Diaby on defense where he kept accumulating hits as the game went one. He showed good mobility and seemed comfortable on the ice. He made good decision defensively and made life hard for his opponents. I didn't notice much from him offensively but he's comfortable with the puck and gets it out of the zone just fine.

VIC #57 LW Veilleux, Tommy (2013) – Played a much better game than the previous time I saw him. He showed a better physical presence and was even used in front of the net on the power play where he did a good job hanging in there. Still would like to see more from him in terms of puck possession and skating.

SHE #2 D Neill, Carl (2014) – Played a simple game but made some good plays with the puck from his zone and in the offensive zone. You could see he likes to join the rush and give his teammates options. He has overall good mobility and footing. He still has ways to go in one on one situation with his gap control and stick work. You could see he was a bit confused with speedy players coming at him and had to catch up on them. Unfortunately it seems his coach used in two sequences, at the beginning and the end of the game with a big pause in the middle.

SHE #9 C Audette, Daniel (2014) – Only played a couple of shifts before he apparently left the game with an injury. But he did a great play on the man advantage worth noticing: He showed excellent vision and accuracy with a long cross-ice pass that was perfect for his defenseman and led to a goal.

SHE 33 G Flinn, Jack (2013) – Had an excellent outing and stole quite a few goals from Victoriaville. He had excellent rebound control and made great reads that allowed him to position properly. He covers a lot of the net with his huge frame and his long legs allowed him to make some key saves. He was in control the whole time and never panicked in front of the repeated Victoriaville attacks.

Scouts Notes:

Despite big lack of depth and talent, Sherbrooke started the game better than Victoriaville and had a better level of execution. They also outworked their opponents and it lead to them taking the game 4-2. Victoriaville had trouble getting their transition play going and they had trouble generating offense when their first line (Halley-Danault-Maillet) was off the ice. The players that stood out the most were Diaby and Coté for their physical presence and goaltender Jack Flinn for his great game. Veterans Phillip Danault and Philippe Hudon also had a good game. Danault was faster than anyone on the ice and you could see he was always a step ahead of everyone. Hudon did a great physical job and imposed his presence around the net where he picked up a goal.

Sept 7, 2012 Chilliwack Chiefs vs. Penticton Vees (BCHL)

CHI #6 LD Roberts, Eric(2013) A good skating defenseman who had an unnoticeable game tonight. Did not make a huge mistake, but did not do anything spectacular either. Roberts got better as the game went along, especially with his gap control and his ability to anticipate the play. He seemed to be chasing too much rather than contain opponents, especially around the boards and the corners. He is a little below average with the puck. He has an average shot and an average outlet pass. He needs to improve on all facets of his game to have a chance of being a pro hockey player.

CHI#14 RW Plevy, Austin(2013) Quick, grinding forward played a very good game for the Chiefs. Showed off a lot of energy all game long, and brought a nice 2 way game tonight. Plevy is very shifty around the boards, and possesses some nice speed to get away from defenders. He had an end to end rush, deked through a couple of defenders and drew a penalty at the last second. He then scored on the PP on a quick, low wrist shot off the half wall. Showed some grit all game long and was a pain to play against. He tried to land a hit whenever he could. He needs to get stronger on his skates, and contain opponents in the defensive zone instead of taking a run at them all the time. Could work on his offensive skills more as well. Plevy has committed to Merrimack.

CHI#28 RW Forster, Garrett(2013) A small, 2 way forward who had an average game. Forster is not particularly fast or strong. His best skill is his vision. He made some very impressive plays in the offensive zone that created some good scoring chances for the Chiefs. He had a wonderful one timer opportunity, but fanned on it completely. Must be better in his own end, especially with his stick. He often fails to cover the correct passing lane, giving the other team some good options while he is on the ice. Forster must also be more willing to be hit and make some sacrifices for his team in front of the net. Has a tendency to get to the net, then slowly move to the side of the net for a scoring chance if possible.

PEN#8 LW Gropp, Ryan(2015) A big speedy forward who seems to be a complete package. He is a very good skater given his size, and showed off some soft hands throughout the game. He is very good in the offensive zone, and displayed some nice vision too. Gropp must become more physical to take advantage of his size along the boards. He is very smart without the puck, and positions himself well to take away passing and shooting lanes. He needs to work on his finishing touch to pick up more points as the season goes along. he creates many opportunities, he just has a difficult time finishing them.

PEN#18 RW Depourcq, Cody(2014) A small forward who got better as the game went along. Only stands 5'6, and his size was definitely an issue at the beginning of the game, but made a few adjustments and became more effective for his team. He used his feet more to try to fend off opponents, and made plays a second or two quicker. For a small player, his skating is quite awkward, and really needs to work on his strides and overall speed. Despite being so short, Depourcq goes into the corner and in front of the net without any fear, and competes extremely hard for pucks. He puts himself in good position often times without the puck, but still has some work to do defensively, particularly along the boards.

Scouts Notes: Penticton dominated the entire game, but did not make the most of their opportunities. I was quite impressed with Austin Plevy(2013) tonight. Really liked his approach to the game and how good his compete level was. Still has to polish up his overall game, but he still has time to develop. Ryan Gropp(2015) also caught my eye for his combination of size, speed and skill. Not many players can put those three things together at once. Needs to put on some strength and be able to play at a higher pace to be successful. Troy Stecher(2013) of Penticton also had a good game. Born in 1992, a good puck moving defenseman, but his skating is an issue. Not very big either to make up for it.

FINAL SCORE: 2-1 Penticton

Sept 7, 2012, Victoria Grizzlies vs. Coquitlam Express (BCHL)

VIC#6 LD, De Jong, Nolan(2013) Big defenseman who had a quiet, but effective game tonight. Moved the puck very well in any given situation and looked very poise while doing so. Looks like a good skater, but he could improve his overall speed skating forwards and backwards. Would like to see him be more physical along the boards and use his body more to his advantage. Possesses a good, active stick. Knocked away a few passes going cross ice, and takes away passing lanes well. Committed to Cornell University.

VIC#31 G, Rouleau, Brady(2013) Tall, athletic goaltender who had a great game for the Grizzlies. He was very quick going post to post and made a couple of huge saves to keep his team in the game. Tracks the puck well and looks through traffic quite easily. Battles for loose pucks to the end. Needs to improve on his rebound control. Had a few go right up the middle and could have ended up being great scoring chances for Coquitlam. Possesses active hands, but blocker side seems to be his weak side as he could not control rebounds well, and had a few scary moments where the puck could have squeezed by a few times.

COQ#97 RC, Barzal, Mathew(2015) 15 year old who was recently the #1 overall pick in the WHL Bantam Draft had a good game for Coquitlam. Barzal received more and more ice time as the game went along. He looked a little nervous to begin with, making decisions too quickly and not using his excellent vision. Did not look out of place tonight at all. Did not dominate the game, but he did not back down either. So smart without the puck. Positions himself perfectly whether he's the first guy in the forecheck, or acting as F2 or F3. Picked off a few passes throughout the game and created some good scoring chances. Creates a lot of room for his teammates with his ability to draw defenders to him. Took a lot of stick work from the opposition, but did not react negatively once. Just kept playing his game. He had some memorable moments using his body to fend off bigger, older opponents to take the puck to the net. A very good skater who reaches top speed in a hurry. Needs to work on getting faster though. Will be very fun to watch for years.

COQ#74 LW, Pryzbek, Zachary(2013) Hulking power forward who made his presence felt by dishing out some big hits tonight. Really used his 6'4 frame to his advantage. Showed off some nice hands coming off the half wall a couple of times. Needs to work on his skating, particularly his speed and strides. Pryzbek looked quite lost in the defensive zone and must stay aware of his surrounding much more to take away passing and shooting lanes, and to make sure his point man does not sneak through for a back door play. Must get rid of inconsistent stretches in his game. He had a very good first period, then disappeared in the second, then showed some life in the third. Committed to Brown University for 2013.

COQ#18 LC Hennig, Jace(2013) A quick, skilled forward who had a good game tonight. Created some good chances with his vision and speed. Showed off some above average stickhandling skills in tight. Sometimes tried to do too much, but mostly around the 3rd period when the team could not bury their chances. Showed a high level of commitment by backchecking hard to break up odd man rushes a couple of times. He is not afraid to go in front of the net and sacrifice his body. Needs to get stronger be more effective along the boards.

Scouts Notes: This game was a very good goaltending match up. Both goalies came out to play today. Coquitlam was the much better team, but they just could not capitalize on the number of chances they received. Mathew Barzal (2015) will be an interesting player to watch as he gets more comfortable with the level of play, and have a pair of wingers that he plays with all the time instead of ro-

tating into different combinations. John Siemer(2013) of Coquitlam was a turnover machine. Tried to do too much on his own, and made very poor decisions with the puck.

FINAL SCORE: 1-0(OT) Coquitlam

Sept 8, 2012, Prince George Spruce Kings vs. Merritt Centennials (BCHL)

PG#14 RW, Luedtke, Jeremiah(2013) Small forward whose best attribute is his speed. However, other parts of his game must improve significantly. Made a number of bad reads throughout the game, and committed a lot of turnovers. Had a few in the neutral zone that turned into an odd man rush the other way. Below average strength, particularly around the boards. Luedtke has a difficult time staying on his feet when an opponent is all over his back. He cannot get inside positioning on an opponent with a puck to take it away. Has below average instincts with and without the puck.

PG#21 RD, Eden, Mitch(2013) Smooth puck moving defenseman who had a very good game for Prince George. Made solid reads with the puck all game long. Looked very poise with the puck as well. Quite strong around the boards and on his skates. He was good in his own zone. Used his stick effectively and was in the right position most of the time. Has a tendency to get too aggressive at times. Also needs to improve on his passing skills. It is generally good, but could be better, especially in traffic. Not the fastest skater, but has some quickness to him. Size is a bit of a concern. Only stands at 5'11.

MER#4 RD, Chanter, Dylan(2014) Big defenseman who had some good moments in the game. Definitely more of a home stay defenseman. Maintained good gap control with his stick and did well to angle opponents to the wall. The problem occurs when forwards are coming at him in full speed. Has a difficult time keeping up with them and needs to improve on his lateral movement. Made some good outlet passes throughout the game, but needs to improve on his puck handling skills. Must improve his shots and make decisions quicker to prevent a crowd from forming in the slot and take the shot away. Looks very raw and a little awkward at 6'3, but some potential seems to be there.

MER#19 RW, Cuglietta, Diego(2013) Good skating forward who displayed some good skills at times. Not very strong on his skates, and lost many battles along the boards. Not very good at reading the play and handling the puck. Must learn to bear down, and make good plays when the opportunities are given. Has a weak wrist shot that must be improved. Not too bad in his own end, but positioning was an issue a couple times. during the game.

Scouts Notes: This game was there for Prince George to take right from the start. They looked much more faster and physical than Merritt. The only impressive player from this game was Mitch Eden(2013). He looked very confident out there, and played a solid game. Could be a late round pick up in the 2013 NHL Entry Draft. Dylan Chanter(2014) has some potential to develop into a good defensive defenseman. He certainly has the physical tools. He just needs to work on his skating and look comfortable in his own skin. Other than those two players, both teams do not have very good players.

FINAL SCORE: 4-1 Prince George

Sept 8, 2012, Salmon Arm Silverbacks vs. West Kelowna Warriors (BCHL)

SA#4 RD, Bowen, Dylan(2013) 2 way defenseman had a quiet, but good game. Did not receive much ice time, but when he was on the ice he made some good plays defensively. Moved the puck effectively. Was not fancy, but got the job done. Bowen was in good position defensively for most of his shifts. Got caught overcommitting once in the corners and turned into a mini 2 on 1 down low. A good skater but could improve on his overall speed. Made some good tight turns around the corners. Looks quite raw, but some potential was evident.

SA#8 LW, Klonarakis, Michael(2013) Speedy winger who spends most of his time around the perimeter. Needs to attack the net more and be aggressive to put up some more points. Showed off some skill a few times during the game going down the wing and deking out a few defenders. Needs to be stronger along the boards. Largely ineffective all game.

WK#8 RD, Plant, Adam(2013) Small offensive defenseman who had a very good game. Finished off a nice goal on the PP, coming down from the point on a back door play and snapping one home very quickly. A very good skater, who must use his speed to his advantage to make up for his lack of size standing at only 5'9. Made some solid passes all game long and quickly got the attack going for his team. Needs to improve on his strength and be harder to play against, especially in front of his net. Committed to Harvard.

WK#9 LW, Pope, David(2013) Big, speedy forward who was a presence all game long. Really used his speed and size to his advantage. Has a good slap shot and was set up numerous times on the PP. Likes to go down the wing and try to cut to the middle. Displayed above average hands. Likes to play the game at a high tempo and looks comfortable doing so. Could be better along the walls and show more desire to retrieve pucks. Defensively, took away shooting lanes effectively, and gave opposing defensemen very little time to make plays.

Scouts Notes: Salmon Arm got dominated in every facet of the game. They committed too many turnovers, looked much slower and got manhandled consistently. They did not respond to Salmon Arm's pressure once. Would have liked to see Dylan Bowen(2013) receive more ice time. Out of all Salmon Arm defensemen, he probably had the most effective night. Made good decisions with the puck and played well in his own end. Definitely has some potential to his game. Probably will never be a flashy player, but looks very dependable. If Alex Plant(2013) was a few inches taller, he would be a legitimate prospect for the 2013 NHL Entry Draft. David Pope(2013) looks to have some potential to his game. Has a good mix of size and offensive skills to his game.

FINAL SCORE: 6-0 West Kelowna

Sept 8, 2012, Cowichan Valley Capitals vs. Trail Smoke Eaters (BCHL)

CV#7 LC, Cooper, Steen(2014) Speedy forward who plays a grinding style of game. Likes to get in on the forecheck and throw his body around. A pest to play against, was in the middle of a scrum numerous times. Has awkward strides, looks too upright and very choppy. Creates offense by going to the net with the puck. Shifty around the boards, protects the puck well given his size. Not very good at reading the play, and made some poor decisions with the puck. Will probably never be depended on to create plays.

CV#25 LD, Bechtel, Rylan(2013) Aggressive defenseman who loves to take the body. Got caught a number of times trying to land a big hit and they resulted in great scoring chances for Trail. Likes to take gambles, and they pay off when he successfully jumps the play, but is also often detrimental to his team's efforts. On the PK, was caught running around too much and left the man in front of the net wide open which resulted in a goals against. Needs to learn how to contain the opposition. Has average offensive instincts. Would make good plays in one instance, then a terrible one the next. Will be difficult to play his type of game at the next level when he is only 5'10.

Scouts Notes: Trail is an awful hockey team. They were dominated by a Cowichan Valley team who are average at best. Keyler Bruce(2013), a '92, was probably the best player in the game. A good 2 way forward who created offense with his solid play along the boards. I don't see Steen Cooper(2014) and Rylan Bechtel(2013) as NHL prospects at this present time, especially with their lack of size.

FINAL SCORE: 8-1 Cowichan Valley

Sept 9, 2012, Vernon Vipers vs. Powell River Kings (BCHL)

VRN#9 LC, Tambellini, Adam(2013) Power forward who looked very good today. Used his speed and size to create offense all game long. Powell River had a very difficult time stopping him. Loves to cut to the net and try to score off of a rebound. Not afraid to take hits to make a play. Strong along the boards, but could be much stronger given his size. Quarterbacks the PP and looks very good doing so. Makes good decisions with the puck and does not try to do too much by himself. Quite reliable defensively. Committed to North Dakota for 2013.

VRN#14 RW, Hadley, Ryan(2013) 1993 born forward was Vernon's best player today. Played a solid game created a lot of offense with Tambellini. A bruising forward who displayed above average hands in tight. Very good along the wall and is tough to knock off the puck. Created a partial breakaway by breaking through the middle between two oppositions and scored. Received an assist by spinning off a defender in the corner and then taking the puck to the net and left a rebound for Tambellini. Could improve his play in his own zone. Not very good in coverage, as he is not very aware of his surroundings.

PR#22 RC, Richardson, Evan(2013) 1993 born forward who was the offensive catalyst for Powell River. A very good skater, especially in tight situations. Handles the puck very well in any situation and has very good vision. Only problem is his size as he is listed as only 5'8. Tries to play a much bigger game, and has mixed results. To receive any kind of an opportunity to play in the NHL, Richardson must have elite skating and playmaking skills. Committed to Boston College for 2013.

Scouts Notes: This game was quite entertaining. It displayed a lot of offense and physical play. Adam Tambellini(2013) was very good in this game. His combination of speed and size is quite rare. It would be interesting to see how he does against better competition. Will probably be the highest picked player from the BCHL in the 2013 NHL Entry Draft. It is a real shame that Evan Richardson(2013) is not any bigger. His offensive game was very good today. Powell River relies on him for most of their offensive output.

FINAL SCORE: 4-3 Powell River

Sept 9, 2012, Coquitlam Express vs. Cowichan Valley Capitals (BCHL)

COQ#4 LD, Biega, Marc(2013) A solid defensive defenseman who can move the puck quite well. Biega's best attribute is his positioning. He stayed patient in his own end and never was caught chasing or being too aggressive. A good skater who was able to get out of trouble with his calm approach to the game and ability to change directions. A good puck mover, but made a couple of mistakes on breakouts. Offensively, reads the play well but needs to improve on his shot to be more of a threat.

COQ#6 RD, Marks, Cameron(2013) A flashy defenseman, Marks is a very impressive skater not just with his speed, but his ability to make tight turns and change directions. Oozed confidence all game long. Very good with the puck all game long and made good reads with and without the puck. Good along the boards, but could get better. Handles the puck well in any situation and gets the attack going in a hurry. Defensively, was in good position for most of the game. Had an active stick, and was very good at keeping opponents to the outside. Committed to University of New Hampshire for 2014.

COQ#97 RC, Barzal, Mathew(2015) Flashy forward was depended on to play more of a 2 way game today, and looked pretty good doing so. Was not a liability defensively at all. Read the play very well and showed off some impressive strength. Offensively, was around the net all game long to try to bang home a rebound. When he had the puck, he had the right ideas but just could not execute them as well as he would like. He took a beating all game long, but withstood all of it and just played his own game. Still looks like he is making some adjustments to his game to get used to the speed and physicality of the oppositions.

CV#15 LW, Jarvis, Eli(2013) A small forward who had an inconsistent game. At times, looked very good in the offensive zone and along the boards with his stickhandling skills and vision, and at other times really struggled to get the puck and do anything with it. Needs to improve on his skating, especially since he is only 5'9. He often has the right ideas to create scoring chances like a give and go, but is not quick enough to make the plays work. Competes hard in all areas of the ice. Defensively, could be much better at covering the point

Scouts Notes: Coquitlam showed up with a good performance today. I was quite impressed with Cameron Marks(2013) and his level of confidence. Looked like a veteran out there. Definitely somebody to keep an eye on for the rest of the season to see what kind of improvements he can make. Would like to see him play against better competition. Marc Biega(2013) was also quite good. Just kept making plays after plays in the game, with or without the puck. Mathew Barzal(2013) was not spectacular, but was not bad either. Definitely a big jump in competition to go from bantam to Junior A. He is hanging in there and looked comfortable in the later stages of the game. Will be interesting to see if he is granted exceptional status to play in the BCHL for the rest of the year.

FINAL SCORE: 3-0 Coquitlam

Sept 9, 2012, Prince George Spruce Kings vs. Langley Rivermen (BCHL)

PG#21 RD, Eden, Mitch(2013) Did not have as great of a game as he did against Merritt, but still managed to put up 3 assists in the game. His positioning and decision making were not as good as the previous game which negatively affected his defensive game. Offensively, was very good moving the puck again, and created time and space for his forwards with his passes. Would wait an extra second or two to draw in opponents, then hit the open man with speed to get the attack going. Showed off a good shot from the point.

LAN#14 LW, Butcher, Ben(2013) A hulking forward who displayed some good offensive instincts. Made a few good plays in the corners to create room for himself with his stickhandling. Needs to really work on his skating to be able to take it to the net. Overall speed is not very good, and is detrimental to his game. Stays too up right, and strides are too long. Listed at 6'2, and looks like he is still adjusting to his body. Not bad along the wall, but could improve his strength and be able to stay up on his feet more often than not. Not too big of a factor in this game.

LAN#17 LD, Pellah, Bo(2013) A smooth puck moving defenseman who had a very good game. So smart with the puck, and uses time and patience to his advantage. Not afraid to stickhandle and try to beat opponents one on one. Definitely has the skills to do so. A very good skater, could turn from one direction to another in a hurry. Pushes the pace of the game very well. Needs to bulk up and get much stronger. Was listed as 5'11, 139 lbs last year, but this year listed as 6'1, 165 lbs. Defensively, above average in terms of positioning, but play along the walls could improve a lot.

Scouts Notes: A bit of a wild game with back and forth scoring all game. Really impressed with Bo Pellah(2013). His puck moving skills were by far the best out of any 2013 NHL Entry Draft eligible defensemen from this weekend. I was able to talk to his old major midget coach and he said Pellah has moments once in a while where he tries to put on a stickhandling clinic and gets caught and pays for it. Did not see that today, but could be evident later. Both teams looked a little sluggish in the neutral zone and in their respective defensive zones without the puck after a long weekend. Will be interesting to keep an eye on Mitch Eden(2013) for this season. I was impressed with his play this weekend. Currently see him as a late round pick in the NHL Entry Draft.

FINAL SCORE: 6-5(OT) Prince George

September 9, 2012, Drummondville Voltigeurs vs Victoriaville (QMJHL)

(Pre-Season)

VIC #5 D Vance, Troy (Dallas Stars prospect) Vance didn't have his best game and kept multiplying the turnovers going out of his zone. His ratio of good plays versus bad plays wasn't very good. He still showed his great hands and ability to rush the puck a few times. He made some great plays just before turning the puck over. It looks like he was trying to do too much in those situations.

VIC #12 C/W Rehak, Dominik (2013) – Best game I've seen so far from him. He looked much more comfortable. Didn't generate a lot of speed but he was a constant threat when the puck was nearby him in the offensive zone. His quick hands and good decision making proved to be helpful and got him two assists along with his goal. He had a quick release on a loose puck for his goal. You could see he is still adapting to the physical game the way he reacts when he gets banged up (he looks surprised).

VIC #19 C Savage, Félix-Antoine (2014) – He doesn't get a lot of ice time and I've been watching him for a few games trying to get a read on him. He skates well and follows the play on both ends of the ice but he doesn't seem comfortable with the puck. He tries to rush his decisions as if he was trying to keep up with the speed of the game. He would benefit keeping the puck a little longer and let the play develop around him instead of making sloppy plays too quickly. You could see he works hard and tries to win battles but he isn't strong enough right now to be really effective.

VIC #20 RW Ayotte, Mathieu (2014) – Didn't factor much into this offensive contest. He is at his best with the puck on his stick where he seems to be in a comfort zone. He had a couple flashes where he showed maturity the way he is able to hold onto the puck before making the right play. It looks like he is a fairly decent skater too but he didn't get many opportunities to show it in this game. His skinny 140 pound frame isn't helping him either when he has to win a battle along the board or carry the puck through traffic. I liked the fact he wasn't a quitter even though he's clearly disadvantaged with his weight.

VIC #79 D Pomerleau, Tristan (2014) – Very undersize (5,09 – 170) but I thought he had an excellent game. He was an offensive sparkplug when he was on the ice with his speed and quick puck-moving ability. He also did well on the power play cycling the puck around to his teammates. He still has to learn how to use his speed and stick to defend properly but he limited the mistakes and was mostly effective in his own zone.

DRU #9 LW Archambault, Olivier (Montreal Canadiens prospect) – Archambault didn't have a good game. Only had a few chances with his speed and he ended up doing his usual stuff, getting stuck between a couple opponents because he wouldn't pass or dump the puck. Most of the time when he gathers momentum with the puck in an open space, you think he's going to do something great only to end up turning the puck over. I'm not sure if it's a matter of trust towards his teammates or limited vision. But still, his speed and great hands can be a deadly weapon for him.

DRU #55 C Balmelli, Lukas (2013) – Second time I've watch him and it's hard to get a read on him because he skates around but doesn't get into the action much. He moves around pretty easily and he's never too far from the action but never really gets into it. He also lost quite a few battles for the puck. It's still to be seen what he can do when he has the puck on his stick.

Scouts Notes: A game filled with goals and penalties that was ultimately won 9-5 by Victoriaville. Dominik Rehak (1-2) had a great game alongside veterans Philippe Maillet (3-3) and Angelo Miceli (3-1). I like his instincts in the offensive zone and his quick hands allows him to finish the job most of the time when he sees an opportunity. It's still early pre-season but his game is coming along pretty well and he seems to have a very legit package as a player. Like I mentioned it was the second time watching Swiss import Lukas Balmelli and on the first occasion I didn't even bother filling in a report because I didn't see him at all on the ice. Tonight he was there in term of speed of the game but he didn't factor at all into the action. We'll see how he adapts to the North American game as the season goes on. Adaptation early in the season is not always easy for import players.

September 19, 2012, Dubuque Fighting Saints v Tri-City Storm (USHL)

DUB #4 RD Downing, Michael (2013) - Downing is a pretty good skater for a big guy. He knows where he has to go and what he's supposed to do in those situations. He struggled a little handling 2 on 1 situations in this game. Michael retreats off the blueline in order to ensure he's in proper defensive positioning. However sometimes backed off too early and the puck left the zone in situations where it would have been easy for him to hold the line. Downing got hit hard by a clean check behind the net on the first shift of the second period. Downing returned late in the period for two shifts, then left the game again, this time for good.

DUB #9 LW Malone, Seamus (2014) - Malone was, without question the best forward for Dubuque in today's game. He shows great skating ability, good vision and excellent playmaking abilities. He made quick decisions with the puck and created scoring chances with his passing ability. He had a chance in alone and was stopped, he stuck with the rebound and was able to score on it. He scored his second goal in a 3 on 1 situation, wound up and blasted it past the goaltender. Malone created offensive chances consistently shift after shift. He is a little small, but considering his skills, he should be an interesting prospect for the 2014 NHL Entry Draft.

TC #7 LD Cecere, Garrett (2013) - Used regularly on the power play. He moved the puck fairly well both up ice and in the offensive zone throughout the game. He was used in a lot of big game situations despite being the youngest defenseman on the team.

TC #8 LW Moore, Trevor (2013) - Moore was hands down the best forward in this game for Tri-City. Without Moore there's little chance they would have got a point. Despite his size, Moore is very strong. He won battles along the boards and did not hesitate to become involved in the more physical aspects of the game. Trevor is very composed with the puck. He protects the puck very well considering his size and fought off checks very well. This was on display for Moore's first goal of the game, with a defender all over him, he fought him off to score the tying goal. Once again Dubuque would take the lead later on in the gam, and once again Moore would tie the game up due to Moore's willingness to drive to the net. When he wasn't scoring, Trevor was agitating the Fighting Saints' players throughout the game.

TC #27 RC L'Esperance, Joel (2013) - Joel was a little slow getting going but as the game progressed he showed a lot of what we liked out of him in U.S. Select 17 Camp in Rochester. He has great size and likes to skate with the puck. This was so clearly evident when he was at his own blue line, under 10 seconds left, and he was able to rush and protect the puck 150 feet down the ice, get the puck on net which subsequently allowed Tri-City to tie the game with less than a second left. He appeared to be at his best when battling in the slot area. His reaction time is OK and knows what to do in that position. Joel is a player who due to his size, and what we've seen so far has a decent chance of hearing his name on draft day.

TC #31 LW DiBenedetto, Joey (2013) - DiBenedetto, who spent the last two years playing hockey in Las Vegas, showed great energy and physicality early on in this game. He controls the puck fairly well down low, and when given an opportunity he created some offensive chances.

Scouts Notes: A very exciting back and forth game saw Dubuque and Tri-City require a shootout to decide this game. It really felt like the Seamus Malone (2014) vs. Trevor Moore (2013) show. Once one scored, the other responded. The two combined for 4 of the 6 goals scored in this game. 2014 Eligible Dylan Gambrell showed some flashes of talent throughout the game; particularly in puck playing situations. Kyle Eastman (2013), Garrett Gamez (2013) and Peter Halash (2013) all showed very similar games for Tri-City. All of them cycled the puck effectively and used their good size to play a physical style of hockey throughout this game.

Sept 19, 2012, Cedar Rapids vs. Des Moines (USHL)

CR#6 LC, McLaughlin, Dylan(2013) A good playmaking centre, had an effective game in the offensive zone. Was able to create a good scoring chance consistently throughout the game. A good skater, and uses his speed to his advantage to get some separation from opponents and be a in a good position to receive a pass and make plays happen. A few times on the rush, McLaughlin drew defenders to him, then made a simple pass to his line mates for them to attack an open lane that he was able to create with his intelligence and speed. Needs to improve his play in the defensive zone, especially positioning. Not always in shooting lanes. Also needs to improve his strength, especially along the walls. Had a difficult time winning battles along the boards.

CR#22 RW, Oglevie, Andrew(2013) A very speedy forward, creates offense mostly with his skating abilities and desire to go to the net and create havoc. Drew a couple of penalties because of his speed. Had a very good scoring chance after splitting the defense, but lost the handle of the puck. Hands still have some catching up to do with his feet. Goes to the net hard, and created a goal by going to the net down the slot and attracting a defensemen on a 3 on 2, and gave his teammate a lot of room to work with and to score off the wing. Not very strong along the boards or in his own end. Oglevie got beat off the wall time and time again, does not seem to play with the same amount of energy in his own end as he does in the offensive zone.

DM#10 LW, Voltin, Luke(2013) 2 way forward who had an okay game. Definitely needs to be quicker making decisions with the puck. Holds on to it for too long, especially on the PP, and is caught in a bad position and turns it over. Showed a good combination of size and speed, but was invisible for much of the game like all of his teammates. Needs to improve on his stickhandling as well. One positive part of his game was his play in the defensive zone. Played with determination in his own end, and kept his head on a swivel and looked quite aware of the play and kept himself in the right position at all times.

DM#23 RW, Galt, Ryan(2013) Small speedy forward created some chances with his feet. Did not have a great game with the puck like most of his teammates. Just was not able to beat defenders and have some open looks for a shot or a pass. Not very strong along the boards, was beat for the puck almost every single time. Best moments in the game came on forechecks, where he was able to read the play well and intercept passes to quickly get a counter attack going.

DM#26 RW, Marnell, Michael(2013) Explosive skater, was able to create a few chances with his speed. Showed off great breakaway speed time and time again. Just was not able to finish on any of the chances however. Needs to work on his hands judging from this game. Made a few great passes to set up teammates for a scoring chance, but were not able to finish. Needs to improve the velocity on his shots, and strength to be able to come away with pucks in any situations. In defensive zone, was a little hesitant at times to commit to a player, and would be caught in no man's land, not taking a lane to take away anything. Needs to find the right areas, and use his skating more to get in front of a shot or be in a position to take away passes.

SCOUT'S NOTES: Cedar Rapids overwhelmed Des Moines all game long with their offensive abilities. The Buccaneers just did not have an answer defensively. They gave up glorious scoring chances time and time again. Quite impressed with Dylan McLaughlin and his playmaking abilities. Set up his teammates for good scoring chances time and time again. Considering the bad game Des Moines had, Michael Marnell looked quite good all game long. Such an impressive skater, time and time again just exploded through the defense and created some chances, but was not able to finish.

FINAL SCORE: 7-1 Cedar Rapids

Sept 21, 2012, Green Bay Gamblers vs. Fargo Force (USHL)

GB#9 RC, Schmaltz, Nick(2014) A creative forward who made some good plays in the offensive zone. Displayed some good hands and vision. He has the ability to see a play one step ahead of his opponents and give his teammates good scoring chances. Schmaltz possesses good speed. He got pushed around too easily, and needs to be stronger with his stick and on his feet.

GB#16 LC, Weis, Matthew(2013) Had a good game in both ends of the ice. Really liked his offensive game today. Created good chances and put himself in good positions to score consistently. Weis looked confident with the puck and looked dangerous whenever he had it. He is a good skater, and quite good in tight areas to get away from opponents. Defensively, Weis had some moments he would like to forget. A couple of times, instead of using his feet and getting good position against an opponent, he would lazily try to use his stick and create a turnover, which never really worked. When he is moving his feet and getting in the proper areas, that is when he is effective in his own zone, especially because he is not overly big.

GB#22 LW, Lemieux, Brendan(2014) Skilled forward who impressed with his offensive game. Showed off some nice hands in traffic a few time to create some good scoring chances. Looked confident with the puck, and consistently made good plays with it. Good vision all game long. Not afraid to take on anybody, and was going to fight an opponent but the refs stepped in because they took off their chin straps. Above average skater, but needs to work on his overall speed. Also needs to work on his play in the defensive zone. Got caught in a bad position a few times, and was not able to take away shooting lanes from the point.

FG#21 RC, Harms, Brendan(2013) Offensive threat for Fargo on this day. Made good things happen with his skating abilities and vision. Made good passes in traffic and off the rush. Took his time with the puck, and it presented him with some holes to expose in the d-zone coverage. Needs to work on his shot selection and needs to shoot more. Did not show any elite level of skills. Competed hard at all times, and backchecked hard and was able to break up a couple odd man rushes. Needs to work on his strength along the boards and overall positioning without the puck.

FG#27 RW, Booth, Michael(2014) Played a good game on this day. Made some good plays in the offensive zone, but also some bad ones. Was inconsistent with his reads. Liked to force some plays and cause turnovers as a result. A good skater, and was able to use his speed to his advantage a couple of times. Not a fancy player by any means. Defensively, looked okay. Could get stronger on his feet and along the boards. Stayed patient and watched the shooting lanes well, but needs to commit more to sacrificing his body for his team.

SCOUT'S NOTES: This was a game that Green Bay took control of from the start. They were just too good with the puck for Fargo, and took advantage of their depth. Really liked Nick Schmaltz's game on this day. The offensive talent is clearly there, just needs to get quicker and faster. Gabe Gertler of Fargo was one of their best players in the first period, but got ejected from the game because of a spearing penalty in front of the net in the offensive zone. Very undisciplined penalty to say the least. Matthew Weis also made a good impression. One of Green Bay's go to players for offense.

FINAL SCORE: 3-0 Green Bay

September 21, 2012, Chicoutimi Saguenéens vs. Québec Remparts (QMJHL)

QUE #10 LW Duclair, Anthony (2013) – Didn't really standout to me despite the three goals. Duclair struggled with his speed early in the game and never really adjusted. He had trouble with his puck reception at high speed and was poke checked a lot. We only got to see him once or twice going full speed on his wing and creating a direct chance to the net. So he was far off from his own standards in term of impacting the game with his speed. He still got the hat trick with two easy tap-ins and a wrap-around from behind the net. He was positioned perfectly for his first goal in a 2 on 1 situation. He also did a good job using his speed to come out of a corner in the offensive zone and crashed to the net, thus creating some scoring chances. I also liked how he managed the puck in periphery in the offensive zone and how he was able to spot teammates. This showed to me he had good vision and was also comfortable passing the puck. His best offensive sequence to me came late into the game when he went from his own zone to the offensive zone with blazing speed and cut right through the middle at the last second to get the defender away. He looks like a wide-receiver in football out there when making his cuts to get open. Other than that, he didn't really standout in terms of physical implication and battles. Had a couple fights for the puck here and there and one or two hits, but I've see higher commitment from him previously.

QUE #19 C Etchegary, Kurt (2013) – Real hard working player. He didn't really standout offensively but he was in the way, getting involved the whole game. His skating looked like average to me, where he had good speed but not enough to create anything offensively. He showed confidence on a 2 on 1 situation with Erne by his side and opted for a wrister that went in for his first goal of the game (goalie Gibson was down on his knees pretty quick). He has very average skills with the puck and will rely more on puck protection than his hands to move the puck around. Playing with skilled players, he does the right things the right way to get his share of points and be effective. I think overall he had a good game, but didn't show enough abilities to say he should get drafted. It should be noted that Etchegary is playing with an injury that will require surgery in the near future that will put him out for a long period of time.

QUE #25 C Grigorenko, Mikhail (Buffalo Sabres Prospect) – Looked like the same old Grigorenko from last year out there. He was floating around and looked flat. Gave the puck away a few times in the neutral zone and didn't generate anything with his speed. He did some good things in the offensive zone with his excellent hands. Extremely good wrist shot on his goal. Overall, I thought he didn't have a good complete game but he was able to compensate with his skills in the offensive zone to get his name on the scoreboard.

QUE #27 C Shea, Brandon (2013) – Shea played an honest game. He did a good job using his size and long reach to play defense and cut passes. He doesn't have a great explosion but skates pretty well in straight lines. This last point made him easy to defend as he didn't show any creativity to elude himself either. I wouldn't say it was a negative outing for him, but it wasn't positive either.

QUE #73 RW Erne, Adam (2013) – He was simply the best player on the ice. He just showed an ever better version of the player he was last year. His skating is heavy and he's hard to move but it doesn't prevent him from going fast. He showed very good explosion and used his speed all night long to get things going in the neutral zone and to go around defenseman. He displayed the same intelligence on the ice as last year, where he takes the right decision, whether it's shooting, passing or dumping the puck. On one occasion he drew all three forwards on him going at high speed in the neutral zone and was able to pass the puck at the last second to his teammate standing alone by his side. He also looks far more comfortable with the puck and he uses his hands a lot more to go with his speed. His variety of movement with the puck makes him much harder predict. I also liked how hard he plays without the puck. He gave some solid hits and one that was devastating late in the game. He also showed his real heavy shot even though he only got one goal in the game.

QUE #94 W Sorensen, Nick (2013) – Played an OK game. I love his skating, it's just flowing nicely and he can move fast. Did a great job on Erne's fist goal passing the puck; fantastic play by both of them on a 2 on 1. It seems that the puck didn't "bounce" for him in this game. He showed good effort and involvement to get the puck but he didn't get many chances to showcase his abilities and speed on the rush. But when he had the occasion, he did well. I thought he was bounced around a little along the boards and he needs to be more aggressive and also lower himself when working in corners. It will help him win more battles even though he's not very strong. Based on this game alone, his wrist shot seemed a little weak but accurate. One thing I also noticed is how he tried a lot of "set" plays on the power play without looking if his option was open. It seems that he just assumed his player was at a certain place when he wasn't. Will have to look into that more to see if it's a trend or just some occasional mistakes that he made tonight.

CHI #17 LW Tremblay, Simon (2013) – I barely noticed him and had to look closely to find him on the ice. He plays a simplistic game and is used as a grinder. It looks like he hustles but he was caught up by the speed most of the time and he wasn't able to hit his opponents. He took a couple of quick shots on goal, but nothing dangerous. I saw him holding the puck for a longer period of time only once at the beginning of the game and he ended up losing the puck to a defender in the offensive zone.

CHI #27 C Dauphin, Laurent (2013) – First time I noticed him was in the third period when he was coming down the wing with good speed and passed the defender with a great move that left his opponent wondering what just happened. He seems to have excellent hands to go with good speed. He ended up playing a good third period with more confidence and got two assists. Looking forward to see if he can create more of those chances throughout a whole game.

Scouts Notes: The game started a little slow and neither team was able to move the puck from their zone. Quebec's talented group of forward started to pace the game up and was able to get the lead halfway through the first period. They didn't look back after that. The game finished 9 to 4 in favor of Quebec. Chicoutimi's very thin defense and Quebec's lethal offense was an equation for horror for the visiting team. Chicoutimi tried a comeback in the third period when it was 8-2, but it was too late. Adam Erne impressed me big time with a complete package that he was able to use throughout the whole game to mess with Chicoutimi's defense. His combo of speed, quick hands and physical ability was just awesome to watch. Duclair showed his huge potential with his 3 goals despite a bad game. He was dangerous in the offensive zone and he barely used his speed. That goes to show he can do a lot more and I'm looking forward to that. Sorensen left me with the thought of wanting to see more out of him. He did some nice things but looked sluggish at times. I still liked the implication even though things were not turning his way tonight. Etchegary had a good game but I'm not sure he showed enough upside to be considered for the draft. Brandon Shea has the physical tools and hockey sense to play the game at a higher level. He didn't show he had the speed to do it and the offensive abilities to be a premium player either. I could see him getting drafted if he brings a little more tempo to the game than he did tonight. I'd like to see him hustle more with the two-way style that he's trying to play. Chicoutimi's players were barely noticeable except for Laurent Dauphin who played fairly good in the third period and showed good things. Simon Tremblay as a bottom line player didn't do enough applying pressure and using his body. He needs a little more speed to do it against a team like Quebec.

September 21, 2012, Rimouski Oceanic vs Sherbrooke (QMJHL)

Pre-Season

RIM #3 D Kostalek, Jan (2013) – Good confidence with the puck and he showed he can take advantage of open spaces in the neutral zone by carrying the puck there by himself. Kostalek looked like a very fine passer and was very effective on the transition throughout the game. He showed good decision making and made smart offensive plays from the neutral and the offensive zone. I also liked his defensive play; he has good mobility and covered his opponents really well. He even had the confidence to pinch and give some good hits in the neutral zone. He also had a fight in the middle of the game after jumping to hit an opponent. Kostalek also did a good job in the offensive zone, especially on one occasion where he beat the defender with quick hands and got a good shot on goal.

RIM #15 LW DeLuca, Anthony (2013) – Very good with the puck on his stick and he protects it well. I was not crazy with his implication in this game. He doesn't skate very hard without the puck and just waits for it to come to him. His skating is also below NHL standards. He didn't use his hard shot as much as I expected him to. He was not much of an offensive factor.

RIM #23 C Gauthier, Frédérik (2013) – I thought his skating looked pretty good for a big guy and he was fairly dynamic. He had a couple of nice sequences with the puck in the neutral zone. He had enough speed to come close to the offensive zone but had to dump the puck. He showed off his passing skills with good decision making and accurate passes. What stood out the most his is play without the puck. He is very conscious of his positioning and he did a good job blocking shots on the PK and cutting passing lanes with his long reach. He was also very active on the back check in the neutral zone. He was not overly physical but he did a good job using his size to create space around him and to move the puck. Gauthier scored a nice goal late in the game after he made a good defensive play, he came down the wing and scored on a good wrist shot. Overall, he didn't standout with high offensive upside, but he was present in all phases of the game and he made the difference for his team.

RIM #55 D Morin, Samuel (2013) – He likes to punish his opponent whenever he can. Physically strong. He also made a good use of his long reach to clear loose pucks in front of his net and to contain his opponents. I thought his positioning was a little off on the PK. He stood far from the action at times and was slow to react in those situations. He looked a little more comfortable moving around than he did last year and his footing looked good on 1-on-1 situations where he relies mostly on his long reach to stop his opponents. The more I see him, the more I think he is limited offensively and at his best when he keeps it simple.

SHE #7 D Lysenko, Vladislav (2013) – He made a mistake trying to handle the puck in his zone that resulted in a turnover for Rimouski's first goal. Showed fairly good skating while moving the puck from his end but he doesn't seem to be the type to rush the puck very far up the ice. He makes a good use of his body to protect the puck. Plays a very tight gap in his zone and likes to play man-to-man. He left a couple passing lanes open playing like this on the penalty kill. He did a good job keeping his opponents away from his crease, pretty physical. Also liked the fact he was willing to sacrifice his body to block shots.

SHE #10 LW Torok, Tomas (2013) – I'm not really crazy about his game, he looked the same the last three games I saw from him. He showed decent speed and what looked to be a good pair of hands but didn't generate anything offensively with it. Great wrist shot that hit the post at one point. Had a good sequence late in the game where he controlled where he controlled the puck behind Rimouski's net and made a good pass to a teammate in front of the net.

Sep 21 2012, Québec Remparts @ Chicoutimi Saguenéens, (QMJHL)

QUE #10 LW, Duclair, Anthony (2013): 3 goals, 1 assist. Has elite burst of speeds, is able to distance himself from almost any D on the ice. Has quick hands and likes to cut around the net with speed for wrap-around attempts. Makes himself open on 2-on-1 with his speed and has a really strong finishing touch. High level of offensive execution. Needs to work harder in his defensive zone; was a bit inconsistent in his effort in his own end. He cut a couple of Chicoutimi odd-man rushes with great efforts to come back hard; but also made some poor decisions with the puck such as passes through the center that resulted in turnovers; also glided on a couple of shifts in his zone. No real physicality showed although he seems a lot bigger than last year and that helps for his puck protection skills.

QUE #27 C, Shea, Brandon (2013): Lacked energy on every shift. Didn't seem to engage mentally in the game. Poor performance on faceoffs and no physical implication. He kept things simple along the boards, cycling the puck. He has great reach and physical strength, average skating abilities.

QUE #73 RW, Erne, Adam (2013): Improved speed compared to last year, showed excellent burst of speed on the first goal with Sorensen, taking the Chicoutimi D off guard in the neutral zone. He loves to throw the body on the forecheck; needs to be careful not to put himself out of the play by doing so. Has an excellent quick released shot and knows how to hide himself in the slot. He can play the board game and he can play when things open up because he has a good mix of size, speed and skills; he excels in all 3. He was dominant in his battles and was able to create a lot by protecting the puck and passing the puck to teammates.

QUE #19 C, Etchegary, Kurt (2013): Smart player that has really good hockey sense. Did a lot of the little details you need to do to be a successful pro hockey player, great positioning in the neutral zone, smart sticks, great work ethic and compete level. He has good strength even though a bit smallish. Scored a good goal on a 2-on-1, choosing the right option when shooting. He plays the system really well and has above-average level of skills.

QUE #94 RW, Sorensen Nick (2013): Lots of speed and energy displayed by the Danish player. He set-up his own goal by bringing the puck up with speed in the neutral zone and making a great 2-on-2 play with Adam Erne. He's a dynamic player who understands the game pretty well, he works hard on the boards and plays a skilled North-South game. He created multiple chances in the offensive zone by supporting the puck carrier and placing himself in positions where he could be open. He has all the tools to be a great 2-way forward. Blocked a couple of shots, was used in defensive situations and responded well.

CHI #27 C, Dauphin, Laurent (2013): Talented, he makes things happen. He will crash the net a lot for a skilled player, it makes up for a good mix. He won most of his draws and most of them against Mikahil Grigorenko, got hit, but never backed down, positioned himself well in the slot on the powerplay, undressed a couple of defenseman and gave the effort throughout the majority of the game. He'll need to mature a bit, he used fanciness in a couple of occasions near the blue lines and got beat on the boards, but he could develop into something special.

Sep 22 2012, Gatineau Olympiques @ Chicoutimi Saguenéens (QMJHL)

GAT #27 LW, Poirier Émile (2013) : Not a good game from him, you can still see glimpses of what he can be, but he had a tough time getting good shifts after good shifts. A good shape, he works really well on the boards and that's where he was at his best, when the puck is cycling, he gets creative and knows how to create confusion in the opponent's defensive squad. He has quick hands and sees the ice well. Not an explosive skater by any means, his top speed is good. He needs to be better in his own zone, with his frame he could be better at getting the puck out.

GAT #44 LW, Reway, Martin (2013) : Has an elite-level of pure talent. Just a blast to watch him dangle with the puck, really quick and unpredictable with the puck in the offensive zone, he caused many headaches on some particular sequences in Chicoutimi's zone. He likes to twist and turn and he is an agile skater. His game is still pretty raw and small, he's still shy on the boards and sometimes lost in the system in his own zone. Had a tough time winning the battles against bigger guys and doesn't adjust well to a north-south type of game. It will be interesting to see the progression this season.

CHI #27 C, Dauphin, Laurent (2013) : Caused troubles by driving the net, made Lukas Sedlak score a goal, and caused many penalties by making the defensemen work down low. He is really strong when lowering his center of gravity and driving with the inside shoulder. He sees the ice really well and understands where to be to have succes, he doesn't shy away from scrums. He made a couple of fancy plays that didn't work but they didn't cause any turnovers.

September 21, 2012, USA U18 v Sioux City Musketeers (USHL)

USA #4– Butcher, Will (2013) - The further away from his own net Butcher gets, the more reliable he is with the puck. Butcher rushed the puck effectively on the power play and moved it well in the offensive zone in general. He made some mistakes with the puck in the neutral zone as well as his own zone trying to do too much in areas he should be making the smart simple play. He did well late in the game with a one goal lead not forcing anything and using his skating ability to skate the puck out of trouble and getting the puck deep. It was held deep by a forward and killed a lot of time, but it all started with Butcher's play out of the zone.

USA #7 RC Compher, J.T. (2013) - Compher came out flying in the first few shifts really showing his skill. He scored the first goal of the game as he was well positioned, took a bouncing rebound, quickly calmed it down and put it in while under heavy pressure. Compher's play declined throughout the game and re-emerged late in the game winning a number of big draw's for the

USNTDP. One of these went right to Tyler Motte breaking up a tie game in the final 10 minutes giving USNTDP a 5-4 win. He also came up big very late as Sioux City pressured for the tie game forcing turnovers.

USA #10 RW Allen, Evan (2013) - Allen showed good skating and elusiveness for a player at 5'10" and over 200 lbs. He made some nice passes throughout the game. One frustrating part was watching him dive pretty blatantly when the opportunity came up, however he was successful in drawing the penalty but it was pretty clear.

USA #11 RD Hamilton, Trevor (2013) - While Trevor wasn't very flashy at all, he impressed throughout this game. He made a great play on a 2 on 1 when his defensive partner jumped up. He showed great lateral movement to get in ideal positioning then made a textbook play to break up the chance. He was excellent making smart plays with the puck all game long. A solid first pass, and also hit tape to tape on long distance passes as well. He uses the glass to clear the zone very well when under sustained pressure.

USA #12 RC Labanc, Kevin (2014) - Labanc is a good skater who showed some elusiveness through traffic. He moved the puck well and made good decisions around this. He was great shorthanded forcing a lot of turnovers, got a partial shorthanded break and generally was effective defensively as a whole.

USA #14 LW Motte, Tyler (2013) - Motte was good on the penalty kill. He provided great pressure and found ways to kill a lot of time off the clock. Overall he was pretty quiet throughout the game, but he scored the game winner going right to the net off the draw, stick on the ice and he made no mistake. In the final minute he tried to dive to draw a penalty. It didn't work and lead to a Sioux City rush up the ice and scoring chance.

USA #16 RD Santini, Steven (2013) - Santini possesses a very good skating and size combination. He likes to use his size to impose himself along the boards and towards oncoming skaters. He has the skating to execute reads on passes to intercept and also to rush the puck up ice when the option is available. Santini constantly moved the puck up ice intelligently throughout the game. He makes hard accurate passes and constantly making the right decision. He, along with a lot of players on his team appeared to get lazy later on in the game, especially with the puck. This resulted in a number of turnovers and allowed Sioux City to get back into the game. Took a really bad penalty getting way too excessive defending his goaltender, by knocking the forward down then dragging him all over the slot forcing the official to call him.

USA #22 RW Fasching, Hudson (2013) - Fasching is easily at his best when he's below the circles in the offensive zone. He controls the puck and cycles extremely well. He regularly won battles along the boards, this included battles against some big players. He used his physicality in open ice and along the boards to force turnovers. Fasching is very difficult to move from the front of the net. He did a great job killing the clock in the final minute with a 5-4 lead in Sioux City's zone preventing them from being able to pull the goaltender.

USA #24 LW McCarron, Michael (2013) - McCarron is a pretty solid skater with very big size at 6'5" – 228lb. McCarron goes for the hit whenever possible and is consistently a factor playing a very physical game. He goes hard to the net and sets up shop at the top of the crease which gave Sioux City fits. It also resulted in an eventual goal for McCarron. His temper got the best of him after he got rocked by a clean hit and took away his focus for a little while in this game. Not many players can really give him a hard time physically, but he doesn't seem to handle his emotions too well when there is a player who can. Overall he played better than we have seen out of him in the past.

SCM #22 RW McGlynn, Connor (2013) - Showed good puck movement on the rush. McGlynn was a force all night long in front of the net. He was constantly and reliably going hard to the net with his stick on the ice. This saw him score three goals in this game (although one was negated). All due to him driving to the net, stick on the ice and not giving up on the play. In addition to this, he made a great play behind the net showing great patience to set up a teammate for another goal. Connor was directly involved in 3 of Sioux City's 4 goals and was really the main reason they had a chance in this game. He also had a few great opportunities he just missed on late in the game to try to tie things up.

SCM #26 LD Heinrich, Blake (2013) - Heinrich had an overall solid game with a few hiccups. He was good on the penalty kill and was particularly efficient clearing the zone. He moved the puck well on the powerplay and has a good shot from the point. He made a few turnovers, one was particularly bad in the neutral zone and just looked lazy on the play. He showed some nice moves rushing the puck on occasion beating opponents on the rush giving himself a good scoring chance.

Scouts Notes: This game looked like it was going to be a blowout when USA took a 3-0 lead over Sioux City. The USNTDP dominated early on however took their foot off the gas and allowed Sioux City, who never gave up right back into the game. The Musketeers overcame 3-0 and 4-1 deficits to tie the game at 4-4. However Tyler Motte (2013) scored the winner. Dawson Cook (2013) looked good early on for the penalty kill. However he was knocked down and went awkwardly into the boards. He left the game and did not return. Anthony Louis (2013) wasn't very noticeable tonight but he did a great job going hard to the net over and over again. This eventually resulted in a goal for him. Sean Malone (2013) caught Sioux City on a bad line change, showed good hands and scored on the break. Michael Babcock (2013) isn't a regular with the U.S. Development Program, in fact he is Canadian. However having lived in the U.S. for the past 10 years or so due to his father being the head coach of the Detroit Red Wings allowed him to play with the program at the fall classic. He showed great forechecking ability and really appeared to want the puck more than those he battled with on a regular basis.

September 21, 2012, Belleville Bulls @ Sarnia Sting (OHL)

BEL #14 LD Subban, Jordan (2013) - Jordan remained fairly restrained for the first half of this game. He wasn't rushing the puck as much, instead making solid passes up ice and moved it calmly and effectively on the power play. As the game progressed, Subban started rushing the puck into the offensive zone more frequently and also looked more pinching in from the point during sustained pressure in the offensive zone.

BEL #20 RW Lemmon, Mack (2013) - Lemmon's skating has improved a lot. He still loves to hit and works extremely hard. The skating improvements if anything has helped him use these attributes more frequently. He showed some flashes of puck skills making some good passes on the rush. While we love the edge Mack plays with, he desperately needs to understand where that line is between an agitator and a liability. Twice in this game he made a selfish or undisciplined move that cost his team. The first came with a power play coming to Belleville, Mack attempted to force an opponent to fight to the point where he received his own two minutes negating the power play. The second came when he smashed a Sarnia defenseman in the face right in front of the official. This gave Sarnia a power play with six minutes remaining in the 3rd period, Bulls up 2-1. It didn't cost his team in this game, but in the future it could be a very costly mistake.

BEL #23 LC Petti, Niki (2014) - In his first career OHL game, Petti jumped right into the action after it took him a few shifts to warm up. He was willing to engage physically and overall was he is a very good skater. As he got more comfortable he started showing flashes of his offensive potential and almost scored a highlight reel goal showing great agility. Overall it was a successful debut for Niki.

BEL #30 G Subban, Malcolm (Boston) - If it was possible, Subban's reflexes may have actually improved over the last 6 months or so. He made some absolutely unbelievable saves that most goaltenders would have no chance on. He was outstanding in second chance opportunities. His rebound control continues to be a major issue, but he was outstanding on second and third chance opportunities. While the Bulls controlled a lot of the pace tonight, there is no way they would have come out with the victory if not for Subban's play.

SAR #2 RD Chapman, Joshua (2013) - After being hit clean, Chapman unnecessarily retaliated by hitting him from behind taking a very selfish penalty early on in this game. Joshua delivered some good open ice hit one of which resulted in Chapman engaging in a fight against an older but smaller opponent. He fought to a draw in that one. He reads plays well, but his reaction time is a struggle at this stage of his development.

SAR #3 LD Nemecek, David (2013) - Nemecek was willing to battle right front the start however he won some and lost some. He played a physical game, but this too was very inconsistent on a shift by shift basis. He made a good defensive play in a 2 on 1 situation. Nemecek has some good attributes but needs to play more consistent if he wants to move up the rankings.

SAR #9 RD DiPaolo, Mike (2013*) - In a fast paced start with a lot of back and forth, DiPaolo was the first one to really lay a big hit to ramp up the physical play. His skating needs improvement although he is built so solid, has such a big wingspan and is adequate enough in that department that he is still tough to beat. DiPaolo prides himself on his physical play, but he didn't go out of position looking for the big hit tonight. His puck play was unnoticeable, which is probably a good thing for DiPaolo because it means he's keeping it simple and that would be his best course of action.

SAR #11 RW Hargrave, Brett (2014) - Hargrave got off to a slow start, and was very quiet to stat things off. However what seemed to wake him up was the older players on Belleville really trying to push him around and going after him. At one point a 20 year old forward for Belleville tried to level Hargrave and it looked like he ran into a wall. This shift really got Hargrave into the game, he began competing more and showing his strength. He was losing a fair share of battles, but as he gains confidence he will start to show his dominance in this area at the OHL level. He really appears to be feeling things out right now.

SAR #21 LC Nikandrov, Daniel (2013) - Nikandrov didn't do much offensively, but he consistently battled hard in the corners, getting pucks deep and winning his share of battles all night long.

SAR #71 RW Goldobin, Nikolai (2014) - Goldobin was very uninvolved for most of the game unless the puck came to him. There was a few flashes in the offensive zone. He was willing to get back defensively, but anything that involved battling for possession he looked very passive, primarily in the neutral zone. He has the skills and the hands, but he needs to play with a little less fear if he wants to make an impact on the smaller rinks.

Scouts Notes: Opening night of the OHL Regular Season for both of these teams. Belleville sat all of their 1996 players except 1st round selection Niki Petti (2014). Belleville came out flying early on dominating. Both goaltenders were outstanding and posted highlight reel saves. Malcolm Subban (Boston) made some particularly unbelievable saves. If it was any other goaltender Sarnia likely would have won 5-2. Instead Belleville posted a narrow 3-1 win, one of those goals being an empty netter. J.P. Anderson (San Jose) playing in his first regular season game since shoulder surgery and it was a beauty. He kept Sarnia in this game and came up huge when they were trying to claw their way back. All in all a very good game that had a little bit of everything and it came right down to the final seconds.

September 22, 2012, Muskegon Lumberjacks v Lincoln Stars (USHL)

MUS #17 LW Tiffels, Frederik (2013) - Frederik is a very good skater with great speed and he couples this with strong acceleration. He likes to do everything fast. He makes quick decisions with the puck moving it up ice, or distributing it in the offensive zone. He has great hands and he uses this both to handle the puck along the boards, and to protect it waiting for options to open up. He makes very quick decisions but can also slow things down and outwait the opposition. He did this and it resulted in a second period goal. Tiffels is smart with great hockey sense and vision. He was a constant threat in the offensive zone all game long.

MUS #19 LW Alferd, Riley (2013) - Went to the net fairly regularly with his stick on the ice. He showed quick hands and good moves when controlling the puck. Shook off a few checks effectively when controlling the puck.

LIN #4 LD Willett, Daniel (2014) - At 5'7" Daniel is going to have a very uphill battle in his attempts to become an NHL defenseive prospect. Despite his size, he tries to take the body on the opposition. However he was able to create very little impact. He keeps calm with the puck when opponents are bearing down on him. He doesn't try to force passes with the puck and made the smart play rather than the risky or high reward play. He did on the other hand try to force shots through from the point on the power play. Some of which he really didn't need to push because his team was leading in the third period.

LIN #7 LD Pittman, Zack (2013) - This was not Zack's best performance. He struggled 1 on 1 defensively. On one play he turned the puck over on the power play and had to hook and hold the opposing player to prevent a breakaway. It resulted in a penalty shot anyways. Zack is a good skater at his size, but gets caught in the offensive zone forcing offensive forwards to cover his defensive position for him.

LIN #9 RC Lettieri, Vinni (2013) - Lettieri is very small, but he's also a very good skater. He showed good two-way play tonight especially when his team had the lead. He maintained good positioning even cheating towards the defensive side to make sure he would be there. He also covered the points well with the lead. Showed off a few flashes of skill before that.

LIN #27 LW Johnson, Luke (2013) - Johnson protects the puck well when working along the walls. He is a decent skater who makes good, quick, accurate passes. Considering his high regard for the draft, his performance was slightly underwhelming in this game.

Scouts Notes: To be honest this was a bit of a sloppy game for the most part from start to finish. Tiffels really showed off his potential in this game and was easily the best skater on either team. Ross Olsson (2013) who is fairly well regarded for the draft had a bit of an underwhelming performance. He did make a great pass 2 on 1 to set up the tying goal in the second period. Lincoln took the lead on a huge rebound then sealed the deal on a very weak goal clinching a 3-1 win.

September 22, 2012 Portland Winterhawks @ Seattle Thunderbirds (WHL)

SEA #17 RD Theodore Shea (2013)- Shea played a strong game, the smooth skating defenseman was joining rush trying to spark any offense Seattle could muster up. He played tight in his defensive zone forcing the shooter to the outside keeping the play along the boards where he was strong through out the game.

SEA #33 LD Hauf Jared (2013)- Jared had a decent game, nothing to brag about he could of used his 6'5 frame with more physicality through out the game. He was caught watching the play multiply times and was unable to recover due to being very slow footed. Jared needs to used his size and reach to his defensive advantage and improve his skating and foot speed.

SEA #2 LD Smith Jeret (2013)- Jeret play a solid game defensively, he didnt really stand out with any flashy play. He was the quite blueliner who played the body, chip pucks and did the little things tonight. His skating and overall skill set does need improvement, but is a player to watch this year he may surprise some people.

SEA #19 LW Sheen Riley (2013)- Riley was a little spark plug all over the ice tonight, using his quick flash to lead the rush, or his shifty skating to sneak into scoring areas unoticed. He showed good offensive instincts with hawk like vision tonight. I was impressed with his play, only down side, he is not very big.

SEA #32 RD Green Taylor (2014)- Taylor not only has Chara's size but also his condor reach. This kid is a giant, and should be using his size to punish his opponents. His overall game tonight was not very good, he got caught pinching and watching all game, but you cant teach size. This young stay home d-man need to improve his skating and overall play. Excited to watch his development over this season.

PORT #3 LD Jones Seth (2013)- Jones played a overall decent game tonight, he joined the rush looking to help the offensive threat. At times it looked like jones was set on cruise control, going through the motions. I would of like to see him be more physical. His hockey abilities are top notch, he shows a good understanding of both side of the puck.

PORT #27 RW Bjorkstrand Oliver (2013)- Oliver started out kinda flat during the 1st period, then caught on fire in the 2nd and 3rd. I was impressed with his offensive instincts, his ability to slide into the quite areas of the ice unoticed and deliver a nasty wrister or pin point pass. Oliver notched 2 goals and 1 assist +3 tonight. Many have him ranked low, but he may surprise you this year and sneak up to the upper rounds.

PORT #19 C Petan Nicolas (2013)- Petan was the best player on the ice tonight   (1g 3a +4), he used his speed all night causing havoc on seattle defense, petan is slick and slimy always winning loose pucks and battles along the boards. His quickness with dazzle you and his ability to handle pucks in traffic makes your head spin. Petan may be small but has the total package. Ty Rattie (St Louis) has found his wing man for the year.

PORT #4 RD Hanson Joshua (2013)- Josh didnt stand out to much, but thats because he was doing the little things to help his team win. Josh is a stay home d-man who i would call the silent professional. I dont see much offensive production with josh, but you got a rugged player who will do anything for his team. His skating needs some work and could play more physical.

Port #29 RD Vorobyev Kirill (2013)- Kirill was another player who i didnt notice much. He has good skating ability and love to join the rush. He does get caught low in the offensive zone trying to create to much. He has all the right tools, just need to get out the filer and start sharpening.

Scouts Notes: Seattle started out strong in the 1st period taking control of the game and knocking Portland back on their heels scoring the first goal. Then the sleeping giant work up, and Portland evened up the score. Seattle forgot a complete hockey game is 3 periods and didn't show up for the last two. Petan and Bjorkstrand took over the game and all Seattle could do was watch the show. Portland put nothing short of a beat down, peppering Seattle goalies for 44 shots and 6 goals. Final Score Portland 6 Seattle 2

September 23, 2012 Prince George Cougars @ Everett Silvertips (WHL)

PG #9 LW Bolduc Carson (2013) Carson didnt really stand out. He was 3 steps behind the play most of the game when he saw ice. His overall play needs development. Not much interest here.

PG #27 C Forsberg Alex (2013) Alex was a work horse all night, his fluid skating and crash and bang style cause some havoc for the Tips defense. He has all the tools in the shed just needs some sharpening. He will be a player to watch this season.

PG #32 LW Fontaine Jarrett (2013) Very small, listed at 5'5 Jarrett has trouble protecting the puck and fighting for open space on the ice. His size and strength are huge factors that will need improvement. Not much interest here.

PG #3 D McNulty Marc (2013) Tall and lanky will cover Marc, his skating is decent and show good defensive awareness. His overall play tonight was decent, he control the 1 on 1 battles below the circle using his long reach and body, but struggled to clear the front of his net. Marc is a player to watch and see how he developments.

EVT #8 C Chynoweth Ryan (2013) Ryan works hard but lack the hockey sense and skating. Ryan was physical through out the game but did not see a regular shift. He looked lost at times. Ryan would try to forces passes out of his zone turning over the puck, which eventually lead to a PG goal.

EVT #15 C Bauml Kohl (2013) Kohl was all over the ice tonight, jumping in the offensive rush or laying down to block shots. He played a hard nose grinder style game. I see potential with Kohl it will be interesting to see how he play this season.

EVT #16 C Stadnyk Carson (2013) Not sure if carson showed up to play, his defensive awareness was no where to be found tonight, he forced the puck and would panic under pressure. I dont see much interest with Carson.

EVT #17 RW Lofthouse Trent (2013) I can see the skill set with Trent. His plays with a edge to his game and does not mind getting involved with the rough stuff. Trent played physical the whole game creating time and space for his line mates. He will need to work on his puck handling and skating. Potential draft pick but low rounds.

EVT #23 D Foulk Griffen (2013) Panics under pressure and just looked lost tonight. He has some upsides to his game hidden some where but did not impress me. I see some potential but only time will tell.

EVT #25 D Mueller Mirco (2013) Mirco played a solid defensive game. He's not a flashy player, just a rugged stay at home style defenseman. Throughout the game he would punish his PG forward with his body, his closed down the ice forcing PG to turn over the puck multiply times. Mirco plays well under pressure. Lots of potential with this kid, 2nd rounder if he continues to progress this season.

Scouts Notes. This was a back and forth game tonight. Everett came out strong putting the pressure on PG. Everett opened up the scoring with some slick passing. PG fought back to even the score on a weak goal. Everett would add 5 more goals to PG 2 to end the 2nd. Everett came out playing in the 3rd period like they had already wrapped this game up, PG put the pressure on and score 3 unanswered goals to tie the game and eventually force a OT then shootout where they claimed victory 7 to 6.

September 23, 2012, Kitchener Rangers @ Sarnia Sting (OHL)

KIT #73 LW Puempel, Matthew (Ottawa) - Had outstanding position especially on the power play. Combine this with his great shot and it resulted in two goals for him. Constantly in the goal area causing trouble.

SAR #3 LD Nemecek, David (2013) - Held the line in the offensive zone well on a few occasions in the first period. Made some odd plays with the puck in defensive zone throwing it away by moving it much quicker than he needed to.

SAR #14 LW Boucher, Reid (New Jersey) - A really, really bad turnover on his own zone resulted in a goal. He competed and got a high stick in the face for his efforts. But it resulted in a power play goal for. Boucher is hitting on a regular basis which is great to see as it's a necessary element to make him an effective player.

SAR #21 LC Nikandrov, Daniel (2013) - Went right to the net on developing rushes. One of these resulted in his first goal of the season. Daniel goes full speed as hard as he can into corners on a regular basis and was a workhorse for the Sting today.

SAR #77 RD DeAngelo, Anthony (2014) - Has been a little more restricted than usual in terms of taking chances. However as the game went on he made several puck playing miscues trying to do too much. He ended up negating some big chances for the Sting to tie the game up.

Scouts Notes: Goaltending was key in this match-up. A couple of Pacific Division prospects stole the show in John Gibson (Anaheim) and J.P. Anderson (San Jose). Both put on outstanding performances and made this game exciting right to the end. Joshua Sterk (2013) for the Kitchener Rangers showed off his speed going hard into the corners to battle. Justin Bailey (2013) didn't get a great deal of playing time due to the strong depth at forward and him playing his second OHL game. He has massive size and he takes a few steps to get going but once he does he showed a good top speed.

Sep 23 2012, Drummondville Voltigeurs @ Sherbrooke Phoenix, (QMJHL)

SHE #7 D, Lysenko, Vladislav (2013): He loves to hit. He has the uncanny ability to see the play develop and time his hits perfectly like Alexei Emelin does in the NHL. Wether it's open-ice or on the boards, he makes his opponents pay for having their heads down. He's a defensive specialist, blocks shots, protects the crease well, aggressive in his gap control (sometimes too much), likes it rough on the boards and makes the simple plays to get the puck out. He's not an agile skater and doesn't have quick feet. He can get beat on the rush by quick skater or gifted puck handlers while trying to hit them or by trying to close the gap too quickly. He does nothing flashy offensively and doesn't seem really comfortable moving the puck.

SHE #15 D, Deschamps, Jonathan (2014) : I always like to see young kids come in with such a great hockey IQ. He does an excellent job at taking the right decisions in a quick amount of time in his own zone, he sees the ice really well and already seems to adjust pretty well to the Q caliber. He pays attention to the little details, such as positioning his stick, defensive angling and gap control, he just doesn't have all the tools to apply those principles to perfection right now. He needs quicker feet and better lateral movements on his skates. Although he is not a bad skater, he needs to add agility. He has nice offensive tools; crisp passes and a quick wrister that he'll learn to use more often.

SHE #28 C, Audette, Daniel (2014) : Tons of skills, a gifted playmaker with an elite vision, he can dangle wit the bests. He created a lot of magic in that game, undressing defensemen with shoulder fakes, head fakes, quick turns, pure skill, or quickness. He is still pretty small and he's gonna need a lot more experience to adjust to the quickness of the Q game. He needs to be better in the execution of the little details. He missed many opportunities by trying to be too fancy. He is a « pass first » kind of guy, so shooting is not in his mentality. He's going to be even better when he understands the correct time and place to use his skills and when he takes some weight.

DRU #15 D, Brouillard, Nikolas (2013) : Great skater which gives him an edge in all 3 zones. He is tough to beat 1-on-1 because he follows the play really well; he caused a couple of turnovers but was on time for the defensive backcheck because of his skating abilities. He moves the puck well and loves to join the rush even though it's not always clever. He would need to add some pounds to his frame as I don't feel him ready to compete in tight games again well grown men. He has tremendous vision for the breakout pass and is accurate with it. Small offensive D.

Sep 26 2012, Victoriaville Tigres @ Chicoutimi Saguenéens, (QMJHL)

CHI #17 LW, Tremblay, Simon (2013): Really executes what the coach wants him to do. He played a great "in-your-face" type of game. He hits hard, really strong on his skates and makes the simple plays. He caused multiple turnovers Victoriaville's D in the 3rd period when Chicoutimi started pressing the play more, with his speed and good angling as the first forechecker. He got 2 scoring chances whit his quick-release wrist shot, 2 really powerful wristers in the lower part of the net. He's dedicated and aggressive, plays well the PK. Pretty good puck protection, looks a lot smaller than his 6,01 because of his inclined stance. He doesn't have great passing skills and needs to be better in his decisions with the puck but interesting project.

CHI #22 C, Sedlak Lukas (2011 CBJ Jackets draft pick): One of the best games I've seen him play. I think he understands more and more the type of player he needs to become to play pro hockey. 21 on 32 on the faceoffs, many block shots, relentless energy displayed, always the first man back to help is D behind his net when his line is on, 25 minutes TOI, PP, PK, goes in front of the net on the PP and uses his large frame to protect the puck on the wall and retrieve the dump ins, lots of hits, the most physical game I've seen from him. He was able to cause many turnovers with his speed and intelligence, placing the stick at the right place on breakout passes, he sees the ice really well. He wins his battles and makes the safe plays to get the puck out of his zone.

CHI #10 LW, Hudon, Charles (2012 Montreal Canadiens draft pick): If you watch the 3rd period only of that game, you might think Montreal got a steal in the 5th round, but if you watch the whole game, then you see there's still plenty of work to do. He was dominant for the second part of the 3rd period and you can see he has all the tools to be one of the best players in the league when he works this way. He's got an uncanny ability to score goals whether it's by shooting the puck hard, tipping pucks, deking his way through everybody or going to the net for rebounds. When he moves his feet, starts to focus on what he has to do, stops playing the fancy game and gets down to business he is definitely one of a kind, except he lacks consistency. In the first two periods, he was complaining, took bad penalties, made bad turnovers, didn't move his feet to bring the puck in the neutral zone and didn't want to engage mentally into the game. He has all the tools, he just needs to correct his attitude on the ice.

VIC #4 D, Sidlik Petr, (2013*): Stabilizing defenseman. When you see a 18 years old kid take 28 to 30 minutes of ice time, you know he has a very good hockey sense, cause you can't play the energetic, run-around, throw the body, big hits kind of game when you play that much. He sees the ice so well, an exceptional hockey sense, he added lots of muscle this summer and now has more ease in his one-on-one battles. Still an undersized defenseman, he's got really good footwork and always has the good gap control. He likes to be the 4th attacker in the offensive zone, but still reads the play so well he almost never gets caught. I liked the fact that I saw more aggressiveness in his battles in front of the net and on the boards, he made It tough with his stick for players to go through him. He got beat a couple of times near the end of the game, but had so much ice-time, I can understand that. He moves the puck really, has a nice pass quality and he is very smart, he open lanes with little movement.

VIC #3 D, Diaby, Jonathan (2013): Continued his good progression during the summer. He loves to hit and does he ever ! Really punishing hitter, it hurts when Diaby lays the body on you. He's better skating wise than he was last year although he's still far from where he's going to need to be. He was caught off position a couple of times during the game and he doesn't have the great hockey sense you need to have a good game when you're a poor skater on the Olympic sized-ice in Chicoutimi. He's getting more comfortable with the puck and he has a really good low and powerful slapshot.

VIC #15 RW, Ayotte, Mathieu (2014): Really flashy kid. He doesn't have the best skating but he's got quick hands and lots of creativity. He likes to use defensemen as a screen to shoot pucks on goals showing a real goal scorer instinct. Really skinny and not strong, he has good hockey sense as he knows how to create space and passing lanes, he reads the play well and understands hockey, but doesn't have the strength and speed to be a factor in every facets of the game. I liked the skill level he displayed and the hockey sense.

Sept 28, 2012, Shawinigan Cataractes @ Victoriaville Tigres, (QMJHL)

VIC #4 D, Sidlik, Peter (2013*): Sidilk is a very smart player, especially with his stick as it is almost always perfectly positioned to deflect shots out of play or breakup passing lanes. He cuts down a lot of the opposition's space and time with his stick, he moves really well on the ice and reads the play better than most players of his age. He played very well in 4-on-4 situations, as well as when he was a man short on the penalty kill and in general doesn't really make mistakes while he gets in an aggressive position along the boards, demonstrating his ability to read the play. He got caught with bigger players pressuring him a couple of times, as he was much more soft on the puck than the last few games he played in but was still the best defenseman on the ice.

VIC #15 RW Ayotte, Mathieu (2014): What says a lot about this player's offensive capabilities is the fact that he plays the first power play unit on a strong offensive team, demonstrating the fact that his coach is very confident in his play. What he does really well is his ability to find shooting lanes to get his shots through to the net, which is very important with his style of play as he is a shoot first type of player. He plays the game quite intelligently with his stick, which helps to win board battles, and he knows that he won't win most of the battles using size and strength so he is instead forced to use smart stick positioning. He needs to add some size and strength so that he is not knocked off the puck so easily.

VIC #3 D, Diaby, Jonathan (2013): Diaby skates pretty well, which he showed on a great back-check to catch a player after a turnover by a teammate. His forward skating is still more effective than his back-wards skating and he will need to improve on this moving forward. He made a great aggressive pinch on the half-boards which lead to on Victoriaville's 4th goal and he was quite rough on the boards, winning the majority of his battles. Diaby is most effective when he makes simple short passes, however will often try complicated cross-ice neutral zone breakout passes which result in turnovers. He needs to make better decisions on the ice as he plays too often high in the neutral zone and gets caught, giving the opposition some good chances and makes some blind plays just throwing the puck around the boards which also resulted in some costly turnovers.

SHA #6 D, Pozgay, Lukas (2013): Pozgay did not get too much ice time in this game, however still managed to demonstrate some good tools while he was on the ice. He showed some good speed for a bigger player, although it could definitely still improve. He moves his feet quickly and can get the puck moving quickly as well with some good tape-to-tape short passes. He put good physical pressure down-low, however was not too aggressive to put himself out of
position, and did not appear to be caught out of position at any point during the whole game in his 8-10 shifts.

SHA #24 D, Labbé, Dylan (2013): There is still a lot of work to do for this player before he becomes anywhere near a professional player. Starting most importantly with his footwork, he has long powerful strides, but pretty slow feet so it's tough for him to get going with his backward skating and lateral mobility which caused him troubles getting in position in time to get to the front of the net or to stop quick skaters coming down the wing. He's not an aggressive defenseman, rarely throwing the body and he also took an awful lot of time before making decisions with the puck. He is not a great puck handler and seemed to lack confidence in almost everything he did, which caused multiple turnovers throughout the game. He was however able to use his long reach well to cut down the opposition's time and space on the penalty kill.

SHA #80 D, Maheux, Raphael (2014): Maheux Did not get the opportunity in this game to play much, but the hockey smarts were still quite evident in his game. Beginning with his positioning, which was solid most of the time as he made himself available and was communicating well on the ice with his partner. He sees the ice well and was able to read the play well to anticipate plays along the wall to help correct for some mistakes that his defensive partner made. He is a fluid but not overly quick skater and seemed to lack confidence on the power play. It doesn't appear that that is a good role for him at the moment as he missed a couple of easy passes and panicked when he was pressured by Victoriaville's penalty killers.

SHA #94 LW, Campagna, JC (2013*): Campagna was the best player on his team in this game by a mile. He is a good skater and with explosive speed as he took the space that was given in the neutral zone to carry the puck up the ice. He is quite a gifted puck handler as he created magic on a couple of occasions through traffic. He is really agile on skates, can turn on a dime and is not shy to try some creative plays. He is not intimidated or afraid to be hit, and will take a hit to make a play. He is strong on his skates, hard to knock off the puck, but at times chooses to stick handle when it may be more effective for him to just protect the puck from the opposition. There were moments in the game where he can be soft, especially in front of the net where rebounds were available and he needs to have a higher degree of competitiveness in his game. He is able to win battles along the boards in his own end, however he does not like to block shots.

Sept 28, 2012, Québec Remparts @ Sherbrooke Phoenix, (QMJHL)

QUE #10 LW, Duclair, Anthony (2013): Duclair tries too hard to make the pretty play rather than going to the net and staying there looking for the tough dirty goal. He did not appear to be overly invested in this game but was still able
to create some fantastic plays using his elite speed, skill and vision. He did not use his quickness and puck protection as much as we have become accustomed to and still makes some soft plays at times as well that may work in the QMJHL, however might not translate as successfully into the pro ranks. He also lacked having much of a physical impact in this game.

Que #19 C, Etchegary, Kurt (2013): He likes to make the simple plays but can execute them well to have an effective style. He is an average skater but plays with a nice edge, some grit and uses his stick well. He comes back to provide his defense some good support and he wins lots of puck battles along the boards. He needs to keep his emotions in check and not let them take over his game.

QUE #73 RW, Erne, Adam (2013): Erne has a nice hard shot with a quick release. He puts good pressure on the fore-check and likes to angle the play to direct the opposition where he wants them to go which forced many turnovers in the opposition's own end. He is relentless and very disciplined with his stick, as he will never give up on a play and he works hard around the net. He showed excellent vision to find the open man with some great cross-ice passes and I loved to see him work around the net in this game. He likes to play in the slot on the power play and puts good pressure on the point on the penalty kill. He does an excellent job in both situations demonstrating some very valuable versatility. He drives the puck well down the middle to get through the opposition's defense, however he is sometimes predictable with the puck. He also needs to get the puck up out of his own end on the breakout, rather than turning it over along the boards.

QUE #94 LW, Sorensen, Nick (2013): This is a player who may not have the elite skill set as some of the top draft eligible players, however he makes up for that with his speed, vision and work ethic. He is an explosive skater and is really effective on the fore-check. He loves to protect the puck while coming down the wing with speed and he makes his decisions with the puck quickly. He has a great vision of the ice and plays with more physicality than he has in the past as he was able to knock over the puck carrier both along the boards and through center ice. He is nice and strong on his skates and has a good sense of the game, which is why the puck always seems to find him

QUE #27 C, Shea, Brandon (2013): Shea was coming back well to help out his defensemen to provide some good support and was playing with a nice element of physicality in his own end. He is nice and strong on his feet and battles nicely for the puck when he is interested. The problem with his game is there are many times when he seems uninterested with what is happening on the ice. He needs to move his feet more to really get going and play with a higher level of competitiveness.

SHE #15 D, Deschamps, Jonathan (2014): Deschamps has a really nice mix of size, smarts and different intangibles that can really help a team win. He positions himself nicely along the boards to win battles for the puck and he is not intimidated by any rough physical play. He played with a nice element of physicality as he had a few nice hits on Duclair and Grigorenko. He is calm and patient with the puck as he doesn't panic, and he makes pretty good decisions to get the puck out of the zone, making good crisp tap-to-tape passes. There were times when his defensive positioning was too passive and needs to be more aggressive, and has to use his stick more aggressively, as he let 3 cross-ice passes get by him on the penalty kill, this may be due to a lack of confidence. Offensively he missed some good chances with his slap shot, as he did not get his shot off quicker and needs to have more confidence with the puck.

SHE #7 D, Lysenko, Vladislav (2013): Lysenko did not have a good game tonight, as he only had 4 shifts in this game, allowing 2 goals and an odd-man rush in that limited time and was therefore sat for the rest of the game. He was too aggressive in the neutral zone, especially with the quick skaters of Québec, therefore it was easy for them to get by him. He was unable to execute the simple plays, trying to make it more complicated than it needed to be by passing pucks through the center. His decision making was just bad, plain and simple and this was a game that he needs to learn from and be better next time out

SHE #28 C, Audette, Daniel (2014): Audette will still need to mature his game quite a bit to be more of a factor in this league moving forward. He needs to add speed and strength and make quicker decisions as he holds on the puck too long at times which results in turnovers. He is scared of playing in the dirty areas, as he is never in the slot or in front of the goalie's face, as he tries to play on the perimeter and stickhandle his way through opponents. He has some great skills and is a creative player, but needs to stick to a simpler game to be most effective.

SHE #32 D, Neil, Carl (2014): This is quite an interesting player as he has some great tools that should make him successful. He possesses a nice hard shot from the point, he has great size, controls the puck really well and he skates well. His biggest problem is his decision making, as he plays high in the neutral zone and likes to play his gap control aggressively. He has a lot of confidence to do things that many 16 years old wouldn't and he had a great chance by jumping up on a cross-ice pass by the Remparts in the neutral zone and put a great slapshot on net. He likes to join the rush to be the 4th man and provide passing options on the rush. He is an explosive skater but there are times when he doesn't have his head up to look at his options before making his decision on the breakout passes.

September 28, 2012, Rouyn-Noranda Huskies vs. Drummondville Voltigeurs (QMJHL)

DRU #13 RW Gauthier, Guillaume (2013) – The former #2 overall pick in the QMJHL draft never really caught my eye and is far from NHL standards. I thought his effort level was up last night compared from previous viewings. Even though he's not making a big physical impact, I liked his perseverance and the way he worked along the boards trying to use his body. He showed some offensive flair when he had the puck and did a good job distributing it in the neutral zone. He has shown me so far that he was an average skater with slightly above average skills. He is not a difference maker offensively and is not a dynamic skater with the puck. He seems to be at his best around the net where he has good instincts.

DRU #15 D Brouillard, Nikolas (2013) – While Brouillard looked good in pre-season, he didn't really standout in this game. He is still a very good skater but this game showed to me he was not on the very high-end side and he has to be smarter the way he does thing. He has the ability to move the puck out of the zone but he doesn't have that speed that allows him to go coast to coast. His good hands and mobility serve him well but last night he took too much time taking decisions and that limited his options a lot. By taking too much time he had his passing options reduced and had the puck taken away from him and made some turnovers. It would be to his advantage to keep it simple and stop pushing it too much. Defensively, again, his mobility and smart positioning helps him a lot but he struggles when it gets physical. Big forwards can take advantage of that easily coming down the wing and in front of the net. From what I've seen so far, he still has ways to go before making a higher impact, especially at the next level. He needs to use his speed better to impact the game and find a way to be more efficient defensively with his small stature.

DRU #31 G Graham, Domenic (2013) – He didn't play a very good game giving up 3 goals on 11 shots after two periods. He was not tested a lot but he didn't have his usual speed and reflexes and gave up bad goals. He is not very big and needs to do a better job covering angles.

DRU #55 C Balemlli, Lukas (2ND year eligible) – Balmelli looked better than the previous viewings I had on him. He is a decent skater and moves around pretty easily. He was involved both offensively and defensively last night. He did some nice things with the puck and was able to create a few offensive chances. I'd say he has this ability to carry the puck with decent speed and a little above average hands. Moreover, I think he could try to hold on to the puck a little bit longer to let the play develop. His vision seems a little limited in the sense where he gets rid of the puck a little too quickly instead of controlling the play more. He also did a correct job applying pressure in the neutral zone and forcing opponents to do mistakes. I am not sold on him being a legit prospect for the NHL, although he can hang in there in the Q. He looks to be just an average offensive player without much more to his game.

DRU #96 D Weber, Dexter (2013) – He was used as the sixth defenseman for Drummondville and didn't play a lot with all the penalties, but I like what I saw from him. He showed good mobility and quick footing. He was reliable defensively for his team with good positioning and poise. He was calm and used his mobility to make safe plays in his zone. He also looked comfortable with the puck and made the right decisions pretty much every time. He was able to move the puck out of his zone by himself a few times and made solid passes afterwards. He looked good in a scenario where he was used sporadically so I'm looking to see more out of him.

ROU #5 D O'Brien, Andrew (Anaheim Ducks prospect) – I thought he looked really good in this physical game. He is a man among boys and made his presence felt all night long. O'Brien usually goes for the big open ice hit but in this game he used his body a lot behind the net and along the board, both in his zone and in the offensive zone. He crushed a few players and got the momentum going for his time. He is also a surprisingly good skater for his size and he is able to play safe defense. He also has this ability to use his speed to move the puck up the ice and use his body efficiently to protect it. Compared to other viewings, he did a good job limiting turnovers, which is excellent for him. He has this tendency to sometimes overdo things and put his team into trouble. For instance at one time he decided to race for a loose puck in the neutral zone but he ended up not getting it, but it took him a few seconds to realize his mistake and comeback to help in his zone. Sometimes he would just benefit from playing the game more safely.

ROU #7 D Guénette, Justin (2013) – O'Brien's partner didn't play a bad game by any means but he didn't show much upside for the NHL either. He plays a pretty quiet game and tries to be reliable defensively. He has quick feet that allow him to be sound defensively and to follow the play well. I thought he overreacted at times and he has to catch up on players to make defensive plays. On some occasions he just braked to try to play the men but he didn't touch anyone. Guénette didn't do much with the puck either. He made the passes he had to do from his zone and it pretty much stopped there. He does the right thing to do without doing much more. I don't want to make it sound like a bad thing, but like I said, he didn't show much upside.

September 28, 2012, Sault Ste. Marie Greyhounds @ Sarnia Sting (OHL)

SSM #3 RD Ganly, Tyler (2013) - The rookie Ganly had his moments in 1 on 1 situation matching up well showing great strength. He won several battles along the board and is very strong overall. He showed this by standing up for a teammate after they got injured. His progression since minor midget has been very strong.

SSM #11 LW Dempsey, Mitchell (2013) - Mitchell is a good skater for his size, and showed some good moves 1 on 1. He protects the puck well when driving to the net and got multiple scoring chances out of it.

SSM #19 LC McCann, Jared (2014) - McCann went hard to the net, and appears to be still adjusting to the speed of things as many rookies do. He had some tough luck in this game getting tripped on a good scoring chance, and his stick breaking after acquiring ideal scoring position.

SSM #25 LD Nurse, Darnell (2013) - Nurse made good passes up ice and flips the puck out if there is no option. He fired the puck down the ice a little too early without much reason behind it at times. However on the penalty kill this was one of his strong points as he was usually the one clearing the zone. He moves the puck well in the offensive zone and appears to have simplified his offensive game a little. He was very reliable in 1 on 1 situations.

SSM #28 RW Tolchinsky, Sergey (2013) - He has a laser shot but really didn't show much in the first. As the second and third periods came he started to show more flashes of his skill and elusiveness but he is very timid around physical contact at this point.

SAR #2 RD Chapman, Joshua (2013) - Usually made the good defensive play when he was in position, but he really struggled with the puck.

SAR #21 LC Nikandrov, Daniel (2013) - Nikandrov's work ethic is really showing through in this game. He worked in all three zones showing great determination. He was good on the penalty kill particularly forcing turnovers.

SAR #71 RW Goldobin, Nikolay (2014) - Goldobin was much more patient and composed with the puck. He is very elusive starting to show off his hands. This made it possible for him to create offense. He has a very good shot. Goldobin needs to battle more in the neutral zone for pucks and along the wall. Usually he's caught just standing there observing the play.

SAR #77 RD DeAngelo, Anthony (2014) - DeAngelo pinched in from the point on the power play giving Sarnia the lead in the second period. He battled all night long with much bigger opponents and he did fairly well in these situations.

SAR #88 LW Addesi, Jordan (2014) - Extremely hard worker and finished his checks whenever the opportunity arised. He created a few good scoring chances. Addesi appears fully recovered from his shoulder injury in minor midget. In our limited viewings we really liked what we saw in him. He is looking like an excellent fourth round selection.

Scouts Notes: This was a very interesting game. Sault Ste. Marie came out extremely physical to the point they appeared to have the Sting worn down and some players conceding battles. Unfortunately instead of taking advantage of this they became very undisciplined and gave Sarnia many opportunities to take over the game. The Sting in fact took a 2-1 lead into the third period. However after both Andrew Fritsch (Phoenix) and Nick Cousins (Philadelphia) scored within 30 seconds of each other the 2-1 Sarnia leads became a 3-2 lead for the Greyhounds. The SOO held on to take the one goal lead.

Sept 28, 2012, Vancouver Giants vs Everett Silvertips

VAN#18 RC, Ast, Anthony(2013) Very impressed with the improvements he made to his game over the off season. Looks so much stronger on his skates and poised with the puck. Blew past a defender a couple times during the game off the rush down the wing to get a good scoring chance. Also, never seen him be able to walk out of the corner with the puck despite taking a beating until tonight. Needs to work on his shot and the velocity on it. Unfortunately, size is still an issue for him, standing at only 5'8.

VAN#27 RW, Houck, Jackson(2013) Had a good game for Vancouver. Looks much more confident with the puck. Does not treat it like a grenade like he did last year. Was counted on to be the net presence on the power play, and did a good job. Treated his body like a wrecking ball once again, and tried to hit everything in sight. Was almost caught with head down in the neutral zone, and just got out of the way at the last moment. Really liked the energy he played with today.

EVE#7 RC, Mappin, Ty(2014) Good 2 way forward who was more of a presence in the defensive zone than in the offensive zone. Was not much of a threat when his team had the puck. Looked a little out of place, but it was only his 3rd game in the WHL, and was hurt at the start of the season. Quite impressed with his strength along the boards on this day, and his defensive awareness. Consistently in good position without the puck and had good anticipation.

EVE#15 LC, Bauml, Kohl(2013) Played a very good game today. Was trusted in every important situation by the coaching staff, and excelled in those situations, whether it be on a power play or to protect the lead with a couple of minutes left in the game. Very good instincts with the puck, and loved to attack the net. Best asset is his vision and playmaking ability. Needs to work on finishing off plays and his scoring touch. Defensively, is not afraid to sacrifice his body, and displayed that at the end of the game when an opposing defenseman blasted a point shot and he slid and blocked a shot. Good coverage, and understands how to play without the puck.

EVE#25 LD, Mueller, Mirco(2013) Poised, puck moving defenseman who displayed good offensive skills. Opened up the scoring with a big slap shot off the wing on a rush. Stays patient with the puck even when there is a forecheck right in front of him. Makes good, solid passes and puts his teammates in a good position to move the rush up the ice. Biggest problem in his game is in the defensive zone. Mueller was too easy to play against, especially around the boards. Must be tougher, and improve his strength. Also needs to be more aware out on the ice. One of the goals Vancouver scored was through a screen and the shot was tipped, and he essentially screened his own goalie and did not tie up the opponent to prevent the tip.

Scouts Notes: Vancouver controlled the play for much of the game, but their goaltending was far too shaky. Said this since last year, but if Kohl Bauml was a few inches taller, he would be a 1st-2nd round draft pick. Can't deny his talent level. Has a tough time against bigger opponents, but keeps his feet moving at all times. Mirco Mueller is a player to keep an eye on. Good offensive talent from the back end. David Musil had a tough time against any opponent who was streaking down his wing with some sort of speed. Not a good sign for the future.

FINAL SCORE: 5-3 Everett

Sept 29 CCM All-American Prospects Game (Buffalo New York)

Team McClanahan (white)

TeamWhite #3 D Seth Jones – Size is a major plus as Jones looks like a man amongst boys comparable to Zdeno Chara. Jones is also a good skater for being such a big kid, which speaks to a high level of athleticism. Shows patience with the puck and finds the open man with a good first pass. Jones also shows a high level of offensive upside carrying the puck and jumping into the rush on numerous occasions throughout the game. Has a cannon of a shot, showcased on a powerful slap shot from the point which blasted by the goalie for the second team white goal. Occasionally took bad angles with oncoming rushers which did lead to a few scoring chances for team blue. This should improve as Jones matures and the potential is off the charts.

TeamWhite #4 D Will Butcher – Lower end of the size scale for elite defenseman at this level. Butcher stood out in this game being paired with Seth Jones. A smooth skater, Butcher shows good feet and movement laterally and works to keep opposing forwards to the outside and keep them at bad angles. Smart player with the puck does not try to force plays but chooses the safe play to get the puck out of the defensive zone. Occasionally showcases his skating by carrying the puck out of the defensive zone or jumping into the rush.

Team White #15 F Quentin Shore – Good size for a forward at this level. Average skater, is generally in good position to make plays and get him in open areas of the ice. Showed some offensive upside by making crafty plays in the offensive zone and getting the puck to teammates in good spots. Showcased a good net presence and was not afraid to get dirty in front of the net and battle for pucks.

Team White #17 F Cole Cassels – Good size for a forward at this level. Cassels is a good skater and has a decent level of speed. Cassels stood out for his playmaking and vision in this game, consistently moving the puck to open players and putting himself in positions to score. Also helped out in the defensive zone and was a good outlet for moving the puck up the ice.

Team White #16 D Trevor Hamilton – Good size for a defender at this level. Hamilton stood out in this game for a high physical presence. On numerous occasions, Hamilton made a big hit that turned the puck over and led to attacks for his team. Showed good body positioning in the defensive zone which led to the opportunities to throw the body around.

Team White #21 F Mike McCarron – Initially stood out for being a big bodied forward. McCarron disappointed throughout the game by generally not contributing and seemed to be just going through the motions. Good skater but generally just didn't stand out when he was on the ice.

September 29, 2012, Baie-Comeau Drakkar vs. Victoriaville Tigres (QMJHL)

BAC #3 D Vanier, Alexis (2014) – Showed some good potential in this game. He was much better than I expected in the skating department and made his fair share of good plays defensively. I think he was a little overused for a rookie and he eventually made a few mistakes with the puck. He did a good job doing damage control against a speedy and fierce offensive from Victoriaville. Another thing I liked is his confidence with the puck. He never panicked and made some good plays overall (except a few mistakes here and there like I mentioned prior)

BAC #26 RW Ranger, Alexandre (2013) – He caught my eye with his speed and intensity. He has a motor that never stops and he uses his great speed the play the game both ways. I believe his offensive potential is a little limited. He didn't do much with the puck and adopted the "dump and chase" mentality that goes with his team.

BAC #31 G Cadorette, Philippe (2013) – As much as I liked him last year, he didn't have a favorable showing in this game. Gave up 6 goals and he just wasn't there (neither was his defense). He still showed some good reflexes and speed but he didn't play with a lot of confidence. I saw him deep in his crease on a lot of occasions and he didn't confront the shooters much.

BAC #73 G Zykov, Valentin (2013) – Showed some good tools in this one but I can't say he had a very good game offensively. He had some highs and some lows. Zykov isn't a typical Russian skilled player but he showed some decent speed on straight lines and a little above average hands. He didn't look extremely comfortable skating with the puck and he got rid of it quickly or lost it. I liked his presence around the net where he is trying to elude himself to receive a pass or knock in a rebound. He works fairly hard and he's never too far away from the puck and battles for it. The next step in this department for him would be to use his big frame to punish the opponent and give some good hits.

VIC #21 C Danault, Phillip (Blackhawks Draft Pick) – Just a quick note on Danault who had a great night and who's having a great start to his season. He scored a hat trick and he's showing a lot more confidence in his shot than he did in the past. He's also flying all over the ice and is noticeably stronger. His work ethic is still present and he's leading the charge for Victoriaville.

VIC #57 LW Veilleux, Tommy (2013) – Now that Veilleux improved his speed considerably, we get the chance to see him more with the puck. He takes a lot of time before making decisions and doesn't show a lot of hockey sense. His head is down and he doesn't read the play ahead of him. He still displays his intensity on the forecheck and hits like a train. This would be the best aspect of his game right now and the reason why he's playing. He needs to use this strength and translate it to his offensive game. He should use his big body more to drive the net and create chances.

September 29, 2012, Val-D'Or Foreurs vs. Drummondville Voltigeurs (QMJHL)

VDO #2 D Murphy, Matt (2013) – I was really impressed with his maturity and confidence in this game. He played with poise and had an excellent showing. He is an extremely smooth skater and moves really well, whether it's backwards, laterally or forward. One thing I wanted to see more from him last year was using his speed to move the puck and he did just that. His speed is not high-end and he doesn't have the explosion to beat everyone with it, but he has the ability to move the puck out of the zone and accompany his players on the rush. He was also very confident and made some very hard and precise passes. Some were riskier plays but he always had his head up and looked what he was doing before taking a decision. He took them fast and caught his teammates by surprise a couple times. One thing I'd like to see him do more is use his shot in the offensive zone. I believe he only had one shot on goal in the game. Murphy also did a good job defensively, keeping a good gap between him and the attacker and he used his stick to profusion to stop the play. He wasn't overly physical but he used his body to win fight along the boards and clear the front of the net.

VD #8 RW Mantha, Anthony (2013) – Mantha left me a little perplex after this game. He didn't play poorly but didn't show a very complete package either. He didn't generate a whole lot with the puck in the neutral zone and we saw him mostly around the net where he was hunting for rebounds. He still has some explosion when he starts and his full speed is very decent. The area of concern I have with his skating is his balance and agility. He can't turn corners very fast and looked more like a straight line skater. Like I mentioned, he did a good job around the net making his presence felt. He was always there for rebounds and he gave his teammates options. I also thought his work ethic was off tonight as he floated around a little. He also NEEDS to make a better use of his body along the board to win battles. Overall he has above average tools with his good hands and decent skating, but he needs to work more and use his huge frame to his advantage.

VDO #79 LW Zlobin, Anton (1993 born) – Zlobin has always been a favorite at HP and he played a very good game worth mentioning. I thought his speed improved a lot since he came into the league and that compliments his NHL caliber shot extremely well. We saw him go from one end to another with blazing speed more than once. He showed in the past he was more of a one zone player (offensive zone) but now he looks like he can impact the game in a lot more areas with his speed.

DRU #13 RW Gauthier, Guillaume (2013) – Gauthier in this game showed he is at his best with the puck on his stick in the offensive zone and with space around him. He did an excellent job on the powerplay moving the puck, passing and shooting. He showed good vision but only when things were slower and he had time to take his decisions. He also showed his finishing touch with two goals from close range. Although he had a better showing tonight, he still didn't show enough in terms of skating and talent to be worth drafting. His work ethic is off and he doesn't factor much in the defensive zone and the neutral zone.

DRU #15 D Brouillard, Nicolas (2013) – He got outworked physically in this game but again, he relies on mobility to get out of trouble. He had a few good plays bringing the puck to the offensive zone. He also had some bad plays that happened right in front of his net where he wasn't able to clear the puck or lost possession. At one point he decided to go give some help into the corner in his own zone without looking around and left a forward completely by himself in front of the net. He did a good job on the powerplay cycling and moving the puck. He also put a couple of very good low shots to the net. He also showed one more time this tendency he has to hold on to the puck too long when moving it. At one point he had a forward crossing the ice in front him at full speed and waited too long to pass it there and the defender was able to make a play and stop the rush.

Sept 30, 2012, Vancouver Giants vs Spokane Chiefs (WHL)

VAN#8 LD, Morrison, Tyler(2014) Had a very inconsistent game, but mostly not a good showing today. Really liked to join the rush and try to create a mismatch for his team. An above average skater, but got caught flat footed going backwards a couple of times and gave the opposition a couple of good scoring chances as a result. Did not have a good night moving the puck at all. Made some poor decisions when passing the puck and made a number of turnovers. Much too soft to play against in the defensive zone. Got knocked around time and time again around the boards.

VAN#27 RW, Houck, Jackson(2013) Physical forward who was dominant along the walls today. Very good instincts around the boards and controlled the puck with authority. Even without good positioning, he is able to come up with the puck and keep the play in the offensive zone alive. Struggled with the accuracy on his shots all night. Had a few good chances to score down the wing but just was not able to hit the net.

VAN#31 G, Fuhr, Tyler(2013) Made his first start in the WHL, and was quite good. Made a few good saves going post to post. One memorable save was on a 2 on 1 situation, the puck carrier faked a slap shot and made a quick pass for a one timer, but Fuhr was able to just get to the other side and make the pad save. Had a difficult time tracking pucks in traffic. Had a good day controlling rebounds, but could be improved on. Looks calm and poised in net.

SPO#2 RD, Fram, Jason(2013) Played a good, quiet game today. Does not possess any elite skills, but did not make any big mistakes. A good skater, but will not blow past by any quick skaters. Made simple, easy outlet passes accurately and did not put his teammates in any bad position. Defensively, could be better at reading the play. At one instance on the rush, it was a 2 on 2 situation, and for some reason left his side and started to chase the puck carrier instead of staying with the other opponent. Not bad around the boards, but could be much stronger.

SPO#4 LD, McIntosh, Jeremy(2013) A tough, stay at home defenseman had good and bad moments in the game. Was at his best when he was physical along the boards and stayed aggressive on the line. However, his poor skating ability put him in a bad position a couple of times. Got into a good fight in the first period and took the decision at the end. Not very good with the puck, made a few terrible decisions trying to thread a pass in tight in the neutral zone and allowed the opponents to counter attack.

SCOUT'S NOTES: Vancouver was able to pick up their first win of the season with a good team effort. Really liked Tyler Fuhr's game today. Did not face many shots, but was solid when the team needed him. Could see him taking the starting job away if he keeps his play up. Interesting that Anthony Ast was scratched today, don't remember him getting hurt last game, but the Giants are still trying to count their roster down so they did play a number of younger players to get a closer look at their talent. If Jackson Houck could improve his shots and attack the net with more authority he will be a very attractive option in the upcoming draft. Reid Gow of Spokane took a slap shot to his face in the slot when he was on the ice and it knocked off his visor and left blood on the ice at the end of the 2nd period, but came right back on the ice in the 3rd period and was able to finish the game.

FINAL SCORE: 3-2 Vancouver

Oct 04, 2012, Victoriaville Tigres @ Rimouski Océanic. (QMJHL)

RIM #3 D, Kostalek, Jan (2013): This is a player who has the tools and potential to be effective in all 3 zones as he is a strong, fluid skater with good puck moving capabilities and is sound defensively. He had a bit of an up and down game however, and there were times when he had some trouble playing the gap on some of the quicker players on the opposition. He likes to play the game pretty safe and appears to be a pretty smart player all-round.

RIM #11 RW, Bryukvin, Vladimir (2013): Bryukvin possesses some quick hands and has good instincts to create time and space. He displayed a good 2- way game and showed the ability to win the battles on the boards in his own zone. He wasn't overly active in the game and had trouble getting much speed going to be effective.

RIM #15 LW, DeLuca Anthony (2013): This is a player who would really benefit from improving his acceleration, as he does not tend to win many of the races to loos pucks. He plays with a high skill level however and has some highlight reel moves to beat defenders in one-on-one battles. He also has a rocket of a shot that he knows how to use in order to get it to the net to create opportunities. He doesn't have much physical implication in his game as he is a small player that always tries to deke before protecting the puck and playing a hard-nosed style of hockey.

RIM #23 C, Gauthier, Frédérik (2013): This was an excellent game for Gauthier. He played a smart and mature 2-way game and used both his long reach and big frame to cut down the space on the ice. He possesses a really high hockey IQ as he sees the ice like very few players do. He can play an effective cycle game, or he can also beat defenders with his hands to get by them by placing the puck behind and retrieving it with his long reach. He uses his frame very well in all aspects of the game and is always in the right position defensively. He is really good on the draw and is not a selfish player as he knows how to move the puck around to create opportunities for teammates. He could improve his skating still to become somewhat more explosive, however this was overall a really quality game for this prospect.

RIM #55 D, Morin Samuel (2013): More physical down-low than before; seems to have gotten some kind of mean streak; uses short passes on the breakout not willing to try the risky plays; uses the board; has a long stick to deflect many pucks; not the quickest feet can get past by quick skaters; has to work on his game with the puck; defensive D.

Oct. 05 2012, Moncton Wildcats @ Chicoutimi Saguneéens, (QMJHL)

MON #22 LW, Barbashev, Ivan (2014): This was a solid game for Barbashev that may not have shown up on the score sheet, however he had numerous scoring chances including a penalty shot. He played a very Pretty North American style game, as he was the one to initiate contact along the boards and plays with a really high compete level and also displayed nice grit in his battles. He is a fluid skater, using his explosive speed very well to beat the opposition's defenders and get a clean break opportunity at the net. He still needs a bit of polishing in the defensive zone, as he gets himself out of position quite easily but there is definitely a lot to like in how aggressive his play is. He possesses some nice quick hands, which are typical of a Russian player, but he doesn't rely solely on that in one-on-one situations which is really nice to see. He has a decent sense of the game, however he appears to be more of a goal scorer than a playmaker.

MON #26 LW, Jaskin, Dimitri (St-Louis): Jaskin was the best forward in the game. He has incredible size and still skates like few can, especially of his size. He has impressive hands and uses them well to create space and openings. He has some amazing natural talent and combines that with a love to drive the net and create plays from around the crease, as he is normally stronger than his opponents and can protect the puck to draw players on him and then make passes to find the open players or simply go around defensemen then drive the net hard. He is a physical player who loves to get his nose dirty and is also solid 2-way.

MON #43 D, Melindy, James (Phoenix): Melindy looked really slow, made a couple of bad turnovers just throwing the puck around the boards when the opposition and pressure were already coming from that direction and was playing overall really passively. He has a good frame which helps to win his battles on the boards, but again he doesn't seem to be aggressive enough to contain more energetic forwards. He is much more effective when he plays with a mean streak in him.

CHI #17 LW, Tremblay, Simon (2013): This was the best game I have seen Tremblay play this year. He played a solid in your face type of game, pressed hard on the fore-check and had a lot of jump in his skating which gave him the opportunity to force multiple turnovers. He was also very good on the penalty kill, blocking multiple shots and even generating some great rushes by bringing the puck all the way to the other end with a lot of grit. He is the kind of player you notice a lot in a game, as he is always pressuring the puck carrier or working in traffic. He possesses a good quick shot as he comes down the left wing, but he just doesn't have the scoring touch or the high end skills to be on the scoreboard very often.

October 5, 2012, Youngstown Phantoms vs Waterloo Blackhawks (USHL)

WAT #91 LW Taylor Cammarata (2013) - Finesse offensive forward, primarily a playmaker off the wing. Set up on the half wall on the powerplay, drifting between the corner and the point. Killed penalties sparingly. Biggest asset was his vision. On numerous occasions he threaded perfectly timed passes, on-ice and saucer, through tight seams. Immediate instinct was almost always to pass. In certain situations, such as when he quickly reacted to a turnover and one-touched a perfect snap pass to an open teammate in front, his playmaking ability looked outstanding and very natural. In others, like when he readied for a slap shot off the rush then faked, held the puck, and dished it into a crowded slot, he looked to be trying to force a fancier play.

Showed deceptive hands but without a lot of stops and starts with his feet, limiting his effectiveness in evading checks both in the offensive zone and on the breakout. Stickhandling looked best on the powerplay when he had room to work with. Showed great passing ability in maintaining powerplay pressure. Was almost always the first option for his teammates, who tried to get him the puck as often as possible. Flashed the ability to lead an offense. Was the main creative force behind sustained-pressure offensive situations on multiple occasions at even and extra strength, but also had a hard time maintaining poise in the face of physical contact.

Was clearly a target for the opposition and was tightly checked. His strength was a limiting factor. Was pushed off the puck too easily and took too many hits for a finesse player. Did surprise in shaking off contact, but only on a few occasions. On one distinct occasion he tried to wind up for an end-to-end rush and was disoriented by an oncoming forechecker, leading to a costly turnover. Skating is a little awkward and choppy but mostly effective. Good acceleration from side to side. Showed effective burst getting to loose pucks. Had trouble getting to top speed.

Liked to take the puck to the slot in stride, not so much to take a shot as to draw a defender and open up a teammate for a pass. Would benefit from shooting the puck more as when he did put the puck on net he was dangerous. His offensive zone instincts were good overall. Followed his teammates' shots to the net and liked to try to find soft spots in coverage. His second goal came from crashing the net for a rebound.

Was inconsistent overall with his effort, particularly in the defensive zone and on the backcheck. Rarely came back into his own zone, except to restart the offense and when Youngstown maintained pressure. Lost his man in the neutral zone on a few occasions. Sometimes had his head on a swivel in the defensive zone and covered his man well, sometimes seemed disinterested in defense altogether. Had a few shifts where his eyes seemed glued to the puck and his feet stopped moving. Did not show a good effort in getting back to the bench for changes. Tried to do too much on numerous occasions. Showed enthusiasm on the penalty kill but had issues with coverage.

Scout's Notes: Waterloo LD Ian McCoshen (2013) and goaltenders Eamon McAdam (2013) and Calvin Peterson (2013) were all scratched due to a team-imposed suspension. Youngstown RW JJ Piccinich (2014) played an OK game, showing good skill and effort, but needs to improve his skating, while Phantoms RC Austin Cangelosi (Passed over 2012) was the best player on the ice for both teams, with great hands, a dangerous shot, and strong PK work. Waterloo LC Brandon Salerno (2013) impressed with great skating, quick hands, and strong defensive play, while RC Justin Kloos (Passed over 2012) showed speed and skill.

October 5, 2012, Owen Sound Attack @ Sarnia Sting (OHL)

OSA #4 RD Dotchin, Jake (Tampa Bay) - Very good to start the game. Skating is much improved and he continues to look very solid in his own zone. Would like to see him pick up the offensive game a little bit, but really like how he looks early on.

OSA #10 RW Blandisi, Joseph (Colorado) - Showed off excellent elusiveness all game long. Considering his 190lb listing he is a tremendous skater. He scored an outstanding goal as it appeared he got partially tripped up, he stuck with the play and scored the goal. Skating, hands and determination are his ticket to success at the next level.

OSA #24 LD Bigras, Chris (2013) - Bigras consistently stuck with the play effectively in the defensive zone. He is extremely mobile in small areas and uses it to effectively stick with his man turning, stopping and changing directions quickly. He didn't too much offensively in this game but he is very smart in choosing the right time to pinch and when to get back into secure defensive positioning.

OSA #27 RW Nastasiuk, Zach (2013) - Nastasiuk protects the puck very well down low. He is elusive in this area and shows strong skating ability. He also uses this protection ability to create scoring chances for himself and others.

SAR #21 LC Nikandrov, Daniel (2013) - Daniel keeps getting better every game. Works extremely hard, shows good smarts and hockey sense with his positioning and his puck possession. His hands are very quick.

SAR #71 RW Goldobin, Nikolay (2014) - Made some outstanding moves around three Owen Sound players and nearly scored showing highlight reel moves. Outstanding passer and puck mover and looked flawless on the power play today.

Scouts Notes: A very exciting and very close back and forth game between these two teams. Jordan Binnington (St. Louis) was solid tonight in Sarnia sneaking out of the RBC Centre with the win. The Attack gained a 4-3 lead in the first minute of the third period. From there on in they relied very heavily on their top defensive pairing of Nathan Chiarlitti (Free Agent) and Chris Bigras (2013). Chiarlitti who was honored before the game put together about as flawless of a performance as he could have. Bigras also performed excellent in the third period really showing his development in shutdown situations from his rookie year. Both teams put on pretty complete performances but those three (Binnington, Chiarlitti, Bigras) were the best three players in this game tonight. Brett Hargrave (2014) is doing a little better in his battles. Joshua Chapman (2013) did well in a fight against a bigger, older opponent but lost. Also rookie Jaden Lindo (2014) showed well crashing the net to help Owen Sound score their first goal.

October 5, 2012, Portland Winterhawks @ Brandon Wheat Kings (WHL)

POR #3 RD Jones, Seth (2013) - Uses his size intelligently to box out opponents in open ice in his own zone. Played a very simple game for the first half making smart basic passes and rushing to the red line then duping the puck deep in the offensive zone. He showed safe defensive positioning and calm under pressure controlling the puck in his own zone. He has very good positioning challenging oncoming forwards rushing towards his zone. Jones hits hard but doesn't seem to have much of a mean streak and usually only hits when the situation is calling for it. Very smooth skating and surprising shiftiness for his size allowed him to move the puck up ice very well. His game opened up around them midway point and became more aggressive with the puck and also made an outstanding long distance pass from behind his net to the offensive blueline to set up a breakaway. Seth has a good point shot and gets it on net.

POR #9 LC De Leo, Chase (2014) - De Leo got plenty of ice and engages at both ends of the ice forcing turnovers early. He's a good skater and marginally engaged in the offensive zone.

POR #19 LC Petan, Nicolas (2013) - Petan jumps out at you immediately as he steps onto the ice. He handles the puck so smoothly going through traffic. He uses his speed and hands to create offense for himself and others. He knows where to go in the offensive zone and puts himself in great positions to score. Petan was also a key player for Portland defensively. He was a regular on the penalty kill and forced turnovers and pressured defensemen on the point very well. He was also able to create a few very good short handed scoring chances as well.

POR #27 RW Bjorkstrand, Oliver (2013) - Oliver is a very slick passer who seemed to have great chemistry with Petan and made some excellent set up's in the offensive zone early. He has tremendous creativity and he is very quick to rush the puck, or jump up into ideal positioning on the rush.

BDN #2 RD Pulock, Ryan (2013) - Pulock made some smart plays to move the puck up ice. He shows fairly smooth skating ability to rush the puck up ice but had the occasional mental lapse when rushing. Ryan did a very good job holding the line on the power play keeping the pressure on the Winterhawks. When in the offensive zone he comes off the point with or without the puck if there is a lane for him. He did this intelligently and it resulted in him getting a couple shots on goal. Pulock really was a leader tonight when it came to creating offense for Brandon.

BDN #6 LD Nikkel, Ayrton (2013) - Nikkel made some good quick plays up ice while under pressure. Fairly reliable in his own zone forcing turnovers, making good decisions with the puck and at times willing to block shots.

BDN #7 LD Roy, Eric (2013) - Roy has tremendous size and a good stick in the defensive zone. However his reaction time was a little slow and appeared to be affected by his slow first step when needing to make a play that was more than stick length away. He will get down to block shots in his own zone. Appears to lack the realization of his low level skating and attempts to make plays he isn't able to make regularly at this level or got caught up ice and wasn't able to get back into position. Passing is hit or miss on the power play.

Scouts Notes: Portland really dominated this game start to finish. After taking a 2-1 lead into the third period they absolutely controlled the Wheat Kings leading in the shot clock 14-3 to secure the win. Despite the loss a big player in this game was Corbin Boes (2013*) who really kept Brandon in this game. It could have easily been a blowout if not for his play and allowed Brandon a chance to win right down to the final seconds. Portland would get the win holding only their 2-1 lead with Alex Schoenborn (2014) scoring his first goal in the WHL which was ultimately the game winning goal.

October 5, 2012, Acadie-Bathurst Titan @ Baie-Comeau Drakkar (QMJHL)

Acadie-Bathurst
#23 Patrick Zdrahal, RW (2013) Zdrahal played on the Titan's 3rd line with Banville & Zboril. The young Czech forward had a quiet game overall but still showed glimpses of his talent on two particular shifts. On the first shift he made a nice play after entering the Baie-Comeau zone, cut inside between two defensemen but was stopped by the Drakkar goaltender. On the 2nd shift, he showed some great stickhandling skills, deking two of Baie-Comeau's best defensemen in Gabriel Verpelast and Samuel Noreau before losing control of the puck in front of the goalie. Other than that he was not very noticeable in this game.

#24 Adam Zboril, C (2013)   Zboril was as quiet as his linemate Zdrahal minus the two great shifts Zdrahal had. Zboril centered the 3rd line with Banville and Zdrahal, only listed at 5'7", 186 lbs. Didn't stand out in any areas, made one bad turnover in the 2nd period, making a pass to an area with only Baie-Comeau players which led to a scoring chance. Although he is undersized, he showed a willingness to get his nose dirty. I saw him with a strong forecheck presence, battling with the much bigger Alexis Vanier behind the Baie-Comeau net. However, he didn't do anything offensively in this game. His skating looks like it will need work, as he doesn't generate a lot of speed.

Baie-Comeau

#3 Alexis Vanier, Def (2014) Tough game for the young Vanier, who had trouble handling the puck and making passes all night. Was paired with fellow rookie Loik Leveille on the 3rd pair. He has a lot of work to do with his foot speed and agility. Didn't show a lot of confidence with the puck. Big kid who didn't play a physical brand of hockey in this game.

#7 Loïk Léveillé, Def (2015) Léveillé played a relatively good game and was also quarterbacking the Drakkar's first power play unit. He was caught a couple of times with a man behind him and had to take a penalty once because of it. Moves the puck well and is a good skater, kept his game simple rushing the puck, as he crossed the red line he just threw the puck deep. Made a great pass to Zykov for his first goal of the game, great shot/pass in front of the net.

#13 Gabriel Paquin-Boudreau, LW (2013) The 17 year old rookie was playing on the Drakkar's 3rd line but got ice time on the power play. Overall Boudreau was quiet in this game, didn't have possession of the puck often and when he did, he tried to do too much with it. Played a perimeter game as well, stayed too much on the outside.

#16 Felix Girard, C (1994)Girard is in his second year as captain of the Drakkar, and plays with a lot of grit and heart. Played in every situation in this game, and one has to love his puck pursuit on the forecheck. Did a good job on the PK, using his stick to break passes and was also very effective at protecting the puck to run time off the clock. Girard had a very strong game in the faceoff circle, skated well and had a few good scoring chances. Tireless worker, and even at his size, didn't lose too many one-on-one battles.

#25 Thomas Gobeil, RW (2013) Gobeil has limited skill, but a great work ethic. Plays a hard, physical game, likes to initiate contact along the boards. Had 2 or 3 good scoring chances but couldn't finish them. Doesn't have the smoothest hands. His scoring chances came from him driving the net with the puck.

#73 Valentin Zykov, RW (2013) Played on the Drakkar's top line with Gelinas and Gamelin, and saw time on the power play as well. Zykov was great in this game, scoring 3 goals in the process. Zykov is always around the net, as 2 of his goals were scored close to the net and the other was scored from 15 feet out tipping a shot from the point. I also liked his quick release on his shot, which is very quick and a skill that he loves to use Below the hashmark he was dominant, very strong player and tough to contain. Skating will need work, as he doesn't generate a lot of speed in the neutral zone, first couple steps will need work too.

October 6th, 2012 Everett Silvertips @ Seattle Thunderbirds (WHL)

SEA #17 RD Theodore Shea (2013)- Shea played a very strong game adding 2 goals and 1 assist. Shea lead the offensive rush much of the game with his smooth skating. He showed his ability to handle and protect the puck when he dangle 2 Everett D-man then finish with a hard snapper to beat the goalie. Top 5 d-man in the league this year. Has all the tools in the shed lets just see how many he will use this year.

SEA #33 LD Hauf Jared (2013)- Jared had a decent game, He played a strong defensive game, forcing Everetts shooter to the outside and crushing them along the boards. His physical play pick up this game ashe was using his huge frame. His skating and foot speed need work.

SEA #2 LD Smith Jeret (2013)- Had a decent game, showed his defensive potential tonight with some physical play. Need to work on his angling and foot speed. Not much there as far as offensive punch. Could develop into a good shut down d-man

SEA #19 LW Sheen Riley (2013)- Small things come in big packages and thats what riley was tonight. I like this kids and how he plays with a edge every night. He added 2 assists and once again show his offensive vision and ability to thread a needle through traffic. Only down side is his size .

EVT #15 C Bauml Kohl (2013) Kohl didnt show much of anything tonight. Not sure if he took the night off or not. There was no speed or flash or edge to his game tonight. Very flat, could not win the battles along the boards and was forcing the play way to much. I am 50/50 with kohl after this last performance.

EVT #16 C Stadnyk Carson (2013) Not sure if carson showed up to play, his defensive awareness was no where to be found tonight, he forced the puck and would panic under pressure. I dont see much interest with Carson.

EVT #17 RW Lofthouse Trent (2013) I can see the potential Trent. He played a very physical game, but is not showing me much else. Waiting for him to create any offense. I would like to see him use his size and crash the net and grind. Plays timid around the net, need to get strong and bang in those rebounds.

EVT #25 D Mueller Mirco (2013) Mirco played a solid defensive game. He's not a flashy player, just a rugged stay at home style defenseman. He added a assist and show a little offensive flare to his defensive style game. He did show signs of trouble and panic with the aggressive forecheck.

Scouts Notes. The scoring went back and forth between the first and second period with both teams playing aggressive. Seattle was attacking the puck and forcing Everett's defenseman to turn over the puck multiple times but seattle couldn't muster up any scoring chances. The start of the third Everett came out with a punch, making Seattle look dazzled, but just like seattle, everett was unable to muster up any offense. Then the light clicked on for Seattle and Shea took charge leading the offensive purge. Seattle scored 3 unanswered goals in the third deflating any comeback for everett. Final Score Seattle 5 Everett 2.

October 6, 2012, US NTDP Under-18 at University of Wisconsin

USA #4 LD Will Butcher (2013) – Stocky blueliner had a nice game, particularly strong offensively with good carries and creativity. Went end-to-end with poise. Made good breakout passes under pressure. Took hits to make plays in his zone. Good keeps at the blueline on the powerplay. Had one glaring giveaway, but recovered well by getting his stick into the shooting lane.

USA #6 LD Keaton Thompson (2013) – Was blown away by Thompson's effort today. Elite skating, silky smooth on his feet with pinpoint footwork and outstanding balance. Very efficient with his movement. Positioned himself well to give his defensive partner an outlet option whenever possible. Broke the puck out of his zone frequently and had the poise and speed to burn through the neutral zone and take the puck end-to-end. Jumped into the attack appropriately to create numbers without excessive risk. Walked the line well at the offensive zone point. Received passes with his feet moving and head up. Good point play with deceptive fake shots and a quality wrister that he was unafraid to use. Played top pairing on the powerplay and made things happen. Smart about putting the puck into soft space for his teammates. Extremely poised in the defensive zone with a great stick, save for a couple minor lapses that he recovered from well. Great at puck retrieval against the forecheck, made safe plays and quick outlet passes with the puck under pressure. Good coverage against the rush, was difficult to beat with good body positioning.

USA #7 RC JT Compher (2013) – Nice two-way game. Showed great wheels and cycled well in the offensive zone. Showed good hands in flashes. Was willing to take the puck to the slot and showed a hard, accurate wristshot. Backchecked hard.

USA #9 LW Anthony Louis (2013) – Hardworking, undersized offensive forward was outstanding. Was very strong on the forecheck with quick hands and skating, forced turnovers. Great skater that kept his feet moving, played with a lot of jump. Tried to take the puck to the net whenever possible, size was an issue but he was brave. Smart with the puck, made good decisions. Good keeps at the point on the powerplay. Had one glaring giveaway where he not only won the puck back immediately but also got two dangerous shots on net right afterwards.

USA #16 RD Steve Santini (2013) – Loved that he played with an edge and has obvious physical tools, but he was much too aggressive today. By far the most physical player on the ice for either team. Wanted to play the body above all else, taking himself out of position to throw big hits on pinches and at his blueline. Made dazzling contact but left his teammates to deal with outnumbered attacks. Played on the top powerplay pairing but wasn't able to get much going, though he did show off a good one-time shot.

Scout's Notes: USA RW Hudson Fasching (2013) played on the top line. He tried to play a power game and has the tools, but was pushed off the puck too easily and seemed frustrated. Wisconsin handled the NTDP fairly easily with a 5-0 win. USA LC Sean Malone (2013) had a weak game with poor decision-making. Wisconsin RW Morgan Zulinick (passed over 2012) showed good hands and speed all game and scored a beautiful breakaway goal.

October 7, 2012, US NTDP Under-18 at University of Notre Dame

USA #4 LD Will Butcher (2013) – Was more aggressive today than yesterday, with positionally sound but intense coverage in his end. Physical for his size. Safe plays with the puck up the boards to clear danger. Got good shots on net from the point that he fired with his head up looking at the goaltender and traffic in front.

USA #6 LD Keaton Thompson (2013) – What a difference a day makes. Thompson was brutal today. Looked frazzled from the onset. Got totally burned twice, on 1-on-1 and 1-on-2 coverage. Had a few solid shifts with a good, active stick but was frequently exposed in coverage. Had a hard time recognizing his check and an even harder time actually checking, lacked physical assertiveness. Fought the puck most of the time it was on his stick, showed flashes but also had his share of giveaways and poor passes. Poor decisions overall.

USA #9 Anthony Louis (2013) – Skilled forward had another solid game but his decision-making was off. Was quick on the rush and had a great read to get a dangerous shot off on a 2-on-1, but overall tried to do too much offensively. Passed up a golden scoring chance to try to make a fancy pass late in the game.

USA #14 LW Tyler Motte (2013) – Not a great game from Motte. Was too casual clearing the puck out of his end and made a boneheaded blind pass to the middle in the offensive zone that nearly led to a goal against. Was almost directly responsible for Notre Dame's only goal by blowing his coverage.

USA #16 RD Steve Santini (2013) – Safe and steady today, much more poise and control than yesterday. Good wheels, a bit of an awkward skater but he moved well for his size. Great checking, very responsible but still knew when to play the body hard. Outlets were safe.

USA #17 LC Ryan Fitzgerald (2013) – Undersized forward play a strong two-way game. Showed great overall quickness with a good motor. Was creative and dangerous with the puck. Played well on the penalty kill with good coverage up top.

USA #25 Connor Hurley (2013) – Couldn't get much going offensively, but liked his physical play and forechecking ability. Got in with speed and positioned himself well to make life difficult on opposing defensemen. Read plays to get his stick into lanes and force turnovers.

USA #28 LW Shane Eiserman (2014) – Nice two-way game. Played well on the penalty kill and looked good on the forecheck. Flashed a good slapshot. Crashed the crease for rebounds and eventually did put one him.

USA #29 G Thatcher Demko (2014) – Very sharp today, was his team's best player. Showed good rebound control and outstanding lateral agility, though his reactions on one-time shots were a little slow. Had no trouble with deflections and shots through traffic as he tracked the puck very well.

Scout's Notes: The NTDP's best defensive pairing today was LD Clint Lewis (2013) and RD Trevor Hamilton (2013). Neither of them blew me away with any aspect of their game but they kept it safe and simple.

October 9, 2012, Portland Winterhawks @ Regina Pats (WHL)

POR #3 RD Jones, Seth (2013) - Jones made some absolutely flawless long distance passes in this game. He uses his stick very well in one on one situations. Physical along the boards and is relentless there but not very physical unless he needs to be. Handles puck passed into his skates well. He played second unit power play for Portland and used his big point shot to set up a huge scoring chance in overtime.

POR #9 LC De Leo, Chase (2014) - Chase has a very consistent work ethic and forces turnovers regularly. He nearly set up the game winning goal in the final minute of the third period tied 2-2 by sending his linemate on a breakaway with a very nice pass. However he did make a few less than admirable passes while on the power play.

POR #19 LC Petan, Nicolas (2013) - Not the biggest guy on the ice but he protects the puck so well and cam beat multiple opponents regularly. He was able to use his speed to turn a 3 on 2 into a 2 on 1 then made a beautiful pass but got robbed on the finish. Makes opponents freeze up due to his puck skills and shiftiness. Puck movement was extremely smooth and he made an outstanding pass to set up the first goal of the game on the power play. Nicolas plays big minutes in every game situations for Portland. He reads the defensemen on the point very well when his team is short handed allowing him to anticipate their decisions well. He appears to like shooting more than passing but isn't a selfish player.

POR #27 RW Bjorkstrand, Oliver (2013) - Bjorkstrand showed very quick acceleration and skates very smoothly. He pressures the puck carrier in all three zones and forces a large amount of turnovers.

REG #4 RD Burroughs, Kyle (2013) - Burroughs did not have his best game. He is a good skater but can make mistakes when pressured. He's willing to block shots, but his reaction time in general was a little slow. He made a very bad turnover in his own zone resulting in a huge scoring chance for Portland.

REG #5 RD Williams, Colby (2013) - Williams is a pretty smooth skater and shows good elusiveness when skating with the puck. He's comfortable pinching off the point to keep the puck in the zone or into the top of the slot making himself available for shooting options.

REG #18 LW Klimchuk, Morgan (2013) - Great positioning in the offensive zone early but his teammate didn't see him otherwise he would have had a sure goal. He showed good jump in his step and smooth overall skating ability. Very reliable and consistent on the forecheck. He was part of the top power play unit but was moved back and forth between forward and the point.

Scouts Notes: Portland continued their road trip in Regina and this was a very close game with a lot of back and forth action. Portland took an early 1-0 lead. Regina responded with two of their own goals before Portland tied the game in the final five minutes of regulation pushing the game to overtime. With only seconds left Lane Scheidl (2013) scored the overtime winner to give Regina the win.

October 10, 2012, Baie-Comeau Drakkar vs. Victoriaville Tigres (QMJHL)

BAC #3 D Vanier, Alexis (2014) – He didn't get much ice time in this game but he did some interesting things. I really liked how he used his size to its advantage and to punish opponents. He makes it known that it's not going to be easy playing in his zone. He does a good job defending around his net when the play is installed in the defensive zone but he needs to improve his speed to handle 1-on-1 situations at high speed better. In the games I've seen so far, including tonight's game, he also showed he likes to handle the puck and move it a little bit. His puck play looks a little bit risky as he is not really fast and keeps his head down, but the good hands he has shown so far allowed him to elude from the pressure and limit mistakes. While it's obviously not a big part of his game right now, it's an interesting thing to see a young giant like him handle the puck like this.

BAC #26 RW Ranger, Alexandre (2013) – Baie-Comeau's go to guy along with captain Felix Girard to generate speed and energy. Ranger plays extremely hard and brings speed and passion to the game. He's extremely quick to react in all three zones and that makes him very effective in most situations at this level. He can stop and start really quick as well and that allowed him to score the first goal after stopping behind the net and coming back in front with lightning speed to beat the goalie. He didn't show any high end skills to go along with his good speed and doesn't seem to be the type of player to go through the whole ice with dangles and deceptive speed. He skates straight lines very fast and reads the play well to move the puck. As good as a QMJHL player I think he's going to be, I believe his professional potential is limited.

BAC #31 G Cadorette, Philippe (2013) – Cadorette played a respectable game. He didn't standout but was able to make the first save for his team most of the night. Most of the goals scored on him came right in front of his crease where he had time to react and the player all for himself. I can't say he caught my eye in a positive way in the game. He had a decent outing, but nothing more.

BAC #73 G Zykov, Valentin (2013) – Zykov is starting to pick up the pace and adapting to his new environment. The element that caught my eye in this game from him is his hands. He didn't use them much the previous time I saw him, but in this game he was just creating a lot of space by fooling his opponents to go a different direction. He doesn't handle the puck overly fast, but his hands are smooth and solid. It seems those moves he had tonight worked a lot when he was installed in the offensive zone and on the power play. He created a lot of space around him and complimented that by protecting the puck with his body. The next point I want to bring forward with his hands concern 1-on-1 situations in the neutral zone when he is on the rush. He had a lot of those in the first period but although he has decent speed on straight lines, he wasn't able to come out on top and get past the defender or enter the offensive zone. The quality of his play diminished as the game went on and we didn't see much from him in the second half of the game. Finally, like I mentioned in my previous report on him, he demonstrated once again his implication in the defensive zone and along the boards. The point I don't like much is he seems to absorb the impact when he goes for a hit. He launches himself but it looks like he's trying to absorb the shock or bounce off the player instead of hitting him hard.

VIC #3 D Diaby, Jonathan (2013) – Diaby played a decent game. There were stretches where he was excellent and others where it was more difficult. He started the game strong and was extremely effective defending with his long reach. His backwards skating although it improved needs to be better in order to defend properly against faster players. Luckily for him, he is a pretty good skater going forward and that allows him to catch up at times. He also had some rough plays like a 2-on-1 where he didn't defend either option. He just stood there and wasn't able to do anything.

VIC #15 RW Ayotte, Mathieu (2014) – Ayotte played an excellent game and had a lot of scoring chances. He is extremely intelligent and posses very good hands. Even though he lacks size and strength, he can control the puck in tight spaces and has the ability to get out of trouble by spotting a teammate. While he is not an explosive skater, his speed still allows him to skate with the fastest player on his team and be a constant threat. He has a knack to score goals and is very dangerous in close range from the net.

VIC #57 LW Veilleux, Tommy (2013) – I didn't like Veilleux's game tonight. He didn't display his usual hustle and intensity. He didn't go all in for all the length of his shifts. He also didn't impact the game the way he should with his physical play. He was falling more than he was hitting and he often got caught behind the play because of this. He needs to be more in control when he hits in order to, first, reach his target, and secondly, get back in the play. Other than that I didn't see much from him with the puck. He had a couple sequences but that didn't result in anything. His speed and hockey sense just don't allow him to keep the puck for too long.

Scout Notes: Both team played the dump and chase for the most part of this game and we didn't get to see much of individual efforts with the puck. Baie-Comeau clearly outworked Victoriaville and came out on top 4-3. Victoriaville's Dominik Rehak who is eligible for 2013 didn't play a good game. He showed his great hands on sequence early in the game and he didn't play much the rest of the game after making a mistake in the neutral zone. I was also keeping a close eye on Gabriel Paquin-Boudreau who is also eligible this year, but he didn't play a strong game. You could see he has very good puck skills and decent speed, but it wasn't his game and lost puck possession quite often and got demoted to the fourth line at some point.

October 12, 2012, Boston Jr. Bruins vs. Valley Jr. Warriors (EJHL)

BJB #11 LC Ryan Cloonan (2013) – Outstanding raw offensive talent. Was a step ahead of everyone on the ice, including his teammates. His stride is quick and efficient and he showed great burst quickness in addition to the ability to make plays at top speed. Flashy stickhandling ability allowed him to create space for himself and maintain possession for extended periods of time. Carried the puck with authority. Capable of going end-to-end as well as acting as a one-man cycle. Very shifty. Unafraid to drive the middle. Was guilty of trying to do too much on almost every shift. Did not utilize his teammates well. Effort was inconsistent, particularly defensively. On one occasion he showed great burst in puck pursuit and threw a nice hit to separate his opponent from the puck. For most of the rest of the game, he floated and waited for the offense to restart. Convince him to go 100% all the time and he could be a dynamic two-way player.

BJB #24 LD Josh Couturier (2013) – Big body defenseman with an active stick. Still lanky but did not use his size well at all and was pushed off the puck frequently, often by smaller players. Lacked poise against the forecheck and didn't handle the rush well. Major project.

October 12, 2012, South Shore Kings vs. Portland Jr. Pirates (EJHL)

PJP #17 RW Haralds Egle (2014) – Leading Portland in scoring as one of the youngest players in the EJHL. He has an outstanding shot. Absolutely crushed a one-timer for a goal and got great velocity on wristers. Good skater and stickhandler, showed some flashes of brilliance but I got the impression that he tries to play a pretty simple game overall (dumping the puck, making safe passes, etc.). Much more of a professional style than most of the players surrounding him, which illustrated an appreciation for detail that I think will serve him well. Intelligent positioning in the offensive zone. Chippy along the boards. Defense needs work, had issues with coverage and was inconsistent with his backchecking effort. Could see him developing into a pretty good triggerman.

October 12, 2012, Plymouth Whalers @ London Knights (OHL)

PLY #21 RC Hartman, Ryan (2013) - Hartman opened the game with a ton of energy. He played physical finishing his checks when he could and just constantly making things happen all game long. Hartman created chances for his teammates almost every single shift and took advantage of the chances he received. He was quick to go after loose pucks and force turnovers. Work ethic and ability to find a way to make an impact every shift was impressive.

LON #16 LC Domi, Max (2013) - Max was very effective tonight for the Knights. He moved the puck well right from his first shift throughout the game. He forced turnovers particularly in the offensive zone keeping the play going. He showed off his quickness, so shifty that most opponents couldn't keep up with him. He reads the play very well and knows when to pass, when to shoot and when to handle the puck. He was the catalyst for the 3-0 goal for the Knights by moving the puck very well, then going right to the net deflecting it in.

LON #53 LW Horvat, Bo (2013) - Horvat was excellent in tonight's game. He is put out in the slot area on the power play and does a great job. His quick hands helped him pick up the rebound and score the first goal of the game. Worked hard down low consistently winning battles. Bo scored the game winning goal at the midway point of the second period. Horvat showing off why we consider him a first round talent. His combination of skill, work ethic and respectable size

LON #65 LD Zadorov, Nikita (2013) - Zadorov made good passes out of the zone all game long. He was effective for the most part but a lot of his mistakes came when being rushed. Nikita possesses a powerful point shot. He was good more often than not defensively and in one on one situations, but had the occasional miscue.

LON #81 LW Elie, Remi (2013) - Elie played bottom six today and cycled the puck extremely well on a regular basis. He hits hard and picks his spots well. He had a few flashes of skill but got into some trouble when getting fancy and made a few mistakes this way. At his best when he just kept it simple and uses his intelligence.

Scouts Notes: This one started out pretty exciting. Both teams putting together some solid back and forth. Plymouth had a large amount of chances early on, but Kevin Baillie (Free Agent) played the best game I think we've ever seen out of him. He was solid and made a number of big saves. London was able to capitalize on their chances, and it was the 3-0 goal that really deflated the Whalers efforts. London dominated from there on in and wrapped this game up taking it by a 4-1 score.

Oct 12, 2012, Vancouver Giants vs Seattle Thunderbirds (WHL)

VAN#27 RW, Houck, Jackson(2013) Definitely a game he would like to forget. Definitely have seen better games from him this season. Was not very physical on this day, and lost battles for pucks consistently. One memorable play was in his own zone, he had the puck and was fumbling it around his skates and an opponent came to hit him, but Houck saw him at the last moment and dropped his shoulders and laid him out instead. Shots definitely still need to improve. Rarely ever on target.

VAN#29 RD, Zalitach, Reid(2014) Did not receive a ton of ice time today, but looked confident and poised whenever he was out there. Took his time with the puck and did not just throw it away at the first given chance. He would hold onto it and assess the situation then make the right passes. Really liked how he slowed down the game if he had to. Looked like a good skater and did not have any trouble handling quick forwards. Made a good play in the second period to close the gap down the middle to prevent an opponent from driving the slot for a scoring chance. Read the play well consistently.

SEA#17 LD, Theodore, Shea(2013) Showed off some nice stickhandling skills today. Made good first passes out of the zone consistently in this game, but also tried to do too much with the puck at times and commit turnovers as a result. Most obvious play was in the first period when he gained the line, and tried to make this cheeky soft pass to a streaking winger down the wing but got easily intercepted and the play went the other way. Definitely more of a passer than a shooter. Was often on the ice for all 2 minutes of their power plays. Really the only puck moving defenseman on the team. Defensively did not look very good at all. Quite soft around the boards and made no attempts to try to tie up anybody along the wall. Lost his man in the slot a few times and resulted in great scoring chances. His play without the puck really worried me on this day.

SEA#19 LW, Sheen, Riley(2013) Created some offensive chances with good anticipation and played with a lot of speed. On one goal, Sheen was the F3 and read the play very well and came to about the top of the circle to pick off a pass going cross ice and created a mini 2 on 1 chance in which he made a nice move to the net but got stopped then his teammate jammed home the rebound. Liked to get the puck on net and get the defense scrambling. Has some quick hands down low. Problem today was consistency. Would look good for 3-4 shifts in a row, then disappear for a while. Not very strong along the boards.

SEA#33 LD, Hauf, Jared(2013) A big defenseman who had his moments this game. Looked quite good in his own end, but not so good whenever he had to handle the puck. Had a good fight in the first sticking up for a teammate who received a big hit. Has a tendency to panic with pressure and throws the puck away and just takes an icing call if he needs. Does not have the skating abilities to buy himself some time and give teammates a chance to get open. Tried to rush the puck up a couple times and had mixed results. Looked confident with it, then when he had to pass it did not make good passes at all. Defensively, held his position well and used his reach as much as he could.

Scouts Notes: This was a game that featured a lot of sloppy play in general by both teams. Seattle dressed 5 defenseman whose height ranged from 6'2 to 6'7, and were all born in 1995 or after. Many of them looked bad. The only good defen-

seman out of that group is Shea Theodore who played a ton of minutes. Almost never came off during power plays and usually played all 2 minutes of them. Handled the puck well. Don't like the way he plays defense. Very passive style and does not like taking the body at all. Has a pair of really nice hands though. Defensemen Jerret Smith, Kevin Wolf and Taylor Green have a ton of work to do, especially with their skating and use of sticks. Got beat time and time again by third and fourth line forwards wide and could not poke pucks away from them. Got dangled easily. I thought Reid Zalitach played well when he had the chance. Looked very confident and made reads quickly with and without the puck.

FINAL SCORE: 6-4 Seattle

Oct 12, 2012, Prince Albert Raiders vs. Portland Winterhawks (WHL)

PA#10 LD, Morrissey, Josh(2013) Had a quiet, effective game. Was not very noticeable all game long. Made good decisions with the puck and started the attack for Prince Albert quickly. Did not try to move with the puck very much. Kept it very simple. Made one very nice back door pass off the half wall. Looks stronger than last season. Did a good job along the boards to tie up opponents and protect the puck. Made a couple of mistakes in terms of positioning in his own end. On a 2 on 2, Morrissey tried to double team the opponent with the puck for some reason, who then saw an opening and made a quick pass to his teammate and drove the open lane to the net from out wide.

PA#29 LW, Draisaitl, Leon(2014) A rookie import who seems to be thriving with Prince Albert. Playing on their first line and looked very good on this night. Very skilled playmaker who uses his size well and shows off some nice hands. Forces his opponents to respect his skating abilities and passing skills on the rush and backs them off quite a bit. Really liked his creativity all game long. Draisaitl created a number of chances with the puck on his stick. Quite strong along the boards, but could improve this aspect of his game, especially staying on his skates. Looked okay in his own end, but did seem to be out of position a number of times.

POR#3 RD, Jones, Seth(2013) Big defenseman who was clearly a level above everybody else in all aspects of the game tonight. Such a great combination of size, offensive, defensive and skating abilities. Possesses a very lethal wrist shot. Scored from the point by using it in the first period. Very smart with the puck and is able to buy everybody sometime because he is so poised and uses his body very well to fend off forecheckers and find an opening to get the attack going. Very good skater despite his size, looks almost effortless. Nobody could knock him off the puck or put him in a panic mode. Has very good stickhandling abilities. On a 3 on 2, he was able to toe drag and get himself some time and released a heavy wrist shot which nearly went in. Hard to play against because he has such a good reach and keeps everything to the outside. Has a tendency to get a little aggressive and get himself out of positioning, but it is something that is easily coachable.

POR#19 LC, Petan, Nicolas(2013) Another small, highly skilled forward for the Winterhawks. Played with a lot of confidence offensively and created scoring chances consistently. Definitely had the right ideas, just could not execute them perfectly. In the first period, he threaded a pass between 2 opponents to give his teammate a chance for a breakaway, but the pass was just a little too hard. Made a very nice cross ice, backhand saucer pass to set up his teammate for a one timer goal. Uses his skating to his advantage very well. Went for a good skate with the puck a few times and made opponents look silly with his elusiveness. Defensively works very hard. Received quite a few shifts on the PK. Made one excellent play to backcheck hard and deflect away a cross ice pass off the rush that would have resulted in an easy goal. Definitely needs to get stronger on his skates.

POR#27 RW, Bjorkstrand, Oliver(2013) Creative power forward had a good game tonight. Looked to be more of a playmaker than somebody to pull the trigger to finish off a play. Very confident with the puck and takes his time to make the best play. Memorable play in the 2nd period. He dominated the wall for a good 7-10 seconds using his size and tight turns, then finally made a move to the net from the half wall, and fed his teammate a sweet backdoor pass. No doubt that it was elite. Would like to see more consistency in his game. He had a tendency to disappear a few times.

Scouts Notes: A game that was dominated by Portland from start to finish. Whichever team that gets to draft Seth Jones will have a franchise defenseman to build their team around. Made Josh Morrissey look very ordinary. Really liked Oliver Bjorkstrand's game too. Uses his body very well and made some creative plays with the puck. Chase De Leo also had a good game for Portland. Small, shifty centre like Petan. Made some good things happen with the puck.

FINAL SCORE: 5-2 Portland

October 13, 2012, Baie-Comeau Drakkar @ Rimouski Oceanic (QMJHL)

Baie-Comeau
#3 Alexis Vanier, Def (2014) Played a much more physical game than in my previous viewing, had a real good hit on Rimouski's top player Peter Trainor. Even after whistles, he is always involved in a scrum. He has an imposing frame and used it well in that game. Took some chances offensively, was caught a couple of times and he doesn't have the speed to get back.

#7 Loïk Léveillé, Def (2015) Didn't stand out at all in this game, rarely touched the puck. Was paired with Vanier once again, and I'm not sure that is a pairing that helps those two players. With Vanier taking chances offensively, Léveillé stood behind. Léveillé should be the one taking those chances, since he has the skillset made for this.

#13 Gabriel Paquin-Boudreau, LW (2013) Finished the game with a goal, but otherwise this was not a good effort from Boudreau, who was not involved enough in the play. Boudreau is a smallish player and slightly built, but his skating will need work. Made a great play on his goal, stole the puck from Ryan MacKinnon at the Rimouski blueline to wind up on a breakaway, where he beat Philippe Desrosiers high glove.

#16 Felix Girard, C (1994) One has to love Girard's game even though he was not a factor offensively. He played a real physical game with a big hit to start on Kostalek, and another one later on the backcheck. Love his hustle also, his feet were always moving and outworked the bigger Morin to win a puck battle.

#25 Thomas Gobeil, RW (2013) Not much standing out other than his physical game in this one, as he worked hard and threw some good hits. Got into a scrap after one of his teammates got run over, but it was not much of a fight, more of a wrestling match.

#73 Valentin Zykov, RW (2013) The Russian forward had a solid game once again, though his skating is still a question mark to me as his feet look heavy. Showed he has some real quick hands on his goal, jumping on a bad rebound from the Rimouski goaltender. What I love the most about Zykov's game overall and especially tonight: he's always close to the net. On multiple occasions he had a scoring chance simply by following the puck to the net or standing near the goaltender, looking for a rebound or a tip-in. Another thing I like: he might get stopped, but he works to find his rebound in the corner and bring back the puck to the net. If he has to, he will run over the goalie in the process as well. Got hit hard entering the Rimouski zone by big Samuel Morin, but that didn't look to bother him too much as he got up and continued his shift like nothing happened.

#90 Bokondji Imama, LW (2014) Imama didn't get a ton of ice time but made sure to make an impact on all of his shifts. Started the game with 3 big hits in the opening period. Showed good puck protection, using his size to hold on of the puck. In the 2nd period he got hit hard by Étienne Boutet which led to a fight between Boutet and Thomas Gobeil. Later in the game, he came close to scoring his first QMJHL goal but was robbed by Rimouski goaltender Philippe Desrosiers. Was all alone in the slot and took a one-timer, but Desrosiers made a great pad save.

Rimouski
#3 Jan Kostalek, Def (2013) Kostalek played a quiet, effective game in his own end, did a good job with his stick in his own end with breaking passes and blocking the passing lane. Saw him block shots with his partner Samuel Morin on the PK. Played on Rimouski's 2nd power play unit, made some good crisp passes, but didn't generate anything offensively. Got hit hard earlier in the first by Felix Girard but that didn't bother him too much.

#11 Vladimir Bryukvin, RW (2013) He will need to work on his skating ability and mostly on his first-step quickness. In the first period, made some interesting rushes but always stayed on the outside, too much of a perimeter game right now for the rookie Russian forward. Made a nice deke on an opponent in the 2nd period but then made a no-look pass to nobody. Weird play.

#15 Anthony Deluca, LW (2013) It was not a good game from Deluca, who is still trying to figured out the QMJHL. Skating is Deluca's biggest weakness right now; his first three steps need a lot of work and he need to keep his feet moving. Deluca has a shot first mentality but right now he's taking too much time getting his shot though, and not doing much offensively. When he has the puck, he dangles with it too much, or tries some moves that would have worked... in Midget AAA last year. Tries to play a physical game, but was overpowered by bigger players.

#20 Nicolas Hebert, C (2014) Hebert centered the Oceanic's 4th line and was strong in the faceoff circle in this game, which is impressive for a 16 year old not even 10 games into his QMJHL career. Hebert had some good scoring chances in this game and was rewarded with some power play time at the end of the game. He has a great work ethic and is already playing a sound two-way game, but will need to keep working on his first three step quickness.

#23 Frederik Gauthier, C (2013) Not a good game from Gauthier, who was not good at all in the faceoff circle. Didn't do much in the offensive zone and didn't see him get a solid scoring chance all night. However, he was very strong in his own end, as he was very smart in how he used his long stick to block passing lane or passes. Always the first forward to get back in the defensive zone to help out his defensemen out. Also has a long reach which he uses well in defensive situations.

#55 Samuel Morin, Def (2013) Paired with fellow draft-eligible Jan Kostalek in this game, had trouble with his passing game and also had a tough time getting puck out of his zone. Moves well for a big guy, has good agility on his skates. Played with a mean streak, likes to clear the front of his net, whether it's using his size or just slashing opposing players. I like how he uses his long stick to break plays and passes. Had a big hit in the third period on Valentin Zykov, those two were battling all night with solid contact from both sides.

#64 Maxime Gravel, Def (2013) Love Gravel's game tonight, used on the first power play unit for the Oceanic. Love his feet, good skater and very agile. Feet are always moving, very active in his own end. Loves to pinch in the offensive zone, his shots from the point will need more accuracy as they rarely hit the net tonight. Was moving the puck well on the PP, good puck distributor.

October 13, 2012, Niagara Ice Dogs @ Sarnia Sting (OHL)

NIA #21 LC Verhaeghe, Carter (2013) - Skating has shown some improvements but acceleration looked like he was in quick sand. He goes to the net and consistently works hard in the offensive zone. Shows good willingness to get back defensively and compete.

NIA #26 RW Lemmon, Mack (2013) - Mack was a pretty physical presence in this game. He passed up on a few opportunities but he connected on a fair number. He appeared to be getting under the skin of some Sarnia players and was pretty active both physically and with his mouth after the whistle.

SAR #15 LW Brown, Davis (2013) - Davis Brown put on his best performance on the season in our viewings. Used his speed to track down opponents and to get to the corners and win battles on a consistent basis throughout the game.

SAR #71 RW Goldobin, Nikolay (2014) - Showed off his outstanding hands, but needs to shoot the puck a little more. He's an excellent passer but will force it sometimes.

SAR #77 RD DeAngelo, Anthony (2014) - Controlled the puck extremely well and rushed it effectively. He was very consistent skating it out of trouble and avoiding some of the mistakes he has made previously. Scored coming in off the point and sneaking into position by the side of the net.

Scouts Notes: One of the best games of the year. A very back and forth battle between the two teams the lead changed four separate times from a tie to a one goal lead. Never did either team have more than a one goal lead. Daniel Nikandrov (2012) worked very hard out front of the Niagara net and ended up scoring the first goal of the game. It all ended when overage right winger Craig Hottot (Free Agent) scored the overtime winner on a solid cross ice pass by Charles Sarault (Free Agent).

October 13, 2012, Halifax Mooseheads vs. Drummondville Voltigeurs (QMJHL)

HAL #19 RW Falkenham, Ryan (2013) – I kept an eye on this draft eligible and he didn't show much. He skated on the third line and displayed good energy and decent skating but he wasn't much of a factor. We barely saw him with the puck and he didn't standout physically along the boards even though he was involved there. He looks to be destined as an energy player, even at the junior level.

HAL #22 C Mackinnon, Nathan (2013) – I thought he had a poor game given his abilities and what we are used to seeing from him. He started the game slowly and we didn't see much from him in the first period. His line was skipped a few times and he didn't get to manage the puck and use his speed the way he usually likes to do. On two occasions he showed good hockey sense entering the offensive zone and setting up plays for his teammate. I also thought his work ethic was not up there at the highest level. On a couple occasions early in the game he used his great burst to back check and help his teammates and on other occasions he just floated waiting for the puck to come to him. He kept being discreet for the rest of the game although he picked up an assist and a late goal. He had only two good flashes with the puck in the second period where he used his speed in the neutral zone but he wasn't able to do anything against the defender who played the situation perfectly. He got to showcase his hands once where he dangled beautifully through the defender, but again, it didn't lead to any scoring chances. All that being said, I got to see glimpses of his abilities that we are all aware of, but I was expecting him to have better work ethic and to be able to use his speed on a constant basis throughout the game.

HAL #31 G Fucale, Zachary (2013) – Fucale had a slow start to the game and I thought he looked sluggish in front of his net where he gave up two goals in the first period. He quickly went back to his usual form in the second period and was razor sharp. His calm and technique showed on numerous occasions where Drummondville was buzzing around his net but he never broke down. He excels following the puck from close range and made some spectacular save by extending his legs. His rebound control was excellent and he was aware of where the puck was at all time.

HAL #91 RW Frk, Martin (Detroit) – Frk played a solid game in the offensive zone. He was a constant threat around the net and he was working hard down low to get the puck out of corners. We didn't see him skate with the puck much, but he followed the play extremely well to give his teammates options.

DRU #9 LW Archambault, Olivier (Montreal) – Archambault played an excellent game picking up two assists. He was able to generate speed in the neutral zone and he skated with the puck a lot, which I like to see. His great hands can be a great asset for him and he proved it tonight. He can be extremely hard to defend when he uses his speed and skill to move forward. I still think he needs to do more of that and simplify his game to be much more effective. On a few occasions again, he skated with the puck doing big circles in the offensive zone and passing the puck to him using the board, ultimately leading to nothing.

Scouts Notes: Drummondville did a good job limiting Halifax's scoring chances, but goalie Domenic Graham (2013 eligible) didn't follow in the footstep of his team. He allowed three goals in the first period before giving up the net to his backup. Nikolas Brouillard (2013 eligible) didn't do much for Drummondville either. He had a few flashes with the puck from his D zone but nothing more worth mentioning. Same thing goes for Guillaume Gauthier (2013 eligible) that we didn't see a lot of. His work ethic is a concern for me. Dexter Weber (2013 eligible) played an OK game but made a direct turnover in his zone that resulted in a goal. Other than that, a quick note on Luca Ciampini (2012 eligible) who played a good game. His skating got a lot better (still not a great skater) and he worked hard around the net to knock in rebounds.

October 13, 2012, Halifax Mooseheads vs. Shawinigan (QMJHL)

HAL #22 C Mackinnon, Nathan (2013) – Mackinnon played a much better game in my opinion than the previous night in Drummondville. He started the game slow with an ugly play in the defensive zone trying to dangle his way out of trouble but he picked up the pace fast after that. He did the entire job on the first goal starting by winning his puck battle behind the net. He then faked to receive a pass behind the net to let it roll to a teammate and positioned himself in front of the net to cash in the pass from that teammate. Very well done. I also liked his decision making in that game: it was quick and it was good. On one occasion on the powerplay he went with a superb cross-ice pass that surprised everyone. He still didn't display his top notch speed although he was obviously fast, but instead he did a good job using his teammates on the rush instead of trying to do it all by himself. One main quality he also showed in the offensive zone is his ability to attract defenseman. He excels at moving the puck and changing directions to move the defender and create space both for him and his teammates. His work ethic was also a notch higher than the previous night. He worked harder along the boards and in the defensive zone. I also liked how he responded at shots taken at him. He had a hard coverage on him all night long and he didn't let his opponents cross the line.

HAL #79 Andrews, Brent (Nashville) - Andrews played extremely well the last two games (last night and tonight). He plays an excellent 2-way game with smart plays and good hockey tools to go along the way. He moves plenty well around the ice for a big guy and he displayed surprising skills with the puck on 1 on 1 situation. He plays a very simple game but is effective at bringing the puck into the offensive zone and he likes to control the play. His decision making was quick and efficient. His best work came behind the net where he applied pressure and was able to win puck battles. Not overly physical for his size, I didn't see him hit much. He also plays extremely well defensively except for one mistake where he mishandled the puck in his own zone, leading to a Shawinigan goal.

SHA #80 D Maheux, Raphael (2014) – Maheux is a huge defenseman that excels in close range confrontation with his opponents, whether it's deep in his zone or in front of the net. He is very strong on skates and places his body smartly to block his opponents. His skating needs a lot of work, both backwards and forwards. This will allow him to handle one on one situation a lot better. He also displayed surprising puck skills for a young big guy. He is able to move the puck a little and he is a good puck distributor. He also seems to have a strong shot that he can use on the powerplay.

SHA #95 LW Campagna, J.C (1993 born) – He caught my eye with his speed and hands in the neutral zone. He was very elusive but just like the Shawinigan offense, he wasn't able to go past the blue line much. He didn't work really hard but his speed and hands allowed him to standout on a few occasions. I would have like to see him use his speed more and display his offensive talent on a larger scale.

Scouts Notes: This was a particularly boring game between those two teams. Shawinigan did their best defending but Halifax was just buzzing in the offensive zone the whole game. They were not able to generate much offense either. Mackinnon stood out in this game with his superior talent, although he has seen better days. Brent Andrews also played an excellent game. Luca Ciampini and Matthew Boudreau displayed good chemistry cycling the puck in the offensive zone. They were a threat all night. Other than that, it was a very quiet night for everyone on the ice.

OCT 13, 2013, Swift Current Broncos vs. Portland Winterhawks (WHL)

SWF # 2, D, Heatherington, Dylan (2013) Heatherington has some pretty nice size, skating and agility. He displayed some great physicality and aggression in his own end and was clearing the front of his net well. He used his stick really well to knock the puck off the opposition and force them to the outside, as he has such a nice long reach. He showed some great patience, using his stick well on a 1-on-1 battle to keep the opposition from the net, and was reading the play well to pick off a turnover in the neutral zone. He was willing to jump in on the rush to drive the puck down low into the offensive zone, but needs to watch the turnovers both along the boards in his own end, and through the neutral zone as well.

SWF # 10, C, Cave, Colby (2013) Cave was finding some space in the high slot off the rush, and put some really nice pressure on the puck carrier as well. He provided some good support in his own end, and was able to get a cycle going in the offensive zone. He was however taking some long outside shots on an odd-man rush rather than moving the puck or driving it down low, and needs to add some size and strength so that he's not knocked off the puck so easily.

SWF # 25, C, Mackay, Zac (2013) Mackay put some pretty nice pressure on the puck carrier, and was playing physical in his own end, although he needs to add some size and strength. He got in a lane showing a willingness to block shots, and got to the net to get some loose pucks and put some good shots on net from in tight. He has to watch the turnovers in the offensive zone trying to force the puck through the opposition.

SWF # 29, LW, Lesaan, Tanner (2013) Lesaan really likes to get the puck in deep on the dump and chase to start the cycle, and would be better to add some more creativity to his game. He made some pretty good chip plays to start the rush up the ice, and did a good job trying to drive the puck to the net. He put some good pressure on the fore-check, and was cycling the puck well deep in the offensive zone. He was also battling hard for loose pucks in front of the net, but needs to get the puck out of the zone along the boards in his own end.

PRT # 3, D, Jones, Seth (2013) Jones is able to take a hit, hold on to the puck and get it in deep into the offensive zone. He was walking down into the high slot to put some good shots on net, and was willing to jump up and join the rush, but has to hit the net on his shots off the rush. He is calm with the puck and can make some good breakout passes, and did a good job protecting the puck from the opposition. He was unable to hold the puck in the offensive zone at times, and also has to get the puck out on penalty kill clears. He also got caught in deep, leaving the opposition with a 2-on-1 opportunity.

PRT # 12, C, Kopeck, Preston (2013) Kopeck made some pretty good breakout passes to start the rush, and was able to get open in the slot to put a good one-timer on net. He was willing to get to the front of the net and battle for his territory, and had a nice wide drive protecting the puck well to hold on to it under pressure. He was putting some of his own pressure and physicality on the fore-check, and made a nice pass on an odd-man rush to move the puck across for a good chance.

PRT # 19, C, Petan, Nicolas (2013) Petan has some excellent speed, hands and moves to split the defense and make a fantastic pass down low for a tap in goal for his teammate. He has some great offensive instincts, and drove hard to the net with his stick down to knock in the puck for the team's 3rd goal of the game. He has some fantastic hands and puck skills that he can work under pressure, and was battling hard for the puck to win it on the fore-check. He made a nice centering pass to create a good scoring chance, then later showed some amazing vision to find a lane and move the puck across to a teammate off the rush for a one-timer for the team's 5th goal of the game. He needs to watch some of the neutral zone turnovers trying to dangle his way through the opposition, and also let his man get away from him a bit on the inside track on the penalty kill for the 1st goal for the opposition. He also needs to add some size and strength so that he's not knocked off the puck so easily.

PRT # 27, RW, Bjorkstrand, Oliver (2013) Bjorkstrand displayed some good strength and puck protection off the rush, and was distributing the puck pretty well. He made a really good centering pass for a nice chance, and had a good net-front presence as well tipping pucks. He was able to get to the slot with the puck to put some good shots on net, and also put a shot on net from a bad angle to score the team's 1st goal of the game. He made some nice breakout passes to start the rush, and put some really good pressure on the puck carrier to force turnovers. He has some nice hands to get to the net with the puck, and showed some really good moves and creativity.

FINAL SCORE: 6-3 Portland Winterhawks

October 14, 2012, Sault Ste. Marie Greyhounds @ Sarnia Sting (OHL)

SSM #3 RD Ganly, Tyler (2013) - Ganly made some puck mistakes, but showed good physicality along the boards and won battles pretty consistently. Looks improved from where he was at earlier in the season.

SSM #22 LD Spinozzi, Kevin (2014) - Played very physical right off the drop of the puck. He was getting into it with anyone and everyone including the toughest players on the Sarnia team. He loves to hit and does so very hard every chance he got. However he got a game misconduct for a cheap head shot to the head of 5'8" Davis Brown in open ice. Brown did not have the puck. Spinozzi then beat up fellow 16 year old Alexandre Renaud who stood up for his teammate. Expect Spinozzi to get a suspension out of this one.

SSM #25 LD Nurse, Darnell (2013) - Nurse put together a few great rushes up ice, but didn't force anything and took the smart option. He matched up well one on one when the situation came up throughout the entire game and was tough to beat.

SSM #28 RW Tolchinsky, Sergey (2013) - Once again he showed off his outstanding speed and elusiveness. But as his last game he was rather quiet. He showed flashes of his great talent but really didn't do too much again today to convince us he's going to overcome his size at the NHL level.

SSM #29 G Nichols, Justin (2013) - Nichols played outstanding in his OHL Debut. He showed great quickness, reflexes and remained square to the shooter. He faced a ton of action in this game and handled it all very well for it being his first game. Nichols single handedly kept the Greyhounds in this game.

SAR #17 LW Renaud, Alexandre (2014) - Played very physical in today's game which was particularly noticeable early on. Renaud stood up for a teammate who was taken out in open ice, but paid for it in the fight.

SAR #71 RW Goldobin, Nikolay (2014) - Added a little physicality to his game for the first time tonight. He showed off great hands, getting robbed early, but came back the next shift beat the defenseman, then scored a highlight reel goal. Goldobin keeps getting better every single game.

SAR #77 RD DeAngelo, Anthony (2014) - DeAngelo played fairly well today, but put a really risky and unnecessary pass up the middle which directly resulted in a goal for the Greyhounds.

Scouts Notes: A very underwhelming performance by the Sault Ste. Marie Greyhounds at the end of a 3 game in 3.5 day road trip. They struggled right out of the gate and really never recovered. Justin Nichols (2013) really kept the Greyhounds in this game for a little while with his excellent play. Nikolay Goldobin (2014) is really showing his level of improvement with a highlight reel goal. We expect Kevin Spinozzi (2014) to receive an suspension after this game. He lined up Davis Brown (2013) from a mile away. He hit him hard except there were a few issues with the hit. Brown didn't have possession of the puck, as he missed the pass and the hit was to the head of Davis Brown. He remained on the ice for a few moments and left the game without returning. Alexandre Renaud (2014) showed a little bit of his toughness standing up for his teammate, however Spinozzi got a rather decisive win in the fight.

Oct 16, 2012, USNTDP U18 vs Muskegon Lumberjacks (USHL)

USNT #4 D, Butcher, Will (2013) A nice puck rushing defenseman who can also move the puck very effectively. He skates well and some good hands and great vision to see the ice well. He can make his decisions quickly and moves the puck very effectively and quickly and is very willing to join the rush to give more options to his teammates. He can hold the line well and get his shot through and on the net, and has a good shot with a quick release that can be kept low and on the net. He needs to get a bit stronger on his feet so that he is not knocked off the puck too easily.

USNT #22 Rw, Fashing, Hudson (2013) A winger with some great size and plays well along the boards. He battles hard for the puck and is aggressive jumping on pucks quickly. He has some great hands and some excellent moves that could make you dizzy. He brings a nice net front presence and opens up well in the slot for a shot. He moves the puck quickly and protects the puck well and can really play an effective cycle game. He needs to get a little quicker and to keep his head up as he was knocked off the puck by the opposition a few times with his head down. He has some nice offensive instincts and can find space to work with in the offensive zone and makes sure to get the puck on the net, and holds his own territory very well.

USNT #24 RW, McCarron, Mike (2013) Another player with very good size and brings some nice physicality on the fore-check. He opens up well for a shot and shoots the puck well. He drives to the net well and gives his teammates some good options in the offensive zone and will shoot the puck often and from anywhere. He has a nice battle for the puck and drives directly to the net, and can also take a hit well while holding on to the puck. He battles hard in front of the net but needs to get a bit stronger on his puck movement and get the puck out of the zone when he has the opportunity.

USNT #14 C, Motte, Tyler (2013) He did well in the faceoffs in this game and has some great vision, passing and moves the puck well. He protects the puck very well and can drive in to the net from the outside effectively demonstrating some good upper body strength. He has a lot of good moves but sometimes tries to do too much when he has some simpler options available. He also has the tendency to come down too low towards the net and it doesn't give any options to his teammates but to throw the puck on net. He needs to stay a little higher in the slot and find some open space to open up for a pass. He has some good sense with the puck and gets it to dangerous areas but needs to watch his turnovers especially in the neutral zone. Started throwing the puck on net much more often as the game wore on and his team was down.

USNT# 9 LW, Lewis, Anthony (2013) A player who brings great speed to the game. He protects the puck and moves it so well and quickly and demonstrated a great ability to be able to think quickly. He has some good vision and passing and a very high compete level. He is nice and strong on his feet, especially for a smaller forward and is very aggressive and not at all intimidated. He is very nice and agile and has some great shiftiness and unpredictability to his game.

USNT# 19 RW, Kelleher, Tyler (2013) Scored two goals in this game and the first was just an absolute beauty. He demonstrated great vision, some nice moves, good speed and a nice quick release on this play leaving the entire opposition in his dust. He did a good job when he took some face-offs in this game and has such a nice speed to his game. He passes the puck very well and can read the play and anticipate what will happen to cut off passes. He likes to keep the puck moving, has some great agility and consistently finds space to work with. He can really see the ice well, keeps his feet moving and goes hard to the net. At times he tries to force plays when simpler options are available and needs to learn to read those opportunities better.

MUS# 17 LW, Tiffels, Frederik (2013) A player who can move the puck very effectively. He has some exceptional vision and passing and also brings some good speed with him as well. He has a nice all-round compete to his game and likes to throw the puck on net to keep the goaltender on his toes. He can protect the puck well and is agile as well and can get in lanes to break up plays. The vision, passing and puck movement are what most stand out about this player.

FINAL SCORE: 4-2 Muskegon Lumberjacks

October 17, 2012, Indiana Ice @ Green Bay Gamblers (USHL)

IND #4 D Smith, Alex (2013) - Joined rush on 3 on 1 and wired 1-0 goal past the Green Bay Goaltender. Adequate puck movement on the power play but didn't show a powerful shot from the point but got it on net.

GB #5 D Oloffson, Gustav (2013) - He likes to go deep in the offensive zone regularly, but doesn't possess the skating to recover effectively and resulted in odd man rushes. Skating is about average overall. Moves the puck adequately on the power play but wasn't tested by penalty killers. Seems to understand when to get the puck deep and when he can fire it on the net when the puck comes back to the point. Pretty good passer out of his own zone to move the puck up ice.
GB #9 F Schmaltz, Nick (2014) - Shows impressive individual puck skills. He likes to take on defensemen one on one and tends to win those battles more often than not. He prefers to take the puck inside towards the centre of the slot where he shows off his strong wrist shot. Schmaltz was able to draw multiple penalties in this game with his puck handling ability in scoring areas.

GB #16 F Weis, Mathew (2013) - Set up well on a two on one break making himself available for a pass and effectively scored what was the tying goal at the time. He moves the puck very well on the power play getting second unit minutes in this regard. He also handles the puck well cycling the offensive zone and found a lane and fired it at the net. It went off his teammates face in into the net giving Weis an assist. He showed good work ethic even when his team was down three goals forechecking hard and causing turnovers on his backcheck. His energy level appeared to just go up as the game went on. Driven awkwardly into the boards late in the game needing to be helped off the ice.

GB #20 D Wolanin, Christian (2013) - Willing to jump up in the rush fairly often. He protects the puck well when skating deep in the offensive zone. However he got caught deep in the zone, couldn't recover and it resulted in Indiana's second goal of the game. To his credit, he appeared a lot more positionally responsible after this occurred. Above average forward skating and mobility for a 6'1" defenseman but isn't a great backwards skater.

GB #22 F Lemieux, Brendan (2013) - Struggles alittle with his skating in open ice. He will shoot from outside areas but has a powerful shot that resulted in a few rebounds. He really picked up his play early in the second forcing turnovers then creating multiple chances a few shifts. Overall he made a pretty good impact for a 16 year old.

GB #23 F Gross, Jordan (2013) - Gross has very good hands and showed them off regularly. He made a beautiful shooting pass setting up a goal to tie the game up in the first period. He shows great mobility on the point and is an overall strong skater. Plays the point on the power play and he makes quick decisions and showed off a hard shot getting it to the net.

GB #88 D Lindhart, Jake (2014) - Lindhart played a safe reliable defensive game. He made the smart simple plays with the puck and left it at that.

Scouts Notes: A back and forth battle occurred early on as defensive lapses and rough starts by both goaltenders saw 6 goals scored in the first period. Indiana was able to separate themselves but the great chemistry shown by Mathew Weis (2013), Jordan Gross and Kevin Irwin (2013) helped keep Green Bay in this game and were clearly the Gamblers best line. Despite this, they were not able to score again after making it a 5-3 score early in the second period resulting in a win for Indiana. Sam Kauppila (2014) was brought up as an associated player but looked very nervous in this match-up but overall it was an important experience for his development.

Oct 17, 2012, Lethbridge Hurricanes vs. Brandon Wheat Kings (WHL)

LET#6 RD, Erkamps, Macoy(2013) Very impressive showing in all areas of the game. Played with an aggressive mindset tonight. Landed a big hit in the offensive zone when an opponent had his head down along the wall and was going to carry the puck up the ice. Made good reads defensively to get in position and take away passing lanes. Took hits to make plays and get out of trouble. Very poised with the puck. Does not have the skills to go coast to coast and score a goal, but makes great decisions with the puck and can make good passes in all situations. One improvement to make is his overall speed. Could be more of a threat if he can skate with the puck better. No problems with angling or backwards skating.

LET#17 RW, Watson, Jamal(2013) Very speedy forward who had a good game offensively. Created a number of chances with his skating ability. Not many players in the league who are as fast as him. On a few occasions, he was behind an opponent by 5 steps or so for a loose puck and would beat them to it quite easily. Despite this rare ability, does not get to the net as much as he should. When he drives to the net he creates very good scoring chances, but did not see that aspect of his game on this day. Liked his work along the boards. Quite strong on his skates. Was a little inconsistent on this day. Had a great first period, then slowly started to disappear in the game.

LET#21 RC, Merkley, Jay(2013) Forward was an offensive force on this day. Made good things happen with his vision, speed and willingness to go to the net. Scored by tipping home a point shot about knee high. Created some good chances by taking the puck to the net too. Made good decisions with the puck and did not force any crazy passes. Also had a bit of an inconsistent game, but took some shifts off throughout the game.

BDN#2 RD, Pulock, Ryan(2013) Had some flashes of brilliance, but did not make any huge contributions to the game for his team. Was quietly good. Definitely has good offensive instincts. Made a few good plays in the offensive zone to step up and have chances to score from the slot. Showed off his booming slap shot once again. Made a number of good pinches in the neutral zone to take away pucks and get the attack going the other way. Was tough to play against in his own end. Very strong along the walls and was smart without the puck. Did not see him get caught out of position.

BDN#6 LD, Nikkel, Ayrton(2013) Played his usual good defensive game. Kept it simple and did not take any big chances offensively. Connected on some solid hits to separate opponents from the puck. Hard to play against all night long. Really like the poise he plays with in all areas of the ice. Skating was a bit of an issue. Overall speed could get better.

BDN#7 LD, Roy, Eric(2013) Was the best player for Brandon today, hands down. So composed with the puck, and showed off the ability to be able to weave through traffic and skate it out of trouble. Went coast to coast on one play and had a very good chance. Not overly fast, but changed directions in a hurry and caught opponents flat footed. More of the power-play QB than Ryan Pulock. Roy is depended on to make the right passes, Pulock is depended on for his heavy shot. Defensively, was solid. Made good reads to take away passes. Had a tendency to get caught a little wide though. Speed was not a problem off the rush.

Scouts Notes: Lethbridge was able to score some key goals through out the game and did not give Brandon any chances to come back in the game. Curtis Honey of Brandon let his team down and gave up some questionable goals. A very impressive game by Macoy Erkamps. Can't say enough about his overall game. Jay Merkley has made some big strides in his offensive game. Looks much more confident with the puck. Russell Maxwell was passed over during last year's draft, but he is making a lot of noise in Lethbridge and I could see him being a late round pick. Issue with him is size, listed at only 5'8, but does everything for the Hurricanes.

FINAL SCORE: 6-1 Lethbridge

October 18, 2012, Mississauga Steelheads @ Sarnia Sting (OHL)

MIS #10 RW Goldberg, Andrew (2013) - Goldberg played a very physical game tonight. He constantly finished his checks. He handles the puck well along the boards. Andrew was used as a regular on the penalty kill and was fairly effective.

MIS #13 LW MacIntyre, Bobby (2014) - MacIntyre was great taking on defensemen one on one using his speed to beat them fairly regularly. At one point he made a great move created the entire play and got an assist out of it. A great skater who is very elusive he just needs to continue to overcome his size as he can be outmatched at times. However he works extremely hard most shifts.

MIS #15 LW Burnside, Josh (2013) - Burnside is a good shatter who won some key puck battles to keep the puck in the offensive zone. He received some time on the penalty kill and worked pretty hard throughout this game.

MIS #28 LD Percy, Stuart (Toronto) - Percy started out this game very strong. He made a great play in his own zone, then took the puck up ice, waited for the screen then wired it top shelf for the opening goal of this game. He was very effective rushing the puck up ice quickly and consistently.

Stuart has a very dangerous point shot because he has a habit of utilizing the screen very well and knowing exactly when to shoot when the goaltender is screened. He was fairly solid in one on one match-up's however he had one where he got beat really bad while his team was on the power play and it directly resulted in a goal against.

MIS #30 G Martin, Spencer (2013) - Spencer is consistently in the proper positioning. He isn't very quick but compensates for this with great positioning and limited rebounds. When he does give one up he isn't particularly quick on the recovery. This recovery speed, or lack there of is really the only weakness in his game. He has a slightly above average glove hand as well.

SAR #2 RD Chapman, Joshua (2013) - Joshua's one on one play was pretty hit or miss in this game. He got beat one on one on the eventual winning goal due to a lack of skating ability. His skating has seen some improvements but not where you'd like to see it just yet. He plays consistently physical and battles hard in the corners. Fights the puck sometimes on moderate passing situations.

SAR #21 LC Nikandrov, Daniel (2013) - Nikandrov created some chances in the offensive zone while short handed. He took a bit of a cheap shot and responded with three chances around the net in two shifts. He really elevated his game when his team needed it.

SAR #55 RD Murphy, Connor (Phoenix) - Murphy showed some improvements in this game. He won more battles than usual and completes more passes up ice. However it seems like the most critical moments in the game is where he's made his biggest mistakes. He shows good puck protection and patience with the puck in the offensive zone, but sometimes Connor is almost too patient with the puck losing passing options or having the puck taken from home. Still remains as physical and tenacious as a box full of kittens.

SAR #77 RD DeAngelo, Anthony (2014) - Right off the bat Anthony looked good. His first shift he picked up the puck in the slot and skated it out of trouble up ice. He was effective at both ends displaying his skills in this game. He can put together a pretty wide range from good to bad in terms of performances. This was a pretty solid performance for him both offensively and defensively. He still has more trouble than any player I've seen in recent years in junior hockey in terms of keeping his emotions in check when things not going well. He started to both slam his stick on the ice and screaming profanity that was very clear to understand across the rink and 15 rows up when things weren't going his way.

Scouts Notes: Mississauga jumped out early and always seemed to be a step ahead of the Sting tonight. It turned into a very back and forth match-up after the Steelheads got two early goals in this one. However every time Sarnia got something rolling, they would give up a goal to give the two goal lead back to Mississauga. For Mississauga Sam Babintsev (2013) showed off his skating but was quiet until he used his speed to earn a breakaway opportunity but didn't score. For Sarnia, David Nemecek (2013) battled hard early on in his own zone. However MacIntyre blew by him in a one on one situation. The rebound off of this was banged in for a goal. David was pretty quiet after that. Brett Hargrave (2014) worked very hard in the offensive zone. This resulted in a few scoring chances but he kept trying to do too much with the puck. Nikolai Goldobin (2014) showed great hands and patience waiting for things to open up then completed a hard accurate pass to help set up the Sting's first goal of the night. Jordan Addesi (2014) showed physicality and consistent aggressive play despite receiving fourth line ice.

October 19, 2012, Everett Silvertips @ Prince Albert Raiders (WHL)

EVT #7 RC Mappin, Ty (2014) - Mappin skates well and displayed good positional play. He got a good amount of ice on the power play. He also showed a strong forecheck throughout this game.

EVT #12 LW Leedahl, Dawson (2014) - Dawson showed good passing ability throughout this game. He moved the puck intelligently on the rush setting up a couple scoring chances. He also made a great pass up ice reading the play and sending one of his teammates on a partial break.

EVT #25 LD Muller, Mirco (2013) - Mirco had a bit of a difficult game with some bright spots. He got a little bit of ice time on the power play and displayed intelligence with the puck making good decisions consistently. He was also used regularly on the penalty kill. Mirco lost positioning in the defensive zone a few times, although he got back in time to prevent a goal making a goods tick check. He turned the puck over a little in his own zone which kept the play going for Prince Albert. Muller tried some difficult long distance passes but would get picked on these instead of making the safe play advancing the puck.

PA #10 Morrissey, Josh (2013) - Morrissey likes to rush the up ice and shows quick hands while carrying the puck. He protects the puck effectively and doesn't force plays that aren't there. He will sneak off the point on the power play and play deep in the zone but will reset quickly. He did this intelligently resulting in a few great scoring chances. He constantly makes good decisions with the puck and kept the play going on the power play. Unlike a lot of offensive defensemen, Josh doesn't try to force offensive plays by holding the line. Instead he gets back into good defensive positioning. He was great in one on one match-up's tonight forcing opposing forwards to the outside then checking them into the boards ending their rush. He was effective around the corners adding some toughness to his game and battling hard. He made the odd mistake but generally recovered quickly when he did.

PA #22 LW Braid, Chance (2013) - Braid has good size and protects the puck well driving the net creating scoring chances with it. He will finish every hit available to him. Chance engaged in a fight with St. Louis Blues prospect, and tough customer in Nick Walters and absolutely worked him over.

PA #29 LC Draisaitl, Leon (2014) - Draisaitl showed off his offensive skills early and often in this match-up. At the end of a powerplay he slid in around the slot to bury a rebound and score the first goal of the game. He has a powerful shot and can sneak into areas to utilize it. He also showed slick hands in tight deep in the offensive zone.

Scouts Notes: This was an exciting back and forth game. Leon Draisaitl (2014) opened up the scoring early and Prince Albert looked good to open this game. The momentum shifted to Everett and they would go on to score three straight goals. Almost immediately following the third goal, Chance Braid (2013) dropped the gloves for Prince Albert and shifted the momentum after laying a beating on a tough opponent in Nick Walters (St. Louis). Prince Albert would go on to score their second goal but couldn't get the tying marker was Everett slipped one past the Raiders 3-2. Ben Betker (2013) displayed some very good compete in front of his own net clearing the slot area. For Prince Albert Mackenzie Stewart (2013) showed some very solid physical play.

October 19, 2012, Québec Remparts vs. Victoriaville Tigres (QMJHL)

QUE #19 C Etchegary, Kurt (2013) – Etchegary impressed me again with his work ethic and positioning on the ice. He is always in the mix fighting for the puck or cutting passing lines. But this game was the perfect example of the glaring weaknesses he has with the puck, particularly his hands and skating. He lost the puck on a number of times trying to make his way through the neutral zone. He has a very hard time handling the puck while maintaining his speed. With the lack of centers for Quebec, Etchegary was put on the second line where he was forced to play an offensive role that doesn't suit him well at all.

QUE #25 C Grigorenko, Mikhail (Buffalo Sabres Prospect) – I didn't notice Grigorenko until after the first period, but at that point, he played an excellent game in the offensive zone. He showed off his great hands and ability to manage the puck around the offensive zone. His coordination while navigating through heavy traffic was impressive to say the least and it seems that no one could take the puck away from him. Grigorenko also displayed is rocket shot in the third period, though it hit the post. His shot is an asset he doesn't take advantage of in my opinion. He has this tendency to find someone to pass to although he has a clear shooting lane. Other than that it was a very quiet night for him in the neutral zone where he wasn't able to generate speed. His line also struggled defensively. Grigorenko also didn't take all the face-offs against Tigres' captain and first line centre Phillip Danault.

QUE #27 C Shea, Brandon (2013) – Very poor showing by Brandon Shea to the point where there is not much to mention. His work ethic was clearly poor and it showed just in the way he skated. He wasn't dynamic at all and I got to see very little of him with the puck.

QUE #73 RW Erne, Adam (2013) – Erne started the game slowly with the puck and couldn't generate anything with it. The same story applied for the rest of the game, where Victoriaville's defenseman was a stud that night, handling Erne like a charm on almost every single occasion. What I liked about this situation was Erne's reaction. He didn't panic and instead of trying to force plays, he managed to protect the puck very well and hand it over to someone else or simply dump. The way he handled it was very smart and helpful for his team. He also worked very hard behind the net in the offensive zone, getting puck out of corners and even drawing a penalty at one point. He made some great passing plays from that position at well, distributing pucks extremely quickly to teammates in front of the net. On Grigorenko's goal in the second period, Erne took the puck away from a defender in the offensive zone and just exploded with great speed to get a shot on the goalie (Grigorenko took the rebound).

QUE #94 W Sorensen, Nick (2013) – Sorensen had a few flashes with the puck early in the game, displaying his quick and smooth skating. He did a good job entering the offensive zone and using his hands to escape from defenders. I also liked his work ethic, in the sense that while his strength is far from being an asset, he doesn't shy away from physical play and working along the boards. This is something he has shown in all my viewings of him this season. Sorensen had a game of sequences, meaning he was not very constant.

VIC #3 D Diaby, Jonathan (2013) – His weaknesses regarding agility showed a little bit more in this game, especially when going backwards. He is fine most of the time because he is strong on his skates, but he also lost balance going backwards a couple times. You can see he relies again on his long reach to be effective and if he can't stop his opponents with his stick, it gets harder. While he is one of the most reliable D-man in Victoriaville, I still see him as a work in progress who needs to show more consistency in his defensive play.

VIC#5 D Vance, Troy (Dallas) – Vance did a good job moving the puck early in the game and showed why he was considered a very good skater despite his size. His hands are also a valuable asset to him when it's time to move the puck. He had his head up the whole time and made the right decisions. I believe he needs to do this more often and he is at his best when he does that. He also needs to move his feet more when he defends, because he took two bad hooking penalties in this game, on in the offensive zone and the other in the defensive zone.

VIC #57 LW Veilleux, Tommy (2013) – I thought his mobility was a little bit better than the previous games I saw from him. He showed he was also more comfortable with the puck and he was able to hold on to it for a longer period of time, which is a positive thing in his case. I liked his physicality once again but on two occasions he went for the huge hit in the neutral zone and he missed, causing him to be late on the play afterwards. His play is getting better, but I still don't see him getting drafted.

October 19, 2012, Sarnia Sting at Guelph Storm (OHL)

GUE #11 LW Jason Dickinson (2013) – Dickinson still has a lot of filling out to do but his size and skill combination is intriguing. Biggest asset is his reach. Protected the puck well and was difficult to deal with along the boards. Showed confident and assertive stickhandling and a great shot. Was deceptive in outnumbered attack situations, equally capable of using his reach to feather a pass or change his shooting angle to get a shot through. Effort was inconsistent at both ends, particularly defensively. Passive and uninvolved on a number of shifts.

GUE #19 RC Hunter Garlent (2013) – Skilled and gritty, but undersized. His motor never stops. Fearlessly went to the corners and net front with and without the puck and showed intense determination to fight through checks. Flashed great hands along the boards and in tight around the net. Easy player to like as he plays an honest, hardworking game but could stand to add mass and more evasiveness.

GUE #9 LC Robby Fabri (2014) – Skilled player but still has a lot of developing to do. Good hands with a quick-release wrister and he was willing to take the puck to the middle, but is lacking size and as a result was pushed off the puck too easily. Needs to build strength before he can be a real factor at this level.

SAR #7 RD Anthony DeAngelo (2014) – One of a growing number of high-risk OHL defensemen with elite offensive talent. Think Ryan Ellis or Ryan Murphy. Skating is top notch. Quick feet in all zones, particularly when set up on the powerplay. Heavy slapshot. Good wrist shot with a quick release. Flashy, hazardous plays plague his game. Saucer passes to his D partner across the middle over a forechecker's stick while penalty killing won't work as he ranks up. Joined the rush with frequency and showed end-to-end capability as well as the ability to make plays at high speed, but on two occasions he overcommitted himself and was forced to race back to his own zone to try to cover up, leading to overextended shifts and lapses in defensive coverage. Biggest challenge will be to simplify his game without taking away from his gamebreaking ability. Undersized and not aggressive enough. Defensive positioning was good overall, including on the PK, but he was pushed around on numerous occasions and struggled to keep bigger forwards in check.

SAR #71 RW Nikolay Goldobin (2014) Very shifty with fantastic stickhandling and deceptiveness. Had great chemistry with linemate Daniel Nikandrov. Tried to do too much with the puck from time to time and had a hard time dealing with physical play. Didn't show much skill in defense. For skill alone, he's worth keeping a close eye on.

SAR #3 LD David Nemecek (2013) – Big defenseman played a poor game. Lacked poise and was slow with his decision-making. Slow feet. Pucks skills were lacking. Not much here.

Scout's Notes: Sarnia LC Alex Galchenyuk (2012 - MTL) was head-and-shoulders above the competition. Played an outstanding two-way game. Looked as if he was going through the motions much of the time, but dominated when he turned it on.

Oct 19, 2012, Sioux City Musketeers vs. Youngstown Phantoms (USHL)

SCM #3 D, Kapla, Michael (2013) Nice size, and good puck movement showed in this game. He will join in the rush and drive hard all the way to the net, got a great chance in the first period by crashing the net. Kapla is calm with the puck and can pass it out of trouble. He displayed some nice vision as he was finding those passing lanes in the offensive zone and reading the play well to decide when to pinch, coming in to the high slot to provide options.

SCM #14 RW, Lacroix, Cederic (2013) A smaller forward who is versatile and can be used as a forward or defenseman. He has some speed but there were a few times in this game where he would mishandle the puck and lose it and needs to work a bit on that puck control. He was blocking shots and willing to go to the dirty areas and making sure to finish his checks on the fore-check. Lacroix also threw a lot of pucks on net and then drove hard to the net looking for rebounds. He also displayed an ability to move the puck and get it out of his own zone.

SCM #19 C, Guentzel, Jake (2013) This is another smaller forward, but one who was showing some great offensive instincts. He did an excellent job in this game of getting to the slot, finding open space and opening up for passes and then also connecting on the passes to get some great shots off; he scored a real nice opening goal of the game by doing this on the power play. Guentzel was creating space in the offensive zone and moving the puck well to create chances. He had a nice set-up for the third goal of the game by getting the puck to the man in the high slot. He gets to the net looking for the puck, and will drive hard to the net offering an option for a pass. Guentzel also displayed some nice hands, great vision and passing and the ability to think and get the puck to the right areas.

SCM#22 C, McGlynn, Conor (2013) Some nice size and strength and uses his body well to protect the puck. He was able to find space to gain the zone and get a shot off from the wing and used some deception to make some unpredictable passes as well in this game. He was making hits on the fore-check and getting in lanes to block shots, however was on the perimeter for most of the game and simply moving the puck to the middle, and so he needs to cut down the middle towards the net more often to become a more dangerous player. He did this once near the end of the game where he drove hard to the net looking for rebounds and got a good opportunity.

SCM#26 D, Heinrich, Blake (2013) A defenseman who showed himself as a solid weapon in the offensive zone. He was holding the line well, reading the play and making some good decisions as to when to pinch and getting shots through from the point. He will come down to the high slot to provide offensive options to his teammates but then would also work hard to get back and cover his man and keep him to the outside. Heinrich threw around a few big hits in this game as well but needs to watch that he doesn't cross the line when he does so as he took a couple unnecessary penalties with some big hits. He was also able to rush the puck up the ice well and protect the puck and find lanes to skate through and get the puck in nice and deep.

YNG#4 LW, MacSorley, Mac (2013) Watching MacSorley in this game you realize just how strong he is on his feet. He could take a few hits without getting knocked over and really stood his ground. He was aggressive on the puck carrier, willing to go down and block shots and battled hard to clear the front of the net. He had a few bad turnovers along the boards in his own zone trying to get the puck out and needs to ensure he can get the puck out of the zone when he gets it along the wall, and he also needs a bit of work on his passing to make sure that he is passing tape to tape and not behind his teammates as they are skating.

YNG#9 C, Cangelosi, Austin (2013) Cangelosi is a highly skilled forward with some great hands and can really work the puck under pressure. He has some nice speed and displayed some great vision and passing as he was moving the puck well in this game. He was willing to go hard to the net with his stick down and competed hard to win puck battles. He had a few bad turnovers in his own zone up the middle but did recover at least once by clearing the puck in the crease to save a goal against.

YNG#21 D, Mackey, Kyle (2013) Was willing to pinch and join in the rush as a fourth forward a few times in the game and also rushed the puck up the ice often. He was moving the puck well and even driving to the net when he joined the rush. He has some pretty decent size but needs to be stronger on his puck control and can't give up the puck so easily.

YNG#27 RW, Stork, Luke (2013) A physical forward who really likes to throw the body around and finishes his checks on the fore-check. He brought a good net-front presence and was very willing to stand in the dirty areas and look for tips. He was moving the puck well in the offensive zone and crashing the net hard, keeping to a pretty simple game. He needs to keep his head up to avoid the open ice hit when he's rushing the puck up the ice.

FINAL SCORE: 5-1 Sioux City

Oct 20, 2012, Chicago Steel vs Muskegon Lumberjacks (USHL)

MSK#20 D, Brodzinski, Mike(2013) A defenseman who is very calm with the puck and brings that calming presence to the ice for his teammates to feed off of. He gets his shot through to the net for the most part and has some pretty good size and decent skating. He moves the puck pretty well and tries to keep the opposition from high-risk areas. At times he was too aggressive on the puck carrier and this was most evident on a 2 on 1 when he tried to force the puck carrier who passed it over and generated a good opportunity. He needs to relax a little and take the pass away and wait for the play to come to him.

MSK#28 RW, Garland, Conor (2014) A pass first type of player who can move the puck and passes well when he has lanes and options open, however at times tries to force the puck through when the option isn't available and there is a simpler play available. He drives hard to the net and offers teammates options in the offensive zone.

MSK#17 LW, Tiffels, Frederik (2013) A player with some great speed and likes to gain the zone on the outside. He protects the puck well but the most noticeable attribute about this player is his passing. He moves the puck so well and has great vision to see all of his options. He is creative and can read the play very well and will also stop off the wing to distribute the puck. He also likes to come down the wing and get a shot off and then follows up on his shot by going to the net. He has some nice moves, great hands and can move the puck up the ice well. He can make some nice breakout passes and is willing to be physical and get in the way of the opposition.

CHI#25 LW, Dodero, Christopher (2014) Didn't get too much ice time in this game but a player who needs to watch the neutral zone turnovers. He showed his hand too easily and what he was going to do and it was very easy for the opposition to read. He needs to be a bit more deceptive in his game and make some decisions quicker. He plays a pretty simple game.

CHI#8 C, Widmar, Joseph (2013) Some nice speed and good instincts from this player. He drives to the outside very well and then makes a cross ice pass to an open winger so well. He also gains the zone with speed and then can take the defenseman with him to open up a man and generate an opportunity. He has some great vision, some nice passes and has some good hockey sense and offensive instincts. He is also willing to drive hard to the net.

CHI#11 LW, Heil, Christian (1994 Prospect) Some great hands and good speed to his game. He had some excellent moves in this game and has some vision; sees the ice well. He has a quick release on his shot and gets the puck out of his zone well.

FINAL SCORE: 4-0 Muskegan

Oct 20, 2012, Kingston Frontenacs vs Niagara IceDogs (OHL)

KNG#15 LW, Beckstead, Marc (2013) A real high energy up-tempo type of player. He demonstrated some nice hustle and physicality and some good two-way play. He is a decent skater but had too much stop and go in his game and lacked some fluidity. This is a player with great work ethic and he battles very hard every shift for the puck. He has some speed and moves the puck well and is also very strong on the puck. He does not have all the skill in the world but makes up for it with effort and energy. He never quits on a play and keeps a very simple game doing a lot of the little things well.

KNG#17 C, Kujawinski, Ryan (2013) Ryan showed some hockey sense and offensive instincts in this one. He displayed a great ability to get himself open in good scoring positions and finds the open space in the offensive zone. He had a net front presence and a willingness to battle in the dirty areas and was also physical in his own zone. He battled hard for pucks and tied up his man in his own end. Tod Gill used him in many critical situations as well.

NIA#16 LW, Petersen, Trevor (2013) A player whos game is built off speed. He is a very quick skater and wins races for pucks almost effortlessly. He looked much more involved in this game than usual. He was physical and working hard in puck battles, demonstrated a high tempo of play, some great energy and a good level of physicality.

NIA #28 D, Haydon, Aaron (2014) A player with great size, a powerful stride but it is a little bit awkward still and needs a bit of work. He needs to make sure he is getting his shot on net and watch that he isn't too aggressive and put himself out of position when he is deciding to pinch to take an opportunity. He was also way too aggressive on his gap control and needs to relax and let the game come to him. He put himself out of position too many times by trying to force the play unnecessarily and needs to have a bit more patience and play his gaps properly.

NIA #15 RW, Hiddink, Brook (2014) Protects the puck well and can play a good cycle game. He keept his game simple. He moves the puck well and makes his hits, however was out-muscled in a few puck battles and at times looked lost as to his responsibility in his own zone. Not sure he thinks the game very well.

FINAL SCORE: 4-2 Niagara

October 20, 2012, London Knights at Barrie Colts (OHL)

BAR #5 RD Aaron Ekblad (2014) – Ekblad is a presence. He possesses the size (6'4, 213) and skill combination ideal in a number one defenseman. Long stick is a major attribute. He used it intelligently in all three zones, particularly in holding the line and in 1-on-1 situations. His poke-check ability in particular was excellent but he relied on it too much, letting numerous players get by him on the rush without challenging them physically. He showed a tendency to reach for the puck instead of closing the gap to play the body. Part of his tentativeness may have had to do with his backwards skating, which was awkward against speed, putting his timing and gap control off. Moving forward, he showed a long, powerful stride and the confidence to carry the puck, but his decision making with the biscuit was a little rushed overall.

His hands are not the quickest but he used his reach well to evade forecheckers, enabling him to go end-to-end a few times. Great shot from the point, gets a lot of torque from his stick. Overall I would have liked to see more of a killer instinct and a little more agility in all aspects of his game.

LDN #16 LC Max Domi (2013) – Max is intense and hardworking. He demanded the puck on almost every shift and showed no qualms in taking the puck to the net with reckless abandon despite his moderate stature. Showed the ability to lead a rush and an affinity for being the creative force behind an attack. His hands in tight were outstanding and he did great work along the boards and behind the net. Very strong on his edges and showed the ability to bounce off some checks, but had a tendency to challenge opponents physically regardless of their size.

LDN #53 LW Bo Horvat (2013) – Horvat played such a strong overall game that it's easy to imagine him having success as a pro. He did the little things very well, such as winning board battles and his paly in the neutral zone was outstanding. Was very shifty around the net and in tight, flashing good hands and quick stops/starts. Good skater with an efficient stride, got to speed quicker than last season and backchecked hard. Carried the puck with confidence. Showed good puck protection skills and the willingness to take the puck to the net.

LDN #81 LW Remi Elie (2013) – Elie is skating in a fairly limited role for London, but I was impressed with his tempo and physicality. In his best shift of the night he threw four consecutive hits, and then drew a retaliatory penalty when he kept on his gloves and took a punch in the scrum that ensued. Was a menace on the forecheck with his speed and checking ability. Great energy player. Rarely carried the puck but flashed some skill when he did. I think he is a candidate to break out offensively and establish himself as a quality three-zone talent at some point if given the opportunity.

LDN #65 LD Nikita Zadorov (2013) – Had a quiet night. Big and lanky. Surprisingly shifty for his size but awkward on his feet from time to time. Was a bit sloppy with the puck but made the right plays with it. Defensive coverage was sound.

Scout's Notes: London RC Kyle Platzer (2013) had a nice game, with smart offensive zone play with and without the puck.

October 20, 2012, Kitchener Rangers @ Sarnia Sting (OHL)

KIT #55 LD Gilbert, Jared (2013) - Very improved skating ability. Made a lot of solid passes up ice. However he is also very patient and didn't force plays with it. Gilbert was very reliable in all three zones for the Rangers and was effective one on one when necessary.

SAR #9 RD DiPaolo, Mike (2013*) - He did a great job out front of his own net fighting for positioning and making opposing forwards move. Made some solid passes up ice and out of his zone showing more confidence with the puck. He struggled one on one early on making the first move on forwards and getting beat because of it. He made a bad turnover in neutral ice which resulted in a scoring chance against.

SAR #14 LW Boucher, Reid (New Jersey) - Reid has never seen a shooting angle he didn't like as he fired regularly from impossible angles looking off passing opportunities that would give Sarnia a legitimate scoring chance. He did eventually score but it was from a little more promising angle. Boucher whose work ethic was very impressive early on has all but disappeared. He wouldn't work for anything that wasn't a stick length away, and literally just gave up on a defensive play in the third period. The play he gave up on ended up being the game winning goal in this game. You can't put a loss on one skater, but looking back, Sarnia very easily could have escaped with two points if Boucher actually competed on this play. He was in a key position to prevent the goal but he didn't want to work and his team gained zero points.

SAR #71 RW Goldobin, Nikolay (2014) - Nikolay added another great goal to his list by working around two Kitchener defenders then out waiting John Gibson then roofing the puck. Goldobin is showing a lot better work ethic in the neutral and defensive zone playing more aggressive on the puck. Overall this may have been the best game he's played in the OHL thus far.

SAR #36 G Barrick, Brodie (2013) - Showed quick lower body movement. He tended to slide too far on his pads putting him out of position. The first goal of the game was one that he would probably like back. Barrick gave up four goals but some of these were really beyond his control.

Scouts Notes: In what was a fairly even matched first 40 minutes, Kitchener kicked it up a notch and left the Sting in the dust with three unanswered third period goals. Scoring opened with two top 2014 NHL Eligibles when Darby Llewellyn wired a powerful wrist shot top shelf four minutes in. Later in the period Nikolay Goldobin scored a highlight reel goal beating two defensemen, out waited John Gibson (Anaheim) then roofing the puck. Sarnia was able to take over control after two periods, but late in the third, Tobias Rieder (Edmonton) with his excellent positioning buried on a rebound to score the game winning goal.

Oct 20, 2012, Swift Current Broncos vs. Tri-City Americans (WHL)

SC#2 LD, Heatherington, Dillon(2013) Big defenseman who had a good showing tonight. Like the poise he has with the puck and his ability to move it effectively. Made a couple of terrible decisions with it that led to great scoring chances for Tri-City, but apart from them was good with the puck. Good recognition to skate with the puck if there was room instead of just aimlessly passing it. Liked his play in his own zone. Made good reads and took away passing lanes effectively. Biggest concern with him is speed. Struggled a little against opponents who had good sets of wheels, but was able to use his long reach to steer them to the outside.

SC#5 LD, Martin, Brycen(2014) A rookie to the WHL, but looked like a veteran at times when handling pressure. Very impressed with the way he moved the puck even with forechecks hounding him from behind. Rushed the puck effectively as well too. Held onto the puck for too long at times. Still has some adjustments to make defensively, but not too shabby in his own end either. Was quick with his decision making to get in the right areas. Impressed with his strength along the boards. Looks like he needs to work on his overall speed.

SC#27 RD, Zinkan, Bobby(2013) Had a very up and down game today. Kept it simple with the puck and did not try to do too much with it. Made some good passes and did a good job to recognize chances to skate with the puck. Landed a huge open ice hit that was quite impressive. Did a good job of angling opponents to the outside. Definitely has some good instincts for the game, but made a few errors throughout the game. For example, after a face off win, Zinkan chose to take a slap shot with an opponent right in front of him, who easily poked the puck away and got a partial break.

TC#1 G, Comrie, Eric(2013) Did not have to be brilliant today, but made the key saves when he had to. Really liked his focus level today. The Broncos took some shots on him abruptly down the wing or from the corner, but he was up for the task every time and made the saves look easy. Plays aggressively in the crease and loves to challenge shooters. Impressive glove hand. Stirred rebounds away from trouble time and time again. Quick on his knees. Fights hard to look through traffic, and does not let it effect his game too much.

TC#27 LC, Rankin, Connor(2013) 2 way centre had an excellent game tonight. Really liked his overall game. Looked very strong along the boards with the puck and opponents had a very tough time trying to separate him from the puck. Had an aggressive mindset tonight to attack the middle often with the puck. Was always in the middle of piles in front of the net. Had one memorable play when he went coast to coast with the puck. Made opponents look silly with his deceptive moves. Did not take a shift off tonight. Fittingly scored the game winning goal tonight by going to the net and picking up the loose puck and buried it.

SCOUT'S NOTES: Both teams struggled to create great scoring chances tonight. Best player tonight was Connor Rankin by a mile. Was everywhere out on the ice and displayed his solid 2 way game. Liked his composure with the puck. Don't see elite level offensive instincts, but enough to be an effective scorer at this level. Coda Gordon is still too soft to play against. Didn't like his compete level tonight. Brycen Martin will definitely be a player to watch for the 2014 NHL Entry Draft. Really impressed with his level of play tonight. Still has some rough edges around is game, but they are things that are easily fixable. Justin Gutierrez of Tri-City is another player to watch for. Has not recorded a point this season as of this game, but showed very good speed and good offensive instincts to get to the right areas around the ice.

FINAL SCORE: 2-1 Tri-City

Oct 21, 2012, Kingston Frontenacs vs Kitchener Rangers (OHL)

KNG#93 LW, Bennett, Sam (2014) A responsible player who can play effectively in both ends of the rink. He gives support in his own end and pressures the puck carrier forcing the opposition to the outside. He cycles the puck well and can move it quickly, and also has some great hands. He has some moves and can beat a defender 1 on 1 and brings a nice element of speed to the game as well.

KNG#96 LW, Watson, Spencer (2014) Plays a decent cycle game and protects the puck well. He had a nice give and go in the offensive zone and he gets to the front of the net. He puts pressure on the puck carrier and does a good job getting shots on net. He is strong on his feet.

KNG #20 D, McKeown, Roland (2014) A great puck moving defenseman with good size. He has excellent vision and passing and can spot his lanes in the offensive zone. He does a good job in the defensive zone as well getting his stick in lanes to block passes and ties up his man in front of the net. He is willing to join in on the rush and also gets his shot through from the point. He bit too hard on opponent's moves and needs to get a bit stronger on the puck, but with some added size and strength he will be an elite defensive prospect.

KNG#17 C, Kujawinski, Ryan (2013) Sees the ice so well and can pass the puck very effectively. He spots breakout options well and does a good job seeing his opportunities and taking advantage of them. He drives hard to the net, moves the puck quickly and keeps his feet moving. He made quick decisions and showed the ability to work the puck under pressure. He is calm with the puck and can really find space to work with in the offensive zone. Some great hockey sense and offensive instincts were shown in this game.

KIT#16 LW, Pedersen, Brent (2013) He does a good job following up the play to the net and goes hard to the net to get some opportunities. He battles hard for the puck, brings a net front presence and tries to tip the pucks. Has a nice physical element to his game and goes hard on the fore-check.

KIT#19 LW, Sterk, Josh (2013) Carries the puck up the ice really well and can see the play developing in front of him. He has some nice hands and can also move the puck up the ice well through his passing. He likes to drive to the outside and cycles the puck well. He had a nice give and go play to generate an opportunity and can also generate chances off the rush. He offers good support in his own zone and ties up his man well.

KIT#95 LW, Bailey, Justin (2013) Scored two goals in this game, one of them was a beauty and the other just by throwing the puck on the net. He demonstrated some finishing abilities and was moving the puck up the ice very well. He protects the puck well and gets to the slot to get his shot off. He got his stick in lanes in his own zone.

KIT#3 D, Genovese, Cory (2013) A defenseman who keeps a simple game and sticks to the basics. He avoids high-risk plays and gets the puck out of his zone well. He demonstrated some nice puck movement in getting the puck up the ice quickly and also did a good job getting his shots through to the net.

KIT#55 D, Gilbert, Jared (2013) Some great positioning defensively. He has some size and clears the front of his net well and makes sure to get the puck away from dangerous areas. He tied up his man.

FINAL SCORE: 5-2 Kitchener

Oct 23, 2012, Indiana Ice vs. USNTDP (USHL)

IND #4 D, Smith, Alex (2013) In this game he demonstrated some good gap control and forced his man to the outside. He was clearing the front of the net and moved the puck out of the zone up the boards, chipping the puck out of dangerous areas. He was willing to join in the rush and get his shot on net and did a good job finding lanes to skate the puck up the ice. Smith also demonstrated some good vision with a nice first pass out of the zone to spot his breakout options and could make his long pass tape to tape. He got his shots through from the point and kept them low. There was one questionable decision when the opposition had a 2 on 1 against him and he was too aggressive on the puck carrier, in this situation he needs to have patience and watch the pass rather than the puck. Overall he demonstrated some good speed and skating and was able to protect the puck.

IND #8 D, Jacobs, Joshua (2014) In this game Jacobs was physical and challenging the shooter. He had some good gap control and managed to keep his man to the perimeter and directed the play with his stick. He got his stick in the way to tip the puck out of dangerous areas and got down in lanes to block passes with his body. He has some pretty decent size at 6'2 and 192 lbs. and managed to get his shot through and kept down nice and low.

IND #24 LW, Pieper, Bo (2013) A fast high energy player who showed some good positioning in his own zone and gave options for a breakout. He was protecting the puck well and was strong on the puck and able to move the puck well and quickly. He was making sure to put pressure on the puck carrier and kept to a simple dump and chase game when his options are taken away ensuring he is making the safe play.

USNT#12 LW, Lebanc, Kevin (2014) Lebanc had a great game and was finding the score sheet often. He was showing some really nice hands, had some good moves and rushed the puck up the ice welling finding seems to skate or pass the puck. He can pass the puck well and was opening up to give options and shot the puck well, also crashed the net looking for chances. He displayed some great vision to see where the puck should go and cuts well to the middle with the puck, protecting the puck. There was a questionable decision when he took a shot on a 3 on 1 when he could have easily moved the puck around a bit to make it harder on the goalie.

USNT #14 LW, Motte, Tyler (2013) Displayed some clear high-end skill in this game. He has some great moves and can beat a defender 1 on 1 but sometimes tries to do too much and force a play and could be more effective making the safe play and getting the puck in deep. He took a lot of shots from different areas in this game and followed up going to the net for rebounds and is willing to stand in front of the net. He got to the net and had some nice positioning in the offensive zone. He tried to force the play through unnecessarily at one point on the power play and needs to wait for lanes to open up to make his passes.

USNT #4 D, Butcher, Will (2013) A defenseman who has some great vision and can really move the puck well. In this game he was making some great passes and some nice little chip plays off the board. He showed some nice agility and was able to twist and turn his way out of any trouble and can rush the puck up the ice very well. He was getting to the slot to offer options in the offensive zone and had a nice quick release on his shot as well.

USNT #14 RW, McCarron, Mike (2013) McCarron is a winger with some great size at 6'5 and could be quite a dominant force if he added some strength. He demonstrated some good patience with the puck to outwait his defenseman and move the puck across the ice to a scoring area. He was passing the puck well and showing good instincts to get the puck to those dangerous spots. He was driving hard to the net and did a great job getting to the slot and finding space to open up for a pass. He can drive wide and get a shot off looking for a rebound, or get out to the slot to get his shot off. He was protecting the puck well, and made a nice play a few times where he would gain the zone and move the puck to the outside to the side-boards and then drive hard to the net to create some chances.

USNT #14 RW, Kelleher, Tyler (2013) A very highly skilled forward who showed some nice moves and good finish in this game. He displayed some real nice passing and battle for the puck and was able to move the puck to scoring areas. He drove hard to the net and was looking for rebounds and did a good job spotting his options and getting the puck to the open man in the high slot. He is a player who clearly really loves to score and did a good job finding open ice to work with on the Power play and moved the puck quickly into scoring areas. He kept the puck moving well and shot often from just about everywhere.

USNT #14 RW, Fasching, Hudson (2013) This was a great game for Fasching, he played a great two-way game and was showing some excellent potential. He has some good strength and was showing some nice puck battle winning almost every one. He moved the puck really well to high chance dangerous areas and kept the puck moving north on the breakout. He also showed some great hockey sense moving into the slot and opening up to create chances. Fasching was very effective defensively as well back-checking had and knocking the puck off the opposition. He hustled end to end but did cross the line at one point when he took down his man and took a penalty coming back. He was making hits to neutralize the opposition's attack and was very strong on the puck protecting it well as he was very difficult to knock off the puck in this game. He was fore-checking hard and playing a good cycle game and making some moves to create space in the offensive zone.

USNT #28 LW, Eiserman, Shane (2014) Eiserman was working very hard in this game and really hustling and competing in all three zones. He has some nice speed and the sense to read the play developing. He demonstrated some great physicality and finished his checks and was using his body well to protect the puck while driving from the outside. He displayed some real nice hockey sense and puck movement, and brought a good net-front presence as well. Eiserman likes to shoot the puck often and made quite a few good little chip plays to keep the puck moving towards his teammates. He followed up hard to the net but sometimes was mishandling the puck by trying to make too many moves, or had the tendency to go soft on it from time to time. Eiserman needs to watch the turnovers and make sure he can get the puck through when throwing it up the middle, but also did make some good passes in this game and got the puck across on a 2 on 1.

USNT #14 RW, Allen, Evan (2013) What stood out the most in this game for me was his shot. Allen displayed a really great shot a few times in this game and scored a couple goals including one with a minute left to give his team the lead when he just picked the perfect spot in the net. He was also passing the puck very well in this game and getting a lot of good shots off from dangerous areas showing some nice offensive instincts. He can drive well to the outside and really showed this when he drove wide and took the defenseman with him and then made a great no-look drop pass for a great opportunity. He showed some nice speed and vision, especially when he was rushing the puck up the ice and finding lanes to work with. He also showed some nice vision in his passing when he moved the puck to the slot to find teammates, passing the puck very effectively.

Scouts Notes: A game that featured a lot of offense. It appeared both teams were just trying to outscore the others and stopped focusing on defending. The game could have been much higher scoring if it wasn't for some lucky breaks and good saves by the goaltenders. There were players left open in the slot all game for both sides and a lot of good chances coming off the rush as well as from cycles. USA clearly has a very talented offensive group but is going to need to tighten up in their own zone and have some better coverage if they are going to win more often this year.

FINAL SCORE: 6-4 USNTDP

Oct 24, 2012, Vancouver Giants vs Brandon Wheat Kings (WHL)

VAN#1 G, Lee, Payton(2014) First game of the year with Vancouver after getting demoted to Junior B in the pre-season because he lost the back up job. Had a solid game overall. Really liked the confidence he displayed. Very aggressive mindset and challenges the shooters from way out of his crease. Very good glove hand, snatched pucks out of the air with ease. Gave up a very soft first goal. Opponent came down the wing on a 3 on 2, and took a quick shot from around the half wall, caught Lee cheating to the middle. I liked the way he came right back and made some good saves after. Good anticipation and puck tracking abilities. Tried to cheat a couple of times. Needs to depend on his quickness and trust that he will be able to make the save.

VAN#27 RW, Houck, Jackson(2013) Made very good contributions all game long at both ends of the ice. Got the first goal of the game on a broken play, picked up the puck in the slot and took a good wrist shot through a screen. Was at his best when he threw his body around and land some good hits. Liked how he was able to keep himself controlled physically and not take any undisciplined penalties. Played the half wall on the PP and looked comfortable with the puck. Not world class vision or creativity, but kept it simple and made good decisions with the puck. His intensity and overall played dropped in the third period, disappointed at his effort when the team was down by two goals, but that can be said about all of his teammates basically.

BDN#2 RD, Pulock, Ryan(2013) Not impressed with his game today. Made some bad decisions with the puck, looked hesitant in all areas of the ice and was not very physical. Have to keep in mind that the team has gone through a long road trip from Manitoba through British Columbia. Looked strong on his skates initially, but as the game went on, logged a ton of minutes and was easier to knock down. One very notable play on this day was on the power play, he had the puck behind his net and the team was executing their controlled breakout. Vancouver's forward swung low and followed one of Brandon's forward up the ice, but Pulock still decided to pass the puck in that direction anyway, which got picked off easily. Have seen much better games out of him before.

BDN#6 LD, Nikkel, Ayrton(2013) Defensive defenseman who had his moments tonight. Made some very good plays without the puck and read the play quite well. Let his hockey IQ do more of the work than his physicality on this day. Made a lot of good reads and took some risks stepping up in the blue line but none of them came back to hurt his team. Got beat a few times by opponents who drove to the net out wide. Below average puck handler, especially in speed. Makes good decisions with the puck, but will probably never be known for his puck moving abilities.

BDN#7 LD, Roy, Eric(2013) Hulking defenseman who had an inconsistent game. Impressed by his strong play at both ends of the ice, but looked exhausted as the went along. Uses his size effectively in all areas of the ice, and a few times stepped up at the blue line to try to land a big hit, which forced opponents to dump it in. Handled the puck very well, even with pressure. Has some work to do with his skating abilities, but his potential to be an impact player at the pro level is very evident.

Scouts Notes: A very slow game filled with a lot of turnovers. Both teams were unable to generate many chances. I was disappointed with Ryan Pulock and his overall game tonight. Have seen much better performances out of him, but the team has been on the road for 10 days now, and he logs huge minutes every night. Really impressed with Payton Lee tonight. Was unsure how he would look in his first game at the WHL level, but he looked very confident. Will not be surprised if he takes over the #1 job soon. Tim McGauley of Brandon also had a good game. Brought a lot of energy tonight. Looked confident with the puck and made some good plays. Needs a ton of work to do in his own zone. His awareness is quite low, and time and time again let an opponent be wide open in the slot.

FINAL SCORE: 3-2 Brandon

October 25, 2012, Windsor Spitfires @ Sarnia Sting (OHL)

WSR #16 LW Rychel, Kerby (2013) - Kerby was very physical right out of the gate and it continued all game long. He also showed off his laser shot. He went hard to the net and it gave him a few good chances although he didn't score tonight. He went for a big hit and needlessly elbowed a Sarnia player in the head taking a very bad penalty putting his team short handed. Skating has improved but still lots of room to get better. He tries to push his limits as a player at times getting too fancy and it resulted in turnovers. He is a power forward type player who's at his best when hitting, getting into good shooting positions and chipping in defensively. When he decides to try to dangle and beat multiple defenders as he did in this game it usually affects the team negatively, as it did in this game. If he can learn to stick to his strengths on a consistent basis he has a lot of value in the second half of the first round of this 2013 NHL Entry Draft.

WSR #66 RW Ho-Sang, Joshua (2014) - Josh is really improving with his puck distribution. The talent to do it was always there, the willingness was not always there. He shows excellent creativity with the puck and with his passing ability. He could be a very dangerous player combining this with his hard shot which helped him give Windsor a short lived 2-1 lead in this game. Ho-Sang was one of the more valuable players for Windsor in this game as he constantly set up scoring chances for his teammates. He is at his best when not trying to do too much because it simply results in too many turnovers.

SAR #9 RD DiPaolo, Mike (2013*) - Mike was a force to be reckoned with tonight. He won battles right from the start of the game to the end of it. He utilized his size very well pushing around opponents with power. He was very good in one on one situations throughout the game. At one point absolutely destroyed a Spitfires forward forcing him outside then finishing him along the boards. He likes to shoot when he has the time and has a big point shot that he can get to the net. This may be a big game for DiPaolo in sending a message that he's ready for regular big time minutes with the team as Sarnia's blue line has been inconsistently hit or miss this year.

SAR #21 LC Nikandrov, Daniel (2013) - Daniel sacrificed his body on more than one occasion to block shots. Tonight was a good definition of the player Nikandrov is. He won some battles that he maybe otherwise shouldn't have won. He showed off good hands entering the offensive zone, and maintaining puck control in the offensive zone. He also showed excellent defensive instincts and was a key part to the Sarnia penalty kill. Great anticipation of the Windsor power play forcing several turnovers and breaking up offensive plays.

SAR #23 LD Core, Zachary (2014) - Core kept it simple in his OHL debut. He maintained good safe positioning. At one point he got crushed with a big welcome to the league but he got up stuck with the play and it didn't really phase him making the right defensive play moments later.

SAR #55 RD Murphy, Connor (Phoenix) - Murphy looked better than usual in one on one situations. A lot of the time he would either win a battle or force a turnover, then lose the puck, or he would lose the battle then win the puck back a few seconds later. His good, strong, smart point shot is clearly his best asset. He is a threat to score whenever he lets it go. He made some strong puck plays but also had his usual "what was he thinking" moments as well. Connor backed down to a smaller Windsor player (three inches and 20 pounds) after Murphy initiated a discussion where they both nodded, the Spitfire removed his gloves which resulted in Connor Murphy backing behind the official faster than you could blink. He puts on a tough act but then consistently backs down to the smaller players whom he appears to call on. He is starting to gain a reputation around the OHL as the "softest big man in the league" and opponents are testing this theory. An example of this was tonight.

Scouts Notes:

Windsor took the 1-0 and 2-1 leads early on in this game. However they lost their focus and ended up being outworked by the Sting on this night. The momentum shifted back and forth early on. Windsor's Jordan Maletta (2013) opened the scoring by going to the net and putting the rebound in. He finished his checks regularly throughout this game. The teams went back and forth through the first four goals of this game. However it was a huge penalty shot goal scored by Alex Galchenyuk (Montreal) that really changed this game. Both Windsor and Sarnia looked like two different teams going in two different directions after this goal. Nikolai Goldobin (2014) really battled hard defensively impressing in his own zone. He forced turnovers and negated a great scoring chance by Windsor.

October 24, 2012, Saginaw Spirit at Erie Otters (OHL)

ERIE #97 LC Connor McDavid (2015) – Very strong game from the young flashy forward, who has a promising future. Skating is elite. Went from coasting to full-speed nearly instantaneously. Incredible straight-line speed. Got behind the defense a number of times with only one or two quick steps. Tended to leave the zone a bit early to get open for a long pass, which was troublesome at times but did keep the opposing defense honest. Smooth turns, pivots, starts and stops. Very shifty with limited space along the boards.

Elite stickhandler. Liked to pick guys out and try to beat them 1-on-1 with a strong arsenal of moves. Fantastic control at high speed, so much poise. Overdid it at times with the dangles, tried to deke the puck into the net too often. Kept it safer and simpler on the powerplay than at even strength. Defensive coverage was mixed. Was mostly passive and when he did put in the effort, tended to chase the play, especially in his own zone.

ERIE #10 LW Stephen Harper (2013) – Was a high energy force in the mold of Dustin Brown. Forechecked hard and played the body with frequency in all zones, doing damage with hard hits. Skated well and played with a lot of intensity. Showed skills as a triggerman in the offensive zone with a quick slapshot. Liked to set up in the slot on the powerplay. Did great work along the boards in all three zones and showed fantastic determination to win battles where he had no right to be coming out with the puck.

October 25, 2012, Acadie-Bathurst Titan vs. Victoriaville Tigres (QMJHL)

BAT #23 RW Zdrahal, Patrick (2013) – Zdrahal is a very dynamic skater and he can fly in the neutral zone. He is always in movement and his feet move fast. Unfortunately he and his line mates were not able to use their speed to create anything offensively. They created a lot of turnovers and Zdrahal was very slow to get back in the defensive zone. He didn't use his speed to back check. I can't say this was a very positive outing for him outside of his speed. He showed little offensive touch with the puck and I didn't like his work ethic.

BAT #24 C Zboril, Adam (2013) – Very small player and he didn't display much speed. He wasn't a force in the neutral zone but he was effective deep in the offensive zone. He showed good puck control and picked up two assists. I didn't see much upside in his game although he played an all right game offensively.

BAT #29 G McDonald, Mason (2014) – I thought he played a good game and kept his team in the game despite the goals he allowed. He was very aware of his surroundings and made a great pad save early in the game, showing off his quickness. I liked how he stayed focus despite Victoriaville scoring a lot of goals and he kept making saves. He seems to have good tools to work with and I'm looking forward to see more.

VIC #12 C/W Rehak, Dominik (2013)- He didn't have what you could call a good game but he did show some nice tools. He was able to handle the puck through traffic a few times while maintaining his speed. His hands are definitely a strong asset for him. He looks to be a good skater but in most games I saw from him including this one, he struggles to maintain the pace and to really impose his speed offensively. He also one good shot on net that I particularly noticed; it was a good low slapper that the goalie had trouble stopping.

VIC #34 D Beaulieu, Anthony (2013) – Very tall defenseman for Victoriaville, he brings stability on the backline despite being a rookie and he excels defensively in close range situations. He uses his size and reach almost perfectly. If he doesn't, he ends up being in trouble most of the time. He HAS to use his physical advantage to play the game. I like the way he engages his opponents physically with his whole body. He is not a pretty skater but is surprisingly mobile. He projects mostly as a stay at home defenseman and I see him as a very long shot to be drafted (his size will help him).

VIC #57 LW Veilleux, Tommy (2013) – He displayed good energy to start the game on the third line and gave some good checks. He showed off his passing skills on the powerplay at one point, making a good pass. He is slowly getting more comfortable with the puck. I also noticed he anticipates more instead of going all in at full speed every time. He also won a few races for the puck in this game, showing decent speed against an opponent.

October 26, 2012, Sault Ste. Marie Greyhounds at Erie Otters (OHL)

ERIE #97 LC Connor McDavid (2015) – Another strong game from McDavid. Acceleration is elite. Was able to get behind the defense numerous times, but teammates couldn't always find him with a pass. Showed well with and without the puck. Went hard to the net with speed when the lane was open and battled on the boards and in front of the net, especially on the powerplay. Passing was elite. Great vision to find teammates through seams and had the touch and accuracy to deliver perfect passes both on the ice and sauced over sticks. Lacked a shot mentality, passed up scoring chances to dish. Is an absolute menace on the goal line, found teammates in front of the net or cross-crease for dangerous chances with great precision.

ERIE #10 LW Stephen Harper (2013) – Had nowhere near the same energy as last night. Was lost in coverage and slow getting to pucks. Flashed good hands on a filthy toe drag move and scored a goal off a powerplay one-timer but aside from a few select shifts he was uninvolved. Interested to see which player shows up next time I see Erie play.

SOO #25 LD Darnell Nurse (2013) – Nurse is a raw talent with a lot of upside. He's tall and strong but still fairly skinny. Drew the ire of the hometown fans with his chippy play. Perilously tightroped the line between nasty and dirty in front of his net and along the boards in his own zone, like when he tackled a player into his goaltender and crosschecked another headfirst into the boards. Definitely difficult to play against. Somehow he escaped the night with only one penalty, I counted four occasions where he could have received one.

Positioning was good overall but he did get lost a few times. Worst lapse was a giveaway on the PK that led to a goal. Good defending one-on-one and stepped up well to play the body when given the opportunity. Offensive game is still a little rough around the edges but he flashed some skill. Showed a hard slapshot that he liked to one-time off the draw and a good low wrister for rebounds. Had a few great pinches to jump into the attack, one of which led to him scoring the game-tying goal from the slot. Made a couple great stretch passes and played the point well on the powerplay. Puck-rushing ability was a little awkward, he was mostly unsuccessful carrying the biscuit up ice.

SOO #28 RW Sergei Tolchinsky (2013) – Really exciting player. This kid is slick. Listed at a slight 5'7, 160. He looks it. Got absolutely leveled on multiple occasions but showed great determination to pop back up. Fought through a lot of checks where I thought he'd get outmuscled and showed the ability to make smart plays while engaged physically. Great offensive awareness overall. Was a menace along the boards with lightning quick hands and very creative decision making. Was not afraid to go to the corners or take the puck to the net. Was tough to check on the rush as he got to speed quickly and evaded contact well at full flight.

Showed fantastic playmaking ability with some impressive dangles and good awareness of his teammates in outnumbered attack situations. Pass arsenal included well-placed drop passes and saucers into space for his teammates to skate onto. Flashed a great wristshot with a quick release. Forechecked aggressively with good positioning. Backchecked hard, read the play well and utilized his stick to pickpocket or intercept passes when possible. Size is the major question mark but he showed the shiftiness, work ethic, and skill necessary to succeed as undersized player.

October 26, 2012, Guelph Storm @ London Knights (OHL)

GUE #7 LD Harpur, Ben (2013) - The first thing you notice about Harpur is his massive size. Ben is one of the biggest eligible defensemen available. However he struggled in one on one situations fairly regularly. His skating needs improvement and he pivots a little too late most of the time which saw him get beat fairly regularly. His puck play is very unpredictable. He showed some good plays, but also made some plays that didn't make much sense. He scored what was the tying goal at the time with a big hard point shot in the third period. He has some positives to build on, but also requires a lot of work.

GUE #9 RC Fabbri, Robby (2014) - Fabbri has very good speed but really needs to add strength to his frame. He was very capable of getting into good scoring areas with the puck on a few occasions, but just couldn't finish on the prince scoring chances. He took a really unnecessary penalty for holding away from the puck early in the third period seconds after London took a 2-1 lead.

GUE #11 LW Dickinson, Jason (2013) - Jason was extremely impressive in tonight's game and may have been the best player on either team tonight. He shows very good skating with a big frame. He finishes his checks whenever possible. Dickinson showed great defensive zone presence. This leaded into the penalty kill time he received and he was a constant factor in getting the puck down the ice and killing time off the penalties. On more than one occasion Dickinson sacrificed his body to block shots. Shows a lot of hockey sense and awareness in all three zones, but he was relied upon heavily in his own zone tonight.

GUE #17 LW Bertuzzi, Tyler (2013) - Bertuzzi has grown a bit since last season. He is a strong skater who made smart simple plays. He was capable of rushing the puck into the offensive zone but commonly skated himself into a corner without options. He finished on a 2 on 0 breakaway to score the first goal of the game. Overall he looked good despite staring in more of a depth role in this game.

LON #4 LD Liberati, Miles (2013) - Liberati who handles the puck very well using his elusiveness to draw a penalty at one point. He doesn't force passes up ice and waits for the right option to present itself. He has a powerful wrist shot that he is willing to let go from the point. He impressed in the defensive zone battling bigger forwards along the walls and winning battles. He showed well during his time on the penalty kill really sticking with his man well, battling, and negating scoring chances.

LON #65 LD Zadorov, Nikita (2013) - Zadorov showed a cannon of a point shot and isn't afraid to use it. He did a pretty good job on the penalty kill clearing the puck down the ice pretty consistently. He battled effectively deep in his own zone. An effective skater who was willing to skate the puck up ice when the lanes permitted it, and moved it up ice fairly well in this game.

LON #81 LW Elie, Remi (2013) - Remi looked dangerous every time he touched the puck. He has very high hockey sense and displayed this with an outstanding cross ice pass to set up a tying goal in the second period. He played on the point of the Knights' power play tonight and just unloaded a massive blast from the point that the goaltender had to just hope hit him. He unloaded about five of these however none resulted in a goal. He is very good in his own zone working hard defensively, and skates hard the second the play starts going the other way.

LON #91 RW Platzer, Kyle (2013) - Kyle won a lot of battles and works extremely hard every shift. However he ended up throwing the puck away far too much rushing his play with it. Didn't show a ton of skill but there was enough of it to mix in with his great work ethic to make him look like a prospect tonight.

LON #35 G Patterson, Jake (2013*) - Patterson showed great quickness and very good recovery ability. He was constantly strong on the second or third successive chance in close. He usually directs rebounds to the corners well. He seemed to struggle with point shots and was too elaborate with his positioning just outside the crease and kept losing his ideal position in relation to the net.

Scouts Notes: Garret Sparks (Toronto) really stood on his head in order to keep his Guelph Storm in this game. Not only did they escape with one point, but they earned the second in the shootout. London looked great all game long but struggled finishing on some big chances that could have put this game away in regulation. Max Domi (2013) was pretty quiet through forty minutes, however really elevated his game in the third controlling the puck well and creating some chances. Bo Horvat (2013) showed his usual work ethic, and battled hard all game long. Guelph won off of a Brock McGinn (Carolina) shootout winning goal by the score of 4-3.

Oct 27, 2012, Waterloo Blackhawks vs. USNTDP U 17 (USHL)

WAT #3, D, McCoshen, Ian (2013) I didn't like the way McCoshen started this game, however as the game went on his game started to get better. McCoshen is a defenseman with good size and was making some good hits in this game. He got his shot through from the point and was providing a nice setup for one-timers on the power play. He is able to move the puck up the ice for a breakout, and also showed some nice physicality in his own end as he was clearing the front of the net well. He put some good pressure on the opposition with his gap control to make it difficult for the opposition to get some good opportunities and showed a willingness to block shots on the penalty kill. McCoshen was holding the line well in the offensive zone and getting the puck in nice and deep on his dumps when there were no other options available for gaining the zone. Early on I felt he was looking to get rid of the puck in a hurry and didn't show much calmness or patience and was not getting his passes through to move them up the ice.

WAT #29, D, McCrea, Alec (2013) Another big body defenseman, who for his size is actually a decent skater. He was able to move the puck out of the zone for a breakout and was getting his shot through and kept down low from the point. He was physical and winning puck battles in his own zone as well. I felt his decisions to pinch were a bit inconsistent as at some points he held the line and kept the play alive very well, whereas on another opportunity he made a very bad decision to pinch to give the opposition an unnecessary chance the other way. He made some nice hits to separate the opposition from the puck but looked like he had a bit of a panic with the puck in his own zone when he was under pressure.

WAT # 91, C, Cammarata, Taylor (2013) Cammarata has some pretty good speed and hustle, and displayed a willingness to take a hit to make a play. He was moving the puck up well for a breakout and also found some good passing lanes in the offensive zone. What I noticed early on in this game is that he is trying to make a lot of plays up high by passing or shooting the puck rather than driving the play down low towards the net where the real dangerous opportunities happen. Without the puck he was going to the net and I would like to see more of a drive and desire to get to the net with the puck. He had a nice follow up to the high slot on an odd man rush and opened up well for a pass to get a good opportunity, however with the puck I'd like to see a bit more consistency in his passing as he was able to make some real nice passes right on target a few times, but others were no where near the intended target. Cammarata was going in nice and hard to the net and did a good job pulling the puck out from behind the net to get a good opportunity right in front. He did a good job using the passing lanes available on the power play to generate some good chances and got some good opportunities himself from in close in the slot. He has the ability to move the puck out from the boards to scoring areas and followed up some plays nicely to go hard to the net and scored his team's second goal of the game by doing so. Cammarata was taking a lot of outside shots but could also make some good moves to beat defenders and create some room to work with, however at times tried to much and was not effective. He can get on the puck nice and quick and had some great vision and passing to spot the open man in the slot for the third goal of the game. On the defensive end he can make a hit and bring the opponent into the boards to neutralize him and separate him from the puck as well.

WAT # 71, C, Salerno, Brandon (2013) I found that Salerno was in the right position and had the right intentions most of the game, but didn't do too much with it. He was soft on his hits and missed the puck a lot when he went for it and I'd like to see more battle and compete to take the puck from the opposition. He can protect the puck well and cycle it but needs to get stronger on his feet and not fall over every time he is hit or is hitting someone else. He was going to the net and battling in the dirty areas and had some nice pushing and shoving in front of the net, and Salerno needs to do this more often to be most effective. He also looks like he is rushing to move the puck at times and should show some more patience with the puck.

USNT # 48, C, Milano, Sonny (2014) Milano has some real nice speed and some hands to be able to find lanes to rush the puck up the ice. He goes to the net with his stick down and opens up to take passes and by doing this created some great chances in close to the net. He has some amazing moves and the ability to beat defenders clean 1-on-1 and protects the puck very well when driving to the outside. Milano moves the puck in the offensive zone well as he has some great sense and can also get open and into the slot to offer some good scoring options to his teammates. He displayed some great patience in this game, and was passing very effectively but also goes hard to the net and digs and battles for the puck, which is how he scored the first goal of the game by battling from the crease. He can gain the zone and hold up and then move the puck to the dangerous areas as he was moving the puck so well offensively.

USNT # 46, C, Eichel, Jack (2015) For such a young player Eichel is noticeably dominant and was creating chances every time he stepped onto the ice. He is a dangerous player who can beat a defender clean 1-on-1 and is smart about it so that he doesn't put himself out of position with his moves. He can create time and space with his hands and gains the offensive zone with ease. Eichel has some good puck protection and displays a calmness with the puck as well. He can drive well to the outside and made some nice power forward moves by driving wide and then cutting to the middle to create some chances. He has patience with the puck and can see his options that are available.

FINAL SCORE: 3-2 Waterloo

Oct 27, 2012, Sioux City Musketeers vs. Chicago Steel (USHL)

SIC #4 D, Mantha, Ryan (2014) A nice young, big body defenseman who for the most part was very reliable in his own zone. He let his man walk out front a bit too easily on two occasions but other than that played with some good gap control and was very calm and collected on the ice. He has a big reach on his stick and likes to direct the play to the outside with his stick and did a good job both of clearing the puck on the penalty kill and getting his shot through from the point. At times he was a bit too aggressive in puck battles and would find himself out of position. Mantha also did a good job in his own zone of getting down low to block passes by the opposition.

SIC #3 D, Kapla, Michael (2013) Kapla's coach used him effectively in all critical situations in this game and he was able to have a positive impact in both the offensive and defensive zone. He was getting his shot through from the point, demonstrated some calmness with the puck and was moving it really well in the offensive zone. He was moving the puck up the ice to breakout of his own zone well, and also showed some nice communication with his D partner. Kapla was aggressive and physical in his own zone- especially in the puck battles, and demonstrated some great vision finding lanes and making great passes in the offensive zone. He got caught pinching at one point, but did a great job back checking to break up the chance the other way.

SIC #22 C, McGlynn, Conor (2013) McGlynn did a better job tonight of getting to the net and playing more down the middle and in the dirty areas. He showed a willingness to go down and block shots and had some nice big hits on the fore-check- however needs to make sure he doesn't cross the line and take a penalty as he did at one point in this game. He can protect the puck well as he cycles with his big body, but still needs to add some speed to his game. He did a great job in this game when he walked out from the half boards and got a great shot on net and needs to start being more of a force and trying things like this more often.

SIC #14 LW, Lacroix, Cedric (2013) A very fast skater who works hard both ways and was really back checking well in this game. He was chasing down the puck carrier and hitting on the fore-check and battling to get to the net. I would like to see a bit more consistency in his puck battles as sometimes he works hard for the puck and other times almost looks uninterested.

SIC #19 C, Guentzel, Jake (2013) Guentzel had a good game and was gaining the zone well. He showed this best, as he would gain the zone wide and stop up at the half boards to wait for a pass to a streaking player joining the rush. He was protecting the puck well, and standing in front of the net on the power play. He was moving the puck well and demonstrated some nice hands and patience with the puck. He was getting out to the slot to create chances and finding some nice lanes to work with in the offensive zone to make cross-ice passes. Guentzel needs to watch the turnovers near the blue line and just try to get the puck deep instead of trying to do too much when he is out of options and doesn't have support. He got a lot of chances and was finding space to work with in the offensive zone after gaining the zone.

CHI #10 C, Ebbing, Thomas (2013) A good skater who did a good job tonight of gaining the zone and stopping up to pass the puck to a trailing player. He had a net front presence on the power play and was getting to the slot to get some good scoring chances. He had a nice give and go early on in the offensive zone to get to the slot and get a good shot off showing some good offensive instincts. He went in hard on the fore check and was finishing his checks and had a nice battle for the puck. This is a player who is not intimidated and was getting to the net and standing his ground, as well as getting to the slot and opening up for passes.

CHI #28 C, Roos, Alex (2013) A smaller forward but was really passing the puck well. He opens up well for a pass in the offensive zone and connected on the one-timer opportunity. He was also able to walk out front from behind the net quite easily to the slot and got a great opportunity from a dangerous area. He was passing the puck well in the offensive zone and finding the man in the slot and getting him the puck. He brought a net-front presence on the power play and was getting to some good positions in the slot.

CHI #8 C, Widmar, Joseph (2013) Widmar was less of a factor in this game but was still doing some little things well and kept to a simple game. He was putting pressure on the puck carrier, had a nice net-front presence and was battling to hold his territory in the dirty areas. He was taking a lot of outside low-chance shots and needs to try to get the puck to more dangerous scoring areas, and was finishing his checks on the fore-check.

SCOUT'S NOTES: A tight defensive battle in this one that was kept to no score until late in the third period. Both goaltenders were outstanding and the defense did a good job keeping chances to the outside. Chicago got lucky they didn't blow this one as they took a few dumb penalties near the end of the game that almost cost them, and that they didn't go down early as Sioux City really dominated the first half of this game.

FINAL SCORE: 2-1 Chicago

Oct 28, 2012, Green Bay Gamblers vs. USNTDP U17s (USHL)

GBG #5 D, Olofsson, Gustav (2013) A pretty big body who was physical and throwing the body around, especially in his own zone along the boards. For most of the game seemed to be a steady stay-at-home defenseman but did show a willingness to join in the rush from time to time and can definitely skate. He did a good job clearing the front of his own net and showed a nice puck battle. He moves around to give his teammates passing options in the offensive zone and also moved the puck pretty well. He had a few miscues in this game, for example when he unnecessarily followed the puck carrier to the far side on a 2-on-2 rush for the opposition and lost his man he was supposed to be covering who ended up scoring. In this situation he needs to show more patience and let his partner take the far man, even if the puck carrier switches sides- better communication on the ice. Olofsson also mishandled the puck at one point in the neutral zone for a turnover and made a couple inopportune pinches leading to potential chances going the other way.

GBG#20 D, Wolanin, Christian (2013) Another big body defenseman who played a pretty simple safe game for the most part. He was able to get his shot through from the point, and just tried to make the simple chip play most of the time and get the puck in deep. At least twice in this game he jumped up and showed a willingness to join in the rush and was able to get back and was moving the puck pretty well, keeping it moving especially on the power play. Wolanin also had a nice slap-pass to cause some deception of what he was going to do in the offensive zone, but needs to make sure he can get all his passes through in the offensive zone without trying to force it. He also had a bad turnover in his own zone and needs to make sure he knows where he is passing the puck and who is there to receive it rather than blindly throwing the puck around to the other team.

GBG#23 D, Gross, Jordan (2013) Gross played this game with some good gap control, which was most evident when he made a nice stick-check play to knock the puck off the opposition demonstrating that perfect gap. He was willing to take a hit to make a play as well. One thing that was noticeable however was when he came back to his own zone to retrieve the puck and had time and space to break the puck out with no pressure, he decided to just throw it off the glass resulting in a turnover and needs to make sure that he is either rushing the puck or passing it up the ice to teammates to start an effective breakout.

GBG #24 LW, Siroky, Ryan (2013) Siroky was generating chances almost every time he stepped onto the ice tonight. He was competing hard and battling to get to the net an was aggressive going after the puck carrier and putting pressure on the puck. He was making hits on the fore-check in the offensive zone and also had a net-front presence. He had some good positioning in the offensive zone getting to the low slot and in-front of the net but wasn't finding too much open ice and may need to move more towards the high slot. He was getting the puck to high-chance dangerous scoring areas and was physical and finishing his checks all over the ice. At one point was able to just walk out from behind the net into the slot for a good opportunity as well.

GBG #97 RW, Dikushin, Grigori (2013) This was a very up-and down game for Dikushin as there were moments where he looked great and others where I was left wondering what he was thinking. Starting with the good Dikushin was aggressive on the puck carrier and got to the high slot to open up for passes and got the puck on the net well. He got down low and to the net and was moving the puck pretty well in the offensive zone, but at times it was too much and needed to just shoot the puck as he had opportunities from the slot but just overpassed the puck and ended up without a chance at all. He drove hard down the middle towards the net and was rewarded with a goal that ended up being the game winner. He had some questionable decision making by throwing the puck cross ice to no one in particular and at times was overly aggressive on the puck carrier and over-skated himself out of position. He also lost the puck with some poor puck control a few times.

USNT #47 LW, Hitchcock, Ryan (2014) Displayed some nice hands with some good moves and had a great shot as he scored a real nice goal on a 2-on-1 opportunity. He made some nice passes in the offensive zone as he was finding lanes to get passes through and kept the puck moving, and also got the puck to the slot and to dangerous areas and was shooting the puck often.

USNT #46 C, Eichel, Jack (2015) Eichel dazzled me early on with some nice hands making some great moves to beat a defender on a 1-on-1 and then finished it off with a great pass to the right area to get to his teammate without needing to look. However as the game went on it seemed he was trying to do too much on his own, especially when there were other options available and consistently tried to deke his way into the zone every time, which the opposition was able to shut down almost every attempt. He protects the puck pretty well and was gaining the zone to get some decent shots off and also had a great opportunity late in the game but mishandled the puck and fanned on the shot from the slot.

USNT #37 RW, Tuch, Alex (2014) Displayed some real nice speed and was gaining the zone well. He made some good moves in order to create space and got some good shots off from great scoring areas. He also demonstrated a willingness to block shots and was clearing pucks effectively on the penalty kill.

Scouts Notes: A game that Green Bay really dominated and controlled early on, but let USA back in the game with 3 straight goals to tie up the game before Green Bay took over again and finished with a commanding 6-3 win. USA needs to play more as a team rather than as a group of individuals all trying to win the game on their own and use their talents together to make more plays and to gain the zone without trying to deke their way through the entire opposition.

FINAL SCORE: 6-3 Green Bay Gamblers

November 1, 2012, Oshawa Generals @ Peterborough Petes (OHL)

OSH #19 RC Cassels, Cole (2013) - Effective skating, didn't show great acceleration but gets around effectively. Made some good passes and positioned himself well around the slot area getting open. He lost a ton of battles and rarely came out with the puck. Not due to a lack of effort or willingness but a lack of strength. Cassels was pretty reliable in his own zone always getting back and competing.

OSH #71 LC Dal Colle, Michael (2014) - Dal Colle did not look out of place playing on Oshawa's top line. Constantly made the smart play with the puck. He has good quickness and skating ability for his size. Dal Colle is an excellent playmaker who consistently created scoring chances for his team and did so almost every shift. Excellent puck moving ability in all three zones.

PET #8 LD Varga, Steven (2013) - Very hit or miss tonight. He made some very good, solid defensive plays. But he also made some bad reads particularly when he decided to pinch off the point.

PET #16 LD Murphy, Trevor (2013) - Struggled right off the bat. Puck mistakes in his own zone and lack of positioning resulted in scoring chances against. Struggled moving the puck up ice and rushed his passes despite having plenty of room to make a decision.

PET #17 LW Betzold, Greg (2013) - Overall an OK skater. First few steps need work but he has slightly above average speed for hiss size. Gets the puck deep and chases it. He wins battles regularly and has a big frame with lots of room to add muscle. Made a few great plays to create scoring chances for a Peterborough team that really struggled tonight. Betzold drew power plays with his good hands and strong puck protection ability. Showed a few flashes of great passing ability. Got better with every shift after struggling early he looked a lot better in the final two periods.

PET #35 G Giugovaz, Michael (2013) - Very good quickness and made good on second chance opportunities. He gives up a ton of rebounds and this quickness is essential for him. Leaves his glove hand down and out of positioning, not ready for the shot and Oshawa made him pay for this. Moves well side to side but lost his positioning. Really struggled handling the puck making no less than a half dozen puck playing mistakes and turnovers.

Scouts Notes: Right from the drop of the puck the Peterborough Petes were completely outmatched. It took them over ten minutes to record their first shot. They caught up eventually on the shot clock however Oshawa was able to land 53 shots in total. Really the only Petes' players who elevated their game were

Greg Betzold (2013) and Alan Quine (Detroit). Both really improved after a slow start. Quine in part because this was his first game back from injury. The Petes have some injury woes particularly with Nicholas Ritchie (2014) but the team did not look very good all game long. Daniel Altshuller (Carolina) wasn't tested often but when he was he stood up to the challenge.

Oct 27, 2012, Medicine Hat Tigers vs. Regina Pats (WHL)

MH#9 LW, Shinkaruk, Hunter(2013) Dynamic forward who had an excellent game tonight. Displayed a high level of creativity when making a pass or trying to score. Has a deceptive release to his shot. Scored a beautiful goal by going around the net, did a spin-o-rama by the faceoff circle and went backhand top shelf. Very smart without the puck, was able to find soft spots in coverage. Has a goal scorer's instincts that is difficult to teach. Was often the first one to loose pucks. A very good overall skater. Quite strong on his skates, opponents had a difficult time knocking him off the puck. By far the best performance by a draft-eligible forward I have seen this year.

REG#4 RD, Burroughs, Kyle(2013) Defenseman who played a quiet, but solid game at both ends of the ice. Really liked the way he kept his game simple and did not try to do too much. Works hard in his own end, especially around the boards. Maybe only 5'11, but seems to be much bigger because of his strength. Likes to be aggressive and not give opponents much time to make a play. Used his stick well on a number of occasions to knock away passes and shots. Offensively, made good outlet passes to start the attack. Does not have the hockey IQ to jump into plays and be a threat. Could improve on his point shots as well. Biggest deficiency in his game is skating. Must improve his overall speed to make up for his lack of size. On a number of times, he was in trouble when an opponents would carry the puck towards the outside and cut back to the slot.

REG#18 LW, Klimchuk, Morgan(2013) Speedy forward had a very good game offensively. Used his skating abilities to his advantage all game long and was a big factor. Liked the way he took the puck to the net, a big change from last year when he was more of a perimeter player. Scored on a broken play by going to the net, picking up a loose puck and quickly putting it in the net. Has a very impressive wrist shot. Scored from the high slot cutting to the left and shooting across his body, top shelf. Has good vision, but definitely more of a goal scorer. Needs to make some adjustments defensively. Looks lost on forechecks and cannot contain puck carriers to one side of the ice and loses the middle to opponents consistently.

Scouts Notes: This was a fun game to watch. There were a lot of good scoring chances created by skilled players on both sides. Hunter Shinkaruk has solidified his position has the best draft eligible forward from the WHL. Can do it all, and will be fun to watch in the NHL for years to come. Morgan Klimchuk was no slouch either. Impressed with his game on this day, and just how confident he looked with the puck on his stick. Colby Williams, a defenseman for Regina also had a good showing. Looks very poised in all areas of the ice and made some great plays defensively. Definitely has a good level of hockey sense. Will be a player to watch later on. Curtis Valk of Medicine Hat has found some great chemistry with Shinkaruk. He's not Emerson Etem, but looks very good. It is more evidence that Shinkaruk can make others look great playing along with him.

Oct 27, 2012, Edmonton Oil Kings vs. Kelowna Rockets (WHL)

EDM#13 RW, Baddock, Brandon(2013) A big forward who used his size to his advantage in the offensive zone to create some havoc. Protects the puck well and was difficult to control in front of the net. Not much of a playmaker, and his vision is below average. Just seems to be a little nervous with the puck. Made one impressive play in the first period by softly chipping the puck past a defenseman off the boards and went around him and had a very good scoring chance off the rush. However, his speed is not very good. He was fortunate to catch that opponent off guard, other wise did not see any indication that he is a good skater.

EDM#27 RC, Lazar, Curtis(2013) A forward who displayed some high level of hockey sense in both ends of the ice tonight. Made a few great plays without the puck in the defensive zone to disrupt scoring chances and intercept passes. Had a level of understanding in his own end that is rare to see in forwards at his age. Lazar was able to find the right areas to go to in the offensive zone to get open and be in a position to get the puck and make good plays. He read the defensive coverage well and found holes in them quickly. The issue in his game tonight was his skill level. Just did not see any high level of vision, shooting abilities or speed. He was quite average all game long, and even looked like he was a step behind the play when the tempo was high.

KEL#2 RD, Lees, Jesse(2013) Offensive defenseman who did not look very good tonight at all. Looked quite overwhelmed with the level of play. He looked particularly bad along the boards. Do not remember a single time where he came off the walls with the puck on his stick. Lees had a hard time reading the play without the puck and was caught out of position time and time again. Had a difficult time handling speed as well. Best attribute of Lees is his passing ability. Makes very good tape to tape passes and gets the attack going for his team quickly.

KEL#4 RD, Bowey, Madison(2013) Dynamic defenseman who looked very confident in all areas of his game tonight. Made a number of outstanding reads in the neutral zone to jump the play and intercept passes to get a quick counter attack going for Kelowna. Always looking to push the pace and take some risks. However, I would not call him reckless because many of those risks are high percentage plays. He only tried to intercept passes when there was a backchecker nearby and would be able to cover for him. Has a good point shot, but could improve his velocity on them. Makes very good first passes out of the zone. A very good skater who was able to close in on his opponents quickly and land some good hits.

Scouts Notes: Both teams played a very good game tonight, but Edmonton clearly had more depth and skill in their line up which allowed them to come out on top. Liked the way Griffin Reinhart played tonight. Looked like he was in control of every situation and made very good reads. People would like to see him be more physical, but he does not have to use his body when he is in great position to take away passes and block shots all the time. I was quite disappointed with Curtis Lazar and his game on this night. His high level of hockey sense was quite evident, but I do not see him making much of an impact offensively as a pro. Just do not see any elite level of skill. Also liked Madison Bowey's performance tonight. His aggressive approach to the game has not been matched by any other draft eligible defenseman from this year. Kelowna is a factory for defensemen who make it to the NHL, and Bowey does not look not an exception to that trend.

FINAL SCORE: 5-3 Edmonton

Oct 31, 2012, Portland Winterhawks vs. Everett Silvertips (WHL)

POR#3 RD, Jones, Seth(2013) Had a great game at both ends of the ice. Special talent to be able to control the game like he does. On a countless number of occasions, Jones would be able to knock a player off the puck, use his body to protect it, look up and make a nice pass to get the play started. He makes the game look almost too easy. Scored a beautiful goal by intercepting a pass in the neutral zone, skate it down the middle, then deke a defender, get around him, and bury it in tight. Eluded opponents consistently with his great skating abilities. May not be the fastest player, but he does not have to be with his size. His strength is ability to change direction in a hurry and turn on a time. Hard to find a hole in his game.

POR#9 LC, De Leo, Chase(2014) Small forward who had a very effective game tonight. Made so many good things happen with the puck and kept Everett on their toes with his speed. Scored from the slot with a very impressive wrist shot. Patient with the puck and lets the play come to him before making a decision. Around the net all game long and was not afraid to take the body. Needs to get stronger on his skates to be able to take hits, and improve his overall strength level to be able to fend off bigger opponents.

POR#27 RW, Bjorkstrand, Oliver(2013) Power forward played a good aggressive game tonight. Always looked to attack the net with the puck by using his speed and puck protecting skills. Showed off some nice hands off the rush and in tight. Scored in front of the net by getting a good touch on the puck on a pass from behind the net despite having an opponent on his back. Very good at getting positioning in front of the net. Uses his head to go to a soft spot in coverage and make himself a target for passes. Needs to improve on his play in his own zone. Not always in the right spot, has a tendency to cheat and not cover the point man effectively. Looks to play much bigger than his actual size.

EVE#15 LC, Bauml, Kohl(2013) Had a very good game for Everett. Every time I watch him, I have a hard time believing that he is only 5'8 tall. Plays aggressively and attacks the net hard. Makes up for his lack of size with hockey intelligence, speed and skill. Read the play perfectly on a forecheck, picked off a cross ice D to D pass and got a great breakaway chance. Scored in tight by controlling a rebound then going backhand quickly. Made good plays with the puck and put his teammates in good areas to make plays. Most impressive aspect of his game is his grit and determination. Dove in front of shots consistently. In the first period made a huge block on a Seth Jones one timer on a PK. Willing to do anything to give his team a chance to win.

EVE#25 LD, Mueller, Mirco(2013) Smooth skating defenseman who moved the puck quite well tonight. Made smart decisions and did not try to take any gambles and risk a turnover. Very interesting combination of size, skating and offensive abilities. Just has to make some strides physically. Got pushed around far too often this game considering that he is 6'4. Did not look bad in his own end. Stayed in position and read the play well. Really liked the poise he played with at both ends of the ice.

EVE#30 G, Lotz, Austin(2013) Had an excellent game today. Stats do not tell the story at all. Portland scored beautiful goals that he did not have a chance on any of them. Very good at controlling rebounds and keeping them in front of him. Looked through traffic extremely well. Very quick laterally and recovers from his knees back to his feet in a hurry. Loved the way he competes in the crease for loose pucks. Mentally looks strong. Would come back after giving up goals to make saves look routine consistently. One flaw in his game is his puckhandling. Not very good at passing the puck.

Scouts Notes: Portland looked very good in this game. They peppered Austin Lotz with shots throughout the game, and could only beat him when plays worked out perfectly. Seth Jones controlled the play consistently. He made Ryan Murray look average at best. Has offensive abilities that Murray will probably never develop. Came away impressed with Kohl Bauml again. Does not matter that he is 5'8, the kid can flat out play. Does not get enough credit for arguably being Everett's best forward.

FINAL SCORE: 5-2 Portland

November 2, 2012, Val d'Or Foreurs @ Victoriaville Tigres (QMJHL)

VDO #2 LD Murphy, Matt (2013) - Murphy commits very early in one on one situations which turned up some mixed results as he got burned pretty bad a few times. One of these directly cost his team a goal. He won some battles but his reaction time and positioning were inconsistent at best. He worked effectively but lack of positioning hurt him at times. Adequate puck moving abilities in the offensive zone and made some good decisions from there. He scored on a shot from the point. It wasn't a very powerful shot but it made it through a lot of traffic.

VDO #8 RW Mantha, Anthony (2013) - Did a lot of floating around when his team didn't have the puck and when they did he was quick to jump up ice. Anthony was a bit of a liability on the penalty kill focusing more on trying to get a chance to score than actually killing the penalty. He used his size effectively delivering several solid checks along the boards throughout this game. Great positionally on the power play. Mantha shows excellent passing ability and consistently made difficult passes look easy. Has a good shot, not great but likes to shoot far more than pass. Could be a very, very dangerous offensive threat if he even realizes what a good playmaker he is and is able to choose the right times to shoot and pass.

VDO #26 LC Dunn, Vincent (2013) - Played with a lot of determination, contributing at both ends of the ice. Not afraid of a little physicality. Dunn kept getting better and better as the game went on. He scored a nice goal in the third period picking up a loose puck, made a little move and scored to give Val d'Or a temporary lead in the third period. He made a great pass with only two minutes left to once again break the deadlock this time setting up the game winning goal.

VIC #3 LD Diaby, Jonathan (2013) - Diaby was very solid defensively making smart plays both with his stick and with his body in one on one situations. He really picked up his physical play as the game went on asserting himself. He eventually engaged in a fight in this game. He appeared uninterested in the fight in a very close game in the third period as he was playing huge minutes for the Tigres, but he eventually dropped the gloves and faired well in the tilt.

VIC #12 LC Rehak, Dominik (2013) - Moved the puck fairly well and had several moments where he created some scoring chances, however they were unsuccessful. Competed hard in the corners and showed off some very good hands.

VIC #34 LD Beaulieu, Anthony (2013) - Made a few very good passes up ice under pressure. He made a really good play in the third period pinching from the point and set up what was the tying goal at the time. He really struggled in the skating department but minimized it's effect by regularly maintaining safe positioning.

VIC #57 RW Veilleux, Tommy (2013) - Tommy is a good skater who had a few flashes offensively. He protects the puck well, but thrives in the role of the antagonist. He consistently got under the skin of the Val d'Or players and got them focused on him. Dropped the gloves at one point and faired well.

Scouts Notes: Val d'Or and Victoriaville played an excellent game tonight. A lot of energy and physicality throughout this match-up and a lot of back and forth on the scoreboard. It appeared to be going to overtime, however Anton Zlobin (Pittsburgh) scored on a pass from Vincent Dunn (2013) to put the game away with only two minutes remaining.

November 2nd 2012, Val-D'Or Foreurs vs. Victoriaville Tigres (QMJHL)

VDO #2 D Murphy, Matt (2013) – Despite finishing the game +5 with a goal and an assist, Murphy had a lot of ups and downs in this game. He played a really aggressive style while defending that caused him trouble more than once. He tried to jump on loose pucks quiet often, losing those races by a couple seconds on a few occasions. He was able to do damage control most of the time and won his fair share of puck battles, but he needs to asset the situation better before taking a decision. A breakaway lead by Dominik Rehak from Victoriaville ensued after he tried to pinch in the neutral zone and he was driven hard and didn't look good on Victoriaville's fourth goal by Jean-François Leblanc. I also thought he was laid back a little around his net and he had a late jump when following or engaging an opposing player. Overall I would say his speed and awareness were more present in the previous viewings I had from him. I thought Murphy did a good job using his shot though, firing a good one from the blue line to score the first goal of the game. He had little space and time but still managed to release a quick and accurate slap shot. He also made a couple of smart and simple plays with the puck that were effective to help his team move the puck forward. He didn't do anything out of the extraordinary with the puck, but he has shown he can be effective with it.

VDO #8 RW Mantha, Anthony (2013) – Mantha showed some flashes of what he can do with the puck early in the game. He had his moments with it and brought a little bit of heat to the Tigres' goalie. He moves around pretty well for a player of his size and his hands are excellent. I thought he cheated a lot in the neutral zone early in the game, waiting for pucks to come out of his territory instead of working to get them out. One thing I particularly liked was his physical play, which was absent in the previous viewing I had from him. He delivered some very hard hits tonight. I would also like to see him in movement a lot more, instead of floating and picking his moments to accelerate. In my mind, that would make him much more efficient and would give him much more occasion to come down the wing to exploit his ability to shoot and even distribute the puck. He surprised me at one point in the third period when he made a great pass to a teammate while leading the rush. Mantha also showed in this game he loves to shoot the puck. He has a heavy shot and used it a lot, but he also missed quite often. I would say Mantha played an honest game because of the tools he showed, but I would like to see him play a more complete game, using those tools a lot more. I believe he lacks "puck-possession skills", meaning he doesn't have much impact on the game in the defensive and neutral zone. He is still very dangerous in the offensive zone and with the tools he has, his game could mature into a more complete one.

VDO #26 C Dunn, Vincent (2013) – Dunn displayed his usual style of play, skating hard and working hard on the ice. He surprised me with his speed on straight lines and he was able to work both ways of the ice. What caught my eye was his game with the puck in this game, something he didn't always show the previous times I saw him. He wasn't a game breaker by any mean, but he was comfortable with the puck and made some very good plays. One moment in particular where he made a beautiful pass from behind the net to Anton Zlobin who cashed in on it to give Val-D'Or the lead late in the third period.

VIC #3 D Diaby, Jonathan (2013) – Diaby was finally able to bring that consistency I was talking about in my previous reports. He was a stud on the blue line from first to last minute and made a great job keeping the danger at distance. He was extremely calm when engaging opponents and did a good job as usual using his stick and body to stop them. His gap control was excellent and he didn't overdo things, which is something he has a tendency to do. His speed and footing looked good tonight and he was able to follow the play fairly well. The big defenseman even showcased his skills with the puck, firing a good shot from far distance that resulted in his first goal of the season. He also did a good job applying pressure behind his net and crushing opponents with his body. Late in the game he started being a little too aggressive around his net, leading to a few mistakes. Those were the only setbacks for him in this game in my opinion. He also got in a fight if you could say late in the game. Cedrick Henley from Val-D'Or left him no choice but to drop the gloves even though he clearly wasn't interested in fighting, in what looked like a disguised attempt to take him out of the game for a while.

VIC #12 C/W Rehak, Dominik (2013) – Rehak played on the fourth line in this game and saw very little action. He didn't capitalize on his playing time; therefore I had very few occasions to watch his game. He had one strong moment with a breakaway on Matt Murphy but he wasn't able to score. The slide continues for him, as it's been a long time since he played a good one.

VIC#34 D Beaulieu, Anthony (2013) – Beaulieu tried his best and worked as he always does but I would say he had a hard time. It seems that he is always on the edge of making a mistake. His size and reach served him well as usual and he made a few good things, but the mobility question inevitably came up at some point during the game. You could also see he is clearly not comfortable playing with the puck. He is happy to get rid of it as quick as he can. I believe it's a good project to work with for Victoriaville, but as far as the NHL draft is concerned, he is just not there in his progression.

November 3, 2012, Halifax Mooseheads vs. Drummondville Voltigeurs (QMJHL)

HAL #22 C Mackinnon, Nathan (2013) – Mackinnon got to showcase his speed in pretty much all situations tonight. His burst is sensational when coming down the wing and he did a good job using it. He can come out of corners just as quick and he seems to be one step ahead of the defender the whole time. I thought he also does a good mixing up his body along with his speed, making it even harder to stop him with the strength he has in his legs. One thing I particularly liked compared to other viewings I had from him earlier this year was his intensity. He gave some good checks and he was involved in all phases of the game. He used his great explosion to back check and make some plays in the neutral zone. His hands are also something to watch for: he likes to use them and they're extremely quick!

HAL #27 LW Drouin, Jonathan (2013) – What a pair of hands he has! Whenever he touches the puck, you know something is going to happen. He showed very good speed tonight with his feet in movement at all time and that makes for a deadly combination with his hands. He loves to dangle and can make his way through traffic with this attribute alone. He is extremely creative and I thought he did a good job using his line mates instead of limiting it to him. He has to be careful though and try not to do too much with his skills. I also really liked his work ethic in this game. He didn't mind using his body to drive or to work along the boards. He wasn't a physical force of course, but just the fact that he tried every time means a lot. He also didn't back down from the aggressions he took. He didn't mind responding and letting people know he wouldn't accept it. I think his play is just getting better every time I see him. He has outstanding puck skills to go along with good vision and excellent skating. Plus he shows good work ethic and that he is willing to take on the physical challenge. One particular play that was impressive in this game is when he received a long stretch pass from behind that I thought would end up to nothing. He was in full stride and he was able to get the pass from behind straight on to his stick and he fired a rocket from the wing for the goal.

HAL #31 G Fucale, Zachary (2013) – Fucale didn't see a lot of action in this game and the danger came by sequences. He looked a little bit slow to react on Drummondville's first goal. He then made some good saves with good technique and good positioning in front of his net. On other occasions he looked a little bit sluggish in front of the net. He used to show me more consistency within a game in my previous viewings. Overall it wasn't a bad start but he can do even better than that.

DRU #15 D Brouillard, Nikolas (2013) – Brouillard made some good and some bad plays in this game. He joined the rush A LOT, acting as a fourth forward most of the time. He showed off his great hands on numerous occasions while moving the puck. At one point he went very quickly to his back hand to get a good scoring chance but missed. He still needs to polish his game in his zone, especially being so undersized. He is exposed a lot when comes the time to fight for the puck behind the net and when he has to clear the front of the net.

DRU #39 G Guindon, Louis-Philip (2013) – This is the player who saved the day for Drummondville, preventing the score from growing bigger than 5-1. He managed to make some spectacular saves with sharp and quick reflexes. He had a lot of traffic in front of him the whole night and he kept finding a way to make saves. I thought he looked good in front of the crease and I'm looking forward to see more of him.

November 3, 2012, Halifax Mooseheads @ Drummondville (QMJHL)

HFX #22 RC MacKinnon, Nathan (2013) - MacKinnon showed off his tremendous hands beating multiple guys early on. He has very quick reaction time to the play around him and seems to see the game at a superior level as he can figure out where he should go or what he should do almost instantaneously. He forced a fair amount of turnovers with his forecheck and played in all game situations. He worked very hard to get back defensively and contributing in his own zone. Nathan made an outstanding pass to set up the eventual winning goal midway through the second period. He took a beating after the whistle and didn't really let it affect him. He was quite the antagonist hooking opponents sticks under his arm, not selling the hook but he would do things to try to tempt them to commit legitimate penalties.

HFX #27 LW Drouin, Jonathan (2013) - Drouin showed excellent hands and kept forcing a great deal of turnovers particularly in the offensive zone. He has outstanding playmaking ability and vision. He combines this with a quick and powerful shot and the knowledge when to use his passing and when to use his shooting. Drouin got pushed around a little but he eventually pushed back, standing up for himself and responding physically. Drouin scored an outstanding goal late in the second period. He made it 3-0 when he took a pass off the wall at full speed, didn't break stride then wired the puck top shelf. Jonathan took an awkward hit in the third period injuring his leg and didn't look the same after. In his final shifts there was a limp to his skating, however he kept getting put on the ice despite the fact his team was winning 5-1 late in the game and the pain that was very evident every time he put pressure on his one leg.

DRU #11 LW Ratelle, Joey (2014) - Joey got some power play time and showed off his skills and hands. He is a pretty smooth skater with great agility. He was willing to play a physical style of game despite not having a great deal of size.

DRU #15 LD Brouillard, Nikolas (2013) - Brouillard shows exceptional hands and has the ability to make highlight reel plays with the puck. Unfortunately this was combined with questionable decision making and hockey sense. At times Nikolas made some very nice plays, but too often he would make plays that didn't make much sense.

DRU #39 G Guindon, Louis-Philip (2013) - Guindon showed good quickness, but kept losing his positioning and used far too much unnecessary movement. This cost him the first goal of the game. He flashed an impressive glove on a few occasions making a few great saves.

Scouts Notes: We were hoping for a bit of an even matched game, but the Halifax Mooseheads dominated from start to finish. Drummondville only registered 15 shots and only 3 in the second period. Halifax showed the ability to dominate pretty much every area of the game en route to a 5-1 victory. Zachary Fucale (2013) showed good quickness but this wasn't much of a game to evaluate Fucale. He was legitimately tested maybe two or three times.

Nov. 3, 2012, Sudbury Wolves vs. Ottawa 67s (OHL)

SDB #9 LW, Desrochers, Danny (2013) Showed himself to be a real blue collar hard working type player in this game. He was going down and showing that willingness to block shots on the penalty kill and was really working hard for the puck. He is a good skater and quick and puts lots of pressure on the puck carrier. He worked hard both ways tonight and was just keeping his game simple and making the safe plays by getting the puck in deep.

SDB #14 RW, Baptiste, Nicholas (2013) A quick player and was getting to the inside lane and driving hard to the net. He was protecting the puck well and was also aggressive and showing some nice physicality. Baptiste was very aggressive on the fore-check and moved the puck to good scoring areas and showed a good willingness to block shots. He competes hard for the puck and displayed some great hockey sense, especially when he was able to keep the play alive and make some passes after he was knocked down to the ground. He put a lot of pressure on the puck carrier and forced turnovers and drove hard to the net taking the defenseman with him. There were a few no-look passes in the offensive zone that he made which resulted in turnovers and I would like to see him move the puck just a bit quicker as well in the offensive zone but overall a very good game from Baptiste.

SDB #15 LW, Kubalik, Dominik (2013) Kubalik showed some real nice hands tonight and was making moves to create space and beat defenders. He did some nice work on the fore-check by making his checks and getting out to the slot with the puck. He did a good job in the puck battles and was able to get in front of the net to make some tips as well. He showed some great vision and passing by finding the open man in the slot for a great opportunity and was also able to get himself to the slot to get some great scoring chances. In his own zone he made some hits being physical and moved the puck up well and quickly for a breakout.

SDB #21 LW, Kahun, Dominik (2013) In the first period of this game he had a good moment where he used some deception by faking a shot to create some time and space for himself and then got to the slot with the puck for a good opportunity. He had some nice puck movement by moving it quickly, and also displayed some gifted hands by making some good moves. He had some real nice passes to the slot to find an open man and moved the puck up the ice well for a breakout. There were a couple times when he would try to make too many moves by gaining the zone and just needs to get the puck in deep at least.

SDB # 94 LW, Silk, Brody (2013) I did not think this was Silk's best game, however the coach kept using him in critical situations near the end of the game when his team was looking to tie up the game. He cycled the puck well and could protect the puck and went hard to the net battling to get there. For the most part he kept to a pretty simple dump and chase game and I would like to see a bit more battle and compete to get the puck and for him to watch the neutral zone turnovers as well.

SDB # 24 D, DeHaan, Evan (2013) What I liked about his game was that he showed he could move the puck up or rush it up the ice. He got it out of the zone well and also showed some good patience with the puck and got it through on the net from the point. He had some good gap control and was keeping his man to the outside and was using his stick effectively to check the puck away. There was a moment in the 3rd period where he got caught watching the puck and got beat clean for a good opportunity and needs to make sure that he isn't letting the opposition get those chances in such good scoring areas.

OTT # 20 C, Monahan, Sean (2013) Monahan really showed tonight why he is expected to get drafted so high this year. He just simply took control of this game and was a key factor in every one of Ottawa's goals and could have had a few more points as well. He showed some real nice patience with the puck and got some great opportunities from the slot. He is a quick skater and comes down off the wing well and really showed a deadly shot as well. He picked his spot for the opener of the game and then made a great give and go play to finish off the second goal of the game too. He was used effectively on both the power play and the penalty kill and moved the puck up the ice well for a breakout. He created some good space with some moves and finishes his hits on the fore-check. He was able to cycle the puck well to come out off the boards to the slot to get some good shots off and is able to get away from the defense in the offensive zone to get himself wide open in some good scoring positions, showing some real nice hockey sense. He has some great confidence and takes command when he has the puck as he looks like he really has a purpose. On the third goal of the night he made a beautiful feed cross-ice showing some nice vision and passing abilities as well.

OTT # 28 LW, Brown, Connor (2013) A very tough kid, and showed this with a great fight in the third period. Another blue-collar type player who is physical on the fore-check and keeps to a pretty simple game. He really finishes his checks and goes to the dirty areas and drives hard to the net.

OTT # 11 D, Vlajkov, Mike (2013) Typically a defenseman but used offensively in this game. He was moving around well in the offensive zone to get open and reading the play well showing some good hockey sense. He communicates with his teammates and was back-checking working hard both ways up the ice and put some real good pressure on the puck carrier.

Scouts Notes: A really exciting high tempo game which Ottawa had control with a 3-1 lead in the last couple minutes and Sudbury came back to score 2 late goals including one in the last 30 seconds to send the game to a shootout. Sean Monahan was definitely the player of the game as he was creating opportunities every single shift and put up a few good points. He made it very difficult for Sudbury to contain him and looked much better than the last time I saw him play.

FINAL SCORE: 4-3 Ottawa

Nov 4, 2012, Rimouski Oceanic vs. Halifax Mooseheads (QMJHL)

HAL # 22, C, MacKinnon, Nathan (2013) MacKinnon has excellent hands and agility that he showed with the puck to create some room to work with in the offensive zone. He displayed some really explosive speed on the rush into the offensive zone, but was taking outside shots quite a large amount of the time rather than driving the puck to the net. He was hustling hard and had played with some good 2nd efforts for loose pucks and rebounds in front of the net. He did a nice job of getting the puck to the front of the net off the cycle to get a good chance and draw a penalty and made a really nice saucer pass to lead a man into the offensive zone. He was cutting to the middle off the wide drive for a good chance in tight and stuck up for himself after a hit along the boards but ended up taking a double minor which proved to be costly for his team. He also missed the net on some shots from the high slot and had a really bad turnover on a no-look pass behind him in overtime. In the shootout however he showed really nice hands and fakes for a great chance.

HAL # 27, LW, Drouin, Jonathan (2013) Drouin was moving the puck down low then driving towards the net on the power play to provide scoring options in tight. He was distributing the puck well on the power play, made a really nice saucer pass in the offensive zone and also made an excellent pass to find an open man down low beside the net. He got a good cycle going in deep in the offensive zone and showed his fantastic hands and agility to avoid the opposition's pressure. He has a great shiftiness to his game with the puck but in the shootout just made a pretty simple back-hand move that the goaltender handled easily.

HAL # 31, G, Fucale, Zachary (2013) This was a game of two tales for Fucale. The first two periods he played really well, was directing shots to the corner and playing at the top of his crease to make a save and hold on to avoid rebounds. He was able to read the play well to follow the puck then made an excellent save on a tough shot from the slot off a pass from behind the net. The 1st 2 goals of the game were tough to blame him, however the 3rd goal was scored short-side on a shot from the slot that he could have had but did not get across quick enough to make the save. He then gave up another goal short-side on the 4th, however it was tipped top shelf on a shot from the point. He gave up a bad goal on a shot from the point for the opposition's 5th goal of the game as well. In the shootout he showed some good patience, especially on the 1st save to make a good blocker save and followed the player well on the 3rd shootout attempt as well to stay with the deke and make the save. He was beat clean on a back-hand move on the 6th shootout attempt but for the most part was cool and calm in the shootout.

RIM # 3, D, Kostalek, Jan (2013) Kostalek made a nice pass to lead a man into the offensive zone with speed and was able to skate the puck up the ice on the rush to get it in deep into the offensive zone. He played his man with a good element of physicality, was finishing his hits on the puck carrier and was getting in lanes to pick off passes for the opposition in front of his own net. He was clearing the puck out of the zone well on the penalty kill, picked off a penalty kill clear by the opposition to rush the puck back into the offensive zone from the neutral zone, but needs to watch the neutral zone turnovers on the transition, and he also panics with the puck at times and just throws it away. He lost his man in front of the net as well trying to follow the puck behind and the opposition ended up scoring.

RIM # 11, RW, Bryukvin, Vladimir (2013) Bryukvin was putting good pressure on the puck carrier and used his stick well on the back-check to knock the puck off the opposition. He has nice hands to walk around defenders off the rush to get to the slot for good shots and made a really nice breakout pass to start the rush. He made an excellent move in the shootout to get the goalie moving left to right, but then he still managed to make the save. He has to watch the neutral zone turnovers on puck mishandles.

RIM # 15, LW, Deluca, Anthony (2013) Deluca put great pressure on the puck carrier to force turnovers in the neutral zone and made a nice pass on the rush through the neutral zone to lead a man into the offensive zone with speed. He used his stick well to knock the puck away from the opposition and was cutting towards the middle in the high slot to put a shot on, but has to get his shots through to the net. He was protecting the puck well on the wide drive then cutting to the net, and showed some pretty nice speed and quickness on the rush through the neutral zone. He has to watch neutral zone turnovers on breakout passes and was taking some bad angle shots on the power play instead of moving the puck to dangerous scoring areas instead. He also mishandled the puck and lost his shootout attempt altogether.

RIM # 24, RW, Joly, Micheal (2013) Joly was protecting the puck well on the wide drive then was cutting towards the net off the rush. He showed some nice hands and patience with the puck on a 2-on-1 chance trying to get the puck cross-crease to a teammate. He did a great job reading the play to pick off a turnover at the offensive line for a shot opportunity from the high slot, got a good cycle going in deep in the offensive zone and was getting to the net pretty well looking for loose pucks and rebounds. He was taking long outside shots off on the rush and needs to watch the neutral zone turnovers holding on to the puck too long, and also on bad breakout passes.

RIM # 64, D, Gravel, Maxime (2013) Gravel was holding the offensive line well and had a nice hard shot that he got through to the net from the point with consistency. He got his stick in a lane to deflect the opposition's shot out of play, was calm with the puck but can also move it quickly. He went down to block a shot in his own end in front of the net and was able to make a good pass to start the breakout in the neutral zone. He was skating the puck up the ice to get it in deep but had a bad turnover on a puck mishandle in the neutral zone and also shot the puck directly at the goaltender's chest in his shootout attempt.

RIM # 81, RW, Fortier, Simon (2013) Fortier protected the puck well along the wall but has to get it out of the zone on the penalty kill. He put some good pressure on the puck carrier and also pressured the point well on the penalty ill. He got a good low shot off on the rush to try to generate a rebound for a man driving hard to the net and got a good cycle going in deep, however was for the most part taking long outside shots off on the rush.

FINAL SCORE: 6-5 Rimouski Oceanique (Shootout)

November 4, 2012, Val d'Or Foreurs @ Gatineau Olympiques (QMJHL)

VDO #2 LD Murphy, Matt (2013) - Murphy looked very good rushing the puck up ice. He also moved the puck well on the power play and finds a way to get his shot through. Good size, and decent speed when he gets rolling. He generally doesn't read defensive plays quickly enough. There were turnovers galore in his own zone and he constantly threw the puck right up the middle. Because it became such a habit Gatineau used this to create scoring chances. He tried to force the play very early in one on one situations and got beat early and often.

VDO #8 RW Mantha, Anthony (2013) - Mantha showed just enough effort in this game to get by. He was used in all game situations, and looked fairly good on the penalty kill. He was effective in stealing the puck and clearing the zone. At one point flying down the wing for a great shorthanded chance. Mantha protects the puck well and shows effective skating at his size. He has a good shot and landed strong accurate passes whenever necessary.

VDO #16 RC Aube-Kubel, Nicolas (2014) - Looks bigger than his size. Nicolas absorbs contact very well and too the hits to make the play. He shows a fair amount of aggression himself and landed some very solid hits. He works hard down low despite being one of the younger players on the ice he won a lot of battles. Shows good shiftiness and hands to beat multiple defenders. Great puck protection resulted in him scoring a goal. Nicolas also scored the game winning goal very early in the third period working hard in the goal area eventually scoring the winner. He has a great work ethic.

VDO #26 LC Dunn, Vincent (2013) - Vincent dropped the gloves his very first shift of the game and beat up a Gatineau player pretty good. A good accelerator who works hard along the boards and wins battles. He shows some good skills at one point taking a really bad pass and almost instantaneously turned it into a tying goal in the first period. His work ethic created scoring chances as the game went on. He showed at several points of this game he wanted the puck more than anyone else. Struggled with the occasional turnover.

GAT #12 LD Beauregard, Mickael (2013) - Beauregard is about the furthest thing from flashy. But that is meant to be a compliment. He moved the puck fairly well making the simple smart decision. Good gap control in one on one situations and didn't get beat. He was also solid in two on one situations. He prefers to use his size but concedes to using his stick when necessary. Mickael reads the play well showing good hockey sense and delivered a few solid hits.

GAT #27 LW Poirier, Emile (2013) - Poirier is a player we haven't had the best reviews of this season, but he certainly impressed us today. He showed good positioning around the slot and it resulted in him scoring the opening goal of the game. He made some very nice plays to create chances early on in the second period but it was his good positioning and one-timer from the top of the slot that gave him what was the tying goal at the time. Less than two minutes later he took the puck while short handed, showing great puck protection and gave Gatineau a 3-2 lead after two periods. He is a smooth skater who changed directions quickly. He gets good penalty kill time and covers the point well. Despite the loss, Poirier scored all three goals for Gatineau and put together a great performance.

Scouts Notes: A very even match-up between two teams who were unusually well rested for a Sunday afternoon game. Because of this we were able to see these two teams match-up very well. Emile Poirier (2013) gave Gatineau a huge lift by scoring three goals in just over 24 minutes. Unfortunately for the Olympiques the Foreurs made some adjustments and scored two goals in the first 1:45 of the third period to take a one goal lead and added an empty net goal with no time left on the clock to take a 5-3 victory.

Nov 5, 2012, Czech Republic vs. Russia (World Junior A Challenge)

CZE # 4, D, Kokes, Martin (2013) Kokes was playing his man pretty hard and physical along the boards to take the puck and clear it out of the zone on the penalty kill. He is calm and patient with the puck and can make the good 1st pass out of the zone to start the breakout. He used his stick well to knock the puck from the opposition but has to get his shots through to the net on his chances from the point and also needs to watch some of the high risk passes up the middle in his own zone.

CZE # 10, C, Kampf, David (2013) Kampf had great speed and put really good pressure on the puck carrier. He displayed great agility to twist from the opposition's pressure then moved the puck up along the boards to start the breakout. He was distributing the puck well through the neutral zone and protected the puck nicely along the wall to get the cycle going deep in the offensive zone. He made a really good pass on the rush after gaining the offensive zone to find a trailing player in the high slot for a good opportunity.

CZE # 13, RW, Vrana, Jakub (2014) Vrana played with great speed off the wing to put a good shot on net on the rush. He was hustling hard, competing well and was able to beat the defense on the wide drive with his speed after taking a pass into the offensive zone to wrap the puck around the net and score. He made a really nice centering pass on the rush to find a man driving hard to the net and had fantastic hands and agility to walk into the slot for a good shot opportunity. He did a really nice job of finding lanes to move the puck back to the high slot in the offensive zone and had some explosive speed rushing the puck up the ice but needs to watch the turnovers forcing passes through the opposition. He played with a nice element of physicality by closing off his man along the boards to separate him from the puck.

CZE # 16, D, Pryochta, Filip (2014) Pryochta likes to jump up on the rush to join the attack and is able to make a good 1st pass out of the zone to start the rush. He is a good skater and has some nice speed to skate the puck up out of his own end. He missed his target on a couple breakout passes resulting in turnovers and has to play his man harder along the boards as the opposition spun away from him far too easily in the defensive zone.

CZE # 22, RW, Pasternack, David (2014) Pasternack is a pretty good skater who can distribute the puck well to lead his man into the offensive zone with speed to allow him to come in and score. He made a great cross-ice pass in the offensive zone to find a man far side on the rush for a great opportunity and was moving the puck well to get it out of the zone to start the breakout. He put good pressure on the point on the penalty kill and got his stick in lanes to deflect shots out of play.

CZE # 23, LW, Rob, Lubos (2013) Rob was distributing the puck well in the offensive zone on the power play, is strong on the puck and protects it well along the boards. He goes to the net looking for loose pucks and rebounds and brought that nice net-front presence on the power play. He made a great long pass to find a man at the far blue line to spring him into the offensive zone and was able to make a nice pass to find a trailing man in the high slot.

RUS # 12, LW, Leschenko, Vyacheslav (2013) Leschenko did a good job of getting to the net and battling for loose pucks and rebounds on the power play. He got the puck in deep off the rush to get the cycle started and opened up well in the high slot to take a pass then found an open man down low in front of the net for a goal in tight on the power play. He did a good job of getting his stick in lanes to block passing lanes in his own end on the penalty kill and put great pressure to force turnovers on the fore-check. He needs to watch the neutral zone turnovers on some of his breakout passes.

RUS # 17, C, Okulov, Konstantin (2013) Okulov put good pressure and physicality on the fore-check and protected the puck well along the wall to get an effective cycle going in deep. He did a good job of holding the puck in the offensive zone to keep the attack alive and was able to make a really nice cross-ice pass in the offensive zone to find a man driving hard to the net with his stick down. He has to hit the net on his shot opportunities from the high slot and needs to watch the neutral zone turnovers trying to skate through the opposition. He also has to keep his head up on the rush to avoid being rocked in open ice.

FINAL SCORE: 6-1 Russia

Nov 5, 2012, QMJHL vs. Russia (Subway Super Series Game 1)

QMJ #8 RW, Mantha, Anthony (2013) Showed some good qualities in both ends of the rink and was used effectively as a forward on the point on the power play. At one point was the last man back and did a good job defensively in his own end. He does a good job up high as the trailer and playing the high slot providing options to his teammates and also had some nice puck movement in the offensive zone on the power play. He opens up well for a pass and can get off a one-timer with space in the high slot and made a few good passes, but one especially to move the puck cross ice to the scoring area to find a man right in the slot. He got lots of shots off from up high and did pretty well with some physicality on the fore-check. He competed and battled for pucks for the most part and showed some aggression in his game, this was most evident near the end of the game when he got checked from behind and took a few swings with his stick at the back of the opponent's legs, but needs to make sure that he is keeping his emotions in check and not taking dumb penalties. Mantha also got open and drove well to the net in the third period for a great opportunity. There were a few moments where he mishandled the puck and resulted in turnovers, even in his own zone and needs to try to be stronger on the puck and more sure of what he wants to do with it.

QMJ #22 RW, MacKinnon, Nathan (2013) As this game started MacKinnon looked nervous and mishandled the puck a few times and made some questionable passes. The first real problem was when he made a drop pass while entering the offensive zone that resulted in a turnover and ended up in his own net for Russia's opener of the game. As the game went on he looked more comfortable and became a bit more of a factor and showed some nice speed and protected the puck real well. He opened up well in the offensive zone to get a good shot off and also was willing to drive down hard to the net. MacKinnon displayed some great vision and passing to find a man down low in the slot, and later in the game had an incredible give and go, and then spun around to get away from the defender and finished with a no-look pass right on the stick of Mantha for an excellent opportunity. MacKinnon battled hard for the pucks and competed both ways making sure to back-check and cover his man. He showed some willingness to make a hit on the fore-check and got himself to good high-scoring areas, battling to get to the net. He did a good job on the face-offs for the few that he took in this game and is pretty strong on his feet, also showed some pretty good hands but needs to watch the neutral zone turnovers that started to pile up as the game went on. He was also able to rush the puck up the ice well and found some lanes to skate into.

RUS #23 RW, Zykov, Valentin (2013) What I really liked about his game was that he showed no fear and was very willing to go to the dirty areas. He protected the puck well and battled for the puck and drove hard to the net, standing in front of the goalie tipping pucks and creating problems for the goaltender. He is an agile player who has some moves and can get away from a defender and did a great job driving out to the front of the net from behind. He gets out open in the slot and finds space to work with and got some good opportunities off. He is very strong on the puck, protects it so well and consistently got out to the front of the net down low with the puck. Zykov displayed some nice hands and took a great drop pass to get a shot off as the trailer and pick his spot to score in this one.

Scouts Notes: This was not a good game for Quebec as they looked really sloppy defensively and did not get much goaltending help. There were a lot of turnovers and bad mistakes made and the offensive weapons on the team such as MacKinnon did not step up to be as much of a factor as was expected of them. Russia's top snipers were fully on display and really made the most of their opportunities.

FINAL SCORE: 6-2 Russia

Nov 5, 2012, Team USA vs. Team Canada East (World Junior A Challenge)

USA # 4, D, Downing, Micheal (2013) Downing used his stick really well to knock the puck from the opposition and keep them to the outside. He played his man hard and physically along the boards and protected the puck well from the opposition's pressure, displaying great strength on the puck. He was distributing the puck well on the power play and jumped up on the rush to get in deep with the puck, but has to watch that he doesn't cross the line on his hits along the wall and take penalties. He is calm with the puck, moves it around well in the offensive zone but has to get his shots through to the net on chances from the point.

USA # 6, D, Heinrich, Blake (2013) Heinrich was moving the puck around well to break it out of the zone and start the rush. He is calm with the puck and was able to get his shot through to the net from the point for a teammate to score on the rebound. He got the puck in deep off the rush to get the cycle started but needs to get his shots through to the net with more consistency. He played his man pretty hard and physical along the boards and displayed great agility to twist from the opposition's pressure in his own end to move the puck up along the boards.

USA # 8, D, Walsh, Jared (2013) Walsh came down low in the offensive zone to provide scoring options and likes to jump up on the play to join the attack on the rush. He is a pretty good skater and was able to drive the puck wide, protecting it well to get it in deep, then after losing it he hustled hard to get back and recover. He moved the puck around well on the odd-man rush, then got the puck back in tight for a good shot opportunity next to the net. He also opened up down low next to the net on the power play in the offensive zone.

USA # 10, C, Cammarata, Taylor (2013) Cammarata displayed a great quickness and agility with the puck to twist from the opposition's pressure. He was driving to the net with his stick down looking for opportunities in tight and was distributing the puck nicely from the point on the power play. He was able to get a cycle going in deep in the offensive zone and walked out into the slot showing some nice hands on the power play to get a shot off and score. He was hustling hard for loose pucks, showing great speed and was able to use his speed to rush the puck up the ice end-to-end. He battled hard for the puck along the boards and was distributing it well on the rush through the neutral zone.

USA # 14, C, Fitzgerald, Ryan (2013) Fitzgerald battled really well for the puck right in front of the net then put a shot on to score. He was driving to the net really well to pick up a loose puck in tight to score on a rebound as well. He put some nice pressure on the fore-check and displayed great quickness and agility to his game. He got a good cycle going and went to the net looking for loose pucks and rebounds and had the agility to get away from the opposition with the puck and draw a penalty. He again went hard to the net to score on a rebound in tight and was getting involved with the opposition after whistles.

USA # 20, C, Ebbing, Thomas (2013) Ebbing put some excellent pressure on the puck carrier and battled well for the puck along the boards to force turnovers on the fore-check. He opened up well in front of the net to provide scoring options in tight and got a good cycle going deep in the offensive zone, then got to the front of the net. He hustled hard for loose pucks as well in order to draw penalties.

CAN # 19, RW, Buckles, Matt (2013) Buckles was hustling hard for loose pucks and put some nice pressure and physicality on the fore-check. He played with a good effort and work ethic and battled hard for the puck along the boards. He has to keep his head up though as he got rocked pretty hard on an open ice hit.

FINAL SCORE: 9-1 USA

Nov 6, 2012, Barrie Colts vs. Peterborough Petes (OHL)

BAR #17, C, Scott, Justin (2013) Scott demonstrated some nice physicality tonight and was pressuring the puck carrier well. He opened up for a pass well in the neutral zone and then was able to make a good wide drive while protecting the puck and put a good shot on net. He wrapped the puck around from behind the net and then drove the puck to the net. He went to the dirty areas, made hits on the fore-check and was blocking shots in his own end. He got the puck out of his own end and was making hits as well. In his own end he turned the puck over a few times by mishandling or not being strong enough on the puck and needs to get a bit stronger on his feet.

BAR #18, C, Bradford, Erik (2013) Bradford was blocking shots and had a nice net-front presence on the power play and trying to tip shots, and also showed some nice speed and drive to the net. He put the puck on net and then would drive hard to the net which is how he scored his team's first goal of the game, and also got another opportunity by getting in all alone behind the opposition's defense and showed some great strength to draw a penalty shot by driving hard to the net. He missed the penalty shot by trying to go 5-hole. Bradford was able to move the puck up the ice well for a breakout through the neutral zone and got down low next to the net to open up for a pass on the power play in the offensive zone. At one point though he tried to force the puck down low in the offensive zone, which resulted in a turnover.

BAR # 7, D, Yuil, Alex (2013) Able to hold the line and had a strong battle for the puck in his own end protecting the puck along the boards. He missed his assignment by leaving a man wide open in his own end on Peterborough's 3rd goal of the night and needs to make sure there is no one left open in those dangerous areas when he offers extra support on the man with the puck.

PET # 17, LW, Betzold, Greg (2013) He got an opportunity down low next to the net and showed some nice hands and patience with the puck to try to beat the goalie. He made some nice lead passes to teammates in the neutral zone and then drove hard to the net with speed. He protected the puck well and is an agile and shifty player and was able to move the puck under pressure. He was able to get the puck out of his zone with some good little chip plays to teammates, and made a great read on the penalty kill to intercept a pass and get a breakaway. On the breakaway he drove hard to the net to draw a penalty shot which he missed on a nice move to go forehand.

PET # 18, C, Tanus, Jonatan (2013) Some great shot blocking was shown in this game both by going down to block shot on the penalty kill and standing in the way of point shots. He pressured the puck carrier all over the ice and was physical and kept his man to the outside in his own zone. He was able to take a long pass well and reading the play to pick up on a turnover in the neutral zone. At times he looked unsure of where to be in the offensive zone, and also took some weak low-chance shots from the outside and needs to try to drive the puck down low. He also did a good job getting his stick in lanes to block passes.

PET # 8, D, Varga, Steven (2013) A good skater who showed some nice agility and shiftiness in his skating. He can move the puck up nicely for a breakout and got a nice shot on a one-timer from the point. Varga let his man get open behind him in the neutral zone for a long pass breakaway for the opposition and lost the puck in a couple battles, I would like to see him get a bit stronger on his feet.

PET # 16, D, Murphy, Trevor (2013) Murphy made a beautiful play by opening up and taking a pass on the power play and then showed great vision to spot man down low and get him the puck for the team's second goal of the night. He was jumping up and willing to join the rush as an extra attacker and displayed some nice hands and the ability to work under pressure. He also had a nice puck clear on the penalty kill and was physical, but made a low hit on Scheifele and took a penalty and needs to make sure he isn't crossing the line. His point shots were also inconsistent as he was able to get some through and on net kept down low, but then other times they were blocked and cleared out of the zone and so Murphy needs to try to be able to consistently get his shots through from the point.

FINAL SCORE: 5-3 Barrie Colts

Nov 6, 2012, Mississauga Steelheads vs. Kitchener Rangers (OHL)

MIS #15, LW, Burnside, Josh (2013) Burnside was able to read the plays tonight to pick up on some turnovers and also realized when the defenseman was giving him a bit of space and used that space to walk into the slot for a good opportunity. He had a pretty good two-way hustle going, back-checking to take care of his own end and was putting some good pressure on the puck carrier to try to rush the opposition and force a turnover. He was cycling the puck pretty well in the offensive zone and then going to the front of the net, and also made a good attempt to break through the defense and cut to the net but just lost control of the puck. Burnside was really pressuring well on the fore-check and held the line nicely to keep the puck in play in the offensive end. At one point just threw the puck up the ice to no one unnecessarily and would like to see him avoid these panic moments.

MIS #18, RW, Babintsev, Sam (2013) He didn't get a whole lot of ice time tonight but had some net-front presence on the power play and likes to sit next to the net waiting for that chance down low. Je was moving the puck around pretty well and chasing down the puck carrier and putting on some good pressure.

MIS # 20, D, Graves, Jacob (2013) A good sized defenseman who can hold the line and get his shot through on target some of the time. He is willing to block shots and made some good pinches to keep the play alive. He likes to make some nice chip plays up the boards to his teammates to move the puck up and out of the zone and showed some pretty good puck protection in his own end by pinning it against the wall and was also demonstrating a good level of physicality. He had a bad turnover behind the net in his own end and got knocked down by a big hit in a puck battle, and he also missed his assignment in his own zone to leave Sterk wide open next to the net and Kitchener eventually score on the opportunity. In this play he needs to read the open man in front of the net rather than giving unnecessary extra support along the boards. When Graves jumps up to join the attack he needs to at least hit the net on his opportunities and from the point has to make sure he is getting his shot through every time.

KIT # 19, C, Sterk, Josh (2013) Sterk had a real nice game tonight and was moving the puck around so well in the offensive zone. He was able to play both a cycle game and a finesse game effectively and was really great under pressure as well. He was good and physical on the fore-check and stepping up when given space to get a great shot from the slot. He showed some nice moves and some real nice hands and stick skills and showed the speed, determination and hustle to be the first on pucks. He got open down low next to the net and was able to create space and dangle his way through traffic under pressure. He was physical and aggressive in his own end but needs to make sure he doesn't go too far and take penalties when doing so.

KIT # 95, RW, Bailey, Justin (2013) Bailey scored a goal in this one where he was protecting the puck well along the boards and then made a great pass down low to find Sterk open next to the net. He then followed up the play and went to the slot where the puck popped out and got the rebound to score a nice goal from the slot. He put some good pressure on the puck carrier and showed some physicality and was able to hold the puck in the offensive zone. He demonstrated some great strength by protecting the puck and walking out front with ease to draw a penalty and had a nice net-front presence on the power play where he was right up in the goaltender's face. Bailey can tie up a man well to take the puck and is really strong and hard to knock off the puck once he has it.

KIT # 3, D, Genovese, Cory (2013) For the most part Genovese is pretty calm with the puck and moving it to safe areas. He is able to move the puck up the ice and keep his man to the outside, however I would like to see him attacking the puck with his stick rather than trying to reach around his opponent. He made a bad giveaway by passing the puck to no one in his own end and also missed his target on a pass for a breakout.

KIT # 55, D, Gilbert, Jared (2013) Gilbert did a great job rushing the puck up the ice to gain the zone with some end-to-end skates. He can move the puck well to create some time and space and can pass the puck up well. He keeps the puck moving nicely for a breakout and was also willing to come down low and join the attack. He had a nice shot on target kept down low from the point as well. Gilbert gave a bit too much space to the shooter on a couple of occasions and needs to jump up to challenge the shooter and take away their time and space.

FINAL SCORE: 3-2 Kitchener Rangers

Nov. 6, 2012, USNTDP U18 vs. Team Finland U18 (U18 Four Nations)

USA # 6, D, Thompson, Keaton (2013) Thompson is a big body defenseman with a great shot from the point, and was distributing the puck really well on the power play. He was jumping in on the attack showing some great hands and driving hard to the net with the puck to create a fantastic opportunity. He was also stepping up into the high slot to take a drop pass and put a great shot on net from scoring position off the rush, and used his hands on the rush to get the puck in deep into the offensive zone. He made some good passes to move the puck up to start the rush, and did a nice job holding the puck in the offensive zone.

USA # 9, LW, Louis, Anthony (2013) Louis displayed some fantastic hands on the rush beating defenders and getting in tight with space for a fantastic opportunity. He made some nice long passes to break the puck out to create a nice chance off the rush, and had a really nice drive to the net with the puck and made a nice play to move the puck out front to a teammate for the team's 2nd goal of the game. He showed his great hands and agility in tight but was trying to force the puck through the opposition at times. He made a really great centering pass to find a man streaking in towards the net for a great chance, and made some great moves to get by defenders, cut to the slot and put a great shot on to score the team's 3rd goal of the game.

USA # 19, RW, Kelleher, Tyler (2013) Kelleher has some great speed, hands and agility that were on full display this entire game. He did a great job opening up on an odd-man rush to take a pass and put a great shot on net, and had a nice net-front presence as well to bang in a rebound to open the team's scoring in this game. He was walking into the slot off the sidewall to put shots on net on the power play. He put some nice pressure on the fore-check to force a turnover and make a centering pass to an open man out front. He had some great speed and puck protection on a wide drive, and displayed some fantastic hands and patience to make a drop pass and find an open man in the slot for a great opportunity. He has to watch the turnovers trying to be too fancy, and as well the neutral zone turnovers holding on to the puck for too long.

USA # 24, RW, McCarron, Mike (2013) McCarron started this game off with an excellent pass to spring a man for a break through the neutral zone to create a great opportunity. He then took the puck off a rush and put a nice low shot on net from the outside to try to generate a rebound. Later he put a nice shot on net and the team opened the scoring on the rebound. He was protecting the puck nicely on the wide drive and cutting towards the net driving hard with his big body. He displayed some really great strength and puck protection along the wall, and was able to take a hit and hold on to the puck. He uses his strength and size extremely well to his advantage, and also made some really nice little chip plays to break the puck out of the zone to start the rush. He was also putting some good pressure on the puck carrier.

FIN # 3, D, Lintuniemi, Alex (2013) Lintuniemi is a big body defenseman who did a good job of reading the play and stepping up to pick off passes through the neutral zone. He did a really nice job rushing the puck up the ice with some great hands to gain the offensive zone and drive the puck down low. He is a pretty good skater for such a big body, is calm and patient with the puck and willing to jump up and join the attack. He is also willing to step in off the point into the high slot on the power play to put shots on net.

FIN # 5, D, Honka, Julius (2013) Honka got down in lanes to protect the net and block shots from in tight, and was also getting down to breakup plays for the opposition and keep them from the inside track. He made some nice breakout passes to start the rush on the breakout, and was stepping up to read the play and pick off passes through the neutral zone. He has a good shot that he put on target from the point, and showed some nice puck protection and agility to twist away from the opposition and avoid their pressure. He was able to make some nice moves to get the puck in deep into the offensive zone as well, but has to watch some of the high risk dangerous drop passes in his own end.

FIN # 18, D, Ainali, Aleksi (2013) Ainili had a really nice fore-check finishing his hit on the boards and forcing a turnover, then made a great pass out front to find an open man to score the team's 1st goal of the game. He is able to protect the puck really well along the wall from the opposition's pressure. He has some hands and agility to his game and some decent size, and was stepping in on the power play to put some good shots on net.

FIN # 28, RW, Ojamaki, Niko (2013) Ojamaki made some really nice moves to get by a defender to get in towards the net for a good shot, but still could have drive the puck more towards the net for a better chance from in tight rather than the longer shot that he took. He found some space in the slot to open up and take a pass to put a one-timer on net to open the scoring of the game. He has some speed that can really get going at times, but has to watch some of the long shots that he takes off the rush.

FINAL SCORE: 3-1 USNTDP U18

November 6, 2012, Team Sweden vs. Team Switzerland (U18 Four Nations)

SWE #4 LD Hagg, Robert (2013) - Struggled early but picked his game up as the game went on. Turned over puck over a few times being too fancy and panicking under pressure. His puck play was hit or miss as the game went on. Strong point shot. Stuck with his man well in corners. Has tools but lacked the mindset. Showed some ability to rush the puck end to end.

SWE #6 LD Cederholm, Anton (2013) - Laid some very good hits along the boards. Showed a good stick one on one and handled these situations well. Showed some passing ability launching some accurate long distance passes.

SWE #9 LD Westlund, Wilhelm (2013) - Has a solid point shot which he seemed to always be able to get through the traffic. He was able to do this in overtime and his teammate (Leon Bristedt) deflected it in for the game winning overtime goal.

SWE #13 RC Liljendahl, Tobias (2013) - Showed great hockey sense making smart plays all game long. He didn't try to force plays choosing the smart safe option. Good hands for a big guy and uses his size well to protect the puck and delivers hits.

SWE #20 RW Bristedt, Leon (2013) - Despite his size, Bristedt was excellent in today's game. He shows great patience with the puck. He is very elusive and a smooth skater. Works hard along the boards and isn't afraid to go hard to the net and has good hands. In overtime Bristedt delivered a massive hit deep in Switzerland territory forcing a turnover, then went right to the front of the net just in time to deflect the point shot in to win the game in overtime for Sweden.

SWE #21 LW Nylander Altelius, William (2014) - Very good skating ability and showed good elusiveness on multiple occasions. He has quick hands, a very powerful shot and a lot of skill. Sometimes he tries to do too much with the puck.

SWE #27 RD Hansson, Niklas (2013) - Hansson looked impressive on a 5 on 3 penalty kill using both his size and stick very well. Has a decent shot and was able to get it on net. Really struggled at times with his puck playing ability.

SWE #28 RW Karlsson, Anton (2014) - Cleaned up rebound out front of the net to score the big tying goal to send the game to overtime. Has good size and really likes to hit. He seemed to struggle a little with skating although it was still average.

SUI #14 LD Baltisberger, Phil (2014) - Very intelligently moves the puck up ice. Uses his size very well when battling for positioning. Very effective in his own zone sticking with his man and playing a reliable defensive game.

SUI #17 RW Fiala, Kevin (2014) - Fiala has excellent hands. He shows great patience to go with these hands to score what was at the time the tying goal. Could be a player to watch as the tournament progresses.

SUI #22 LC Wieser, Tim (2013) - Good skater with an excellent shot. He was very easy to knock around. He seemed scared of his own shadow most of the time. Bare minimum contact put him down and he appeared to dive a couple times as well.

SUI #27 LD Busser, Xeno (2013) - Showed very good passing ability. Was able to complete the long distance passes as well as cross ice passes. One of which allowed him to set up a go ahead goal in the third period.

Scouts Notes: A very back and forth game to open the Under-18 Four Nations Cup. Sweden appeared surprised at times by the play of Switzerland. The game went very back and forth in momentum and score. Eventually Sweden came through in Overtime taking a 5-4 victory. In addition to the player reports Sweden's Victor Crus Rydberg (2013) showed impressive strength along the boards. He has great vision and made things happen with his passing ability. On the other end of the ice Switzerland's Marc Aeschlimann (2013) made several great defensive plays in his own zone showing that he was without question Switzerland's best defensive forward.

November 6, 2012, Team Finland vs. Team USA (U18 Four Nations)

FIN #5 RD Honka, Julius (2014) - Very composed with the puck even under pressure. A good skater who is shifty and always chooses the right options on the rush. Very high level of hockey sense and reads the game quickly. He is likely smaller than listed at 5'10" and his size is really the only thing keeping him out of the first round of the 2014 NHL Entry Draft.

FIN #7 RD Makinen, Atte (2013) - Big physical defenseman punished USA players all game long. He plays very tough on opponents. Finishes his checks whenever possible. Very effective for Finland in one on one situations.

FIN #11 RC Ojantakanen, Kasperi (2013) - Cycles the puck vey effectively. Won battles and finished checks hard. Plays a very North American style of game. He also shows flashes of speed and skill. Definitely a player to watch as the tournament moves on.

FIN #24 RW Kapanen, Kasper (2014) - Good skater who was willing to hit. Puck movement hit or miss and he made some solid passes. Unfortunately he also struggled with some bad turnovers in this game as well.

USA #4 LD Butcher, Will (2013) - Reminded us how not afraid he is to pinch in from the point on a very liberal basis. He made some good plays in the offensive zone. Will also possesses a dangerous shot from the point and usually gets it on net. He will take a space given and turn it into an end to end rush.

USA #9 LW Louis, Anthony (2013) - Shows great patience with the puck. He scored a beauty goal using his speed and hands to beat defenders making it 3-1. Goes hard to the net and sets up shop whenever possible. He's pretty small and can be a little inconsistent, but he played great today.

USA #13 LC Malone, Sean (2013) - Malone has a powerful release on his shot. He takes up strong positioning in the slot area and battles there effectively. Showed a good ability to deflect pucks regardless of the defensive coverage that was being applied to him.

USA #15 RW Hayden, John (2013) - Protects the puck well using his huge frame to hold off defenders. He used this ability to create a few scoring chances for himself. Played physical and also crashed the net on a regular basis.

USA #16 RD Santini, Steven (2013) - Santini showed both his physical and his puck moving skills in this game. Put together a very level performance where he didn't make a big difference one way or the other.

USA #22 RW Fasching, Hudson (2013) - Fasching used his size well to intimidate opposing players and kept forcing turnovers. Took a very lazy penalty in the third period.

USA #25 LW Hurley, Connor (2013) - Hurley regularly goes exactly where he's supposed to be on the ice. He is a very strong skater who works relentlessly hard. He lost his positioning a few times, but it was more based on a defensive first mentality rather than an unawareness.

USA #28 LC Eiserman, Shane (2014) - Eiserman showed tremendous and relentless physicality all game long. He works hard and likes to assert himself regularly. Crashes the net hard whenever he can on the rush. He was pretty reliable defensively as well.

Scouts Notes:

Team USA dominated from start to finish wrapping up day one of the Under-18 Four Nations Cup with a 3-victory. However thanks to a fantastic performance by the diminutive yet lightning quick Juuse Saros (2013). USA outshot Finland by more than a two to one ratio. Saros was the story in net but Thatcher Demko (2014) stepped up for Team USA when the team needed him. USA's Michael McCarron (2013) showed a tenacious fore check all game long and contributed well on the penalty kill.

Nov 7, 2012, Russia vs. QMJHL (Subway Super Series Game 2)

RUS #15, LW, Nichushkin, Valeri (2013) Some great speed displayed and a good hustle for pucks. He has some great hands and was moving the puck around well and making some great hits on the fore-check. He showed some great strength and puck protection and got out to the slot from behind the net. He was able to take a hit well and continue to drive down low. Nichushkin was also pressuring the puck carrier, finishing his hits and battling hard for the puck on the fore-check.

RUS # 23, RW, Zykov, Valentin (2013) Zykov was showing some physicality in his own end and putting some good pressure on the puck carrier tonight. He was competing for the puck, able to get it out of his own end and dumping the puck keeping to a pretty simple game. He protects the puck well and takes some long passes nicely for breakouts. He had at least one good opportunity from the high slot and missed the net and needs to make sure that he can hit the net from these areas.

QMJ # 2, D, Murphy, Matt (2013) A pretty big body who was calm and moving the puck up the ice well for a breakout. He has to watch the turnovers and try to keep the opposition to the outside as he let his man walk out too easily to the slot.

QMJ # 8, LW, Mantha, Anthony (2013) Mantha was passing the puck really effectively tonight and getting himself to the front of the net. He did a good job going to the net with his stick down and got to the front of the net on the power play. He made a great pass attempt to find a man in the slot on a back hand pass and made a nice pass to find a man down low. He was opening up well for a pass to be able to get a one-timer off on the power play and then made a great cross-ice feed to spot a passing lane and get the puck to a good scoring area. Mantha has some nice hands and made some good moves to create some time and space for him self. There were a couple turnovers in the offensive zone by trying to make some passes and needs to just make sure he is keeping these to a minimum.

QMJ # 22, C, MacKinnon, Nathan (2013) Mackinnon had a much better performance in this game and was getting the puck to some really great scoring areas. He had a good hustle for pucks and did a good job gaining the zone and then getting into a good scoring position. He has some nice quick hands and clear stick skills and was able to walk out front and throw the puck out front to some dangerous areas. He made a great feed on a 2-on-0 with Huberdeau in the second period for a goal, but going the other way was very effective as he had a real nice back-check and compete to get the puck and showed some physicality as well but needs to make sure the doesn't cross the line by taking penalties as he got a checking from behind penalty in the second. MacKinnon also showed some real nice vision and passing to spot a trailing man and find the lane to get him the puck. He also made a great pass to find Huberdeau down low cross-ice on the power play for a goal late in the second period. MacKinnon was driving well to the net to offer an option and take a defenseman with him. He did a great job in the slot battling for the puck to score a goal on the power play in the third period. He showed some great hands and nice moves and is clearly very strong on his feet as he made a great power forward move to cut to the middle from the outside after beating his man. Mackinnon did a great job on the face-offs tonight and was pushing the puck in front of him to create some great speed on the rush. At times he was tying too much to force the play and gain the zone with some moves and needs to just get the puck deep when he is out of options.

QMJ # 28, C, Carrier, William (2013) Carrier did a nice job moving the puck up for a breakout and was protecting the puck well. He got a good cycle going and was physical on the fore-check. He showed a willingness to block shots and is strong on his feet and able to keep the puck in the zone knocking it off his opponents.

FINAL SCORE: 5-2 QMJHL

Nov. 7, 2012, Team Sweden vs. Team Finland U18 (U18 Four Nations)

SWE # 4, D, Hagg, Robert (2013) Hagg has a nice big booming shot from the point that he was getting on net often in this game, and was used best as his shot was tipped for the team's 2nd goal of the game. He was distributing the puck well on the power play and was able to get his one-timer off for a good chance on net. He displayed some good physicality along the boards, and was even able to knock his man over at times to separate him from the puck. He made some pretty nice passes to move the puck up and start the breakout off the rush, and was stepping up on the rush to lead the attack and put a good shot on net.

SWE # 6, D, Cedarholme, Anton (2013) Cedarholme is a nice big body defenseman who is calm with the puck and has a good hard shot from the point. He was cycling the puck well to keep the attack alive in the offensive zone, and made some nice passes up the boards to start the breakout. He did a really good job stepping up on his man to close him off along the boards and take the puck to rush it back up the other way. He was also putting a nice low shot on target off the rush on a long shot, and did a nice job holding the puck in the offensive zone. He has some really great agility and puck protection to avoid the opposition's pressure and then move the puck up along the boards to start the rush.

SWE # 17, C, Gunnarsson, Fabian (2013) Gunnarsson has some nice hands and moves to beat a defender for a great chance in tight. He was able to take a pass with speed through the neutral zone to get to the slot for a shot but missed the net on the opportunity. He also has to watch some of the turnovers trying to dangle his way into the offensive zone.

FIN # 5, D, Honka, Julius (2013) Honka was distributing the puck very well on the power play to set up some good one-timer shots, and made some nice long passes to find a man at the far blue line to spring a man for a break. He was able to skate the puck up the ice to gain the offensive zone to put a shot on net, and also had some nice shots from the point but has to get them through to the net with more consistency. He also had a bad turnover in his own end to give up a chance and then took a penalty right after to take away their chance on the play.

FIN # 13, C, Antonen, Joose (2013) Antonen had a really nice wide drive with the puck to gain the offensive zone, displaying some pretty decent speed as well. He made a great pass to set-up a one-timer on the power play for the opening goal of the game, then made almost an identical pass later on to set-up a one-timer again for the 2nd goal of the game as well on the power play. He was stepping into the high slot on the power play to put shots on net, and was protecting the puck well to get it in deep into the offensive zone. He also did a good job on the fore-check winning the puck battle to keep the attack alive.

FIN # 24, LW, Kapanen, Kasperi (2014) Kapanen displayed some great hands early on to draw a penalty, and made a great pass to set-up a one-timer chance on the power play. He has some really nice agility with the puck, but has to watch the turnovers trying to dangle with the puck in his own end. He has to be a bit stronger on the puck along the boards as well. He put some good pressure on the fore-check and was getting back to his own end to provide some good support in his own zone.

FIN # 28, RW, Westermarck, Felix (2013) Westermarck protects the puck really well on the drive to the net with the puck to create a good chance from in tight. He is able to rush the puck up the ice, but has to get the puck in deep rather than holding on to the puck for too long and turning it over in the neutral zone. He was battling hard along the boards to try to hold the puck in the offensive zone as well.

FINAL SCORE: 3-2 Team Sweden

Nov. 7, 2012, Team Switzerland vs. USNTDP U18 (U18 Four Nations)

SWT # 10, LW, Pfranger, Ramon (2013) Pfranger was rushing the puck up the ice well, but needs to keep his head up so that he is not knocked over through center ice. He did a nice job on the back-check, closing his man off along the boards with some pretty good physicality. He had a great battle for the puck in tight in front of the net, and picked up the puck right in the slot to put a nice shot on net to score the team's 2nd goal of the game. He was protecting the puck well on the wide drive to gain the offensive zone.

SWT # 17, C, Fiala, Kevin (2013) Fiala was great in the puck battles in his own end, then moving the puck well on a good pass to start the breakout. He did a really great job all night getting the puck up out of his own end along the boards. He has some great moves and hands to weave his way in and out of the opposition, and some fantastic hands and moves, but at times tries to do too much on his own resulting in turnovers through the neutral zone. He has some really nice agility to distance himself from the opposition, and fantastic moves to get some space and in behind the opposition's defense for a good chance from in tight. He was distributing the puck pretty well in the offensive zone on the power play, but was also trying to force pucks through the opposition at times. He provided some good support coming back in his own end to take the puck away from the opposition.

SWT # 21, C, Fuchs, Jason (2013) Fuchs did a good job gaining the offensive zone on the wide drive to get the cycle going. He also just threw a puck towards the net for a shot that was deflected in for the team's 1st goal of the game.

USA # 4, D, Butcher, Will (2013) Butcher is such a great smooth skating defenseman, with the ability to rush the puck up the ice with ease. He displayed some great agility to twist away from the opposition's pressure, and was reading the play to see an opportunity to step in to the low slot to take a pass and put a shot on from in tight to generate an excellent chance. He has some great hands to get around defenders off the rush and displayed some fantastic puck distribution on the odd-man rush to get the puck to scoring areas. He was also able to get his shots through from the point.

USA # 10, RW, Allen, Evan (2013) Allen had a nice net-front presence to take a rebound and bat the puck in for the team's 1st goal of the game, and showed some good hands and agility to twist away from the opposition. He had a good wide drive, protecting the puck well along the boards, and was able to walk out from behind the net into the slot to put a good shot on net. He did a great job of moving the puck down low then driving to the net with his stick down to take a pass and put a great shot on net, and was able to find some good lanes to move the puck across in the offensive zone on the power play to create some excellent chances. He has to watch some of the turnovers trying to force the puck through the opposition, and also lost a handle of the puck right in scoring position in overtime.

USA # 14, LW, Motte, Tyler (2013) Motte displayed some fantastic hands to beat a defender clean and get a nice break for a good chance from in tight. He made some good breakout passes to start the rush through the neutral zone, and was getting the puck to the net well. He was driving well to the net with his stick down looking for opportunities, and used his excellent speed and moves to get in to the offensive zone with some space to get a good shot on net. He has great agility and puck protection, but at times was trying to force the puck through the opposition resulting in turnovers.

USA # 15, RW, Hayden, John (2013) Hayden started this game with some great hands and moves to split the defense and get a lane to drive the puck to the net. He was battling for pucks really well in tight in front of the net, and displayed some great puck protection and agility along the wall in the offensive zone. He was getting the puck to the net, and had a really nice net-front presence battling for territory in tight. He was driving well down the middle towards the net with his stick down, and had a great wrap-around attempt to drive the puck to the net, with a nice cycle in deep in the offensive zone. He has to watch some of the turnovers along the wall trying to move the puck out of his own end.

USA # 22, C, Fasching, Hudson (2013) Fasching did a great job reading the play to pick off a neutral zone turnover, and was coming back really well on the back-check. He did a great job getting in tight to the net and opening up to take a pass for some good chances. He did a nice job of holding on to the puck in the offensive zone, and was moving the puck down low then driving to the net with his stick down. He was battling on the back-check to take the puck and then rush it back up the ice. He got to the slot and opened up well for one-timers, but lost control of the puck a few times in good position in the offensive zone. He also missed the net on some good chances, and needs to pick up the tempo of his play a bit to be more effective.

FINAL SCORE: 5-4 Team Switzerland

November 7, 2012, Team Sweden vs. Team Finland (U18 Four Nations)

SWE #4 LD Hagg, Robert (2013) - Made smart simple plays with the puck in his own zone. But he showed when he's given space he can rush the puck and knows when to pass it off. Doesn't seem to hit unless he feels he absolutely needs to. However on one play he made a textbook stop eliminating time and space from the opponent in a one on one situation then crushed the opposing forward into the boards. He had his misses one on one due to impatience rushing the situation, making the first move allowing the forward to beat him. He got beat with this late in the game with a one goal lead however a big save was made. Hagg showed off some excellent long distance passes in this game and was very accurate. Possesses a very hard and usually pretty accurate point shot.

SWE #9 LD Westlund, Wilhelm (2013) - Rushed the puck effectively and protected it well with his good sized frame at one point drawing a penalty with it. Showed good patience and intelligence with the puck. Makes a lot of smart simple decisions with and without the puck in his own zone. Showed good determination at the offensive blueline falling but maintaining focus and made smart plays with the puck.

SWE #11 LW Henriksson, Alexander (2013) - Henriksson was a consistent threat in the offensive zone. He has a laser of a shot and protects the puck well using his strong frame. He used a strong forecheck to force turnovers on a fairly regular basis.

SWE #13 RC Liljendahl, Tobias (2013) - Slow acceleration but builds up to good speed, especially for his size. Good end to end rush while short handed, beating multiple defenders in the process. Very effective on the penalty kill on a consistent basis.

SWE #15 RC Crus Rydberg, Victor (2013) - Played with a ton of energy in all three zones. Played very well in all game situations. On the penalty kill he forced a lot of turnovers and created headaches for Finland when trying to set up. On the power play he always seemed to have ideal positioning. Quick decisions with the puck and was willing to take a hit to make the play. Great work in the final minute of the game to keep Finland pinned in their own zone leading by a goal.

SWE #20 RW Bristedt, Leon (2013) - Leon is extremely shifty in open ice and is near impossible to contain once he gets going. What made him even more dangerous is the rate in which he forced turnovers in open ice. He plays with a never quit attitude and works extremely hard. Showed good passing in all three zones. He is very dangerous in the slot due to both his quick release and his great ability to deflect pucks. Great work in the final minute of the game to keep Finland pinned in their own zone while leading by one goal.

SWE #21 LW Nylander Altelius, William (2014) - Nylander has a very high level of puck skills and is very tough to contain. He made some excellent passes on the rush. However he also had his moments where he made some plays that really didn't make much sense, and resulted in turnovers.

SWE #27 RD Hansson, Niklas (2013) - Hansson showed good body positioning to contain forwards in his own zone. He was effective clearing his own zone on the penalty kill. He had good accuracy making solid long distance passes. Niklas moves pretty good while holding down the offensive line moving around and opening himself up for passing lanes.

SWE #28 RW Karlsson, Anton (2014) - Karlsson showed great work ethic and battles hard for loose pucks. He was always visible on the power play shooting the puck, protecting it or making the smart pass. His hockey sense is at a very high level at a young age. He's a good skater who has a great forecheck on the penalty kill forcing Finland to make mistakes. Anton made a great move in a one on one situation then fired a bullet to score the game winning goal with 2:29 left in the third period. The very next shift he came out and did a great job in the final minute in the offensive zone keeping Finland pinned not allowing them to create any offense.

FIN #5 RD Honka, Julius (2014) - Honka impressed us yet again with his outstanding hands and puck control skills. Honka is extremely intelligent and has a very high level of hockey sense. Size remains the only real concern for this talented defenseman.

FIN #7 RD Makinen, Atte (2013) - Makinen improved on his physical play shown yesterday. While he wasn't quite as physical today he was very tough along the boards. He started to show flashes of his puck handling skills throwing multiple solid tape to tape passes while under pressure.

FIN #13 LW Antonen, Joose (2013) - Good speed with very quick acceleration which is impressive for a 6'2" forward. He rushes the puck up ice effectively. He handles the puck very well in traffic. He had a few moments where he struggled with his decision making.

FIN #31 G Saros, Juuse (2013) - Saros has exceptional quickness and he is very technically sound. He gets his pads down then gets back up remarkably quick. Good vision through traffic and he has lightning quick recovery. He is pretty good with the puck. He doesn't rush decisions and makes the intelligent play with it.

Scouts Notes: Another very close game for Sweden and another great performance by Jusse Saros (2013) made for a great game today. Finland actually took the lead through forty minutes however Sweden got one early and one late in the third to pull out the victory. For Sweden Anton Blidh (2013) landed several massive hits in this game and asserted himself on a regular basis. He showed a few flashes of good playmaking ability. For Finland Saku Kinnunen (2013) was a very good puck mover but it was his cannon of a one-timer that gave Finland the temporary lead in the second period. Niko Ojamaki (2013) was very dangerous in one on one situations beating defensemen regularly.

November 8, 2012, Des Moines @ Sioux City Musketeers (USHL)

SC #4 D Mantha, Ryan (2014) - First shift he saw his teammate take a questionable hit and he immediately dropped the gloves and won the fight. However this was the end of his night as he received a game misconduct for instigating.

SC #14 D Lacroix, Cedric (2013) - Lacroix likes to put the puck on the net from the point willing to sacrifice a little speed to ensure it gets through to the net. He is an extremely smooth backward skater which allows him to match up very well one on one against oncoming forwards. He has a good stick and generally only lost a battle when he would over pursue the puck carrier.

SC #18 D Pionk, Neal (2013) - Joined Sioux City as an associated player for this game. Got beat on his first shift but made a great stick check to recover. He jumps up in the rush as quickly as he can but was able to get back into position when the puck was turned over in this situation. He shows a decent stick in his own zone and was used in all game situations. He made the smart safe play with the puck in his own zone under pressure. Jumped up on odd man rush and followed up for a great scoring chance.

SC #19 F Guentzel, Jake (2013) - Very good skater with a hard forecheck. His team was shorthanded almost the entire first 10 minutes of the game. He was tenacious forcing turnovers and was able to create a few minor scoring chances during this time as well. He showed very quick and intelligent puck movement on the powerplay. Positionally he always seems to know exactly where to go. He showed great hand/eye coordination and seemed to unload on multiple one-timers. Including ones that he didn't have time to set himself properly. One of these resulted in the 2-2 goal for Sioux City.

SC #22 F McGlynn, Connor (2013) - McGlynn didn't see much ice in the first but finished his checks regularly and showed very intelligent passing on the rush. When he didn't have passing options he usually opted to protect the puck and rush down the right wing. Uses his size well when battling for positioning. Fore checked effectively and finished checks when he did. Backcheck was hit or miss but he made some important turnovers when he did jump back.

Scouts Notes:

Des Moines opened up the game early with a 5 on 3 power play. They would score on both of them taking over a 2-0 lead. However Sioux City was able to shift the momentum late in the first period responding by scoring 6 of the next 7 goals. There were several fights in this game and some players seemed to become more consumed by fighting than the actual score of the game.

Nov 8, 2012, Russia vs. OHL (Subway Super Series Game 3)

RUS # 29, D, Koledov, Pavel (2013) Koledov showed some nice physicality and aggression in his own end and was sticking up for himself getting involved in some scrums. He was pretty calm with the puck and is a pretty quick skater but mishandled the puck a few times and twice was unable to clear the puck on the penalty kill. He was able to move the puck up and get it out of the zone and spot his option for a breakout. He kept to a pretty simple game and was able to get a shot off quickly from the point and to get it on net.

RUS # 31, D, Zadorov, Nikita (2013) This is a big strong defenseman who shows some pretty good potential but really needs to improve on his skating. He has a nice big reach, and a big body to keep the opposition to the outside. He ties is man up along the boards and has some hands to make moves and create some space to move up the ice. He can rush the puck up the ice, but is probably more effective by passing it, and also showed some nice physicality in his own end and likes to clear the front of his net.

RUS # 15, LW, Nichushkin, Valeri (2013) I found that Nichushkin played a pretty up and down game. He did a few things very well such as showing some real nice speed and he can drive to the outside and move the puck to the front of the net, and also demonstrated some great hands to get himself down low and to the net. He moved the puck pretty well and can protect the puck while taking a hit effectively. He also brought a nice net-front presence on the power play and was willing to come back to help out in his own zone, however he got beat pretty easily on the defensive end and also got checked in the neutral zone and lost control of the puck, he needs to move it quicker and make some quick decisions with the puck.

OHL # 10, C, Monahan, Sean (2013) Monahan made a great feed for OHL's only goal of the game as he pressured the puck carrier and forced a turnover and then showed some nice patience to watch what the defenseman was going to do and then made a great pass across to get it into a great scoring position for Graovac to finish the play. Monahan displayed some nice speed and was gaining the zone well and finding some good passing lanes in the offensive zone. He was strong on the fore-check going in very hard and was finishing his hits and winning puck battles. He can take a pass very well, even if it isn't a perfect pass and will get a lot of shots on net.
FINAL SCORE: 2-1 Russia

Nov 9, 2012, Switzerland vs. Team USA (World Junior A Challenge)

USA # 4, D, Downing, Micheal (2013) Downing displayed really good physicality along the boards to knock his man over and used his stick really well to keep the opposition to the outside and poke the puck loose. He held the offensive line well, distributed the puck well in the offensive zone and was able to find the open man in the high slot He read the opposition's play nicely to pick off a pass in the defensive zone and clear the puck out of his own end on the penalty kill and made sure to get in lanes to breakup plays and passes for the opposition. He got the puck through to the net on his shots from the point but has to watch the turnovers along the boards trying to move the puck out of the zone and he also got involved after whistles and ended up taking a dumb unnecessary penalty.

USA # 6, D, Heinrich, Blake (2013) Heinrich was able to make a nice long pass to spring a man into the offensive zone with speed and acquired a pass in the high slot then took a step in to score on a good shot. He did a nice job of clearing the puck from the front of the net and displayed some good physicality on the puck carrier along the boards in his own end. He was calm with the puck and was able to rush it up the ice well to back off the opposition's defense. He has a nice hard shot that he got through to the net from the point but also had a really bad turnover on a puck mishandle resulting in a turnover behind his net.

USA # 10, C, Cammarata, Taylor (2013) Cammarata made a nice pass on the rush to find an open man down low for a goal and opened up nicely next to the net to put a good shot on. He got an effective cycle going in deep and displayed some really nice quick hands to avoid the opposition's pressure then was able to get to the net for a good chance. He made an excellent pass to find a man in the high slot for a one-timer goal and then made another great pass to find a man down low driving hard to the net. He distributed the puck well from the point on the power play but needs to watch the offensive zone turnovers skating the puck through the opposition rather than chipping the puck in deep.

USA # 14, C, Fitzgerald, Ryan (2013) Fitzgerald had some great speed going in this game and was able to move the puck to get it to an open man next to the net off the rush for a great shot opportunity. He went hard to the net to take a pass in the slot for a nice chance and went to the slot and opened up well to take a pass and score on a one-timer. He was driving the net with his stick down for some good chances in tight but has to watch some of the turnovers trying to skate the puck up out of his zone.

USA # 20, C, Ebbing, Thomas (2013) Ebbing was cycling the puck well in deep in the offensive zone and showed good speed and agility with the puck, but needs to watch the offensive zone turnovers on puck mishandles trying to be fancy. He got to the front of the net and battled well for loose pucks and rebounds.

USA # 21, LW, Johnson, Luke (2013) Johnson had some really good speed and puck movement on his odd-man rush chance then got the puck back in tight for a good shot opportunity. He drove the puck wide with speed to get a good shot off the rush and was able to make a nice centering pass off the wide drive as well to find a man going hard to the net. He made a really good long pass to lead a man into the offensive zone and was cutting to the middle from the wing for some good chances in tight. He has to watch the offensive zone turnovers trying to dangle his way through the opposition.

SWI # 5, D, Frick, Lukas (2013) Frick made a really good pass to lead a man into the offensive zone with speed and got the puck in deep off the rush on some pretty simple dump-in plays. He was aggressive at times when closing the gap on his man however and got beat with ease for a good chance off the rush for the opposition. He put some great pressure on the opposition in his own end and used his stick well to force turnovers. He is able to skate the puck up the ice into the offensive zone making some nice moves and was twisting and turning from the opposition's pressure displaying nice agility to step into the high slot for a good shot opportunity. He needs to watch some of the turnovers trying to move the puck up along the boards to start the breakout.

SWI # 27, RW, Fazzini, Luca (2013) Fazzini is able to make a good long breakout pass to find a man at the far blue line to spring him into the offensive zone and went to the net looking for loose pucks and rebounds. He battled hard for a rebound in front of the net which he put off the post but at least drew a penalty on the play. He had good speed on the rush and drove hard to the net for a good chance in tight, but has to get his shots through to the net on chances from the high slot.

FINAL SCORE: 7-4 Team USA

November 9, 2012, Team Finland vs. Team Switzerland (U18 Four Nations)

FIN #5 RD Honka, Julius (2014) - Honka won several battles for the puck. He pinched in from the point and forced pressure in the offensive zone which resulted in a goal for Finland.

FIN #7 RD Makinen, Atte (2013) - He showed good puck movement up ice and rushed the fairly well using his big size to protect the puck. He fumbled the puck a little at times.

FIN #11 RC Ojantakanen, Kasperi (2013) - Kasperi picked up a loose puck and used his speed to separate from the defender then wired a perfect hard accurate wrist shot glove side to give Finland a 3-1 lead. He shows very good patience with the puck and moves it very effectively.

FIN #24 RW Kapanen, Kasper (2014) - Kapanen used his puck possession to kill off his team's penalty. He forces turnovers and always seems to be around the puck. Kapanen delivered some hard hits despite his size. Played hard, showed creative puck control and patience with the puck.

SUI #14 LD Baltisberger, Phil (2014) - Uses his body positioning very well when in a close race for the puck to win the battles. Good along the boards and is hard to beat down low. He struggled a little with his puck movement in the game today.

SUI #21 LC Fuchs, Jason (2013) - Has good speed with hands rushing the puck well up ice and beating opponents one on one. He passes the puck effectively. Fuchs battles hard in his own zone winning defensive battles.

SUI #27 LD Busser, Xeno (2013) - Busser is a strong puck mover who knows when to pass off when rushing up the ice and was very reliable on the power play. Despite being down a few goals at the time, Busser made a huge defensive play with the goaltender out of position saving a sure goal his first shift of the third period.

Scouts Notes: With Switzerland having a shot at making the Gold Medal Game with a victory and Finland already eliminated from Gold Medal contention, this was expected to be a bit of a rout. It was, but not for the favorite in this match-up. Finland scored early and often to surprise a Switzerland team that simply needed to advance to overtime to ensure a shot at the game depending on how the USA/Sweden game went. Finland took this one 5-1. For Finland Janne Puhakka (2013) was pretty quiet through most of this game but he did do a great job winning a race to the puck beat the defenseman with a nice move then beat the goaltender to make it 5-1.

November 9, 2012, Team Sweden vs. Team USA (U18 Four Nations)

SWE #4 LD Hagg, Robert (2013) - He can generate good speed and likes to use this when on the rush. He has a cannon of a point shot but sometimes tries to force it when he shouldn't. Sweden had trouble keeping the game close particularly due to some suspicious calls and the frequency in which they were made. Down 3-1 and 4-2 Hagg used a wrist shot, then a big blast to score two goals and reduce those two goal deficits to one helping Sweden have a chance in the late stages of the game.

SWE #15 RC Crus Rydberg, Victor (2013) - Very calm and composed with the puck. He shows a lot of patience not rushing plays and letting the options to come to him. He showed great energy on the penalty kill forcing turnovers.

SWE #20 RW Bristedt, Leon (2013) - Used his speed and worked hard in all game situations. He battles relentlessly on the penalty kill. He is very aggressive along the boards despite his size and does well. Bristedt is always all over the puck carrier forcing turnovers and ends up drawing penalties when his turnover turns into a scoring chance for his team.

SWE #21 LW Nylander Altelius, William (2014) - Likes to do everything fast. He is a quick skater who usually makes quick decisions. He has excellent passing ability but has his moments where he makes bad plays trying to be unnecessarily fancy for no reason which negatively affected his team. He can at times particularly on the power play forget that he's playing a team sport.

SWE #27 RD Hansson, Niklas (2013) - Good awareness of the play going on around him. He moves the puck effectively on the power play making smart decisions and battles hard when he's working in the defensive zone.

SWE #28 RW Karlsson, Anton (2014) - Anton always seems to be right in the middle of everything. It's almost as if the play follows him not the other way around. He's very physical and works hard forcing a lot of turnovers in all three zones and in all game situations. He used this turnover ability on the power play turning potential clears to scoring chances for Sweden. On the penalty kill he has good defensive zone positioning and knows what he's doing when setting up defensively.

USA #2 RD Clifton, Connor (2013) - Clifton launched a great long distance pass first shift of the game creating a scoring chance. He tried to get too fancy at one point and turned the puck over leading to a scoring chance against. Very aggressive and effective in one on one situations and takes the body whenever possible.

USA #9 LW Louis, Anthony (2013) - Very quick hands. Anthony is willing to play physical despite his size and forces turnovers with his fore check.

USA #13 LC Malone, Sean (2013) - Sean makes a lot of smart simple plays with the puck around his vision and hockey sense. He has good positioning and goes hard to the net on the rush into the slot with his stick on the ice. He jammed home the opening goal of the game in the slot. He's really not a flashy player just very smart.

USA #25 LW Hurley, Connor (2013) - Works hard and delivers crushing hits and finishes his checks whenever possible. He combines great passing ability with a great shot although he much prefers to pass over shoot. Very tenacious on the penalty kill making smart plays and clearing his zone.

Scouts Notes: USA opened up with a 3-0 lead and it looked like this one could be a route. However Sweden showed great resiliency making it a one goal game on two separate occasions. However every time Sweden made it a one goal game, Sweden seemed to get penalties that may be best referred to as questionable at best. Team Sweden received 10 minutes in minor penalties throughout the 20 minutes of the third period. Team USA used these power plays to score the two goals they would need to secure a 4-2 goal win. Despite the calls, Team USA were the team who lost their composure at times. Particularly Shane Eiserman (2013) who attacked Alexander Henriksson (2013) after he committed an infraction which would have given USA a potentially critical power play. Also Michael McCarron (2013) who sucker punched a Sweden player in the face about five seconds after Sweden scored their 3-2 goal. Had McCarron been disciplined for this action it could have drastically shifted the momentum of the game. Both cases were easily avoidable through self control. Wilhelm Westlund (2013) made a lot of very smart simple plays with the puck. He battles hard when controlling the puck and drew some obstruction calls in the process. Lucas Wallmark (2013) who has been pretty quiet in this tournament worked hard and effectively won battles along the wall and showed some good speed and elusiveness on the rush. For Team USA John Hayden (2013) was very tenacious on the penalty kill. His forecheck forced turnovers killing time throughout the game. Steven Santini (2013) made an impression physically asserting himself all game long. Hudson Fasching (2013) uses his strength very effectively along the boards and out front. He scored the 3-0 goal due to his great positioning out front of the Sweden goal. First few steps still need a lot of work.

Nov 9, 2012, Vancouver Giants vs. Portland Winterhawks (WHL)

VAN#1 G, Lee, Payton(2014) Safe to say that Lee has had much better performance as a Giant in his career. Did not receive much help from his teammates, but out of the 5 goals he gave up, he should have had 4 of them. Looked more and more shaky as the game went along. This could be due to the fact that he was under pressure virtually all game long, and his conditioning level needs to improve. Just looked a little sluggish going down to his butterfly and recovering for any rebounds. Will definitely be interesting how he looks next game.

VAN#27 RW, Houck, Jackson(2013) Normally makes his presence physically even if he has a bad night offensively, Houck just could not get anything going with his body. He was a step or two behind the play all night long, and did not have an opportunity to land any solid hits. He may look great against slower opponents, but tonight was a good example of how he may look when playing against quicker teams with players that have high hockey sense and recognize when they will get hit and gets out of the way. He went after Seth Jones a couple of times, but Jones was able to spin away from his checks along the wall quite easily. Another performance to forget tonight.

POR#3 RD, Jones, Seth(2013) Dominated the game today in both ends of the ice. Picked up a nice assist on the power play when he rushed the puck up the ice and created a 3 on 3 opportunity. Jones drove wide, made a nice drop pass and took 2 defenders with him to the net, which gave his teammate a lot of room from the top of the circle to release a heavy wrist shot and score. Just understands the game very well and looks so poised. Made opponents look silly with his elusive skating abilities and quickness to avoid getting hit along the walls. Will allow him to be durable at the pro level if he can avoid getting hit time and time again. Defensively, used his stick very well to knock away passes and stir opponents to the outside. He does not have to play a physical game often because he is so smart in his own zone.

POR#19 LC, Petan, Nicolas(2013) Had an excellent game at both ends of the ice. May be undersized, but competed hard every second he played tonight. Displayed a high level of vision and moved the puck quickly and efficiently. Rarely ever tried to force plays and turn pucks over. Made one bad decision on the PK, when he carried the puck on a 2 on 2 situation and had it knocked away along the opponent's blue line, and Vancouver quickly started a 3 on 2 counter attack the other way and scored to tie up the game. The shot should have been saved, but when protecting a lead, should have just dumped it in deep and play it safe, especially in the third period. Made up for it 5 minutes later though when he took a pass at the side of the net, protected it well and cut across to score easily. Defensively had a very impressive game too. He read the play quite well and seemed to be in the right position many times to intercept passes and get the play going the other way.

POR#27 RW, Bjorkstrand, Oliver(2013) Have seen better games out of Bjorkstrand this season. Did not use his speed and puck protecting abilities to his advantage tonight. Tried to force plays consistently. For example, he would try to squeeze by 2 defensemen on a 1 on 2 situation. Higher percentage play would have been to dump it in and chase it, especially against defensemen who are not as quick as him. Talked to an NHL scout tonight who said Bjorkstrand has been quite inconsistent in his viewings. Looked great in some games, and struggled at other times. Tonight was a perfect example of that.

Scouts Notes: This game should not have been close, but Brendan Burke had a tough time keeping easy shots out of the net tonight. Like Payton Lee, he got pulled as well when it was 5-5. Mason Geertsen made his home debut for Vancouver and was invisible. Was not physical at all, which is his bread and butter. Dominic Turgeon of Portland had a very good game tonight. Very smart without the puck, and is a face off machine. Won draws cleanly time and time again.

FINAL SCORE: 9-5 Portland

November 9, 2012, Cap-Breton Screaming Eagles vs. Victoriaville Tigres

CAP #12 LW Murphy, Cole (2013) – I thought he was a good asset for Cap-Breton in this game. We got to see very little of him with the puck but he did manage to play an intense game and apply pressure. He had decent mobility moving around and showed good awareness on the pursuit. He didn't look like an NHL prospect to me in this game, but he did good.

CAP #15 C Beaton, Bronson (2013) – His skating prevents him to do pretty much everything. He is extremely slow and couldn't do a whole lot. He showed very little creativity in 1-on-1 situations and therefore didn't generate anything offensively. I thought he played relatively hard and made some good decisions with the puck though. Still nothing there in my mind for the NHL draft.

CAP#21 LW Guevremont, Charles (2013) – He had a good shift early in the game, flying around and making some noise. It didn't carry for the rest of the game, as we got to see very little of him. He was slow to make his decisions with the puck and reacted a few seconds to late. He also lacks skills to set up or finish offensive pieces.

CAP #28 LW Carrier, William (2013) – Carrier didn't look good on the ice tonight. He had heavy legs and was late behind the play on numerous occasions. He also showed poor work ethic and no desire to use the body at all. Carrier has a little above average skating: he reaches a decent top speed quickly but it's not overwhelming by any mean and you couldn't really call it a burst either. The thing he does well is using his hands along with his speed to carry the puck. He excels at finding open ice and protecting the puck to carry it forward. Unfortunately he didn't get to do that a lot and the one time he did, he held on to the puck a little bit too long and couldn't make a play. He is not very creative with the puck although he has good hands and he plays a pretty straightforward game. He also showed some good agility while carrying the puck, working low with good balance. Carrier didn't show anything you would like to see from a typical power forward either. He showed a strong tendency to slow the game down and barely used his body to drive the net and the one time he did, Jonathan Diaby from Victoriaville knocked him down. He also made some poor decisions with the puck in the neutral zone, going with long and soft passes that resulted in turnovers. He did a good job on Cap-Breton's first goal attracting the defenseman Diaby with his hands to slip the puck to a teammate in the slot who had an open net. Other than that Carrier showed good positioning and anticipation in the neutral zone and made some good plays on coverage in the defensive zone. He was often the last player backing up from the offensive zone and he didn't have a physical outing at all. Aside from his good hands and decent ability to carry the puck, Carrier didn't leave a positive impression. Apart from his skating, he needs to show way better work ethic and he needs to use his body and strength to play the game along the boards, in front of the net and with the puck entering the offensive zone. Carrier played in the Subway Series during the week, but it's only 3 games in 8 days, so it shouldn't be an excuse.

VIC #3 D Diaby, Jonathan (2013) – He played an excellent game once again, especially against William Carrier. He was a force along the boards and made a good job shutting down the play quickly when he had the chance to. He maintained a good gap again tonight and his stick work was very effective as usual. One positive play that I particularly noticed was when Carrier entered the zone with his head down with the puck bouncing. Diaby made the read extremely quickly and went directly to him, knowing he couldn't do anything and he had the other options around him covered. It showed good hockey sense to me and confidence in his ability to make the play. On the downside, I think he could make his pivot a little bit faster when he is skating backwards. On one occasion he turned his shoulder and followed the attacker with his back bent and his long reach. He could have made his pivot earlier to follow him face to face instead of giving up his shoulders. Other than that, he has to be careful when he is overmatched in terms of number (ex: 2-on-1 situations). It's exactly what happened on Cap-Breton's goal, where he wasn't sure which player to go to and he ended up being useless. He is far more comfortable when he has only one player to focus on and no decision to make. We also got to see some action of Diaby on the power play. He didn't look out of place although it's clearly not the best part of his game. He kept it simple and made sure to move the puck around efficiently. He also showed some confidence moving the puck around on the blue line while he was pursued.

VIC #12 LW Rehak, Dominik (2013) – Rehak showed some interesting tools but something is missing in his game, preventing him from putting it all together. He is a fine straight line skater with good top speed. His hands are noticeably good, especially when it's time to pass. He can make quick and accurate passes. It seems that he can only use those tools separately and he is not able to use them together. In that regard, he doesn't have the biggest impact of the game although he shows some good signs. I liked the drive and desire he showed tonight. He made a lot of contacts and didn't back down from physical challenges.

VIC #57 LW Veilleux, Tommy (2013) – Veilleux did his usual stuff throughout the game. He skated hard and played an intense physical game. He initiated the contact a lot and applied good pressure. He doesn't do anything bad on the ice but he doesn't standout much either. His game with the puck is still limited and he doesn't create much scoring chances. I thought he did a good job around the net tonight, chasing loose pucks. He had one good scoring chances but fired a weak shot right on the goalie.

Nov. 9 2012, Cape-Breton Screaming Eagles @ Victoriaville Tigres, QMJHL
CB #12 LW, Murphy, Cole (2013): Murphy is a small player may not have explosive speed, but does have some speed to his game. He played a pretty simple game, handling the puck well and winning board battles displaying a nice element of intensity in his game. He was able to create a good scoring chance in tight by protecting the puck around the net and then making a good pass to find a teammate going hard to the net. There is a limit to his upside at the pro level as he does not possess high-end elite skills, and he made a lot of inconsistent decision in his own end leading to a pretty weak overall defensive game.

CB #15 C, Beaton, Bronson (2013): This is a player who needs to improve on his skating, as it is very easy to notice this is the weakest part of his game and it creates some troubles for him as he has a tough time distancing himself from the opposition. He displayed some nice soft hands on a couple of sequences, but was limited to very few offensive flashes during the game as the opposition has a quick team that likes to put pressure on opponents. He needs to be more aggressive along the boards and show some more competitiveness and has to be stronger on the puck. He also has to improve his 2-way game.

CB #28 LW, Carrier, William (2013): Carrier displayed some really nice tools that he had on display in this game, however also showed a worrying lack of competitiveness. He handles the puck really well with some great moves to get around defenders and has some great speed to rush the puck up through the neutral zone, protecting it well from defenders to gain the offensive zone. He has a great slap-shot which is why his team uses him at the point on the power play and also has great mobility and vision to move the puck to open teammates for scoring chances and even a goal. He showed some really good offensive instincts and is able to find lanes to get his shot through to the net, displaying some true goal scorer's instincts. He is strong on his skates, protects the puck well on the wide drive into the offensive zone, however can't turn the puck over trying fancy plays to get past the opposition which happened on multiple occasions in this game when he could have easily chipped the puck in to get it in deep. The most worrying part of his game however was how he gave up on many plays and did not show a willingness to play a physical game or use his body in any way to create time and space. He did not appear to play with any real intensity and needs to get himself more invested into games, he also had some poor body language that did not look like he was really into what was happening on the ice.

VIC #3 D, Diaby, Jonathan (2013): Diaby had a ton of ice time in this game and was continuously going up against the opposition's best forwards. He played a pretty solid aggressive, in your face style of game and showed some impressive speed and quickness for the size that he possesses. He was strong on the penalty kill, protecting the front of the net nicely and getting in lanes to block passes, and also was strong on the wall to protect the puck then clear it out of the zone. He has a mean streak to his game and was also aggressive at a lot of the right moments through the neutral zone to make some nice big hits on the opposition while never seeming to put himself out of position. He played with a good gap control, rarely getting beat 1-on-1 and had a good energy from the drop of the puck until the final buzzer, which was really impressive given how much time he was out on the ice for. He was ok on the power play, moving the puck pretty well for the most part however tried a couple of risky fancy passes, which showed that he may not be suited to play in that situation regularly at the next level. He has a good shot though and uses that at the right times to get it through to the net. He uses the boards pretty often to clear the puck and plays simple in his own zone, the only times he got beat were by quick passing plays where his footwork was too slow to change direction quickly, showing that he still needs to work on his footwork as he can be late at times when he pivots.

VIC #12 C, Rehak, Dominik (2013): Rehak Played a pretty good game, but lacks pretty desirable skating abilities. He has natural hockey sense, puts pressure on the opposition at the right moments and was able to score a goal due to some good positioning at the blue line. He is not afraid of getting involved in scrums, playing physical or going to the dirty high traffic areas to get scoring chances, which is a great sign for a young prospect. He is a gifted puck handler, has good offensive instincts and shows some nice flashes of potential and awareness on the ice.

Nov 10 2012, Acadie-Bathurst Titan @ Sherbrooke Phoenix, (QMJHL)

BAT #9 C, Lafontaine, Raphael (2013): What is nice about Lafontaine's game is that he plays within his capabilities, not trying anything too fancy or extraordinary except the level that he competes at. He is a great leader on the ice, sticking to the details of the game, mostly by hitting, crashing the net and jumping on rebounds. He plays a blue-collar game, chipping and battling on the boards and to his credit he is able to win most of them. He is responsible in both ends of the ice, has a good sense of the game and can play in both special units, in front of the net on the power play and covering the points well on the penalty kill. He scored a goal in this game by jumping on a rebound off a shot from the point.

BAT #23 RW, Zdrahal, Patrik (2013): Zdrahal was invisible for most of the game, as he didn't have much jump in his skating and didn't seem interested in getting involved in the high traffic areas either. He has soft hands and is an agile skater, but doesn't want to get hit. He has good overall offensive tools but lacks character and 2-way game for the time being.

BAT #43 C, O'Brien, Zach (Free agent): O'Brien had a pretty disappointing showing in this game. He is a great puck handler with great skill and a thousand
ways to beat defensemen 1-on-1, but again his work ethic and physical game is quite poor. He is a strong player for his size, protects the puck well, but he doesn't like to get hit and he won't certainly doesn't initiate the physical game. He has an uncanny ability to create time and space for himself, as he is a very shifty player and he can find open ice and teammates easily from just about anywhere. The focus and intensity wasn't where it needed to be in this game, even though he scored a goal on a nice passing play and showed some great acceleration.

SHE #7 D, Lysenko, Vladislav (2013): Lysenko played a superb stay-at-home type of game. He was really physical down low and his decision making on the ice has improved drastically from the beginning of the season. He is a strong player who is still disciplined but makes you pay the price in his own end. He played his gaps pretty well in the neutral zone where he used to try to make a hit at the beginning of the season, showing some great progression in his game. He still has some learning to do as he made a couple of bad plays with the puck, forcing the play on the board when he could've skated the puck out of the zone, but this is still a learning process for him and he should learn how to read the play to make better decisions moving forward. He protects the front of his crease nicely and skates pretty well going forward, however his backward skating could still improve and become more fluid and natural. He ended the game with a pretty good stat line at +3 and 5 hits.

SHE #15 D, Deschamps, Jonathan (2014): Deschamps is a smart player but is just playing with a lack of confidence at the moment. He has some great footwork and is possesses great lateral mobility which allows him the opportunity to follow and contain any skilled forward that handles the puck well, however in this game he was playing his 1-on-1 situations quite inconsistently as he would read the play great one shift and then get beat quite easily the one after. He made some questionable decisions under pressure and his lack of confidence seemed to effect his ice time, as he did not get out on the ice much in the second half of this game.

SHE #32 D, Neil, Carl (2014): Neil has some nice poise with the puck and is really strong on it. He is able to break the puck out of the zone on some good passes and tries things that many defensemen his age would not try, showing some good confidence in his game. He played a pretty solid defensive game, was able to execute the simple plays well and in return he got a lot of ice time. The amount of ice time he received seemed to have an effect on his game as he showed his fatigue in some of the decisions he made and did not have as much energy and jump to his game as he usually does.

SHE #71 LW, Deslauriers, Vincent (2015): This was a tremendous game for a very young 15-year-old player entering the game. He played with lots of energy, had an impressive physical implication for size, worked hard every shift and was rewarded with his first point in the Q. He has very good top speed and showed pretty good offensive instincts at his high pace, finding space to release his shot. He is a pretty good blue-collar player for now, but shows great skill with the puck and potential to be much more than that moving forward as he grows and matures. He is very noticeable even though he is such a young player and lacks experience.

November 10 2012, Halifax Mooseheads vs. Victoriaville Tigres (QMJHL)

HAL #22 C Mackinnon, Nathan (2013) – Mackinnon had a very difficult game. He didn't display his usual jump and Victoriaville's Jonathan Diaby did a wonderful job matching against him. Mackinnon had one flash early in the game where he used his burst down the wing and exploited his body to drive the defenseman to the net, which I liked. Then it took a while to see him use his speed again, but he did it nicely, cutting to the middle ridiculously quick to get a scoring chance. Then I didn't get to see much. He was abused physically at the blue line and didn't display much energy in his puck battles. He had a few sequences in the offensive zone where he looked good using his quick hands, but that was it. Mackinnon was also very weak in the faceoff circle, winning only 11 of 28 against Victoriaville's captain Phillip Danault.

HAL #27 LW Drouin, Jonathan (2013) – Drouin, just like his partner Mackinnon, started the game very slowly but he was able to raise his performance level throughout the game. He tried two long passes in the neutral zone early in the game that resulted in turnovers. Then he managed to get a breakaway on the penalty kill with a great burst of speed but was stopped by the goalie. He also displayed his great passing skills in the offensive zone, spotting a teammate the other way around the zone, passing it through heavy traffic right on the money. In the 2nd period we got to see another Drouin breakaway, created with his very good speed once again. He managed to beat the goalie but couldn't slip the puck in. The fact that his feet are always in movement and very quick well help him get ahead of his opponents. In the second period again, Drouin had yet another breakaway, beating the goalie this time with his quick hands. Drouin also made a nice play on Martin Frk's goal, spotting him in front of the net for the one timer. It wasn't a very difficult pass to make, but it was the right decision to make. Other than that, Drouin wasn't as involved physically as I saw in my other viewings, but this game was a lot about skating and he really get much chances to work along the boards.

HAL #31 G Fucale, Zachary (2013) – Fucale showed he was very cautious with his positioning and about covering angles. He is always searching for the puck and putting himself in the best position as he can. He gave up five goals in this game but there is not much he could do on any of them. On the first goal, he was beat by a beautiful set play on the powerplay. On the 2nd goal he had a pile of players in front of him trying to force the puck him and he was able to get the first save on them. On the 3rd goal he made the save but gave a rebound which resulted in a goal. And on the 4th goal, he saw absolutely nothing. He had his view blocked and a powerful shot came from the blueline. On the fifth goal Victoriaville's Dominik Rehak slipped one past him with a rocket from his far left. He couldn't move laterally a little bit faster to face Rehak, but the shot was just too quick.

VIC#3 D Diaby, Jonathan (2013) – Diaby had a wonderful game against the Mackinnon line. He was on the ice every single time they were out there and he did great. He started off the game with a great physical play on Stefan Fournier behind the net to stop him and recuperate the puck. He managed his 1-on-1s against Drouin and Mackinnon beautifully. He kept a safe gap and used his long reach to keep them from dangling the puck at their will. He forced them to slow down and then he could redirect them the way he wanted to. He kept doing a great job along the board, ending the play quickly with his big body. On one occasion Mackinnon tried to use his speed on him but he had to slow down and opt for a wrist shot from far away. He also used his stick once to poke check Mackinnon and he drilled him with a legal hit. Diaby also played on the power play again tonight. He made a beautiful shot pass from the point to his teammate Miceli for the goal. You can see he is getting more comfortable handling the puck, although like I mentioned several times, it's not his cup of tea. His defensive zone coverage once installed in the defensive zone was good most of the night, but on a few occasions he was at the wrong place and he hesitates a little bit. I did like the fact that he kept going hard after the players even though he got himself out of position.

VIC #12 LW Rehak, Dominik (2013) – Rehak played an excellent game. He showed very good passing skills while in movement and he was able to combine his speed and his hands to create things offensively. He worked very hard in the slot for one of his first goal. Then he positioned himself extremely well to receive a pass and fire a rocket past Fucale. He displayed good energy in this game and was able to use his speed a lot more compared to other outings.

VIC #57 LW Veilleux, Tommy (2013) – All I have in my notes for him in this game is: hitting, hitting, hitting, and fighting. He started the game with one huge hit along the board and another open-ice hit on the same shift to get his team going. On his next shift he got a big hit on Mackinnon in the defensive zone that allowed his team to regain possession of the puck. He then picked up a fight against veteran Trey Lewis, both throwing some hard punches. Veilleux kept doing a good job physically and he brought energy on the ice. I got to see very little of him offensively. He prefers to dump the puck rather than play with it. He did a good job crashing the net on one occasion in the third period.

November 10, 2012, Team Finland vs. Team Switzerland (U18 Four Nations)

FIN #7 RD Makinen, Atte (2013) - Quiet through the first two periods but really picked up his physicality in the third. Usually makes good plays with the puck moving it up ice.

FIN #11 RC Ojantakanen, Kasperi (2013) - Works very hard along the boards, wins more battles than his size may suggest. Plays a physical style of game, finishes his checks despite the size the opposing player. A very good skater who shows off some good moves in open ice and hands. He had a few chances to score but was not able to finish. He has good defensive instincts and battles hard in his own zone, even in the slot area covering for defensemen and clearing the players from the front of the net.

FIN #13 LW Antonen, Joose (2013) - Antonen was quiet for some stretches of this game, but then he exploded with flashes of skill. Impressive skater at 6'2" very quick hands and great moves on breakway to nearly score. Consistently created scoring chances for Finland. However as we got to the third period he seemed to run out of gas well before his line mates. He appeared to wear down within 25-30 seconds of his shift which made him less of a factor.

FIN #19 LW Puhakka, Janne (2013) - Showed some good hands and elusiveness when coming out of the corner with the puck. He weaves through the neutral zone effectively with the puck to acquire the offensive zone. Showed some good passing ability.

FIN #20 LC Koivistoinen, Eetu (2013) - Has great size and made things happen offensively on a consistent basis. He has a powerful shot and a very good skater despite having power forward like size. He moves the puck very well up ice. He is very good out front in the slot always keeping himself available to receive a pass but also screens the goaltender well whenever a teammate is in a good shooting position. He wins races and battles to the puck using his speed and size respectably. Also has a very good turnover rate. Koivistoinen missed some action in this tournament but was able to play in the Bronze Medal game and was one of Finland's best players.

FIN #24 RW Kapanen, Kasper (2014) - Finished his checks wherever possible. Shows decent speed and good hands on rush resulting in some scoring chances. He picked up physical play as the first period went on. Kasper battles well for position out front which resulted in scoring chances.

SUI #10 LW Pfranger, Ramon (2013) - Had an outstanding shift beating two defensemen one of which was all over him. He shook him off then had a great chance to score. He then followed up on the rebound for two more good chances but was robbed by the quickness of Finland goaltender Juuse Saros. Followed up this play with good physicality.

SUI #14 LD Baltisberger, Phil (2014) - Struggled with turnovers in his own zone. In one on one situations he pivoted too late at times which caused him to get beat more than usual. He uses his frame very effectively in puck battles. Very dangerous on power play with simple puck movement and a cannon one timer. He gets his shot off quickly and usually on net.

SUI #21 LC Fuchs, Jason (2013) - Fuchs has quick hands and good mobility. His first few steps are good he's very agile and gets the puck deep.

Scouts Notes: After seeing Finland dismantle Switzerland 24 hours ago, one could expect the rematch to be much of the same right? Well when Finland took a 2-0 lead less than five minutes into the game it looked like we were in for much of the same. However those two goals are all Finland would put together. Switzerland found their game once again and put away five unanswered goals to win the Bronze at the Four Nations Tournament 5-2. Finland's Julius Honka (2014) has shown excellent vision. He makes the right decision nine out of ten times. Niko Ojamaki (2013) banged home a rebound to score the opening goal in the first shift of the game. He also made a nice pass rushing into the offensive zone creating a scoring chance. For Switzerland Kevin Fiala (2014) shows good quickness. He made a great pass cross ice on a well covered two on one to create a great scoring chance.

November 10, 2012, London Knights @ Plymouth Whalers (OHL)

LON #7 LW Pawley, Corey (2013) - Pawley used his speed and stick check to create turnovers early on in this game. He used his great acceleration to win races to pucks and showed great energy to win battles against bigger, stronger players. He made a lot of very solid passes and even created some scoring chances for the Knights.

LON #16 LC Domi, Max (2013) - Domi was pretty quiet tonight. He had good positioning but didn't battle nearly the way he usually does. Received ice in every game situations. He didn't make many mistakes but he just wasn't the impact player he has been in other viewings.

LON #53 LW Horvat, Bo (2013) - Horvat showed great resiliency after losing the puck trying to make a move on the defenseman, he won the race to the loose puck then made a great pass to set up the first goal of the game, which also turned out to be the game winning goal. Horvat put together an average performance for him and added a power play goal with less than five minutes remaining to make the score 5-0 for London.

LON #65 LD Zadorov, Nikita (2013) - Zadorov made an impression early on with his physical play. While he didn't lay up physically he had a little trouble reading a few plays and resulted in a bit of a struggle at points in this game.

LON #81 LW Elie, Remi (2013) - Elie was all over the ice tonight. Always seemed to be in great positioning and will go to the front of the net without hesitation. Excellent coordination to kick the puck up to his stick and make a precise pass all in one movement. He created some good scoring chances but didn't have any points to show from it.

LON #95 RW Jammes, Jacob (2014) - Jammes with only a handful of OHL games under his belt certainly did not look intimidated by the bigger, older Plymouth Whalers. He had a ton of energy and was relentless with his effort. He won battles regularly and threw himself in front of shots to block them. Jammes did all of this on a very consistent shift by shift basis. He also showed several flashes of good playmaking/passing abilities as well.

PLY #18 LW Vanderwiel, Danny (2013) - Vanderwiel is a big physical ball of energy. He likes to hit and finishes his checks whenever possible. He shows good skating for his size and worked very hard consistently throughout the game.

PLY #19 LW Bratina, Zach (2014) - Played physical right off the start. He is very conscious of his great size and won battles in the corners on a regular basis.

PLY #21 RC Hartman, Ryan (2013) - Hartman really showed a contrasting game tonight. He shows a lot of energy and he's the kind of player who can make anyone who sleeps on him, pay with his quick hands and good moves, even if he's starting from a standing position. Ryan shows good speed and skating ability. He likes to shoot much more than pass and tonight that seemed like the better option. He was very hit or miss with his decision making with the puck. He made some good plays but also threw the puck away. This happened a few times on the power play and resulted in the puck being iced by London. At one point he had a great chance to score short handed. He got stopped and took his time getting back. This extra man down in the defensive zone saw London scoring a power play goal before he got back into position.

Scouts Notes: While this game looked pretty even matched off the start, London was able to capitalize on their chances in the first period and open up with a 2-0 lead. After Matt Rupert (2013*) completed his natural hat-trick early in the second period, the Plymouth Whalers started to really lose their composure. London was able to exploit this continuously opening the gap further and further without compromising their defensive positioning. The end result was a 5-0 victory for the Knights.

Nov 10, 2012, Czech Republic vs. Russia (World Junior A Challenge)

CZE # 4, D, Kokes, Martin (2013) Kokes was able to make some good 1st passes out of the zone to start the rush and was distributing the puck well on the power play to find the open man in the high slot, as well as an open man down low next to the net. He picked off some passes to hold the puck in the offensive zone and got his stick in lanes in the defensive zone to deflect passes out of plays and breakup chances for the opposition. He also was able to pick off passes on the penalty kill and got in lanes to block shots in front of the net then cleared the puck out of the zone.

CZE # 13, RW, Vrana, Jakob (2014) Vrana was pressuring the puck carrier pretty well and showed good speed on the wide drive then tried to cut towards the net with the puck. He showed great hands and moves to get around defenders but needs to drive the puck to the net more often rather than trying to play on the outside. He was moving the puck well in the offensive zone, distributing it well and got a good cycle going in deep and showed nice quick hands from the point on the power play to walk into the slot and put a good shot on. He had great speed to rush the puck up the ice but has to watch the turnovers trying to be too fancy at times. He also needs to get the puck out of the zone on penalty kill clearing attempts.

CZE # 16, D, Pryochta, Filip (2014) Pryochta is calm with the puck and moves it up well on the rush. He is a pretty good smooth skater and was able to step into the high slot to open up, take a pass and put a good shot on. He was jumping up on the play to lead the attack down low, get a cycle going and held the offensive zone pretty well. He is able to skate the puck up the ice to get it in deep into the offensive zone as well.

CZE # 23, LW, Rob, Lubos (2013) Rob displayed some pretty good agility with the puck to twist from the opposition's pressure, and protect it on the cycle. He had good strength on the puck to hold on to it under pressure and went to the net looking for loose pucks and rebounds. He played the puck carrier with an element of physicality along the wall and was moving the puck around nicely on the power play by passing it down low then drove hard to the net. He opened up well on the power play next to the net to take a pass and score from in tight and made a nice pass to find an open man right in front of the net. He did however take far too many long outside shots on the rush.

RUS # 12, LW, Leschenko, Vyacheslav (2013) Leschenko was protecting the puck well along the wall then moved the puck out to the high slot to find a teammate for a good shot opportunity. He was getting the puck to the net either by moving the puck or driving it and was able to draw a penalty by driving the puck to the net. He also went hard to the net with his stick down to take a pass and deflect the puck to score from in tight. He was able to make a nice long pass to find a man at the far blue line to spring him into the offensive zone and showed nice speed on the rush to bring the puck up the ice but has to watch the turnovers on puck mishandles. He has some nice quick hands and good moves but also needs to watch the turnovers trying to dangle his way through the opposition.

RUS # 17, C, Okulov, Konstantin (2013) Okulov was protecting the puck well along the wall and got a good cycle going in deep. He stepped off the boards into the high slot to put a hard slap shot on and was moving the puck and distributing it well on the power play in the offensive zone. He won the puck in some board battles then displayed a nice shiftiness to get to the slot for shots and was able to find the open man in the high slot for a goal. He made a great pass on the rush to find an open man in the slot for a great chances and was moving the puck up well on the rush to lead a man into the offensive zone with speed. He also drove to the net with his stick down to take a pass for a great chance in tight off the rush.

RUS # 24, D, Baldaev, Viktor (2013) Baldaev is able to move the puck to find an open man down low and was also getting the cycle going in deep. At times he panicked with the puck and just tried to get rid of it and also needs to get his shots through to the net on chances from the point on the power play, as he was shooting the puck into the opposition, allowing them to block it then rush it back up the ice with ease for good opportunities.

FINAL SCORE: 4-1 Russia

Nov. 10, 2012, USNTDP U18 vs. Team Sweden (U18 4 Nations Gold Medal)

USA # 3, D, Savage, Scott (2013) Savage has a really great hard shot from the point that he can get through on target, and also is able to get his shot off well on a one-timer. He is pretty mobile on the point, and willing to come down to the high slot to provide scoring options in the offensive zone. He also used his stick well to knock the puck away from the opposition.

USA # 10, RW, Allen, Evan (2013) Allen started the game out taking a pass in the high slot, walked down low into the slot on the power play and put a fantastic shot on net for the team's 1st goal of the game. He was opening up really well in the high slot with space in the offensive zone to provide options, and was cycling the puck nicely down low. He drove hard to the net with his stick down, and was also able to walk right into the slot for a great shot opportunity. He distributes the puck on the rush, and was opening up really well to take a pass in scoring position for a great chance. He has some nice speed, distributing the puck well on the odd-man rush, and made an excellent pass across on a 2-on-1 for a great scoring chance. He had a great cross-ice pass on a breakout to spring a man into the offensive zone. He still needs to get a bit stronger on his feet.

USA # 19, C, Kelleher, Tyler (2013) Kelleher has some really nice hands and agility to work the puck under intense pressure to create some room for himself to make a play. He did a great job opening up in the high slot to put a nice shot on a one-timer on the power play, and some nice speed and puck distribution on an odd-man rush. He had a nice break to draw a penalty, taking a great feed but was caught by the defenseman on the opportunity. He had a good drive to the net to battle for rebounds and put some great shots on from in tight.

USA # 28, LW, Eiserman, Shane (2014) Eiserman was battling really well for pucks in tight in front of the net, and displayed some really great puck protection and strength on the wide drive. He had some great speed to get on a loose puck to take the puck for a break, and then cut to the net on an excellent power forward move to create a great chance. He was protecting the puck well along the wall to draw a penalty, and had a really nice pass to find an open man back door for a nice opportunity. He forced a turnover in the neutral zone to take the puck for a break with speed, but hit the post on the opportunity and also drew a penalty on the play. He was driving well to the net with his stick down, battling for loose pucks, and had some great speed to rush the puck into the offensive zone, but has to hit the net on his chances. He was getting to the slot for good shot opportunities off the rush, but also decided to take a poor shot on a 2-on-1 opportunity instead of trying to move the puck to a better scoring area.

SWE # 4, D, Hagg, Robert (2013) Hagg did not have his best game of the tournament tonight, especially in one play where he had an absolutely terrible turnover on a drop pass at his own blue line to give the opposition a break on net. He did however have a nice one-timer from the point on the power play, but has to get his shot through to the net. He has some good agility to avoid the opposition's pressure, and then made some great breakout passes. He was jumping in on pinches to hold the puck in the offensive zone and keep the attack alive. He has a good ability to skate the puck up the ice, but needs to move the puck a bit quicker instead of holding on too it for too long. He was blocking shots in his own end, and distributing well on the power play. He was unable to handle a pass through the neutral zone resulting in a bad turnover as well.

SWE # 9, D, Westlund, Wilhelm (2014) Westlund was distributing the puck well on the power play, and has a good one-timer from the point, but needs to keep it down low on net. He did a good job closing his man off along the boards and finishing him off with a nice big hit to separate the man from the puck. He used his stick really well to knock the puck away from the opposition, and displayed some nice physicality in his own end along the boards on the puck carrier.

SWE # 14, RW, Blidh, Anton (2013) Blidh put some great pressure on the puck carrier on the fore-check, and displayed a good element of physicality. He was taking some long outside shots off the rush rather than driving the puck down low to the net. He was unable to handle some long breakout passes, and had a bad turnover through the neutral zone trying to dangle his way through the opposition.

SWE # 23, C, Johansson, Mikael (2013) Johansson has some pretty good strength and puck protection, but lost a handle on the puck a few times resulting in turnovers. He got to the slot and opened up well to take a pass and put a great shot on net. He was protecting the puck so effectively when rushing it up the ice and into the offensive zone, and put some great pressure on the opposition to force turnovers. He also made a really nice little chip play to make a great pass and spring a man into the offensive zone for a good opportunity.

FINAL SCORE: 3-1 USNTDP U18

November 11, 2012, Sudbury Wolves @ Sarnia Sting (OHL)

SUD #14 RW Baptiste, Nicholas (2013) - Baptiste made an impression right off the bat. First shift he evaded two checks and got a shot on goal. He then won a battle for the puck and nearly scored. He likes to use his speed on the rush but didn't over do it knowing when to pass off to an open teammate. He took the body along the wall but sometimes reacted too slowly positionally in the offensive zone a few times. Struggled a little when taking on defensemen one on one. Nicholas played all game situations and looked pretty good on the penalty kill.

SUD #15 LW Kubalik, Dominik (2013) - Kubalik may be from Czech Republic but with his style of play it would be just as easy to assume he was from somewhere in Ontario. Kubalik has good size and finishes his checks with authority and had no less than ten hits in this game. He shows a very hard forecheck and his work ethic shows tremendous consistency. With the puck he's capable of beating defensemen one on one. He has a good shot and he's very smart positionally on the rush. He knows where to go and how to keep himself available for passes.

SUD #94 LW Silk, Brody (2013) - Brody forced offensive zone turnovers to keep the play going for Sudbury. He makes simple plays cycling the puck very well and making an impact offensively. He had about a half dozen scoring chances, many of which were right into the slot area but he couldn't finish. At one point he kept getting the puck on the same play in prime scoring positioning. The third time he fumbled the puck losing it, but it went right to Josh Leivo who finished the play in a hurry. He contributed quietly, but just couldn't make anything happen when the scoring chances game to him. Silk played in all game situations.

SAR #2 RD Chapman, Joshua (2013) - Chapman likes using his size whenever possible. He sticks with forwards much better than he has in the past. Chapman was a regular on the penalty kill. Midway through the first period he unleashed a pretty hard slap shot from the point, tying the game for Sarnia just over a minute after Sudbury took a 1-0 lead. Joshua got caught flat footed watching Alex Galchenyuk stickhandle in neutral ice which resulted in a 2 on 0 breakaway for Sudbury when they forced the turnover.

SAR #13 LW Dundas, Justice (2013*) - Dundas has been very impressive this season and one of the most improved players on the Sting line-up. He showed off very good speed and puck protection then made great pass to Galchenyuk to tie the game up at 2-2. With his ability to drop the gloves, play a physical style and now adding some hands and speed into his game, he may be a very attractive option to an NHL team late in the draft or as a free agent invite.

SAR #74 LW Carnevale, Alex (2013) - Battled hard and won along the boards. Showed some patience with the puck and made some good passes after winning battles. Goes to the net with his stick on the ice when team acquires the offensive zone. Didn't do too much but seemed to play within his role very effectively.

SAR #77 RD DeAngelo, Anthony (2014) - Rushes the puck at will against the Wolves. He's at his best when passing off because he can sometimes hold onto the puck for far too long and get picked off. He cost his team a two minute penalty because he ignored the referee's warning for re-entering the play after losing his helmet. A very easily avoidable penalty in what was a tie game at the time.

Scouts Notes: A very exciting back and forth game between the Sudbury Wolves and Sarnia Sting. Both teams wrapping up their weekend on a Sunday afternoon. The teams exchanged goals in the first period but it was Reid Boucher (New Jersey) finishing on a chance created by Alex Galchenyuk (Montreal) that gave the Sting the eventual 3-2 edge and they held on for the victory. Nikolay Goldobin (2014) who seems to come out with at least one highlight reel play per game made a great play evading two checkers from standing position, then make a great cross ice pass high in the offensive zone to Joshua Chapman (2013) to set up the 1-1 tying goal. Brett Hargrave (2014) looks much more confident with the puck taking his shots and moving it a lot better. For Sudbury Danny Desrochers (2013) didn't get much ice on the fourth line but showed a lot of what we liked in his minor midget year playing physical, and showed improved, effective skating ability too. Evan de Haan (2013) the brother of New York Islander prospect Calvin de Haan is a bit smaller. He shows very good skating ability, and effective point shot, but he gets pushed around a lot due to a lack of size.

November 11, 2012, Cap-Breton Screaming vs. Québec Remparts (QMJHL)

QUE #10 LW Duclair, Anthony (2013) – He was among the very few who had a positive game today, even though he didn't played his best hockey. He started the game with a very good burst to get a breakaway but couldn't capitalize. He also showed some good positioning in the neutral and blocked a shot. The game was played in sequences and so was Duclair's game. He showed glimpses of his speed at times, making a good use of his body to move down the wing. He showed good puck distribution in the offensive zone and made some very smart passes. He also displayed his very good hands in traffic, where he stays low and well balanced on his skates. His play in the defensive zone wasn't bad but he did create a turnover there at one point. Overall he did some nice things, but I would like to see him more dynamic with the puck and more along the boards.

QUE #45 G Fortin, Zachary (2013) – He was shaky the whole game. He wasn't square in his net on a few occasions, moving too far sideways. He gave up A LOT of rebounds, going mostly right in the slot. He also struggled catching high pucks with his glove hand. Based on this game alone, he did not look good and left me with a very bad impression. Not the kind of performance by the goalie that give the team confidence.

QUE #73 RW Erne, Adam (2013) – This is probably the worst game I have seen from Erne since he joined the Remparts. He didn't display his usual speed and hustle that makes him effective both in the neutral and offensive zone. He had trouble going wide on the defenseman like he usually does. I thought he did a good job using his teammates though when he couldn't get it done by himself. He wasn't much of a factor either without the puck in the neutral zone, where he usually excels. Erne used me to bring a lot of tempo to the game, with good anticipation, hustle and physical play, something he didn't display tonight. He still made some alright plays in the offensive zone, but nothing out of the ordinary. His best moment came early in the game where he made a wonderful pass to Duclair who was in front of the net. It was a hard pass to make and he showed very good vision to see the little space he had to reach his teammate.

CAP #27 LW Carrier, William (2013) – Let's put it this way: he was awful. He looked like he carried a piano on his back and didn't want to be there. He was extremely passive and showed no speed whatsoever. We barely got to see him skate with the puck and he had no explosion at all. He ended up dumping the puck most of the time. There was no hustle in his game when he didn't have the puck and there was very little involvement from him physically. He played the point on the powerplay where I thought he didn't move his feet enough to be productive. He stand still the whole time, thinking options around him would open. He also looked very bad when he had to play defense on the power play and he fell on his butt. He did score a goal at the end of the game to tie it up. He entered the zone at a normal speed and fired an OK shot that slipped between the legs of the goalie. He seemed to have a little regain of energy from that moment on, but didn't do much else worth mentioning.

November 12, 2012, Russia @ OHL Game #4 Subway Super Series

RUS #15 LW Nischushkin, Valeri (2013) - First few steps are a challenge but generates very good speed. His skating style could be best compared to that of Alex Galchenyuk's in last year's draft year. Valeri forced turnovers on a regular basis in all three zones. He has a laser of a shot but didn't use it.

RUS #24 RC Yakimov, Bogdan (2013) - He has tremendous size and doesn't hesitate to try to use it along the walls and in the corners. He battled in all three zones but lost at times he probably should have own. He didn't have a great game but didn't receive a lot of ice either.

RUS #29 RD Koledov, Pavel (2013) - Koledov was very reliable again for Team Russia and has been arguably their best defenseman in this event so far despite spending a fair amount of time on the third pairing. He won a surprising number of battles along the boards against bigger OHL players. He shows good hockey sense and knows where he should be positionally at all times. Effective at clearing the zone when there is heavy pressure in the defensive zone without icing it and makes the smart pass up ice and on the point in the offensive zone.

OHL #16 LW Rychel, Kerby (2013) - Kerby made a point to finish his checks wherever and whenever possible. He forced turnovers and kept his game pretty simple throughout delivering some of the biggest and hardest hits in this game. Counted around twelve solid hits throughout the game.

OHL #61 LC Domi, Max (2013) - Domi took a good path to the front of the net while on the power play but took an unnecessary penalty negating it while unnecessarily interfering with a Russian defender. He showed quick handling through traffic and uses his low centre of gravity to protect puck in traffic despite taking contact emerging with the puck. Had a couple moments where he created a few chances.

Scouts Notes: Team OHL came out physical, determined and clearly looked like the better team all game long. Ryan Strome (NYI) opened up the scoring with a tremendous shift. He sent a pass from inside his blueline up to a teammate to send them on a break for the net. He went full speed up ice and went right to the net where he picked up the puck and scored the opening goal. He certainly left a positive impression on this game. Tom Wilson (WSH) also left an impression with his physically intimidating play and intelligent contributions at both ends of the ice. Frankie Corrado (VAN) scored the eventual game winning goal going to the net and scoring a nice goal which was assisted by Strome. After Jordan Binnington (STL) shut the door on Team Russia, it appeared Jake Paterson (DET) would team up with him to help Team OHL shutout Russia for an unprecedented third straight Subway Super Series game in Sarnia (Also in 2003 and 2006) however with 36 seconds left in the game Nail Yakupov (EDM) made no mistake with the split second of time and space he was given to get a shot off. Team OHL tied the series with Team Russia heading into the final two games against Team WHL with a 2-1 win in Sarnia tonight.

November 15, 2012, Oshawa Generals @ London Knights (OHL)

OSH #14 RW Latour, Bradley (2013) - Bradley hit everything he could and won battles regularly. His skating didn't look good. But if he can improve on his skating, he shows the potential and the mindset to be a very good grinder/physical player.

OSH #19 RC Cassels, Cole (2013) - Cole is a very good skater. He wins races to the puck and battles hard. He was very reliable defensively for Oshawa for the most part. He is a key component to their penalty kill and breaks up offensive chances. He struggles a little when he has the puck in good scoring areas. He generally just throws the puck into the slot and hopes for the best when he does acquire it down low, sometimes after doing a great job winning a battle.

OSH #71 LC Dal Colle, Michael (2014) - Dal Colle shows tremendous work ethic. He gives everything he's got every single shift. Michael has a great combination of size and speed. He closes gaps quickly and hits hard. He's always in good position, or en route to ideal positioning. Dangerous combination of shooting and passing abilities, however he much prefers to pass over shoot. Dal Colle made an unbelievable defensive play to break up a big scoring chance and save a sure goal for London with a minute left and the Generals up by a goal.

LON #2 LD Maatta, Olli (PIT) - Unfortunately Olli showed us a lot of what we saw out of him last season. He struggled moving the puck in all three zones. Still throwing the puck into the skates of his teammates, and icing or turning the puck when he's about to get hit. But as we've seen before he emerges from these mistakes to make a great play to set up a scoring chance. Outside the odd play here and there it was all panic with the puck. To his credit although he doesn't win as many battles as we'd like to see he never quits on a play. He comes out every shift and works hard and certainly gets an A for his efforts.

LON #4 LD Liberati, Miles (2013) - Miles got some power play time and created chances with his patience and passing ability. He put a good point shot on net which directly resulted in a goal for the Knights and an assist for Liberati scoring the first of four unanswered goals starting the Knights big comeback run. He did a lot with the little amount of ice he was given, which resulted in the Knights' coaching staff rewarding Miles as he was given a lot more ice in the critical moments of the game.

LON #16 LC Domi, Max (2013) - Domi was absolutely dominant tonight. But it didn't start out so promising for him. He had two breakaway chances earlier on in the game and he fell both times. He made an outstanding behind the back pass to send his linemate on a breakaway. Max looked like he was on a mission and he really set the tone early in the third leveling a much bigger guy. His competiveness and willingness to pay the price out front rewarded him with the first of four unanswered goals for the Knights. He scored again with less than five minutes left making it a one goal game thanks to his great positioning at the side of the net. Finally, he made a great play in which he assisted on the third and tying goal with 22 seconds left on the clock. London isn't even close in this game if Max Domi doesn't put on this kind of performance.

LON #53 LW Horvat, Bo (2013) - Very opportunistic offensively. He doesn't create offense on a consistent basis but he exploits openings that few see. Horvat battled at both ends of the ice showing great competiveness. He had a sure goal taken away from him with a minute left down 3-2 but he kept working, regrouped then regained his original positioning making no mistake with 22 seconds left to tie the game.

LON #65 LD Zadorov, Nikita (2013) - Threw a few solid hits but at times chases the hits. He panicked with the puck at times when he was going to be hit turning it over in the defensive zone or just icing the puck despite better options being available.

LON #81 LW Elie, Remi (2013) - Very physical and protected the puck well but couldn't get anything going offensively in the first. He started to get more critical ice in the final two periods as a reward for his compete level in trying to help the Knights get back in the game. He rushed the puck very well on the power play making smart passes. At one point London tried to create a play on the power play directly designed to get Elie's one timer off.

Scouts Notes: Oshawa absolutely dominated the Knights through 40 minutes. Jake Patterson (2013*) came in to relieve Kevin Baillie (Free Agent) and really kept the Knights in it after three early goals. While this game looked over entering the third period, London somehow found a way to score four unanswered goals; three in regulation and one in overtime for the win. To add a little controversy, the *final three goals scored by London came off of three very questionable penalty calls on Oshawa in the final eight minutes of the game.*

Nov 12, 2012, Team OHL vs. Russia (Subway Super Series Game 4)

OHL #16, LW, Rychel, Kerby (2013) Rychel played a real physical high-energy game tonight displaying the ability to be able to adapt his game in order to be effective when he isn't the top scorer on the ice. He showed some nice physicality on the fore-check and was battling hard for the puck and competing to get to the net. He was hustling and working hard to back-check and be responsible in his own end and even had a nice stick-lift in the offensive zone to take the puck from the opposition and force a turnover. He can accelerate really well and was moving the puck well, especially on a nice give-and-go with Tyler Graovac later in the game. Rychel showed some good patience with the puck and was finishing his hits and did a good job getting his stick down in lanes and reading the play to force neutral zone turnovers, however mishandled the puck on one of them and lost it. He also had some trouble staying on his feet as he fell down a few times with absolutely no pressure and was not as offensively able tonight as I am used to seeing him play.

OHL #61, C, Domi, Max (2013) Domi is a real hard working player who doesn't quit on a play and makes sure he finishes all of his hits. He works hard for the puck and can protect the puck as well and also brought a nice net-front presence on the power play. He was real nice and physical in this game but took a dumb penalty early on in the 1st period on the power play in the offensive zone and needs to make sure he is keeping his game in line and refraining from doing so. Domi put some good pressure on the puck carrier and had the sense to move the puck to dangerous areas and get to the slot. He was moving the puck pretty well and did a good job finding the man in the slot. He was hustling back to his own end and getting the puck in deep as well as reading plays and blocking passes. He also showed the ability to open up for a pass down low next to the opposition's net. It was good to see Domi play more of that shut-down high-energy role that he may be forced to play at the next level if his skills and scoring can't translate.

RUS # 29, D, Koledov, Pavel (2013) A defenseman who likes to use his stick to direct the opposition. He is calm with the puck and can protect it but needs to watch the neutral zone turnovers. He is able to move the puck up for a breakout and gets the puck out of the zone nice and safely. Koledov is also willing to pinch to pick up the puck and get a good opportunity from the high slot. He was also reading the play and aggressively jumping up to hold the line and keep the play alive. He was willing to lie down to block shots and passes and was able to clear the puck and get it out a few times on the penalty kill. He can protect the puck and was winning most of the puck battles and got involved in a few scrums after the whistle to protect his goalie. I felt on the defending side he was too aggressive on the puck carrier and didn't show much patience to wait for the play to come to him, however this could also be the way that the coach is asking his defensemen to play so it is hard to point that all at him. I felt he was following his man up too high in the slot and I would prefer my defenseman not to follow the man higher than the circles in his own end, and also thought he got caught a few times watching the puck rather than taking the man.

RUS # 15, LW, Nichushkin, Valeri (2013) A really fast player who showed that great speed tonight in this game and was finding those lanes to skate through to rush up the ice. Nichushkin does a really good job of making the typical power forward move by gaining the zone wide and then cutting in to the front of the net really showing no fear and making some dangerous plays to create opportunities. He is so strong on the puck and also displayed the ability to move it under pressure and showed a willingness to bring a nice net-front presence. He was not trying to do too much and just got the puck in deep when he was out of options and was putting some good pressure on the puck carrier as well. The only thing I would like is for him to be a little more physical and finish his hits and try to make some more hits on the fore-check to try to keep the puck in deep.

FINAL SCORE: 2-1 OHL

Nov 14, 2012, WHL vs. Russia (Subway Super Series Game 5)

WHL # 2, D, Pulock, Ryan (2013) What jumps out at me first about Pulock's game is his shot from the point. Many times in this game Pulock was offered a great opportunity and got a great shot off from the point that was kept down low and on target and was a nice strong shot. He can hold the line well to keep the puck in play and was moving the puck around well in the offensive zone on the power play. He can think and make the safe play to get the puck in deep instead of forcing what isn't there and was blocking shots in his own end. Pulock can pass the puck out for a breakout and was effective with both the long and short passes.

WHL #19, C, Shinkaruk, Hunter (2013) I really liked Shinkaruk's game tonight and felt that he brought the perfect blend of physicality, compete and skill to be a really effective player. He was making his hits on the fore-check and had a good net-front presence as well showing the willingness to stand in the dirty areas. He has some explosive speed and can find lanes to move the puck up and expose the defense at times by doing so. He is able to take a hit and hold on to the puck still to make a play showing some good strength and balance and was physical himself all over the ice. He can protect the puck well and has a quick release on his shot and has a real goal scorer's shot as he can pick his spot and showed this on his goal in the shootout. He battled hard for pucks and would tie up the opposition to take the puck from them and then showed some good patience with the puck. He also had a really nice high speed give-and-go to get the puck to the net and was moving the puck well on the power play and was not at all scared or intimidated to take a hit.

WHL # 28, C, Lazar, Curtis (2013) Lazar showed some good speed and hustle to be the first to the puck at many times and he puts some great pressure on the puck carrier forcing him to make plays. He cycles the puck well and was reading plays to take some neutral zone turnovers from the opposition. He goes to the net with his stick down and opens up well to take a pass, but also displayed some of his own great vision and passing to find an open man in the slot. He has some really nice speed, battle and compete for the puck and was also willing to be physical.

RUS # 29, D, Koledov, Pavel (2013) Koldeov was a bit inconsistent with his breakout passes tonight as he was making some real beautiful plays to find the breakout man on some long passes and was seeing some good lanes as well to move the puck up but also missed on some of his passes as well and late in the game did not look before passing in his own end and passed to no one which turned into a good opportunity for the opposition. Koledov showed an ability to take some bad passes well and keep the puck active and in play and also has some decent speed to his game. He showed some good puck protection and a willingness and ability to rush the puck up the ice, but needs to make sure that he is getting his shots through from the point.

RUS # 15, LW, Nichushkin, Valeri (2013) As soon as you see Nichushkin, the first thing that jumps out at you is his amazing speed. He gains the zone so well wide and can move the puck to some good areas. He puts on some great pressure to force turnovers and was also showing some physicality on the fore-check which is something I felt his game had been lacking earlier in the series. He can beat everyone to the puck, and can protect it so well, as he had a great spin move to get a great shot on net late in the 2nd period.

FINAL SCORE: 1-0 WHL

Nov 15, 2012, Russia vs. WHL (Subway Super Series Game 6)

RUS #29, D, Koledov, Pavel (2013) Koledov is nice and calm with the puck and was willing to take a hit to get the puck out. He was making some real nice long passes for breakouts and in his own end showed some nice stick work to check the puck away from the opposition and keep them on the perimeter. I would like to see him get a bit stronger on his skates.

RUS #15, LW, Nichushkin, Valeri (2013) A very highly skilled player who can make some great power forward moves by cutting in to the middle off the wing while protecting the puck and getting the puck to those dangerous scoring areas. He was getting some good shots from in close but also took a few from the outside and was really gaining the zone with some great speed. He moved the puck around well in the offensive zone and was able to take the puck off the boards to the slot in the middle to get some good shots off. He is very strong on his feet and tough to knock off the puck, and defensively does a good job pressuring the puck carrier. There were a few times where he holds on to the puck for too long and loses it and needs to keep it moving a bit quicker, and also mishandled the puck a couple times and had one bad drop pass in the offensive zone that resulted in a turnover.

WHL # 28, C, Lazar, Curtis (2013) Lazar is a quick forward with some size and can do a lot of little things well to help the team win. He is not a liability and doesn't make too many mistakes. He brings some nice speed and can drive wide well and has the strength to stay on his feet when the opposition tries to knock him off. He gets a nice low shot on net from the outside to try to generate rebounds and can get himself open in the high slot to open up for a pass and connected on the one-timer for a great opportunity. He pressures the puck carrier and finishes all his checks on the fore-check. Lazar is also able to move the puck up the ice for a breakout and showed the vision and passing to spot the open man in the high slot and get him the puck.

WHL # 4, D, Reilly, Morgan (2012 draft pick Toronto) There is so much that jumps out at you when you watch Reilly play that make him such an exciting and dynamic player. He has some great speed, amazing hands, great vision and hockey sense and can pass the puck extremely well. He has moves to create space and can find lanes to pass or skate through, and showed this on one play later in the game where he took the puck up the ice and made two toe-drag plays to beat defenders and get a good shot on net. He can rush the puck or pass it up the ice and reads the play to jump in and keep the play alive. He made some great long passes and in his own end he uses his stick to direct the opposition and check the puck away. He plays right on the edge and never gives up on a puck or a play, but this play concerns me that he might be dealing with a lot of injuries over the course of his career by this style. He can hold the line well and gives some good pass options to his teammates in the offensive zone, and does a really good job of keeping his man to the outside. A few times he mishandled the puck or turned the puck over in the neutral zone, but every time he works hard to get the puck back and battles every time he loses it.

FINAL SCORE: 5-2 Russia

Nov 16, 2012, Peterborough Petes vs. Kingston Frontenacs (OHL)

PET 17, LW, Betzold, Greg (2013) Betzold's highlight moment of the game was when he picked up the puck in the neutral zone and made a great move to beat the defender 1-on-1 and then made a great feed to spot Nosad going to the net down low for the team's second goal of the game. He was protecting the puck well along the boards and was hard to knock off the puck and was going hard to the net. For the most part he kept to a pretty simple game and also took a penalty early on in the game by running the goalie.

PET #18, C, Tanus, Jonatan (2013) Tanus was able to read the play pretty well tonight and picked off a turnover by the opposition in the neutral zone. He was physical on the fore-check and had a nice puck battle as well to take the puck in the neutral zone off the opposition and move it up to a teammate. He was trailing the play well on the odd-man rush to provide an option up high and was also willing to block shots and get his stick in lanes to block passes in his own end. He needs to make sure he is getting the puck out on the penalty kill as he had 2 opportunities and failed on both and was a bit weak on the puck at times as he took some really weak long outside shots.

PET # 21, RW, Nosad, Stephen (2013) Nosad was getting some good speed off the wing to gain the zone tonight and drove down off the wing to get some decent shots on net. He was lifting sticks and battling to get the puck out of the zone and was making some nice safe dump plays for the most part.

He had a really nice drive to the net with his stick down to score his team's second goal of the game on a feed from Betzold and also got a nice cycle game going on the fore-check. He was putting some good pressure on the puck carrier and was battling to keep the puck in the offensive zone. Nosad also had a real nice clear of the puck on the penalty kill at one point.

PET # 16, D, Murphy, Trevor (2013) What Murphy does really well is his long pass up the ice for a breakout, and at one point made a beautiful pass up for a breakaway. He can take a hit and still get the puck out of the zone, and was also showing some physicality of his own in his defensive end. He was willing to come in deep and join the attack but needs to watch the offensive turnovers by trying to force the play through. He also took too much time getting the puck on net a few times and lost the puck and his man got away from him in his own zone right next to the net to score Kingston's second goal of the game.

KNG # 15, LW, Beckstead, Marc (2013) Beckstead is very willing to go to all the dirty areas and had a nice net-front presence on the power play and got a good tip on the point shot for the team's 3rd goal of the night. He also scored another goal from in tight by battling and competing for the puck in front of the net and showed some good hand-eye coordination to knock the puck in from in tight late in the game. He made some nice lead passes and then went hard to the net to get rebounds and got some good opportunities off this. He is really most effective in tight around the nice. Beckstead also had a nice fore-check by holding the puck in the zone and played a simple dump and chase game at times with some good physicality shown on the fore-check. He can get the puck out of his zone and move it up the ice well for a rush and is able to take a hit and hold on to the puck.

KNG # 17, C, Kujawinski, Ryan (2013) I really love Kujawinski's hockey sense and compete level and his battle in both ends of the rink. He has a great two-way hustle to come back on the back-check and take his man but also has some real nice offensive instincts to chip in with some goals. He has nice speed and the ability to take the puck away from the opposition in the offensive zone and is so good at getting in between the defense to take a pass and get a good opportunity on net. He did this a few times and scored once by getting in right behind the defense and made a nice move to score the teams first goal and took a great feed off his backhand. He is also good at feeding the puck down low and then going hard to the net and made a great drive to the net on an odd-man rush opportunity. He showed some great sense to get to the net and open up to always be open for a pass in good positioning. He put some good pressure on the puck carrier and was hustling to be the first to pucks and did a nice job moving the puck up the ice to teammates. He is also creative and tried a nice back pass to an open man but was broken up and in retrospect was probably too many passes and should have just put the shot on net. He made a nice read to pick up a turnover in the neutral zone and then made a great pass to spot Jenkins streaking in the far side for the team's 4th goal of the night. He also displayed some nice vision and passing to find the open man in the high slot and was making some good lead passes to the slot. He offered some good support in his own end and is clearly a responsible defensive player with great offensive upside.

KNG # 27, RW, Dupuy, Jean (2013) Some real nice physicality was demonstrated from Dupuy and showed this early on with a real nice hit. He ran the goalie and took a penalty in the first period and needs to refrain from crossing that line. He also made a nice wide drive to gain the zone and then throw the puck on net for a teammate to create a good opportunity in close, and did a great job also of walking off the boards into the high slot for another chance.

KNG # 61, LW, Fitzmorris, Mitchell (2013) When Fitzmorris loses the puck on a turnover he battles to get the puck back and puts in that extra effort to recover. He was blocking shots in his own end and had a nice net-front presence in the offensive zone. He also got a good cycle going and was able to protect the puck and take a hit and also displayed some real nice speed in this game.

FINAL SCORE: 7-4 Kingston Frontenacs

Nov 16, 2012, Sault Ste. Marie Greyhounds vs. Brampton Battalion (OHL)

SSM #11, LW, Dempsey, Mitchell (2013) Dempsey is your prototypical blue-collar hard working grinding forward. He made his hits on the fore-check and did a great job on the back check by grinding his man out along the boards to take the puck and show that element of physicality. He was cycling the puck well and able to move the puck down low to find an open man next to the net. At times he looked unsure of what to do with the puck in the offensive zone and looks like he needs some more confidence to his game.

SSM #18, C, Halagian, Nick (2013) This is another player who also looked as though he is really lacking confidence. Many times he would swipe at the puck or go for it and just missed all together and even mishandled the puck and lost it on simple dump-ins where he just didn't get anything on it. He was able to show a net-front presence and a willingness to block shots and kept to a pretty simple game. He also was able to take a hit and keep going to drive the puck down deep in the zone and in his own end was able to get the puck out most of the time.

SSM # 28, RW, Tolchinsky, Sergey (2013) Watching Tolchinksy's game tonight he reminded me of Mikhail Grabovski in many ways. He has good speed and keeps down low and is very agile and shifty to make moves and beat defenders. He hustles hard for the puck and back-checks and was physical all over the ice. He opens up well to give passing options in the offensive zone and moves the puck to good dangerous scoring areas. He had a nice give and go to gain the zone and was really moving the puck effectively on the power play. He protects the puck well and has some great vision and passing to find the open man in the slot and also drives well to the net. Late in the game he had a really great wide drive and beat a defender with a move, then protected the puck and moved it to the front of the net with a backhand to find the streaking man perfectly. He came back to his own end every shift and was responsible defensively and had some good stick lifts to take the puck away. He also had some great sense to throw the puck low and on net from the outside looking for rebounds.

SSM # 25, D, Nurse, Darnell (2013) Nurse has the great combination of being effective defensively and the ability to move the puck up the ice to create an attack. He can rush the puck or pass it up the ice, and in the offensive zone is willing to walk in and join the attack. He made some nice passes up the ice, and protects the puck as he rushes it up while making some head fakes to make moves and find space to gain the zone by skating the puck end-to-end. He showed a willingness to go down and block shots and made a great diving play in his own end to knock the puck away from the opposition. He is a good skater and has some great size and does a good job stick-checking the puck away and clearing it on the penalty kill. He doesn't let his man have the inside lane, and was finding some nice passing lanes in the neutral zone to move the puck around. He likes to gain the red line and dump the puck in to keep it safe, but also had a bad turnover on a long pass attempt up the ice. He played with a good gap control defensively and was able to ride his man off the puck showing he is also a strong player.

BRM # 21, LW, Paul, Nick (2013) Paul is a tall lanky forward who shows good size potential but needs to add some strength and weight to his frame. He made some good passes to find a trailing man open in the high slot and was also cycling the pucks well down low and then going to the net. He did a great job on the 1st goal of getting open in the high slot and then getting a nice shot off to open his team's scoring. He had a nice net-front presence and was tipping pucks and making life difficult for the goaltender and was also able to walk out front from behind the net to get a nice shot on net from the slot. On the penalty kill he got in lanes to block passes and was showing some willingness to be physical and finish his hits on the fore-check, and then cycled the puck and was protecting it well deep in the offensive zone.

BRM # 26, RW, Santos, Matthew (2013) A quick skater who is surprisingly physical for not being a strong filled out player. He also has some decent potential for good size but needs to add some strength and weight to a good frame. He made some nice passes that generated some good chances, first on a 2-on-1 for a great opportunity and then later spotted Paul in the high slot to feed him with a great pass showing some real nice vision for the first goal of the game. He was playing a good cycle game and protecting the puck and drives hard to the net. He showed some pretty good speed and

physicality on the fore-check and able to move the puck up the ice nicely for some breakouts. He puts some good pressure on the puck carrier and was reading the play well to try to break up passes.
FINAL SCORE: 4-3 Brampton Battalion

November 16, 2012, Owen Sound Attack @ London Knights (OHL)

OS #22 RW Lindo, Jaden (2014) - Jaden uses his size extremely well along the boards and is far ahead of the developmental curve in terms of physical maturity.

OS #23 LD MacDermid, Kurtis (LAK) - Made a very lazy play out front of his own net which directly resulted in a 1-1 goal for London. He then showed his willingness to drop the gloves but got TKOed by Kevin Raine.

OS #24 LD Bigras, Chris (2013) - Bigras showed very smart puck decisions in all three zones. He can rush the puck up the ice and possesses a good point shot. His shot was deflected in on the power play to give Owen Sound a 1-0 lead. He usually makes the right play with the puck but did have a few turnovers. He's successful about 8-9 times out of 10

OS #27 RW Nastasiuk, Zach (2013) - Nastasiuk shows good defensive zone presence covering passing lanes very effectively. Pretty good along the walls. He battled effectively out front of the London goal deflecting home the 1-0 goal.

LON #4 LD Liberati, Miles (2013) - Liberati looked to build on a good performance the previous night. During the first shift he won a one on two battle in the corner emerging with the puck. He then took it end to end evading an opposing player on the way up ice to create a great scoring chance. Miles was steady at both ends of the ice possessing average size but most of the time he just wants it more than anyone else. Unloaded a big one timer on the power play early in the third period to give London the 3-2 lead scoring the game winning goal.

LON #16 LC Domi, Max (2013) - Max Domi really fueled the Knights at times with his hockey sense, vision and determination. He is elusive with the puck and created chances but at times his linemates couldn't finish on the opportunities. He made some very good cross ice passes in the offensive zone.

LON #53 LW Horvat, Bo (2013) - Horvat had great positioning in the offensive zone and kept doing the work to get in prime position but kept missing on his chances. He worked very hard along the boards, won battles and consistently was a positive for the Knights, he just couldn't put anything up on the scoreboard.

LON #65 LD Zadorov, Nikita (2013) - Zadorov struggled at times with his puck play. However he worked extremely hard down low, won more battles than he usually did and physically looked like the defenseman that he should be considering his size.

LON #81 LW Elie, Remi (2013) - Sacrificed his body to block shots. Great defensive positioning helped him break up potential offensive plays and send the puck in the other direction. He worked hard all night long although he didn't get as much ice, and didn't have the chances in the offensive zone he usually generates. Regardless he was still a positive impact defensively.

LON #35 G Patterson, Jake (2013*) - Follows the play very well and shows a good quick glove hand. Sometimes seemed to over thinking his positional play which occasionally saw him outside of ideal positioning.

Scouts Notes: A very even matched game by the top two teams in the OHL's Midwest division. They exchanged goals and the lead three different times and after two periods it appeared that this game may need to be solved in overtime. However

Miles Liberati (2013) unloaded a massive one-timer early in the third period to give London a 3-2 lead. The Attack would never come back and a series of mental mistakes by Owen Sound collectively through the period negated a few chances, and opened things up for London. The Knights won the game 5-2 but the final score doesn't give justice to how incredibly close this match-up was for the majority of the match-up.

November 20, 2012, Leamington Flyers @ Sarnia Legionnaires (GOJHL)

LEM #17 LC Manchurek, Joe (2014) - Manchurek has good size and great skating ability. His decision making with the puck is pretty even between passing and shooting but he is a much, much better passer. He had multiple chances but didn't finish. Two of them were right in the slot and he missed the net by a mile. On the other hand he made some pretty slick passes that wound up creating chances for his line mates. He lost some battles that he should have won for someone his size (6'1") didn't seem the slightest bit interested in the physical part of the game. He showed a good knack for forcing turnovers especially in the offensive zone. Took part in the shootout but didn't score. Manchurek is a 4th round pick of the Oshawa Generals in the 2012 OHL Priority Selection Draft. .

LEM #31 G Mancina, Matt (2014) - Mancina looked very good tonight. Everything seems to come naturally to him. He's very technically sound, his movement is very compact with no excess movement. He directs all his rebounds into the corner very effectively. Plays angles and posts very well with good side to side movement. There are very few flaws in his game. He likes to set himself last second so he could leave himself vulnerable if someone surprises him. Also he holds his stick sideways which can expose his five hole. In the shootout he made a great play to pokecheck on the first shot. He got beat pretty bad five hole second shot, and the third he got beat by an excellent move. Mancina is a 3rd round pick of the Guelph Storm in the 2012 OHL Priority Selection Draft.

LEM #11 LW Friesen, Alex (2015) - Friesen comes into the game at only 15 years old but was one of Leamington's best players. Alex opened up with a lot of energy and in his second shift of the game he made an excellent behind the back pass to set up the opening goal of the game. Alex has great speed and can handle the puck in his skates and didn't break stride knocking it up to his stick and advancing into the offensive zone. He has quick hands and likes to do everything fast. Friesen really took the most out of this experience. He played with a lot of excitement and looks like he's shot out of a cannon every time he steps on the ice. He has good positional awareness and instincts for a great chance to score in overtime. Although He only got one assist in this game he very easily could have had 2 or 3. He created two sure goals but in both cases his linemates couldn't finish. Alex is eligible for the 2013 OHL Priority Selection and while his point totals are not great, anyone who saw this performance would need to give him atleast some kind of consideration.

SAR #9 RC Tyczynski, Hunter (2014) - Good puck protection to shake a hit and get a good scoring chance. Got some good power play ice. Played very physical and has a good sized frame to finish his hits. Tyczynski is a 13th Round pick of the Barrie Colts in the 2012 OHL Priority Selection.

SAR #14 RD King, Jeff (2014) - King is very defensively responsible especially for a smaller, younger defenseman like himself. He has been very reliable. He's a good skater but lacks a top speed you'd expect out of a 5'10" – 155lb. defenseman. He has good hands and doesn't rush the puck as much as we'd like to see instead passing it off. Despite being 16 Jeff is used in first unit power play and penalty kill although there are stronger defensive defensemen on the team King holds his own. He showed great shot selection from the point not forcing them through. He nearly turned over the game winning goal in overtime by throwing the puck right across the Sarnia crease. King was the third shooter for Sarnia in the shootout and pulled an excellent forehand, backhand move to score the shootout winner.

SAR #26 RD Vandervaart, P.J. (2013) - P.J. was physical right off the start of the game. He was able to push older opposing players off the puck, with one hand at times. He shows a good stick when puck carrier is below the goal line getting his stick down and following him well eliminating options. He likes to finish his opponent physically but knows when to just use his stick instead. Went to protect teammate who took a high stick late in the second period. Vandervaart is very focused on the defensive side of the game often looking like he has little interest in controlling the puck. However he did a good job identifying a scoring chance and pinched in from the point with a great chance but the puck was thrown into his skates.

Scouts Notes: A very good game at the Jr. B level on a Tuesday night. Leamington battling for top spot in the conference opened up with great jump to their game and it allowed them to take a 2-0 lead which they carried late into the second period. However with a late second period goal then another for Sarnia with less than three minutes left in regulation pushed this game to an overtime where there were many chances on both sides. It eventually took a shootout to decide this game. Jeff King (2014) pulled off an excellent shootout move that likely would have beat most OHL goaltenders ended up being the winner as Sarnia beat Leamington 3-2.

Nov 17, 2012, Belleville Bulls vs. Plymouth Whalers (OHL)

PLY #21, C, Hartman, Ryan (2013) Hartman showed that he is a pretty hard working prospect and has the ability to make things happen offensively. He was breaking the puck out well, both with the ability to make some nice long passes for breakout and made a couple good chip plays as well to move the puck around the defender and get it on the stick of a teammate. He made a great pass out front to find the open man in the slot and was really moving the puck well in the offensive zone. He hustled to get to loose pucks and was blocking shots as well. Hartman was rushing the puck up the ice and showed some pretty good speed to gain the zone. He had a fight early on to demonstrate he can stick up for himself. Hartman also had a few turnovers in the offensive zone by trying to force plays through and at one point had a nice odd-man rush but then stopped up in the offensive zone and really did nothing with it and ended up losing the puck and the opportunity all together.

PLY #22, LW, Mistele, Mathew (2014) Mistele needs to find a way to get down to dangerous scoring areas with the puck. He was able to get a lot of outside shots from up high and he brought a net-front presence in the offensive zone without the puck, but never managed to get to the inside track with the puck. He was cycling the puck well and standing in front and next to the net on the power play. He moved the puck up for a breakout and showed some good battle for the puck on the fore-check.

BEL # 8, C, Berisha, Aaron (2013) Berisha was able to read the plays both offensively to pick up a pass off the board and defensively to cover for a defenseman who jumped up and made a good defensive lay by poke-checking the puck away from the opposition to nullify the rush the other way. In the offensive zone I felt a few times he was trying to force his passes through which resulted in some turnovers and at times was also standing in no-mans land not really offering anything to his teammates and really not in a place where he could be effective.

BEL # 13, RW, Kuptsov, Sergey (2013) Kuptsov didn't get much ice time tonight but was able to walk out front from the side boards to get a nice shot from the slot. There was also another moment where he tried to drive wide but mishandled the puck and lost it into the corner, as he was not able to handle the pressure being put on him by the opposition.

BEL # 14, D, Subban, Jordan (2013) Subban is a quick defenseman capable of rushing the puck up the ice effectively and finding some nice skating lanes to get the puck up. He uses his stick well to take the puck away from the opposition and showed some good two-way hustle to get back after he got caught on a pinch. He can pass the puck or rush it up the ice and showed a pretty decent battle for the puck in his own end. He did a good job jumping in and holding the line and was also willing to come in deep to join the attack. Subban showed some good moves to beat defenders as well. At times he was soft on the puck and threw it away displaying a bit of a panic in his game and I would like to see him get a bit stronger on his feet. He gave a bit too much space on Plymouth's first goal of the game and also missed the puck at the blue line by trying to hold the line ineffectively with his skates and allowed an opportunity to go the other way. He scored the game winner in overtime by just throwing the puck on net from the side boards.

FINAL SCORE: 3-2 Belleville Bulls

November 18, 2012, Halifax Mooseheads vs. Val D'or Foreurs (QMJHL)

VAL # 2, D, Murphy, Matt (2013) Murphy is a good skater, is strong on the puck and can make a good 1st pass out of the zone to start the breakout. He is able to skate the puck up the ice on the rush effectively, made a few nice passes on the rush to lead a man into the offensive zone with speed however did miss his target on a couple neutral zone passes and needs to make his passes with more consistency. He was distributing the puck well from the point on the power play and used his stick very well to poke the puck loose, knocking it off the opposition to take away their opportunity. He did a nice job tying up his man along the wall in his own end, but has to add some strength to keep the opposition from gaining the inside track to the net so easily.

VAL # 4, D, Rioux-Legault, Guillaume (2013) Rioux-Legault played his man hard and physical along the boards in his own zone and is able to hold the offensive line and get a cycle going in the offensive zone. He has some nice hands to rush the puck up through the neutral zone and gain the offensive end, but then has to watch the turnovers forcing passes through the opposition.

VAL # 8, RW, Mantha, Anthony (2013) Mantha displayed great speed off the wing and was protecting the puck well on the wide drive to draw a penalty, but can't keep trying to force passes through the opposition. He was hustling really well on the back-check, played the puck carrier really hard and physical to knock his man over and put good pressure on the puck carrier to force turnovers. He was skating well and had nice quickness to get in deep with the puck off the rush and showed great hands to cut to the middle off the rush to put a good shot on net. He opened up really well in the slot to take a pass and put a quick shot on but was robbed by the goalie. He protected the puck well along the boards, was cutting to the net off the wide drive for good chances and went hard to the net looking for loose pucks in front. He made some excellent moves to get by defenders then made power forward moves to get towards the net and found lanes to move the puck cross-ice in the offensive zone on the power play to set-up a one-timer goal. He showed great speed through the neutral zone to poke the puck loose past the opposition for a break opportunity and opened up really well in the slot to take a pass and put a great shot on to score.

VAL # 11, RW, Gray, Mason (2013) Gray showed nice physicality on the puck carrier along the wall, played a pretty simple dump and chase game to get the puck in deep and took a pass off the rush to put a shot on from the high slot, however needs to hit the net on his opportunities. He put good pressure on the puck carrier on the fore-check, as well as good pressure on the point in his own end and finished his hits to knock his man over. He got the puck in deep off the rush, but needs to watch the offensive zone turnovers.

VAL # 26, C, Dunn, Vincent (2013) Dunn put really good pressure on the puck carrier, played his man with an element of physicality and got a good cycle going in deep. He was getting involved with the opposition after the whistle and was thrown out of the game for an apparent racial slur directed at an opponent. He also needs to watch the offensive zone turnovers trying to force passes through the opposition.

HAL # 22, C, MacKinnon, Nathan (2013) MacKinnon displayed really good speed and puck distribution through the neutral zone on the rush and showed good strength by playing the body to keep the opposition to the outside. He had some explosive speed through the neutral zone to get a shot off from the high slot and was going to the net off the rush looking for loose pucks and rebounds. He did a really good job of cutting to the middle on the rush to draw a penalty and he played the game with a nice element of physicality. He opened up really well in the high slot to put a great one-timer on off the rush and showed incredible hands and moves to split the defense and come in on a break to draw a penalty and make a good move on the goalie for a nice chance in tight. He also had a great look to move the puck for a man driving the puck down low and made another good pass to find an open man in the high slot off the rush, who then moved the puck down low for a goal. He had great hands and agility with the puck under pressure and went hard to the net with his stick down looking for a pass in tight to the net.

HAL # 27, LW, Drouin, Jonathan (2013) Drouin had some great passes to find the open man out front in the slot and went hard to the net to take a pass right in tight for a tap-in goal. He made a really nice pass to move the puck cross-ice to a teammate far side in the offensive zone for a good opportunity and then made another fantastic back-hand pass on the rush to find a teammate in the high slot for a great one-timer chance. He has an excellent quickness and hustle to his game and he put pressure on the puck carrier but has to watch the neutral zone turnovers trying to dangle through the opposition. He has great speed on the wing, took a bad pass off his skate to come into the offensive zone off the rush with hands to walk around the opposition to put a shot on from the slot and scored 5-hole. He showed his amazing hands to walk around defenders to get to the slot and put some great shots on net and was able to read the play well to pick off turnovers on the opposition's breakout passes. He needs to watch the offensive zone turnovers by forcing passes through the opposition and also needs to watch some of the neutral zone turnovers trying to dangle his way through the opposition.

FINAL SCORE: 4-3 Halifax Mooseheads

Nov. 18, 2012, Barrie Colts vs. Sudbury Wolves (OHL)

BAR # 18, C, Bradford, Erik (2013) Bradford showed a good work ethic to win some puck battles and take the puck and put some great pressure on the fore-check. He had some nice battles in the corner and in one instance took the puck and the team eventually scored on the attack generated from the turnover. He had a nice back-check and stick lift to take the puck off the opposition and did a pretty good job as well on face-offs tonight. He did mishandle the puck resulting in a turnover in the neutral zone and has to watch the turnovers by trying to force passes through in the offensive zone. He had a nice use of his stick and also made a great lead pass to a teammate for a breakout and a good chance was created.

BAR # 24, D, Webster, Micheal (2013) Webster played with some pretty decent gap control and used his stick well to check the puck away from the opposition on their rush. He tends to make the safe plays and get the puck in deep, but needs to get his shot through from the point and I would like to see a bit more patience in his game and to wait for the play to come to him rather than chasing the play around the ice.

SDB # 9, LW, Desrochers, Danny (2013) Desrochers is a pretty decent skater with nice speed to his game. He was putting good pressure on the puck carrier, had a nice fore-check and got a decent cycle going. He makes the safe plays and dumps the puck in deep and showed a nice willingness to block shots a few times as well. He offered good support in his own zone and was battling hard for pucks and also had a nice clear on the penalty kill.

SDB # 14, RW, Baptiste, Nicholas (2013) I feel that Baptiste's best asset is his skating and his speed and his willingness to drive to the net showing no fear. He is a good skater with great quickness and agility and above average puck skills. He showed some creativity and a nice work ethic as well. He had a net-front presence and was looking for rebounds and showed he was not intimidated to drive to the dirty areas as he walked out front from behind the net. When he is out of options he can dump the puck in to get it in deep and gets to the puck quickly on the fore-check, he then showed a nice battle to take it and was protecting the puck to come out and move to a teammate for an opportunity showing some nice agility and speed in doing so as he could twist and turn away from the opposition. He is pretty calm and patient with the puck and did a nice job getting the puck out and deep on the penalty kill, he was also willing to get in the way of the opposition's shots. On the penalty kill he also put some nice pressure on the point man and was getting his stick in lanes to direct the puck out of play and tip shots away. He had a real nice puck protection and cycle game going deep in the offensive zone and made a really great feed down low to spot an open man next to the net driving for an opportunity and later made another good attempt to throw the puck across to the middle man driving hard on the net. Baptiste had a bad turnover in the neutral zone resulting in a goal for the opposition and turned the puck over along the boards as he was unable to get it out of the zone.

SDB # 15, LW, Kubalik, Dominik (2013) Kubalik had some pretty good puck protection and got a nice cycle game going. He finished his checks pressuring the puck carrier and made some pretty good passes to move the puck up the ice. He made a nice saucer pass to try to move the puck to a teammate out front, and was reading the play to pick off neutral zone turnovers and hold the line in the offensive zone.

SDB # 21, LW, Kahun, Dominik (2013) Kahun made a great feed to the front of the net to find and open man on the power play for the team's 1st goal of the game. He also did a real nice job waiting up high and opening up to take a pass on an odd-man rush and then put a great shot on net to pick hi spot and score the team's 2nd goal of the game. He made a great pass to find Leivo open all alone in the slot for a one-timer opportunity and made another nice pass to find Silk open in the high slot also for a one-timer opportunity. He also put some great pressure on the puck carrier to take the puck but missed the net on the opportunity, and was able to take a pass through the neutral zone well but then tried to force a pass through in the offensive zone resulting in a turnover. He has to watch the turnovers in the offensive zone by not looking where he is moving the puck and also has to watch the turnovers in his own zone by trying to break the puck out. He made a very questionable decision on a pass to no one in the offensive zone resulting in a turnover that went the other way for a great chance.

FINAL SCORE: 7-2 Barrie Colts

Nov 18, 2012, Kitchener Rangers vs. London Knights (OHL)

KIT # 3, D, Genovese, Cory (2013) Genovese is a good sized defenseman who is calm with the puck and moving it around the boards nicely. He was hitting well and showing some nice physicality in his own end, finishing his checks however struggled to hold the line at times in the offensive zone by missing the puck.

KIT #16, LW, Pedersen, Brent (2013) Pedersen had a pretty good game tonight showing some good skating as well as some nice quickness and agility. He displayed a good level of hockey sense in the offensive end with a great pass out to the slot to find an open man. He put some nice pressure on the fore-check, working hard and finishing his hits and was controlling and protecting the puck well in the offensive zone He showed some nice aggression as well getting involved in scrums after the whistle but has to make sure he isn't taking penalties and hindering the team by doing so.

KIT # 19, C, Sterk, Josh (2013) Sterk showed a nice work ethic in this game and some creativity with a few of his passes offensively to move the puck around. He can protect the puck effectively and cycle it around in the offensive zone, and did a great job getting open down low to score the team's second goal of the game displaying some nice hockey sense with his ability to find that open space. He was skating pretty well and showed some moderate quickness and agility as well in this one.

KIT # 95, RW, Bailey, Justin (2013) This is one of the best games that I have seen Bailey play this far into the season. Some of his passes were really impressive, he was skating well and showing some great quickness to his game and displayed a really high level of offensive sense by creating a ton of chances for his team. He started with a great pass to find an open man next to the net for the team's first goal of the game, and followed to find Sterk all alone in the slot as well for the team's second goal of the game. He was passing the puck well in the offensive zone moving the puck to some dangerous areas in the slot and showed some great hands and stick skills to walk out to the slot under pressure. He took some long wide shots and would like to see the puck driven down low and Bailey also has to watch some of the turnovers on puck mishandles as well.

LND # 65, D, Zadorov, Nikita (2013) Zadorov is a big hulking Russian defenseman, however is much more physical than you might expect. He was hitting very well tonight and playing his gap control pretty well using his stick to direct the opposition. He could get a bit faster, but is not too slow for his big frame. He made some nice passes up the ice on the breakout and has some moves to his game by protecting the puck and walking out to the slot for some shots, but has to get those shots on net. He got his stick down in lanes to tip the opposition's shot out of the zone, and made some nice big hits along the boards, as well as some open ice hits in his own end. He has a strong body, with the ability to take a hit and still make a play.

LND # 4, D, Liberati, Miles (2013) A bit of a smaller quicker defenseman who had a nice rush to come down deep and showed some hands to create space and get a real nice opportunity in the slot. He handles the puck in some dangerous areas in front of his own net which could lead to some unnecessary scoring chances the other way or heart-attacks for his teammates. He showed however a calmness with the puck and the ability to hold the line in the offensive zone.

LND # 53, C, Horvat, Bo (2013) Horvat to me projects to be a forward who can play a very good shut-down penalty kill role at the next level, as this seems to be his specialty at this current stage. Don't get me wrong he can chip in offensively and has some nice hands, puck skills and creativity to make things happen in the offensive zone, but it is his work ethic, determination and ability to read the play in the defensive zone that makes him such an effective player. He does just an amazing job reading the play, blocking shots and using his stick defensively to direct the opposition's attack and clearing the puck on the penalty kill. He makes some nice hits in the neutral zone to force some turnovers and puts good pressure on the fore-check and finishes his hits. He showed some good puck protection on the fore-check and was able to find some nice passing lanes in the offensive zone to move the puck around, and showed some real nice hands in deep for a great chance.

LND #91, RW, Platzer, Kyle (2013) Platzer was working hard and hitting well tonight, and got a really effective cycle game going with his line with Jammes and Elie. He was driving down the middle hard to the net, and was able to find a lane to make a good pass back to the point as well. He also picked up a turnover right in the slot to score the team's 3rd goal of the game.

LND # 95, RW, Jammes, Jacob (2013) Jammes displayed some good speed and pressure on the fore-check, but was taking some weak long shots and has to try to drive the puck down low. He got a great cycle game going in the offensive zone, and did a great job blocking a pass deep in the zone to force a turnover which the team scored the third goal of the game off of.

LND # 81, LW, Elie, Romi (2013) Elie showed some good puck movement I the offensive zone, great puck protection and cycle going with his line, and had a net-front presence trying to tip pucks in front of the net. He was able to pick up some neutral zone turnovers and get the puck in nice and deep and then tried to move out front where his teammates were, but the opportunity got broken up. He moved the puck to the slot to some dangerous areas for the most part, and got a good breakout rush going as well.

LND # 16, LW, Domi, Max (2013) Domi had a solid game where he was able to show some nice puck skills, creativity and a strong work ethic. He displayed a good shot and real nice scoring touch and offensive instincts that you just can't teach. He started off by showing some great hands, vision and passing to find a man next to the net for the team's first goal of the game, and then got open down low right next to the net for an opportunity, and then got a second chance which he made no mistakes and scored a real nice goal off of. He drives hard to the net and was working well under pressure but has to watch the neutral zone turnovers.

LND # 17, RW, Griffith, Seth (2012 Boston Bruins Draft Pick- Round 5) Griffith displayed a great work ethic and offensive instincts tonight, opening up really well to take a pass next to the net and score the team's first goal of the game, and put some good pressure on the fore-check to take the puck in deep. He also showed a willingness to go to the dirty areas with a nice net-front presence.

FINAL SCORE: 4-3 London Knights

Nov 18, 2012, Windsor Spitfires vs. Owen Sound Attack (OHL)

WND # 13, RW, Maletta, Jordan (2013) Maletta showed some good physicality on the fore-check and was able to walk out to the slot from the boards, and showed a willingness to go to the dirty areas. He did a good job reading plays to break up passes and get his stick in lanes and is able to get the puck in deep and start a pretty decent cycle. He was taking some outside long shots and was forced wide too easily generating no opportunity off the rush, and I would like to see him try to drive the puck down the middle or down low to the net, and to hit the net from his opportunities in close.

WND #16, LW, Rychel, Kerby (2013) Rychel started this one with a good fight right off the hop. He had a net-front presence on the power play and a nice look to move the puck to a man right in close to the net and just barely missed on his target. He showed some good speed and was moving the puck up to a teammate and driving hard down the middle to the net and showed some good physicality as well on the fore-check. He can accelerate well as he gets right up on to his toes and digs his skates in and comes back on the back-check to lift sticks and take the puck from the opposition. Rychel displayed some nice hands under pressure and was calm and patient with the puck moving it around well in the offensive zone. He had a nice slap-shot for a great chance in the high slot however also had a great opportunity right in front of the net at the end of the game to tie the game up and missed the net. There were also times he would try to force the play through the opposition at times resulting in turnovers.

WND # 44, D, Bateman, Adam (2013) Bateman was able to gain the zone wide with ease and get the puck in deep and was showing a nice battle for the puck in corners along the boards to come out with it. He did a nice job walking down to the high slot to get a shot off as well, but has to get his shot through from the point. When he turns the puck over he back-checks hard to recover and was able to knock the puck away from the opposition.

OWS # 21, LW, Gabor, Gilbert (2013) What Gabor was really excelling at tonight was his physicality and pressure he was putting on the fore-check. He was protecting the puck well and showed a nice battle and compete for the puck in front of the net and was going to the dirty areas. He likes to get down low and try to cycle the puck around behind the net, and battled to take the puck off the opposition on the fore-check and then find a man in the slot with a pass for a good chance. He made a good long pass for a breakout, but has to watch the turnovers in his own end and took a bad unnecessary penalty right at the end of the game when his team had the lead.

OWS # 27, RW, Nastasiuk, Zach (2013) Nastasiuk showed that he is a pretty quick player and was hustling to be the first on pucks, and then protected the puck pretty well down low. He was willing to go down to block shots and was putting pressure on the puck carrier. He is strong on the puck and hard to knock off, showing a nice drive down low to the net looking for pucks and rebounds. He drives hard to the net with his stick down looking for opportunities and providing options for teammates and did a nice job walking out front from behind the net but then fanned on his opportunity. He also had a nice pass down low to find a man next to the net for an opportunity and made a nice pass along the boards to move the puck up and create a rush as well.

OWS # 24, D, Bigras, Chris (2013) A defenseman who can rush the puck up the ice and comes down low with the puck to lead the attack. He moves the puck up along the boards safely to get the puck out of his own end and did a nice job getting down and getting his stick in lanes to block passes and break up opportunities. He is able to pas the puck up the ice effectively for the most part, however was off target on some breakout passes, and showed a good element of physicality in his own end along the boards. He was inconsistent with his shooting from the point, as he was able to get some shots through from the point and many others were blocked and has to try to get those pucks in deep and on net.

FINAL SCORE: 1-0 Owen Sound Attack

Nov 18, 2012, Sarnia Sting vs. Sault Ste. Marie Greyhounds (OHL)

SAR #74, LW, Carnevale, Alex (2013) Carnevale was making the safe plays all night as he would dump the puck in deep and goes for the chase, going for the hit on the fore-check. He is not really an offensive threat, or creative making any plays but knows his role. He needs to make sure he can get the puck out of his zone and to pick up the tempo of his game a bit.

SAR #21, C, Nikandrov, Daniel (2013) Nikandrov showed some nice hands in attempt to drive the puck down low. He has some stick skills and a drive to the net with some decent skills with the puck but at times tries to do too much and loses the puck. He can move the puck up well on the rush and showed some good speed through the neutral zone. He was also able to find lanes to move the puck around on the power play and had a net-front presence. He has a nice reach with his stick and uses it well to take the puck in battles.

SSM # 11, LW, Dempsey, Mitchell (2013) Dempsey was getting a good cycle game going in the offensive zone and was putting some good pressure on the puck carrier to take the puck and move it to the middle for some opportunities. He goes hard to the net with his stick down showing a good drive and had a pretty good breakout going as well.

SSM # 16, C, Kirkup, Ryan (2013) Kirkup is a really agile and quick forward who was protecting the puck and finding passing lanes in the offensive zone. He is able to twist and turn his way out of trouble and showed a nice work ethic going hard for the puck but needs to get a bit stronger on his feet.

SSM # 18, C, Halagian, Nick (2013) Halagian did a good job cycling the puck deep in the offensive zone and showed a good drive hard to the net. He made a nice drop pass feed to create a chance and put some good pressure on the defense when he was on the penalty kill, however at times was a bit too aggressive and put too much pressure on leaving someone wide open, however did not result in anything and was able to clear the puck on the penalty kill.

SSM # 28, RW, Tolchinsky, Sergey (2013) Tolchinsky is a really highly skilled player with some great quickness and agility. He has great puck skills, high offensive instincts and a nice scoring touch. He works hard all over the ice, can breakout well and puts some good pressure on the fore-check. He showed some real nice speed coming in along the wing and good stick skills to beat a defender 1 on 1 with a great move. He makes some nice passes and shows patience with the puck. He can protect the puck well with some nice hands and a net-front presence was shown as he scored his team's 4th goal of the game. He was able to make a nice saucer pass to move the puck back to the point, and got himself open down low next to the net on the power play.

SSM # 3, D, Ganley, Tyler (2013) Ganley showed he was able to find some space with a nice rush up the ice and was protecting the puck to get it in deep. He jumped up in to the slot to take a few shots and was able to get it through for the most part but fanned on a one-timer early on in the game. He also had some nice clears to get the puck out on the penalty kill.

SSM # 25, D, Nurse, Darnell (2013) Nurse has already established himself as an elite defender and showed why with a great game tonight. He had some nice rushes up the ice showing good speed and protecting and is really calm with the puck as he can find some good lanes to skate the puck up the ice. He showed really good gap control and then would finish his man with a nice hit as he showed great strength and hitting all night long. He got his shots through from the point and was jumping up into the slot to join the attack. There was one moment where he missed his assignment in his own end on the penalty kill near the end of the game to leave the opposition all alone next to the net and they scored on the opportunity and he has to make sure he isn't too aggressive on the puck carrier and is able to cover his man.

SSM # 37, D, Clutsom, Mac (2013) Clutsom demonstrated a nice shot from the point getting it through and on net, and played with a nice gap control defensively, using his stick to knock the puck away. He was also making some good safe plays and getting the puck in deep on the dump.

FINAL SCORE: 9-2 Sault Ste. Marie Greyhounds

Nov. 20, 2012, Kingston Frontenacs vs. Ottawa 67s (OHL)

KNG #15, LW, Beckstead, Marc (2013) Beckstead had a pretty good cycle game going deep in the offensive zone and put some nice pressure on the puck carrier and showed some good physicality on the fore-check. He doesn't have all the puck skills in the world but plays a good grinder role bringing that great net-front presence and a drive down the middle towards the net, and also did a nice job getting open down low next to the net on the power play. He found some good passing lanes to move the puck back to the point in the offensive zone, and was able to walk out from behind the net into the slot for a nice backhand opportunity. He showed some good hand-eye coordination and a battle in front of the net to knock the puck in for the team's second goal of the game and then made a great feed to spot a man driving the net down low to score the team's 3rd goal of the game. He had a jump in his step all night showing a good work ethic and was really putting some nice pressure and physicality on the puck carrier. He mishandled a pass through the neutral zone as well that resulted in a turnover and has to try to corral those pucks a bit better.

KNG # 17, C, Kujawinski, Ryan (2013) Kujawinski is a pretty quick skater with an elite offensive hockey sense. He can cycle the puck well in the offensive end and moves around to find open space well and shows some real nice puck protection. He comes back to his own end as well to offer support and is willing to drive to the net and open up to take passes. He is calm and patient with the puck and opened up well to take a one-timer next to the net but fanned on the shot. He displayed some nice quickness, agility and hands and was hustling hard showing that great speed and desire for loose pucks. If he turned the puck over he would battle to get it back and also have a net-front presence trying to tip pucks. He has some good hands but mishandled the puck and lost it by trying too many moves in the offensive zone and had some trouble tying up his man in front of his own net resulting in a goal for the opposition.

KNG # 27, RW, Dupuy, Jean (2013) Dupuy displayed a good responsible game in his own end tonight offering some good support on the back check and showing some nice aggression on the puck carrier. He was real nice and physical on the fore-check, and got a good cycle going in the offensive zone with some nice puck protection and also had a net-front presence. He took some long shots that were pretty weak and from the outside and missed the net and they really weren't good decisions or shots to say the least.

KNG # 61, LW, Fitzmorris, Mitchellp (2013) Fitzmorris is another blue collar player o this team who was cycling the puck well in the offensive zone and also had a real nice wide drive while protecting the puck to gain the zone. He is calm and patient with the puck and really does a good job pressuring the puck carrier and challenging him with his stick. He forces turnovers with his pressure but has to hit the net as he missed the net on a real weak outside shot on a rush up the ice and later had another opportunity and missed the net again. He battles hard for the pucks in the corners and was blocking shots as well on the penalty kill.

OTT # 20, C, Monahan, Sean (2013) Monahan started this game off quickly with a real bang taking a great feed on an odd man rush to score a one-timer 24 seconds into the game. He did a good job spotting a man in the high slot and getting him the puck and also did a great job getting out to the slot with the puck and finding some nice space to get a good shot off from scoring areas. He put some great pressure on the puck carrier and then picked up a turnover in the offensive zone along the boards and walked out to the slot for a great chance as he was just finding open ice all night long. He showed some good skating and speed and came back to offer support in his own end. He did a nice job holding up after gaining the zone and spotting a trailing man high with a nice pass and was hustling hard to be first on loose pucks. He was willing to stand in front of the net on the power play and just needs to watch some of the turnovers in the offensive zone by trying to force the puck through some areas.

OTT # 28, LW, Brown, Connor (2013) Brown was hitting really well tonight and had some great physicality and pressure on the fore-check. He made a real nice big hit on the fore-check early on and was showing some nice aggression to his game. He got a pretty nice cycle game going and was moving out front to the net, and did a nice job getting to the net looking for rebounds. He made some open ice hits as well and was clearing the puck well on the penalty kill.

OTT # 5, D, Desautels, Matthieu (2013) Desautels had his moments where he was using his stick well but then others where he just let his man walk around him too easily and get to the net. He also has to watch his stick as he took a tripping penalty early on just being careless with his stick and later was trying to rush the puck up the ice but was outskated and stripped of the puck.

OTT # 11, D, Vlajkov, Mike (2013) Vlajkov did a nice job reading the play to spot his opportunity to jump down low off the point to get a shot and score from the slot on a rebound. He showed some decent physicality in his own end and used his stick well to challenge the puck carrier or the shooter. He did a nice job getting his shot through from the point on the penalty kill and made a nice long pass up the ice as well for a breakout. At times he rushes a bit when he is under pressure and has to watch the suicide passes up the ice to teammates not recognizing where the opposition is coming in from.

OTT # 18, D, Davis, Taylor (2013) This was probably the best game I have seen Davis play this year. He was making some nice passes up the ice for breakouts and did a nice job defensively to close the game and take his man down to take the puck. He was also squeezing his man out along the boards and showing a good element off physicality and was able to protect the puck to avoid the pressure put on from the opposition. He did a nice job holding the line in the offensive zone and tying up his man in his own end. He was reading the play to step up and anticipate a pass to pick off a turnover in the neutral zone and was blocking shots in his own end on the penalty kill. He showed some nice aggression after the whistles to defend his goaltender and was using his stick well to check the puck up to teammates and away from the opposition. He has to watch the turnovers along the boards in his own end and watch where he is passing it and to get the puck out on his clears on the penalty kill whenever he can.

FINAL SCORE: 5-3 Ottawa 67s

Nov 20, 2012, Medicine Hat Tigers vs Everett Silvertips (WHL)

EVT #15 C Bauml Kohl (2013) Kohl was creating scoring chances for Everett all night. He stuck his nose into every ones business. With his speed and smarts he was cutting off passes and threading the needle. Kohls only downside is his size. I wish this kid was about 40lbs heavier and 3" taller and he would be a top power forward in the draft.

EVT #16 C Stadnyk Carson (2013) Was impressed with Carson play tonight. He played a crash and bang style that seem to work against the Tigers defense. Carson added two goals tonight. On Carson second goal he beat the the Tigers D-man wide with speed and forced his way to the net and put the biscuit home from a beautiful feed from Everett's Oslanski. Carson showed some soft hands in traffic and veteran poise through out the game. His defensive play needs work, he get caught running around and watching the puck a lot tonight.

EVT #25 D Mueller Mirco (2013) Mirco had solid defensive game. He control the play along the boards tonight with some aggressive hitting and stick work. He shut down the middle of the ice with presences. Micro was moving the puck very well tonight finding the seams with limited mistakes. He stepped up his game with the absent of Ryan Murray. He got sloppy at times during when he was caught in a couple shift changes.

MED #5 D Lewington Tyler (2013) One of the better Defenseman on the ice for the tigers tonight. I enjoy his aggressive style along the wall forcing Everett players to move the puck quickly not allowing them time to set up. His foot speed needs improvement, his 1 on 1 play and open ice gap control needs work. I don't see much for a draft prospect but could go in very late rounds.

MED #12 D Becker Kyle (2013) The best defenseman on the ice for the tigers. His skating allowed him to buy time and space to moved the puck with poise, finding outlets through traffic and Everetts forecheck. Kyle had good gap control through the zones and rarely got beat on any offensive rush. His physical play needs to find another gear, tends to be soft in the corners using his stick check more then the body at times. Needs to pick up his play in front of his own net, allowed Everett to walk right in on his tender a few times and showed no emotion.

Scouts Notes: Very low scoring game, players on both sides seemed to be lost or didn't want to make a game changing mistake. The hitting was sub par from both teams and most of the game lacked any speed. Everett's Trent Lofthouse and Griffen Foulk seemed to be going through the motions most of the night, just a heartbeat for Everett's bench. Medicine Hat has some strong players born in 95 and 96 should be interesting come next season. Top rated Tigers player Hunter Shinkaruk was not suited up.

Nov 21, 2012, Kootenay Ice vs Seattle Thunderbirds (WHL)

SEA#17 LD, Theodore, Shea(2013) Shea was putting on a show with stickhandling skills tonight. His smooth skating help him gain distance to thread a first good pass out of the zone during the game, but at times he tried to do to much with the puck resulting in a couple turn overs. His play in front of his net and along the boards was disappointing most of the game. I didn't see any physical part to his game and he allowed Kootenay to walk the puck right to the net.

SEA#19 LW, Sheen, Riley(2013) Riley used his speed and hands to put up a 4 point game. He used his quick hands in front and his speed along the boards to give Kootenay havoc all night. He was productive every shift through out the game in the offensive zone. His strength along the board was a big weakness tonight when he would get tied up, but when given some space to work he would burn you with his speed. His defensive play seemed to be on another planted tonight, he didn't work at all, he was set on offensive mode most of the night.

SEA#33 LD, Hauf, Jared(2013) A big defenseman for Seattles back end who shows flash's of skill at times. He used his condor reach most of the game keeping the speedy forwards out of the scoring areas, but he didn't use his size or strength to punish his opposition. Very slow footed and was making bad pinches most of the night.

KTY #25 LW Prochazka Jakub(2013) Played a decent game, showed flashes of skill most of the game. He used his skating to created scoring chances and was productive on both side of the puck most shifts. He plays a typical European style with not much physical play or grit.

KTY #23 C Reinhart Sam(2014) Sam shows a high level of Hockey IQ and vision, he was setting up his line mates most of the game. Sam was thinking the game a few steps a head of his teammates which tend to make his game slow down to there level. Sam is a very dynamic player who will be turning head all year long.

Scouts Notes: Seattle's Defensemen Taylor Green, Jerret Smith and Kevin Wolf are works in progress, especially since their skating and skill level are sub par for this level. All three got beat by speed shift after shift. This was a high scoring impact game from both teams. The aggressiveness from both teams tonight made for very poor defensive decision making causing both sides to turn over the puck leading to scoring chances. Seattle's Riley and Delnov were the impact players both putting up 4 points.

Final Score 7-4 Seattle

November 22, 2012, London Knights @ Sarnia Sting (OHL)

LON #4 LD Liberati, Miles (2013) - Liberati appeared confident and comfortable joining the rush fairly regularly on this game. He made very good passes and quick smart decisions with the puck.

LON #16 LC Domi, Max (2013) - Status quo for Max in tonight's game. Again showing excellent positioning in the offensive zone playing with relentless effort and determination. He uses his elusiveness in open ice extremely well but didn't over do it by passing off to line mates when necessary.

LON #53 LW Horvat, Bo (2013) - Horvat was silenced once again offensively but he was able to contribute in other ways. Although he received no points for it, he won battles on the power play in the offensive zone and was the difference between keeping the pressure on with the man advantage or a cleared zone several times. He worked very hard throughout the game and is hard to beat along the boards.

SAR #2 RD Chapman, Joshua (2013) - Chapman isn't afraid of going to war in the corners and behind the net. He is very aggressive but loses too many battles. Great play at one point getting his stick down blocking a pass saving a great scoring chance. He matched up pretty well 1 on 1 but sticks with his man too long which opens things up in the lower half of the offensive zone. At one point the Knights exploited this getting a 2 on 1 in the slot scoring what was the eventual game winning goal.

SAR #71 RW Goldobin, Nikolay (2014) - Showed off his hands as usual, but also his ability to shoot the puck. He has always been an excellent passer but he has a cannon of a shot using it to score the Sting's third goal of the night putting them within two of the Knights. He really was leading the charge towards creating several chances in the third period giving Sarnia a shot at getting back into this game. He drew multiple penalties with his calm and composed puck possession and rushing abilities.

SAR #77 RD DeAngelo, Anthony (2014) - DeAngelo was a little hit or miss tonight. He made some very good plays with the puck in the offensive zone both passing the puck and shooting it. He showed his end to end rushing ability but generally just threw the puck away afterwards.

SAR #94 LC Galchenyuk, Alex (Montreal) - Galchenyuk played great tonight in a losing effort. He shows tremendous hockey sense, ability to exploit any holes given by London and great creativity. He made some excellent passes and unloaded a laser shot with one second left on the clock in the second period to make it a 5-2 deficit.

Scouts Notes: London came out right off the drop of the puck and dominated this game. They managed to beat Sarnia 5-2. They took a 3-1 lead out of the first period and chased starting goaltender J.P. Anderson (San Jose) 25 minutes into the game as they took a 5-1 lead. The Knights let off the gas and Brodie Barrick (2013) came in and played 33 minutes of shutout hockey giving Sarnia a chance. The Sting did not stop working and ended up dominating the second half of this game controlling the play, drawing penalties but took a lot of perimeter chances and really only challenged Jake Patterson (2013*) a few times. Notable for London, Remi Elie (2013) showed some creativity at a few points in this game, but didn't do much outside battling hard and grinding it out.

November 23, 2012, Moose Jaw Warriors @ Edmonton Oil Kings (WHL)

MJW #7 RD Doucette, Braiden (2013) - Stuck with his man very well in one on one. Not overly smooth possessing the puck but gets the job done.

MJW #15 RW Hansen, Carter (2013) - Carter did not show off exemplary skating ability, but he does work extremely hard. Especially along the walls and in the corners.

MJW #19 RC Point, Brayden (2014) - Outstanding speed, not afraid to crash corners and work for the puck. Excellent hands and creativity created scoring chances while he was out there.

MJW #32 RD Morse, Spencer (2013) - Smooth backwards skating in transition. Makes good quick decisions with puck in his own zone. Good vision good mobility. One of Moose Jaw's best defensemen tonight.

MJW #1 G Paulic, Justin (2014) - Shows great composure in high pressure situations. Very little excess movement. Very calm and composed on breakaway. Can get caught out of position at time. Recovery is a little slow side to side not great either. Slow reflexes a few soft goals he probably should have had.

EDM #27 RC Lazar, Curtis (2013) - Very good at moving into slot hovering undetected. Very intelligently positions himself available for scoring chances. Slightly above average skating. Was set up on a breakaway but was stopped after making a great move. Always likes to drive the net offensively. Effective forcing turnovers at a high rate.

Scouts Notes: To open the game the Moose Jaw Warriors did a great job sticking with the highly regarded Oil Kings, but as the game reached the midway mark, Edmonton really started to pull away and in the third period just dominated to seal the victory. Griffin Reinhart (NY Islanders) scored the game winning goal and did a great job shutting down Moose Jaw's offense. Brandon Potomak (2013) showed great outside speed driving the wings and took the puck end to end in a losing effort.

November 24, 2012, Peterborough Petes @ Sarnia Sting (OHL)

PET #17 LW Betzold, Greg (2013) - Betzold created scoring chances early on in this game, and was fairly consistent in his ability to create offensive chances for his team. Does a good job out front of the opposing net screening the goaltender, which lead to Peterborough's first goal of the game. Betzold forechecks hard but eases up once he gets close to the puck carrier giving him a little extra time. He has slightly above average skating and did win some races to the puck. He protects the puck well in the offensive zone and can get his shot off with defenders all over him. Laid a few solid hits. Betzold went hard to the net the last shift of the third period and pulled off a nice move to score Peterborough's second goal.

PET #20 LW Ritchie, Nick (2014) - Great physicality, got called on a double minor essentially for a clean hit. Sarnia scored two goals on this power play. Early in the second Ritchie had good patience with the puck then unleashed a powerful shot to put Peterborough on the scoreboard. Ritchie showed he has some good moves and slick hands making some creative passes.

SAR #21 LC Nikandrov, Daniel (2013) - Showed good work ethic all game long. He battles and engages physically. One of the guys on the ice who seems to want the puck more than others. Deflected a point shot in to 8-2 Sarnia.

SAR #71 RW Goldobin, Nikolay (2014) - Tried to force passes too often. Even with his great playmaking ability he is getting a little predictable at times because he's so focused on the pass. He looked good but really needs to shoot more often.

Scouts Notes: Right from the very first shift of the game it was all Sarnia. Alex Galchenyuk (Montreal) scored a beautiful goal off a turnover in the slot on his first shift and it was all uphill for Sarnia from there. After Sarnia took a 3-0 lead through 20 minutes, Peterborough pulled Andrew D'Agostini (2013*) in exchange for Michael Giugovaz (2013). However when Giugovaz gave up three goals on three shots the Petes reverted back to D'Agostini down 6-0 early in the second period. Sarnia eventually walked away with a 8-2 win. Jonathan Tanus (2013) is a good skater. He battles hard and isn't intimidated by bigger players despite his size. Alan Quine (Detroit) struggled today giving up a large amount of turnovers, some of which resulted in goals against.

November 24 2012, Chicoutimi Saguenéens vs. Victoriaville Tigres (QMJHL)

CHI #17 LW Tremblay, Simon (2013) – He has very limited skills with the puck and didn't show much in terms of speed. He plays more of a defensive game on the third line. He didn't catch my eye in terms of intensity and physical play either. His work ethic is all right, but nothing out of the extraordinary. He did some good work on the penalty kill late in the game and was able to score a goal. He doesn't profile as a "draft worthy" prospect.

CHI #19 Tremblay, Tristan (2013) – Plays pretty much the same style than Simon Tremblay, but on the fourth line. His speed prevents him from playing a better grinding game and using his big body more. He didn't get a lot of ice time and there is not much to be said about his game. He could become a good defensive player in the QMJHL with more speed.

CHI #27 D Dauphin, Laurent (2013) – He started the game very slowly and I got to see very little of him with the puck until the second period. Then he picked up the pace and showed is great ability to control the game and slow it down. He doesn't have overwhelming hands but he's comfortable handling the puck on the move and he can hold on to it for long periods of time while the play develops. I particularly liked his vision and smartness on the ice. He reads the play ahead of him very well and he is able to find open ice where to skate or teammates to pass to. He finished the night with a lucky goal and two assists. He didn't blow me away with his offensive upside, but his passing play is precise and the puck possession aspect of his game is very good as well. His skating is a little bit above average but his game doesn't revolve around it. I also liked his anticipation without the puck in all three zones: he is in good place to receive pucks and to create turnovers in defensive or neutral zone. His anticipation compensates for the lack of physical play or puck battle that he didn't display in this game.

CHI #32 C Grégoire, Jérémie (2013) – First and foremost, his skating looked awful. He tries hard and moves his feet a lot but he just can't get that explosion. His top speed looks to be average at best. It prevents him from playing the hardnosed game he likes to play, both offensively and defensively. I got to see very little of him with the puck but he did the small details well. He positioned himself properly in the offensive to fire shots from close range and was very intense in his physical battles behind the net or along the boards. He's extremely strong and won most of them. He gave some hard checks as well and I saw him driving the net hard a couple times. His hustle and intensity still makes him a valuable player, but his skating could prevent him from being drafted as he is on the inside looking out right now.

CHI #39 D Tremblay, Carl (2013) – Started off the game with some good puck moving. He skates fairly well and made some good decisions moving forward with the puck. He played an honest overall game but he had some difficulties with his defensive coverage. His ice time also diminished in the second half of the game. On one occasion he was beat for a breakaway and he never saw the play develop from the offensive zone. He was alone at the blue line and the play developed on his right but never saw it and he couldn't catch up. He displayed some all right tools in this game but I don't view him as a legit prospect.

VIC #3 D Diaby, Jonathan (2013) – Diaby played an almost mistake free game. As always, he used his long reach and body to be extremely effective. He reads the 1 on 1 situation correctly and adapts really well. Even when he was beat wide, he made some good pivots and kept following his player around the net to prevent him from doing anything. The one glaring mistake he made was with Dauphin coming at him with speed and he had to hold him, which resulted in a penalty. He also displayed his underrated hard slap shot on the power play tonight. It takes him some time to wind-up, but when he does, it's a very hard shot.

VIC #12 C/W Rehak, Dominik (2013) – Rehak had about three or four shifts in this game playing on the fourth line. Displayed his speed on a straight line once but that was about it.

VIC #22 Rhéaume, Michael (2013) – Recently called up by Victoriaville, he had his moments in this game. He was bounced between lines and didn't get as many shifts as other forwards, but he showed excellent speed. The 5'8 forward can outburst his opposition when he has space and he did just that on a breakaway for a nice goal. He struggled when he had pressure on him and he wasn't able to use his speed, making some questionable decisions. He precipitated his decisions and gave the puck away too often. While is speed was impressive, is size is a big issue and he didn't impress me enough for now to mention him as a legit prospect.

VIC #34 D Beaulieu, Anthony (2013) – He made some good plays defensively with his long reach but also struggled handling speedy forwards. He had an up and down kind of game. He looked particularly bad with the puck, where he takes a lot of time to set up before he can take any decision or make any play. I believe he lacks too much to be considered as a prospect.

VIC #57 Veilleux, Tommy (2013) – Tommy opened the scoring with a goal. He took a slow shot from far away and when we all thought the play was dead; he went to the net and insisted numerous times on a shaky goaltender to slip the puck past him. I didn't really like his hitting game in this one. His timing was off and he launched himself into the boards more than anything else. He also got himself out of the play quite a few times by going too hard for a hit. He did connect a couple of times in the open ice but that was it. I liked the hustle he put into it, but I think it was more useless than helping his team in this game, especially with the penalties he took.

Nov 25, 2012, Kelowna Rockets vs Everett Silvertips (WHL Regular Season)
EVT #15 C Bauml Kohl (2013) Kohl didnt play his best game. He looked slow and out of place tonight. He was holding the stick a little to tight, forcing the puck through traffic causing turns overs. He had a few good shifts with some spark of offense but was shut down through out the game.
EVT #16 C Stadnyk Carson (2013) Carson played a physical game tonight, playing the body more then in recent games. It seemed like he was going out of his way to make contact with the puck carrier more then playing positional hockey to take away time and space. He was caught flat footed and watching the play most of the night.

EVT #25 D Mueller Mirco (2013) Mirco played his usual game, he was solid in his zone taking away space from the speedy rocket forwards. Every shift was consistent tonight with good body contact and stick checking. Micro was only minus -1 tonight after the shooting gallery the rockets put on everett.

KEL #6 D Wheaton Mitchell (2013) This kid has good size and showed it tonight with his puck protection and ability to make a good first pass out of the zone. He used the body well against Everett forwards not giving much space to work. His skating is OK, needs to work on his lateral movement. Finish with a +4 and showed some good offensive spark.

KEL #4 D Bowey Madison (2013) Had a good overall game, in the second he released a top cheddar bomb that Everetts goalie didnt even see. His skating ability allows him to create time and space. He showed some good hands and ability to draw the puck off the wall and put in on net. He controlled all 1 on 1 battles along the boards winning the battles. Just a work horse every shift. Bowey could add some size to his frame.

Scouts Notes: Kelowna controlled the tempo of the game all night putting a pounding on Everett. Kelowna's Nyberg and Baillie both had productive games showing good offensive skills and Rigby netted 3 for the hat trick. Everett's Lofthouse need some work on his skating, as he was a step behind most of the game, Betker played physical and was awarded with a good amount of ice time. Everett's Leedhal netted his first WHL goal, lots of talent and a player to watch.

Final Score: 8-2 Kelowna

Nov 25, 2012, Owen Sound Attack vs. Mississauga Steelheads (OHL)

OWS #18, LW, Pezzetta, Stefano (2013) Pezzetta was not much of a factor in this game but was at the least making the safe plays and dumping the puck in to get it deep. He had a few bad turnovers in his own end and was getting out muscled and out battled for the puck. I would say that his breakout, speed and work ethic were all poor tonight.

OWS #27, RW, Nastasiuk, Zach (2013) What Nastasiuk does well is protect the puck and drive hard to the net. He showed a good battle to try to win puck battles after losing the puck and showed a few nice attempts to drive to the net and get the puck in deep. He also drove hard to the net without the puck with his stick down looking for rebounds and did a great job opening up next to the net short side to take a pass and drive to the net with the puck. He showed some really amazing puck protection behind his net, as he is so strong and hard to knock off the puck and then moved it out front to an open man from behind the net under pressure. He got his stick in the way to block shots from the point as well and may not be the quickest player but he knows his role and in general will make the safe play.

OWS # 24, D, Bigras, Chris (2013) Bigras demonstrated the nice ability to rush the puck up out of his own end, but was also capable of making some good passes up the ice for a breakout. He didn't have the strongest shot but was at least getting it through and on net from the point and was forcing turnovers with some good pressure and then was willing to come up and join the attack to offer options. He used his stick well to try to force the opposition to the outside and direct their traffic and was passing the puck well all night long.

MIS # 10, RW, Goldberg, Andrew (2013) Goldberg didn't have the greatest game tonight as he struggled to handle passes resulting in some turnovers and missed his target on a pass up the ice for a breakout as well. He was out muscled off the puck too easily and needs to get a bit stronger on his feet. He moved the puck out front for teammates nicely but at times was trying to force through traffic or would take a weak low chance shot from the outside and was just throwing pucks on net not being overly creative.

MIS # 15, LW, Burnside, Josh (2013) I really liked Burnside's game tonight as he was making a lot happen all night long. He was skating well and was probably the fastest player on the ice showing that great quickness and agility. He put some good pressure on the fore-check and was breaking the puck out well and had a great net-front presence on the power play demonstrating that willingness to go to the dirty areas. He had good puck protection and was able to take a hit and hold on to the puck and made some good cross-ice passes after gaining the offensive zone. He was directing the opposition well defensively, and in the offensive zone could spot lanes to get himself open and offer options to his teammates to take some passes.

MIS # 18, RW, Babintsev, Sam (2013) Babintsev had his moments tonight but overall I felt his play was a little inconsistent. He showed some good physicality in his own end to separate his man from the puck and put some good pressure on the fore-check. He did a nice job blocking shots by reading the play and getting in lanes and had a net-front presence on the power play as well. He cycled the puck well to make some safe plays down deep but at times turned the puck over in the offensive zone trying to force the puck through the opposition. He had some long weak outside shots and got an opportunity from the slot but missed the net and has to watch the neutral zone turnovers as well.

MIS # 19, RW, Teskey, Scott (2013) Teskey was not very noticeable for most of the night tonight and didn't get too much ice time but was pretty defensively responsible to cover for his defenseman who went on a pinch. Unfortunately the play went back the other way and he let his man walk out front way too easily and it resulted in a goal for the opposition. He also made a good attempt to get the puck out of the zone but has to watch the neutral zone turnovers.

MIS # 20, D, Graves, Jacob (2013) Graves has a nice big frame for a defenseman and I would like to see him use it a bit more by being more physical in his own end when he has the opportunity. He did make some nice passes up the ice for a breakout and was dumping the puck in deep and then joining the rush to go in after it. He is capable of taking a hit and still making a play and was protecting the puck in his own end and battling to take it off the opposition, using his stick and body to wedge his man out and take the puck. He only had one shot opportunity from the point and fanned on the shot.

FINAL SCORE: 6-1 Owen Sound Attack

November 26 2012, Drummondville Voltigeurs vs. Victoriaville Tigres (QMJHL)

DRU #4 RW Grenier, Alexandre (2013) – He had very limited ice time playing on the fourth line. He came out with energy every shift he had and tried to apply pressure with intense body checks. He moved around all right for a big guy, but that was about it.

DRU #8 C Auger, Jeremy (2014) – Auger showed good speed throughout the game as he is always in movement and moving his feet. He didn't create much offensively, but he was always around the puck trying to keep it in movement with his speed. The 5'7 forward struggled with battles and back checks in my opinion. He lacked desire a little and the size factor didn't help him obviously.

DRU #11 LW Ratelle, Joey (2014) – Ratelle displayed some good puck handling abilities in this game. He showed he was comfortable with the puck and patient enough to let the play develop. He wasn't a major factor either, but he did good things with the puck. He was involved physically in the game and played fairly intensively, but his soft play in the defensive and bad positioning caused some turnovers.

DRU #13 RW Gauthier, Guillaume (2013) – He didn't really impress me as a prospect, but he did nice things with the puck. You don't get to see him much throughout the game, but he is a very good puck handler with quick hands. Most often, his tunnel vision prevented him from creating anything and his speed isn't a big factor in his game either.

DRU #15 D Brouillard, Nikolas (2013) – Brouillard had his moments offensively in this game, carrying the puck often and putting good shots on net. He has a nice package of speed, hands and creativity when he joins the rush and that makes him effective entering the offensive zone. He fired an average shot from the top of the circles that went through traffic for the goal. He also fired some good low shots on target. He also showed good vision to spot teammates across the ice. He didn't have many battles defensively, but you could see it's easy to make him back up and create space to shoot or pass the puck. His size and puck battles defensively are also negative aspects of his game.

VIC #3 D Diaby, Jonathan (2013) – I thought Diaby played a little bit of a sketchy game defensively, but he was effective and reliable as you would expect. He played a good game with the puck and did a good job using his speed and body to move the puck forward. He also had ice time on the power play and again, did surprisingly well. He moved the puck around l and scored a nice goal with his wrist shot. Most of the time he was patient enough to let shooting lanes open, but on one occasion he fired right in the legs of his opponent. He needs to make a better job at getting himself in the right position to receive passes from his teammates as he was a few seconds late at time, but I believe more experience on the power play will help him do that. Diaby also picked up a fight against Matt Boudens, where both went for a safe fight but landed some good punches.

VIC #12 C/W Rehak, Dominik (2013) – Rehak started the game on the fourth line, before being bounced on the top two lines and then going back on the fourth line. Therefore, he didn't get much ice time but did some all right things with the puck. He skated with it a couple times but his head was down and the opposing defense stopped him quick. He was also in a rush to fire shots when he entered the offensive zone, resulting in weak or out of targets shots.

VIC #22 Rhéaume, Michael (2013) – He was always in movement in this game and tried to get things going for his team. He drew a penalty in his offensive zone with his speed and effort. He had some good moments with the puck and tried to keep it simple despite his great speed and hands, which served him well. He got a breakaway again tonight, but wasn't able to score.

VIC #57 Veilleux, Tommy (2013) – Tommy had an average game. He didn't hit as much as usual and was a few step late on most plays. He struggled with coverage and was slow on the back check. He was still able to give some devastating checks. He needs to get his top speed going if he wants to be effective in his grinding and defensive role, not to mention offensively. I liked the job he did on the power play, blocking the view of the goalie.

November 27, 2012, PEI Rocket vs. Drummondville Voltigeurs (QMJHL)

PEI #1 G Bibeau, Antoine (1994 born) – Bibeau's game was overall solid, but his strong performance was overshadowed by two very bad goals he let in. On one goal, he was down on his knees quickly and let a soft backhand shot slip behind him. On another one, he gave up an easy goal between his legs. Other than that, he showed good athleticism moving from side to side and used his long legs to cover the bottom of the net. While his rebound control was good most of the time, it got himself in trouble on the 4th goal by Drummondville.

PEI #26 C/W Pépin, Alexis (2014) – Extremely solid player on his skates and he loves to throw his body around. His skating needs some polishing, but didn't look too bad for a big young player (6,2 – 196). The thing he needs to do better is to keep his feet in movement at all time to have a better reaction time and get his speed going faster. He didn't do much with the puck tonight and he precipitated his decisions, but he seems to have a strong shot.

PEI #27 D Graves, Ryan (2013) – I was not a fan of his game tonight. His skating didn't look to good both in terms of actual speed and footing. His coverage in front of the net was also deficient and he forgot to cover player quite a few times. His bad coverage led to Drummondville's first goal. I also didn't like his puck battles along the board, where he couldn't use his huge physical advantage. His play with the puck wasn't much better either. He tried to do too much at times and it killed the momentum for his team when he gave the puck away. He also displayed a very strong but inaccurate shot. He also did good using his long reach to cut plays in the neutral zone.

DRU #11 LW Ratelle, Joey (2014) – A forward in next year's draft, Ratelle showed very nice things with the puck in this game. He had his chances throughout the game and showed good puck handling. He wasn't able to capitalize on any of his chances, but you can see he is getting more comfortable carrying the puck as the season goes on. He also had a physical edge in this game and gave some solid checks. He needs to work on his play in the defensive, both with and without the puck. He tried to do too much on one occasion and turned the puck over.

DRU #15 D Brouillard, Nikolas (2013) – Once again his size was a big disadvantage for him in the defensive zone as he lost multiple battles deep in its zone. He also had a few good moments with the puck using his speed but that was it. The outcome of his game wasn't so bad because he was able to limit costing mistakes, but he didn't look like a prospect to me.

DRU #39 G Guindon, Louis-Philip (2013) – Guindon had a fairly good game and his reflexes were present in this one. The thing I noticed the most though aside from his reflexes is his rebound control. He struggled to keep the puck close to him when making a save or redirecting it out of harm's way. This lasted the whole game and came close to costing him some goals.

Nov 28, 2012, Vancouver Giants vs. Moose Jaw Warriors (WHL)

VAN#1 G, Lee, Payton(2014) Held the fort of the Giants for much of the night. They were outplayed for much of the game and couldn't generate any offensive chances. Showed off his flashy glove hand all game long. Liked the way he battled through traffic this game. Let in a soft first goal, but did a good job to bounce back from it. Above average rebound control, but could not do so on the second goal which was ultimately the game winner with 5 minutes left in regulation. Very quick on his feet and moves laterally well. Difficult to see him lose the starter job anytime soon.

VAN#16 RC, Popoff, Carter(2013) Hard working centre had a good game for the Giants. Made a number of good defensive plays to help out his defensemen. Showed a lot of determination along the boards and fighting for loose pucks, but his lack of size was often a factor. Shifty along the boards, but does not have great speed in open ice. Showed that he lacks offensive abilities and intelligence. Very ineffective on the PP as the slot guy and could not find much open space.

VAN#44 LD, Geertsen, Mason(2013) Steady defensive defenseman who, other than his goaltender, was the only player that really showed some kind of intensity on the Giants tonight. A good skater given his size, but could not stir Morgan Rielly to the corners off the rush on the second goal against. Other than that, was difficult to play against. Was very physical, but also did a good job to stay disciplined. Liked his defensive awareness in this game. Stayed between the dots on the PK, and only chased if there was an opportunity to get to a loose puck. Made good, smart outlet passes all game long as well. Limited offensive abilities.

MJ#19 RC, Point, Brayden(2014) Agile forward who had a bit of an inconsistent game tonight. Played a ton and received a lot of time on the PP but just could not get much going offensively. Needs to work on staying on his feet along the boards. Too easy to knock down. Size is definitely a factor. His lack of reach makes it difficult for him to protect the puck. However, his offensive abilities are definitely evident. Looks confident with the puck on his stick and possesses good vision. Needs to add more speed and grit to his game to ever have a chance of becoming a pro.

MJ#23 RC, Gore, Bryson(2013) Two way forward who played a good game tonight. Liked the intensity he brought to the game. Did not let the lack of size be a factor to his game. Looked strong along the boards and was able to come away with the loose puck a few times. Threw his weight around often as well. Does not have elite offensive abilities, and all of his chances offensively came from pure hard work. Has a nose for the net and is always around looking for rebounds. Played well without the puck as well. Stayed in good position in the defensive zone and took away passing and shooting lanes effectively.

Scouts Notes: This was not a very good game for both teams. Morgan Rielly of Moose Jaw was by far the best player on the ice for both teams. Such a fantastic overall skater. Had some issues handling bigger opponents though. Payton Lee was very good, but just could not make the 2 stops that he had to for his team. A little concerned with the drop of Jackson Houck's performance. Lack of speed makes him ineffective since his game is largely based around physical play. Had no chance to hit Rielly behind the net or get to a dump in first. Really liked Mason Geertsen's game. Only player on the Giants that seemed to have a pulse tonight. Vancouver had 3 good scoring chances tonight, 1 which they scored on and 2 that were breakaways. The team looks extremely disinterested. Disappointed with Brayden Point's performance. Needs to be stronger and much more quicker. A little surprised that he's been able to put up the amount of points that he has so far.

FINAL SCORE: 2-1 Moose Jaw

November 29, 2012, LaSalle Vipers @ Sarnia Legionnaires (GOJHL)

LAS #12 RC Jones, Blake (2014) - Jones showed a very good compete level in the corners and battled effectively in front of the net. He has an OK shot but struggled with accuracy at times. His skating is below average despite being 5'9". Jones is a 14th Round pick of the Erie otters in the 2011 OHL Priority Selection.

LAS #73 LD Brown, Graeme (2014) - Good skater with decent size. He has good mobility and overall skating in all areas. He is capable of skating the puck out of trouble and rushing it end to end. He also skates well backwards. On many occasions Brown was left out for long shifts but he showed the endurance to handle this effectively. He was usually the first out in all game situations he had good positioning on the penalty kill and negated rebound opportunities. Good puck mover who completes most of his passes but did have his share of turnovers. Most of them come when he's trying to create scoring chances in the offensive zone. Brown is a 3rd Round pick of the Windsor Spitfires in the 2012 OHL Priority Selection.

SAR #9 RC Tyczynski, Hunter (2014) - Tyczinski has good size and looks very comfortable rushing the puck. He has been a pretty steady presence for the Legionnaires and plays a pretty simple but competitive game. Tyczynski is a 13th Round pick of the Barrie Colts in the 2012 OHL Priority Selection.

SAR #14 RD King, Jeff (2014) - King plays a very equal two way game and is used regularly in all game situations He made some good defensive plays to break up scoring chances and blocking shots. He moves the puck fairly confidently up ice. However considering his size his skating doesn't quiet appear to be where it should be. King is a 10th round pick of the Sarnia Sting in the 2012 OHL Priority Selection.

SAR #26 RD Vandervaart, P.J. (2013) - Started out much in the same way he has the past few games opening very physical. He set the tone early after two big hits as his teammates appeared to become more physical as well. Usually only gets beat on quick transition turnover plays as he's advancing up the ice but on the second play he dove to break up what would have been a 2 on 0 and completely negated it. He rarely gets beat one on one when he's in position. His physicality intimidated LaSalle on a few occasions. He postured to throw a hip check at which time the LaSalle player just poked the puck ahead conceding it to Vandervaart. Later on his captain got hit with a questionable hit. The next time he was on the ice with the opposing player he went after him tripping him up then challenging him to a fight. The player in question despite playing physical all game wanted nothing to do with

P.J. and couldn't get away from him and back to his bench fast enough. Unfortunately he took a minor penalty on the play and it resulted in a power play goal against his team.

Scouts Notes: A very entertaining game tonight between two teams battling for 6th place in the conference. Both teams went back and forth and the momentum shifted many times. A very physical game and one where the goal difference was never more than one goal until the final five minutes of the game when LaSalle scored to put the game away with a 4-2 victory.

November 30, 2012, Saginaw Spirit @ Sarnia Sting (OHL)

SAG #18 LW Perklin, David (2013) - Perklin struggled today getting outworked for pucks and losing one on one battles. He has good hands but couldn't get many things rolling. He played a little stronger in the second period creating scoring chances with passing but didn't have a great overall game.

SAG #21 RC Lodge, Jimmy (2013) - Lodge is an excellent skater and at 6'2" this is clearly his biggest asset. He forces turnovers in the offensive zone and turns them into scoring chances. He uses his speed whenever he can to fly back to the defensive zone in transition and is very responsible in his own zone. He has good size but has a very, very thin frame and has a lot of room to add muscle. He doesn't show any interest in the physical game. He has a long way to go development wise but could pay off big for whichever team selects him.

SAG #83 LD Prophet, Brandon (2014) - Prophet's progression in the OHL has been a very sharp curve. He came into the league with NHL ready size, but as a 16 year old he makes some very smart plays one on one. He moves the puck very intelligently up ice and doesn't make many mistakes. Consistently physical and aggressive.

SAG #91 RW Moutrey, Nick (2013) - Moutrey looked great throughout this game. It all started when the puck dropped where he took the puck, he beat a defensemen driving down the wing. After getting his shot off he went to the net where the rebound was put on goal. Moutrey tipped it in to give Saginaw a 1-0 lead 27 seconds in. He uses his quick hands, combination of size and speed to consistently create chances for the Spirit throughout the game. He is creative with the puck and shows good hockey sense. Because of this he played a huge amount of the third period for Saginaw trying to get them back into the game. He uses his size to impose his will along the boards and wins a lot of battles. He plays a very physical game in general. Moutrey projects to be a power forward, but thanks to his skating and hands may do much better than your average power forward.

SAR #11 RW Hargrave, Brett (2014) - Good puck protection although skating is slightly below average. Considering his size and age this isn't much of a problem. He showed good net presence banging in the eventual game winning goal with only 11 seconds left in the second period.

SAR #14 LW Boucher, Reid (New Jersey) - Everything he shot seemed to go in. He was fed with a good pass two on one just one minute into the game to score. He had good positioning on the power play which made him available for passes and resulted in his second goal. He then scored just over midway through the game to have a hat trick and score what was the tying goal at the time.

SAR #71 RW Goldobin, Nikolay (2014) - Very good skater who has improved a lot this year. He's extremely creative and made some excellent passes, although he should use his powerful shot a lot more than he does. Doesn't like to hit but will forecheck.

SAR #74 LW Carnevale, Alex (2013) - Creating more chances playing on the third line. He forced turnovers and played with a lot of energy and a decent amount of physicality. Fairly consistent since joining the Sting with his hard work.

SAR #77 RD DeAngelo, Anthony (2014) - Got beat early one on one played physical on the next shift one on one. Not rushing puck as much good puck movement. Got called for a pen that was really just DeAngelo making a very good play in one on one coverage. He didn't like the call and although it was a bad one Anthony unnecessarily threw a bit of a fit on the referee for the call.

Scouts Notes: When the opening minute supplied a 1-1 game you could get the feeling that this game was going to be a high scoring match-up. Both Jake Paterson (Detroit) and J.P. Anderson (San Jose) struggled a bit in this match-up, particularly in the first half of the season. Garret Ross (Chicago) who was a positive impact in this game for Saginaw unleashed a laser to give Saginaw what seemed like a commanding 3-1 lead. However Sarnia answered with 6 of the next 7 goals to give themselves a 7-4 victory in a game that wasn't particularly the most technically executed game on either side. Maybe the only group that was on the same page was Sarnia's top line of Alex Galchenyuk (Montreal), Reid Boucher (New Jersey) and Charles Sarault (Free Agent). All three scored goals in the first period, and they supplied 6 of Sarnia's 7 goals. For the Sting Davis Brown (2013) showed great skating ability and great work ethic winning battles and playing effectively along the boards. For Saginaw Terry Trafford (2013*) who was passed over in last year's draft showed an excellent forecheck forcing turnovers. He has to be one of the best skaters in the entire OHL. Unfortunately he has very little offensive skill to speak of.

Dec 1st, 2012, Portland Winterhawks vs Everett Silvertips (WHL)

EVT #15 C Bauml Kohl (2013) Kohl played on and off tonight. He had couple good offensive shifts were he controlled the flow. He played a solid defensive game, blocking shots and taking away time and space, he force Portlands defense to turn over the puck but couldnt turn it into a productive offensive rush. Kohl has the tools to be a dominate player but is lacking the size to add that extra punch to his game.

EVT #16 C Stadnyk Carson (2013) Carson look like a man on a mission tonight hitting everything that touched the puck. I liked the physical aspect of his game tonight but needs to learn when to deliver contact as he took himself out of the play most of the night. His offensive play is starting to come around as he was getting more creative with the puck, and willing to take a pounding in the scoring areas.

EVT #25 D Mueller Mirco (2013) Mirco played his usual game, he was very consitent with his play tonight, not allowing anyone to skate through the scoring areas. He used some good angles to keep Portlands speedy players to the outside and was standing them up at the blue line most of the game. He rushed the puck a couple shifts which caught me by surprise as hes not much of a offensive minded player.

PORT #3 LD Jones Seth (2013)- Jones played a good game tonight, he joined the rush looking to help the offensive threat almost every shift. At times it looked like jones was on a mission , controlling his defensive zone with good stick checks and body positioning. I would of like to see him be more physical along the boards and use his size. His hockey senses are top notch, he shows a good understanding of both side of the puck. Jones look like a man playing with boys for a few shifts, he dominated both sides of the puck. I was impressed with his play tonight.

PORT #27 RW Bjorkstrand Oliver (2013)- Oliver came out flying during the 1st period, then caught on fire in the 2nd and 3rd. I was impressed with his offensive instincts and skating , his ability to slide into the shallow areas of the ice unnoticed and deliver a nasty wrister or pin point pass was top notch. This kid is a gamer and works every shift.

PORT #19 C Petan Nicolas (2013)- Petan started slow tonight, but his game picked up through out the the last two periods, he used his speed causing havoc on the defense, petan was very slick along the boards winning the battles. He showed his creativity with the puck showing why he is 3rd in league scoring adding a assist. Petan needs to add some size to his smaller frame, as he got pushed around trying to find the scoring areas of the ice.

Scouts Notes: Portland's Hanson and Vorobev played flat tonight, both theres games picked up through out the night, Ty Rattie (St.Louis) dazzled notching a goal and assist tonight and Pouliot (Pitts) added a pretty goal and was solid most of the game. Everett's lofthouse had a couple good shifts but was unnoticeable for much of the game.

Final Score 4-1 Portland

Dec 1, 2012, Green Bay Gamblers vs. Indiana Ice (USHL)

IND # 15, LW, Talcott, Alex (2013) Talcott got to the front of the net looking for loose pucks and rebounds. He put good pressure on the fore-check and played the puck carrier with a nice element of physicality. He was able to cycle the puck in deep and went to the net nicely with his stick down to provide scoring options. He needs to have a bit more battle and compete for the puck and also has to watch the turnovers along the boards by not being strong on the puck.

IND # 24, LW, Pieper, Bo (2013) Pieper put some good pressure on the puck carrier and was battling nicely for territory in front of the opposition's net. He was also using his stick well to knock the puck free off the opposition and force turnovers but was repeatedly taking long outside shots on the rush with teammates and options available. He also needs to move the puck or drive it down low on the rush rather than shooting into sticks and having his shots deflected out of play.

IND # 61, D, Valiev, Rinat (2013) Valiev read the play pretty well to pick off a neutral zone turnover and was hustling well for loose pucks. He made some nice chip plays to move the puck up along the boards and tied up his man pretty well in front of the net. He made a nice pass in the offensive zone to find an open man in the high slot ad was coming down into the high slot himself to provide scoring options and to join the attack. He was a bit aggressive going for a hit along the boards as a man got in behind him for an excellent opportunity and he also needs to watch the offensive zone turnovers trying to force passes through the opposition. He showed good agility with the puck to twist from the opposition's pressure, but has to get his shots through to the net on his chances from the point.

GBG # 5, D, Olofsson, Gustav (2013) Olofsson was jumping in on the pinch to hold the puck in the zone and keep the attack alive. He played his man hard and physical along the boards and used his stick well to knock the puck away from the opposition. He was able to skate the puck up the ice, protecting it well to get it in deep into the offensive zone and got a cycle going in deep. He cleared the puck out of the zone on the penalty kill and just needs to try to get his shots through to the net better on chances from the point.

GBG # 16, C, Weiss, Mathew (2013) Weis was moving the puck up pretty well on the breakout and displayed some nice hands to make moves and get around defenders. He made an excellent pass on the rush to find the open man down low next to the net and was distributing the puck well on the rush through the neutral zone too. He did a great job of coming back to tie up his man in front of the net and lift his stick to take away their opportunity but just needs to watch the offensive zone turnovers trying to force passes through the opposition.

GBG # 23, D, Gross, Jordan (2013) Gross was able to skate the puck up the ice pretty well to get it in deep and was distributing the puck in the offensive zone to find an open man down low off the rush to score. He was moving the puck up pretty well on the breakout out of the zone and did a good job clearing the puck out of the zone on the penalty kill. He was able to get some shots through to the net form the point but needs to do this more consistently.

GBG # 24, D, Siroky, Ryan (2013) Siroky got a nice cycle going and was physical on the puck carrier, finishing his hits along the boards on the back-check. He has some hands as he tried to get around defenders to drive the puck in towards the net and was also driving to the net well without the puck with his stick down. He got himself to the front of the net and battled for both territory and loose pucks but just needs to hit his target on his breakout passes more often.

GBG # 97, LW, Dikushin, Grigory (2013) Dikushin got the puck in deep on some pretty simple plays and was getting the cycle going in deep in the offensive zone. He put good pressure on the puck carrier on the fore-check and got himself to the front of the net. He was forcing turnovers and at one point was able to take the puck then move it to the front of the net for a teammate to score. He got in behind the opposition's defense to take a pass with speed then come in on a break and made a great move for a good chance in tight and was competing well along the boards to win puck battles. He has to watch the turnovers along the boards trying to move the puck out to start the breakout and also through the neutral zone on puck mishandles. He was also taking a lot of long outside shots off on the rush.

FINAL SCORE: 6-3 Green Bay Gamblers

Dec 4, 2012, Guelph Storm vs. Kitchener Rangers (OHL)

GUE # 11, LW, Dickinson, Jason (2013) Dickinson has some good speed to his game and was battling hard for pucks on the fore-check. He was making some good passes and moving the puck well in the offensive zone on the power play. He put some good pressure on the point on the penalty kill and was willing to get in lanes to block shots and passes. He had some good puck protection along the boards in the offensive zone and was coming back to his own end to offer some support. He made a nice little chip play to pass the puck up the ice and had a really nice battle for the puck deep in his own end. He did a nice job opening up in the high slot to take a pass and put a shot on net but needs to be stronger on the puck and to watch turnovers and get the puck in deep when no options are available. He made a real nice feed down low to spot a man short side next to the net for a great chance and did a good job closing the gap and forcing a turnover with some good pressure. He had a nice wide drive but was squeezed off the puck and made a great diving play to knock the puck out of the zone with his stick on the penalty kill. He also had a nice backhand move to score in the shootout.

GUE #19, C, Garlent, Hunter (2013) A smaller player who is not easily intimidated and is a good skater with nice quickness and agility. He has good speed and was back-checking hard. He put good pressure on the fore-check and was driving hard to the net. He did a nice job holding the offensive zone and made some good passes up the ice for breakout. He had a nice cycle game going deep in the offensive zone and opens up well on the power play and can find a lane to offer a one-timer option from the high slot. He took a long pass well but then cut up after gaining the zone and needs to drive the puck down low.

GUE # 7, D, Harpur, Ben (2013) Harpur did a good job closing the gap and keeping the opposition from driving to the middle with his body. He joined the rush to get the puck in deep and lead the attack and had a good shot opportunity from the point but fanned on the shot. He also made some high risk passes through the neutral zone trying to move the puck up on the rush.

KIT # 16, LW, Pedersen, Brent (2013) Pedersen started this game with some great speed and a drive to the net to pick up a rebound and score the team's first goal of the game. He was putting the puck in deep and then went hard on the fore-check to pressure the puck carrier with some physicality. He also had some nice puck protection and a cycle deep in the offensive zone. He has good hands and a drive down low towards the net and was back-checking hard coming back to breakup chances on the opposition's breakaways. He had a great wide drive and cut to the middle for a nice chance in overtime but missed the net and at times turned the puck over in the offensive zone by trying to force the play. He made a great move to score in the shootout.

KIT # 95, C, Bailey, Justin (2013) Bailey put on some good pressure in the offensive zone and had a hard drive to the net. He held up at the line after gaining the zone to try to move the puck to a trailing man for a chance. Bailey had a bad turnover right up the middle through the neutral zone and also has to watch the turnovers in the offensive zone and was outmuscled in a puck battle in the offensive zone as well.

KIT # 3, D, Genovese, Cory (2013) Genovese made a nice pinch to hold the puck in the offensive zone early on and has a nice reach with his stick to check the puck away in his own end. He showed some good physicality finishing his hits along the boards and did a nice job getting his stick in shooting lanes to block shots.

KIT # 55, D, Gilbert, Jared (2013) Gilbert has some good size and was battling for the puck along the boards in his own end. He can work the puck under pressure and gets it out of the zone well. He did a good job stepping up to challenge the puck carrier and knock the puck away with his stick. He has some good puck protection in his own end and made some nice passes up the ice for breakouts. He had a nice use of his stick to poke the puck out to a teammate and used it as well to knock the puck away from the opposition and then move up for a breakout. He missed his target a couple times on the breakout and had a bad turnover up the middle through the neutral zone.

FINAL SCORE: 3-2 Guelph Storm

Dec 4, 2012, Portland Winterhawks vs. Everett Silvertips (WHL)

POR#19 LC, Petan, Nicolas(2013) Showed why he is one of the points leaders in the league tonight. So quick with his decision making when he has the puck and combines it with his high level of hockey sense to make it very difficult for opponents to try to stop him. Showed willingness to go into the tough areas to win puck battles with sheer determination. Only listed as 5'9, but he tried to play much bigger than that. Played with determination that is rarely seen by guys as small as he is. His speed allows him to beat defenders wide and have a wide lane to the net to either take a shot for himself or pass it off to his teammates to school.

POR#27 RW, Bjorkstrand, Oliver(2013) Speedy winger had a very good first half of the game, then disappeared for much of the other half. Definitely at his best when he is moving his feet and making tight turns along the boards to lose opponents and feed the puck to an open teammate for a goal. Really liked the way he was always looking towards the play instead of facing the boards and not knowing where his teammates were and what the situation looked like. Showed off a good wrist shot as well. Defensively, still looks like he has some learning to do. Had a tendency to lose track of where his point man was and not be in the right position to block shots or take away passing lanes.

EVE#25 LD, Mirco, Mueller(2013) Big, offensive defenseman who played one of his better 2 way games tonight. He was engaged physically, which was something he did not do too much of at the beginning of the year. Might have something to do with the rivalry, or he has made an effort to add a physical element to his game. Liked the way he used his stick to knock away passes tonight consistently. Has a big slap shot from the point that he is not afraid to use. Really liked how quickly he moved the puck tonight. Made nice, crisp passes too. Needs to cut down on his turnovers though. Has a tendency to force plays or try to carry the puck and get it stripped and have a counter attack going towards his own end.

EVE#30 G, Lotz, Austin(2013) Goaltender gave up 7 goals tonight, but looked very solid overall. Got very little help all night long, and realistically he should have gotten 1 of them. Did a very good job of looking through traffic to make saves. Not only was he able to consistently look through the number of bodies in front of him, but he also did a very good job to hold onto rebounds or push them to the corners. Displayed quick, active arms, but his blocker hand could be better. He is quick on his feet and quick to recover after going down to his butterfly stance.

SCOUT'S NOTES: This was a fun game to watch with the number of goals it had. Brendan Leipsic of Portland scored 4 times tonight, and was on another level from everybody else. Played the game very as usual, and was rewarded in a big way tonight. Brendan Burke of Portland really struggled in net tonight. Gave up a number of soft goals, and looked shaky whenever Everett would throw pucks at him.

FINAL SCORE: 7-5 Portland

Dec 5, 2012, Kelowna Rockets vs. Swift Current Broncos (WHL)

KEL#4 RD, Bowey, Madison(2013) Very agile defenseman who displayed his high level of hockey sense, and combined it with his skating abilities to be a big factor in the game tonight. He joined the rush a couple of times after knocking the puck off of an opponent's stick to start a counter attack. He read the play very well consistently, and opponents had a difficult time carrying the puck into Kelowna's zone with possession if they were coming through Bowey's side. He is very strong on his skates, and engaged physically along the boards and came away with the puck often. He was in good position throughout the game and let the play come to him instead of chasing the puck mindlessly. Did a good job to control his energy. Would like to see him carry the puck more as he liked to stay on the safe side on the breakout and just make passes to his forwards even when there were lanes to attack. Could have used his shot more from the point too.

KEL#6 RD, Wheaton, Mitchell(2013) A big defenseman who was Bowey's defense partner tonight and was more of the stay at home defenseman. Was simple with the puck and did not try to be fancy. Very strong on his skates and was a force along the boards and in the slot. Read the play quite well. Would like to see him use his size more and land some more hits and be harder to play against. Not the greatest skater, but certainly held his own on the rush and did a good job to keep opponents to the outside. Gave forwards some room to come down the wing to compensate for his speed.

SC#2 LD, Heatherington, Dillon(2013) Another big defenseman who played in this game, and was surprisingly mobile given his size. He lacks explosive speed, but showed that he can skate at a high level. Made one bad turnover along the offensive zone blue line which turned into a 2 on 1, but he was able to come back and break up the play. Was hard to play against in the defensive zone with his hockey sense, speed and physicality. Did not show much offensively, but made good first passes out of the zone consistently. Logged a ton of minutes, but was good throughout the game in all situations.

SC#5 LD, Martin, Brycen(2014) Rookie defenseman in the league and looked very poised when he was on the ice and played a very good game. Really liked his play with the puck as he was able to make some great passes. One memorable pass came in the second period when he made a long stretch pass from his goal line to the offensive blue line to hit his teammate tape to tape for a breakaway chance through the forecheck. Really liked his play in the defensive zone as well, especially along the boards. He displayed very good strength and displayed good awareness without the puck in the slot. Would like to see him have a more active stick on the rush and be able to take away passes and shots. Definitely a player to watch for in the future.

SC#28 LW, Gordon, Coda(CALGARY) Drafted by the Flames last year, and fans should be concerned with his lack of physical play and impact he made in the game overall. Plays on the first line for the Broncos, but was ineffective in the offensive zone. Just floated around the ice often and was not able to get good positioning in the good scoring areas. Did not see the goal scoring abilities tonight that he displayed last year. Defensively is a mess. Not always in the right position and was not effective with his body at all.

Scouts: This game was filled with a lot of goals and poor defensive play on both sides. Madison Bowey really shined for Kelowna as their best defenseman in this game. Was solid at both ends of the ice and did not try to force any plays. Also like the progress Damon Severson has made in his game. A draft pick of New Jersey, looks much more composed in his own zone and in consistently good position. Has seemed to have taken away a bit in his offensive game, but definitely needed to in order to be an effective defenseman. Impressed with Dillon Heatherington tonight. Not convinced yet that he will provide much offense as a pro, but can definitely be a force in his own end. Calgary should be worried with Coda Gordon's play. Was shockingly ineffective tonight when he is counted on by his team to produce points.

FINAL SCORE: 6-5 Kelowna

Dec 05, 2012, Lethbridge Hurricanes vs. Edmonton Oil Kings (WHL)

LET#6 RD, Erkamps, Macoy(2013) Smart, puck moving defenseman had a very solid game tonight. Makes up for his lack of size with his hockey sense in both ends of the ice. Made one very good play to take a slap shot wide to the net, which bounced right to the slot to his teammate for a very good chance to score. Time and time again, made smart, accurate breakout passes. A good skater, who handled speed of opponents with ease. Defensively, could be stronger along the boards, but tried to keep opponents honest in the neutral zone by jumping into the play to land an open ice hit a few times. Has a good active stick to knock pucks away and to steer opponents to the outside. Showed off good awareness without the puck to be in good, consistent position all game long. Nothing particularly flashy about his game tonight.

LET#14 LD, Pilon, Ryan(2015) Big, rookie defenseman who showed good flashes of brilliance tonight. Biggest concern in his game is the lack of urgency he plays with. A couple of times, he was too nonchalant with the puck, and got it taken away as a result. Otherwise, he moves the puck quite well, and already quarterbacks the first unit PP for Lethbridge. He likes to get shots on net quickly, and rarely got a slap shot off, but when he did, he let go a rocket from the point. Pilon has nice feet for a tall player, and gets around in tight areas quite well. He engages physically along the walls, but still has some muscle to put on.

LET#21 RC, Merkley, Jay(2013) Speedy forward was invisible for most of the night offensively, but made some impact in his one zone. He read the play pretty well and was able to cause some turnovers throughout the game. He used his stick effectively to tip away shots a few times too. The key for him to being successful is to keep moving his feet and using his speed to his advantage. He is not particularly great along the boards, and does not have great hands or vision to create offense that way. He managed to score a goal in tight by controlling a bouncing puck and quickly releasing it on net.

EDM#27 RC, Lazar, Curtis(2013) Very intelligent forward who showed off some great intangibles to his game tonight. Got better as the game went along and was really the only player on his team competing in a game that was arguably already lost. Not terribly quick or skilled, but without the puck, it's quite obvious that he thinks the game well. He is always looking around to be aware of his surroundings and to try to be in the right position defensively and offensively. Showed off his high compete level on his first goal by outbattling an opponent in front of the net to get good positioning and to beat him to the slot for an easy goal.

SCOUT'S NOTES: Lethbridge dominated this game from start to finish and put together a solid effort from all of their players. Came away impressed with Cur-

tis Lazar's game tonight. He was really the only player that competed from start to finish and was the only player that showed some intensity and focus. Giorgio Estephan played in his first WHL game with Lethbridge and looked quite good. He got more playing time as the game went on, and even scored a goal off of a rebound. Definitely a player to watch for in the future. Impressed with the improvements Russell Maxwell has made in his game since last year. Basically carrying Lethbridge offensively now. Stands at only 5'8, so he will have to take his game to another level again to get noticed by NHL teams.

FINAL SCORE: 6-2 Lethbridge

Dec 5, 2012, Belleville Bulls vs. Peterborough Petes (OHL)

BEL # 8, C, Berisha, Aaron (2013) Berisha showed some good hands, skating and hockey sense tonight. He was getting a pretty good cycle game going and going hard to the net showing some nice puck protection. He was able to make his passes up the ice for a breakout on the rush and had some good speed and pressure put on the puck carrier. He was pressuring well on the fore-check and was able to move the puck around well including a couple real nice centering passes to find an open man in front of the net. He did a nice job opening up in the slot to take a shot on an odd-man rush to score the team's 1st goal of the game and was finding open space to work with in the offensive end.

BEL # 13, RW, Kuptsov, Sergey (2013) Kuptsov displayed a nice hustle to get on loose pucks and was showing some good physicality as well including a real nice big hit in his own end to knock over the puck carrier. He did a pretty nice job finding a lane to move the puck back to the point on the power play and is a pretty good skater but has to get the puck in deep, and he has to make sure he is hitting the net on his shots coming in off the rush. I would also like to see a bit more battle for the puck in front of the net.

BEL # 14, D, Subban, Jordan (2013) Subban was most effective tonight jumping in off the point to spot his opportunities and get some good shots off from the slot, as he did this about 3 or 4 times and was able to score the team's 2nd goal of the game as well on this type of play. He displayed some nice stick work and aggression in his own end and was tying up his man very well. He did a nice job walking up into the slot with the puck to get a good shot on net and was passing the puck up well for breakouts. He is very agile and quick and can make some nice chip plays in his own end to buy some time and space. He moved the puck around well in the offensive zone and was getting his shot through from the point. He can pass or skate the puck up the ice on a rush and showed some nice hands to get the puck in deep. He got in the way of some of the opposition's plays to breakup their opportunities but has to watch the turnovers through the neutral zone and in his own end as well by trying to force the plays through unnecessarily.

PET # 17, LW, Betzold, Greg (2013) Betzold showed some nice speed, pressure and physicality on the fore-check. He got a nice cycle game going and had a good give and go to get to the front of the net for a great opportunity. He chose to dump the puck in deep when he was out of options and also had a nice drive to get down low towards the net on the rush. He is a quick skater who likes to dump and chase and then to cycle the puck but also has some nice hands and moves that he showed to drive the puck down low and then some good puck protection to walk out to the slot for a shot on net. He did a good job getting his stick in lanes to breakup passes in his own end on the penalty kill and did a nice job pressuring the puck carrier. He displayed a good battle and drive to get to the net, but has to get his shots through off the rush and watch that he isn't trying to force his passes through in the offensive end.

PET # 18, C, Tanus, Jonatan (2013) Tanus had a really nice feed to spot Nosad open all alone in front of the net for a great opportunity, but other than that there was not too much that impressed me about his game tonight. His shots got blocked trying to get them through and on net and he missed his target on a few passes through the neutral zone resulting in turnovers. He showed some good patience with the puck but then did nothing with it and I would also like to see more battle for pucks in front of the net.

PET # 21, RW, Nosad, Stephen (2013) Nosad had a great chance early on with a 2-on-1 opportunity and opened up well to take the feed but then fanned on the opportunity. He did a nice job getting open all alone in front of the net to get a good shot off and made a nice centering pass as well later on to find a teammate all alone in the slot. He showed a good hustle to get on loose pucks and was driving to the net with his stick down looking for chances. He had a nice attempt to move the puck across to a man open down low next to the net and was pressuring the puck carrier as well. He turned the puck over a few times though in this game and at times was just weak in his passes up along the boards in the offensive zone.

PET # 8, D, Varga, Steven (2013) Varga made a few good passes up the ice for breakouts but still needs to watch some of the neutral zone turnovers. He had a nice battle for the puck along the boards in his own end and was getting his stick in the shooting lane to tip shots out of the way. He showed some nice stick work to poke the puck out to break it out of the zone, but he has to hit the net on his shots from the point.

FINAL SCORE: 3-2 Belleville Bulls

Dec 6, 2012, Peterborough Petes vs. Kingston Frontenacs (OHL)

PET # 17, LW, Betzold, Greg (2013) Betzold has some really nice speed and hustle to his game. He works for loose pucks and drives hard to the net. He was passing the puck pretty well out of his own end to start a rush through the neutral zone and displayed some nice creativity as well on a drop pass to a teammate for a good chance. He battles for pucks down low in the offensive zone and had a great give and go feed to move the puck out front to a man in the slot for the team's 1st goal of the game. He was getting open down low in the slot on the power play and also did a great job opening up for a one-tier from down low. He was physical on the puck carrier on the fore-check, showing his great speed and hitting again as he actually broke the glass on one of his hits. He was picking off turnovers deep in the offensive zone for at least on great shot from in tight and had a nice wide drive with speed and cut to the net for a great chance in overtime. He made one bad play clearing the puck over the glass and had to take a delay of game penalty but had a pretty solid game all-round tonight.

PET # 18, C, Tanus, Jonatan (2013) Tanus was putting some good pressure on the puck carrier and finishing his checks. He made a pretty decent little chip play to get the puck out of the zone and start the rush and was cycling the puck pretty well in the offensive zone. He battled hard for the puck and showed some decent puck distribution through the neutral zone. He showed he is willing to get involved in scrums with some good aggression and was able to skate the puck up the ice with ease and get a decent long shot on net from the high slot. He was also willing to drive the net hard looking for rebounds. He has to watch some of the turnovers along the boards in his own end.

PET # 21, RW, Nosad, Stephen (2013) Nosad showed some nice speed and was putting good pressure on the fore-check, he displayed his passing abilities with a nice pass to find a man open in the high slot from behind the net. He also put some nice pressure on the puck carrier to force a turnover in the offensive zone and then walked out to the slot from a good shot. He was driving down the middle with his stick down, but he has to watch the turnovers by trying to force the puck into the zone with his moves.

PET # 8, D, Varga, Steven (2013) Varga likes to stand around the front of his own net clearing the dangerous area and keeping the opposition to the outside. He was moving the puck out of the zone safely along the boards and was showing some good physicality in his own end by keeping his man to the outside and taking him down along the boards. He showed some great quickness and agility and was getting down in lanes and using his stick to block passes in the defensive zone. He has to watch some of the turnovers along the boards by just being soft on the puck at times.

KNG # 15, LW, Beckstead, Marc (2013) Beckstead was much less of a factor in this game than I am used to seeing. He was passing the puck pretty well, both up through the neutral zone to break the puck out and also made a real nice cross-ice feed to find an open man in the slot for a great shot on net. He was protecting the puck and cycling it deep in the offensive zone but has to watch some of his turnovers along the boards in his own end.

KNG # 17, C, Kujawinski, Ryan (2013) Kujawinski showed some of his nice battle for pucks tonight in the corners and was bringing the puck out to the slot for some good chances on net. He was cycling the puck pretty well in the offensive zone and had a nice attempt on a feed across on a 2-on-1 but was broken up by the defenseman. He was following up the play driving to the net for some excellent opportunities on the rebounds. He also would drop the puck and drive hard to the net showing that nice drive down the middle, and was also putting some good pressure on the fore-check. He had some really good quick puck movement through the neutral zone to gain the offensive zone with speed and was putting shots on net from the high slot, which the team scored on one of the rebounds. He was cycling the puck and made some real nice little chip plays to move the puck around and then going hard to the net showing some nice offensive instincts.

KNG # 27, RW, Dupuy, Jean (2013) Dupuy is a pretty tough kid which was shown in his fight tonight. He was physical and finishing his checks on the puck carrier and did a good job closing off his man in the defensive zone and putting some good pressure on the puck carrier.

KNG # 18, D, Hutchinson, Ryan (2013) Hutchinson played with some great physicality tonight by closing the gap on his man and forcing him to the outside and then finishing his check along the boards. He was getting in lanes to block shots on the penalty kill and used his stick well to knock the puck off the opposition. He hauled down his man on a breakaway and took a penalty tonight, and also needs to watch the turnovers moving the puck up along the boards.

FINAL SCORE: 3-2 Peterborough Petes

December 6, 2012, Rimouski Oceanic vs Sherbrooke Phoenix (QMJHL)

RIM #11 RW Bryukvin, Vladimir (2013) – Bryukvin had some nice flashes with the puck, showing good speed and quick hands. He was able to go through traffic easily at times and showed off good passing skills when he had to make a play. He set up a very nice play to Anthony DeLuca on one occasion. He also hits surprisingly hard even though he doesn't do it a lot.

RIM #15 LW DeLuca, Anthony (2013) – He is a very weird and slow skater. He skates very large but he has no explosion and his feet are heavy. Therefore, I didn't see much from him with the puck and he was very slow to get back from the offensive zone. He scored a nice goal in front of the net with what seems to be his only weapon: his shot.

RIM #23 C Gauthier, Frédérik (2013) – Gauthier displayed all his smartness once again in this game. He wasn't a strong presence offensively, but he was always there to make plays or to create turnovers. When he had the puck, he kept it simple and passed the puck along to his teammates. He also did a good job cycling the puck in the offensive zone. Without the puck, I really liked how he goes hard to the net and that created a lot of space for his teammates. He is very aware of what is going on during the play, whether he has to cover for a defenseman who is playing deep or simply play great defense. On the penalty kill he got the puck out of the corner in the offensive zone and was able to get it out all by himself. On the power play he made a back check from the offensive to defensive zone, stole the puck away from the other team and was able to re-organize the power play. He also showed some good puck protection skills on couple occasions. He also seems to be a precise passer as his passes are hard and on the money most of the time. In addition, he gave a very solid check to

Jonathan Diaby, which is something I hadn't seen from him before. I also liked his competition level: he did a great job with his coverage in the defensive zone all night but on one play, while he was covering a player in front of the net, he couldn't get a hold of his stick and the forward almost scored. Gauthier looked pissed that he missed his defensive play. This is something that I like to see.

RIM #55 D Morin, Samuel (2013) – Morin had another good game for Rimouski. He was very physical and didn't leave much room for his opponent to work with. He won most of his physical battles and did a good job using his stick. He really limited his mistakes and kept it simple, which made him very efficient. He was also able to move the puck forward and play on the transition very well. Again, he kept it simple there and made sure he didn't turn the puck over. One thing I also noticed is that his feet don't always follow his body when he battles for the puck behind his net. It looks like he is trying to push his opponent against the wall, but his feet don't always follow his upper body while doing it. This resulted in a loss of balance and less power to win his battles.

VIC #3 D Diaby, Jonthan (2013) – Diaby had a solid game from start to finish. He wasn't in control like he usually is, but he was a force on the backhand and most of his plays were effective. He was able to impose his physical presence and gave some hard checks. He also scored a pretty goal from the blue line with a wrist shot that went through traffic. One thing I didn't really like was his decision making without the puck. At times he was too hesitant or too aggressive and that lead to him losing battles or letting the other team get the puck. His lack of puck handling abilities was also displayed on the power play. He really has to keep it simple when he gets the chance to play there. He also did a nice job using his speed to move the puck out of the defensive zone. Once again, he is a very surprising skater going forward.

VIC #12 C Rehak, Dominik - This was a positive outing for Rehak so to speak after a number of disappointing games. He wasn't great but e showed he has very fast feet when he has space to move, but it gets trickier when his opponents close on him. It seems that he loses all his abilities when he is surrounded or about to get hit. He did a nice job going to the net for a goal. He finished a good check at one point, but it was the only one I saw from him in the game.

VIC #34 D Beaulieu, Anthony – Just a quick word to say that his play was bad. His play with the puck was deadly to his team, to the point where he was benched early in the game. We didn't get to see him much after that.

VIC #57 LW Veilleux, Tommy – Veilleux had a few isolated good moments, but I didn't like his game much. He looked slow out there and ended up down on the ice far too often. He did a good job protecting the puck in the offensive zone at one point, which is one of the first time I see him do that. He also made a pretty pass from behind the net to his teammate in front of it at one point. While trying to pump his team up, he invited a small player from the other team to drop the gloves, but wasn't able to get the edge over him in the fight.

December 7 2012, Moncton Wildcats vs. Victoriaville Tigres (QMJHL)

MON #4 D Sweeney, Jacob (2013) – Sweeney started off the game on the first pair of defenseman and saw his ice time go down quickly. He didn't look too bad in close range battles in the defensive zone but he didn't look comfortable moving at greater speed. He tried to compensate for his lack of speed by being very aggressive with his gap, but that didn't pay off. I also thought he struggled to use his massive body to move opponents from the front of his net.

MON #8 RW Garland, Connor (2014) – Garland played his first game in the QMJHL tonight and showed some very good tools. His skating and acceleration definitely compensate for the lack of size he has. He wasn't always in the right place to receive the puck from his defenseman and that prevented him from using his skating tool more. He also showed some very good hands and ability to play with the puck in traffic. He also loves to shoot the puck and it paid off at some point in the game as he recorded his first goal.

MON #22 C/LW Barbashev, Ivan (2014) – I was very impressed by Barbashev's play tonight. He's an excellent skater who can carry the puck for an extended period of time with very good speed and excellent hands. He showed he could beat opponents with his burst of speed alone and other times he did it with his quick and precise hands. He also showed he has an excellent wrist shot. He used the defenseman as a screen and fired a strong shot off the post once. His play without the puck was also very surprising: he was very active defensively and didn't mind using his body at all. In fact, he was one of the most physical player in this game, giving some very hard checks. Barbashev looks very promising for next year's draft as he is a very complete player with high end tools.

MON #26 LW Jaskin, Dimitri (STL Blues) – Jaskin is one the best physical player I've seen in the QMJHL this season. He looks ready to play professional hockey in that regard. He was a force along the boards and deep into the offensive zone. He can out power opponents to get the puck or to create a path to the net. He protects the puck very well and his hands make him a lethal threat within close range of the net. He looks to be more of a patient player with the puck than a dynamic skater. He didn't produce anything with his speed but he was patient in the neutral zone and he let the play develop.

VIC #3 D Diaby, Jonathan (2013) – Diaby played an average game. He wasn't bad but he didn't show the physical aspect of his game tonight and he was physically abused by Jaskin deep in his zone. He didn't live up to the physical challenge Jaskin presented to him and lost quite a few battles. He was more discrete, but he managed to limit mistake and play good enough to play his regular turn.

VIC #57 Veilleux, Tommy (2013) – Veilleux didn't have a very strong game but he did enough to get noticed. He didn't hit as much as usual but he was present in front of the net. He also picked up a fight that helped his team gain momentum. I was expecting him to bring more speed and physical play in this game but he didn't. He managed to score a goal early in the third period: he was alone in front of the goalie and went with a good high shot to beat the goalie.

Dec 7, 2012. Guelph Storm vs. Owen Sound Attack (OHL)

GUE#7 D Ben Harpur (2013). Ben had a fairly strong game on the Storm blue line. Was very effective using his long stick to keep defenders to the outside and stood up to attackers at his blue line forcing passes and quick decisions from the Attack forwards. Cut down on the mistakes in this game, only really making one questionable pass along the boards in the defensive zone. Was a steady presence and did not seem rushed or panic handling the puck. Had a strong 1-on-1 vs. Dan Catennaci not allowing the speedster to get a step on him, and using good body positioning to knock him off the puck. Needs to work on his offensive zone instincts, and would benefit from getting shots off quicker when walking to the middle from the side wall.

GUE#11 F Jason Dickinson (2013). Jason was very steady in this contest, rarely making a mistake or being caught out of position. Jason is a player that Guelph consistently trusts in all situations and showed good instincts getting into passing lanes on the penalty kill. Had a strong game in the offensive zone, consistently generating scoring chances around the Attack net. Would like to see offensive consistency and a stronger scoring touch in order to move him into the elite conversation. Some nights the offensive skills are evident and some they are not. Was very involved physically in this game, throwing solid body checks in open ice, and finishing every available hit along the boards. Is not the biggest guy, but uses good vision and positioning to put himself in position to make contact.

GUE#20 F Justin Auger (2012). Skating has improved for Justin from last year, allowing him to be more involved in the offensive zone. Uses his big body size well, leaning on smaller players to win puck battles and being strong along the half wall. Was strong in this game being hard on the puck, and was effective on the fore-check creating turnovers down low and generating a few solid scoring chances. Sometimes seems to be out of position skating down the center of the ice with his centerman, clogging up the middle and really cutting down passing opportunities.

OWE#24 D Chris Bigras (2013). Chris was very effective in this game using his body to win corner battles for the puck and really put a pounding on forwards in front of the net. Initiates physical contact whenever the situation arises, and is not shy about mixing it up with opposing forwards. Chris saw time in all situations for the Attack and showed some nice offensive instincts on the power play utilizing a strong shot to get pucks through screens and towards the net area for tips or rebounds. Did not show any panic handling the puck in the defensive zone and was good at reading the play before deciding to slow things down to regroup or to speed things up for quick offensive counter attacks.

OWE#27 F Zach Nastasiuk (2013). Was not the best game for Zach tonight against the Storm. Used his body effectively to shield the puck when trying to maneuver around the offensive zone. Skating was not very strong in this game, and would really benefit from showing effective edge work and gaining an extra burst of speed to beat defenders. Did not really show any instances of offensive flash in this game and was rarely noticed in the offensive zone.

December 7, 2012, Windsor Spitfires @ Sarnia Sting (OHL)

WSR #8 LD Murphy, Trevor (2013) - Murphy looks like a different defenseman in a Windsor Spitfires jersey. He battled very effectively in his own zone maintained his positioning and didn't force or rush his passes in his own zone. He made a great play midway through the game to use his speed to save what would have been a breakaway and negate the chance. He was used on the power play and was effective making decisions on the point. In the third period he shot the puck over the glass when pressured giving Sarnia a power play.

WSR #13 RW Maletta, Jordan (2013) - Wasn't very visible in this game as he spent a lot of time playing on the perimeter of the play.

WSR #16 LW Rychel, Kerby (2013) - Kerby has a hard very powerful shot, certainly among the better shots of those available in this year's draft. However he sometimes chose some bad angles in which to shoot from. This included on breaks and on the rush. He played a very physical and energetic game. Shows average skating ability and a decent amount of hockey sense in his own zone receiving ice in all game situations.

WSR #66 RW Ho-Sang, Josh (2014) - Ho-Sang had good positioning at the side of the net in the offensive zone early in the game and was rewarded with the opening goal of the game. He was able to create a few chances throughout this game and was able to use his speed however he was unable to put up more than just the one point. He struggled with his willingness to play defensively and was unimpressive in the moments he did play defensively. As he already has all the natural offensive talents this will be an important area of focus for his development.

WSR #81 LC Verbeek, Ryan (2014) - Verbeek plays a very physical game. He likes to finish his hits and does so on every possible opportunity available to him. Because of his style of play his good hands are a little unpredictable at times but has the ability to handle the puck very well and shows some potential offense as he develops into a bigger role for Windsor.

WSR #80 G DeKort, Jordan (2013) - DeKort covers so much net with his big 6'4" frame. He follows the play extremely well and is tough to beat first shot. He has long legs which he utilizes but kicks out a lot of rebounds into the slot. Fortunately for Windsor their defense did a good job collectively clearing rebounds out of the goal area.

SAR #11 RW Hargrave, Brett (2014) - Hargrave appears to be getting a little quicker. He uses his hands and protects the puck well on the rush. He showed good intelligence on the rush patiently allowing the play to develpp then set up a goal early in the third period which gave Sarnia the temporary lead. Brett uses his size well to protect the puck in the offensive zone.

SAR #71 RW Goldobin, Nikolay (2014) - Goldobin shows great patience and excellent hands. Down on the goal line Nikolay was abile to bang home the tying goal in the second period for the Sting.

SAR #74 LW Carnevale, Alex (2013) -Carnevale shows great forechecking ability. This forecheck resulted in turnovers, some of which he was able to turn into scoring chances. He really gives his all on a regular basis both on a shift by shift and on a game by game basis. Slightly above average skater.

SAR #94 LC Galchenyuk, Alex (Montreal) - Alex as usual created chances but was surprisingly held pointless in this game. He played a lot more physical than usual and was very effective in doing so. We hope this becomes more of a recurring trend for him because he is very effective when he finishes his opponents using his body.

Scouts Notes:

A tightly contested match-up between two divisional rivals, Windsor came out with the lead early. However Sarnia scored in the second to tie it up then again early in the third to take the lead. It appeared they would walk out with the victory, however Ben Johnson (New Jersey) was able to take advantage of a scoring chance created by Trevor Murphy (2013) with less than 8 minutes left on the clock to send the game to overtime and the eventual shootout. Finally in the seventh round of the shootout local product Ryan Verbeek (2014) scored the winner for Windsor.

Dec 7, 2012, Guelph Storm vs. Owen Sound Attack (OHL)

GUE # 11, LW, Dickinson, Jason (2013) Dickinson was showing some really good speed and chemistry early on with Garlent. He had a good opportunity by driving the net with his stick down on an odd-man rush but fanned on the shot. He had some really great speed and skating through the neutral zone and then he made a nice drop-pass to find Garlent in the high slot for a chance. He showed some nice puck protection and cycle going and displayed some really nice hands to get the puck in deep. He was winning battles by competing hard and distributing the puck well in the offensive zone. He has to hit the net on his shots coming in off the wing but was protecting the puck really effectively behind the offensive net. He put some nice pressure on the puck carrier to get the puck out of the zone on the penalty kill and was making some real big hits finishing his checks along the boards on the fore-check. He offered some good support in his own zone to come back and tie up his man and had a nice net-front presence as well. He was using his stick to poke the puck down low and start a cycle and showed some nice skill and agility to avoid a check and take the puck. He has to watch the turnovers by trying to force passes through in the offensive zone to a man who is already covered.

GUE # 16, LW, Milne, Brody (2013) Milne was battling hard for the puck in the corner on the fore-check and put on some pretty good pressure on the puck carrier to try to force turnovers. He had a nice back-check to cover his man in his own end and was driving the net pretty well. He is a bit of an awkward skater but was hitting and showing physicality on the puck carrier. He protects the puck well but has to watch the turnovers by trying to force passes through.

GUE # 19, C, Garlent, Hunter (2013) Garlent made some nice chip plays to move the puck up the boards for a breakout and was opening up well to take passes with speed through the neutral zone. He made a great feed to find Dickinson for a chance early on and also did a nice job opening up in the high slot but couldn't get his shot off. He had a net-front presence looking for rebounds and made another great feed to find Dickinson in the high slot. He went hard to the net to put in the puck for the team's 1st goal of the game and was coming back to his own end to offer support. He showed some good speed and puck movement in the offensive zone and did a nice job taking passes in full speed and then dropping the puck to a teammate and then driving the net. He put some nice pressure and physicality on the fore-check, cycling the puck well and competing for the puck along the boards. He missed the puck on a pass to breakout on the power play wasting some valuable power play time. He showed some really nice hands to walk out to the slot and made a real nice feed to a man down low near the net for a god chance. He made a nice pass to spot an open man in the high slot for a one-timer opportunity.

GUE # 7, D, Harpur, Ben (2013) Harpur did a nice job holding his territory ad keeping his man to the outside. He was willing to jump up and join the rush and showed some good stick work to poke the puck away from the opposition. He tied his man up well in his own end and made some nice chip plays to move the puck up to the forwards for the rush. He showed some pretty good aggression in battles after whistles and was physical and finishing his checks along the boards in his own zone. At times he gave his man a bit too much space on the rush and needs to close the gap a bit better.

OWS # 27, RW, Nastasiuk, Zach (2013) Nastasiuk is a strong player with some great size and uses his size well to protect the puck and battles to take the pucks away. He goes hard on the fore-check and has a net-front presence as well. He drives hard to the net with his stick down looking for opportunities. He showed some good physicality on the fore-check and came back hard to offer support in his own end. He battled hard on the back-check to take the puck from the puck carrier and take down his man but has to watch he doesn't take penalties by doing so. I would like to see him get a bit quicker and play at a faster pace and he has to watch some of the turnovers in the offensive zone.

OWS # 24, D, Bigras, Chris (2013) Bigras has both great skating and passing to move the puck up the ice effectively on the rush. He is calm with the puck and can make the nice long passes up the ice to hit his man for a breakout on the rush. He showed nice speed and hustle to get back on pucks in his own end and good passing to move the puck out of the zone. He was willing to come down low to join the attack and showed the sense to stand next to the board battles and direct the play to come out with the puck. He did a good job tying up his man in his own end but at times he had some trouble also tying up his man on the penalty kill in front of the net resulting in a goal for the opposition. He let his man walk around him a bit too easy on the rush up the ice as well and has to watch the turnovers at the line in the offensive zone.

FINAL SCORE: 4-1 Guelph Storm

Dec 7, 2012, Sarnia Sting vs. Windsor Spitfires (OHL)

SAR # 15, LW, Brown, Davis (2013) Brown showed some good speed tonight to rush the puck all the way up the ice and get a good shot on net. He did a nice job getting open down low near the net for a one-timer but fanned on the shot. He was making some nice passes up the ice for breakouts to allow his team to gain the zone with speed, and was putting on some good pressure on the fore-check. There was one pass he was unable to control through the neutral zone on the breakout but for the most part was breaking out fairly well. He had a nice drive to the front of the net with his stick down to deflect the puck in the net for the team's 2nd goal of the game, but has to watch the turnovers in the offensive zone by forcing the passes through.

SAR # 21, C, Nikandrov, Daniel (2013) Nikandrov has some really good size but needs to fill his frame out a bit and add some strength. He was however getting a pretty good cycle game going deep in the offensive zone and showed a willingness to go to the dirty areas and battle in front of the net. He had some good drives to the net with his stick down looking for opportunities and was opening up well to offer options in the offensive zone. He has some pretty good hands and stick skills with the puck and was finding open space to work with. He found some open space to take passes through the neutral zone and then could find a lane to pass the puck cross-ice back to the point after gaining the zone deep. He does a good job holding on to the puck after gaining the zone and showing patience to move the puck to a trailing man streaking in to the zone. He displayed some great vision and offensive sense to move the puck to some good scoring areas as well. There were times when he would pass the puck to no one however resulting in turnovers and a few times had some trouble settling the puck down after he would take passes.

SAR # 74, LW, Carnevale, Alex (2013) Carnevale was going to the net and trying to tip pucks and was also able to get open all alone in front of the net to take a pass for a good chance in tight. He made a great cross-ice pass to find Brown open as well for a one-timer opportunity. He took a bunch of low-chance shots off the rush and was just trying to get the puck in deep, and also has to watch some of his neutral zone turnovers where he would miss his intended target.

WND # 16, LW, Rychel, Kerby (2013) Rychel had his speed and hustle on full display tonight as he was really skating hard and finishing his checks on the fore-check. He was able to find some space to work with to get out to the slot for a shot on goal and got a pretty good cycle game going in the offensive zone as well. He found some space to get open in the slot and had a real nice slap shot taken from the high slot. He was battling for the puck and had a nice stick lift to take the puck but needs to watch he isn't taking penalties. He had a nice net-front presence on the power play and was battling for pucks in front of the net looking for those grinder type goals.

WND # 13, RW, Maletta, Jordan (2013) Maletta was playing some dump and chase hockey tonight going hard after the puck and moving it out to the slot for a teammate and then crashing the net for rebounds. He had a nice drop pass for a good chance and showed some nice hands to get out to the slot and put a nice shot on net. He also made a real nice pass to spot a man down low next to the net, and later had a nice centering pas to try to move to an open man in the high slot. He has to hit the net on his chances off the rush though.

WND # 19, RW, Studnicka, Sam (2013) Studnicka had a great backhand feed out to the slot to an open man for a nice scoring chance early on. He was driving pretty well to the net with his stick down looking for rebounds and also had a nice clear on the penalty kill. He has to watch some of the turnovers especially along the boards in his own end.

WND # 8, D, Murphy, Trevor (2013) Murphy is a pretty agile defenseman who can move the puck around pretty well. He showed some nice puck protection in his own zone and was using his stick well to check the puck away from the opposition. He also showed some nice physicality and was passing the puck up nicely on the rush. He was hitting often along the boards and stepped up to challenge the puck carrier at the line with his stick to try to hold the zone. He has to hit the net on his shots from the point.

WND # 44, D, Bateman, Adam (2013) Bateman used his stick well tonight forcing the opposition to drive to the outside and to block shots and swipe the puck out of dangerous areas. He has to watch the neutral zone turnovers and the turnovers by forcing passes through as well.

FINAL SCORE: 3-2 Windsor Spitfires

Dec 8, 2012, Kingston Frontenacs vs. Barrie Colts (OHL)

KNG # 17, C, Kujawinski, Ryan (2013) This was not Kujawinski's best game. He did have some nice puck movement on an odd-man rush for a good chance and was also offering good support in his own end. He had a nice wide drive to gain the zone and then was throwing the puck to the middle. He got open down low next to the net and was looking for rebounds and had a great chance from in tight on one of those rebounds. He has to tie up his man better in his own end as he left him open to score early in this game and has to watch the turnovers along the boards moving the puck out of the zone. He was able to get his stick in lanes a few times to break up some plays defensively.

KNG # 15, LW, Beckstead, Marc (2013) Beckstead showed some nice puck protection and was getting a good cycle game going deep in the offensive zone. He was putting some great pressure and physicality on the fore-check and did a good job getting his stick in lanes to intercept passes and break the puck back up the ice. He likes to dump the puck in and just get it in deep and showed some nice puck movement moving the puck up the ice on the rush. He has a nice shot on net coming in off the wing and was hustling and competing hard to get on loose pucks. He did a great job opening up for passes and then made an excellent cross-ice feed to find a teammate for an excellent scoring chance but was robbed by the goaltender. He was following up plays and driving hard to the net to get rebounds and put the 2nd shots on net. He pressured the puck carrier on the fore-check to get his stick in lanes to deflect passes and shots out of the way.

KNG # 61, LW, Fitzmorris, Mitchell (2013) Fitzmorris is able to cycle the puck really well and showed some great puck protection in this game. He was back-checking hard to tie up his man and showed a real good hustle on his back-check to offer support in his own end. He was showing some nice aggression in scrums after whistles to stick up for teammates and was nice and physical pressuring on the fore-check. He cleared the puck on the penalty kill and had a nice 2-on-1 opportunity as well but missed his target on the pass. He also passed the puck up the ice on the rush through the neutral zone fairly decently.

KNG # 95, C, Povorozniouk, Sam (2013) Povorozniouk was putting some nice pressure on the puck carrier to force turnovers on the fore-check. He battles hard along the boards and was able to hold the offensive zone really well. He showed some good hands to make moves and create a bit of space and later on showed his great hands again as he drove the puck down low to the net. There were times though when he tried too many moves and lost the puck at the blue line and he has to make sure he is hitting the net on his shots off the rush. He came back to offer good support in his own end to force some turnovers, then took the puck and moved it up the ice on the rush well to start an attack the other way.

KNG # 7, D, Hutchinson, Ryan (2013) Hutchinson displayed some pretty good hitting and physicality in his own end. He was getting his stick in lanes to block shots and passes and was making sure to hustle back on the back-check after he got beat to lift the opponent's stick to breakup the opportunity. He was protecting the puck well along the boards in his own end and showed a nice first pass out of the zone for a breakout. He was very aggressive on the puck carrier at times and I would like to see him wait for the play to come to him a bit, and then there were other times when he gave his man too much space and then they scored Barrie's 2nd goal of the game. He has to watch that after he gets beat he isn't taking penalties and not to bite too hard on the opposition's moves down low leaving them with lots of space after getting beat. He also held on to the puck a bit too long at times and should get rid of it when he has the chance.

BAR # 17, C, Scott, Justin (2013) Scott put some good pressure on the fore-check going hard for the puck, and was also driving well down the middle towards the net. He had a nice net-front presence and was finding some space in the offensive zone to get a shot on net although it was a pretty weak shot. He did a nice job dropping the puck to a trailing man and then crashing the net, but when it comes to his cycle game he has to watch some of the turnovers he is making.

BAR # 18, C, Bradford, Erik (2013) Bradford displayed some pretty nice speed and agility, and was protecting the puck well under pressure. He put some good pressure on the puck carrier to try to force the turnover and was also putting good pressure on the fore-check deep in the offensive zone. He battled hard for pucks in front of the net, showing a nice willingness to go to the dirty areas and was going hard to the net looking for loose pucks and rebounds.

BAR # 7, D, Yuil, Alex (2013) Yuil was using his stick well to try to check the puck off the opposition. He made some pretty good passes up the ice for breakouts and had a pretty nice shot from the point kept down low and on net for rebounds which the team scored on the rebound. He holds his ground really well, holding the opposition to the outside and did a good job squeezing his man out along the boards in his own end. He was caught watching the puck and swinging at it a little bit much on a 1-on-1 rush and I would like to see him try to use his body to force his man to the outside in that situation. He has to watch some of the turnovers by trying to force the puck through the opposition and also needs to watch some of the turnovers along the boards in his own end by being soft on the puck.

BAR # 24, D, Webster, Michael (2013) Webster had a really nice diving play to go down and block a pass across the ice for the opposition. He held the offensive line pretty well and made some pretty good passes up the ice for breakouts as well. He was willing to come down low on the attack and was showing some good physicality in his own end. He used his stick well to keep the opposition to the outside and poke the puck away and was showing some nice aggression getting involved in scrums. He did a good job skating the puck up the ice but has to get his shot through on net on those rushes and also needs to watch the suicide passes up along the boards in his own end. He also needs to watch the interference penalties hauling down his man after the puck is dumped in past him.

FINAL SCORE: 6-2 Barrie Colts

Dec 8th, 2012, Vancouver Giants vs Everett Silvertips (WHL)

EVT #17 RW Lofthouse Trent (2013) Trent was the best player on both teams tonight. He was like a pin ball hitting every gianst player who touch the puck. Trent show me a glimspe of his offensive potential tonight netting 3 goals. He used his size to create time and space inside the scoring areas finally and he made the most of it. His game was strong tonight ive been waiting for him to break out this year, but once again not impress with his skating.

EVT #24 D Oslandski Landon (Free Agent) Landon is a overager who has been playing very solid this year. Tonight he added a pretty one time goal on the PP from a nice feed from his partner Mueller. He was leading the rush out of the zone and setting the tempo of the game for Everett defense.

EVT #25 D Mueller Mirco (2013) Mirco played nothing short of consistent tonight once again. He was animal along the boards winning battles and making a crisp first pass out of the zone. He added two assists and was joining the rush all game. I did not see any flaws in his game tonight.

VAN#8 D Morrison Tyler (2013) I didnt see much in his game tonight, he showed some skill on certain shifts. His skating is decent "Not Great". He looked like he was watching the game instead of playing as he got beat wide a few times and turn over the puck atleast every other shift.

VAN #27 RW Houk Jackson (2013) Jackson has all the tools in the shed, but couldnt put them to use tonight. He showed some greasy hands down low beating the D with a couple dangles. Has good awarness and was driving the net hard all night. I see the potential, he's needs to shoot the puck more instead of looking for a pass. He forced a few passed through traffic causing turn overs which lead to a Everett goal.

VAN #44 D Geertsen Mason (2013) Mason is a gamer, he was throwing his weight around tonight. He was tough in front of his net clearing the scoring areas for his tender. His play along hte boards was good, making the first pass out of the zone most of the time. He does like to cheat some time and got beat by speed. Needs to watch his pinching and seal off the boards better. He was one of the better players for the giants tonight

Scouts Notes: Everett came out on a mission tonight to beat up Vancouver and that is just want they did. From the opening faceoff Everett was checking and winning races to loose pucks and controlling the boards. Everett's Carson Stadnyk and Ben Betker both had solid games. Betker had a good tilt with Vancouver's Scott Cooke dropping him with a solid right. Vancouver just couldn't find the spark tonight.

Final Score: 4-1 Everett

December 8, 2012, PEI Rocket vs. Victoriaville Tigres (OHL)

PEI #1 G Bibeau, Antoine (1994 born) – Bibeau is a goaltender that reads the play well when it moves around him and he has good reactions. His rebound control was good early in the game as he made some key saves. His athletic ability and the fact that he stays square when he confronts the shooter help him to be effective. He had a lot of bodies in front of him all night long and most goals scored on him were hard to stop.

PEI #27 D Graves, Ryan (2013) – Graves delivered a very poor performance in this game. His defensive coverage was not very good. He was not in control and had to try to recover from his mistakes on a lot of plays. He tried to rush his decisions a lot and a lot of his passes from his zone didn't reach the target. He had some good opportunities to use his shot, but again, tried to go too quick and wasn't able to put it on target. Graves needs to simplify his games both offensively and defensively as he tends to get himself out of position and to create a lot of turnovers with the puck.

VIC #3 D Diaby, Jonathan (2013) – Diaby had an average outing. He wasn't dominant with his body but he was able to limit mistakes. The most glaring aspect of his game that caught my eye was his lack of hockey sense. He has a hard time making decisions when he faces two or three forwards. If he has one player to cover, he plays it almost perfectly every time. But when his opponent has options, he struggles to make the right decision. He also did a good job finding shooting lanes on the power play with his patience. He showed his heavy shot again, but I thought they were a little bit high.

VIC #57 LW Veilleux, Tommy (2013) – Veilleux did a good job driving the net in this game to create some scoring chances. He made some simple but effective plays with the puck and that suits him well. His lack of speed and offensive abilities prevents him from doing much with the puck so he needs to use his body more and chip the puck deep in the offensive zone. I didn't see him hit much in this game, which is a minus for him. He needs to bring that every game.

December 8, 2012, Boston Jr. Bruins vs. New York Apple Core (EJHL)

BJB #11 LC Ryan Cloonan (2013) – Such a frustrating prospect. As far as a raw talent, I think he's on par with Ryan Fitzgerald. He flashes the ability of a top-50 prospect. So explosive when he asserts himself. Read and intercepted passes with a quick stick and counterattacked up the ice with outstanding acceleration and stickhandling ability. Anticipated the breakout from his end and, when his teammates found him with speed, was an absolute handful to deal with. Great passer, gave his teammates good looks. Looked a step ahead of everybody on the ice when he turns it on.

Showed an aversion to shooting the puck. Not sure if he's trying to make the pretty play or if he was told to use his teammates better. Was absolutely a puck hog when I saw him earlier in the year, less so now. Whatever the case, he got himself into great shooting positions before dishing the puck off; because his linemates can't keep up with his skill, these passes tended to be mishandled and cause the play to collapse.

Without the puck, he looked bored. Coasted a lot. I got the impression that he's not very involved in the game mentally. Passive defensively. His coach played him on the PK, I would guess in an attempt to round out his game. His PK positioning was good but he wasn't aggressive enough in coverage. Very undersized, intrigued as to how he'd play with another 40 lbs to work with.

BJB #24 LD Josh Couturier (2013) – Great frame but he's a terrible defenseman. Too aggressive, slow feet, chases the puck, awful positioning, boneheaded penalties.

NY #21 LW Mike Laffin (2013) – Small, feisty player who did good work along the boards and in front of the net. Showed some good passing ability, drawing coverage and then finding seams. Nice wrist shot. Set up at the low circle on the powerplay and acted as a triggerman. Guilty of being too stationary, waiting for the puck to come to him rather than rotating around to attract defensive attention and give his teammates an option. Was really only effective on the powerplay.

December 8, 2012, South Shore Kings vs. Jersey Hitmen (EJHL)

SSK #20 LC Brandon Shea (2013) – Bull-in-a-china shop type but lacks skating ability and finesse. Not a pro prospect for me, though he's a good player at this level.

December 8, 2012, Middlesex Islanders vs. Philadelphia Revolution (EJHL)

ISL #12 LW Zachary Sanford (2013) – Big kid with room to fill out. He's a very, very raw talent but with upside. Some good individual play but really wasn't a team player at all. Did an extremely poor job of getting himself open for outlet passes, which limited his offensive-zone time on almost every shift. Much too stationary. Has the size to be a dominant player at this level, but was inconsistent with his effort. Physical, but in bursts. Capable of absolutely leveling guys but too many fly-bys.

Has a hard wristshot, accuracy was a bit off. Flashed some great vision with his passes, but did not utilize his teammates well. Tried to bull the puck into the zone with frequency with mixed results. Great skater, outstanding stride, especially for a player of his size. Good work along the boards, used his reach and body well. Did not assert himself with consistency. Potential riser, see him as a 4th rounder right now.

ISL #44 RW Luke Kirwan (2016) – This is a kid to watch. Late '97 birthdate playing with kids up to five years his elder. Showed a lot of good things as far as natural skill and intelligence. Good hands, keeps his feet moving with the puck at all times. Already very mature of stature and uses his size well to protect the puck, dipped his shoulder and took the puck to the middle without hesitation. Used his teammates well, putting pucks into space for them to skate onto and effectively cycling. Was mostly ineffective in the second half of the contest. Whether that's conditioning or work ethic I couldn't tell, but obviously he has plenty of time to work out his kinks. Has the potential to develop into a dominant forward.

Scout's Notes: Big Islanders LD Robby Klein (2013) and Dakota Ford (2013) showed poorly, with slow feet and poor decision-making.

December 8, 2012, Portland Jr. Pirates vs. Rochester Stars (EJHL)

PJP #17 RW Haralds Egle (2014) – Like Egle as a prospect but he had a poor showing. Early on, was very active, forechecking hard and showing a good stick to intercept passes. Didn't PK at all, so when his team went short for about 7 minutes straight thanks to a slew of penalties, he sat and sat. Afterwards, looked fairly lax and disinterested. A few flashes of good patience with the puck and quick hands, showed off a nice stride, but played uninspired. Go end-to-end trying to go through the whole opposing team, give the puck away, slink back, skate slowly to the bench. Rinse, repeat. Too overzealous when he shouldn't have been, too casual when he shouldn't have been. Didn't show any of the shooting ability and boards skills that impressed me in the past.

December 8, 2012, Valley Jr. Warriors vs. New York Apple Core (EJHL)

VAL #27 LC Ryan Fitzgerald (2013) – Hard to believe a player of Fitzgerald's talent is playing at the EJHL level. I saw him suit up for the NTDP earlier in the year against NCAA competition and he was capable, solid even, at that level. Plays a very smooth game. Perhaps his best skill is his awareness. Always seemed to have a good impression of time/space/pressure. So deceptive with his hands, both in open ice and along the boards. Good body control allows him to change direction and burn defenders. Looks effortless much of the time. Good on the draw, refined technique and wins cleanly to his defensemen.

Uses his reach well, both with the puck and defensively to intercept passes. Positioning is outstanding in all three zones, has an internal compass that allows him to be consistently involved in the play. Keeps his head up at all times. Great speed and acceleration, can blow by guys when he turns on the jets. Precise with his passes, which are appropriately timed and receivable. Great finishing ability. Picks his spots with his wrist/snap shot (5-hole, over pad, high corners, etc.). Corrals tough passes and releases shots in one motion, making him effective even when his teammates don't put the puck in the right spot.

The only negative was that he was overzealous at times. On the PK at the end of the third period in a 3-3 game, he tried to be the hero and took a penalty in the offensive zone after giving the puck away on an end-to-end rush. Hard to say how he'll adjust to playing with talented teammates, as he seems to be fairly accustomed to being "the guy" on Valley. Not sure if he has the size to be a top-six NHL center and not sure how well his game will translate to the wing.

VAL #22 LW Devin Tringale (Passed over 2012) – Was passed over this past summer as the CSS 79th ranked skater after an MVP-quality Mass HS season that saw him lead Lawrence Academy to a state championship. Not sure why, but that certainly brings up a red flag.

He's a good player, but he plays choppy. Gets by more on work ethic than skill. Strong on his skates, goes hard to the net. Very determined. Showed the ability to navigate traffic well, both with stickhandling and passing ability, but with somewhat jerky motions. Moved the puck well under duress.

Finishing ability was lacking. Flubbed one finish on a partial breakaway where he deked and had an empty net. Had a glorious empty net rebound chance that he shot into the goalie's glove. In fairness, he scored the OT winner in the game I saw, but he shanked the shot and it happened to go in five-hole. I'm not sure that I see him being drafted this year, but I'm interested to see how he plays at Harvard.

Dec. 9 2012, Cape-Breton Screaming @ Chicoutimi Saguneéens (QMJHL)

CB #2 D, Leduc, Loic (2012 NYI 4th round pick): Leduc is a big player who is very useful on the penalty kill. He is a mean defenseman down-low, throwing devastating body checks and intimidating his opponents. He has a nice long reach on his stick and plays with some nice aggression, but is still pretty slow and needs quite a bit of improvement on his footwork to start the transition, as he uses the boards exclusively to get the puck out on some pretty simple chip plays. To play at the next level he will need to improve all his skating abilities as he will get beat easily by faster skaters and he needs to choose his moments better on when to be aggressive on the puck carrier as he left some players alone in the slot at times trying to force the play or make a hit.

CB #15 C, Beaton, Bronson (2013): Beaton had a pretty good game tonight, showing some nice skills with the puck down low and protecting the puck well to come around the net out front to put a good shot on net, then jump on rebounds in a hurry. He uses his body and strength nicely to win battles along the boards and create space for himself. He has some pretty nice agility but very poor top speed, which makes it difficult for him to get around opponents with the puck. He also does not win many races to loose pucks and his physical game is much less effective. His efforts seemed inconsistent but he still possesses some nice offensive potential.

CB #28 LW, Carrier, William (2013): Carrier scored a nice goal on the power play in this game with a wicked wrist shot that was impressively accurate through traffic. He has some top-end skill and talent

and is really strong on the puck when he protects it in the offensive zone, as it seems impossible even for big defensemen to knock him off the puck when he leans on them with his outside shoulder. He has many desirable offensive tools such as: good top speed , nice explosiveness, strong shooting abilities in all areas (wrist-short, snap shot, slap shot or backhand) and has some really nice passing skills, although he probably wouldn't be characterized as a playmaker. He doesn't seem to take a lot of pride in defensive play, as he won't give the 2nd effort to
get to a loose puck in the defensive zone or engage physically on a regular basis to win the puck back for his team. He also didn't show the required intensity or compete in his game that it will take to be effective at the next level.

CB #41 G, Honzik, David (2011 VAN 3rd round pick): Honzik was just tremendous in this game. He is a goalie that has trouble with his consistency but can steal games on his own when he's hot, and this was the case in this game. He possesses some of the best hand reflexes amongst QMJHL goalies and was able to rob Charles Hudon with the glove on at least 3 occasions, showing great confidence in front of his net. He was pretty aggressive, showing amazing quickness and athleticism on lateral butterfly slides and he is a high energy goalie who won't always be perfect technically, but his natural abilities and agility took over in this game. His rebound control could be better but this is a small technical detail that could be corrected easily. He made this great performance (shutout 3-0) after being pulled against that same Chicoutimi team a week earlier in Cape Breton, showing a great ability to rebound from a tough outing and that when he wants to be the difference maker, he can be.

December 9, 2012, Sault Ste. Marie Greyhounds @ Sarnia Sting (OHL)

SSM #3 RD Ganly, Tyler (2013) - Tyler's puck play has absolutely come miles since the start of the season. He shows great patience and seems to make the smart play every time. He can get up the ice decently well for a big guy. Ganly showed a willingness on more than one occasion to stand up for his teammates. Ganly will be moving up the draft ranks with play like what we saw today combined with his size and willingness to use it.

SSM #13 RW Schiller, Landon (2013) - Schiller was overly aggressive a few times early on in the game, which resulted in him sitting in the penalty box and his team killing his penalty. He made up for it, in a way, when he refused to fight a 16 year old forward who eventually forced Schiller into a fight after Landon hit a Sarnia player from behind. This somewhat made up for his undisciplined penalty earlier on. But where Ganly was more than willing to stand up for his teammates, Schiller did the opposite in this game despite both having good size.

SSM #19 LC McCann, Jared (2014) - McCann seems to stalk the slot area almost like a predator waiting for the right time to jump into position and get the scoring chance. His positional awareness in general is extremely impressive and is indicative of his great hockey sense. He has an absolute cannon of a shot although at times he seems to prefer passing over shooting. In general Jared turned the puck over too much in this game, some of which resulted in scoring chances against.

SSM #20 RW Mallette, Trent (2014) - Trent slips in and out of traffic very effectively due to his small size and strong agility. Trent went right to the net and banged home a rebound to tie the game up in the first period.

SSM #25 LD Nurse, Darnell (2013) - Nurse had the undesirable task of taking on Alex Galchenyuk most of the game. He used his stick a lot when matched up against #94 but gave him plenty of space to maneuver and generally didn't take the body on him in this match-up. At one point he actually had to trip up Galchenyuk to stop him. He was much more physical 1 on 1 against other players for the Sting. He was aggressive and worked well along the boards all game long. He made plenty of smart passes up the ice. He is a good skater who has impressive mobility for his size, but isn't quite as smooth skating backwards at times. Darnell with smart with the puck all game long and was equally effective in the offensive and defensive zones.

SSM #27 LC Cousins, Nick (Philadelphia) - Nick usually does a great job of agitating the opposition and helping his team offensively. However today he was more focused on trying to blatantly sell penalties and embellishing rather than being an effective contributor to his team. This game was close right into the final 5 minutes or so of this game. So Nick showing off his offense rather than the display he was putting on could have made all the difference in this game.

SSM #28 RW Tolchinsky, Sergey (2013) - Tolchinsky showed tremendous speed, but really didn't do too much in this game. You can see the skill and elusiveness but he was neutralized regularly and couldn't really get anything going.

SSM #30 G Murray, Matthew (Pittsburgh) - This was probably the best game I've ever seen Matt Murray play. He was the reason his team was in the game up until the final five minutes or so. He was strong positionally, not the quickest but always where he needs to be and reset himself well. He has above average quickness and glove hand. His rebound control was a real struggle in this game, but it fortunately didn't hurt him as much as it has in the past. This will be the key to his development. Not only trying to limit the rebounds, but directing them into non threatening areas. He made several spectacular saves in this game.

SAR #2 RD Chapman, Joshua (2013) - Chapman was on his best on what was basically a six minute penalty kill. He made several great plays to break up Greyhound scoring chances and keep the game tied.

SAR #15 Brown, Davis (2013) - Davis worked hard all game long and was rewarded late in the third period when he got the puck and fired an absolute laser to make it 4-1. While he's not the biggest guy on the ice, he's got one of the most powerful shots on the team.

SAR #71 RW Goldobin, Nikolay (2014) - Nikolay can thread passes through such small areas and his vision is nothing short of exceptional. He made a great pass to set up the first goal of the game for Sarnia.

SAR #77 RD DeAngelo, Anthony (2014) - Anthony lost his temper yet again early on in this game. He tried to fight someone who has a few more scraps on his fight card. Anthony got turned down on his invitation but wouldn't let it go which resulted in a 10 minute misconduct. He let the opposition get under his skin too easily and became focused on his own personal agenda instead of what was best for the team. DeAngelo was about par for the course when it comes to turnovers. There were plenty but he forced about as many turnovers for his team, as he did turning it over to the opposition.

SAR #94 LC Galchenyuk, Alex (Montreal) - Galchenyuk was very dangerous today creating chances every time he stepped onto the ice. Less than two minute after Sarnia made it 2-1 he absolutely turned Alex Gudbranson inside out and fired a laser past Murray. This gave Sarnia a 3-1 lead and was really the backbreaker for the SOO with less than 7 minutes left.

Scouts Notes: A very tightly contested Sunday afternoon match-up between Sault Ste. Marie and Sarnia opened up with both teams registering chances, but it was Daniel Nikandrov (2013) who drove hard to the net, receiving a great pass from Nikolay Goldobin (2014) to score the Teddy Bear Toss goal and giving Sarnia a 1-0 lead. After Trent Mallette (2014) tied the game up moments later it was Matthew Murray (Pittsburgh) who took over the next 40 or so minutes of the game. Making several spectacular saves Murray kept the Greyhounds in it until the final 10 minutes. Nick Halagian (2013) took an undisciplined penalty which initiated Sarnia's breakthrough of three goals in six minutes en route to a 4-1 Sarnia win.

Dec. 11 2012, Rouyn-Noranda Huskies @ Val D'Or Foreurs, (QMJHL)

VDO #2 D, Murphy, Matt (2013) : Pretty good offensive game, not so much defensively. He lost his puck battle on the first goal behind the net and then was late to come in front of the net for crease protection. He showed his great forward speed and puckhandling abilities on multiple occasions, joined the rush numerous times to create odd-man rushes. He didn't always watch for his defensive position while joining the rush. His decisions on breakouts should be taken quicker too as pressure has time to come on him before he makes his choice of play. He tried a lot of risky passes on breakouts which sometimes looked fantastic in terms of transition and other times caused turnovers and great chances for opponents. He can distance forchecker easily with great first steps in his own zone and wins his footraces most of the time, just can't manage the puck right when he gets it. His footwork gives him a great help 1-on-1 playing the gap, but sometimes he can be too passive with his stick and let a player go past him easily even though he skates him well. He needs to work on physical play too, could be a lot more physical down-low.

VDO #8 RW, Mantha, Anthony (2013) : One of the smartest games I've seen a prospect all year. He had 10 to 15 takeaways during the whole game using his long strides, great active stick and superb hockey sense. He was just a blast to see on PK, the positioning of his stick and his very long reach made him look like a potential PK specialist. He can just press you so quickly and get time and space away in the blink of an eye. He creates time and space well for himself, good speed, pretty good hands and he is strong like a horse, he kept the puck in battles against 2 opponents on multiple occasions and it looked easy. He didn't waste shots on net, most of the times the puck hit the net when he decided to shoot, just a great offensive hockey sense. He loves to use his great wrister from the right circle on the powerplay, where he creates a lotof plays. Mantha is also able to distance himself from coverage in order to put himself in a scoring area. His biggest weakness is that he glides a lot, wether it's on backcheck or in his defensive zone, he needs to keep his feet moving to be in perfect position to block a shot or to cover a D's mistake. He can look pretty lazy on some plays and can become fancy, his focus isn't always at its best. He could be more physical too, especially when he is closing in on an opponent quickly on the forecheck. Physicality and agressive play doesn't seem natural for him right now. He is not afraid of being hit though and is pretty slippery in fact through checks.

VDO #26 C, Dunn, Vincent (2013) : He is tenacious on the forecheck, very intense player, always at 110% in his effort level. He has great top speed and acceleration, he is able to close in quickly on his opponents when pressuring them. An above-average puckhandler, he has very good passing abilities. He was able to create superb passing plays off the cycle and from the rush throughout the game showing great poise and offensive vision on multiple occasions. He has a nose for the net and doesn't hesitate to go in the high traffic areas to collect rebounds. He plays with an agressive edge in his battles, likes the rough stuff even though he's not the biggest player out there. He plays a North-South game with speed and intensity. He worked hard in his own zone too, willing to block shots and hit his opponents, but seemed lost on some occasions. He needs more experience on the little details to execute in order to cut down on turnovers and help his D start the transition.

ROU #7 D, Guénette, Justin (2013) : Solid game all-around. Dillon Fournier wasn't playing in the game and veteran Mathieu Brisebois got injured on a hit by Mantha, so Guénette got more quality ice time then he usually gets. He's not overly big, but plays safe and is able to bring his man on the wall. Likes to be physical and be the aggressor in a 1-on-1 battle, which is always something good to see from a small D. He has good hockey sense which helps him take away a lot of space and time from opponents, reads the play very well, steps up aggressively into a play when he sees an opportunity. He doesn't hesitate to join the rush when he can, he is not the most gifted skater or puck handler but he is effective in his decisions and moves the puck simply and effectively. He seems like a strong kid although he got beat by bigger players on a couple of plays, Mantha was a big test for him and I liked how he used his smarts and stick positioning to keep him out of the slot when he couldn't have the edge physically on his opponent.

Dec 12, 2012, Red Deer Rebels vs. Calgary Hitmen (WHL)

RD#4 LD, Fleury, Haydn(2014) Big, puck moving defenseman who really made his presence felt tonight at both ends of the ice. Was able to use his hockey sense to make very good plays with the puck and get the attack going quickly for Red Deer. He was also able to create turnovers in the neutral zone a couple of times by jumping the play. He has a long reach he uses effectively and keeps opponents to the outside. Time and time again, Fleury was able to poke pucks away on the rush and slow down Calgary's attack. He engaged physically along the boards and was able to use his body to win puck battles, but has to improve his balance on his skates to stay on his feet more often. Would like to see him shoot more from the point as well.

RD#8 RD, Doetzel, Kayle(2013) Defensive defenseman who played a quiet solid game tonight. Liked his overall skating abilities as he was able to comfortably handle speed. He was good at dealing with the forecheck and did not panic with the puck on his stick. Did not show great vision, but kept the plays simple and gave his teammates a chance to attack Calgary. Doetzel protected his net well and was tough to play in front of the net. He was physical all over the ice, but was careful to not get caught out of position. Would like to see him use his stick more and be able to knock passes and shots away on a consistent basis.

RD#27 RW, Bellerive, Matt(2013) Quick moving forward who had ups and downs in his game tonight. Overall, committed far too many turnovers in all areas of the ice. Tried to be too cute with his passes and thread the needle time and time again. Showed off some impressive speed and agility out in open ice. Needs to get much stronger along the boards to be able to keep plays alive and handle bigger players off the cycle. Likes to shoot the puck, but missed the net far too many times.

CAL#2 RD, Thrower, Josh(2014) Aggressive defenseman who plays the game quite similarly to his older brother Dalton Thrower. Really made an effort to finish his checks and be a pain to play against along the walls. Would get caught out of position from time to time trying to be too aggressive without the puck, but was able to recover because of his skating abilities. Thrower is able to quickly change directions to stick to his man and prevent them from being a threat in the offensive zone. He displayed good intelligence for the game in the defensive zone when he was not caught running around in his own zone. Offensively, he made very good passes out of the zone and was not afraid to shoot the puck from the blue line if there was an open lane.

CAL#25 RC, Chase, Greg(2013) Forward had an inconsistent game tonight. Looked good when he was using his speed and skating abilities to take the puck to the net and be aggressive. However, he committed a few questionable turnovers throughout the game. It seemed like he would just lose focus once in a while and just blindly throw a pass to nobody or tried to be too cute with the puck. He was good in his own zone and did not make any big mistakes.

SCOUT'S NOTES: This was a game played very tightly by both teams. They could not generate much offensively, and defensemen on both sides were able to keep much of the play to the outside. I was impressed with 15 year old call up Adam Musil for Red Deer, who is the younger brother of David Musil. He was very smart with and without the puck, strong along the walls and definitely held his own all game long. He created a couple of scoring chances and almost scored by tipping a slap shot from the point in the slot. Haydn Fleury received a lot of ice time and really thrived all game long. Definitely a player to keep an eye on for the next year and a half.

FINAL SCORE: 2-1 Calgary

December 12, 2012, Kelowna Rockets @ Lethbridge Hurricanes (WHL)

KEL #2 RD Lees, Jesse (2013) - Lees handles the puck very well along the wall in his own zone and dangerously sacrificed himself to block shots. However he had a world of trouble trying to clear the zone on the penalty kill. Jesse shoots a ton from the point.

KEL #4 RD Bowey, Madison (2013) - Madison possesses excellent mobility and an exceptional first step. He rushes the puck using his speed and is about as automatic as they come in terms of puck rushing ability. He uses his mobility, strong vision and makes quick decisions from the point on the power play where he generally gets second unit ice. He pinches off the point at intelligent times to make plays with the puck or shoot it and he is generally very smart with the puck in the offensive zone. While Bowey is strong with the puck, he has work to do when he doesn't have the puck on his stick. Defensively he was inconsistent. He made the occasional strong one on one play with his stick but got beat multiple times.

KEL #6 RD Wheaton, Mitchell (2013) - Mitchell really struggled today. He can get caught out of position at times and isn't a very good skater but has great size.

KEL #24 RC Baillie, Tyson (2014) - Baillie protects the puck very well when moving down low in the offensive zone. He plays an effective physical game but did take an unnecessary penalty clearly elbowing an opposing player to the head

LET #6 RD Erkamps, Macoy (2013) - Erkamps got off to a slow start in this game. He got beat one on one pretty regularly early on. He turned the puck over quite a bit one of which involved the puck being thrown right into his own slot. At about the midway point Macoy picked up his physical game and every other area of his game seemed to follow along. In addition to him finishing his checks regularly, he skated well with more confidence with the puck. He made some very important plays for his team in the offensive zone in the third and showed off some very slick puck skills.

LET #9 RD Topping, Joel (2013) - Made some good plays in his own zone breaking up passes and showed good positioning on a two on one break. He tries to skate the puck out of trouble but would get caught trying to do this with Kelowna players close to him.

LET #14 LD Pilon, Ryan (2013) - Pilon showed pretty good mobility for his size. He does a great job holding the line on the power play and has a very hard shot and gets his shots through traffic. Ryan dropped the gloves standing up for his teammate after taking a bit of a cheap shot.

LET #21 RC Merkley, Jay (2013) - Merkley showed pretty good passing on the rush, but he also has a good shot and uses it rather liberally. He showed a good forecheck and took away time and space from opponents but didn't finish. Jay will battle defensively and work in his own zone. He showed off his passing ability in the offensive zone setting up the only goal of the game for his team. He creates offensive chances and was used in the final minute down 2-1 and hits the goal post picking up the puck in the slot.

Scouts Notes: This was a very tightly contested mid week match-up. One where each team had to battle for every inch and where both teams had tremendous scoring chances stolen from them by goalies Jordon Cooke (2013*) & Ty Rimmer (Free Agent). Lethbridge put together tremendous pressure in the final few minutes but with a 2-1 lead, Kelowna put away an empty net goal to secure a 3-1 win in the final 15 seconds.

Dec 12, 2012, Ottawa 67s vs. Belleville Bulls (OHL)

BEL # 8, C, Berisha, Aaron (2013) Berisha was driving well to the net and picked up a nice rebound early on to score the team's 1st goal of the game. He was aggressive and physical on the puck carrier and hustling to get on loose pucks. He was getting out to the high slot with some space to put a nice shot on net after opening up to take the pass and also did a great job of getting to the front of the net for chances. He was all around the net battling and looking for those chances and driving down the middle to the net. He was protecting the puck to rush it up the ice and made some nice passes as well through the neutral zone for the breakout, but has to get his shots on net off the rush. He also needs to watch some of the turnovers at the offensive blue line.

BEL # 13, RW, Kuptsov, Sergey (2013) Kuptsov was protecting the puck and cycling it well deep in the offensive zone. He had some nice speed and puck protection coming down off the wing to gain the zone wide and was getting to the front of the net looking for opportunities. He brought that nice net-front presence with him picking up some loose pucks and also was passing well as he did a nice job spotting a man cross-ice on a feed in the offensive zone. He also was able to stop quickly showing his agility to avoid pressure and hold up at the blue line and then move the puck to a man driving the net for a good chance. I'd like to see a bit more of a battle in his game as he was outmuscled for the puck in corners in the offensive zone.

BEL # 14, D, Subban, Jordan (2013) Subban has some nice hands and speed and that great ability to rush the puck up the ice. He also likes to sneak down low to get some opportunities in the slot for some great chances and is very calm with the puck, but he needs to make sure his shots are getting through from the point. He finds lanes very well to either skate or pass the puck up the ice to gain the offensive zone with ease and showed some nice puck distribution on the power play. He is able to spot a man down low next to the net for some good chances in tight and can make some perfect tape-to-tape passes through the neutral zone. He has to watch some of the turnovers in the offensive zone by trying to shoot the puck through the opposition.

OTT # 28, LW, Brown, Connor (2013) Brown showed some of his physicality tonight by finishing his checks on the fore-check and was cycling the puck well in the offensive zone. He tried to force the pass through to the front of the net a few times from behind and needs to look for some open lanes to get passes through. He battled hard for the puck in front of the net and was opening up next to the net looking for some chances. He also did a nice job of opening up to take a pass on a 2-on-1 to put a pretty decent shot on net, and was also opening up in the high slot to provide options, and was moving the puck to an open man in the middle. He likes to get the puck in deep on a dump and chase to start the cycle, and was out battled a few times deep in the offensive zone and needs to come out with the puck more often.

OTT # 5, D, Desautels, Matthieu (2013) Desautels has some pretty good hands and agility to get away from the opposition's pressure. He was getting down in lanes to try to block passes and is a quick player with nice speed displayed with the ability to move the puck up and out of the zone well on that 1st pass. He uses his stick well to check the puck away from the opposition, and showed some good speed coming back and getting in lanes to breakup passes. He was breaking up opportunities with his stick and keeping his man to the outside for the most part. He needs to watch some of the turnovers along the boards in his own end.

OTT # 11, D, Vlajkov, Mike (2013) Vlajkov was really physical in his own end trying to separate his man from the puck and throwing his man into the boards. He used his stick well to check the puck away and did a nice job of taking away the forward's space and forcing him to the outside. He was jumping down low to put some shots on net and keep the attack going, but needs to watch some of the turnovers along the boards moving the puck out of his own end and also needs to watch the turnovers up the middle through the neutral zone.

OTT # 18, D, Davis, Taylor (2013) Davis didn't have too great of a game tonight as he was turning the puck over along the boards and had a bad turnover right up the middle in his own end resulting in the opposition's 2nd goal of the game. He is calm with the puck and can move it up and out of the zone under pressure, and uses his stick to keep his man to the outside. He did however lose a step on his man who drove wide around him for a good chance.

OTT # 24, D, Guy, Nevin (2013) Guy was just looking to pressure the opposition on the fore-check and keep pressure on the puck carrier and to try to get the puck in deep whenever he could by dumping and chasing after it. He kept to a pretty simple game tonight.

FINAL SCORE: 2-0 Belleville Bulls

Dec 13, 2012, Erie Otters vs. Niagara IceDogs (OHL)

ERI # 7, C, Evans, Jake (2013) Evans is a pretty quick skater and showed his great speed on multiple occasions in this game as he tried to get the puck in deep. He played a dump and chase game for the most part and got some decent cycles in the offensive zone. He showed some good strength as he is hard to knock over and did a good job getting in lanes to block shots on the penalty kill. He has to get his shots on net from the slot and get the puck out on the penalty kill on his clearing attempts, and also tried too many moves at one point trying to gain the offensive zone and should keep it simple and stick to getting the puck in deep.

ERI # 10, LW, Harper, Stephen (2013) Harper was able to find some open space in the high slot to get off some shots and was getting a nice shot through from the point on the power play. He kept his shot down low trying to generate rebounds and opened up well in the slot to get shots off but has to hit the net on his opportunities. He was battling hard for the puck in deep and protecting the puck well deep in the offensive zone. He was driving to the net and passing the puck to some dangerous areas getting it through the crease. He put some good pressure on the puck carrier and was able to force some turnovers by being aggressive on the point on the penalty kill and then rushing the puck back the other way. He showed some great strength to drive the puck down low and get a shot off from in tight and was showing his great speed to gain the offensive zone and use his hands and puck skills to create space and get chances from the slot. He can take a long pass well in full speed to gain the zone and was finding some good lanes to pass the puck back to the point from the corner and the team scored the 2nd goal of the game off this play.

ERI # 19, D, Kuleshov, Artem (2013) Kuleshov is a big body defenseman who has a nice hard shot from the point that he can get on target as the team scored on a tip of one of his shots. He made some good passes up through the neutral zone but still has to watch some of the turnovers. He also got beat by being too aggressive on his man along the boards and the other team got a good chance from the play.

NIA # 12, LW, Difruscia, Anthony (2013) Difruscia has some good speed to his game and displayed this as he blocked an opponent's shot and then rushed the puck back up the ice with speed and put a good shot on net. He was passing the puck up the ice pretty well and was clearing the puck on the penalty kill. He can take a hit and still make the play and is not easily intimidated getting involved in scrums showing some nice aggression defending his goalie. He had a nice wide drive and cut to the middle for a good back-hand chance as well and the only issue I had with his game tonight were some of the struggles getting the puck out of the zone along the boards.

NIA # 16, LW, Petersen, Trevor (2013) Petersen was putting some good pressure on the puck carrier and was nice and physical on the fore-check. He found some open space in the slot to open up and get off a nice one-timer on net and had a good shot on net as well later from the high slot. He had a pretty nice cycle game going down low and was getting some nice shots on net and protecting the puck well along the boards. He was also taking some long shots off the rush and I would prefer to see him drive this puck down low for better chances.

NIA # 21, C, Verhaeghe, Carter (2013) Verhaeghe had some nice speed coming out of the neutral zone and was distributing the puck well moving into the offensive end. He can protect the puck to rush it up through the neutral zone to gain the offensive zone and was also opening up in the slot for a shot but has to get his shot through. He was able to drive the puck wide with some decent protection and put good pressure on the fore-check as well. He was also willing to get in lanes to block shots.

NIA # 26, RW, Lemmon, Mack (2013) Lemmon is a physical blue collar type role player on this team who battles hard for the puck and is aggressive and getting in opponent's faces. He had some nice big hits on the fore-check and was forcing turnovers with some great pressure on the fore-check as well. He got down in lanes to block shots and drives the net well. He was able to get open for a shot from the slot but has to hit the net on his opportunities and needs to watch some of the penalties as well with his big hits. He can break the puck out of his zone effectively as well to move it up through the neutral zone.

NIA # 4, D, Kelly, Broderick (2013) Kelly is a smaller defenseman but very willing to jump up and join the rush. He was jumping in off the point as well into the slot for a nice shot on net and had a nice drive wide to gain the zone and lead the attack down low. He also made some nice little chip plays to move the puck up along the boards and was physical in his own end and using his stick to keep the opposition to the outside. He let his man get away from him a bit and scored their 1st goal of the night and has to watch his man in the defensive end and keep him tied up as best as he can.

FINAL SCORE: 4-2 Erie Otters

Dec 13, 2012, Oshawa Generals vs. Barrie Colts (OHL)

OSH # 10, RW, Urbanic, John (2013) Urbanic displayed some of his nice hands tonight with some good moves and some good passing as well to move the puck up through the neutral zone. He did a nice job of getting open in the slot and opening up for a pass but needs to have a bit of a quicker release on his shot. Later in the game however he was able to take a drop pass and get a nice shot off from the high slot. He displayed his puck skills tonight and has some good speed as well trying to drive the puck into the slot, but needs to get that shot through. He was pressuring the puck carrier and was physical finishing his hits on the fore-check as well. He has to watch some of the turnovers in deep by trying to force the puck to a teammate in front when no lane is available to him.

OSH # 14, RW, Latour, Bradley (2013) Latour was driving the net well and had a real good wrap-around attempt to drive the puck down low. He was cycling the puck fairly well and getting to the net and also showed some nice puck protection on a real power-forward move to fend off the defenseman and get a shot from in tight, but has to hit the net from there. He was finding some open space in the slot to get shots off and was pressuring the puck carrier and using his stick to direct the play.

OSH # 19, C, Cassels, Cole (2013) Cassels was able to cycle the puck pretty well down low and was moving around to get to the net. He was distributing the puck well dropping to a trailing man and then driving hard to the net and showed that nice net-front presence. He made some nice big hits on the fore-check to try to force turnovers in deep. He also made a nice fake-shot and drop pass to create a good chance and showed some nice hands and puck protection to get the puck in deep and then found a lane to move the puck back to the point from behind the net. At times he was out battled and lost the puck and I'd like to see more battle for that puck.

OSH # 7, D, Carlisle, Chris (2013) Carlisle is an agile good quick skater, but is a smaller defenseman. He was jumping up joining the rush and the attack in deep and is able to find lanes to skate the puck up the ice and then distribute it. He was tying up his man pretty well in front of his own net and was battling hard for the puck and then moving it up and out of the zone. He showed some nice hands and puck distribution in the offensive zone and scored on a shot from the point on a high floater shot, but I would still like to see him keep this puck down low for rebounds even though it worked out this one time. He also needs to watch the turnovers up through the middle of the ice and along the boards as well.

BAR # 17, C, Scott, Justin (2013) Scott is not the quickest skater, but he gets the puck in deep and makes his hit on the fore-check. He had a nice drive hard to the net with his stick down and was throwing pucks on net from just about everywhere. He was pressuring the puck carrier hard and making sure to finish all his checks.

BAR # 18, C, Bradford, Erik (2013) Bradford is a really fast skater who was pressuring the puck carrier well and showing a nice element of physicality. He had a net-front presence on the power play and was passing the puck up the ice well to start the rush. He had a wide drive and then threw the puck towards the middle to try to hit the man driving the net. He made a really great lead pass to spring a teammate for a breakaway and got a great chance but hit the post on the chance. He showed some nice hands to move the puck down low near the net for a great chance in tight and was also opening up well down low next to the net to take a one-timer feed and score the team's only goal of the game. He got his stick in lanes on the penalty kill to break up chances and rush the puck back up the other way and made a great feed to hit a man with speed gaining the zone for a great chance to tie up the game late. He has to watch where he is passing the puck as he passed to a man without a stick at one point and also needs to hit the net on his shots off the rush.

BAR # 7, D, Yuil, Alex (2013) Yuil is another smaller defenseman who is willing to jump up and join the attack down low. He made some nice passes to move the puck up and out of the zone along the boards, and was coming down low to the slot for a nice shot but missed the net on his chance. He had some pretty good battles for the puck along the boards in his own end and was using his stick to get it in the shooting lane and deflect the puck out of the way. There were a few times he jumped up into the slot for some shots.

BAR # 24, D, Webster, Michael (2013) Webster did a pretty nice job of holding the line under pressure and was making some nice chip plays up the boards to start the rush. He was also jumping down low into the play to keep the attack alive on the cycle and was able to take a hit and still move the puck out of the zone. He has to watch some of the suicide passes up through the neutral zone for wingers and also missed his target a couple times on passes up for breakout.

FINAL SCORE: 3-1 Oshawa Generals

Dec 14, 2012, Plymouth Whalers vs. Sudbury Wolves (OHL)

PLY # 18, LW, Vanderwiel, Danny (2013) Vanderwiel was finding some lanes to rush the puck up the ice and drive the puck down low. He was taking some outside low-chance shots and was for the most part just trying to get the puck in deep. He was pressuring the puck carrier with some good speed trying to force turnovers and was battling hard for pucks in front of the net.

PLY # 21, C, Hartman, Ryan (2013) Hartman hustles hard for loose pucks and drives the puck to the low slot to get shots on net from in tight. He protects the puck really well and battles hard in front of the net for the puck. He had a net-front presence on the power play and was finding some space in the high slot to get some shots off. He did a great job pressuring the puck carrier to force turnovers and rush the puck back up the other way and made a pretty nice slap pass to hit a man cross-ice in the offensive zone. He needs to hit the net on his chances from the slot on the power play and also missed his target on a pass up the ice for a breakout.

PLY # 23, RW, Sills, Connor (2013) Sills was driving the net pretty well going to the dirty areas and had a nice net-front presence as well. He was pressuring the puck carrier on the fore-check but was mishandling the puck on the cycle in the offensive zone turning the puck over.

PLY # 6, D, Jones, Mitch (2013) Jones was stepping up off the blue line to get off a nice shot from the point. He was protecting the puck well from pressure but has to watch the turnovers around the boards in his own end. He got in a good fight showing that willingness to stick up for himself but was taken down pretty unanimously in the fight. He did a nice job protecting the puck and has a nice hard shot from the point but has to get it through.

SDB # 9, LW, Desrochers, Danny (2013) Desrochers was protecting the puck well getting a good cycle game going deep in the offensive zone. He was moving the puck to the front of the net from the side boards trying to hit the man streaking in and was pressuring the puck carrier on the penalty kill. He was physical along the boards in his own end to force turnovers and had some nice chip plays up the boards to move the puck up to break out of his own zone.

SDB # 14, RW, Baptiste, Nicholas (2013) Baptiste is such a quick agile player who is physical and pressuring well on the fore-check. He had a net-front presence on the power play and battled hard for the puck in the corners and showed some really nice hands and a great spin move to protect the puck and get a shot off from the slot. He found some open space in the high slot to open up and get a shot off but has to hit the net. For the most part however he was getting his shot on net and following up for the rebound. He did a great job on the power play of getting to the slot and opening up for a one-timer and score the team's 3rd goal of the game, he then again later opened up again in the slot for a one-timer chance on the power play but missed the puck. He can stop on a dime to move away from his man and made a great pass to find a man in the slot for an excellent chance. He was playing with some real high energy and displaying his great speed up the ice protecting the puck and then made a great one-handed pass to find a man down low for a great one-timer chance.

SDB # 15, LW, Kubalik, Dominik (2013) Kubalik had a great game tonight showing his great speed off the rush. He did a great job taking a pass through the neutral zone with speed and then drove to the net cutting with a great back-hand shot to score the team's 4th goal of the game. He was finding some open space in the slot on the power play in the middle of the opposition's box, and coming in off the wing with speed and dropping the puck and then driving the net hard. He also had a great give-and-go to get the puck down deep for a great chance for Leivo from in tight and was passing the puck well through the neutral zone to lead the rush. He showed some nice physicality on a big hit along the boards and had a nice net-front presence as well opening up well in the slot. He also made a really amazing saucer pass to feed Harris for the team's 7th goal of the game.

SDB # 16, C, Harris, Jacob (2013) Harris was all around the net in this game and battling hard in front of the net for the puck. He found some open space to get open in the slot for a great chance early on but fanned on the shot. Later on he took a pass really well in the offensive zone to drive the net with the puck, and was getting open in front of the net with tons of space to take a pass and score the team's 6th goal of the game. He also showed some great hand-eye to bat the puck out of the air on a 2-on-1 and score the team's 7th goal of the game. He was offering some good support coming back to his own end and tying up his man keeping him away from the net. He was battling to lift the opponent's stick and take the puck forcing the turnover and then showed some real nice speed up the ice pressuring on the puck carrier. He has some nice agility to make some moves and create space, but has to watch some of the turnovers in the neutral zone by mishandling the puck.

SDB # 24, D, DeHaan, Evan (2013) DeHaan did not look like his regular self tonight as he had some trouble holding on to the puck early on in his own end. He was moving the puck up pretty nicely on the breakout and did a great job stepping up for an excellent shot from the point to score the team's 5th goal of the game. He was getting in lanes to break up plays and move the puck up the boards to break it out and is calm with the puck moving it around the boards. He showed his hands and agility to get his shot off from the high slot and was walking down low with the puck but has to hit the net from down low.

FINAL SCORE: 7-3 Sudbury Wolves

December 14, 2012, Guelph Storm @ Sarnia Sting (OHL)

GUE #3 LD Pedan, Andrey (NY Islanders) - Andrey's skating really hasn't improved nearly as much as we hoped it would, now in his third OHL season. Andrey has a powerful shot but he really struggles with the puck in general, trying to force things that just weren't there. His decision making and hockey sense in general is below average and his development just isn't working the way I'm sure the Islanders were hoping it would.

GUE #4 LD Finn, Matt (Toronto) - Matt played a great game and was excellent in both the offensive and defensive zones. He uses his body very well to box out opponents in both zones. Defensively he's willing to block shots and gets into passing lanes very well. In the offensive zone he's very smart with the puck and created several good chances in the offensive zone. He let go of a powerful point shot to make it 2-4 in the final minute of the game. Consistency was one of the biggest concerns last season entering the draft. While the jury is still out on that area of his game, tonight Matt put on a great performance and showed why he was in the discussion for the first round of the 2012 NHL Entry Draft.

GUE #7 LD Harpur, Ben (2013) - Harpur moves fairly well up and down the ice for a big guy. But he wasn't overly involved in this game.

GUE #9 RC Fabbri, Robby (2014) - Robby showed great creativity with the puck and created several scoring chances for himself and others. He worked hard throughout the game. He utilized his strong positioning and was opportunistic to score with just 11 seconds left in the first period to tie the game for the time being at 1-1. Fabbri gets his shot off quickly. Fabbri got off to a slow start this year but really looks like he's turning things around in his rookie season.

GUE #11 LW Dickinson, Jason (2013) - Dickinson was fantastic in this game. He shows a great combination of size and skating ability. He works hard to create offensive chances on a regular basis. He shows great patience with the puck and makes smart decisions when entering the offensive zone with the puck. Every time he touched the puck he was a threat to score or create a goal. Jason is just as smart defensively as he is offensively. He possesses great defensive positioning and is very aware of the play going on around him. He has very good hockey sense in all areas of the game and seems to keep getting better and better every game.

GUE #19 RC Garlent, Hunter (2013) - Hunter works very hard and plays with a ton of energy. He is a very good skater and shows great quickness and agility. He controls the puck well in the offensive zone and has good hockey sense.

SAR #21 LC Nikandrov, Daniel (2013) - Nikandrov was very solid defensively and on the penalty kill taking away passing lanes and blocking shots. He has good work ethic and even created a few offensive chances for his team.

SAR #71 RW Goldobin, Nikolay (2014) - Goldobin's vision is exceptional and he sees things that most players just don't. He has outstanding passing ability and a very high level of creativity.

SAR #77 RD DeAngelo, Anthony (2014) - Anthony had several strong end to end rushes in this game, however at one point he tripped himself trying to make a move resulting in the puck going the other way. He had his moments in 1 on 1 defensive situations winning a few match-up's. DeAngelo shows pretty good hockey sense in the offensive zone, but it drops off the closer he gets to his own net as he made some very questionable plays with the puck in his own end.

SAR #94 LC Galchenyuk, Alex (Montreal) - Galchenyuk was on the right point for the power play early on blasting the second goal of the game. Then he made an outstanding pass to set up the eventual game winning goal. Alex played a little more physical than we're used to seeing as he has the size for it.

Scouts Notes: Guelph's defense had all they could handle with Sarnia's top line as Alex Galchenyuk (Montreal), Charles Sarault (Free Agent) and Reid Boucher (New Jersey) combined to score all four goals for the Sting in a 4-2 victory. The three of them combined to put up 9 points. Davis Brown (2013) three game scoring streak was snapped in this match-up as well. He got pushed around a little early, but he was the one giving the hits later on in this one.

Flood-Marr Holiday Hockey Tournament (December 14th-16th 2012):

Andover #2 LD Connor Light (2013) – Intimidating two-way defenseman. Good skater, can skate the puck out of danger and join the attack. Went end-to-end when given space, strong through neutral zone with puck, normally gained line and dumped deep. Pinched like a freight train, very decisive and picked his spots well. Hard to play against, took body hard and protected his net front. Hard to beat on rush, good positioning and long stick, angled off well. Overaggressive at times. Hurt himself midway through tourney throwing a big hit where opponent unfortunately made contact with his head.

Andover #9 LC Eddie Ellis (2013) – Highly skilled center but inconsistent with effort. Disappeared for periods at a time. Defensive coverage was consistently iffy, floated and fixates on puck. Tantalized with upside but inconsistency was an issue. Top 50 talent when at his best. When on his game: Instinctual offensive player with intimidating skill, speed, and intensity. Strong skater, very agile and deceptively quick. Great passes, found seams with crisp hard feeds and was capable of well-timed dishes into space and drop passes. Used his reach to protect well or change direction of shot/attack. Had arsenal of dangles. Head-up shooter, quick release and good velocity on wrist/snap shots. Good on powerplay, very active. Forechecked hard. When off his game: Unsure on skates, indecisive, overzealous. Slow. Whiffed on scoring chances. Gave the puck away in all three zones trying to do too much. Frustrated.

Andover #15 LD Michael Kim (2013) – Physical two-way defenseman with good instincts and skill. Good skater, quick feet and edges, very strong on his feet. Exploded into space with puck thanks to quick first steps. Physical on the boards and in front, defended well against much bigger players with good positioning. Did damage with hits, finished hard. Battler, won 50/50 pucks with frequency. Strong neutral zone play on both sides of the puck. Active stick, chopped and poked well. Good lane coverage. Blocked shots in key moments. Very capable puckhandler. Strong against forecheck, good decisions and outlets. Joined rush and went end-to-end when given space. Had one hero shift where he burned three players and ripped a slapshot home. Played the point well but can also think like a forward in the offensive zone, useful when team was behind or needed boost. Good pinches. Quick wrister and hard slapshot. Can play both sides (LD/RD). Floated a lot in the neutral zone and defensive zone (walks line between efficient and lazy). Worked harder in some games than others. Not the biggest guy but loved the way he played in this tournament.

Deerfield #19 LW Alex Gonye (Passed over 2012) – Skilled offensive forward who was not always involved enough. Good skater, stride was smooth and efficient, but lacked explosiveness. Stickhandled well in tight and fed pucks through sticks/legs. Capable of great individual efforts 1-on-1 or even 1-on-2. Good stick in neutral and defensive zones. Defensive effort was inconsistent, often seemed to be waiting for offense to restart. Did not go to dirty areas with frequency. Still lanky.

Hotchkiss #8 LW Tyler Hill (2013) – Big skilled forward who's still rough around the edges. Was a tale of two players in tourney. Early on, was tentative with iffy balance. Used size in bursts through middle, down outside, and along boards but was not decisive or aggressive. Feet were slow and puck control was lacking, hands looked unpolished. Later in tourney came into his own. Showed surprising shiftiness, great burst quickness with the puck on his stick. Used his reach and quick hands to dangle in neutral zone and inside blueline, creating numerous scoring opportunities for himself. Wrister was hard and accurate, released quickly and deceptively. Worked hard in corners, played physical along the boards, very difficult to get off puck, fought through checks. Good PKer and in defensive zone, utilizes his reach, a little stationary. Even at the top of his game had some issues. Lacked killer instinct overall (reminds of Brian Boyle but with more upside). Was used on the point on the powerplay and was dreadful, exposed by PK forwards for multiple SH scoring chances. Major project but intrigues with skill, speed for size, and intimidating strength when utilized. Injured in knee-on-knee collision towards end of tourney.

Hotchkiss #25 LD Wiley Sherman (2013) – Big, steady two-way defenseman with upside. Skating was a strength, especially for size. Good stride, speed, edges. Calming presence, good keeps at point and good decisions with puck in defensive zone. Safe in his end, puck off glass under pressure and simple passes. Good point shot, wrist and slap. Rock defensively late in games, coach made concerted effort to keep him on ice in last couple minutes.

Kimball Union #10 LW AJ Greer (2015) – Raw but budding power forward. Good hands in tight. Worked well in cycle. Strong on the boards. Went hard to the net. Played well on the PK, responsible defensively. One to watch for the future.

Milton #18 RC Anthony Sabitsky (Passed over 2012) – Consistently Milton's best offensive player in this tournament. Quick skilled forward with good finesse skill. Was able to penetrate the high slot with speed on the rush on numerous occasions thanks to quick stickhandling maneuvers. Made some outstanding passes, both from standstill and at high speed. Good puck recognition in traffic, picked pucks out of crowds. Great wrist shot, quick release with good velocity and accuracy.

Milton #26 RD Conner Wynne (2014) - Shifty, gifted offensive defenseman. Good passer, quick outlets. Great on the powerplay, ran the ship: on one occasion the coach yelled "Conner, stay out the whole time!". Overpowered and outsmarted by bigger and older players. Should improve with experience.

Nobles #27 RW Colin White (2016) – One of the top prospects in his age group, already committed to BC this past spring. Power forward type, not huge (yet?) but he protected the puck well and played with great drive. Great shooter, good variety and selection. Will be more effective as he matures, but was already a top player at this level as a freshman and impressed last year as an eighth-grader playing up.

Salisbury #9 LD Will Toffey (2013) – Very smooth offensive-minded defenseman. Played the full rink. Fantastic skater, great edges, good acceleration. Comfortable with the puck at high speed. Made quick, crisp outlet passes and found seams on the powerplay. Jumped into the attack frequently, protected the puck well and got the puck deep when he runs out of space. Frequently chased the puck deep in such instances, usually made good contact but sometimes overcommitted himself. Tended to be a little overzealous offensively. Projects as a two-way player but needs some work in his own end as he tends to be too lax in front of his net. Physical on the boards, tough to play against in bursts. Too aggressive on the PK, took himself out of position. Made up for lapses with reflexes, but that won't work at higher levels.

Salisbury #22 LD Ryan Segalla (2013) – Two-way defenseman with a mean streak. Very physical, tough to play against, finished every check. Good stick in his zone, very active in lanes. Protected the net front. Smooth skater, good stride and strong on his feet. Hard wrister and slapshot, quick release. Made good decisions with the puck at the point. Took himself out of position to play the body often. His reads were questionable overall, especially against the rush and with the puck in his own end. Liked to go end-to-end and had the ability to get by forecheckers but tended to make one move too many, had trouble when forced to make a decision against strong pressure. Outlet passes were frequently risky. Discipline was a concern, multiple boarding penalties and lost his cool on a couple occasions. Tantalized with upside but his over-aggressiveness was a concern.

Westminster #11 LC Sean Orlando (2013) – Shifty two-way talent. Great vision, moved the puck well in the cycle and made great reads with the puck in the neutral zone. Quick hands, very difficult to defend against on the rush and hard to check on the boards. Good wrist shot, hard and accurate. Played the whole rink, responsible defensively. Tried to do a little too much at times.

Westminster #16 RW David Hallisey (Passed over 2012) – Honest, hard-working two-way player. Good feet, quick first steps and strong on his skates. Worked well in a cycle, difficult to deal with in front of the net. Took the puck strong to the outside and protected well. Very aware of his teammates and made hard, accurate passes. Good stick in the neutral zone. Finished his checks. Backchecked hard. Should have success at the college level, played a pro-style game.

Westminster #24 LW Mario Benicky (2013) – Big power forward type with upside. Bullish on the boards and a menace in the low slot. Acceleration was lacking but has a good stride and when he builds up speed, watch out. Good work protecting the puck down the wing. Surprisingly quick hands for a big guy. Good passer, good decisions with puck in outnumbered attack situations. Freed his stick up in front of the net for passes. Worked well in cycle. Had shifts where he was much too stationary in the offensive zone. Slow first few steps are a concern.

Dec 15, 2012, Coquitlam Express vs. Powell River Kings (BCHL)

COQ#17 LC, Rockwood, Adam(2014) Quick forward who was at his best tonight when he was moving his feet along the boards to get away from defenders. Liked the way he played without the puck in his own zone, and was quite dependable to take passing and shooting lanes away. Worked very hard in all areas of the ice. Has good vision in tight. Just needs to work on making decisions with the puck at a quicker pace. Has the tendency to wait too long for the perfect play, and by then the room he had is gone and a puck battle ensues as a result.

PR#24 LD, Ripley, Luke(2013) A big, defensive defenseman who had an average game tonight. Has very good speed, but struggles at times moving laterally. Needs to work on his footwork. Got caught standing still a couple of times in the neutral zone, resulting in odd man chances for Coquitlam. Possesses a good first pass out of the zone and is quite poised with the puck, but has limited offensive abilities.

PR#27 RD, Burns, Jordan(2013) Offensive defenseman who struggled without the puck tonight. Makes very good passes and is poised with the puck. Got the power-play going efficiently, but needs to work on his shots from the point. Defensively, he is not very strong on his skates or along the boards, so he turned over the puck a number of times. He was often caught out of position, and gave up a number of chances, especially in tight. Needs to really work on his defensive game to ever have a chance of making it to the pro level.

Scouts Notes: There was a lot of sloppy plays in this game. Many players have to learn to manage the puck better and limit the number of turnovers. Heard some good things about Luke Ripley before attending this game. His skating ability is impressive, but he got caught too many times in the middle of nowhere which resulted in great scoring chances, and the overtime goal. Still quite raw, but if he can learn to think the game better, he could be a good pro in the future. Brandon Morley was quite impressive tonight for Coquitlam. Played with an edge and went to the dirty areas to score, and sacrificed his body to block shots time and time again. Problem is his size, only stands at about 5'7.

FINAL SCORE: 3-2(OT) Coquitlam

Dec 15, 2012. Guelph Storm vs. London Knights (OHL)

GUE#9 F Robby Fabbri (2014). Robby really stood out in this game and was probably his best game yet at this point in the season. Came out flying in the first period and was really effective skating with the puck through the neutral zone and getting it deep into the offensive zone. Skating was a plus in this game and showed instances of speed beating a few defenders on races to pucks. Robby is especially effective in the offensive zone participating in a strong cycle game and then cutting to the middle from the half wall before unleashing a strong wrist shot on target. Saw time in all situations for the Storm in this game, and was effective in the face-off circle winning the majority of draws.

GUE#11 F Jason Dickinson (2013). The strongest part of Jason's game is his vision and positioning and this was especially on showcase in this game. Jason consistently seems to be in the right positions to make plays and is very rarely caught in a bad position. Never lets defenders get positioning on him so that in the case of a turnover he is always in a strong spot to win the puck back. Jason had a strong game on the Power Play, finding open lanes and setting up teammates in strong positions to score. Did not make any noticeable mistakes and is a steady presence that Guelph consistently relies on in big situations.

GUE#19 F Hunter Garlent (2013). Hunter was especially effective on the Power Play tonight, unleashing an absolute laser from the top of the circles beating the Knights goaltender top shelf. Showcases a strong skating ability to position himself in strong scoring areas of the ice. Needs to consistently keep things a little bit simpler and got caught trying to force some passes in instances where he was trying to make things look fancy. Hunter is undersized although this does generally not hamper his ability of working the puck into the corners or down low in the offensive zone. Helped out on breakouts in the defensive zone when the defenders needed assistance.

LDN#53 F Bo Horvat (2013). Bo was one of the better players on the ice in this game. Bo initially stood out for excellent work on the Penalty Kill, diving into shot lanes and blocking a number of pucks. Was effective at forcing bad passes and causing the offense to regroup in the neutral zone. Bo displayed a strong net presence in the offensive zone, consistently getting into the face of the Storm goaltender and is especially adept at going to the hard areas of the ice to make plays. Bo also saw time on the Power Play unit for the Knights banging home a goal on a goal mouth scramble. Showed flashes of elite speed and skating ability, beating Storm defenders to the outside on numerous occasions in this game and winning the majority of races to the puck.

Scouts Notes: Max Domi was suspended for this game after a cross checking major during the game the night before. Also missing for LDN was a number of players at their respective World Junior camps

Dec 16, 2012, Prince Albert Raiders vs. Brandon Wheat Kings (WHL)

PA#10 LD, Morrissey, Josh(2013) Had a solid game at both ends of the ice tonight. Was consistently physical and landed a couple of open ice hits in the neutral zone. Morrissey did a very good job to keep opponents to the outside on the rush and used his stick effectively to take away any cross ice passes in transition. He read the play well without the puck in coverage and never really got caught out of position. Offensively, did well to get shots through traffic and on net. Unleashed a good one timer a couple of times as well. Moves the puck well and got the attack started for his team quickly on a consistent basis. He was patient with the puck, and did not try to force any passes through heavy traffic.

PA#19 RC, Gardiner, Reid(2014) Rookie forward received a lot of key ice time tonight and performed quite well. Impressive on the PK, particularly on the controlled forecheck where he was able to anticipate and create a number of turnovers. Possesses above average skating abilities, and will need to work on his speed in the future. Offensively, still needs to make decisions with the puck at a quicker pace, and limit the turnovers he caused.

BDN#2 RD, Pulock, Ryan(2013) Defenseman had an inconsistent game tonight. A few times during the game he was caught out of position and gave opponents a couple of open lanes to the net, but his positioning got better as the game went, particularly on the rush. His stick could have been more active to knock away passes as well. Made one really bad soft clearing attempt in the slot which led to a goals against. Very strong on his skates and along the boards. Was very hard to knock down. Made a couple of very nice rushes with the puck and displayed some impressive speed.

BDN#6 LD, Nikkel, Ayrton(2013) Defensive defenseman who had a good game in his own zone. Showed off his good strength and ability to read the play without the puck to be in good position on a consistent basis. Really liked how physical he was all game long, and he was hard to knock off the puck along the walls. Was inconsistent when he had to move the puck. At times he got the attack going quickly, and at other times would hold onto the puck for too long and tried to be too fancy. In one instance, he turned his back toward the play and tried to make a backhand pass for some reason.

BDN#7 LD, Roy, Eric(2013) Was the most consistent defenseman for Brandon tonight. Roy was very good with the puck and moved it quickly and was quite creative with it at times. He was good along the boards, but needs to raise his intensity level more and try to win more battles for loose pucks. He was also a little casual in his own end at times. Defensively, he had a good active stick to take away passing lanes.

Scouts Notes: This game had a very good pace to it. I was impressed with Josh Morrissey's physical game. He was smart to not get caught out of position and made calculated risks in the neutral zone. He is starting to become more and more well rounded. Ryan Pulock must be more consistent with his game, and have better starts too.

FINAL SCORE: 3-0 Prince Albert

Dec 15, 2012, Barrie Colts vs. Plymouth Whalers (OHL)

BAR # 17, C, Scott, Justin (2013) Scott was cycling the puck really well in the offensive zone and protecting the puck along the boards. He was just trying to get the puck in deep and is calm with the puck and willing to take a hit to make a play. He was protecting the puck to get to the slot for a great chance but has to hit the net on the opportunity. He was passing the puck well through the neutral zone to breakout and taking some long shots but needs to get them through on net.

BAR # 18, C, Bradford, Erik (2013) Bradford was showing some physicality early on moving the puck up on the rush and showing some pretty good speed into the offensive zone. He had a good net-front presence and was protecting the puck deep in the offensive zone and cycling the puck well. He did a nice job rushing the puck up the ice and putting the shot on net off the rush. He was physical on the fore-check pressuring the puck carrier trying to force turnovers. He was getting down to block shots and showed some nice agility to avoid the opposition and get the puck in to the offensive zone, he was also displaying some good aggression in this game.

BAR # 7 D, Yuil, Alex (2013) For a smaller player Yuil shows some good physicality in his own end on his man. He keeps his man to the outside with his body and displays some pretty good aggression. He closes his man off along the boards then makes his hit to separate him from the puck and is pretty calm with the puck skating it up the ice. He steps off the point to take his shot from the high slot but missed the net far wide and needs to get that shot on target, but also did a nice job blocking shots in his own zone.

BAR # 24, D, Webster, Micheal (2013) Webster showed some good aggression along the boards and was jumping in to pinch and keep the play alive. He can pass the puck out of the zone nicely along the boards to get it up to the neutral zone but still needs to watch some of the turnovers along the boards by just throwing the puck around the boards in his own end. He showed some decent speed to get back to his own end to get on pucks first and did a nice job also of squeezing his man out along the boards in the defensive zone to take the puck away.

PLY # 21, C, Hartman, Ryan (2013) Hartman started this game off with a great pass to the slot from behind the net to find his man for a good chance. He was reading the play well to pick off turnovers all night in the neutral zone and was also pressuring well on the fore-check to force turnovers in the offensive zone as well. He was throwing the puck on net low to try to generate rebounds and was finding good lanes to skate the puck up into the offensive zone and then was protecting the puck to drive it in deep and get a shot off. He was pretty physical on the fore-check and battling hard to drive the puck to the net and was using his speed to get on loose pucks. He made a great pass to a teammate on an odd-man rush for a great chance and was finding passing lanes on the power play to move the puck back to the point. He also made a great cross-ice pass in the offensive zone and showed some of his great hands and moves to get the puck down low with some space. He has to watch some of the turnovers as he had a bad one at the far blue line and the opposition rushed the puck back for a breakaway to score the 2nd goal of the game, and needs to watch the turnovers trying to skate the puck out of his own zone as well.

PLY # 18, LW, Vanderwiel, Danny (2013) Vanderwiel was coming back to offer some good support in his own end and showed a nice willingness to block shots on the penalty kill. He was getting down to block shots from the point and put some good pressure on the point on the penalty kill as well. He was driving to the net well and opening up to offer options and showed some great speed driving hard to the net looking for loose pucks as well. He has to be able to get the puck out of his own end along the boards.

PLY # 23, RW, Sills, Connor (2013) Sills was sticking to a pretty simple dump and chase game tonight just trying to get the puck in deep. He has to get the puck out along the boards in his own end and missed his target on a few passes up the ice resulting in some turnovers as well.

PLY # 6, D, Jones, Mitch (2013) Jones was using his stick well to get it in lanes and breakup pass opportunities for the opposition. He was passing the puck pretty well under pressure to get the puck out of the zone but has to watch some of the neutral zone turnovers on the long passes. He had some good short breakout passes and was calm and patient with the puck for most of the game until late in the game when his team was pushing it looked like he panicked with the puck and fanned on the outlet pass and then mishandled the puck right after.

FINAL SCORE: 2-0 Barrie Colts

Dec 15, 2012, Niagara IceDogs vs. Sudbury Wolves (OHL)

SDB # 16, C, Harris, Jacob (2013) Harris did a nice job tonight in the battles by digging for pucks and coming out with it and then moving the puck to the front of the net. He was driving hard to the net looking for tips and trying to create traffic and was getting in lanes on the penalty kill to block shots. He put some nice pressure on the fore-check and was driving the puck down low hard on the wide drive. He put shots on net from just about everywhere and had some chances from the top of the circle which the team scored on one of his rebounds but he has to make sure he is hitting the net on his chances off the rush.

SDB # 14, LW, Baptiste, Nicholas (2013) Baptiste showed some great work ethic tonight in his battles and protects the puck really well on the wide drive with speed. He was cycling the puck in deep and competing hard to get to the front of the net. He was paying the price and willing to stand in front of the net on the power-play and was trying to tip pucks. He had some great speed and pressure on the fore-check and was reading the play well to force a turnover deep in the offensive zone. He put some good pressure on the point on the penalty kill but also needs to watch the turnovers himself as he turned the puck over trying too many moves in the offensive zone. He has some real quickness, speed and agility to his game and was finding some space to work with in the high slot, but needs to get his shots through.

SDB # 15, LW, Kubalik, Dominik (2013) Kubalik has some speed to his game rushing the puck up the ice and was hustling and battling hard for pucks in the corner. He was able to hold the offensive zone well along the boards and was finding some open space and opening up in the slot for a one-timer from in tight. He also had another chance and opened up for the one-timer in the high slot but fanned on his shot. He was turning the puck over by forcing the play in the offensive zone and has to hit the net on his shots off the side-wall as well.

SDB # 24, D, DeHaan, Evan (2013) DeHaan had a game tonight that he would probably like to forget as he did not look like himself tonight. He was not rushing the puck up the ice or really looking effective much at all. He was outmuscled a few times for the puck in his own end and mishandled the puck as well resulting in a turnover. He was able to hold the line pretty well in the offensive zone and did show some decent physicality as well.

NIA # 12, LW, Difruscia, Anthony (2013) Difruscia showed some real nice willingness to battle through the dirty areas tonight with a great net-front presence and really took a beating for standing there. He was coming back to his own end giving some good support and was taking passes well through the neutral zone and then distributing it to gain the offensive zone. He showed some nice aggression in his game but was smart and didn't retaliate as he was able to draw a penalty and was putting some good pressure and physicality on the fore-check. He also found some open space right in front of the net for a good chance as he drove the net hard.

NIA # 26, RW, Lemmon, Mack (2013) Lemmon got a pretty nice cycle game going deep in the offensive zone and was battling hard in the corner on the fore-check to take the puck by force. He had a nice net-front presence and was protecting the puck well. He showed his typical aggression by getting involved in scrums after whistles and was very physical by running over his man and taking the puck to rush it back up the ice. There were some moments where he was a little weak on the puck around the boards in his own end.

NIA # 16, LW, Petersen, Trevor (2013) Petersen did a nice job tonight of getting to the slot with some space and then opening up for a one-timer. He was passing the puck well up through the neutral zone on the rush and then drove the net hard with his stick down. He was also getting some space in the high slot for a great shot on net but has to hit the net on his opportunity. He then found some open space down low and opened up for a one-timer from in close and got open again in the slot for a chance and was stopped at point blank. He was aggressive and forcing turnovers on the back-check.

NIA # 7, LW, Kopta, Ondrej (2013) Kopta was putting some good pressure on the fore-check and finishing his hits nice and hard. He was very physical along the boards all over the ice and also made a really nice feed up through the neutral zone for a long breakout.
FINAL SCORE: 3-2 Niagara Ice Dogs

December 16, 2012, Kingston Frontenacs @ London Knights (OHL)

KGN #17 LC Kujawinski, Ryan (2013) - Kujawinski covers a lot of ground despite a bit of an awkward skating stride. He had some good chances in the offensive zone but got stopped every time. Ryan showed strong defensive play and forced a large amount of turnovers in his own zone helping his team out defensively.

KGN #18 RD Hutchinson, Ryan (2013) - Hutchinson was physical right off the bat and didn't let up. He threw a bit of a questionable hit midway through the first which saw Brett Welychka initiate a fight with Hutchinson. Ryan faired well as he was clearly the bigger and stronger combatant.

KGN #27 RW Dupuy, Jean (2013) - Dupuy played very physical throughout the game. He had a very good fight against a bigger and older opponent in Paxton Leroux.

KGN #55 LD Watson, Matthew (2014) - Looked very good in one on one situations despite being a little undersized for a defenseman to break up offensive chances for London.

KGN #95 RC Povorozniouk, Sam (2013) - Sam scored a temporary tying goal in the first period as he pulled a nice move on the defenseman then unleashed a pretty good shot. Povorozniouk showed slightly above average skating ability and was very smart positionally in the offensive zone. He has above average hockey sense and read plays fairly well.

KGN #96 LW Watson, Spencer (2014) - A bit of a homecoming for Watson as he is from the London area. He showed tremendous determination in the slot area. Strong positionally in the offensive zone and was dangerous on several occasions despite not posting any points. Spencer fights off checkers very well he's extremely elusive and tough to contain.

LON #4 LD Liberati, Miles (2013) - Miles struggled a little with some defensive miscues. However he was very good on the rush carrying the puck up ice. He makes the smart pass, but is also very patient and won't rush plays that aren't there. He seemed to pivot a little too late at times in one on one situations, but fortunately can recover due to utilizing his stick very well in these situations.

LON #53 LW Horvat, Bo (2013) - Horvat scored the second goal of the game for the Knights making a nice move in the goal area then showing great patience to make the goaltender make a move then beating him. He showed excellent hockey sense in the offensive zone and while he didn't always execute on chances, he gains a lot of them thanks to the level of hockey IQ he has. He also showed good creativity with the puck at times.

LON #81 LW Elie, Remi (2013) - Remi's first few steps have noticeably improved. He has pretty smooth hands in the slot and is calm in traffic. He had great positioning and was rewarded with a few great scoring chances but couldn't finish. He showed a smart first pass into the offensive zone to advance the play in the best possible spot. Elie does a lot of these little things well.

LON #91 RW Platzer, Kyle (2013) - Kyle was placed on defense due to injuries and players away at World Junior camps. Kyle is definitely not a defenseman. It was very obvious. He was caught out of position early and often resulting in scoring chances. Kyle is a very hard working forward but he was on quite the adventure in this game. You can't really take much value out of this game as a scout except that it's safe to say no NHL team will draft Platzer and move him to defense.

Scouts Notes: The Knights looked to continue their streak and got off to a great start taking an early 2-0 lead. Kingston showed great resiliency coming back with three unanswered goals to take the lead. London would tie it up again. But Kingston would score and take a 4-3 lead into the second intermission. After Kingston scored with less than 12 minutes left in the game to make it 5-3, we saw a series of rather questionable calls and non calls. As Kingston blocked a shot with 5 minutes left and appeared they would have a clear cut breakaway but he was tripped up. There was no call, London picked up the puck and Ryan Rupert (Toronto) scored a nice power play goal to tie the game up and sending it to overtime. After both teams had a few good chances in overtime, it was Seth Griffith (Boston) who unleashed a blast to score and win the game for London in overtime. A combination of the Knights never quit attitude and a few questionable calls/non-calls in the final 10 minutes of this game will see the Knights go into the Christmas break holding onto their consecutive win streak.

Dec 18, 2012, Indiana Ice vs. USNTDP U18 (USHL)

IND # 9, LW, Salvaggio, Jason (2013) Salvaggio showed some pretty good speed and puck distribution on the rush to gain the offensive zone. He battled hard for the puck and was moving it around well in the offensive zone and then driving hard to the net. For the most part he kept his game pretty simple on a dump and chase game, however was able to hustle hard to win a race to the puck to nullify an icing then take the puck out front to the slot to put a shot on and score the team's 2nd goal of the game.

IND # 15, C, Talcott, Alex (2013) Talcott put some really good pressure on the puck carrier, and was holding on to the puck well deep in the offensive zone on the cycle. He got the puck in deep to start the cycle and was protecting it as he twisted away from the opposition then move the puck to an open man in the high slot for a good chance.

IND # 24, RW, Pieper, Bo (2013) Pieper was getting the puck in deep on the cycle and showed some decent puck protection, but he still needs to get bigger and stronger to be more effective. He was getting to the front of the net to open up to provide scoring options, however off the rush his offensive instincts left something to be desired as he was not opening up well, allowing the goaltender to read that the shooter would have to shoot since the pass was not available. He put some good pressure on the puck carrier and got his stick in lanes to breakup plays and knock the puck off the opposition.

USNT # 7, C, Compher, J.T. (2013) Compher showed some really explosive speed to blow by the defensemen and take a break for an excellent shot put on net to score the team's 2nd goal of the game. He put some good pressure on the puck carrier, and displayed some nice support coming back to help out in his own end. He had great speed on the wide drive, was protecting the puck well and can cycle it effectively, and also found some space to work with and opened up in the offensive zone to provide scoring options. On one of his wide drives he made a nice centering pass to an open man right in front of the net for a good chance from in tight, and made an amazing spin and ass to find a man across the crease for a really good chance from in tight later on in the game. He had some really nice speed on the rush finding lanes to gain the offensive zone, and had a great wide drive then cut to the net late in the game but hit the post on the opportunity. He was getting down to block shots and tie up his man in his own end. At times he decided to cut up high with the puck instead of driving it down towards the net, and has to watch the neutral zone turnovers as he had a really bad one that the opposition took to come back and tie up the game late.

USNT # 4, D, Butcher, Will (2013) Butcher can protect the puck well from pressure and move it up the boards to start the rush. He has some great speed and an excellent ability to find lanes to skate the puck up the ice and gain the offensive zone. He was jumping up on the pinch to keep the attack alive, and displayed some good patience and calmness with the puck. He can distribute it well on the power play and moves around to provide options, and was jumping in on the rush to come down low into the offensive zone and move the puck to a man in the slot. He came in wide on the rush to put shots on, but has to hit the net on his chances.

USNT # 14, LW, Motte, Tyler (2013) Motte has some really great agility to twist away from the opposition's pressure, and drives to the net with his stick down. He showed some good speed and movement to get to the slot and open up to take passes. He protects the puck well on the wide drive, and can rush the puck up the ice effectively with speed. He made a good drop pass off the rush to find a man in the high slot, and was taking the puck in tight right next to the net for a great chance in tight late in this game. He hustled hard to get back and battle for the puck in his own end, and has some really nice hands but has to watch the turnovers trying to dangle his way through the opposition instead of getting the puck in deep.

USNT # 19, RW, Kelleher, Tyler (2013) Kelleher opened up really well on the odd-man rush to put a great shot on from good scoring position to score the opener of this game. He did a great job rushing the puck up the ice then moving the puck to an open man in the high slot for a good opportunity. He was making a good first pass out of the zone, and then a nice centering pass to find a man in the slot. He took the puck with great speed on the wide drive for a good shot that hit the post, and displayed some great agility to twist away from the opposition. He battled hard for the puck along the boards and was distributing the puck nicely with speed through the neutral zone. He stood up his man to take away his space and force a turnover, and showed some nice hands as well.

USNT # 22, RW, Fasching, Hudson (2013) Fasching was finishing his checks along the boards and protecting the puck well on the cycle in the offensive zone. He displayed some decent speed to skate the puck into the offensive zone of the rush, and had a really nice net-front presence on the power play. He made a nice centering pass to find a man streaking down the middle towards the net, and then later on made a nice tip in front of the net to score the team's 3rd goal of the game. He also was hustling hard to get on loose pucks deep in the offensive zone, and was able to take a pass down low next to the net for a great chance from in tight.

USNT # 28, LW, Eiserman, Shane (2013) Eiserman did a nice job of going hard to the net with his stick down. He can take a bad pass off the rush, but after he gained the zone at times he was taking low-chance shots from the outside rather than driving the puck towards the net for chances from in tight. He made a really excellent long pass to hit a man in behind the opposition's defense for a break to get a great chance on net, and showed some pretty good puck protection along the wall deep in the offensive zone. He was clearing the puck on the penalty kill, but just lost the puck on a mishandle at one point deep in the offensive zone along the boards.

FINAL SCORE: 4-3 Indiana Ice

December 20, 2012, Quebec Remparts @ Victoriaville Tigres (QMJHL)

QUE #10 LW Duclair, Anthony (2013) - Duclair was fearless going through traffic while handling the puck. He capitalized on a puck playing mistake in the offensive zone to score Quebec's first goal and bring them within one of Victoriaville late in the first period. He did a good job following up on a great play by Adam Erne to score once again to tie the game. Duclair finished with three points (2G, 1A) factoring into all of Quebec's goals tonight.

QUE #73 RW Erne, Adam (2013) - Skating wise Adam's first few steps are not bad but he needs to add another gear to his top speed. Despite this he shows impressive moves with the puck and an outstanding shot. He's very physically strong, hits hard finishing his checks when possible. Adam set up two goals in this game showing a good passing ability for one, and made an outstanding move to set up the other.

VIC #3 LD Diaby, Jonathan (2013) - Good skater for his big size. He delivered some very solid hits throughout this game. He was also very reliable defensively for the most part of this game.

VIC #12 LC Rehak, Dominik (2013) - Rehak made a great play at the side of the Quebec net to give Victoriaville the lead, and what would ultimately be the game winning goal. He works hard defensively but made some mistakes in his own zone resulting in scoring chances against.

Scouts Notes: A bit of a sloppy performance overall by both teams who, to be fair were missing personnel due to the upcoming World Junior Championships and injuries. Not to mention the upcoming Christmas break. However 2013 prospects in the line-up for Quebec really gave their team a chance to win this back and forth game. Adam Erne (2013) and Anthony Duclair (2013) were arguably the best players on the ice tonight. Both put on outstanding performances allowing Quebec to score three consecutive goals giving them a temporary lead. However Victoriaville answered with three straight of their own to escape with a 5-3 win.

Dec 27, 2012, Germany vs. USA (2013 WJHC)

GER#10 LC, Draisaitl, Leon(2014) Undeniably Germany's best player on their team. Highly skilled and possesses very good vision. Quarterbacked the power play and did a pretty good job doing so. He was able to read the play quite well and dished the puck efficiently. Needs to work on his acceleration and his top speed. Really liked his strength along the walls, and was able to buy some time to let the play develop, and used his playmaking abilities to make good passes off the wall. Should shoot the puck more, and improve on his release. Defensively, still looks like he has some work to do in terms of anticipating and being in good position to prevent plays from happening..

GER#21 LW, Kahun, Dominik(2013) Good skating forward who showed some above average hands in open ice. Needs to be much stronger on his skates to maintain balance even as he gets bumped, particularly along the walls. Made decisions with the puck too slowly, and looked like he wanted to wait for the perfect play, but would get the puck taken away from him or would commit a turnover because opponents had time to get back into position.

USA#3 RD, Jones, Seth(2013) Played a strong, consistent game tonight. Made a couple of bad decisions with the puck at the beginning of the game, but he quickly got rid of that part of his game and made good passes with the puck. He took a lot of shots in the first period, then his fake slap shots froze opponents which gave him all the time in the world to make a great pass on the PP for a goal. Scored a very nice goal in the slot by perfecting locating the puck top shelf, glove side on a wrist shot. Showed off his mobility and quick feet on the blue line. He made very good use of his body to protect the puck off the rush. Defensively, was physical all over the ice, but let the play come to him. Looked poised in all situations.

USA#21 RW, Hartman, Ryan(2013) Dynamic forward who played a very aggressive game tonight. Loved to take the puck to the net in tight and create havoc. A very quick skater who was able to draw a couple of penalties because of his speed. While his team was winning 4-0, really liked the way he backchecked to break up an odd man rush. Scored a goal on a 2 on 0 by finishing off a rebound. Got more ice time as the game went on, and responded well with good play in the offensive zone using his hands and feet.

Scouts Notes: This was a game that was dominated by USA from start to finish. Despite that, Leon Draisaitl shined for Germany. By far the most skilled player in Germany. Used his body effectively and was really the only player in Germany that was able to create offensive chances. The team as a whole looked tired from playing Canada the night before. There was no push back from them all game long. Alex Galchenyuk was very good in this game. Scored a very nice goal in the slot and showed off his quick release and shooting accuracy. Also liked the way Mike Reilly moved the puck for USA. The Columbus prospect kept it simple, and skated with the puck when given some room.

FINAL SCORE: 8-0 USA

Dec 28, 2012, Czech Republic vs. Finland (2013 WJHC)

CZE#15 LW, Vrana, Jakub(2015) Skilled forward who did not look out of place playing with older players. Displayed a high level of hockey sense with and without the puck. Always looked to be where the puck will go instead of reacting to the play. Needs to get stronger on his skates to be able to handle physical play, but showed the ability to make quick lateral moves to lose defenders. Engaged well physically all game long. Still has to work on the rough edges of his game, like keeping his stick on the ice on the forecheck to be ready to pick off passes when he is in the right position to do so.

CZE#19 LC, Hertl, Tomas(San Jose) Best player for the Czech Republic tonight. Showed off his soft hands in traffic time and time again tonight. Loved to deke out a few opponents from the corner to walk to the slot and try to score. Skating has improved since last year. Really liked his compete level all game long in both ends of the ice. Also showed off a quick one timer, but just could not finish. Possesses a good combination of size and skill that is difficult to come by.

FIN#5 RD, Ristolainen, Rasmus(2013) A smart, dynamic defenseman who had an excellent game tonight. So poised and confident with the puck, and has an aggressive mindset out on the ice. Loves to jump into the play, and looks like a forward at times as he leads the attack. Makes great first passes out of his own zone, and whether it be in tight or a stretch pass, was able to consistently hit his teammates tape to tape. Fun to watch his creativity. Another impressive aspect of his game was just how good he was defensively. He kept opponents to the outside consistently, used his big frame along the boards to win board battles and was in good positioning throughout the game.

FIN#16 LC, Barkov, Aleksander(2013) Big, skilled forward who did not stand out much tonight. Clearly very strong along the boards, but was not able to create offense after coming away with the puck. Showed off his playmaking abilities in tight, and was able to make quick decisions. Has to limit the number of turnovers he commits though. Controls the puck well in tight situations. A good skater for his size, and was able to combine it with his hockey sense to be very good in his own zone. Just was not able to create any good scoring chances throughout the game.

FIN#28 LW, Lehkonen, Artturi(2013) Quick, skilled forward who was another Finnish player that struggled to do anything offensively tonight. Very good skater who was not able to use his speed to his advantage tonight to create scoring chances. Not very strong along the boards, and needs to work on his balance on his skates. Was invisible for much of this game. Did not make any glaring mistakes, but did not do anything great either.

Scouts Notes: Czech Republic really controlled this game from the start. They just worked harder all game long and it allowed them to win this game. Tomas Hertl looks like he has improved his skating since last season, and it allows him to be even more dangerous with his skill and size. Best player on Finland tonight was Rasmus Ristolainen. Was constantly involved in the play and made good plays with the puck.

FINAL SCORE: 3-1 Czech Republic

Dec 28, 2012, Sweden vs. Switzerland (2013 WJHC)

SWE#10 LW, Wennberg, Alex(2013) 2 way forward who played on the 4th line tonight, but really made a physical presence when he did get on the ice. Very good along the boards and displayed good strength on his skates. A good skater who was able to get around quickly and deliver good hits on the forecheck. Was not able to show much offensive abilities tonight other than in the third period where he made a smart play to tip a faceoff ahead of the opposing centre, and created a 2 on 1 opportunity then made a nifty back hand pass to his linemate who was not able to finish off the play unfortunately.

SWE#14 LD, Hagg, Robert(2013) Big, poised defenseman who provided a calm presence for his team in the backend. Other defensemen on Sweden made bad decisions with the puck and committed a number of turnovers, but Hagg was able to stand out and make good passes. He did seem a little too casual with the puck at times, and in one instance in the 2nd period, he just missed the puck along the boards, which led to a great 2 on 1 opportunity. Hagg played a good physical game tonight, and just narrowly missed landing a big hit in one of his first shifts on a transition. He has a good active stick without the puck, but did let a cross ice pass go through his area which led to a goal against. Like his mobility given his size.

SWE#19 RC, Lindholm, Elias(2013) 2nd line centre for Sweden, and logged a lot of minutes tonight in all situations. He was able to create a lot of time for his teammates to get opened with his ability to protect the puck, but they just could not find an open area to go to for him to hit them with a pass. He drew a couple of penalties because of his agility off the wall to quickly spin away from his check to the net. He did not do much offensively tonight, but was able to contribute to the game with his defensive play. He worked very hard along the boards and seemed to come away with the puck so often. He blocked shots, took away passing lanes and was physical without the puck consistently. Saved a goal in overtime with his work ethic off the wall to get to the slot and tie up an opponent to prevent them from scoring.

SWI#5 LD, Mueller, Mirco(2013) Arguably the best defenseman for Switzerland tonight. Really impressed with his overall defensive game. Was able to use his body consistently to rub out opponents along the walls, and his long reach to his advantage all game long to stop Sweden's attack. His offensive game suffered a little bit because he was so defensive minded today and he did not jump into the play as he usually does. Liked the way he used his skating abilities along the walls to make quick starts and stops, and not allow any opponent to walk out to the slot. Would have liked to see him receive more ice time.

Scouts Notes: Sweden is very fortunate that Switzerland is not a very skilled team and could not capitalize on the number of good scoring chances they received. The Swedes came out very flat, and essentially just maintained that all game long. Extremely impressed with Filip Sandberg tonight. Despite being only 5'9, he protected the puck so well against bigger opponents, and was really the only player on Sweden that played with a high level of intensity all game long. Was rewarded with his second straight player of the game award. Went undrafted last season, but if he keeps up this kind of performance, he will surely catch the attention of at least one NHL team. Disappointed with the play of Jacob De la Rose tonight. Possesses a good combination of speed and size, but lacked intensity to do anything with it. Received less ice time as the game went along.

FINAL SCORE: 3-2 Sweden (SO)

December 28, 2012, Peterborough Petes @ Kingston Frontenacs (OHL)

PET #17 LW Betzold, Greg (2013) - Betzold created scoring chances in each of his first few shifts but his linemates couldn't finish. When in doubt he'll get the puck deep and whenever the puck is deep he showed the ability to win races and puck battles. He is a regular on the power play and showed great net presence on the power play. At one point due to his great battling at the top of the crease the puck hit off him and into the net for the first goal of the game (however Betzold did not get credit for the goal.) After around the midway point of the game Betzold really disappeared for the remainder of the game.

PET #21 RW Nosad, Stephen (2013) - Nosad played regularly in all game situations and used his good speed and determination to win races and battles for the puck to keep the play going in the offensive zone. Stephen was all over loose pucks and turned them into scoring chances. At one point he took a feed from Alan Quine on a 2 on 1 rush. He pulled a nice little forehand/backhand move to score the second goal of the game for Peterborough.

KGN #17 LC Kujawinski, Ryan (2013) - Kujawinski controlled the puck well. He made smart passes in all three zones particularly while on rushes. He seems to be at his best on the rush when he has support because he has the ability to make a move, but usually opts to make the pass, many of which show some slick hands and resulted in scoring chances. Kujawinski is one of those players who just seems to look better on home ice than on the road.

KGN #95 RC Povorozniouk, Sam (2013) - Povorozniouk had a great fight in what was a pretty even match-up. He was able to take and give several shots. Sam shows great determination going into corner winning battles and turning them into scoring chances. He has slightly above average skating ability and good creativity creating a couple scoring chances playing on the top line tonight.

Scouts Notes: The Frontenacs played with only 16 skaters tonight with many of their top players at the World Under 17 Challenge and several of those players were call ups. So with a fairly depleted line-up they went up against the Petes who had pretty close to their full line-up and iced a full line-up. Peterborough absolutely dominated the first period but we left the period tied 0-0. Both teams were able to get on the scoreboard in the second, but the Steven Trojanovic (2013*) goal with just 40 seconds left in the second period to make it 4-2 Peterborough really seemed to be the backbreaker for Kingston. The Petes outshot Kingston 15-3 in the third period to secure a 5-2 win.

December 29, 2012, Team Ontario vs. Team USA – (World U17)

ONT #5 RD Ekblad, Aaron (2014) - Ekblad showed off his massive slap shot from the point but also showed the intelligence to pinch into a shooting position and score the opening goal of the 2013 World Under 17 Challenge. Ekblad showed off his passing ability making a great long distance pass out of his zone to create a great scoring chance. Aaron struggled a little in one on one match-up's all game long due to his lack of mobility.

ONT #6 LD Middleton, Jacob (2014) - Middleton was hands down the best defenseman in this game. He shows very good skating especially for his size. He uses it in his own zone with the puck to buy time and allow options to open up. He made solid, hard tape to tape passes all game long. Middleton landed some big hits and battles hard drawing penalties with his compete level. Middleton was excellent in one on one situations using both his size and stick to break-up plays.

ONT #9 LC McDavid, Connor (2014) - McDavid made a great pass to set up the first goal of the game as he was controlling the puck behind the net under pressure and recognized Ekblad as he was pinching in. McDavid scored an absolute highlight reel goal utilizing both his tremendous speed and elite hands to give Ontario a 4-1 lead. After USA scored three unanswered to tie the game up McDavid quickly responded pulling another unbelievable move to create the 5th goal of the game for Ontario.

ONT #11 LW Bennett, Sam (2014) - Bennett rushed the puck very confidently with good speed. He showed a great back check to help maintain the momentum Ontario built through most of this game. He scored what was almost a very big goal for Ontario giving them a one goal lead in the third tapping in a great play created by McDavid.

ONT #12 LC McCann, Jared (2014) - McCann showed some great passing ability and created many chances for Ontario in the game. Some of which his teammates just couldn't finish on, but De Sousa was able to finish on a short handed set up by McCann. Jared showed a great compete level all game long winning battles and forced turnovers. He was a regular on the penalty kill clearing the zone very effectively.

ONT #16 RW Ho-Sang, Joshua (2014) - Ho-Sang displayed very shifty moves with speed while controlling the puck. He fired a wrister that just slipped behind the goaltender to regain a one goal lead in the second period.

ONT #17 LW Dal Colle, Michael (2014) - Michael had good presence and positioning in the defensive zone. He was also very strong on the penalty kill. He showed off his passing abuility at different times throughout this game and wound up finishing with one assist.

ONT #22 RW Lindo, Jaden (2014) - Lindo was great on the penalty kill at one point protecting the puck from three American players killing a lot of time off the clock. Lindo used his size and strength throughout the game.

USA #46 RC Eichel, Jack (2015) - Eichel is a very smooth skater who rushes up and down the ice well and changes directions on a dime. He has excellent hands in goal area beating a defenseman then slipping the puck past the goaltender to initiate USA's three unanswered goals. He also finished the run by firing a wrist shot from point blank to tie the game. Simply put, USA is not in this game if Jack Eichel isn't in the line-up as he really sparked their offense.

USA #48 LW Milano, Sonny (2014) - Milano possesses great speed and very good moves. Combined he can make highlight reel type plays look easy. He provided great follow up on the rebound to score the goal that would send this game to Overtime. Sonny then proceeded to score the only goal in the shootout to give USA at 6-5 win.

USA #51 RW Wilkie, Chris (2014) - Wilkie used his speed to create scoring chances. He also showed great presense in the slot area and in the corners throughout this game.

USA #52 LC MacInnis, Ryan (2014) - MacInnis has great size and generates a good top speed, but really needs to improve his first few steps. He likes to rush the puck up ice whenever he can and displayed a good shot to score USA's third goal of the game.

Scouts Notes: Although Team USA has been playing together all season, it was Team Ontario who really came out flying to open the World U17 Challenge opening up a 4-1 lead. However USA answered scoring three straight to tie the game up midway through the third. The tie was short lived as Ontario would score to make it 5-4 just 22 seconds later. Sonny Milano responded a few moments later to tie the game at 5-5 then scored the shootout winner to give Team USA a shocking and exciting 6-5 victory to open the tournament. In addition to the reports above, for Ontario Spencer Watson (2014) showed off his great speed and handled the puck extremely well through traffic. Dante Salituro (2015) was also able to show off his great skating ability although USA was able to neutralize him as he looked poised to break out a few times. For USA Brandon Fortunato (2014) showed off excellent skating ability from the defensive position and rushed the puck up ice successfully on the power play, but also while at even strength. Alex Tuch (2014) has an extremely powerful shot and although he didn't register a point he was dangerous a few times in this match-up.

December 29, 2012, Team Pacific vs. Team Russia – (World U17)

PAC #5 LD Martin, Brycen (2014) - Martin skates very well for 6'3". He moves the puck on the power play very well and is quick and decisive with his passes. He makes good decisions with the puck in all three zones and all game situations. Brycen has a good hard point shot which was deflected for a goal. On another occasion he faked a point shot then sent a slap pass over to be tapped in for a goal. He shows great offensive instincts all throughout this game. Martin showed some good physicality and ultimately got penalized for playing too physical. He sticks with his man very effectively along the wall.

PAC #7 RD Mayo, Dysin (2014) - Mayo was tenacious along the boards all game long battling hard. He plays a very tough physical game, eventhough he definitely has room to get stronger. He got beat in one on one match-up's not squaring up well to oncoming forwards. He also made a few bad plays with the puck in his own zone.

PAC #10 RC Bleackley, Conner (2014) - Bleackley showed great shiftiness and was very elusive with the puck shaking off checks. He always seems to always be in the right spot when scoring chances occur. Early in the game down two goals he followed up on the rush and scored Pacific's first goal of the game. He has a good shot and used it to score his second goal of the game.

PAC #15 LW MacMaster, Tanner (2014) - Tanner possesses outstanding hands and shows them off when working through traffic. He is so calm with the puck under pressure and in traffic. He made an excellent move on an odd man rush after an excellent give and go he buried the puck backhanded.

PAC #16 RW Revel, Matt (2014) - Revel showed great physicality throughout this game and threw as many hits as he possible could. His compete level was good, unfortunately he misread a lot of plays in this game.

PAC #18 RW Virtanen, Jake (2014) - Virtanen made a great move to split the defense and score the 6th goal of the game for Team Pacific. He also delivered a few very hard hits in this game but for the most part looked very lazy and was rather quiet except for a few good shifts.

RUS #10 RW Zinoviev, Ilya (2014) - Zinoviev showed a lot of playmaking ability in this game. He set up several scoring chances early on for Russia. He set up the first goal of the game and followed up with a deflection for Russia's second goal. Zinoviev worked hard to win battles on the penalty kill.

RUS #11 LC Nikolishin, Ivan (2014) - Nikolishin is very smart with the puck but can overhandle it at times. He doesn't pass often but when he does he shows he's pretty good and accurate. He was constantly involved in Russia's offensive chances. He has a hard shot and unloaded one on the powerplay to bring Russia within one goal in the third period. Later on he tried to help his team again by rolling around on the ice faking an injury while Team Pacific was on a big rush. However when the sell job wasn't working he just got up and rejoined the play as if nothing happened.

RUS #12 LD Lyamkin, Nikita (2014) - Lyamkin displayed extremely smart decision making with the puck. He knows when to pinch and when to maintain smart safe positioning. He's very reliable with the puck and always seems to choose the smart option. He has a hard point shot. He showed well defensively in one on one battles but he got outmuscled at times against the wall in more physical situations.

RUS #14 LW Vovchenko, Daniil (2014) - Vovchenko is very slippery and difficult to contain. He has good speed and created a few scoring chances. He also possesses a hard shot. He forced turnovers on a regular basis.

RUS #17 LW Yazkov, Nikita (2014) - Yazkov showed great moves in one on one situations protecting the puck well. Late in a tie game he pretty clearly tried to dive to give his team a power play but he apparently was unable to convince the officials.

RUS #18 RD Nasybullin, Eduard (2014) - Nasybullin made some great reads when rushing the puck up ice. He fired a seeing eye shot through traffic to complete Russia's comeback in this game and tie it up at 7 with about two minutes left in regulation. Throughout the game he was consistently strong along the boards despite his size.

RUS #19 LC Fazleyev, Radel (2014) - Fazleyev created some good scoring chances for his team. He made some good plays with the puck down low, then cycled into great positioning to finish on a scoring chance. He forces turnovers regularly and showed intelligent positioning in this game.

RUS #20 G Tretiak, Maxim (2015) - Tretiak has tremendous size and frame. He also most certainly has blood lines on his size. He covers the net well, but his reaction time was rather unimpressive.

Scouts Notes: Day one at the World Under 17 wrapped up with a rather wild one between Pacific and Russia. After Team Russia opened up with a 2-0 lead and were dominating puck possession and the pace of the game, Pacific was able to come back to score 6 of the next 7 goals to take a commanding lead in this game. Russia didn't give up and put together another dominant performance in the third showing great resiliency and sending this game to overtime. In overtime a point shot from Brycin Martin (2014) was deflected by Joe Hicketts (2014) on the power play to win the game 8-7 for Team Pacific. In addition to the reports above, Brandon Hickey (2014) did a good job in one on one situations and played physical. Alexander Mikulovich (2014) utilizes his big frame and takes the body on a regular basis.

December 29 2012, Team Sweden vs. Team Ontario (World U17 -Exhibition)

SWE #3 D Lagesson, William (2014) – Lagesson was Sweden's best defenseman in this game and was effective in different areas of the game. He did a good job using his body to separate the opposing players from the puck and he won quite a few battles deep in his zone. He was very aggressive on 1-on-1 battles and he took a bad penalty doing it. I also thought he moved very well around the ice and he showed it by joining the rush a few times. He seems to have some interesting tools and the upside to play a solid two-way game.

SWE #7 D Mattsson, Adam (2014) – Mattson is a big defenseman who showed good shutdown qualities in this game. His size obviously serves him well most of the time, even though he was pushed around a couple times behind his own net. He did a good job using his stick defensively to keep his opponents at bay. He was also effective at blocking shots. You could see he was overwhelmed at times by Team Ontario's quick and well executed plays.

SWE #16 D/C Pettersson, Markus (2014) – Petterson is listed as a defenseman and played a few shifts on the backhand and on the power play, but was used as a forward for most of the game. He came out as one of the best player in this game from Team Sweden. He looked very sharp out there and played a complete game. He is very confident with the puck and does a good job carrying it around the ice. He also showed excellent vision as he spots teammates quick and is able to get the puck to them with precise passing. He worked very hard into the slot area and didn't mind taking a beating to stay there.

SWE #18 F Karlsson, Anton (2014) – Karlsson excelled when he had the puck on his stick and showed good abilities. He is able to move the puck forward with excellent speed and hands. He likes to control the puck and he did a good job cycling it on the power play. I wasn't a big fan of his overall performance as he struggled without the puck and wasn't very active with his feet, whether it was in the neutral zone or on the back check.

SWE #20 F Nylander, William (2014) – Nylander was absolutely electric with the puck. He has a great burst of speed and can be quite deceptive. That skating ability matches with an excellent pair of hands that allow him to navigate through traffic without much problem. He was at his best when he was in motion on the transition and received good passes from his defensemen. Not only was he agile on his feet, but he also showed good vision and seemed to know when to let the puck go. He showed off his good shot as well when he scored Team Sweden's second goal.

SWE #22 F Timashov, Dmytro (2014) – Timashov is fairly small (5'8) but extremely dynamic whenever he touches the puck. He can really fly around the ice and is very agile. He has quick feet and he has great balance that allows him to change direction quickly. He really pushed it to the limit and doesn't mind skating on the edge of his skates. I thought he tried to force things at times, trying to skate his way through heavy traffic for example. He caused a turnover at one point that could have been avoided. He is also not a force along the boards and was pushed around fairly easily.

ONT #5 D Ekblad, Aaron (2014) – I thought Ekblad was very mature the way he played and showed great confidence. He excelled defensively and didn't mind cutting plays right at the middle of the ice when he had the chance to. He uses his stick effectively and always seems in the right position to make a defensive play. He delivered a devastating open ice hit at one point as well. He also showed a good ability to move the puck on the transition. He looked good carrying the puck, handling it with smooth and solid hands.

ONT #6 D Middleton, Jacob (2014) – Middleton played a solid game on defense as well. He was reliable defensively with some good physical plays. He also did a very good job joining the rush, picking his moments smartly. He showed good all-around mobility and took the right decisions most of the times. That paid off for him as he scored two goals for Team Ontario.

ONT #7 D De Sousa, Daniel (2014) – De Sousa didn't get as much ice time as other defenseman, but he caught my eye with his smart play with the puck. He showed good mobility and carried the puck around very well. He did a good job spotting his teammates and displayed some solid passing skills. He moved the puck well on the blue line when his team was installed in the neutral zone and picked up a goal on a good wrist shot from far away.

ONT #9 F McDavid, Connor (2015) – It's an absolute disaster for the other team whenever he touches the puck. He started the game slow but quickly got his rhythm back. He is a fantastic player to watch with the puck. Even though he didn't look overly fast, he skates very fluidly and is extremely elusive. His overwhelming hands allow him to manoeuvre the puck through anything that shows up in front of it. I liked how he used his body to shield the puck and how he was able to shift it back from one side to another without losing his momentum. He also applies the same technique with his hands around the net, as he can fool the goalie in no time. He had plenty of chances throughout the game and ended up scoring a goal. He was also a good puck distributor and showed good vision and creativity to set up plays.

ONT #12 F McCann, Jared (2014) – I thought McCann played a fantastic two-way game. Even though he lacks a little bit of explosion, his top speed looked good and he was extremely strong with the puck and did a good job using his body to protect it. He was very patient and made some really smart plays. He takes very good decisions on the ice, both with and without the puck. He also showed some good hands when entering the offensive zone, making up for the lack of speed at times. He also displayed a very strong shot. I really liked how complete he was as a player and how hard he competed.

ONT #14 F Petti, Niki (2014) – Petti caught my eye with his intensity and dedication on the ice. He was always in the mix, trying to make a play or to force a turnover. He applied a lot of pressure on Sweden's players. I thought he moved around smoothly and started to show some nice things with the puck as the game went on. I'm looking forward to see more of him.

ONT #16 Ho-Sang, Josh (2014) – Ho-Sang displayed some very good speed in the game and great elusiveness. He was able to match his speed with his great hands to get pass the defenders. He opened up a lot of space for his team by attracting opposing players with his hands and was very dynamic offensively. He kept pushing hard even when he had pressure on him and was able to draw a penalty at one point. He seemed to be a bit selfish when he had the puck, but it didn't lead to any mistake in this game. I'm looking forward to see more of him to see if this is a tendency.

ONT #17 Dal Colle, Michael (2014) – I really liked Dal Colle in this game. He played a solid two-way game with good intensity and brought speed to his team. He applied a lot of pressure and was a strong presence everywhere on the ice. He seems to be able to get good reads on what the opponent is doing. His skating looked very good and allowed him to be effective without the puck. He also did some nice things along the boards to win a few puck battles. Unfortunately, I didn't get to see much of him in terms of puck possession.

Dec 29, 2012, Sweden vs. Latvia (2013 WJHC)

SWE#8 LD, Arnesson, Linus(2013) Defensive defenseman played a good game quietly. Kept his passes simple, and thrived in the defensive zone with his skating ability and size. Used quick starts and stops to keep up with opponents along the wall, and then would do a good job to pin them along the wall and take them out of the play. Took one unnecessary holding penalty in the second period. Has a good active stick, and does a good job to keep opponents to the outside. Offensively, made good first passes out of the zone and really limited the number of turnovers he committed.

SWE#10 LW, Wennberg, Alex(2013) Received more ice time tonight, and was quite effective for his team. Stuck to his physical game, which led to offensive opportunities for him and his teammates. Displayed some good playmaking abilities off the wall. Provided a good screen on the PP, and retrieved dump ins effectively, which was a problem for Sweden on their PP against Switzerland. Always finished his checks and made his presence felt. A few times, he was able to display some good agility by spinning away from his check away from the wall to get a lane to the net. Scored late into the game from the slot by letting go a laser wrist shot.

SWE#19 RC, Lindholm, Elias(2013) Dynamic centre had a much better offensive game tonight, while not sacrificing his efforts in his own end. Showed off his play with the puck and his aggressive mindset to take the play to the net and try to jam home a rebound. Displayed his impressive vision from all over the offensive zone, whether it be from behind the net, off the wall or on the rush. He showed the ability to make any type of passes. Most impressive part of his game is just how strong he is on his skates, and he would be able to control the puck quite easily despite getting bumped. Has very soft hands, which is especially noticeable in traffic. Gave his all in this game in all areas of the ice.

LAT#10 RW, Bukarts, Rihards(2014) An underaged forward who is one of the most skilled forwards on Latvia. Really liked his hockey sense, skill level and physicality. Needs to work on his skating abilities, but seems to be well on his way to develop into a good prospect for the 2014 NHL Entry Draft. He knocked off an opponent from the puck in open ice and get a transition attack going. He has good instincts, and was in good position to receive passes. However, he needs to get better with reading the play in his own end. A couple of times, he should have covered his opponent in the slot, but just stuck to the point man, who was not much of a threat at that time. He also needs to use his teammates better and not try to do everything by himself all the time. In terms of speed, he had deceptive agility off the wall and was able to lose his man a couple of times by spinning away from them.

Scouts Notes: Sweden came out quite flat in this game, but they got better as the game went along. Filip Sandberg was promoted to the top line and immediately injected some life into his line mates. He was able to draw 4 penalties tonight because of his puck protecting abilities. On a 5 on 4 PK, he actually drew 2 penalties at once, a holding off the wall, and an elbowing as he was trying to take the puck to the net. Only concern is his ability to finish off plays, and if he can keep this up against stronger players as a pro. Teodors Blugers was the best player for Latvia tonight. Scored a nice goal on a 5 on 3 PP in tight by going far side top shelf. Good all around game. Jacob De la Rose was invisible once again. Did not play much tonight.

FINAL SCORE: 5-1 Sweden

December 30 2012, Team Sweden vs. Team Finland (World U17)

We had yet another game where Team Sweden outmatched their opponent with a much better and complete hockey club. They took the game 7-3 over Team Finland with two empty-net goals at the end.

SWE #9 F Franzen, Gustaf (2015) – Franzen played an underrated yet very effective role for his team. He made some smart defensive plays on the penalty kill and created his share of turnovers in the neutral. He was able to take the puck away from the other team and get his team on the transition. He plays a simple game with the puck and is an all right skater. He was able to go down the wing and exploit the outside lane of the defenseman a couple times. His biggest asset is his smartness: he reads the play well and knows where to go to be effective, with or without the puck.

SWE #18 F Karlsson, Anton (2014) – Karlsson had some good flashes in this game, noticeably with his puck possession skills. He was able to carry the puck for extended period of times and slow the game down. He has to ability to circle and protect the puck in the offensive zone while letting the play develop. His hands are solid but he needs to show better vision as he turned the puck over once without even looking who he was passing to. He also went with a shot on a 2-on-1 when his teammate had the net open.

SWE #19 F Karlsson, Jacob (2015) – Karlsson played the same complete game than in the previous viewings we had on him, plus the offensive impact. He was excellent with the puck in the offensive zone and he had a good finishing touch on the power play. He made a very nice pass on a 2-on-1 for a goal and distributed the puck properly throughout the game with good vision. He has very good hand-eye coordination and can receive passes from everywhere without a problem.

SWE #20 F Nylander, William (2014) – Nylander simplified his game in this one and
used his skills in a much smarter way. He was very creative with the puck once again and took over the offensive zone numerous times. He got to show his excellent vision with great passes, noticeably on the power play. We also had a better look at his shot with a strong release on his wrist shot and a very good low slap shot. Nylander was also effective at the point on the power play. He was moving a lot and it opened a lot of holes in Finland's defense. If he is able to play a smart and straight forward game like this with consistency, his high end tools and talent should take him far.

SWE #22 F Timashov, Dmytro (2014) – Timashov had his first off game of the tournament. He didn't make anything bad, but he wasn't able to generate a lot of speed like he did in the previous games. He also showed a lacked of control with the puck, creating a few turnovers and getting knocked off the puck.

FIN #4 D Tuulola, Joni (2014) – Tuulola looked to be Finland's best defensemen despite his team's struggles. He showed very good mobility getting the puck out of his zone and his poised when handling the puck in the offensive zone. He showed some sights of physical play defensively, but he relied mostly on his mobility to be effective.

FIN #20 F Lamsa, Teemu (2014) – Lamsa had some very interesting flashes in this game. He has a big body and showed good speed coming into the offensive zone. He doesn't have the greatest explosion, but does all right once he hits full speed. He did well when he had open ice coming in the neutral zone but struggled more when pressured.

FIN #22 F Honkanen, Manu (2014) – Honkanen showed a good two-way game and excelled with the puck. He has the ability to protect it and made some very good decisions with it to set up plays. His speed served him well carrying the puck and we liked his involvement in battles along the boards.

FIN #24 F Kapanen, Kasperi (2014) – Kapanen didn't leave a great impression, but had an honest game with some good tools. He is not overly dynamic with the puck but exploited the wing well with his speed and a straightforward approach. He reads the play well but doesn't explode or react fast enough all the time. His effort was inconstant as he was invisible for extended period of times and very good in others.

December 30, 2012, Team Sweden vs. Team Finland (World U17)

SWE #7 LD Ollas Mattsson, Adam (2014) - Adam is very poised with the puck, always keeps is head up ice and chooses smart safe options with the puck. He chooses the right lanes to skate through but his skating really needs work. Adam showed some really good physicality throughout this game.

SWE #17 LC Kempe, Adrian (2014) - Kempe has good size and is very shifty. He picked off a pass and finished for a 4-2 lead. Adrian was very reliable on the penalty kill blocking shots and getting in passing lanes. At one point he got in front of a shot, and got up and stuck with the play despite being in very obvious pain. He made another interception and scored on an empty net. Then promptly completed the hat trick with his second empty netter of the game.

SWE #20 LW Nylander Altelius, William (2014) - Nylander does a good job at high speed controlling the puck, making a move or two and gets scoring chances because of it. He played on the point on the power play and distributed the puck a lot more in previous viewings but still will use any excuse he can to shoot the puck. He did this on a 5 on 3 power play and showed off a laser to put the puck in the back of the net.

SWE #22 LW Timashov, Dmytro (2015) - Timashov showed off some very good hands in this game. But he made a few bad reads while on the power play which resulted in some turnovers and time killed off the power play.

SWE #23 RW Lindblom, Oskar (2014) - Lindblom had some good scoring chances but for some reason showed no urgency to finish. This was really not Lindblom's best performance but he still wound up with a goal in this game along with two assists. Both assists were second assists on the power play.

SWE #26 LW Kovacs, Robin (2015) - Kovacs showed off some very good puck movement uses angles and the wall very well to progress the puck teammates when necessary.

FIN #2 LD Niku, Sami (2015) - Made a really unnecessary no look behind the back play created scoring chance for Sweden. Made some pretty bad decisions pinching off the point at really bad times. He made a bad puck playing mistake which directly resulted in Finland sealing the game with an empty net goal.

FIN #7 RD Sopanen, Eetu (2014) - Sopanen intelligently likes to sneak off the point on the power play when the puck is sustained deep in the zone to open up a shooting option. He scored late in the first period doing this by pinching into the slot for a one-timer. He showed great puck movement on the power play but made a really bad pass in his own zone directly through his own slot which resulted in Sweden's game winning goal.

FIN #26 RW Rantanen, Mikko (2015) - Rantanen opened the scoring early in the first period with good positioning in the slot. He added an assist in the opening frame assisting on Finland's goal. He added another goal after having a pass blocked showing the presence of mind to fire a hard shot on the net scoring to keep Finland in the game. Mikko was a huge contributor for Finland offensively in this game and he moved the puck very well in the other two zones helping them rush the puck up ice.

FIN #28 LW Lammikko, Juho (2014) - Lammikko made a great pass from the corner early on to set up the first goal of the game. He won battles for the puck then was able to immediately turn them into scoring chances.

FIN #1 G Kahkonen, Kaapo (2014) - Kahkonen shows great side to side movement with good size and covers his angles well.

Scouts Notes: After Finland opened the scoring Sweden responded with 3 quick goals to take the lead. Finland then was able to score in the final seconds of the first period to keep this game within one. After exchanging goals, Sweden was able to make the score look a little more lopsided than the actual game burying two empty net goals. In addition to the reports above, for Sweden Filip Karlsson (2014) displayed very good puck movement on the powerplay. Daniel Muzito Bagenda (2014) displayed a very good forecheck and was able to force turnovers on a regular basis. For Finland Julius Nattinen (2015) showed some very strong physical play along the boards. Waltteri Hopponen (2014) and Antti Kauppinen (2014) both forced a lot of turnovers while on the penalty kill.

December 30, 2012, Rimouski Oceanic @ Victoriaville Tigres (QMJHL)

VIC #3 LD Diaby, Jonathan (2013) - Diaby was only only physical tonight but he handled some pretty big forwards with ease in one on one situations and crushed them. He was good in general in one on one situations and stood up for his teammates. Tonight was a career night for Diaby offensively as he set up the opening goal of the game with a nice simple pass to set it up. He unloaded a shot from the point to give Victoriaville a commanding 3-0 lead. He let another shot from the point fly which helped set up the 5-1 goal. He made a great read to join the rush but Desrosiers absolutely robbed him. As the game went on the Tigres' started to slide and Diaby got rocked along the boards as he was caught napping which resulted in a big scoring chance.

RIM #11 RW Bryukvin, Vladimir (2013) - Vladimir showed a very reliable defensive game and got in good defensive positioning and he was quick to get back when the puck was turned over. He's an above average skater with a good shot and he made some nice passes finding the open man cross ice.

RIM #23 LC Gauthier, Frederik (2013) - Gauthier wins tough battles along the boards and is smart with the puck when coming out of the corner. He moves the puck very well and created some great chances not only on the power play and even strength. He made a nice play to help set up Rimouski's first goal of the game. He has a pretty good shot as well. Gauthier showed excellent defensive zone awareness and had ideal positioning in his own zone seemingly all game long. He was able to break up many scoring chances tonight. Frederik played with a full face shield as he's still recovering from injury which may have prevented him from being as physical as he could have been. Skating definitely needs work.

RIM #55 LD Morin, Samuel (2013) - Morin put together a very hot/cold performance tonight. There were many moments where we were both impressed with his play, and frustrated with it. Morin follows the play along the wall very well and wins battles using his strength and his board play is very effective. However he can lose his positioning giving away too much access to the slot which resulted in scoring chances. Morin plays very physical and uses his size appropriately. He usually shows a powerful shot but tonight he scored sneaking a weak one past Victoriaville's goaltender. He gets the puck to the net effectively and had one of his point shots banged home for a goal. Morin landed some solid breakout passes. Morin can be caught standing still sometimes in one on one situations which resulted in forwards blowing by him. His skating is average at best but needs work as does his quickness. His works fairly hard and hits even harder.

Scouts Notes: Victoriaville looked determined to make a statement tonight opening up a 5-1 lead early in the second period. With a 5-3 lead in the final two minutes of the game, it appeared the Tigres would go on to victory, however Rimouski scored two unanswered goals then completed the unthinkable comeback to win the game 6-5 in a shootout.

December 31, 2012, Team Pacific vs. Team Sweden – (World U17)

PAC #2 RD Gagnon, Ryan (2014) - Gagnon jumped up in the rush well and scored the tying goal for Pacific. He made a bad clearing attempt on the penalty kill resulting in a big scoring chance against.

PAC #3 LD Hicketts, Joe (2014) - Hicketts showed good physicality for force turnovers, won a ton of battles and was very aggressive. Which was even more impressive considering his size. He likes to shoot the puck from the point.

PAC #12 RW Duke, Reid (2014) - Duke played very physical and works hard along the boards and out front of the net going to war in the slot. He made some great plays and created some good scoring chance. He shows elusiveness with the puck and good hands and always seems to get himself into good scoring areas.

PAC #15 LW MacMaster, Tanner (2014) - MacMaster has tremendous hands and showed them off whenever he was able to get close to the puck. He handles the puck very well in tight areas and created scoring chances for both himself and his teammates.

PAC #17 RC Point, Brayden (2014) - Brayden shows quick hands and battles through traffic to get open for scoring chances. He showed great moves in one on one situations to nearly score a highlight reel goal.

PAC #1 G Lee, Payton (2014) - Payton's vision through traffic was not good today. He was also a little slow moving side to side and with his recovery.

SWE #7 LD Ollas Mattsson, Adam (2014) - Adam played physical right off the bat in this game and made a massive open ice hit. He always seems to make the smart plays both positionally and with the puck. These attributes hold a little more importance because His skating could really use some improvements.

SWE #9 RC Franzen, Gustaf (2015) - Franzen showed great determination and focus under pressure. He utilized his puck skills to score Sweden's third goal.

SWE #18 RW Karlsson, Anton (2014) - Karlsson showed great positioning and won battles down low and gets into prime scoring areas. He shows great vision and makes quick decisions with the puck. He is elusve and difficult to stop in one on one situations and displayed a powerful shot to score two goals for Sweden in this game the second of which was the game winner. Anton plays with tremendous desperation on the penalty kill. He would block shots and cleared the zone extremely well.

SWE #20 LW Nylander Altelius, William (2014) - Nylander dictates the play well on the power play but will also take shots that don't have much chance getting through to the net firing it into opponents skates instead of utilizing good passing options. He made some really great plays at the line on the power play. He utilizes his excellent skating ability to go end to end at will and is extremely elusive

SWE #22 LW Timashov, Dmytro (2015) - Timashov went on a nice end to end rush displaying elusiveness and puck control. He shows very slick passing ability and consistently created scoring chances. At one point he made a great pass, cycled around and got into great scoring position but the goaltender made a nice save.

SWE #26 LW Kovacs, Robin (2015) - Kovacs showed some great passes throughout this game to set up scoring chances. He showed excellent second effort on a partial break for a big scoring chance.

SWE #28 LD Englund, Andreas (2014) - Englund used his size and played physical finishing checks regularly along the board. He also made a lot of smart simple plays with his stick to break up plays in his own zone.

SWE #29 RW Muzito Bagenda, Daniel (2014) - Daniel is extremely effective down low in the offensive zone on the cycle. He is relentless forcing the opposition to turn the puck move and made a consistent positive impact on his team with his work ethic today.

Scouts Notes: This was a very tightly contested match-up to open the games on the day of New Years' Eve. Until the final 5:15 where Anton Karlsson (2014) and Oscar Lindblom (2014) scored within 30 seconds of each other to put two insurance markers on the board and put this game away. In addition to the reports above, for Pacific Matt Revel (2014) played with excellent physicality throughout tonight's game. While Jake Virtanen (2014) was pretty quiet most of this game, he had a few really good shifts showing intense competitiveness and picked up a rebound and banged it home for a goal. For Sweden, Adrian Kempe (2014) showed off excellent positioning in the offensive zone along with a hard shot.

December 31, 2012, Team Quebec vs. Team USA (World U17)

QUE #2 RD Neill, Carl (2014) - Carl showed quick puck movement on the power play. However he also made some very risky plays with the puck in his own zone.

QUE #7 RD Leveille, Loik (2015) - Leveille showed great coverage matching up with American forwards and consistent defensive zone coverage.

QUE #12 RW Simard, Tomothe (2015) - Team Quebec didn't get a lot of offensive chances, but Simard seemed to be in on a lot of them. He creates chances forcing a few turnovers. He made a good play on the rush taking a bad pass in his skates and kicking it up to his stick without breaking stride then created a scoring chance from it. Simard showed off some physicality leveling an American player with a crushing hit.

QUE #16 RW Aube-Kubel, Nicolas (2014) - Nicolas displayed excellent hands in this game. He controls the puck well creating scoring chances on a consistent basis for Team Quebec. He forechecked hard forcing a surprising amount of turnovers. At one point he made a great move right off the draw to get the puck, drive the net and bang the puck in scoring the only goal for Quebec today.

QUE #18 RC Pepin, Alexis (2014) - Pepin was noticeable throughout this game due to his tremendous physical pressense. He was constantly crushing American players left and right. He was relentless along the boards winning battles and leaving with the puck. He forced several turnovers both with his stick and asserting himself physically in open ice.

QUE #30 G Billia, Julio (2014) - Despite allowing five goals in this match-up, Billia was outstanding. He showed lightning quick recovery and very quick reflexes. He has the ability to make some highlight reel saves and did so throughout this game. Julio shows awareness of his lack of size by getting out and cutting down angles effectively.

USA #36 LD Fortunato, Brandon (2014) - Brandon made some very good plays up ice with the puck. He moves it quickly and efficiently and looked very good on the power play. One of his great passes lead to USA's second goal of the night. However Brandon really struggled defensively particularly with containing forwards in his own zone.

USA #37 RW Tuch, Alex (2014) - Alex has a rather awkward skating stride but generates pretty good speed for his size. He was dominant at times down low skating with the puck protecting it well along the walls. He has a powerful shot, but it was a couple passes that created the best scoring chances from him today.

USA #39 LC Larkin, Dylan (2014) - Dylan handles puck extremely well in traffic. He showed very good intelligence on the rush knows when to make an evasive move and when to pass off and go hard to the net. He protects puck well possessing a very hard shot. He also showed off his great skating and acceleration.

USA #41 LD Billitier, Nathan (2014) - Nathan really showed off his excellent quickness and mobility tonight. He has exceptional speed in every direction. He rushed the puck extremely well in this game, but also made some nice passes up ice as well. He has very quick hands controlling the puck well. Billitier is willing to play physical when necessary. He needs to add strength but he was effective and was willing to use both the body and his stick one on one.

USA #44 LD Bliss, Ryan (2014) - Ryan showed pretty good mobility and movement on the blueline. He made some nice passes through traffic to create scoring chances. He showed good patience with the puck outwaiting goaltender to score the fourth goal of the game.

USA #46 RC Eichel, Jack (2015) - Jack protects the puck well in order to create time and space for himself. He has great positioning out front of the net resulting in the first goal of the game. Jack possesses excellent skating ability and quickness. He has a very powerful shot which he gets off quickly and impressive puck skills. His hockey sense is very good at both ends of the ice. Jack took a big hit from behind the net leaving the game in the first period. He returned briefly in the second but would leave the game shortly after that.

USA #48 LW Milano, Sonny (2014) - Sonny displays good hands in tight areas. He is able to get his shot off or pass the puck accurately when heavily covered. He made a great play in the second while falling he still found a way to set up his linemate. Sonny shows great overall puck control and can make things happen fairly consistently.

USA #51 RW Wilkie, Chris (2014) - Chris pressures the puck carrier very well and it resulted in turnovers. He shows great hands and patience with the puck. He also displays good passing to create scoring chances. He scored the final goal of the game showing his patience then firing a laser of a shot in the slot to score displaying a lot of power in his release.

USA #57 RW Poganski, Austin (2014) - Austin showed off some great moves first beating the defenseman one on one then making a great move on the goaltender. He shows the ability to slip in and out of traffic fairly well and can still find ways to get a shot off when he has the puck or receives a pass in heavy traffic.

Scouts Notes: USA came out and dominated the game and the pace from puck drop to the final whistle. Quebec however remained in this game much longer than expected thanks to some excellent goaltending provided by Julio Billia (2014). However just after the midway point of the game USA was able to score two quick goals and would slowly put this game away from there. In addition to the reports above, Jared Fiegl (2014) showed some great, consistent work ethic in this game. Particularly on the penalty kill. Jonathan MacLeod (2014) stood out by making some very good plays in one on one situations.

January 1, 2013, Team Pacific vs. Team Finland – (World U17)

PAC #4 LD Stadel, Riley (2014) - Riley showed good ability to acquire the red line and get pucks deep. He also showed the willingness to play physical.

PAC #5 LD Martin, Brycen (2014) - Brycen showed off excellent skating and puck skills today. He can rush it end to end seemingly at will and controls the puck extremely well. He is very smooth and elusive. His defensive play saw a few lapses and Saarela blew by him on the outside for the firs goal of the game.

PAC #6 RD Thrower, Josh (2014) - Josh showed excellent physicality all game long. He finishes his checks whenever possible along the boards, played tough in the corners and in puck battles and landed a couple huge open ice hits.

PAC #10 RC Bleackley, Conner (2014) - Conner displays great moves in one on one situations. He has good anticipation to force turnovers in the offensive zone or capitalize on puck misplays by the opposition. He played a great two-way game tonight battling hard in the defensive zone and had good hockey sense in his own end. Conner looked a little lost on the cycle at times.

PAC #16 RW Revel, Matt (2014) - Matt was able to force turnovers and turn them into scoring chances. He shows good moves one on one and a very nice pass set up Team Pacific's first goal of the night.

PAC #17 RC Point, Brayden (2014) - Brayden is a little small, but shows nice moves to beat defenders. He protects the puck well for his size and can create scoring chance for himself and others. This game went to the shootout and Brayden made a great shootout move to score the shootout winner.

PAC #18 RW Virtanen, Jake (2014) - Jake had an excellent game tonight and played a huge part in Pacific's victory. Early on he showed great individual effort to burn the defenseman then scored a very nice goal. On his very next shift he walked into the shot and fired a wrister to post two goals less than 12 minutes into the game. He rushed the puck effectively with slightly above average skating ability, but did get caught trying to do too much at times. He displays pretty good puck skills and would fight hard to get the puck back when he would turn it over.

PAC #20 RW Sandu, Tyler (2014) - Tyler showed very well on the cycle keeping the puck moving in his team's possession. He also made some nice moves while driving down the wing to get a good shot off.

FIN #6 LD Keskitalo, Miro (2014) - Miro is a very smooth skater and moved the puck well. He has good size but needs to get stronger. He showed a willingness to take the body when the option presented itself. He also competed along the boards. Miro was a shot blocking machine tonight taking a few blasts. At one point he got hit where there wasn't much padding, Miro got up on one foot stuck with the play and continued competing despite being in obvious pain.

FIN #19 RW Kiviranta, Joel (2014) - Kiviranta showed a great forecheck and created turnovers. He was effective in all three zones and used regularly on the penalty kill. He has good hands and positioning in the offensive zone. Joel unloaded a one-timer to bring Finland within one goal in the final 10 minutes of the game.

FIN #20 RC Lamsa, Teemu (2014) - Teemu has good size and landed some big hits in this game. He is strong on his skates and battles hard maintaining positioning. Teemu unloaded a one timer to score Finland's second goal of the game initiating a run of 3 goals in the final 14 minutes of the game to send it to overtime.

FIN #24 LW Kapnanen, Kasperi (2014) - Kasperi asserted himself early while forcing turnovers. He was dangerous high in his own zone taking away time and space and stealing the puck creating a few scoring chances. He really showed off his passing ability moving it well all over the ice. Kasperi ended up scoring a bit of a weak goal late in the game to tie it up and send it to overtime.

FIN #25 RW Saarela, Aleksi (2015) - Aleksi has excellent speed and absolutely blew past a Team Pacific defender early in the game the score a beautiful opening goal of this game. He displays quick hands and agility on a consistent basis and needs to be watched as he can very quickly become a dangerous player on the ice. He has outstanding acceleration displaying a great first few steps and is able to almost immediate separate from most players.

Scouts Notes: Team Pacific scored 3 goals in two and a half minutes midway through the first period and eventually opened up a three goal lead. Up 4-1 with less than 15 minutes left it looked like Pacific would cruise to an easy victory. However Team Finland remained resilient and clawed back to tie the game up at 4. After a scoreless overtime, Brayden Point (2014) and Jake Virtanen (2014) scored in the shootout to get the victory. In addition to the reports above, for Team Pacific Joe Hicketts (2014) made several excellent long distance passes all game long creating offense for his team. Brandon Hickey (2014) provided solid physical play in one on one situations. Reid Duke (2014) batted the puck out of mid air from the side of the net to score the fourth goal of the game. For Team Finland, Jere Huuhka (2015) regularly blocked shots on the penalty kill. Atte Makinen (2014) provided a consistent forecheck for his team. Jaakko Halli (2014) played one on one battles very well in this game. Waltteri Hopponen (2014) made some solid passes to move the puck up ice quickly.

January 1, 2013, Team Russia vs. Team Sweden (World U17)

RUS #7 RW Svechnikov, Yevgeni (2014) - Svechnikov finished checks on a pretty regular basis. He showed some very good moves in one on one situations and in one of those he beat the defenseman and the goaltender with a great move to score a big goal early in the third period to keep Russia in the game.

RUS #11 LC Nikolishin, Ivan (2014) - Ivan showed off his strong defensive play. He was diving in front of point shots showing a consistent willingness to block shots. On the penalty kill he did a good job at the top of the point getting in passing lanes and created a few offensive chances off of turnovers. Nikolishin showed great speed flying up the ice but he made some questionable passes after some great rushes. Ivan is certainly a player who will test his limits with the puck and did so constantly. Some of these paid off for him, some of them didn't.

RUS #12 LD Lyamkin, Nikita (2014) - Nikita was consistently lined up with some of Sweden's top players. He engaged physically trying to wear them down and was able to skate with them neutralizing them effectively during his shifts this game.

RUS #14 LW Vovchenko, Daniil (2014) - Vovchenko showed good aggression on the penalty kill. However he was very risky with the puck and his decisions with the puck in the neutral zone.

RUS #18 RD Nasybullin, Eduard (2014) - Eduard was noticeable on a few occasions making some very good breakout passes and was very solid in a two on one situation.

RUS #23 LW Lazarev, Maxim (2014) - Lazarev had some highs and lows in this game. He made a nice play to protect the puck then beat the goaltender to score a goal that helped Russia stay in this game. However he had a few lazy passes and turnovers in his own zone, one of them resulted in a goal for Sweden.

RUS #27 LD Sergeyev, Dmitri (2014) - Sergeyev made some very good plays in one on one situation particularly using his stick well. He used his strength along the walls to win battles and to contain forwards.

RUS #28 LD Mikulovich, Alexander (2014) - Mikulovich played very well defensively on the rush breaking up plays. He handled a two on one very effectively. He also made some good one on one plays. Alexander showed off his physicality standing up at the line making a big hit.

SWE #4 LD Forsling, Gustav (2014) - Gustav is slightly undersized for the defensive positioning but he proved to be very effective in one on one situations using both his stick and his body to shut down the opposing forward properly and effectively. He battles very hard and is quick to get onto the wall and compete. He's calm under sustanined pressure and we don't see any panic in Forsling in his own zone. Gustav likes to show off his skating ability and will jump up on the rush. He also rushes the puck quite effectively himself. At one point he made a mistake becoming too focused on one forward on the opposing team. It drew him way out of position and resulted in a goal in his own end.

SWE #6 LD Johansson, Emil (2014) - Emil rushed the puck effectively into the offensive zone on occasion. Great wrist shot on partial break to score Sweden's fifth goal.

SWE #7 LD Ollas Mattsson, Adam (2014) - Adam was noticeable on the penalty kill making good plays picking off passes and clearing the puck down the ice. He seemed to always make the smart play with the puck and showed some strong physicality. Adam's skating needs improvement.

SWE #9 RC Franzen, Gustaf (2015) - Gustaf was moderately effective offensively in this game. He shows great hands and moves on the breakaway but he got absolutely robbed. He makes a lot of great passes to set up scoring chances. At one point he picked off a bad pass and turned it into an assist with a nice pass.

SWE #18 RW Karlsson, Anton (2014) - Anton shows great hands while under pressure in the offensive zone particularly in high traffic area. He showed this off on Sweden's third goal of the game. Anton also showed off his passing ability and he made one excellent play in particular while penalty killing sending his linemate on a short handed breakaway. Karlsson was clearly targeted by Team Russia as he was heavily covered all game long which opened things up for his teammates.

SWE #20 LW Nylander Altelius, William (2014) - While we haven't seen Nylander pass as much as he should in the past, he was moving the puck more frequently today showing that he is in fact a very talented puck mover. He made a great cross ice pass through traffic to set up Sweden's second goal of the game. William controls the puck very well and eludes contact regularly. He made a great individual play to score the final goal of the game beating both the defender then the goaltender both one on one. William was caught being a little undisciplined 200 feet from his own net.

SWE #23 RW Lindblom, Oskar (2014) - Oskar really showed off his hands in this game. He fired a laser top shelf late in the second period to give Sweden a two goal lead. Later on he scored an outstanding goal with little space to roof the puck backhanded with almost no space to elevate the puck. Oskar also moved the puck effectively. If it had to do with offense Oskar was involved in it, but we didn't notice him much away from the goal area.

Scouts Notes: There was a bit of back and forth in this game. Sweden opened with a 3-0 lead however Russia came back and made it close. Russia hung in until the final minutes of the game when Oscar Lindblom (2014) and William Nylander-Altelius (2014) scored beautiful back to back goals in a 47 second span. Both teams showed a lot in this game. In addition to the reports above, for Russia

Ilya Zinoviev (2014) showed off great passing ability on a consistent basis in this game. For Sweden Robin Kovacs (2015) displayed great hands at multiple points in this game.

January 2, 2013, Team Russia vs. Team Finland (World U17)

RUS #7 RW Svechnikov, Yevgeni (2014) - Svechnikov showed off his offensive ability in this game. He displays great moves rushing the puck up the middle evading checkers and getting the puck in the offensive zone. Late in the first he scored an outstanding goal beating Finland's defenseman one on one then pulled a great move to score. He later deflected the puck in to score his second of the night. While he can put the puck in the net, he's made some excellent passes to set up goals as well. Almost every goal Russia scored today Yevgeni was involved to some extent with. The only things we didn't like in this game is he seemed to lack strength although he worked pretty hard along the wall and was willing to hit. He also would bang his stick on the ice looking for a pass although he was heavily covered.

RUS #11 LC Nikolishin, Ivan (2014) - Ivan showed off his hands and quckness working around defenders effectively. He moves the puck extremely well especially on the power play making quick decisive plays. He seems to have a knack for making excellent long distance passes putting the puck tape to tape. Ivan was penalized for diving in the third period, a penalty that could have been very harmful to Russia as this was a very close game. Ivan has had a constant issue with diving, rolling around, pretending he's hurt every single game we've seen in this tournament and it's getting incredibly ridiculous. Apparently the referees agreed.

RUS #12 LD Lyamkin, Nikita (2014) - Constantly right on opposing forwards in his own zone. Plays his man and his position very well. He likes to take the body but needs to get stronger. He was caught out on the ice for a very long shift resulting in a series of mental errors which ended with the puck in the back of his net.

RUS #13 RW Pilipenko, Kirill (2015) - Kirill did a great job winning the race to the puck then setting up a nice scoring chance. He utilized his wrist shot for the fifth goal of the game.

RUS #14 LW Vovchenko, Daniil (2014) - Vovchenko is a very good skater with even better acceleration. He was able to draw a penalty using his speed driving to the net. He's pretty small but apparently no one has ever told him. He hits with energy, he's relentless on the forecheck and works extremely hard along the wall winning battles against bigger and stronger defensemen. He was able to force puck playing mistakes and turn them into scoring chances. His work ethic was tremendous in today's game.

RUS #18 RD Nasybullin, Eduard (2014) - Eduard displayed great physical play along the boards all game long. He has a huge shot from the point which he uses regularly on the power play. He has good overall hockey sense in all three zones. He's a pretty good skater who carries the puck effectively.

RUS #23 LW Lazarev, Maxim (2014) - Lazarev has a big shot and used it to score Russia's second goal of the game after one timing a great pass. Maxim is undersized and appeared intimidated in physical situations and uninterested in any part of the physical game.

RUS #27 LD Sergeyev, Dmitri (2014) - Dmitri shows good patience with the puck allowing lanes to open up and making the smart accurate play. This plays a part in him constantly moving the puck up ice well.

FIN #2 LD Niku, Sami (2015) - He gets the puck on net effectively on the powerplay. Sami got caught up defending a few two on one breaks and committed way too much to the shooter early on essentially giving the second player on the rush a free shot point blank once the pass was made.

FIN #19 RW Kiviranta, Joel (2014) - Kiviranta handles the puck very well under pressure and unleashed a good wrist shot for Finland's second goal of the game.

FIN #24 LW Kapnanen, Kasperi (2014) - Kapanen pressured the puck carrier on a regular basis making him capable of forcing turnovers throughout the game. One of these turnovers resulted in the fourth goal of the game for Finland.

FIN #25 RW Saarela, Aleksi (2015) - Aleksi showed the ability to be dangerous cross 200ft. winning battles deep in his own zone then rushing the puck end to end. He finished on a great two on one pass to score Finland's third goal while short handed helping put them back into the game with only ten minutes left.

FIN #26 RW Rantanen, Mikko (2015) - Mikko picked off passes in the netural zone effectively. He also showed very good hands in the goal area in today's game.

Scouts Notes: Finland has had big third periods all tournament long and this was no different. Russia was up 4-1 and 5-2 and with 10 minutes left Finland scored two big goals to make it a 5-4 game. Despite great pressure they were unable to get the tying goal and lost a narrow one goal decision. In addition to the reports above, for Team Russia Nikita Yazkov (2014) made a great move to beat the goaltender on a breakaway to score the fourth goal of the game for Team Russia. Sergei Svetlakov (2014) showed off great hands down low in the offensive zone. He wasn't a standout in the game but made several good plays on one particular shift to create multiple chances. Alexander Mikulovich (2014) battled well along the boards. For Team Finland Atte Makinen (2014) banged home the opening goal of the game. He also did a great job on the penalty kill. Waltter Hopponen (2014) made a great pass on a 2 on 1 break to set up a goal to try to get Finland back into the game.

January 2, 2013, Team Pacific vs. Team West (World U17)

PAC #6 RD Thrower, Josh (2014) - Josh has a great point shot and unloaded a blast to tie the game late in the first period. In the second Josh saved a sure goal while on the powerplay in the slot playing his man very well.

PAC #12 RW Duke, Reid (2014) - Reid did a great job on the power play forcing turnovers on potential clearing attempts keeping the play going and helping put on pressure in the offensive zone.

PAC #15 LW MacMaster, Tanner (2014) - Tanner showed off great hands in this game. He didn't give up on the play and followed up on his initial chance to score the 3-2 goal for team Pacific.

PAC #17 RC Point, Brayden (2014) - Brayden displayed great puck control in the offensive zone. He protects it well for his size. He made a few solid plays passing off when he was covered then driving to the net. Point unleased a great wrister from the slot to score Pacific's second goal on the power play.

PAC #18 RW Virtanen, Jake (2014) - Jake displayed a great forecheck to create turnovers. He shows an extra gear in his skating ability when necessary. He also displayed excellent puck control.

WST #4 LD Pilon, Ryan (2015) - Ryan moves the puck effectively on the point. He was effective in his own zone showing a very good stick on the penalty kill. He battles well in his own zone consistently. He's willing to ice the puck when his team is pinned deep in their own zone to get a line change.

WST #17 RW Glover, Austin (2014) - Austin provided strong pressure on the forecheck, but wouldn't finish with any contact.

WST #18 LW Gardiner, Rhett (2014) - Rhett was constantly involved in scoring chances for Team West. He has good hands and created opportunities for himself and others. He is also able to force turnovers which he also turned into scoring chances. He sets up around the crease and was able to finish in the goal area. Rhett displayed good physicality in this game and above average skating ability. He's very creative with the puck possessing a good hard shot.

WST #31 G Edmonds, Ty (2014) - Ty moves well and covers the lower part of the net effectively. He used this ability to make several excellent saves in this game with his flexability. He displays good reflexes and agility. Edmonds was a huge part in Team West staying in this game and taking it to overtime. He leaves a lot for shooters to see and can at times play a little deep in his crease.

Scouts Notes: Despite Pacific looking for a spot in the semi-finals, it was Team West who put the pressure on Team Pacific with some strong defensive play. They either had the lead or kept it close all game long. Team West took this game to overtime but it was Brandon Hickey (2014) from Team Pacific who scored the overtime winner to give his team the victory. In addition to the reports above, for Team Pacific Joe Hicketts (2014) rushed the puck effectively in this game. For Team West Reid Zalitach (2014) provided good physical play along the boards. Jordan Thomson (2014) showed good physicality throughout the game. He also made a good play with his stick to save a potential goal. Adam Brooks (2014) displayed good hands and passing ability in this game.

Jan 2, 2013, Vancouver Giants vs. Kamloops Blazers (WHL)

VAN#27 RW, Houck, Jackson(2013) Physical forward had a good game for the Giants tonight. He moved his feet quickly all game long and was able to get involved into the game by using his body on the forecheck. Looks rejuvenated from the 2 week break in the WHL schedule. His line was not able to generate much of a cycle because his line mates are not very strong along the boards like him. Would be interesting to see him play with better players and see the impact he may be able to make. Made one crucial mistake on the PK that costed his team a goal. He was far too late to pick up a man in front of his own net on a play that came down low. Could be smarter out on the ice.

VAN#44 LD, Geertsen, Mason(2013) Did not play much in the first half of the game because he took an unnecessary 10 minute game misconduct after a fight between 2 other players, in which he skated over to Kamloops' penalty box and started to trash talk the opponent. Had some trouble with speed along the boards, especially with quick starts and stops. Played a good physical game, and showed some sound defensive abilities everywhere along the ice. Received a lot of ice time during the 2nd half of the game and did quite well. Definitely one of the strongest player on the Giants, and was depended heavily on the PK all night long.

KAM#14 RW, Needham, Matt(2013) Speedy forward who had an average game tonight. Showed some good instincts for the game overall at times, but really struggled along the boards. He was knocked off the puck consistently, and just was not able to use his feet to his advantage to get away from checks. Liked his game more when he did not have the puck. Had a good forecheck going a few times to land a hit along the boards and create a turnover. He was able to block a shot from the point on the PK, get a 2 on 1 going which created a shorthanded goal for his teammate. Needham caused a few turnovers with the puck, and just did not make great decisions with it. He also missed a chance to score on a wide open net when a shot was blocked and just bounced towards him, he could not settle it and take a good shot.

KAM#21 LW, Ully, Cole(2013) One of the better forwards for Kamloops tonight. Was able to use his quickness to his advantage to find open areas in the offensive zone and get the rush going for his team with his speed. Showed off above average hands a couple of times by stickhandling through opponents. Was not anything overly fancy, but rather he combined it with his agility to get around them. Needs to work on his decision making with the puck as he turned the puck over when making passes a number of times. Not a big player, but worked hard along the boards and was able to out-compete opponents for the puck consistently.

Scouts Notes: This was a close game with not much offense from both teams until the 3rd period when Kamloops really dominated and took the lead and never looked back. I thought Tim Bozon, a draft pick of the Montreal Canadiens, got better as the game went along. Showed his nice touch around the net by finishing off a great pass to get on the scoresheet. Matt Needham needs to make better decisions and have better hands to compensate for his lack of size. Not good enough along the boards either. Jakub Stukel played his first WHL game for the Giants and got more and more ice time as the game went along. Was even out on the ice when they pulled the goalie to try to tie the game up. Thought he played a smart game. Needs to get faster and stronger, but he was going to the right areas, and did not look overwhelmed by the pace of play.

FINAL SCORE: 4-2 Kamloops

Jan 3, 2013, Canada vs. USA (2013 WJHC)

CAN#23 RC, MacKinnon, Nathan(2013) Like much of the tournament, MacKinnon was not able to provide much impact for Canada tonight, largely due to the poor quality of ice time he received throughout the night. He was not able to utilize his speed or offensive abilities for most of the game. He was counted on to be good defensively and provide a physical presence, which produced mixed results for him. He did not provide much physicality, which is not too much of a surprise because he is counted on to score points with his club team in Halifax. Defensively, he worked hard along the boards, but made a couple of mental errors. He was caught focusing on the puck too much, and in one point in the 1st period, an opponent got a very good scoring chance right in the slot, who should have been his job to stop. When he had the puck, he displayed very good strength on his feet and was very hard to knock off the puck.

CAN#29 LW, Drouin, Jonathan(2013) Played on the top line tonight, and had an average game. Showed some very good speed and vision, but was not able to create any great scoring chances. In one play, Drouin and his linemates had a 3 on 2 opportunity, and he drove the middle with the puck, sucked in both defenders, and quickly made a pass to his teammate who had a good lane to the net, but just did not score on the opportunity. He had a good chance to score from in tight, but missed the net with his snap shot. I liked the jump he played with in this game, and the way he used his body out in open ice to separate opponents from the puck. By the time the score was 4-0 for USA, he was starting to try to do too much by himself, which was not successful. Really liked the way he backchecked all game long, but also made some mistakes without the puck, particularly with his stick positioning. Just needs to be more aware of where his stick is and be more active with it.

USA#3 RD, Jones, Seth(2013) Had an excellent game for the Americans tonight. He brought a good mix of poise and physical play to the game. He looked unfazed by Canada's forecheck all night long, and was patient with the puck, and used his body to protect it and buy some more time to make a play. He made solid, crisp passes to his teammates, and did not commit a turnover tonight. He displayed some good soft hands all night with his ability to effortlessly control hard passes on his stick to be quickly ready for his next move. Jones also made good decisions on shot selections. He did not try to rip a slap shot everytime from the point, but would take a quick wrist shot if the situation is right. Without the puck, Jones really took advantage of his reach and strength to make opponents ineffective offensively for most of the night. He did get caught late in the 3rd period on the PK for trying to land a hit along the boards, in which he missed and it turned into a mini 2 on 1 situation down low. He is a very effortless skater, and was not in danger of getting beat once all game long.

USA#21 RW, Hartman, Ryan(2013) 2 way forward had a good game overall. Did not do anything particularly well to be really noticeable, but played the game with a lot of tenacity and discipline. For much of the game, his line did not create any great scoring chances, but did a good job in their own end to prevent Canada from scoring. Hartman was good along the boards, and impressed me with his ability to not get too focused on the puck, which kept the point man on his wing ineffective for most of the game. They just did not have a clear lane to shoot, all thanks to his attention to detail. He had a couple of moments where his stick could have been in better position to take away passes though. Offensively, his best chances came in the third period when he was able to find the soft spot in coverage and take some good shots on net. Showed off a quick release on his wrist shot. He took no risks with the lead, and played a safe game.

Scouts Notes: The Americans absolutely dominated the game tonight. They competed much harder throughout the night, and it showed on the score board. Surprised at the lack of offensive productivity from Ryan Nugent-Hopkins in this game. Just got out hustled and outworked for the puck consistently. John Gibson played a solid game, and made the saves when necessary. Columbus Blue Jackets got a good defenseman in Mike Reilly. Thought he played a strong game again tonight for his team.

FINAL SCORE: 5-1 USA

January 3, 2013, Team Ontario vs. Team Pacific – (World U17)

ONT #5 RD Ekblad, Aaron (2014) - Ekblad unloaded a blast from the point to score Ontario's second goal of the game. He made a very smart play on a two on one break to help out his goaltender and potentially save a goal.

ONT #9 LC McDavid, Connor (2014) - McDavid showed off his outstanding talent as usual. Great hands in close. He also picked up the puck behind the net, faked out the goaltender to score.

ONT #22 RW Lindo, Jaden (2014) - Great work by Jaden to fight off checkers while standing in the slot to bang home Ontario's third goal of the game. He displayed very good physical play throughout this game.

PAC #5 LD Martin, Brycen (2014) - Brycen made some puck playing errors early on unbecoming of his performance in this tournament. He came in off the point to one time Pacific's third goal of the game on the power play.

PAC #14 RC Mappin, Ty (2014) - Ty played an agitating style all game long in order to get under the skin of his opposition. He outworked opponents in battles to acquire the puck.

PAC #18 RW Virtanen, Jake (2014) - Virtanen drives the wing very well displaying close to power forwards size but great speed for this size. He protects the puck then fires it with a lightning fast shot. Jake scored an outstanding goal to force a turnover then beat the goaltender with speed on the wrap around. He also showed off his passing ability making a great pass to set up Pacific's second goal of the game on a two on one. He showed good creativity and puck skills. Jake also played physical and displayed a high compete level.

Scouts Notes: Team Ontario entered the World Under 17 Challenge as one of the favorites with a ton of talent. However they were looking to salvage fifth place on the second last day of the event. Team Pacific just wouldn't quit and this game went back and forth for the entire 60 minutes. In the final 90 seconds of the game, just as this match-up looked like it was heading to overtime, Conner Bleackley (2014) scored to give Pacific a 7-6 lead and would go on to win this game. In addition to the reports above, for Team Ontario Niki Petti (2014) was quiet in this game although he provided some good physicality during a few moments. Tanner MacMaster (2014) did a great job at the side of the net to score Pacific's fourth goal of the game. Ryan Graham (2014) rushed the puck up ice then unloaded a powerful shot to score Pacific's first goal of the game.

January 3, 2013, Team Russia vs. Team USA (World U17)

RUS #7 RW Svechnikov, Yevgeni (2014) - Yevgeni utilized his speed and elusiveness on a regular basis. He battled out front of the net providing a great screen to help Russia score what ended up being their goal winning goal.

RUS #10 RW Zinoviev, Ilya (2014) - Ilya battles hard in his own zone. He made a great pass cross ice to set up Russia's second goal of the game.

RUS #11 LC Nikolishin, Ivan (2014) - Ivan can be caught making lazy plays with the puck. He finished on a great pass to tie the game up late in the second for team Russia. He looked great on the penalty kill especially late in the game clearing the zone multiple times on arguably the biggest kill of the game.

RUS #12 LD Lyamkin, Nikita (2014) - Team USA pressured Russia's goaltender throughout this game, Nikita was really called upon to clear out the front of the net and play tough protecting his teammates and really stepped up his physicality this game. He was excellent on the penalty kill stripping the puck then skating with it killing a lot of time with his puck control. He made a lot of great plays just making the smart simple decision not trying to do too much. He's a good skater who's willing to hit.

RUS #18 RD Nasybullin, Eduard (2014) - Eduard shot the puck at will from the point making a few bad shooting decisions. He did get his shot through on Russia's first goal getting it deflected on the way to the net. Eduard showed nice passing ability in this game. He made good passes to start the rush up ice. He also set up Russia's fourth goal of the game.

RUS #23 LW Lazarev, Maxim (2014) - Lazarev displayed great skating to rush the puck up ice effectively. He uses this speed to burn defensemen outside but has the moves to cut in if defensemen try to force him outside. He displays the ability to make great passes to create chance but also the talent and puck skills to do it himself. He forced turnovers in all three zones, some of which resulted in scoring chances. Lazarev was constantly involved in the offense in this game and was the biggest reason among the forwards helping Russia win this game.

RUS #28 LD Mikulovich, Alexander (2014) - Alexander made some effective passes up ice to set up an odd man rush. He used his positional play very well defensively in order to break up several potential scoring chances for team USA.

USA #48 LW Milano, Sonny (2014) - Sonny read plays extremely well and made some very smart passes. One of which set up the opening goal for team USA. Sonny embellished a little bit at one point, and it worked setting up a power play for team USA. He then went out of said power play and scored USA's fourth goal of the game keeping them in this match-up right to the end.

USA #51 RW Wilkie, Chris (2014) - Chris was an excellent presence in the slot in this game and throughout the tournament. He used this presence to score USA's first goal of the game, then made a great finish off a great pass to score USA's second goal of the game. Chris is listed smaller than he looks and has a great frame. Chris got a little frustrated in the final seconds after the loss was secured and took an unnecessary cheap shot at a Russian player who wasn't looking to engage.

USA #53 RD Wesley, Joshua (2014) - Joshua made a great play blocking shots out front but on one play he kinda negated it by throwing the puck out of play resulting in a penalty. He struggle din the slot at times taking too long with the puck which resulted in a scoring chance against.

USA #31 G Birdsall, Chris (2015) - Chris made some excellent glove saves in this match-up. He is very technically sound and presents himself very well to shooters. He displays good patience not being lured into making an early move and generally follows the puck carrier well maintaining his positioning.

Scouts Notes: As we enter the Semi-Finals of the World Under 17 Challenge, USA and Russia met in an excellent match-up of two very equally talented teams. USA jumped out to an early 2-0 lead, but 13 seconds later, Russia would bring it back to a tie game before Austin Poganski (2014) made a great deflection off a point shot to put USA back up 3-2. This time Russia would not only tie the game but take a commanding lead. USA made it a one goal game, but Russia's Yevgeni Svechnikov (2014) scored an empty net goal to secure the victory for Russia. In addition to the reports above, Daniil Vovochenko showed great elusiveness and was very shifty in small areas.

Jan, 4, 2013, Chicago Steel vs. Green Bay Gamblers (USHL)

CHI # 10, C, Ebbing, Thomas (2013) Ebbing drove hard to the net looking for loose pucks and opportunities. He got to the front of the net to tip a puck on the power play and score and was also able to skate the puck up the ice to gain the offensive zone on a nice end-to-end rush, then distributed the puck effectively in the offensive zone. He had a good back-check to breakup the odd-man rush for the opposition, was clearing the puck up out of his own end on the penalty kill and got a nice cycle going to move the puck down deep in the offensive zone. He set up a teammate well in the high slot for a nice one-timer opportunity and made a great pass to find a man in the slot off the rush, then got to the slot to pick up the rebound for a good opportunity from in tight.

CHI # 17, RW, Polino, Patrick (2013) Polino put some pretty good pressure on the puck carrier, had a good wide drive into the offensive zone but was taking long outside shots off the rush instead of driving the puck to the net. He moved the puck around well in the offensive zone on the power play, got a nice cycle going and got down low to the net with the puck for a nice chance from in tight beside the net. He just needs to try to drive the puck more towards the net, as he takes a lot of his shots from the outside never really getting past the opposition's defensemen.

CHI # 28, LW, Roos, Alex (2013) Roos put great pressure on the puck carrier on the fore-check to force turnovers. He did a nice job of reading the play to pick off a pass in the high slot then put a good shot on net and had an excellent drive to the net with his stick down to take a pass for a good chance from in tight. He opened up nicely on an odd-man rush to take a pass and put a good shot on and was distributing the puck well in the offensive zone on the rush. He possesses great agility and puck protection abilities but has to be stronger on the puck along the boards and has to watch the turnovers trying to force passes through the opposition in the offensive zone.

GBG # 20, D, Wolanin, Christian (2013) Wolanin was capable of reading the play to pick off a neutral zone turnover and then get the puck in deep. He made some good breakout passes to start the rush, moved the puck well to the high slot then jumped down low driving the net with his stick down.

GBG # 23, D, Gross, Jordan (2013) Gross was distributing the puck very well through the neutral zone for his team to gain the offensive zone with ease. He was jumping up on the rush to lead the attack down low and made a really great centering pass to a man driving the net. He made a good 1st pass out of the zone to start the rush, displayed excellent speed to gain the offensive zone on the wide drive and was coming down low into the slot to put shots on. He was able to get a cycle going in deep in the offensive zone, got in lanes to breakup plays for the opposition in the defensive zone and put nice pressure on the puck carrier to force turnovers.

GBG # 81, C, Winborg, Adam (2013) Winborg did a good job of moving the puck back to the point then going to the net for opportunities on the point shots. He was battling well for the puck through the neutral zone to win it off the opposition forcing turnovers, but has to hit the net afterwards on his shots off the rush.

GBG # 97, LW, Diksuhin, Grigori (2013) Dikushin can drive to the net very effectively with his stick down looking for loose pucks and opportunities. He put good pressure on the fore-check and was distributing the puck nicely through the neutral zone. He has to get his shots through on net however from the high slot, or at the very least get the puck in deep off the rush. He was able to take a hit and still hold on to the puck to make a play, opened up nicely in the slot to take a pass and put a good one-timer on from scoring area and has hands and a shiftiness to create a bit of space to put shots on from the slot. He put good pressure on the point, challenging the shooter and displaying a willingness to block shots and was coming back well on the back-check to breakup plays for the opposition. He has to watch the neutral zone turnovers by holding on to the puck for too long.

FINAL SCORE: 4-2 Green Bay Gamblers

Jan 4, 2013, Fargo Force vs. Omaha Lancers (USHL)

OMA # 2, C, Moy, Tyler (2013) Moy kept to a fairly simple game tonight getting the puck in deep on the dump and chase and was finishing his hits on the fore-check. He displayed some pretty good puck skills but needs to get his shots through on net, and was able to make a really good pass to find a man open down low next to the net for a great chance. He showed some really good speed to get a break with some excellent puck protection to draw a penalty shot, but lost a handle on the opportunity that he was given. He was getting in lanes for some really good shot blocking as well in his own end, especially on the penalty kill.

OMA # 3, LW, Worden, Nash (2013) Worden is typically a defenseman but played this game as a winger tonight. He was able to skate the puck into the offensive zone with some really effective puck protection, and coming down low to get to the net and put some good pressure on the puck. He was physical on the fore-check, playing a good dump and chase game finishing his hits hard along the boards. He was able to make a pretty decent stretch pass cross-ice to start the breakout, but still needs to watch some of the turnovers through the neutral zone. He also came back well for some good support in his own end.

OMA # 11, RW, Gaudreau, Matthew (2013) Gaudreau played much better tonight than I have seen so far, and reading the play very well to pick off turnovers in the offensive zone along the boards to walk into the slot for a good shot. He was throwing shots on net from just about everywhere in the offensive zone, and did a very good job finding lanes to skate the puck up into the offensive zone. He was holding the puck in the offensive zone to keep the attack alive, and was distributing the puck well on odd-man rushes to move the puck to good scoring areas. He is calm and patient with the puck, moving it out well on breakout passes, clearing the puck on the penalty kill and coming back to his own end to tie up his man.

OMA # 27, RW, Melanson, Drew (2013) Melanson put some really good pressure and physicality on the fore-check to take the puck off the opposition. He was pressuring the point as well on the penalty kill to force a turnover and clear the puck out of the zone, and coming back well to tie up his man in his own end. He was back-checking well, getting his stick in passing lanes to knock it off the opposition and take away their opportunities, and put a good hard shot on net off the rush. He needs to watch the turnovers in the offensive zone trying to force the pass through the opposition instead of waiting for lanes to open up, and needs to watch the turnovers moving the puck up along the boards as well.

FRG # 8, C, Guertler, Gabe (2013) Guertler protects the puck very well to get the puck into the offensive zone, but skated himself into a corner a few times. He has a nice net-front presence, and was getting open down low next to the net on the power play. He did a good job holding the puck in the offensive zone, and was able to get a nice quick shot off the draw from the high slot. He was getting the puck in deep for the most part, but needs to watch the high risk passes through the neutral zone up the middle, and the turnovers trying to force the puck through the opposition in the offensive zone.

FRG # 10, LW, Dedenbach, Jared (2013) Dedenbach was keeping it simple for the most part just trying to get the puck in deep, but also displayed a bit of creativity along the side boards to get some shots off on net. He made some good little passes to start the breakout with some nice speed, but also had some trouble getting the puck out of his own end along the boards at times. He put some decent pressure on the puck carrier.

FRG # 21, C, Harms, Brendan (2013) Harms made some nice passes to move the puck up out of his own end for breakout, and then drove hard to the net with the stick down, although his skating could use a bit of work. He was battling hard for the puck in front of the net, and cycling it well deep in the offensive zone. He was patient with the puck to hold up at the line and put a shot on from the high slot, but needs to hit the net on the opportunity. He put good pressure on the fore-check, finishing his hits, and made a great pass to find a man streaking in behind the defense for a break as well. He can rush the puck up the ice, and did a really good job opening up in the slot to take a pass and get a shot off on net that almost squeaked through.

FINAL SCORE: 4-1 Fargo Force

Jan 5, 2012, Waterloo Blackhawks vs. Cedar Rapids Roughriders (USHL)

WAT # 3, D, McCoshen, Ian (2013) McCoshen showed some good physicality and battle for the puck in his own end. He hustled back to recover in his own end after turnovers, and was getting the puck in deep into the offensive zone. He made some nice passes to move the puck up on the rush to jump in to join the attack, and was jumping down low as well to provide scoring options in the offensive zone. He is calm with the puck and has a good shot that he can get through from the point, I would still like to see him add some speed to his game. He can hold the offensive line well and clears the puck on the penalty kill as well.

WAT # 29, D, McCrea, Alec (2013) McCrea was reading the play to pick off turnovers through the neutral zone and got in lanes to blocks shots in his own end. He was moving the passes up well o the breakout to start the rush and jumping in to the high slot to put shots on the power play. He stepped into the high slot for some good chances and did a great job closing off his man and taking the body.

WAT # 91, LW, Cammarata, Taylor (2013) Cammarata can distribute the puck and then drives to the net with his stick down. He put some good pressure on the fore-check, was coming in off the wing to put a shot on then picked up his own rebound in the high slot to score the team's 1st goal of the game. He is a smaller forward with some great agility to create some space for himself, and was able to make a nice pass to move the puck to a man in the slot for a good chance from in tight. He did a great job to find a lane and made an excellent cross-ice pass to a man in the slot in the offensive zone and was finding some space to work with in the slot. He made a really nice pass to set up a man in the high slot for a great chance on the power play, and displayed a good element of creativity to get shots off from under pressure. He distributes the puck well and can make that good 1st pass out of the zone to start the breakout. He made a good drop pass to tee-up a one-timer chance, but needs to watch some of the more dangerous passes that he makes that result in turnovers.

WAT # 71, C, Salerno, Brandon (2013) Salerno displayed some good speed off the rush to gain the offensive zone then move the puck to a man streaking don the middle towards the net. He was finding lanes to rush the puck up the ice effectively and was able to make a really nice centering pass to an open man in front of the net for an excellent chance from in tight. He put some good pressure on the fore-check, and was making some nice passes to lead a man for a breakout. He battled to get to the net in the offensive zone and battled hard for pucks as well. He needs to watch some of the turnovers trying to force the pass through the opposition, and still needs to get bigger and stronger as well.

CED # 22, RW, Oglevie, Andrew (2013) Oglevie has some really good speed to his game, pressures the puck carrier well and was nice and physical on the fore-check. He was able to take a long pass at the far blue line to walk in and put a great shot on from a good scoring area to score the team's 2nd goal of the game. He was able to walk into the slot to take a pass and put a quick shot on from in tight. He has some great speed and hustle to get on loose pucks, and the agility to twist away from the opposition then make a great pass to a trailing man in the slot for a great chance.

CED # 26, D, Kuster, Clark (2013) Kuster is a big body defenseman who was getting in the way to block shots in his own end. He holds the offensive line well and cycles it deep into the offensive zone, and was pinching to keep the attack alive, but has some trouble getting his shot through from the point.

CED # 6, C, Mclaughlin, Dylan (2013) Mclaughlin was coming back for support down low in his own end, put some good pressure on the puck carrier an was getting his stick down in lanes. He played more of a dump and chase style and needs to add a bit more creativity to his game.

FINAL SCORE: 6-1 Cedar Rapids

Jan 5, 2012, USNTDP U18 vs. MSOE Raiders

USNT # 7, C, Compher, J.T. (2013) Compher drove hard to the net with his stick down to take a pass for a good chance from in tight. He can protect the puck well along the boards deep in the offensive zone, and showed a really good hustle to get on loose pucks. He battles to take the puck on the fore-check, and showed a pretty effective cycle as well. He put some relentless pressure on the puck on the penalty kill, and has some really nice agility to twist away from the opposition. He also displayed a good element of pressure and physicality on the fore-check.

USNT # 10, RW, Allen, Evan (2013) Allen started this game by making a great cross-ice pass to Kelleher off the rush through the neutral zone to spring him for a break and open the scoring. He displayed some really great quick hands to get the pass down low, then made a great pass to Kelleher again for a one-timer for the team's 3rd goal of the game. He protects the puck very effectively on the cycle along the boards, and was able to make a nice lead pass for a man to gain the offensive zone with speed off the rush. He opened up well to take a pass and score an easy one from the slot for the team's 7th goal of the game, and also made a really good drop pass for a good chance off the rush. He showed some nice patience to stop up at the line to try to move the puck to a man cross-ice, but still needs to watch his turnovers trying to dangle his way through the opposition.

USNT # 12, LW, Lebanc, Kevin (2013) Lebanc showed a really nice hustle and battle for the puck along the boards to force at turnover, and was able to make a really great pass out to the slot to find Motte for the team's 5th goal of the game. He put some really great pressure on the puck carrier on the fore-check, and can protect the puck very well off the rush. He missed the target on a long breakout pass resulting in an icing however.

USNT # 14, RW, Motte, Tyler (2013) Motte put some really nice pressure on the puck carrier deep in the offensive zone, and was getting in lanes to try to block shots from the point. He was able to get open in front of the net to take a pass and put a good shot on to score the team's 5th goal of the game. He has a nice net-front presence, screening the goalie and looking for rebounds and loose pucks. He displayed some really nice speed on the rush but decided to take an outside shot on the odd-man rush instead of moving it to a better scoring area.

USNT # 19, C, Kellher, Tyler (2013) Kelleher started the game by taking a nice pass with speed through the neutral zone to rush the puck into the offensive zone and made a really nice move to open the scoring from in tight. He opened up nicely down low next to the net to put a on-timer on and score the team's 3rd goal of the game as well. He showed some nice speed and pressure on the fore-check and was distributing the puck well off the rush, as he can make some really good little passes to gain the offensive zone with speed. He did a great job opening up in the slot to take a pass and put a shot on from in tight, and made a really nice no-look pass to Allen for the team's 7th goal of the game. He has to watch the turnovers trying to force the puck through the opposition.

USNT # 22, RW, Fasching, Hudson (2013) Fasching puts great pressure on the fore-check and finishes his hits hard along the boards. He had a really nice open ice hit to knock his man over, and showed a really great battle to take the puck and get it out of his own end on the penalty kill. He can get the puck in deep into the offensive zone off the rush, and was also unable to get a shot off under pressure by the opposition.

USNT # 28, LW, Eiserman, Shane (2013) Eiserman displayed some pretty good strength and puck protection on the rush up the ice. He made some nice hits on the puck carrier along the boards to separate his man from the puck. He can make a really good 1st pass out of the zone to start the rush, and was taking low shots on net off the rush to try to generate rebounds for a man driving the net on the far side. He missed the net on a chance off the rush, and has to get his shots through from scoring areas when he gets the opportunities.

USNT # 4, D, Butcher, Will (2013) Butcher was able to take the puck in the neutral zone on a turnover and displayed some really nice patience with the puck. He was getting the puck in deep on the rush, and found some space in the slot to open up and take a pass then put a great shot on to score the team's 2nd goal of the game. He displayed some really good physicality on his man along the boards to separate him from the puck, and had some really good speed to get the puck up out of his own end. He put a great shot on from the point to score short-side for the team's 4th goal of the game, and did a really good job holding the offensive blue line. He was also able to make a great long pass to find a man at the far blue line for a chance off the rush.

FINAL SCORE: 7-2 USNTDP U18

Jan 10, 2012, Owen Sound Attack vs. Niagara IceDogs (OHL)

OWS # 24, D, Bigras, Chris (2013) Bigras was jumping in on the attack, showed some great skating and puck movement then was driving hard to the net. He made some nice passes out of the zone to start the rush, then battled hard for the puck in the offensive zone to keep the attack alive. He was able to skate the puck up the ice on the rush, and protected the puck well to skate the puck out of his own end. He showed some nice agility to twist away from the opposition, and opens up well to provide options in the offensive zone. He got in lanes showing a willingness to block shots, and showed some really good gap control to keep his man to the outside. He had a really nice shot from the point to score the team's 2nd goal of the game and was clearing the puck nicely on the penalty kill.

OWS # 27, RW, Nastasiuk, Zach (2013) Nastasiuk put some nice pressure on the point in his own end, and a nice battle along the boards behind the offensive net. He hustles hard for the puck, and displayed a good willingness to get in lanes to block shots. He is calm with the puck, but still needs to pick up the pace to his game a bit. He showed some good support to come back to his own end to tie-up his man. He made a really great centering pass to find a man in the slot, and made a really nice drive to the net with the puck.

OWS # 18, LW, Pezzetta, Stefano (2013) Pezzetta is a real high energy up-tempo player who competes hard both ways. He has a really good net-front presence, and battles hard for the puck along the boards. He is hard and physical to play against, and showed some really excellent speed on the back-check to take the puck and take away the chance for the opposition. He hustles hard all over the ice and was picking up the puck in the offensive zone for some good chances from the high slot on some good shots.

NIA # 26, LW, Lemmon, Mack (2013) Lemmon puts some really nice pressure on the puck carrier and was getting down in lanes to try to block passes on the penalty kill. He pressures well on the fore-check and finishes his hits along the boards and also had a nice net-front presence in the offensive zone. He had a good wide drive, but then off the drive at times made some no-look passes to no one. He has a good work ethic and battle for the puck, and makes sure that he is a pest to play against. He is aggressive and getting involved after whistles, but at one point fell down in his own end trying to rush the puck out of his own end resulting in a turnover.

NIA # 21, C, Verhaeghe, Carter (2013) Verhaeghe did a pretty good job rushing the puck up the ice on the wide drive, but then was trying to force the pass through the opposition in the offensive zone. He made a really nice saucer pass later on to create some space, and was protecting the puck well in the offensive zone to draw a penalty. He can find lanes to rush the puck up the ice, and drove hard to the net looking for loose pucks and rebounds. He got his stick in lanes to deflect passes out of the way as well.

NIA # 24, RW, Fitzmorris, Mitchell (2013) Fitzmorris is a really high energy up-tempo player who finishes his checks and put some good pressure on the puck carrier. He pressures the point on the penalty kill and was getting down in his own end to block shots. He has some good speed to his game, but still needs to add some size and strength. He followed up the play well to get to the slot on rebounds for chances from in tight, and uses his stick well to challenge the shooter and knock the puck away.

NIA # 9, RW, Maletta, Jordan (2013) Maletta made a great pass to an open man in the slot for a great chance from in tight, and is able to take a hit and make a play to get the puck in deep. He protects the puck well deep in the offensive zone, and has a nice net-front presence. He drove hard down the middle towards the net with his stick down, and drove hard to the net as well right off of an offensive zone faceoff for a great chance from in tight late in the game.

FINAL SCORE: 3-2 Niagara Ice Dogs

Jan 11, 2012, Omaha Lancers vs. Dubuque Fighting Saints (USHL)

OMH # 2, C, Moy, Tyler (2013) Moy is a defensive forward who was putting some good pressure on the point on the penalty kill, and getting in lanes trying to block passes. He came back for some good support in his own end and was communicating well with his teammates. He was blocking shots from the point and came down low to keep his man from getting to the net. He put good pressure on the puck carrier and had a great wide drive but decided to take a weak long outside shot off the rush.

OMH # 11, RW, Gaudreau, Matthew (2013) Gaudreau put some good pressure on the puck carrier and battled to get the puck into the offensive zone. He was putting shots on from just about everywhere in the offensive zone, and came back to his own end to provide some good support and get in lanes to tip the puck out of the way. He needs to watch the turnovers trying to skate the puck up through the neutral zone, and he has to watch them as well on long passes up through the middle of the ice. He didn't display a great element of creativity as he was just dumping the puck to get it in deep, and has to hit the net on chances off the rush as well.

OMH # 27, LW, Melanson, Drew (2013) Melanson has some really good speed to his game and hustles hard to get on loose pucks. He showed great work ethic and hustle to put pressure on the puck, and is able to get the puck in deep off rushes. He was finishing his hits on the puck carrier along the boards, but I would like to see a bit more battle for the puck along the boards.

OMH # 3, D, Worden, Nash (2013) Worden is a pretty big body defenseman who has some decent skating and can skate the puck up on the rush and get it in deep into the offensive zone. He played with a pretty good gap control to force the opposition to dump the puck in behind him, and has a hard shot from the point but needs to get it on net. There were also times where he looked a little lost to his role in his own end.

DUB # 9, RW, Malone, Seamus (2014) Malone did a really nice job finding a lane off the rush to move the puck across for a great assist on the team's 2nd goal of the game. He has pretty nice hands, agility and cycle deep in the offensive zone and finished off the play with a great pass to find a man open in front of the net for a great chance in tight on the power play. He was excellent at finding space and opening up to get great shots off from the slot. He opened up on the rush as well to put shots on from scoring positions, and just needs to watch some of the turnovers through the neutral zone. He was also able to pick off neutral zone turnovers but needs to make his decisions with the puck quicker.

DUB # 4, D, Downing, Michael (2013) Downing can make a good 1st pass out of the zone to start the rush, and is able to step up through the neutral zone to pick off a turnover. He showed some good physicality along the boards in his own end, but needs to watch some of the turnovers along the boards trying to move the puck up out of his zone. He also needs to watch some of the turnovers in the offensive zone trying to force the pass through the opposition, and has to try to hit the net on shots from the point.

DUB # 7, D, Ford, Keegan (2014) Ford is calm with the puck and had a really nice hard back-check to close off the opposition's opportunity. He can jump in on the pinch to keep the attack alive, and was also willing to come down into the high slot to provide scoring options. He can move the puck up out of the zone to start the rush, and was willing to come down low to the net on the power play to get a great chance from in tight. He is patient with the puck and is able to get it through on net from the point, and was jumping up on the rush to get the puck in deep into the offensive zone. He needs to watch some of the turnovers trying to move the puck up out of his own end along the boards.

FINAL SCORE: 5-3 Dubuque Fighting Saints

January 11th, 2013. London Knights vs. Ottawa 67's

OTT#20 F Sean Monahan (2013 Late 94). Monahan was the lone bright spot for a greatly overmatched 67 squad in this game. Sean showed his elite offensive talents in the offensive zone winning puck battles and getting into strong scoring positions with ease. He is strong and using his body to shield the puck coming off the cycle and uses solid footwork to take strong steps towards the net. Seems to always know where the puck is going and works hard to find open lanes to the net. He showed strong resilience and constantly battled to the last whistle when the 67's were clearly out of the game. Showed solid defensive positioning and is just as strong away from the puck as he is with it. Sean showcased his scoring sense working hard in front of the net to finish his chances.

LDN#16 F Max Domi (2013). Domi stood out with a strong offensive performance in this game. He displayed strong skating ability and good speed constantly beating defenders both wide and up the middle. Max displays confidence when skating with the puck and is not afraid to carry through traffic in the neutral zone before sparking the offensive attack. He shows creativity with the puck in the offensive zone and uses shiftiness along with his strong skating to constantly keep defenders guessing. Max utilized his strong wrist shot and vision to score two nifty goals for the Knights finishing off some nice passing plays from his linemates. Domi had a strong game as a playmaker as well, connecting with linemates for a number of scoring opportunities as well as putting pucks on net for good rebound opportunities.

LDN#53 F Bo Horvat (2013). Bo was excellent for the Knights in this game, showcasing improved skating ability by beating defenders to the puck and displaying quick bursts of acceleration once gaining control of the puck. He is an underrated playmaker and showed flashes of great vision in this game with numerous passes through traffic setting his linemates up in great scoring positions. Horvat drives the net with the puck and was not afraid to get into the corners or front of the net to battle for pucks. He also displayed a strong finishing ability beating the 67's goaltender with a quick release wrist shot.

LDN#81 F Remi Elie (2013). Remi also had a strong game for the Knights, getting in strong on the fore check forcing defenders to turn over pucks and make quick decisions that benefitted the Knights. Elie is a solid skater and is good at getting pucks deep and battling in the corners and along the half wall to gain puck possession. He also displays an extremely underrated set of offensive tools, scoring a nice goal with a heavy wrist shot in space. If he was on a club that was not as deep as the Knights he would find himself on a much higher line. Remi never stops moving his feet and looks like a professional with the little things he does with and without the puck. He also is responsible in the defensive end and works hard to get himself into shooting lanes on the penalty kill.

Jan 12, 2013, Vancouver Giants vs. Kelowna Rockets (WHL)

VAN#8 LD, Morrison, Tyler(2014) Played a good game for Vancouver today. Received limited minutes on the third pairing, but Morrison showed some good hockey sense throughout the game to jump into the play and join the rush a number of times. A decent skater who will need to work on all areas of his mobility to compensate for his smaller stature. Also needs to work on all areas of his defensive game. Not very strong along the boards or in front of the net. He also looked nervous out on the ice, mishandling the puck a couple of times and taking too long to do something with the puck. Made a few bad outlet passes as well.
VAN#27 RW, Houck, Jackson(2013) Had a good productive game offensively tonight. Was moved from the half wall to the front of the net on the power play and looked so much more comfortable. Scored two goals by banging home rebounds. Was more energized and used his physical game to his advantage. Skating is still a bit of an issue and is not a elite offensive player by any means, but got his job done tonight with hustle .

VAN#44 LD, Geertsen, Mason(2013) Big, physical defenseman had a good game tonight. Did not make any huge glaring mistakes out on the ice and limited his turnovers. Logged a ton of ice time in all situations of the game, and definitely looks much more fluid out there in his own end. Not a great puck mover on the PP, but it's an indication of the lack of talent Vancouver has this season. An above average skater for his size, who compensates his lack of mobility with good positioning. Was hard to play against along the boards, and made a nice blocked shot on the PK by sliding over to block a one timer.

KEL#2 RD, Lees, Jesse(2013) Offensive defenseman who really struggled all night long. Definitely a good puck mover and showed some skills in the offensive zone, but had a difficult time in his own end or whenever he did not have the puck. One example is on the transition, it was a 1 on 1 situation and the opponent was skating down the wing, but for some reason Lees pivoted towards the slot and held the lane down the middle instead of closing the gap and funneling the opponent towards the boards to stop him at his tracks, which resulted in a great scoring chance for Vancouver. He was consistently late coming off the wall to cover the slot, and ran around clueless in his own zone consistently, which resulted in a number of Vancouver goals.

KEL#4 RD, Bowey, Madison(2013) Dynamic player who was one of the best players for Kelowna tonight. He made very good passes out of the zone, and if he did not see a play, he would show off his elite skating abilities and skate the puck out himself and start the attack. He made a few risky plays with the puck that needs to cut those out of his game. Was solid on the power play tonight. Would have liked to see him shoot more, but when he did take a shot he missed the net a couple times. Needs to work on velocity and accuracy of his shots. Made a number of good passes to display good vision. Was a step ahead of teammates at times, as he located an open lane back door a few times throughout the game and made some great passes cross ice, but his teammates just were not in proper position to take advantage of a good scoring chance. Defensively, he had a great active stick, and showed good angling techniques all game long. He covered for his defense partners a number of times throughout the game. Most memorable event in his game was when he took a really bad hit from behind, and I expected him to get up angrily and retaliate, but instead he just got up, gave the opponent a few words and just quickly skated to the bench, in a game that they were winning 3-2. Very good composure and discipline in an event where majority of players his age would have taken a bad penalty.

Scouts Notes: Kelowna scored 2 goals in 2 minutes to start the game, but quickly faded away and did not play very hard other than a few players. Madison Bowey really impressed tonight in all areas of the game. 2014 eligible forwards Rourke Chartier and Tyson Baillie were quiet for most of the game, but did have some good moments in the offensive zone with their offensive abilities. Just did not put together a full game effort tonight. Jackson Houck showed that he belongs in front of the net to be effective and not along the walls to try to create plays for Vancouver. Was much more effective tonight with that change in his game than the last few months where he was depended on to be the catalyst in the offensive zone.

FINAL SCORE: 4-3(OT) KEL

January 12, 2013, Ottawa 67's @ Sarnia Sting (OHL)

OTT #5 RD Desautels, Matthieu (2013) - Matthieu showed a couple good defensive plays to break up offensive chances. His skating ability is considered average.

OTT #11 LD Vlajkov, Michael (2013) - Vlajkov shows basic puck moving abilities. He has a cannon of a point shot. The speed he reaches while skating is average at best but his quickness and backwards skating are still below average. He's improved slightly but it's still not where he needs to be as a potential NHL prospect.

OTT #20 LC Monahan, Sean (2013) - Sean definitely had an off game, and the 67's as they commonly do went the way of Monahan's play. He looked really tired right off the start of the game. He turned the puck over far too much in this match-up. He was also shooting the puck from the perimeter when he got the chance. He did show good positioning on the power play and displayed his vision with passes. However it looked like he just skated a marathon earlier in the day and just couldn't seem to get it going. The majority of our viewings of Sean have been very good, so we think this is worth overlooking as long as this doesn't become a trend.

OTT #21 LD Middleton, Jacob (2014) - Jacob skates very well for his size. He sticks with his man well in one on one situations. He also shows puck rushing ability. Jacob works hard and won battles in all three zones. He even showed the ability to drop the gloves. He squared off against Alex Renaud and took a few good shots early, but hung in there and eventually landed the TKO punch.

OTT #22 RW Urbanic, John (2014) - Urbanic had an excellent game tonight and was a huge factor on the 67's penalty kill. John always seemed to have ideal positioning while killing penalties. He was able to intercept passes and clear the zone as well as use these turnovers to gain short handed scoring chances. At one point he got taken down on the breakaway. He showed good moves and a good shot but couldn't score. In 5 on 5 action Urbanic displayed solid physical play. He was also well positioned in the offensive zone resulting in a couple scoring chances. His skating is slightly above average at this point.

OTT #26 RC Salituro, Dante (2015) - Salituro showed some good moves on defenders to beat them. He also possesses a good wrist shot which he used to score Ottawa's first goal of the game.

OTT #33 LW Kuptsov, Sergey (2013) - Sergey had a pretty good game tonight. He won some battles against some bigger defensemen and was able to create scoring chances early on. He displayed good passing ability and made some quick decisions with the puck to keep the play going in the offensive zone. His skating still appears to be an issue moving forward.

SAR #5 RD Hore, Tyler (2014) - Tyler protects the puck surprisingly well when he rushes the puck up the ice. He's not the quickest player but he gets it done with his size and puck control. He was strong on the penalty kill tonight clearing the zone regularly.

SAR #11 RW Hargrave, Brett (2014) - Hargrave drove hard to the net all game long on the rush with his stick on the ice. Good positioning in the offensive zone to get his shot off. Brett is doing better along the wall in battles.

SAR #17 LW Renaud, Alexandre (2014) - Renaud was willing to drop the gloves against the older Middleton. He delivered some good shots and faired well until he got dropped at the end of the fight.

SAR #21 LC Nikandrov, Daniel (2013) - Nikandrov dominated in the faceoff circle all night long. This was primarily against Monahan as he was sent to shutdown his line all night.

SAR #88 LW Addesi, Jordan (2014) - Jordan provided a good work ethic all game long. He regularly finished his hits and won battles.

Scouts Notes: Sarnia hosted Ottawa in the middle of their western road swing and controlled this game from start to finish. Sarnia jumped out to an early 2-0 lead then dominated the second period leading in shots 16-3 and lead 4-0 after 40 minutes. Thanks in part to Nikolay Goldobin (2014) who made a great play to set up Sarnia's fourth goal. Sarnia would eventually escape with a 5-1 victory.

Jan 13, 2013. Guelph Storm vs. Kingston Frontenacs (OHL)

GUE#7 D Ben Harpur (2013). Ben had a solid game on the Storm blue line in this matchup. Ben showed strong puck skills skating along the blue line in the offensive zone and was generally effective at getting shots through towards the net, although would benefit from getting his shot off a little quicker. Ben used solid footwork and back skating ability to keep defenders to the outside on the majority of rushes he faced in this game. Ben was especially effective at holding the defensive line in the offensive zone, keeping a number of pucks in play and not giving opposing forwards room to skate the puck out. Ben did occasionally get caught standing around in the defensive zone, and against a stronger opponent this could be a bigger problem.

GUE#11 F Jason Dickinson (2013). Jason was especially effective showcasing his offensive skills in this game. Smooth skating ability allows him to sometimes get lost in the offensive zone and then all of the sudden the puck is on his stick in an open lane to the net. Jason had a strong drive to the net on the power play and showed some good puck skills in tight beating a defender with a nice deke. Jason also was very strong coming off the half wall before deciding to either move the puck to an open teammate or put a strong shot on net. This type of offensive contribution is something that Jason should strive to do with more consistency. Physicality was also a strong aspect of Jason's game in this matchup and he caught two unsuspecting Frontenac forwards with strong hits along the boards and in the neutral zone.

GUE#19 F Hunter Garlent (2013). Hunter had an average game against the Frontenac. Needs to work on his skills in the face-off circle as his numbers were below average in this game. Hunter needs to work to consistently make strong reads and try to cut down on forcing passes into tight locations when other lanes are open. Hunter showed some strong offensive skill in the offensive zone, and scored a goal on a beautifully tipped point shot. Hunter is a pesky water bug type skater and is constantly zipping all over the ice. This is effective because he is upon opposing defenseman deceptively quick, but sometimes this puts him out of position if the defender can make a strong read.

KGN#17 F Ryan Kujawinski (2013). Ryan had a strong game for the Frontenacs in this matchup. Scored a nice rebound goal early in the game, finding the puck in goal mouth scramble towards the side of the net. Ryan showed strong offensive instincts working with linemates to generate a number of quality offensive chances. Showcased solid vision and a strong passing ability to jump start these offensive chances. Ryan was very strong in the face-off circle rarely losing a draw and constantly battling to win the puck when the draw was a tie. Did not showcase an elite level of speed, and would be more effective cutting to the net if he could beat defenders consistently wide.

KGN#95 F Sam Povorozniouk (2013). Sam had a really strong game in the offensive zone for the Frontenac. Seemed to be able to slip around defenders and constantly found himself in open positions with great scoring opportunities. Showcased good instincts by reading his linemates well and knowing where to set up in front of the net. Was unable to finish any of his chances and with an improved scoring touch would have had at least two goals in this game. Needs to work on his positioning in the defensive zone, and needs to be stronger along the wall chipping out pucks with consistency.

January 13, 2013, Shawinigan Cataractes @ Rimouski Oceanic (QMJHL)

Shawinigan
#2 Raphael Maheux, Def (2014): Maheux got a regular shift at even-strength, moved the puck well out his zone and helped the Cataractes' transition game. Made a great play blocking the stick of Michael Joly who had a great scoring chance at the side of the net. However, he has slow feet and will need to work on that as he continue to progress.

#8 Patrick Koys, LW (2014): Koys has been hyped a lot the last couple of years but judging from this game it was all hype, even though he scored a goal. He was not noticeable at all tonight. His goal was scored without him getting a shot on net, as he happened to be going to the net and his teammate's shot hit him in the leg to go behind the Rimouski goaltender. There is a lot of work left to be done with his skating and on his shot. Also need to get a hell of lot stronger to compete more.

#24 Dylan Labbé, Def (2013): Labbé showed some good and bad things in this game. The good: his puck movement ability and lack of shyness joining the rush. The not-so-good: by joining the rush he got caught a couple of times. However, he played on his off side all game long, and it didn't seem to bother him.

Rimouski

#3 Jan Kostalek, Def (2013): Kostalek doesn't play many bad games. He was solid once again for the Océanic, as he played with Kevin Gagné. One has to love his compete level when he battles in the corner. Really tough to beat one-on-one, doesn't get beat often. Didn't generate a lot of offense as he let his even-strength partner Gagné do this job. Was also not used on the power play, but was used regularly on the PK. Does a nice job on the PK, getting in shooting lanes, and blocking shots.

#15 Anthony DeLuca, LW (2013): DeLuca played on a line with veterans J- F Plante and Alexandre Lavoie. Opened the scoring by taking a pass in the neutral zone, trying to beat a defenseman on the outside but took a 180 degree turn instead to fire a quick wrist shot around the faceoff circle to beat the Shawinigan goaltender. As he gets more involved in the play, I see that his play has improved from earlier viewings. Threw a big hit in the 3rd period on the forecheck. Deluca may be only 5'9", but is over 200 lbs.

#23 Frederik Gauthier, C (2013): Gauthier was very good in every facet of this game. He finished with 2 assists, backchecked hard as usual to help his defensemen out and won some key faceoffs at the end of the game to preserve a one-goal lead. Played on the top line with Peter Trainor and Anthony Beauvillier and used his size well today, winning positions in front of the net and protecting the puck. He had a nice chemistry with Francis Beauvillier, finding him twice for goals in this game. The first one was after a turnover in the offensive zone leading to a 2-on-0 and all Gauthier had to do was give the puck to Beauvillier for an easy goal. On the 2nd goal, Gauthier set up Beauvillier in the slot after recovering a puck along the boards.

#24 Michael Joly, RW (2013): Joly was quiet in the first period but was superb in the 2nd & 3rd periods. Was a constant threat on the Rimouski 3rd line. Although he's not the biggest guy, he does a pretty decent job to protect the puck; on one occasion he came out of the corner with it and used his size to protect it, taking a shot on net while doing a 180. He is not afraid, either, as he threw a great hit in the 3rd period. Missed a ton of scoring chances in this game, as his line was everywhere in the 2nd & 3rd period. Joly might not get drafted because of his size and speed, but he had amazing hands. Should score a lot of points at the QMJHL level.

#55 Samuel Morin, Def (2013): Morin played with Ryan MacKinnon at even strength & Maxime Gravel on the Oceanic's 2nd PP unit. His passing game was on and off today, as he did miss a lot of passes. Made a horrid pass late in the 3rd period to his D-partner in the offensive zone, which almost caused a turnover and a breakaway. Played a strong physical game with a couple of good hits and did a good job of clearing the front of the net. Has a long reach and he likes to use his stick to break play or passes.

#64 Maxime Gravel, Def (2013): The rookie blueliner was paired with team captain Casey Babineau, which also meant Gravel was playing on his wrong side. Also got 2nd PP unit time with Samuel Morin, but didn't do anything to stand in this game both offensively and defensively. He needs to work on the accuracy of his shots and passes as they were off today. Quick feet.

Jan 16, 2013, Vancouver Giants vs. Tri-City Americans (WHL)

VAN#8 LD, Morrison, Tyler(2014) Had a very poor game tonight, especially without the puck. At the beginning of the game, he threw the puck right up the slot to an opponent, who scored as a result. He had a tough time handling the rush with his poor positioning and could not keep opponents to the outside. He constantly ran around his own zone and put himself in bad positions around the ice. He needs to get stronger on his skates and on the puck. He was too soft along the walls.

VAN#29 RD, Zalitach, Reid(2014) Like most of his teammates, struggled all game long. Generally good with the puck, but struggled with making passes throughout the night. He got exposed tonight in his own zone, as he had a tough time reading the play and did not have a good stick at all. One notable play was on a controlled breakout by Tri-City, they had a winger cut to the middle and was given a perfect pass and went right by Zalitach and scored. Showed very poor awareness out on the ice all night long.

VAN#44 LD, Geertsen, Mason(2013) Big defenseman had a bad game tonight. Really struggled with the speed of some of the forwards on Tri-City. Got deked out badly on a goals against and showed his poor lateral movement. He played a physical game, but just was not much of a factor. With the puck, Geertsen mismanaged it a few times by holding onto it for too long and getting it stripped away from him. He needed to make better decisions with the puck as well.

TRI#26 RW, Williams, Brian(2013) Had a great start to the game with his line mates and continued to build on that momentum for much of that game until about half way through the third period. He scored a minute into the game by picking up a bad outlet pass and sniping it home from the top of the circle. Williams was quite aggressive on the rush all night long and consistently tried to stickhandle through opponents. He had mixed results, but did show off above average hands and speed. Was shifty along the walls, and defenders had a tough time trying to contain him.

TRI#27 LC, Rankin, Connor(2013) Centre had a good game tonight in the offensive zone. Was able to create a ton of chances with his line mates by hard work and speed. Needs to work on protecting the puck better along the walls. A good skater, but needs to improve his agility and overall quickness. Rankin showed off some good passing abilities and vision off the rush and along the walls. He made quick decisions with the puck and looked poised. Rankin did not look as great in his own zone. He did a good job to back check on rushes, but took a penalty in the first period because he was on the wrong side of the play. In the third, he looked absolutely lost in the slot down low, which resulted in a goals against.

TRI#39 LW, Bowles, Parker(2013) Winger had a very good game for Tri-City tonight. Scored a highlight reel goal in the first period by dancing around Mason Geertsen with his speed and stickhandling abilities. He looked to have gained a lot of confidence off of that play and displayed a lot of energy all game long. He is not very fast, but he has the ability to quick change directions. He also finished off a 2 on 1 play with a good one timer. Bowles needs to get much stronger along the boards, and learn to use his body to protect the puck better.

SCOUT'S NOTES: This was a bad game to watch overall. Tri-City really dominated the game, and Vancouver was not read to play at all. Every player on the Giants looked defeated and were not able to generate much offense other than in the third period when the Americans decided to take the rest of the night off. Mason Geertsen showed that if he is not in proper position on the rush defensively, he will get burned consistently by speed. Definitely needs to work on his lateral mobility. The line of Parker Bowles, Connor Rankin and Brian Williams had a great game. They were able to generate a lot of offense consistently, but they were also handed those opportunities on a silver platter.

FINAL SCORE: 9-5 TRI

Jan 16, 2013, Team Cherry vs. Team Orr (CHL Top Prospects Game)

ORR # 3, D, Jones, Seth (2013) Jones jumped up on the rush early on to take a pass in the slot and put a shot on, which the team scored on the rebound for the 1st goal of the game. He was reading the play extremely well to pick off turnovers in the offensive zone, and was leading the rush down low, following up the play and going to the net for chances in tight. He picked off turnovers in his own end to rush the puck up the ice with speed, displayed some nice hands to get around the opposition, move the puck up and jumped in on the attack. He did a good job forcing his man to the outside and playing him physically along the boards, and used his stick really well to deflect pucks out of the way.

ORR # 73, RW, Erne, Adam (2013) Erne followed up the play early in the offensive zone to score the team's 1st goal of the game. He displayed some really nice chemistry with Dauphin all night, which was most evident on an incredible wide drive getting past the defensemen and made an excellent pass to find Dauphin for a great chance. He made some nice passes up to start the breakout off the rush, and made a great pass as well off the rush to find a man crashing the net for a great chance from in tight. He was able to put a great hard shot on net off the rush, and displayed some really excellent hands at time playing at a real high tempo. There was another play that he exhibited some incredible speed off the wing to blow by a defenseman and then cut in towards the net with a wide drive for an excellent chance.

ORR # 14, C, Dauphin, Laurent (2013) Dauphin was a player who really jumped out at me in this game right off the hop when he showed some good hands on a wide drive and made a great pass to find Jones in the slot for his team to open the scoring of the game. He was driving to the net with his stick down to take a pass off the rush for a great chance from in tight, and was able to just take the puck in the neutral zone and walk into the slot with ease to score the team's 2nd goal of the game. He found space in the slot to open up and put a great shot on net off the one-timer, and was also able to work the puck under pressure. He got open off the rush and took a pass from Erne but just hit the post on the opportunity. He put good pressure on the puck carrier on the penalty kill, but needs to watch some of the neutral zone turnovers.

ORR # 20, C, Monahan, Sean (2013) Monahan was not very noticeable whatsoever in the 1st period, but I felt he started off the 2nd period with more of a jump to his game. He was forcing turnovers in the offensive zone and got to the slot with lots of time and space to put shots on net. He was coming back to his own end for some good support and was finishing his hits along the boards. He made a really nice pass up through the neutral zone to gain the offensive zone with speed and drove hard to the net with his stick down looking for the rebound for an excellent chance from in tight. He was also putting some good pressure on the puck carrier.

ORR # 65, D, Zadorov, Nikita (2013) Zadorov was just a huge, physical beast in this game playing physical all over the ice with some real big hits and clearing the front of his net making it a tough place to stand. At times he was a bit over-aggressive stepping up to make the hit putting himself a bit out of position though and needs to watch that he isn't taking penalties as well. He was able to make some good breakout passes, and was jumping up to join the attack off the rush at times as well. He did a really good job forcing his man to the outside, closing him off along the boards and getting in lanes to take the puck away on passes.

CHR # 22, C, Mackinnon, Nathan (2013) Mackinnon got open early on in the high slot to open up, take passes and put some good shots on net. He has some nice moves and agility to create some space for himself in the neutral zone and has some really good strength and puck protection on the rush. He can create room with all his agility, and made a really nice pass to a man in the slot on the power play for a great chance but was stopped at point blank. He had a good net-front presence and displayed some aggression getting in battles in front of the net, and displayed some nice support coming back to his own end using his stick to check the puck off the opposition. He can move the puck down low and drive to the slot, and made a really incredible end-to-end rush with speed displaying excellent hands to drive the puck towards the net late in this game. It wasn't all good for MacKinnon in this game as he turned the puck over a few times in the neutral zone, and missed his target on some breakout passes as well. He also has to hit the net on his shots off the rush.

CHR # 27, LW, Drouin, Jonathan (2013) Drouin had a bit of trouble in this game, mishandling the puck a few times and made some high risk passes through the neutral zone that resulted in turnovers. He did display some really nice hands and patience with the puck to fake a shot and walk into the slot for a nice chance, and made some nice chip plays to start the breakout. He was able to walk into the slot on the power play and could find some lanes for cross-ice passes on the power play. He took the puck on a great pass to make a move and get by the defenseman and made an excellent pass through the crease for Hartman in tight for a really nice opportunity. At times however in this game he was trying to overpass the puck instead of shooting it when he had some good opportunities from scoring areas.

CHR # 4, D, Subban, Jordan (2013) Tonight was the tale of two games for Subban. One was his offensive capabilities and the ability to move the puck effectively, and the other his defensive lapses. Starting with the good, he showed some really good speed jumping up on the rush to get to the net for a good chance from in tight on a nice shot, and made a really great pass to spot an open man down low next to the net. He has some really nice agility and shiftiness to his game and can twist away from the opposition with ease. He had a nice one-timer shot from the point but needs to hit the net on his chances. He was jumping in on the rush down low to get to the net, but was caught on the pinch giving the opposition a 2-on-1 chance the other way. He also gave Dauphin a bit too much space to work with in the slot giving him a clear shot on net which he scored on. He was soft on the puck at times, and also let his man walk around him too easily as well, and needs to watch some of the turnovers in the offensive zone.

FINAL SCORE: 3-0 Team Orr

Jan 18, 2013, P.E.I. Rocket vs. Baie-Comeau Drakkar (QMJHL)

PEI # 27, D, Graves, Ryan (2013) Graves got in lanes to breakup passes and take away the puck from the opposition in his own end. He read the play in the neutral zone to pick off turnovers then moved the puck in deep into the offensive zone. He was able to protect the puck from the opposition's pressure and then move it up out of the zone to start the breakout. He needs to get the puck out of the zone on his clearing attempt opportunities.

BAI # 10, C, Gregoire, Jeremy (2013) Gregoire put some good pressure on the fore-check and played with an element of physicality. He was battling hard to get to the net from behind for a good shot from in tight. He made a nice give and go play in the offensive zone to get to the side of the net to put a good shot on, and brought a nice net-front presence in the offensive zone. He got a good cycle going in deep then got to the front of the net to provide scoring options for his teammates. He was distributing the puck well on the rush into the offensive zone and was forcing turnovers by pressuring the puck carrier.

BAI # 13, LW, Boudreau, Paquin (2013) Boudreau got a good cycle going in deep in the offensive zone and had some nice speed on the rush to drive the puck wide. He hustled really well for loose pucks, put good pressure on the puck carrier on the fore-check, and was able to get the puck out front for a man driving to the net. He distributed the puck really well on the rush into the offensive zone with speed but was taking lots of long outside shots on the rush.

BAI # 26, RW, Ranger, Alexandre (2013) Ranger got the puck in deep on some pretty simple dump-in plays and was putting good pressure on the point to get in lanes and block shots in his own end. He battled really well for loose pucks but was playing on the perimeter for the most part in the offensive zone then trying to flutter passes through rather than trying to drive the puck to the net. He needs to be stronger on the puck along the boards and has to get the puck out of the zone on his clearing attempts. He also has to watch the turnovers along the boards trying to move the puck up to start the breakout.

BAI # 73, RW, Zykov, Valentin (2013) Zykov went to the net looking for loose pucks and rebounds and he opened up really well in the high slot to take a pass and put a good shot on off the rush. He got right in front of the net to the slot for some good shots and showed fantastic hands to get around defenders on the rush then dish the puck off to a man beside the net for a goal. He got to the front of the net and battled for territory and was also battling well for the puck along the boards. He went to the net with his stick down and got to the front of the net to pick up a rebound and score from in tight. He made a really good wrap-around attempt to jam the puck in for a good opportunity in tight and he was able to skate the puck up the ice end to end with some nice moves to gain the offensive zone. He needs to watch the turnovers in the offensive zone trying to dangle his way through the opposition and also can't try to force passes through either.

FINAL SCORE: 3-2 Baie Comeau Drakkar

Jan 18, 2013, Halifax Mooseheads vs. Quebec Remparts (QMJHL)

HAL # 22, C, MacKinnon, Nathan (2013) MacKinnon opened up well in the high slot to take a pass and put a one-timer on net. He displayed some great strength and puck protection and was able to make a really great cross-ice pass in the offensive zone to find an open man off the rush for a good chance. He got a great cycle going in the offensive zone and opened up well in the slot off the rush to score on a one-timer. He made an excellent pass to spring a man into the offensive zone with speed.

HAL # 27, LW, Drouin, Jonathan (2013) Drouin has excellent agility with the puck to twist away from the opposition's pressure and was able to make a really nice pass to set-up a one-timer from the high slot. He has some fantastic speed, is able to distribute the puck really well on his rush up the ice and was able to use his hands and agility to get to the slot to put shots on net. He was able to make a good pass on the rush to find a man driving hard to the net for a tap-in goal and also made a nice pass to set-up a one-timer goal from the point.

HAL # 24, D, Murphy, Matt (2013) Murphy was able to make a great breakout pass to start the breakout and lead a man into the offensive zone with some good speed, however did miss his target on a few passes. He closed the gap well on the opposition, then used his stick to knock the puck free and had a big open ice hit to knock his man over. He came down low into the slot on the power play to provide scoring options in tight and opened up well to take a pass and put a good shot on from the slot. He was able to get a cycle going in deep in the offensive zone and made a great cross-ice pass in the offensive zone to find an open man driving hard to the net. He shot the puck into a shin pad of the opposition from the point which allowed them to rush the puck back up the ice with speed, however he hustled hard to recover and knock the puck from the opposition.

HAL # 31, G, Fucale, Zachary (2013) Fucale made lot's of big saves early on both from shots from the slot and dekes in tight. He was able to follow the puck on a pass across to stop a one-timer as well and was coming to the top of his crease to challenge the shooter. He was directing rebounds behind him to the corner and had a really strong push across to make a huge save on a deke attempt on a breakaway. He did a good job making a save from the point to ensure there was no rebound and made a good save on a one-timer but then couldn't handle the rebound and the opposition scored.

QUE # 10, LW, Duclair, Anthony (2013) Duclair displayed nice speed and quickness with the puck to rush it up the ice, distributing it well. He had some great agility and moves to get to the slot for an excellent shot on net and was able to rush the puck up end-to-end to get to the slot for a shot opportunity. He made a great drop-pass on the rush to set up a man in the slot with time and space for a good opportunity and used his stick well to poke the puck loose from the opposition. He had some fantastic speed on the wide drive then made a good centering pass for a man driving hard to the net and he used some really nice quick hands to get around the opposition. He has really nice hands but has to watch the turnovers on missed target passes.

QUE # 73, RW, Erne, Adam (2013) Erne had a pretty good hustle and battle for loose pucks and was able to make a nice pass to find a man driving hard to the net. He played the puck carrier with an element of physicality and displayed good speed and puck protection on the wide drive into the offensive zone. He has some dynamic speed and hands to blow by defenders wide then cuts towards the net for a good shot attempt. He is able to cycle the puck well but needs to protect the puck a bit more effectively so that it is not knocked off him so easily.

QUE # 91, C, Boivin, Alexandre (2013) Boivin played the puck carrier with an element of physicality along the wall and put some nice speed and pressure on the fore-check. He made a nice pass out of the zone to lead the breakout and was finishing his hits along the boards well. He has to watch the turnovers forcing passes through the opposition.

QUE # 94, RW, Sorensen, Nick (2013) Sorensen protected the puck well along the wall and showed great agility with the puck to twist from the opposition's pressure. He put some good pressure on the puck carrier and used his stick well to knock the puck away from them. He showed great speed and hands on the wide drive to get in deep with the puck and was driving hard to the net with his stick down for chances in tight. He was taking long outside shots on the odd-man rush opportunity.

FINAL SCORE: 11-2 Halifax Mooseheads

Jan 18, 2013, Vancouver Giants vs. Victoria Royals (WHL)

VAN#1 G, Lee, Payton(2014) Lee looked quite shaky in this game, and gave up a few soft goals. It seems that his confidence is starting to go downhill because he has not looked the same for the last couple of weeks. He gets very little help from his teammates on most nights, but tonight he failed to keep his team in the game. The biggest indication of that was his glove hand. Lee has one of the best glove hand in the league, but he did not catch the puck cleanly and confidently a few times tonight as he usually does. He was beaten down low on average shots tonight, and his body language looked like he was defeated.

VAN#44 LD, Geertsen, Mason(2013) Had a much better performance tonight than his previous game. He was in better position in the defensive zone and off the rush to keep opponents to the outside and to not get beat to the net because of his lack of foot speed. Geertsen showed a lot of energy consistently, which at times was detrimental to his game. He tried to join the rush a couple of times, and really was a non factor. He would get the puck on a 3 on 2 down the wing, and did not make good decisions with it at all which resulted in turnovers and an odd man rush going the other way. He needs to save that energy for the defensive zone to punish opponents with his body checks.

VIC#2 LD, Hicketts, Joe(2014) Smooth skating defenseman had a good game tonight, particularly in his own zone. Hicketts is a good skater with good speed, but his strength is his ability to use his edges to turn away from opponents and go around opponents, and he was able to show off that skill consistently throughout the game. He was very poised with the puck tonight and did not panic, but did not accomplish much whenever he tried to carry the puck himself. He has an average shot from the point that definitely needs to be improved. He was very good in his own end tonight with his angling skills and active stick. His size was detrimental to tonight however. He was easily knocked off the puck consistently, and he was quite weak along the boards. Hicketts will need to be an elite defenseman in all other areas of his game if he will have any chance of playing as a pro one day.

VIC#5 LD, Kanzig, Keegan(2013) Big defenseman who had a quiet night tonight. He was not particularly noticeable in his own end other than when he had to try to get from point A to point B. A below average skater in all aspects. He looked quite stiff and awkward whenever he tried to get around the ice. He gave big gaps on the rush to ensure that he does not get burned by speed. He showed some mean streak tonight, but was not much of a factor. Kanzig needs to really improve his play with the puck, specifically his outlet passes and decision making. He made a couple of 5 foot passes that were more like rockets, which went all the way down the ice for an icing.

Scouts Notes: This game started off a little slow with a number of turnovers back and forth. Victoria was able to get a few soft goals past Payton Lee, and as a result Vancouver was never really able to generate much of a come back. Tyler Soy made a good impression tonight. He was Victoria's first round draft pick last year and showed some good hands, speed and work ethic. Impressed with his play in the defensive zone. He stuck to his man well, and used his stick quite effectively. He was rewarded with a goal in the last minute of the third period. Brett Kulak had one of his better games of the year tonight. He has developed his stickhandling abilities and was able to create a couple of good chances in the offensive zone. Still needs to work on his speed.

FINAL SCORE: 6-2 VIC

January 18, 2013, Erie Otters @ Sarnia Sting (OHL)

ERI #7 LC Evans, Jake (2013) - Jake finishes his checks whenever possible. He is a regular on the penalty kill and works hard. He pressured defensemen on the point effectively.

ERI #10 LW Harper, Stephen (2013) - Stephen is a very smooth skater who rushes the puck up ice well. He constantly beat defensemen for Sarnia by going wide with speed. He is one of the better skaters coming out of the OHL for this year's draft despite having good size. Stephen played the point on the power play and displayed a very good point shot. He threw the occasional solid hit, but didn't seem to like being tested physically very much at all. He also took his time getting back defensively.

ERI #19 LD Kuleshov, Artem (2013) - Artem played a quiet, simple, reliable game for the most part. He made the smart, quick play to get the puck out of the zone while he was in the slot. He battles effectively enough in the corners. His skating does need improvement.

ERI #23 LC Crisp, Connor (2013*) - Connor's night was long and filled with physical battles around the crease. Erie received seven power plays and every time they went on the man advantage, Connor was positioned in the slot battling for space and although he didn't always win these battles he found a way to get scoring chances and screen the goaltender. Connor made smart plays with the puck making good passes and protecting the puck when he needed to gain extra time. He picked off a bad pass in the offensive zone to fire a hard wrister for Erie's 3rd goal of the night. He then showed great hands in a crowded goal area to flip the puck past Sarnia's goaltender with 20 seconds lef ton the clock to make it 6-7 and give Erie a chance in the final seconds.

ERI #97 LC McDavid, Connor (2015) - Connor's talent was definitely on display in this game. He's excellent shifty and explosive. McDavid creates scoring chances quickly and frequently. He's not afraid to go places he'll get hit to make the play. He didn't hesitate to get into battles and compete along the boards. He even finished a few good checks. Connor didn't show much urgency on the backcheck but did break up plays once he got into the defensive zone.

SAR #2 RD Chapman, Joshua (2013) - Joshua won some long physical battles out front of his own net on the penalty kill. There was a little bit of selling to try to get power plays in this game and at one point Chapman decided to join in. However he was unsuccessful and it lead to a scoring chance for Erie.

SAR #7 RD DeAngelo, Anthony (2014) - Great pass on shorthanded rush to set up Sarnia's first goal of the night. DeAngelo uses his great skating ability to create time and space in his own zone to let passing options open up. He wasn't rushing the puck as frequently as he has in the past and moved the puck instead which seemed to work for him at the time. DeAngelo did a great job coming off the point to deflect the third goal of the game.

SAR #21 Nikandrov, Daniel (2013) - For the second straight night, Nikandrov was used to shut down the opposing top line. This time in Connor McDavid, however he had a little more difficult time containing his skillset. McDavid didn't score but he was able to create chances. Nikandrov provided a little offense and was able to score Sarnia's winning goal in the final two minutes of the game.

Scouts Notes: It was a wild game in Sarnia tonight. The Otters made it through forty minutes with a lead and looked great. However there was a lack of defensive support from many forwards on Erie and that played a big part in Sarnia being able to escape with a come from behind victory thanks to sustained pressure in the offensive zone. A few players looking to get drafted came up big late as Daniel Nikandrov (2013) scored with just under two minutes left to give Sarnia a 7-5 lead. However Connor Crisp (2013*) was able to finish in the goal area with 20 seconds left to make it 7-6. Erie pushed in the final seconds but the game would end with the wild 7-6 final score.

January 18, 2013, Halifax Mooseheads at Quebec Remparts (QMJHL)

HFX #27 LW Jonathan Drouin (2013) – Deceptive playmaking forward with elite upside. Skating is outstanding w/ quick cuts, first step quickness, and good top speed. Made plays in full flight. Elite stickhandling, good arsenal of effective 1v1 moves. On one rush, went through/around the entire Quebec team with synergy of hands and footwork. Saw seams and anticipated plays, outstanding vision with puck. Was patient with puck but sometimes frustratingly so. Could have utilized his teammates better. Good stick defensively in neutral zone but didn't always backcheck fully and sometimes left his zone too early. Arguably the most explosive player in this draft class, came away very impressed. Don't see how he slips out of the top 3.

HFX #22 RC Nathan MacKinnon (2013) – Straightforward and determined offensive talent. Consistently double-teamed, fought through checks and stood up for himself in altercations. Showed good skill with puck in flashes (stutter step + burn D, no-look pass tape-to-tape, etc). Quick release with great velocity, dangerous to score from anywhere in zone. Created space for himself with speed in offensive zone, hard to check. Had a hard time taking the puck end-to-end like he wanted save for one outstanding rush. Didn't produce much on the night despite his team's huge win. Similar impression as I had in the Top Prospects Game: just don't see the #1 overall talent, but he's obviously an outstanding player.

QUE #10 LW Anthony Duclair (2013) – Boom or bust dangler. Looked completely disoriented in the defensive zone. Chased the puck, was lazy with his stick, let guys buzz around him, and left the zone early without the puck. Backcheck was 50/50, seemed to know that he was supposed to but only did it about half the time. Great puck control, bought time/space with quick hands. Mostly worked the perimeter but did cut to the middle on occasion… Good body control, very athletic. Good decisions in 1v1 and outnumbered attack situations. Could have utilized his teammates better.

QUE #73 LW Adam Erne (2013) – Complete forward who played an honest game. Strong skater, good speed down the outside and tough to knock off the puck. Skated faster with the puck than without. Protected the puck well. Made some heady passes at high speed and on the PP. Hard slapshot. Physical and chippy after whistles. Good compete level especially considering the score. Questions about his offensive upside at the next level, but I liked his overall game.

QUE #94 RW Nick Sörenson (2013) – All-around forward with some touch, was hard to get a read on in the blowout loss. Good skater, smooth stride and strong on his skates, but didn't show top gear and lumbered a bit. Showed good hands in bursts with smooth saucer passes and some 1-on-1 ability. Nice cross-body one-time finish on his goal. Used his hands and reach well, played much bigger than his size with the puck.

January 19, 2013, Val-d'Or Foreurs at Blainville-Boisbriand (QMJHL)

VDO #8 RW Anthony Mantha (2013) – Fairly enigmatic goal-scoring forward with high upside and two-way ability but inconsistent effort. Wanted to be "the guy" every time he was on the ice, called for the puck incessantly. Wingspan is his biggest asset, great puck protection skills. Skill in bursts with smart passes and great decisions in 1v1 or 2v1 situations, but lacked deception. Mostly straightforward, not a lot of flash or explosiveness. Strong skater for his size, good first steps, gets to top speed quickly with an efficient stride. Was outstanding on the forecheck when he put in the work with a good combination of body and stick checking, but more of an opportunist. Tended to deflate when the breakout moved past him, relying on reach rather than positioning in the neutral and defensive zones with a lot of puck-watching. Primarily perimeter play in his own zone. Ran hot and cold, involved on some shifts and invisible on others. Showed a nasty side with two dirty hits late. Has the tools to be a dominant player.

BLB #62 LW/C Danick Martel (2013) – Sparkplug two-way forward with good skill. Undersized but no-quit attitude, went to dirty areas. Quick release, powerful and accurate wristshot. Some dangling ability, made plays. Backchecked hard. Size is biggest limiting factor. Don't think he'll be drafted, but he's a good player at this level.

Jan 19, 2013, P.E.I. Rocket vs. Chicoutimi Sagueneens (QMJHL)

PEI # 27, D, Graves, Ryan (2013) Graves did a nice job protecting the puck along the boards to draw a penalty and was able to make a good pass up through the neutral zone on the rush. He got the puck in deep into the offensive zone on a pretty simple dump-in play, got his shots through to the net on opportunities from the point and also got in lanes to breakup passes and pick off turnovers. He did a great job of playing the body to keep his man to the outside then separate him from the puck, and was also able to pick off passes in the offensive zone to put shots on net.

CHI # 11, LW, Guevremont, Charles (2013) Guevremont protected the puck nicely along the boards, got a good cycle going in deep and put a low shot on net off the rush to try to generate a rebound. He did a good job of tying up the opposition in his own end and put great pressure on the puck carrier to force the turnover then take the puck in on a break to drive the net with some good moves for a great opportunity in tight. He was distributing the puck well on the rush up the ice and got the puck in deep on some pretty simple chip in plays. He did however turn the puck over at times by not being strong enough on the puck.

CHI # 17, LW, Tremblay, Simon (2013) Tremblay played his man physically to knock the puck over in open ice and was getting involved with the opposition after whistles. He went hard to the net and battled really well for territory and loose pucks in front. He showed good speed and distributed the puck well on the rush up the ice.

CHI # 25, RW, Gobeil, Thomas (2013) Gobeil went to the net well and opened up nicely on the power play to provide scoring options down low. He got a good cycle going in deep and found lanes on the power play to move the puck to an open man in the high slot. He hustled well for loose pucks, was physical on the puck carrier along the boards in his own end but needs to get the puck out of the zone on his chances along the boards. He opened up nicely in front of the net.

CHI # 27, LW, Dauphin, Laurent (2013) Dauphin had nice speed on the rush and was able to get the puck up out of his zone to start the breakout. He put good pressure on the point on the penalty kill and had some nice quick hands to get around defenders through the neutral zone. He went hard to the net to battle for loose pucks and rebounds, opened up well in the high slot to take a pass and put a shot on and also had a nice shot from the high slot to score. He had some great moves to help drive the puck to the net and displayed great agility and creativity with the puck, however still needs to watch some of the turnovers trying to force passes through the opposition. He was able to find a man in the slot on some good passes from the sidewall and opened up well next to the net for a great chance on a one-timer.

CHI # 39, D, Tremblay, Carl (2013) Tremblay kept his man to the outside on the rush and got in lanes in front of his own net to try to breakup passes and plays for the opposition. He played his man hard along the boards, which helped to force him to the outside.

CHI # 64, RW, Pouliot, Samule (2013) Pouliot put good pressure on the puck carrier and was moving the puck up out of his zone to start the breakout pretty effectively. He distributed the puck well on the rush through the neutral zone and hustled hard for loose pucks.

FINAL SCORE: 5-2 Chicoutimi Sagueneens

January 20, 2013, Owen Sound Attack at Ottawa 67s (OHL)

OS #24 LD Chris Bigras (2013) – Positionally sound two-way defenseman with outstanding defensive IQ and a lot of offensive potential. Head on a swivel in the defensive zone, always kept his feet moving. Physical when necessary, steps up at the blueline and protected the net front, tough along the boards when the opportunity presented itself to separate player from puck. Very safe with the puck in his end and on the breakout. Good outlets, accurate and receivable passes. Carried the puck with poise, quickly turning up ice off intercepts and dumping the puck from center to clear danger, sometimes deking around a player or two in the process. A lot to like here as far as hockey sense.

OS #27 RW Zach Nastasiuk (2013) – Upside two-way forward with inconsistencies. Good reads overall, intelligent player. Skates well, strong on his feet. Worked hard around the net/slot on the powerplay and was very aggressive on the PK, good special teams positioning. Flashed a bullet wrister on his goal. Didn't bring a strong physical presence, needed to get more involved on the boards. Tools are there to be a solid 3rd line forward, maybe 2nd line upside, but was lacking real fire.

OTT #20 LC Sean Monahan (2013) – Two-way forward who really doesn't have much to work with on this Ottawa roster. Wasn't flashy but solid overall. Good, strong skater, but was lacking in real burst. Patient with the puck, good protection. Carried the puck with poise. Acted as powerplay quarterback and often started the breakout at even strength by winding up in his own end. Very aware of passing lanes, found teammates with precise dishes. Defensively responsible, made sure the puck was clear before leaving the zone and if his team needed a change, made sure to get it deep. Good wrister with a quick release.

January 20, 2013, Halifax Mooseheads @ Blainsville-Boisbriand (QMJHL)

Halifax
#22 Nathan MacKinnon, C (2013): MacKinnon was pretty good in this game, showing why he's an elite skater in this year's NHL draft class. In first period, he used his speed to draw a penalty, pretty amazing to watch him gain top speed with two or three strides. Plays in all situations for the Mooseheads and was used on the penalty kill with Jonathan Drouin. Scored a goal just by being close to the net after a MacKenzie Weegar shot went through the Armada goalie, touched MacKinnon's leg and went into the net for a lucky goal. Did a great job on the PK today, using his speed and strength to keep the puck and kill time on the clock. Overall he was average in the faceoff circle but won a big one with a one-goal lead with a minute left in his zone to keep the Mooseheads on top.

#24 Matt Murphy, Def (2013): Murphy was quiet in this game and that his is style. Was paired with Mackenzie Weegar and moved the puck well. Didn't get involved in the offensive zone, he let his partner do this. Just took care of things in his own end and cover for Weegar who like to jump in the play. Didn't see any stand out play in the physical game department too.

#27 Jonathan Drouin, LW (2013): Drouin showed once again why he's going to be a top pick in June, scoring the tying goal after taking a great feed from Marty Frk and beating Étienne Marcoux on the backhand. On that goal he showed how quick his hands are. Put on a stickhandling display all game long, in some case less is better as he turned the puck over a couple of times trying to deke too much. He can basically do whatever he wants with the puck on his stick. What I like about Drouin is that he's fearless, he will go in the corner or in front of the net if he has to. His skating has improved a lot since last year, he can gain top speed much faster and change direction quickly.

#31 Zachary Fucale, G (2013): Fucale played well most of the game, gave up 3 goals in a quick span in the third period but was able to stay focused and lead the Mooseheads to a victory. On the 3 goals I thought Fucale would like to have two of them back; the first one was a rather weak shot that went through him. For the 2nd goal, he was out of position in his crease and the Armada player bounced the puck off his back from behind the net. Earlier in the game I thought he was staying too deep in his net to make saves, he also has a tendency to go down quickly on his knees. I like how he's square to the shooter and never seems to panic. Very calm in his crease.

#48 Luca Ciampini, LW (undrafted 1994) : His line was good at cycling the puck in the offensive zone, Ciampini did a good job of protecting the puck using his body, as he likes to distribute the puck down low. Also liked to see him slow down the play to find his open linemate. Skating still needs a lot of work as far as speed and agility goes. Could use more burst in his step to make him more dangerous in the offensive zone. Tried to play physical on the much bigger Yasin Cissé and took the worst of it.

#52 MacKenzie Weegar, Def (2013): Weegar had a super game, scoring the game-winning goal late in the third period. Loved how he didn't hesitate going on the attack late in the game like this. He had little bit of a lucky goal as he tried a pass on a 2-on-1, the puck went back to him and he had an open net to shoot at. Made some strong decisions with the puck, pinched many times to become the 4th forward and, as I recall, only got caught once but was quick enough to come back and cancel the odd-man rushes. Played physical in his own zone when he had to and also took a heck of a hit from Cedric Paquette, but popped right up and continued his shift. I like how he plays the man instead of the puck on a couple of occasions in one-on-one confrontations.

Blainville-Boisbriand
#11 Marc-Olivier Roy, RW (2013): Roy played a solid two-way game, made numerous takeaways in the neutral zone which led to a counter attack. Used his great speed to beat defensemen wide but didn't generate a good enough shot to beat Fucale. Didn't take many good shots tonight, had some chances but either his shots were weak or in the crest of the goalie. His goal was scored from the right faceoff circle, a rather weak shot that Fucale would like to have back, but it was a smart decision by Roy to put the puck on net with traffic coming. Didn't shy away from the physical game, but his lack of strength showed in some physical confrontations.

#15 Philippe Sanche, LW/RW (2013) Played a regular shift on the Armada's 2nd line and also was used on the point on the power play with team captain Xavier Ouellet. You can see why they use him there thanks to his great vision and passing ability. At his size, he's struggling to win puck battles in the corner against much bigger opponents at even strength. Most of his scoring chances tonight came from 10-15 feet from the net. He's willing to pay the price in front of the net.

#57 Christopher Clapperton, LW (undrafted, 1994): Still playing with his usual linemates Paquette and Roy, played a real high-energy, intense game from the get-go. Strong presence on the forecheck as he loves to finish his checks. Doesn't have the quickest acceleration, but I love how he keeps his feet moving. Also played on the team's 1st PP unit but didn't generate a lot of offensive opportunities for himself during that game.

January 21, 2013, Erie Otters at Plymouth Whalers (OHL)

ERIE #10 LW Stephen Harper (2013) – Not sure what's going on here. Saw Harper play one outstanding game earlier in the year when he was hitting everything in sight, involved everywhere on the ice, and scored a goal. The last two times, including this one, he's been lazy, lazy, lazy. I don't know if his heart's not in it because Erie is such a terrible team, but his effort is dreadful. I don't think I saw him make contact this entire game and he looked incredibly sluggish with the puck on his stick.

ERIE #97 LC Connor McDavid (2015) – It could be that McDavid is suffering from the same kind of disinterest as Harper, or it could be that Plymouth checked him well, but aside from a few flashes of talent McDavid was invisible in this game. Erie badly needs to surround him with some players to work with, because as it stands his only options are to try to take the puck end-to-end or dish it off to someone who's going to give the puck up, and that has to be disheartening for him.

PLY #21 RW Ryan Hartman (2013) – Was really impressed with Hartman's game. I have not seen a better draft-eligible penalty killer this year. He moved like he was on a track, very fluid and always conscious of where he should be without having to look at his feet. Showed some skill with the puck too on a nice snapshot finish on a breakaway. Was also noticeably strong on the puck on the boards, fighting through checks and protecting well and actively participating in cycle play.

Jan. 22 2013, Gatineau Olympiques @ Chicoutimi Saguenéens, (QMJHL)

GAT #7 D, Deslauriers, Jean-Simon (2013): This is a smaller defenseman, but he has good mobility and doesn't hesitate to jump up and join the rush. He is able to move the puck well and is starting to come into his own defensively, using his speed to get to the puck first then make the right play. He is also more tenacious in his battles, is improving in his net-front coverage and playing more against talented players. His defensive zone coverage is also getting more aggressive using what foot speed he can to be most effective.

GAT #8 D, Carrier, Alexandre (2014): Carrier is such a smart player, his footwork is great, and he is able to read and anticipate the play like he's a veteran. He is able to find teammates quite easily with his passes, rarely turns the puck over in his own end, and he steps up nicely when a player is having trouble handling the puck to force a turnover. He ended the night with a +3 rating.

GAT #27 LW, Poirier, Émile (2013): Poirier showed the superb explosiveness and blazing speed that he possesses tonight. He is able to get past most defensemen in just a couple strides and he has a great forehand-to-backhand move, which he makes quickly to put defenders on their heels to blow past them. He used his speed to go behind the net and set up a teammate very well with a nice pass right on the tape that resulted in a goal. He also managed to get a breakaway with a great anticipation on the penalty kill to pick off a pass, as he sees plays develop well and is used in many defensive situations by his
coach. He cheats in the neutral zone on some occasions, but it didn't cost him this time in this game, however he needs to watch those types of plays moving forward. He could be more constant in his effort as he had many nice flashes but was quiet on many occasions too. He is a great player on the rush and possesses a superb release on his wrist shot that is able to fool goaltenders.

GAT #44 LW, Reway, Martin (2013): Reway is a small but elite offensive talent. He has an uncanny ability to turn quickly, slow down the play and create space for himself. He appears to have eyes in the back of his head, as he is an elite passer who can find teammates on great passes through sticks and skates. He made a perfect pass 2-on-1 to Mikael Langlois who scored the 4th Gatineau goal and was controlling the play well on the power play displaying some great creativity. He plays with intelligence and skill most of the time, however will loose a couple of battles along the boards trying to avoid checks.

CHI #27 C, Dauphin, Laurent (2013): Dauphin was kept very quiet in that game. Gatineau was putting a lot of pressure on the puck carrier through the neutral zone and Dauphin had trouble finding space to work with, which showed a lack of speed. His normal offensive execution wasn't there either as this was a bad game all-round for him and he lost a lot of battles for the puck which is uncharacteristic for him. This was just an off-night it seemed.

Jan. 22 2013, Gatineau Olympiques @ Chicoutimi Saguenéens, (QMJHL)

GAT #7 D, Deslauriers, Jean-Simon (2013) : Small but has good mobility and doesn't hesitate joining the rush. He has an above-average skillset and moves the puck well. He's starting to come into his own defensively using his speed to get to the puck first and choose the right play. More tenacious in his battles, he's getting better in his net front coverage and playing talented players, getting more agressive in coverage, with his footspeed he can.

GAT #8 D, Carrier, Alexandre (2014) : Ended the night with a +3 rating. So smart, the footwork is great, he reads and anticipates like he's a veteran. Will rarely do a turnover in his own end, finds his teammates easily. Steps up easily when a player has troubles handling the puck.

GAT #27 LW, Poirier, Émile (2013) : Showed the superb explosiveness and blazing speed he posesses. Can get past most D's with just 2 strides has a great forehand to backhand move that he does quickly to put defenders on their heels. He used that speed to go behind the net and set up Adam Chapman very well with a nice pass on tape that resulted in a goal. He got a breakaway with a great anticipation on the PK, sees plays develop well and used in many defensive situations by his coach. He cheats in the neutral zone on some occasions, but it didn't cost him in the game. Could be more constant in his effort as he had many nice flashes and was quiet on many occasions too. Great player on the rush, he posesses a superb release on the wrist shot.

GAT #44 LW, Reway, Martin (2013) : Small but elite offensive talent. He has an uncanny ability to turn on himself, slow down the play and create space for himself. Seems to have eyes all-over his head, finds teammates through sticks and skates, an elite passer. He will loose a couple of battles trying to avoid checks, tries to play with smarts and skills most of the times. He made a perfect pass 2-on-1 to Mikael Langlois who scored the 4th Gatineau goal. He controls the play well on the powerplay and has great creativity. Still a diamond to be polished though.

CHI #27 C, Dauphin, Laurent (2013) : Was kept very quiet in that game. Lost a lot of battles which is uncharacteristic for Dauphin. Gatineau was putting a lot of pressure in the neutral zone on the puck carrier and Dauphin had trouble finding space in neutral zone, showing maybe a little lack of speed. Offensive execution wasn't there either. Bad game for him.

January 23, 2013, USHL Top Prospects Game (Muskegon, MI)

3 D Ian McCoshen Made some nice outlet passes, got shots on net, and threw some big hits, so there was a lot to like about him, but his decision making under pressure got him in trouble a couple times. Overall the good definitely outweighed the bad, but he can play better.

4 D Michael Downing Was not particularly impressed with his reads or coverage tonight. A couple badly flubbed clearances and positional errors. Has ideal size and plays with an edge but had some problems with the puck. Got leveled by a much smaller Justin Kloos. I can see the two-way potential here but he was off by a step.

5 D Gustav Olofsson Rangy two-way defenseman. Took care of his own end first. Tough to play against. Good reads, very physical on the boards and against the rush. Could rush the puck and play the point on the power play. Looks like he has room to get even stronger.

11 F Jason Cotton For a guy who came into this game with zero goals on the season, Cotton really impressed. Nice finish on his goal, but that wasn't his only contribution offensively. Worked hard in the slot all game and went to the corners without hesitation. Showed some impressive poise with the puck, acting as the PPQB on one occasion. Would like to see him do it in a regular season game but I think a lot of scouts will at least give him a second look after this performance.

12 F Ross Olsson Was inconsistent with his effort. Physical on the forecheck, then weak on the back check. Made a move to pull the puck from behind the net and get a shot, then passed up a great shot opportunity. Flashed some great skill for a player of his size but would've liked to see more hustle and decisiveness.

15 F John Hayden Real gritty two-way forward. Showed good touch in the offensive zone tonight, was the catalyst for much of Team East's offense. Tough on the boards, wins battles and protects the puck well. Backchecks hard. Proved tonight that he's willing to fight when needed.

23 F Connor McGlynn Workmanlike game. Limited upside but have to admire the effort. Great work on the forecheck and backcheck and strong in front of the net in the offensive zone.

27 F Luke Johnson Skilled player but had trouble fighting through checks. Nice that he defended his teammate by picking a fight with Michael Downing, but bugged me that he refused to take off his lid and fought with a visor on.

28 D Blake Heinrich Aggressive defenseman who played a pretty solid game overall. Made some flashy plays on defense, including a diving pokecheck that stopped an outnumbered attack and a strong stand up hit that knocked the forward clean off his feet. Pretty capable in his own end as well, kept his stick active and got his body in front of shots and passes. A bit short but sturdily built.

35 G Eamon McAdam Had a great night. Very athletic goaltender. Positionally sound and showed the ability to make desperation saves including one unbelievable goal-line glove stop. Communicated well with his teammates, barking commands and warnings to help.

91 F Taylor Cammarata Gets knocked because of his size a lot but I think he's way too skilled not to have success as a professional. So shifty and unpredictable. Created space for himself with deceptive stickhandling, kept his hands and feet churning with the puck. Kept his head up and always looked to make plays. Some outstanding passes tonight. Didn't get the chance to show off his shot tonight but he was in good spots for one-timers on a frequent basis.

Jan 23, 2013, Team East vs. Team West (USHL Top Prospects Game)

Prospects Breakdown:

EST # 10, C, Ebbing, Thomas (2013) Ebbing displayed some really nice hands and some good speed on his wide drive to put a good shot on net. He was protecting the puck well along the wall in the offensive zone, and was cycling the puck really well. He was moving around nicely to get to the slot and opening up to provide some good scoring options, and made a really good centering pass to find an open man in front of the net. He has to watch turnovers through the neutral zone on breakout passes as well as puck mishandles.

EST # 15, LW, Hayden, John (2013) Hayden showed some incredible hands and agility early on to weave in and out of the opposition and get to the slot for a great scoring chance and drew a penalty on the chance. He had a nice net-front presence in the offensive zone going to those dirty areas, and demonstrated he is also a tough kid having a pretty good fight. He protects the puck really well and showed some creativity to get to the slot for a shot. He did a great job holding the puck in the offensive zone and was forcing turnovers with some good pressure. He was firing shots on net from everywhere, and had a really battle for pucks in front of the net to pick up a rebound and score the team's 1st goal of the game.

EST # 17, LW, Tiffels, Frederik (2013) Tiffels has some pretty good hands and agility and did a good job trying to move the puck to an open man out front of the net for a good chance. He has some fantastic speed and a good drive down the middle towards the opposition's net. He used his hands to get around the opposition and was able to make a great pass to find an open man down low for a chance from in tight. He needs to get stronger on the puck along the boards.

EST # 22, C, Stevens, John (2013) Stevens is a big body with some great puck protection and a really nice cycle deep in the offensive zone. He had a really nice net-front presence on the power play, and was able to get open down low next to the net to make a fantastic pass to an open man through the crease for a great shot but was robbed by the goalie. He has some great strength and protection to get in behind the defense with the puck for a great chance in tight on a break. He was driving to the net with his stick down to get to the slot for a shot, but has to hit the net on his chances. He was also moving the puck to good scoring areas but has to watch turnovers in the offensive zone, and also needs to watch turnovers trying to dangle the puck through the opposition.

WST # 8, C, Moore, Trevor (2013) Moore has some good speed and showed some great hands on the wide drive. He was able to take a pass in the slot to put a great shot on net to score, but the goal was called off. He was protecting the puck well and cycling the puck in deep in the offensive zone along the wall. He made some good breakout passes to start the rush, and was making some nice moves to get around defenders in deep into the offensive zone with the puck. He made a great pass to a man cross-crease for a nice chance in tight. He was opening up well in the slot for a nice opportunity, but has to get his shot through to the net. He put some good pressure on the puck carrier to take the puck forcing a turnover, and was reading the play to pick off turnovers in the offensive zone.

WST # 19, C, Guentzel, Jake (2013) Guentzel started this game making an excellent feed to find McGlynn right in front of the net to open the scoring for the game. He also made a really great pass to set-up a man in the high slot for a nice chance on a good shot. He was driving well to the net with his stick down to provide scoring options, and showed some good patience with the puck to walk around the net for a good shot on net.

WST # 24, RW, Melanson, Drew (2013) Melanson made a great drive to the net with his stick down looking for loose pucks and rebounds. He displayed some really good speed to gain the offensive zone and get the puck in deep, but at other times he needs to be able to get the puck in deep instead of making moves at the blue line. He made a great centering pass to find an open man in the slot, and was cycling the puck well deep in the offensive zone. He protects the puck really well and was battling for loose pucks in front of the net.

WST # 91, LW, Cammarata, Taylor (2013) Cammarata has some really good speed to gain the offensive zone on a wide drive, and was able to walk into the slot on the power play off the rush for a great shot that he rang off the cross-bar. He made a really nice pass on a 3-on-1 to create an excellent chance in tight, and displayed some excellent passing and vision to find an open man in the slot to create some good chances. He was able to hold up off the rush after gaining the offensive zone to move the puck to a trailing player, and was distributing the puck well on the power play. He needs to watch turnovers trying to force passes through the opposition, and also had a really bad turnover trying to be fancy in his own end giving up a huge chance for the opposition.

FINAL SCORE: 2-1 Team West

Jan 24, 2013, Cape Breton vs. Quebec Remparts (QMJHL)

CAP # 8, D, Nicholson, Gareth (2013) Nicholson displayed great strength and puck protection in his own end to avoid being knocked off the puck. He made a nice big hit along the boards on the puck carrier to knock his man over and was able to get his shot through to the net kept down low from the point. He has to get the puck out of his zone on clearing attempts on the penalty kill and needs to watch the turnovers on puck mishandles in his own end.

CAP # 12, LW, Murphy, Cole (2013) Murphy is able to make a good pass to start the breakout out of his own zone and was getting the puck in deep on the rush by making the simple play. He got to the front of the net but has to watch the turnovers on the rush into the offensive zone trying to pass pucks through the opposition.

CAP # 15, C, Beaton, Bronson (2013) Beaton went hard to the net to battle for territory and look for loose pucks and rebounds. He protected the puck well on the cycle and is able to get the puck in deep off the rush. He made a great pass off the cycle to find a man out front and was moving the puck around well in the offensive zone. He put great pressure on the fore-check and opened up well in the high slot for a one-timer chance, but then fanned on his shot attempt. He moved the puck around well on the odd-man rush to draw a penalty and played his man hard and physical in his own end. He has to get his shots through to the net on chances from the high slot and also needs to watch the turnovers trying to force passes through the opposition.

CAP # 23, C, Lyle, Michael (2013) Lyle had great hustle for loose pucks and was protecting the puck well on the wide drive. He displayed nice strength on the puck to take a hit, hold on to it then walk out to the slot from behind the net to score 5-hole. He showed good speed on the rush then drove the puck wide but took a long outside shot off the rush. He was also able to skate the puck up the ice but then lost it trying to skate his way through the opposition.

QUE # 10, LW, Duclair, Anthony (2013) Duclair was able to put a good shot on net to generate a rebound that the team scored on, and displayed some really good strength, puck protection and agility with the puck. He made a nice give and go play in the offensive zone to move the puck to a man driving hard to the net off the rush and also found lanes on the power play to move the puck back to the point. He was able to make a good pass to find an open man down low next to the net and was battling well for the puck along the boards and hustling for any available loose pucks. He made a good chip pass to move the puck past the opposition to start the breakout and was able to move the puck to find a man in tight to the net for a great opportunity after twisting away from the opposition's pressure.

QUE # 73, RW, Erne, Adam (2013) Erne got the puck in deep off the wide drive and was able to get a good cycle going in the offensive zone. He had great hands to step out to the slot with the puck for a good shot attempt and made a really nice pass cross-crease for a teammate for a great chance in tight. He demonstrated really nice quickness and agility with the puck and distributed the puck on the rush through the neutral zone. He went to the net for a good chance right in front of the net and showed some of his great speed on the wide drive then made a nice centering pass to find a man in front.

QUE # 91, C, Boivin, Alexandre (2013) Boivin had really good speed on the rush into the offensive zone, was hustling for loose pucks and driving hard to the net. He was competing really well, battling for his territory in front and was able to make a really nice long pass to find a man at the far blue line to spring him into the offensive zone. He was able to take a hit and hold on to the puck in deep to make a play, protected the puck well along the boards in the offensive zone and got in lanes to breakup a pass in his own end then moved the puck up well to start the breakout.

QUE # 94, RW, Sorensen, Nick (2013) Sorensen made a nice lead pass to spring a man into the offensive zone with speed and was driving to the net with his stick down to provide options off the rush. He was able to make some good passes to start the breakout out of his own zone and made an excellent cross-ice pass on the rush into the offensive zone for a great shot opportunity. He was distributing the puck well on the rush to gain the offensive zone with speed and opened up nicely in front of the net to take a pass and put a good shot on from the slot. He has to watch the offensive zone turnovers on missed pass attempts and needs to move the puck rather than taking long outside shots.

FINAL SCORE: 4-1 Quebec Remparts

January 24, 2013, Plymouth Whalers at Windsor Spitfires (OHL)

WSR #16 LW Kerby Rychel (2013) – I have mixed feelings on Kerby. I think his skating is a major issue, even though it's much improved this year. He lacks explosiveness in his feet, which I think hampers a player with a two-way skillset. That aside, the kid works his ass off. His feet are always moving in the right direction. His play with the puck is so-so. Not the kind of guy I'd want carrying the puck on any line. At his best as a complementary forward that can crash and bang around the net. Good hands in the paint. Pretty good shot overall, can really let wristers go. Have seen him drop the gloves twice in two games, so that's nice to see.

WSR #66 RW Joshua Ho-Sang (2014) – Boy does this kid have some hands. Dangles with the best of him and has OHL superstar offensive talent. That said, his overall game is very, very lacking. The defensive side of his game was nonexistent. A lot of the time he didn't even come back into his own zone and he's lazy on the forecheck. Tunnel vision with the puck, didn't utilize his teammates as well as he could have. Not by a longshot. Risky passes, risky 1v1 moves, much too fancy overall. Not sure if the sense is there.

PLY #21 RW Ryan Hartman (2013) – Pretty quiet night, but showed that he can still be valuable even when he's not buzzing. Has consistently brought his skating legs every time I see him. Stride is great, always moves his feet. Fought and threw a couple hits. Showed off some 1v1 skill. Great defensive play. Such a strong all-around player. Don't see how he makes it out of the first round.

PLY #22 LW Matthew Mistele (2014) – Kid is an enigma to me. Not because he plays an up-and-down game or anything like that, but because in the two games I saw him play in the last few days (Erie + Windsor) I would not have noticed him were I not looking for him. Certainly not what you'd expect from a guy who's scored the most points in a Whaler uniform this year. He's got a good frame but I think he's still got room to add size/strength. Did not see him throw his weight around at all. Did back check but was a little lax in his defensive zone in the Windsor game, but I guess I can understand that in a blowout win. Skating is OK, good stride but didn't show much burst. First goal vs. Windsor was as a trailer, just went to the net and potted home the rebound. Lorentz did all the work. Second goal, Lorentz brought it up the wing, dished across to Uvira who got the shot off, and it went off Mistele's skate and into the net. I would call him an opportunist. Gets by largely on positioning. Seems to understand the game very well and as a result, doesn't have to put in a balls-to-the-wall effort to get results. Fairly average overall as far as specific talents (puck skills, finishing, etc.) but you can't argue with the production.

Jan. 24 2013, Rouyn-Noranda Huskies @ Val D'Or Foreurs, (QMJHL)

VDO #8 LW, Mantha, Anthony (2013) : Overall impressive showing from the big forward. He shot 12 pucks on net, had a 3 goals 1 pass night and probably could've had 2-3 more goals easily. He has a superb hockey mind and gets open easily in the offensive zone, offensive execution is off the charts, will rarely miss the net when he shoots towards it wether those are backhands, wrist shots or one-timers. His first goal was a thing of beauty, using speed and strength to beat the defender protecting the puck, cutting in front of the Rouyn goalie and coming back on the forehand putting the puck behind the red line with his long reach. He showed more intensity in his one-on-one battles than usual, starting to get more physical. He doesn't spend much strides trying to go where the puck is but will rely on smarts to get where the puck will be before his opponent. I thought he started to chea little bit more in the 2nd part of the match trying to get to the neutral zone before his team would recover the puck in defensive zone.

VDO #16 RW, Aubé-Kubel, Nicolas (2014) : Showed the great speed he posesses on the rush, great vision but tends to play a little too fancy. He's really quick coming off a battle on the boards and making a play, sees the ice very well. Has a terrific skillset and good at making space for himself.

VDO #20 C, Richard, Anthony (2014) : Energic and even though he's really small, he is not easy to get away from in a 1-on-1 battle. He has quick hands but not always in control, tenacious around the net and executes well the defensive aspects of the game, takes a lot of pride in helping D's.

VDO #26 C, Dunn, Vincent (2013) : Showed off the rough and tough he can play. Not the biggest guy, but has a ton of heart, superb passing skills on the rush. Was part of a ton of scrums and rough stuff, he fought with 2013 prospect Justin Guénette in a great tilt. Getting better in his own zone, can take the wrong decision sometimes, but is willing to work twice as hard to correct that mistake. Nice mix of physical play, hard work and offense. Could shoot more on net, tends to watch for passes too much.

ROU #7 D, Guénette, Justin (2013) : Plays steady smart game. Not a lot of upsides, not naturally skilled with the puck or really big but strong on the puck, makes good reads quickly, reacts well under pressure and will play the rough game well. Offensively will make good short passes, moves well to get open, has an above-average shot. Built like fire hydrant.

ROU #25 LW, Andrighetto, Sven (2013*) : The 19 years old undrafted forward is just a constant threat in the offensive zone. Has a great shot, releases it quickly, reaches top speed in 2 strides which helps him create space for himself easily. Great puckhandler, really slippery, goes through checks and defensive players with ease. Puck seems to be glued on his stick when he carries it to neutral zone. Was still able to get chances on net even though the game was really physical, which showed that he doesn't fear physical play, knows how to be a factor in those games too.

ROU #30 G, Bélanger Alexandre (2013) : The big goalie really seemed off his game. The reflexes were slow and didn't seem to be able to track a puck in traffic. Sometimes for young goalies, it's tough to be consistent which is the case for Bélanger who's the starter every game for Rouyn right now, some up nights, some down nights. This was a down night, got beat on the glove side (a strength normally) 3 times on 4 goals allowed. A little slow to react and the focus wasn't there.

January 25, 2013, Sioux Falls Stampede at US NTDP Under-17 (USHL)

USA #37 RW Alex Tuch (2014) – Big forward played a nice power game. Went fearlessly and heavily into board battles and won difficult pucks. Was strong on the penalty kill with good positioning. Flashed a nice wristshot and a little bit of flair with the puck.

USA #38 RW Anders Bjork (2014) – Had a mixed game, mostly negative. Decision-making was poor. Gave the puck away in his zone. Defensive coverage was sloppy. Made a few smart reads, especially stepping up in the neutral zone to force turnovers. Skating wasn't there. Slow release on his shot.

USA #39 LC Dylan Larkin (2014) – Poor game today. Needs to get stronger. Was weak on the backcheck and pushed off the puck too easily. Made poor decisions on the powerplay in the offensive zone. Took a needless penalty. Positioning on breakouts was strange, on one instance skated right into his teammate, causing a turnover. Clearly has some skill, as he showed off good hands and a nice wrister.

USA #41 LD Nathan Billitier (2014) – Good skater but undersized. Transitioned smoothly and moved well. Some nice puck skills with good stickhandling and smart outlet passes. Was slow to loose pucks and could have battled harder on the boards.

USA #43 RD Ryan Collins (2014) – Big, lanky defenseman. Still pretty awkward. Was strong in front of his net and covered shooting and passing lanes well with an active stick. Made safe plays with the puck to clear his zone. Let go a bomb from the point but didn't show much else offensively.

USA #45 RD Louis Belpedio (2014) – Undersized offensive defenseman with very quick feet. Made smart decisions on the breakout with passes and carries and made the safe play off the glass when he had no options. Needs to bulk up, was overpowered often in his zone.

USA #46 RC Jack Eichel (2015) – Very impressive player. So strong on his skates and on the puck, can beat guys with skill or by taking the puck wide and shrugging off contact. Outstanding skater, accelerated quickly and carried the puck with poise at speed. Nice 1-on-1 skill, great stickhandler. Play away from the puck could use improvement. Left his zone before his team had possession and floated on some shifts, especially in the neutral zone.

USA #48 LW Sonny Milano (2014) – Finesse forward showed a lot of skill. Passing was excellent including nice flat saucers on the powerplay and long cross-ice and stretch feeds. Showed a lot of patience with the puck on the boards, protecting well with finesse. Great 1-on-1 skill. Was decked on one play trying to be too fancy.

USA #52 LC Ryan MacInnis (2014) – Massive kid but still very lanky. Showed good offensive zone instincts and positioning, going hard to the net with and without the puck and finding soft spots in coverage to set up for shots. Good about sensing pressure coming and quickly finding an open teammate. Took the puck strong down the wing. Flashed a big slapshot. Backchecked and played the body well defensively, was physical in his zone. Got dumped on one shift, at times looked off-balance.

Scout's Notes: USA LW Jared Fiegl (2014) was very physical. USA RD Jack Glover (2014) had a poor showing, with weak coverage and poor offensive decisions. USA LD Brandon Fortunato (2014) moved the puck well and was a major asset on the powerplay. USA LD Jonathan Macleod (2014) was injured, but was physical in limited minutes beforehand.

Jan 25, 2013, Kelowna Rockets vs Seattle Thunderbirds (WHL)

SEA#17 LD, Theodore, Shea(2013) Shea was putting on a show with stickhandling skills tonight. His smooth skating help him gain distance to thread a first good pass out of the zone during the game, but at times he tried to do to much with the puck resulting in a couple turn overs. His play in front of his net and along the boards was disappointing most of the game.

SEA#19 LW, Sheen, Riley(2013) Riley used his speed and hands to put up a 2 point game. He used his quick hands in front and his speed along the boards tonight. He was productive every shift through out the game in the offensive zone. His strength along the board was a big weakness tonight when he would get tied up, but when given some space to work he would burn you with his speed.

KEL #4 D Bowey Madison (2013) Had a good overall game, in the second he released a top cheddar bomb that Everetts goalie didnt even see. His skating ability allows him to create time and space. He showed some good hands and ability to draw the puck off the wall and put in on net. He controlled all 1 on 1 battles along the boards winning the battles. Just a work horse every shift. Bowey could add some size to his frame.
Scouts Notes: Kelowna controlled the tempo most of the game, but the play was back in forth all night with Seattle putting up a good fight. Seattles huaf and green play good on the blue line, showing some potential and skill. But it was not enough for Seattle as Kelowna was able to bang one home in OT to take the game.
Final Score: 4-3 Kelowna

January 25, 2013, Plymouth Whalers @ Sarnia Sting (OHL)

PLY #2 LD Peters, Alex (2014) - Protects puck well with size, however he holds on too long, trusting his size too much being knocked off the puck. He played a very simple defensive game tonight.

PLY #18 LW Vanderwiel, Daniel (2013) - Daniel forechecks hard and battles hard in the offensive zone. He goes to war every chance he can along the boards and in the corners and is very good at winning battles. He provided a lot of physicality with a big open ice hit as well as finishing his checks along the boards. He plays with a ton of heart and desire displaying strong positioning in all three zones. Vanderwiel was like a third defenseman whenever Sarnia had the puck in Plymouth's zone. Never took a shift off all game long.

PLY #22 LW Mistele, Matthew (2014) - Mistele displayed solid positioning in the offensive zone. He was constantly available for pass in a place he could get a good shot off. He kept it simple getting the puck deep, playing smart positionally. He was able to force a turnover on the power play and turn it into a scoring chance. He took an unnecessary tripping penalty almost 200ft. from his own net after losing the puck.

SAR #5 RD Hore, Tyler (2014) - Tyler was very good with the puck tonight. He made quick decisions with the puck on the point. He received power play ice time and moved the puck intelligently and quickly. He rushes the puck rather effectively despite not being a great skater. He looks off bad options and shows patience and he's surprisingly elusive for his size generating average speed, but his skating will need to improve especially backwards. He matches up well in one on one situations against opposing forwards and will only get more effective with better skating. Tyler didn't play an overly physical game but he stood up for his goaltender after getting run.

SAR #7 RD DeAngelo, Anthony (2014) - Tonight may have been rock bottom for DeAngelo. The skilled defenseman opened by slamming his stick graphically showing his frustration after not finishing on a scoring chance. He also turned over the puck in his own zone early in this game. He didn't check his man in the slot, who got multiple chances and eventually scored. He missed assignments all over the defensive zone and was out for three straight Plymouth goals. After the third goal Anthony didn't see the ice again for the rest of the game presumably being benched. Note: Anthony was scratched from the line-up the following night in Plymouth for non injury reasons.

SAR #21 LC Nikandrov, Daniel (2013) - Daniel had great defensive positioning all game long. He was up against Plymouth's top line and did a great job. He spent a lot of time covering for an offensive defenseman for Sarnia practically playing defense for long stretches of his shift. He also was well positioned on the penalty kill. He was successful because he wasn't try to do too much. He had a high and a low handling the puck. One was a great pass to set up a scoring chance on a break, the other he made a mistake forcing a pass that wasn't there in his own end.

SAR #71 RW Goldobin, Nikolay (2014) - Nikolay fired Sarnia's second goal top corner in a hurry after making a great play when he lost control of the puck, quickly getting it back and scored before defense could react. He showed commitment to his own zone in this game getting back defensively.

Scouts Notes: Sarnia jumped out to a big 2-0 lead in what is a big battle for the West Division title. Plymouth wasn't going to go down without a fight scoring three of the next four goals before Reid Boucher (New Jersey) scored with 10 minutes left. However Garrett Meurs (Colorado) tied it up with five minutes left preserving a point for Plymouth. Boucher and Charles Sarault (Free Agent) scored in the shootout to give Sarnia the victory tonight.

January 26, 2013, Dubuque Fighting Saints at US NTDP Under-17 (USHL)

DUB #4 LD Michael Downing (2013) – Played a great two-way game with an edge. Joined the attack frequently and intelligently. He covered back well and the one time he got caught up ice, it wasn't his fault. Was very involved in the offense and even ended up below the offensive goal line a few times. Read passes well in the neutral zone and stepped up to intercept them, transitioning into attack immediately. Picked on Jack Eichel the whole game, chirping him every time they were out on the ice together. Was aggressive at 4-on-4 and made great decisions. Had a major misplay on a 1-on-2 outnumbered situation. Took a dirty slashing penalty.

USA #36 LD Brandon Fortunato (2014) – Undersized defenseman had another strong offensive game. Powerplay work is outstanding. Broke the puck out with fluid skating and showed good awareness to get the puck through the neutral zone without just dumping it in. Moved his very feet quickly for loose pucks and while under pressure. Evaded contact with nifty stickhandling.

USA #37 RC Alex Tuch (2014) – Played a great game. Spent a lot of his time around the net, making life difficult on the goaltender and defensemen trying to get him out of the play. Backchecked hard, played the body well. Showed some flashes of skill with a great toe drag and subsequent dangerous shot. Has a nice wrister.

USA #40 LW Jared Fiegl (2014) – Kind of a cannonball type. Fiesty but didn't show much as far as finesse. Took the puck hard down the outside and powered to the net. Played the body hard but overdid it on a dirty check from behind.

USA #45 RD Louis Belpedio (2014) – Size was an issue today. Was outmuscled in his defensive zone and as a result had a hard time making smart decisions with the puck, leading to giveaways. Flashes of skill but needs to play stronger.

USA #46 RW Jack Eichel (2015) – Another impressive game from Eichel. Played with a determined game with a fluid combination of power and skill. Strong on the puck with excellent stickwork and puck protection. Stickhandling was precise with attention to detail. Got a lot on shots, even when he had poor foot positioning. Backchecked hard and showed pickpocket ability. Knocked pucks out of the air with good hand-eye. Was one step ahead of his linemates at times, hitting their sticks with passes before they realized they were coming.

USA #47 LW Ryan Hitchcock (2014) – Skill player was noticeable on a few shifts. Quick feet, gave an honest effort. Was a threat to score shorthanded through hard work and finesse. Came in on a defender in a 1-on-1 situation and beat him clean thanks to pure determination, looking like he was about to lose the handle and fighting through the check.

USA #48 LW Sonny Milano (2014) – Very useful player. Hands and skating were excellent in tight. Worked very well in the cycle, creating space with stickhandling. Protected the puck with finesse, passing it to himself along the boards and dodging checks. Wasn't afraid to go hard to the net and scored a goal on a rebound.

USA #49 RD Jack Glover (2014) – Had a strong game today. Played actively, always on his toes and reactive to the play. Still very lanky but strong. Kept his stick in lanes and played the body well. Showed some offensive upside with a great play where he pinched down, took control of the puck, drew a defender with poise and found an open teammate with a precise pass for a golden chance.

USA #52 LC Ryan MacInnis (2014) – Played OK, but was very sluggish on his feet today. Skating was labored. Penalty killed well and blocked shots. Got himself into position for good shots, finding space in the high slot and around the crease. Missed an empty net off a great feed.

USA #53 RD Joshua Wesley (2014) – Not a very strong effort. Made a few glaring lapses in coverage. Liked to keep his crease clear but overdid it, losing focus on play around him. Flashed a big slapshot but not much offense otherwise.

USA #55 RW Joe Wegwerth (2014) – Loved his game today. Gritty, physical player who's tough to play against. Laid out completely to block a shot and was chippy all the time, during the play and after whistles. Offensive upside seems limited as he had a hard time maintaining possession.

Scout's Notes: USA RD Ryan Collins (2014) was physical in front of his net and along the boards. Credit to DUB Keegan Ford (2014) for standing up for his teammate and fighting pesky USA LC Blake Christensen (2014).

Jan. 26 2013, Québec Remparts @ Halifax Mooseheads, (QMJHL)

HAL #22 C, MacKinnon, Nathan (2013) : There are a lot of things that I liked about the game he played and many that I didn't like too. I liked the way on some occasions he just kept the play simple on the rush, he just put the puck behind the Québec D's and used his blazing speed and explosiveness to get first to that puck and come to the net. He's a natural goal scorer and a real competitive guy, shows frustration when he looses the puck. He made his way easily through Québec players behind the net. I thought he could have passed the puck a little bit more to teammates, sometimes puts all the pressure on his shoulders and starts trying to do all by his own. I didn't like the way that he still was trying fancy stuff, trying to get through players, stuff that didn't work, when the game was 3-2

Québec at the end of the game, showing a lack maturity. He has an amazing skillset and lightning quick hands, but doesn't always seem to be in control of what he does, sometimes will dangle and loose the puck by himself, something that hapened at really bad times on the powerplay in the 3rd. The intensity and work ethic is always there with MacKinnon, sometimes the decisions are not good with and without the puck. Defensively was responsible in the game and with the speed he has, he comes to help D-men pretty deep and puts pressure quickly with a great active stick.

HAL #24 D, Murphy, Matt (2013) : Murphy was again a rollercoaster ride to watch, sometimes playing great shifts and sometimes really poor ones. Can be pretty dangerous at the blue line, finds lanes well and has good breakout passes, but in his own zone, he wants to be too agressive and puts himself out of position, can lay the body pretty well but needs to do it smartly.

HAL #27 LW, Drouin, Jonathan (2013) : Was again the best player overall on the ice. He finds space where there doesn't seem to be. He slows down the play when no options are available, executes everything to perfection almost offensively. He jumped on a rebound for his goal and will go in high traffic areas to get goals, his compete level has improved tremendously in the last year. He wins his battles and made some superb defensive plays anticipating them very well and being smart. Speed is great and the puck seems glued to his stick even though he's at top speed carrying the puck. I think he does a better job at using his skillset smartly than MacKinnon.

HAL #52 D, Weegar, Mackenzie (2013*) : Impressive showing from Weegar, an Ontarian free agent signing from Halifax at the start of the season. He moved the puck very well in the offensive zone with crisp simple passes, made great breakout feed to forwards on tape, rarely missed a breakout pass, was physical down-low while playing tons of minutes espcially in the 3rd period. His positioning was good most of the times keeping track of where are his teammates and where he should be, never leaving the slot coverage. I'd like to see him get more shots on net instead of always passing when he's doing the puck-moving duties. He's a bit small but really strong and smart.

HAL #31 G, Fucale, Zachary (2013) : Seemed shaky throughout most of the game. Gave away bad rebounds and seemed to fight with the puck. Had a hard time tracking pucks through traffic and gave away a bad goal between the legs from the blue-line in the 3rd period. He's not nearly agressive enough and seems to have a hard time keeping focus when the other team doesn't have many shots.

QUE #10 LW, Duclair, Anthony (2013) : One of the best defensive games I've seen Duclair play. He made some superb backchecks against MacKinnon and came back to help his D's, in a game where the neutral zone was very important because of the speed of Halifax, Duclair played his role well and took a lot of pucks away from the Halifax offense by being tenacious and being smartly positionned. He was disciplined in the way he played and got rewarded by being on the ice at the end of the game protecting a lead and scoring the Empty Net goal. Offensively was average, being at its best when he used his puck protection skills to cruise around the offensive zone passing the puck when the option shows up and using the passing skills he posesses to find teammates. He also tried to get through players too many times instead of putting the puck behind them and chasing it down-low, considering he has, he would have much more success on some occasions. But big improvements in the work ethic and defensive game.

QUE #73 RW, Erne, Adam (2013) : Played a typical Adam Erne game with less physicality than usual. He used his speed well wide a couple of times to get space and lanes to get to the net which I always like to see. Played smart hockey and responsible hockey in the neutral zone and in his own end, taking away tons of space quickly with his skating abilities. He showed the versatility of his game playing a more defensive role in that game and responding well. Was strong on the walls and puck protection skills are great.

QUE #94 RW, Sorensen, Nick (2013) : Quick passer, he made a couple of nice plays from the slot, one that resulted in Verret's goal. He has a pretty good offensive hockey sense, but I thought he was a notch lower than usual in terms of energy and intensity. He didn't compete well on the walls, not playing a physical game and was distant from the play trying to anticipate instead of supporting his teammates. He sees the ice well and great awareness but can't rely only on his talent to be successful.

January 27, 2013, Dubuque Fighting Saints at US NTDP Under-17 (USHL)

DUB #4 LD Michael Downing (2013) – Was invisible for most of the first period, but showed up well after. Chirped frequently, really got into it with the US team. Kept his head up and tracked the play well, solid positioning. Made the odd mistake but covered for them with effort. Was great on the powerplay, roving around the zone and dropping down to threaten at the back door. Night was cut short when he scrapped with Joe Wegwerth halfway through the 3rd.

USA #46 RW Jack Eichel (2015) – Quietest game of the weekend, but still played well. Skating was noticeably excellent again, stride is strong and efficient. Was strong on the puck down the wing and showed the awareness to find teammates off the rush while still at speed. Great touch to lift the puck on shots from in tight. Was a threat to score 1-on-2.

USA #47 LW Ryan Hitchcock (2014) – Nice game from the shifty, undersized forward. Helped his defensemen down low and liked to break the puck out himself. Transition game was smooth, was able to forced turnovers and immediately kickstart the offense with acceleration or quick passes. Flashed a great wristshot, strong with good placement. Was pushed off the puck too easily.

USA #48 LW Sonny Milano (2014) – Showed great skill again today along the boards. Cycling game is top end. Was able to maintain control in the zone for extended periods of time. Stickhandling was excellent with nice dangling ability, dragged the puck quickly and precisely around opponents. Burned end-to-end with great speed 4-on-4. Did a little too much at times and didn't deal with contact well on the occasion that he did get pinned down.

USA #49 RD Jack Glover (2014) – Excellent tools but decisions were mixed. Was physical on the boards and tough in front of his net. Instinctively identified his checks and activated. Great awareness in his zone. Had a tougher time against the rush. Got beat on a criss-cross play closing too early and in another situation, positioned himself right but took a needless penalty. Was evasive with the puck with quick feet against the forecheck but had one brutal giveaway in his end that led to a partial breakaway. Really like his upside despite the mistakes.

USA #55 RW Joe Wegwerth (2014) – Another workmanlike effort from Wegwerth. Was safe in his zone and showed good offensive positioning today but lacked finish. Got into a scrap with Michael Downing in the third that ended his day early.

Scout's Notes: RD Joshua Wesley (2014) had a weak showing, with relaxed coverage and mental errors. RD Ryan Collins (2014) was too weak in front of the net for a player of his size.

Jan 29th, 2013, Portland Winterhawks vs Everett Silvertips (WHL)

EVT #15 C Bauml Kohl (2013) Kohl played on and off tonight. He played a decent defensive game, blocking shots and chipping pucks but not enough to stop the Hawks speedy forwards. The lack of size and strength is his biggest weakness along the boards battling for loose pucks.

EVT #16 C Stadnyk Carson (2013) I like his game, but looked lost tonight. Struggled to do much of anything. Had a couple rushes but tried to skate up the middle and split the D just to turn over the puck. He struggled to get the puck out of his own zone and looked like he had on his blinders tonight.

EVT #25 D Mueller Mirco (2013) Mirco play was consitent tonight, pushing Portlands top snipers to the outside. Played strong along the boards, made good first passes out of the zone but seemed to struggle clearing the slot and boxing playesr out insde the paint tonight. He rushed the puck a couple shifts and was joining the offensive rush, his offensive talents are starting to show more each game.

PORT #3 LD Jones Seth (2013)- Jones played solid through out the whole game, he joined the rush looking to help the offensive threat almost every shift. The big swift blueliner used his stick well and showed good defensive presences. He was calm and cool with the puck hitting tape to tape stretch ice passes. He QB the power play and dazzled with his vision adding 2 PP assists. Jones seems to shy away from the body contact, i noticed when pressured hard on the forecheck he tends to panic with the puck.

PORT #27 RW Bjorkstrand Oliver (2013)- Oliver was a work horse tonight, good crash and bang style of play. Won the race for looses puck and was just dominate over Everetts defense. Kid has ton of raw skill.

PORT #19 C Petan Nicolas (2013)- Petan was the best player on the ice. This little mighty mouse was slick and unoticed, slipping into the scoring areas untouched. Petans hands are greasy in tight and dangled the D with ease. He showed his offensive creativity adding 1 goals and 2 assists. Petan needs to add some size to his smaller frame.

Scouts Notes. Portland's Hanson and Vorobev played decent defensive games tonight, Ty Rattie (St.Louis) dazzled notching 2 goals. Portland dominated from the drop off the puck. Everett was unable to keep up with Portland speed and puck movement.

Final Score 6-0 Portland

Jan 30, 2013, Vancouver Giants vs. Prince Albert Raiders (WHL)

VAN#27 RW, Houck, Jackson(2013) Had an excellent game offensively, and was able to score 2 goals while creating a number of scoring chances. Both of his goals came from great work in front of the net and outmuscling opponents to rebounds and quickly getting shots off. Liked how he was able to get good positioning in the slot by the far post. Had a good jump to his steps tonight, but might have had something to do with Prince Albert looking exhausted at the end of a long road trip. Brought his physical game as usual and was able to wear down opponents on the forecheck as the game went along.

VAN#44 LD, Geertsen, Mason(2013) Geertsen had a good game in his own end tonight by being responsible with the puck and getting in good position. He made good reads to knock away passes and shots tonight, and he was very tough to play against because of his physicality. He took advantage of tired opponents and just punished them along the walls all night. On the only goals against, he screened his own goaltender and was caught in no man's land. His check was behind him by the post waiting for the rebound, so he really should have just gotten out of the way and look to take away any rebounds. Logged a ton of minutes tonight, and did not look tired at all.

PA#10 LD, Morrissey, Josh(2013) Smart defenseman who looked exhausted tonight. The Raiders only dressed 5 defensemen for this game, and Morrissey had to log a ton of minutes at the end of a very long road trip. He had to play on the right side a few times during the game and struggled. Just did not look very accustomed to playing on his off side. He was very poised with the puck, and limited the number of rushes he made and the number of times he joined the rush. He did not bring much of a physical game tonight, but did crash the crease a few times throughout the night to start a scrum. As the game went on, he had a tendency to chase the puck and a couple of times left the slot wide open which resulted in good scoring chances. He was missing some explosiveness in his steps tonight. Really liked the way he skates and his abilities to quickly shift directions and turn on a time.

PA#29 LC, Draisaitl, Leon(2014) Big, skilled forward who did not have a great game tonight. Was a step behind everybody in terms of skating. Just looked sluggish and his legs looked like they weighed a 100 pounds each. He was quite weak along the boards, and needs to use his big frame better to protect the puck along the walls. He was also soft tonight, and passed up on a hit a few times during the game. He showed off his great vision a few times during the game, particularly on the power play.

SCOUT'S NOTES: Prince Albert looked exhausted from the drop of the puck. They were on the road for 19 days and just did not have any gas left. Vancouver really took advantage of it, and pounced on them early and often with tenacity and physical play. I was disappointed in Josh Morrissey's performance tonight. Would have liked to watched him when he was less tired and when he does not have to play as many minutes as he did. He looked good in the first period, and then everything just went down hill from there. He tried to force plays when his team was trailing. Mark McNeill had an up and down game tonight. He showed off his quick release and laser beam of a wrist shot on the only goal that the Raiders managed to score.

FINAL SCORE: 5-1 Vancouver

Jan 30, 2013, Saint Johns Sea dogs vs. Victoriaville Tigers (QMJHL)

VIC # 3, D, Diaby, Jonathan (2013) Diaby did a nice job of picking off a pass to force a turnover then clear the puck up out of the zone on the penalty kill. He used his body really well to keep the opposition from gaining the inside track to the net and used his stick well to knock the puck away from the opposition. He put good pressure on the puck carrier but can't follow him up too high in his own end and put himself out of position. He got his stick in lanes in front of the net to try to block passes and breakup plays and used his stick to force the opposition to the outside. He needs to watch the offensive zone turnovers by forcing passes through the opposition.

VIC # 12, C, Rehak, Dominik (2013) Rehak protected the puck well from the opposition's pressure and was able to move the puck back to the point for a good shot opportunity for his defenseman. He was distributing the puck well on the rush through the neutral zone and got to the slot then opened up to take a pass but fanned on his shot opportunity. He needs to watch the offensive zone turnovers on bad passes that the opposition was able to pick off.

VIC # 25, RW, Chenier, Carl (2013) Chenier protected the puck really well on the wide drive and put good pressure on the fore-check but can't take offensive zone penalties. He also has to watch the turnovers by forcing passes through the opposition.

VIC # 55, D, Trickett, Mark (2013) Trickett was able to protect the puck along the boards in his own end to avoid the opposition's pressure then moved the puck up to start the breakout. He is pretty calm with the puck and has nice hands and moves to skate the puck out of his own end then move the puck up on the rush making some good passes through the neutral zone. He held the offensive line well and was able to get a cycle going in deep in the offensive zone. He needs to hit the net on his shots from the high slot.

VIC # 57, LW, Veilleux, Tommy (2013) Veilleux got the puck in deep off the rush to get the cycle going in the offensive zone and he battled well for the puck. He was able to get the breakout started with some good passes out of the zone and put great pressure and physicality on the fore-check to force turnovers then move the puck out front to a man in the slot. He protected the puck on the wide drive into the offensive zone, but still needs to add some size and strength so that he's not knocked off the puck so easily.

SJS # 6, D, Doucet, Jeremy (2013) Doucet was jumping up on the pinch to try to hold the puck in the offensive zone and keep the attack alive, as he played the puck carrier with a nice element of physicality. He was able to get the cycle going off his pinch and used his stick and pressure to take the puck and force turnovers. He was hustling for loose pucks but has to watch the turnovers up along his own boards just throwing the puck up on a panic play. He also needs to watch the turnovers up along the boards in his own end, and needs to get his shots through to the net on chances from the point, rather than shooting into shin pads.

SJS # 27, LW, Cooper, Oliver (2013) Cooper got a cycle going in deep and went to the front of the net to open up and take a pass. He picked off a pass in his own end to rush the puck back up the ice with speed to get it in deep and did a good job of stepping up on his man in the neutral zone to pressure him and take the puck away, forcing a turnover. He did a great job of getting in lanes to pick off passes on the penalty kill then clear the puck out of the zone and he also got in front of his own net to deflect pucks out of danger. He put good pressure on the fore-check but needs to get the puck in deep more often on the rush rather than turning the puck over in the offensive zone on some bad passes.

SJS # 37, LW, Anderson, Stephen (2013) Anderson made a nice pass on the rush to start the breakout then he drove hard to the net with his stick down looking for chances in tight. He distributed the puck well on the rush up the ice, and then got beside the net for a good shot opportunity, however it was from a bad angle and he had better options to move the puck to a more dangerous area. He did an excellent job reading the play to steal the puck on a turnover in the neutral zone, then he came in on a break opportunity for a great chance on a good move and shot. He came back for support in his own end and put good pressure on the puck carrier. On the rush he went to the slot and opened up well to take a pass and score on a one-timer.

FINAL SCORE: 2-1 Victoriaville Tigers

Jan 31, 2013, Youngstown Phantoms vs. USNTDP U18 (USHL)

USA # 6, D, Thompson, Keaton (2013) Thompson made some great 1st passes out of the zone to start the rush, and did an excellent job of holding on to the puck under pressure. He made some nice moves to skate the puck up the ice, and was able to get his point shot off quickly and through to the net. He did a good job distributing the puck off the rush into the offensive zone, and is a pretty good smooth skating defenseman, but turned the puck over in his own end holding on to the puck too long. He also got beat wide with speed standing still in his own end.

USA # 7, C, Compher, J.T. (2013) Compher showed some great speed and hands on an end-to-end rush, and was protecting the puck really well on the wide drive, but at times was trying to force the puck through the opposition to get it to the front of the net. He put some good low shots on net off the rush on the wide drive, and was also driving to the net with the puck. He has some pretty good hands and agility under pressure, and a nice net-front presence on the power play. He was able to find a man on an excellent pass right in front of the net, and was battling hard for loose pucks in front of the net. He was going to the net to tip pucks, and has some exceptional speed and puck distribution through the neutral zone. He put some good shots on net from the high slot, and was moving the puck well on the odd-man rush leading to the team's 2nd goal of the game. He protects the puck really well, but needs to watch the turnovers trying to skate the puck into the offensive zone.

USA # 10, RW, Allen, Evan (2013) Allen did a nice job driving the puck to the slot to put a good shot on net, and was protecting the puck well. He was able to take a pass right in front of the net for an excellent chance in tight, but then later was unable to handle a pass off the rush resulting in a turnover and an odd-man rush opportunity for the opposition. He has some nice hands in order to get to the slot with the puck, and was moving it around really well in the offensive zone. He also made a really good pass to lead a man into the offensive zone with speed.

USA # 22, LW, Fasching, Hudons (2013) Fasching has some nice hands under pressure, and is able to get the puck in deep off the rush. He was battling well for the puck along the boards, and protecting the puck nicely on the wide drive. He got a good cycle going in deep in the offensive zone, and used his stick well to pressure the puck carrier. He also displayed some good moves and hands skating the puck up the ice, but missed his target on some weak passes through the neutral zone.

YNG # 9, C, Cangelosi, Austin (2013) Cangelosi is a smaller forward, but was coming back and providing some great support in his own end. He made some great breakout passes to start the rush, and also some really good passes to find an open man in the slot. He battles for the puck and uses his body to get the inside track to the net and put a good shot on from in tight. He put some really good pressure on the fore-check to force turnovers and keep the attack going. He was cycling the puck well in the offensive zone, and has some really good quickness and agility with the puck. He opened up down low next to the net on the power play to take a pass and put a good shot on net, and made a great pass to set-up a one-timer on the power play for the team's 1st goal of the game. He has some great hands and moves cutting towards the inside lane off the rush, but needs to watch the offensive zone turnovers without looking first.

YNG # 27, C, Stork, Luke (2013) Stork is able to get a pretty decent cycle started, and has some good size, and physicality to finish some big hits along the boards. He put good pressure on the puck carrier, and was getting his stick in lanes in his own end to try to breakup passes and plays. He can distribute the puck well on the odd-man rush opportunity.

FINAL SCORE: 3-2 USNTDP U18

Feb 1, 2013, Swift Current Broncos vs. Edmonton Oil Kings (WHL)

SWI # 2, D, Heatherington, Dillon (2013) Heatherington is able to move the puck up on the breakout to start the rush and put some good pressure on the puck carrier in his own end to force turnovers. He got the puck in deep into the offensive zone on some pretty simple dump-in plays and was also able to lead the rush up the ice by skating the puck out of his own end. He used his stick well to knock the puck from the opposition, he is calm with the puck and can make some good little chip plays to avoid the opposition's pressure to start the breakout. He did a great job of getting down in lanes to block passes and breakup plays for the opposition and also went down in front of his net to block shots. He was nice and physical on the puck carrier to take the puck away from the opposition and showed great speed to skate the puck up the ice end-to-end to get a shot off from the high slot. He did a nice job of holding the offensive blue line, however in his own end he was unable to tie up his man or clear the rebound out of play and the opposition scored.

SWI # 10, C, Cave, Colby (2013) Cave put some nice pressure on the fore-check and got his stick in lanes to breakup plays for the opposition through the neutral zone. He distributed the puck well on the rush and did a nice job of trying to cut to the middle to drive the puck to the net from the side boards. He made a great pass from behind the net for a man open right in front, however needs to move the puck down low more often when he's under pressure as he did get caught trying to hold on to the puck instead to make a play and lost the opportunity all together. He got in a lane in front of his net to pick off a pass to breakup the opposition's chance and start the rush back up the ice, and he was playing the puck carrier with a nice element of physicality. He needs to watch the turnovers up the middle through the neutral zone on some of his breakout passes.

SWI # 12, LW, Merkley, Jay (2013) Merkley got the puck in deep on a pretty simple dump and chase play and he put good pressure on the fore-check. He was able to get a cycle going in deep in the offensive zone and showed nice speed on the rush into the offensive zone to come in on the goalie and make a great move for a really good opportunity in tight. He was also playing with a nice edge to his game.

SWI # 20, LW, Bosc, Denis (2013) Bosc got a nice cycle going in deep off the rush by just chipping the puck in deep. He played with a pretty nice level of compete; however it would still definitely benefit him to add some size and strength so that when he is hit, he is not separated from the puck so easily. He did a nice job of using his body to protect the puck from the opposition and was able to really get going on the rush with some good speed on the wide drive, then made a great centering pass for a man driving the net.

SWI # 25, C, MacKay, Zac (2013) MacKay put good pressure on the puck carrier at the point and also through the neutral zone, but at times was overly aggressive and got beat quite easily leaving himself out of position on the play. He got his stick in lanes to breakup passes and plays for the opposition in his own end and he went to the net well looking for loose pucks and rebounds in tight. He did a nice job of getting the puck in deep off the rush and also got involved with the opposition after whistles.

EDM # 12, C, Benson, Cole (2013) Benson protected the puck effectively and showed nice strength and agility to twist away from the opposition's pressure and start the cycle. He was able to get a nice effective cycle going along the boards in the offensive zone and also distributed the puck well on the rush. He got open down low in the slot to take a pass for a good opportunity, but the defenseman for the opposition made a great diving defensive play to take away the chance all together.

EDM # 23, LW, Kulda, Edgar (2013) Kulda was able to rush the puck up the ice, but needs to watch some of the turnovers on puck mishandles. He displayed nice strength and puck protection along the wall in the offensive zone and got an effective cycle started. He was however taking some low-chance long outside shots off on the rush.

EDM # 27, C, Lazar, Curtis (2013) Lazar displayed really good strength on the puck to avoid being knocked off it as he rushed into the offensive zone, and also showed great agility to avoid a hit and still hold on to the puck to make a play. He got to the front of the net to battle for territory looking for loose pucks and rebounds and got a good cycle going in deep in the offensive zone. He battled so well for a loose puck in front of the net to score on a rebound in tight, and later again went to the net and banged at a loose puck to knock it in and score from right in front of the net. He opened up well in the high slot off the rush to take a pass and put a good shot on net and was able to take a bad pass off his skate on the rush in full stride. He displayed great agility and creativity with the puck to distance himself from the opposition and was also physical and had a big hit to knock over the opposition in open ice through the neutral zone. He took a long outside shot on the rush that was weak and missed the net rather than moving the puck to the front of the net to create a scoring opportunity.

FINAL SCORE: 3-0 Edmonton Oil Kings

Feb. 1, 2013, Waterloo Blackhawks vs. Green Bay Gamblers (USHL)

GBG # 5, D, Olofsson, Gustav (2013) Olofsson made a really good lead pass to start the breakout on a quick transition, and is calm with the puck moving it up out of the zone well on the penalty kill. He took a pass to lead the rush down low, then moved the puck to a man driving the net out front. He used his stick well to knock the puck away from the opposition, and has a nice hard shot that he kept down low on target from the point.

GBG # 16, C, Weis, Matthew (2013) Weis made an excellent pass in the offensive zone to find a man down low cutting towards the net for a good chance from in tight. He was getting the puck in deep into the offensive zone off the rush, and made a really nice pass to find an open man in the high slot off the rush. He was driving hard to the net with the stick down looking for opportunities in tight, and was able to get the cycle started pretty well deep in the offensive zone.

GBG # 24, LW, Siroky, Ryan (2013) Siroky put some really nice pressure and physicality on the fore-check, and made some nice moves and puck protection on the rush to gain the offensive zone and try to drive the puck to the slot. He has some pretty good agility, was cycling the puck well, but took some long high shots off the rush instead of moving the puck or driving it down low.

GBG # 81, C, Winborg, Adam (2013) Winborg put some great pressure and physicality on the fore-check and was battling hard for the puck along the boards. He was driving the net well with his stick down, and made a good centering pass to try to find a man out front, but it was picked off by the opposition.

WAT # 3, D, McCoshen, Ian (2013) McCoshen made a good pass to move the puck up out of the zone on the breakout, and has a really nice hard shot on net from the point. He is calm with the puck and moves it quickly to avoid the opposition's pressure, but needs to watch the turnovers in his own end along the boards. He was jumping up on the attack driving the net with his stick down, ad was skating the puck up the ice well on the rush to put a good shot on net. He needs to add a bit of strength so that he's not knocked over so easily.

WAT # 71, C, Salerno, Brendon (2013) Salerno showed some good speed on the rush to drive the puck to the net, but was knocked off the puck and lost his opportunity. He is able to take a pass at full speed through the neutral zone to gain the offensive zone with speed, but missed his breakout pass in the neutral zone resulting in an icing.

WAT # 91, C, Cammarata, Taylor (2013) Cammarata made a really great pass to spring a man into the offensive zone with speed, and opened up well in the slot to take a pass for a good chance, but has to hit the net on the opportunity. He made an excellent drop-pass to create room for a teammate in the slot, then drove hard to the net looking for chances. He was able to take a pass in behind the opposition's defense to go in on a break, then made a really nice move to score the team's 2nd goal of the game. He made some really good lead passes to start the rush, and showed some great creativity in the offensive zone. He had a really nice shot from the high slot on the power play, which the team scored on the rebound, and showed some good agility and puck protection in the offensive zone. He spreads the defense out wide really well skating east to west, rather than north south a lot of the time, and was holding the puck in the offensive zone nicely. He has some really quick hands to avoid pressure from the opposition.

FINAL SCORE: 6-4 Green Bay Gamblers

Feb 1, 2013, Red Deer Rebels vs. Lethbridge Hurricanes (WHL)

RDR # 8, D, Doetzel, Kayle (2013) Doetzel put good pressure on the puck carrier and was battling well for the puck to try to win it off the opposition. He showed great agility and puck protection to avoid the opposition's pressure then moved the puck up out of the zone along the boards. He played the puck carrier with a nice element of physicality and was playing his man pretty hard, tying up his stick well but can't cross the line and take penalties on the play.

RDR # 21, C, Johnson, Wyatt (2013) Johnson put great pressure on the puck carrier in the offensive zone and went to the net pretty well looking for loose pucks and rebounds. He did a good job of tying up his man on the back-check in tight in front of the net and was battling well for pucks along the boards. He put good pressure on the point in his own end and was protecting the puck well on the wide drive trying to cut to the middle towards the net for a good chance, but was unable to get by the defender. He was cycling the puck nicely in deep in the offensive zone and did a good job trying to jam the puck into the net on a wrap-around attempt from behind. He did a nice job of skating the puck up the ice to get it in deep in the offensive zone and he went hard to the net looking for loose pucks and rebounds.

RDR # 27, RW, Bellerive, Matt (2013) Bellerive got to the front of the net really nicely on the power play looking for loose pucks and rebounds and was battling for his territory. He was able to get the puck in deep into the offensive zone off the rush but was taking lots of long outside shots and he needs to hit the net on his shots from the high slot off the rush at the very least.

LET # 6, D, Erkramps, Macoy (2013) Erkramps stepped up into the high slot to provide teammates with pass options to take the pass and put a good shot on. He did a nice job of protecting the puck from the opposition's pressure and displayed a great speed, quickness and agility. He did a really good job of taking away the opposition's opportunities in front of the net and made a nice pass through the neutral zone to lead a teammate into the offensive zone with speed. He had a nice shot from the point that was tipped in for a goal however he needs to watch the neutral zone turnovers when he is not strong enough on the puck and also on passes along the boards trying to move the puck out of the zone. He got caught in behind the net and was unable to help out in a scramble in front that resulted in a goal for the opposition.

LET # 10, D, Henry, Adam (2013) Henry used his body so well to stand up his man and separate him from the puck. He forced his man to the outside really nicely on the rush and was able to make a good 1st pass out of the zone to start the breakout. He protected the puck well on the wide drive into the offensive zone to get a cycle started in deep and made a pretty nice pass to find a man in the slot from up high. He jumped in on the rush to join the attack and provide scoring options in the offensive zone and held the offensive line pretty well in order to get his shot through to the net on chances from the point on the power play. He needs to watch some of the offensive zone turnovers on puck mishandles.

LET # 17, RW, Watson, Jamal (2013) Watson put great pressure and physicality on the fore-check and did a really good job of protecting the puck on the wide drive then he cut to the front of the net. He got the puck in deep on some pretty simple dump and chase plays but at times was overly patient with the puck off the rush waiting to make a play and the opportunity was taken away. He has to watch the turnovers up the middle on some pretty soft passes.

LET # 22, D, Hackman, Lenny (2013) Hackman made a nice pass to move the puck up out of his own end along the boards on the breakout and battled well for the puck along the wall behind his own net. He had a nice clear out of the zone on the penalty kill and got his shot through to the net from the point to generate a rebound for a good opportunity.

LET # 26, RW, Blomqvist, Axel (2013) Blomqvist got in lanes and put good pressure on the point to block a shot. He did a good job of driving the puck to the net from the side of the goal and was able to protect the puck along the boards in behind the opposition's net to get a cycle going. He tied up his man in his own end but can't take penalties on those types of plays. He was putting good pressure on the fore-check, had a nice net-front presence on the power play getting in the goalie's face and tipping pucks in tight and he got to the front of the net with his stick down battling for his territory.

FINAL SCORE: 3-2 Lethbridge Hurricanes

Feb 1, 2013, Vancouver Giants vs. Kelowna Rockets (WHL)

VAN#39 LC, Foster, Thomas(2014) Rookie forward had a good game tonight. Not particularly fast, but he was able to beat opponents to the net and created some good chances in tight. He showed some good toughness to drive to the net and take a beating for most of the night. Foster was in good position at both ends of the ice tonight, and was quite responsible in his own end. He picked up open guys down low and did a good job to not let them get open for too long to have good scoring chances. He still has a lot of work to do in all areas of his game, but it was nice to see him show some progression in his development from the beginning of the year where he looked absolutely lost.

VAN#44 LD, Geertsen, Mason(2013) Had a much tougher time tonight than against Prince Albert. He made a few bad turnovers, and one led directly to a goal. Was not as noticeable physically tonight, particularly along the walls. His gap control was good, and did not get beat wide. Geertsen was able to use his stick really well to knock away pucks. He did a good job of protecting the slot. Offensively, he pinched down to keep the play alive a number of times during the game and did not get caught once on a bad gamble. He needs to get the puck through traffic more, and keep the play simple to be effective. Definitely not going to be featured on a power play on a good team.

KEL#4 RD, Bowey, Madison(2013) Dynamic defenseman had more of a quiet game tonight with than puck than usual. Did not rush the puck up as he usually does tonight, but just made solid passes to get the attack going. He was smart with the puck and did not turn over the puck. Really like how he always has his head up to be aware of his surroundings. Made some positioning mistakes in the game, particularly in the slot. He would gamble and try to take away the pass to the slot from the wall by creeping towards the passer, and they would get through a few times which resulted in some good scoring chances for the opponents. However, he was in good position more often than not. Had a very active stick and broke up a couple 2 on 1 plays. Really like his aggressiveness on the blueline, and his skating abilities allow him to come back and get into position.

KEL#24 RC, Baillie, Tyson(2014) Skilled forward had a bit of an up and down game tonight. Showed that he definitely needs to improve his game along the walls and be stronger on his skates. He got knocked down too easily throughout the game. He could not generate anything down low. However, he was very dangerous on the rush. He finished off a 2 on 1 by taking the pass and quickly releasing the puck, and made a very nice pass on a 2 on 1 opportunity to give his teammate an easy tap in goal. Defensively, competed hard without the puck and provided a lot of help down low. Could get faster, and will need to because of his lack of size.

SCOUT'S NOTES: Vancouver came out hard tonight, but it just was not enough against Kelowna, who have been on an absolute tear lately. Colton Sissons was great at both ends of the ice. Not a flashy player, but very strong along the boards and just executes. So impressive defensively. Like how he has improved his speed since last year. Zach Franko of Kelowna displayed some impressive stickhandling abilities. Just could not finish off plays however. Tyler Morrison of Vancouver looked awful defensively.

FINAL SCORE: 5-1 Kelowna

Feb 1, 2013, Moose Jaw Warriors vs. Medicine Hat Tigers (WHL)

MJ#23 RC, Gore, Bryson(2013) Small, 2 way centre played a good game tonight using his speed to create good scoring chances. Scored a nice goal off the rush on a counter attack in the neutral zone as he received a pass and quickly blew past by 2 defenders and finished off the play quite nicely. Offensive abilities were inconsistent tonight. There were times when he would be able to make good plays in speed, like quickly tapping an errant outlet pass from his skate to his stick to continue to skate in full speed, then not be able to hand a simple pass in the neutral zone. Scored a goal by tipping a shot from the slot. Offensive instincts were not very good tonight. Went to the net, but was not able to capitalize on any opportunities, nor was he able to get away from traffic and find an open area on the ice to receive a pass for a scoring chance. A regular on the PK, as he played with good intensity tonight.

MJ#27 RW, White, Torrin(2013) A small, quick forward who looked invisible tonight other than when he scored his 2 goals. Very similar to each other as he just took a loose puck in the slot and quickly snapped them upstairs. A huge liability in the defensive zone tonight. He committed far too many turnovers off the wall, and looked lost on the d-zone coverage and could not maintain shooting lanes. Needs to play with much more intensity without the puck. Quite weak along the walls tonight as well.

MJ#19 RC, Point, Brayden(2014) The offensive leader on this team tonight. Created a lot of good scoring chances with his speed, intensity and offensive instincts. Point was consistently in good position to receive passes and to continue to keep the pressure up in the offensive zone. He was very quick out on the ice and made it difficult for opponents to knock him off the puck. Pretty strong on his skates as well. Always seemed to be around the net tonight and fought through traffic quite well. Showed his willingness to win tonight on a consistent basis. Most memorable play was when he was in the slot on even strength, and he was covered by 2 opponents who tried to check his stick, but he was able to fight them off and get a nice shot away. Made a nice play on a quick 2 on 1 opportunity as he looked like was going to shoot until the last moment, and slid the puck under the opposing defenseman's stick for an easy goal.

MH#5 RD, Lewington, Tyler(2013) Puck moving defenseman who stuck to his game tonight and struggled at times without the puck. Quite poised with the puck in any types of situation, and makes it easy for his team to break out of their zone. Not a particularly good play maker from the point, as he keeps the play simple. There were times when he was able to use his stick effectively to deflect away shots off the rush, then there were times when his stick was positioned poorly and opponents had an easy shot on net. Possesses above average speed, so he will have to continuously use his reach to drive opponents to the outside. Had bad gap control at one point, which costed his team a goal. The opposing forward just drove to the net past him and had an easy lane to the net. Was quite good along the walls and used his body well.

MH#7 RD, Jensen, Spenser(2013) Defensive defenseman had a bit of an off game tonight in his own end. Did not maintain good position off the rush and was beaten to the net a few times. Was a physical presence along the walls tonight, and really used his size to his advantage. Jensen was not afraid to block shots and made a few key blocks on the PK tonight. Not particularly great at reading the play tonight and played a really safe game, especially because he is an average skater, and Moose Jaw had a number of small, but quick forwards playing. Limited game tonight offensively. Made simple passes to his forwards, and was not involved offensively very much.

SCOUT'S NOTES: The Warriors played a very grinding game, and their counter attacks proved to be the difference tonight. They attacked with a lot of speed, which the Tigers had difficulty containing. Really liked the game that Brayden Point played tonight. He was all over the ice and played with a lot of intensity despite his size.

FINAL SCORE: 8-4 Moose Jaw

February 1st, 2013. Guelph Storm vs. Windsor Spitfires

GUE#7 D Ben Harpur (2013). One of the better games for Harpur so far this season. He used his long stick effectively to keep attackers to the outside and did not allow any good net drives along his side of the ice. Ben was very solid holding the offensive blue line and keeping pucks deep in the offensive zone instead of giving up the line easily and allowing quick Windsor counter attacks. He showed confidence controlling the puck along the offensive blue line and picked shot opportunities well. Harpur was also very effective in the defensive zone making smart safe passes on the breakout instead of forcing the stretch through traffic. He does occasionally get caught watching the play in the defensive zone, but when he is able to get into the corners he is good at using his size as an advantage to knock opponents off the puck.

GUE#11 F Jason Dickinson (2013). Dickinson was the best storm forward on the ice in this game. He displayed a good understanding of offensive zone positioning and seems to always find little openings to attack. Jason utilized solid puck movement to create give-and-go's with his line mates generating a number of offensive chances. He is a very smooth skater and shows confidence skating with the puck through the neutral zone, gaining the offensive line with ease. Dickinson especially stood out in this game for his strong physical presence, finishing a number of checks in both open ice and along the boards, helping to set the tone and pace for the Storm. He does need to improve on his offensive scoring touch, as he was unable to solve DeKort with a number of quality scoring chances.

GUE#20 F Justin Auger (2012). Auger had a strong game utilizing his size to essentially dominate the board battles in the neutral and offensive zone especially. Once he gains possession of the puck in the offensive zone, he is very hard to knock off of the puck and is adept at controlling the puck helping to create scoring chances with strong drives to the net. Justin shows confidence skating with the puck although he does need to work at moving the puck quicker as he missed a few streaking teammates throughout the game. Auger also needs to improve his foot speed although he does move fairly well for such a big kid once he gets a head of steam going.

WSR#16 F Kerby Rychel (2013 Late 94). Rychel was the offensive catalyst for the Spitfires in this matchup. Kerby possesses a fantastic quick release wrist shot which was especially on display beating Sparks with a dynamic wrister from the slot. He always seems to get into the slot and is an elite scorer with the puck on his stick in tight. Rychel also scored a dynamic goal skating down the wing before sending a rocket high over Spark's glove. Foot speed is occasionally noticeable when Rychel is in races for the puck, although he overcomes this negative with a strong scoring touch and elite vision and game sense. He shows a ton of confidence and wants the puck on his stick in the slot when the game is on the line.

WSR#66 F Joshua Ho-Sang (2014). Ho-Sang is a very strong skater and is especially adept at carrying the puck with confidence through the neutral zone. Joshua also showed creativity and playmaking ability in the offensive zone, setting up Rychel with a nifty passing play. His high level of confidence is also sometimes his downfall as he occasionally tries to make too fancy plays which end up as turnovers in the neutral zone. He possesses an elite wrist shot but needs to learn how to get into better scoring positions to really make use of it.

WSR#80 G Jordan DeKort (2013). DeKort absolutely stood on his head in this game, and was a major factor in the Windsor win. Jordan was a brick wall throughout the game and did not seem flustered with the high number of shots coming his way. He controlled rebounds very effectively and constantly battled to smother loose pucks in his crease area. DeKort showed a strong lateral ability making a number of sliding back door saves to help preserve the win. He flashed a solid glove hand, and was not afraid to come out of his net and stop the pucks for the Spitfire defenders on long dump-ins.

Feb 1st, 2013, Tri City Americans vs Everett Silvertips (WHL)

EVT #23 F Aasman Logan (2013) Big kids who just played a muck and grind style game. He notched the only lone goal for the tips. Played a solid defensive game, chipping and moving the puck out of the zone with limited turn overs at the blue. His offensive game was up close and personal hitting every Tri player who came near the puck, won most of the battles along the boards and show good vision.

EVT #5 D Betker Ben (2013) I like his game, was very physical for 3 periods, tough along the boards winning battles. Played with a hard work ethic and toughness most of the game. His defensive game need some development but has all the tools in the shed. When he was pressured with the puck he tends to panic and make bad decisions.

EVT #25 D Mueller Mirco (2013) Mirco played a strong physical game, he showed his toughness tonight in front punishing any Tri player standing in the slot. His game is consistent from game to game. Solid defensive game from Mirco.

TRI #15 Stromwall Malte (2013) Played with offensive finesse, Showed good creativity and vision with the puck. Had the Ams only goal and was finding the soft areas of the ice, had multiple scoring chances through out the game. His defensive game tonight was off, tends to move the puck to quickly and didnt show patients coming out of the defensive zone.

TRI #27 Rankin Connor (2013) Played a overall decent game, showed good patients and creativity with the puck. Offensive minded player who needs to play more of a two way defensive game. Has the tools just need to put them to work.

Scouts Notes: Everett's Bauml and Petryk both had good games, moving the puck well and creating good scoring chances off the rush. Tri Gutierrez had a good tilt with Evt Zipp. The game was pretty much back and forth action through out 3 periods of play with Tri just out shooting Evt 26-22. The game went to a shoot out with Tri coming out on top.

Final Score: 2-1 Tri City

Feb 2nd, 2013, Kamloops Blazers vs Everett Silvertips (WHL)

EVT #23 F Aasman Logan (2013) Played a typical grinder game, battling away in the corners for loose pucks and pushing around the Kamloops d-man. Had a good tilt with Kamloops Lipon with lipon getting the upper hand. His defensive game was subpar tonight.

EVT #5 D Betker Ben (2013) Betker played a good two way defensive game, he moved the puck well and was forcing Kamloops top players to turn over the puck. He was physical along the boards and was reading the ice well tonight.

EVT #24 D Oslanski Landon (Free Agent) Played a strong offensive game from the blue line. Notched 2 goals for Everett and was paired with Mueller in shutting down Kamloops top line most of the night.

KAM #34 F Lipon JC (2013) Showed good creativity and vision with the puck, played strong along the boards. Has a good offensive minded game, but i do question the defensive side. Seemed to get a little lazy in his own zone tonight.

KAM #33 D Cross Landon (2013) Notched two assists from the swift skating blueliner. Smart defensive game from Cross tonight, moved the puck with a solid first pass out of the zone and shut down Evt players along the boards. Needs to play a more physical game in front of the net.

Scouts Notes:

Another back and forth game tonight with Kamloops out shooting Everett 33-30. Everett's Leedahl and Hayer both had good two way games. Kamloops Colin Smith (COL) had a good game using his offensive mind and speed to create good scoring chances for Kamloops top line. Both teams play with passion, with Kamloops winning in the shoot out.

Final Score: 3-2 Kamloops

Feb 2, 2013, Brandon Wheat Kings vs. Regina Pats (WHL)

BRN # 2, D, Pulock, Ryan (2013) Pulock protected the puck really well to hold on to the puck under pressure and take a hit while not losing control of it. He had some real nice hands and moves with the puck and a nice shot from the point on the power play that was tipped in for a goal. He read the play really well to pick off a turnover in the neutral zone and jumped up to join the rush to take a pass in the high slot, however needs to hit the net on his opportunities. He made a fantastic pass to find a man driving the net for a goal and also came down low into the slot on the power play to provide teammates with good pass options.

BRN # 7, D, Roy, Eric (2013) Roy distributed the puck well from the point on the power play to set up one-timers from the high slot and he showed some nice patience with the puck to wait for lanes to open up to put shots on, however still has to get his shots through to the net with more consistency. He displayed some good agility to twist from the opposition's pressure and fantastic puck protection on the wide drive, then got to the front of the net to pick up his own rebound to score. He used his stick really well to knock the puck off the opposition and was clearing the puck well on the penalty kill. He has to watch some of the turnovers on his breakout passes up the middle through the neutral zone.

BRN # 15, LW, Palmer, Jack (2013) Palmer is able to get the puck in deep in the offensive zone off the rush and did a pretty good job of trying to cut to the front of the net off the wide drive. He put some good pressure on the fore-check and displayed great hands in tight under pressure, then moved the puck around well to get it to the front of the net for teammates. He went hard to the net to battle for loose pucks in front for an excellent chance in tight and he got a decent cycle going in deep in the offensive zone. He has to watch the turnovers trying to move the puck up out of the zone along the boards.

BRN # 23, C, McGauley, Tim (2013) McGauley made a great cross-ice pass in the high slot on the power play to set-up a one-timer goal and he was distributing the puck really effectively in the offensive zone to find the open man. He had a good clear on the penalty kill and protected the puck well in the offensive zone to draw a penalty. He came back to his own end for some good support, put pressure on the puck carrier and tried to get hi stick in lanes to deflect passes out of danger. He went to the net well looking for loose pucks and rebounds and protected the puck effectively on the wide drive, however needs to make sure he has a teammate behind him on his drop pass attempts.

REG # 2, D, Hand, Tye (2013) Hand made a good pass to move the puck out of the zone to start the rush and was able to protect the puck well from the opposition's pressure. He is calm with the puck, likes to make the safe, simple play as he doesn't try anything too fancy, and he also got in a pretty good fight, taking his man down.

REG # 4, D, Burroughs, Kyle (2013) Burroughs displayed great agility with the puck and made a really nice long pass to find a teammate at the far blue line to spring him into the offensive zone. He did a nice job of tying up his man in the defensive zone and made a fantastic chip pass up along the boards to spring a man into the offensive zone for a break opportunity. He stepped up on a pinch to play the puck carrier with an element of physicality and to keep the attack alive, and he also found seems in the high slot on the power play to move the puck across on some good cross-ice passes. He needs to get his shots through to the net with more consistency.

REG # 5, D, Williams, Colby (2013) Williams is able to move the puck out of the zone to start the breakout and has a nice hard shot from the point that he got on net as it was tipped in for a goal. He displayed nice physicality on the puck carrier to stand up his man and knock him of the puck and he used his stick well to knock the puck free off the opposition and keep them to the outside. He was able to skate the puck up the ice into the offensive zone but needs to watch the turnovers trying to hold on to the puck for too long. He stepped up on the pinch to hold the offensive zone and keep the attack alive and he got in lanes to block shots in his own end. He stepped up on the rush to join the attack in the offensive zone to get a cycle going and he did a really good job of holding the offensive line and putting pressure on the puck carrier.

REG # 18, LW, Klimchuk, Morgan (2013) Klimchuk opened up well in front of the net to take a pass for a good shot opportunity and he has some decent speed but for the most part was just trying to make the simple plays and get the puck to the net. He battled well for pucks along the boards on the fore-check and got in behind the opposition's defense to take a pass and come in for a pretty good shot attempt. He is able to protect the puck along the wall and get a cycle going in the offensive zone but he needs to be stronger on the puck so that it is not taken away from him so easily. He also has to hit the net on his shot opportunities from the high slot and he was taking lots of long outside shots from the blue line with options available to him down low instead to move the puck.

FINAL SCORE: 5-2 Brandon Wheat Kings

Feb 2, 2013, Sioux City Musketeers vs. Sioux Falls Stampede (USHL)

SIF # 16, C, Valesano, Conner (2013) Valesano put some excellent pressure and physicality on the fore-check. He had nice speed and pressure on the puck carrier to force turnovers, was able to make some good breakout passes to start the rush and was getting a good cycle going in the offensive zone. He has to watch the turnovers on breakout passes up the middle and was also playing on the perimeter for the most part trying to flutter passes through to the man in the front.

SIF # 17, LW, Calderone, Tony (2013) Calderone had a nice net-front presence on the power play and got a pretty nice cycle going in deep in the offensive zone. He was taking long outside shots off on the rush, but at least was following up the puck well, going hard to the net looking for rebounds. He also moved the puck down low then opened up in the slot to take a pass, but has to get his shot through to the net. He took a pass in the high slot then stepped in to put a great shot on to score on the power play and made an excellent pass by finding a lane in the offensive zone to move the puck to an open man right next to the net.

SIF # 23, LW, Ahlgren, Jake (2013) Ahlgren got in lanes to block shots from the point and put some good pressure on the puck carrier. He made a nice pass to lead a man into the offensive zone with speed and then hustled hard to drive to the net looking for a rebound on the play. He protects the puck well from the opposition along the boards and showed really good speed, hustle and some great moves to beat a defender on the wide drive. He was taking long outside shots on the rush that were not even on net and also was unable to hit the net on his shots from the high slot.

SIC # 3, D, Kapla, Michael (2013) Kapla was able to protect the puck well from the opposition's pressure and had a nice hard shot that he got through kept down low from the point, however needs to hit the net with more consistency. He was able to make a good breakout pass on the rush out of the zone up the middle to lead a man into the offensive zone, and also stepped up into the high slot on the rush to take a pass and score on a great shot. He had one really dangerous drop pass at the offensive line that almost resulted in a great break opportunity for the opposition.

SIC # 19, C, Guentzel, Jake (2013) Guentzel put good pressure on the puck carrier on the fore-check and was cutting to the middle in the high slot off the rush for a really good shot opportunity. He went hard to the net and opened up really well to provide a scoring option on the rush, and also showed some nice speed on the odd-man rush to move the puck across to a teammate for a great opportunity. He made a nice pass on the rush to find a trailing player in the high slot and displayed excellent vision to spot an open man in the high slot on a great pass and the team scored on the play. He also made a fantastic back-hand move in the shootout to score the winner. He has to watch some of the turnovers along the boards in his own end and also had a bad pass in the offensive zone that the opposition picked off for a turnover.

SIO # 22, LW, McGlynn, Connor (2013) McGlynn did an excellent job of opening up next to the net to take a pass and put a one-timer on to score and later again went to the net with his stick down to open up in the slot and take a pass to rip an excellent shot on to score. He had a nice net-front presence in the offensive zone, getting to the net to tip pucks and put good pressure and physicality on the puck carrier on the fore-check, using his body and strength well after to protect the puck along the boards. He was a little over aggressive with his stick at one point and took a bad offensive-zone tripping penalty and also missed the net just barely on his shootout attempt.

SIC # 26, D, Heinrich, Blake (2013) Heinrich got a good cycle going in deep in the offensive zone and was distributing the puck well from the point on the power play. He opened up nicely in the high slot to take a pass and put a good shot on net, and also got in a fight and took his man down. He has to hit the net on his shots from the point with more consistency, and also needs to tie-up his man in front of the net as he was caught puck watching and the opposition got the rebound and scored. He also needs to watch some of the neutral zone turnovers on breakout passes.

SIO # 28, LW, Torok, Tomas (2013) Torok put nice pressure on the fore-check and was finishing his hits along the boards. He came back to his own end for some good support, got his stick in lanes to try to block passes and also used his stick well to knock the puck off the opposition. He played the puck carrier with a nice element of physicality but has to watch the offensive zone turnovers by trying to force passes through the opposition. He was also taking long outside shots when there was an open man available down low.

FINAL SCORE: 5-4 (Shootout) Sioux City Musketeers

February 6, 2013, Kitchener Rangers @ Guelph Storm (OHL)

KIT #16 LW Pedersen, Brent (2013) - Brent displayed great puck protection ability driving the net creating chances and also drew a penalty shot, however he didn't score. Brent was a little snake bitten tonight having multiple chances. He missed pretty much an open net after Guelph's goaltender misplayed the puck. He did made a great pass sending Josh Leivo up ice and went to the net to help Kitchener score their 5th goal of the game. Brent's skating appears to have improved and will continue being an area he needs to improve. He also showed adequate hands.

KIT #95 RW Bailey, Justin (2013) - Bailey's first few steps are a bit of a struggle. He generates efficient agility and speed when he gets going but it can take several steps. Justin is built solid and protects the puck fairly well and has quick hands. His reaction time is well above average which has helped him a few times, this includes deflecting pucks while taking up space out front of the net. He made a great pass out front but his teammate got robbed. Justin has been very smart with the puck in the offensive zone tonight.

GUE #7 LD Harpur, Ben (2013) - Ben was at his best making good simple plays in the neutral zone with the puck. He has a pretty good point shot. Took wide route to the puck in his own zone. He struggles a little with a lack of mobility due to his size. He was caught out of position a few times, one of these times he chased Kitchener forward hard but couldn't catch him and they scored. He had his moments in one on one situations, but kept getting beat when he tried to step up which resulted in scoring chances for Kitchener.

GUE #11 LW Dickinson, Jason (2013) - Jason competed very hard defensively in tonight's game. He was pretty quiet but effective in his own zone. Calm under pressure. He was used on the second power play unit and he got one good chance to score. However he got stick checked before he could finish the opportunity.

GUE #17 LW Bertuzzi, Tyler (2013) - Bertuzzi is very good along the boards. He plays a simple but smart game, he competes hard and wins. He helped Guelph score their second goal by getting the puck on net hard with a low shot causing the rebound and Justin Auger finished for the goal.

#19 – RC – Garlent, Hunter – 5'9" – 164lb. – 2013 Eligible
Played the point on the power play regularly. He made a great shot block to save a scoring chance.

Scouts Notes:

Both teams came out fighting for every inch with home ice in the playoffs potentially on the line in this games. However early on in the second period Kitchener started to pull away. Guelph put up a fight and kept it close but the Rangers provided consistent pressure and eventually in the third period were able to break away and secure the 5-2 victory. Hunter Garlent (2013) was noted for playing the point on the power play regularly. He also was willing to block shots making one in particular that may have saved a big scoring chance.

February 6, 2013, USA vs. Finland (5 Nations Tournament)

USA #4 LD Will Butcher (2013) – Played a pretty strong game. Was very involved in the offense, taking any opportunity to join the rush and pinch in the offense zone. Overcommitted a couple times but recovered with excellent skating. Buzzed with the puck and drew a lot of attention. Good work at the point on the powerplay, acted as the triggerman. Defensive zone play was OK, good stick but he chased the play too often.

USA #6 LD Keaton Thompson (2013) – Started strong and finished flat. Showed poise with the puck early, carrying well and getting it deep when pressured. Shot the puck at the right times but had trouble getting them on net. Later in the game began to lose composure. Turned the puck over multiple times with poor puck decisions. Not a great way to start the tournament.

USA #7 RC JT Compher (2013) – Worked hard on every shift. Was strong on the penalty kill. Skating was excellent, accelerated quickly. Showed flashes of skill with a nifty drop pass on a criss-cross and a beautiful dangle behind the net.

USA #15 RW John Hayden (2013) – Played a strong all-around game. Was strong on the puck down the wing, shaking off contact and maintaining control. Took the puck to the net dangerously from below the goal line. Pursued loose pucks and played the body well.

USA #16 RD Steve Santini (2013) – Showed a bit of offensive flair today, carrying strong thru the middle and dealing well with attention, on one instance drawing a penalty. Was safe and sturdy in his end with good physical play. Kept things pretty simple overall.

USA #19 RC Tyler Kelleher (2013) – Team USA's best offensive player today. Scored two goals and was dangerous most shifts. Hands were excellent, was very elusive and patient through center and in the offensive zone. Cycle work was good, Finns had a hard time pinning him down. Showed determination to score on a loose puck.

USA #22 RW Hudson Fasching (2013) – Had a rough go of it. Forced the play with frequency and took bad shots from severe angles. When he did get chances to score, he couldn't finish. Looked totally snakebitten. Carried the puck with his head down too often, leading to turnovers. Balance was shaky, did not look comfortable on his feet.

USA #24 RW Michael McCarron (2013) – Skated well today but couldn't get anything going offensively. Has a good stride for his size and kept his feet moving. Backchecked hard. Was strong on the puck but lacking in creativity. Carried the puck down the wing, took a weak shot from the outside, and hoped for a rebound. Over and over.

FIN #12 LW Artturi Lehkonen (2013) – Played a strong two-way game. Forced turnovers in the neutral zone and on the forecheck with a good stick and smart positioning. Took the puck to the net with a great power move, don't think it's his game but he was effective with his body today. Fanned on his best scoring chance. Skated alongside Juuso Ikonen and Aleksi Mustonen, their line was outstanding.

FIN #14 RW Juuso Ikonen (2013) – Small player with a lot skill. Made things happen with the puck, very creative and elusive. Kept the defense honest with his stickhandling and cycled well with his linemates. Took a boneheaded offensive-zone hooking penalty on the powerplay at a key juncture of the 3rd period when his team had the opportunity to salt the game away.

FIN #24 LW Kasperi Kapanen (2014) – Started off the game as a threat on every shift but had a tougher time as the minutes passed. Tried to do too much by himself and didn't utilize his linemates well enough. Had one notable giveaway that he recovered from well with a hard backcheck. Finished his checks on occasion but defensive play needs work.

FIN #32 G Juuse Saros (2013) – As much as the Americans failed to take advantage of their chances, Saros was huge for the Finns in this one. He made 36 saves on 38 shots and a few of them were robbery. Great quickness post to post, a quick glove, and great fundamentals. No real weakness except for his size.

Scout's Notes: LW Tyler Motte (2013) and LW Evan Allen (2013) also played well for the Americans. G Hunter Miska (2013) was shaky in net. LC Aleksi Ainali (2013) was productive for the Finns, and LD Teemu Vuorisalo (2013) was strong in his own end.

February 6, 2013, Sweden vs. Czech Republic (5 Nations Tournament)

SWE #3 LD Robin Norell (2013) – Liked his game today. Not a real upside guy but sturdy and physical. Stood guys up at the blueline with big hits, including one massive hipcheck. Solid positional play in his end with plenty of rough stuff. A little undersized but he's dense.

SWE #4 LD Robert Hägg (2013)– Had a mostly poor game today. Forced the play with risky passing and shots that were consistently wide or blocked. Lacked a physical presence early but did pick up his coverage in the third. Should have dominated this Czech team, can play much better.

SWE #5 RD Rasmus Andersson (2015) – For a double underager, he played very well. Was always looking to join the rush and pinch in the offensive zone, did so with effectiveness though he was a bit overeager at times. Scored on a beautiful wrister against the grain that he banked in off the corner where the post meets the crossbar. Defensive coverage needs some work, lacked assertiveness on the boards.

SWE #9 LD Wilhelm Westlund (2013) – Disappointing showing. His coverage was loose around the net and his positioning was consistently off by a step. Made questionable decisions with the puck in his end.

SWE #12 LW André Burakowsky (2013) – Very strong showing. Skated with good agility and showed good offensive instincts with nice passing and stickhandling. Had a couple takeover shifts where he skated circles around the Czechs in their own zone. A little overambitious with the puck at times (ex. trying to split the defense in a 1-on-2) but I liked his creativity. Good work on the penalty kill.

SWE #19 RW Jacob de la Rose (2013) – Excellent all-around game from the rangy forward. Was consistently physical and involved in all three zones. Good penalty killer with an active stick and smart positioning. Strong skater with a nice stride, though he lacked extra gear. Flashed a strong wrister and great footwork to get shots off quickly. Scored on a freak deflection and added two assists. Took two minor penalties.

SWE #26 LW Jakob Forsbacka-Karlsson (2015) – The young forward played with a lot of jump and jam and was able to make an impact playing fourth line minutes. Was given penalty killing responsibility and did not disappoint, hustling for loose pucks and to get in shooting lanes. Won himself a breakaway with quick feet and made a great move, but was denied.

SWE #29 LC Lucas Wallmark (2013) – Contributed well offensively with three assists, but his skating is still a concern. Shows great footwork in the offensive zone but has a hard time getting through center ice with a labored stride. Great hands and vision, very smart player. A shame his feet are holding him back.

CZE #13 LW Jakub Vrana (2014) – Skilled player with plenty of upside. Showed good speed through the middle with and without the puck. Tried to break away behind the defense and was successful once, had his teammates been able to get him the puck. Decisive player, played without hesitation. Went hard to the net and showed off a good selection of shots with a deceptively quick release, though accuracy was lacking. Made one elite skill play where he spun off a defender and got a backhand shot off in one motion.

CZE #22 RW David Pastrnak (2014) – Showed off great individual skill and flair with the puck. Dangled a few guys out of their jocks but lacked a finishing touch. Very agile and difficult to contain. Could have utilized his teammates better.

Scout's Notes: LC Elias Edström (2013) scored a nice goal on a wonderful individual effort.

Feb. 6 2013, Blainville-Boisbriand Armada @ Chicoutimi Saguenéens, (QMJHL)

BLB #11 RW, Roy, Marc-Olivier (2013) : Played an average game, pretty speedy player with quick feet, handling the puck well at top speed. He got a goal pushing a wrap around's rebound behind the Chicoutimi goalie. He has a high level of offensive hockey sense, but also has a tendency to get a little lazy and try to take the easy way out on plays. He finds teammates easily, has a good vision of the ice and will outsmart a lot of his opponents. He is 6,01 but looks a lot smaller, not very big and bending on his knees a lot when skating. Some tools here, but not sure his game would translate well to a professionnal hockey game as he doesn't chip and chase, doesn't win a whole lot of battles and creates mostly on speed and by finding soft ice.

BLB #16 D, Ouellet, Xavier (2011 2nd round, Detroit Red Wings) : Played half the game on forward and half the game on defense. He had a good showing while putting an average level of effort into the game, dominating with his high level of skills, speed and strength. He's got all the tools to play professionnal hockey. He made a lot of difficult plays look easy throughout the game, he has long strides when he's trying to reach his top speed, got open easily in the neutral zone with that speed. He still makes a couple of unnecessary plays in his own zone, try to make a breakout through players and through sticks which resulted in turnovers, I think he can get a lot better in his puck management in his own zone, but the potential is undeniable.

BLB #54 D, Marti, Christian (2013*) : Big stay at home D, already 19 years old but played a steady defensive game. Everything he does is pretty sound defensively, from bringing his man well to the boards, being physical down-low but rarely getting caught out of position, strong and safe in his decisions with the puck. I also liked the discipline he showed too during the game, which is sometimes tough for big men on an olympic sized ice when you're trying to be physical and agressive down-low. He makes good first passes and not afraid to carry the puck to neutral zone if he has skating room. The skating is good, could get better, but the footwork enables him to follow his opponent's well and adjust to the twisting and turning forwards without hooking. I really liked the level of maturity.

BLB #93 G, Marcoux, Étienne (2013*) : Didn't get a lot of scoring chances during the game but was again good in his style. A goalie that his not perfect by any means, but he competes hard, tracks pucks well and anticipates plays quickly. He is athletic and will make saves when he looks beat, not a typical butterfly goalie. Was especially challenged in the lower part of the net, which gave him no problem with the quick leg movements, directing rebounds in the corners.

February 6th, 2013. Guelph Storm vs. Kitchener Rangers (KIT 5-2)

GUE#7 D Ben Harpur (2013). Harpur struggled a little in this game and looked a step slow at points on the transitions from backward to forward skating and vice versa. He did show decent speed and utilized his long reach effectively to keep a number of pucks in the offensive zone on wraps around the boards. Harpur has to utilize his reach better in the defensive zone and be careful about watching pucks instead of closing the gap against rushing opponents. Ben displayed a strong wrist shot from the point but needs to work at getting it on target more often.

GUE#11 F Jason Dickinson (2013). Dickinson had another solid all-around performance in this game. He is very strong away from the puck and constantly works to keep plays in front of him and support the Storm defenseman in the defensive zone. Jason was especially effective on the penalty kill, getting in front of shots and getting his stick into passing lanes to disrupt the Ranger timing. He did struggle in the face-off circle and is more suited as a winger with space to move up and down the wing. Dickinson displays a smooth skating stride and shows great offensive awareness generating a number of quality scoring chances. Offensive finishing touch needs improvement.

GUE#17 F Tyler Bertuzzi (2013). Bertuzzi was very effective on the fore-check in this game and is constantly finishing checks in the corners and along the boards. Tyler is constantly working and moving his feet whenever he is on the ice and is very good at forcing opposing defenders into bad decision making. He excels in the classic shit disturber role and is very good at getting under opponents skin and drawing penalties especially after whistles. He shows no hesitation standing up for teammates and is effective at setting the pace for the Storm. He does show solid speed when he is giving space to move up and down the wing and skating with the puck. Size is an issue as he may be on the shorter side to continue to play the same role at the next level against men.

KIT#15 F Ben Thomson (NJ). Thomson had a strong offensive performance for the Rangers scoring a beautiful goal and setting up another with a nice assist. Ben works hard to get himself into quality scoring positions and is slippery enough to sneak behind defenders to get in on breakaways. He is not the smoothest skater, but overcomes this with solid vision and offensive awareness. There is room for improvement on his finishing touch as he did generate a number of offensive chances that went unfinished. Ben is not afraid to get into the faces of his opponents and uses his body well battling in front of the net for loose pucks.

KIT#19 F Josh Sterk (2013). Sterk was effective at getting in hard on the fore-check and showed good offensive awareness slowing plays down and picking solid dump and chase opportunities. He worked hard to battle for loose pucks in the slot and did show a strong wrist shot when given space. He works hard down low in the defensive zone and is reliable at moving pucks up ice on the breakout.

KIT#95 F Justin Bailey (2013). Bailey showed a good work ethic in the offensive zone battling for loose pucks and was very effective at finding lanes to drive to the net with the puck. He is strong at keeping his feet moving and showed a burst of speed capable of beating unsuspecting defenders. Justin was very good at getting his stick on pucks in this game, breaking up a number of plays in the defensive zone as well as looking for tips in the offensive zone. Bailey does need to work at showing more urgency on the power play as he tried to make some plays look too fancy which resulted in turnovers. He shows a strong wrist shot and needs to get into better scoring positions when given a power play opportunity. Bailey is reliable in the defensive zone and was constantly working to chip pucks into the neutral zone.

February 7th, 2013. Sault Ste. Marie Greyhounds vs. Brampton Battalion

BRA#21 F Nick Paul (2013). Paul was very good at taking a strong outside step to beat defenders off the rush, and showed no hesitation driving to the net with speed. He showed good confidence skating with the puck through the neutral zone and was not afraid to carry it through traffic. Nick works hard up and down the walls and is reliable at getting pucks out of the defensive zone. Showed solid foot speed especially on one rush beating a defender with a quick burst up the middle. He needs to consistently keep making hard plays and getting pucks in deep as he tried to be too fancy high in the offensive zone leading to a quick turnover and counter attack for the Greyhounds on one particular occasion.

SSM#3 D Tyler Ganly (2013). Ganly plays a very simple defensive minded game. He is reliable in the defensive zone and is constantly working in the corners to win puck possession and to keep attackers pinned deep. Tyler makes a solid first pass but needs to show more confidence skating with the puck himself. He lined up a few rushing attackers but needs to work on strength to be more consistent in separating them from the puck. Ganly also needs to work at getting his shot from the blue line off quicker and look to position himself in better spots for one timer or back door opportunities.

SSM#25 D Darnell Nurse (2013). Nurse had a strong game in the shutdown defender role for the Greyhounds. He is exceptionally strong at finishing checks along the boards and in the corners and makes life very hard for opposing forwards on his side of the defensive zone. He utilizes a long stick and works hard to keep attackers to outside lines while getting his stick on the puck to knock it free. Darnell is a strong skater and closed gaps very quickly on rushing forwards in this game. He shows a solid first pass coming out of the defensive zone and is not scared to skate the puck out of the defensive zone when pressured. Nurse did occasionally appear as if he wanted to jump into the offensive rush but his offence still has room for improvement.

SSM#28 F Sergey Tolchinsky (2013). Tolchinsky had a strong offensive performance for the Greyhounds in this game. He is deceptively fast and can skate for miles while stick handling with the puck. Sergey is very shifty and is good at getting himself in and out of danger very quickly. Size is his biggest issue although in this game he utilized his smarts to evade checks and deke around defenders. Sergey showed off a laser of a wrist shot beating the Battalion goaltender top shelf from the middle of the slot. He needs to work on his defensive positioning and really work at getting stronger chipping pucks out along his wall.

SSM#55 D Ryan Sproul (DET). Sproul showcased his elite offensive skills on a number of occasions in this game. Not only with a heavy slap shot from the point, but strong playmaking skills and creativity leading to three assists. He is a very strong skater and shows impressive confidence carrying the puck and generating the offensive rush from the backend. Sproul did struggle at times in the defensive zone and he needs to ensure strong play in his own end before flying the zone on the counter attack as a fourth forward.

February 7, 2013, Finland vs. Czech Republic (5 Nations Tournament)

FIN #3 LD Alex Lintuniemi (2014) – Big defenseman played a strong game in his own end. Was physical against the cycle and did a good job of timing his hits. Good stick against the rush. Stepped up well at the blueline, including one beautiful hipcheck on a player who had his head down.

FIN #8 LD Mika Ilvonen (2013) – The main source of offensive creativity from the back end for the Finns today. Nice shots for tips and rebounds. Didn't have much success rushing the puck but wasn't overzealous about it. Made smart outlet passes. Scored on a good pinch where he had the goalie swimming and made no mistake.

FIN #10 LC Aleksi Mustonen (2013) – Small stature was not an issue today. Took the puck hard to the middle and wasn't afraid to get in front of pucks for tips. Hands are quick. He was very shifty and difficult to pin down along the boards.

FIN #12 LW Artturi Lehkonen (2013) – Offensive flair was evident but only in flashes. Surprisingly apt at using his reach despite his limited size. Scored on an absolute snipe of a shot.

FIN #14 RW Juuso Ikonen (2013) – Played well in the offensive zone today. Showed excellent hand-eye on a very dangerous redirect from the high slot. Passed the puck well and kept his feet moving to get himself open. Shot release was quick but accuracy was off. Had trouble with coverage in the defensive zone, was overpowered on the boards and had trouble tracking his man.

FIN #24 LW Kasperi Kapanen (2014) – A few bursts of flash but another unproductive day for Kapanen. Showed great speed and hit the crossbar on one highlight-reel play where he turned on the jets and let go a wonderful shot off a cut. Hands were excellent, very shifty. Passes were intelligent, found tight seams, but his linemates had a hard time taking advantage of them. Looks as if he's being limited by linemates and as a result trying to do too much by himself.

FIN #26 LW Felix Westermarck (2013) – Big forward had an OK day, but his offensive game was limited. Took the puck down the wing and crashed the net. Got control of the puck down low and tried wraparounds. Too predictable.

CZE #13 LW Jakub Vrana (2014) – Fairly quiet game. Showed flashes of poise carrying the puck, including a couple determined rushes where he navigated traffic well. Was too risky with the puck in the defensive zone.

CZE #22 RW David Pastrnak (2014) – The main offensive catalyst for the Czechs today. Stick skills were borderline elite with great dangles and detailed passes, including a beautiful long bomb lead pass that set up a breakaway and another backdoor feed that led to a near-empty net chance, both of which his teammates were unable to convert on. Used his reach well and showed great body control. Very dangerous as a shooter with a hard one-timer and a sneaky wrister. Was a threat to score shorthanded with strong skating and the awareness to shoot through defenders to screen the goalie.

Scout's Notes: RW Kasperi Ojantakanen (2013) scored a beautiful goal with a great individual effort and RW Joel Kiviranta (2013) played a strong two-way game. G Juuse Saros (2013) was again excellent in net with 26 saves on 27 shots. The Finns gave the Czechs six powerplays with some poor penalties, but the Finns didn't allow a powerplay marker as the penalty kill was strong and Saros shut the door. RW Ondrej Kase (2014) played well on the Czech first line, showing some flair with the puck and good skating.

February 7, 2013, Sweden vs. Russia (5 Nations Tournament)

SWE #4 LD Robert Hägg (2013) – Not a great effort in this one. Was too passive in his end for much of the game, chasing the play and looking lost in coverage. Was too careless with the puck and had a hard time getting it up to his forwards. His best shifts were on the penalty kill, where he was physical in front of the net and showed an active stick.

SWE #5 RD Rasmus Andersson (2015) – Showed some good things today, but he's very raw. Went end-to-end with poise and speed, did well to navigate traffic without giving the puck away. Dealt well with forecheck pressure. Good point play in the offensive zone, smart passer. Stepped up at the blueline when appropriate and made good contact.

SWE #8 LD Carl Dahlström (2013) – Big defenseman was shaky early with poor reads and decisions, but righted the ship and ended up playing a decent game. Made safe plays with the puck in his zone. Moved well for his size and was strong on his feet.

SWE #19 RW Jacob de la Rose (2013) – The big two-way forward was one of the few bright spots up front for Sweden today. Was dangerous off the rush with quick hands and an excellent wrist shot that he was able to get on net through traffic. Also showed good protection skills down the outside. Good vision in the offensive zone, shot and passed appropriately. Forechecked well and also came back to cover in his own zone. Reminds me of Ottawa 67s forward Sean Monahan.

SWE #28 LW Anton Karlsson (2014) – Played a strong two-way game. Went hard to the net with and without the puck. Buzzed with the puck on his stick in the offensive zone with good footwork, drawing defenders and subsequently finding open teammates with passes. Laid a couple big hits. Forechecked and backchecked hard.

RUS #2 LD Rushan Rafikov (2013) – Big blueliner played a nice, physical game. Was difficult to beat wide and made life difficult on Swedes brave enough to come into his corner. Pinched physically and decisively, led with the stick but made sure to make contact on 50/50 pucks. Good shots from the point though his offensive game was lacking overall.

RUS #4 LD Rinat Valiyev (2013) – Offensive-defenseman had a nice game. Scored a shorthanded goal on a hard, accurate shot from far out. Pinched actively. Showed a good stick in his zone and coverage was strong.

RUS #19 RW Pavel Buchnevich – Flashed a lot of skill today. Was difficult to contain with his combination of strong skating and dangling ability. Scored on a beautiful move where he made the Swedes look silly. Played too individually.

RUS #27 RW Valeri Nichushkin (2013) – Great game from the big Russian, who dazzled frequently. Skates well for his size and when he got moving with the puck, he was like a freight train. Protected the puck well and took it hard to the slot or net frequently. Made beautiful tape-to-tape passes and flashed a great selection of shots, including a strong backhand. Backchecked, played the body, and intercepted pucks in the neutral zone with good awareness.

RUS #29 LW Vladimir Tkachyov (2014) – Small playmaking winger had a great game. Flashy speed and stickhandling, was very effective at darting around opponents to create space and buy time. Missed a golden chance with a slow shot release but later flashed a nice one-timer. Forechecked well with good footwork and stick positioning.

Scout's Notes: 8-2 final in favor of Russia, though the shots were 38-31 in favor of Sweden. Swedish G William Silwerfeldt Öhman (2013) and Jonas Johansson (2014) were both shaky. Quiet games from most of Sweden's top forwards, including LC Lucas Wallmark (2013) and LW Andrei Burakowsky (2013), who was benched for most of the third period. LC Viktor Crus-Rydberg (2013) has yet to really show up in the team's first two games. LW Jakob Forsbacka-Karlsson (2015) had another solid game in a supporting role and scored a goal. Nichushkin's linemates LW Nikita Shatski (2013) and LC Ilya Ivanov (2013) played well but don't project as draft prospects, as they're small and one-dimensional offensive forwards.

February 7, 2013, Sarnia Sting @ London Knights (OHL)

SAR #2 RD Chapman, Joshua (2013) - Josh made some very good plays down low in the defensive zone to break down some of London's scoring chances

SAR #7 RD DeAngelo, Anthony (2014) - Anthony was a little excessive showing off his fancy moves. It negated his own offensive rush and nearly resulted in a breakaway for London. He moved the puck very well otherwise. He also displayed the quickness of his wrist shot when he scored the overtime winner to give Sarnia a big upset win.

SAR #21 LC Nikandrov, Daniel (2013) - Daniel made some very smart plays with the puck not trying to be too fancy just making the play that needed to be made to get the play going. He did struggle a little as the game went on making a few mental errors. However he came up big with about six minutes left up by one keeping London pinned deep in their own zone for pretty much his entire shift. This killed off valuable time in London attempting to get something going. At the end of the day Daniel went home with two well earned assists including one on the overtime winning goal.

SAR #71 RW Goldobin, Nikolay (2014) - Nikolay did a great job sticking with the play to bang home the rebound to his one-timer for the first goal of the game in the final seconds of the first period on the power play. In overtime he made an unbelievable play working around two defenders then making a highlight reel pass to set up the game winning goal in overtime.

LON #16 LC Domi, Max (2013) - Max identified a hole near the slot and slipped in scoring the first goal of the game on the power play showing quickness and confidence with the puck. He was a little quiet in the second period but on his first shift after Sarnia tied the game he looked almost possessed on the ice creating three outstanding set-up's and eluding Sarnia defensemen. His shifts following this were also excellent as he showed excellent determination and drive to help his team get this game tied up. Max showed off a very good shot in this game.

LON #53 LW Horvat, Bo (2013) - Bo displayed great positional awareness in the offensive zone competing well along the boards. He seems to be able to blend into the play around him at times much in the same way Sean Monahan does. He displayed excellent positioning but is also more than willing to battle effectively along the boards.

LON #65 LD Zadorov, Nikita (2013) - Nikita showed his skating and puck rushing ability early on getting the puck up ice and on net. Despite this he played a more consistent, simplified game. He finished his checks more consistently in the past and didn't run around. He was also very solid along the wall battling hard. Unfortunately he deflected a point shot into his own net for Sarnia's third goal on the night.

LON #81 LW Elie, Remi (2013) - Remi put together an excellent performance tonight. He was excellent on the back check getting back quickly on broken plays and finished his checks whenever possible. He was smart with the puck making good passes and cycling the puck well. He was consistently in good position in the offensive zone and moves moderately well. He has an absolutely cannon of a shot. Remi received a penalty for what was essentially a clean hit.

Scouts Notes: London opened up a quick 2-0 lead and appeared to have a solid grasp on this game. Sarnia however scored late in the first then scored twice in the third period to take a 3-2 lead. London was able to respond with just 4:09 left to tie the game and send it to overtime. Sarnia was able to gain the extra point in overtime just 33 seconds in off a great play created by Nikolay Goldobin (2014) and finished by Anthony DeAngelo (2014). 5'9" Davis Brown (2013) decided to drop the gloves with the much bigger Justin Sefton (San Jose) as expected Sefton overpowered Brown in the fight, however not before Davis landed a few good shots at the start of the fight. Alex Carnevale (2013) was noted for displaying a great work ethic throughout tonight's game.

February 8, 2013, Owen Sound Attack @ London Knights (OHL)

OS #7 LC Catenacci, Daniel (Buffalo) - Daniel scored am absolutely beautiful short handed goal winning the race to the puck, fighting off a defenseman then finished while in mid air to score the first goal of the game.

OS #24 LD Bigras, Chris (2013) - Chris made some very good plays in one on one situations. His backwards skating is very strong. Chris received a roughing penalty in the final 5 minutes of the third period. When he got out of the box he went right into the defensive zone and made a few huge shot blocks to help preserve a 4-3 win in the final moments of the game.

OS #27 RW Nastasiuk, Zach (2013) - Zach was a regular on the penalty kill although he worked hard in all game situations in his own zone. He came up huge late in the game when killing off a 5 on 3 getting in passing lanes and blocking passes which would have set up scoring chances.

LON #16 LC Domi, Max (2013) - Max displayed excellent vision and puck movement on the power play tonight for London. Although it wasn't his best game, he was still a positive impact for the Knights.

LON #53 LW Horvat, Bo (2013) - Bo displayed how quick and powerful his release is by scoring the first goal of the game on a nice set up by Alex Broadhurst. He showed great work along the boards in the defensive zone winning battles and adding in some physicality. Excellent work ethic on penalty kill on two separate rushes he stole the puck then pinned it to kill a bunch of time off of Owen Sound's power play.

LON #65 LD Zadorov, Nikita (2013) - Will do his best to send puck around the boards smartly in his own zone. Although he did turn the puck over a little early on in the game. He rushed the puck a bit in this game but kept it safe. He made some very good plays in one on one match-up's maintaining good positioning and letting forwards come to him before he hit them instead of chasing them as he did earlier on in the season.

Scouts Notes: This was an excellent performance put together between the top two teams in the Midwest Division. It was a constant back and forth battle that saw both teams lead, and saw the lead change four different times and at least once a period. Owen Sound was able to hold on for a 4-3 win only after holding off an outstanding consistent attack by London in the final five minutes of the game. Steven Janes (2013*) scored two goals including the game winner in exactly the same fashion. Out front of London's net deflecting booming point shots provided by Cody Ceci (Ottawa)

February 8, 2013, Finland vs. Russia (5 Nations Tournament)

FIN #2 LD Jimi Kuronen (2013) – Defense-first blueliner who played a positionally-sound game, save for a couple major lapses. Showed a good active stick and was smart dealing with outnumbered attack situations.

FIN #3 LD Alex Lintuniemi (2014) – Big, physical defenseman had a nice two-way effort. Threw a number of big hits, including one on Nichushkin that absolutely leveled him. Scored an opportunistic goal with a great pinch that put him in the right place at the right time.

FIN #5 RD Julius Honka (2014) – Small offensive blueliner was very active today. Showed a lot of poise carrying the puck and evaded the forecheck well. Nice outlet passes. Joined the rush and pinched aggressively but appropriately. Scored on an ice one-timer and had a few good low shots for tips and rebounds. Battled in his own zone but was noticeably overpowered by bigger players.

FIN #7 RD Atte Mäkinen (2013) – Rough game from the big blueliner. Was physical in his end but too aggressive and as a result completely blew coverage at times. Took a boneheaded tripping penalty late in the third with his team trying to get back into the game. Passing and stickhandling were shaky and led to giveaways.

FIN #10 LC Aleksi Mustonen (2013) – Shifty little forward had a nice game. Controlled the puck well on the boards and showed off quick feet and hands in the cycle. Was good with the puck behind the net. Kept his head on a swivel and tracked the play well. Showed off a nice snapshot and intelligent passing. Defensive coverage was positionally strong and he forechecked well, utilizing his speed.

FIN #12 LW Artturi Lehkonen (2013) – Mostly good today. Showed good offensive flair but at times tried to do too much with the puck. Great passer, especially on the powerplay where he was difficult to predict. Flashed a nice wrister and pursued rebounds hard. Scored on a nice one-timer from the slot. Read the play well in all situations, positioning was smart.

FIN #14 RW Juuso Ikonen (2013) – Very nice offensive effort from Ikonen. Showed good puck control in traffic and flashed dangling ability. Had the foresight to make plays off turnovers with smart passes while the play was still in transition. Was determined with and without the puck, moving his feet and fighting through checks. Great skater with quick feet, liked to stutter step to burn the defense.

FIN #24 LW Kasperi Kapanen (2014) – Was quick and elusive as always. Showed fantastic speed down the wing and made some intelligent passes, was most impressed with his short feeds. Great footwork kept the other team guessing. Showed good hands on the backcheck to strip players of the puck. Had a tendency to chase the play defensively and blew his coverage drastically at times.

RUS #7 LD Ivan Teterin (2014) – Stocky defenseman showed OK today. Consistently stood the Finns up at the blueline with strong contact. Physical on the boards and in front of his net. Lacked poise in his zone with the puck, was very shaky.

RUS #8 RD Artyom Zub (2014) – Played smaller than his size and decisions were poor. Was weak in front on the penalty kill, leading to scoring chances against where the goalie was screened. Much too aggressive standing up at the blueline at the wrong times.

RUS #19 RW Pavel Buchnevich (2013) – Great offensive effort. Showed great positioning in the offensive zone with and without the puck. Lightning quick release on his shot made him a threat to score from almost anywhere in the zone. Scored a nice breakaway goal. Was strong on the puck. Nice powerplay passing.

RUS #25 LD Vladislav Gavrikov (2014) – Didn't stand out much overall, but was very impressed with one particularly ballsy play where he injured his shoulder and stayed on the ice, maintaining smart positioning in spite of serious pain. Other than that, has a nice frame and had a couple useful pinches.

RUS #27 RW Valeri Nichushkin (2013) – Another fantastic game for Nichushkin. Skating is excellent, moves very quickly for a big man. Offensive vision is top-end, outstanding passing. Great selection of shots with great low wristers for rebounds, a hard one-timer, and the ability to get great lift on quickly-released shots near the net. Liked to camp the backdoor on the powerplay. Went hard to the net frequently, was very bullish and intimidating with the puck and backed defenders off when he came at them. Strong on the penalty kill and played the body from time to time to good effect.

RUS #29 LW Vladimir Tkachyov (2014) – Tkacyhov showed a lot of creativity and poise with the puck today. Carried the puck through center elusively. Made guys look silly with great dangles, including one where he beat a defenseman at the dot for a great scoring chance. Overdid it at times, trying to go 1-on-3 and giving the puck away without getting a shot, or at the very least getting it deep. Showed great skill along the boards, patiently spinning away from checks and buying time for his teammates to get open. Great finish on a one-timer.

Scout's Notes: Russia's fourth line of LW Kirill Shmurygin (2013), C Ruzal Galeyev (2013), and RW Nikita Setdikov (2013) was very strong, the three showed great chemistry, were dangerous offensively, and defended well. LW Nikita Shatski (2013) and LC Ilya Ivanov (2013) played well again in one-dimensional offensive roles.

February 8, 2013, Czech Republic vs. USA (5 Nations Tournament)

CZE #13 LW Jakub Vrana (2014) – Didn't show much against a strong US defense. Put in a good forecheck effort from time to time and made a few nice plays with the puck, but for the most part was kept in check. Was again too fancy in his defensive zone with the puck, creating problems for his team.

CZE #18 RW Ondrej Kase (2014) – Showed great skill in flashes. Great speed through center with the puck and showed the ability to change gears with one step. Burned US defender Keaton Thompson with wonderful burst quickness, drawing a hooking penalty. Had a great wrist shot where he spun off a check and placed it well that showed a bit of his upside.

CZE #22 RW David Pastrnak (2014) – Great individual skill but didn't utilize his teammates well. Went end-to-end and dangled selfishly. Was determined to make things happen. Scored on a beautiful snipe off an individual effort. Was too casual with the puck in his zone on the powerplay, leading to a great shorthanded chance against.

USA #2 RD Connor Clifton (2013) – Very strong game from Clifton. Skating was excellent with fluid movement forward and back. Was active in the attack and took the puck end-to-end with poise, though decision-making once he gained the zone was hit or miss. On one particular occasion, showed great awareness to make a risky jump up into the play while shorthanded and ended up with a breakaway. Turned quickly up the ice with the puck on turnovers to catch defenders off guard. Shots from the point were hard and placed well for rebounds. Good hits in the neutral zone and at the blueline. Physical on the boards.

USA #4 LD Will Butcher (2013) – Loved Butcher's game today. Offensively was very strong, carrying the puck with poise end-to-end and pinching up physically and intelligently. Showed off good hands and a quick release wrister. Found the net from the point with shots through traffic. Coverage in his zone was strong, especially against skill moves off the rush. Played the body well on forwards trying to cycle.

USA #7 RC JT Compher (2013) – Nice two-way game today, showed a lot of creativity offensively. Scored a nice goal off the goaltender's back. Was strong on the puck and good behind the net. Flashed a great variety of shots with a hard slapshot, nice chipped backhand from the top of the circles, and a strong wrister from the slot. Showed the ability to spin and shoot quickly and on target. Acted fast on turnovers, turning quickly up ice to catch defenders flat footed. Didn't have to do much defensively as his line played a lot in the Czech half of the ice.

USA #13 LC Sean Malone (2013) – Really came to play today. Was strong in front of the net in the offensive zone and fought for rebounds and loose pucks. Took the puck to the net with determination and fought to score until the whistle blew. Scored a great breakaway goal where he went to the backhand and roofed it perfectly.

USA #14 LW Tyler Motte (2013) – Played a nice two-way game. His skating was excellent with good burst quickness and agility. Was strong on his stick, fighting off slashes to maintain control and take the puck to the net. Scored a nice goal chopping at a loose puck with one hand. Was determined on the penalty kill and kept the point men very honest with quick feet and good positioning.

USA #15 RW John Hayden (2013) – Was physical today but lacked touch. Took the puck hard to the net but didn't show much as far as stickhandling ability, though he protected well. Laid a couple outstanding hits and was generally tough to play against.

USA #16 RD Steve Santini (2013) – Santini was fired up today and played a great game. Was involved on every shift. Played the body aggressively in the neutral and defensive zones. Showed good poise with the puck, fighting off the forecheck well and taking it end-to-end on one occasion with good protection. Pinched into the attack occasionally. Had a few shifts early where he chased the play in the defensive zone, but righted the ship quickly.

USA #24 RW Michael McCarron (2013) – Looked good today. Used his size well with great puck protection. Made one outstanding offensive hit while shielding the puck that knocked a defender clean off his feet. Covered back defensively and was useful on the forecheck with his long reach. Moved well and showed good awareness to hustle into the attack to create numbers.

USA #28 LW Shane Eiserman (2014) – Nice two-way game. Scored on a good tip and was active in an effective cycle. Had a good showing on the penalty kill with good pressure up ice to kill time. Forechecking was strong with good contact and smart positioning.

Scout's Notes: USA RW Kevin Labanc (2013) is a good player being held back by his skating. RW Hudson Fasching (2013) was fighting the puck all game and tried to do too much by himself. LW Evan Allen (2013) showed good speed and made a few nice offensive plays. G Evan Cowley (2013) took over the starting job from

Hunter Miska and was solid when necessary, making 18 saves on 19 shots. Nice game from RD Trevor Hamilton (2013) who posted two assists. He's been keeping it simple and makes few mistakes, but is not a future NHL defenseman to me. Czech G René Svoboda (2013) was strong in net, making 49 saves on 54 shots.

Feb 8, 2013, Halifax Mooseheads vs. Moncton Wildcats (QMJHL)

HAL # 22, C, MacKinnon, Nathan (2013) MacKinnon had some great speed in this game to rush the puck up the ice and find lanes to gain the offensive zone, and was also able to find an open man in the high slot for a good chance. He put some good pressure on the puck carrier on the fore-check to force a turnover, and was also able to make a play while being pressured and hauled down to move the puck to an open man down low. He opened up well in the slot to take a pass and put a great shot on from point blank, and showed some good speed and puck distribution through the neutral zone. He displayed his explosive speed to blow by defenders and then made a fantastic pass to the slot on a 2-on-1 for the team's 2nd goal of the game. He did a great job splitting the defense to get in tight behind them, and was able to avoid a check along the boards and still hold on to the puck. There was one play however where he lost track of his man in his own end, and he got away to the slot to score the opposition's 1st goal of the game.

HAL # 24, D, Murphy, Matt (2013) Murphy is calm and patient with the puck, and was moving it around pretty well in the offensive zone. He did a good job putting pressure on the puck carrier to take away his time and space, and then showed some of his own agility to avoid the opposition's pressure. He was willing to jump in to lead the attack down low, and get a cycle started in the offensive zone. He did a good job holding the puck in the offensive zone, and starting the cycle, but mishandled the puck in his own end, turning it over to give the opposition their 5th goal of the game.

HAL # 27, LW, Drouin, Jonathan (2013) Drouin started the game making a great pass to find an open man in the slot, and used his great hands to walk out to the slot from behind the net. He has such fantastic hands to get to the slot, but needs to let the shot go when he has the chance. He has some really good quickness and agility, and was able to take a pass down low right next to the net, but missed the net on the opportunity. He is able to take a pass so well, displaying some exceptional skill, then made another great pass to find MacKinnon open in the slot. He also made a great pass to spring MacKinnon for a break through the neutral zone, and has some nice quick hands to distribute the puck with speed off the rush. He drove hard to the net with his stick down, but was unable to take the pas in tight, and then later was able to take a pass right in front of the net and had a wide-open opportunity, but fanned on his chance. He was able to create some space with his hands and open up the slot, and then made a nice drop-pass to create a good opportunity right at point blank. There were times he was turning over the puck trying to force the pass to a man who was covered, and needs to watch the turnovers trying to do it by himself and dangle through the opposition. He also had a bad turnover right up the middle in his own end.

MNC # 4, D, Sweeney, Jacob (2013) Sweeney showed some pretty decent physicality in his own end along the boards, and was moving the puck up out of the zone along the boards pretty well. He can skate pretty decently, but needs to watch some of the neutral zone turnovers on bad passes, and I would also like to see some more crisp tape-to-tape passes on the breakout.

MNC # 22, LW, Barbashev, Ivan (2014) Barbashev displayed a pretty good element of physicality on the fore-check, and was also able to take a hit and still make a play. He made some good chip plays to move the puck up out of his own end, and also put some good pressure on the puck carrier. He was driving to the net with his stick down, and has some nice hands and puck protection, but has to watch the turnovers trying to hold on to the puck for too long in the offensive zone. He had a nice net-front presence on the power play, and was able to make an excellent pass across on an odd-man rush to create a great opportunity in tight. He was able to get open down low next to the net on the power play, and was able to get open in front of the net to take a pass and made a decent move but the goaltender saved it. He was unable to handle some long hard passes through the neutral zone, and also needs to watch the neutral zone turnovers on no-look passes. He needs to watch some of the turnovers just throwing the puck away up the boards as well.

FINAL SCORE: 8-5 Moncton Wildcats

February 9, 2013, Sweden vs. Finland (5 Nations Tournament)

FIN #12 LW Artturi Lehkonen (2013) – Didn't figure into the scoring for the first time and had a harder time creating offense today. Got leveled at open ice and though he took the puck to the net and went to the corners bravely, found a lot of physical opposition and struggled to fight through it. Very crafty on the rare occasions that he was given space, but the Swedes played him pretty tight.

FIN #14 RW Juuso Ikonen (2013) – Good all-around game from Ikonen. Was scrappy along the boards and after the whistles. Played good defense though he can't cover well on the boards with his size. Made a beautiful saucer pass that showed great vision and scored on a strange one-timer that floated in from deep. Took a brutal hooking penalty trying to forecheck on the powerplay.

FIN #24 LW Kasperi Kapanen (2014) – Quiet game. Had a few solid shifts but for the most part was checked tightly and couldn't get anything going. Did show good backchecking ability when he felt like it.

FIN #28 LW Niko Ojamäki (2013) – Played a good game. Showed quick hands in the offensive zone and was unafraid to take the puck to the middle. Nice backhander and a hard slapshot. Laid a big hit in the neutral zone.

SWE #3 LD Robin Norell (2013) – Nice two-way game, very safe and steady. Played the body well and covered intelligently in his zone. Outlet passing was safe and on the tape, including a couple nice stretch feeds through traffic.

SWE #4 LD Robert Hägg (2013) – Should be better at this level with his skillset and experience. Shot the puck into his teammates and didn't show poise carrying it. Safe and physical in his own zone with smart reads to get the puck out of danger.

SWE #8 LD Carl Dahlström (2013) – Mixed game. Big defenseman moved well but didn't play with poise in his end. Panicked with the puck on his stick and was too aggressive in coverage. Positioning was off by a step. Point shots lacked velocity. Did have fleeting shifts of physical dominance on the boards.

SWE #12 LW Andre Burakowsky (2013) – Poor effort from game 2 carried over into this one. Was not a factor. Stickhandling was shaky and he was indecisive with the puck. Looked uncomfortable.

SWE #15 LC Viktor Crus-Rydberg (2013) – Really came to play today. Scored a beautiful goal on a breakaway and added two helpers with great passes in the offensive zone, including one particularly nice setup from behind the net. Flashed a hard one-timer. Was physical in his defensive zone and kept his stick active to cover passing lanes. A little overaggressive in coverage at times, missed an all-or-nothing poke in a 3-on-4 situation, which led to a goal against.

SWE #19 RW Jacob de la Rose (2013) – Strong defensive game, but his line had a hard time creating anything. Threw his weight around well, a couple of his hits were monstrous. Was active with his stick in neutral and defensive zone coverage. Wristshot was again strong today but hard a hard time getting offensive zone penetration and had to depend on one-and-done shots from the rush and the perimeter.

SWE #26 LW Jakub Forsbacka-Karlsson (2015) – Another strong game from the young Swede, who added his second tally of the tournament. Have been impressed with his effort and two-way play in every game.

Scout's Notes: Finns RW Joel Kiviranta (2014) and RD Julius Honka (2014) played strong two-way games. LC Aleksi Mustonen (2013) was an occasional factor but only in the offensive zone.

February 9, 2013, Owen Sound Attack @ Plymouth Whalers (OHL)

OS #24 LD Bigras, Chris (2013) - Bigras made two great plays early on in his own zone showing quick reaction time to break up scoring chances against. He put together a strong effort tonight on the penalty kill and deflected passes very well. He quieted significantly offensively from earlier on in the year. However down two goals he showed he can still rush the puck end to end. He was a very good skater in all directions.

OS #27 RW Nastasiuk, Zach (2013) - Zach scored the first goal of the game early on after putting the puck in the net while in a crowded slot. He had a few good chances around the slot and from in close and possesses a hard shot. He displayed good backcheck on a regular basis and competed hard on the penalty kill. Skating needs improvement.

PLY #18 LW Vanderwiel, Daniel (2013) - Daniel won battles early and often. He displayed excellent work ethic all game long and was utilized regularly on the penalty kill for Plymouth.

PLY #21 RC Hartman, Ryan (2013) - Hartman came out with his usual excellent high energy competitiveness helping his team overcome a slow start. He shows good hands in traffic and had more than his chances to score. He registered 4 assists in this game, some came off rebounds of scoring chances he had, others were off of intelligent passes. He also showed good patience with the puck creating a short handed break as well. During that rush he was able to also draw a penalty and get both sides back to even. Hartman had a great game and although playing on the first line helps, he's helping his teammates just as much if not more than they're helping him.

Scouts Notes: Owen Sound came out very strong tonight just 24 hours after matching up with the #1 team in the OHL, now take on the #2 team in the Western Conference. They lead both 2-0 and 3-2 to open the game. Plymouth really picked up the physicality and while Owen Sound was able to come close to matching this, Plymouth was able to take this physical jumpstart and use it to open up some chances and were able to score five unanswered goals to give the Whalers a 7-3 victory.

February 10, 2013, Barrie Colts @ Sarnia Sting (OHL)

BAR #5 RD Ekblad, Aaron (2014) - Ekblad shows quick footwork but doesn't move anywhere particularly fast. He blocks shots in his own zone. He was able to blast a big point shot of his own for Barrie's second goal in this game.

BAR #18 LC Bradford, Erik (2013) - Bradford is a good skater who jumps up ice quick and provided an excellent two-way presence for the Colts today. He is a regular on the penalty kill. He displays a very active stick and pressures the puck carrier very well. He forced a lot of turnover while short handed. He also created a short handed breakaway for himself, he force the opposition to take a penalty to slow him down. He was very strong in his own zone all game long. He also provided a consistent forecheck 5 on 5 and showed the ability to make quick, intelligent decisions in the offensive zone to set up scoring chances. However he wasn't given many opportunities in this game to show what he could do offensively, the flashes we got were promising.

BAR #21 LW Lemieux, Brendan (2014) - Lemieux is a very aggressive forward who finished his checks regularly throughout today's game. However his aggression also got him into some trouble taking an undisciplined penalty in the second period. He protects the puck well and likes to use his size. He also possesses a powerful shot.

BAR #24 LD Webster, Michael (2013) - Webster is not a flashy player, he keeps it pretty simple and gets the job done. He battles and competes physically. He also gained an assist by setting up Aaron Ekblad's goal.

SAR #2 RD Chapman, Joshua (2013) - Chapman made a smart play with the puck on the penalty kill to send it back to his defensive partner to kill extra time instead of rushing play. He made several other key defensive plays on the kill all game long. He uses his long reach to protect the puck when he's pressured in his own zone. He played very physical in this match-up. This was one of Josh's better games this season.

SAR #7 RD DeAngelo, Anthony (2014) - DeAngelo made a good pass at the point of the point to help Sarnia score their firs goal of the game on the power play. Then in the second period he threw a small tantrum after getting called on a penalty, which was clear as day, but it prevented a scoring chance for Barrie. His temper tantrum caused his two minute penalty to become a four minute double minor. Barrie scored on this penalty to take the lead for the time being. Fortunately Sarnia received a power play not long after this, and DeAngelo scored with a one timer from the point. This game was a perfect example of why DeAngelo is an important player to watch beyond his stats. Yes he had a multi point game, but he drastically lacks mental toughness and blasting the referees can hurt and embarrass the team when he's slamming his stick and yelling at the referee. He also had some defensive lapses that didn't help. He's able to offset these with his offensive talent at the junior level.

SAR #71 RW Goldobin, Nikolay (2014) - Goldobin made some excellent plays displaying his great hands especially late in the game trying to give his team some chances to score. He has a quick shot and was very dangerous at the most important part of this game.

SAR #88 LW Addesi, Jordan (2014) - Addesi did a great job to fight and battle through traffic for a scoring chance. He played with a lot of aggression finishing his checks whenever possible.

Scouts Notes: This game was absolutely wild giving us 6 different lead chances. Sarnia was able to keep up with Barrie throughout this match-up, but every time they seemed to take control in this match-up, Barrie would build momentum once again. It was one of the more exciting games to watch. Brett Hargrave (2014) did a great job protecting the puck and driving hard to the net simultaneously then roofing it for Sarnia's third goal of the game. Davis Brown (2013) competed hard all game long and showed great determination to win battles and races to the puck.

February 10, 2013, Czech Republic vs. Russia (5 Nations Tournament)

CZE #4 LD Martin Kokes (2013) – Two-way defender had an OK game today. Showed quick feet and cleared the front of his net well. Stride is OK but his skating is not efficient. Offensive game was limited, as it has been all tournament. Decision-making was iffy in all situations, especially with the puck in the defensive zone.

CZE #13 LW Jakub Vrana (2014) – Nice game today. Was probably the biggest factor in the Czech upset with two assists, both primary on nice setups, and a beautiful goal that he wristed in off the post from the slot on the rush. Skating was excellent with a lot of burst and good agility. Backchecked hard.

CZE #22 RW David Pastrnak (2014) – Couldn't keep his emotions in check today. Got a roughing penalty in the 2nd period and ended up getting a game misconduct for taunting the Russians after time expired. Wasn't much of a factor in the game. Only noticed him when he telegraphed a pass directly onto a Russian stick.

RUS #2 LD Rushan Rafikov (2013) – Big, bruising defenseman was nasty to deal with today. Physical in front and on the boards, threw his weight around with abandon. Ended up getting a double minor for roughing and abuse of officials in an altercation with Pastrnak, putting his team short. Was frustrated with his team sitting in 3-0 hole at that point but can't have that. Showed a good low point shot but offensive upside seems limited.

RUS #6 LD Nikolai Demidov (2014) – Weak game. Coverage was poor, was caught out of position often and played too aggressively. Was casual with the puck in his end.

RUS #19 RW Pavel Buchnevich (2013) – Was frustrated early when Czechs took the lead and never really settled in. Took shifts off, was too casual with the puck and floated defensively. Had a shift where he buzzed with good forecheck work on the PK but otherwise was kept in check. Took two unnecessary minor penalties.

RUS #21 RW Nikita Setdikov (2013) – Was promoted to the third line today and showed skill in flashes. Used nifty stickhandling to evade checks and had the poise to carry the puck end-to-end through traffic.

RUS #27 RW Valeri Nichushkin (2013) – Has been excellent in every game in this tournament, today was no exception. Carried the team on his back as best he could. Extremely poised and strong on the puck, took advantage of space and showed the ability to either finesse around or power through traffic. Went end-to-end with great skill. Scored on a hard one-timer and added another with a great forehand finish, getting lift in tight. His two goals came in the third period when his team was trying to claw back into the game. Backchecked hard. Took a very dirty slashing penalty, showing a bit of a feisty side.

RUS #29 LW Vladimir Tkachyov (2014) – Nifty skill today, but was not a huge factor. Quick release on a snapshot and good speed down the wing. Set up Nichushkin with a pretty cross-crease pass for a great goal.

Scout's Notes: The Czechs took a commanding 3-0 lead into the third period and were able to hold on for a surprising 4-3 win, though the Russians had locked up first place in the tournament before the game even started. Czech G René Svoboda (2013) was strong for most of the game but just did enough to win in the end, giving up three third period goals, though the goals were not really his fault as the Czechs were scrambling. LD Rinat Valiyev (2013) scored a nice goal pinching into the attack but was quiet otherwise. RW Artyom Prokhorov (2013) played a nice game from the fourth line.

February 10, 2013, Sweden vs. USA (5 Nations Tournament)

SWE #3 LD Robin Norell (2013) – Was strong for most of the game, with strong defensive-zone positioning, good awareness all over the ice, and smart pinches, but struggled towards the end when the result hung in the balance, with over-aggressiveness and puck troubles in his zone.

SWE #4 LD Robert Hägg (2013) –Hägg was excellent today. Nice to see him finally come to play, unfortunate that he waited until the last game. Used his size well with big hits and physical coverage in his own end, very rarely strayed out of position and kept his stick active to take away shooting and passing lanes. Showed off his booming slapshot from the point and made great outlets, including a fantastic stretch pass that led to a breakaway.

SWE #5 RD Rasmus Andersson (2015) – His size was a factor today. Needs to bulk up as he was pushed around in coverage. Was calm with the puck in his zone and made smart outlets but had a hard time carrying out of the zone in the face of a strong forecheck. Flashed a great one-time shot from the point.

SWE #8 LD Carl Dahlström (2013) – Played well today. Was physical on the boards, overdid it once with a dirty boarding penalty but used his size well. Showed poise carrying the puck up ice and made smart passes. Stepped up to squeeze at the blueline and read the play well, using his active stick to intercept passes.

SWE #9 LD Wilhelm Westlund (2013) – Showed good offensive upside today. Was strong on the puck and carried it capably. Defensive zone coverage was iffy, wasn't physical enough.

SWE #26 LW Jakub Forsbacka-Karlsson (2015) – Yet another great game for the youngster, who set up behind the net frequently today and showed smart setup skills from there. He's definitely one to watch for the future.

SWE #29 LC Lucas Wallmark (2013) – Scored a nice goal with quick hands in front of the net, but was again unimpressed with his skating. He was sluggish, particularly without the puck.

USA #6 LD Keaton Thompson (2013) – Not a great showing. Hands were slow and he tried to do too much with the puck, leading to turnovers. Had one especially brutal giveaway where he gave the Swedish forward a partial breakaway and had to take a hooking penalty to recover. Was shaky in his own end, had a hard time recognizing his man for coverage. Wrister from the point in the offensive zone was good, that's about it for the positive.

USA #10 LW Evan Allen (2013) – Scored the overtime winner on a nice goal but was concerned with his puck skills today. Can rifle them with the best of this draft class but lacked poise in carrying, as a result couldn't do much to create offense. Acted as a complementary player for a majority of the tournament, save for a shift or two of skill.

USA #13 LC Sean Malone (2013) – Another strong game from the stocky center. Was strong on his skates in front of the net and battled for pucks. Showed off a nice wrister with a quick release. Backchecked hard and played the body in the defensive zone.

USA #16 RD Steve Santini – Quiet game, but solid. Good coverage and intelligent reads. Aside from one big hit, he was hardly noticeable.

USA #22 RW Hudson Fasching (2013) – Wow, what a game. Showed up today in a big way. Was not rewarded on the score sheet but was excellent offensively. Skating was forceful, powerful stride with good acceleration. Flashed a quick wrister and had a great redirect on the powerplay that clanked the pipe. Puck control was poised and smooth, good hands in traffic. Protected well along the boards and won battles. Intelligent passing. Active stick defensively to break up plays and played the body hard, including one huge hit.

USA #24 RW Michael McCarron (2013) – Another physical game where McCarron was simple-minded offensively. Filled the agitator role with plenty of borderline contact during the play and after the whistle that elicited a lot of attention. Has a hard wrister but was limited to outside shots. Good, physical defensive coverage and smart stickchecking.

USA #28 LW Shane Eiserman (2014) – Another solid two-way game. Strong on the forecheck and in the neutral zone with good contact. Was patient with the puck along the boards and won battles. Shot needs work.

Scout's Notes: Along with Fasching, LW Tyler Motte (2013) was also promoted to first line. He was quiet all tournament but showed speed today. RW John Hayden (2013) and LW Anthony Louis (2013) were demoted to fourth line and didn't do anything of note. Quiet tournaments from LD Gage Ausmus (2013) and LD Clint Lewis (2013), who along with RD Trevor Hamilton (2013) played mostly mistake-free hockey but all showed little upside. Ausmus is the best of the bunch as he can play physically and joined the attack from time to time. RW Jacob de la Rose (2013) had a quiet but solid game on the Swedish top line, while his linemate LW Andre Burakowsky (2013) was again invisible.

Feb. 10, 2013, Cedar Rapids Roughriders vs. Green Bay Gamblers (USHL)

GBG # 5, D, Olofsson, Gustav (2013) Olofsson is able to rush the puck up the ice, skating well, but needs to watch some of the neutral zone turnovers on missed passes. He has some pretty good size, is calm with the puck and moving it up out of the zone pretty well. He stepped up on his man to challenge him, but got beat giving the opposition an odd-man rush, which they scored on. He was coming down deep into the offensive zone on the attack, and was getting some good shots through on the net. He was tying up his man, and winning puck battles in his own zone, and blocking shots in his own end in front of the net. He also read the play well to come down into the slot in the offensive zone to provide good options.

GBG # 16, C, Weis, Matthew (2013) Weis did a good job opening up in the high slot to take a pass and put a good shot on net, but has to hit the net on his opportunity. He displayed some nice physicality to knock over his man in open ice and take the puck, and showed his hands and puck skills on a great move to get in tight to the net with the puck. He took an unnecessary cross-checking penalty kin the neutral zone.

GBG # 23, D, Gross, Jordan (2013) Gross got the cycle started well in the offensive zone, and was able to get his shot through to the net, although it was not the hardest shot. He did a good job moving the puck up out of the zone to start the rush, and is able to skate the puck up on the rush and get it in deep. He was playing his man pretty hard with an element of physicality along the boards, and used his stick to get in a lane and knock the puck off the opposition. He had a great point shot on the power play to score the game winner in overtime.

GBG # 97, LW, Dikushin, Gregory (2013) Dikushin did a good job going hard to the net looking for loose pucks and opportunities in tight. He was able to take a long pass through the neutral zone and move it up to lead a man on the rush into the offensive zone with the puck. He showed some nice agility on the rush to avoid the opposition's pressure, and was able to make a great pass to find a man crashing the net for a great opportunity in tight. He made a really nice long breakout pass to start the rush and find a man at the far blue line, and showed some good support coming back on the back-check to steal the puck off the opposition.

CED # 15, RW, Petrash, Corey (2013) Petrash is able to get the puck in deep off the rush to get the cycle started, but needs to watch the turnovers trying to move the puck out of his own end along the boards. He was also out-muscled off the puck along the boards.

CED # 22, LW, Oglevie, Andrew (2013) Oglevie was able to get open down low next to the net, but was unable to score on the opportunity. He got a pretty nice cycle game started deep in the offensive zone, and made a really great long pass to spring a man on a break at the far blue line. He took a pass with great speed driving hard to the net to take a pass and score the team's 3rd goal of the game on a nice move, and then showed his great hands and moves again later, but needs to hit the net on chances form the slot. He also put good pressure on the fore-check, battling well for the puck, but needs to look first when moving the puck.

CED # 26, D, Kuster, Clark (2013) Kuster was able to take a hit to make a play, and move the puck up the boards o the breakout to start the rush. He opened up well to put a one-timer on net on the power play, but then fanned on the shot. Later on he had a good hard shot that he got through on net from the point, and was distributing the puck well on the rush through the neutral zone. He was willing to jump in on the rush to join the attack, but then defensively let his man get towards the inside track which lead to the opposition's 3rd goal of the game.

FINAL SCORE: 4-3 Green Bay Gamblers

Feb 11, 2013, Rimouski Oceanic vs. Moncton Wildcats (QMJHL)

RIM # 3, D, Kostalek, Jan (2013) Kostalek played the body well to make a hit and knock his man off the puck and also got his stick in lanes to breakup the opposition's passes through the neutral zone to force a turnover then rush the puck back up the ice. He did an excellent job of tying up the opposition in front of the net to keep them away and take away their chances and was playing the body to keep the opposition to the outside. He took the puck on the wide drive to come in and score on a shot from a bad angle and got the puck down low to start the cycle in the offensive zone. He played his man with great physicality to knock him over but needs to get his shots through to the net on chances from the high slot and also needs to watch the neutral zone turnovers on breakout passes.

RIM # 7, D, Leclrec, Mathieu (2013) Leclerc was able to move the puck down low to get the cycle started, but he needs to get stronger on the puck along the boards in his own end and he also has to watch the turnovers in his own end, especially those that result in great opportunities for the opposition.

RIM # 11, RW, Bryukvin, Vladimir (2013) Bryukvin put good pressure on the puck carrier on the fore-check and was hustling well to get on loose pucks. He was coming back to provide support and cleared the puck from the front of the net to get it out of danger. He showed great speed on the rush to drive the puck wide into the offensive zone and he went to the net to take a pass for a good chance in tight. He was playing the body pretty hard and physical in front of his net.

RIM # 15, LW, DeLuca, Anthony (2013) DeLuca was hustling well on the back-check and was able to move the puck back to the point to set up a one-timer goal on a point shot. He was able to move the puck up along the boards to start the breakout and was distributing the puck well in the offensive zone on the power play. He showed good speed on the rush to get in deep with the puck and was driving the puck wide well, but has to cut towards the middle on his shot to get to a more dangerous scoring area for his opportunities.

RIM # 23, C, Gauthier, Frederik (2013) Gauthier had some really good agility to twist the puck from the opposition's pressure and played the puck carrier with a nice element of physicality. He was driving to the net with his stick down and had a nice net-front presence on the power play. He was protecting the puck well on the wide drive and could get the puck up the ice with ease to get it in deep in the offensive zone. He did a really good job of tying up his man on the back-check to take away the opposition's opportunity, and hustled hard on the back-check to use his stick to pressure the opposition and rush them to make a play, however he can't cross the line and take a penalty on the play. He was forcing turnovers through the neutral zone by putting pressure on the opposition but has to watch his own turnovers up the middle trying to get the puck out of the zone.

RIM # 81, RW, Fortier, Simon (2013) Fortier got down low with the puck to get the cycle started and he was hustling well for pucks along the wall. He used his body nicely to get the inside track to the puck.

MNC # 4, D, Sweeney, Jacob (2013) Sweeney used his stick really well to knock the puck off the opposition on their rush and held the offensive zone nicely to get a cycle going in the offensive zone. He is calm and patient with the puck and can get his shots through to the net from the point. His breakout pass was a bit too hot for forwards to handle at certain points.

MNC # 12, C, Johnson, Stephen (2013) Johnson did a nice job of pressuring the puck carrier in his own end and used his stick to knock the puck free off the opposition. He got a good cycle going in deep in the offensive zone and did a good job of driving hard to the net with his stick down looking for loose pucks and rebounds. He drove the puck to the net really well to create opportunities in front and got a good cycle going in deep. He needs to watch the turnovers moving the puck up along the wall in his own end and by trying to force passes through the opposition.

FINAL SCORE: 2-0 Rimouski Oceanique

Feb 15, 2013, Sioux City Musketeers vs. Tri-City Storm (USHL)

TRI # 7, D, Cecere, Garrett (2013) Cecere did a pretty nice job in this game of tying up his man in front of the net. He was able to make a really nice long breakout pass to find a teammate at the far blue line to spring him into the offensive zone and was physical on the puck carrier along the wall. He showed some good agility to twist and turn from the opposition's pressure and was able to find a lane and an open man down low on a great pass on the power play. He also had a nice hard shot that he kept down low from the point on the power play and was holding the offensive line well by reading the play to pick off passes then move the puck down low for a teammate to score on one occasion. He used his stick really well to knock the puck from the opposition and breakup their play, however at one point was unable to catch an opponent as he drove hard down the middle to split the defense for a good opportunity.

TRI # 8, LW, Moore, Trevor (2013) Moore had some great speed and pressure that he put on the puck carrier and he opened up really well in the slot to pick up a loose puck and put a good quick shot on net. He put nice pressure on the fore-check and showed nice sped rushing the puck up the ice into the offensive zone to get a good shot off from the high slot. He opened up well to take a pass beside the net for a good one-timer chance and displayed great quickness and agility with the puck. He protects it well along the boards and was also protecting the puck well on the wide drive to beat defenders. He was putting pressure on the fore-check, was physical on the puck carrier along the boards to force turnovers and had excellent speed on the rush then made a good drop pass once to create room for a teammate to get a good shot off from the high slot.

TRI # 11, C, Cotton, Jason (2013) Cotton was coming back well to his own end to provide support and get in lanes to try to block passes. He did a good job of driving hard to the net looking for loose pucks and rebounds and put some really good pressure on the puck carrier. He has to tie up his man however on the back-check as he let his man get away and then get a good shot off to score.

TRI # 13, LW, Gamez, Garrett (2013) Gamez had some really nice speed and quickness and a great drive to the net with his stick down to provide scoring options. He went to the front of the net for a nice net-front presence on the power play and was distributing the puck well in the offensive zone to get it back to the point, then he drove hard to the net. He took a pass down low in front of the net then made a good back-hand move to score and was able to rush the puck up into the offensive zone to get a shot off from the high slot, however he had better options to move the puck instead.

TRI # 27, RW, Lesperance, Joel (2013) Lesperance played with a nice element of physicality on the puck carrier along the boards and was using his stick well to poke the puck loose from the opposition. He made a couple nice passes to move the puck out of the zone on the breakout, however needs to do it with more consistency as he also missed his target on some long breakout passes as well. He took the puck off the sidewall to get to the slot for a good shot and put some nice pressure on the point, getting in lanes to block shots. He also had a nice net-front presence on the power play to screen the goalie and tip the point shot to score, and was battling hard to get to the front of the net. He has to keep his head up as he got rocked in neutral zone and knocked over on a huge open ice hit and he also got beat by the opposition's speed at one point and was forced to take a tripping penalty. He also needs to tie up his man and take a stick on his back-check.

SIO # 14, RW, Lacroix, Cedric (2013) Lacroix came back well for some nice support and was hustling hard for loose pucks and battling well for it. He was able to get the puck up out of his own zone along the boards and put good pressure on the puck carrier while playing with a good effort and work ethic.

SIO # 22, LW, McGlynn, Connor (2013) McGlynn was protecting the puck well and showed good strength on the puck to hold on to it under pressure. He did a great job of driving hard to the net with his stick down and put a good low shot on off the rush to try to generate a rebound. He had a nice net-front presence on the power play, put good pressure and physicality on the fore-check and got his stick in lanes to block passes and breakup plays for the opposition, as well as knocking it away from them.

SIO # 28, LW, Torok, Tomas (2013) Torok was distributing the puck pretty well on the rush through the neutral zone and put some nice pressure and physicality on the fore-check. He had a great battle for the puck along the boards and played the puck carrier hard and physical. He made a nice move on the drive to the net to get in tight for a good opportunity, however needs to watch the turnovers in the neutral zone by holding on to the puck too long trying to skate his way through the opposition.

FINAL SCORE: 5-3 Sioux City Musketeers

Feb 15 2013, Val D'Or Foreurs @ Chicoutimi Sagueneens, (QMJHL)

VDO #8 LW, Mantha, Anthony (2013) : Uninspiring performance from Mantha who looked like he played because he had to, not because he wanted to; he had a couple of nice shots on goal, showing the accuracy and quick release on it; didn't want to get physical, didn't win the battles; he doesn't waste a motion going where the puck is, preferring to anticipate plays; has tons of smarts and probably relies too much on smarts and talent instead of efforts. Big body, but got knocked off the puck by young Chicoutimi D's who wanted the puck more than him.

VDO #16 RW, Aubé-Kubel, Nicolas (2014): Little chunks of ice-time here and there, showed good puck handling skills in tight space and great skating abilities. Didn't win his battles and had a tough time bringing his plays somewhere.

VDO #20 C, Richard, Anthony (2015): Superb energy displayed; pretty small but still has plenty of time to grow before his draft year; very good 2-way player with good offensive abilities mixed with great grinding; not afraid of anybody and willing to be physical; has quick feet, gains speed quickly.

VDO #26 C, Dunn, Vincent (2013): He played the left wing in the game which suited him well, can be more energetic deep in the offensive zone, throwing the body, he is willing to backcheck and do the little details in his own zone. Great passer he sees the play develop well and although the skill set is not elite, his pretty fast hands and quick passing skills helps him a lot creating chances for teammates. He is in every scrum and willing to drop the gloves with anybody, aggressive kid.

CHI #27 C, Dauphin, Laurent (2013): Put on his grinder boots for the game and it paid off, had many good chances around the crease, charging the net. He won his battles and showed great strength all-around. Sometimes keeps the puck for too long and limits his options by taking too much time, dangles well in tight spaces. I'd like to see him get more physical in scrums and on the forecheck.

Feb. 23 2013, Sherbrooke Phoenix @ Chicoutimi Saguenéens, (QMJHL)

SHE #7 D, Lysenko, Vladislav (2013) : He was physical on all his presences. Sometimes a little too much, getting undisciplined, but I like the agressiveness he showed on the boards, recovering the puck most of the times with a good shoulder check. He was really tough to get around, stepping up well at the blue line and showing good footwork when he adjusted his speed for a good gap control. He likes to use the hip check to break his opponent's momentum getting into the offensive zone. He was safe when playing the puck, holding his blue line well, shooting at the right moments, chipping it back behind the net when the shooting lane is blocked. He stayed positionnally disciplined in his hits distribution, not getting out of his way to lay the body. Strong showing.

SHE #15 D, Deschamps, Jonathan (2014) : Didn't play much and when he was used was afraid to make a mistake, keeping the play simple, not doing anything particularly good or bad. He's always putting himself in a position where he's on the defensive side of the puck, which his a good sign at 16 years old. His footwork is not particularly great, although his 1-on-1 coverage down-low is pretty good. Needs to get better with the puck.

SHE #28 C, Audette, Daniel (2014) : Smallish center with above-average skating, good passing skills and puckhandling abilities. He glided a lot during the game and had troubles handling physical pressure from opponents. He has a lotto learn to get from a good offensive player to a great hockey player. For the moment is strickly efficient in the offensive zone.

SHE #32 D, Neil, Carl (2014) : Great puck-mover, has a high level of offensive hockey sense, strong slapshot and is confident when he has the puck on his stick. He started a beautiful 3-way play from the point on the powerplay with a tape-to-tape cross-ice pass, was very solid on the walls, strong player. The biggest problem with Neil is the decisions he take with and without the puck. He has questionnable defensive hockey sense, tries risky plays, makes passes through center when he should use the boards, a mistake that resulted in the game's 4th goal. He really needs to step up in that area as he has a lot of good tools to be a good D in the future, size, footwork, passing skills, shot…

SHE #71 RW, Deslauriers, Vincent (2015) : Small but hardworking gritty forward, he really showed a lot of energy and intensity in the game. He makes his way to the net even though he's surely not as strong as most D's he faced during the game. You can not hate that kind of player as coach or scout, at 16 years old, he's already showing tremendous work ethic, attention to little details and willingness to take a hit to make a play. I don't think he has a ton of puckhandling abilities, more of a North-South player with an agressive edge, he'll surely need to get bigger and even taller to be on the radar at his draft year.

CHI #7 D, Léveillé, Loik (2014) : Offensive defenseman with a lot of puckhandling abilities, heavy wrist shot and quick feet. He has a ton of potential with the puck and already playing big minutes at 16 years old getting better in his defensive hockey sense. His instincts to join the rush and position himself in open spots are just great. He finds open men easily, posesses quick hands and he is able to bring the puck up very well. He made a good shot on goal through traffic to earn his goal. He plays well defensively without the puck, blocking shots, bringing his man on the walls, but that should get even better when the speed and strength are improved. His puck management in his own zone can be a bit akward sometimes, trying to complexify plays and breakouts more than what they need to be, try to use his talent with the puck to get it out of the defensive zone. Diamond that needs a little bit of polishing.

CHI #12 C, Sylvestre, Sébastien (2013*) : This guy is playing with a ton of confidence and looking great as Chicoutimi's 1st line center. He is taking a lot of pride at blocking shots and executing the little details in his own zone well. He has great speed, elite skills with the puck and impressive strength that he displayed again tonight by protecting the puck on the walls. He goes in front of the net to collect garbage goals and has a superb release on the wrist shot. Very disciplined and starting to get more physical too, not big hits, but some good bumps on the forecheck. He is not a sellfish player and could shoot the puck even more on net, trying to pass the puck too often, sees plays that others don't see and executes at a high level.

CHI #27 C, Dauphin, Laurent (2013) : Didn't like what I saw again from Dauphin, 2 lazy penalties and a lot of predictable plays in the offensive zone. He got pushed off the puck easily on many occasions and he's looking like a tired player at the moment. Mentally and physically he's not on the level he was earlier in the season, taking up big minutes and not giving up on plays. He's having some problems with the level of energy and it's winding down his game.

CHI #30 G, BIlia, Julio (2014) : Superb game. He played very well at crucial times when the game was tied. He especially showed amazing reflexes with both hands, making a great glove save on a breakaway and made a superb blocker save in the 2nd period on a shot coming from the slot. He follows the play well, stays calm and controlled the rebounds very well, never giving up any of those in the slot. He keeps his calm and cool attitude at all times and starting to get more confident when he's getting out of his blue paint to play the puck, communicating with teammates well. He's not the tallest but with reflexes, quickness and great attitude, he has a great potential.

February 15th, 2013. Guelph Storm vs. Owen Sound Attack (OHL)

GUE#7 D Ben Harpur (2013). Not the best night for Harpur in this game. Ben looked lost at times in the defensive zone and was caught standing and watching the play develop instead of initiating contact. He was on for a goal against and was outworked in front of the net battling for rebounds. He was taking some bad angles against opposing rushers and did not hold the offensive or defensive blue line with much effort. Ben was effective at getting his stick into lanes and picked off a few passes. He showed a good first pass breaking out of the defensive zone but would benefit from skating the puck out of the zone when given space. Displayed a strong shot from the point but needs to work at keeping it on target for tips and rebound chances.

GUE#11 F Jason Dickinson (2013). Dickinson continued to display a stronger physical presence in this game and was very solid finishing a number of big hits along the boards and in the corners. He showed a willingness to battle for free pucks and did not step down from opposing defenders. Jason also had some strong shifts on the penalty kill, getting his stick into lanes and willing to block shots up high. He used a quick burst of speed to gain the offensive blue line with ease and worked well with his linemates generating offensive chances. Jason was unable to find the back of the net but displayed a quick release wrist shot when given space in the slot. Dickinson needs to improve his work in the face-off circle as he struggled to win draws when stepping into the centerman role.

GUE#17 F Tyler Bertuzzi (2013). Bertuzzi was excellent at setting a physical tone early in the game, and uses a strong burst of speed to close gaps and punish opposing players for holding into the puck too long. He is constantly working and moving his feet on every shift, and is always looking for checks to finish. Tyler is exceptionally strong at getting under opponents skin and is great at drawing penalties after whistles. He is very strong on the fore check and is good at getting turnovers for the Storm in the defensive zone. Bertuzzi works hard in front of the net to bang away at rebounds and does not back down from bigger players. He did show a tendency to run around on occasion and needs to ensure that he keeps in the right position instead of always looking for the big hit.

OWE#24 D Chris Bigras (2013). Bigras had a very strong game for the Attack in both the offensive and defensive zones. Chris shows exceptional confidence skating with the puck through the neutral zone and was good at skating with the puck out of trouble in the defensive zone when pressured. He showed excellent awareness constantly keeping his head up and looking for passing outlets. Bigras scored a beautiful goal sneaking back door behind the unsuspecting Storm defenders displaying a strong understanding of the offensive zone. He showed great recovery speed and was quick to get back whenever he did jump into the offensive rush. Chris works hard in the defensive zone and is excellent at keeping attackers in front of him and uses a combination of smarts and strength to win puck possession.

OWE#27 F Zach Nastasiuk (2013). Nastasiuk had an up and down game versus the Storm. Zach's feet were not moving very well early in the game and he was forced to take a bad penalty due to a lack of speed and bad positioning. His game got stronger as the game progressed and he had an exceptional shorthanded rush but was unable to beat the Storm goaltender. He showed good offensive playmaking abilities by setting up a nice goal for the Attack. Zach also displayed a quick release wrister from the high slot that hit the post late in the game. Nastasiuk works hard and generally gets into good positions in both the offensive and defensive zones, but his feet sometimes let him down and he needs to improve on this area.

February 15, 2013, Rouyn-Noranda Huskies @ Drummondville Voltigeurs (QMJHL)

Rouyn-Noranda
#2 Allan Caron, Def (2014) Good size with average mobility, played a physical game in his own end. Played on the Huskies 3rd pair of defensemen. Didn't do much as far as moving the puck or even in the offensive zone.

#7 Justin Guenette Def (2013) Guenette for the most part was quiet in this game, made a spinorama move at the Drummondville blueline to escape an opponent in the 3rd period was his only flash of the game. Has quick feet and can move the puck well but didn't have possession of the puck often in this game. Play on his opposite side with Redgie Bois, got run over a couple of times in this game. Needs to get stronger.

#10 Jean-Sébastien Dea, C (2013) Dea centered the Huskies' 2nd line between Gabriel Desjardins and Marcus Power but played on the first powerplay unit. Scored a very nice goal by getting to a loose puck in the faceoff circle and skating with it in the slot untouched and taking a nice wrist shot high glove side on Guindon. He has a real quick release on that shot. Usually strong in the faceoff circle, but Dea struggled in that facet today. A couple of times in this game he showed that he's a capable stickhandler, making defensemen look not so good. Also very patient with the puck. Made a bad pass in the offensive zone that was intercepted by Nikolas Brouillard that came close to costing a goal to the Huskies.

#12 Gabriel Slight, RW (2013) The first thing you noticed with Slight was his big frame and how much space he takes up on the ice. At even strength, he was used on a 3rd or 4th line but he got to play on the first power play unit. There is no secret as to why he's playing there, as he's used in front of the net to create traffic in front of the goalie. Took a dumb penalty while playing on the powerplay after a whistle, made some other iffy plays with the puck on the man advantage. Skating will need a lot of work, as he has heavy feet and doesn't generate any speed. Does a good job using his size for protecting the puck and is effective if his line cycles the puck well.

#25 Sven Andrighetto, RW (Undrafted 1993) Andrighetto was great today, played in all situations of the game. He was always on the ice with Nikita Kucherov whether it's at even strength, power play or penalty kill. On the power play he's used on the point with Mathieu Brisebois, you can see his vision is top notch from there. An effortless skater who loves to rush the puck in the offensive zone. Makes the players around him better thanks to his great playmaking ability. Beautiful skater, very agile on his skates. In this game I saw him made some real strong plays by backchecking ; he has become an excellent two-way forward these last two years under Andre Tourigny. Very dangerous on the power play, controls the play from the backhand and made an excellent pass for a Kucherov goal.

#30 Alexandre Belanger G (2013) Belanger was shaky in the first period and rebounded well in the 2nd and struggled late in the 3rd, giving up 3 goals in the last 10 minutes. Didn't look very confident making saves in the first period, was deep in his net and his rebound control was off. Looked a lot more confident in the 2nd period, as he was more square to the shooters. Would probably love to have 2 of the 5 goals he gave back; for the first one he didn't hug his post enough and on the 4th goal with seconds left in the game he should have stopped that shot from the top of the faceoff circle. Doesn't look confident with the puck on his stick, has some work to do with his puckhandling skills.

Drummondville

#11 Joey Ratelle (2014) Ratelle had a tough game, took a 4 minute penalty for high sticking early in the first period and had a horrid turnover right on Marcus Power stick which lead to a goal. Didn't get much ice time after this.

#15 Nikolas Brouillard Def (2013) Brouillard had a strong offensive game with 3 goals and an assist in this game. Scored twice in the last minute to send this game to overtime. Brouillard saw a lot of ice time, excelling at quarterbacking the Voltigeurs powerplay. For his first goal he took a good wrister from the left faceoff circle and beat the goalie high. On the 2nd goal, with heavy traffic in front of the Rouyn-Noranda net, he made a nice play of just throwing the puck on net and somehow the puck went in. Seconds later, Brouillard completed his hat trick with 1 second left in the game, taking a slapper from the faceoff circle. Came close to scoring a 4th goal in overtime after intercepting a pass from J-S Dea in his zone and flying all the way to the Huskies net. Showed great acceleration on that play, didn't see that kind of speed the rest of the game. Had some struggle in his own end against the big Rouyn-Noranda forwards, got manhandled along the board by them also. His lack of strength really showed there.

#31 Domenic Graham G (2013) Graham came in in relief at the start of the third period, played well and made some real good saves to keep the Voltigeurs in this game. Unlike Belanger and Guindon, Graham is good at handling the puck and made at least 3 nice stretch passes. Kudos to him for stepping up and helping his team come back in this game after being down by 3 after 40 minutes.

#39 Louis-Phillippe Guindon G (2013) Guindon was pulled after the 2nd period after giving up 4 goals on 15 shots. Earlier in the game, he made some good saves, including one on Marcus Power on a breakaway, where he was patient and made Power make the first move. Can't blame him on the first goal, as Dea beat him with a perfect shot from the slot. On the 2nd goal, a perfect pass from Andrighetto to Kucherov at the side of the net made its way behind him. On the 3rd goal, Marcus Power got another breakaway and beat Guindon five-hole, I would have liked to see Guindon keep his stick on the ice as that would have likely stopped the puck. On the 4th goal, Andrighetto took a shot from the point, and Guindon left a big juicy rebound in front of the net so that Brisebois had an an easy tap-in. Like his opposing goalie, Guindon has a lot of work to do with his puckhandling skills, his rebound control was off in that game: a perfect example was on the 4th goal.

February 16, 2013, Oshawa Generals @ Sarnia Sting (OHL)

OSH #14 RW Latour, Bradley (2013) - Bradley went to the net early and was rewarded picking up a rebound and quickly put it in. He competes hard and shows some good creativity with the puck. Bradley was also utilized on Oshawa's penalty kill and put forward an effective effort.

OSH #19 RC Cassels, Cole (2013) - Cole plays a very up and down style of game. He doesn't really do anything exceptional and pretty much stuck to the defensive side of the game. Cole was very effective and useful on the penalty kill. His skating is above average.

OSH #34 RW Smith, Hunter (2013) - Hunter is built like a house and finishes his checks. His skating and puck skills are well below average. He has some raw potential that may be appealing to a few teams, but will need some time and attention to reach his potential.

OSH #71 LW Dal Colle, Michael (2014) - Playing high in defensive zone but was able to identify and negate offensive chances in his own end. He absorbs contact effectively and is willing to go into the corners. His skating needs improvement and he didn't play as big of a factor as expected in this game.

SAR #2 RD Chapman, Joshua (2013) - Chapman has been getting noticeably better with the puck in his own zone with more accurate passes and handling the puck with more confidence. However he still had the occasional brain cramp.

SAR #7 RD DeAngelo, Anthony (2014) - DeAngelo displayed excellent passing and shooting selection while on the power play. Anthony was much smarter overall in this game, but the excessive spin-o-rama got him in a little trouble later on in this game.

SAR #21 LC Nikandrov, Daniel (2013) - Nikandrov was effective forcing turnovers in all three zones. He put forward a great effort short handed but also multi-tasked directing traffic making sure everyone was in position at the same time. He blocked several shots in this game. Despite the fact Daniel is a strong defensive forward, he displayed very good puck control tonight.

SAR #71 RW Goldobin, Nikolay (2014) - Goldobin displayed precise passing up ice and moved the puck intelligently. He forced turnovers in the defensive zone helping Sarnia limit scoring chances against. He didn't look as productive on a line with Boucher and Sarault as he has with Nikandrov and Latta. There's only so much puck to go around and with Boucher and Sarault's chemistry, Goldobin is very much in the background on that line.

Scouts Notes: Oshawa came out very strong in the first 20 minutes of this game. Sarnia being able to escape with a 1-1 tie may have set the tone and helped give them the momentum to win this game. J.P. Anderson (San Jose) put together one of his best performances all season long making several huge saves for the Sting while stopping 40 of 42 shots. Brett Hargrave (2014) has noticeably improved his hands and is calmer with the puck than in the past.

Feb 16, 2013, Cedar Rapids Roughriders vs. Green Bay Gamblers (USHL)

CED # 6, C, McLaughlin, Dylan (2013) McLaughlin battles really well for the puck to win it off the opposition and force turnovers. He made a really good pass across down low to create a good chance in tight, and has the hands as well as puck protection in deep in the offensive zone. He has to keep his head up to watch out for the big hit coming his way.

CED # 22, LW, Oglevie, Andrew (2013) Oglevie distributes the puck effectively on the rush up the ice, then was driving hard to the net with his stick down. He can make a good first pass out of the zone to start the rush and has the puck protection and agility to keep the puck from the opposition's pressure. He made some good cross-ice passes to find teammates off the rush and used his body to win puck battles and protect the puck effectively. He gets to the net looking for loose pucks and opportunities and did a good job on the wide drive keeping the puck from the opposition then moving to a man driving hard to the net. He has to watch the turnovers holding on to the puck too long in the high slot and needs to drive the puck to the net rather than taking long outside shots off the rush.

CED # 26, D, Kuster, Clark (2013) Kuster did a good job of holding the offensive line and has a good hard shot from the point. He got his stick in lanes to breakup passes for the opposition on their odd-man rush opportunities and was closing off his man well along the boards to separate him from the puck. He got down showing a willingness to block shots and was putting good pressure on the puck carrier in the defensive zone.

GBG # 16, C, Weiss, Mathew (2013) Weiss put good pressure on the puck carrier to force turnovers and got a good cycle going deep in the offensive zone then got to the slot to open up and provide options. He has great speed on the rush coming down on the wing and was distributing the puck nicely to create room in the offensive zone. He protects the puck well from the opposition's pressure and is really creative with his passes in the offensive zone. He has really good agility to twist away from the opposition and was taking passes to put great shots on net from the high slot to score.

GBG # 23, D, Gross, Jordan (2013) Gross has a great ability to rush the puck up the ice, was finding lanes to gain the offensive zone and has some great vision to find an open man in the offensive zone with excellent passes to create scoring opportunities. He is able to make a good first pass out of the zone and was holding the offensive line nicely. He puts good pressure on the puck carrier in the defensive zone and has the hands to get around the opposition and avoid their pressure. He needs to get his shots through to the net from the point with more consistency.

GBG # 81, C, Winborg, Adam (2013) Winborg put good pressure on the fore-check and displayed nice physicality on the puck carrier. He made a great pass to find a man out front of the net to score, and put a great shot on net from the side-wall trying to generate a rebound for a man out front. He was getting the puck in deep into the offensive zone to start the cycle.

GBG # 97, LW, Diksuhin, Grigori (2013) Dikushin had a pretty good drive to the net with his stick down and was opening up in the high slot to take passes, but then was trying to force the puck through the opposition. He has some hands, moves and creativity but also turned the puck over holding on to the puck too long trying to be fancy. He was pressuring the puck carrier really well on the fore-check to force turnovers in deep and was willing to get in lanes to block shots in his own end. He has to watch the neutral zone turnovers by not being strong on the puck, and also had a wide-open net opportunity but panicked and fanned on the shot.

FINAL SCORE: 4-3 Green Bay Gamblers

February 16, 2013, Des Moines Buccaneers vs. Sioux City Musketeers (USHL)

DMB # 2, D, Schueneman, Corey (2013) Schueneman made a nice long pass out of the zone to find a man at the far blue line to spring him into the offensive zone. He did a nice job holding the offensive line then moved the puck down low to create a great scoring chance on the power play. He is able to skate the puck up the ice to gain the offensive zone and made some good chip plays to create space for teammates with the puck. He got his stick in lanes to try to block passes in the defensive zone, was protecting the puck well on the rush and was also able to take a hit and still hold on to the puck to make a play.

DMB # 3, D, Drake, David (2013) Drake got a good cycle going in the offensive zone and he used his stick really well to force the opposition to the outside and create some trouble for them by knocking the puck away. He was a little over-aggressive at times trying to pick off turnovers and was beat by the opposition's speed and passing.

DMB # 9, C, Jenkins, Jack (2013) Jenkins had good speed, hustle and put good pressure on the puck carrier. He came down on the wing then cut to the middle on a great move for an excellent chance in tight, but has to get stronger on the puck along the boards so that he's not knocked off it so easily. He put good pressure on the fore-check and used his stick well to poke the puck loose and force turnovers. He made a really nice pass to find an open man in the high slot for a good shot opportunity and was playing the puck carrier with a nice element of physicality.

DMB # 10, C, Voltin, Luke (2013) Voltin got a good cycle going in deep and was able to find lanes to move the puck back to the point on the power play. He made an excellent pass to move the puck cross-crease to a teammate for a goal in tight on the power play. He also showed some nice hands and agility while protecting the puck from the opposition's pressure. He put good pressure on the fore-check and played with a nice element of physicality. He displayed nice patience with the puck, however has to get shots through to the net on opportunities from the high slot and also needs to watch turnovers moving the puck up along the boards out of the zone.

DMB # 23, LW, Galt, Ryan (2013) Galt put good pressure on the fore-check and was able to move the puck up out of the zone pretty well to start the breakout. He got a good cycle going in deep and opened up pretty well in the slot to provide scoring options. He made a nice pass to tee-up a one-timer in the high slot and opened up fantastically in front of the net on the power play to take a pass and put a really good shot on net for an excellent chance. He has some nice hands and moves to gain the offensive zone trying to get to the slot, but has to watch the turnovers trying to dangle through the opposition. He also has to get shots through to the net from the high slot and needs to be stronger on the puck along the boards.

DMB # 24, D, Shiplo, Luke (2013) Shiplo was making some pretty simple plays to get the puck in deep off the rush and was able to rush the puck up the ice, however it would be better for him to pass it out of the zone more often instead of skating then dumping the puck in. He has a nice shot that he got through to the net from the point, but needs to keep his shot down low. He was skating well and put a great shot on from the point to score. He also had a really bad turnover skating the puck up through the neutral zone that resulted in the game winner for the opposition.

SIO # 19, C, Guentzel, Jake (2013) Guentzel opened up really well in the slot for a great one-timer chance and picked up a loose puck in the high slot then took a step in to rip a fantastic shot on from scoring position. He made a really nice pass to find an open man in the slot from behind the net for a great chance and opened up right in front of the net to tap in the puck for a goal, however it was waved off. He picked off a pass at the blue line to come in on a break and draw a penalty as he got tripped and put nice pressure on the opposition on the fore-check. He again opened up in the slot to take a pass and put a back-hander on to score and put a nice low shot on net to generate a rebound for a teammate far side for an easy goal. He made a fantastic diving play on a drive to the net for a loose puck and a good opportunity in tight off the rush and just needs to watch some of the turnovers trying to force passes through the opposition and also turnovers by not being strong enough on the puck along the boards.

FINAL SCORE: 3-2 Sioux City Musketeers

Feb 17, 2013, Calgary Hitmen vs. Regina Pats (WHL)

CAL#18 RW, Virtanen, Jake(2014) Physical forward had a good game throwing his weight around and making a difference with his aggressiveness. Showed what he can do if he moves his feet and stays engaged in the game. Tried to do a little too much fancy stickhandling off the rush and in 1 on 1 situations which never really worked, and resulted in turnovers. Received some ice time on the PK, and showed that he can be responsible in his own end without the puck. Showed off an impressive release on his shot a couple of times.

CAL#25 RC, Chase, Greg(2013) Quick playmaking forward showed good vision when given time out in open ice. Made a nice spin and behind the back pass toward the net off the wall that awkwardly bounced off an opponent to his teammate for an easy goal. Has good patience with the puck to read the play and to make the play. Needs to shoot more and show some more physicality along the walls and to go to the net to get some scoring chances for himself. Had a good stick in the defensive zone, particularly on the PK. Does not panic without the puck, and does a good job to help down low when necessary.

REG#5 RD, Williams, Colby(2013) Good puck moving defenseman who had a very up and down game. Showed good poise with the puck all night long, but had some trouble making the right decisions at times, particularly on the power play. Good at starting the rush, but when he is in the offensive zone, he almost always throws it down the walls without taking a look or walking the line even when he has time to do so. An above average skater, but needs to get faster considering his size as he is only 5'11. He likes to engage physically, and works the walls pretty well. Also showed a good stick to knock away pucks from entering the slot.

REG#10 LC, Brooks, Adam(2014) Fast centre who seemed to be in defensive situations for most of the game. Really needs to work on his strength and give opponents a more difficult time to knock him off the puck in open ice. Needs to slow down the game for himself and make better decisions with the puck. Showed some good speed down the wing with the puck, but could not do anything with the play afterwards. Missing an offensive component to his game.

REG #18 LW, Klimchuk, Morgan (2013) Dangerous sniper showed off his wicked shot on the power play tonight. Came off the half wall to drive the net from the right side, and went short side, top corner on his wrist shot. Had very little room but placed his shot perfectly. Showed very good energy tonight and liked his combination of speed and willingness to be physical. Not a player that will put fear into opponents for his physical play by any means, but will certainly finish his checks and be difficult to play against. A couple of times, he managed to find a soft area in coverage in the slot or around the net to get some good scoring chances, but was robbed on a couple occasions. Not much of a playmaker.

Scouts Notes: This game was dominated by Calgary in all areas of the game. Their defense gave Regina very little scoring opportunities, and outworked them for the puck everywhere. Calgary's group of defensemen are all big and physical, and matched up well against Regina's smaller but quick forwards. Jake Virtanen showed what he can do when engaged into the game without the puck. Very impressed with his physical abilities. Just needs to use his teammates more.

FINAL SCORE: 5-2 Calgary

February 18, 2013, Plymouth Whalers @ Sarnia Sting (OHL)

PLY #21 RC Hartman, Ryan (2013) - Hartman was very good all game long for the Plymouth Whalers. He works very hard regardless of the score and was always found either in the slot or cycling the puck in the offensive zone. He's always moving and protects the puck really well. Ryan has excellent hands and can steal the puck in the offensive zone to create scoring chances. He was rewarded for the time he spent in the slot, banging home a rebound for a goal. He also makes very good passes for scoring chances. Despite spending a lot of time in the offensive zone, Hartman did a great job pinching for defensemen and getting back in his own zone.

SAR #2 RD Chapman, Joshua (2013) - Covers passing lanes well but can over pursue forwards and lose his positioning which happened on Plymouth's fourth goal. He lost defensive positioning on two goals in total tonight. Joshua's skating has improved.

SAR #3 LD Nemecek, David (2013) - Nemececk's skating speed is pretty good but he looks very awkward when moving around. He has shown the ability to make good plays with the puck, but he tends to take too long to make decisions and can get stripped of the puck. He shows a willingness to hit and is pretty effective at it, but he definitely needs to fill out his frame and get stronger.

SAR #7 RD DeAngelo, Anthony (2014) - DeAngelo moved the puck effectively early on in the game. However as Plymouth began pulling away with this game he lost his focus. He fired the puck down the ice without being pressured and unnecessarily turned the puck over too much.

SAR #21 LC Nikandrov, Daniel (2013) - Daniel finished his checks early on. He was getting back into defensive positioning well. He was also able to utilize positioning in the offensive zone to gain a few scoring chances.

Scouts Notes: Plymouth put together an absolutely dominant performance today in Sarnia. They outshot the Sting 51-15. This included an 18-1 shot count in favor of the Whalers in the third period. Sixteen different Whalers found their way onto the scoresheet. This included a hat trick by Stefan Noesen (Ottawa). On a positive note for Sarnia, Matteo Ciccarelli (2015) provided a good forecheck and finished his hits despite the size of the opposition. Jordan Addesi (2014) put together an excellent forecheck in a losing effort for the Sting. He hits opponents hard every opportunity he gets.

February 20, 2013, Choate Rosemary at Loomis-Chaffee (New England Prep School)

CHO #12 RD Cory Gottfried (2013) – Solid if unspectacular two-way defenseman. Aggressive and physical in his end. Good poise and feet with the puck and some smart passes. A few coverage issues.

CHO #14 LW Owen Powers (2013) – Big, lanky power forward type. Used his size well to protect the puck and made plays. Went hard to the net with and without the puck. Came back to help out his defense and played the body along the boards. Still needs to fill out and work on his skating. Not quite a D1 type player yet but the tools are there.

CHO #15 RW Charley Borek (2014) – Played an OK game. Good complementary offensive forward. Not massive (not small either) but very sturdy. Worked hard in the offensive zone, made plays in traffic and along the boards. Some flashes of skill.

CHO #16 RD Brendan Russ (2014) – Strong offensive defenseman with some good defensive instincts, particularly for a sophomore. Played a fairly mistake-free game with good reads all around. Very smooth and efficient. Great skater forward and back, can burn up ice with the puck when given space and did well to cover against speed to the outside facing the rush. Attacked the puck carrier with an active stick but was careful not to overcommit. Good pinches and outlets, helped start the offense and keep it going. Could be an intriguing player if he grows a little bit.

LMC #6 RD Zach Giuttari (2014) – Not polished but had a great game. Defense-first player, very honest. Good size, will be better once he fills out further. Liked to play the body but wasn't overaggressive. Stepped up and squeezed off at the blueline. Good stick against the rush and to take away passing lanes once offense set up in his own zone. Showed good awareness in the neutral zone in tracking forwards and cutting off passes. Mixed bag offensively, scored on one nice wrister and liked to put the puck on net but accuracy and power were iffy. Could stand to be more physical in front of his net and improve his skating.

LMC #9 RD Matt O'Donnell (2013) – One of the top offensive defensemen in prep by the numbers, looked good today. Junior, uncommitted for school. OK size, might hold him back at college/pro. Very strong skater, agile with great acceleration. Quickly joined the rush and recovered well when the play went the other way. Good, hard point shot that he consistently got on net. Smart pinches and good keeps. Safe outlets, tried to keep it simple in his end. Active stick in the neutral and defensive zones. Could stand to be more physical and had some issues with coverage.

LMC #12 LW Alex Esposito (2014) – Skilled player with quick hands. Showed off top-end flash with some nifty moves to burn defenders. Good skater but was lacking an extra gear, something to improve on that will help him tremendously. Not huge and tended to favor evasiveness over protection. Good snapshot, showed finishing touch. Had some issues leaving his zone before the puck, defensive game needs work overall. One to watch for NHL draft next year.

LMC #21 RW Cory Swift (2013) – Undersized but showed off sharp goal scoring instincts. Shot-first mentality on the attack. Flashed a great slapshot. Crashed the net for rebounds, scoring twice on putbacks.

Scout's Notes: Joe Caffrey (2014), Jeremy Germain (2014), and Luke May (2013, late '94 birthdate) also played strong games for Choate Rosemary.

2013 NHL DRAFT BLACK BOOK

February 21, 2013, Sault Ste. Marie Greyhounds @ Sarnia Sting (OHL)

SSM #3 RD Ganly, Tyler (2013) - Uses his size very well and he is physically strong. He was good on one on one match-up's in this game. Tyler also shows strong positioning and he wins battles. Skating has also improved. He did make some puck playing mistakes but corrected them. In one case in his own end the draw was won to him and he made a mistake rushing it out of the zone for icing. He got the puck again on the ensuing draw and corrected his mistake showing patience and got the puck up ice well. He made some excellent long distance passes to give his team some breakout opportunities. He generally looks off bad options and lets the right play open up. He dropped the gloves against a smaller opponent, but didn't fair as well as expected.

SSM #19 LC McCann, Jared (2014) - Jared has an excellent, consistent work ethic and showed good moves and intelligent passes on the rush. He also showed good two-way effort always quick to get back into position and get back defensively. He visualizes options very well but at times was off with the actual execution. He's great on the power play displaying good shooting/passing selection and has a very hard shot. He made a great play at the line to save which lead to a scoring chance.

SSM #20 RW Mallette, Trent (2014) - Despite his size he loves to play a physical game and hits very hard despite being smaller than most of the players he hits. He showed good hands making a nice little backhand move and snuck the puck by the goaltender for Sault Ste Marie's second goal.

SSM #25 LD Nurse, Darnell (2013) - Darnell is a lot more controlled when rushes occur for his team. Instead of joining he waited for the play to move up ice before he moved up ice hanging back and leaving a passing option open for his teammate. He has a very good point shot that is hard, low and easy to deflect. Nick Cousins deflected his point shot on the first goal of the game. Nurse was used regularly on the second power play unit for the Greyhounds. He did show puck rushing ability on the power play, but would at times skate himself into a corner or get into some trouble when he held the puck too long. Darnell wasn't tested too much defensively in this game.

SSM #28 LW Tolchinsky, Sergey (2013) - Tolchinsky showed yet again he is one of the best pure skating talents in this draft. He accelerates on one step and uses it to drive the wing whenever possible. He's always dangerous with the puck in the offensive zone especially in open space. He scored Sault Ste. Marie's fifth goal of the game after a great move to beat defensemen. Zero physicality from Tolchinsky and he looks very tiny out there.

SAR #5 RD Hore, Tyler (2014) - Tyler looked good overall tonight but got himself into a little trouble trying to do too much. He knows how to get mobile and will get space when there are no passing options and made intelligent passes. He also received some time on the penalty kill and did relatively well.

SAR #7 RD DeAngelo, Anthony (2014) - Early on a fancy no look pass in his own zone went right into the hands of the Greyhounds and helped them sustain offensive pressure in the Sarnia zone. He would jump up in the rush trying to help Sarnia put some offense on the board. He crashed the net a few times until a bigger defenseman on the Greyhounds challenged him. Despite the no look puck playing mistake in his own zone earlier on in the game, he continued to do these things. While he's more than willing to get into the offense, while the team was down two goals he showed little to no urgency to get back defensively after jumping up in the rush. A frustrating game for Anthony, however not based on a lack of skill, just seemed more so out of pure frustration.

SAR #11 RW Hargrave, Brett (2014) - Hargrave had possibly his best game of the season in a losing effort. His hands are very improved. He's a lot better in front of the net and handles the puck in ways he didn't earlier in this year in the offensive zone. He looked much stronger along the wall and at one point an opponent had to grab a hold of him just to slow him down. He covered for pinching defensemen and made a great defensive play to save a sure goal.

SAR #71 RW Goldobin, Nikolay (2014) - Goldobin made an absolutely beautiful behind the back pass to set up a big Craig Duininck one-timer for Sarnia's first goal of the game. He didn't touch the puck and create quite as much as he has in the past, but he showed flashes when he got the opportunity to do something.

Scouts Notes: A huge match-up with playoff positioning implications opened with a lot of back and forth between these two teams. Sarnia was outmatched physically but kept working and were really in this game for the first 40 minutes. Nick Cousins (Philadelphia) scored two goals in this game, both of them were backbreakers. One came with 28 seconds left in the second period to give SOO a 3-1 lead. The second came after Sarnia looked to make a comeback. He then set up the 5-2 goal followed by scoring the 6-2 goal to put this game away. Nick Halagian (2013) was passive in his first few shifts, but later made a great steal and move for a great scoring chance, but he hit the post. Ryan Sproul (Detroit) made a great play to steal the puck, carrying it in and unload a massive shot for Sault Ste. Marie's fourth goal. Jordan Addesi (2014) showed excellent forecheck using his stick and his size very well.

February 22, 2013, Erie Otters @ Sarnia Sting (OHL)

ERI #10 LW Harper, Stephen (2013) - Harper was able to show off his best assets when gaining the red line and dumping the puck in the corner. He has great speed and won the races. He played physical in the corners and protected the puck. He played the point on the power play and has a very powerful shot. His ice time increased as his the blowout ensued.

ERI #11 RW Hodgson, Hayden (2014) - Hodgson was one of the few Otters on this night who worked hard for the entire 60 minutes. He scored Erie's first goal of the night by winning a race despite average skating ability, protecting the puck then showing his powerful shot. He got first unit power play time and was rewarded later spending time on a line with Connor McDavid.

ERI #12 RW Betz, Nick (2013) - Betz was unfortunately not very noticeable in this game despite his massive size. It not that he doesn't use it, he just doesn't use it nearly enough to be as effective as his potential suggests. He displayed adequate hands when in the slot area.

ERI #15 LC Pettit, Kyle (2014) - Pettit stands strong in the slot with great size. He had a great scoring chance but couldn't finish. He absolutely leveled Davis Brown in open ice, who responded by instigating a fight. He got the edge in this fight and was the only player on Erie to finish with a plus in the plus/minus column.

ERI #19 LD Kuleshov, Artem (2013) - Not a strong performance by Kuleshov. He was quiet early on getting beat one on one. He made a lazy play with the puck in the neutral zone and had to take a hooking penalty on Goldobin to try to slow him down, but he still got a breakaway chance.

ERI #23 LC Crisp, Connor (2013*) - Connor was great playing in front of the net regularly doing a great job creating a screen. He played top power play minutes for Erie and protects the puck very well in the offensive zone while making quick decisions with the puck.

ERI #97 LC McDavid, Connor (2015) - Picked up puck in open ice in his own end and absolutely flew up ice showing a great move then beating defenseman wide. He has exceptional vision and had it on display in the offensive zone. He showed a great backcheck even when Sarnia was running away with the game.

SAR #5 RD Hore, Tyler (2014) - Hore made some solid one on one defensive plays. He made a lot of smart simple plays in this game. He protects the puck well and likes to rush the puck. He makes good decisions with the puck most of the time, however did try to force shots from the point through screens that just ended up out of the zone.

SAR #7 RD DeAngelo, Anthony (2014) - DeAngelo walked in from the point and absolutely wired a wrister past the goaltender for Sarnia's third goal. He was effective offensively all game long skating well showing off his speed and puck skills. He was pinching a lot despite the lead and got caught up ice on one of Erie's goal. He still struggled with trying to be too fancy and at one point Erie got a lot of momentum from a series of turnovers.

SAR #11 RW Hargrave, Brett (2014) - Brett made a decent little move to slip the puck five hold. He was good on the power play gaining a lot of ice. He protected the puck well and was constantly making things happen in the offensive zone.

SAR #22 RC Ciccarelli, Matteo (2015) - Matteo possesses above average speed but he has a very, very awkward skating stride. He puts in work, competes and will go into corners to battle. He will need to improve some puck decisions.

SAR #71 RW Goldobin, Nikolay (2014) - Goldobin showed great positioning, especially on the power play. He displayed his outstanding shot twice in this game for two goals. Both of them around the top of the slot and both found their way top shelf in a hurry. The first was the game winning goal.

Scouts Notes: Sarnia has had a frustrating past few games, and they too all of their frustrations out over the course of 60 minutes against the Erie Otters. It all started 15 seconds into the game where Reid Boucher (New Jersey) scored his first of four goals on this night. While Boucher put up 6 points, Charles Sarault (Free Agent) put up 7 assists on this night. The second line wouldn't be outdone as Nikolay Goldobin (2014) celebrated his reunion with Nikandrov and Latta by posting 2 goals and 5 points. Nick Latta (2013) and Daniel Nikandrov (2013) combined for 6 points tonight. Anger boiled over for the Otters in the end as Dane Fox (2013*) after receiving a clean hit from David Nemecek (2013) and chased him down throwing his gloves off and landing a few cheap punches before the Czech defenseman (who has never been in a fight), knew how to respond. Fox received the instigator and will be sitting out at least two games if not more for forcing the rookie defenseman into a fight.*

February 22, 2013, St. Paul's at Dexter (New England Prep School)

DEX #12 RD Charlie Donners (Passed over 2012) – Best player on the ice for both teams. Shifty, evasive offensive blueliner who lacks size but played a dynamic game. Top end skater, accelerated quickly and changed directions seamlessly. Carried the puck with a lot of poise and was difficult to pin down, but really needed to simplify things as he tried to do too much. Pretty effective defensively despite his stature. Physical at times and positionally solid. A really strong DI prospect who'll probably be a wait-and-see type player for NHL teams.

DEX #16 LC Ryan Donato (2014) – North-south offensive forward. Not huge but good size that he used well. Liked to take the puck strong down the outside, good protection and strong on his feet. Accelerated quickly to get the defense on their heels and showed a lot of poise with the puck. Strong on the boards, difficult to play against. Good finisher with a great shot that he wasn't shy with.

Scout's Notes: Despite being outshot 30-18, Dexter did a great job of finishing their chances. Mark Webber (2013) also had a nice game for Dexter.

February 27, 2013, Westminster at Belmont Hill (New England Open Quarterfinal)

WES #10 LC Vincent Gisonti (Passed over 2012) – Very strong game, consistently intense on a shift-to-shift basis. Great skater with top end acceleration. Outstanding stride, very efficient and strong on his feet. Fantastic stickhandler, navigated neutral-zone traffic with pinpoint precision. Good shot, quick release. Great cycle work, his line (w/Mowery and Holdaway) had a lot of chemistry. Showed a lot of poise with the puck. Worked hard on the forecheck, backcheck, and in his own end. D-zone coverage was effective.

WES #11 LC Sean Orlando (2013) – Flashed some things earlier in the year but was mostly invisible tonight. Bad body language, seemed frustrated that he couldn't get it going.

WES #16 RW David Hallisey (Passed over 2012) – Love this kid. Not a big guy but he plays a really complete game and competes on every shift. Real heart-and-soul player. Tonight was no different. Nice skater, moves his feet and really gets going quickly. Hard to stop when he gets up to speed. Great hands, navigates through forecheckers. Great penalty-killer, backchecks, forechecks, plays the body. Does it all. Committed to Princeton where I think he'll have a lot of success.

WES #20 W Ethan Holdaway (Passed over 2012) – PG year '94 forward who really came on strong at the end of the year, including a five-point performance and a couple game-winners. He was really strong in this game, figuring on all of his team's scoring with two goals and an assist. Scored the GWG in overtime on an extremely impressive finesse player where he beat a defender, deked the goalie out of his jock, and slid it into the empty net. Don't think he's a pro prospect but he had a great game. Slick, fairly one-dimensional forward. Didn't show much in his end but didn't play there often as his line dominated possession.

WES #24 LW Mario Benicky (2013) – Lanky winger who plays a pretty good power game. Liked to take the puck strong down the wing and to the net with mixed success. Not the most creative or adaptable player, straightforward thinking with the puck. Slow feet, skating needs work. Useful defensively. Saved a goal with a hard backcheck and frequently helped out in his end. Good stick on the PK, long reach made him useful. Was gassed at the end of every shift and skated casually to the bench, not sure if it's conditioning or lack of effort but something's up there.

BEL #10 RD Charlie Barrow (2014) – Not the biggest kid at 5'10 but recently hit a growth spurt and could get bigger. Very, very smooth. The catalyst for the offense and powerplay. Outstanding distributor of the puck, intelligent outlets. His footwork was quick and agile which gave him a lot of flexibility and evasiveness. Very aware and reacted quickly to pressure.

BEL #15 RW Will Golonka (2013) – Nice player who was the focal point of the forward group for Belmont. Did a lot of good things with his speed and stickhandling, made a few guys look silly with dangles and showed poise with the puck. Showed a good awareness of transitional opportunities by burning up ice quickly on turnovers and making good outlet passes off turnovers. Scored the game-tying goal with less than a minute left. Did show some defensive awareness but mostly an offensive player.

BEL #20 RW Mike Leary (2013) – Not a dynamic player or much of a pro prospect but he had a nice game. Good footwork, stride was above average but not the most efficient. Some smart shots, flashed a nice wrister and the awareness to place the puck for tips and rebounds. Good effort on the backcheck.

Scout's Notes: This was an outstanding hockey game and a big upset for Westminster, who won it 3-2 in overtime. Both goaltenders, BEL Ryan McConnell (2013) and WES Zac Hamilton (2013) were solid and the game had some heavy ebbs and flows. After Will Golonka tied the game with under a minute left, Ethan Holdaway won it in overtime on an outstanding individual effort.

Feb 22, 2013, Vancouver Giants vs. Kamloops Blazers (WHL)

VAN#1 G, Lee, Payton(2014) Definitely had a game to forget tonight. Gave up a goal 10 seconds into the game after a bad defensive break down, and just could not really recover from it mentally. He looked slow to go down on his butterfly, and did not have the same compete level to fight for pucks in traffic as he usually does. Let in a few soft goals tonight, and got pulled in the 2nd period. Looks like his confidence level is quite low at this point.

VAN#27 RW, Houck, Jackson(2013) Houck had an up and down game tonight. Created very little offensively, but made his presence known at times with his physical play on the forecheck. Looked good on the penalty kill tonight with his stick positioning and knowing when to apply pressure on an opponent and when to hold his position. Houck was not much of a factor on the power play with his net front presence, mostly because his teammates could not get anything to the net.

KAM#12 RW, Souto, Chase(2013) Quick skating forward had a good offensive game tonight. He was able to find his way around the ice well and create chances in the slot. Showed off above average hands, nothing fancy but looked very comfortable with the puck and his ability to control the puck in speed and in traffic. He needs to release the puck a lot quicker when he has an open lane to the net. He had a couple of good scoring chances, but took too long to shoot, which got blocked or deflected. Defensively, Souto was good enough to cover his point and not be a defensive liability. Did not get any PK time though.

KAM#21 LW, Ully, Cole(2013) Good two way forward who had a very good game in the offensive zone. Scored two goals by showing off his quick release. Did not hesitate to shoot when he had opportunities, and just got pucks on net. First goal was a bit of a weak one right off the wall, but the second one was a good one in the slot. Ully was very involved out on the ice tonight in all zones. He was in good position without the puck, and constantly moved his feet. Still needs to work on his play along the wall.

KAM#34 RW, Lipon, JC(2013) Skilled forward who played on the edge tonight. In the first period, he almost took a terrible, undisciplined penalty as he was going for a line change, he went to Vancouver's bench and just pushed an opponent into an opened door for no apparent reason. Thankfully for him, the officials missed it. In the near end of the second period, he took a really bad hit from behind, and laid on the ice for 5 seconds, then got up angrily and picked a random opponent and just threw massive punches at him, which costed him 17 PIMs. Then in the late third period, he took a terrible kneeing penalty and got into another fight to end the game. He spent a good portion of the game sitting in the penalty box tonight. When he was on the ice, he showed off a great shot. Had a nice velocity to his shot, but just missed the target a couple of times. He created a goal at the start of the game with his good forecheck. A good skater with his speed and ability to change directions quickly. Was out on the ice in all situations. Defensively, battles hard along the boards, but needs to work on his shot blocking.

SCOUT'S NOTES: Vancouver gave up a goal 10 seconds into the game, and it was basically over from that point. Did not like the undisciplined play of JC Lipon tonight. He had a short fuse, and luckily for his team they were able to win without him on the ice on this day. Vancouver came out with a poor effort and did not show much of a push. Almost all of their shots were from the outside, and nothing dangerous. Liked Cole Ully's game tonight. Kept his game simple and just got pucks on net. Tim Bozon had a very inconsistent game. Made one excellent play on a 2 on 1 for a great assist, but other than that really struggled at both ends of the ice tonight for Kamloops.

February 22, 2013, Sherbrooke Phoenix @ Baie-Comeau Drakkar (QMJHL)

Sherbrooke

#3 Vladislav Lysenko, Def (2013) The Russian rearguard played a very physical game in his own end, as he threw multiple devastating checks. Loves to step up at his blueline to deliver those big hits, but can get caught being too aggressive. The 3rd period is where he really stepped up his physical game and had some great battles against Jeremy Grégoire. Will need to make his decisions quicker with the puck, can make good passes out of his zone when he has the time, but gets in trouble versus a strong forecheck.

#15 Jonathan Deschamps, Def (2014) Quiet game for Deschamps, didn't make many plays with the puck. Played with Lysenko during this contest, had trouble dealing with Petr Straka's outside speed on one shift. On Baie-Comeau's 2nd goal he forgot a man in front of the net who tipped the puck behind his goaltender. On another shift he showed good strength versus Gabriel Paquin-Boudreau to win a puck-battle in Sherbrooke zone. Overall, he played fairly well in his own zone.

#28 Daniel Audette, C/LW (2014) Audette played LW on the top line with two overagers (Steve Lebel & Alex Comtois). Showed that he loves to have the puck on his skates and make plays, but sometimes tries to do too much with the puck and over-handles it. Made a beautiful backhand pass to send his linemate Lebel all alone in front of the goaltender for a goal. Has a tough time in the corners, as he's undersized and not strong enough to win puck battles. Got hit real hard by Baie-Comeau defenseman Gabriel Verpaelst. Audette skates well and if he can generate speed though the neutral zone he's even more dangerous. Also not afraid, even at his size.

#32 Carl Neil, Def (2014) Neil played on the Phoenix's first power play unit, made some good passes on the power play but will need to work on the accuracy of his shot, as it was either blocked or missed the net. Neil likes to take risks and got caught multiple times with a man behind him while on the PP, but doesn't have the foot speed to get back quickly enough. He also had to take a penalty on one of those plays. In the 3rd period he had a real tough shift in his own end where he was stuck in his zone for a about a 2-minute shift, unable to get the puck out of his zone.

#71 Vincent Deslauriers, RW (2014) Deslauriers played on Sherbrooke's 2nd line, but didn't stand out in this game. His line was not noticeable.

Baie-Comeau

#3 Alexis Vanier, Def (2013) Played on the 3rd pairing, didn't get much ice time and was noticeable. Skating and foot speed still need tons of work.

#10 Jeremy Grégoire, C (2013) Grégoire played an okay game, had a great battle with Lysenko in the 3rd period both as players were challenging each other with some big hits. Skating still needs work, as he just doesn't generate a lot of speed, and his first three steps will need some work too. Not a good stickhandler either. Generates most of his scoring chances 5-10 feet from the net, either by crashing the net or standing in front to tip shots or get rebounds. Played a consistent physical game all night long on the Drakkar's top 2 lines and got a regular shift on the power play. Great game in the faceoff circle as well, as he won 20 of 30 draws.

#13 Gabriel Paquin-Boudreau, LW (2013) Played on the top line with Girard and Zykov, looks to have improved his top speed from my earlier viewing of him this season. Can generate a lot more speed though the neutral zone. His hands are real quick and he is also very agile on his skates as he took a pass on one a skate and was able to push the puck from his skate to his blade (wouldn't be surprised if he has a soccer background). Still has a slight frame which made it hard to win puck battles against bigger players along the boards, doesn't play a particularly physical game. On his line all the dirty work is done by Girard and Zykov. Paquin-Boudreau was used in the shootout, where he tried a backhand deke that was stopped by the Sherbrooke goaltender.

#16 Felix Girard C (undrafted 1994) Girard had an insanely good game in the faceoff circle, only losing 3 of 21 . Girard used his speed well to put pressure on a young defense for Sherbrooke. Scored a goal by going to the net and scoring on a rebound. Most of his scoring chances in that game came from in close, and he did a great job cycling the puck with his 2 linemates. Girard is very smart without the puck, knows what do in the defensive zone and is always the first forward in his line to get back and help out his defensemen.

#73 Valentin Zykov Rw (2013) Zykov was good in this game, in the first period he escaped a big hit from his countryman Lysenko along the boards, took the puck to the net and went to get his rebound in the corner, only to create another scoring chance right after. I like that even though he's stopped once, he continues to work and make things happen. He's very dangerous on the power play, whether it's in front of the net, a set-up on the half-wall or waiting for a pass in the slot. His passing game is also very underrated; he sees the ice well and can find his teammates well. Would like to see Zykov finish his checks more, as he can take punishment along the boards or in front of the net but doesn't dish any. Scored the shootout winner while roofing the puck on his backhand, a beauty of a goal.

Feb 26, 2013, Seattle Thunderbirds vs. Edmonton Oil Kings (WHL)

SEA#17 LD, Theodore, Shea(2013) Offensive defenseman who had a nice game with the puck, but had some struggles in his own end. Really like his skating abilities, especially how quickly he can change directions and catch opponents flat footed. Looked poised with the puck at all times, and by far the best puck handling defenseman on Seattle. Makes quick decisions with the puck, and knows when to make an outlet pass and when to carry it if he has no options to create time and room for teammates. Lost the puck a few times in the neutral zone while trying to do too much, which resulted in good scoring chances the other way. Needs to do a better job getting pucks on net and try to use his shot more. Seems like he can get a little predictable as the game goes on. Defensively, Theodore has some work to do in terms of reading the play. Engaged with the body when necessary, but could get stronger along the boards. Needs to have a better stick in his own end.

SEA#32 LD, Green, Taylor(2013) Towering defenseman who had a quiet, but effective game tonight. Really like how his overall game has developed throughout the season. Still needs to really work on his skating, but other parts of his play have steadily improved, especially his poise with the puck. Looks much more calm handling it and making decisions compared to the start of the year when he looked extremely nervous. Made good, simple plays with the puck and really limited his turnovers. Defensively, his best assets are his long reach and physical play. He may be a couple of steps slower than other players, but he makes it up with his long reach and good positioning, but he can still be a liability in his own end. Sacrificed his body a couple of times to make huge blocks.

SEA#29 LW, Lipsbergs, Roberts(2013) Originally a 2012 draft eligible forward, but was passed over by all teams. Showed a good offensive game tonight and combined it with good work ethic in all areas of the ice. A good skater who can get from point A to point B in a hurry. Has good overall skills with the puck. Often the first one to the corners for loose pucks, and not afraid of body contact. Created a few good scoring chances throughout the night, but did not get much help from his teammates.

EDM#27 RC, Lazar, Curtis(2013) 2 way centre had a very good game tonight. Very impressed with his play without the puck tonight. Consistently finished his checks, and looked very strong along the walls. Showed his fearlessness by blocking a number of shots throughout the game, and did whatever it took to help his team win. Stuck up for his teammate who took a bad hit along the walls and got involved in a fight. Above average skater who can improve on his speed, but his intelligence allows him to read the way and anticipate where he needs to be out on the ice. Offensively, worked hard along the boards and had a few good chances in the slot and was finally rewarded in the 3rd period on the PP when he got a rebound right in front of the net and quickly finished it off. Did not show much vision out on the ice, and not many scoring chances by himself.

EDM#37 RD, Mayo, Dysin(2014) 16 year old defenseman showed very impressive poise in tonight's game. So calm with the puck even with pressure from forecheckers, and effectively moved the puck. Was consistently in good position, and looked quite solid in his own end. Not particularly physical, but used his intelligence to take away passing lanes and steal pucks along the walls when given the opportunity. Not afraid to take off with the puck if he sees open ice.

SCOUT'S NOTES: Edmonton dominated this game as soon as the puck dropped. Their depth was too much for Seattle to handle. Jerret Smith, a defenseman for Seattle who is draft eligible for this year's NHL Entry Draft had an up and down game. There were times when he looked poised and in control, then at other times his game would come apart and make a number of bad mistakes. Curtis Lazar looked very good tonight at both ends of the ice. Needs to work on his vision to be more dangerous. Impressed with the development of Taylor Green. Unsure if he will be drafted, but made good improvements. Feel like Dysin Mayo will be a player to watch for in the 2014 NHL Entry Draft. Not particularly noticeable, but showed good overall play.

FINAL SCORE: 6-2 Edmonton

February 26, 2013, Lincoln Stars vs. Sioux City Musketeers (USHL)

LIN # 7, D, Pittman, Zack (2013) Pittman protected the puck pretty well from the opposition's pressure to move it up out of his own end. He is able to move it up on breakout passes along the boards and can make a pretty good 1st pass, however at times turns the puck over by panicking with it and he still has to get stronger on the puck as he was worked off it fairly easy in his own zone.

LIN # 9, LW, Lettieri, Vinni (2013) Lettieri was able to get a decent cycle going in deep, was hustling really hard to get on loose pucks and protected it well. He put some good pressure on the fore-check however lost the puck on a mishandle in the offensive zone which allowed the opposition to clear the puck out of their end and he has to watch the unnecessary penalties through the neutral zone being overly aggressive.

LIN # 27, C, Johnson, Luke (2013) Johnson showed really nice speed and protected the puck well on his rush up the ice to gain the offensive zone, then got a good shot off from the high slot. He opened up really well in the slot on the power play to take a pass and put a great one-timer on from scoring position for a really good opportunity. He made a great pass on the rush to find a man driving hard to the net for a great chance in tight and went to the net and opened up well on the rush to take a pass in behind the opposition and tap the puck into the net. He put some nice pressure on the fore-check, and put a nice low shot on net from the side boards to generate a rebound and a teammate at the far side of the net picked up the loose puck to score. He was able to get open right in front of the net to take a pass for a great chance in tight, however has to get the puck out of the zone on battles along the boards and he would be more effective if he drove the puck to the net rather than taking long outside shots from the blue line.

SIO # 3, D, Kapla, Michael (2013) Kapla did a good job of holding the offensive line and getting his shot through to the net from the point. He was able to find the open man in the high slot on a good pass, was strong on the puck and protected it nicely from the opposition's pressure. He put an excellent shot on from the point to pick the top corner and score and made a really nice pass to find the open man down low for a one-timer goal on the power play. He is able to make a good 1st pass out of the zone to start the breakout.

SIO # 14, LW, Lacroix, Cedrik (2013) Lacroix showed great physicality on the puck carrier and put good pressure on the fore-check. He was pressuring the puck carrier, finishing his big hits along the wall and tied up his man well in his own zone after a great back-check. He was hustling hard to get on loose pucks, used his body well to protect it from the opposition and did a good job going hard to the net looking for loose pucks and rebounds. He did an excellent job of going hard to the net, but has to hit the net on his shots off the rush and needs to watch the neutral zone turnovers on breakout passes.

SIO # 26, D, Heinrich, Blake (2013) Heinrich put some nice physicality on the puck carrier along the boards and tied up his man well. He used his stick effectively to keep the opposition to the outside and held the offensive line pretty well to keep the attack alive. He did a good job of skating the puck up into the offensive zone to get it in deep on the rush but has to hit the net on his shots from the high slot. He also has to watch the offensive zone turnovers trying to force passes through the opposition rather than waiting for a lane to open up. He was jumping up on the rush to get in deep with the puck to start the attack but also needs to watch neutral zone turnovers on breakout passes.

SIO # 28, RW, Torok, Tomas (2013) Torok was nice and physical on the puck carrier and was able to rush the puck up the ice, however could definitely pick up some speed to his game. He was distributing the puck well on the rush to gain the offensive zone and was hustling hard and battling well for loose pucks. He put some pretty good pressure on the fore-check and was able to make a nice pass off the boards to find an open man in the high slot. He got a cycle going in deep in the offensive zone, played for the most part a pretty simple dump and chase game, and got involved with the opposition after whistles. He was taking long shots off the rush but at least kept it low to try to generate a rebound for a man in front of the net.

FINAL SCORE: 8-5 Lincoln Stars

Feb 27, 2013, Brandon Wheat Kings vs. Swift Current Broncos (WHL)

BDN#2 RD, Pulock, Ryan(2013) Had a good, quiet game tonight. Cut down on the number of rushes he made the puck compared to his other games, and looked more composed without the puck. Very good along the walls today and physically dominated opponents in front of the net. Played inside the dots and let the play come to him for most of the night. He was close to landing a couple of big open ice hits in transition. Read the play well in the offensive zone and made good pinches when appropriate, especially on the PP. Drew a penalty by protecting the puck well along the boards. Was on the ice for 2 goals against, but was not his fault. Made a couple of positional mistakes, but played one of his better games in a long time.

BDN#7 LD, Roy, Eric(2013) Defenseman who has very good size, but was much too soft tonight. Roy got bumped off the puck too easily all game long, and looked scared to take a hit. Has the potential to be a very good puck moving defenseman, but made too many gambles trying to make long stretch passes. He was in bad position all game long, and looked lost in his own end. He would chase plays behind the net and disregard the slot which could have resulted in great scoring chances. Showed off some good skating abilities with the puck. Uses his edges well and turned on a dime comfortably with the puck a few times to lose opponents on the breakout.

SC#2 LD, Heatherington, Dillon(2013) Big defenseman who has steadily developed his game as the season has progressed. Biggest concern at the start of the year was his mobility, which he has been able to really improve. His acceleration and overall speed has really improved, but still has some work to do in terms of footwork in tight areas and quick starts and stops. He lets the play come to him without the puck, and uses his reach and size in his own end. Heatherington's play with the puck has improved, and makes good, simple decisions to just move the puck and not try to do anything fancy. He looks more confident moving the puck, but has very average hands and offensive instincts.

SC#5 LD, Martin, Brycen(2014) Offensive defenseman who had a good game in both ends of the ice. Really like the poise he plays with and without the puck. He scored the OT winner by jumping into the play as a trailer, making a nice move to the slot and quickly releasing the puck top shelf. Impressive play from a rookie in the league. Defensively, he is not afraid to be aggressive between the bluelines and trying to start a quick transition play. He still has to get stronger along the boards and using his stick more effectively, but he definitely has the hockey intelligence to play in his own end. Martin is already the team's power-play quarterback, and does a good job moving the puck. He does not depend on himself to carry the puck and gain the line, but makes solid passes to his forwards and makes good decisions consistently.

SCOUT'S NOTES: This was a sloppy game overall by both teams offensively. Nobody could really generate much offensive pressure all game, and there were a lot of turnovers in the neutral zone and lacked scoring chances. Ryan Pulock had one of his better games in recent memory. He looked much more composed, and played a solid all around game. Eric Roy looked extremely soft. He is a big defenseman, but played like he was 5 inches shorter and 30 pounds lighter than he actually is. Needs to take hits to make plays and be stronger on the puck. Dillon Heatherington's skating abilities have come a long way, but still needs to be better in tight areas. Brandon's forwards lacked creativity and scoring touch. They dump and chase, but had difficulty retrieving pucks and creating chances.

FINAL SCORE: 3-2(OT) Swift Current

February 28, 2013, Holderness at Rivers (New England Small School Quarterfinal)

HOL #2 LD Terrance Amorosa (2013) – Sort of a Mr. Everything for Holderness, must have played over 35 minutes and was on the ice for the entirety of every powerplay. Good PPQB work with accurate short passes and a good selection of shots from the point that he frequently got on net through traffic. Intelligent outlets in all situations. Smart and steady with the puck, with a bit of a hero streak. Cleared the puck off the boards or lifted it out when he had to, but liked to skate it and was pretty successful overall in bringing it up ice. Not really dynamic but an effective stickhandler who protects well. Play of the game came when he went end-to-end through/around four Rivers players and snapped the game-tying goal home just over the pad with under four minutes remaining. Strong, efficient skating stride forward and back. Changed directions quickly to jumpstart offense or cover back. Defensive-zone play was mixed, had some trouble identifying his man on occasion but cleared the net and was physical on the boards. Overall, a very effective player. Could be on the NHL radar for this year.

HOL #18 LW Alexander Spina (2013) – Small, dynamic forward who played with a lot of intensity. Fantastic skater, exploded off the blocks and went pedal-down on numerous occasions. Created two breakaways for himself, one by winning a footrace to a loose puck and another by catching the defenseman flat-footed. Finishing ability was lacking. Quick on his edges and very deceptive, which made him hell to deal with on the forecheck. Physical, especially for his size. Finished checks and battled on the boards. Effective at this level and could be a good college player, but not much here beyond that.

RIV #10 LC Miles Gendron (2014) – Real solid prospect, very rough around the edges but there's a lot of promise here. Tall and lanky but showed strong puck protection skills that I think improve as he bulks up. Managed the puck well, especially in his own end where he could be depended on to dissolve pressure with smart passes or by carrying the puck out himself. Made some beautiful passes in the offensive zone, including one highlight-reel play where he came in hard down the wing on a 2-on-1 rush, drew the check to him at the dot, spun off, and set up a one-timer goal with a perfect blind pass. Played the point on the powerplay, hard tape-to-tape passes and good low shots for tips and rebounds. Strong, efficient stride. Heavy on his skates with the puck, light and active on them without it. Quick for his size, good cuts. Forechecked, backchecked, killed penalties. Physical in his end when the opportunity presented itself. Defensive zone coverage was hit or miss, didn't show strong awareness but did front to block shots on a consistent basis. Like the rest of his team, he backed off completely for the third period and overtime. Still made the odd smart play, but very little energy.

RIV #15 RW Joseph Sacco (2014) – Nifty skill forward, not the biggest or most physical kid but he played with energy. Skilled at navigating traffic, strong skater with the puck and difficult to knock off or contain. Burst acceleration created opportunities. Good release on his shot. Shot-first on the night, looked off passes to put the puck on net which wasn't always the right move and resulted in some weak shots that ended the play. Good backchecker, tied up in the slot and tracked his man well. Defensive zone positioning was OK, put in the effort and blocked shots. Tenacious stickchecking made him useful without the puck in all three zones.

RIV #18 RD Austin Rook (2015) – Hulking kid, ideal size at a very young age. Had a brutal third period. He was a major reason his team blew their two-goal lead and eventually lost. Lazy in his end, mostly stood in front of the net with his stick off the ice chewing on his mouth guard and watching the play. On the occasion that he tried to get involved, chased the play and didn't get involved physically. Slow feet, got caught flat-footed numerous times. Had a hard time keeping the puck in at the point and an even harder time recovering defensively. Have no idea why the coach kept putting him out late, he looked completely disinterested. Was told he suffered a concussion earlier in the season, maybe that has something to do with it.

Scout's Notes: Rivers played a physical, high-energy game to close the second period up 3-1, but wilted in the third. Holderness pressed and pushed them back onto their heels, and their intensity disappeared. Two goals by Terrance Amorosa knotted the game, and the momentum was such that the game-winner at the 7:33 mark was basically a foregone conclusion. Rivers is a young team that has plenty of young talent, they should be very competitive next year. Shots were 36-27 in favor of Holderness.

March 1, 2013, Sarnia Sting @ London Knights (OHL)

SAR #2 RD Chapman, Joshua (2013) - Chapman got outworked in puck battles tonight. However he never let up competing hard all night and sticking with his man. On the penalty kill he got his stick in passing lanes regularly and was physical out front of the net making sure his goaltender was able to see the puck. He was also willing to sacrifice his body to block shots.

SAR #5 RD Hore, Tyler (2014) - Tyler was solid physically tonight along the boards in his own zone winning more than his share of battles. He finishes his check and shows pretty solid physicality but can sometimes chase the puck carrier a little too much losing positioning. He protects the puck well in the defensive zone and gives him extra time to open up options and moves the puck effectively. He broke up a lot of plays with his stick and was very reliable in the defensive zone tonight.

SAR #7 RD DeAngelo, Anthony (2014) - DeAngelo showed off his excellent puck handling skills tonight especially when skating with it working around multiple defenders rushing the puck into the zone. Nothing is done simply by DeAngelo, even simple plays at the lines he's able to create something. His fancy moves provided mixed results sometimes advancing the play for Sarnia, others turning it over. Anthony took a very unnecessary tripping penalty deep in the defensive zone

SAR #21 LC Nikandrov, Daniel (2013) - Nikandrov made a smart play with the puck on the power play with the goalie out of position nearly banking it in off him instead of trying to force a low percentage pass. He competes hard every shift and he will take the hit to keep the play going. He showed smart positioning in every zone. He was a regular on the penalty kill and made some huge plays. At one point he saved what appeared to be a sure goal for London.

SAR #71 RW Goldobin, Nikolay (2014) - Goldobin showed excellent hockey sense throughout this game, particularly when moving the puck. He has excellent hands and used them to create scoring chances multiple times tonight putting up an assist in this game.

LON #2 LD Maatta, Olli (Pittsburgh) - Nice work reading the play and coming in off the point to score London's first goal with a strong backhander.

LON #4 LD Liberati, Miles (2013) - Miles got caught jumping up ice too quickly when his defensive partner, who isn't a very good puck carrier lost control of the puck. It resulted in a odd man break for Sarnia and they scored. Liberati attempted but just couldn't recover in time because he was caught too far up. Miles made a great play later on in a 2 on 1 situation where he read the pass and broke it up at a key point in this game.

LON #16 LC Domi, Max (2013) - Right from the opening of this game, Domi showed off his talent. His second shift he generated great speed going through the neutral zone then made a beautiful cross ice pass to set up a big chance. He is extremely elusive and has quick reflexes. His passes are hard and accurate and makes smart decisions in all three zones. HE created chances all game long and was probably the best player on the ice period. He can at times overhandle the puck but still makes plays happen. Domi scored the tying goal with just 29 seconds left to tie the game and send it to overtime.

LON #53 LW Horvat, Bo (2013) - Horvat was very noticeable in the faceoff circle tonight winning a lot of big draws. He also drew two power plays for the Knights in the first half of this game due to his puck control abilities. He also created some good scoring chances for his team.

LON #65 LD Zadorov, Nikita (2013) - Zadorov had an OK game tonight. He was reliable for the most part minus a few puck playing mistakes. He skates well with the puck and when he's successful he lets options open up. He came off the point with less than four minutes left in the third and wired a wrister to bring the Knights within one goal in this game.

LON #81 LW Elie, Remi (2013) - Elie cycled the puck very well all game long. He has intelligent positioning in all three zones and his offensive zone positioning earned him a couple scoring chances. He's relentless on the forecheck and will finish hits whenever possible. He also shows very good two-way competitiveness working hard in his own zone. He was rewarded for his hard work with an assist.

Scouts Notes: Sarnia came out strong and seemed to have the Knights number in the second half of this season. They carried a 3-1 lead into the final five minutes, but like we've seen so many times with the Knights this year, they're relentless in the final five and were able to score twice to send this game to overtime. The game eventually went to a shootout where Alex Broadhurst (Chicago) was able to score the shootout winner.

March 1st, 2013, Gunnery vs. Kent (New England Open Semifinal)

GUN #8 LD Nicholas Quillan (2014) – Good two-way defenseman, leaned offensive side. Showed a good stick overall with poise carrying the puck up ice and nice outlets. Good work on the PP moving the puck around and getting the puck on net when the lane was available. Last decisions were sometimes questionable (i.e. pinched to keep the puck in, deked a check, and then get off a poor shot; turned the puck over with good coverage, eyed a nice long outlet option, and then waited to long to get the pass off). Instincts were there. Good coverage vs. the rush with strong skating and some physicality, average-sized for a defenseman but he didn't back down.

GUN #15 LC Ryan Dmowski (2015) – One of the top players of his age group in New England. Big kid who played a mixed game. Good board work using his size to protect and work a cycle. Neutral zone coverage was intelligent, forced a couple turnovers and turned the play back the other way. Played the body all over the ice, including the defensive zone. On the downside, lost a couple battles in important moments. Skating wasn't the prettiest and could use work.

GUN #19 RC Joey Fallon (2014) – Great little sparkplug. Size will be an ongoing issue but tenacity definitely was not. Was consistently active shift to shift. Great skater, very agile and kept his feet moving. Particularly nice work shorthanded in pressing the defense and following up clearances, on one shift killed nearly 20 seconds by himself along the offensive zone boards through sheer effort.

Played the body. Backchecked hard and recognized his check. Dangerous shooter with a quick release, nearly scored on a great wrister against the grain and had another high quality chance off a beauty snapshot on a loose puck. Pursued rebounds and wasn't afraid to go to dirty areas.

KEN #14 RC Mitchell Allen (2013) – Tall, lanky forward with upside. Still very raw at this point. Strong skater, especially for his size. Good acceleration and control with good straight-line speed when given space to get going. Was prone to floating. Good backcheck when he put in the effort, got back quickly and forced turnovers. Intelligent, accurate passes in all situations, especially on the powerplay where he showed good awareness of open seams. Flashed some power forward skills with great reach and strength down the wing and to the net. Finish was lacking, missed on two top quality chances.

Scout's Notes: A few other noteworthy players – Gunnery winger Christopher Cobham (2014) is tall and lanky, might be a player when he fills out. Kent center Jimmy Ricciardi (2013) is undersized but talented and had a nice night. Kent left wing Anthony Rinaldi (2013) is a big kid who played a good all-around game.

March 1st, 2013, Salisbury vs. Westminster (New England Open Semifinal)

SAL #9 LD Will Toffey (2013) – Played a good two-way game but lacked the same type of gamebreaking ability I saw at the Flood-Marr Tournament. Still, lacked any defined flaws in his game. Strong skating forward and backward, took the puck end-to-end and recovered quickly. Defended the rush very well, played patient when necessary but showed he could step up to take the body. Great point work in the offensive zone, showing off a hard slapshot, the ability to get the puck on net quickly with snap and wrist shots, and good distribution skills on the powerplay. Made a few errors with the puck in his end trying to do too much when a simple bank of the glass would have been the right play. Quality player overall.

SAL #22 LD Ryan Segalla (2013) – Nice two-way game, aggressive and physical overall. Mean in front of his net and along the boards with a couple huge hits where he knocked guys clean off their feet. Strong on the puck in his end, kept things pretty simple most of the time with quick outlets or banks off the glass. When given a lot of space, showed a little bit of his offensive side carrying the puck up ice but was unproductive with it in this game and either lost the handle or had to dump it. A couple glaring errors. Indecisive in a 1v1 situation where the forward came in with speed, had a hard time figuring out the proper gap and almost got beat clean to the outside. Noticed this in previous viewings as well. Also had one really, really brutal D-zone turnover right in front of the net that left me scratching my head. Tools are there, still some question marks with sense.

WES #10 LC Vincent Gisonti (Passed over 2012) – He's really impressed me lately. Outstanding skater in all aspects. Bow-legged stride keeps him strong on his feet and he can accelerate with the best at this level. Great forechecker who attacked the defense aggressively. With the puck, showed off quick hands and the ability to carry the puck through traffic with speed and poise. Made a number of impressive skill moves but wasn't afraid to take the puck hard to the net. Great snapshot. Consistency was disappointing in this game. Took a few shifts off in the first two periods. Very strange to see a guy go balls out for five shifts, look totally flat for another, and then get right back on the horse. Had a stinker of a third where he was lazy in the neutral and defensive zones.

WES #11 LC Sean Orlando (2013) – Another mediocre showing from Orlando, who hasn't looked nearly as involved down the stretch as when I saw him earlier in the year. Showed off his excellent release numerous times but had a hard time carrying the puck, seemed to be fighting it every time it was on his stick. Backchecking was weak and he passed up hits in the neutral zone.

WES #16 RW David Hallisey (Passed over 2012) – Another great, complete game. Hard forecheck and backcheck work, effective on the PK, and played the body in all three zones. Showed off great skating, particularly with stops/starts and in transition. Flashed offensive upside with nice passes and a strong wrister. Lots of energy and a real strong work ethic. A couple errors (brutal line change, held on to the puck too long on occasion) but mostly without flaws.

Scout's Notes: Twins and Yale recruits Evan and Mitchell Smith (2014) play a great brand of hockey for Salisbury. Much like the Sedins, they are the offensive catalysts of the team and show great synergy along the boards and on the rush. Not the greatest skaters but they rarely get beaten to loose pucks.

March 1, 2013, Calgary Hitmen vs Swift Current Broncos (WHL)

SC #2 D, Heatherington, Dylan (2013) – used his body well to cut off Colton Mayer driving to the net after catching Heatherington's partner off guard in transition. Strong on his feet. A long reach that he uses well. Good size. Positioning came and went. As a result of poor positioning, Heatherington tends to reach quite a bit with his stick in desperation, essentially eliminating his strength advantage on most forwards. Is willing to use his body to stop shots and cut off passing lanes.

SC #5 D, Martin, Brycen (2014) – Great size and mobility for a 16 year old. Played key minutes paired with Richard Nedomel. A big defenseman that can play at both ends of the rink. Plays a pretty safe game and makes a great first pass. Could stand to improve his positioning along the walls. Got caught taking a bad penalty by reaching around to grab a guy when he could have easily pinned him along the boards and gained control of the puck. As he starts playing smarter, he can rely less on his physical size (which is also still developing).

SC #10, Cave, Colby (2013) – Strong game from the quick centerman. A versatile player, Cave can play up and down the lineup. He can play at both ends of the rink, is fast, and has a little sandpaper in his game.

SC #12 W, Merkley, Jay (2013) – Good two-way play. Slowed the play down numerous times by cycling back through the neutral zone, collecting the puck to draw a checker and then passing back to his own defensemen deep in his own zone. Good awareness with the puck, but didn't show much offensive play on the night. Good up and down his wing. Did a lot of things well, but nothing great.

Cal #18 W, Virtanen, Jake (2014) – Good puck possession skills. Improved vision. Starting to use his teammates better. Was kept to the perimeter early on against the big Swift Current defensemen. Has tremendous acceleration that he uses to switch directions and drive wide around defenders.

Cal #31, Shields, Mac (2013) – Did not play.

Mar. 1st 2013, Moncton Wildcats @ Rimouski Océanic, (QMJHL)

MON #3 D, Racine, Jonathan (2011 3rd round, Florida Panthers) : He was matched against the most offensively productive line on the Rimouski team and he did a good job of chriping, hitting and trying to get into the head of these players. He played a tough game to play for opponents, which means brining them to the outside, roughing them up and starting the scrums after whistles. He took good decisions with the puck, using the boards a lot and never giving easy turnovers to Rimouski. A well rounded, defensive D.

MON #8 RW, Garland, Conor (2014) : Small forward, with great skillset and elusiveness. He was only noticeable in the offensive zone. He has a natural goal-scoring instinct, finding soft ice easily when he is in control of the puck. He has a quick release on the wrist shot. Was knocked off his feet and hit very hard a lot of times and he'll need to bulk up a bit if he wants to stay healthy while playing in traffic like he does at the moment.

MON #22 LW, Barbashev, Ivan (2014) : Plays a mature physical two-way game, which is surprising for a Russian player with the skillset he has and the youth he has. He is a great passer and has a high hockey IQ. Takes away a lot of pucks from the opposition with his anticipation and great defensive instincts. He still lacks the high end speed to be at the level of his 2 linemates (Philip Danault and Dimitri Jaskin) and glided a little bit too much in his own end in the 3rd period relying only on hockey sense and not efforts which gave Rimouski's D a couple of easy point shots while Barbashev was late coming in for the shooting lane coverage. He's not afraid of physical play and is able to stickhandle through sticks and skates easily to gain space.

MON #26 RW, Jaskin, Dimitri (2011 2nd round, St-Louis Blues) : He's NHL ready in all areas of his game, the most NHL ready player I've seen this year in the Q. He wins his battles easily, he got multiple chances by beating players on the walls and cutting quickly in the slot shielding the puck using his big body. He's a man among boys in most of his battles. He will back check hard, will be physical and start the play from his own zone, never cheating in neutral zone. He showed a lethal release on the wrist shot and natural goal scoring instincts. He didn't try to get cute, using his skillset to get through players, always playing a North-South type of game using his big frame.

RIM #3 D, Kostalek, Jan (2013) : Loved the consistency and level of competition in his game, especially shifts where he played against the big Barbashev-Danault-Jaskin line where he was maybe a little overpowered but still found a way to use smarts, good positioning to prevent scoring chances. He showed a great intelligence on most plays where pressure was on him, he makes quick reads and takes the right decision. He showed good agressiveness on the boards and will take a big hit in order to make a play. He has an average skillset and could get more comfortable with handling the puck through traffic. His footwork is pretty good but could get even better to follow laterally players. He skates well, has a good speed and wins a lot of footraces. He got a couple of good chances to let the slapper go on the powerplay and made a good job of getting the puck low on net for rebounds and not causing turnovers shooting the puck from the blueline especially on the 2nd PP unit where Moncton liked to press. Plays a huge amount of time on the ice and is able to do so because of the smarts he has.

RIM #15 LW, Deluca, Anthony (2013) : He played a more physical game than I'm used to see from the small sniper. De Luca had a couple of nice flashes offensively, carrying the puck with skills and some good speed down the wing and getting his nose dirty in front of the net. He's a work in progress, getting better in his work ethic and defensive work than he was at the start of the season, but there's still a lot of room for improvement, decisions with and without the puck, hockey sense.

RIM #21 D, Gagné, Kevin (Signed by Anaheim Ducks) : Great free agent signing by the Anaheim Ducks. He's small but posesses every quality you want from a puck-mover. He has amazing foot speed, great skillset and has a superb offensive vision. He will join the rush a lot but has the speed to recover if there's a turnover. His major problem is without any doubt, physical strength and size and it was easy to notice against a guy like Jaskin during the game, not being able to do anything against the big Czech on the walls except skating with him and containing him. His speed gives him an edge in 1-on-1 situations which makes him tough to beat as he is quick popecheck the puck while maintaining a proper gap. Offensive defenseman with amazing skating abilities, but with a physical team like Moncton cycling the puck down-low, it was tough for him which could be a little bit worrying for the pro level.

RIM #23 C, Gauthier, Frédérik (2013) : He played a solid 2-way game but didn't seem as comfortable as usual with the puck and seemed to lack energy, which is the case for many of these young players when the end of the season is around the corner. He was still a force down-low to help his D and is really a defense first player, the smarts are there and he wants to produce offensive by being good in defense. He is a good body and shields the puck well in his battles and when he's confronted by an opponent, not afraid to take a hit or a slash to make a play. He made a couple of bad plays with the puck one was a soft pass to his D that caused a Moncton breakaway and a couple plays where he got pressured carrying the puck with slow moving feet. I'd like to see him display more explosiveness and more agressiveness around the opposition's net. He is lacking offensive production at the moment and I'd like to see him play with more hunger, but you can't deny smarts and defensive cautiousness.

RIM #30 G, Desrosiers, Philippe (2013) : I liked many aspects of his game like the way he played the puck well behind his net, the way he controlled rebounds well and absorbed high shots into his glove and chest without giving any juicy rebounds. He stayed calm and focused even though Moncton crashed his net. He was a little bit quick on the kness though and playing the butterfly a little too deep in his crease on some occasions, giving space for shooters to pick. I'd like him to be more agressive in front of his net, gave way too much of an easy chance to Mark Tremaine on a breakaway, getting on the knees very quickly and also would be more easy to track pucks through traffic if he was more agressive. Anticipation is good and he made a number of good saves on Jaskin by playing well technically and anticipating plays, starting his push a split second before the pass.

Mar 1, 2013, Vancouver Giants vs. Lethbridge Hurricanes (WHL)

VAN#6 RD, Atwal, Arvin(2014) Defenseman whose game has come a long way this season. Probably played his best game of the year at this level. Managed the puck pretty well and limited his turnovers. A good skater with good speed and good footwork in tight areas. Played with an edge as usual along the boards, and got into a nice fight too. Played on the power play and still struggled with making reads, but the coaching staff have enough confidence in him to put him out there in offensive situations, although some of it has to do with the lack of depth on the team.

VAN#13 RC, Baer, Alec(2015) Rookie forward who was recruited out of Minnesota and playing in his first game, and did not look out of place at all. Received top 6 minutes 5 on 5, and had a very impressive showing. His positioning in the defensive zone was quite good, and he competed hard along the walls. Baer is a good skater who displayed good speed out in open ice. He looked very poised with the puck, and trusted in his skills and hockey sense to play a good game. He made an impressive move in the neutral zone and got a breakaway, and was tripped for a penalty shot. He made a backhand move and lost the puck, and looked a little nervous on such a big stage. Definitely a player to watch for in the future.

VAN#26 LW, Vickerman, Taylor(2014) Another player who probably had one of his best games of the year tonight. Vickerman used his big frame to his advantage and created havoc in front of Lethbridge's net. He was able to score a goal off of a rebound in front of the net. He drove to the net a few times and showed some grit and puck protecting ability, something that he was missing for most of the year. It seems like his game is starting to click and has gained some confidence.

LET#6 RD, Erkamps, Macoy(2013) Puck moving defenseman who had a good game tonight. Played a ton of minutes and wore down a little bit as the game went along. Erkamps got beat physically along the boards in the offensive zone on the power play, which directly led to a goals against. Offensively he stayed simple with the puck, and made good, solid reads and looked poised doing so. He needs to improve his velocity on shots, but he does a good job of getting shots on net. He is fairly mobile, but he can improve on his lateral movement. He has a bit of a physical element to his game, as he likes to line up opponents to try to land open ice hits. He was not afraid to get into scrums to protect teams throughout the game.

LET#14 LD, Pilon, Ryan(2015) Big defenseman who showed that he can play a solid game at both ends of the ice. Only concern is his intensity level. Just does not seem to play the game with much urgency with and without the puck. Still has some improvements to make in terms of little details, but definitely on his way to becoming a very impressive prospect in the future. He does not looked particularly fast, but he made a nice rush at the early parts of the game that led to a good scoring chance. Pilon made a very impressive slap pass on the power play that also led to an excellent chance. He made good passes all night long. Has an impressive reach that he uses to knock away pucks, but needs to improve his use of his stick. On a rush from Vancouver, his poor stick check allowed an opponent to drive to the net which led to a goals against. He is physical when necessary along the boards and in scrums, but still think his intensity level can be higher.

SCOUT'S NOTES: This was one of the best games that Vancouver has played all year. They were rewarded for their efforts tonight, and many players stepped up to play a great game. Very impressed with Alec Baer. It seems like they have found their #1 centre for the future. Looked very good at both ends of the ice. Really believe that Russell Maxwell will at least get an invite to a prospects camp by an NHL team. He is undersized, but showed some very good offensive abilities tonight, especially in the slot to finish off plays and to create good scoring chances for teammates. His play has improved immensely since last year. Disappointed with Jamal Watson and Reid Duke of Lethbridge tonight. Both got very little accomplished, and did not play with much purpose on the night.

FINAL SCORE: 5-4(OT) Vancouver

Mar 1, 2013, USNTDP U18 vs. Muskegon Lumberjacks (USHL)

MSK # 17, LW, Tiffels, Frederik (2013) Tiffels plays with good speed and agility and will hustle to get on loose pucks, using his body to protect it well and get a good cycle going in deep in the offensive zone. He also came back really well on the back-check to close off his man along the boards and take the puck. He pressures the puck carrier pretty well on the fore-check, was getting to the front of the net and displayed some physicality in his game as well. He has fantastic hands and moves to get by defenders on the rush, displayed really good passing and creativity, however needs to be stronger on the puck along the boards.

MSK # 19, LW, Alferd, Riley (2013) Alferd displayed a good element of physicality on the fore-check, and put pretty good pressure on the puck carrier. He can cycle the puck pretty well, possesses pretty quick hands and has a good quickness and acceleration to get on loose pucks with speed. He was moving the puck down low then driving to the slot with his stick down, but mishandled the puck on an odd-man rush giving up the opportunity.

MSK # 20, D, Brodzinski, Mike (2013) Brodzinski possesses great hands to rush the puck up into the offensive zone and was finding lanes to get to the slot to put great shots on net. He is calm with the puck, protecting it from the opposition's pressure and battles well for the puck however can't cross the line by taking penalties. He is able to get the puck in deep into the offensive zone, but has to watch the turnovers holding on to the puck for too long.

USA # 2, D, Clifton, Connor (2013) Clifton has a nice hard shot from the point and is able to read plays to get in lanes to pick off turnovers through the neutral zone. He holds the offensive zone well, jumps down low with the puck to lead the attack and will cut to the net on a good power forward move to create a great chance in tight. He rushes the puck up the ice well, finding lanes to gain the offensive zone. He possesses great speed and puck distribution on the rush, however needs to hit the net on his opportunities.

USA # 7, C, Compher, J.T. (2013) Compher protects the puck very effectively along the wall deep in the offensive zone and has good speed to come in off the wing for shots, but needs to drive the puck towards the net or to the middle rather than taking long outside shots. He puts good pressure on the fore-check, reads the play to force turnovers in the offensive zone and possesses great strength while protecting the puck to get to the slot for shots. He gets to the net looking for loose pucks and rebounds, has a great reach to control the puck and plays with a good element of physicality in the defensive zone, keeping his man to the outside.

USA # 10, RW, Allen, Evan (2013) Allen was able to make a great pass to find an open man in the slot to create a really good chance. He read the play to stay back and cover for a defenseman when he got caught on a pinch and displayed great speed on the rush through the neutral zone, finding lanes to get up the ice with the puck on an end-to-end rush. He was able to find lanes in the offensive zone as well to move the puck around, but needs to watch some of the turnovers trying to force passes through the opposition.

USA # 22, RW, Fasching, Hudson (2013) Fasching plays with good speed, hustles to get on loose pucks and puts really good pressure on the fore-check. He also opened up really well in the offensive zone on the power play to take a pass and put a good one-timer on net.

FINAL SCORE: 3-1 Muskegon Lumberjacks

Mar 1, 2013, Moncton Wildcats vs. Rimouski Oceanic (QMJHL)

MNC # 4, D, Sweeney, Jacob (2013) Sweeney was calm with the puck, has a good element of agility to his game and was able to make a good 1st pass out of the zone. He was strong on the puck, protected it well from the opposition's pressure and moved it around pretty nicely in the offensive zone.

MNC # 12, RW, Johnson, Stephen (2013) Johnson kept to a pretty simple game in this one. He was putting the puck in deep on the dump, then pressuring the puck carrier on the fore-check. He was also able to get a decent cycle started.

RIM # 3, D, Kostalek, Jan (2013) Kostalek possesses great size, is really strong on the puck and was protecting it well from the opposition's pressure. He can make very effective short or long passes to start the breakout, as he was able to find a teammate at the far blue line a few times for good opportunities. He stepped up to challenge the shooter in his own zone to get in the way of shots and was strong on the puck when holding on to it. He has a good hard shot from the point, but needs to get it through to the net with more consistency and to hit the net when he does.

RIM # 11, RW, Bryukvin, Vladimir (2013) Bryukvin did not get much ice time in this game, but when he did he found space to work with in the offensive zone and opened up really well to take a pass and put a nice one-timer shot on net.

RIM # 15, LW, DeLuca, Anthony (2013) DeLuca showed some really nice hands, especially on a 1-on-1 move to get in towards the net with the puck, however he needs to drive the net with the puck rather than fading back to the outside and trying to make a fancy play from the perimeter. He possesses pretty good speed and agility with the puck, was distributing it well and moved the puck to the front of the net to create chances from in tight. He was also willing to have a net-front presence when he did not have the puck and was protecting it nicely along the wall deep in the offensive zone. He distributed the puck well on the rush through the neutral zone, did a great job coming out of the corners with the puck while protecting it then was able to make a great centering pass to find an open man out front. He also displayed some decent physicality at times on the fore-check.

RIM # 23, C, Gauthier, Frederik (2013) Gauthier displayed a really good battle to get to the net while looking for loose pucks and rebounds. He had a great net-front presence, battling for his territory and was able to get a really good cycle going in the offensive zone. He came back for some excellent support in his own end to tie up his man, got in lanes to block shots, and came down low to clear the puck away from the net to take away a good scoring opportunity for the opposition. He has good size and strength, is tough to knock off the puck and uses his body really well to get the inside track to the puck and win the battles. He has to watch some of the turnovers moving the puck up along the boards on the breakout however.

RIM # 30, G, Desrosiers, Phillippe (2013) Desrosiers did a good job of controlling his rebounds for the most part in this game, and came out to the top of his crease to challenge the shooter. He read the play to follow a deflection in tight to make a real good save, and showed a lot of aggression when a player got pushed into him and he took a really unnecessary penalty that resulted in a goal. He battled through traffic at times to find the puck and make saves, however had some trouble a couple times as well on point shots when there was a lot of traffic right in front of him. He mishandled the puck a few times trying to play the puck behind the net, resulting in turnovers, and there were moments when he was moving around way too much in the net when the puck was moved East to West putting himself out of position and he really needs to keep himself more controlled in the net in these times. He was also way off mark in the opposition's breakaway, giving away half the net, which resulted in the game winning goal for the opposition.

RIM # 81, RW, Fortier, Simon (2013) Fortier showed a pretty good battle along the boards to win the puck on the fore-check and then get a good cycle going in the offensive zone. He was reading the play to pick off neutral zone turnovers, but needs to watch his own turnovers by holding on to the puck for too long on the rush.

FINAL SCORE: 4-2 Moncton Wildcats

Mar 1, 2013, Sioux Falls Stampede vs. Green Bay Gamblers (USHL)

SIO # 8, LW, Mansfield, Ian (2013) Mansfield has fantastic speed, and was able to pick up the puck on a great back-check to lift the opposition's stick then rush into the offensive zone with speed, making nice moves to cut to the net on a power forward move then the team scored on the rebound. He battled and competed well for the puck, got it in deep into the offensive zone and was hustling hard to be first on loose pucks. He was able to get a pretty good cycle going in the offensive zone, but has to get the puck up out of his own end on the opportunities along the boards.

SIO # 16, RW, Valesano, Connor (2013) Valesano put really good pressure on the fore-check, and made some good little chip plays to create room in the offensive zone. He was cycling the puck well and possesses nice hands and moves on the rush to get to the slot and put good shots on net. He needs to watch the turnovers up along the boards in his own zone.

GBG # 5, D, Oloffson, Gustov (2013) Oloffson put really good physicality on the puck carrier along the boards in his own zone and was able to make a pretty good first pass out of his own end. He was coming down low to join the attack then made his hits on the fore-check. He was distributing the puck well on the power play in the offensive zone, but needs to get his shots through to the net from the point and has to work harder in puck battles as he lost his battles in the corners behind the net resulting in turnovers.

GBG # 16, C, Weiss, Mathew (2013) Weiss has good speed, comes back well on the back-check playing physically on the puck carrier, tying up his man well in the defensive zone and clearing the puck from the front of the net. He had really good speed on the wide drive then cut to the net on a great move for a fantastic chance in tight off the rush. He put good shots on net off the rush and moved the puck across on a 2-on-1 opportunity to create a great chance. He did a good job off the rush to get the puck in deep and draw a penalty and was opening up really nicely in the high slot to provide scoring options. He has really good agility to avoid the opposition's pressure, was distributing the puck well on the odd-man rush, but has to watch the neutral zone turnovers holding on to the puck too long.

GBG # 20, D, Wolanin, Christian (2013) Wolanin used his stick really well to force the opposition to the outside and made a really good long pass to find a teammate at the far blue line off the rush. He was getting his shot through from the point and jumped up on the rush to provide options in the high slot to take a passes and put shots on net. He distributed the puck well through the neutral zone, but has to watch the turnovers on dangerous passes up the middle in his own zone. His man got around him a bit easily on the rush along the wall, and another got in behind him to get to the net and take the puck to score.

GBG # 24, C, Siroky, Ryan (2013) Siroky has nice speed and hustles to get to the net looking for opportunities in tight. He has good strength and puck protection to hold on to the puck while taking a hit and was able to get a really quick shot off from the high slot right off the draw. He made a really nice long pass to spring a teammate at the far blue line for a good chance.

FINAL SCORE: 2-1 Sioux Falls Stampede

March 2, 2013, Moncton Wildcats @ Quebec Remparts (QMJHL)

Quebec

#10 Anthony Duclair, LW (2013) Duclair had a good game overall and lot of jump in his step. Used his speed well on Quebec's 1st goal, where he exploded in the neutral zone to beat a defenseman wide, drove to the net, went to get his rebound behind the net and found Adam Erne all alone in front for an easy tap-in. Duclair is most dangerous on open ice, but still struggled with his decision-making with the puck and the passing game. Had a nice give-and-go with his centerman Kurt Etchegary in the 3rd period, where Duclair came close to scoring.

#19 Kurt Etchegary, C (2013) Works hard in all three zones. Plays in all situations, finishes his checks. Not the most natural skilled player, but he has a lot of will and determination. His skating will need some work, as he needs more explosion in his first three steps. Made a real nice give-and-go play with his linemate, where he made a sweet pass to Duclair who couldn't bury it. On Quebec's 2nd goal he made a nice, no-look back-end pass to his right winger, Frederic Bergeron.

#73 Adam Erne, LW (2013) Erne started the game slowly. His line had possession of the puck often in the Moncton end, but were lacking imagination with it. His play improved when he started getting involved physically. He was used on the half-wall on the Remparts' power play, whereas I would prefer to see him being used in front of the net, where he would be more useful. Scored the Remparts' first goal just by going to the net and following a great rush by Anthony Duclair, who gave him an easy tap-in with an open net. Can create scoring chances by using his good speed on his off-wing and driving the net hard, which I wish he would do more often. It is very hard for defensemen to contain him with his speed and size. Was used as a centerman on the power play when the faceoff was on the left side, while Sorensen or Shaw took the faceoff from the right side. Did relatively well in the faceoff circle.

#94 Nick Sorensen, RW (2013) Was really skating well in the first period, but like Erne, not much was happening offensively for him in that period. A number of times, I saw him backcheck very hard in this game, which I really liked. He took faceoffs on the PP when they were on the right side. Overall, however, this was a quiet game for Sorensen, who made some good plays without the puck but didn't do much with it.

Moncton

#8 Connor Garland, RW (2014) Garland got limited ice time at even strength, but made the 2nd power play unit with Barbashev. Very small but quick, not very strong on the puck or his skates. Can get knocked off the puck easily but did battle hard in this game. Made some nice reads in the defensive zone.

#22 Ivan Barbashev, LW (2014) Barbashev played a good, quiet all around game with Jaskin and Danault. Not afraid to get physical along the boards. He and Jaskin can really find each other on the ice, but didn't do much offensively in this game. Played well defensively and was also used at center on the 2nd power play unit.

March 2nd, 2013, Kents Hill vs. Holderness (New England Small School Semifinal)

KH #19 RD Logan Day (2013) – Great offensive defenseman at this level but don't think there's much more to him than that. Big and poised with the puck, loved to join the attack and act as a forward to create numbers. Great passer and very decisive at the point on the powerplay. Strong one-timer and showed the awareness to shoot low for rebounds. Active stick. Skating is an issue, moved well when running the point offense but otherwise lacked mobility and had a hard time in particular against the rush. Not agile. Defensive zone positioning was fairly pedestrian.

KH #4 RC Mark Dufour (2013) – Drummondville property but committed to Union. Good player that has room for improvement. Agile for his size. Good control of his feet, stopped on a dime. Lacked real top end speed, needs to work on his straight line skating. Consistently went hard to the net and stopped up there for rebounds or to screen. Good work on the boards. Slow to shoot, got into good shooting positions but passed up good opportunities. Showed good hands in flashes with some evasiveness and touch on passes.

HOL #2 LD Terrance Amorosa (2013) – Had a mixed game. I love his physical tools and what he brings to the table for this Holderness team but question his situational decision-making. Had a great start with safe outlets, smart coverage, and physical defensive play. Was good on the PK and tracked the play well in all situations. Showed off strong skating and poise carrying the puck in end-to-end rushes. Wanted the puck and got off good shots. Showed off good passing ability on the rush and powerplay. As Holderness started to lose hold of the game, he tried to put the team on his shoulders. Progressively tried to do more and ended up doing far too much. Tried to beat multiple defenders with the puck. He has nice hands but looked off his teammates too frequently. Was much too aggressive in outnumbered and 1v1 situations, didn't seem to trust his goaltender to make the save. He was able to save Holderness against Rivers with this kind of effort but not tonight.

Scout's Notes: Kent's Hill won this one handily by a score of 5-1. Kent's Hill defenseman Francesco Tolfa (2013) showed tools but had more than his share of trouble in his own zone.

March 2nd, 2013, Brooks vs. Tilton (New England Small School Semifinal)

BRO #28 RD Connor Moore (2015) – On the smaller side but skilled offensive defenseman who played surprisingly well in his own end. Very strong on his skates and moves with agility. Battled physically in his end, did well to cover bigger players. Was quick to recover loose pucks and clear zone. Showed some good touch with the puck though he was prone to trying to do too much. Flashed shooting ability with a great slapshot, particularly one he took on a loose puck, and some good wristers that he got through on net. Nice work running the powerplay.

TIL #9 RD/F Andrew Sullivan (2013) – Good offensive defenseman. Lacking size. Smart with the puck and a great skater. Strong point shot that he got through traffic. Went end-to-end on a few occasions with poise and was evasive against the forecheck in his own zone. Showed some nice individual ability without being selfish.

Scout's Notes: Connor Moore's older brother KJ Moore (2013) also had a nice game. He was smart, gritty, and involved in the offense, but not especially fluid.

March 2nd, 2013, Cushing vs. Exeter (New England Big School Semifinal)

CUS #8 RD Connor Brassard (2013) – Tall two-way defenseman, bulky but looks like he still has room. Can see why he was Q drafted. Showed good skating and surprisingly quick hands for his size. Lots of poise with the puck. Took a brutal double-minor late that almost cost his team the game, otherwise decisions were good.

CUS #10 RC Shane Kavanagh (2013) – Hard not to love the way this kid plays. Aggressive, uptempo two-way center. Average-sized (5'11ish) but laid a few guys out with massive hits. Skating is outstanding, very nimble with good top speed and strong on his feet. Good stick on the PK. Strong on the forecheck and difficult to beat. Effectively combined speed and strength to break down the wing and go hard to the net with frequency. I have some concerns about his durability with the way he plays, and how well his game will translate when he matches up against stronger players, but he showed a lot of heart and some flashes of talent to go with it.

CUS #12 RW Thomas Aldworth (2013) – Really liked Aldworth's game. He's tall and lanky. Played with a lot of intensity though decision-making was a bit of an issue for me. Strong skater with really good edges in the offensive zone to work in a cycle. Chippy with a couple big hits. Aggressive and capable defensively, good compete level along the boards and a huge asset shorthanded where he showed great awareness to kill time, going end-to-end once when given space and playing keepaway with his defense on another occasion. Great hands, quick and agile and showed the ability to beat guys 1v1. Passing was iffy, a couple blind dishes and one brutal drop pass to no one. Would benefit from simplifying overall, will have to if he hopes to advance. Good raw skills, played a complete game.

CUS #13 RC Cameron Askew (2016) – Stocky kid, didn't stand out much. Played a relaxed game overall, liked to carry the puck up ice but wilted at the first sign of pressure and either coughed it up or threw a weak shot on net. Would have liked to see him get more involved physically. Skating needs work, strong on his feet but lacked agility. Stride is OK but he wasn't putting in the effort to really pump his legs. Not dynamic overall. Flashes of skill (i.e. receiving tricky passes in flight and intelligent short passes) but if I wasn't making an effort to look for him, I could have gone the whole game without really noticing him.

EXE #12 RD Spenser Young (2015) – Upside offensive defenseman. Undersized at about 5'10. Needs to bulk up. Great skater, quick feet and very elusive. Showed great skill with the puck. Went end-to-end with a lot of deceptiveness and poise. Made a few highly skilled passes, tape to tape with air. Good powerplay QB, distributed well and managed attack from point. Had one particular takeover shift that blew me away where he was two steps ahead of everyone. A little too fancy, tried to do too much by himself. Defensive coverage was poor overall. Too aggressive, especially in outnumbered situations. Took himself out of position with missed all-or-nothing attempts. Not strong enough to handle bigger players.

EXE #13 LD Peter Christie (2016) – Showed a lot for a freshman blueliner. Similar to Young, shifty offensive defenseman. About 5'11 as a late '97 so he'll likely grow. Evaded checks well and made some beautiful outlet passes look easy. Great patience and poise with the puck in his own end. Coverage was mostly strong. Good against speed, closed quickly and timed his contact.

Scout's Notes: Lanky 6'2 defenseman Richard Boyd (2013) played a simple and solid game for Cushing. Defended well with grit and showed a nice first pass.

March 2nd, 2013, Avon vs. Thayer (New England Big School Semifinal)

AVN #11 LW Mason Krueger (2013) – Man could this kid shoot the puck today. Two high-quality snipes, one from the high slot and the other from near the dot. The latter was an absolute bullet that he placed with very little room for error. Foot speed was an issue, looked sluggish and had a hard time carrying the puck up ice. Some upside but needs work.
AVN #14 LC Nicholas Hutchison (2013) – Big kid at around 6'2, 180. Showed some smarts and raw combination of size and skill but only in bursts. Overall was pretty awkward on the day with a number of misplays. Didn't look totally comfortable out there. Think there's more here.

THA #9 LW Lincoln Griffin (2016) – Top '97 talent playing well against bigger, older competition. Had a very productive freshman season and has continued strong play as sophomore. Northeastern commit for 2016. Dynamic skater with high-end acceleration and good straight-line speed. Very shifty and agile, played with a lot of jump. Showed off some nifty hands though tried to do too much on a number of shifts, got hammered once and gave the puck up twice with unnecessary dangle attempts. Despite that, did manage to utilize his teammates well on a number of occasions with shots for rebounds and intelligent passes. Showed two-way ability with good PK coverage and some strong backchecking, though his focus was on attacking most of the time.

March 3rd, 2013, Avon vs. Cushing (New England Big School Final)

CUS #7 LD Richard Boyd (2013) – Not sure he's a high upside guy but played a polished and decisive game. Very smooth skater, especially for his size at 6'2. Evasive against the forecheck and covered the rush well. Smart with the puck in his end and made good decisions to get it up ice, whether by safe outs off the glass or long stretch passes when available.

CUS #8 RD Connor Brassard (2013) – Played a nice two-way game. Very physical in his own end. Made himself difficult to play against, stepping up to take the body at the line when opportunity knocked and battling on the boards. Blocked shots and cleared the front of his net. Didn't carry much in this game but did pinch into the attack at the right times and showed evasiveness with the puck. On one occasion he pinched and got the puck deep, noticed the forward who was supposed to cover him went for a change instead, and quickly reversed direction to cover back appropriately. Very heady play that showed a lot of awareness.

CUS #10 RC Shane Kavanagh (2013) – Love this kid but his day got cut short predictably. For the first half of the first period he was all over the place. Scored a goal and was really buzzing, making plays with the puck and making his presence felt with his stick and body without it. Laid out three guys on one shift, then had Avon's Nick Hutchison take a run at him near the penalty box (there's no glass on that side). Got bent over the boards awkwardly and looked like he might have broken his arm. Tried to come back twice but was in too much pain to play. Gutsy effort but this game illustrates his downside.

CUS #12 RW Thomas Aldworth (2013) – Had another strong game today. Poise with the puck is his biggest asset, went end-to-end on numerous occasions with good use of reach, protection, and outright strength down the wing. Smooth skater with a nice stride, very efficient and quick. Footwork was precise overall. Excellent wristshot. Very deceptive hands. Backchecked hard and played the body. Needed to shoot the puck more.

CUS #13 RC Cameron Askew (2016) – Better than yesterday, but still not a great showing. Flashed some skill on the powerplay, quick stickhandler for his size and some heady passes. Went hard to the net on a couple occasions. Biggest issue was that he didn't keep his feet moving. Crashed the net in a 2-on-2 situation and got behind the defenseman, but stopped skating when the puck came off his teammates stick and ended up being just too late to finish the play. Defensive zone play was dreadful, floated and chased the play around, didn't really seem to have any clue of where to be. Gave the puck away a few times trying to do too much and rarely backchecked with any kind of vigor. Poor on the draw, needs to work on that.

AVN #11 LW Mason Krueger (2013) – Good raw skills but needs work. His shot was exceptional again today, dangerous with snap/slap shots from anywhere below the top of the circles. Made some heady passes and looked good in cycle work. Fought off hits and made himself difficult to cover. Defensive game needs improvement, stickchecks were weak and he reached too often. Needed to keep his feet moving as he's not a strong enough skater to coast when he's out there.

AVN #14 LC Nicholas Hutchison (2013) – Played an excellent, intimidating game. Injured Cushing's Shane Kavanagh by taking a dirty run at him (for which he received no penalty) after Kavanagh had been (cleanly) physically dominating his teammates all game. Chippy after whistles, talked a lot of trash and didn't back down from anybody. Leveled a few players with his big frame in all three zones. Very sturdy on his feet and difficult to knock off the puck along the boards or when he took the puck hard down the wing. Drove the net with reckless abandon. Showed some flashes of skill with nifty dekes and a quick release. Needs to work on his skating but showed a lot of good things today.

Scout's Notes: Michael Turner (2014) had a nice game for Cushing. Big power forward with a good skill set who needs to work on his skating.

March 3rd, 2013 Kent vs. Salisbury (New England Open Final)

KEN #4 RD Bennett Morrison (2014) – Big defense-first kid, had a mixed game today. In his own end he was very solid and played mean. Was strong on the boards and in front and very difficult to beat wide on the rush. Skating needs work as he doesn't move smoothly. Offensive instincts were good but hands were lacking, i.e. pinched at the right times but misplayed or turned over the puck afterwards. Puck skills are lacking, hands just aren't well coordinated.

KEN #14 RC Mitchel Allen (2013) – Got the impression that there's more to give here. Raw talent was there but effort and focus were not. Great skater, smooth stride and a high top speed. Stickhandling is good, protects the puck well to the outside and can make skill moves. Went end-to-end with poise and navigated traffic well. Inconsistent with physical and defensive play. Capable of strong neutral zone coverage but too often skated by hits. Had a few shifts where he was a presence, closing hard and pickpocketing. Would have liked to see more of that. Spent energy trying to kickstart the offense from his zone when a better checking effort would have kept the puck out of there more often in the first place. Finishing was lacking, including one empty net chance that he needed to put in the net.

SAL #9 LD Will Toffey (2013) – Probably the best game I have seen Toffey play this year, he really stepped up in this one. Skating is top end. Accelerates quickly and stops on a dime. Matched speed against the rush perfectly, was impossible to beat wide today. Good top speed and can handle the puck with poise through traffic with the jets on. Evasive through center, didn't rush the puck a ton today but when he did he made it count. Activates into the attack like a forward, protecting well along the boards when he chases the puck in. Skating ability allows him to get back into position without a hitch. On one occasion he was caught deep and ended up hurdling a player laying on the ice to get back into the play. Beautiful. Was aggressive defensively at the right times. Squeezed off at the blueline when guys tried to beat him wide. Any time it looked like he might be beat, he stayed with it. Never let up on his man. Strong in front of his net and along the boards though he could stand to put on some strength. Good point one-timer that he placed low for rebounds. Nice powerplay and breakout passing. Tried to do too much with the puck on two shifts, which led to turnovers, but other than that no real black marks. Very well-rounded performance.

SAL #17 RC Evan Smith (2014) – Showed fantastic chemistry with his brother as always. Their line had shifts of dominance, cycling and retrieving loose pucks a step ahead of the defense. Evan flashed a great wristshot and outstanding passing. Did good work on the forecheck and penalty kill and played physical for his size. Needs to bulk up as despite being very evasive he had trouble breaking free when the defense was able to pin him down. Not a great skater, which may limit his effectiveness in the future, but he's still a great player from the blueline in regardless of that.

SAL #18 LW Mitchell Smith (2014) – Mitchell was the better finisher today. He potted two opportunistic goals, one on a 2-on-1 and the other off a rebound from a sharp angle. Battled well in the neutral and defensive zones but like Evan, needs to work on his strength and skating. These two are still raw but their hockey IQ is off the charts.

SAL #22 LD Ryan Segalla (2013) – Segalla has consistently impressed me with raw ability and aggressiveness this year, and today he played a tempered and intelligent game. His skating was strong as always, with a powerful stride and efficient footwork. Dealt well with starts and stops in his own zone and timed his contact well. Bulldozed the crease when an opponent got too close to his goaltender. Carried the puck well through the neutral zone without trying to do too much and dealt well with traffic. Took advantage of the space he was given. Showed the ability to make strong outlets if pressured. Showed off his booming slapshot but for the most part today was quiet in the offensive zone. Just very solid overall.

SAL #30 G Callum Booth (2015) – Very nice showing in net. Was impressed by the way he tracked the puck in traffic, very aware and wasn't bothered by bodies in front of him. One minor flaw I noticed is that he liked to crouch down a little too low when tracking the puck, leaving the very top shelf open. Fundamentally sound with his angles, didn't give shooters much to look at especially in outnumbered attack situations. Methodical and calm. Showed great athleticism, made one save where he did a full split to stop a backdoor shot and dealt well with desperation situations in finding the puck quickly to freeze it. Twice swallowed the puck quickly with his glove when it got behind him, preventing what would have been tap-in goals. Biggest issue I noticed is that he had a tough time tracking the play when it went behind his net.

Mar 3, 2013, Regina Pats vs. Brandon Wheat Kings (WHL)

REG#4 RD, Burroughs, Kyle(2013) Puck moving defenseman who had an up and down game tonight. Most notable inconsistent part of his game was his passes. At times he looked really good moving the puck to his forwards, then at times would hesitate to do anything with it and make decisions too late and commit turnovers. It looked like he was thinking too much at times. Logged a ton of minutes and was depended on in all situations. On the power play, had a few open lanes to shoot but almost always looked to pass instead. Defensively, Burroughs was above average along the boards given his size, and tied up opponents quite effectively. Could improve on positioning and staying patient without the puck, but did pretty well in that part of his game. Has above average skating abilities, but something he definitely needs to work on, particularly his lateral movement on the rush because he is a little small.

REG#5 RD, Williams, Colby(2013) Another defenseman for Regina that logged a ton of minutes, but used more for defensive situations. Williams played a quiet, but steady game at both ends of the ice. He was simple with the puck, and will probably never score a coast to coast highlight reel goal, but did an admirable job moving the puck. He also needs to make passes quicker and not overthink the play too much. He forced passes at times which resulted in turnovers as well. Defensively, Williams was in very good position for most of the game, but needs to get stronger along the boards with and without the puck. He has a difficult time tying up opponents and holding onto the puck along the wall. He landed a couple of nice open ice hits, and maintained a good gap throughout the game.

REG#18 LW, Klimchuk, Morgan(2013) A pure sniper who had a number of chances to score tonight by being in great position in the slot and showing off his quick release. Played on the point on the power play for most of the game, and unleashed a few heavy one timers. Recorded an assist by taking a one timer and his teammate tipping the puck into the net. Scored a nice goal by winning a battle along the wall and reversing it behind the net to his teammate, and he circled the zone and opponents were watching the puck, and Klimchuk sensed it and went to the high slot, where his teammate found him for a quick goal off of his snap shot. Liked his effort without the puck all game long. Very quick off the draw to try to win it off the scramble or jump the play to take the puck back when necessary. Blocked a one timer from the point by diving in front of it. Needs to improve on his stick positioning on the power play. A few times his stick was in the wrong position so opponents just picked him apart and went cross ice every time.

BDN#8 RC, Hawryluk, Jayce(2014) Quick, skilled forward who had a good game for Brandon. He showed a lot of hustle and work ethic to chase down loose pucks and be the first one on the forecheck at all times, something that was missing from most of his teammates in this game. He played a smart game at both ends of the ice. He had good awareness without the puck, and helped out his teammates by being in good position and setting very subtle picks to help them get loose along the boards a few times. He possesses a good shot, but needs to be better at shot selection. In OT, he was in a 1 on 1 situation down the wing, and when he should have taken a quick wrist shot or snap shot, winded up to take a slapper, which was knocked away by his opponent before he can get the shot off. He has good hands, and may be able to score a couple highlight reel goals a season with some luck. Like the confidence he plays with.

out of the zone to start the breakout and was battling to get the puck to the front of the net for chances from in tight.

USA # 49, D, Golver, Jack (2014) Glover possesses great size and distributes the puck very well on the power play in the offensive zone. He did a good job of holding the line in the offensive zone and was stepping up to challenge the puck carrier. He jumped up on the rush to come in for a good shot opportunity but missed the net on his chance, he is very calm with the puck but at times was over-aggressive on the puck carrier and got beat.

CHI # 10, C, Ebbing, Thomas (2013) Ebbing was able to get the puck in deep and have a good cycle started. He had fantastic puck distribution and creativity to get to the slot for a great shot opportunity and showed really nice agility to find space to work with in the offensive zone. He was able to skate the puck up into the offensive zone, has some good agility to twist away from the opposition's pressure and had a nice net-front presence on the power play. He also came back for some good support in his own end and showed some physicality on the puck carrier.

CHI # 15, LW, Hill, Tyler (2013) Hill has nice hands and distributes the puck well in the offensive zone off the rush. He made a fantastic pass to find a lane and move the puck to a teammate for a back-door tap-in goal and was protecting the puck very well on the cycle to avoid the opposition's pressure. He made a really good power forward move on the wide drive to cut in towards the front of the net, but he was for the most part continuously taking long outside shots off the rush, most of which missed the net, and also missed his target on some neutral zone passes.

CHI # 17, RW, Polino, Patrick (2013) Polino showed some good aggression getting involved after the whistles and has great speed on the wide drive but missed the net on his opportunity. He put good pressure on the puck carrier, was able to get the puck in deep and was physical on the fore-check and also made a really good cross-ice pass on the power play to move the puck to an open man and the puck ended up in the back of the net. He has to watch the turnovers trying to hold on to the puck for too long, and was also taking lots of long outside shots on the rush.

CHI # 28, C, Roos, Alex (2013) Roos got a nice cycle started in deep into the offensive zone and was able to make a nice cross-ice pass to find a man far side in the offensive zone. He put a good shot on from the high slot to score the opener of the game and made an excellent pas to find a man far side in the offensive zone for a good opportunity. He did a great job of pick off a neutral zone turnover then rushed the puck back up into the offensive zone and was moving the puck up well on the rush into the offensive zone. He made a great give-and-go play to get to the slot to put a nice shot on, went to the net with his stick down for an excellent chance in tight to the net and was reading the play to pick off turnovers in the offensive zone as well. He also used his speed for a good breakaway opportunity that drew a penalty shot, and on the penalty shot he made a great move to score 5-hole. He has to get the puck in deep instead of turning the puck over at the blue line trying to make a move and also had a 2-on-1 opportunity but elected to shoot and the goaltender made the save.

FINAL SCORE: 4-3 Chicago Steel

Mar 5, 2013, Red Deer Rebels vs. Kootenay Ice (WHL)

RD#8 RD, Doetzel, Kayle(2013) Big, physical defensive defenseman had a good game by sticking to his strengths and protecting his own end well. Not a great skater, but quite mobile given his size. Does a good job to turn away from opponents to protect the puck and to stick with opponents when they try to skate past him. Very strong along the walls, and showed his physicality everywhere out on the ice tonight. Made good, simple outlet passes to get the attack going. Not much offensive abilities, but he did read the play well a couple of times to pinch down the walls to keep pucks inside the offensive zone.

RD#9 RC, Bleackley, Connor(2014) 2 way centre who made a much bigger impact in his own end tonight than in the offensive zone. Needs to work on hitting the net with his shots as he is moving with speed. Mishandled the puck a few times throughout the night, but could have been the result of bad ice. However, he does seem to possess only average hands with the puck, as he did not show much puckhandling abilities. Best work done tonight is in the defensive zone with the puck. Was in good coverage all night long and really helped out with defensemen and allowed them to be physical and take some risks to land some hits on opponents as he would cover for them well. Produced a few turnovers as the game went along too.

KTY#14 RW, Descheneau, Jaedon(2013) Small, skilled winger who displays some good chemistry with Same Reinhart. Loves to shoot from everywhere and rarely looks to make a pass. Scored a goal with his quick release in the slot. Scored another goal late in the game as he took a loose puck in the slot and quickly pulled it from his backhand to forehand to score in tight. Had a difficult time protecting the puck due to his small size.

KTY#23 RC, Reinhart, Sam(2014) The offensive catalyst for his team. His teammates could not generate good scoring chances without him. So smart with the puck, and seemed to know exactly where all of his teammates are. He is able to read the play far more quickly than everybody else out on the ice. Has good speed out in open ice, and is hard to control along the boards. Such a sneaky passers around the net, and rarely does it ever get intercepted by opponents. Surprisingly quite strong on the puck, as he has the ability to fend off opponents and buy some time for a play to develop. Possesses an underrated shot, as he has a deceptive release to his shots.

SCOUT'S NOTES: Sam Reinhart could be posting unbelievable stats if he had better players to play with. His intelligence in the offensive zone cannot be matched by any player currently playing in the WHL. Haydn Fleury of Red Deer also had a very good game for the Rebels. He is a 2014 NHL draft eligible defenseman, but is already receiving very tough minutes to play and is trusted in all situations. Polished game at both ends, but just needs to read the play a little better.

FINAL SCORE: 6-4 Kootenay

Mar 5, 2013, Prince George Cougars vs. Tri-City Americans (WHL)

PG#3 LD, McNulty, Marc(2013) Big physical defenseman who provided a nice presence in the defensive zone. Opponents had a difficult time trying to get away from him along the walls as he used his big reach to contain them then pin them along the boards. He went into puck battles hard, and played good intensity throughout the game. Not very good with the puck, as his poise with forecheck pressure is quite poor. Threw the puck away into the neutral zone more often than not. Needs to improve his speed as he is able to maintain a good gap on opponents, but speed forwards had chances to make a move on him and get to the net for a great scoring chance.

PG#14 LW, Witala, Chase(2013) A quick grinder who played a quiet game tonight. He was all over the ice when he was out on the ice and played with a lot of intensity, but was not able to really accomplish too much despite the effort he put into the game. Made one good pass off the half wall to the slot for a good scoring chance. Not particularly strong along the walls, and did not read the play well to get himself free from coverage. Defensively, he was willing to block shots and take a hit to make a play, but did not really do anything special without the puck.

TRI#2 RD, Tomchuk, Wil(2013) Defensive defenseman who played mostly on the third pairing and sometimes on the PK tonight. Provided a physical presence from the backend and was not afraid to mix it up in scrums. Looked a little timid and nervous whenever opposing forward came into the zone with speed. Not a very good skater, as he needs to work on his lateral footwork and overall quickness. Tomchuk was not too bad at reading the play without the puck, as he did not make any huge mistakes, but he also was not able to anticipate plays before they occurred and try to create a turnover. A mess when it comes to handling the puck. Rarely made an actual breakout pass. Glass and out is his favorite play.

TRI#26 RC, Williams, Brian(2013) A quick, offensive minded forward who had a very up and down game. Looked good when he was coming down the wing with the puck, and was able to spin away from hits or throw the puck on the net and hope something good would happen. Displayed good vision at times with slap passes and cross ice passes to create some offensive chances. Did not really look to drive to the net and try to score dirty goals. Turned over the puck a few times trying to make cute plays. Needs to improve his shot off the rush as he seems to not be able to get them on net very often.

TRI#39 LW, Bowles, Parker(2013) Speedy winger really tried to take advantage of Prince George's slow defensemen and carry the puck himself coast to coast to score goals. He played the game with a lot of speed and was not afraid to weave through traffic. He became far too predictable as usual, as he tried to carry the puck again and again with little success. Showed above average hands as he was able to quickly control the puck as he was changing directions in speed. Needs to use his teammates more in these rushes with the puck and keep himself unpredictable. Did not play with much intensity without the puck in the defensive zone.

Scouts Notes: The Cougars did a good job to keeping most of the Americans' offensive play to the outside tonight. Marc McNulty was burned a few times by speed, but otherwise did a good job in his own end and was able to separate opponents from the puck a few times along the walls. Tri-City did not show enough intensity as a team to try to win puck battles and get to the net, which costed them this game in the end.

FINAL SCORE: 3-0 Prince George

March 5, 2013, Quebec Remparts @ Baie-Comeau Drakkar (QMJHL)

Quebec
#10 Anthony Duclair, LW (2013) Duclair had a rough time distributing the puck in this game, as he took too much time to pass to an open teammate or was just trying to go end to end by himself. He was also lazy on some backchecks, including one when the puck was loose and he would have managed to get the puck in just two or three strides but instead, was coasting, allowing Baie-Comeau to take possession

#19 Kurt Etchegary, C (2013) Quiet game for Etchegary, who didn't really stand out. Did a good job helping his defensemen by being the first forward to get back to help out in the defensive zone. Had a tough time in the faceoff circle, was matched up against Felix Girard , though he did win one late in the 3rd period when the Remparts were protecting a one goal lead.

#73 Adam Erne, LW (2013) Erne had a solid game overall, including a good shift were he provoked a turnover at the Baie-Comeau blueline which led to a scoring chance for the Remparts. Made a lot of nice things happen on the Remparts' first goal, started with a heavy hit on the forecheck, then later went around the net with the puck and found Nick Sorensen all alone at the side of the net for an easy goal. Erne's physical game picked up in the 2nd period, and he's at his best when he plays a physical brand of hockey. Late in the game while up by a goal, Erne blocked a shot from the point which left him in some discomfort, but he still continued to hustle on the ice and protect that lead.

#94 Nick Sorensen, RW (2013) Sorensen was quiet in the first period, other than making some good reads in the defensive zone, breaking up some plays from the Drakkar. Play would pick up in the 2nd period, where on his first goal, after being robbed point-blank by Baie-Comeau's goaltender, he was left all alone beside the net and got a great feed from Adam Erne for an easy tap-in. On his 2nd goal, he got a pass in the neutral zone and used his great speed to go between both Baie-Comeau's defensemen and outwaited the goalie for his 2nd of the game. On more than one occasion during this game, Sorensen showed off his great acceleration, including on this 2nd goal.

Baie-Comeau

#10 Jeremy Gregoire, C (2013) Gregoire didn't really stand out in any area in this game but did work hard in all 3 zones. Played on Baie-Comeau's top line with Raphael Bussieres & Petr Straka. Skating is still average at best, he needs to improve it to make things happen offensively and get more room to maneuver. Didn't see too much in terms of physical play in this game.

#13 Gabriel Paquin-Bourdreau, LW (2013) Boudreau, who played on a line with fellow 2013 draft prospect Valentin Zykov and team Captain Felix Girard, had a relatively quiet game offensively. His best chance came in the 3rd period where he couldn't bury Girard's pass after a tic-tac-toe exchange between the 3 members of the line. Showed some good flashes of his skill level, stole the puck in the 1st period with a quick stick from a Quebec defender that led to a Drakkar scoring chance. He also showed some good passing skills, setting teammates up with some sweet little flip passes on the power play.

#73 Valentin Zykov, RW (2013) Zykov was very good again in this game, as he is always very quick to jump on a loose puck in the offensive zone. Very strong on his skates and tough to contain down low. Made some good passing , which is not a well known fact about his game. He loves to play behind the net and takes the puck to the net, and it is almost impossible to stop him with his great strength. He is always around the net and it is tough to move from there. He possesses a very good, quick wrist shot and loves to get it off in a hurry when he's standing in the slot.

Mar 6, 2013, Prince Albert Raiders vs. Calgary Hitmen (WHL)

PA#10 LD, Morrissey, Josh(2013) Offensive defenseman who had a solid game at both ends of the ice tonight. Played a quiet role in the defensive end and did a good job to contain opposing forwards and to keep them to the outside. Did not make any glaring defensive mistakes. A very fluid and quick skater out in open ice and in tight areas. He showed that he can handle quick forwards easily, and was never really in a position to get caught flat footed. A phenomenal puck moving defenseman. Smart with the puck on his stick, and has very good poise. In one instance on the power play breakout, he pulled all the PK opponents to the right side, then fired a long, accurate cross ice pass to the opposing blue line to give him a clear lane to the net for a scoring chance. Played on both PP units for most of the game.

PA#18 RC, Hart, Jayden(2013) Big power forward who showed good physical and puck skills tonight. At his best with the puck when his team is in the offensive zone and he is not moving with great speed. Struggled a bit with stickhandling and passing when skating with the puck in the neutral zone. A good skater given his size, but can do better in tight areas to quickly maneuver his way around traffic and to stick to opponents in the defensive zone. Provided a very good net front presence on the power play. Opponents had a hard time moving him out of the middle and trying to get body position. Defensively, provided good coverage down low as a centre, and used his body well.

PA#29 LC, Draisaitl, Leon(2014) Big, skilled forward had a phenomenal game offensively tonight. Displayed very impressive vision with the puck, and created a number of chances throughout the game for his teammates. Made decisions quickly, and used his body well to protect the puck and stickhandle away from opponents. Drew a couple of penalties because of his puck protecting abilities. Not very quick, but has long strides and covers a lot of ground. Has a nice, quick release to his shots off the rush. Works hard for loose pucks, but needs to make better decisions with the puck at times.

CAL#2 RD, Thrower, Josh(2014) High energy defenseman who provided a nice presence for Calgary. Likes to throw his weight around in the defensive zone, but would like to see him provide the same physical play in the neutral zone. A good skater who can cover for his positioning mistakes and is able to maintain a good gap against forwards off the rush. Likes to pinch in the offensive zone, but needs to be more selective to not get caught. Still has some work to do in terms of positioning and reading the game.

CAL#18 RW, Virtanen, Jake(2014) Very inconsistent game from this skilled power forward. Would look like he is having a difficult time along the boards at times, then make a great play to drive to the net and get a scoring opportunity. In the first period, he had his back against the play with the puck along the half wall, then faked like he was skating to the point, then made a quick turn to the other side for a wide open lane to drive to the net. Created a nice chance, but couldn't finish. A good effort overall, but could have a bigger impact on the game with his skill level and size. Also made some bad decisions with the puck. Seems a little selfish with the puck and tries to do too much by himself.

CAL#25 RC, Chase, Greg(2013) Playmaking forward played a good overall game. Needs to really improve on his play along the walls. Gets outworked and pushed around too easily when battling for pucks. A good skater who uses it to his advantage, and combined with his passing abilities makes him quite dangerous off the rush. Made a few nice plays off the transition. Needs to create more chances more often.

Scouts Notes: This was a good game featuring some talented players on both teams. 2014 NHL Draft eligible Prince Albert forward Carson Perreaux showed some good potential. Big and a good skater, just needs to improve his play with the puck and gain some more confidence. Josh Morrissey and Leon Draisaitl were difficult to handle for Calgary on the PP. Both saw the ice so well and moved the puck so quickly.

FINAL SCORE: 4-3 Calgary

March 8th, 2013. Sault Ste. Marie Greyhounds vs. Guelph Storm

SSM#25 D Darnell Nurse (2013). Nurse was very effective demonstrating a strong physical ability in the corners of the defensive zone, knocking numerous Storm players off of the puck with ease. He did show a tendency to run around a little too much, and occasionally took bad angles giving good options for net drives to the attacking forwards. Darnell displayed a strong hockey sense making smart crisp breakout passes while also stretching opposing defenders hitting streaking forwards in stride when given the option. He is not afraid to carry the puck out of the defensive zone and generally made good reads choosing between the dump in or to keep carrying the puck. Nurse needs to improve his shot from the point as he struggled to find the net through traffic.

SSM#28 F Sergey Tolchinsky (2013). Tolchinsky was one of the lone bright spots for the Greyhounds in this game. He displayed excellent offensive instincts buzzing around the Storm net looking to get his stick on rebounds. Sergey showed excellent patience with the puck waiting for the play to develop or teammates to catch up with him before launching his offensive attack. He can stick handle in a phone booth and is very adept at making defenders miss. He works hard to keep himself out of dangerous areas by constantly keeping his head on a swivel and aware of his surroundings. Tolchinsky does sometimes carry the puck too long, and would benefit from distributing the puck more often with his linemates. He is an excellent skater although majority of the time his strong rushes end up nowhere because he runs out of room and does not move the puck quick enough. Sergey does have a very strong wrist shot and is able to get it off very quick in limited amounts of space.

SSM#19 F Jared McCann (2014). McCann showed flashes of elite speed cutting through the center of the ice winning races to loose pucks and beating flat footed defenders with ease. He is very good at gaining the offensive blue line and shows the patience to slow up and wait for options if the defender is closing the gap on him. Jared is a strong passer and is very good at working the give-and-go with his linemates. He also has a nose for the net and is very good at positioning himself in the slot for quick one timer opportunities. He needs to work on his strength because he was a little easy to knock off the puck in this game.

GUE#11 F Jason Dickinson (2013). Dickinson continued to show a willingness to get physical along the boards and battled hard in front of the net. Jason struggled to get much going offensively in this game, besides one assist early. He was not moving his feet as well as he usually does and it showed in the lack of net drive and getting shut down by defenders on the rush. Dickinson was reliable defensively and was very effective in penalty kill situations shadowing the Greyhound defenders and getting into passing and shooting lanes.

GUE#20 F Justin Auger (2012). Auger had a solid game for the Storm, consistently battling for loose pucks in front of the net and using his size advantage to lean on defenders and create turnovers. Justin works extremely hard along the boards to control puck possession and utilizes his size to shield the puck from defenders. He is great at creating a cycle with his linemates and has the quick step ability to catch opponents off guard with a quick drive to the net. Auger sometimes appears a little selfish with the puck and would benefit from distributing the puck when teammates are in better positions than him. Justin skates well for a big guy and catches defenders off guard with two quick bursts of speed coming down the wing. He needs to work at improving his scoring touch as he produced a number of great opportunities but was unable to find the back of the net.

March 8, 2013, Gatineau Olympiques vs. Val-d'Or Foreurs (QMJHL)

GAT #27 LW Emile Poirier (2013) – Not the smoothest player but was very productive tonight and showed a lot of positives. Had a hat trick in a 13-minute stretch and two assists. Was instrumental in his team coming back from a 6-0 deficit to ultimately win in overtime. He was shifty, creative, and opportunistic with finishing, flashing a good variety of hard, accurate shots regardless of foot positioning. Though not the strongest on the puck when faced with contact, he was elusive and is still gangly so the potential is there to fill out and improve on his protection. Skating stride is choppy but he got from A to B with a surprising amount of acceleration and could handle the puck at high speed. Footwork was inefficient with wide turns and slow starts/stops. Was defensively responsible but did get caught watching the puck repeatedly. Backcheck positioning was strong though he lacked intensity in coverage. High upside here based on hockey intelligence, was very impressed with how he took the game over when his team looked down and out.

VDO #8 RW Anthony Mantha (2013) – The talent here is undeniable but he had a rough night. Each time I see Mantha, I'm a little more concerned about his decision-making and compete level. He scored a breakaway goal to put his team up 5-0 and then relaxed for most of the rest of the game. Seemed to get frustrated and detached when Gatineau started their comeback. Was soft in scrums and didn't backcheck hard. Tried to force the play with the puck off the rush much too often, going for cross-ice passes through too much traffic or attempting weak shots from the outside that were blocked or missed the net. Showed flashes of strong forechecking ability and physical play that left me wanting more.

VDO #16 RW Nicolas Aubé-Kubel (2014) – Works hard but his skating is holding him back for right now. Heavy feet make him slow out of the gate and his top speed is lacking. Footwork in tight is good with agile starts/stops. Played a fairly well rounded game but nothing is advanced yet. Made good decisions for the most part but had a hard time getting things going in the offensive zone.

Scout's Notes: Unbelievable game that finished as an 8-7 shootout victory in favor of Gatineau, who were at one point down 6-0 in the game.

March 8th, 2013, Québec Remparts vs. Victoriaville Tigres (QMJHL)

QUE #19 C Etchegary, Kurt (2013) – Played a sound two-way game. His speed wasn't matching well with the rest of his line mates but he works hard enough to keep the pace and uses his hockey sense well to move the puck. Not overwhelming hands, but strong enough to handle the puck and protect. Fierce competitor and showed a lot of pride when the play got tougher physically. He tried to cross the penalty bench to fight another player and got ejected.

QUE #10 LW Duclair, Anthony (2013) – I was very surprised to see him play a simple game and applying the team system which consisted of a lot of dumping. He didn't mind dumping the puck and working hard to retrieve it. He also made some solid defensive plays and created a few turnovers. It's nice to see he has this type of game in his tool set. He still needs to find consistency: finding a way to bring this type of game every time and matching it with his high-end speed. He didn't factor much offensively tonight but was still very effective.

QUE #73 RW Erne, Adam (2013) – Erne played a strong power forward game I've been waiting to see for a long time. He was disturbing for other players along the boards and he crashed the net hard and often. He used his strength to blast through the offensive zone when he couldn't use his speed and he opened up a lot of space to set up teammates by doing so. I really liked the implication and the physical aspect of his game tonight. He also showed his smartness again with good puck distribution.

QUE #94 W Sorensen, Nick (2013) – It wasn't a very noticeable Nick Sorensen that was on the ice as far as speed and skills are concerned, but a very effective one. He made smart plays all night long and made sure the puck was rolling quickly between him and his teammates. He showed good vision while moving the puck and always seemed in the right spot to make plays. Showed a very good release on the goal he scored on a one-timer from behind the net.

VIC #3 D Diaby, Jonathan (2013) – Fairly quiet night for Diaby. He didn't do anything wrong but wasn't outstanding either. He made some solid defensive plays at times and he missed timing on other occasions. His transition play was fine but a few mistakes were made (passing accuracy). He doesn't look as sharp as he was lately. Corresponds to the time when Victoriaville brought in enforcer Sawyer Hannay to take on the fighting duty. Diaby is still effective, but more discrete in the physical department.

VIC #57 LW Veilleux, Tommy (2013) – His game plan was pretty clear for the night: hit and disturb. He brought a lot of intensity and tried to play into the heads of Quebec's players. He was able to get Etchegary off his game as he got ejected in the third period.

March 9, 2013, Gatineau Olympiques vs. Chicoutimi Saguenéens (QMJHL)

GAT #27 LW Emile Poirier (2013) – Though he didn't have the same output as yesterday, Poirier played another strong game tonight. Stride is still a concern, his upper body and arms sway too much when he skates which compromised his balance, but on the upside that also made him more unpredictable to cover. Skates much better with the puck than without it, the minute it hits his tape he gets the legs going. Showed a lot of speed up the wing and down the outside, not a power forward by any means but did a good job hanging onto the puck when pressured. Backchecked well with a good active stick but had trouble in his defensive zone where he was guilty of chasing the play on numerous occasions. Scrapped towards the end of the game, which I wouldn't have expected from him. Not much of a fighter but good to see him stand up for his teammate.

CHI #27 LC Laurent Dauphin (2013) – Played a very strong all-around game and lacked any noticeable flaws. Stickhandling is high-end and poised, can buy time with handles along the half wall and make guys miss bringing the puck up ice. Good at dealing with traffic and unafraid to take the puck to the net front from the corners or behind the net. Battled hard though he was overpowered on a few occasions. Still very lanky with plenty of room to get stronger. Worked hard on the forecheck and competed for pucks in 50/50 battles. Played the body in all three zones, though he doesn't quite have the bulk to damage with contact. Backchecked hard and fully though he overcommitted badly on two occasions and missed coverage on the trailer. Defensive coverage was strong overall. Made some nice passes though he was mostly depended on to carry the mail and had a lot of success in that role. Good wrister. Had a heroic shorthanded shift where he took a puck off the wrist in his zone blocking a shot, lost both gloves in the process, picked up his stick and gained possession, went end-to-end barehanded, and found Guillaume Asselin in front with a great pass. Great competitor.

CHI #28 LC Félix Plouffe (Passed over twice) – '93 birthdate but he had a really nice game. Big, strong two-way forward. Used his reach and body well, was strong on the penalty kill and in his own zone. Good skater for his size, hunched forward but got a lot out of his legs. Smart with puck though he lacked real finesse. Made good decisions in the offensive zone. Good cycle positioning and forecheck. Assuming he goes undrafted again, could be a flier as a potential fourth liner.

Mar 9, 2013, Swift Current Broncos vs. Brandon Wheat Kings (WHL)

SWI # 2, D, Heatherington, Dillon (2013) Heatherington is able to make a god pass up out of the zone to start the breakout and showed nice speed and skating to rush the puck up the ice. He was physical and used his body well to rub his man out along the boards and take the puck. He got his stick down in lanes to block passes and breakup plays for the opposition and also used his sick to knock the puck away from them. He was picking off passes in the neutral zone and protected the puck well from the opposition's pressure in his own end. He also had a nice hard shot from the point on the power play to score.

SWI # 10, C, Cave, Colby (2013) Cave got the puck in deep to the offensive zone on some pretty simple dump-in plays off the rush and was moving the puck around well on the power play in the offensive zone to set up a shot from the point for a goal. He is pretty calm and patient with the puck as he likes to make the safe plays and battled well for the pucks along the boards. He is able to take a hit and hold on to the puck but needs to hit the net on his chances from the high slot. He was forcing turnovers on the fore-check with a good work ethic but at times in the offensive zone was taking weak outside shots rather than moving the puck to a teammate in a more dangerous scoring area. There were also times when he was under pressure he tried to make a play in the neutral zone rather than just getting the puck in deep and he has to try to make the safe plays as often as possible to be most effective.

SWI # 12, C, Merkley, Jay (2013) Merkley had a great hustle for loose pucks and was battling really nicely for them along the boards. He made a good centering pass for a man out front on the power play and had another fantastic cross-ice pass to find a man down low right next to the net for a tap-in goal. He did a really nice job of pressuring the point and went down showing a willingness to block shots. He also pressured the point on the penalty kill to force turnovers and get the puck out of the zone, but has to watch the offensive zone turnovers forcing passes through the opposition. He also needs to move the puck when he has an open man available in the slot rather than taking an outside low-chance shot from the side-boards.

BRN # 2, D, Pulock, Ryan (2013) Pulock was able to rush the puck up the ice into the offensive zone with ease to get to the high slot for a shot and was able to get some nice hard shots through to the net, however he needs to hit the net on his shot opportunities with more consistency. He made a really nice pass through the neutral zone to lead a man into the offensive zone and he stepped in on a pinch to keep the attack and cycle alive. In his own end however he stepped back a bit too much towards his net giving the shooter too much space to get off a good shot attempt.

BRN # 7, D, Roy, Eric (2013) Roy made some good moves to try to get to the high slot for a shot but he can't turn the puck over trying to dangle his way through the opposition. He stepped into the slot to pick up a loose puck and put an excellent shot on net to score and he was able to skate the puck into the offensive zone, but needs to watch the turnovers again just skating through the opposition. He is calm with the puck and was for the most part distributing the puck well through the neutral zone and into the offensive end as well, however he missed his target on a few of his long breakout passes. He was also able to get the cycle going in the offensive zone.

BRN # 15, LW, Palmer, Jack (2013) Palmer got the puck in deep on some pretty simple dump-in plays off the rush and he put nice pressure on the puck carrier in the offensive zone to force turnovers. He was hustling well to get on loose pucks and used his body effectively to gain the inside track to the puck. He did an excellent job of reading the play to pick off a turnover in the neutral zone then he distributed the puck well on the rush up the ice. He went for a hit pretty aggressively in his own end along the boards and the opposition spun off it pretty easily then drove the net to score. He put good pressure on the point in his own end.

BRN # 23, C, McGauley, Tim (2013) McGauley got to the slot to pick up a loose pucks and put a nice quick shot on net. He protected the puck nicely along the wall on the cycle and put some excellent pressure on the puck carrier, then used his stick to force turnovers. He distributed the puck well on the rush through the neutral zone however was taking long shots on the rush with options available. He needs to watch the offensive zone turnovers on puck mishandles and by trying to force passes through the opposition.

BRN # 26, LW, Maguire, Gordie (2013) Maguire displayed nice strength and puck protection along the boards to get the cycle going in deep in the offensive zone and he went to the net to pick up a loose puck and rebound for a nice easy goal. He showed good speed on the wide drive but has to watch the turnovers on puck mishandles in the offensive zone.

FINAL SCORE: 3-2 Swift Current Broncos

Mar 9, 2013, Vancouver Giants vs. Victoria Royals (WHL)

VAN#26 LW, Vickerman, Taylor(2014) Big winger who had one of his best games as a Giant this season. Looks so much more confident out on the ice, and was rewarded with more ice time as a result. For most of the year, Vickerman really struggled to do anything with the puck, and basically just skated up and down the ice and made almost no impact in games. Tonight, he was strong on the forecheck and good along the boards. He made good plays with the puck and created some chances around the net. A big player for a 16 year old, but still needs to work on his foot speed in general.

VAN#17 RW, Houck, Jackson(2013) Physical player played with a lot of energy tonight and really made a difference for the team. Had a particularly physical period in the 1st and made a difference in the forecheck. Showed his competence around the net by scoring a goal off of a rebound by the far post. Puck was bouncing but Houck managed to control it and a get a quick shot off. Nice presence around the net all game too. Was rewarded with an empty net goal at the end of the game with his good forechecking. Was more effective tonight because Victoria's defensemen were not very quick to move the puck.

VAN#44 LD, Geertsen, Mason(2013) Big, tough defensemen who has had better games before. Definitely needed to manage the puck better tonight and committed too many turnovers. Tried to move the puck too quickly at times. Played his usual physical game in the defensive zone tonight, but could have been smarter without the puck tonight. Tried to do a little too much with his physicality and got out of position a few times.

VIC#5 LD, Kanzig, Keegan(2013) A towering defenseman played a quiet, average game tonight. Very strong along the boards and was a dominating presence with board battles. Did not really stand out with his physical play in the slot, and did not make any glaring mistakes tonight. Just a simple game and did not try to do too much. Kept it very simple with the puck, but could take some time to look for a pass instead of trying to go glass and out so often, especially when he has time. Not a very good skater, but was able to make it up with his long reach throughout the game. Questionable hockey sense that will probably get exploited at the pro level in the future.

VIC#20 LC, Fisher, Logan(2013) 2 way center who was on the 4th line tonight and did very little to impact the game. Does not think the game very well, and does not do anything particularly well with and without the puck. A good skater for his size, and works hard, but questionable skill and hockey sense. Needs to keep his stick on the ice for outlet passes. On a couple of breakouts, a defenseman who pass him the puck but he had his stick in the air and just missed the passes.

VIC#22 LW, Crunk, Taylor(2013) Good skating forward who showed inconsistency with his play with the puck tonight. A hard worker in his own end and not afraid to use his body. Made some nice plays with the puck in the offensive zone, but there were times when he would take unnecessary chances and turn the puck over. Not a great stickhandler either.

Scouts Notes: Vancouver's young players have made some big strides in their game, starting with winger Taylor Vickerman. Definitely a player that may be able to to rise up the draft rankings for 2014 if he can improve his skating, strength and continue to gain confidence in his game. 15 year old Alec Baer for the Giants looked great again. Impressed with his play without the puck in his own end. Another player to watch for 2014 on the Giants is defenseman Arvin Atwal. Not particularly great at anything, but brings a good package of toughness and speed. Needs to work on his play with the puck, but has gotten better.

FINAL SCORE: 3-1 Vancouver

Mar 10, 2013, Youngstown Phantoms vs. Green Bay Gamblers (USHL)

YNG # 8, C, Brown, Cam (2013) Brown displayed fantastic speed and hands to find lanes to rush the puck up on an end-to-end rush, get to the slot and put on an excellent shot from scoring position. He showed his amazing speed again skating the puck up out of his own end on the penalty kill and had great agility with the puck to create some space from the opposition. He was able to get a cycle started in deep in the offensive zone and opened up nicely in the high slot to take a pass and put a good shot on net. There were times when he was trying to force passes through the opposition when spotting an open man next to the net.

YNG # 16, LW, Evancho, Zach (2013) Evancho put good pressure and physicality on the fore-check. He was going hard to the net looking for loose pucks and rebounds and got to the slot to open up, take a pass and put a good shot on off the rush. He was opening up well in the high slot as well to put one-timers on net.

YNG # 21, D, Mackey, Kyle (2013) Mackey displayed great strength and puck protection to be able to take a hit and still move the puck up out of his own zone. He didn't have the hardest shot but got it through to the net from the point, but needs to watch the turnovers up along the boards in the neutral zone.

YNG # 27, C, Stork, Luke (2013) Stork did a great job of getting the puck in deep to start the cycle, and stuck to a fairly simple dump and chase style of game. He was challenging the puck carrier at the point, got in lanes and showed a willingness to block shots. He did however, have an odd-man rush opportunity and mishandled the puck, losing it and the opportunity all together.

GBG # 5, D, Oloffson, Gustav (2013) Oloffson made some pretty nice passes to start the rush on the breakout. He has a great shot from the point on the power play that found the net down low to get tipped and the team scored, then later got his shot through from the point again and it was tipped and the team scored. He used his stick well to keep the opposition to the perimeter and got his stick down in lanes to pick off passes on the penalty kill then clear it out of the zone. He has to watch the bad turnovers in dangerous areas in his own zone, and he also mishandled the puck a few times resulting in turnovers.

GBG # 16, C, Weiss, Mathew (2013) Weiss followed up the play nicely to pick up a rebound in the slot for a good shot opportunity. He got a good cycle started by moving the puck down low then going to the net with his stick down and made a nice pass to set-up a point shot for a goal. He did an excellent job of using his stick to force turnovers then move the puck up the ice on the rush to create a good opportunity and put good pressure on the fore-check as well. He got down to block a hard shot from the point but needs to watch some of his neutral zone turnovers.

GBG # 23, D, Gross, Jordan (2013) Gross was able to gain the offensive zone then get to the high slot to put a good shot on net. He was holding the offensive line extremely effectively to keep the attack alive, was distributing the puck well on the power play to find an open man down low and got a nice shot through from the point that the team batted in to score. He had a good clear on the penalty kill but has to watch some of the turnovers just throwing the puck up around the boards and also on long passes up the ice trying to start the breakout.

FINAL SCORE: 6-3 Green Bay Gamblers

March 13, 2013, New Jersey Hitmen vs. Middlesex Islanders (EJHL Finals Game 1)

ISL #12 LC Zach Sanford (2013) – Can't believe how much better he is now than he was in the fall. Poise with the puck continues to grow. Showed deceptively quick hands and a keen eye, making smart passes and navigating traffic well. Was strong on his stick and his skates, making him very difficult to knock off the puck. Made good decisions in outnumbered attack situations and showed surprising finesse with successful skill moves. Threw a few outstanding hits on the forecheck and in the neutral zone. Skating still needs work as he's very choppy with his feet. Other than that, he's fairly complete.

ISL #44 Luke Kirwan (2016) – Not a great game. His performance illustrated some of his shortcomings. A very talented player no doubt and already effectively uses his size, reach, and stickhandling ability, but had a hard time today getting anything going offensively, particularly when it came to utilizing his teammates. Forced the play much too often. Forechecked and backchecked hard but reads were off. Got beat physically by better-positioned, but not necessarily bigger, players. Showed good skill in 1-on-1 situations. Will be a hell of a player, still putting it all together.

Scout's Notes: Was not impressed with Islanders defenseman Dakota Ford (2013) in previous viewings, but he had a nice game today. Skating looked improved and he brought a nice physical element.

March 13 2012, Gatineau Olympiques @ Rimouski Océanic, (QMJHL)

GAT #11 RW, Kielly, Kameron (2014): Plays a well-rounded 2-way game for a 16 years old. Lacking speed, but has a good reach and uses it well to take away pucks from opponents, was a threat on a couple of occasions in plays around the net, strong on skates and protecting the puck well. His decisions were good with and without the puck. He doesn't have a particularly good skillset but his passing skills are pretty good.

GAT #27 LW, Poirier, Émile (2013): A game with high and lows like most of the times I've seen him play this year. He sees the play develop so well and can play in all situations because of that, penalty killing or powerplay. He showed the tremendous speed and acceleration he possesses, distancing easily even good skaters on Rimouski's D. He loves to bring the puck on slowly on the boards and then taking his speed with one stride cutting in front of the net trying to beat goaltenders with a quick backhand to forehand move. His short bursts of speed are nothing short of exceptional, rarely gets matched by a D when he uses it. I like when he uses those good instincts and bursts of speed to cause turnovers and press opponents in forecheck (neutral zone or offensive zone). He still has a tendency to cheat in order to get free chances on breakaways and odd-man rushes. He has a pretty good skill set and has no problem handling pucks through sticks and skates but gave up on a couple of plays where I would've liked to see him give a second or third effort. He played a game where he didn't want to get hit and when that happened, lost the puck, wants to play a high pace game with space in neutral zone for him to get speed.

RIM #3 D, Kostalek, Jan (2013): A strong presence on the back end. One of the most physical games I've seen Kostalek play. He can play that style safely because of the hockey sense he possesses. He is solid on skates and has great core strength for a 17 years old. Consistency is sometimes a problem for young players, not in the case of Kostalek who's just steady shifts after shifts. Not afraid of getting hit to make a play, he has good puck control and will rarely miss a teammates on a breakout pass. Turnovers are rarely created by Kostalek. He is not a very quick player, but uses stick positioning and little details to control opponents that are quicker than him and keep them to the outside. I don't think he has a huge offensive potential except on the powerplay where he might get points because of his good puck moving abilities and slapshot, but is great in his own zone.

RIM #23 C, Gauthier, Frédérik (2013): Very quiet game for the big center. Lacked energy and intensity. He still did what makes him great, which means getting back in his own zone deep, helping D's, blocking shots and using that big frame to get the puck out, but offensively did almost nothing. Pressure was coming quick and hard on him and when he's not jumping on his feet and lacking energy, his major weakness, skating becomes even worse. He was gliding a lot and seemed out of breathe for a vast majority of the game. But even in bad games, he is willing to do the simple things in his own zone and pay the price for his team, which is a good sign.

RIM #30 G, Desrosiers, Philippe (2013): Strong showing again. Was great at tracking pucks through traffic and especially controlling his rebounds, he absorbs pucks so well even coming from hard shots. He made some great saves at the end of the game when Gatineau were pressing hard to get the tying goal, showing good concentration. I like how he plays the puck with confidence, communicates with teammates and makes good passes, not afraid to take his time before making the good play. Technically the most solid goalie for this year's NHL Draft coming from the Q, such a good butterfly style.

March 13-15, 2013, Beantown Spring Classic (Marlboro, MA)

Very strong tournament with a lot of quality talent on hand and a good quality of play, though players understandably shied away from intense physical contact. Got a look at the pre-draft kids, who were mostly 97s, but spent most of my time there focused on the draft division, which was largely 94s, 95s, and 96s.

F Thomas Aldworth (2013) – Liked Aldworth's game, have not seen him play poorly this year. Showed off good hands and puck protection, he's a good hybrid of power and skill. Worked well on the forecheck and showed an active stick in all three zones. Good skater with a lot of jump. Needs to bulk up but he plays a style suited to the pros and college.

RD Connor Brassard (2013) – Solid if unspectacular. Smooth skater with good hands. Outlet passes were intelligent. Good decisions with the puck overall. Carried when given space and got rid of it without giving it away when pressured. Responsible defensively, took care of his end first.

F Ryan Cloonan (2013) – The Junior Bruins forward is undoubtedly skilled but his drawbacks were very apparent today when playing outside his system and with teammates unfamiliar with his habits. To be direct about it, he's just not a team player. Floated around in his own zone waiting for his team to gain possession, either following the puck unassertively or just hanging out near the blueline. The moment he got the puck, he was magically involved again, but too often tried to do too much by himself and got leveled on numerous occasions. Great skating, great hands, but he has a long way to go before he's considered anywhere near a pro quality talent. His game has not changed much since I first since him at the start of the EJHL season.

F Eddie Ellis (2013) – Seems to have really regressed from the start of the season. Skating today was awful. Lacked any kind of jump or quickness. Decision-making was poor and didn't seem to have a good awareness of other players on the ice. Offensive game was much too simple with weak perimeter shots and low percentage cross-crease passes that didn't get through. He has a lot more skill than he showed. I'm not sure what's going on here.

F Anthony Florentino (2013) – Played well. Some offensive upside in joining rushes when appropriate but mostly held back and kept it simple. Smart reads, good coverage in his end, physical when necessary and strong on his skates. No glaring mistakes.

F Daniel Lafontaine (2013) – Really buzzed out there. Great skater, very agile. Feet and hands were deceptive on the rush and he was able to put dangerous pucks on net from outside the dots. Showed off good offensive instincts with smart passing and good positioning. Went hard to the net without the puck and retrieved loose pucks with vigor. Strong work on the forecheck.

LD Connor Light (2013) – Played well in his own end with strong defensive zone positioning and good play in front of his net. I have had some doubts about his offensive upside and he did nothing to dispel them. Can carry the puck and pinches at the right times but I don't think he has great instincts for the offensive side of the game. Still an intriguing prospect with his combination of size and skating.

F Brian Pinho (2013) – Liked Pinho's game. A skill guy but not soft. Was very strong on the puck with a lot of poise and patience. Difficult to dispossess through center and along the boards. Liked to carry and create offense. Made some highly skilled passes and flashed a good wrist shot.

LD Wiley Sherman (2013) – At times, the hulking two-way defenseman looked a step ahead of everybody else. Awareness was outstanding, he played intelligent hockey. Nasty in front of his net and physical on the boards. Has a strong stride and moved very smoothly. Scored on a bullet wrister from the point through traffic. Smart outlets from his own zone. Showed no real weaknesses.

RD Connor Wynne (2014) – Offensive upside here but he had a tough go of it. Footwork against the rush was poor, needs to pay more attention to detail. Got crushed by a huge hit trying to do too much. Questions about his sense, but admittedly he was one of the younger guys playing in this division.

Scout's Notes: Other draft division players who impressed were two-way D Richard Boyd (2013), physical all-around D Ryan Segalla (2013), pesky F Corey Ronan (2014), and lanky but skilled F Eric Robinson (2013). Draft division players who did not help their stock were slow, hulking F Dwyer Tschantz (2013), who didn't show me enough to offset his lack of mobility; skill F Mitchell Allen (2013), whose decision-making was questionable; and EJHL star F Ryan Fitzgerald (2013), who tried to do too much and seemed overwhelmed by bigger players.

3/14 New Jersey Hitmen vs. Middlesex Islanders (EJHL Finals Game 2)

ISL #12 LC Zachary Sanford (2013) – Another strong game, though shortcomings were better illuminated today. Skating is inefficient and a concern. Also needs to learn to better use his size on the boards. Has the frame to be a power forward but lost too many battles. Tried to do too much with the puck overall. More effective when he focuses on playing a simple north-south game, rather than trying to create. Did show flashes but still very raw.

ISL #17 LD Dakota Ford (2013) – Had another strong game today. Passing was smart and safe, especially in his own zone. Outlets were smooth and receivable. Save for one whiffed clearance on the penalty kill, made no glaring mistakes with the puck. Showed some upside in joining the rush from time to time and showed off strong skating in the process. Covered the rush well and cleared his net front. Stick and head were active.

Scout's Notes: Luke Kirwan (2016) was a scratch for this one.

Mar 14, 2013, Cedar Rapids Roughriders vs. USNTDP U18 (USHL)

USA # 4, D, Butcher, Will (2013) Butcher started the game out by getting his shot through from the point on net that ended up scoring the team's 1st goal of the game. He had good speed rushing the puck up the ice to gain the offensive zone on an end-to-end rush and showed good patience with the puck waiting for a lane to open up to move the puck around. He read the play to pick off a turnover in the offensive zone, then walked into the slot to put a back-hander on net and score. He came down low on the rush off the wing and put a great shot on that rang off the post from in tight.

USA # 7, C, Compher, J.T. (2013) Compher displayed excellent strength and puck protection on the wall to hold on to the puck then make a centering pass to find an open man out front for an excellent opportunity. He had really good speed and hustle for loose pucks, made some good passes to find an open man in the slot and was distributing the puck well on the rush through the neutral zone, then drove hard to the net with his stick down. He put good pressure on the puck carrier on the fore-check as well to force turnovers.

USA # 9, LW, Lewis, Anthony (2013) Lewis was able to pick off a turnover in the offensive zone and opened up really well in the slot to take a pass and put a good shot on net. He displayed great agility with the puck, was opening up on the rush to get a great shot on net from scoring position and got to the slot with the puck to put a quick shot on net. He decided to shoot on a good 2-on-1 opportunity that the goalie saved and also has to watch the turnovers trying to pass the puck through the opposition in the offensive zone.

USA # 19, RW, Kelleher, Tyler (2013) Kelleher has fantastic speed and agility on the rush, was distributing the puck well then going to the slot to open up for a shot from in tight. He made a nice pass to move the puck to an open man on the power play for a one-timer chance and has great agility to avoid the opposition's pressure and create some room to work with in the offensive zone. He followed up the play well to pick up a loose puck in the slot for a shot opportunity and made a really nice pass to spring a man into the offensive zone with good hands to get around the opposition on the rush and get to the slot to put shots on net from scoring position.

CED # 6, C, McLaughlin, Dylan (2013) McLaughlin was back-checking very well, battling hard for the puck and came back to tie up his man well. He put great pressure on the puck carrier, but has to watch the neutral zone turnovers.

CED # 15, LW, Petrash, Corey (2013) Petrash got a good cycle started in the offensive zone, doesn't have all the speed in the world but keeps to a simple game by getting the puck in deep, going hard to the net and battling for loose pucks and opportunities. He has to move the puck a bit quicker rather than holding on for too long and turning it over along the boards.

CED # 26, D, Kuster, Clark (2013) Kuster can both skate the puck up out of the zone to start the rush, or is able to make a good breakout pass to move it out as well. He was jumping down low into the slot to provide scoring options in the offensive zone off the rush. He tied his man up nicely on the back-check to take away the opposition's opportunity. He moved the puck up safely along the boards to get it out of the zone and is able to protect the puck and move it to avoid the opposition's pressure. He has a nice hard shot that he kept down low on target from the point that generated a nice rebound.

CED # 22, RW, Oglevie, Andrew (2013) Oglevie put nice pressure on the puck carrier on the fore-check, got the puck in deep to start the cycle and had great speed and moves to rush the puck up end-to-end to gain the offensive zone. He opened up nicely back-door on the power play for a good opportunity, but needs to pull the trigger and shoot the puck on his opportunity. He was weak on the puck as the last man back, turned the puck over and the opposition got a great opportunity on the play. He has to watch the turnovers up along the boards and needs to have more compete to win the puck battles along the boards. He was shooting into shin pads from the point and therefore needs to get his shot through to the net.

FINAL SCORE: 4-2 USNTDP U18

Mar 15, 2013, Dubuque Fighting Saints vs. Sioux City Musketeers (USHL)

DUB # 4, D, Downing, Mike (2013) Downing displayed some nice strength as he played the puck carrier with good physicality along the wall. He closed off his man nicely, forcing him into the boards and finished his hits along the wall. He is calm with the puck, moving it up pretty well to start the rush and was willing to come down low with the puck into the offensive zone to try to make a play to a teammate in front. He played the body well off the rush to keep the opposition to the outside and had a really good fight as well, he just needs to watch the neutral zone turnovers on breakout passes.

DUB # 24, RW, Kuhlman, Karson (2013) Kuhlman got the puck in deep off the rush and was hustling hard for loose pucks putting good pressure on the fore-check. He had a nice net-front presence in the offensive zone and was finishing his hits on the puck carrier along the boards. He got a pretty decent cycle going in deep in the offensive zone but has to watch the offensive zone turnovers trying to force passes through the opposition.

SIO # 3, D, Kapla, Michael (2013) Kapla did a nice job tying up his man along the boards to win a battle for the puck and was forcing his man to the outside, using his stick to knock the puck away from the opposition. He also used his stick very well to keep the opposition to the outside on the rush and deflect shots out of play. He was able to take a hit and still make a play to get the puck up out of the zone and can make a good breakout pass to start the rush. He is a Douglas Murray type player and would benefit by picking up his foot speed as he lost a few races to get to pucks and needs to get his shots through to the net with more consistency.

SIO # 5, D, Pionk, Neal (2013) Pionk has a nice shot from the point that he kept down low on net and was stepping into the slot to pick up a rebound for a good shot opportunity. He played his man with a good element of physicality and used his stick really well to poke the puck free from the opposition. He also played with great agility to twist away from the opposition to skate the puck up the ice and has good speed and hustle for loose pucks. He plays the body well to keep the opposition from gaining the inside track and was skating the puck up very effectively on an end-to-end rush to get to the slot for a good shot. He needs to watch the turnovers in his own end trying to get the puck up to the forwards and has to get his shot through to the net with more consistency.

SIO # 14, LW, Lacroix, Cedric (2013) Lacroix played with good speed, hustle and battle for the puck, pressuring the puck carrier really nicely. He protects the puck well, plays with a good energy and a nice work ethic and was coming back well to provide support in his own end. He did an excellent job of getting down in lanes to block shots from the point, forced turnovers by putting pressure on the fore-check and was battling to get to the front of the net. He battled hard on a wrap-around attempt trying to jam the puck in to the net from in tight and was reading the play to cover for his defenseman who was stepping up on the pinch.

SIO # 19, C, Guentzel, Jake (2013) Guentzel put some nice pressure and physicality on the fore-check and made a really good drop pass to create some room for a shot in the high slot. He has fantastic agility and puck protection to create room from the opposition then finds lanes to move the puck around in the offensive zone. He put some nice low shots on net to create rebounds for teammates driving hard to the net and made a good 2nd effort to get a rebound chance from the slot. He did a fantastic job of jumping in the air to pick off a turnover in the offensive zone, and then came in to get a shot from the slot to score. He was taking the puck from behind the net to walk out into the slot for a good shot attempt.

SIO # 22, LW, McGlynn, Conor (2013) McGlynn was putting great pressure and physicality on the fore-check and was finishing his hits nicely on the puck carrier. He protects the puck well from the opposition's pressure and was able to put a nice low shot on net on a 2-on-1 chance to try to generate a rebound for a man driving hard to the net. He had a good drive to the net with his stick down looking for loose pucks and rebounds and put some good physicality on the fore-check. He was however taking some long outside shots off the rush instead of moving the puck or using his big frame to drive the puck hard to the net.

SIO # 26, D, Heinrich, Blake (2013) Heinrich is able to make a good 1st pass out of the zone to start the breakout and got his shot through to the net from the point. He was able to skate the puck up the ice end-to-end to get it in deep to start the cycle and showed some nice strength to take a hit and hold on to the puck. He moved the puck down low to get the cycle started in deep in the offensive zone and was stepping up into the high slot to take a pass and put a great shot on net.

FINAL SCORE: 2-1 Sioux City

Mar 15, 2013, Red Deer Rebels vs. Edmonton Oil Kings (WHL)

RD#8 RD, Doetzel, Kayle(2013) Big physical defenseman who had a good game in his own zone tonight. Time and time again he would take hits to make a play. A calming presence from the backend, did a good job to clear pucks out of the zone when the team was in trouble defensively, and did a good job to clear the slot. Likes to use his body along the boards and is quite strong on his skates. Needs to manage the puck better with his outlet passes. Likes to go glass and out, but can learn to take his time and make outlet passes to his forwards instead. A good skater for his size, but can still improve his overall speed.

RD#11 LW, Millette, Cory(2013) Good skating forward who had some good moments offensively in the game. Possesses average stickhandling abilities, but he plays with confidence with the puck on his stick. Not afraid to try to deke opponents, and uses his quickness to his advantage. Had one good play where he faked a shot, froze the defenseman and went quickly around him off the wall to have a good lane to the net, but could not capitalize. Not overly big, but uses his body effectively to protect the puck. In the 3rd period, had one memorable play where he was actually able to fend off 2 opponents at once to have a lane to the net. Not all too reliable defensively, and did not receive PK time tonight.

RD#27 RW, Bellerive, Matt(2013) Another quick forward for Red Deer. Bellerive had an average game tonight in both ends of the ice. He is a very good skater who can get around the ice in a hurry. Showed off some good offensive creativity tonight. Looks confident with the puck on his stick, and is an above average playmaker. Needs to make decisions quicker at times though. Has a good release to his shots off the wing. Really needs to improve on his play along the walls.

EDM#23 LW, Kulda, Edgars(2013) Lightning quick forward who showed some good awareness without the puck today. Impressed with his defensive zone coverage and ability to get to the right areas around the ice consistently in both ends of the ice. Did not get much accomplished with the puck however. Was not afraid to block shots and be a dependable player. Needs to improve on his confidence with the puck and overall handling of it.

EDM#27 RC, Lazar, Curtis(2013) 2 way center who showed his high intelligence for the game and his good overall play. Had 3 excellent scoring chances in front of the net but just could not finish them off, was just robbed everytime by the opposing goaltender. Very good at finding open areas in coverage, and has a nice release to his shots. A good skater who got around the ice quite nicely. Not a playmaker by any means. So strong and determined along the boards. Rare to see him ever get beat for a puck at both ends of the ice. Played a ton on the PK, and did a good job to be in good position. Very good at faceoffs tonight. Compete level was very high in every shift that he played tonight.

EDM#37 RD, Mayo, Dysin(2014) Smooth puck moving defenseman had a very good game tonight. Showed some very nice poise with the puck despite pressure from forecheckers. Just needs to improve on his outlet passes. Not afraid to skate with the puck and push the pace. Good job at angling throughout the game off the rush and kept opponents to the outside. Showed some good strength on his skates. Needs to use his stick better to take away lanes.

Scouts Notes: Edmonton was just too much to handle for Red Deer in the end. Came away impressed with Red Deer's Haydn Fleury tonight. Showed off all the tools to be a very good defenseman as a pro in the future. Particularly liked how he was able to get so many shots on net. Logged a ton of tough minutes for the Rebels. Curtis Lazar had a very good game, but only came away with an empty net goal. Could have had a few more. Impressed again with his play without the puck and compete level.

FINAL SCORE: 3-1 Edmonton

Mar 15, 2013, Vancouver Giants vs. Kelowna Rockets (WHL)

VAN#1 G, Lee, Payton(2014) A promising goaltender at the start of the season, today was a perfect example as to what has happened to Lee's confidence level as the season progressed. He did a good job to keep his team in games early in the season, but just was not able to do that at all as the season progressed, like tonight. His team committed a number of defensive mistakes and they needed Lee to shut the door, but failed to do so. Glove still looks strong, but too many goals are beating him through the 5 hole. Body language after goals against is not good, looks defeated after every one that goes in.

VAN#44 LD, Geertsen, Mason(2013) Really struggled defensively tonight. Looked out of place, and just not focused to play the game. Long pre-game ceremony might have been a negative factor to his game tonight. Looked half a step slower than usual, and was just chasing the play all night, and was thoroughly burned by Kelowna's quick forwards.

KEL#2 RD, Lees, Jesse(2013) Puck moving defenseman had one of his better games in his own end tonight. Made a number of key blocks throughout the game, and held his ground tonight and did not chase the puck as much. Played on the left side for most of the game and had a tough time adjusting to it, but did a fairly good job off the rush. Still looks a little lost in the slot in regards to coverage, but has improved immensely since the start of the season. A good skater and moves the puck quite well. Not overly creative with the puck, but showed good poise and passing abilities.

KEL#4 RD, Bowey, Madison(2013) Lightning quick defenseman who has had better games this season. Really struggled moving the puck tonight, and just was not crisp with his passes. Also made a couple bad decisions with the puck that led to bad turnovers. Took a bad holding penalty along the walls because he stopped moving his feet, something that rarely happens with him because of his skating abilities in tight areas. Perfect example of his struggles tonight came when he got out of the penalty box, he had to cover as a forward, and in the middle of the play in his own end, decided to gamble and go for a line change. The man he was covering was all alone in the slot and scored as a result. Possesses a good shot from the point, and good vision as well.

KEL#24 RC, Baillie, Tyson(2014) A player to watch for the 2014 NHL Draft, Baillie showed his very good skill, hockey sense and willingness to play a physical game tonight despite his lack of size. Made a number of good plays with and without the puck that created scoring chances. Showed nice patience with the puck all night long, and did a good job to spin off his checks along the walls and buy some time to make plays. Loves to drive the net with the puck. Not afraid to mix it up with anybody. For his size, Baillie could certainly improve his overall speed.

Scouts Notes: Vancouver was clearly outclassed by Kelowna tonight. They made mistakes after mistakes and paid for it in the end. Nashville's draft pick Colton Sissons played a great game at both ends of the ice tonight, and showed his potential to be a very good 3rd line centre as a pro one day. Kelowna's goaltender Jackson Whistle played a very good game tonight. He faced 41 shots and while most of them were from the outside, he was great when he had to be. Jesse Lees has made good strides to his game, but I still question his defensive abilities. Don't know if he will last in the professional level.

FINAL SCORE: 6-2 Kelowna

Mar 16, 2013, Sioux City Musketeers vs. Sioux Falls Stampede (USHL)

SIF # 8, RW, Mansfield, Ian (2013) Mansfield was able to read the play well to pick off a turnover in the offensive zone to get a good cycle started. He had nice speed on the rush to drive the puck wide and throw it on net, kept down low for a great rebound opportunity for a teammate right in front of the net. He was able to get his stick in lanes in the defensive zone to block pass attempts and he put good pressure on the puck carrier. He did however turn the puck over in the offensive zone by trying to dangle his way through the opposition in deep and was not protecting the puck very effectively.

SIF # 16, C, Valesano, Connor (2013) Valesano was making the simple chip plays to get the puck up out of the zone and was hustling hard to get on loose pucks to help draw a penalty. He was playing a dump and chase simple style of hockey, put some pretty good physicality on the puck carrier on the fore-check and opened up well on the rush beside the net to take a pass and put a good shot on. He move the puck to a trailing player on the rush then went hard to the net and his teammate scored on the rebound, and just needs to watch some of the turnovers through the neutral zone along the boards on the breakout plays.

SIF # 17, RW, Calderone, Tony (2013) Calderone protected the puck well in deep in the offensive zone and was able to get a pretty nice cycle started. He played a simple dump and chase style, was clearing the puck well on the penalty kill and went hard to the net for loose pucks as he battled hard for the chances. He had a nice net-front presence to get in the goaltender's face to allow his defenseman to score on a point shot, but does not have much speed to his game and was taking long outside shots on the rush when he had a teammate and options available to him.

SCM # 3, D, Kapla, Michael (2013) Kapla came down into the high slot early in this game to take a pass and put a great shot on net. He did a really good job holding the offensive line, had a great shot from the point that was able to find the net and later was able to score on a nice hard point shot to tie up the game in the 3rd. He was jumping up on the rush for a 2-on-1 opportunity but missed his target on the pass across to a teammate. Later he was able to find a lane to move the puck cross-ice on the rush for a good one-timer chance and he had good agility to spin and avoid the opposition's pressure before moving the puck up out of the zone on the breakout.

SCM # 5, D, Pionk, Neal (2013) Pionk was forcing his man to the boards in the defensive zone and played him with a pretty good element of pressure and physicality. He was able to make a pretty good breakout pass to start the rush through the neutral zone and was distributing the puck well in the offensive zone on the power play as well. He was willing to jump up to join the rush and get the puck in deep into the offensive zone, was skating the puck up the ice pretty well and protected it from the opposition's pressure.

SCM # 19, C, Guentzel, Jake (2013) Guentzel has really nice hands and moves to skate the puck up the ice on an end-to-end rush and made a really nice little pass to move the puck to a man down low going hard to the net for a great opportunity. He was protecting the puck well along the boards, got a good cycle game going in deep and made a really great power forward move to cut towards the net off the wide drive to beat a defenseman to the net. He moved the puck around well on the odd-man rush, made a fantastic pass to find an open man down low next to the net and used his body so effectively to protect the puck and then draw a penalty. He played with a great compete to win puck battles, made some nice breakout passes to start the rush but needs to watch some of his neutral zone turnovers.

SCM # 28, LW, Torok, Tomas (2013) Torok displayed really good strength, puck protection and agility to avoid the opposition's pressure. He drove well to the net with his stick down to take a pass and put a good shot on and provided some nice support to teammates to help out in board battles. He was physical on the fore-check, made a really nice short pass on the rush into the offensive zone to move the puck to an open man in the slot and was protecting the puck well to get in towards the net for a good chance. He made some great moves to cut to the middle for a nice shot from the high slot that got through to the net, battled so well for the puck and was distributing it nicely on his odd-man rush chances.

FINAL SCORE: 3-2 Sioux Falls Stampede

March 17 2013, Rimouski Océanic @ Québec Remparts, (QMJHL)

QUE #10 LW, Duclair, Anthony (2013): Up and down game, I don't know if it's Grigorenko's impact on him, but he stopped playing like in the last games I saw him which means a way more simpler game with less fanciness and more speed. He had good shifts but also terrible shifts. On his good shifts, he used his speed and core strength to protect the puck gaining soft ice quicker than his opponents could adjust to it. He showed the amazing offensive hockey IQ he possesses, moving quickly to an open spot after a pass. His explosiveness is amazing, he got a penalty shot using it and also a great chance cutting in front of the Rimouski goalie after shifting easily Rimouski's D. He has great scoring instincts. That's the good part. There was also the lazy part, losing battles on the walls trying to take the easy way out of those battles, turnovers caused off bad passes from near the blue lines and trying to go through players with fancy moves in offensive zone and using purely skills. He is not willing to sacrifice the body or simplify the play to a maximum in order to succeed in his own zone, still maturity to get.

QUE #19 C, Etchegary, Kurt (2013): Played a gritty, steady game and didn't hesitate to come at his teammate's defense at the end of the game when he got hit from behind. He's not afraid of the physical play and will get on his opponent's nerves from times to times. Work ethic is great and even though he's a little bit undersized he was able to win battles against bigger players. He lacks explosiveness and skills to play on an offensive line; he was playing with Dclair in the game and didn't have the skillset and speed to keep up with him. His defensive hockey sense is very good, kind of player that looks good within a tight system. He still got some good chances using good positioning in front of the net, but it was mostly a quiet offensive game for Etchegary.

QUE #20 D, MacIntyre, Duncan (2014): I like what I see from the Nova Scotian game after game. Very fluid in all his movements has a great footwork and can follow most players because of his lateral movements. He closes gaps well and has a solid effective breakout pass. He is confident, anticipates well, solid physically even though he's undersized for a D.

QUE #73 RW, Erne, Adam (2013): He played a tremendous game. He was absolutely fantastic laying the body on the forecheck, in neutral zone, in defensive zone, recording 8 official hits but I thought he had even more than that. All his hits were legal, no contact with the head. He blasted Kostalek and Gagné with two great bodychecks and changed the momentum of the game with those hits as Rimouski were dominating Québec with their transition in the first half of the game. Erne went out of his way on a couple of occasions to hit especially in his defensive zone which could have cost a scoring chance, but you can't deny the effort and energy he brought in. He was able to take away tons of pucks from Rimouski's possession with great backchecks, lifting sticks and displaying super speed and relentless work. He showed good finishing touches on both goals, tipping a puck from a blue-line shot and then scoring on a one-time shot after a superb feed from behind the goal by Grigorenko. He was dominant in all 3-zones and showed also nice vision on a chance he created for Sorensen, winning strongly a battle on the boards in defensive zone and then finding Sorensen all-alone in neutral zone with a backhand feed. He dangles the puck so quickly, great rolling movement of the wrists which enables him to bring the puck from backhand to the forehand very quickly. Great power forward game.

QUE #94 LW, Sorensen, Nick (2013): Lacked energy and intensity in the first half of the game. Gave away the puck a couple of times trying to get the puck out using the center of the ice and being weak in physical confrontations. In the 3rd period, he was great, using speed and explosiveness to make himself available and gain the high slot with ease. He is pretty elusive when he skates like he did in the 3rd and has a natural offensive hockey sense, finds teammates well and even though he doesn't have an elite skillset, his puck protection gives him some time to execute his plays. See-saw game.

RIM #3 D, Kostalek, Jan (2013): Got blasted by Adam Erne behind his net, but then continued his shift and played well, without retaliating showing good toughness. He likes to be aggressive in gap coverage, cut down space quickly go in neutral zone to pope check a free puck and even in coverage he likes to put physical pressure quickly on opponents and bring them to the outside which is a style I like. He still does some mistakes but when he gets more mature, quicker and bigger it's going to be an even more effective style of play. He takes good decisions offensively with the puck, shooting the puck on net when he knows he won't create turnovers. He needs to be better in his footwork has he got beat by Anthony Duclair a couple of times, getting caught taking too much time doing his pivot and also at taking decisions with the puck in his own zone when there's pressure on him. On a control breakout, he's going to take a smart decision, but with pressure, he gave the puck away rimming the puck where there was already a Québec player or trying dangerous plays in front of his net. He needs more composure in his own zone and doesn't need to start panicking when there's pressure on him, needs to stay heads up and choose better plays.

RIM #23 C, Gauthier, Frédérik (2013): He played a very good game, being his usual self in his own zone which means excellent, always getting in good position to help his D, starting the play from his own zone, never cheating and always being proactive and not reactive to what's going on, anticipating so well. He got a goal off a great rush where he displayed good top speed, nice puck protection on the backhand to create a 2-on-1 and a good five-hole shot to score the goal. He corrected a lot of his teammates' mistakes with his defensive backchecks and long reach, taking away space from Québec players with hit. He also used the long reach to gain the slot well and that 6,04 frame helps him generate options offensively too. On the PK, he is reliable and maybe lacking explosiveness on the short bursts of speed, but the smarts will make up for it 9 times out of 10.

Mar. 19, 2013, Tri-City Storm vs. Sioux City Musketeers (USHL)

SIO # 3, D, Kapla, Michael (2013) Kapla was able to take a pass and put a good shot on from the high slot. He has a nice hard shot that he kept down low from the point, however needs to be able to hit the net with more consistency. He showed excellent patience to wait for a lane to open up to move the puck to an open man down low right in front of the net, however at other times was trying to force passes through the opposition resulting in turnovers. He was distributing the puck well in the offensive zone and was willing to jump down low on the attack to provide a scoring option in the slot.

SIO # 19, C, Guentzel, Jake (2013) Guentzel displayed great hands to get by defenders on the wide drive then moved the puck to a trailing player in the high slot. He put great pressure on the fore-check to force a turnover and move the puck to an open man out front. He drove hard to the net with his stick down, got a good cycle game going in deep in the offensive zone and was distributing the puck well on the rush. He opened up next to the net to take a pass and score from a tough angle and also took a pass on a 2-on-1 chance to score on a nice shot. He had great battle, compete and puck protection in the corners and moved the puck around very effectively to create chances in the offensive zone. He used his fantastic hands to get around defenders then move the puck to an open man down low for a goal on a nice shot and was also able to find a lane to move the puck cross-ice for a goal on a good pass He then made another really good pass to spot a trailing man on the rush that the team scored on after he drove hard to the net and took the defenseman with him to open up a lane for the man with the puck.

SIO # 22, C, McGlynn, Conor (2013) McGlynn possesses great speed and strength while protecting the puck to rush it up the ice end-to-end. He showed really nice physicality on the puck carrier and on the fore-check to force a turnover and create a good opportunity. He was able to make a really nice pass on the rush to lead a man with speed into the offensive zone and was driving hard to the net with his stick down.

SIO # 28, LW, Torok, Tomas (2013) Torok did a good job going to the net hard looking for loose pucks and rebounds. He had a really big hit on the fore-check, but can't cross the line and take a penalty in doing so. He also got in a fight and after putting up a bit of a battle was thrown down to the ice.

TRI # 7, D, Cecere, Garrett (2013) Cecere skates pretty decently and was coming down into the high slot to provide scoring options. He made a pretty nice 1st pass up out of the zone and was willing to jump up on the rush to join the attack. He has to watch the turnovers up along the boards in his own end and also had a bad turnover in the neutral zone that resulted in a goal for the opposition.

TRI # 8, C, Moore, Trevor (2013) Moore had pretty good speed through the neutral zone and was able to rush the puck end-to-end to gain the offensive zone. He distributed the puck nicely and was driving hard to the net to take a pass in tight for a good opportunity. He was getting to the net looking for loose pucks and rebounds and opened up well for a one-timer on the power play that he fanned on, but the puck somehow still found the back of the net. He had really nice hands and moves on the rush through the neutral zone and had a really good pass to move the puck to a trailing player in the high slot off the rush. He needs to watch the neutral zone turnovers as well as the turnovers in his own end right up the middle.

TRI # 10, RW, Eastman, Kyle (2013) Eastman had a nice net-front presence and was able to find a lane to make a really good pass and find an open man in the high slot. He opened up nicely next to the net for provide a scoring option down low, but was taking long outside shots off the rush instead of driving the puck to the net.

TRI # 11, C, Cotton, Jason (2013) Cotton was able to take the puck off the side boards and walk into the slot to put a good shot on and score from a great position. He was getting the puck in deep off the rush, showed great physicality on the fore-check, finishing his hits on the puck carrier and pretty much stuck to a pretty simple dump and chase, cycle style of hockey.

FINAL SCORE: 7-4 Sioux City Musketeers

Mar. 19, 2013, Youngstown Phantoms vs. USNTDP U18 (USHL)

YNG # 16, RW, Evancho, Zach (2013) Evancho put good pressure on the puck carrier, was protecting the puck well along the wall and able to get it in deep on the rush. He was driving the puck wide while protecting it, but has to hit the net on his opportunity.

YNG # 21, D, Mackey, Kyle (2013) Mackey was able to make a good lead pass to start the rush out of the zone. He is calm with the puck; able to twist from the opposition's pressure nicely, however he let his man get away from him in front of the net to score an easy goal.

YNG # 27, RW, Stork, Luke (2013) Stork is able to skate the puck up the ice on the rush to get it in deep to start a cycle. He put some nice pressure on the puck carrier coming back to his own zone for good support and showed some excellent pressure and battle for the puck on the fore-check to force turnovers. He did however mishandle the puck through the neutral zone resulting in a turnover.

USA # 9, LW, Louis, Anthony (2013) Louis has fantastic hands that he used to weave in and out of defenders to get to the slot for a great shot, but hit the post on his opportunity. He has really quick hands, distributes the puck well on the rush and was finding lanes to move the puck cross-ice in the offensive zone. He displayed his hands, speed and puck protection on the wide drive, but missed the net on his opportunity from the outside. He was able to make a really nice no-look pass to find an open man in front of the net and did a good job coming back hard on the back-check to provide support.

USA # 15, RW, Hayden, John (2013) Hayden has great hands that he used to get in deep in the offensive zone with the puck. He was able to get to the slot to tip a point shot and score and displayed fantastic strength and puck protection on the rush to get in deep and start the cycle.

USA # 19, RW, Kelleher, Tyler (2013) Kelleher is best described by hands and puck distribution. He has fantastic hands that he used to dangle through the opposition on the rush, get to the slot and put a great back-hander on to score. He has good moves and agility in the neutral zone to avoid the opposition's pressure and was able to get the puck to the front of the net for a teammate who battled hard to score from in tight. He clearly has fantastic puck skills but at times tries to do too much on his own. He did a really good job opening up down low next to the net and was able to make great passes to find the open man down low. He needs to add some size and strength so that he's not knocked over so easily.

USA # 52, RW, MacInnis, Ryan (2014) MacInnis did a good job protecting the puck along the wall, has some great hands and moves but needs to watch the neutral zone turnovers holding on to the puck for too long. He had a nice net-front presence on the power play and got in a lane to block a shot from the point.

FINAL SCORE: 8-2 USNTDP U18

Mar. 21, 2013, Saskatoon Blades vs. Medicine Hat Tigers (WHL)

MED # 5, D, Lewington, Tyler (2013) Lewington uses his stick really well to keep the opposition to the outside and knock the puck away from them. He was also battling well in the corners for the puck and was able to get a cycle going by moving the puck down low in the offensive zone, however later on the play decided to pinch and got beat which allowed the opposition to rush the puck back up the ice. He showed nice agility and puck protection to avoid the opposition's pressure and then made a nice chip play to create some room and get the puck out of the zone. He was also able to get his shot through from the point.

MED # 7, D, Jensen, Spenser (2013) Jensen did a really good job of getting his stick in a lane to deflect the opposition's shot out of play. He was using his sick to keep the opposition to the outside, is calm with the puck and was moving it up out of the zone pretty well. He missed his target on some breakout passes through the neutral zone.

MED # 9, LW, Shinkaruk, Hunter (2013) Shinkaruk had a really nice wide drive and was getting the puck to the front of the net. He put good pressure on the fore-check and opened up really well in the high slot to provide a scoring option. He did a great job of lifting the opposition's stick to take the puck away and was able to start the rush and drive hard to the net. He has really nice hands to get by a defender on the wide drive in towards the net for a good shot and had a fantastic battle and compete for the puck along the boards. He had great speed to take the puck on a break then made an excellent backhand move to beat the goaltender for a nice goal and displayed really fantastic hands to cut in towards the net off the wide drive. There were many plays that he played on the perimeter and just threw the puck to the front of the net and was much more effective when he drove the puck towards the middle. He was walking out from behind the net to the high slot to put a shot on, but I would rather see him move the puck to a teammate in the scoring area.

MED # 22, C, Labelle, Chad (2013) Labelle was cycling the puck pretty well in deep in the offensive zone. He was protecting the puck very well and got out to the high slot to put shots on net. He plays with a good compete level, battles hard along the wall and protects the puck effectively.

MED # 36, C, Cox, Trevor (2013) Cox puts really good pressure and physicality on the fore-check and showed some pretty nice agility and protection of the puck. He made a really nice 1st pass to move the puck up on the rush, opened up nicely in the slot to take a pass and put a great shot on to score the opener of the game. He had a really great give-and-go with speed to take a pass in deep for a good opportunity in behind the defense and made a fantastic pass to find a man driving hard to the net to score. He was driving to the net really well looking for loose pucks and opportunities from in tight.

SAS # 17, LW, Zajac, Nick (2013) Zajac protected the puck really well and was battling hard for it in deep in the offensive zone. He put a nice hit on the puck carrier to knock him off the puck and was protecting it well on the wide drive.

SAS # 38, RW, Stovin, Brett (2013) Stovin showed some pretty nice speed to skate the puck up on an end-to-end rush, however mishandled the puck and lost it at the end. He made a really nice pass to find an open man in front of the net for a good opportunity in tight and was going to the net well looking for loose pucks and rebounds. He has to get the puck out of the zone however on his clearing attempts.

FINAL SCORE: 4-1 Medecine Hat

March 21, 2013, Acadie-Bathurst Titan at Blainville-Boisbriand Armada (QMJHL)

ACB #9 LC Raphaël Lafontaine (2013) – Decision-making and defensive positioning were poor. Didn't do a lot of the little things well tonight. PK positioning needs a lot of work, had a hard time reading the puck carrier and keeping his body in the shooting lane. Lost battles the whole game. Offensively couldn't get anything going. Don't think he got a single puck on net. On one notable occasion he looked off a good pass to try a low percentage shot, which was subsequently blocked and went back quickly the other way. Was strong on the dot.

ACB #23 LW Patrick Zdrahal (2013) – Was one of the few players on the Titan trying to create offense, but didn't show much. Showed good hands and passing when given time and space, but didn't seem willing to work for it and overdid it with unsuccessful fancy plays. Lost battles and lacked energy. At a certain point he seemed magnetically opposed to the puck, as if trying to stay away from it.

BLB #62 LW/C Danick Martel (2013) – Outstanding game from the undersized forward. Very slippery and energetic, showed something on every shift. Boasts quick feet that he keeps churning. Forced turnovers on the forecheck and played well on the penalty kill. Aware of passing lanes, used his stick to take away space. Battled hard. Showed puck skills with patience and good use of reach, though tried to do too much at times. Strong shot with a varied selection. Passing was outstanding. Quick ups on the breakout and off turnovers. Good cycle work with soft setup passes to linemates.

Mar 22, 2013, Portland Winterhawks vs. Everett Silvertips (WHL)

POR#3 RD, Jones, Seth(2013) Had a quiet, but very solid game tonight at both ends of the ice as usual. Showed off his heavy slap shot from the point a few times, and were able to get them on net.

Showed off his very impressive skating abilities with his speed and ability to get away from forecheckers with tight turns. Used his good size to keep opponents away from the puck. Would have liked to see him play with much more intensity in a playoff game, especially as his team was losing. Used his excellent reach on the rush to keep opponents to the outside.

POR#19 LC, Petan, Nicolas(2013) Highly skilled forward who displayed his elite playmaking skills and vision tonight. So patient with the puck and waits until there is an opening to make a tape to tape pass in the offensive zone. Played with a lot confidence, and showed his elite abilities. Impressed with how hard he played the game tonight, as he chased down every loose puck quickly. A few times he was able to knock opponents off the puck along the walls despite his size. Made one very poor decision with the puck in the defensive zone as he tried to make a cute backhand pass to the slot to his teammate, which got picked off easily. Then in the same sequence of play, he was caught watching the puck behind the net and lost his coverage in the slot, who was wide open for a goal. Showed off his quick release in the slot for a goal at the end of the game.

POR#27 RW, Bjorkstrand, Oliver(2013) Made very little impact in tonight's game. Showed some nice offensive instincts and skills a few times throughout the night, but did not do enough to help his team try to win tonight's game. Needs to finish his checks, especially as the playoffs go along to tire out opposing defensemen. Displayed very good speed throughout the night and was able to beat opponents to the puck a few times on the forecheck, but just did not do enough with it after to make an impact. Liked to go down the wing and tried to use his speed to beat opponents to the net. Went to the net for loose pucks, but could not finish them off.

EVE#25 LD, Mueller, Mirco(2013) Played an excellent game in his own end tonight to frustrate opponents all night long. So strong along the boards, and was tough to beat in puck battles. Was able to keep everything to the outside, and made life miserable for opposing forwards in front of the net as he stuck to them like glue and did not give them any chances to get open for scoring chances. Very good at reading the play without the puck, and was rarely caught out of position. Makes very good first passes out of the zone, and does not take unnecessary risks with the puck. If he does not have a play to make, he will simply just put it off the glass and send it into the neutral zone.

EVE#30 G, Lotz, Austin(2013) Faced 58 shots throughout the game and gave his team a chance to win. Looked calm in net, and as the traffic in front of him got bigger and bigger as the game went on, he stayed composed and was able to fight through it to make saves after saves. Liked how he played his angles as he kept making saves off his chest. Has quick feet and reaction time, which served him well in tight as he had to recover time and time again to get to the other post. Gave up many rebounds around the crease throughout the night, opponents just were not in the right areas to score off of rebounds. Also looked like he struggled on wrap arounds as his body got twisted around awkwardly a few times, and his body was not tight enough to the post.

Scouts Notes: This was a game that Portland should have won, but Austin Lotz stood on his head to give Everett the victory to start off the playoff series. Seth Jones will definitely need to play with a little bit more urgency in his game as the playoffs get going. Would have liked to see him play with some more aggression to force the issue a little bit. Very impressed with Mirco Mueller tonight. His intensity level is night and day compared to the beginning of the season. Has adjusted very well to the style of play in North America.

FINAL SCORE: 4-3 Everett

March 22nd, 2013. London Knights vs. Saginaw Spirit

LDN#16 F Max Domi (2013). Domi had an exceptional offensive performance in this game for the Knights. Max showed strong bursts of speed entering the offensive zone and displayed a willingness to carry the puck through traffic while initiating the offensive rush. He was constantly on the puck whenever he was one the ice, and dominated the Spirit defenders throughout the game. Max worked some beautiful passing plays with his linemates and seemed to be able to connect on everything they tried. He showed creativity and patience in the offensive zone both letting plays develop and making plays happen depending on the circumstance. Domi showcased an elite wrister on numerous occasions and displayed quick release capability from the slot and the half wall. Max was excellent on the power play and showcased great vision and puck moving ability.

LDN#71 F Chris Tierney (SJ). Tierney played a really strong complete game for the Knights. He was very strong in the offensive zone and was constantly working hard to win puck battles and control puck possession down low in the offensive zone. Showed great playmaking abilities assisting on three goals for the Knights with a variety of touch passes and set ups. Chris was also reliable in the offensive zone and was excellent at moving and chipping pucks into space for his linemates to start quick offensive attacks. Tierney was all over the ice in the offensive zone and was strong on the power play working to create space for his linemates and displaying great vision and awareness with puck movement.

SAG#15 F Eric Locke (2012). The biggest thing that stood out about Locke's game was hard work and effort. He is constantly moving his feet and out working opponents in battles for the puck. Eric is not the biggest player on the ice but made up for this with smarts and awareness. He constantly finds himself in strong positions to make plays happen. Locke was good at generating offensive chances and was rewarded with a goal late in the game. He shows good awareness and playmaking abilities setting up linemates for great scoring chances. Eric is also extremely reliable in the defensive zone and can be counted on to help out his defenders down low and make smart breakout decisions when needed. He is a strong skater and is deceptively fast beating a number of opponents in races for loose pucks.

SAG#21 F Jimmy Lodge (2013). Lodge was very inconsistent throughout this game for the Spirit. He would have one strong offensive shift and then make some bad turnovers on the next. Jimmy is good at using his size to shield the puck in the offensive zone, but seems indecisive on a number of chances throughout the game. He displayed a strong wrist shot, but needs to keep working to get himself into better scoring situations. He needs to work on his playmaking abilities and move pucks quicker to streaking linemates. Lodge did get into a fight late in the game standing up for one of his linemates, although the fight did not last very long. He showed flashes of potential but needs to work on consistency moving forward.

SAG#83 D Brandon Prophet (2014). Prophet had a solid game on the back end for the Spirit. Brandon made a number of solid body checks both in open ice and along the boards, and really worked hard to make things tough for Knights attackers on his side of the ice. He looked to be in better shape than he was at Christmas time and was able to keep up speed wise with the streaking Knight forwards. He showed a willingness to join the offensive rush but needs to pick his spots better. Brandon was good at walking the point to get into stronger shooting positions and unleashed a strong slap shot when given time to shoot. He needs to work at slowing things down in the defensive zone when controlling the puck and not force passes into crowded areas.

Mar. 22, 2013, Niagara IceDogs vs. Oshawa Generals (OHL)

OSH # 7, D, Carlisle, Chris (2013) Carlisle is able to make a really good 1st pass up out of his zone to start the breakout. He came down into the high slot to provide a scoring option after opening up well and has really good hands and moves to gain the offensive zone on the rush. He was hitting his targets on the breakout passes for the most part, however did miss a teammate at the far blue line. He was able to find an open man down low next to the net on the power play but needs to get his shots through to the net. He was also taking long outside shots from a bad angle that didn't get through to the net on the rush.

OSH # 14, RW, Latour, Bradley (2013) Latour put good pressure on the puck carrier and was able to take the puck and force turnovers. He distributed the puck well on the rush, then drove hard to the net and was able to make a nice pass through the neutral zone to lead a man into the offensive zone with speed. He opened up in the slot to take a pass right in front to score on a great shot and was able to get a nice cycle going in deep in the offensive zone. He needs to finish his hits along the boards, be hungrier for pucks in his battles and watch the neutral zone turnovers as well.

OSH # 19, C, Cassels, Cole (2013) Cassels was protecting the puck well along the boards, cycling it well and has a nice hard shot from the point on the power play, but has to get his shot through to the net. He had a 2-on-1 opportunity but elected to shoot and the goaltender made the save. He got a great cycle going by moving the puck down low then drove hard to the net with his stick down and has really nice hands and agility in tight to avoid pressure from the opposition.

NIA # 4, D, Kelly, Broderick (2013) Kelly is able to protect the puck from the opposition's pressure and move the puck up along the boards. He was getting his shot through to the net from the point, but has to be kept down low to generate a rebound or opportunity in tight and needs to get his shot through with more consistency.

NIA # 9, C, Maletta, Jordan (2013) Maletta put really good pressure and physicality on the fore-check and was able to get to the slot to pick up a loose puck and put a good shot on. He was physical on the puck carrier in his own end, got in lanes to block passes and then take the puck back up the ice to drive wide for a good shot. He protects the puck nicely, is able to get a good cycle going deep in the offensive zone but needs to watch the turnovers trying to force passes through the opposition.

NIA # 12, LW, DiFruscia, Anthony (2013) DiFruscia protects the puck really well on the wide drive, trying to get it to the net and was opening up to take a pass right in front of the net, but fanned on his opportunity. He did a really good job blocking a shot from the point on the penalty kill to force a turnover and get the puck up out of his own end. He put really good pressure and physicality on the puck carrier on the fore-check, and was getting in lanes on the penalty kill to block shots.

NIA # 21, C, Verhaeghe, Carter (2013) Verhaeghe had a really strong game as he was able to move the puck up to start the rush, was lifting the opposition's stick to force a turnover in the offensive zone then drove hard to the net with the puck. He made a really good pass to find an open man in the slot and showed really good strength and puck protection along the wall. He was able to pick up a loose puck in the slot to put a great shot on net to score the team's 2nd goal of the game, had really nice hands and moves to create space from the opposition and was skating the puck up the ice very well to gain the offensive zone on an end-to-end rush. He did a really good job finding an open man in the slot for a great opportunity and was clearing the puck out of the zone on the penalty kill. He put really good pressure and physicality on the fore-check but has to watch the turnovers trying to skate through the opposition and needs to get the puck out on chances along the boards.

FINAL SCORE: 5-2 Oshawa Generals

March 23rd, 2013. Owen Sound Attack vs. Sault Ste. Marie Greyhounds

OWE#24 D Chris Bigras (2013). Bigras had a solid game defensively for the Attack. He was excellent at making smart and simple breakout passes and was good at slowing things down in the defensive zone allowing his forwards to get into open passing lanes. Chris showed tremendous confidence skating with the puck when pressured in the defensive zone. He kept his game simple and did not risk any chances by jumping into the offensive rush. Bigras was good at finding the net through traffic with his shots and displayed good playmaking ability on the power play setting up his teammates in strong shooting positions.

OWE#27 F Zach Nastasiuk (2013). Nastasiuk had a strong offensive performance for the Attack. He scored two big goals for the Attack. He was constantly around the net in the offensive zone and was rewarded with the first goal of the game off a nice rebound opportunity. He needs to work at improving his skating stride which would really add another element to his game with some bursts of speed. Zach is constantly working hard and is reliable along the boards in the defensive zone at chipping pucks into the neutral zone and out of danger. He also was solid on both special teams in this game, moving the puck well on the power play and working to get into shooting and passing lanes on the penalty kill.

OWE#31 G Jordan Binnington (STL). Binnington was exceptional for the Attack in this game. He faced over 40 shots and rarely seemed flustered or phased. Jordan showed great lateral ability making a number of huge back door saves. He bounced back quickly after allowing some goals and worked hard to keep the Attack in the game. He was great at controlling rebounds and was steady when coming out of his net to play the puck. Jordan made a number of nice glove saves and worked to make himself appear bigger than he is to take away most of the net. Binnington was also very solid at coming out and challenging shooters, really cutting off all shooting angles coming down the wing.

SSM#17 F David Broll (TOR). Broll was effective at setting the physical tone and presence for both the game and the series in this game. He dropped the mitts both in the first and second period and really worked to spark the Greyhounds. David uses his size to dominate smaller opposing defenders and can really punish the opponents with some crunching body checks. Broll skates well for a bigger guy and really worked up a head of steam when given space to skate up and down the wing. He showed little offensive punch in this game and needed to get into better scoring positions in front of the net to really utilize his size effectively.

SSM#25 D Darnell Nurse (2013). Nurse struggled a little bit in this game in the defensive zone and really lacked much pop or aggression in the corners or in front of the net. He was making smart breakout passes but did not seem too interested in skating with the puck out of the defensive zone. Darnell was good at utilizing an active stick to keep defenders wide and was good at getting his stick into lanes and intercepting passes. He showed a willingness to block shots and do whatever it took to keep the Attack shots from getting on target. Nurse was solid on the penalty kill and did not over pursue for pucks along the walls and in the corners. Darnell also picked his spots well when choosing to jump into the offensive rush and generated a couple of chances that were unable to find the back of the net.

March 23, 2013, Mississauga Steelheads at Belleville Bulls (OHL)

MISS #15 LW Josh Burnside (2013) – Had some great shifts tonight, but was inconsistent and didn't really show much as far as upside. Body positioning on PK was good but was too inactive with his stick. Defensive zone coverage was mixed, reads were OK but was not always involved enough on boards. On strong shifts, buzzed with good forechecking and active cycling but lacked touch with the puck in opportune moments. Showed flashes of good acceleration and straight-line speed but footwork lacked detail overall.

BELL #14 RD Jordan Subban (2013) – One-dimensional offensive-defenseman had a mixed game. Powerplay passing was strong and outlets were smart. Shot the puck frequently and hit the net about half the time. Received the puck smoothly with his feet moving. Pinched up a few times but seemed very conscious of his defensive responsibilities, sometimes to a fault. Had a tendency to take himself out of the play by getting sucked back when his team was sustaining pressure. Kept his feet moving but footwork was choppy. Gap control against the rush was off. Did not kill penalties at any time. Skated on the second unit powerplay and third pairing at even strength. Played sheltered minutes. Wasn't impressed.

Scout's Notes: Goaltender Spencer Martin (2013) backed up Tyson Teichmann for Mississauga.

March 24, 2013, Sudbury Wolves at Brampton Battalion (OHL)

BRAM #9 LW Brandon Robinson (2014) – Burly forward who played with a lot of jam, though was very inconsistent. When he was involved he was very difficult to knock off the puck. Showed strength down the wing and good protection skills along the boards. Won battles in the offensive zone and took the puck hard to the net when given a lane. Stickwork was OK for a player of his size though he's never going to be considered a dangler. Skating needs work, lacked footspeed and agility.

BRAM #19 LW Blake Clarke (2014) – Flashed talent but lacked intensity and decision-making was poor. Slow to pucks and lost as many battles as he won. Tried to do too much with the puck on the breakout, carrying it into traffic without foresight. Didn't finish checks in the neutral zone. Chased the play in the defensive zone and overcommitted on the backcheck. Was brutal when his team pulled their goalie for a 6-on-5 advantage, trying to be the hero but having the opposite effect.

BRAM #21 LC Nick Paul (2013) – Big kid, played a mixed game. Was in the right spots most of the time but didn't seem to know what to do when he got there. Positioned himself well on PK but didn't get his stick into lanes. Backchecked but coverage was poor. Was strong on the puck and played the body hard from time to time. Good work in the cycle using his size to protect. Showed off a nice wrister.

SBY #14 RW Nicholas Baptiste (2013) – Played a very nice two-way game with a lot of energy. Backchecking in particular was excellent. Churned his legs to get back and was involved in his own zone though his positioning needs work. Was active with a good stick on the penalty kill. Good forecheck work. Not the prettiest skater but he moves very well. Great edges. Showed a nose for the net with determined drives to the crease. Flashed skill on the powerplay with nice passing a great finish. Patient with the puck and kept his head up. Intelligent overall. Was outmuscled in battles from time to time. Don't know how much upside there is here but I think he's a safe bet to make it in some capacity.

SBY #15 LW Dominik Kubalik (2013) – Showed talent flashes but was mostly quiet in this one. Played point on the powerplay and moved the puck well. Had a couple shifts with good forecheck pressure where he finished his checks but was inconsistent with defensive play overall. Did show a good stick in the neutral zone to cut off passing lanes. Carried the puck through center with poise but for the most part tried to do too much with it and didn't deal well with defensive pressure. Made one excellent skill play to beat a defender and get to the net but needs to simplify his game overall.

SBY #21 LC Dominik Kahun (2013) – Not a great showing from the undersized pivot. Is skilled with the puck and showed some shiftiness but was punished physically along the boards and one point, received a pass with his head down and was absolutely laid out. Don't think that there's NA pro potential here.

SBY #94 LW Brody Silk (2013) – A heart-and-soul type, played a high-energy game from the third line and made his presence known often. Good skater, very active on his feet and in the play. Forechecked hard, backchecked hard. Great effort in his own zone at even strength and on the PK but his positioning needs work. Went hard to the net in the offensive zone and worked well in the cycle. Puck skills are lacking but he played a pro-style game.

SBY #16 RC Jacob Harris – Scored on a beautiful snapshot but was mostly uninvolved otherwise. Was weak in battles and skating was poor, lacking in agility and acceleration.

Scout's Notes: Sudbury D Jeff Corbett (2013) was playing a stable game before he was injured towards the end of the first period. Brampton D Dylan Blujus

(TBL - 2012) was outstanding. Big, intimidating defenseman who used his size well and showed offensive upside with good decisions and a strong point shot. Pretty fiery start saw Brampton coach/GM Stan Butler ejected before the midway point of the first period. Things calmed down after that. Brampton outshot Sudbury 34-17, but the Wolves pulled out a 5-4 victory by scoring the only third period goal and hanging on for dear life.

March 24, 2013, Guelph Storm at Kitchener Rangers (OHL)

GUE #9 LC Robert Fabbri (2014) – Wasn't very noticeable. Skill is there but he needs to bulk up badly. Offseason will be key for him as he could carve out a major role next season. For the moment he's a complementary offensive player that has an effective shift from time to time, but not the guy you want playing any kind of crucial minutes in an important playoff matchup.

GUE #11 RW Jason Dickinson (2013) – Rough game for Dickinson, who had a strong first period but really tailed off as the stakes rose. Early he pursued the puck hard and got involved in scrums, backchecked, and utilized his size to protect the puck well. At one point towards the midway point of the game, he was checked hard along the boards and it seemed to fall apart from there. Don't know that it was necessarily the catalyst but it was the point when I started to notice how poorly he was playing. Puck poise was completely lacking. Was a step behind the play in all three zones. (ex. Backchecked hard but long after his man was out of reach.) Positioning on the penalty kill was good but he was too passive with his stick.

GUE #17 LW Tyler Bertuzzi (2013) – Bertuzzi seems like a hard-nosed, straightforward player, but I was impressed by some of the little things he did tonight. In particular, his shot was outstanding. Can wire dangerous slapshots off the rush and had a nice wrister that he placed well through traffic. Was determined to loose pucks and went hard to the net. Other aspects are lacking. He moves his feet but he's a poor skater. Lacked poise with the puck, passing was brutal on a few occasions. Took a boarding penalty on a real cheapshot and got a roughing double minor late in the third mixing it up with Kitchener goalie John Gibson that put his team short in the midst of a comeback attempt. Can imagine him as an NHL fourth liner some day. Can also imagine him as a LNAH goon. Needs to find the balance between playing a gritty game and keeping his emotions in check.

GUE #19 RC Hunter Garlent (2013) – I liked Garlent earlier in the season, when he was an absolute sparkplug, but he had a weak game today. Was surprised to see how poor his compete level was for loose pucks on multiple occasions. Was weak on the puck and on one occasion was knocked clean off his feet on an innocent looking hit. Decisions with the puck were poor, giveaways and wide-angle shots.

KIT #95 RW Justin Bailey (2013) – Mixed game for Bailey, had a few good shifts but was mostly a non-factor. Skating is awkward but he's strong on his feet. Showed poise with the puck in neutral zone traffic but tried to do too much at times. Got a couple good shots on net from the high slot. Active stick on the forecheck forced a few turnovers. Shifts were too long and he lacked compete at the end of many of them.

Mar 24, 2013, Fargo Force vs. Green Bay Gamblers (USHL)

FAR # 8, C, Guertler, Gabe (2013) Guertler is a smaller player but came back to his own end to provide some good support. He was distributing the puck nicely on the rush to move it up and start the breakout and was reading the play to pick off a turnover in the neutral zone to rush the puck back up into the offensive zone. He did a good job of driving the puck hard towards the net to create chances in tight and put some good pressure on the puck carrier on the fore-check. He had great agility with the puck to twist from the opposition's pressure and create some room to work with and put some great pressure on the puck carrier to force turnovers.

FAR # 10, LW, Dedenbach, Jared (2013) Dedenbach was battling hard for the puck in the corners, tying up his man nicely in the defensive zone. He put some good pressure on the point on the penalty kill and was also pressuring the puck carrier on the fore-check.

FAR # 21, LW, Harms, Brendan (2013) Harms was distributing the puck pretty well on the rush into the offensive zone but has to watch some of the turnovers trying to move the puck up out of his own end. He had a nice net-front presence, battling well for territory and opened up nicely in the slot to take a pass and put a good one-timer on net. He was cycling the puck well in the offensive zone to generate chances from the point and made a really nice pass to find an open man in the high-slot from the sidewall. He missed his target on the long breakout pass to start the rush and has to watch the offensive zone turnovers trying to get the puck to a teammate down low. He also has to watch the turnovers up the middle through the neutral zone and when he tries to dangle his way through the opposition.

GBG # 5, D, Olofsson, Gustav (2013) Olofsson was playing his man with some nice physicality along the boards. He played with a pretty good battle to hold the offensive line then got his shot through to the net kept down low from the point. He used his stick really well to knock the puck from the opposition and keep them from getting to the front of the net and closed his gap on his man well to force a turnover and take the puck from him. He was willing to come down into the high slot to provide scoring options.

GBG # 16, C, Weis, Matthew (2013) Weis had some fantastic puck movement in the offensive zone off the rush and did a good job getting to the net looking for loose pucks and rebounds. He got a pretty nice cycle going in deep in the offensive zone and did a really good job poking the puck forward away from the opposition in his own end to come into the offensive zone with speed and put a really good shot on from beside the net for a great opportunity. He got in lanes on the penalty kill showing a willingness to block shots then clear the puck out of the zone. He put some great pressure on the puck carrier to force turnovers in the neutral zone to rush the puck back up the ice and had some fantastic puck movement in the offensive zone off the rush. He has to be hungrier for the puck along the wall and needs to watch the turnovers trying to dangle his way into the offensive zone.

GBG # 20, D, Wolanin, Christian (2013) Wolanin got his stick in a lane to deflect the shot out of play and picked off a neutral zone turnover then jumped up on the rush to gain the offensive zone and get the cycle started in deep. He protects the puck well from the opposition's pressure then moved it up along the boards to start the rush. He was jumping down low into the slot to pick up a loose puck on a rebound for a great shot opportunity.

GBG # 24, RW, Siroky, Ryan (2013) Siroky put some good pressure on the fore-check and opened up well in the high slot to provide scoring options. He was protecting the puck well from the opposition's pressure and made a really nice little chip play to move the puck to the middle for a man in the slot for a good shot off the rush. He has to watch the turnovers on breakout passes out of his own end into the offensive zone.

FINAL SCORE: 2-1 Fargo Force (O.T.)

Mar. 24, 2013, Saginaw Spirit vs. London Knights (OHL)

LND # 16, C, Domi, Max (2013) Domi was flying in this game, playing with really nice speed and the vision to spot an open man in the offensive zone. He had absolutely incredible hands to dangle his way through defenders to get the puck to the slot for a good shot on the power play and showed really great agility, puck protection and strength. He was making great passes to find the open man in front of the net, distributed the puck well from the point on the power play and had a pretty nice hard shot that he got on net. He was able to make another really fantastic pass to find an open man down low on the power play for a great opportunity and used his fantastic speed on the rush to get by a defender on a nice chip play then put a great shot on net that he rang off the post. He doesn't give up on a play, and showed this when he lost his stick and still made an excellent kick pass to an open man in front and had a really nice give-and-go play in the offensive zone to get in tight for a good opportunity. He was opening up well in the slot off the rush to take a pass and put a good shot on, but has to hit the net on his opportunities and even though he has the vision to spot the open man, he has to make sure there is a lane to get him the puck instead of forcing passes through the opposition. He was reading the play well to pick off turnovers and used fantastic speed repeatedly to blow by defenders and put good shots on that he could have scored on a few.

LND # 53, LW, Horvat, Bo (2013) Horvat showed really nice speed on the wide drive and got the puck to the front of the net for teammates. He did a nice job of getting in lanes on the penalty kill to block shots and had a nice net-front presence on the power play as well. He went hard to the net with his stick down to open up for chances in tight, but was unable to connect on 2 of the opportunities. He was able to take a pass at the far blue line to come into the slot and put a nice low shot on along the ice and also took a nice pass in the slot on the power play to put a good backhander on net. He went hard to the net to take a pass in tight and score on a good deflection and then also picked up the puck in front of the net to score and tie up the game as the buzzer sounded to send the game to overtime. In overtime he had really nice hands to cut in towards the net off the wide drive for a great chance and also had the puck in the slot with some space but elected to pass the puck down low instead of shooting it.

LND # 65, D, Zadorov, Nikita (2013) Zadorov protected the puck well in behind his net to avoid the opposition's pressure and was moving the puck up pretty well to start the rush at times, however there were many others when he missed his target on passes and needs to be able to make the strong 1st pass out of the zone with more consistency. He had some really excellent vision to move the puck to an open man down low on the power play after a lane opened up and has a nice hard shot from the point, but has to hit the net with more consistency as well. He was coming in down low to keep the cycle going on the power play and also jumped in on the rush but turned the puck over and got caught in deep which lead to an odd man rush for the opposition. He also got caught watching the puck and was beat in tight for a good chance for the opposition.

SAG # 8, RW, Alexeev, Audrey (2013) Alexeev had some pretty nice hands on the rush through the neutral zone to get to the high slot for a shot, but has to hit the net on his opportunity. He put good pressure on the puck carrier on the fore-check, was finishing his hits and was able to take the puck then throw it out front to a teammate in tight. He had really nice speed and a nice drive to the net without the puck looking for opportunities.

SAG # 15, C, Locke, Eric (2013) Locke showed fantastic speed in this game to get a bunch of break opportunities, especially short-handed and put some good shots on net on those chances. He put some decent pressure and physicality on the puck carrier, had a pretty good battle for the puck and was competing to get his shots off. He had a nice hustle to get on loose pucks and opened up nicely in the slot to pick up a rebound and get a good shot on net. He was getting involved aggressively but can't be crossing the line and taking penalties, especially in the offensive zone. He was getting in deep with the puck with his great speed and was opening up on the power play to put one-timers on but there were a lot of times when he was taking long outside shots that missed the net completely. He has nice hands on the wide drive to cut in towards the middle for a shot and was putting good pressure on the puck carrier to force turnovers. He has to watch the turnovers trying to force passes through the opposition unnecessarily.

SAG # 21, C, Lodge, Jimmy (2013) Lodge was able to protect the puck well from the opposition's pressure to move the puck up out of the zone to start the rush. He made a nice pass on an odd-man rush opportunity but his teammate was unable to connect on the play. He also put a fantastic shot on from a pretty tough angle beside the net to score the team's 2nd goal of the game.

SAG # 91, RW, Moutrey, Nick (2013) Moutrey did a good job of getting to the net looking for loose pucks and rebounds. He was moving the puck pretty well in deep on the cycle, had a nice net-front presence on the power play and has great hands and moves but lost the puck trying to dangle his way through 3 players when there was a ton of open space due to some 4-on-4 play. He is calm with the puck and able to get it up out of the zone on the penalty kill and was throwing pucks low on net to try to generate rebounds off the wide drive. He was distributing the puck well on the rush, got to the slot to put a good shot on and was protecting the puck on the rush to get a good backhander shot off. He was able to make a really good centering pass form the sidewall for a man driving hard to the net and was basically throwing pucks on net from just about everywhere in the offensive zone.

FINAL SCORE: 3-2 London (2nd OT)

Mar 24, 2013, Youngstown Phantoms vs. USNTDP U18 (USHL)

YNG # 16, LW, Evancho, Zach (2013) Evancho provided some good support in his own end coming back and clearing the front of the net. He put good pressure on the fore-check and was able to get a cycle started in deep in the offensive zone.

YNG # 21, D, Mackey, Kyle (2013) Mackey was stepping into the high slot to provide scoring options in the offensive zone and used his stick nicely to keep the opposition from the front of his net. He has to watch the turnovers along the offensive zone blue line as well.

YNG # 27, C, Stork, Luke (2013) Stork showed his really good speed to get on a loose puck and put some good pressure on the fore-check. He was moving the puck around pretty well in the offensive zone and was willing to play with an element of physicality. He put nice pressure on the puck carrier and showed nice speed coming into the offensive zone with the agility to stop-up quick, create some space then move the puck to a trailing player in the high slot off the rush for a good shot opportunity. He put nice pressure on the point on the penalty kill, got in lanes showing a willingness to block shots from the point, but has to hit the net on his chances off the rush.

USA # 6, D, Thompson, Keaton (2013) Thompson stepped up into the high slot to take a pass and put a good shot on. He was nice and calm with the puck, even under pressure from the opposition and jumped up to hold the offensive line but got caught on a pinch in deep. He was getting his shot through to the net from the point and was able to make a good breakout pass to lead his man through the neutral zone with speed.

USA # 7, C, Compher, J.T. (2013) Compher was walking out from the side wall to drive the puck to the net for a good chance in tight and found lanes on the power play to move the puck cross-ice for good opportunities. He had some fantastic speed on the wide drive to blow by a defender then throw the puck low on net for a teammate to score. He distributed the puck well from the point on the power play and opened up really well in the high slot on the power play to take a pas and put a one-timer on to score. He took a pass down low right next to the net on the power play to put a great shot on to score and showed good speed and hustle for loose pucks. He drove well to the net looking for loose pucks but has to watch the turnovers trying to dangle his way through the opposition, especially on the power play.

USA # 15, LW, Hayden, John (2013) Hayden had a fantastic battle for a loose puck, hustling well and using his body to protect the puck to get it in deep on the penalty kill. He had a good hard drive to the net with his stick down looking for loose pucks and rebounds and put some good pressure on the fore-check to force turnovers. He pressured the point well to poke the puck loose for a break opportunity and made a really nice back-hand move on his chance. He battled hard for loose pucks and rebounds in front of the net and drove hard to the net to get a rebound and score from in tight. He protected the puck really well on the wide drive and found a lane to move the puck back to the point for a great chance. He was able to take a hit and still get the puck in deep and played with some nice physicality on the fore=check. He needs to watch the turnovers trying to move the puck out of the zone on the breakout.

USA # 24, RW, McCarron, Shane (2013) McCarron put some really nice physicality and pressure on the fore-check and used his body well to protect the puck from the opposition, finding lanes to move the puck cross-ice in the offensive zone. He was distributing the puck well on the odd-man rush then drove hard to the net with his stick down. He had some really nice physicality put on the puck carrier in his own end and made a nice pass to find an open man in front in tight to the net. He went hard to the net with his stick down to take a pass and deflect a shot to the net but missed the net on his opportunity. He got a good cycle going in deep in the offensive zone and showed some really good strength and puck protection in deep in the offensive zone.

FINAL SCORE: 4-2 USNTDP U18

March 26, 2013, London Knights at Saginaw Spirit (OHL)

LDN #16 LC Max Domi (2013) – Domi is a highly skilled sparkplug of a player and played an outstanding game, but he also let his emotions get the better of him tonight. Didn't like Max's skating in earlier viewings but his feet looked good tonight. Not the strongest straight-line skater but he was quick and shifty enough that he could back off defenders and showed good pace down the wing. Stickhandling was elite, overdid it at times but with his low center of gravity and elusiveness, he was extremely difficult to get the puck from when he got his feet moving anywhere on the ice. Every time I've seen him play, he's knocked pucks out of the air with unbelievable hand-eye, and tonight was no different. Corralled and settled passes very quickly, especially on the powerplay where he took advantage of time and space to move around the offensive zone and create holes in coverage. Flashed a hard one-timer and a great wrist shot. Took a boneheaded slashing penalty and after the whistle, proceeded to mug a Saginaw player. Was lucky he didn't spend more time in the box tonight. His feistiness is a plus but needs to keep it reigned in.

LDN #53 LW Bo Horvat (2013) – Not a great game from Bo. Did a lot of the little things well tonight with hard backchecking and good physical play, but tried to do too much with the puck on a consistent basis. Frequently stickhandled into traffic and tried to make fancy plays. Was slow off the blocks and didn't show enough jump in outnumbered attack situations. Can play much better when he keeps it simpler.

LDN #65 LD Nikita Zadorov (2013) – Solid, clean night for Zadorov. His puck skills against the forecheck were outstanding, with safe outs to his teammates or smart clearances off the glass. Adjusted well on the fly, getting sucked back at times against the rush and immediately recognizing and stepping up. Recovered well from the one glaring giveaway he made with a desperation reach to break up a golden scoring chance. A couple nice pinches but he wasn't especially involved offensively. Skating was good.

LDN #81 LW Remi Elie (2013) – Outstanding game from Elie who has impressed me more with each viewing. Fantastic forecheck work, laying the body on defensemen and getting his sticks in passing lanes to create havoc. Tracked the play well in all three zones and kept his feet moving. Showed good board work on the puck and flashed offensive upside with smart cycling, passing, and shooting, including a great finish on a goal where he batted the puck in out of mid-air. Skating is quick and efficient. Hard not to love this kid.

SAG #15 LC Eric Locke (Passed over 2012) – Bit of a waterbug. Wasn't very effective. Quick feet and good hands but he's undersized and was knocked off the puck easily and often. Good coverage on the PK getting in shooting lanes and some flashes of good forecheck ability but when he's unable to create offensively like tonight, he's not very valuable.

SAG #21 RC Jimmy Lodge (2013) – Good puck skill but he looked a step behind the play for most of the game. Skated well with the puck but his movement away from it was too passive, save for brief flashes (ex. showed good burst going hard to the net and in one particular 1-on-3 situation). Smart passing on the powerplay to find seams and avoid sticks. Backchecked and forechecked well but without consistency. Good defensive zone positioning but needed to battle more. A few boneheaded passes concerned me. Still very raw.

SAG #91 RW Nick Moutrey (2013) – Thought Moutrey had an OK game in the losing effort. Power forward type with some upside. Puck protection skills were good and showed the ability to will his way through defensemen. Brought the puck down the wing hard into the zone. Got alone on the breakaway once and made a nice move. Didn't score but was impressed with the flash of talent and speed. Not quick overall but his skating wasn't an issue. PK positioning was good but he lacked urgency. Overcommitted too much in his own zone at even strength chasing the play. Played the body very well in the neutral zone, laid guys out a couple times with huge hits including one where he forced a turnover that led to a scoring chance.

March 26th, 2013. Guelph Storm vs. Kitchener Rangers (OHL)

GUE#3 D Andrey Pedan (NYI). Pedan struggled early in the game, turning over the puck in the neutral and offensive zones on questionable decisions. He was trying to force passes at points or get too fancy and hold onto the puck too long. Andrey had a very strong third period and scored two huge goals sparking the Storm comeback. He is very offensive minded and was able to get hard wrist and slap shots on net through traffic. He walks the blue line effectively and was constantly looking for opportunities to jump back door and create offensive chances. Pedan is a strong skater and had enough speed to keep pucks in at the blue line after being wrapped hard around the boards from the opposite side. Andrey was effective at using an active stick to keep rushing attackers to the outside. He did not show much of a physical presence and would benefit from getting bigger to go with his tall frame.

GUE#9 F Robby Fabbri (2014). Fabbri had an exceptional game for the Storm. He was constantly moving his feet and utilizing a mix of awareness and creativity to create offensive chances for himself and his linemates. He displayed strong offensive instincts in finding loose rebounds and getting into strong scoring positions but was unable to beat the Ranger goaltender. Robby was very strong in the face-off circle and was on the ice for a number of key face-offs late in the game. Fabbri worked very hard to battle in front of the net and kept the play alive in the final minutes eventually assisting on the game winning goal. He is a strong skater and shows confidence carrying the puck deep into the offensive zone before slowing things down giving his linemates enough time to get into open scoring positions. He is responsible in the defensive zone and was efficient at moving the puck out of dangerous areas quickly.

GUE#11 F Jason Dickinson (2013). Dickinson was skating very well in this game, beating a number of Rangers defenders with a quick outside step. He also continued to display a willingness to finish checks and made life tough for opposing Ranger forwards cutting through the middle of the ice. Jason showed great vision and awareness constantly finding passing lanes to move the puck to his linemates. He had trouble displaying any offensive consistency and would create chances one shift then not get any for a few shifts between. He was good at getting into positions to lay the body checks but needs to add some bulk to his frame to really become effective. Dickinson was relentless on the penalty kill and is constantly in quality positions to get into shooting lanes and intercept cross ice passes.

KIT#24 D Ryan Murphy (CAR). Murphy had a strong offensive game for the Rangers. He is such an effortless skater it appears at times as if he is just floating across the ice. Ryan displays a high level of confidence skating with the puck and is very good at making opponents miss in space. He is a great playmaker and is constantly coming up with creative new ways to move the puck to his linemates. Murphy showed no hesitation from jumping into the offensive rush and was effective in generating scoring plays. Ryan was able to win puck battles against the Storm forwards using a combination of anticipation and smarts, although he rarely uses the body and can get off his game if fore checked hard in the corners.

KIT#31 G John Gibson (ANA). Gibson was absolutely outstanding for the Rangers. He showed calm and collectiveness facing a number of quality scoring chances for the Storm. John was very good all game long except for a late game collapse with five minutes to play after getting beat by a bouncing shot from the point. He was very strong with his lateral movements and made a number of spectacular sliding saves keeping the Rangers ahead for the majority of the game. Gibson controlled rebounds well and was very effective at directing pucks into the corners and behind the net allowing his defenders to set up with some space. John was very good at never giving up on plays and ultimately was beat by a few bad bounces late in the game. Gibson was good at getting out of his net and moving the puck up the ice to create mismatches on line changes for the Rangers.

March 27 2013, Moncton Wildcats vs. Victoriaville Tigres (QMJHL)

MON #4 D Sweeney, Jacob (2013) – I was not really impressed by his play. He is huge and takes quiet some place in front of the net and can make some defensive plays with his stick. He is heavy on his feet and is not dynamic defender. Play with the puck was all right but he is limited in what he can do.

MON #8 RW Garland, Connor (2014) – Played limited minutes on the 4th line but was able to bring energy and intensity. He was in an offensive role last time I saw him and he did a good job translating his speed on a checking line. He likes to agitate and run his mouth after the whistle. Got into the Tigres' heads a little.

MON #22 LW Barbashev, Ivan (2014) – I had the chance to watch Barbashev play earlier in the year and he displayed all his offensive tools on that occasion. While he was more discrete offensively in this 1-0 game, what stood out to me was his intensity and physical play. He likes to apply pressure when he doesn't have the puck and he finishes most of his checks. And he makes quiet an impact with those hits that are very solid. He still showed some good puck skills, most noticeably his quick and solid hands. Barbashev also has the ability the rush the puck with good speed and explosion, but he didn't show it too often in this game.

VIC#3 D Diaby, Jonathan (2013) – Not his best game and looked sluggish out there. He was apparently playing with an injured ankle, which would explain why. He battled his lack of speed by using his reach and body but Moncton was able to beat a few times on 1-on-1 situations. He also had some weak coverage on the penalty kill and his decision regarding who to cover was not the best. He played on the power play again in this game and had some issues moving the puck along the blue line but displayed once again his strong but not completely accurate slap shot. One area Diaby still needs to work on his is play with the puck: he needs to secure his decisions even more because he made quite a few dangerous plays tonight.

VIC #4 D Sidlik, Petr (2012 eligible) – He got passed over in last year's draft but the more I see him play, the more I like him. He stood out as one the best D in the QMJHL this year and tonight's game was no exception. He played solid defensive hockey and showed very good poised. He is calm when engaging defensively and makes solid decision. He worked hard along the boards to retrieve puck and makes quick and solid decisions on the rush. Not really a puck-moving defenseman though. I like the total package he brought on the ice again; he played in every situation possible and is very reliable. He took a big hit from behind protecting the puck and the lead late in the game.

VIC #57 LW Veilleux, Tommy (2013) – Crashed and banged as usual. He brings high-intensity but lacks speed. Needs to be more careful after the whistle as well, he took a bad penalty at a bad moment again tonight. Not much of a prospect here.

March 29th, 2013. Owen Sound Attack vs. Sault Ste. Marie Greyhounds (OHL)

OWE#7 F Daniel Catenacci (BUF). Catenacci had an exceptional offensive performance for the Attack. He flashed exceptional speed cutting through the middle of the ice and was very shifty and elusive once crossing into the offensive zone. Daniel showed confidence controlling the puck through the neutral zone and was able to generate a quick burst of speed when given open space to skate. He drove the net on a number of occasions and was rewarded with two goals off of rebound and hard work chances. He showed good offensive awareness in getting into open areas of the ice and was constantly moving his feet to create turnovers in the neutral zone. Daniel does need to work at becoming more reliable in the defensive zone and not force cross ice passes into tight spaces resulting in turnovers in the neutral zone.

OWE#9 F Gemel Smith (DAL). Smith also had an exceptional performance in this game scoring two goals and assisting on two others. Gemel was all over the ice in the offensive zone and constantly seemed to be on the puck whenever he was one the ice. Both of his goals were generated off of great positioning and never giving up on a play jumping on rebound chances in the slot. He displayed a good level of playmaking skills as well finding open teammates in scoring positions and putting pucks on net to generate rebounds. Gemel was also very good at playing a strong physical presence and likes to finish checks in the corners. He was very strong standing in front of the net and keeping defenders busy. Smith also was effective getting under the skin of his opponents and worked to draw penalties from scrums after the whistle.

SSM#25 D Darnell Nurse (2013). Nurse struggled in this game in the defensive end. He got caught watching on two instances that turned into goals for the Attack. Darnell made some bad reads and ended up giving the Attack forwards chances to move into open scoring lanes. He also did not seem to have as much of a physical presence as normal and was caught standing around at points in the defensive zone. He was good at transitioning from forward skating to backwards skating when facing oncoming rushes but put himself out of position by choosing to close the gap on the wrong forward on occasion. Darnell worked hard to move opponents from in front of the net and did not let the bad start bring down his whole game. He was solid on the penalty kill and showed a willingness to get into the lane and block a number of shots from the point.

SSM#28 F Sergey Tolchinsky (2013). Tolchinsky continued his offensive output in this game putting up one goal and one assist. He displayed a strong wrist shot from in tight that he was able to get over the Attack goaltender. Sergey showcased his strong stickhandling skills in the neutral zone but needs to work at utilizing his linemates. He turned the puck over at times trying to make plays too fancy resulting in scoring chances and goals for the Attack. He needs to get pucks deep into the zone rather than trying to stick handle by himself waiting for something to develop. Sergey also needs to be more reliable in the defensive end and work at winning puck battles along the boards against bigger defenders. Tolchinsky is very shifty and elusive although adding some strength would help keep him on the puck from attacking defenders.

SSM#55 D Ryan Sproul (DET). Sproul had a strong offensive game for the Greyhounds. He scored on an absolute laser from the low slot that beat the Attack goaltender high glove. Ryan is constantly skating with the puck and is very good at generating a quick offensive counter attack once intercepting the puck in the defensive zone. He has a long stick and was good at knocking pucks off opponent's sticks. Sproul did manage to throw a big body check in open space, but would benefit from consistently adding a physical element to his game. Ryan is very offensive minded and would sometimes flee the zone before the puck was completely in Greyhound possession. He is very strong on the power play and constantly gets into positions for one-timers. Sproul generally made good decisions on breakout passes and was effective at stretching a long pass to a streaking teammate.

Mar 30, 2013, Sioux City Musketeers vs. Omaha Lancers (USHL)

OMA # 2, C, Moy, Tyler (2013) Moy is able to make a good pass through the neutral zone to start the breakout on the rush with speed. He got the puck in deep on a nice dump and chase then put some good pressure on the fore-check. He displayed good strength and battle for the puck along the wall and made a really good pass on the power play to move the puck cross-crease to a teammate for a goal down low. He was able to get a nice cycle started in deep, had the speed to rush the puck into the offensive zone and put nice pressure on puck carrier.

OMA # 3, D, Worden, Nash (2013) Worden was jumping in on the attack to put some pressure on the fore-check and was distributing the puck nicely on the rush into the offensive zone. He was distributing the puck well on the rush into the offensive zone but has to watch the turnovers on puck mishandles through the neutral zone and lost a battle for the puck along the boards in his own end which resulted in a great opportunity and almost a goal for the opposition.

OMA # 11, LW, Gaudreau, Matthew (2013) Gaudreau was getting the puck in deep on dump and chase style of hockey and was reading the play well to pick off a turnover in the neutral zone then bring the puck back into the offensive zone on the rush. He did a nice job getting the puck up out of the zone and got down showing a willingness to block shots in his own end. He put great pressure on the point and displayed a nice element of physicality on the puck carrier along the boards. He also put a big hit on the puck carrier to knock him over and when he lost the puck he battled really hard on the back-check to take it back, however can't cross the line and take a penalty in doing so. He also can't take an unnecessary penalty by jarring after the whistle.

OMA # 27, LW, Melanson, Drew (2013) Melanson displayed some good physicality on the puck carrier along the wall and put in some good effort on the back-check to take the puck from the opposition. He showed great speed and hustle on the rush to get in deep with the puck, got a good cycle started and provided some good support in puck battles. He needs to watch the turnovers in the offensive zone trying to force passes through the opposition.

SIO # 19, C, Guentzel, Jake (2013) Guentzel showed some nice speed on the rush to fight off a check and get the puck into the offensive zone. He was looking to move the puck cross-crease to a teammate on the power play however the puck got deflected into the net for his goal, then he opened up really well down low next to the net to score on a nice one-timer shot. He had a great give and go play to move the puck down low and drive hard to the net and later drove hard to the net to deflect a shot from in tight to score his 3rd goal of the game. He had some nice hands and moves on the rush into the offensive zone and displayed good speed on the wide drive as well as a fantastic pass to find an open man in the slot on the power play for a goal.

SIO # 20, C, Peterson, Avery (2013) Peterson has some nice quick hands and was distributing the puck well to move it to an open man driving to the net in the offensive zone. He stepped into the high slot to take a pass and put a great shot on net that the team scored on the rebound, however the goal was waved off, and he also took the puck off the side wall to put a nice quick shot on net that seemed to catch the goaltender by surprise. He had a really good wide drive to put a good shot on to try to generate a rebound for a man in front.

SIO # 22, C, McGlynn, Conor (2013) McGlynn had a good battle for the puck along the boards and was getting it in deep to start the cycle. He drove hard to the net looking for loose pucks and rebounds and was moving the puck around well in the offensive zone to get the puck back to the point for a shot opportunity. He has some good hands and moves to get around defenders on the rush through the neutral zone and protected the puck really well on the wide drive but was taking outside shots. He used his hands again later to create some space in the offensive zone but has to get his shots through to the net on opportunities from the high slot and was taking lots of long shots off on the rush. He also has to pick up his foot speed to be more effective.

SIO # 26, D, Heinrich, Blake (2013) Heinrich was holding the offensive line well on the power play and was willing to come down low into the offensive zone to keep the attack alive. He displayed some good physicality on the puck carrier along the wall and had a really nice hit on the puck carrier to knock him over and take the puck away. He is calm with the puck, protecting it well from the opposition's pressure and also has the agility to twist away from them. He did a great job stepping up on the rush to split the opposition's defense to come in for a break opportunity. He needs to get his shots through to the net with more consistency.

FINAL SCORE: 5-1 Sioux City Musketeers

Apr 1, 2013, Mississauga Steelheads vs. Belleville Bulls (OHL)

BEL # 8, RW, Berisha, Aaron (2013) Berisha was battling really well for the puck and showed nice agility to twist from the opposition and protect the puck from them. He also put some nice pressure on the opposition on the fore-check.

BEL # 14, D, Subban, Jordan (2013) Subban is able to make a good 1st pass up out of the zone to start the breakout and had a really nice shot that he kept down low on net from the point. He displayed some excellent speed and hands to skate the puck up the ice end-to-end to get to the slot and put a good shot on net and later opened up in the high slot on the power play to put a hard one-timer on net that he rang off the post. He had some nice speed and puck movement on the rush up the ice through the neutral zone but has to be a bit stronger on the puck in his own end.

MIS # 10, RW, Goldberg, Andrew (2013) Goldberg is able to get the puck in deep off the rush and put some good pressure and physicality on the fore-check. He got a pretty good cycle going in deep in the offensive zone and was pressuring the puck carrier pretty well to force turnovers. He has to pick up the speed and tempo of his game and needs to be stronger on the puck along the boards.

MIS # 15, LW, Burnside, Josh (2013) Burnside had some really good speed to skate the puck into the offensive zone off the rush and get it in deep to draw a penalty. He used his body really effectively to beat the opposition to the puck and had a nice net-front presence on the power play. He hustled hard and battled for pucks in the corners, playing with a good energy and opened up right in front of the net on the slot to take a pass and put a good shot on net. He went hard to the net looking for loose pucks and rebounds and picked off a turnover in the high slot to take a step in and put a great shot on net. He got a pretty nice cycle started deep in the offensive zone and had a nice net-front presence on the power play to tip a point shot and score. He showed some great speed on the wide drive off the wing but has to hit the net on his opportunities. He also lost the puck on a mishandle along the boards by not being strong on the puck.

MIS # 18, RW, Babintsev, Sam (2013) Babintsev was distributing the puck well, as he moved the puck back to the point on the power play. He made a good pass to move the puck out of the zone to start the rush on the breakout and was able to skate the puck up into the offensive zone then moved it to an open man in the high slot. He found lanes to move the puck around in the offensive zone to get the puck to an open man in front of the net and had some really good speed on the wing to put a low shot on net trying to generate a rebound for a man in front. He had a really good drive down the middle towards the net with his stick down and got a good cycle started in deep in the offensive zone. He had some good speed and put nice pressure on the fore-check and used his speed to rush the puck up the ice but has to watch the neutral zone turnovers trying to dangle his way through the opposition.

MIS # 20, D, Graves, Jacob (2013) Graves did a great job of edging the opposition to the boards to take the puck and force a turnover. He had a fight in the 1st period in which he threw a few good punches but lost the fight overall and demonstrated his toughness again later on his ability to take a hit and still make a play to move the puck up out of the zone. He is calm with the puck, protects it well from the opposition's pressure and played the puck carrier with a nice element of physicality along the boards. He was able to make a nice 1st pass out of the zone for a quick transition and protects the puck pretty well along the boards.

FINAL SCORE: 3-1 Belleville Bulls

Apr 1, 2013, Portland Winterhawks vs. Everett Silvertips (WHL)

PRT # 3, D, Jones, Seth (2013) Jones was distributing the puck really well to lead a teammate into the offensive zone with speed. He had a nice hard shot that he got through to the net from the point on the power play and showed great strength and puck protection to hold on to the puck under intense pressure from the opposition. He can make a good 1st pass out of the zone to start the breakout and took a pass in the slot then drove to the net to put a great back-hander on to score. He had great speed and puck distribution through the neutral zone on the rush and great strength to knock his man off the puck. He stepped down into the slot on the power play to pick up a loose puck and score again on a good shot and just needs to watch the turnovers on passes up along the boards in his own end.

PRT # 12, C, Kopeck, Preston (2013) Kopeck made a really nice chip pass to lead a teammate into the offensive zone with speed and demonstrated good speed to rush the puck up the ice into the offensive zone then got a good cycle started in deep. He has a good quickness to his game, put good pressure on the puck carrier and also had a nice wrap-around attempt trying to drive the puck into the net. He had a really good give-and-go play to get in beside the net for a good shot opportunity, was distributing the puck well on the rush and did a good job tying up his man in the board battles along the wall in his own end.

PRT # 19, C, Petan, Nicholas (2013) Petan had great speed and agility to gain the offensive zone and create some space to work with. He made a really nice drop pass then drove hard to the net looking for loose pucks and rebounds. He showed his great hands and speed in the neutral zone to find lanes and gain the offensive zone and protects the puck well, battling for it along the wall. He got a nice cycle going in deep in the offensive zone and opened up well in the high slot to put a nice quick shot on net however, he has to hit the net with more consistency on his shot opportunities off the rush. He has excellent hands and moves that he displayed on an end-to-end rush to create some space and get towards the slot for a good opportunity, but has to get stronger on his feet so that he is not knocked off the puck so easily by bigger, stronger defensemen.

PRT # 27, RW, Bjorkstrand, Oliver (2013) Bjorkstrand had an excellent game with 2 goals and 2 assists as he was moving the puck around well in the offensive zone, was playing the puck carrier with some great pressure and physicality and made a really nice long pass to find a man at the far blue line to lead him into the offensive zone. He had a fantastic drive to the net to get a rebound and bat the puck into the net from in tight and showed excellent speed and hands on the wide drive to walk around defenders towards the net for another good chance in tight. He made a great pass to find an open man back-door for a great opportunity and protected the puck well getting a good cycle going in deep. He showed really good strength and puck protection and was able to find a man driving hard to the net with some good passes. He took a pass down low in tight to the net to make a great back-hand move for an excellent chance in tight and drew a penalty on the play and opened up really well in the slot on the power play for a great one-timer opportunity. He got to the slot to pick up a rebound and score on the power play and also got a very good cycle going which his team ended up scoring off the cycle on a great play.

EVE # 2, D, Nikkel, Ayrton (2013) Nikkel was able to get the puck up out of the zone to start the breakout and made a really nice pass to find a man at the far blue line to lead him into the offensive zone. He got in a lane to block a shot in front of the net but at one point gave his man far too much time and space in his own end to get a shot opportunity. He also tried to play his man physically along the wall but the puck carrier spun away from him fairly easily for a good chance. He used his stick well to put pressure on the puck carrier, but got beat far too easily on a wide move as his man got to the slot for a good shot opportunity off the cycle.

EVE # 15, C, Bauml, Kohl (2013) Bauml put some pretty nice pressure on the puck carrier and made some nice chip plays to create space for himself and teammates to work with. He had nice speed and puck distribution on the rush through the neutral zone, some great hands to walk around defenders on good moves, but has to get stronger on his feet so he's not knocked off the puck so easily and can't keep taking long outside shots off the rush when he has teammates and options with him.

EVE # 16, C, Stadnyk, Carson (2013) Stadnyk put some nice pressure on the puck carrier but had a really bad turnover up the middle in his own end that resulted in a great opportunity for the opposition.

EVE # 25, D, Mueller, Mirco (2013) Mueller is a nice big body defenseman who had a good clear on the penalty kill and a nice hard shot on target from the point on a one-timer. He is calm and patient with the puck, able to skate the puck up the ice to gain the offensive zone and was also able to make a good 1st pass out of the zone to start the rush. He made good decisions with the puck, doesn't panic under pressure and is a good skater with great hands to rush the puck up into the offensive zone to get to the high slot and put a nice shot on net. He played his man with some good physicality along the wall and got in lanes in front of the net to block shots

FINAL SCORE: 5-1 Portland Winterhawks

Apr 2, 2013, Waterloo Blackhawks vs. Green Bay Gamblers (USHL)

WAT # 3, D, McCoshen, Ian (2013) McCoshen is pretty calm with the puck, gets his shot through to the net and doesn't rush or panic to make a play. He distributes the puck effectively on the power play and got a nice hard shot through to the net that the team scored on the rebound. He got in a lane to block a shot from the point on the penalty kill and showed some good physicality on the puck carrier along the boards in his own end. He protects the puck well from the opposition's pressure then can move it up out of the zone to start the breakout.
WAT # 71, C, Salerno, Brandon (2013) Salerno has a really nice quickness to his game and a great ability to rush the puck up the ice to gain the offensive zone. He was distributing the puck well off the rush then going hard to the net with his stick down looking for loose pucks and rebounds but took a ton of long outside shots off the rush when he had teammates and options available. He also needs to add some size and strength to be more effective and has to finish his this along the boards on the fore-check.

WAT # 91, C, Cammarata, Taylor (2013) Cammarata started the game out by picking up the puck in tight in front of the net and made a great move to get the goalie out of position and the team scored on the rebound. He got a good cycle going deep in the offensive zone and put some nice pressure on the puck carrier. He has a really nice hard shot from the point on the power play and later picked up the puck in the high slot to take a step in and put a great shot on from scoring position. He distributed the puck well in the offensive zone to tee-up a one-timer from the point but he needs to watch some of the neutral zone turnovers by not being strong on the puck.

GBG # 16, C, Weis, Matthew (2013) Weis got a good cycle going in the offensive zone and was distributing the puck well, but can't move the puck to a man who's already tied up. He put good pressure on the puck carrier on the fore-check and was able to make a good breakout pass to move the puck out of the zone to start the rush. He has to move the puck or drive it down low rather than taking long outside shots off the rush.

GBG # 20, D, Wolanin, Christian (2013) Wolanin is calm with the puck and is able to make a good pass through the neutral zone, but has to make the good first pass with more consistency. He was jumping up on the rush to join the attack and provide scoring options and was able to rush the puck up the ice to gain the offensive zone and draw a penalty. He had a really good battle for the puck, showed nice strength and puck protection and was jumping up to put pressure on the fore-check. He also got his shot through to the net from the point and got in a pretty good fight later on throwing some good punches. He has to watch some of the turnovers by just throwing the puck up the boards.

GBG # 23, D, Gross, Jordan (2013) Gross did a nice job of reading the play to pick off a turnover by the opposition through the neutral zone and had a nice hard shot on net from the point. He was distributing the puck well in the offensive zone on the power play and can spot the open man but has to have a harder pass to get it through open lanes before sticks get in the way. He was able to skate the puck up the ice end-to-end but then took an outside shot that was deflected out of play and he needs to get the puck out of the zone on penalty kill clearing attempts. He also got caught watching the puck behind his own net and left a man open in front that ended up scoring on the play.

GBG # 24, RW, Siroky, Ryan (2013) Siroky picked up the puck in behind the net in the offensive zone for a great centering pass to a teammate in front for a goal. He came back for support in his own end, playing his man with some nice physicality along the boards and opened up really nicely in the slot to take a pass and put a good shot on net. He was also physical on the puck carrier on the fore-check.

GBG # 97, LW, Dikushin, Grigory (2013) Dikushin got in a lane to block a shot from the point then rushed it back up the ice to get a good shot on net. He put some nice pressure on the fore-check but was taking long outside shots off the rush that didn't get through and also held on to the puck too long waiting to make a play in the neutral zone and was knocked over off the puck.

FINAL SCORE: 7-4 Waterloo Blackhawks

April 5, 2013, Calgary Hitmen vs. Red Deer Rebels (WHL)

CAL # 6, D, Harmsworth, Colby (2013) Harmsworth put some nice physicality on the puck carrier behind his own net to knock his man over. He made a great long pass to find a teammate at the far blue line to spring him into the offensive zone with speed and cleared the puck well on the penalty kill. He is calm with the puck and can protect it well from the opposition's pressure.

CAL # 25, C, Chase, Greg (2013) Chase battled hard for the puck along the boards and was distributing it well through the neutral zone. He put some good shots on net from along the boards to try to generate rebounds for a man out front and was opening up well down low next to the net on the power play to take a pass and put a great shot on for a couple excellent opportunities. He is strong on the puck, protects it well to get it up out of the zone on the rush and made a great pass to find a man down low driving to the net. He got a pretty good cycle going in deep in the offensive zone but fanned on a few shot opportunities and lost the puck.

CAL # 28, LW, Peterson, Elliott (2013) Peterson demonstrated great speed and hustle to be the 1st on the puck to pick up a loose puck in front of the net to score off the rush on his first shift of the game. He put some nice pressure and physicality on the fore-check to force turnovers and played the game with a good work ethic and battle for the puck. He battled hard, was able to get a good cycle going in deep and was going down low to take a pass for a chance in tight, however would have been more effective if he went directly to the net rather than skating into a corner with the puck. He protected the puck well along the wall and showed great strength to draw a penalty, however has to get the puck out of the zone on his chances on the penalty kill.

RDR # 8, D, Doetzel, Kayle (2013) Doetzel displayed good physicality on the puck carrier early on to knock his man over in behind his own net. He was able to make a good 1st pass out of the zone to start the breakout and displayed great strength to be able to take a hit and still hold on to the puck. He used his stick well to keep the opposition from gaining the inside track to the net but he has to get his shots through to the net from the point with more consistency.

RDR # 11, LW, Millette, Cory (2013) Millette drove well to the net with his stick down to deflect a shot on net from in tight. He protected the puck nicely and was able to get a good cycle going however needs to watch the offensive zone turnovers trying to force passes through the opposition. He had a good opportunity to pick off a turnover in his own end, but mishandled the puck as it went through him, giving the opposition a break opportunity that resulted in the game-winning goal.

RDR # 21, C, Johnson, Wyatt (2013) Johnson displayed good strength and puck protection to get the puck up out of the zone. He was battling hard to get to the net looking for loose pucks and rebounds and had a nice quick shot that he put on net right off the draw. He showed good speed, hustle and physicality on the puck carrier and nice speed on the rush to follow up his shot to pick up rebounds in the slot for some good opportunities. He has to watch some of the offensive zone turnovers on bad passes.

RDR # 27, RW, Bellerive, Matt (2013) Bellerive was distributing the puck well in the offensive zone to create space for himself and teammates to work with. He got a good cycle going in deep in the offensive zone, protected the puck well from the opposition and did a good job of rushing the puck up the ice. He had a nice net-front presence on the power play, battled hard for pucks in front and even got his stick on the puck in front to poke it loose to a teammate who batted the puck in to score on the power play. He put some good pressure and physicality on the fore-check, was physical and had a really big hit in open ice, however it ended up crossing the line and costing the team a 5-minute major penalty.

FINAL SCORE: 2-1 Calgary Hitmen

Apr 5, 2013, Kitchener Rangers vs. London Knights (OHL)

KIT # 16, LW, Pedersen, Brent (2013) Pedersen has some nice hands and moves, a good net-front presence and showed great strength and puck protection with the ability to hold on to the puck under pressure. He needs to watch the turnovers up along the boards trying to get the puck out of the zone to start the breakout and has to be stronger on the puck.

KIT # 95, RW, Bailey, Justin (2013) Bailey put really good pressure and physicality on the fore-check and got a good cycle going in deep. He showed nice sped with the ability to rush the puck up the ice and gain the offensive zone and has a really good quickness and puck distribution on the rush. He put a really good low shot on net off the rush to generate a rebound for a man in front and can read the play to jump up and pick off a turnover in the neutral zone and also got in a lane to block a shot from the point. He has to watch the neutral zone turnovers on puck mishandles.

LND # 16, C, Domi, Max (2013) Domi protected the puck really well along the wall, showed good strength on the puck and got a good cycle going. He displayed patience with the puck, was able to rush it up the ice effectively and put good pressure on the puck carrier on the fore-check. He had a couple good give and go plays, one to set up a man in the slot for a good shot opportunity and later had a similar play on an excellent saucer pas to find a man driving hard to the net for a great chance in tight. He made some really good breakout passes to start the rush, made a really good long pass to find an open man at the far blue line on the breakout and an excellent drop pass to create some space for a man in the slot for good shot off the rush. He showed his nice hands and agility to get around defenders and get to the slot for a shot, however it was deflected out of play and he had a bad turnover in the offensive zone trying to move the puck back to the point off a draw. He has great speed and quickness on the rush and went hard to the net to take a pass for a great chance in tight.

LND # 53, C, Horvat, Bo (2013) Horvat got a nice cycle going in deep in the offensive zone and was able to make a good 1st pass out of his own end to start the rush. He put nice pressure on the puck carrier, made a nice pass to find an open man in the high slot from beside the net and had a great 2nd effort for the puck. He was going hard to the net looking for loose pucks and rebounds and was able to find a lane to make a great pass and move the puck cross-ice in the offensive zone off the rush. He picked up the puck in the high slot for a great shot attempt, was blocking shots from the point and pressured the puck carrier well, but can't cross the line and take penalties by doing so. He also has to watch some of the offensive zone turnovers.

LND # 65, D, Zadorov, Nikita (2013) Zadorov was protecting the puck well along the boards from the opposition's pressure then moved the puck up along the boards safely to start the breakout. He used his stick well to knock the puck from the opposition and stepped up to make a huge open ice hit to knock his man over, however it allowed the opposition to come in on an odd-man rush. He was jumping up on the pinch to hold the zone, keep the attack and cycle alive and played with great physicality along the boards. He was soft on the puck along the boards in his own end resulting in a turnover, which the opposition scored on.

LND # 81, LW, Elie, Remi (2013) Elie picked up the puck in the high slot to put a good shot on and got a great cycle going in deep to try to drive the puck to the net. He showed great speed on the rush to get in deep with the puck on a dump and chase then got a good cycle going. He made a really nice big hit on the fore-check and a good pass to find a man going hard to the net that was just barely out of his reach.

LND # 91, RW, Platzer, Kyle (2013) Platzer put some nice pressure on the fore-check and displayed good agility and puck protection. He got a good cycle going and stepped out from behind the net to put an excellent shot on to score from a tough angle. He did a great job on the back-check to take the puck away from the opposition in the neutral zone but has to watch the offensive zone turnovers passing the puck through the opposition and was taking long outside shots off the rush that he missed the net on some of his opportunities.

FINAL SCORE: 4-1 London Knights

April 5, 2013, Sudbury Wolves vs. Belleville Bulls (OHL)

SDB # 9, LW, Desrochers, Danny (2013) Desrochers was battling really well for the puck to force turnovers in the neutral zone and was keeping his game simple by getting the puck in deep. He put really good pressure on the puck carrier to force turnovers in deep, finished his hits nicely on the puck carrier along the boards and was holding the offensive zone well by reading the play to pick off turnovers.

SDB # 14, RW, Baptiste, Nicholas (2013) Baptiste opened up really well in front of the net to take a pass and put a good shot on. He showed nice speed rushing the puck up the ice, but has to watch the turnovers trying to skate through the opposition and also by trying to force passes through. He has a nice net-front presence on the power play and made a great pass to lead a man into the offensive zone, then opened up in the high slot to take the puck back to put a shot on but has to hit the net on his opportunities. He showed good speed on the wide drive to put a shot on, however it would be better for him to drive the puck to the net. He continuously displayed fantastic speed and quickness on the rush into the offensive zone and put great pressure and physicality on the puck carrier on the fore-check. He was able to use his agility to twist from the opposition's pressure, but kept taking long outside shots.

SDB # 15, LW, Kubalik, Dominik (2013) Kubalik came back well to provide support in his own end and played his man hard along the boards. He got in lanes showing a willingness to block shots, put good pressure on the puck carrier at the point and likes to cycle the puck. He made a great pass to find a man in the slot for a great opportunity and the team ended up scoring on the play. He also made another great pass to set-up a one-timer in the high slot off the rush.

SDB # 16, C, Harris, Jacob (2013) Harris made a nice pass to move the puck out of the zone and start the breakout. He put good pressure on the point on the penalty kill and was clearing the puck up out of the zone. He put nice pressure on the puck carrier to pick up a turnover in the neutral zone, also put good pressure on the fore-check and was hustling hard for loose pucks. He came back pretty well on the back-check and was distributing the puck well from the point on the power play.

SDB # 21, LW, Kahun, Dominik (2013) Kahun displayed nice speed on the rush off the wing to step in towards the net and put a great shot on. He made a good pass to move the puck up out of his zone to start the breakout and showed some nice agility to rush the puck up the ice, stop up quick then made a good drop pass to create some space in the offensive zone. He got the puck in deep off the rush, displayed good speed to put pressure on the puck carrier and also to rush the puck up the ice and drive hard to the slot, however has to watch the turnovers trying to skate through the opposition. He also got beat down low on some great moves that resulted in him being forced to take a penalty to stop the opposition.

SDB # 24, D, DeHaan, Evan (2013) DeHaan stepped up in the neutral zone to pick off a turnover to rush the puck up the ice and draw a penalty. He was able to skate the puck up on the rush, made some good breakout passes and used his body and stick well to keep the opposition from driving towards the net. He made a really good long pass to spring a man at the far blue line but still has to get stronger as he was muscled off the puck far too easily as the opposition took the puck then moved to the front of the net to score.

BEL # 8, RW, Berisha, Aaron (2013) Berisha showed good strength and puck protection and got a good cycle going in deep. He protected the puck well and had a great drive to the net from behind for an excellent chance in tight to the net on his wrap-around attempt. He was hustling hard for loose pucks and made a good pass out of his zone to lead a man on the breakout for a teammate to score an empty netter.

BEL # 14, D, Subban, Jordan (2013) Subban has a great ability to skate the puck up the ice on the rush, and is willing to jump up into the high slot to provide scoring options in the offensive zone. He had nice hands and moves to rush the puck up into the offensive zone, but has to watch the turnovers trying to dangle through the opposition. He stepped down low into the slot to take a pass, reading the play well on the pinch then made a move to get to the middle and put an excellent shot top shelf to score. He had great speed and hands on the rush up the ice, split the defense then drove hard to the net and was also able to get a cycle going in deep with the puck. He made a really good diving play to block a pass and knock the puck away on the opposition's odd-man rush.

FINAL SCORE: 4-1 Belleville Bulls

April 5, 2013, Val D'or Foreurs @ Blainsville-Boisbriand Armada (QMJHL)

Val-d'Or

#8 Anthony Mantha, RW (2013): Not a good game from Mantha, who didn't do anything at 5-on-5 all night and didn't record any shots in the first 2 periods. Threw some hits here and there, but had no real impact on the game. A miss on defensive zone coverage led to a goal against, and he was seen floating in the neutral zone waiting for a stretch pass. Played on the top line with team captain Cedric Henley and 2013-eligible Vincent Dunn. Got ejected late in the 3rd period after taking his opponent's helmet off during a useless fight at the end of the game. This leads to an automatic 1 game suspension in the QMJHL.

#16 Nicolas Aube-Kubel, RW (2014): Aube-Kubel had a nice first period playing on the Foreurs 3rd line. He had 2 good scoring chances on the same shift and brought some good energy to a team who was not in this game from the drop of the puck. Looked to have good chemistry with fellow rookie Anthony Richard, and made a brilliant deke while gaining the offensive zone on an Armada defenseman but couldn't finish it, and he showed flashes of what he could do more of next season. He didn't get much ice time in the 3rd period, not sure if this was due to an injury.

#20 Anthony Richard, LW (2015): Richard brought some good energy on the Foreurs' 3rd line with Aube-Kubel; he is small but a quick skater. Youngest player in the QMJHL this season (December 20th 1996), but didn't get much ice time in 2nd or 3rd period, Val-d'Or was down earlier in the game and in this case, their coach was likely decide to go with his veterans.

#26 Vincent Dunn, LW (2013): Even though the Foreurs were never in this game, Dunn showed some good stuff in the agitating department. Didn't stop being a pain to play against, whether it was from a good hit or slashing opposing forward after a whistle. He also liked to target good players from the other team to agitate; he had a big hit against Armada captain Xavier Ouellet that could have been called for a head shot. The Foreurs had very few good scoring chances all night, but Dunn had at least 2-3 of them. He is the type of player that goes in the hard areas of the ice and is willing to pay the price in front of the net.

Blainville-Boisbriand

#11 Marc-Olivier Roy, RW (2013): Roy had a strong game for the Armada with 4 points, scored on his first shift where the Foreurs couldn't get the puck out of their zone and Roy jumped on a rebound in front of the net to put the Armada up 1-0. Roy, like most of his teammates, has a great work ethic and is a good skater. Played on the team's top line with Cedric Paquette and Christopher Clapperton. Not afraid to get his nose dirty as well. His best play of the night came midway through the 2nd period on the PK, as he first beat a defenseman wide and cut to the net but lost control of the puck, then made a strong backcheck effort to get the puck back in his zone and deked 2 Val-d'or defenders and set up Paquette for an easy tap-in goal. Scored his 2nd goal from a one timer on the PP late in the 2nd period.

#15 Philippe Sanche, LW/RW (2013) Watching Sanche, you would think a pee-wee player was on the Armada, as he is very tiny at 5'5", 150 lbs, but Sanche has a lot of hustle and heart. Easy to contain in one-on-one matchups in the offensive zone versus bigger defenders. A little bulldog, knocked 6'4", 200 lbs Skyler Spiller on his behind with a good hit in the game which drew a lot of reaction in the crowd. Chances are very slim he gets drafted, but it will be interesting to follow his progression over the next couple of years.

#57 Christopher Clapperton LW (2013, undrafted last year): Clapperton had a great game with his 2 linemates Paquette and Roy. The product of the ESND Albatros is a little bulldog who does a lot of good work along the boards and wins a lot of one on one battles. Not an explosive skater, which explains him being passed over in last year's NHL draft. If he could improve his speed I could see an NHL team take a chance on him late in the draft or as invitee. He's a good goal scorer with good hands and also can agitate opposing teams with his nonstop motor. In this game he did a lot of dirty work for Paquette and Roy, winning puck battles in the corner which led to one of the 2 goals from Paquette.

#71 Nikita Jevpalovs. LW (2013): The Latvian forward has been a revelation in the 2nd half of the season for the Armada after struggling in the first half of the season. Scored 2 goals in this game, first he got puck in the slot and fired a quick wrister glove-side and on his 2nd goal he tipped a shot from Xavier Ouellet while standing in front of the goalie. Jevpalovs has brought a nice scoring touch on the Armada's 3rd line with Marcus Hinds and Danick Martel.

April 5, 2013, Calgary Hitmen vs Red Deer Rebels (WHL)

RD #4, Fleury, Haydn (2014) – Highly mobile 16 year old defenseman with size. Very nice speed. Balanced could improve and it should as he fills out a bit. Fleury makes good stretch passes and is willing to join the rush. Defensively, Fleury needs to improve his consistency. His positioning and stick placement along the walls caused him to reach a bit for the puck and player at times when he could have simply bumped or pinned his opponent and then retrieved the puck.

RD #8, Doetzel, Kayle (2013) – Very steady defensively tonight. Very good size and mobility. Used his stick well and will play the body as needed. Even when pressured, Doetzel seemed calm and composed in his end. First pass is alright, but he really needs to develop his play with the puck.

RD #9, Bleackley, Conner (2014) – Looks to be a little bigger and stronger than he was early in the year and looks more confident as a result. Was leaned on heavily with his team down a goal late in the game. Was often chosen to take key offensive faceoffs throughout the game and did well to win the majority of them. A very good (and elusive) skater. Bleackley has very soft hands and is able to make plays with the puck in traffic. Likes to use his skating to create a little bit of space for himself to make a quick pass to one of his wingers. Picked up an assist on the night. A cerebral player, Bleackley is strong at both ends of the ice and generally is very well positioned on the ice relative to the situation. This player has high upside.

RD #11, Millette, Cory (2013) – Solid on his skates. Worked well along the side boards to get the puck out of his zone. In the offensive zone, he would seemingly get lost in a crowd of people yet several times ended up having the puck on his stick for a good chance. Could improve his first few steps. A solid player, but his development looks to be a bit stalled. Doesn't seem to have improved a lot since his successful rookie season.

RD #23, Gaudet, Brady (2013) – A heady, mobile defenseman. Has a bit of grit. Makes a good first pass and has the skating ability to create offense, but Gaudet isn't interested. He likes to keep things simple and just move the puck. Under-sized as a defensive defenseman as he isn't punishing and needs to make himself harder to play against. Guilty of a couple gaffes in his own end with and without the puck that led to some chances for Calgary on the night.

RD #27, Bellerive, Matt (2013) – Bellerive is a good energy player that can provide some physicality and pop a few goals too. That looked to be how he was playing on this night as well before he took a major penalty for kneeing Pavlo Padakin (and ending his night) about midway through the game. Assisted on Red Deer's lone goal on the night.

RD #35, Bartosak, Patrick (2013) – Kept his team in the game and was easily the most important player on the ice. Red Deer lost a close game 2-1, but Bartosak made 40 saves in the loss and he thwarted numerous high quality chances. He's not the biggest goalie at 6'0-6'1, but showed an excellent compete level and good reflexes. Actively challenged shooters without being too aggressive. Could stand play his angles a little better, but he was great at making saves and limited his rebounds.

Cal #18, Virtanen, Jake (2014) – Improved vision – tunnel vision earlier in the year. Willing to go through guys, even when he has the puck. Drove hard to the net and didn't shy away from bigger players. Soft hands. Passes could be a bit more accurate. Good release on the wrist shot, but again could improve accuracy. Very good speed which he used to challenge defenders ability to skate with him.

Cal #25, Chase, Greg (2013) – Chase had a pretty quiet night. He received an unsportsman-like penalty for yapping and was the beneficiary of a couple nice passes. He didn't generate any offense on his own tonight. His skating looked to hold him back a bit as he fell behind the play a few times. He really needs to work on his acceleration and agility.

Cal #31, Shields, Mac (2013) – Did not play.

Scouts Notes: Calgary severely outplayed the Rebels on the night. Despite high shot totals for the Rebels, very few were high quality chances. At the other end, Bartosak was very busy and made numerous big saves to keep his team in the game

Apr 7, 2013, Kelowna Rockets vs. Kamloops Blazers (WHL)

KEL#4 RD, Bowey, Madison(2013) Dynamic defenseman had a good game at both ends of the ice. Was able to use his speed to his advantage to carry the puck and try to make a difference off the rush. Went through traffic in the third and got a good scoring chance in the slot. Jumped into the play once and as a trailer was able to get open and create another chance to score. Did a good job on the PP on the point to set up plays and displayed good vision. Defensively, made one memorable play where off a 2 on 2 rush, he quickly closed the gap as the opponent was skating to the blue line and landed a nice hit along the walls to separate him off the puck. Tried to do too much without the puck at times and was caught running around.

KEL#6 RD, Wheaton, Mitchell(2013) Big defensive defenseman played with a shoulder injury tonight that requires surgery, but did a good job in his own end and to use his body effectively. Played a physical game along the walls and really made his presence felt down low. Wheaton used his long reach to take away passes, and protect the puck whenever he was able to get a hold of it in the defensive zone. He provided a very limited presence offensively, and made average outlet passes. Wheaton was beaten to the inside on rushes, and will need to get into better positions and be better at using his stick to knock away pucks at times.

KEL#26 RC, Linaker, Cole(2013) Played mostly as a 4th line centre during the regular season, but was given more playing time tonight due to injuries and did a good job of filling in for his teammates. He was all over the ice and made his presence known around the net offensively and with solid hits and high level of intensity in the defensive zone. Linaker had a couple of nice chances to score in tight, but just was not able to finish. He was also not very strong on his skates, and will need to improve on staying on his feet even when being knocked around by opponents physically to maintain puck possession and positioning without the puck.

KAM#14 RC, Needham, Matt(2013) Quick, playmaking centre had a very good game tonight in all areas of the ice. Nice to see him play with good intensity, something he was missing often during the regular season. Really looked like he wanted the puck on his stick and fought hard for loose pucks. He was often the first one in on the forecheck and he may lack some size, but hit opponents with a purpose and was able to create a turnover a couple of times. Made smart, quick decisions with the puck and looked poised whenever he was handling the puck.

KAM#21 LW, Ully, Cole(2013) Speedy, 2 way winger was excellent at both ends of the ice. Impressed with the number of turnovers he created in the neutral zone with his good stick positioning and ability to read the play. Ully was quick to start the counter attack and looked dangerous off the wing with his speed. Was not afraid to cut to the middle in the high slot to get shots off. Was hard to knock down along the walls with his quickness and strong lower body strength. Was a monster on the PK with his stick and willingness to block shots. Backchecked hard at all times. Big reason why the Blazers won tonight.

Scouts Notes: The Blazers played a very inspired game tonight. It really started with JC Lipon and his line mates. They were able to create offense by creating turnovers and using their speed and skills off the rush to get good chances. Very impressed with Matt Needham tonight. He needs to play with the purpose he showed in this game on a regular basis. Cole Ully was great again as usual at both ends of the ice. I was curious to see how much impact Mitchell Wheaton could have with his injured shoulder, but handled himself quite well out on the ice.

FINAL SCORE: 5-1 Kamloops

April 7, 2013, Sudbury Wolves vs. Belleville Bulls (OHL)

SDB # 9, LW, Desrochers, Danny (2013) Desrochers was battling really well for the puck to force turnovers in the neutral zone and was keeping his game simple by getting the puck in deep. He put really good pressure on the puck carrier to force turnovers on the fore-check, finished his hits nicely on the puck carrier along the boards and was holding the offensive zone well by reading the play to pick off turnovers.

SDB # 14, RW, Baptiste, Nicholas (2013) Baptiste opened up really well in front of the net to take a pass and put a good shot on. He showed nice speed rushing the puck up the ice, but has to watch the turnovers trying to skate through the opposition and also by trying to force passes through. He had a nice net-front presence on the power play and made a great pass to lead a man into the offensive zone, then opened up in the high slot to take the puck back to put a shot on, but has to hit the net on his opportunities. He showed good speed on the wide drive to put a shot on net, however it would be better for him to drive the puck down low towards the net. He continuously displayed fantastic speed and quickness on the rush into the offensive zone and put great pressure and physicality on the puck carrier on the fore-check. He was able to use his agility to twist from the opposition's pressure, but kept taking long outside shots.

SDB # 15, LW, Kubalik, Dominik (2013) Kubalik came back well to provide support in his own end and played his man hard along the boards. He got in lanes showing a willingness to block shots, put good pressure on the puck carrier at the point and likes to cycle the puck. He made a great pass to find a man in the slot for a great opportunity and the team ended up scoring on the play. He also made another great pass to set-up a one-timer in the high slot off the rush.

SDB # 16, C, Harris, Jacob (2013) Harris made a nice pass to move the puck out of the zone and start the breakout. He put good pressure on the point on the penalty kill and was clearing the puck up out of the zone. He put nice pressure on the puck carrier to pick up a turnover in the neutral zone, also put good pressure on the fore-check and was hustling hard for loose pucks. He came back pretty well on the back-check and was distributing the puck well from the point on the power play.

SDB # 21, LW, Kahun, Dominik (2013) Kahun displayed nice speed on the rush off the wing to step in towards the net and put a great shot on. He made a good pass to move the puck up out of his zone to start the breakout and showed some nice agility to rush the puck up the ice, stop up quick then made a good drop pass to create some space in the offensive zone. He got the puck in deep off the rush, displayed good speed to put pressure on the puck carrier and also to rush the puck up the ice and drive hard to the slot, however has to watch the turnovers trying to skate through the opposition. He also got beat down low on some great moves that resulted in him being forced to take a penalty to stop the opposition.

SDB # 24, D, DeHaan, Evan (2013) DeHaan stepped up in the neutral zone to pick off a turnover to rush the puck up the ice and draw a penalty. He was able to skate the puck up on the rush, made some good breakout passes and used his body and stick well to keep the opposition from driving towards the net. He made a really good long pass to spring a man at the far blue line but still has to get stronger as he was muscled off the puck far too easily as the opposition took the puck then moved to the front of the net to score.

BEL # 8, RW, Berisha, Aaron (2013) Berisha showed good strength and puck protection and got a good cycle going in deep. He protected the puck well and had a great drive to the net from behind for an excellent chance in tight to the net on his wrap-around attempt. He was hustling hard for loose pucks and made a good pass out of his zone to lead a man on the breakout for a teammate to score an empty netter.

BEL # 14, D, Subban, Jordan (2013) Subban has a great ability to skate the puck up the ice on the rush, and is willing to jump up into the high slot to provide scoring options in the offensive zone. He had nice hands and moves to rush the puck up into the offensive zone, but has to watch the turnovers trying to dangle through the opposition. He stepped down low into the slot to take a pass, reading the play well on the pinch then made a move to get to the middle and put an excellent shot top shelf to score. He had great speed and hands on the rush up the ice, split the defense then drove hard to the net and was also able to get a cycle going in deep with the puck. He made a really good diving play to block a pass and knock the puck away on the opposition's odd-man rush.

FINAL SCORE: 4-1 Belleville Bulls

April 8, 2013, London Knights vs. Kitchener Rangers (OHL)

KIT # 19, C, Sterk, Josh (2013) Sterk opened up well right next to the net to take a pass and roof his shot for a good goal in tight. He had great speed, pressure and physicality put on the fore-check and used his speed nicely to rush the puck up the ice into the offensive zone. He was finishing his hits along the boards, even knocking over his man at times but took an undisciplined retaliatory penalty and needs to keep himself from taking selfish penalties that might cost the team.

KIT # 95, RW, Bailey, Justin (2013) Bailey displayed nice speed through the neutral zone to get in deep in the offensive zone and get by a defenseman to draw a penalty. He had nice speed skating the puck into the offensive zone then took a nice low shot from the high slot off the rush. He picked off a neutral zone turnover and showed nice strength to win the battle for the puck and avoid being knocked off it. He had fantastic speed on the rush then made a toe-drag move to get a good shot off from the slot, however later lost the puck on a mishandle at the offensive blue line.

LND # 16, C, Domi, Max (2013) Domi showed nice speed on the rush to gain the offensive zone and get to the high slot to put a good shot on net. He showed great agility to spin off the opposition and avoid their pressure and was distributing the puck well to find a man in the high slot off the rush. He went hard to the net to try to deflect a shot from in tight and showed good physicality on the puck carrier. He made a really nice give and go play through the neutral zone to gain the offensive zone with speed for a good shot attempt and had great speed on the wide drive off the rush then made a good centering pass to find a man in front of the net. He had a nice hard one-timer that he got through to the net from the point on the power play, however has to watch the offensive zone turnovers trying to force passes through the opposition and also missed his target on a couple breakout passes. He also had a bad pass into the middle in the offensive zone with no one there, resulting in an easy clear for the opposition.

LND # 53, LW, Horvat, Bo (2013) Horvat made a nice breakout pass on the rush through the neutral zone and was hustling and battling hard to get on loose pucks. He was getting in lanes to block shots on the penalty kill and clearing the puck out of the zone, but at times was over aggressive going for blocks which left a lane open through the middle for the opposition to move the puck cross-ice for a one-timer goal. He also turned the puck over off the rush in the offensive zone on the power play allowing the opposition to clear the puck out of the zone and needs to watch the offensive zone turnovers on bad passes. He was however able to pick off a pass and clear the puck out of the zone on the penalty kill.

LND # 65, D, Zadorov, Nikita (2013) Zadorov was able to make some good breakout passes for teammates at the far blue line and was playing physical including a really big hit to knock his man over along the boards. He showed nice strength to clear the puck and man from in front of the net and was protecting the puck well from the opposition's pressure. He showed good patience with the puck, but has to get his shot through to the net on his chance from the point. He made a nice pass to find an open man all alone right in front of the net late in the game and was getting involved in scrums after whistles but has to watch the turnovers on some of his breakout passes along the boards in order to start the rush properly with more consistency. On the opposition's 3rd goal of the game he was also not quite quick enough to clear the big rebound which allowed the opposition to shoot on an open net and score.

LND # 81, LW, Elie, Remi (2013) Elie got in lanes showing a willingness to block shots on the penalty kill and was putting good pressure on the fore-check. He showed good strength to stay on the puck and not be knocked off it and was able to make a great pass to find an open man in the slot for a good shot opportunity. He played the puck carrier hard and physical along the boards and showed nice hands and moves to get around defenders then cut to the net for a good opportunity in tight. He had a bad turnover by trying to be fancy and cut to the middle going through the opposition in the offensive zone and has to watch turnovers on no-look drop passes in the offensive zone.

FINAL SCORE: 6-2 Kitchener Rangers

Apr 9, 2013, Gatineau Olympiques vs. Halifax Mooseheads (QMJHL)

GAT # 7, D, Deslauriers, Jean-Simon (2013) Deslauriers did a nice job of getting in lanes to block shots in front of the net and was jumping up on the pinch to hold the offensive zone and keep the attack alive. He distributed the puck well from the point on the power play and made an excellent pass to find an open man in front of the net for a great chance. He held the offensive line well to keep the cycle alive and was making some good passes to find the open man down low on the power play, but missed the target on a few of his breakout passes. He did not clear the front of his net very effectively at one point and the puck ended up in the back of his net and was physical on the puck carrier but at times was too aggressive and followed his man up too high leaving an open man down low.

GAT # 14, RW, Kelly, Brent (2013) Kelly kept to a pretty simple game tonight, just getting the puck out of the zone and in deep into the offensive zone. He got in lanes to block shots but has to be stronger on the puck so that he is not muscled off it so easily.

GAT # 27, LW, Poirier, Emile (2013) Poirier continuously displayed excellent speed off the wings then great hands to cut toward the net to put shots on from in tight in scoring position on some really nice power forward moves. He was battling to get to the slot to provide scoring options and picked up the puck at the blue line to blow by the defense, come in on net and make a great back-hand move to score. He had dynamic speed on the rush to blow by defenders then move the puck cross-crease to a teammate for an excellent chance in tight and opened up in the slot to take a pass and put a good shot on. He also went hard to the net on the power play to pick up a rebound and score and took a pass down low right in front of the net to make a great move but was unable to score on the play. He showed great strength on the puck, some really nice patience to wait for lanes to open up to shoot and was pressuring the puck carrier all night.

GAT # 44, LW, Reway, Martin (2013) Reway put good pressure on the fore-check to force turnovers and did a nice job picking up a drop pass in the slot off the rush to put a good shot on. He was driving to the net with his stick down to take a pass for a great opportunity in tight and was protecting the puck well on the wide drive. He battled hard for the puck on the fore-check to force turnovers, was really strong on the puck to draw penalties and showed excellent hands and moves to get around defenders towards the slot for some good chances. He has really quick hands to avoid the opposition's pressure and good speed on the rush to cut to the middle then drop the puck for a good shot opportunity for a teammate from the slot. He made an excellent pass to find a man down low in front of the net, however needs to watch the neutral zone turnovers and also has to make better decisions with the puck on the power play, as he elected to shoot from the point on a 5-on-3 advantage with no lane available.

HAL # 19, RW, Falkenham, Ryan (2013) Falkenham got a good cycle going in deep, was protecting the puck nicely along the boards and was also able to take a hit and still hold on to the puck to make a play and get the puck in deep. He put nice pressure on the puck carrier on the point on the penalty kill and on the fore-check and was hustling hard on the back-check. He kept to a pretty simple game, taking long outside shots from the high slot, getting in lanes to block shots and clearing the puck out of the zone on the penalty kill.

HAL # 22, C, MacKinnon, Nathan (2013) MacKinnon has nice quick hands and was distributing the puck really well through the neutral zone. He has explosive speed to gain the offensive zone then stop up quickly showing his great agility before moving the puck to an open man in the high slot. He went hard to the net to provide scoring options down low and found lanes in the offensive zone to move the puck around to an open man in the high slot for a great one-timer chance. He made an excellent cross-crease pass on the power play to find a teammate for a tap-in goal and also made a nice pass to set-up a one-timer from the point on the power play. He opened up well in the slot to take a pass and put a great shot on and had a nice net-front presence as well. He needs to watch the neutral zone turnovers trying to dangle his way through the opposition.

HAL # 24, D, Murphy, Matt (2013) Murphy displayed nice speed and hands on the rush up the ice to gain the offensive zone and get to the high slot for a good shot attempt. He made an excellent long pass to spring a man at the far blue line into the offensive zone for a good opportunity and showed great hands and moves to avoid the opposition's pressure, then move the puck up to start the breakout. He got down in front of the net showing a willingness to block shots but made a really bad pass in his own end right up the middle resulting in a turnover.

HAL # 27, LW, Drouin, Jonathan (2013) Drouin made an excellent pass on the power play to find a lane to get the puck to an open man in the slot beside the net for a great shot opportunity. He has fantastic hands, puck protection and strength on the puck to hold on to it under pressure. He was clearing the puck on the penalty kill, playing physical to force turnovers then take the puck and cycle it down low. He opened up really well in the high slot for a great one-timer chance, displayed great speed to rush the puck up the ice then find an open trailing player in the high slot. He had a fantastic cross-ice pass off the rush in the offensive zone to create an excellent chance and showed really good vision on the rush to spot the open man trailing in the high slot.

FINAL SCORE: 4-2 Halifax Mooseheads

Apr 9, 2013, Barrie Colts vs Oshawa Generals (OHL)

BAR # 7, D, Yuil, Alex (2013) Yuil displayed great agility to twist from the opposition's pressure to make a play and put a nice low shot from the point to score. He used his stick well to knock the puck off the opposition and got the puck in deep off the rush on some pretty simple dump-in plays. He is strong on the puck, protects it well and uses his body effectively to keep the opposition from gaining the inside track to the net. He also played the puck carrier pretty hard and physical along the boards.

BAR # 18, C, Bradford, Erik (2013) Bradford did a good job of tying up his man in front of his own net and he went down to get in lanes and block shots. He showed nice speed and hustle for loose pucks and was competing well in the corner for the puck. He did a good job of driving to the net with his stick down and tying up his man along the boards in his own zone. He put some good pressure on the fore-check, got the front of his own net to direct a shot out of play and was able to twist away from the opposition's pressure.

BAR # 24, D, Webster, Michael (2013) Webster uses his body well to protect the puck from the oppositions pressure and was clearing his man from the front of the net well to give the goaltender a view of the shot coming. He showed some nice hands and moves through the neutral zone to draw a penalty and displayed some nice physicality on the puck carrier along the boards. He holds the offensive line well, is able to get a cycle going in the offensive zone and was jumping up on the rush protecting the puck nicely on the wide drive into the offensive zone. He did however take a pretty unintelligent interference penalty on a play after he got beat on in the neutral zone.

OSH # 7, D, Carlisle, Chris (2013) Carlisle was able to make some nice chip plays along the boards to avoid the opposition's pressure and was distributing the puck well from the point in the offensive zone. He has a pretty nice hard shot from the point, which he was able to get through to the net, however needs to be able to do so with more consistency. He displayed nice speed to skate the puck end-to-end but then decided to take an outside shot and missed the net wide. He also followed his man on a play behind the net leaving the front of the net open for the opposition to walk in and score and has to watch the turnovers along the boards in his own end. He can't keep shooting the puck into shin pads from the point, as he needs to find lanes to the net and also has to get stronger on the puck along the boards so that he doesn't lose it so easily and allow the opposition to get in towards the net for good chances in tight.

OSH # 14, RW, Latour, Bradley (2013) Latour put excellent pressure and physicality on the fore-check and played with a great work ethic, hustle and compete for the puck. He finishes his hits on the puck carrier along the boards, including one really big hit to knock his man over in behind his own net. He is strong on his feet, hustles for loose pucks and was driving to the net and willing to play in dirty areas. He moved the puck well on the cycle and was forcing turnovers on the fore-check.

OSH # 19, C, Cassels, Cole (2013) Cassels made a nice pass to find a man in the slot from the side-boards and showed some great hands and moves to gain the offensive zone wide off the rush. He opened up nicely in the slot to take a pass and put a one-timer on net and did a great job on the back-check of tying up his man who was driving the net. He was clearing the puck out of the zone on the penalty kill, cycling the puck nicely in deep and was physical on the fore-check. He also got his stick in lanes to deflect shots out of the way as well as breaking up passes and opportunities for the opposition. He got in behind the defense on the penalty kill for a break opportunity and made a great back-hand move for a good chance. He has to watch some of the neutral zone turnovers trying to dangle his way through the opposition.

FINAL SCORE: 4-2 Barrie Colts

Apr 10, 2013, Gatineau Olympiques vs Halifax Mooseheads (QMJHL)

HAL # 22, C, MacKinnon, Nathan (2013) MacKinnon was cycling the puck well in the offensive zone and showed good strength and puck protection along the boards. He had some dynamic speed on the rush through the neutral zone but then decided to take an outside back-hand shot rather than drive the puck to the net. He displayed excellent strength to take a hit and still hold on to the puck to make a play, moving it to an open man in the high slot and also had great speed on a 2-on-1 then made a great cross-crease pass to provide a tap in goal for his teammate. He was coming into the offensive zone with speed and some excellent hands to split the defense and drive the puck to the net for a great chance in tight, but was also able to make an excellent pass to find a man driving down the middle. He had a nice net-front presence, was battling hard for pucks along the boards but has to watch some of the turnovers when he tries to force passes through the opposition.

HAL # 24, D, Murphy, Matt (2013) Murphy was able to make some good passes to move the puck up out of the zone to start the breakout and was getting in lanes to block shots in front of his own net. He was also getting in lanes to block passes in front of the net, battled hard for the puck behind the net and was able to protect it well from the opposition's pressure. He needs to hit his target on the breakout passes with more consistency and needs to watch the turnovers up along the boards in his own end. He also had a bad turnover at the blue line, which allowed the opposition to rush the puck back up the ice to score.

HAL # 27, LW, Drouin, Jonathan (2013) Drouin has really nice quick hands and a shiftiness to get around defenders, then made an excellent centering pass to find a man in front of the net. He made a really nice give-and-go play on the power play to get to the slot for a shot and found a lane in the offensive zone to get the puck to the high slot for a good chance on a one-timer. He has a really nice quickness and agility to get in tight to the net with the puck for great opportunities and some excellent hands, speed and moves through the neutral zone to get around the opposition and draw penalties. He was distributing the puck well on the rush through the neutral zone and showed great speed and pressure on the puck carrier. There was also one fantastic play that he made to find a man back-door on the power play for a great chance and he was driving hard to the net with his stick down to provide options in tight. He got in lanes to block passes and breakup plays for the opposition and made a great long pass to find a man at the far blue line to spring him into the offensive zone. He did have one bad turnover however up the middle through the neutral zone.

HAL # 31, G, Fucale, Zackary (2013) Fucale started the game off a little bit shaky giving up a pretty bad rebound in front of his net which allowed the opposition to score the 1st goal of the game. He bounced back though and used his sick nicely to clear the puck from the front of his net when his team was in danger of letting in another goal and he read the play well to make an excellent save on a point blank shot right in front of the net. He came to the top of his crease to challenge the shooter and save a slap shot with no rebound and for the most part when there were rebounds he kicked them out to the corners. He did direct one rebound however back out to the slot and the opposition picked it up to score the 3rd goal of the game. Late in the game he made a nice quick glove save to stop a shot from the high slot and hold on to the lead.

GAT # 7, D, Deslauriers, Jean-Simon (2013) Deslauriers displayed nice quickness and agility with the puck and was distributing it well on the rush through the neutral zone. He tied up his man well who was driving hard to the net and was able to make some good passes out of the zone to start the breakout. He was jumping up to join the attack down low and made some nice moves to step around a defender to get a shot through to the net. He has to be stronger on the puck at times and needs to watch some of the turnovers up the middle through the neutral zone. He also stepped up and was caught watching the puck as the forward came in behind him to take a pass for a great opportunity.

GAT # 27, LW, Poirier, Emile (2013) Poirier displayed great speed to blow by defenders then cut to the net on a great power forward move for a good chance in tight. He was battling hard for loose pucks in front of the net and was physical making some big hits on the puck carrier along the wall. He made a nice drop pass off the rush to create space for his teammate to shoot the puck then went hard to the net looking for loose pucks and rebounds. He was using his speed well to beat defenders and get to the net for chances in tight and also made some nice back-hand moves for good opportunities from the slot. He cut to the middle in the high slot off the rush for a good low shot and opened up well in the slot to take a pass for a slap-shot chance.

GAT # 44, C, Reway, Martin (2013) Reway showed some of his great skating, speed and pressure that he put on the puck carrier. He was distributing the puck well on the rush through the neutral zone and displayed a nice agility to twist from the opposition's pressure then made a great pass to lead a man into the offensive zone with speed off the rush. He was physical on the puck carrier at times and made some good cross-ice passes in the offensive zone, finding lanes to move the puck, but has to move the puck a bit quicker on the rush rather than skating into the opposition trying to make a fancy play. He was also taking long outside shots off the rush and turned the puck over in the neutral zone trying to dangle his way through. He missed the target on a few of his breakout passes on the rush and had a really bad turnover at the offensive blue line trying to be fancy. He was getting involved with the opposition after whistles showing some good aggression but ended up taking a dumb extra penalty in doing so.

GAT # 88, LW, Kennedy, Jordan (2013) Kennedy put some good pressure on the fore-check, was strong on the puck and protected it well from the opposition, then was able to make a good pass to find an open man in front of the net for an excellent opportunity. He is a pretty good skater and can cycle the puck well and was getting to the front of the net for that nice net-front presence. He played the puck carrier with some good physicality along the boards and also got the front of the net to pick up a rebound and score from point blank. He opened up well in the slot to take a pass and put a good shot on but has to get his shots through to the net on his opportunities and also needs to watch the turnovers along the boards in his own end.

FINAL SCORE: 5-3 Halifax Mooseheads

Apr 20, 2013, Finland vs. Russia (World U18 Championships)

FIN#2 LD, Kuronen, Jimi(2013) Undersized, poised defenseman had an up and down game. Looked very comfortable with the puck, but his outlet passes were quite inconsistent. Needs to work on hitting his teammates with a better pass at all times. Was able to get away from the forecheck of Russia time and time again, and if he can improve on moving the puck, can be a dangerous aspect of his game. Defensively, Kuronen did a good job of being physical, but he needs to be better at reading the play. Good example is on the PK, there was a mini 2 on 1 situation down low and he had help from his forward to take away the pass, but he was so focused on taking away the passing lane that the opponents with the puck in the slot down low scored easily. Could be better at positioning overall.

FIN#12 LW, Lehkonen, Artturi(2013) Quick winger who received a lot of ice time tonight, but was not able to generate many offensive chances. Lehkonen was far too easy to knock down, and his play along the walls and in the slot really suffered as a result. Displayed soft hands and good skating abilities out in open ice, but if there was any physical play involved, he was invisible. Took shots from everywhere and looked for rebounds. Needs to drive the net with more authority without the puck and be a target for his teammates off the wall. Defensively, his awareness without the puck was quite poor. Was not able to make any good defensive plays and was quite soft along the walls.

RUS#27 LW, Nichushkin, Valeri(2013) Big power forward had a dominant game tonight with the puck. So strong and so big that opponents had a very difficult time knocked him off the puck. In one memorable sequence, he took the puck from the wall and cut to the high slot with 3 Finnish players on his back, but he was still able to get a shot off on net. Dangerous combination of speed and strength. Loves to skate with the puck up the ice, and his speed and quickness is very impressive to watch. Lacked playmaking ability in his game tonight. Basically unstoppable along the walls tonight.

Made such quick starts and stops, and turned on a dime with the puck when necessary to drive to the net.

RUS#2 LD, Rafikov, Rushan(2013) Physical defenseman had a good game at both ends of the ice tonight. Very strong along the walls, and not afraid to use his body to separate opponents from the puck. Read the play quite well in his own end, and made a number of good plays throughout the night. Needs to work on his gap control in the neutral zone, and his speed to be able to be more aggressive. Offensively, Rafikov was average with the puck. Needs to work on being more consistent with his outlet passes, particularly the speed of his passes. Made one really good play to join the rush, get a shot off in the slot, then follow up with the play and pick up his own rebound and then hit the post.

SCOUT'S NOTES: This was a good back and forth game, but Russia eventually took over with their bigger forwards and better execution overall. Valeri Nichushkin was clearly the best player out on the ice tonight. Was nearly unstoppable when he protected the puck with his body. Juuse Saros of Finland was very impressive with his lightning quick lateral speed. Looked very poised in net and made a number of great post to post saves. Concern is his lack of size. Teams could expose him by shooting up high. Disappointed with Arturri Lehkonen's game. Would like to see him create more chances with the puck and be more productive with the ice time that he receives.

FINAL SCORE: 3-1 Russia

April 23, 2013. Team Russia vs. Team Czech Republic (World U18 Championships)

RUS # 6, LD, Demidov, Nikolai (2014) Demidov had a strong game on the blue line for Team Russia. He showed strong offensive awareness picking pinch opportunities well including jumping up into a 2 on 1 and scoring a key goal when the game was tight. Nikolai was skating well and was good at utilizing an active stick to keep oncoming opponents wide. He was good along the boards and worked hard battling for loose pucks in the defensive zone. Demidov showed no panic when controlling the puck while being pressured by Czech fore checkers and consistently made smart outlet passes allowing for quick counter attack opportunities. Nikolai lacked much of a physical presence in this game and would really benefit from finishing checks in the corners and becoming tougher in front of his own net.

RUS # 10, LW, Tolchinsky, Sergey (2013) Tolchinsky flashed the great skating skill he showed all season long playing in the OHL. He generated a good burst of speed with just a few short strides and showed the ability to break away from opposing back checkers. Sergey showcased these skills on one specific penalty kill where he blocked a shot before stepping around the defender and breaking away into a breakaway before slipping the puck past the Czech goaltender. He earned numerous chances for himself but was unable to finish on any others besides the breakaway. Sergey showed a nice level of offensive creativity and was not scared from trying new moves or passes working well with his linemates to generate consistent offensive pressure. Tolchinsky showed good playmaking abilities and vision and constantly displays a strong puck handling ability. He was good at keeping his head up and ensured that he dodged most checkers coming his way.

RUS # 21, RC, Tkachyov, Vladimir (2014) Tkachyov had a solid offensive game for Team Russia. He was good at reading the play and generally put himself in position to create or capitalize on turnovers in the offensive and neutral zones. Vladimir was good at putting consistent pressure on the Czech defenders and was able to create one specific turnover down low before setting up his line mate for an easy goal in the slot. He also was good at getting into scoring positions and was able to pounce on a loose puck in the slot before slipping a nice low shot past the Czech goaltender. Tkachyov showcased a strong wrist shot and was good at getting it off quickly in traffic with a nice release. He needs to work on his defensive zone positioning and needs to consistently help out defenders down low when needed.

RUS # 22, LW, Barbashev, Ivan (2014) Barbashev had a strong game doing the little things that do not show up on the score sheet but are important in winning games. He had strong penalty kill shifts and was effective at getting into shooting and passing lanes creating a number of turnovers and bad Czech passes. Ivan consistently carried the puck with confidence through the neutral zone generating nice speed while opening things up for his line mates. He was very good at gaining the offensive blue line and worked hard to back opposing defenders deep into the zone. Barbashev was consistent in generating offensive opportunities although was unable to get on the score sheet. He constantly moves his feet in the offensive zone and gets into strong scoring positions in front of the net looking for tips or rebounds.

RUS # 27, LW, Nichushkin, Valeri (2013) Nichushkin stood out in this game especially for his strong playmaking abilities, consistently finding open line mates and moving the puck quickly up the ice to generate scoring chances. He is constantly putting pressure on the puck in the offensive zone and barely missed connecting on a number of quality scoring chances. Valeri is very good at gaining the offensive zone with ease and shows the utmost confidence when carrying the puck. He uses his size to both shield defenders from the puck and to lean on smaller defenders in front of the net while battling for rebounds. Nichushkin is adept at gaining the offensive blue line and then slowing things down by putting on the breaks along the half wall allowing for his teammates to catch up and drive the net creating lanes. He shows no panic when controlling the puck and has the ability to stickhandle out of trouble when pressured. Only negative in this game for Nichushkin was that at times he appeared to be disinterested and showed a lack of compete or effort if the puck was on the other side of the ice. He needs to work at bringing the high compete and skill level for the duration of every shift.

CZE # 3, RD, Kostalik, Jan (2013) Kostalik was the best Czech defender on the ice. He showcased a strong slap shot from the blue line and was generally good at getting it on net through traffic. Jan was good at standing tall at the offensive blue line and generally did not leave the blue line early against a quick skating Team Russia. He showed a willingness to play a physical game and was able to finish a few hits along the boards and in open ice. He is good in the corners and uses his stick well to knock pucks free. Kostalik generally made smart outlet passes but sometimes needs to work at moving pucks quicker to beat fast fore-checking opponents. His footwork was a little slow at points and he needs to work on quickening up his transitions from forwards to backwards skating.

CZE # 7, LW, Zacha, Pavel (2015) Zacha had a very impressive game against opponents who were generally two years older. He is very good at using his size against older opponents and is great at shielding the puck while competing in board battles down low in the offensive zone. Pavel saw majority of time with the 1st Power Play unit and showed great vision and awareness connecting on a number of great passing plays with his linemates. He was constantly working hard to win loose pucks and never quit on a play. Zacha was also very effective on the penalty kill getting into lanes and was responsible for setting up a beautiful shorthanded goal for Team Czech with a fantastic pass to a streaking teammate. He consistently worked hard when he was on the ice and was great at keeping his feet moving allowing himself to create a number of turnovers.

CZE # 13, LW, Vrana, Jakub (2014) Vrana stood out in this game for his quick bursts of speed, beating a number of Russian defenders wide coming in off the rush. He is a strong skater in all three zones of the ice and was good at forcing defenders deep into the defensive zone with elusive speed and stick handling ability. Jakub was good at getting shots on net coming down the wing and was effective at using screens and traffic to create a number of scoring chances for his linemates. He showed good understanding of positioning in the offensive zone and read the play well getting himself into the slot before beating the Russian goaltender with a quick release. He needs to work on improving his strength as he was generally easy to knock off the puck when pressured along the boards or in the corners of the offensive zone.

FINAL SCORE: 5-2 Team Russia.

April 24, 2013, Calgary Hitmen vs Edmonton Oil Kings (WHL)

Edm #13, Baddock, Brandon (2013) - Good size and pretty good speed for that size. First few steps need work. Tried to be involved physically by finishing his checks whenever possible. Limited minutes.

Edm #23, Kulda, Edgars (2013) - Strong, pro-style game. Not the biggest guy, but he showed good puck possession skills and good lower body strength. Made a nice cross-ice pass through traffic.

Edm #27, Lazar, Curtis (2013) - Showed good speed and was able to create chances off the rush. Provided a nice low slot screen on Gernat's goal that he didn't get a point on. Had numerous chances early on. Good release on a hard snap shot. Very aware of the play around him. Filled lanes well and was always aware of when he needed to cover for a pinching teammate. Wore an 'A'.

Edm #30, Jarry, Tristan (2013) – DNP.

Edm #37, Mayo, Dysin (2014) - 16 year old was used on the PK. Good all-around game. Pinched at opportune times. Good hand-eye co-ordination in coralling a waist-high clearing attempt. Good gap control and had an active stick. Solid in his own end. Anticipated the play very well.

Cal #2, Thrower, Josh (2014) - Was used as both a forward and a dman tonight. Provided good energy in limited roles.

Cal #10, Lang, Chase (2014) – DNP - Scratched.

Cal #18, Virtanen, Jake (2014) – DNP – Suspension

Cal #25, Chase, Greg (2013) - Needs to lengthen his stride. Lacks high end speed. Made several passes through traffic. Got an assist driving to the net.

Cal #28, Peterson, Elliot (2013) - Strong two-way game tonight. Filled lanes well and was rewarded with a goal as a trailer on a play. Needs to improve his first step along with his top speed.

Cal #31, Shields, Mac (2013) - Did not start, but played most the game after Brossoit was pulled for good at the end of the 1st period. Was square to the puck. Played a little too deep in his net. Coughed up a few bad rebounds. Protected the corners well. Quickness could improve.

Scouts Notes: A game after a large Calgary win, Edmonton came out strong and potted four goals in the first half of the opening period to cruise to a big win.

April 8, 2013, Baie-Comeau Drakkar vs. Victoriaville Tigres (2nd round playoff)

BAC #10 C Grégoire, Jérémy (2013) – Still struggled with speed just like in my last viewing of him, but he managed to play an excellent game. He was great without the puck and was just everywhere trying to apply physical pressure. He played hard along the boards and was a force in front of the net. He scored a goal driving the net cashing in the rebound. He seems to be a good leader on the ice with good work ethic and physical ability. Not a bad player with the puck as he flashed his hands a few times but his speed really concerns.

BAC #13 LW Paquin-Boudreau, Gabriel (2013) – His game came in flashes but he sure showed impressive abilities. He is very dynamic with the puck and showed excellent skating ability. He is sneaky when he explodes and uses his quick hand to manoeuvre through traffic. His set of skills seems to be fairly high-end even though he is very small. The one big problem is he wasn't able to bring it all consistently throughout the game.

BAC #23 RW Straka, Petr (Overage player) – Just a few words to say I'm very impressed with his progression from his draft year until now. He brings tremendous speed on the ice and found his rythm as a goal scorer. Extremely dangerous whenever he touches the puck and lethal shot. Much smarter on the ice and better vision as well.

BAC #73 LW Zykov, Valentin (2013) – His skating looked much better than it did earlier in the year. He moves around plenty well although he is not an explosive player. The best part of his game that he showed tonight was his puck protection and positioning in the offensive zone. No one is able to take the puck from him when he decides to cycle it in the offensive zone and behind the net. He is rock solid and does a good job using that to let the play develop and take a shot or make a pass. He likes to go to the net and position himself to receive a pass. He has a very strong shot.

VIC #3 D Diaby, Jonathan (2013) – His play with the puck from the backend was just not there consistently. Sometimes you wonder why he would try such a play. On other occasions he makes great read and gets the puck out of the zone well. Not much else to say: he played a very safe overall game but needs to sharpen it up both offensively and defensively if he wants to be considered in the high rounds of the draft (mostly needs to work on decision making).

April 17, 2012, Youngstown Phantoms @ Green Bay Gamblers (USHL)

USHL Eastern Conference Semi-Finals Game #1

YOU #12 F Piccinich, J.J. (2014) - J.J. was pretty quiet throughout this game with the exception of a few flashes. He showed some good hands in a few one on one match-up's showing that at this level he can beat defenders with his hands. He was able to get a few scoring chances for both himself and his teammates. J.J. wasn't engaging nearly enough in battles as he should and spent a little too much time waiting for the puck to come to him rather than going in there and taking it.

YOU #18 F Connor, Kyle (2015) - Connor drove the net hard with the puck. He has very good skating ability for his size and can look explosive if given space. Kyle put a few good shots on goal, but was able to score Youngstown's only goal of the game setting up and blasting the one-timer.

YOU #30 G Romeo, Sean (2013) - Sean did a good job getting centred to the puck as the game went on and showed patience outwaiting shooters and making the key save without giving up much in terms of rebounds. Sean got off to a bit of a slow start on this one. There was one, maybe two goals that he probably would like to have back however one he really didn't have much of a chance on. On all of these goals his reflexes looked a little slower than they should have and may have accounted for the one or two he could have had back.

GB #5 D Olofsson, Gustav (2013) - Gustav showed early on the ability to use his size in puck races to box out opponent and win the race to the puck. Gustav consistently made the smart pass. Whether it was up ice, laterally on the rush or in one of the three zones, he was moving the puck well. At one point he let a great long distance pass fly to set up a breakout. He also made quick decisions on the power play, even when heavily pressured. Olofsson moved pretty well in terms of his agility. However his acceleration and speed were slightly below average. He was able to rush the puck up ice evading checks and got the puck on net. In the offensive zone he shows excellent puck protection holding on for several seconds letting options open up while maintaining puck control. His strengths are primarily on the offensive side of the game. He was aggressive defensively jumping up and intercepting the puck. This is working at this level but he's going to have to pick his spots a little more often at higher levels. He is strong and can hit hard but he just wasn't finishing his checks often, rather option to poke at the puck along the boards, although it worked.

GB #9 F Schmaltz, Nick (2014) - Schmaltz was constantly dangerous in this game. He is so smooth with the puck in one on one match-up's and through traffic. He constantly showed off his skating and puck skills in the offensive zone. He displayed his great vision on multiple occasions and created plays and scoring chances fairly consistently for Green Bay. When there were no options on the power play he would skate around the offensive zone, creating space, opening options up and then making a great feed to give his teammates great chances to score.

GB #23 D Gross, Jordan (2013) - Jordan made some good plays to break up a few potential rushes for Youngstown. He made some good plays with the puck, but his overall puck play was hit or miss.

GB #24 F Siroky, Ryan (2013) - Ryan is an above average skater and is always hovering around the net. He helped on a few offensive chances, but also made some solid plays on the back check as well.

Scouts Notes: Green Bay jumped out of this match-up early and never looked back opening up a 3-0 lead in this game. Youngstown put on some pressure and was the only team to score in the final forty minutes. However it wasn't enough to match Green Bay who seemed to always possess ideal positioning for the breakouts that Youngstown provided. They also were able to clear the garbage out from the front of the net preventing Youngstown from being able to cause issues on rebounds. Nicholas Schilkey (2013*) was all over the ice tonight. He was creating chances left and right, using his speed, and going hard to the net. He has a good shot and really looks like one of the best NHL Draft re-entry players in the USHL this season.

April 18, 2012, Youngstown Phantoms @ Green Bay Gamblers (USHL)

USHL Eastern Conference Semi-Finals Game #2

<u>Youngstown Phantoms</u>

#12 – F – Piccinich, J.J. – 5'11" – 176lb. – 2014 Eligible Early in the third period J.J. got into great positioning to get open for a pass in scoring area. However his teammate fired the puck at the net at net. He reacted quickly and jumped on the rebound to score the tying goal.

#18 – F – Connor, Kyle – 6'0" – 160lb. – 2015 Eligible
Kyle was pretty quiet for most of this game. He was able to create some offensive chances in the third period. He made a great move to beat the defenseman, he got caught behind the goal like but centred the puck but his teammate couldn't finish.

<u>Green Bay Gamblers</u>

#5 – D – Olofsson, Gustav – 6'2" – 185lb. – 2013 Eligible Gustav almost always seems to be making the right pass moving it hard and accurate. He is a little too aggressive when trying to jump up on the rush. When the puck is turned over this has left his team outnumbered down low. He struggled defensively particularly on the penalty kill. On the first penalty kill he got caught out of position and wasn't physically battling out front. He was also out of position on the game winning goal which was also a penalty kill. As things started to fall apart for Green Bay, Olofsson started making more mental errors.

#9 – F – Schmaltz, Nick – 5'11" – 160lb. – 2014 Eligible Nick was very quiet in the first period and early on in the second he was trying to do too much. He scored Green Bay's second goal of the game making a great play. He faked a shot passing the puck down low then went straight for the net slipping between defenders and jumped on the rebound. Nick constantly challenged defensemen one on one, sometimes he won sometimes he didn't but he was constantly testing defenders. When Green Bay was struggling in the third, Nick began to make a few mistakes. Nick was very good in the faceoff circle winning more than half of his draws, and some important faceoffs.

#23 – D – Gross, Jordan – 5'10" – 178lb. – 2013 Eligible Jordan made some effective passes, but this was not his best performance. He got walked in the first period in a one on one match-up. In the third period he got stripped of the puck deep in his own zone. This directly resulted in Youngstown's fourth goal of the game.

#24 – F – Siroky, Ryan – 5'11" – 190lb. – 2013 Eligible Ryan provided a consistent and effective forecheck. He dropped the gloves in the third period after receiving a bit of a questionable hit.

#88 – D – Linhart, Jake – 5'9" – 152lb. – 2014 Eligible Jake scored the opening goal of the game by joining the rush, making a quick pass to set up his teammate then finished on the pass back. He did a good job a few times in this game holding the offensive line and keeping the play going. He also finished his checks well and looked a little bigger than his listing.

Scouts Notes: Green Bay opened this game up very well and looked great. However they experienced a defensive collapse while on the penalty kill and left the first period with the game tied. In the second period they were dominant but were only able to escape with one goal. In the third Youngstown came out flying and scored three unanswered goals to steal game 2 and tie the series up 1-1. Alex Kile (2013*) was constantly making plays happen and creating offense for his team. Nicholas Schilkey (2013*) displayed very quick hands and is a very smooth skater. He's also willing to get back defensively and does everything working in every area of the game.

April 23, 2013, Baie-Comeau Drakkar at Blainville-Boisbriand Armada (QMJHL)

BLB #11 RW Marc-Olivier Roy (2013) – Listed at 6'0 but lanky and plays smaller than his size. Physical game was inconsistent. Laid a guy out on one play and mixed it up after, but skated by a lot of hits in the neutral zone. Defensive zone coverage was mixed, wasn't aggressive enough in board battles. Skating is strong, not flashy but he moves well with good acceleration. Didn't seem to be pushing his legs as hard as he could. Solid passer overall and utilized his teammates well. Was an asset on the powerplay in particular with fluid puck movement and the ability to sauce a pass through traffic. Good tools just not sure where he fits in as an NHL player as his game isn't fully defined at the moment.

BLB #62 LC Danick Martel (2013) – Not a big kid by any means but when he's on his game he's a real sparkplug with a lot of presence. Had an off night as compared to previous viewings. Tried to do too much, was slow to loose pucks, and didn't show much jump at all.

BAC #10 RW Jérémy Grégoire (2013) – Bulky and played with a lot of jam. Skating needs work as a he had a hard time getting from A to B but was very useful along the boards and in front of the net, especially on the powerplay. Good forecheck work, liked to play the body, and was involved in scrums.

BAC #13 LW Gabryel Paquin-Boudreau (2013) Was passed over in the 2011 Q draft and selected 10th overall in 2012. Had a strong season. Didn't notice Boudreau much at all. Not a big kid and the Armada defense was so strong that he was rendered mostly ineffective. Positioning was good but teammates had a hard time getting him the puck and when he did have opportunities, he couldn't get shots on net. Needs to bulk up and work on his skating, which is not very fluid. Was very chippy in post-whistle antics all game and ended up getting a double match penalty and suspension for his participation in a fight in the last five minutes.

BAC #16 RC Félix Girard (Passed over 2012) – Played a strong two-way game. A little undersized for a pivot but worked his ass off. Active on his feet. Scrappy and intelligent, defensive game was very sound. Involved physically with hits and physical play after whistles. Didn't start taking much stock of him until late second period as he's a '94 re-entry but will take a closer look tomorrow.

BAC #73 RW Valentin Zykov (2013) – Hot and cold game. Obvious talent but was much too lax in the first two periods. Strong skater but didn't keep his feet moving and mentally looked a step behind play. Made extra moves with puck, lost board battles, and missed assignments in the defensive zone.

Got his legs in the third. Showed a lot of jump and some real quick hands as well, navigated traffic very well. Flashed a nice variety of quality wrist and snap shots and was dangerous on most third period shifts. Too little too late, would have liked to see him play a more complete game.

April 24, 2013, Baie-Comeau Drakkar at Blainville-Boisbriand Armada (QMJHL)

BLB #11 RW Marc-Olivier Roy (2013) – Looked like a tweener. Showed a lot of skill and poise in the offensive zone when given time and space, especially on the powerplay, but didn't show the ability to create space for himself. Went to dirty areas and did battle but had a hard time against bigger players. Hustled with his feet but not a dynamic skater. Defensive coverage was mostly average to poor, though he had a couple good PK shifts. Not sold.

BLB #62 LC Danick Martel (2013) – Had a better game today than yesterday. Not a great skater but he was really hustling out there. Showed good defensive zone positioning and was very involved in coverage. Size is an issue. Had trouble battling against and covering bigger players. Got leveled in the offensive zone on an innocent looking play and had a hard time fighting through checks. Had some good opportunities but couldn't finish and made questionable decisions with the puck. Good Q player but I don't think he's draftable.

BAC #10 RW/C Jérémy Grégoire (2013) – I like a lot of the things he brings but overall I thought Grégoire was sluggish. Plays a well-rounded game that includes strong fore- and backchecking. Played the body well, forcing turnovers and helping out defensively. Needed to keep his feet moving. Considering his lack of footspeed, the only way he's effective is if he keeps his motor going and he took a few shifts off in that regard. Was able to carry the puck through center but don't think he projects as an offensive player at the next level as he had a hard time evading defensive pressure. Missed one absolutely golden, empty-net chance that might have changed the tide of the game.

BAC #16 RC Félix Girard (Passed over 2012) – I really liked Girard's game tonight. He brought it on every shift. Biggest asset was his defensive game. He was very responsible, backchecking fully, battling on the boards in all three zones, and maintaining an active stick and intelligent positioning on the PK. Showed a lot of forecheck ability with big hits that forced turnovers in the offensive and neutral zones. Skating is not pretty but he kept his feet moving and played with a lot of jump. Offensive upside is lacking but he does have a great shot. Picked the far corner with a beautiful wrister coming down the off-wing and flashed a heavy slapshot when given space. Discipline could be an issue, took a number of unnecessary minor penalties in games 3 and 4 and seemed to be frustrated going to the bench after misplays. Don't see how he gets passed over again, looks like a good 4C and should be able to quickly transition to pros.

BAC #73 RW Valentin Zykov (2013) – Zykov played a strong game. Was much more consistent than yesterday when he only showed up for the third period. Loved his compete level. Showed top-end forechecking ability, pressuring defensemen with speed and physicality and winning countless battles through sheer determination. Laid some heavy hits without a lot of speed behind them and on one occasion, legally pinned a guy on the boards so hard that he couldn't even move his arms. Fought through checks and battled in front of the net to gain inside position. Scored a goal hustling to a loose puck off a rebound. Drove the net hard when appropriate. Navigated traffic well in the neutral zone and was useful on the breakout. Strong enough to shrug off hits, skilled enough to make guys miss, and fast enough to beat guys wide. Stickhandling is precise and effective though he was guilty of doing too much on occasion, including one brutal instance where he tried to beat three defenders and ended up taking a penalty in the process. The next time he came in outnumbered in a 1v2, he made the smart play and got a shot on net to get the offensive zone faceoff. Skating is strong, particularly laterally. Strong pivots and changes of direction, a lot of jump overall. Great wrist and snap shots, high velocity with a quick release. Seemed to have a good idea of where to be in the defensive zone but had his eyes glued to the puck at all times, rarely tracked his point man. Baie-Comeau didn't activate defensemen often so it wasn't a huge issue tonight but a lot of interceptable passes back to the point got by him.

Calgary Hitmen vs Edmonton Oil Kings (WHL)

Edm #23, Kulda, Edgars (2013) - Played a pro style game. Hard on the puck, gritty on the walls and made hard accurate passes. Played a very North-South style game. Cycles the puck well. Willing to take a hit to make a play. Defensively aware. Showed good lower body strength by being able to skate through checks and maintain both his balance and the puck. Heavy wrist shot - accuracy could improve. Drove hard to the net, was consistently around the puck and won a lot of of battles for loose pucks. Held the puck for too long a couple times eventually resulting in turnovers. His game has really come along as the season has progressed - he has nearly as many points in the playoffs as he did in the entire regular season.

Edm #27, Lazar, Curtis (2013) – Played center. Good speed on forecheck. Great rush that he finished off with a fantastic wrist shot that beat Driedger low glove side. Supported his defensemen well deep in his own end. Made good first passes and had a reasonably good burst to start moving up ice with the play. Good top speed and is able to control the puck at high tempo. A good skater with room to improve.

Edm #30, Jarry, Tristan (2013) - DNP.

Edm #37, Mayo, Dysin (2014) - Crisp, accurate cross-ice passes. Right hand shot. Over-handled the puck a couple times in his own end resulted in turnovers. Struggled a bit when he couldn't find an outlet.

Cal #10, Lang, Chase (2014) - Scratched.

Cal #18, Virtanen, Jake (2014) - Returning from suspension. Started the game as LW on Calgary's #1 line. Ended up playing on a couple different lines throughout the game. Got in the lane and blocked a shot leading to a two on two chance where he thread a nice pass to Sylvester at top speed while a defender had Sylvester tightly covered. Great speed, but wasn't able to create much off the rush. Often went overly wide waiting for help to come, but just ended up running out of real estate before throwing the puck on net for low percentage plays.

Cal #25, Chase, Greg (2013) - Played LW and RW on the a few different line combinations tonight. Lowe hit him hit hard in the first period when Chase was looking for a loose puck in a battle with his head down. Took numerous penalties and wasn't going to be pushed around. Good effort on the walls, but strength needs to improve especially against the bigger Oil King defenders. Great play in overtime to stall for time in the attack zone before drawing a defender and leaving dropping a pass to Macek for the game winner.

Cal #31, Shields, Mac (2013) – DNP

Game Notes: A highly entertaining match between the top two teams in the WHL's Eastern Conference. Edmonton came out strong and controlled the play for much of the game. Edmonton found success by stretching Calgary's defense and creating space for their skilled forwards in the neutral zone. Calgary fought back from a couple goals down in the third period to extend the game into overtime. After surviving an onslaught of pressure from the Oil Kings late in the third period and into overtime, Greg Chase made a smart play in creating time for his teammates to join the play before drawing a defenseman to him while dropping the puck to Brooks Macek for the game winner.

Part 8
CREDITS

I want to thank all the people who helped put this book together. Our scouts worked harder than ever this season. Our media staff once again provided great content for our website.

Thank you to scouts Ryan Yessie, Charles An, Simon Larouche, Samuel Roberge, Kevin Thacker, Dylan Liptrap, Josh Deitell, Scott McDougall, Matt Gordon, Robert Blaine, Ron Berman and Jerome Berube.

This book is a result of travels to many rinks around the globe. We began our journey towards the 2013 NHL Draft the day after he 2012 NHL Draft in Pittsburgh. We drove from Pittsburgh to Rochester and our 'book' on the 2013 prospects was born. Ten months later I travelled to Sochi, Russia to attend the World Under 18 Championship. It's an event that signals that the end of the season is near.

As I write this, I just completed attending day one of the 2013 NHL Combine in Toronto. It's an event I enjoy attending and due to the our late release date this season, we are able to include information from combine week in our books.

I also want to give stick taps for the contributions of Steven Perko, Michelle Sturino, Laura Barney, Steve Fitzsimmons, Melissa Perri, Leslie Treff and Adam Schnepp who contributed this year to provide our website with interviews and draft features.

A shout out to those who prefer to remain behind the scenes but helped us with editing and all the other little details that are necessary to put a book like this together.

Thanks to media staff from around the NHL, CHL, the USHL and to Hockey Canada who help us out and are a pleasure to deal with.

Finally, thanks my NHL Scout friends who help make the season so enjoyable. Whether it's killing time before games, killing time on long layovers in airports or helping me using their years of experience with things as simple as travel visas, I both appreciate it, and enjoy your company.

Mark Edwards
Founder & Director of Scouting

www.ingramcontent.com/pod-product-compliance
Lightning Source LLC
Chambersburg PA
CBHW062122160426
43191CB00013B/2171